The Encyclopa...
Dictionary of Psychology

Edited by

Graham Davey
University of Sussex, UK

Hodder Arnold
A MEMBER OF THE HODDER HEADLINE GROUP

First published in Great Britain in 2006 by Hodder Arnold, an imprint of
Hodder Education, a member of the Hodder Headline Group,
338 Euston Road, London NW1 3BH

www.hoddereducation.com

Distributed in the United States of America by
Oxford University Press Inc.
198 Madison Avenue, New York, NY10016

© 2006 Hodder Arnold

Hodder Headline's policy is to use papers that are natural, renewable and
recyclable products and made from wood grown in sustainable forests.
The logging and manufacturing processes are expected to conform to the
environmental regulations of the country of origin.

The advice and information in this book are believed to be true and
accurate at the date of going to press, but neither the authors nor the publisher
can accept any legal responsibility or liability for any errors or omissions.

British Library Cataloguing in Publication Data
A catalogue record for this book is available from the British Library

Library of Congress Cataloging-in-Publication Data
A catalog record for this book is available from the Library of Congress

ISBN-10 0 340 812 389
ISBN-13 978 0 340 81238 9

1 2 3 4 5 6 7 8 9 10

Typeset in 9 on 10pt Plantin by Phoenix Photosetting, Chatham, Kent
Printed and bound in Great Britain by Martins the Printers, Berwick-upon-Tweed.

What do you think about this book? Or any other Hodder
Education title? Please send your comments to the feedback
section on www.hoddereducation.com

Contents

Preface

Psychology is one of the most popular disciplines for undergraduate study throughout the world, and there is no sign of its popularity waning. Add to this the burgeoning interest in psychology in schools, on access courses and among lay people generally, and this *Encyclopaedic Dictionary of Psychology* provides a substantial resource for those attempting to study and understand the discipline.

This volume is specifically designed to provide an accessible resource of psychological knowledge and definitions at a number of different levels. It is structured with eight separate sections representing the eight core areas within the discipline. These cover the important content areas of Developmental, Social, Cognitive and Biological Psychology, Personality and Individual Differences, and Abnormal, Clinical and Health psychology, as well as sections on Conceptual and Historical Issues and Research Methods and Statistics in psychology. As such, it covers all aspects of the discipline that a student is likely to encounter when studying psychology from school level, through undergraduate study to postgraduate level.

It also includes entries at a number of different levels of complexity, with important concepts and facts receiving the kind of detailed attention necessary for the reader to comprehend and understand the relevant issues. All entries are up to date, reflect the current state of psychological knowledge and are selected as being relevant to the contemporary psychological curriculum. In particular, it is the complete back-up resource for the student studying psychology at undergraduate, graduate or sub-degree level.

Entries are compiled at four different levels of complexity. The Level 1 entries are up to 1000 words long and tend to correspond to major areas of inquiry within psychology or describe in detail the most important concepts that the student is likely to encounter during their psychological studies. Level 1 entries are supported by references and suggestions for further reading, and, in many cases, by illustrative figures, tables and photographs. Level 2 entries consist of definitions and descriptions of up to 350 words, once again with references and suggestions for further reading. Level 3 and 4 entries consist of more basic definitions of 150 and 20 words respectively, and provide the reader with instant descriptions and explanations of basic terminology and psychological processes. In total there are over 1500 entries at these different levels of description and explanation, so the volume is significantly more than just a dictionary, but is truly encyclopaedic in its attention to detail.

Each core content area in the volume has been compiled and edited by an internationally distinguished psychologist who specialises in that area, and contributions have been written by individual scholars and researchers from a range of countries, all of whom are at the cutting edge of progress in their specialty. Each section has an introduction to that core area by the relevant associate editor, and, where appropriate, additional commentaries on recent developments given by eminent psychologists from a range of different countries worldwide.

Professor Graham Davey
Brighton, July 2004

How to use The Encyclopaedic Dictionary of Psychology

- Entries are divided into eight separate sections which reflect the eight main areas of study in psychology: Conceptual and Historical Issues, Biological Psychology, Cognitive Psychology, Developmental Psychology, Social Psychology, Personality and Individual Differences, Abnormal, Clinical and Health Psychology, and Research Methods and Statistics.
- Entries in each section are in alphabetical order.
- Go to the section in which you expect to find the term or phrase you wish to consult.
- If the term is not in the first section you consult, go to the main index at the back of the book and this will direct you to the section and page on which that or a related entry can be found.

- You can expand your understanding of a particular entry by picking out terms and phrases used in that entry and following these up by using the main index.
- The references listed after the more important entries point the reader to a wide range of books and journal articles that will further expand the reader's understanding of a particular entry.
- All entries are cross-referenced, so if the entry you have consulted includes terms or phrases that are covered elsewhere in the book, these will be highlighted in capitals.

List of editors and commentators

Editor

Professor Graham Davey, University of Sussex, UK

Associate editors

Professor Richard Bentall, University of Manchester, UK (Abnormal, Clinical and Health Psychology)

Dr Colin Cooper, The Queen's University of Belfast, UK (Personality and Individual Differences)

Professor Steven J. Cooper, University of Liverpool, UK (Biological Psychology)

Professor Nick Emler, University of Surrey, UK (Social Psychology)

Dr Andy Field, University of Sussex, UK (Research Methods and Statistics)

Dr Chris Moulin, University of Leeds, UK (Cognitive Psychology)

Dr Alison Pike, University of Sussex, UK (Developmental Psychology)

Professor Graham Richards, Director of the British Psychological Society History of Psychology Centre, London, UK (Conceptual and Historical Issues)

Commentators

Professor Kent C. Berridge, University of Michigan, Ann Arbor, USA (Biological Psychology)

Professor Nathan Brody, Wesleyan University, West Hartford, CT, USA (Personality and Individual Differences)

Professor Fergus Craik, Rotman Research Institute, Toronto, Canada (Cognitive Psychology)

Dr Kirby Deater-Deckard, University of Oregon, USA (Developmental Psychology)

Professor Marcel van den Hout, University of Utrecht, The Netherlands (Abnormal, Clinical and Health Psychology)

Dr Beth Manke, California State University, Long Beach, USA (Developmental Psychology)

Dr Kimberley J. Saudino, Boston University, USA (Developmental Psychology)

Dr Andrew S. Winston, University of Guelph, Canada (Conceptual and Historical Issues)

List of contributors

Professor Dominic Abrams, University of Kent, UK (*DA*)

Professor John Archer, University of Central Lancashire, UK (*JA*)

Mr Russell Ary, California State University, Long Beach, USA (*RA*)

Dr Susan Ayers, University of Sussex, UK (*SA*)

Dr Robin Banerjee, University of Sussex, UK (*RB – Developmental Psychology*)

Professor Richard Bentall, University of Manchester, UK (*RB – Abnormal, Clinical and Health Psychology*)

Professor Hans-Werner Bierhoff, Ruhr-Bochum University, Germany (*H-WB*)

Professor Gerd Bohner, University of Bielefeld, Germany (*GB*)

Dr Peter Bull, University of York, UK (*PB*)

Dr Esther Burkitt, Victoria University of Wellington, New Zealand (*EB*)

Professor Bram Buunk, University of Groningen, The Netherlands (*BB*)

Ms Beth Carls, MindOH!, Houston, Texas, USA (*BC*)

Ms Sonia Chawla, Boston University, Massachusetts, USA (*SC – Developmental Psychology*)

Professor Xenia Chryssochoou, Panteion University of Social and Political Sciences, Greece (*XC*)

Ms Amber Clemens, California State University, Long Beach, USA (*AC*)

Ms Joanne Coldwell, University of Sussex, UK (*JC – Developmental Psychology*)

Dr J. C. Cole, University of Liverpool, UK (*JC – Biological Psychology*)

Professor Martin Conway, University of Durham, UK (*MC*)

Dr Colin Cooper, The Queen's University of Belfast, UK (*CC*)

Professor Steven J. Cooper, University of Liverpool, UK (*SC – Biological Psychology*)

Dr Rhiannon Corcoran, University of Manchester, UK (*RC*)

Dr Duncan Cramer, University of Loughborough, UK (*DC*)

Dr Rudi Dallos, University of Plymouth, UK (*RD*)

Professor Graham Davey, University of Sussex, UK (*GD*)

Dr Mary A. Dolan, California State University, San Bernadino, USA (*MD*)

Professor Nick Emler, University of Surrey, UK (*NE*)

Dr Edel Ennis, University of Portsmouth, UK (*EE*)

Ms Allison Ewing, University of Arizona, USA (*AE*)

Ms Susan Fenstermacher, Boston University, Massachusetts, USA (*SF*)

Dr Andy Field, University of Sussex, UK (*AF – Research Methods and Statistics*)

Dr Alexandra Forsythe, The Queen's University of Belfast, UK (*AF – Personality and Individual Differences*)

Mr Jeffery R. Gagne, Boston University, Massachusetts, USA (*JG*)

Dr Robin Goodwin, Brunel University, London, UK (*RG*)

Dr Aiden Gregg, University of Southampton, UK (*AG*)

Ms Sahar Haghighat, California State University, Long Beach, USA (*SH – Developmental Psychology*)

Dr J. C. G. Halford, University of Liverpool, UK (*JCGH*)

Dr Donncha Hanna, The Queen's University of Belfast, UK (*DH*)

Dr Anna Harrison, Royal Holloway, University of London, UK (*AH*)

Dr J. A. Harrold, University of Liverpool, UK (*JAH*)

Professor Richard Hastings, University College, North Wales, Bangor, UK (*RH*)

Dr Susan Hempel, University of York, UK (*SH – Research Methods and Statistics*)

Dr Graham Hole, University of Sussex, UK (*GH*)

Mr Fred C. Holtz, University of Oregon, USA (*FH*)

Dr Nick Hopkins, University of Dundee, UK (*NH*)

Dr Peter Kinderman, University of Liverpool, UK (*PK*)

Dr Silvia Krauth-Gruber, University of Paris V René Descartes, France (*SK-G*)

Dr Mansur Lalljee, University of Oxford, UK (*ML*)

Professor John Levine, University of Pittsburgh, Pennsylvania, USA (*JL – Social Psychology*)

Professor Jacques-Philippe Leyens, Catholic University of Louvain, Belgium (*JP-L*)

Dr Ruth Lowry, The Queen's University of Belfast, UK (*RL*)

Dr J. E. Lycett, University of Liverpool, UK (*JL –* Biological Psychology)

Dr Beth Manke, California State University, Long Beach, USA (*BM*)

Dr Pearl Martin, University of Queensland, Australia (*PM*)

Professor Robin Martin, University of Queensland, Australia (*RM*)

Dr Chris McConville, University of Ulster, Coleraine, UK (*CM* – Personality and Individual Differences)

Professor Carol McGuinness, The Queen's University of Belfast, UK (*CMG*)

Dr Margaret McRorie, The Queen's University of Belfast, UK (*MM*)

Professor Gerold Mikula, University of Graz, Austria (*GM*)

Dr Jeremy Miles, University of York, UK (*JM*)

Dr Chris Moulin, University of Leeds, UK (*CM –* Cognitive Psychology)

Professor John Nezlek, College of William and Mary, VA, USA (*JN*)

Professor Sik Hung Ng, University of Hong Kong, Hong Kong (*SHN*)

Dr K. V. Petrides, Institute of Education, University of London, UK (*KP* – Personality and Individual Differences)

Dr Kathleen Petrill, Ashland University, OH, USA (*KP* – Developmental Psychology)

Dr Alison Pike, University of Sussex, UK (*AP*)

Professor Stephen Reicher, University of St Andrews, UK (*SR*)

Professor Graham Richards, British Psychological Society History of Psychology Centre, London, UK (*GR*)

Professor Constantine Sedikides, University of Southampton, UK (*CS*)

Professor Noel Sheehy, The Queen's University of Belfast, UK (*NS*)

Dr Frank Siebler, University of Bielefeld, Germany (*FS*)

Dr Alastair D. Smith, University of Bristol, UK (*AS*)

Dr Michael Smithson, Australian National University, Canberra, Australia (*MS* – Developmental Psychology)

Dr Mary Stewart, Heriot-Watt University, Edinburgh, UK (*MS* – Personality and Individual Differences)

Dr Edward J. Sutherland, University of Leeds, UK (*ES*)

Dr Sara Tai, University of Manchester, UK (*ST*)

Dr Annabel S. C. Thorn, University of Bristol, UK (*AT*)

Dr Brenda Todd, University of Sussex, UK (*BT*)

Professor Paul A. M. Van Lange, Free University of Amsterdam, The Netherlands (*PVL*)

Professor Mark Van Vugt, University of Kent, UK (*MVV*)

Dr Glen Waller, St George's Hospital Medical School, UK (*GW*)

Dr J. Ward-Robinson, University of Liverpool, UK (*JW-R*)

Dr Dawn Watling, University of Sussex, UK (*DW*)

Dr Alison Wearden, University of Manchester, UK (*AW*)

Section 1

Conceptual and Historical Issues

Introduction

Psychology still faces numerous, seemingly perennial, conceptual, theoretical and philosophical problems, several of which (like the 'mind-body problem') many had once thought were either solved or irrelevant. Often inherited from philosophy, and frequently debated since Psychology's mid-nineteenth century scientific debut, their speedy resolution in the course of its future growth and progress was confidently expected. This did not happen. If anything the menu of problems has expanded, while others have intensified rather than approached closure. Our sensitivities regarding ethical aspects of research and professional practice have also burgeoned since the 1980s. Much of this pertains in some way to the nature of the relationships between Psychology and its host societies or those participating in its research, and those about whom it theorises. History of Psychology has, in consequence, been profoundly transformed from an exercise in chronicling 'great' theories and psychologists to a discipline concerned with analysing Psychology's past in relation to such matters, while the importance of philosophical Psychology has been similarly reinforced.

We might then summarise this section's themes as follows:

1. Enduring, partly philosophical, puzzles such as the 'mind-body problem'.

2. Long-standing theoretical debates, e.g. the 'nature versus nurture' controversy and holistic versus analytical modes of theorising.

3. Methodological issues such as 'experimenter effects', though most are dealt with in other sections.

4. Recently renewed debates about Psychology's scientific status, currently hingeing around the (loosely termed) 'social constructionist' thesis that psychological phenomena are products of specific, historically mutable, social and cultural conditions, rather than 'natural'. This raises doubts about Psychology's status

as a 'natural science'. (One factor here is how we understand the nature and role of language itself.)

5. The aforementioned ethical issues, many arising within Psychology (and other human sciences) in ways which cannot occur in physical sciences such as meteorology or astronomy, for example.

While often resisting easy solution, some of these matters can at least be greatly illuminated by historical scrutiny and analysis of how Psychology actually *has* previously operated, thereby providing debates with some empirical grounding and parameters. This, it has to be said, invariably demonstrates that sweeping generalisations rarely stand up, or at best require major qualification. From the 1950s to the 1980s Psychology had many passionate critics, both within and beyond its ranks, who variously attacked it as a 'tool of the system', dehumanising, sexist, racist or, from the other end of the ideological spectrum, a communist or liberal conspiracy. Whatever truths such assaults contained, they were usually mounted in polemical and simplistic terms, typically selecting supportive evidence while ignoring the full picture. Self-monitoring and attention to what psychologists are, and have been, up to is essential for Psychology's future success, but this must itself be done in as rigorous a fashion as any other research. This need not compromise one's broader values, but can avert sterile enmity and prevent psychologists falling into the same psychological traps of stereotyping, dogmatism, projection and unthinking conformity they have identified as so ubiquitous in everyone else.

Note

Throughout this section 'Psychology'/'Psychological' (capitalised) are used when referring to the discipline, 'psychology'/'psychological' when referring to its subject matter. This enables the relationships between the two to be discussed without cumbersome circumlocution.

1

References

History:

Danziger, K. 1997: *Naming the Mind: How Psychology Discovered its Language.* London: Sage. **Leahey, T. H.** 2000: *A History of Psychology: Main Currents in Psychological Thought.* Englewood Cliffs: Prentice-Hall. **Richards, G.** 2002: *Putting Psychology in its Place: A Critical Historical Overview.* London: Psychology Press. **Shamdasani, S.** 2003: *Jung and the Making of Modern Psychology. The Dream of a Science.* Cambridge: Cambridge University Press.

Conceptual:

Chalmers, D. J. (ed.) 2002: *Philosophy of Mind: Classical and Contemporary Readings.* London: Oxford University Press. **O'Donohue, W. and Kitchener, R. F.** (eds) 1996: *The Philosophy of Psychology.* London: Sage. **Stich, S. P. and Warfield, T. A.** 2002: *The Blackwell Guide to Philosophy of Mind.* Oxford: Blackwell. **Valentine, E. R.** 1992: *Conceptual Issues in Psychology.* London: Routledge.

Full bibliographic details of sources cited in the entries may be found in one or other of these texts. Full references have been given only where this is not the case.

Professor Graham Richards

Recent trends in historical and conceptual issues: a North American perspective

History of Psychology emerged as a distinct sub-discipline during the late 1960s and developed with the formation of organisations (Division 26 of the American Psychological Association, Cheiron: The International Society for the History of Behavioral and Social Sciences, European Society for the History of the Human Sciences), journals (Journal of the History of the Behavioral Sciences, History of Psychology, History of the Human Sciences), and specialised graduate programmes. These institutional changes undergirded an increase in quantity and a change in the quality of research in the History of Psychology. Scholarship tended, or at least aspired, to be more historicist and less presentist, more external and less purely internal, more critical and less celebratory, and more reliant on primary than on secondary sources. These trends accelerated in the 1990s and were encouraged by extensive contact and cooperation between psychologists who turned to the study of their history and historians of science and culture who took an increasing interest in psychology as a discipline, practice and social phenomenon. Thus History of Psychology became a truly interdisciplinary enterprise.

Two clear trends emerged from this cooperation. First, there is increased emphasis on the analysis of Psychology's history in its social context, that is, the examination of the broader social changes in which the evolution of psychological research and practice are imbedded. The study of individual lives, laboratories and theories has not vanished, but has been supplemented by a richer analysis of how governments, war, funding, immigration, social mores and economic change helped shape North American Psychology. The study of the reciprocal relationship between Psychology and popular culture is now an important area of historical inquiry.

A second trend had to do with the relationship between historical inquiry and fundamental conceptual issues. In general, historians had no investment in the idea that Psychology was a science, had made scientific progress or was beneficial to humanity. Moreover, many of those psychologists who took up the study of the history of the discipline had serious questions regarding the nature and aims of modern Psychology. As a result much historiography of the past decade has examined the 'taken for granted' categories and methods and the historical process by which these practices emerged. Kurt Danziger's seminal book, Constructing the Subject, *provided the best and most important example. For some historians, social constructionism (see entry) in one form or another provided a framework for these critiques. More generally, the full armamentarium of the postmodern was brought to bear on historical problems.*

Describing recent trends in conceptual issues is more difficult, but as Richards (above) correctly notes, many of the discipline's oldest themes persist, albeit in new forms. For example, evolutionary explanations for complex human action, increasingly popular in the past decade, have kept alive a form of the nature-nurture debate, perhaps more intensely fought in North America than elsewhere. Some writers even hoped that an evolutionary perspective, conceived primarily in adaptationist terms, would serve as the long-awaited unifying paradigm for Psychology. The dream of conceptual unification persisted into the new millennium, despite the reality of conceptual fractionation. In Clinical Psychology, for example, conventional positivist notions of illness and therapy continue to vie with 'human science' conceptions, emphasising narrative and 'lived experience'. A very substantial number of social psychologists embraced social cognition as a general framework, and argued that the manipulation of appropriate variables in the laboratory would reveal fundamental, transituational and perhaps even transcultural processes, despite the severe critique of this aim in previous decades. Those who rejected this conceptualisation of the 'social' as a cognitive problem often promoted the study of language and discourse as the appropriate alternative. Direct confrontation was rare, as the creation of sub-communities with their own organisations, meetings and journals has permitted parallel, non-interacting conceptual worlds. The degree of present conceptual confusion (or diversity, depending on one's view) is further illustrated by the survival of both psychoanalytic theory and behaviour analysis long after their obituaries were published.

For many areas of inquiry, the very real success of neuroscience produced a new form of scientific envy. Perhaps all that was needed was to properly conceptualise human emotion and experience as brain activity, revealed via the now ubiquitous MRI. Much conceptual baggage could then be jettisoned. Yet, basic questions about the nature of the mind and the special nature of human beings persisted – questions fundamentally philosophical in nature. Historians knew what the problem was: the late nineteenth-century debate over whether Psychology would be strictly Naturwisssenschaft, Geisteswissenschaft *or a strange amalgam of both had never been settled, and perhaps never will be.*

Dr Andrew S. Winston

A

agency Agency has become a problematic concept within the context of debates about FREE WILL, responsibility, REDUCTIONISM and computer simulation, and provides these with an underlying common focus. At the heart of the issue lies the simple question of who, what or where is the actor, or source, of any human action: 'who did it?' Where, in any given case, we locate the agency from which a behavioural event originates, will determine who we hold responsible, who we absolve from responsibility and to what degrees we do so. Clearly, without such a concept, ethical and moral judgements would be impossible, indeed meaningless. Philosophically and scientifically, however, there is a profound difficulty. Agency is not, like colour or even being introverted, an empirically demonstrable property of a 'system' or 'object', whether it be a rock or a human being. This seems to entail that whether or not a system (e.g. a computer or android) possesses agency is not a straightforward factual scientific issue that can be settled by whether or not the system exhibits particular specifiable features. The criteria we use in practice to decide whether something (including a human being) is an 'agent' appear, ultimately, to lie in the kind of social relationship which we have with it. It is in this sense that the significance of the famous Turing test should perhaps best be understood, although it was not the spirit in which Turing himself proposed it. For most purposes 'agency' may be considered as virtually synonymous with 'intentionality', a more technical term used in much contemporary discourse on these matters, Searle's 'Chinese Room argument' (Searle 1980) being the most widely known instance. Clearly without some concept like agency human behaviour would be meaningless; it is thus hard to envisage how Psychology can do justice to its subject matter without taking it into account. On the other hand, since it is not an objectively existing 'natural' phenomenon, but exists only in the context of socially created rules of moral conduct, it is equally difficult to see how it can be incorporated into a natural scientific Psychology. [See also COGNITIVE PSYCHOLOGY and SCIENTIFIC STATUS OF PSYCHOLOGY]

American Psychological Association (APA)

Principal professional organisation for psychologists in North America. Founded by G. S. Hall (1892), initially with 31 members, it reached 640 members by 1940, then dramatically expanded, following wartime reorganisation, to 88,500 plus 70,500 'affiliate members' in 2000. In 1937 a rival AAAP (American Association of Applied Psychologists) was founded, but was incorporated into the APA in 1944, when 19 'divisions' were established. In 1946 its house journal *American Psychologist* was launched. There are currently (2004) 53 divisions, from 'Addictions' to 'Theoretical and Philosophical Psychology' and 7 regional associations. The APA supports over 50 journals and has its own publishing imprint. Its history has not lacked internal controversy, its sheer breadth often precluding it from adopting clear-cut positions on contemporary social issues (e.g. the Civil Rights campaign of the 1950s–1960s). Moreover, during the latter twentieth century the APA suffered some defections by psychologists who felt it had become too 'soft' at the expense of experimental Psychology.

anthropocentrism Viewing phenomena from a human-centred perspective, typically in terms of their utility to humans. Thus animals may be seen as having been created solely for human benefit (once a common Christian assumption), or a forest's value solely as a source of timber. This should not be confused with ANTHROPOMORPHISM.

anthropology and Psychology

Psychology and anthropology have had a chequered historical relationship. In some respects their remits would appear to have considerable overlap but this has proved deceptive. In Britain, following a short period of harmonious collaboration between anthropologist A. C. Haddon and the psychologists C. S. Myers and W. H. R. Rivers on the 1898 Cambridge Torres Straits Expedition, Rivers himself became preoccupied with anthropological research, laying the foundations for the study of kinship (a central theme in anthropology) and teaching young anthropologists such as A. R. Brown. By the early 1920s, however, the anthropologists were quite explicitly differentiating themselves from Psychology, and the British 'structural-functionalist' school of Brown, Evans-Pritchard and Malinowski pursued a quite independent tack. Malinowski did, however, turn to Psychological topics on occasion, usually from a broadly psychoanalytic direction. In the USA relations were less fraught, notably under Franz Boas at Columbia University, leading to the culture and personality school [see ETHNICITY AND RACE ISSUES] of the 1930s–1960s. A major difference between the British and US situations was that British anthropologists worked in distantly located corners of the Empire, while the North Americans mainly worked with Native Americans, which greatly facilitated collaboration between the two disciplines in field research. The study of cross-cultural differences has frequently brought the two together subsequently, but despite the existence of somewhat vaguely defined subdisciplines, variously called 'Psychological Anthropology', 'Anthropological Psychology' and 'Cross-cultural Psychology', the two camps have rarely since met at the theoretical level. During the late nineteenth and early twentieth centuries many psychologists relied on anthropology for information regarding 'primitive thought', with the French anthropologist Lévy-Bruhl being a favoured source (though not among the CAMBRIDGE SCHOOL or British anthropologists). With the rise of Lévi-Strauss's 'structuralism' in the 1950s, French anthropology, too, went its own way. For the historian it would appear that the boundary between the two disciplines was never rationally defined, but emerged from somewhat arbitrary historical circumstances and personality clashes. Psychology studies PARENTING (see s. 4), anthropology kinship; Psychology studies perception, anthropology colour terminology; Psychology studies NON-VERBAL COMMUNICATION (see s. 5), anthropology studies dancing . . . this is, on the face of it, very odd, and some future rapprochement between the two is surely to be desired.

anthropomorphism Ascription of human psychological traits to non-humans. Especially important in relation to animal behaviour [see LLOYD MORGAN'S CANON], where ascribing such traits to other species has always been tempting. Avoiding anthropomorphism is not, however, straightforward, since precisely which psychological traits and phenomena *are* uniquely human may be the very point at issue.

anti-psychiatry movement A 1960s GROUP (see s. 5) of mainly British PSYCHOTHERAPISTS (see s. 7) who assailed institutional PSYCHIATRY (see s. 7) as dehumanising and oppressive. Leading figures were R. D. Laing, David Cooper and Morton Schatzmann, with widespread growth movement support. The movement focused attention [see COUNSELLING PSYCHOLOGY AND THE GROWTH MOVEMENT] on the social factors involved in MENTAL ILLNESS (see s. 7), the arbitrariness of much psychiatric labelling and the ineffectiveness of much pharmaceutically based treatment and electroconvulsive therapy. Taking patients' experiences as meaningful, they held that, allowed to run their course in supportive conditions, mental illnesses would 'cure' themselves. Drawing on G. Bateson's 'double-bind' notion and EXISTENTIALIST concepts they explained SCHIZOPHRENIA (see s. 7) as a rational response to irrational circumstances, primarily contradictory family communication patterns. The schizophrenic became a scapegoat, carrying everyone else's madness. By the mid-1970s this was losing credibility. The movement may seem embedded in history as a typical 1960s excess, but whatever its shortcomings it irreversibly changed attitudes to mental illness and left a legacy of pragmatically useful insights.

apperception Now obsolete, but once commonplace as a term referring to the total field of CONSCIOUSNESS (see s. 3) as something actively achieved and sustained. From Leibniz down to people like William James, it actually underwent numerous subtle variations in meaning and connotation.

Applied Psychology Unit (APU) Established in Cambridge in 1944 by F. C. Bartlett, with K. W. Craik as director and Medical Research Council (MRC) backing, the APU rapidly established a reputation as a centre for cutting-edge research which, while tackling concrete practical problems, used these as a base for advanced theorising, generally of a cognitivist character. Later directors included H. P. Mackworth, D. Broadbent and A. Baddeley, while R. Gregory and E. C. Poulton were among the many leading British psychologists associated with it. Refounded in 1998 as the MRC Cognitive and Brain Sciences Unit (CBU), under which its agenda has shifted towards clinical studies of brain functioning. During most of its lifetime the APU undertook government-funded research on topics such as cockpit design, performance under extreme conditions, road safety and vigilance, generally in situations involving human–machine interaction. Its unique character lay in its bringing together intellectually elite teams to work on serious practical psychological problems with ample funding resources.

arts and Psychology 'Psychology of Art' has never attained any real presence as a sub-discipline, but this is misleading. Psychology and the visual arts have historically encountered each other at numerous points, the direction of impact varying. Painters have, for example, often paid attention to contemporary theorising on colour perception, notably Turner, *vis-à-vis* Goethe's ideas, and Georges Seurat, the pointillist, in relation to late nineteenth-century theories, while psychologists studying perception have equally often found in the visual arts a source of both data and ideas. Escher's 'impossible' images and Bridget Riley's 'op-art' regularly figure in perception textbooks. Children's art has attracted much attention ever since James Sully's foray into the topic in 1895, being subsequently used variously as an index of INTELLIGENCE (see s. 4 and s. 6), a diagnostic tool and a route for tracking COGNITIVE DEVELOPMENT (see s. 4). In Britain during the 1910s–1930s there was also a solid, if small-scale, tradition of the Psychological study of aesthetics, the leading figure being C. W. Valentine. The greatest contributor to the field however was Rudolph Arnheim, who studied under Wertheimer at Berlin where he did a dissertation on expression. His theoretical allegiance to the Gestalt school largely determined his approach to the nature of art to which he devoted the rest of a long career, which took him to Italy, Britain and finally the USA in 1940, where he joined Sarah Lawrence College. His 1932 *Film as Art* was the first major Psychological study of film, followed in 1936 by *Radio: An Art of Sound*. His *magnum opus* was *Art and Visual Perception: A Psychology of the Creative Eye* (1967, revised 1974). Music, too, has long attracted Psychological attention. For C. S. Myers it was a lifelong interest alongside industrial Psychology, and in the USA Carl Seashore's *Psychology of Music* (1938) integrated the results of a Psychological career devoted to music research, which also yielded the most widely used early Psychological TEST (see s. 6) of musical ability. The major British figure in this field is John Sloboda, director of the Unit for the Study of Musical Skill and Development at Keele University and author of *The Cognitive Psychology of Music* (1985), plus four subsequent books on the subject.

associationism Philosophical doctrine that all mental contents are created by linking together atomic sensations according to a few basic laws of association, e.g. contiguity, succession and contrast. During the latter nineteenth century this was reformulated into the idea of 'ASSOCIATIVE LEARNING' (see s. 2), leading to the classical LEARNING (see s. 3) theories of BEHAVIOURISM.

B

behaviourism Strictly speaking, a Psychological school founded by North American psychologist J. B. Watson, Watson (1913) being considered its founding manifesto. Its key features were (a) rejection of mentalistic concepts in favour of those referring to observable behaviour; (b) the notion that 'behaviour', by analogy with 'genetics', was a phenomenon in its own right (thus abandoning ANTHROPOCENTRISM); (c) insistence on rigorously scientific laboratory-based research methods and quantitative analysis of data; (d) the goal of creating a practical body of expertise in predicting and controlling behaviour; (e) an underlying theoretical assumption that behaviour was primarily determined by the environment (excepting the innate responses of fear and pleasure). It thus rejected the study of CONSCIOUSNESS (see s. 3) and was hostile towards philosophy. Watson's curious life and career have received extensive attention. Behaviourism was developed during the late 1920s and into the 1950s by numerous psychologists who focused on 'LEARNING' (see s. 3) as the key p/Psychological issue, including Guthrie, Tolman, Hull, Skinner, Mowrer, Hilgard and Spence, while the ideas of the Russian PAVLOV were rapidly incorporated (notably his concept of 'conditioning'). Each took behaviourism in their own idiosyncratic direction, Skinner's version becoming the most parsimonious and Hull's the most baroque. Excepting Skinner, this tradition foundered during the early 1960s with the advent of COGNITIVE PSYCHOLOGY and other shifts in disciplinary interests. This was reinforced by growing evidence against its doctrinaire environmentalism coming both from ethology (see s. 2, ETHOLOGY AND SOCIOBIOLOGY and HUMAN ETHOLOGY) and experiments within its own tradition. It nevertheless left a legacy of practical expertise which continues to evolve in areas such as BEHAVIOUR THERAPY (see s. 7) and behaviour modification, as well as helping raise the discipline's scientific rigour and standards of research to those in other disciplines. It is, though, misleading to claim that behaviourism ever entirely dominated US Psychology. While Pavlov initiated a similar movement in the Soviet Union, doctrinaire behaviourism failed to gain much foothold in Britain and western Europe until the late 1940s and 1950s, and even then its success was short-lived. Ironically, however, it raised a number of important theoretical and philosophical issues pertaining to the nature of LANGUAGE (see s. 2), REDUCTIONISM and scientific method, which remain on the agenda.

Berlin school This term usually refers to the Berlin-based school (as distinct from Leipzig and Würzburg) of German psychologists during the later nineteenth and early twentieth centuries, Carl Stumpf's (1848–1936) arrival in 1894 being a key event. Stumpf's primary Psychological interest was in music and tone perception, while philosophically he tended towards a phenomenological position, and E. G. Boring sees him as closely related to Brentano and Husserl. *Tonpsychologie* (1883, 1890), pre-dating the Berlin move, is considered his most important Psychological work. His contemporary as professor of philosophy, Wilhelm Dilthey (1833–1911), should also be included in this group as the proponent of a complex vision of Psychology as both a historical and, in a sense, cognitive discipline, as against a natural science. The Gestalt psychologists Koffka, Kohler and Wertheimer all trained in Berlin under Stumpf, but aside from their concern with phenomenology, owed little to him and should not be classified here.

body-mind problem (BMP) The longest-standing issue in modern western philosophy, the BMP still eludes a solution agreeable to all parties. The question is simply how the mind, or CONSCIOUSNESS (see s. 3), is related to the physical body. Four classic positions may be identified (with numerous internal variations): dualism, idealism, materialism and parallelism. The mid-twentieth-century British linguistic philosopher Gilbert Ryle (1949) may be credited with adding a fifth, which we may call 'linguistic error'. These can be briefly summarised as follows.

Dualism. This was proposed by René Descartes in his 1660 *Passions de l'Âme*, and inaugurated the debate in its modern form. Descartes held that body and mind were different substances, body being extended and mind unextended. This enabled him to advance a physicalistic account of the material world, leaving mind aside as a uniquely human spiritual phenomenon. His solution to how they interacted was notoriously unsatisfactory however; mind and matter interact in the pineal gland of the brain. While few subsequent philosophers accepted Descartes' version of dualism, there being no coherent way of explaining how non-extended and extended substances could ever interact, it initiated a tradition of dualist theorising which continues to the present.

Idealism. Identified particularly with George Berkeley (1710), this is the classic 'it's all in the mind' theory. All versions hold that there is really only one substance, mind, and that the physical world either, as for Berkeley, exists in the mind of God, is somehow an illusion produced by the mind, or exists but is unknowable as it really is. Idealism can be formulated in numerous highly sophisticated ways. The ontological primacy of mind can almost be viewed as a truism, since everything knowable or experienceable must, first, be present in consciousness. One common pitfall of idealism is solipsism, the notion that everything exists in *my* mind. The principal difficulty, however, is that ultimately idealism merely brackets off the entire problem, still leaving the question 'what is the relationship between what seems to be in the mind and what seems to be the material world?' There are some affinities between western idealism and Buddhist doctrines.

Materialism. The converse of idealism, materialist positions hold that there is really only matter. Mind may be explained as either an organic process characteristic of highly evolved organisms or, as T. H. Huxley proposed, an 'epiphenomenon' – a side effect of organic processes exerting no effect on them. Popular among many scientists over the last two centuries, materialism, like idealism, can also be accused of merely bracketing off the real problem. Huxley's epiphenomenalism seems to most to be implausible, since we surely experience ourselves as 'mentally' causing much of our behaviour and indeed doing so on the basis of the mental consequences we foresee ensuing.

Both idealism and materialism are varieties of monism, holding there to be only one 'substance'.

Parallelism. Two broad sub-versions of this can be identified. First, that proposed by Spinoza (1677) of 'double-aspect monism', holding that there is one substance (for Spinoza, an immanent God) which is experienced either as matter or as mind. The second is a version of dualism which argues that there are indeed two substances, but they are non-interacting and events in each proceed in parallel. There have been many formulations of this since Malebranche (1674–6) and Leibniz (1714) first advocated it in their radically different ways. While avoiding some of the difficulties of idealism and materialism, parallelist theories have never convincingly solved (a) how mind and body interact, or appear to do so; and (b) the ontological status of mind itself (the nature of its 'existence').

A common feature of these classical positions, which came increasingly to the fore over the last century, was that it was quite unclear what real consequences followed from any of them. In short, they appear to lack EMPIRICAL (see s. 8) or testable implications. Many philosophers, notably the logical positivists and the later linguistic school, thus claimed that they were really meaningless. This yielded fruit in perhaps the first genuinely new move in the debate for centuries, Gilbert Ryle's *The Concept of Mind* (1949). For Ryle the entire issue was the product of a linguistic error. He famously accused all previous philosophers of adopting the image of 'the ghost in the machine'. The nub of the entire issue was that they had made a 'category mistake'. Simplifying a complex and subtle argument, a category mistake occurs when we ascribe the wrong kind of ontological status to something – thus (Ryle's example) Oxford University does not have the same kind of existence as Balliol College, All Souls College etc. These colleges have a physical existence; collectively they comprise 'Oxford University'; the latter does not exist as a distinct physical thing separate from them. Pursuing this argument with brilliant linguistic virtuosity, Ryle proposed, in effect, that so-called mental phenomena were ultimately behavioural phenomena described in a certain way. Within Psychology he was widely read as having endorsed a version of BEHAVIOURISM. While undoubtedly brilliant, Ryle's work failed to convince everybody, although some of its shortfalls were addressed by the late U. T. Place in 1956, in a paper proposing what he called the 'mind-brain identity' theory.

Psychology, while inheriting the BMP from philosophy, early on attempted to sidetrack the problem, addressing mental phenomena in a pragmatic, empirical fashion and ignoring the ontological philosophical enigma of the status and nature of mind (a major exception being the European phenomenological and existentialist tradition of Husserl and Sartre). The topic returned to Psychology's agenda in the 1980s following the rise of ARTIFICIAL INTELLIGENCE (see s. 3) and computer simulation, which posed the question 'can computers think?'. Since then a number

of people such as John Searle, Roland Penrose, Stephen Pinker and Max Velmans have continued, not entirely unprofitably, to wrestle with the BMP, but its resolution still seems some way off. It should be noted that it overlaps with other issues such as AGENCY, how we ascribe personhood, and REDUCTIONISM.

boundary work   A term recently introduced into history of science to refer to the study of how boundaries between disciplines, fields of research and theoretical schools are created, defined, sustained, changed and breached over time.

brain function and neuropsychology   The studies of brain functioning, deploying sophisticated brain-activity imaging techniques, with which we are familiar today, have a deep historical background. It was only towards the end of the eighteenth century that the localisation of the mind or CONSCIOUSNESS (see s. 3) in the brain became universally accepted among pioneer physiologists. How it then operated within the brain became a crucial question. The issue's subsequent history has seen a continuous oscillation between theories proposing high levels of 'localisation of function' and their opponents (see s. 2,

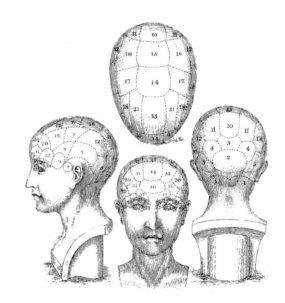

brain function and neuropsychology *Diagram of phrenological 'organs'. Frontispiece of G. Combe,* Elements of Phrenology *(1836). Centre for History of Psychology, Staffordshire University*

LOCALISATION OF BRAIN FUNCTION). The 'localisers' lineage begins with Franz J. Gall's phrenology [see BRAIN FUNCTION AND NEUROPSYCHOLOGY] in the late eighteenth century and resumes later in the nineteenth century in the work of Broca, Fritz and Hitzig and David Ferrier, after a phase of scientific rejection. In the mid-twentieth century Wilder Penfield and his associates used brain-stimulation techniques to explore localisation in a far finer-grained fashion than had been achieved hitherto, while the use of electroencephalography (EEG) (see s. 2, ELECTROENCEPHALOGRAM) began to make an impact from the 1940s onwards. Current studies tend to support a fairly high level of, albeit flexible, localisation and the areas of the brain controlling LANGUAGE (see s. 2), vision, bodily movements, emotional arousal, memory etc. are now well known. The significance of hemispheric lateralisation and asymmetry has also been progressively elicited over the last three decades, although subject to a degree of popular mythologisation. A lineage of anti-localisers may also be discerned, however, from Flourens (1824), whose research played a leading role in undermining phrenology's scientific credibility, to Karl Lashley in the 1930s, who argued for high levels of generalisation of function on the basis, primarily, of evidence supplied by his research on rats. Research in this field has at times (e.g. regarding Colin Blakemore's research on perception) become ethically controversial in so far as it involves intrusive experimentation on live animals. While flourishing as an area of high-tech research, particularly the field now known as 'cognitive neuropsychology', its practitioners can become susceptible to an almost evangelical REDUCTIONISM. The guiding conceptual frameworks for brain-functioning and neuropsychological research have, for the last two decades, primarily derived from connectionist and parallel distributed processing theories within COGNITIVE PSYCHOLOGY.

British Psychological Society (BPS) Principal professional organisation for British psychologists, founded in 1901 as The Psychological Society at a meeting at University College London called by James Sully, 'British' being added in 1905. It received a royal charter in 1965. Membership expanded rapidly after 1919 following a change in admissions criteria introduced by C. S. Myers, but then remained static at around 300 to the end of the 1930s. Expansion renewed after 1945, rising, with no signs of abatement, to 40,000 (January 2004). Membership is open to those completing Society-approved courses. It has numerous sub-disciplinary divisions and sections and gives official 'chartered' status to professional psychologists, exercising disciplinary powers over allegations of professional misconduct. Activities range from conferences to publication of journals and advising government bodies and inquiries. Its headquarters are in Leicester, with a subsidiary London office, but there are seven regional branches, some with their own offices.

C

Cambridge school This term usually refers to the Cambridge-based psychologists of the first half of the twentieth century. Initially the leading figures were W. H. R. Rivers and C. S. Myers, the latter being the driving force in developing Psychology at Cambridge, often funding this himself. F. C. Bartlett, a protégé of Rivers and Myers, became the leading figure after World War I (Myers having left to establish the NATIONAL INSTITUTE OF INDUSTRIAL PSYCHOLOGY). During the 1940s Kenneth Craik joined Myers in conducting war-related research, laying the basis for a British version of COGNITIVE PSYCHOLOGY. This resulted in the establishment of the APPLIED PSYCHOLOGY UNIT and separation from the university Psychology department itself. The key features of the school's approach were, in the earlier years, a somewhat 'social' orientation, which gave way to a hard-headed experimentalism and lack of interest in the kind of PSYCHOMETRICS (see also s. 6) being developed in London by Burt and Spearman (the LONDON SCHOOL).

celebratory history A pejorative term to describe histories which aim simply to celebrate 'great' past events and people [see GREAT MAN APPROACH TO HISTORY]. This is now considered at best naïve and at worst grossly misleading, although it cannot be denied that celebration is one of history's cultural functions.

Chicago school Identified, along with the COLUMBIA SCHOOL, as a major centre for FUNCTIONALISM at the beginning of the twentieth century – due initially to John Dewey's presence, from 1894, alongside sociologist/social psychologist W. I. Thomas. Its leading exponent was J. R. Angell, whose functionalism first gained prominence in opposition to E. B. Titchener's STRUCTURALISM. The school produced several subsequently prominent US psychologists, including J. B. Watson, founder of BEHAVIOURISM. G. H. Mead, another member, went to Chicago with Dewey, but his major work fits uneasily into the 'functionalist' category. The label is shared with the school of sociology, initiated by Thomas, developed by Mead and, during the 1920s–1930s, led first by R. E. Park, then by H. Blumer and E. Hughes. Committed to field studies, and linked with anthropology, this yielded the theoretical approach of 'symbolic interactionism', to have a major impact on SOCIAL PSYCHOLOGY in the 1950s. The boundary between these two 'Chicago schools' is thus unclear after 1920.

child and developmental Psychology Psychological concern with the child is rooted in various educational works dating back to the Renaissance. Subsequent key early landmarks include John Locke's *Some Thoughts on Education* (1692), J.-J. Rousseau's *Emile* (1762) and, in the late eighteenth and early nineteenth centuries, a flurry of texts by Pestalozzi, the Edgworths, Herbart and Froebel, as well as Itard's paper on Victor, 'The Wild Boy of Aveyron' (1799). Evolutionary doctrines of 'recapitulation' gave the child a profounder scientific interest, its growth and maturation being thought to re-enact the stages of human evolution itself. Practical concerns also rose dramatically in the late nineteenth century with the demands of urbanised industrial living and the resulting pressures to expand formal education, thus providing a major 'market' for the newly emerging discipline of Psychology. G. S. Hall in the USA, James Sully in Britain and Wilhelm Preyer in Germany were leaders in the field at this time. The method of keeping observational diaries of children became widely popular, C. Darwin himself producing one of the earliest (1877). Recapitulationism soon declined, but the new doctrines of BEHAVIOURISM and PSYCHOANALYSIS reinforced the field's perceived importance. Piaget in Geneva, A. Gesell in the USA, W. Stern and K. Koffka in Germany and C. W. Valentine in Britain dominated the field during the 1920s–1940s, while J. Bowlby's controversial 'attachment theory' (1969) synthesized psychoanalytic and new ethological perspectives. The latter twentieth century saw a growing focus on the dyadic nature of the parent–child relationship, much work on acquisition of GENDER IDENTITY (see s. 4) and research use of methodological innovations such as the video camera. Erica Burman (1995) and John Morss (1996) have also criticised the 'developmentalist' orientation, which they see as concerned with the child only in terms of its maturation into adulthood rather than as a viable complete person existing in the present. Psychologists' underlying images of the child have always varied; besides the NATURE-NURTURE ISSUE, optimistic vs. pessimistic underlying orientations might be identified. Some historians have tracked how psychologists' shifting views frequently enter popular child-rearing texts, raising questions regarding the nature of the linkage between social pressures and Psychological theorising.

Burman, E. 1995: *Deconstructing Developmental Psychology*. London: Routledge. **Cleverley, J. and Phillips, D.** 1988: *Visions of Childhood: Influential Models from Locke to Spock*. London: Allen & Unwin. **Morss, J. R.** 1996: *Growing Critical. Alternatives to Developmental Psychology*. London: Routledge.

clinical Psychology Although the term was coined by the North American Lightner Whitmer in 1896, the rise of clinical Psychology as now understood largely took place after the 1930s in the USA and 1950 in the UK. Its early fortunes in the USA were particularly chequered. While British PSYCHOTHERAPISTS (see s. 7) were always prominent within the BRITISH PSYCHOLOGICAL SOCIETY, its 'Medical Section' being formed in 1920, their interests and orientations tended to be broadly psychoanalytic in character. By the 1930s Psychological involvement with MENTAL ILLNESS (see s. 7) was rapidly extending in a new direction: the production of diagnostic psychometric questionnaires and other instruments, the mid-century seeing a plethora of these being introduced. The psychologists involved were not generally directly engaged in

233 (Sunday.) Seemed to miss his father in bed last night. Looked all round & then gazed at me with dreadfully puzzled & sad look. The same thing had happened but not quite so noticeably in the study after his bath. Crept quite quickly today on forearms & knees — I think moving arms first. Very wet day so he got rather cross. Cleared up at 4 & he went out, his cross expression changed to smile of bliss when Annie came with hat on & he came in after an hour a different boy.

234. greatly interested in his arm & hand under water in bath. Gazed at them moved them about & lifted out over & over again. Saw him playing with coloured balls on side of playground for first time (Annie says he did yesterday. Holds himself up on one arm & reaches up with other arm frequently when tired.

child and developmental psychology *Page from the child observation diaries of English psychologist C. W. Valentine, probably undertaken during the early 1920s. BPS History of Psychology Centre*

treatment, but worked in supportive and research-oriented roles. These 'clinical psychologists' had to find a niche in a field where professional boundaries between Psychology, PSYCHIATRY (see s. 7) and psychotherapy were already sensitive and tangled. For some years their contributions were largely limited to supplying tests and low-status 'occupational therapy' services. During the 1950s, however, psychologists such as J. Wolpe and H. J. Eysenck began developing a 'BEHAVIOUR THERAPY' (see s. 7) based on LEARNING (see. s. 3) theory principles. In Britain an especially fraught 'boundary' battle ensued at the Maudsley Hospital, Eysenck's base, and within the BPS Medical Section. One upshot was the creation of a BPS Division of Clinical Psychology (now its largest subsystem), the *British Journal of Clinical Psychology* being launched in 1961. Since then, clinical Psychology has greatly expanded on several fronts, aided by the inability of the psychiatric services alone to cope with demand for treatment of non-psychotic conditions. During the late 1960s and the 1970s new theoretical approaches began appearing, such as PERSONAL CONSTRUCT THEORY (see s. 6) (Kelly 1955), clinical applications of which were pioneered by D. Bannister and Fay Fransella (1971). As postgraduate training came on-line after the late 1960s, clinical Psychology boomed in popularity as a career choice, and within the NHS clinical Psychology teams became commonplace within psychiatric institutions and general hospitals. In both the USA and Britain clinical psychologists' roles have become quite diverse, combining assessment and diagnosis with therapeutic work, and branching into sub-specialisms, e.g. concerned with anorexia, child abuse and addiction. (See also s. 7, CLINICAL PSYCHOLOGY)

cognitive Psychology Often described as a 'revolution' (identified above all with G. A. Miller), cognitivism's emergence owed much to the previous GESTALT school and Piaget's developmental studies. Although learning theory's prominence in US Psychology had led to a relative neglect of cognition, the 'revolution' was theoretical rather than in choice of topic, lying in the rise of Norbert Weiner's CYBERNETICS (see also s. 3) and information theory during the 1940s and the birth of the computer. These provided a clutch of concepts – 'information' (technically redefined as a quantifiable phenomenon), 'feedback' and 'programming' – for analysing psychological phenomena and broke an impasse regarding purposive and complex behaviour in which BEHAVIOURISM had become stalled. Miller, Galanter and Pribram's 1960 *Plans and the Structure of Behavior* is generally taken as cognitivism's 'manifesto'. Britain saw a parallel development at the APPLIED PSYCHOLOGY UNIT in Cambridge, where Kenneth Craik, working on military research concerned with human–machine interaction, formulated a similar position, the two meeting in D. Broadbent (1958), which introduced the 'flow-chart' diagram. With U. Neisser's textbook *Cognitive Psychology* (1969), cognitivism came of age, thereafter dominating much Psychology until the present, reconceptualising humans as complex information-processing systems governed by both innate ('hard') and acquired ('soft') 'programmes'. ARTIFICIAL INTELLIGENCE (see s. 3) and computer simulation flourished, reviving philosophical questions about the nature of CONSCIOUSNESS (see s. 3). The Turing test (after A. M. Turing who

proposed it in 1950) argued that an inability to differentiate between the responses to questions of a hidden human and a hidden computer meant the computer had to be considered conscious. The spirit of this 'test' (which has numerous problems) permeated much cognitivist work during the 1970s and 1980s. Rummelhart and McClelland's (eds) *Parallel Distributed Processing* (1986) introduced 'PDP' to a wide professional readership, further advancing cognitivist theorising. With the forging of connections with physiologists which yielded cognitive neuropsychology, some US cognitivists split from Psychology, joining cross-disciplinary departments of cognitive neuroscience. Cognitivism's triumph, however, must be weighed against numerous criticisms e.g. neglect of the social, irrelevance to many psychological questions people consider important, REDUCTIONISM and that it is exploring a computer metaphor which, computers being products of human psychology, is circular in character. Its enormous contributions to our understanding of topics from space perception to memory remain undeniable even so. (See also s. 3, COGNITIVE SCIENCE)

Columbia school Columbia school FUNCTIONALISM differed from the CHICAGO SCHOOL's in adopting a more free-ranging concept of Psychology's remit, less concerned with theoretical issues and often more practical in orientation. In some respects it came to typify the somewhat eclectic, pragmatic character of US Psychology during the 1920s–1930s. Its leading figures included J. McK. Cattell (during the early 1900s), E. L. Thorndike and R. S. Woodworth. As well as promoting orthodox experimental Psychology (Woodworth's 1938 *Experimental Psychology* becoming the standard undergraduate textbook for several decades), the school was particularly concerned with developmental and educational Psychology (Thorndike being a major pioneer of the latter). Among the prominent psychologists associated with the school are J. F. Dashiell, W. F. Dearborn, F. L. Goodenough, H. L. Hollingworth and T. L. Kelley. This is not to be confused with the culture and personality school [see ETHNICITY AND RACE ISSUES], also centred on Columbia, which emerged within anthropology rather than Psychology before linking with neo-Freudian Psychology.

commensurability Theories or levels of explanation and decription are commensurable to the extent that propositions in one can, in principle, be translated into propositions in the other, or more weakly, if there is no essential incompatability between them. The opposite is 'incommensurable'.

contingency/contingent Basically this refers to the occurrence of a phenomenon being dependent on the fortuitous existence of a specific set of circumstances rather than being necessary or predetermined.

counselling Psychology and the growth movement Although not without antecedents, particularly in religious pastoral care, counselling Psychology has, since the 1980s, been a major growth area within Psychology, although academic Psychology is far from monopolising counsellor training and accreditation. Its rise is an interesting cultural development, largely rooted in the so-called 'growth movement' of the 1960s and 1970s.

During the 1950s a number of humanistic psychologists, most notably Abraham Maslow and Carl Rogers, began shifting psychotherapy away from the broadly psychoanalytic approach. Influenced by existentialism, neo-Freudianism and Jung's 'individuation' concept, they viewed their task as enabling people to, in Maslow's terms, 'self-actualise'. The appeal of this soon extended beyond the mentally ill to 'normal' people, who saw in it a route for addressing and overcoming non-pathological psychological problems. The next two decades saw a veritable explosion of widely differing 'alternative therapies', such as Fritz Perls's Gestalt therapy, Janov's primal therapy, 'encounter groups', Ellis's 'rational-emotive therapy' (forerunner of cognitive-behavioural therapy), psychodrama and transactional analysis. The boundary between these and more bizarre or cultist movements, sometimes religious in character, became increasingly blurred, and their leaders could, occasionally, drift into assuming cult-leader status. In Britain there were close connections with the ANTI-PSYCHIATRY MOVEMENT. All this nonetheless helped normalise the seeking of professional help with one's psychological problems, acceptance of 'psychotherapy for normal people', reversing the older perception of seeking such help being a matter of shame and EMBARRASSMENT (see s. 5). Recognition of such problems as POST-TRAUMATIC STRESS DISORDER (see s. 7) further reinforced this. The late 1970s and 1980s saw major moves to control what had become a somewhat anarchic situation, ripe for exploitation, as well as a growing presence of counselling within mainstream health services and large organisations. In Britain BPS accredited counselling courses are now a familiar postgraduate option, paralleled by others approved by the British Association of Counsellors (BAC), membership (or eligibility for it) of one of these organisations now being mandatory for most employment purposes. Governmental regulation of the wider field remains relatively weak, and in most countries little prevents anyone setting themselves up as a 'counsellor', should they so wish.

crime and Psychology

For late nineteenth-century eugenicists like Cesare Lombroso, criminals were paradigm examples of human degeneration, usually physically marked by other 'stigmata', such as facial asymmetry, lack of ear lobes and, in women, undue hairiness. 'Criminal Psychology' and its successor, forensic Psychology, have subsequently exhibited the co-existence of radically different, even opposed, approaches. Some continued trying to identify criminal PERSONALITY (see also s. 6) types. Others located the source of criminality in childhood traumas and pathogenic family RELATIONSHIPS (see s. 5). The more socially oriented, working with sociologists, meanwhile stressed the roles of social deprivation and criminal subcultures. Factors like undiagnosed dyslexia, malnutrition, sex abuse and an extra Y chromosome have also been proposed as predisposing individuals to certain kinds of criminal behaviour. It is easy, in all this, to overlook two simple facts. First, white-collar crime is almost totally ignored. Second, 'crime' is not a natural category, since a behaviour's criminality depends on the existence of a man-made law against it – this can have serious implications when comparing crime rates across CULTURES (see also s. 5) and times: nobody in Britain dealt illegal drugs during the nineteenth century: no British 'juvenile

crime and Psychology *Teenage 'delinquent' of the 1920s immortalised in the frontispiece to Cyril Burt,* The Young Delinquent *(1925). BPS History of Psychology Centre*

delinquents' are so labelled on the grounds of curfew violation. Of course, some behaviours are almost universally held to be criminal, but the legality of many varies widely across time and place. Few psychologists would now accept 'criminality' as a meaningful unitary category or seek monocausal explanations for it. Most of the factors identified above may be implicated some of the time for some types of offence. Psychologists also attempt to identify and devise effective ways of preventing reoffending. As with education [see EDUCATIONAL PSYCHOLOGY] Psychological work in this context is inevitably affected by cultural and institutional factors, its value often being challenged. Over recent decades forensic Psychology has expanded its remit into other areas (though some were anticipated much earlier), including reliability of witness testimony, offender profiling, jury-room behaviour, police training and police interviewing procedures. While undoubtedly having much to offer in this area, Psychology still faces an uphill battle on many fronts, while psychologists themselves have not always been as critical of prevailing social assumptions as they might have been.

culture A more problematic term than is often realised (one authority identifies over 160 definitions!). Within anthropology the concept's theoretical value caused heated controversy during the middle of the last century due to a tendency to treat culture as something separate over and above the individual members of a SOCIETY (see s. 5). (See also s. 5, CULTURE)

cybernetics and systems theory It is generally accepted that COGNITIVE PSYCHOLOGY would not have been possible without the immediately prior theoretical breakthrough, achieved by Norbert Wiener, to which, in 1948, he gave the name 'cybernetics'. This had been preceded by a decade in which the ways in which COMMUNICATION (see s. 2) systems operate had been subject to intense investigation by Wiener, C. Shannon, J. von Neumann, K. Craik (in the UK) and others. This resulted in a complete reconceptualisation, at a very high level of generality, of the nature of complex systems, including the introductions of the notions of positive and negative feedback (Wiener's own major contribution), 'information' (given a technical mathematical meaning) and 'programming'. This was closely related to the development of electronic computers. The adoption of this perspective by psychologists was almost immediate, and to some extent psychologists and neurologists had been involved from the outset (e.g. K. Craik). (See also s. 3, CYBERNETICS)

THE FOUR PIONEERS OF CYBERNETICS GET TOGETHER IN PARIS: left to right: W. Ross Ashby, W. McCulloch, Grey Walter and Norbert Wiener.

cybernetics and systems theory *Four founders of cybernetics. From P. De Latil,* Thinking by Machine *(1956). BPS History of Psychology Centre*

D

demand characteristics   Features of an experimental design which covertly direct subjects or participants to respond in the way desired by the experimenter or which confirm the experimenter's HYPOTHESIS (see s. 3 and s. 8). (See also s. 8, DEMAND CHARACTERISTICS)

E

ecological Psychology Adumbrated by Gardner Murphy's work in the 1930s, ecological Psychology has more recently emerged at the confluence of SOCIAL CONSTRUCTIONISM, humanistic Psychology and MUTUALISM. It seeks to correct the ANTHROPOCENTRISM of humanistic Psychology by viewing humans as necessarily integrated into the total planetary life system. Theoretically, like mutualism, it attempts to transcend simple organism vs. environment distinctions. Taking contemporary 'green' anxieties seriously, ecological Psychology views much human distress as originating in a severance of connections between humans and the natural world. However, there currently appears to be something of a divergence in emphasis between those who view ecological Psychology as a project aimed at integrating Psychology with wider green concerns about the planetary situation and those focusing on it as a theoretical project in the tradition of W. James's pragmatism and J. J. Gibson's ecological theory of perception.

educational Psychology Education is at the confluence of several, often incompatible, interests. 'Fulfilment of the child's potential' is a goal platitudinously accepted by all; in reality, governmental needs for standardisation and certification, economic demands for workers with certain kinds of training, teachers' own ideals and pastoral care, can easily come into conflict. Educational Psychology operates in the midst of this. Its roots lie in

educational Psychology *Educating the muscles. From R. Schulze,* Experimental Psychology and Pedagogy *(1912). Centre for History of Psychology, Staffordshire University*

works cited in CHILD AND DEVELOPMENTAL PSYCHOLOGY. By 1900 there was growing demand for Psychological EXPERTISE (see s. 3) in education; educational Psychology thus became one of Psychology's earliest sub-disciplines, working in three broad areas:

1. Performance assessment and evaluation. Binet and Simon's first INTELLIGENCE (see s. 4 and s. 6) test (1905) aimed to differentiate children with low ability from those simply underperforming. Imported to the USA by H. H. Goddard and to the UK by C. Burt, the test rapidly became widely popular and educational tests of specific ABILITIES (see s. 6) soon followed. While Binet-type tests were administered individually, 'group tests' (see s. 6, ABILITY: GROUP TESTS OF) had appeared by 1920. Testing is now entrenched in education systems worldwide. Originally welcomed as identifying 'natural ability' and countering effects of class and privilege, anxieties are now spreading that the testing 'tail' is wagging the educational 'dog'.

2. Research into teaching methods. Psychologists were always concerned with teaching techniques, studies using experimental vs. control groups originating in this context. Fields such as mathematics and second language learning were completely reformed as a result, while the merits of 'streaming' by ability remain a focus of concern. Work in this area is often guided by theoretical allegiances, behaviourist, psychoanalytic, Piagetian and GESTALT ideas all figuring during the early twentieth century, as cognitivist ones do today. There are intrinsic tensions between this task and the previous one.

3. Diagnosis and treatment of educational difficulties. Once based within the education system, the educational psychologist's task assumed a semi-clinical character, primarily concerned with individual children displaying problem behaviour within school settings, ranging from specific learning difficulties like dyslexia to bullying, ADHD and AUTISM (see s. 6). While using testing techniques for diagnosis, the educational psychologist must also recommend and/or undertake procedures for dealing with these, frequently in conjunction with social work and psychiatric services.

emotion and motivation This coupling established itself as a Psychology course descriptor during the 1930s, but is rather a catch-all category for a wide range of topics. Psychologists have studied 'EMOTION' (see s. 6) from every conceivable direction – from physiological to social constructionist. Despite this they appear to have been covertly constrained in two respects. First, in generally studying only extreme emotions (fear, anger, DEPRESSION (see s. 7), guilt and love), they ignored the milder ones, like boredom, nostalgia, slight amusement and irritation, which suffuse most ordinary waking lives. Second, perhaps related to this, they tended to accept, until recently, the older philosophical assumption of a polarity between emotion and reason, casting emotions as irrational irruptions into our otherwise rational behaviour. This is rejected by modern moral philosophers (e.g. Mary Midgley 1979). After all, our emotions ultimately give our lives any point they may have. The best-known early THEORY (see s. 8) was the 'James-Lange' theory, elaborated by W. James (1890). This held that emotions came *after* behaviour and physiological events – we are afraid because we are running, not the other way round. Although counter-intuitive, this retains a certain phenomenological plausibility (e.g. we often only feel the depth of our distress on bursting into tears). The long-held consensus, however, was that physiological experiments by Walter Cannon (1915) disproved it. Turning to 'MOTIVATION' (see s. 6), K. Danziger (1997) shows how in the 1920s this supplied a bland, theoretically neutral, term giving spurious coherence to highly diverse inquiries into, and theories of, the sources of behaviour. Alternatives ('will', 'instinct', 'conation' and 'desire') possessed connotations unacceptable in the prevailing US Psychological climate, seeing behaviour originating from an inner subjective source. The growing priority in educational and applied Psychologies was, however, with finding techniques to socially control behaviour, requiring reconceptualisation of its source as something amenable to external manipulation. (Danziger's historically documented case cannot, however, be fully summarised here.) 'DRIVE' (see s. 2) also enjoyed a vogue in learning theory, but note the mechanistic nature of this as against 'will', for example. The theoretical-historical point being made here is that while 'motivation' now seems a perfectly natural term, its current meaning was unknown before the 1920s and owed its emergence to quite identifiable contextual factors. It is not, in short, a 'natural category'. (See also s. 2, MOTIVATION AND EMOTION: BIOLOGICAL BASES)

empiricism Philosophical position which holds that all knowledge derives ultimately from sensory experience [see also ASSOCIATIONISM]. In philosophy of science it refers to the positivist belief in the primacy of data-gathering over theorising, or recasting THEORY (see s. 8) as no more than an economic way of summarising EMPIRICAL (see s. 8) data.

epistemology Branch of philosophy concerned with the nature of knowledge – how it is obtained, whence it comes and how it should be evaluated. Commonly used to refer to discussions regarding the merits and nature of scientific research methodologies and the status of the knowledge they yield.

ethical issues in professional practice Being engaged in work directly affecting the well-being of others, which frequently involves face-to-face encounters, psychologists in professional practice can face a range of ethical issues. They also have obligations to employers and fellow psychologists. Without undertaking an exhaustive survey, some issues which commonly arise are the following.

1. Relationship between psychologist and client/patient in a therapeutic context. Besides the long-acknowledged requirement of confidentiality on the psychologist's part, less easy to formalise are the boundaries of what the psychologist should professionally address in such encounters; restriction of the relationship within professional boundaries and management of external encounters; management of situations where personal emotional RELATIONSHIPS (see s. 5) form; and how quality of professional performance can be monitored. Sexual relations between psychologist and client/patient are prohibited in all official codes of practice, at least for the duration of the professional relationship.

2. Conflicts of interest (related to point 3 in ETHICAL ISSUES IN RESEARCH). When a psychologist is employed or commissioned by an organisation, either as an industrial psychologist or in a pastoral/counselling ROLE (see s. 5) dealing with individual employees, potential for conflict of interest is clearly present. The first scenario has long been of concern within industrial and applied Psychology. In the latter case INDEPENDENT (see s. 8) counsellors and therapists providing services to employees should take pains to clarify the confidential character of their work. In some organisations anonymous feedback systems enable the psychologist to 'whistle-blow' without risk to the client.

3. Social and political function of professional practice. Leaving aside ideological questions as such, professional psychologists, especially if working outside academia, should keep a weather-eye on the wider interests their work serves within SOCIETY (see s. 5) at large.

We may aspire to make Psychology a discipline with a unified ethical value system, like medicine, but because psychologists themselves represent a diverse SAMPLE (see s. 8) of the population, their VALUES (see s. 5) reflect at least some of the plurality of values present in that population. Medicine's uncontentious ethical value is the cure of illness and injury, but Psychology enjoys no such position. 'Enhancing human well-being' may be a fine slogan, what it means in practice is perennially debated.

ethical issues in research The latter twentieth century saw a marked rise in sensitivity to ethical issues within Psychology generally. Regarding research this has a number of facets.

1. DECEPTION (see s. 5 and s. 8) and debriefing of participants. While disclosure of an EXPERIMENT's (see s. 8) purpose might undermine its VALIDITY (see s. 6 and s. 8), deception should be minimised. Under most professional codes, researchers must debrief participants and monitor any negative reactions.

2. INFORMED CONSENT (see s. 8) of participants (or guardians). This should be as fully informed as possible regarding the nature of the research. Confidentiality of any personal information obtained should be guaranteed and research reports made anonymous.

3. Research programme goals. The underlying purpose of a research programme may be ethically challenged, even if conditions (1) and (2) are met, e.g. if it is attempting to demonstrate differences between social groups (however defined) which would be detrimental to one of them, or aims at enhancing the social POWER (see s. 5) of a particular GROUP (see s. 5).

4. Use of animals. In medical research this has always been considered necessary for finding cures for human illnesses. This is harder to sustain in Psychology, though sometimes the borderline is blurred. For decades animals were routinely submitted to procedures which would be excluded under most present-day guidelines.

5. Acceptability of research procedures. Even if other conditions are met it may happen that some feature of the research situation risks damaging or upsetting participants. Procedures should thus be open to peer assessment in order to minimise this risk.

6. Legal issues regarding the research topic and rights of participants if the behaviour under examination is illegal and/or participants' levels of SELF-DISCLOSURE (see s. 5) render confidentiality itself unethical, e.g. research on paedophilia or effects of illegal drugs. (See s. 2, DRUG ADDICTION)

7. Issues related to the validity of instruments and apparatus. To maintain research standards only those methods should be used which are already acknowledged as valid, or the validity of which is readily demonstrable.

Ethical issues thus arise from numerous directions, quite rightly constraining a researcher's liberty to conduct whatever research he or she likes. This is a continuously evolving field. Most professional organisations publish extensive ethical guidelines covering the points raised here, and others.

ethnicity and race issues Only a small proportion of Psychology explicitly concerns issues of race and ethnicity, but this has been one of its most contentious fields. Psychological work on race falls into four categories. Due to its controversial character we will focus mainly on the first of these.

1. Race differences. This emerged fairly seamlessly in the late nineteenth century from long-standing white cultural assumptions about and STEREOTYPING of the characteristics of other 'races'. After 1860 evolutionary theory provided a seemingly scientific rationale for belief in race differences, being interpreted as implying that races were at different evolutionary stages – this is now usually referred to as 'scientific racism', but was not homogeneous. Herbert Spencer held that 'primitives' allocated more energy to 'lower' functions and would perform better on these and be more emotional. In G. Stanley Hall's 'recapitulationist' model, 'lower races' were reconstrued as 'adolescent races' which would eventually achieve white-like 'adulthood'. Francis Galton saw things in simpler

hierarchical terms, believing many 'lower races' to be stuck in evolutionary blind alleys. In France, Gustav Le Bon claimed races were in effect different species (a view previously popular during the early 1800s, known as polygenism) and that real communication and understanding between them was impossible. A major step in Psychological research on the topic was the Cambridge Anthropological Expedition to the Torres Straits of 1898, involving leading British psychologists W. H. R. Rivers, C. S. Myers and William McDougall, plus the anthropologist A. C. Haddon, the expedition's leader. Field research on psychophysical phenomena such as perception, hearing and reaction time was conducted for the first time, using the latest scientific equipment and techniques. The results were far from clear-cut but clearly failed to confirm Spencer's theory. Rivers and Myers soon abandoned belief in race differences, but McDougall continued to affirm their reality. R. S. Woodworth's research at the 1904 St Louis Exposition on various groups who happened to be present (including Japanese Ainu and several 'pygmies' from the Congo) was similarly inconclusive, although F. G. Bruner, who conducted

ethnicity and race issues *W. McDougall's crudely racist use of a photograph of an African in* National Welfare and National Decay *(1921), London: Methuen, page 183 (published in the US as* Is America Safe for Democracy?*).*

EXPERIMENTS (see s. 8) on hearing, believed he had shown primitive inferiority – refuting Spencer but supporting race differences. The major factor in the USA, however, was the so-called 'Negro education problem', followed shortly by the wave of east and south European immigration (and, on the West Coast, Chinese). Attention shifted from psychophysical performance to 'higher' functions and, with the advent of INTELLIGENCE (see s. 4 and s. 6) testing, empirical study of race differences in intelligence, which expanded rapidly after 1913. The emphasis moved from theoretical evolutionary 'scientific racism' to data gathering. Results of the 1917 US Army Alpha group intelligence tests reinforced the genre dramatically, apparently showing gross 'Negro' inferiority to American-born whites and lesser, but significant, south and east European inferiority also. A 'race Psychology' sub-discipline emerged during the 1920s, expanding to tackle topics like fatigue-proneness, colour preferences, INHIBITION (see s. 3), memory, musical ability and infant development. By contrast, following the Torres Straits Expedition, British and European psychologists did little further empirical research on race differences (and that tended to be of Jewish and European 'racial' groups). However controversial elsewhere, actual empirical research on 'race differences in intelligence' was (and remains) almost exclusively North American, even apparent exceptions often being US funded or undertaken by US psychologists. After 1930 race Psychology virtually collapsed. Its leader, T. R. Garth, concluded it was methodologically impossible to demonstrate that innate race differences existed, while Otto Klineberg published several devastating critiques. Whether they existed or not, control for environmental factors was apparently impossible, while in-group variation always accounted for more VARIANCE (see s. 8) than between-group variation. The cultural climate had also shifted with the rise of Nazism in Germany and the Depression. Although race-differences research continued at a low level, only with the Jensen controversy of 1969 did the issue resurface on a significant scale. There have since been several oscillations in the genre's fortunes, but as conceptual, theoretical and methodological, not to say ethical, objections have continued to mount, only a minority of psychologists now consider it meaningful.

2. Psychological issues facing non-Europeans in white CULTURES (see also s. 5). An interesting feature of 1930s US Psychology is the sudden rise of applied Psychology studies of problems facing African-Americans and immigrants with regard to SELF-ESTEEM (see s. 5 and s. 7), being victims of PREJUDICE (see s. 5) etc. These were typically undertaken in social work and educational contexts, and the psychologists were themselves occasionally African-American. It has only been since the late 1960s, however, that this type of research has extended beyond the USA, as immigration has increased elsewhere and problems facing immigrants and their descendants have become more obvious. The increasing presence within Psychology of people from ethnic minorities has re-inforced this.

3. Cross-cultural Psychology. From the late 1920s into the 1950s, a 'culture and personality school' emerged and flourished at Columbia University, of which Margaret Mead, Ruth Benedict and Abraham Kardiner are the best-known representatives, and undertook much research exploring the psychological differences between different cultures. Influenced by Freudian ideas regarding child development, they adopted an environmentalist position, seeing these differences as products of different child-rearing practices. While explicitly anti-racist, this approach ironically came to reinforce notions of deep-rooted psychological differences, especially after the mid-1940s, most notably in creating a new, disempowering, 'damaged Negro' stereotype in the 1950s. Cross-cultural Psychology continues as a sub-discipline, but has abandoned the agenda of this early period.

4. Race prejudice and ATTITUDES (see s. 5). Several historians have noted the sudden 'flip' in the 1930s from 'race differences' to 'race prejudice' as the primary target of attention. The history of this genre is closely tied up with that of attitude theory in general within SOCIAL PSYCHOLOGY (see, generally, s. 5). It has been criticised for locating the source of race problems within individual people's psychologies rather than in socio-economic factors, although this charge cannot be levelled at G. W. Allport's *The Nature of Prejudice* (1954), the most comprehensive analysis of the issue. In recent decades this topic has continued to be of major concern, and numerous theories and definitions of racism have been proposed.

It should finally be noted that the extent to which Psychology itself is, wittingly or unwittingly, racist in character continues to be a matter of widespread debate and concern.

Howitt, D. and Owusu-Bempah, J. 1994: *The Racism of Psychology. Time for a Change.* Hemel Hempstead: Harvester-Wheatsheaf. **Richards, G. D.** 1997: *'Race', Racism and Psychology. Towards a Reflexive History.* London: Routledge. **Tucker, W. H.** 1994: *The Science and Politics of Racial Research.* Urbana and Chicago: University of Illinois Press. **Winston, A. S.** (ed.) 2003: *Defining Difference. Race and Racism in the History of Psychology.* Washington, DC: American Psychological Association.

ethology and comparative Psychology

Evolutionary THEORY (see s. 8) cast animal behaviour in a radically new light as promising to illuminate human evolution. The question of what, if anything, is unique about humans acquired intense urgency, Darwin's *Expression of the Emotions in Man and Animals* (1872) assuming the status of a founding text. In Britain D. A. Spalding, G. Romanes and J. Lubbock pioneered the field, followed, in the 1890s, by C. Lloyd Morgan [see LLOYD MORGAN'S CANON]. With the rise of environmentalist theories like BEHAVIOURISM and attacks on the 'instinct' concept during the 1920s, comparative Psychology declined, although white rats assumed a central role in experimental research. Kohler's *The Mentality of Apes* [see GESTALT PSYCHOLOGY – see also s. 3] was a significant exception. In Germany, however, an alternative tradition was initiated by zoologist

PLATE III. SULTAN MAKING A DOUBLE-STICK

ethology and comparative Psychology *The famous chimpanzee Sultan joining two sticks together. From W. Kohler,* The Mentality of Apes *(second edition, 1927). Graham Richards*

J. von Uexküll, who introduced the concept of the *Umwelt*, referring to the world as it existed for a particular animal. Others outside Psychology, such as J. Huxley and S. Zuckerman in the UK, also advanced the study of animal behaviour in natural settings. From these the ethology (see s. 2, ETHOLOGY AND SOCIOBIOLOGY and HUMAN ETHOLOGY) movement, identified with K. Lorenz and N. Tinbergen (see s. 2, TINBERGEN'S FOUR WHYS) in the first instance, emerged after World War II in the theoretical context of the 'new synthesis' – a consolidation of the 'NATURAL SELECTION' (see s. 2) model achieved by geneticists and naturalists during the 1930s, with a new conceptual vocabulary. In the 1970s this was largely transformed into SOCIOBIOLOGY. In the 1960s US psychologist H. Harlow returned to the laboratory to explore ethological hypotheses about the mother–infant relationship ('ATTACHMENT' – see s. 4) in a famous series of studies. Naturalistic animal studies now have a permanent place in the spectrum of research techniques in relation to numerous topics. A divergence in the goals of animal research nonetheless covertly persists. Somewhat simplistically we may identify these as:

1. Minimising human-animal differences by equating apparently distinctively human behaviour to that found in animals.

2. Minimising human-animal differences by humanising animals (e.g. teaching primates sign language).

3. Denying any essential innate character to either (as behaviourists did).

Finally there is the deeper question of the nature of the intense psychological significance animals have for humans. This remains relatively under-researched, being so pervasive that perhaps we take it for granted.

eugenics Coined by Francis Galton (1883) for the use of selective breeding to improve the human race by encouraging the 'fittest' to breed or discouraging the less fit from doing so. Flourished during the years around 1900, eugenics societies being founded in Britain, the USA and various European countries (D. Pick 1989). Initially it appeared to be a logical corollary of evolutionary THEORY (see s. 8), reinforced by the notion of degeneration, and was popular among thinkers of all ideological hues. In the USA compulsory sterilisation of people with learning difficulties and MENTAL ILLNESS (see s. 7) became widespread during the 1920s. Right-wing eugenicists introduced a racial component, especially in Germany and the USA, its co-option by the Nazis legitimating extermination of Jews, gypsies, gays and the handicapped. After 1945, therefore, it fell into disrepute. More recently SOCIOBIOLOGY sometimes verged on reviving eugenics, while the Singapore government explicitly adopted 'positive eugenics', rewarding the highly intelligent for having more children.

Pick, D. 1989: *Faces of Degeneration. A European Disorder c.1848–c.1918.* Cambridge: Cambridge University Press.

evolution and Psychology Evolutionary theory provided Psychology with its first unifying theoretical framework during the late nineteenth century, nearly all psychological phenomena from EMOTION (see s. 6) to child development, and PSYCHOPATHOLOGY (see s. 7) to crowds, being amenable to 'scientific' evolutionary analysis. The early twentieth century saw a decline in the popularity of traditional evolutionary approaches (particularly with regard to EUGENICS and the 'instinct' concept), but both psychoanalysis and W. McDougall's work were based on evolutionary premises. A major revival came after World War II with the wide popularity of the ethology (see s. 2, TINBERGEN'S FOUR WHYS) of K. Lorenz and N. Tinbergen [see ETHOLOGY AND COMPARATIVE PSYCHOLOGY] (see also s. 2, ETHOLOGY AND SOCIOBIOLOGY and HUMAN ETHOLOGY), whose studies of animal behaviour led them to redefine 'instinct' as referring to unlearned species-specific behaviour. Concepts like 'IMPRINTING' (see s. 2), 'displacement activity' and 'innate releasing mechanism' were soon being applied to humans, Bowlby's 'attachment theory' being an early example. By the 1970s concepts from evolutionary biology such as 'KIN SELECTION' (see s. 2) and 'INCLUSIVE FITNESS' (see s. 2) were also being incorporated, culminating in E. O. Wilson's *Sociobiology* (1975). SOCIOBIOLOGY initially presented itself as a challenge and alternative to much of Psychology, but by the 1980s psychologists interested in human evolution were applying Psychological concepts (e.g. Piaget's) to palaeoarchaeological evidence such as stone tools. At this point the scene was highly multidisciplinary, with palaeontology, palaeoarchaeology, physical anthropology, primatology, sociobiology and Psychology all striving for an input into the study of human psychological evolution (Richards 1987). The 'origin of language' topic, long marginalised, also reopened in the mid-1970s. Around 1990 'EVOLUTIONARY PSYCHOLOGY' (see s. 2) emerged, but in the USA this centred predominantly on sociobiological theory and was less interested in human evolution than in evolutionary explanations for problematic or controversial contemporary human behaviour. In Britain a more ethological strand was pioneered by A. Whiten and R. Byrne (1988) and Byrne (1995), who used field studies of primates to explore the evolutionary roots of human INTELLIGENCE (see s. 4 and s. 6). The topic has long been dogged by ideological anxieties inherited from the nature vs. nurture [see NATURE-NURTURE ISSUE] debates of the 1950s and 1960s, in which 'nativism' was cast as inherently rightwing. There is also a risk of re-enacting the late nineteenth-century usage of 'recapitulation' as an explanation for everything, this time composing plausible 'just so' stories around 'inclusive fitness'.

Byrne, R. 1998: *The Thinking Ape: Evolutionary Origins of Intelligence*. Oxford: Oxford University Press. **Byrne, R. and Whiten, A.** (eds) 1988: *Machiavellian Intelligence. Social Expertise, and the Evolution of Intellect in Monkeys, Apes and Humans*. Oxford: Clarendon Press. **Richards, G.** 1987: *Human Evolution: An Introduction for the Behavioural Sciences*. London: Routledge and Kegan Paul. **Richards, R. J.** 1987: *Darwin and the Emergence of Evolutionary Theories of Mind and Behaviour*. Chicago: Chicago University Press.

existentialist Psychology Existentialism is primarily a philosophical rather than Psychological school. Nonetheless the work of J.-P. Sartre and others during the 1940s and 1950s did address psychological issues such as EMOTION (see s. 6), imagination and perception. Existentialist insistence on the individual's total responsibility for what they become through actively creating their identities by their actions, and explorations of how this imperative is evaded, hampered and damaged, greatly appealed to a number of British and US psychologists and PSYCHOTHERAPISTS (see s. 7) such as R. D. Laing and Abraham Maslow. There is nonetheless an overlap with humanistic Psychology in the way the term is used within anglophone Psychology. Strictly speaking it should probably be restricted to the French group. As a distinct movement its duration was fairly short, having virtually disappeared by 1970, but its doctrines have retained an important (often covert) presence in many of the intellectual milieux in which psychologists work.

F

faculty Psychology Analysis of the mind into a set of innately fixed 'faculties' (e.g. thinking, sensation, will, emotion). Usually refers to older Aristotelian, scholastic and rationalist philosophical accounts, or to phrenology and the Scottish realist school. Possesses pejorative connotations when used of modern Psychological theories.

false memory syndrome (FMS) The apparent recovery (usually during psychotherapy) of memories of events (typically of childhood sexual abuse) which never actually happened. This became a focus of controversy during the late 1980s and the 1990s, driven by a wave of cases (especially in the USA) in which patients/clients of PSYCHOTHERAPISTS (see s. 7) mounted lawsuits against close relatives on the basis of these 'recovered memories'. Opponents claimed that these were implanted or suggested by the therapists. False memory syndrome foundations were established on both sides of the Atlantic to promote this interpretation. Coming at a time when child sexual abuse had become a major cultural preoccupation, a balanced judgement proved elusive; fear of absolving genuine abusers being offset by that of devastating injustices being done to those wrongly accused. While the controversy itself has somewhat subsided, the reality of FMS, or the proportion of 'recovered memories' to which it applies, remains unresolved.

falsificationism Doctrine formulated in Karl Popper in rejecting 'verificationism', which held that the meaning of propositions lay in how one verified them. Instead, we should ask what would count as *falsifying* them. Unless this condition is met a proposition or THEORY (see s. 8) is meaningless or tautological. Reflexive application of this principle to itself has, however, obvious paradoxical consequences.

Frankfurt school During the 1920s and early 1930s Frankfurt University's Institute of Social Research hosted a multi-disciplinary group of intellectuals and social scientists including Theodor Adorno, Max Horkheimer, Walter Benjamin, Herbert Marcuse and Erich Fromm, whose legacy endures, J. Habermas and K. O. Apel being its post-World War II heirs. Their 'Critical Theory' initially aimed at revitalising the Marxist tradition, opposing capitalism while sceptical about contemporary party-line Communist thought, and viewing PSYCHOANALYSIS fairly sympathetically. Moving to the USA after the rise of Nazism they adapted in various ways, soon having to downplay their Marxism in the post-1945 cold war climate. Their main immediate Psychological contributions were Adorno et al. (1950) *The Authoritarian Personality* (rooted in earlier work by Fromm), Fromm's neo-Freudian works e.g. *The Sane Society* (1955) and *The Fear of Freedom* (1942), and Marcuse's *Eros and Civilization* (1955) and *One Dimensional Man* (1964). 'Critical Theory' provided an important source for later social constructionist strands of Psychological thought.

free will The philosophical issue of whether humans possess 'free will' has long presented a challenge to those espousing an essentially deterministic scientific worldview, particularly when they seek 'scientifically' to study humans themselves. It should be observed from the outset that the issue originated in Christian theology (it does not appear to have arisen in non-Christian CULTURES (see also s. 5) in a comparable form). Theologically the paradox lay in reconciling the central belief that people exercise moral choice (otherwise notions of sin and judgement become untenable) with belief in God's omnipotence. With the rise of science the issue mutated into one of reconciling a belief in the universal operation of immutable laws of 'cause and effect' with our belief that we exercise control over our own conduct – if this was untenable the principle of moral responsibility on which social order depended was subverted. The free will vs. DETERMINISM (see s. 3) controversy has persisted ever since. Two points may be made which might suggest a way beyond this impasse. First, reiterating what is said under AGENCY, it is misleading to view free will as an EMPIRICAL (see s. 8) property of human nature; it is rather a moral concept arising within the rules we have created in order to manage social life [see also SOCIAL CONSTRUCTIONISM]. Second, following on from this, our actual *use* of the concept in everyday life clearly does not equate it to 'random', as would be the case if it really was opposite to 'determined' in the scientific sense. Random behaviour would appear insane, just as completely 'determined' behaviour would appear robotic. Rather, it refers to our considering ourselves sources of our own actions in pursuit of ends which we have autonomously chosen. But these ends are not arbitrary; they arise from our efforts at integrating our value systems, TEMPERAMENTS (see s. 4) and perceived social obligations. Exercising our free will does not exempt us from the need to account for what we do in terms of 'reasons'. Significantly, when we find all the options are entirely equally balanced we typically do *not* exercise our free will, but hand the choice to fate by tossing a coin!

functionalism 'Functionalism' is one of the worst weasel words in the vocabulary of the human sciences. Depending on context it can refer to:

1. A school of US Psychology which, drawing on the earlier positions of W. James and J. M. Baldwin, began in the early 1900s (J. R. Angell being its first major exponent), initially associated with the CHICAGO SCHOOL and COLUMBIA SCHOOL. This argued that psychological phenomena could be explained in terms of the uses, 'functions', they served for the organism. While at source an evolutionary notion, this could readily be translated into environmentalist terms. Versions of this, in practice fairly pragmatic, approach dominated mainstream US Psychology for much of the twentieth century as it could incorporate lessons from

BEHAVIOURISM while retaining CONSCIOUSNESS (see s. 3) as part of Psychology's subject matter and avoid dogmatic environmentalism.

2. There is a link, albeit somewhat complex, between this and the mathematical sense of 'function' referring to the co-variance of two VARIABLES (see s. 8). Thus experimental and PSYCHOMETRIC Psychological research which sought to identify the covariance of psychological phenomena might also be termed 'functional'.

3. In ANTHROPOLOGY and sociology the term denotes approaches which, again, seek to explain social and cultural phenomena (e.g. food taboos) by identifying the purpose they serve (e.g. avoidance of dangerous foods). This leads to a distinction between 'manifest' and 'latent' functions – the latter being those of which the actors themselves are unaware (e.g. the latent function of Himalayan monasticism and polyandry might be to prevent population expansion beyond that which limited resources can carry).

4. In both senses 1 and 3 it can be used as an oppositional term to STRUCTURALISM, although this term itself means something different in the two contexts.

Functionalism thus varies between denoting a specific historical school within Psychology, a general theoretical orientation differently nuanced in Psychology and anthropology, and a mathematical relationship. In its theoretical senses it is often criticised as excluding the possibility of arbitrary, irrational and simply useless behaviour by assuming that a latent level of functionality must underly it.

funding   At the teaching level little academic attention is paid to the role of funding in determining Psychology's (or any other discipline's) development and agendas. Yet without funding little research would be undertaken, except by the independently rich. It is, however, via funding that SOCIETY (see s. 5) signals which issues it considers important and urgent, thus exerting profound effects on the discipline's agendas in any given place and time. There are numerous funding sources, though, which goes some way to preventing the stifling of diversity and independent initiative. At one extreme we have those funded by individual clients, such as the PSYCHOTHERAPIST (see s. 7). While perhaps limited in scale, this leaves them with a free hand, theoretically. Unsurprisingly many of the most original, bizarre and radical theories have come from this direction. At the other extreme is funding by specific government agencies, and between these a range of governmental, philanthropic and commercial sources, plus universities themselves. Some historians have attempted to unravel more deeply the impacts of, for example, the Laura Spellman Rockefeller Foundation on US developmental Psychology and the Carnegie Foundation on race-related research. A funding relationship does not imply that the funded party is simply doing the funder's bidding – there are negotiations and trade-offs between the interests of the different parties, while what funders usually want is 'the truth', however unwelcome, not echo-like confirmations of prior assumptions or beliefs. Nor are governmental bodies homogeneous; most countries have general funding bodies like the Arts and Humanities Research Board (in the UK) and the National Research Council (in the USA) to support academic research across the board, while the Home Office and Ministry of Defence will have much more constrained interests and exert more direct control. In fields such as INDUSTRIAL AND OCCUPATIONAL Psychology, where funding is supplied by commercial organisations for research into topics they themselves define, psychologists may also face such ETHICAL ISSUES as whether they are on the 'side' of management or the employees. Funding effects remain little explored as yet, despite some forays, but their often covert existence needs to be kept in mind, even if they are not all inherently sinister.

G

---

ganzheit German word meaning 'totality' or 'whole', adopted by some German psychologists in the 1920s who rejected GESTALT PSYCHOLOGY (see also s. 3) but wished to emulate its molar character.

gender and sexuality issues Psychology's historical treatments of sex differences and of the nature of sexuality are particularly convoluted. Regarding sex differences and 'the psychology of women', five overlapping phases may be identified. First, the nineteenth-century use of evolutionary ideas to support traditional western STEREOTYPES (see s. 5) – often, in fact, less ancient than might be assumed. (Images of women as either sexually indifferent or uncontrollably voracious and essentially passive and irrational, only strongly emerged in the late eighteenth century within the new, devoutly Christian and patriarchal middle classes.) Claims that women's brains were smaller, that they were

less evolved than males because their reproductive function kept them closer to 'nature', and that they devoted more energy to the emotions than the intellect, became widespread. Women's relatively 'primitive' character also rendered their criminality peculiarly sinister for such as the Italian Cesare Lombroso. Such ideas peaked in O. Weininger's *Sex and Character* (1906). By the 1890s heyday of feminism, however, works such as Havelock Ellis's *Man and Woman. A Study of Human Secondary Sexual Characters* (1896) were challenging or moderating much of this. The second phase, from around 1900 to the 1930s, was marked less by abandonment of traditional stereotyping as its modulation into a less evaluative tenor. The sexes' 'complementarity' was now stressed, and positive aspects of female traits lauded. Within Psychology Freudian and Jungian ideas were soon reconceptualising the issue, de-emphasising physiological theories in favour of psychological ones. For Freudians

gender and sexuality issues *Beatrice Edgell (1871–1948), eminent British psychologist of the 1920s and 1930s who established psychology at Bedford College, London (then an all-woman college of the University of London) and was a president of both the British Psychological Society and the Aristotelian Society. BPS History of Psychology Centre*

Volume 6 Number 1
Spring 2004

Psychology of Women Section
Review

The British Psychological Society

gender and sexuality issues *Regular newsletter of the Psychology of Women Section of the British Psychological Society, founded in 1988.*

differences originated in differing early developmental scenarios and parental RELATIONSHIPS (see s. 5), while Jungians viewed everyone as psychologically androgynous. The notion that normal women were sexually indifferent was also abandoned. In the USA K. B. Davis's 1929 *Factors in the Sex Life of Twenty-Two Hundred Women* provided the first large-scale EMPIRICAL (see s. 8) data on this, adumbrating the famous 1953 Kinsey Report. The essentially 'natural' character of stereotypical traits remained, however, a deep-rooted assumption, e.g. in L. M. Terman and C. C. Miles' *Sex and Personality. Studies in Masculinity and Femininity* (1936), in which a psychometric questionnaire was developed (this assumption persisted even in the ubiquitous Minnesota Multiphasic Personality Inventory, 'MMPI', in the 1950s). Significant moves on this front came with a third phase, from around 1930 to the mid-1960s, beginning with Margaret Mead's *Coming of Age in Samoa* (1928), *Growing up in New Guinea* (1930) and, crucially, *Sex and Temperament in Three Primitive Societies* (1935), which challenged the universality of European sex roles. The last major work in this tradition was Eleanor Maccoby's edited volume *The Development of Sex Differences* (1967). While far from party-line, many such writers incorporated psychoanalytic ideas. At the end of the 1960s the nearest thing to a revolution in approaches to sex differences came with 'second wave' feminism, following such key, though non-Psychological, texts as Betty Friedan's *The Feminine Mystique* (1963), and consolidated in Germaine Greer's *The Female Eunuch* (1970). This continued into the 1990s. It is difficult to summarise since it yielded a variety of feminist positions, not all mutually consistent, and, moreover, brought several dilemmas into clearer focus even while subverting traditional stereotyping. One core question, shared with race differences, is a tension between denial and affirmation of difference. Each seems appropriate and liberating in certain circumstances. Another development was the differentiation between 'sex' (biological) and 'gender' (psychological), which concedes that biological differences with psychological sequelae exist, but views individual sexual orientation, the nature and meaning of these sequelae and the behaviours and traits considered, gender-typical, as 'socially constructed'. Another outcome was a methodological critique of Psychology's research methods as privileging a stereotypically male mode of orienting to the world (and especially to women); a coldly objectifying, dehumanising 'MALE GAZE' (see S. Harding's *The Science Question in Feminism*, 1986, for an exposition of this problem). Finally it should be noted that many feminist psychologists, like Nancy Chodorow and Juliet Mitchell, were centrally concerned with critiquing and revising PSYCHOANALYTIC THEORY (see s. 6) from feminist perspectives. The beginnings of a fifth phase can now perhaps be detected in the disciplinary institutionalisation of a specific sub-discipline, 'The Psychology of Women', concerned less with sex differences than with psychological issues particularly relevant to, or currently preoccupying, women e.g. premenstrual tension, EATING DISORDERS (see s. 7), integration of work and home life, and the menopause. The post-1970 situation should be understood against a huge increase in women's representation within Psychology (being the majority on British undergraduate courses for at least two decades). As a discipline Psychology was always relatively more accessible to women, but as in other sciences they remained a clear minority until the latter twentieth century. (There is now a historical literature on women psychologists, e.g. A. N. O'Connell and N. F. Russo (eds), *Women in Psychology. A Bio-Bibliographic Sourcebook*, 1990.) Whether the future holds further developments within the feminist tradition or a period of 'normalising' retrenchment and recoupment of older positions is uncertain, but lines of division between feminists and their opponents, once clear-cut, have become irretrievably blurred, and few psychologists any longer wholeheartedly identify with the latter.

Turning more briefly to human sexuality in general, most nineteenth-century Psychological writers tended uncritically to endorse prevailing cultural attitudes, which had, unfortunately, become highly conflicted during the post-1830 period. Varieties of sexual 'deviance' were obsessively catalogued, most famously in Krafft-Ebing's *Psychopathia Sexualis* (1886), while diatribes against the evils of masturbation were routine in popular advice manuals for the young. Explicit (non-medical) discussion of sexual matters, though, had become taboo and was felt to be disgusting and corrupting. The rise of PSYCHOANALYSIS after 1900 and Havelock Ellis's series, *Studies in the Psychology of Sex*, contributed to the increasing erosion of this taboo. By the 1920s younger Psychological writers were rejecting Victorian censorship, often deploying Freudian arguments about the dangers of REPRESSION (see s. 7) and ignorance, albeit couching their views as decorously as possible. In Britain Marie Stopes' pro-contraception campaign in the 1920s breached the norms of what had hitherto been publishable, and when eminent Methodist preacher and PSYCHOTHERAPIST (see s. 7) Leslie Weatherhead published his remarkably frank *The Mastery of Sex through Psychology and Religion* (1931), older restraints had clearly been irrevocably broken. If restraints on discourse had gone, many older attitudes remained; homosexuality was a pathology, sex outside marriage was wrong and masturbation was strongly to be discouraged even if no longer considered positively perilous. It is hard in all this clearly to differentiate specifically Psychological from wider cultural developments. The mid-century academic landmarks, the Kinsey Reports of 1948 and 1953 on sexual behaviour in the human male and female respectively, and W. H. Masters' and V. E. Johnson's *The Human Sexual Response* (1966), both originated outside Psychology. What is perhaps only becoming clear retrospectively is that by the 1960s concerns about sexual morality were paling into insignificance in the light of recent historical traumas and prospects of nuclear war. Tangentially the ethologists were also throwing sexual behaviour into a different perspective, e.g. casting doubt on the alleged abnormality of homosexual behaviour and sex for non-reproductive purposes. When, during the 1970s, homosexuality ceased being considered pathological, Psychology was only reflecting changed social attitudes initiated by the gay liberation movement. If a trend is discernible since then it has been a continued decline in the willingness of psychologists and psychotherapists to pathologise any but the most extreme forms of sexual 'deviance', while the internet has enabled even those with the most bizarre tastes to 'normalise' these by finding fellow-spirits. So far

Psychology has surely failed to engage really productively in analysing the contemporary social psychological situation with regard to human sexuality.

Geneva school Term generally applied to the Geneva group of developmental psychologists based at the Institut Rousseau and led by Jean Piaget, whose own later work extended into broader theoretical and philosophical realms. E. Claparède should perhaps be assigned to this 'school', as a pioneer developmental psychologist and early supporter of Piaget. Piaget's 'stage' theory of child development was among the most influential Psychological theories of the twentieth century, although its impact in the USA was somewhat delayed. Among Piaget's colleagues, associates and collaborators at various periods were Barbel Innhelder, Alina Szeminska, Howard Gruber and D. E. Berlyne. Piaget's work is now retrospectively viewed as anticipating the approaches to child development adopted by COGNITIVE PSYCHOLOGY, and had a particular influence on Jerome Bruner.

Geneva school *Jean Piaget (1896–1980), leader of the Geneva School. BPS History of Psychology Centre*

Gestalt Psychology German theoretical school led by Max Wertheimer which flourished from 1911 to the mid-1930s. The key features of this were its holistic, anti-reductionist orientation and its incorporation of scientific ideas from contemporary physics, most centrally the notion of the 'field'. Gestalt Psychology was primarily concerned with identifying the laws or principles governing how behaviour and phenomenological experience are organised (such as 'figure-ground distinction', 'contrast' and 'closure'). This led it to pay particular attention on the one hand to visual perception and on the other to problem solving and cognition. While holistic, Gestalt THEORY (see s. 8) was underpinned by a belief that the structure of subjective experience was isomorphic with underlying physiological processes, which led W. Kohler into speculations about brain processes. Gestalt Psychology petered out during the post-World War II period, following a time during which its proponents, exiled in the USA, had influenced US Psychology in a number of respects, notably within SOCIAL PSYCHOLOGY and studies of PERCEPTION. The complex relationship between their work on problem solving and the subsequent rise of COGNITIVE PSYCHOLOGY has been explored in D. J. Murray (1995). For Wertheimer and his leading colleagues, K. Koffka and Kohler, the project of Gestalt Psychology was ultimately to rescue Psychology from what they saw as the philistine aridity of reductionist BEHAVIOURISM, and doing so within the most sophisticated scientific terms available. Their work left several iconic legacies in Kohler's studies on chimpanzee problem solving on Tenerife, published in English in 1925, and numerous VISUAL ILLUSIONS (see s. 3) such as the faces/vase figure. The relationship between Gestalt Psychology and Fritz Perls' Gestalt therapy is fairly tenuous, and they are very different in spirit. The clearest English-language statement of the theory is K. Koffka (1935), while M. Wertheimer's posthumously published *Productive*

Gestalt Psychology *Version of the well-known faces/vase figure used to demonstrate figure-ground reversal effect. From R. L. Gregory, Eye and Brain: the Psychology of Seeing (1966). BPS History of Psychology Centre*

Thinking (1945) has enduring value as an intrinsically stimulating work. In the USA M. Henle was a major figure in conserving and promoting the Gestalt legacy during the latter twentieth century. An attempt by W. Metzger to revive its German fortunes in revised form after World War II failed, not least because he had remained in Nazi Germany and was thus personally compromised. (See also s. 3, GESTALT PSYCHOLOGY)

Ash, M. G. 1996: *Gestalt Psychology in German Culture 1890–1967: Holism and the Quest for Objectivity*. Cambridge: Cambridge University Press. **Koffka, K.** 1935: *Principles of Gestalt Psychology*. New York: Harcourt Brace; London: Kegan Paul, Trench & Trubner. **Murray, D. J.** 1995: *Gestalt Psychology and the Cognitive Revolution*. New York: Harvester-Wheatsheaf.

graphology The study of how handwriting reveals the writer's character. Attempts at rendering this scientific began in the late nineteenth century, and it remained popular in Germany in the 1920s and 1930s. While not fallacious, the phenomenon still resists scientific analysis largely due to the sheer number of FACTORS (see s. 8) involved.

Graz school Austrian school of Philosophy/Psychology seen as a precursor to GESTALT PSYCHOLOGY (see also s. 3). Its leading representatives were A. Meinong (at Graz 1889–1920) and C. von Ehrenfehls (there only from 1885–89). Both were concerned with 'form perception' or 'form qualities' in PERCEPTION and the difficulty of reconciling this with elementistic theories.

Great Man approach to history View, strongly espoused by Thomas Carlyle, that history is determined by the actions of 'Great Men'. Now rejected by historians because it ignores so many other factors and, additionally, has negative ideological connotations. Unlike CELEBRATORY HISTORY it does, however, embody a particular explanatory thesis.

PLATE V

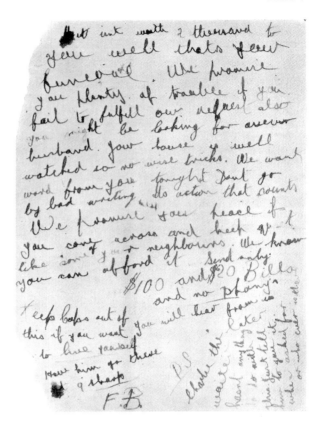

ANOTHER ANONYMOUS LETTER OF BLACKMAIL
(Page 2)

graphology *A blackmailer's letter analysed in Robert Saudek, Anonymous Letters; A Study in Crime and Handwriting (1933), a serious attempt at bringing scientific methods to bear on graphology.* BPS History of Psychology Centre

H

Harvard school   The term 'Harvard school' does not denote a group sharing a common theoretical orientation, but rather a succession of major psychologists, beginning with William James and his successor Hugo Munsterberg, who have been based there, although only in 1934 did E. G. Boring establish Psychology as a department independent of philosophy. These include the social psychologist G. W. Allport, the PERSONALITY (see also s. 6) theorist H. Murray, S. S. Stevens (leading mid-twentieth-century psychophysicist), B. F. Skinner (the idiosyncratic but enormously influential behaviourist), Jerome Kagan (the developmental psychologist) and G. A. Miller (the pioneer cognitivist). Unsurprisingly the school has rarely presented a harmonious picture, but the prestigious status, wealth and liberal heritage of Harvard University provided an atmosphere in which creative and independent-minded psychologists were often able to flourish. This tradition continues today, with the diverse figures of Daniel Schachter, Stephen Kosslyn and Steven Pinker all being current faculty members.

hormic Psychology (W. McDougall)   William McDougall (1871–1938) was the best known British psychologist of the early twentieth century, his 1908 *Introduction to Social Psychology* becoming one of the most successful Psychology texts ever (23 editions by 1936). In 1920 he was invited to Harvard, but his Psychology was at odds with contemporary US developments. In 1927 he moved to Duke University for the remainder of his career. He called his position 'hormic Psychology'; it was, though, a school with but one member. His two central tenets were belief in mind-body dualism and insistence on the validity of teleological or 'purposive' explanations. Both set him apart from his contemporaries. A prolific populariser and controversialist, McDougall remained prominent, but his creativity waned after his emigration. His advocacy of EUGENICS and pro-race-differences argu-

ments further damaged his reputation, but the breadth of issues he addressed and the numerous 'anticipations' found in his works suggest he is owed a reappraisal.

hormic Psychology (W. McDougall) *William McDougall in a haughty pose. BPS History of Psychology Centre*

idiographic methods   The case history was long central in medical research, figuring prominently in late nineteenth-century Psychological work emanating from psychiatric contexts. The term 'idiographic method' is now used to refer to methods, such as this, where individuals are explored in depth, as opposed to NOMOTHETIC METHODS using large numbers of participants/subjects. They enjoyed some renewed popularity among US PERSONALITY (see also s. 6) theorists during the late 1930s–1950s, Henry Murray, John Dollard and G. W. Allport being among the keenest. LONGITUDINAL RESEARCH may also possess a somewhat idiographic character, even if involving large numbers of cases, since it provides extensive data of various kinds on individuals accumulated over long periods of time. It would be erroneous to see the issue as being which method is more scientific (as was once commonly assumed); rather each is appropriate for tackling certain kinds of question. Much large-scale research in any case combines elements of both. (See also s. 8, IDIOGRAPHIC)

industrial and occupational Psychology
Anticipated by 'Taylorism' in the USA and wartime studies of FATIGUE (see s. 7), these appeared across Europe and North America as major facets of a new applied Psychology after 1918. There was tension from the outset between those adopting the managerial perspective of increasing productivity and efficiency and those who wanted to create harmonious working environments where all parties' interests were acknowledged. The former predominated in the USA, the latter in Britain and Europe (where industrial relations had reached potentially revolutionary levels of hostility). In Britain the major pioneer was C. S. Myers' NATIONAL INSTITUTE OF INDUSTRIAL PSYCHOLOGY (NIIP). In the USA the most influential research was the 'Hawthorne Experiments', 1927–32, conducted by Elton Mayo but only fully reported in Roethlisberger and Dickson (1939). This has been a focus of controversy ever since, a thorough critical historical account being Gillespie (1992). By the 1930s occupational or vocational Psychology was separating from industrial Psychology, and then benefited from World War II involvements in military selection. This field has been less controversial, although certain methods recently used for selecting high-level managers perhaps verge on the edge of the ethically permissible. These fields did not simply 'apply' knowledge obtained from academic Psychology; on the contrary they provided considerable input into fields such as MOTIVATION (see s. 6) and cognition. During the post-1945 period the status of industrial Psychology appears to have declined in the UK and its institutional base atrophied, the NIIP folding in 1975. Practised predominantly in the commercial world it suffered further from the confidential nature of much of its research. The high-status APPLIED PSYCHOLOGY UNIT survived, however, largely by shifting from military to other governmentally funded fields as the former declined,

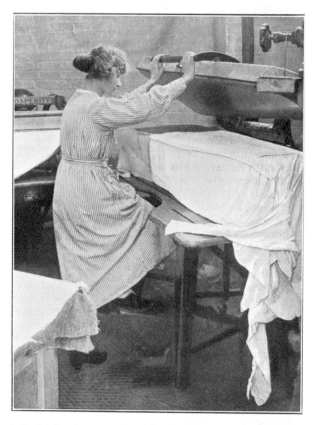

industrial and occupational Psychology *Early industrial psychology: analysing the movements of a laundry worker. From May Smith,* Some Studies in the Laundry Trade *(1922). BPS History of Psychology Centre*

while at the University of Sheffield a Social and Applied Social Psychology Unit also managed to swim against the tide. The current situation is variegated and hard to summarise. Often accused of being an area where Psychology simply 'serves the system', the reality is that both industrial and occupational Psychology have at times been agents of change and sources of criticism, and sometimes simply reflected rather than positively 'served' the status quo.

influence   The unqualified use of the term 'influence' in historical (or any other) discourse is to be avoided since it explains nothing. The precise level and nature of the 'influence' in question always needs to be spelled out.

institutionalisation of Psychology   No scientific discipline can really be said to have established itself until it has acquired an institutional character of some sort. Historical interest in this has been a prominent theme in history of science over the last three decades. Institutionalisation may take several forms: a professional society, the publication of a journal, a presence within the university system – preferably specialist departments and laboratories – a recognised system of professional accreditation and certification of membership or an officially recognised research institute. These may be reinforced by such activities as holding conferences and producing expert reports on topics within its field of expertise which are of broader concern. The key features of institutionalisation are that it (a) creates a community of practitioners who mutually recognise each other as peers, (b) polices entry into this community and conduct within it, and (c) formalises the discipline's cultural presence and gives it a voice in public life. A further, psychological consequence of this is that it creates a professional IDENTITY (see s. 4 and s. 5) for those within the discipline. The history of a discipline in terms of relevant texts thus usually extends back much further than its history as a formal, institutionalised enterprise or project. Nonetheless institutionalisation does not simply happen overnight with the founding of a single society or journal, for example. It would be more accurate to think in terms of degrees or levels of institutionalisation. In the case of Psychology we may identify a number of events marking its gradual institutionalisation into an internationally organised, professionalised discipline.

The first indication of something like a community of psychologists tends to be the appearance of a specialist journal. In Britain the journal *Mind* in 1876 is often seen in this light, although philosophy remained a major concern of its founders, *The British Journal of Psychology* not being launched until 1903. In Germany Wundt's foundation of *Philosophische Studien* in 1880 has perhaps a better claim, despite its name, to being the first Psychology journal in the modern sense. The *American Journal of Psychology* first appeared in 1887 and in France the *Revue Psychologique* started in 1895. After 1900 the number of different journals expanded rapidly, serving the emerging sub-disciplines and theoretical schools. More literally, 'institutional' is the creation of university departments and laboratories. Here again Wundt's creation of a laboratory at Leipzig University in 1876 has long been acknowledged as experimental Psychology's founding event (although William James had introduced a small demonstration laboratory at Harvard in 1874). Although often remaining subordinate to philosophy, laboratories, and occasionally departments, of Psychology began springing up throughout Europe and North America during the 1880s and 1890s. Examples of laboratories include, in the USA and Canada: Johns Hopkins (1883), Columbia (1891), Wisconsin (1888), Toronto (1889); in Britain: University College London (1897) and Cambridge (1898); in France: Sorbonne (1889); in Belgium: Louvain (1891); and in Germany: Breslau (1894) and Würzburg (1896), numbering about 23 by 1900, in which year even Buenos Aires saw a laboratory being founded. National societies were founded alongside these developments, such as the AMERICAN PSYCHOLOGICAL ASSOCIATION (1892) and the BRITISH PSYCHOLOGICAL SOCIETY (1901). While international societies did not appear until the mid-twentieth century, an international dimension was present from the beginning: the First International Congress of Psychology (in Paris) was held in 1889, and they have

been held at regular intervals (usually four years) ever since, the 22nd being held in Leipzig in 1980. Non-academic organisations, such as the NATIONAL INSTITUTE OF INDUSTRIAL PSYCHOLOGY, and the incorporation of Psychological services into the health system (e.g. child guidance clinics) represent a further level of institutionalisation, signifying the penetration of Psychology into the CULTURE (see also s. 5) at large. Finally, recent decades have seen a growth in formal accreditation by professional societies, such as the British Psychological Society's introduction in 1987 of 'Chartered' status for specialist practitioners in different non-academic fields. This formal endorsement of an individual's status can then be used by potential employers, and gives the Society powers to discipline and suspend individuals. However necessary, institutionalisation nevertheless comes at a price, particularly for a heterogeneous discipline like Psychology. The heaviest of these is that it can come to act as a brake on theoretical innovation and reflexive critique, as professional organisations, research organisations and academic departments have to negotiate with contemporary socio-political realities, while having to some extent a vested interest in maintaining the status quo and stifling more fundamental criticisms, whether of the predominant theoretical parties or of the discipline's social roles. This can produce frustrating delays in facing the inevitable, e.g. in Psychology, resistance to the setting up of subdivisions or sections representing women, gay and lesbian or ethnic minority concerns. This merely exacerbates tensions to no purpose. The effect of institutionalisation is then to introduce a social organisational dimension to the way a discipline develops and operates, with all the accompanying internal politicking and bureaucracy that inevitably entails. For the aspiring professional psychologist it is well to bear this in mind and devote at least some energy to understanding this facet of the situation.

intelligence and ability testing Since the Binet-Simon intelligence test was invented in 1905 intelligence and ability tests have become standard features of modern western CULTURES (see also s. 5), used in contexts from education to vocational guidance. Initially useable only on a one-to-one basis and taking long to complete, intelligence tests developed rapidly from the 1910s into the 1930s. The original use of the mental age to chronological age ratio as a measure of intelligence, inappropriate for people beyond their mid-teens, was replaced by using degree of DEVIATION (see s. 8) from population NORMS (see s. 8), while group tests largely replaced individual tests. Despite the success of IQ (see s. 6) testing, theoretical controversy persisted. British psychologist Charles Spearman, who pioneered FACTOR ANALYSIS (see s. 6 and s. 8), strongly advocated a general intelligence factor '*g*', with which more specific types of intelligence (mathematical, verbal, spatial, etc.) correlated. In the USA L. L. Thurstone and T. L. Kelley disagreed, arguing for a multitude of individual types of intelligence. The issue, centring on technical statistical questions regarding the nature of factor analysis, cannot be pursued here. The notion that we possess a measurable IQ in any case proved irresistible. This is not very helpful in many circumstances, however, and greatly stimulated by educational demands, hundreds of tests of specific ABILITIES (see s. 6) soon proliferated alongside general IQ tests. IQ testing has

intelligence and ability testing *An early American intelligence test: Healey's 1911 'Picture Completion Test'. Centre for History of Psychology. Staffordshire University*

subsequently figured centrally in the controversy surrounding the NATURE-NURTURE ISSUE (especially in relation to race differences), as well as being the subject of intense and sustained methodological and conceptual arguments too complex for summarisation here, while some of the ways it has been used in education have become the target of ideological attack. Intelligence and ability tests may undoubtedly serve as quick and effective assessment and diagnostic instruments. Their development also shed much light on the complex nature of human 'intelligence'. There have, though, been some who have sought to treat '*g*' as the engine of all human achievements. Over the last few decades the trend has been in a more Thurstone-type direction, particularly since R. J. Sternberg (1990), and with the introduction of the idea of 'EMOTIONAL INTELLIGENCE' (see s. 6). [See also ABILITY: INDIVIDUAL TESTS OF and ABILITY: GROUP TESTS OF, s. 6]

Sternberg, R. 1990: *Metaphors of Mind: Conceptions of the Nature of Intelligence*. Cambridge: Cambridge University Press.

internalist vs. externalist history 'Internalist' history of science studies the internal development of a discipline or research tradition as a rational, progressive process. 'Externalist' history explores the numerous 'contextual' factors which variously facilitate, hinder and guide scientific work. Introduced by sociologist Robert K. Merton in 1938 (who ironically opposed later strong

'externalist' approaches), this distinction has now been largely superseded.

introspection In Psychology 'introspection' generally refers to the methodology of the nineteenth-century German Psychological pioneers Wilhelm Wundt, Gustav Fechner and their successors, including the Englishman E. B. Titchener, who carried their approach to the USA (although his fidelity to their doctrines is much debated) and the WÜRZBURG SCHOOL of Oswald Külpe and his associates. The key assumption was that scientific knowledge of the nature of CONSCIOUSNESS (see s. 3) (particularly the basic elements or processes of feeling and sensation) may be acquired by disciplined procedures of self-observation. This belief, less formally articulated, also underlay the Psychology of William James and other North American pioneers. After 1900 introspectionism suffered numerous blows, from BEHAVIOURISM (which insisted that only observable behaviour could be the objective focus of scientific study) and PSYCHOANALYSIS (which challenged the accuracy of subjective reports), to irreconcilable divisions among the introspectionists themselves. Radical behaviourists aside, psychologists did not, however, entirely reject 'consciousness' or 'mind' as a legitimate field of study, but strove to devise methods other than introspective reporting to gain scientific access to it. The key methodological problem is that only the experiencer has access to the phenomena of consciousness, thus its 'objective' scientific scrutiny seems impossible. On the other hand, a Psychology without consciousness appears to be a contradiction in terms, and in truth we can only actually feel we understand Psychological texts and propositions by an introspective effort at grasping their meaning. Moreover, in so far as the discipline strives to solve human problems and address psychological distress, its ultimate goal is to enable people to achieve particular states of consciousness. While introspection, as a method of research, has long been abandoned, many of modern Psychology's methods thus remain centred on people's testimonies as to their experience, whether in answering psychometric questionnaires or, more directly, in EXPERIMENTS (see s. 8) on memory. If the controversy regarding 'experimental introspection' is long over, the underlying question of the nature of consciousness *per se* persists as a perennial conundrum within philosophical Psychology [see BODY-MIND PROBLEM], controversies regarding computer simulation and artificial intelligence, and EVOLUTIONARY PSYCHOLOGY (see s. 2), where the evolutionary function of consciousness remains unresolved.

L

Lamarckism The THEORY (see s. 8) that acquired characteristics can be inherited. This was finally rejected by geneticists around 1920. The late eighteenth-century French scientist Lamarck, after whom it is named, did not in fact propose it in the simple sense in which it is now understood.

language and psycholinguistics The Psychological study of LANGUAGE (see s. 2) has, given the psychological paramountcy of the phenomenon, been strangely varied and fitful. A number of themes may be discerned, but it would be misleading to suggest that the development of most of these displays a smooth, continuous, progressive character. The closest to doing so has been the study of children's acquisition of language, which began in the late nineteenth century with work by James Sully and E. von Meumann, continued with E. Claparède and J. Piaget during the first half of the twentieth century and has remained a major topic within CHILD AND DEVELOPMENTAL PSYCHOLOGY ever since. More chequered has been the career of the 'thought and language' debate. The traditional image was that language was no more than a tool we use for communicating pre-existing thoughts and ideas. Though it had long been acknowledged that our language for referring to psychological, mental phenomena was all ultimately metaphorical, this insight was rarely followed through, beyond being seen as grounds for warning the unwary against being misled by physical analogies. There are two major facets to this topic. The first is whether, or how far, language is necessary for human thought – would we be able to think at all without it? The second is how far the parameters of what is thinkable are set by the language we have available. The 'Sapir-Whorf HYPOTHESIS' (see s. 3 and s. 8) proposed in the 1930s, but brought together in J. B. Carroll (ed.), *Language, Thought and Reality* (1956), argued in strong terms that their different kinds of GRAMMAR (see s. 4) affected the ways in which people with different languages thought. There are certain paradoxes in the strong version of this (since formulating it and illustrating it seem to entail negating it), but equally some almost common-sense grounds for believing that it must have at least a grain of truth. After several decades of routine dismissal by cognitivists, the thesis, in reformulated terms, is now again being taken seriously (D. Gentner and S. Goldin-Meadow (eds) 2003). The 'thought and language' issue has surfaced at various points: Ogden and Richards' *Meaning of Meaning* (1923), R. Brown's *Words and Things* (1958), several other US writers such as G. A. Miller in the early cognitivist climate, British linguistic philosophy in the 1940s and 1950s, and subsequently in the contrasting contexts both of AI and computer simulation and social constructionist theorising. In 1957 N. Chomsky's *Syntactic Structures* effectively revolutionised Psychological ideas concerning the nature of language and language acquisition by proposing that there existed an innate 'deep' grammatical structure underpinning all human languages. This initiated a great expansion of research in the field of psycholinguistics, which lasted into the 1970s, but despite its apparent profundity it was unclear quite what the concrete implications of Chomsky's THEORY (see s. 8) were. Two further, quite different, strands must also be mentioned. First, the study of language pathologies, on the borderline with physiology and PSYCHIATRY (see s. 7). Following E. Broca's 1861 discovery of the 'speech area' in the left hemisphere of the brain there has been a constant, if sometimes slow, advance in the identification of speech pathologies in relation to brain damage, yielding a lengthy catalogue of APHASIAS (see s. 3) and AGNOSIAS (see s. 3). This continues, today's researchers employing advanced magnetic resonance scanning techniques. Other language pathologies, such as stammering and stuttering (not quite synonymous in fact) and, since the 1970s, dyslexia, should also be included in this strand. Second, there are the studies of social class and subcultural differences in language use, exemplified in the work of B. Bernstein (which differentiated between 'elaborated' and 'restricted' codes) and the more wide-ranging investigations of M. A. K. Halliday. This is often termed sociolinguistics and overlaps to some degree with social Psychological research on the nature of conversation and everyday discourse. Mention might also be made of the revival during the 1970s of the 'language origins' debate, long in abeyance due to the apparent impossibility of it yielding to scientific investigation. While still unresolved, this has since produced numerous stimulating hypotheses and made some genuine progress when considered in conjunction with palaeoanthropological and fossil evidence. S. Pinker's best-selling *The Language Instinct* (1994) was a highly successful attempt at integrating this. The nature of psychological language itself, though, has still received relatively little attention, despite its theoretical importance (but see G. Richards 1989 and K. Danziger 1997).

One perennial difficulty for psychologists working in this field is the multi-disciplinary nature of scientific and academic concern with language. They find themselves operating at the intersections between linguistics, philosophy, literary criticism and neurophysiology, for example. This renders the establishment of a coherent Psychological discipline of 'Psychology of Language' extremely difficult. The fact that language is the very medium in which much Psychological research is conducted only gives the situation a further twist. Failure to grasp philosophical insights into the nature of language and meaning has on occasion led psychologists badly astray, as for example in late 1930s and 1940s US social Psychological studies, which showed that whether people agreed or disagreed with a proposition could be affected by who they believed made it (Jefferson or Karl Marx being used). This was interpreted as evidence of the ease with which they could be 'influenced' by the status of a 'source', as if the meaning of the proposition was somehow self-evidently contained within the words themselves.

S. Asch, coming from a more sophisticated philosophically informed direction, completely demolished this view, demonstrating what seems retrospectively obvious, that we quite rationally interpret the meanings of statements in the light of what we know of the persons who make them (S. Asch 1952). In conclusion, language should not be viewed as one psychological phenomenon among many which psychologists have sought to investigate, but rather as a pervasive background issue which can force its attention on psychologists engaged in many different kinds of research. It is in any case impossible to constrain the investigation of language within the boundaries of Psychology alone.

Asch, S. 1952: *Social Psychology*. Englewood Cliffs: Prentice Hall. **Danziger, K.** 1997: *Naming the Mind. How Psychology Discovered its Language*. London: Sage. **Gentner, D. and Goldin-Meadow, S. (eds)** 2003: *Language in Mind*. Cambridge MA: MIT Press. **Richards, G.** 1989: *On Psychological Language*. London: Routledge.

lateral thinking Term introduced by the popular writer Edward de Bono to refer to creative approaches to problem solving. Largely derivative from the earlier insights of the Gestalt school.

Leipzig school Invariably identified as the site where modern experimental Psychology began. Under Wilhelm Wundt, Leipzig became Psychology's international hub from the 1870s to the 1890s, particularly after his creation of a laboratory in 1879. Committed to psychophysical and experimental introspective methods, Wundt sought to identify the structure and processes of CONSCIOUSNESS (see s. 3) itself, eschewing interest in 'higher' processes and viewing social behaviour as belonging in the *Geisteswissenschaften* rather than *Naturwissenschaften* (his huge *Volkerpsychologie*, 1900–20, addressing these). Many later eminent British and North American psychologists undertook Ph.D. theses there during this period. Despite this pre-eminence, Wundt's concept of Psychology languished after 1900, the British *émigré* E. B. Titchener becoming almost its sole USA-based advocate, while in Germany it was attacked by the WÜRZBURG SCHOOL and many others, often his ex-students, such as E. Meumann. Theoretical shortcomings aside, its lack of practical application would surely have sabotaged Wundtian Psychology's fortunes in the new century.

Lloyd Morgan's canon In its full 1903 version: 'In no case is an animal activity to be interpreted in terms of higher psychological processes, if it can be fairly interpreted in terms of processes which stand lower in the scale of psychological evolution and development.' What this actually meant is now hotly contested.

London school Early twentieth-century British Psychology is often seen as divided between the London school and CAMBRIDGE SCHOOL. The former is identified primarily with the circle centred on C. Spearman and C. Burt at University College London, along with kindred spirits based elsewhere, such as G. Thomson and W. Brown. The distinctive feature of the London approach was its advocacy of PSYCHOMETRICS and the use of statistical methods like FACTOR ANALYSIS (see s. 6 and s. 8) as research tools (although Francis Aveling of King's College, a close associate of Spearman, was an exception). This it inherited in part from Francis Galton and Karl Pearson, also both closely associated with University College. H. J. Eysenck, who studied under Burt, subsequently continued this tradition in the UK. As Psychology spread to other academic sites this Cambridge vs. London polarity had ceased, by around 1950, to represent the structure of British Psychology, although their own differences in character persisted.

longitudinal research Research which tracks the performance of participants or subjects over an extended period, typically used in developmental and EDUCATIONAL PSYCHOLOGY. While expensive and protracted, this is perhaps the only way in which connections between early life circumstances and adult character can be empirically explored with any rigour. The numbers of participants in such research can also be extremely high, giving the results added RELIABILITY (see s. 6 and s. 8). Usually participants are seen at intervals of between one and five years. Once in train, the momentum of longitudinal research projects tends to accumulate and their duration can become almost open-ended. Longitudinal research may be said to originate in the use of child-observation diaries in the late nineteenth century. L. M. Terman's research on 1470 gifted children broke new ground in scale and duration, beginning in the early 1920s, the last follow-up study appearing in 1959. Numerous longitudinal studies are currently under way.

M

---

male gaze Introduced by feminist writers during the 1970s to refer to the way in which men typically look at women as potential sexual objects rather than individuals. Feminist psychologists have argued that this has often unconsciously affected the tenor of male psychologists' discourse regarding PERSONALITY, for example (see also s. 6).

Marxist Psychology While Marxism largely rejects Psychology as a bourgeois attempt to explain behaviour in terms of individuals' internal processes rather than in terms of socio-economic causes, it does contain a Psychological theory of its own, most fully expounded by L. Sève (1978). This views the psychological as an internalisation of the social (conflicts within the socio-economic sphere becoming internalised as psychological conflicts). Thus individuals are 'historically produced'. Marx's account of 'alienation', found in his earlier writings, has also proved valuable in conceptualising how individuals become psychologically disconnected from their social worlds in urban, industrialised societies. The Marxist view of human uniqueness as lying in the fact that humans 'convert nature into culture' by labour also has psychological implications. Along with the related FRANKFURT SCHOOL tradition, Marxism has fed into contemporary 'critical' and social constructionist thinking, particularly in European contexts. Of Soviet psychologists, only Lev Vygotsky can really be considered as seriously exploring Marxist insights.

Sève, L. 1978: *Man in Marxist Theory and the Psychology of Personality*. Brighton: Harvester.

measurement and statistics The role of measurement in the development of science cannot be overestimated. At every stage it has been marked by improvements in techniques of measurement, expansion of the range of phenomena which may be measured and new methods of analysing the data obtained. There is even a hint of superstition in the widespread faith that measurement can also guarantee 'scientific objectivity'. Thus, while quantitative methodologies are not absolutely necessary in scientific research, there has been ever-present pressure to bring qualitative studies into the quantitative fold. Psychology, for a long time insecure about its scientific status, was especially eager to take this path from the mid-nineteenth century onwards. Given all this it is easy to overlook some underlying conceptual issues. Consider first the widely quoted statement by North American psychologist E. L. Thorndike that 'everything which exists must exist in some quantity and can therefore be measured'. This apparently robust proposition raises two major issues: it treats 'existence' as unproblematic and the converse is not necessarily true – not everything which is measurable necessarily exists (you may think you are measuring x but in fact be measuring y). 'Quantity' carries physical connotations of volume and density, but most of the things Psychology studies do not possess such proper-ties. So what kinds of measurable property can psychological phenomena have? This question vexed Immanuel Kant to the extent that he rejected the very possibility of a science of mind. We are now, however, quite accustomed to converting psychological phenomena into numbers by measuring such things as duration, success/failure rates on tasks, questionnaire responses, frequency of occurrence and other means which we accept as indirect indices of the scale and character of the psychological phenomena we are studying. One problem arising from this for Psychology is that it is sometimes unclear that the phenomenon being studied exists independently of the technique being used to measure it. Consider 'ATTITUDES' (see s. 5) for example. Since we tend to comply when asked questions we will readily agree to play the game of rating our preferences and OPINIONS (see s. 5) on everything from biscuits to the government. The psychologist then converts our responses into numbers indicating the strength of our 'attitude'. But these 'attitudes' may not be INDEPENDENT (see s. 8) 'things' existing prior to the measuring exercise; it could be this very exercise which brings them into being. Moreover, *what* is being measured may not be self-evident from the measurement, indeed may not be specifiable at all 'objectively', apart from the VALUES (see s. 5) etc. of the measurer. This is not just a matter of construct VALIDITY (see s. 6 and s. 8). Thus whether I am measuring 'AUTHORITARIANISM' (see s. 5) or 'strong-mindedness', 'adjustment' or 'CONFORMITY' (see s. 5), even perhaps 'intelligence' or 'obsessionality' (on the grounds that only an obsessional could be bothered solving the more complex test items about who lives next to whom in a cul-de-sac, for example) will depend on my prior theoretical assumptions and values. Measuring length with a ruler raises no such problems. There has been a further tendency over Psychology's history for the introduction of new measurement technologies to stimulate their use. Psychologists then look for questions to ask which can be addressed by the new technique. The risk here is that the research agenda comes to be set by methods available rather than methods being developed to address a research agenda arising from the genuine theoretical importance or practical urgency of the phenomenon in question. To sum up this general point: in Psychology the relationship between 'measurement' and what is being measured is rarely as straightforward as it is in the physical sciences, a situation exacerbated by the problematic ontological status of much which it strives to measure. The ability to obtain measurements, e.g. from questionnaires, does not even imply that the 'thing' which you are measuring actually exists. What may sometimes be going on is that people are indicating what they assume to be the correct usage of a word, its ideal 'referent', rather than a 'dimension of PERSONALITY' (see also s. 6) or objectively existing psychological TRAIT (see s. 6). Thus there are many facets to being 'creative', and we might quantify a person's 'creativity' by tallying how many of these they display. But this may mean no more than assessing how close they come to being the ideal or perfect referent for the term 'creative' as used in our LANGUAGE (see s. 2). Thorndike's dictum is a little over-glib. After all, even centimetres presumably 'exist', but it would be nonsense to ask how many of them!

We can now turn to a few more specific matters relating to statistics (this is confined to noting a few central conceptual points, since statistics is fully addressed in s. 8). First, there has been renewed debate in recent years regarding how 'significance' is assessed and the criteria for identifying it, notably in connection with 'size effects'. This centres on the fact that the greater the SAMPLE (see s. 8) size the smaller an effect needs to be to achieve statistical significance, but if this effect only becomes apparent with very large sample sizes it is likely, in reality, to be fairly trivial and inconsequential. There is thus a tension between ensuring sample sizes large enough to be representative and the need for significance measures to reflect genuinely important effects. Second, the long-standing caveat that correlations do not in themselves indicate causal connections needs to be kept in mind, since it continues to be overlooked on occasion. Third, it is worth pointing out that the practice of ignoring 'OUTLIERS' (see s. 8) (highly deviant data) in statistical analysis in Psychological research is the precise opposite of what obtains in some other fields of research, where the aim is to identify precisely such outliers (e.g. in particle physics) – does this need rethinking? To close, it should be stressed that mathematicians and statisticians continue to engage in levels of theoretical debate and controversy about techniques such as FACTOR ANALYSIS (see s. 6 and s. 8) and MULTIPLE REGRESSION (see s. 8). While this is generally invisible and incomprehensible to psychologists other than specialists in mathematical Psychology, it is a reminder that statistical analysis does not provide quite the rock-solid basis for evaluating research data that is often assumed. The very nature of measurement is indeed attracting growing attention among philosophers and historians of science.

memory A tradition of memory theories runs unbroken from the ancient Greeks to the present. While rarely 'scientific', let alone Psychological, they do all appear to be rational attempts at understanding the same thing. Two kinds of metaphor were long deployed in describing memory, namely those of containment and inscription, though these were sometimes supplemented by others, like Robert Hooke's 'resonance' theory (1705) (see D. Draaisma 2000). Psychologists largely retained these metaphors in updated forms, videotapes replacing wax tablets and circuits supplanting boxes. Memory research was long cramped by a narrow experimental approach concentrating on verbal memory, typically of nonsense syllables, and theoretically framed in associationist terms – the legacy of H. Ebbinghaus's (1885) ground-breaking, if obsessional, research. During the 1930s psychologists began appreciating that rote memorising of nonsense syllables did not, as assumed, isolate the essence of the phenomenon in some pure form, but was totally unrepresentative of the way memory worked in everyday life. The only early Psychological concept which endured was William James's distinction between long-term and SHORT-TERM MEMORY (see s. 3). Over a dozen varieties of memory are now recognised. These include autobio-

graphical, episodic, long-term, short-term, verbal and working 'memories', some with subdivisions such as vocabulary vs. syntactic verbal memory. Memory research was fundamentally affected by the rise of COGNITIVE PSYCHOLOGY, D. Broadbent being among the first to see the possibilities of analysing memory in terms of information channels and storage. Entries elsewhere cover contemporary memory research (see s. 2, MEMORY: GENETIC STUDIES and s. 3). Among many theoretical and conceptual issues which might be identified are:

1. How far memory is purely 'internal' and how far it involves social processes.

2. How far the function and use of memory varies in different social contexts (e.g. verbal rote memory in non-literate vs. literate societies).

3. The reliability of memory – how far memories accurately represent past events as opposed to being reconstructions of these, subject to distortion, selection and invention.

4. How to construe memory pathologies, which sometimes seem to challenge our central assumptions about the nature of personal IDENTITY (see s. 4 and s. 5).

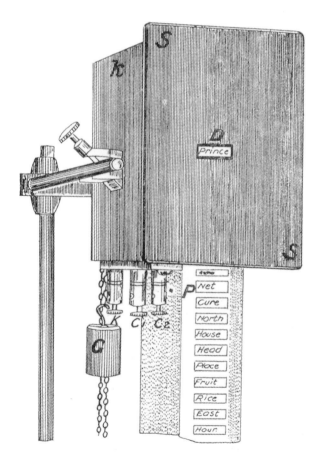

memory *Early memory research apparatus. From R Schulze, Experimental Psychology and Pedagogy (1912). Centre for History of Psychology, Staffordshire University*

Memory remains one of the most intrinsically mysterious of all psychological phenomena, despite being one of the most familiar.

Draaisma, D. 2000: *Metaphors of Memory*. Cambridge: Cambridge University Press.

mental and moral science

During the nineteenth century the transition between traditional philosophy and Psychology was marked by a genre variously called mental and moral science or mental and moral philosophy, especially strong in the USA and rooted in the Scottish 'realist' or 'common sense' school. [See PHILOSOPHY AND PSYCHOLOGY]

molar

Aside from dental connotations, the term is often used to denote the opposite of 'atomic' or 'molecular', akin to 'holistic', but refers less to a theoretical approach than to the level of the phenomenon being addressed.

moral relativism

Doctrine that there are no absolute moral VALUES (see s. 5) transcending CULTURE (see also s. 5) and time, arguably inferred from the high degree of cultural variation, especially in relation to sexual morality. The number of contemporary thinkers genuinely espousing this in a strong, nihilistic form is probably very low.

multiple personality disorder (MPD, DID)

Once called 'dissociation of PERSONALITY' (see also s. 6), the first case studies date from 1905 ('Miss Beauchamp' and 'Hannah'). A syndrome in which an individual possesses more than one personality. Rare, usually involving only two to four 'alters' until the mid-1970s; thereafter, an increase in the USA led to the 1980 coining of the term MPD (officially replaced in 1994 by 'DISSOCIATIVE IDENTITY DISORDER' (see s. 7) – DID). There ensued a curious explosion of cases (almost all female) and numbers of alters – averaging 24 by 1990, one 1991 case exceeding 1000. One website suggests 1 per cent of the US population is affected. It remains a largely North American phenomenon. As with FALSE MEMORY SYNDROME, suspicion grew that DID was created by PSYCHOTHERAPISTS (see s. 7) themselves, although scepticism has been less intense. Generally considered an extreme POST-TRAUMATIC STRESS DISORDER (see s. 7), arising from early sexual abuse, it can raise questions of legal responsibility, and 'sufferers' may have vested interests in maintaining the diagnosis. The subtlest contextualised analysis is I. Hacking (1995). (See also s. 7, DISSOCIATIVE IDENTITY (MULTIPLE PERSONALITY) DISORDER)

Hacking, I. 1995: *Rewriting the Soul. Multiple Personality and the Sciences of Memory*. Princeton: Princeton University Press.

mutualism

Since the late 1980s a GROUP (see s. 5) of British psychologists, A. Costall, J. M. M. Good, A. Still and the anthropologist Tim Ingold, have been developing a theoretical alternative to SOCIAL CONSTRUCTIONISM which avoids what they consider the unidirectional, mechanistic character of the 'construction' metaphor. Drawing on the US pragmatist tradition of John Dewey and the 'ecological' perceptual theories of J. J. Gibson, they argue that psychological realities are constituted by the mutual interactions of individuals with their social and physical environments; indeed the internal and external may be considered almost as interpenetrating. They consider this to be a more viable alternative to orthodox COGNITIVE PSYCHOLOGY, and one which integrates the insights of social constructionism with a sophisticated evolutionary perspective. Closely linked to ECOLOGICAL PSYCHOLOGY, of which it may be considered a component theoretical branch.

Still, A. W. and Good, J. M. M. 1998: The ontology of mutualism. *Ecological Psychology* 10, 39–63.

N

narrativism THEORY (see s. 8) that some or all psychological phenomena are created or constructed 'narratively', i.e. by the stories we tell and believe about ourselves. Associated with Rom Harré, this links with other approaches of SOCIAL CONSTRUCTIONISM in SOCIAL PSYCHOLOGY and PERSONALITY theory. Usually applied to our ideas of 'SELF' (see also s. 4 and s. 5) and the meanings of our life experiences.

National Institute of Industrial Psychology (NIIP)
Founded by C. S. Myers and industrialist H. J. Welch in 1920, the NIIP effectively inaugurated British industrial Psychology, though it partly emerged from the Industrial Fatigue Research Board established during World War I and its successor, the Industrial Health Research Board. Almost all major British psychologists became involved with it during the inter-war years, as it implemented a somewhat Utopian project of bringing Psychology's benefits to the workplace. Its journal *Industrial Psychology* (founded 1922) reported research spanning the spectrum of applied Psychology topics, bar market research and advertising. For complex reasons related to the post-World War II business environment, funding difficulties and developments within applied Psychology, its fortunes declined from the 1950s until its demise in 1975. During its heyday it provided a major route by which Psychology penetrated British culture, and a context for much creative work in the fields of vocational guidance, ergonomics, PERSONNEL SELECTION (see s. 6) and work-place organisation.

nature-nurture issue
The oldest and most enduring of Psychological debates is the 'nature vs. nurture' (or 'heredity vs. environment') controversy. Rooted in older philosophical engagements between 'empiricists' (who held that mental contents originate in experience) and 'rationalists' (who argued for innate ideas and faculties), it rapidly acquired an EMPIRICAL (see s. 8) scientific character in nineteenth-century Psychology, introduction of the phrase itself usually being credited to Francis Galton (1876). It will be helpful to begin by reviewing the various contexts in which the controversy has arisen. One of the earliest concerned visual perception – do we learn to perceive shapes, movement and distance? Or are these abilities innate, biologically determined? This was addressed as early as the late seventeenth century by John Locke, having been raised by his contemporary, Molyneux. 'Molyneux's question', as it became known, was whether a congenitally blind person would see the world correctly immediately on being given sight. It returned as a major Psychological issue in the nineteenth-century dispute between H. Helmholtz and E. Hering. For Galton it arose in relation to INTELLIGENCE (see s. 4 and s. 6). In the context of evolutionary THEORY (see s. 8), heredity acquired much practical urgency for those, like Galton, concerned with the quality of the human 'stock', intellectual ability being of paramount concern. Establishing how far intelligence is genetically or environmentally determined has remained a preoccupation for many psychologists and, beyond them, for those concerned with education, social policy and political IDEOLOGY (see s. 5). A third major area where it surfaces is regarding sex differences [see GENDER AND SEXUALITY ISSUES] – how far do these genuinely reflect innate biological differences and how far are they produced by child-rearing practices and cultural NORMS (see s. 5 and s. 6)? A fourth topic figuring prominently during the 1940s–1970s was 'AGGRESSION' (see s. 5). Again, some, like Konrad Lorenz, argued that humans were innately aggressive, while others, like Bandura and Ross, claimed it was largely learned. However, in principle, the debate can be extended to virtually any psychological topic from MENTAL ILLNESS (see s. 7) and PERSONALITY

nature-nurture issue *Portrait of Francis Galton (1822–1911), Charles Darwin's cousin, who effectively launched the nature-nurture controversy in its modern form. BPS History of Psychology Centre*

(see also s. 6) to EMOTION (see s. 6) and criminality. Indeed all these have generated nature vs. nurture literature and research.

While superficially straightforward, it has become increasingly apparent since the 1970s that the nature vs. nurture polarity is problematic in several ways. First, geneticists such as R. C. Lewontin have shown that *general* answers to such questions are impossible. Every gene (or rather every ALLELE (see s. 4) of every gene) is unique regarding its level of plasticity in response to non-genetic (i.e. environmental) FACTORS (see s. 8) from conception onwards, and this plasticity itself can vary over time. Moreover only *specific* environmental factors are involved, not some general 'environment', thus 99 per cent of 'environments' may have no effect, but 1 per cent very significant ones (e.g. the teratological effects of prenatal exposure to thalidomide). Nor should we think in terms of a single 'ideal' outcome, but rather in terms of environment determining which of various equally viable 'tracks' the organism takes. Since few psychological phenomena can conceivably be determined by single specific genes, the situation becomes even more complex. The two factors can only be unravelled for specific genes, using genetically homogeneous SAMPLES (see s. 8), across a finite environmental range – a task so technically complex it has only been approximated for a few fruit-fly genes. This picture renders the ostensibly sensible 'interaction' compromise difficult to sustain in any meaningful fashion. IDENTICAL TWINS (see s. 4) aside, humans are all genetically unique, which effectively rules out such research for ever. A more general question is what we mean by 'environment'. Scientists, not least psychologists, frequently insist on operationally defining their terms, but although 'heredity' may be so definable, 'environment' simply refers to everything else from the weather to social class. It is difficult, therefore, to see how heredity and environment can be considered 'INDEPENDENT VARIABLES' (see s. 8) when one is only definable as everything that is not the other.

There is, however, a statistical measure, the 'H' or 'HERITABILITY' (see s. 4) score, which partly surmounts these problems. By obtaining cross-generational measurements we can calculate how much of the total within-POPULATION (see s. 8) VARIANCE (see s. 8) is due to heredity (between 0 and 1.0). The interpretation of this is fraught with difficulties, though. In the case of intelligence, for example, heredity presumably determines upper capacity, 'environment' determining how closely this is achieved. In shifting from the population to the individual it thus remains impossible to partial out the two factors, since we only have their actual 'intelligence' (assuming IQ – see s. 6 – tests are valid), not their genetic potential. While we might assume someone with an IQ of 160 is operating at nearly their full potential, someone with an IQ of 100 may have fallen very short or hardly at all. In comparing two populations, 'H' is no guide either, being based on individuals' *relative* positions *within* a population. Diet changes, for example, might increase the average height of a whole population. Even though the 'H' score for height is high, the tallest parents tending to have tall children, it cannot illuminate the reasons for differences in average height *between* populations.

While heredity's role in determining many psychological phenomena is extremely important, and a valid topic to research, the nature vs. nurture image, aiming only to parcel out their contributions in a general fashion, is clearly inadequate to the sheer complexities of the issue. For any chance of success, research has to be on specific GENOTYPES (see s. 2) in specific environments in relation to specific psychological phenomena. This is likely to be facilitated by advances in genetics, which promise to enable us to tackle things on a case-by-case basis.

But why, given its inadequacies, has the nature vs. nurture formula persisted? Without offering a definitive answer, two points may be suggested as relevant. First, it is simple and apparently comprehensible, one of the few issues within Psychology which the general public feel they can readily grasp, and providing an easy starting point for media discussions. Explaining why its simplicity is illusory is difficult, and the outcome disappointing for audiences wanting unambiguous answers. Second, the debate might conceivably serve a useful function within Psychology itself, as a unifying theme to which ever-more diverse sub-disciplines can relate, a common topic to which all feel they are contributing. The death of the nature vs. nurture debate has been being announced periodically since at least the 1930s. A further such announcement now is likely to prove similarly premature.

New Psychology This expression arose in two distinct contexts. It was first used by E. C. Sanford to refer to the new experimental, laboratory-based Psychology (inspired by, if rarely adopting the theories of, W. Wundt's LEIPZIG SCHOOL and O. Külpe's WÜRZBURG SCHOOL), which took hold in the USA during the late 1880s and 1890s, generally being taken to mark the founding of 'scientific' psychology in North America. This typically studied basic psychophysical phenomena like REACTION TIME (see s. 3), PERCEPTION and MEMORY. After 1918, however, it was adopted to refer to the work of such as William McDougall, W. H. R. Rivers, Pierre Janet and, above all, Sigmund Freud's psychoanalytic school. This was seen as 'new' precisely because it addressed the depths of human nature rather than confining itself to psychophysical matters, using clinical rather than experimental methodologies (although McDougall was an exception and Rivers used both). Use of the phrase in this latter sense petered out in the 1930s.

nominalism Doctrine that general terms or concepts refer only to individual things, as opposed to belief in the existence of 'universals'. A major issue in medieval philosophy, the issue can still reappear in new guises.

nomothetic methods Umbrella term for the study of people *en masse* rather than individually [see also IDIOGRAPHIC METHODS]. Most standard experimental and questionnaire-based research methods are nomothetic in character, seeking to identify population NORMS (see s. 5 and s. 6) and general directions of relationship between psychological phenomena. In addressing such questions the individual case ceases to be especially important, and those deviating too far from the 'norm' or failing to fit the general pattern can be ignored as 'OUTLIERS' (see s. 8). While facilitating statistical analysis and enhancing the

RELIABILITY (see s. 6 and s. 8) of findings, nomothetic methods are nonetheless inappropriate, or at least insufficient, for tackling a wide range of questions, requiring in-depth, often long-term study of individual cases. It can also be argued that problems can arise about the way in which participants (or 'subjects') relate to the questionnaire or experimental task, rendering covert 'experimenter effects' more likely. Nomothetic methods nevertheless remain the norm in experimental Psychology. (See also s. 8, NOMOTHETIC)

O

Ockham's razor So called after the medieval nominalist philosopher William of Ockham (or Occam) who spelled it out – the principle of parsimony, that is to say, choosing the simplest possible explanation or avoiding unnecessary complexity.

ontology Branch of philosophy which studies the nature of being or existence. This concern has figured more prominently in mainland European (especially French and German) than in British and North American philosophy. In the twentieth century the best-known exemplar of this was existentialism. [See also EXISTENTIALIST PSYCHOLOGY]

operationalism Methodological doctrine that concepts should be definable in terms of publicly observable criteria for correct usage. Introduced by the North American philosopher Bridgman (1936) and enthusiastically adopted by US experimental psychologists. Distinct from, though with affinities to, contemporary doctrines in logical positivism, it was seen as averting meaningless metaphysical abstraction.

P

paradigm Defining exemplar of a category. The concept was popularised by Thomas Kuhn (1962) as referring to the theories or methodologies governing scientific practice during phases of 'normal science', these being embodied in paradigm texts or experiments. Whether paradigms exist within Psychology or whether it remains 'pre-paradigmatic' is much debated.

parapsychology Study of 'paranormal' psychological phenomena like telepathy, extrasensory perception (ESP), psychokinesis (movement of objects by the power of the mind), spiritualism, clairvoyance, etc. This field played a surprisingly important role in establishing Psychology in the nineteenth century, the Society for Psychical Research, founded in 1882, pioneering scientific Psychological methods in evaluating these phenomena, while funds from the American Society for Psychical Research helped G. S. Hall establish the AMERICAN PSYCHOLOGICAL ASSOCIATION. The best known twentieth-century work was J. B. Rhine's during the 1930s and 1940s, while in 1983 Arthur Koestler's will endowed a Chair in Parapsychology at Edinburgh University. Most research has focused on ESP and, to a lesser degree, telekinesis. Its controversial nature has led to standards of methodological rigour becoming among the highest in experimental Psychology, but results forever hover tantalisingly around statistical significance. More recently the study of 'out-of-body experiences' has attracted much attention.

Pavlov school I. P. Pavlov, a physiologist, was the discoverer of the 'conditioned reflex' and creator of a Russian school of Psychology directly comparable to BEHAVIOURISM. Images of his conditioning EXPERIMENTS (see s. 8) on canine salivatory responses became iconic in introductory Psychology texts. By 1920 behaviourists had widely adopted his technical vocabulary. Successfully navigating the revolutionary upheavals of 1917, Pavlov became the leading officially approved Soviet psycholo-

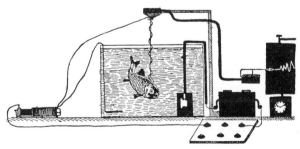

A Fish answers the telephone

Pavlov school *How to condition a fish. From the Pavlovian Y. P. Frolov's* Fish Who Answer the Telephone *(1937). Centre for History of Psychology, Staffordshire University*

gist, developing a general Psychological theory, including the higher mental processes. His followers included A. G. Ivanov Smolensky (who extended his ideas into PSYCHO-PATHOLOGY – see s. 7), Y. P. Frolov (author of a book now famous for its title: *Fish Who Answer the Telephone*, 1937), E. A. Asratyan (his biographer) and B. M. Teplov. Pavlov's reputation somewhat overshadowed those of his forerunners, V. M. Bekhterev and I. M. Sechenov, whose work was similar in spirit. In the 1960s, H. J. Eysenck and J. A. Gray adopted much of Teplov's Pavlovian behaviourism in preference to C. L. Hull's less physiologically elaborated US version.

perception The study of perception, particularly visual perception, has always figured prominently among Psychology's central research topics. It is, moreover, a topic which is very wide-ranging, from psychophysiological research on the neurological basis of perception at one extreme to the effects of social and PERSONALITY (see also s. 6) factors on it at the other. Until the latter decades of the twentieth century, a number of perennial topics and issues can be traced running through psychologists' work in this field.

1. The 'direct' vs. 'indirect' debate, inherited from philosophy. Do we see the world directly or is what we see an internal, indirect representation of it? While this initially strikes one as a very profound question, on closer analysis of what it means – or could mean – its coherence tends to evaporate and the issue reduces to a linguistic one about what is meant by 'direct' and 'indirect'.

2. The 'innate' vs. 'learned' issue (an aspect of the wider controversy surrounding the NATURE–NURTURE ISSUE). This has proved somewhat more productive in that a number of 'hard-wired' or innate perceptual mechanisms have now been identified which set the parameters within which variation can occur.

3. More specifically, the two topics of colour perception and space perception largely dominated perception research during the nineteenth century, notably the Helmholtz vs. Hering controversy over colour perception.

4. The use of VISUAL ILLUSIONS (see s. 3) as stimulus material in exploring numerous topics. Some of these pertain directly to the physiology of perception, others to higher-level processing or even effects of social and personality factors.

From the 1960s onwards the field came to be dominated by two theoretical approaches, both in some respects stemming from GESTALT PSYCHOLOGY's investigations during the 1920s and 1930s. One was J. J. Gibson's 'ecological approach', which adopted a latter-day 'direct' or 'realist' position, the other, the **cognitivist** approach, viewing perception as a fascinatingly complex information-processing system. (See s. 3)

What nobody has yet succeeded in coming to grips with, though, is how the increasingly well-understood physical and physiological processes can actually generate the conscious subjective experiences of colour and shape themselves.

personality Astrology, Galen's 'four humours' doctrine and PHYSIOGNOMY all testify to an age-long fascination with classifying and analysing human diversity. The terms 'TEMPERAMENT' (see s. 4) and 'character' were traditionally used to refer to this diversity, while the term 'personality' has had dozens of different meanings (surveyed by G. W. Allport 1937). Only in the 1920s did Psychology opt for the term 'Personality' to label the field (also known as 'INDIVIDUAL DIFFERENCES' – see s. 6). Both theoretically and methodologically the study of personality has been perhaps the most diverse of all Psychology's fields of inquiry. It is customary to differentiate between 'type' and 'TRAIT' (see s. 6) theories, the former classifying people into a small number of types, the other seeking to analyse variation into, often more numerous, 'traits', preferably quantifiable. Typologies themselves vary widely depending on their basis: the German K. Langer used dominating interests, W. Sheldon body or 'somatotypes', C. G. Jung a complex permutation of extroversion vs. introversion with dominant 'function' (thinking, feeling, intuition, sensation), while Freudians have used terms such as 'anal retentive', 'oral aggressive' and 'phallic narcissist', based on fixation at the various developmental stages. Trait the-

orists such as R. B. Cattell and H. J. Eysenck used factor analytic (see s. 6 and s. 8, FACTOR ANALYSIS) techniques to identify the basic 'dimensions' of personality, Cattell's tally eventually mounting to about 18, while Eysenck more parsimoniously proposed 3 (EXTROVERSION (see s. 6) vs. NEUROTICISM (see s. 6), stable vs. neurotic, and 'PSYCHOTICISM' (see s. 6)). Henry Murray's was one of the most elaborated theories, proposing a large catalogue of 'needs' (need for achievement, 'nAch', being the best remembered), while a number of binary distinctions, such as field dependent vs. field independent and internal vs. external 'locus of control' have also been explored. Methodologically it is a field where the NOMOTHETIC METHODS vs. IDIOGRAPHIC METHODS distinction has most manifested itself. While questionnaires of many kinds have been used to research and quantify personality differences, other techniques such as PROJECTIVE TESTS (see s. 6), colour preferences and Kelly's 'repertory grid' are also widely employed. After the 'grand theorising' of the earlier twentieth century, the coherence of 'personality' as a sub-disciplinary project has somewhat waned over the last two decades, becoming diffused into other topics where individual differences are of concern in a less general fashion. (See also s. 6, PERSONALITY)

Allport, G. W. 1937: *Personality. A Psychological Interpretation.* New York: Henry Holt.

philosophy and Psychology Historically the boundary between Psychology and philosophy is difficult to draw. Western philosophy has constantly addressed such topics as the structure of the mind, perception, EMOTION (see s. 6), LEARNING (see s. 3) and memory, extending

personality *Picture used in Henry Murray's projective 'Thematic Apperception Test' of 1943. BPS History of Psychology Centre*

on occasion to the mind of the child, social relations and the nature of LANGUAGE (see s. 2). The menu of doctrines created by the mid-nineteenth century constituted the point of departure for the first psychologists such as Alexander Bain and Wilhelm Wundt, while the discipline called MENTAL AND MORAL SCIENCE (or philosophy), which flourished in the USA until the 1880s, straddled both camps. Psychology did not, however, *replace* Philosophy. The trend of English-speaking philosophy during the twentieth century was to abandon grand system-building, choosing instead to cast a critical, analytical eye both on traditional philosophy and Psychology's efforts at tackling once philosophical topics in a 'scientific' fashion. While not necessarily hostile, many philosophers felt Psychology was frequently naïve and unappreciative of deeper conceptual difficulties. More evangelically materialist psychologists like J. B. Watson, meanwhile, saw philosophy as pointless metaphysical wrangling. If, to crudely generalise, relations between the two were cool from *c.* 1900–60, at least in English-speaking countries, they began reconverging thereafter. The work of linguistic philosophers from Wittgenstein onwards illuminated the nature not only of language [see LANGUAGE AND PSYCHOLINGUISTICS] but also of a number of other conceptual issues within Psychology associated with the rise of COGNITIVE PSYCHOLOGY and AI projects, including the AGENCY or 'intentionality' problem. Thus philosopher J. R. Searle was able to publish his key 'Chinese room' argument in the highly prestigious journal *The Brain and Behavioural Sciences* (1980). In mainland Europe the Psychology-philosophy divide remained less clear-cut than in Britain and North America. The phenomenological tradition of E. Husserl, leading into mid-twentieth-century existentialism [see EXISTENTIALIST PSYCHOLOGY], had explicitly cast itself as being as much Psychology as philosophy. The current situation resembles a division of labour more than rivalry. The philosophical approach is widely accepted as one way of doing Psychology, hence the sub-discipline 'Philosophical Psychology', while philosophical critiques *of* Psychology are also acknowledged as valuable, hence the emergence of a field called 'philosophy of Psychology'. This surely signifies that the interdisciplinary boundary remains blurred.

physiognomy The belief that a person's character or PERSONALITY (see also s. 6) is evident from their face. Physiognomy was especially popular during the Renaissance and revitalised in the 1770s by the Swiss pastor J. C. Lavater, who published a lavishly illustrated set of volumes elaborating on the thesis. Not to be confused with phrenology [see BRAIN FUNCTION AND NEUROPSYCHOLOGY].

presentism Viewing the past from a position centred on the present. Although unavoidable, this leads to problems when writers are unaware of how far their assumptions, VALUES (see s. 5) and agenda reflect their own present historical context, assuming instead that they are somehow 'objective'. Sometimes takes the form of PROGRESSIVISM.

progressivism Viewing history as an essentially progressive process. In history of science this is particularly tempting, but may produce a version of PRESENTISM, which assumes that we now *know* the truth. All past events are evaluated simply in terms of their role in its discovery. Has obvious affinities with CELEBRATORY HISTORY.

psychoanalysis and related schools Sigmund Freud's psychoanalytic theories, first formulated in the 1890s and undergoing continual development until his death in 1939, were the single most culturally influential Psychological doctrines of the twentieth century. This impact was reinforced by the number of related, but distinct, theories proposed (a) by apostates from Freud's own teachings, including C. G. Jung (never an entirely orthodox follower), A. Adler, W. Reich and W. Stekel; (b) by divergent approaches within mainstream psychoanalysis such as Melanie Klein's; and (c) by numerous 'neo-' and 'post-' Freudians, especially in the USA, such as E. H. Erikson, K. Horney and E. Fromm. Despite this

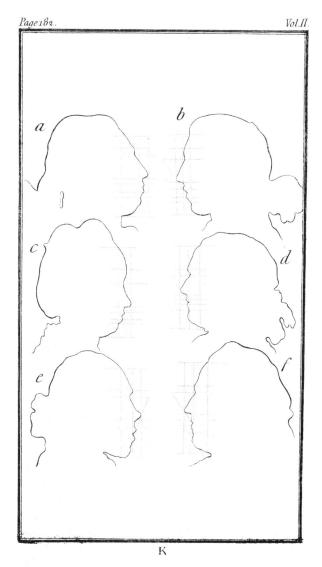

Page 182.　　　　　　　　　　　　Vol. II.

K

physiognomy *Attempt at analysing facial profiles from J. C. Lavater,* Essays on Physiognomy *(Vol. 2, 1797). Centre for History of Psychology, Staffordshire University*

psychoanalysis and related schools *Probably the most famous group photo in Psychology's history. Psychoanalysts Sigmund Freud, Carl G. Jung, Ernest Jones, A. A. Brill and Sandor Ferenczi alongside William James, G. S. Hall, E. B. Titchener and numerous other eminent American psychologists at the 1909 Clark University Twentieth Anniversary celebration at which both Freud and Jung lectured. BPS History of Psychology Centre*

popularity, academic and experimental psychology increasingly kept psychoanalysis of all hues at arm's length from the mid-1930s onwards. Numerous attempts were made to experimentally test Freudian hypotheses during the late 1930s–1950s, but none proved entirely conclusive in either direction. The history of this broad school has considerable regional variations. In Britain it enjoyed exposure and popularity, combined with notoriety, during the 1920s to mid-1930s, but had subsided in status by the end of the 1950s; in the USA, by contrast, following an early burst of interest in the 1910s and 1920s, its heyday of popularity came from the late 1940s to early 1960s. In France the reputation of Pierre Janet somewhat kept it at bay until the mid-twentieth century, when Lacan and others developed quite distinct theories of their own. Curiously an 'Aryanised' version flourished for a while in Nazi Germany. The centrality of sex aside, the appeal in anglophone countries rested in part on the novel terminology introduced to translate Freud's works, which possessed a fascinating technical character absent in the original German, but the underlying hunger for a new 'scientific' account of human nature after World War I was also crucial. While fairly few psychologists or therapists any longer espouse strict psychoanalytic positions, and academic Psychology has effectively evicted it, it is now too late to undo the often enriching legacy of psychoanalysis and its related schools, firmly embedded in everyday language to a degree many are unaware of.

psychohistory Use of a broadly psychoanalytic theoretical framework to analyse historical figures and past social phenomena. Inspired by Freud's 1910 *Leonardo Da Vinci*, this project flourished primarily from the 1950s to 1970s. Erik H. Erikson's *Young Man Luther* (1959), F. E. Manuel's *A Portrait of Isaac Newton* (1968) and Bruce Mazlish's *James and John Stuart Mill* (1975) were among its most successful biographical studies, while Z. Barbu's *Problems of Historical Psychology* (1960) and Everett E. Hagen's *On the Theory of Social Change* (1962) were ambitious ventures into sociological and social Psychological territory. While Mazlish has continued to promote psychohistory, it declined, partly due to the fall in popularity of psychoanalytic theory after the 1960s and partly because it came to be viewed as anachronistically imposing modern concepts retrospectively on those it studied. Most now view psychohistory's efforts as often brilliantly insightful but often also bizarrely forced in their interpretations.

psychometrics The sub-discipline concerned with developing instruments with which to measure psychological phenomena, although this definition needs to be narrowed somewhat since it largely excludes physiologically mediated methods. In practice, if not in principle, it might be defined as the sub-discipline concerned with questionnaire design. Historically, psychometrics has been primarily concerned with INTELLIGENCE (see s. 4 and s. 6), ability, attitude and PERSONALITY TESTING (see s. 6). The process of questionnaire design involves a number of stages. First, the nature of the questionnaire itself (e.g. whether using rating scale, binary choice or multiple choice items). Most basic formats were in place by the end of the 1940s and many during the 1930s (notably the Thurstone, Likert and Gluckman modes of scaling). Second, the validation of the questionnaire, involving eliminating superfluous, non-discriminating and inappropriate items and establishing its RELIABILITY (see s. 6 and s. 8) (e.g. by 'split-half' and/or test-retest methods). Third, the STANDARDISATION (see s. 8) of the test, which establishes POPULATION (see s. 8) response NORMS (see s. 5 and s. 6). Psychometrics is also concerned with developing statistical techniques, such as FACTOR ANALYSIS (see s. 6 and s. 8), for exploring the interrelation-ships between tests of different kinds, thus becoming actively involved in research and theory testing, as for example in studies of intelligence (such as J. P. Guilford's) and PERSONALITY (see also s. 6) (such as R. B. Cattell's). At this point psychometrics becomes engaged with some of the deeper theoretical issues surrounding MEASUREMENT AND STATISTICS. One problem has been clarifying precisely what the numerical scores on psychometric tests actually signify – how can we be sure that the scale is actually one of equal intervals? In what sense are they genuinely quantitative (e.g. is a person with an IQ (see s. 6) of 125 actually 25 per cent more intelligent than someone scoring 100)? How far is the unitary character of what is being measured actually an artefact of the test design procedure itself? While not com-mitted to specific theoretical positions, psychometrics has an intrinsic tendency to support nativist theories of intelli-gence and TRAIT (see s. 6) approaches to PERSONALITY, while it is obviously a NOMOTHETIC METHOD. Not all questionnaire and testing methods can be comfortably classified as psychometric in character; repertory grid, Q-SORT (see s. 6) and PROJECTIVE TESTS (see s. 6), for example, have evolved, often in reaction to what were felt to be the limitations of orthodox psychometrics. (See also s. 6, PSYCHOMETRICS)

psychophysics The earliest field of experimental Psychological research, most famously in G. Fechner's 1859 *Der Psychophysik*, psychophysics is concerned with basic sensory and motor phenomena such as reaction times, size and weight perception, DISCRIMINATION (see s. 3 and s. 5) (e.g. the 'two-point threshold' – at what distance apart two stimulation points on the skin are perceived as separate) and ATTENTION (see s. 3) span. It was in this context that the basic forms of experimental design were introduced, while the use of high-tech brass instruments in laboratory settings, to which such research lent itself, played a major role in establishing Psychology's early credentials as a legitimate natural science. At the end of the nineteenth century the advent of rotating cylinder recording techniques enabled the studies of FATIGUE (see s. 7) and other topics involving the monitoring of muscular movement to be added. (Other contemporary innovations included 'Politzer's Hörmesser' and 'Zwaardmaker's olfactometer' for measuring auditory acuity and sense of smell respectively.) During the twentieth century the overt prominence of psychophysics rapidly declined, overshadowed by the appeal of higher-level phenomena such as LEARNING (see s. 3) and MOTIVATION (see s. 6), while PERCEPTION became a distinct field of research in its own right. If no longer figuring at centre stage as a clearly defined sub-discipline, the techniques psychophysics introduced are, however, routinely used in numerous areas of ergonomics and applied Psychology where questions of vigilance, attention, reaction time and human–machine interaction need to be addressed, while with the advent of informa-tion theory in the 1950s, many came to be integrated into COGNITIVE Psychology. Fechner's original concern was with the relationship between the objective scale or intensity of a stimulus and the sensation as subjectively experienced, an issue he saw as related to the BODY-MIND PROBLEM. While the 'Weber-Fechner Law' which this yielded has proved resilient within a limited range of circumstances, the underlying philosophical aspiration soon disappeared. In some respects, psychophysics was the nearest to being an unproblematic 'natural science' of all Psychology's sub-disciplines, and left an enduring methodological legacy.

R

reductionism The explanation of phenomena existing at one level in terms of the laws governing a 'lower' one, e.g. biological phenomena in terms of chemical processes. While such reductionism has long been a tendency of the physical sciences since it ensures a general continuity and coherence in the physical world, eliminating mysteriously new factors having to be introduced at each 'higher' level, it raises a number of difficulties, both in general and for Psychology in particular. One is that it presupposes an unambiguous hierarchy from 'lowest' or 'simplest' to 'highest', 'most complex'. While in some respects uncontroversial, e.g. biological phenomena do appear to be more complex or 'higher' than chemical ones, this clarity breaks down on closer scrutiny. Were it merely a hierarchy of size, subatomic physics would be the easiest of all disciplines to master, while twentieth-century developments like systems theory and fractal geometry cannot readily be fitted into any hierarchy as they cut across numerous different 'levels'. Nor can fairly conventional disciplines like geology and meteorology be easily placed, since they involve integrating processes of a variety of different types. From a conventional standpoint Psychology would come 'above' biology (and perhaps 'below' sociology and anthropology). Within Psychology the commonest forms of reductionism are those which seek fully to account for psychological phenomena in physiological terms. At this point, however, a second problem arises which we may term 'loss of meaning'. Can psychological phenomena be so reduced without sacrificing their psychological meaning? If so, does this mean that a distinct psychological level of meaningfulness is ultimately illusory and that psychological, 'mentalistic' discourse could, in principle, be fully replaced by a physiological one? This issue has taxed many psychologists and was a central concern of the Gestalt school [see GESTALT PSYCHOLOGY] in the 1920s and 1930s, who attacked BEHAVIOURISM most strongly on precisely this issue. Reduction from psychological to physiological is not the only issue; reduction of the 'social' to the 'individual' has also been questioned by critics of North American SOCIAL PSYCHOLOGY, for example. It is one thing to explain 'wetness' 'chemically' in terms of the molecular structure of H_2O, another to explain 'love' or 'doubt' by describing brain events. And, conversely to the previous example, some have protested at what they see as the reduction of the psychological to the social by social constructionists. There are, in short, a plurality of modes of reductionism at play within Psychology, most obviously the physiological, genetic, individualist and social versions. The strongest reductionist proposals are often said to advocate 'eliminative reductionism', that is to say they seek to eliminate the need for any higher level of analysis. This entails that no loss of meaning occurs in the translation from the higher to the lower level. It is on this point that strong reductionism within Psychology faces the greatest resistance. According to the Gestalt psychologists such an approach is profoundly mistaken; we should instead start from the other direction, with 'wholes' in all their complexity. The broader argument is that the meaningfulness of psychological phenomena and human experience is something which only emerges at the psychological (or socio-psychological) level and simply disappears if we attempt to reduce these to 'lower' terms. Psychology's task is thus to identify and explore the 'laws' governing events at this level in their own terms, even while acknowledging that they do not occur in isolation from those at other levels. A PAIN (see s. 2 and s. 7), for example, is typically the direct result of a physiological event, but its immediate *psychological* meaning – symptom of impending heart attack, punishment for one's sins, sign of ageing or whatever – cannot be reduced to physiological terms. And even if one is correct in understanding it as heralding an impending coronary, this is testimony to one's psychological knowledge and astuteness rather than one's physiology *per se*. Psychological propositions cannot be eliminatively reduced to physiological ones for the simple reason that, as logicians would say, the 'truth conditions' of the two differ. This is clearest in relation to psychological propositions couched in physiological terms, such as 'you're being a real pain in the neck' or 'you make me sick'. In neither case would even the most subtle physiological examination of neck or vomiting mechanisms have any bearing on their veracity. Such a line of reasoning can take us into deep linguistic philosophical waters but the immediate implication is only that the biology/psychology boundary cannot be treated as similar in kind to the biology/chemistry or chemistry/physics ones, where the continuum now appears essentially complete and where choice of 'level' is a matter of pragmatic appropriateness to the question in hand. This is not, however, to claim that reductionism of any form has no place within Psychology. An interesting case in point is the way psychologists during the 1960s and 1970s were able to use ethological concepts to cast various human behaviours in a new, often subversive light – military epaulettes were clearly the equivalent of dominant gorilla shoulder-hair bristling for example. Earlier, psychoanalysts had, more controversially, attempted to 'reduce' religious behaviour and belief by explaining them as symbolic expressions of unresolved infantile needs and fixations (generally sexual in nature, of course). In these instances what we have is a reduction *into* Psychological terms of the meanings of psychological phenomena hitherto explained or given meaning in non-psychological, lay or folk-Psychological, terms. This is quite distinct from attempts at reduction across disciplinary boundaries.

Although often viewed pejoratively, reductionism is, therefore, a rather complex issue. The reductionist imperative in the physical sciences was undoubtedly fruitful and eventually succeeded in dispelling the 'vitalist' view that 'living matter' was essentially different in kind from the non-living and that a new 'force' was required to explain it. For Psychology, however, its value is more ambiguous. Even as a general principle the image of a self-evident hierarchy of the sciences on which it depends is now perhaps obsolete, while strong 'eliminative' reductionism would appear to threaten the very legitimacy of the Psychological level of analysis itself, or marginalise it as a lay person's comforting illusion.

reflexivity   The property of being in some way self-referential. In Psychology and other human sciences this becomes theoretically important in so far as these disciplines are part of the very subject matter which they study [see SCIENTIFIC STATUS OF PSYCHOLOGY]. Psychology, for example, is reflexive in several senses: it is produced by its own subject matter; it produces and changes its own subject matter; its practice is an instance of its own subject matter (i.e. it is itself a human behaviour) and in some sense part of its own subject matter (e.g. Psychological research on perception is now a collective aspect of the human perceptual system). Writers have often commented that Psychological theories should be able to explain their own production. This list is not exhaustive. Similarly, sociology as an institutionalised discipline is a component of its subject matter – social structure and organisation. The concrete implications of all this are not at all clear however, although they obviously have a general bearing on how psychologists should conceptualise their activities.

reification   Ascribing a misleading or invalid, concrete, thing-like status to the referent of an abstract concept. Important in Psychology since it is something to which psychologists are especially prone due to the abstract nature of mentalistic concepts.

religion and Psychology   There is a widespread, quite erroneous, assumption that Psychology and religion have generally been antagonistic or indifferent to each other. Restricting attention to Christianity, their linkage is evident in the origins of US Psychology within North American 'mental and moral philosophy'. Rooted in the Scottish 'realist' tradition, this promoted an orthodox Protestant (usually Presbyterian or Congregationalist) position, both pious and philosophically sophisticated. While often hostile to evolutionary thought and scientific materialism, its later representatives, like Noah Porter and James McCosh, drew extensively on early European Psychology. Their moral agenda was largely retained by early North American psychologists who, moreover, were mostly committed believers, some having initially trained for the ministry. W. James's *The Varieties of Religious Experience* (1902) is this period's classic text. A sub-discipline of Psychology of religion then flourished into the 1920s, G. S. Hall being a major figure, invariably adopting positions supportive of religious belief. The two parties also met over the matter of psychotherapy and mental distress. In the pre–1914 Boston Emmanuel Movement, and in Britain between the two world wars, ministers and religious writers were often leading popularisers of Psychological ideas and incorporated them into pastoral care, the Methodist Leslie Weatherhead being Psychology's most prominent British advocate. The seemingly 'religious' character of C. G. Jung's later works reinforced this. Numerous mid-twentieth-century psychologists (e.g. Gordon Allport in the USA and R. H. Thouless in Britain) were also devout Christians. While

Psychology of religion declined from the 1930s, Psychological interest in the social psychology of religion, PERSONALITY TRAITS (see s. 6) of believers and religious 'cults' continued, and from the 1960s many psychotherapeutic movements returned 'spirituality' to the agenda. Historians like J. A. Belzen and Martin Kusch have recently begun unravelling the complex relationships between the characters of regional Psychologies and their Protestant vs. Catholic contexts, and exploring the role of religious background in the thought of individual psychologists. That some psychologists have been deeply hostile to religion is undeniable, and many of the religious reciprocated this, but the Psychology–religion relationship is both profound and complicated, and eludes facile generalisations. Taking Judaism, Buddhism and 'psychic research' into account would reinforce this reading.

A

TREATISE

ON

SELF KNOWLEDGE:

SHOWING THE

NATURE AND BENEFIT

OF THAT

IMPORTANT SCIENCE,

AND

THE WAY TO ATTAIN IT.

By JOHN MASON A. M.

WITH QUESTIONS ADAPTED FOR THE USE OF SCHOOLS.

Revised Stereotype Edition.

BOSTON·
JAMES LORING, 132 WASHINGTON STREET.

religion and Psychology *This 1833 American edition of the Englishman John Mason's pious* A Treatise on Self Knowledge *indicates by its added questions 'for the use of schools' an early concern with psychological issues among religious educators in the United States. Centre for History of Psychology, Staffordshire University*

reversal theory Seeking a middle path between behaviourist and phenomenological approaches to the relationship between 'arousal' and 'hedonic state' (roughly, pleasure vs. pain), British psychologist Michael Apter began formulating his 'reversal theory' in the late 1970s, since when it has undergone much development and enjoyed substantial success in certain areas of applied Psychology (e.g. sport Psychology) and, to some extent, psychotherapy. The THEORY (see s. 8) centres on a distinction between two 'metamotivational states': the 'telic' (or 'purposive') and 'paratelic' (akin to 'play'). High arousal is unpleasurable in the former, but pleasurable in the latter (and vice versa for low arousal). A common strategy therefore is to switch states when arousal becomes unpleasantly high or low, producing ANXIETY (see s. 6).

Individuals differ in degree of dominance of metamotivational state, a scale now having been devised to measure this. Other 'metamotivational' pairs have also been identified, such as mastery vs. sympathy in interpersonal relations. (See also s. 6, REVERSAL THEORY)

Apter, M. 1989: *Reversal Theory: Motivation, Emotion and Personality*. New York: Routledge.

rhetoric 'Rhetoric' commonly refers to emotional or theatrical speech or discourse devoid of rational argument. Technically, however, it refers to the art of PERSUASION (see s. 5), by whatever means – any convincing piece of discourse convinces by virtue of its successful rhetoric. Some have argued that we cannot really get beyond this.

S

scientific status of Psychology Psychology long struggled for recognition as a bona fide science, and its fortunes largely depend, in today's cultural climate, on sustaining this status. Notwithstanding this, there are several plausible grounds on which its orthodoxy as a natural science is challenged. These are not necessarily fatal, however, since the upshot may be that its status somehow transcends rather than excludes it from this category. During the nineteenth century there were already heated debates in Germany over whether Psychology belonged among the *Naturwissenschaften* or *Geisteswissenschaften*. This division has no direct parallel in English, but loosely corresponds to that between natural science and disciplines such as history and linguistics.

Without seeking here to promote any particular answer to the question, the following reasons for doubting Psychology's orthodox status should be considered.

1. Some earlier writers strongly argued for Psychology's foundational status as the basis for all other sciences. All sciences, the argument runs, are products of human reason, therefore scientific understanding of the laws governing the human mind itself must ultimately underpin these. Only such an understanding can protect us from error and fallacious reasoning in other scientific inquiries. The implication some drew from this, however, was that the nature of mind could not be captured by analogies drawn from the discoveries of other sciences, to do so being in effect explaining the greater by the lesser. The 'foundationalist' view may, in some sense, be traced back to John Locke's *An Essay Concerning Human Understanding* (1690). While never refuted, this argument was discreetly abandoned by 1900. It is, though, noteworthy that Jean Piaget's final ambition has been read as something similar – providing a scientific Psychological account of the nature of knowledge itself, while it continued to be one of C. G. Jung's central theoretical concerns. In so far as this position remains sustainable it would imply that Psychology is to some degree a 'transcendent' or superordinate discipline.

2. The directly reflexive [see REFLEXIVITY] relationship between Psychology and its subject matter is unique. It is a direct product and expression of this subject matter, it historically contributes to changing it and may, from the proverbially Martian perspective, actually appear to be part of it (e.g. experiments on PERCEPTION are now part of humanity's total system of perceptual processing, child-rearing research is a component of our child-rearing systems etc.). Quite what this implies in practice is unclear, but again it suggests that Psychology is not quite as other sciences. These seek to control, or at any rate predict, the physical universe. Psychology, by contrast, appears to be a process by which we continually change ourselves. While figuring infrequently in most twentieth-century English-speaking Psychology, it is interesting that, again, Jung was especially conscious of this problem, as S. Shamdasani (2004) has shown.

3. Pursuing this last point, while Psychology does indeed often seek to 'predict and control' human behaviour, its goals extend more widely. Enhancing mutual understanding and emancipating us from factors which covertly control us also figure prominently on its agenda. There are obviously some differences in these respects between studies of visual perception and COUNSELLING PSYCHOLOGY, for example. The natural sciences are almost exclusively engaged in prediction and/or control. Semtex does not consult chemists in order to overcome its explosive tendencies.

4. As is discussed under REDUCTIONISM, the meanings of psychological-level phenomena cannot readily be reduced across the psychology/biology boundary without a radical loss of meaning. This contrasts with the situation obtaining between physical sciences.

5. Some critics would take the reflexivity argument somewhat further and argue that Psychology is totally embedded in the contemporary social and psychological circumstances in which its practitioners work. On this account it only ever reflects current psychological preoccupations, serves the prevailing social system (or at most criticises it within socially acceptable limits), and diverts people from attending to the 'objective' socio-economic sources of their distress. It is difficult to see how this critique could apply to *all* Psychology. Historically, Psychology's character has always been highly variegated wherever and whenever it has existed. Yet the very fact that it can plausibly become the target of such criticism itself implies that it is a different kind of beast to orthodox natural sciences. Even if 'socially constructed' to an unexpectedly great extent, nobody attacks them in comparable terms.

All these points command serious attention. They do not, directly at least, pertain to the broadly 'scientific' character of Psychology's research methodologies (although many of these may be disputed individually) or institutional and organisational subculture. Their long insecurity in this respect compelled psychologists to pay scrupulous attention to such matters. What is in question is quite where Psychology fits into the grand scheme of things, and how to construe its possession of features above and beyond those of the natural sciences.

A final observation can be made of a rather different kind. This is that the question of what it *is* to be scientific has become rather unclear over the last half-century. Much of this confusion resulted from historians and philosophers of science deploying arguments that are Psychological in fact, if not always in name. Reacting against the logical positivists who had striven to formulate the logical criteria for good scientific practice, they empirically studied how past scientists had actually behaved, how discoveries were made and agreed upon, how arguments were won or lost and the like. Perceptual, cognitive and social psychological factors were all addressed. The upshot was that even the best scientific practice appeared to depart dramatically from the formal criteria previously advocated. Some psychologists also entered the debate, a sub-discipline of Psychology of science nearly emerging in the 1980s. The implications of this are paradoxical. Scientific behaviour surely falls within the purview of Psychology as the 'science of behaviour', but its conclusions actually call into question many of science's long-cherished assumptions regarding its own character. Psychology is therefore in the odd situation of earnestly endeavouring to be a respected member of a club whose rules it feels scientifically bound to dispute.

scientism 'Scientism' or 'scientistic' are used pejoratively in cases where a scientific style is adopted to render plausible ideas which the user of the terms believes to be devoid of scientific basis. Many might thus describe claims that quartz crystals heal by focusing and transmitting 'cosmic energy', for example.

self The concept of the 'self' has presented difficulties for Psychology ever since William James's classic exploration of the topic in *Principles of Psychology* (1890). G. H. Mead, to some degree continuing James's work, provided a complex account of the social origins of the self in his *Mind, Self and Society* (1934). C. G. Jung, by contrast, viewed the self as developing from the integration of the various psychic polarities which he identified (extroversion vs. introversion, animus vs. anima etc.) into a unified whole. Mainstream psychoanalysis has tended to downplay the concept, although the Kleinian D. W. Winnicott differentiated between the 'authentic' and 'inauthentic' selves – which in turn has echoes of the existentialist notion of 'authenticity' [see EXISTENTIALIST PSYCHOLOGY]. Postmodern psychologists have, for their part, tended to criticise the notion of an enduring core self as a myth, or at best a narrative [see NARRATIVISM] creation which we constantly revise. (See also s. 4 and s. 5, SELF)

social constructionism Umbrella term for a variety of theoretical positions claiming that psychological phenomena, the psychological meanings of behaviour and the categorisation systems used to refer to these are products of social processes rather than 'natural'. The underlying assumption is, to oversimplify, that phenomena exist in two different senses. First, in a physical sense as objects or properties of the natural world, which we can accept as falling into 'natural categories'. It does not cause too many difficulties to accept that the animals vs. plants distinction is a natural one, or that mammals, birds, fish and reptiles are broad natural categories of animal life; similarly, with physical properties such as hard and soft, wet and dry, etc. Scientists elaborate and refine these and clarify their boundaries. While some levels of cross-cultural variation in categorisation often occur, for practical purposes we readily accept that such categories reflect really existing differences in the world. While it is possible to make a radical social constructionist case even for these, as some late

twentieth-century philosophers and historians of science have done, we can leave this to one side for present purposes. A second sense in which phenomena exist is in the social, cultural and economic one. These typically emerge from the systems of rules we create to govern and give meaning to social life. These range from simple things like games (e.g. 'serving a double fault', 'being offside') and the phonetic significance of letters of the alphabet (there is no 'natural' reason why letters 'mean' the sounds they represent), to law and economics (e.g 'taking out a mortgage' can only happen within particular economic and legal systems – mortgages could never exist without the concept of 'private property' or in societies where money had not been invented). For Psychology the question therefore arises as to whether the phenomena it studies, either individually or *in toto*, are of the former or latter kind. This clearly has important ramifications for the SCIENTIFIC STATUS OF PSYCHOLOGY, since the natural sciences are concerned with phenomena presumed to be of the first kind. Historically, although there were numerous anticipations in many national traditions, an explicitly 'social constructionist' school only emerged in the 1970s, most notably in the first instance in social Psychology, with the work of Kenneth Gergen (1973). During the last quarter of the twentieth century this developed, more successfully outside the USA, into the major theoretical rival to COGNITIVE PSYCHOLOGY. In Europe it drew upon a number of existing schools of thought and ideas both within and beyond the discipline. To list these briefly: (a) the Marxist doctrine that psychological phenomena are subjective internalisations and reflections of externally existing social relations [see MARXIST PSYCHOLOGY]; (b) the British tradition of F. C. Bartlett earlier in the century which focused on how psychological phenomena were given meaning and structure within social relationships; (c) the North American minority tradition of G. H. Mead's theory concerning the social origins of the SELF (see also s. 4 and s. 5); (d) broader sociological theories like symbolic interactionism, Garfinkel's 'ethnomethodology' and the study of social roles; (e) the support which anthropological research appeared to provide for 'cultural relativism'; (f) the British linguistic philosophy school of Wittgenstein, Ryle and Austin which, while its implications were somewhat ambiguous, greatly facilitated the exploration of the extent to which reality was constituted by LANGUAGE (see s. 2); (g) the German FRANKFURT SCHOOL; (h) feminist critiques of the 'naturalness' of received sexual STEREOTYPES (see s. 5); (i) the French postmodernist school of Derrida and his associates. Harré's NARRATIVISM and Billig's development of the linguistic argument by a re-examination of the nature of RHETORIC subsequently added new nuances. More could undoubtedly be cited, and the background rise of social constructionism within philosophy of science from the 1960s onwards was certainly a factor in creating an intellectual climate in which 'constructionist' approaches could flourish. This sheer diversity of directions from which such views were developing has nevertheless impeded the formulation of a theoretical position agreeable to all parties within the movement. Two dimensions of variability might be discerned: one might be termed ideological vs. philosophical, reflecting the extent to which adoption of the position is motivated by wider ideological political concerns as against being considered simply the logically inescapable conclusion to be drawn from the nature of language or historical evidence, for example; the second could be called 'comprehensive vs. partial', reflecting whether the doctrine is held to apply to all psychological phenomena or whether exceptions are acknowledged. Not all opponents of this position have come from the pro-'natural science' direction. The British mutualist group, for example, consider the metaphor of construction to be misleading and opt for a more thoroughgoing image of perpetual mutual construction going on in the interactions between individuals, SOCIETY (see s. 5) and the natural world [see MUTUALISM]. While remaining the minority tradition within contemporary Psychology, positions being most vehemently polarised within SOCIAL PSYCHOLOGY itself, social constructionism continues to make headway. Within history of Psychology it has been especially influential as a thesis generating numerous interesting questions and insights which have radically reshaped the field during the last two decades. Elsewhere, the initial emotional heat, in which the 'natural science' camp viewed social constructionism as nihilistic relativism and the latter viewed the former as dehumanising REDUCTIONISM, has begun abating and more sober investigations into the extent to which phenomena such as MEMORY are socially constructed have been embarked upon. As indicated at the outset, there are few grounds for dismissing the notion that social construction *can* play a role in creating or defining psychological phenomena; the issues are the extent to which it actually does so, and whether, as an image, the 'construction' metaphor itself may not be misleading and limiting in some respects.

social Darwinism   Use of evolutionary concepts, particularly 'the survival of the fittest', to justify and 'naturalise' socio-economic ideologies of competition and struggle. Actually owes more to Herbert Spencer (who coined the phrase) than to Charles Darwin. Usually applied to such late nineteenth-century doctrines as EUGENICS, but also to some interpretations of SOCIOBIOLOGY.

social Psychology   Social Psychology's varied character, reflecting its social contexts, was apparent from the start: in France G. Le Bon's *The Crowd* (1896) was concerned with the behaviour of people *en masse* and how leaders could control it; in the USA, however, it is usually dated from N. Triplett (1897), a study of effects on cyclists' performance of being watched. Theories of 'group mind' and CROWD BEHAVIOUR (see s. 5) dominated European social Psychology into the 1920s (e.g. W. McDougall's *The Group Mind*, 1920), while North American interest lay in individuals' social relations and ATTITUDES (see s. 5) towards social issues. Triplett's study notwithstanding, US social Psychology was primarily descriptive until the late 1920s, after which experimental and attitude-measurement techniques burgeoned. While for Le Bon public opinion was irrelevant – effective leaders could manipulate it as they wished – North American preoccupations with public opinion led in a quite different direction. During the 1930s a split nevertheless emerged between individual-oriented laboratory research and more politically engaged field research related to real-world social problems, Gardner Murphy and G. W. Allport being leading figures. A third, minority element was G. H. Mead's analysis of the essentially social emergence of the

'SELF' (see also s. 4 and s. 5). In 1936 the liberal Murphy and Allport camp established the SOCIETY FOR THE PSYCHOLOGICAL STUDY OF SOCIAL ISSUES (SPSSI). Thereafter, US social Psychology became increasingly variegated, continued elaboration of 'attitude theory' co-existing with studies related to CONFORMITY (see s. 5), small-group dynamics, role theory and child-rearing, the Civil Rights campaign and cold war supplying much of the backdrop. In Britain the field remained underdeveloped until Michael Argyle (Oxford), Henri Tajfel (Bristol) and Hilde Himmelweit (London School of Economics) began developing a British strand after 1950. With Tajfel's efforts at forging a distinctive European approach, British and mainland European social Psychology increasingly diverged from the North American version. The 1970s saw a near collapse of the attitude measurement paradigm and, following a 'crisis' (now much debated by historians), social Psychology bifurcated into two mutually antagonistic schools: the experimentalist tradition continued by cognitive social Psychology and represented by genres such as ATTRIBUTION (see s. 5) theory, and the social constructionist [see SOCIAL CONSTRUCTIONISM] strand in a sense continuing the spirit of the SPSSI.

Society for the Psychological Study of Social Issues (SPSSI)   Originally founded in 1936 by psychologists addressing the social issues facing 1930s North America, the SPSSI affiliated to the AMERICAN PSYCHOLOGICAL ASSOCIATION in 1937, being reconstituted as its Division 9 in 1945, while retaining an autonomous status, founding the *Journal of Social Issues* in the same year. Membership now exceeds 3500 and remains open to non-APA members. It has often, especially from 1945 to the early 1970s, provided the major forum for liberal Psychologists, which sometimes brought it into conflict with other APA constituencies. It continues to address issues related to gender, public health and ethnicity from a Psychological perspective. The semi-detached position of the SPSSI enables it to take positions on controversial social and political issues, which the APA as a whole has perennially found it problematic to achieve. Nonetheless there is a feeling in some quarters that its original radicalism has gradually dissipated.

sociobiology   Term coined by E. O. Wilson in the title of his 1975 book which sought to initiate what was virtually a new sub-discipline. This emerged from the ETHOLOGY (see s. 8) tradition of Lorenz and developments in evolutionary theory (see ETHOLOGY AND COMPARATIVE PSYCHOLOGY, s. 2, ETHOLOGY AND SOCIOBIOLOGY and HUMAN ETHOLOGY) over the previous two decades. These centred on the ideas of 'KIN SELECTION' and 'INCLUSIVE FITNESS' (see s. 2), arguing that animal social behaviour could be explained in terms of how it served the survival and propagation of the animal's genes, an approach pioneered by W. D. Hamilton. This was promoted with great zeal in the late 1970s and 1980s as a new PARADIGM, some claiming that it would replace behavioural and SOCIAL PSYCHOLOGY. Opponents saw it as SOCIAL DARWINISM reborn and promoting a right-wing ideological agenda. By the early 1990s controversy had simmered down and subtler reformulations of the doctrine emerged. EVOLUTIONARY PSYCHOLOGY (see s. 2), as developed in the USA by Tooby and Cosmides, remains theoretically committed to the sociobiological approach [see EVOLU-TIONARY PSYCHOLOGY].

stereotyping Introduced by journalist Walter Lippman in 1922 (though has older meanings), stereotyping refers to the ascription of a standard set of psychological attributes to all members of a particular social GROUP (see s. 5) (e.g. black people, women, aristocrats, Germans, gays). Became widely used in later Psychological studies of PREJUDICE (see s. 5).

structuralism A term, like FUNCTIONALISM, with a plurality of meanings, only more so. The most important are as follows:

1. In Psychology the term was adopted by E. B. Titchener to characterise his Wundtian concept of the discipline as concerned with identifying the structure of CONSCIOUSNESS (see s. 3). This was opposed to functionalism as advocated by Angell.

2. In linguistics it refers to the movement inaugurated by F. De Saussure which shifted attention away from etymological, philological and historical questions to the analysis of how LANGUAGE (see s. 2) was structured in the present.

3. In anthropology the term was first adopted by the British School of Evans-Pritchard, Radcliffe Brown and Malinowski, etc. to refer to a similar shift from interest in 'evolution of SOCIETY' (see s. 5) questions towards an analysis of its present-day character. For them, however, this and the functionalist perspective were complementary. In the 1950s the French anthropologist C. Lévi-Strauss developed another structural anthropology centred on identifying what were, in effect, the cognitive structures in terms of which 'primitive' peoples understood the world.

4. Meanwhile, N. Chomsky's work in linguistics, concentrating on 'syntactic structures', was also being described as structuralist, even though differing from De Saussure's structuralism.

5. In 1968 J. Piaget published his short book *Structuralism*, in which the term ambiguously comes to refer both to the subject matter of Psychological study and the kind of THEORY (see s. 8) which best explains it. Basically he conceives of 'structures' as dynamic, self-adjusting systems governed by certain rules or principles which determine their development (exemplified in his own stage model of children's intellectual maturation). Structural systems develop by the recursive operation of these rules on their previous products; thus it is erroneous to view their mature features as genetically determined in any strict sense. This is thus contrasted to both 'sequentialist' and hereditarian genetic approaches. He saw GESTALT PSYCHOLOGY (see also s. 3) as pioneering this structuralist mode of theorising. There are affinities between this concept and the old Aristotelian notion of 'formal causes'.

The term is thus to be used and read with caution.

T

topological Psychology (K. Lewin) A variant of GESTALT PSYCHOLOGY (see also s. 3) developed in the USA by the exiled German psychologist Kurt Lewin during the late 1930s and 1940s. This sought to analyse behaviour in terms of fields of forces, which could be diagrammatically depicted. These mapped the form (topology) of the vectors at work in the organism's 'life-space' and their relationship to those operating within the organism. It is difficult to summarise at all adequately the full subtlety of Lewin's approach, which he applied in a wide range of psychological fields, including social Psychology, PERSONALITY (see also s. 6) and LEARNING (see s. 3). Especially fruitful were his long exchanges with E. C. Tolman, whose 'purposive BEHAVIOURISM' had gone some way towards addressing Gestaltist criticisms. Each appears to have found their sparring rewarding for their own work. While Lewin certainly had an impact on his North American contemporaries, topological Psychology as such did not survive him.

typology The classification of instances of a phenomenon into a set of discrete 'types'. In Psychology most commonly used in relation to PERSONALITY (see also s. 6), varieties of MENTAL ILLNESS (see s. 7) and COGNITIVE STYLE (see s. 6, COGNITIVE STYLE AND LEARNING STYLE) (e.g. convergent vs. divergent thinkers). Typologies are categorical, rejecting the notion of a continuum or intermediate zone.

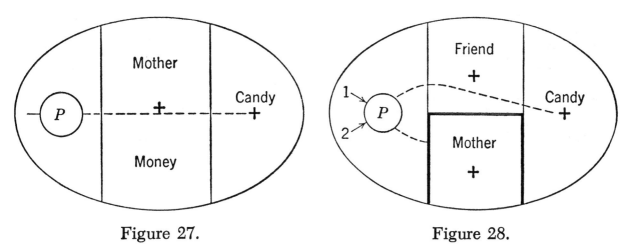

Figure 27.   **Figure 28.**

topological Psychology (K. Lewin) *Lewinian 'topological' diagrams (of a child wanting to buy candy and finding its mother refuses to give it money). From C. S. Hall and G. Lindzey,* Theories of Personality *(1957). BPS History of Psychology Centre*

U

utilitarianism British ethical theory advanced by Jeremy Bentham and James and John Stuart Mill during the first half of the nineteenth century, usually summed up as holding that the 'good' was what achieved 'the greatest happiness of the greatest number', and leaving aside questions of aesthetic value, for example.

V

Vienna circle (*Vienna kreis*)   Name generally given to the Vienna-based group of philosophers (most notably Rudolf Carnap, Otto Neurath, Friedrich Waissman, Carl Hempel, Herbert Feigl and Moritz Schlick) who promulgated logical positivism during the 1920s. Inspired by L. Wittgenstein's early work, and B. Russell's writing on the logic of mathematics, they attempted to resolve outstanding philosophical issues by adopting an anti-metaphysical, logical approach to questions of meaning and the nature of science. A. J. Ayer became their main British follower. However, their central 'verification criterion' of meaning proved unsustainable, Karl Popper's 1934 *Logik der Forschung* (*Logic of Scientific Discovery*) providing a major critique, particularly effective as coming from an insider. In 1936 many moved to the USA where efforts at promoting a 'Unified Science' project continued. Logical positivism was widely held to endorse behaviourist approaches within Psychology and reinforced its 'hard science' camp into the 1960s. It eventually foundered as unresolvable paradoxes reintroduced several old metaphysical issues.

Vienna school   Used from *c.* 1910–30 to refer to Freud and his fellow Vienna-based followers, usually as opposed to Jung's ZURICH SCHOOL.

Völkerpsychologie   German term with affinities to the English social Psychology, but possessing other connotations. In particular it carries resonances of 'spirit of the people' or 'nation', implying an inner psychological collectivity.

Vorstellung   German word (plural: *Vorstellungen*) variously translated as 'presentation', 'representation' and 'idea', much used in nineteenth-century German Psychology. It combines connotations of 'perception' and 'concept' and refers in a general way to the contents of CONSCIOUSNESS (see s. 3).

W

war and Psychology Psychology's relationships with war and the military are complex and far-reaching. A basic dilemma is that if war is pathological psychologists should seek its causes and cures, but as loyal citizens will, in wartime, promote their country's victory. Psychology has been affected both by direct involvements in war and, indirectly, by the effects of military-sourced FUNDING. Several episodes illustrating the first are well known – the World War I work on 'shell-shock' and invention of the US Army Alpha group INTELLIGENCE (see s. 4 and s. 5) tests, and the APPLIED PSYCHOLOGY UNIT (APU)'s World War II research into psychophysical aspects of military equipment design. World War II also saw PERSONNEL SELECTION (see s. 6) techniques developed in most participating forces, 'Psychological warfare', and,

war and Psychology *Radar-related psychological research funded by the US Office of Naval Research figured prominently in the work of the Johns Hopkins University Psychological Laboratory (the oldest in the country) during the post-World War II period. This 'restricted' research report is from 1948. BPS History of Psychology Centre*

in Britain, pioneering work on GROUP THERAPY (see s. 7) for psychologically damaged servicemen and on war's effects on children (see N. Rose 1990). Extensive though a full catalogue of such cases would be, they are probably the iceberg's proverbial tip. The AMERICAN PSYCHOLOGICAL ASSOCIATION's Military Psychology Section (19) web-page reports the military to be the largest single US employer of psychologists. During the cold war the US Office of Naval Research funded research at virtually every US university, while other services also commissioned extensive Psychological research. British levels of military funding were far lower, but the APU, perhaps the country's most prestigious and theoretically innovative Psychological institution, was largely supported from this source into the early 1970s. The rise of COGNITIVE PSYCHOLOGY and important developments in the Psychology of perception during the 1940s–1970s owed much to such military backing. One must thus infer that Psychology's status within North American universities, and the subcultural consequences of close collaboration with the military, were not insignificant. Since the 1920s psychologists have also produced works diagnosing war's psychological causes from a variety of theoretical directions, including psychoanalytic, ethological and behaviourist. N. O. Dixon's *The Psychology of Military Incompetence* (1976) provided a classic exposé of military culture, if not being explicitly anti-war. The topic as a whole remains largely unresearched – were twentieth-century psychologists too immersed in cultural climates dominated by war (recent, ongoing, or threatened) to appreciate the profundity of its impact?

Rose, N. 1990: *Governing the Soul: The shaping of the private self.* London: Routledge.

Weltanschauung German term meaning, roughly, 'world-view'. How the world or universe is experienced in its totality. Thus one might talk of an 'evolutionary' or 'Roman Catholic' *Weltanschauung*, but also of 'Renaissance' or 'late nineteenth-century North American' *Weltanschauungen*, as well as those of individuals.

Wehrmachtpsychologie Contrary to popular belief, Psychology did not fade in Germany with the advent of the Third Reich; on the contrary, it expanded rapidly, a major factor being the recruitment and training of psychologists by the German army, the Wehrmacht, '*Wehrmachtpsychologie*', for purposes of training and selection. In many respects their work closely resembled that of psychologists employed by the North American and British armies for similar purposes (indeed was perhaps more 'advanced' than the latter for several years). Although attempts to use 'racial' criteria for selection were initially explored, these proved useless and more orthodox aptitude tests were developed. This episode is fully explored in Ulfried Geuter's *The Professionalization of*

Psychology in Nazi Germany (1992), a landmark historical study and prophylactic against complacency regarding the moral character of the discipline.

Würzburg school The major anti-Wundtian school of German Psychology from the 1890s through the first decade of the twentieth century, the Würzburg school was led by Oswald Külpe. It took issue with Wundt on several theoretical issues. The two most important were the 'imageless thought' question – Külpe and his followers holding, contrary to Wundt, that imageless thought was possible, indeed necessary to account for the inadequacies of introspective accounts of thought in terms of images and sensations alone; and the presence within all thought of an *Aufgabe* or orienting tendency which precedes the thought process itself. The school effectively pushed experimental introspection to the limit by extending it to the higher thought processes, but by doing so brought its inherent limitations to the surface and subverted the Wundtian primacy of CONSCIOUSNESS (see s. 3). This is, however, too technically complex an episode for brief summarisation.

Z

Zeitgeist German word meaning 'spirit of the time'. Used by E. G. Boring to refer to the way in which Psychology can reflect contemporary concerns, though now considered inadequate as an explanation for the roles of contextual factors.

Zurich school Commonly used from the 1910s to 1930s to refer to C. G. Jung and his followers in promulgating 'analytical psychology' as against 'psychoanalysis'. [See also VIENNA SCHOOL]

Section 2

Biological Psychology

Introduction

Alongside the rapid accumulation of research findings in the brain sciences, with close links to research on the endocrine and immune systems, biological psychology in all its aspects occupies a key position in contemporary psychology. It illustrates the very important point of the necessarily close relationships between psychology and other empirical sciences which comprise the neurosciences. In this section, the contributors not only single out basic facts drawn from anatomy, physiology, pharmacology and other disciplines, but also set out basic concepts, methodologies and approaches.

Biological psychology finds much of its empirical origins in nineteenth-century physiology and neurology. In the middle of the twentieth century, however, much of experimental psychology was led by behaviourists, especially influential in the USA, who wanted to break with the past and forge a new discipline. The behaviourists first divorced themselves from philosophical ideas of the mind and expunged all reference to mentalistic concepts, including consciousness itself. Psychoanalytic theory was cold-shouldered. They went further in separating psychology off from neuroanatomy and neurophysiology, asserting that the study of observable behaviour required no explanations couched in terms of brain structure and function. The overthrow of behaviourism in the 1950s and 1960s by the new cognitive psychologists saw the reintroduction of mentalistic concepts (attention, perception, thinking, etc.), but still excluded neuroscience (Leahey 2000). Seduced by analogies with general-purpose computers and by the rise of artificial intelligence studies, cognitive psychologists thought that psychology should deal exclusively with 'software' problems, leaving all the 'hardware' issues to be sorted out by the brain scientists. This computing metaphor is falling out of fashion, and twenty-first century psychology will achieve closer integration with the other brain sciences (Churchland 2002).

The biological psychology tradition, however, was not completely extinguished in the mid-twentieth century, and continued its development in the forms of physiological psychology and human neuropsychology. To a first approximation, biological psychology fell into two broad camps: in the first, attention was focused on the functions of the cerebral cortex, home to the so-called higher mental functions, which included perception and attention, cognition and memory, and intelligence. Neuropsychologists and neurologists examined the psychological effects of brain injury, which encouraged the view that there was at least some degree of localisation of function within the cerebral cortex and closely associated subcortical structures. Wilder Penfield, at the Montreal Neurological Institute, applied electrical stimuli to the exposed human cortex, and upheld the idea of specialised functions, localised to regions of the cortex. Brenda Milner, at the MNI, embarked on her famous series of studies with the patient with anterograde amnesia. H. M. Roger Sperry, a professor of psychobiology at the California Institute of Technology, working with his associates Michael Gazzaniga and Jerre Levy, investigated the psychological characteristics of 'split-brain' patients, in which the twin cerebral hemispheres had been surgically disconnected. Their work stimulated the idea of division of labour between the two hemispheres, but, most intriguingly, suggested that the mind itself could be separated into two, with 'split-consciousness' (Gazzaniga et al. 2002). Sperry was awarded the Nobel Prize for Physiology or Medicine in 1981 for his startling and influential discoveries.

The second such camp was physiological psychology, or behavioural neuroscience as it is now styled to emphasise the place of psychology within the overall scheme of neuroscience research. In the main, this work relied upon the use of animals in research, and focused upon subcortical structures, such as hippocampus, limbic system, basal ganglia and, pre-eminently, the hypothalamus. Here, the psychological topics of interest were emotion and motivation, reward and aversion. With the current interest in human emotions understood in terms of brain structures and mechanisms, a new field has emerged, to complement cognitive psychology, and is called affective neuroscience (Damasio 2003; LeDoux 1996; Panksepp 1998; Rolls 1999). Professor Kent

Berridge sketches the origins and future directions of this new field of endeavour.

Affective neuroscience owes its modern understanding of how emotion is embedded in the brain to an earlier series of waves of discoveries and conceptual developments that occurred over the past century regarding brain organisation of affective processes. A first wave was Sherrington's and Hughlings-Jackson's demonstrations in the early 1900s of levels of function. Levels of function is the idea that brain systems of motivation and emotion (and other functions) are organised hierarchically as a series of layers that ascend the brain. At the lowest levels, there are concrete affective response elements contained in brainstem, and at higher levels lie modulating affective controls in hypothalamus and ventral forebrain, and finally more abstract and cognitive modulation mediated chiefly by highest cortex and upper forebrain.

Second credit belongs to a host of discoveries between 1930 and 1960 of the affective behavioural effects of local brain lesions or stimulation in hypothalamus or limbic ventral forebrain. These showed that local manipulations of brain systems, nestled at the base of the forebrain, often seemed to turn on or off aspects of hunger, sex, fear, aggression and other motivations, or of affective pain or reward. This wave of discoveries was contributed by pioneering neuroscientists such as Cannon, Hess, Ransom, von Holst, Stellar, Teitelbaum, Epstein, Olds, Valenstein and others.

The third wave, between the 1970s and the present, added neurochemical specificity to neuroanatomical specificity in manipulating and identifying brain substrates of affective psychological processes. Very recently, neurochemical specificity has extended also to genomic specificity, as new techniques have allowed neuroscientists to activate or turn off genes inside neurones that code the production of specific neurotransmitters, receptors, transporters or other neuronal molecules that influence the function of their containing brain systems. Many contemporary affective neuroscientists have contributed to this neurochemical and genomic wave.

Finally, a fourth wave of human neuro-imaging studies from the 1990s to today is adding information about activation of brain structures in humans to the affective neuroscience knowledge base previously grounded in animal biopsychology studies. The human neuro-imaging wave has permitted confirmation in humans of what was previously known for certain only for animals. More importantly, it has also opened the door for examining sophisticated forms of brain interaction between affective processes and cognitive, social and cultural aspects of human psychological processes.

In future, success in affective neuroscience will be aided by more productive connections that can integrate across the diverse themes represented by these waves. Fundamental questions about brain, motivation and emotion remain to be understood. These include: How is pleasure, pain or any other affect generated by brain systems? How do different brain systems mediate specific motives such as fear or hunger? To what extent do different specific motives and emotions share neural substrates? How can we relate new understanding of cellular functions in neurones to psychological processes mediated by affective brain systems? How does human cognition interact with basic affective processes to regulate and cognitively dampen unwanted emotional reactions? Or to cognitively generate emotions in the absence of external eliciting events? Modern affective neuroscience hopes to provide better answers to these questions.

Psychology no longer has to be separationist to establish its own identity; no doubt it had to go through its own adolescence. Future work in biological psychology, under complementary banners of cognitive and affective neuroscience, will not only seek closer working relationships – both empirical and theoretical – with other neuroscience disciplines, but will also contribute in an important sense to our 'rediscovery' of consciousness (Weiskrantz 1997) and of the self (LeDoux 2002).

References

Berridge, K. C. 2004: Motivation concepts in behavioral neuroscience. *Physiology and Behavior* 81, 179–209. **Churchland, P. S.** 2002: *Brain-Wise: Studies in Neurophilosophy.* Cambridge MA: The MIT Press. **Damasio, A.** 2003: *Looking for Spinoza: Joy, Sorrow, and the Feeling Brain.* Orlando: Harcourt, Inc. **Gazzaniga, M. S., Ivry, R. B. and Mangun, G. R.** 2002: *Cognitive Neuroscience: The Biology of the Mind* (2nd edn). New York: W. W. Norton. **Leahey, T. H.** 2000: *A History of Psychology: Main Currents in Psychological Thought* (5th edn). New Jersey: Prentice Hall. **LeDoux, J.** 1996: *The Emotional Brain: The Mysterious Underpinnings of Emotional Life.* New York: Simon and Schuster. **LeDoux, J.** 2002. *Synaptic Self: How Our Brains Become Who We Are.* New York: Viking Penguin. **Panksepp, J.** 1998. *Affective Neuroscience: The Foundations of Human and Animal Emotions.* New York: Oxford University Press. **Rolls, E. T.** 1999: *The Brain and Emotion.* Oxford: Oxford University Press. **Weiskrantz, L.** 1997. *Consciousness Lost and Found: A Neuropsychological Exploration.* Oxford: Oxford University Press.

Professors Steven J. Cooper and Kent C. Berridge

A

acetylcholine (ACh)

(ACh) is synthesised from acetyl coenzyme A (CoA) and choline, a reaction catalysed by choline acetyltransferase (ChAT). It is hydrolysed by acetylcholinesterase (AChE) to liberate choline. ACh is a neurotransmitter in the peripheral nervous system, acting at autonomic ganglia, at parasympathetic postganglionic synapses and at neuromuscular junctions. In the mammalian CNS, cholinergic neurones fall into two broad categories: local circuit cells and long-projection neurones. There are two major constellations of the latter. There is a basal forebrain cholinergic system, with cells in the medial septal nucleus, diagonal band, substantia innominata, magnocellular preoptic field and nucleus basalis. This system projects to the entire nonstriatal telencephalon. The second is the pontomesencephalotegmental complex, which projects extensively to the thalamus, basal ganglia, tectum, brainstem, cerebellum and cranial nerve nuclei. Two classes of ACh receptors have been distinguished: the *muscarinic* receptor (mAChR) and the *nicotinic* receptor (nAChR). Muscarine mimics the effects of ACh at the former, and nicotine at the latter. Atropine is a classical antagonist at muscarinic receptors, and d-tubocurarine blocks nicotinic receptors (Cooper, Bloom and Roth 2003).

It has been proposed that forebrain cholinergic systems are essential to a variety of cognitive processes, particularly LEARNING (see s. 3) and MEMORY (see s. 1), and the cognitive deficits associated with ageing depend, at least in part, on loss of function of those forebrain systems. This HYPOTHESIS (see s. 3 and s. 8) was extended to ALZHEIMER'S DISEASE (see s. 3), suggesting that degeneration of these forebrain systems underlies the memory deficits associated with the disease. While these hypotheses have inspired a great deal of research, recent work suggests that forebrain cholinergic systems are involved in attentional mechanisms (Reiner and Fibiger 1995).   *SC*

Cooper, J. R., Bloom, F. E. and Roth, R. H. 2003: *The Biochemical Basis of Neuropharmacology* (8th edn). Oxford: Oxford University Press. **Reiner, P. B. and Fibiger, H. C.** 1995: Functional heterogeneity of central cholinergic system. In Bloom, F. E. and Kupfer, D. J. (eds), *Psychopharmacology: The Fourth Generation of Progress*. New York: Raven Press.

action potentials (APs)

A neurone's resting MEMBRANE POTENTIAL will remain stable provided the neurone is not stimulated. Introduction of a depolarisation will raise the potential. Unless the depolarisation passes a critical level, called the threshold, this change in potential is proportional to the amount of stimulation, and the membrane potential will return to the resting level as soon as the stimulation has ceased. These are referred to as graded potentials or POSTSYNAPTIC POTENTIALS. Generally these

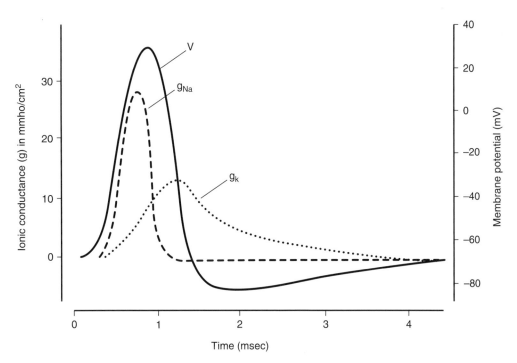

action potentials (APs) *The action potential: time course of changes in membrane voltage and the underlying changes in membrane conductance to sodium ions, Na⁺ (g_{Na}) and to potassium ions, K⁺ (g_k). The initial depolarising phase is due to Na⁺, and the later repolarising phase to an increase in K⁺ conductance.*

potentials are produced in dendrites. If the threshold is passed, the membrane produces a disproportionately large response, which is referred to as an action potential. An action potential is a brief propagated change, the size of which is INDEPENDENT (see s. 8) of the stimulus magnitude. This is referred to as an ALL-OR-NONE response. Increases in stimulus strength are reflected by changes in the frequency of action potential firing. However, there is an upper limit to this frequency, which is determined by the refractory period (Noonan et al. 2003). This is the period immediately following initiation of the action potential.

Action potentials occur in axons. They are conducted in a chain-reaction fashion and travel rapidly along the axon, maintaining a uniform size as they advance. The action potential travels by stimulating the changes in membrane potential that initiated it, at successive locations along the axon. The flow of current associated with the changes in membrane potential depolarises adjacent segments of axons, resulting in action potential firing in each of these segments in turn. Therefore, analogous to a fire burning along a fuse, the action potential regenerates itself at successive points. The refractory period ensures that this regeneration, and thus the movement of the action potential, occurs in only one direction. During the refractory period, the membrane is resistant to stimulus. Consequently, changes in current associated with the newly stimulated action potential are unable to initiate a second action potential at the previous segment of membrane.

The conduction speed of an action potential depends on the diameter of the axon it is travelling along, with speed increasing with axon diameter. Conduction speed ranges from 5 m/s in axons 2 mm in diameter to 120 m/s in axons 20 mm in diameter. The myelin sheath on larger mammalian axons also speeds up conduction. The myelin is interrupted by nodes of Ranvier. Myelin insulates the axon, offering considerable resistance to the flow of ionic current through the membrane. Consequently, the action potential jumps from node to node. This is referred to as saltatory conduction. To conduct impulses as fast as a myelinated axon does, an unmyelinated axon would require 10 times the diameter and thus 100 times the volume. The importance of myelin sheathing in promoting rapid conduction of action potentials explains the gravity of diseases that attack myelin, such as multiple sclerosis (Weinshenker 1998). *JAH*

Noonan, L., Doiron, B., Laing, C., Longtin, A. and Turner, R. W. 2003: A dynamic dendritic refractory period regulates burst discharge in the electrosensory lobe of weakly electrical fish. *Journal of Neuroscience* 23, 1524–34. **Weinshenker, B. G.** 1998: The natural history of multiple sclerosis: update. *Seminars in Neurology* 18, 301–7.

adenosine triphosphate (ATP)
The molecule that provides the cell's energy source. Energy is released by hydrolysis to ADP (adenosine diphosphate), which is converted back to ATP in the mitochondria. *JAH*

adrenaline
Secreted by the adrenal medulla. It stimulates heart rate and regulates metabolism essential for the fight-or-flight response. *JCGH*

adrenocorticotropic hormone (ACTH)
Secreted by the anterior hypothalamus in response to hypothalamic CRH. It triggers the release of the 'STRESS (see s. 7) hormone' cortisol. *JCGH*

all-or-none
Referring to the fact that the amplitude of an action potential is INDEPENDENT (see s. 8) of the magnitude of the stimulus once threshold is reached. *JAH*

amino acid transmitters
Quantitatively, the amino acids constitute the major neurotransmitters in the CNS, and are subdivided into two general classes: the excitatory amino acid (EAA) transmitters and the inhibitory amino acid transmitters, which reflect their respective actions on postsynaptic neurones. Glutamate (Glu) is the main EAA transmitter (Cotman et al. 1995), while γ-aminobutyric acid (GABA) is the major inhibitory transmitter. Glycine (Gly) is another inhibitory neurotransmitter present in the brainstem and spinal cord (Paul 1995).

Until relatively recently, two kinds of EAA receptors were distinguished: the NMDA (N-methyl-D-aspartate) receptors and the non-AMPA receptors (called kainate and quisqualate, respectively). However, at least five different types have now been distinguished: NMDA, kainate, AMPA (α-amino-3-hydroxy-5-methylisoxazole-4-propionic acid), AP4 (1,2-amino-4-phosphonobutyrate), and ACPD (1-aminocyclopentrane-1,3-dicarboxylic acid). Three of these receptors mediate the depolarising actions of Glu (NMDA, kainate, AMPA), whereas the AP-4 receptor is an inhibitory autoreceptor. The fifth receptor, activated by ACPD, has been identified as a metabotropic Glu receptor (mGluR).

Most neurones in the mammalian CNS possess receptors for GABA, and these fall into two varieties: the GABA_A type, which are the more prevalent, and the GABA_B, which are less so. GABA_A receptors are IONOTROPIC RECEPTORS, while GABA_B receptors are classed as METABOTROPIC RECEPTORS. Gly is found in the brainstem and spinal cord, and has more limited function than GABA. Strychine is a Gly antagonist. Gly has also been shown to act as a modulator at the NMDA-RECEPTOR COMPLEX. *SC*

Cotman, C. S., Kahle, J. S., Miller, S. E., Ulas, J. and Bridges, R. J. 1995: Excitatory amino acid neurotransmission. In Bloom, F. E. and Kupfer, D. J. (eds), *Psychopharmacology: The Fourth Generation of Progress*. New York: Raven Press. **Paul, S. M.** 1995: GABA and glycine. In Bloom, F. E. and Kupfer, D. J. (eds), *Psychopharmacology: The Fourth Generation of Progress*. New York: Raven Press.

analgesia
INHIBITION (see s. 3) or suppression of PAIN (see also s. 7) experience. *SC*

androgens
Secreted from the adrenal cortex and from the testes in males. Androgens control growth and development, particularly of sexual characteristics, and influence both sexual behaviour and AGGRESSION (see s. 5). *JCGH*

animal electricity
At the centre of nineteenth-century controversy between Galvani, Volta and others, whether animal nerves and muscle have intrinsic electrical activity or not. *SC*

anterior commissure A small fibre tract that lies at the front end of the corpus callosum and acts to connect the two cerebral hemispheres. *JAH*

anterior pituitary The anterior pituitary develops from embryonic tissue near the roof of the mouth that migrates upwards to join the posterior pituitary below the hypothalamus. The hypothalamus communicates with the anterior pituitary via hormones. These hormones are carried to receptors in the gland by an isolated system of blood vessels (called the portal system). Some of these hormones are stimulatory (termed releasing factors), causing the anterior pituitary to secrete hormones of its own. Stimulatory hypothalamic hormones include gonadotropin-releasing hormone (GnRH) and CORTI-COTROPHIN-RELEASING HORMONE (CRH). Other hypothalamic FACTORS (see s. 8) are inhibitory, blocking the release of anterior pituitary hormones (e.g. dopamine). The hormones secreted by the anterior pituitary are peptides and protein ranging in amino-acid chain-length from 39 to 220. They stimulate various physiological processes by acting on target organs or on other endocrine glands and so are termed trophic hormones. Trophic hormones include LUTEINISING HORMONE (LH), FOLLICLE-STIMULATING HORMONE (FSH) and ADRENOCORTICOTROPIC HORMONE (ACTH) (Brook and Marshall 1996). *JCGH*

Brook, C. and Marshall, N. 1996: *Essential Endocrinology*. London: Blackwell Science.

anti-Müllerian hormone (AMH) Produced by the embryonic testes of males, AMH prevents the development of female internal genitalia from the Müllerian ducts, which instead wither (defeminising effect). *JCGH*

associative learning The associative analysis of LEARNING (see s. 3) is simply that MENTAL REPRESENTATIONS (see s. 3) of (external) events may become connected, and that the subsequent presentation of one of the events will – via its new association – activate the mental representation of the other. This statement is an incomplete account; for example, will the pairing of two events *always* result in associative learning? [See REDUNDANCY EFFECTS: OVERSHADOWING AND BLOCKING] How could associative learning accommodate learning about the presence of one event and the *absence* of another event? [See INHIBITORY CONDITIONING] A full reply to these questions is beyond the scope of this entry, but it will be possible to give some indication of what is learned during associative learning. Examples will be drawn from the study of Pavlovian conditioning in animals (Pavlov 1927/1960).

Consider a standard Pavlovian conditioning EXPERIMENT (see s. 8) in which a brief tone signals delivery of a small amount of food (I will refer to these events as a 'signal' and its 'outcome'). Over the course of training, the signal comes to elicit some overt response. Even in this simple case there are two possible associative structures:

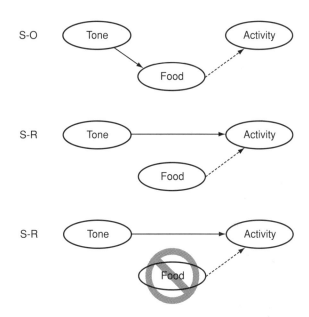

associative learning *Two possible associative structures underlying associative learning in a Pavlovian conditioning preparation. Hungry rats undergo training in which a tone is used to signal delivery of a small amount of food. The measure of learning is a general increase in activity (in anticipation of the food delivery). Assume first that food alone elicits activity (the arrow with a dashed line). It follows that there are two ways that the representation of the tone could be associated with the activity behaviour: (a) (top, S-O) the presentation of the tone could activate the representation of the food (by new associative learning, which consequently generates activity behaviour (a pre-existing association); (b) (middle, S-R) the representation of the tone could be associated directly with the generation of activity behaviour. Predictions from these two accounts have been tested by altering the value of the food after associative learning (e.g. by allowing the rats to consume so much of the food that they are no longer interested in it). It is often found that this treatment reduces the activity to the tone. This is precisely the finding anticipated by the S-O structure but it is not anticipated by the S-R structure.*

associative learning *Redundancy effects: overshadowing and blocking.*

Treatment	Stage 1	Stage 2	Final test of activity to tone alone
Excitatory conditioning	—	Tone → food	High
Overshadowing	—	Tone + light → food	Moderate
Blocking	Light → food	Tone + light → food	Low

Designs for experiments to show the redundancy effects: overshadowing and blocking. In all three procedures, hungry rats undergo training in which a tone is used to signal delivery of a small amount of food and they are all tested for their learning about this tone-food relationship in a final test. The measure of learning is a general increase in activity (in anticipation of the food delivery). For the overshadowing procedure, the tone is paired with the food in the presence of a second stimulus, a light. This light (which is not presented on the test) reduces the level of activity seen to the tone in its test. The effect may be exaggerated (blocking) by first using the light (during Stage 1) as a signal for the food.

1. (S-O learning) The representation of the signal could be associated with the outcome directly (thus the presentation of the signal will activate the outcome's representation which, in turn, will generate responding).

2. (S-R learning) The signal's representation could be associated *directly* with the response (i.e. responding could be generated bypassing the outcome's representation altogether).

It may not seem obvious which of these alternatives is correct, but evidence speaking to the issue is provided by a variety of sources.

One popular technique for discriminating between S-O and S-R accounts is 'outcome revaluation'. Following establishment of Pavlovian conditioning, value of the outcome may be altered and the effects of this on responding to the signal assessed. For example, if rats are given pairings of a tone and sucrose pellets they will come to respond during the tone in anticipation of the desirable outcome. But consider, what would the effect be on responding to the tone if the outcome were made less desirable? This has been tested by allowing rats to consume the sucrose pellets to the point of satiation after Pavlovian conditioning. The finding has often been that the responding to the tone is reduced; this finding is incompatible with the S-R account of learning because the representation of the sucrose pellets is not included in that learning structure. The finding is what would be anticipated on the basis of the S-O account: the current behaviour towards the sucrose pellets can be transmitted to the tone signal.

Further support for the S-O account is provided by demonstrations of 'sensory preconditioning'. One of the most robust techniques for sensory preconditioning involves first giving rats 'cocktails' to drink. These cocktails are composed of two flavours, such as salt and bitter. Rats are afterwards given an injection of a compound that makes salt highly desirable. In the final TEST (see s. 6), rats are offered a drink that tastes of the bitter flavour only; their consumption of this is increased. This change in consumption may be understood if it is assumed that the original pairing of the salt and bitter flavours resulted in the formation of an association between the two and that the current attractiveness of the salt is transferred to the bitter flavour by the association.

In some circumstances evidence of S-R learning may be found, however. For example, associative learning may also be obtained using a SECOND-ORDER CONDITIONING (see s. 3) procedure. Here responding to a signal (Signal 2) is established, not by its pairing with a standard outcome such as food, but instead with a previously established signal (Signal 1). After second-order conditioning is established to Signal 2, responding to Signal 1 can be modified; for example, by presenting it in the *absence* of the outcome that it originally announced. It is rather obvious that this treatment will result in a reduction ('EXTINCTION' – see s. 3) of responding to Signal 1; but what will the effect of this treatment be upon responding to Signal 2? At least in some circumstances, Signal 2 appears to be effective still in its capacity to elicit responding. This type of finding is inconsistent with an S-O mechanism but is what would be predicted on the basis of an S-R account.

The final type of associative structure that will be considered here has been described as 'hierarchical'. Suppose that a rat receives pairings of one signal (Signal 1) and an outcome in one distinct environment (E1), and pairings of another (Signal 2) in another environment (E2). Learning about each signal will progress normally in their respective environments; but what will happen if each signal is presented in the 'wrong' environment? That is with Signal 2 in E1 and Signal 1 in E2. It is often found that this change of environment results in a *reduction* in responding to the signals (rather similar to the way that we may find it more difficult to RECALL (see s. 3) information learned in a new setting). One suggestion is that the initial training results in the establishment of S-O associations for the two signals but that they are, at least in part, dependent upon the presence of the environment that learning has occurred in. It has been suggested that the environments' representations are hierarchical to the S-O associations and that they are necessary to allow their full activation. *JW-R*

Hall, G. 2004: Associative structures in Pavlovian and instrumental conditioning. In Pashler, H. and Gallistel, R. (eds), *Stevens' Handbook of Experimental Psychology, Vol. 3: Learning, Emotion and Motivation*. **Honey, R. C.** 2000: The Experimental Psychology Society Prize Lecture: Associative Priming in Pavlovian Conditioning. *Quarterly Journal of Experimental Psychology* 53B, 1–23. **Mackintosh, N.** 2003: Pavlov and Associationism. *The Spanish Journal of Psychology* 6, 177–84. **Pavlov, I. P.** 1927/1960: *Conditioned Reflexes*. New York: Dover Publications.

autonomic nervous system (ANS) – parasympathetic branch

The parasympathetic nervous system is also known as the craniosacral system, as its preganglionic neurones arise from the brain (cranial nerves) and the sacral spinal cord (Akasu and Nishimura 1995). These preganglionic cells innervate ganglia that are dispersed throughout the body, usually near the organs affected, rather than in a chain near the spinal cord. As the parasympathetic ganglia are not linked directly to each other in a chain they sometimes act more independently than sympathetic ganglia. For many bodily functions the parasympathetic and sympathetic divisions act in opposite directions, resulting in accurate control. For example, parasympathetic activity decreases heart rate, increases digestive rate and generally promotes energy-conserving, non-emergency functions. As parasympathetic postganglionic axons release the neurotransmitter ACETYLCHOLINE (Perry and Talesnik 1953), while most sympathetic postganglionic axons release noradrenaline, certain drugs may excite or inhibit one system in preference to the other.

JAH

Akasu, T. and Nishimura, T. 1995: Synaptic transmission and function of parasympathetic ganglia. *Progress in Neurobiology* 45, 459–522. **Perry, W. L. and Talesnik, J.** 1953: The role of acetylcholine in synaptic transmission at parasympathetic ganglia. *Journal of Physiology – London* 119, 455–69.

autonomic nervous system (ANS) – sympathetic branch

The sympathetic nervous system consists of two paired chains of ganglia, called the sympathetic chain, that run along each side of the spinal column in its central (thoracic and lumbar) regions (Reuss, Johnson, Morin and Moore 1989). Short axons connect these ganglia to PREGANGLIONIC CELLS located in the same regions of the spinal cord. Consequently, these ganglia are controlled by neurones in the CNS. Postganglionic axons [see POST-

GANGLIONIC CELLS] extend from the sympathetic ganglia to innervate smooth muscles in organs and the walls of blood vessels. Generally, sympathetic activation prepares the body for action – it accelerates breathing, increases blood pressure, enhances heart rate and decreases digestive activity. As the sympathetic ganglia are closely linked they often act 'in sympathy' with one another to function as a single system. However, it is also possible to activate one part of the sympathetic nervous system more than others.

Typically, autonomic organs receive both sympathetic and parasympathetic input. However, sweat glands, the adrenal glands, muscles that constrict blood vessels and the muscles that erect the hairs of the skin have sympathetic input only.   *JAH*

Reuss, S., Johnson, R. F., Morin, L. P. and Moore, R. Y. 1989: Localization of spinal cord preganglionic neurons innervating the superior cervical ganglion in the golden hamster. *Brain Research Bulletin* 22, 289–93.

B

behavioural genetics Behavioural genetics is the study of how genes influence the behaviour of organisms. INDIVIDUAL DIFFERENCES (see s. 6) in a wide variety of psychological and physiological traits can be attributed to both environmental and genetic differences. HERITABILITY (see s. 4) is the statistical term used to define the amount of TRAIT (see s. 6) variability in a specific POPULATION (see s. 8) which is due to the genetic differences between individuals in that population. As the influence of genetic FACTORS (see s. 8) on a given trait increases, the heritability of that trait increases. This differentiates it from INHERITANCE (see s. 4), which is used to define the transmission of traits within biological relatives.

Most research in psychology focuses on species-typical behaviour, which defines behaviour by the norm for that species. This approach involves directly manipulating specific genes in order to interfere with normal processes. All members of a species are considered genetically similar except for rogue mutations which produce dysfunction. Single gene disorders, such as PHENYLKETONURIA (PKU), are viewed as aberrations in the population. However, these disorders are rare, and more common disorders are characterised by multiple genetic and environmental factors. In fact, the genes responsible for normal variation in the population are usually responsible for the disorder. Individual differences are defined as differences between individuals within a species. This approach considers variation within a population as normal, with dysfunction representing the extremes of the NORMAL DISTRIBUTION (see s. 8). The genes involved in such variation are called QUANTITATIVE TRAIT LOCI (QTL) because they produce dimensions rather than dichotomies, such as single gene disorders (Plomin et al. 2003). In a single gene disorder, mutation in the single gene is both necessary and sufficient for the development of that disorder. Multiple genes incrementally contribute to the development of the disorder and act as probabilistic risk factors rather than necessary and sufficient risk factors. This contribution is typically expressed as an EFFECT SIZE (see s. 8) to the VARIANCE (see s. 8) of the trait. For example, gene A may contribute 3 per cent of the variance in a complex trait and when added to the contributions of other genes may account for 50 per cent of the variance in that trait. This approach will probably never identify all the genes responsible for the trait because some effect sizes may simply be too small to detect.

There are two main methods of experimentally manipulating genetics in animals, selective breeding and transgenics. Traditionally, species have been altered by mating pairs of animals that express certain characteristics. Over successive generations of selective (in)breeding, specific strains of animals are created. There are two types of strain, inbred and outbred (Li et al. 1993). Inbred strains result from the breeding of SIBLINGS (see s. 4) for at least 20 generations so that the genetic variation within that strain is minimal: they are effectively genetic clones of each other. Outbred strains result from the breeding of non-related animals that share a common ancestry so that they represent a normal, genetically diverse population. However, outbred strains can still be defined by shared characteristics, such as coat or eye colour. Within outbred strains it is possible to create (inbred) strains that have certain behavioural characteristics, such as the Tryon maze dull/bright or alcohol (non-)preferring strains. These strains are created by testing for a behavioural characteristic (e.g. maze learning or alcohol drinking) and then breeding pairs of animals that display it. Over time (inbred) strains can be created that display opposite behaviour on that characteristic. Differences between these strains can then be investigated.

Transgenic animals have had their genetic make-up deliberately altered to produce a desired outcome. For example, 'knockout mice' have had (a) specific gene(s) rendered dysfunctional so that they do not express the consequences of inheriting those genes (van der Staay and Steckler 2001). The 'knockout mice' are then compared to the 'wild-type mice' that have not been genetically manipulated in order to test for differences, e.g. receptor 'knockout mice' do not have specific neurotransmitter receptor sub-types when compared to their 'wild-types'. With the sequencing of the genome this type of work is likely to expand exponentially, adding significantly to our understanding of behavioural genetics.

The study of behavioural genetics has been one of the most dramatic developments in psychology in recent times. It bridges the gap between the behavioural and biological sciences and has led to important breakthroughs in the treatment of major disorders, such as ALZHEIMER'S DISEASE (see s. 3). Fundamentally, genetics play a key role in our behaviour.   JC

Li, T.-K., Lumeng, L. and Doolittle, D. P. 1993: Selective breeding for alcohol preference and associated responses. *Behavior Genetics* 23, 163–9. **Plomin, R., Defries, J. C., Craig, I. W. and McGuffin, P.** 2003: *Behavioral Genetics in the Postgenomic Era.* American Psychological Association: Washington, DC. **van der Staay, F. J. and Steckler, T.** 2001: Behavioural phenotyping of mouse mutants. *Behavioural Brain Research* 125, 3–12.

behavioural pharmacology [See PSYCHOPHARMACOLOGY]

brain lesions and neuropsychology A LESION is a wound or injury, and is made experimentally in order to understand the normal function of the brain structure which has been damaged (Carlson 2004). If the experimental animal can no longer perform a task or exhibit a response, it is inferred that the structure in question contributes in some way to the behaviour. Various lesion methods are available: making radio frequency lesions, which can destroy a circumscribed region within the brain; excitotoxic lesions produced by local application of an excitatory amino acid (e.g. kainic acid), which destroys nerve cell bodies selectively; knife-cuts using microknives to sever fibre pathways in the brain; injection of 6-hydroxy-dopamine (6-OHDA), a neurotoxin which selectively damages catecholamine-containing nerve cells (dopaminergic and noradrenergic). To position these lesions with sufficient accuracy, STEREOTAXIC SURGERY has to be employed and follow-up HISTOLOGICAL METHODS used.

In human neuropsychology, considerable information has been obtained from patients who sustain injury to the brain, as a result of impacts, gunshot wounds, tumour growth, infections, stroke, epilepsy and neurodegenerative disorders (Halligan, Kischka and Marshall 2003). Cognitive psychology of language, ATTENTION (see s. 3), MEMORY (see s. 1) and EMOTION (see s. 6), has been considerably informed by neuropsychological data, although evidence is at its most informative when the lesion damage is relatively localised and neuroanatomically identifiable. *SC*

Carlson, N. R. 2004: *Physiology of Behavior* (8th edn). Boston: Pearson. **Halligan, P. W., Kischka, U. and Marshall, J. C.** 2003: *Handbook of Clinical Neuropsychology*. Oxford: Oxford University Press.

brain microdialysis Chemical substances can be introduced into specific sites of the brain, or withdrawn from brain tissue, using a technique called microdialysis. Dialysis occurs when fluids are separated by a semipermeable membrane, which allows some selected molecules to pass through. Using STEREOTAXIC SURGERY, a microdialysis probe can be positioned in a specific brain region; fluid is pumped through the probe and the dialysate is then collected and analysed. The method is very sensitive and can be used to detect neurotransmitter release in a specified brain region (Westerink 1995). For example, Bassareo and Di Chiara (1999) have investigated the release of dopamine (DA) in the nucleus accumbens when rats consume an unfamiliar, palatable food. *SC*

Bassareo, B. and Di Chiara, G. 1999: Modulation of feeding-induced activation of mesolimbic dopamine transmission by appetitive stimuli and its relation to motivational state. *European Journal of Neuroscience* 11, 4389–97. **Westerink, B. H. C.** 1995: Brain microdialysis and its application for the study of animal behaviour. *Behavioural Brain Research* 70, 103–24.

brain stimulation: electrical and chemical
Although electrical stimulation of the exposed cortex helped to identify motor cortex, much of the important electrical stimulation literature of the twentieth century includes excitation of subcortical structures, most particularly the hypothalamus (Valenstein 1973). The Swiss

brain scientist, Walter Hess, worked extensively on the effects of stimulating the hypothalamus and related structures in the awake cat: not only isolated physiological changes were noted, such as blood pressure and respiratory responses, but also more holistic 'emotional' responses – flight, rage and defensive reactions. In the 1950s, two North American scientists, influenced by prevailing LEARNING (see s. 3) THEORY (see s. 8), made decisive contributions. Neil Miller and his colleagues at Yale University demonstrated that electrical brain stimulation could be aversive and animals would learn to escape or avoid it. In contrast, Olds, at McGill University, showed for the first time that electrical brain stimulation could have positive effects, and could serve as a powerful reinforcer in learning PARADIGMS (see s. 1). Thus was born the idea of the REWARD SYSTEM of the brain. Subsequently, electrical stimulation of the hypothalamus was shown to elicit motivated feeding and drinking responses, and sexual behaviour. These findings concentrated attention on the hypothalamus to investigate neural bases of reward, MOTIVATION (see s. 6) and EMOTION (see s. 6) (Rolls 1999). (See s. 1, EMOTION AND MOTIVATION)

A perceived shortcoming of the electrical stimulation method was that it was indiscriminate; nerve cell bodies and axons beneath the stimulating electrode would all be stimulated. In contrast, it was argued, chemical stimulation methods could be more selective. Methods were developed to allow delivery of small quantities of chemicals (in solution or suspension) into specific regions of the brain via permanently implanted cannulae (Myers 1974). This approach became popular as more was discovered about the brain's many varieties of neurotransmitters. Either the transmitters themselves, or drugs which mimic or in some way modify the actions of specific neurotransmitters, could be injected directly into specific sites in awake animals and the effects observed. Not only could chemical stimulation elicit motivated responses, but it could also have a strong reinforcing effect. This laid the ground for the discovery that addictive drugs acting in the brain at specific locations could act as reinforcers, and so induce and maintain drug self-administration (Wise 1996). *SC*

Myers, R. D. 1974: *Handbook of Drug and Chemical Stimulation of the Brain*. New York: Van Nostrand. **Rolls, E. T.** 1999: *The Brain and Emotion*. Oxford: Oxford University Press. **Valenstein, E. S.** (ed.) 1973: *Brain Stimulation and Motivation*. Glenview IL: Scott, Foresman. **Wise, R. A.** 1996: Neurobiology of addiction. *Current Opinion in Neurobiology* 6, 243–51.

C

---

cauda equina The collections of lumbar and sacral nerves that extend from the end of the spinal cord and run in the spinal canal before their exit from the spinal column. *JAH*

cell-assembly Term coined by the psychologist Donald Hebb to refer to hypothetical collections of nerve cells, or systems, which become associated with each other, and in turn facilitate each other's activity. *SC*

cell morphology (internal) The cell body of a neuron is typically 20 µM in diameter. It contains the same organelles that are found in all animal cells. The most important are the nucleus, the rough endoplasmic reticulum (ER), the smooth ER, the Golgi apparatus and the mitochondria. These are retained within the cell by the neuronal membrane, which lies over an intricate internal SCAFFOLDING (see s. 4) to give the cell its shape.

The nucleus contains the genetic material of the cell. Not far from the nucleus is the rough ER, which consists of enclosed stacks of membrane dotted with globular structures called RIBOSOMES. This is a major site of protein synthesis in neurones (Moore and Steitz 2003). The remainder of the cell is filled with stacks of membrane lacking ribosomes. This is the smooth ER and the membrane stacks lying furthest from the nucleus are termed the Golgi apparatus. They play roles in the processing, sorting and packaging of proteins and the regulation of internal concentrations of substances. Mitochondria are also very abundant organelles in neurones. They play a role in the generation of ATP – a chemical energy store for the cell.

These organelles are enclosed within the neuronal membrane, which also acts to exclude substances from the cell. Properties of the membrane endow neurones with the ability to transfer electrical signals throughout the body. The membrane lies over the cytoskeleton, which maintains the shape of the cell. The cytoskeleton consists of microtubules, microfilaments and neurofilaments. Components of the cytoskeleton are also responsible for the rapid transport of material throughout neurones. *JAH*

Moore, P. B. and Steitz, T. A. 2003: The structural basis of large ribosome subunit function. *Annual Reviews of Biochemistry* 72, 813–50.

cell morphology and neurophysiology The fundamental unit of nervous tissue, like that of all other organs, is the cell. The cells of the nervous system can be divided into two broad categories: NEURONES (nerve cells) and a variety of supporting cells, called GLIAL CELLS in the central nervous system and *satellite cells* in the peripheral nervous system. Supporting cells are more numerous than nerve cells, outnumbering them by a ratio of 3:1. While nerve cells are specialised for electrical signalling over long distances, supporting cells are not capable of electrical signalling. However, they provide physical and functional support (Reddy et al. 2003). They form a physical matrix that holds neuronal cells together (glia means glue), they absorb dead cells and other debris and play a role in the passage of chemicals required for the neurones to operate.

In most respects, the structure of neurones resembles that of other cells. They contain all the organelles essential to the function of all cells. Nevertheless, their morphology reflects the fact that they are highly specialised for intercellular communication. Extending from the central cell body of a neurone are variable numbers of small thin fibres that may extend over short or very wide distances. These determine its connections with other neurones and thus determine how it will contribute to the

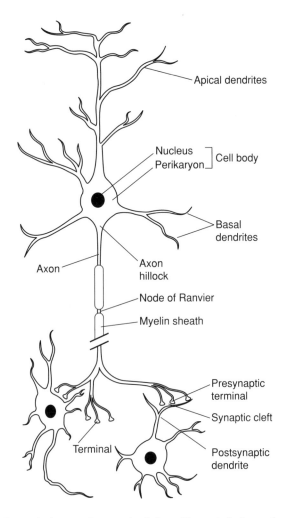

cell morphology and neurophysiology *The main features of a typical neurone.*

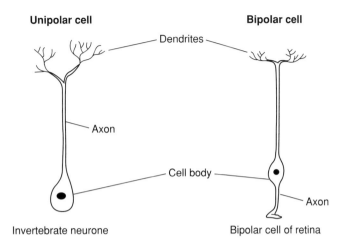

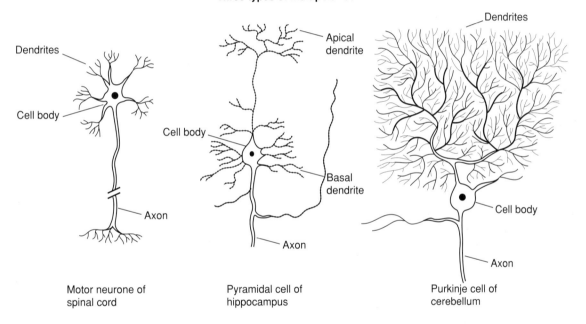

cell morphology and neurophysiology *A unipolar cell, a bipolar cell and three types of multipolar cell.*

overall function of the nervous system. The fibres are termed either dendrites or axons. Dendrites form the information-receiving structures of the neurone. They are stimulated by sensory input from other neurones and relay this information to the remainder of the cell (Williams and Stuart 2003). The dendrite receives information via SYNAPSES, specialised junctions, the POSTSYNAPTIC side of which lies on the dendrite's surface. In most cases the axon is much longer than the dendrite. It is the information-transmitting structure of the neurone. Most neurones have one axon of constant diameter. However, this may have many branches providing input to multiple cells. Interaction with other cells occurs via specialisations at the end of the branches, which form the PRESYNAPTIC

component of a synapse. Some, but not all, axons are covered in an insulating material called a myelin sheath. This is formed by specific glial cells, namely oligodendrocytes and Schwann cells (Arroyo and Scherer 2000), and acts to increase the speed of transmission of neural signals. Some mature neurones do not have an axon. These can only convey information to other neurones immediately adjacent to them.

Neurones can be classified on the basis of the shapes of the cell body, dendrites and axons. Each type of neurone is specialised for particular interactions. Multipolar neurones have many dendrites and a single axon. Most neurones of the vertebrate brain are multipolar. Nerve cells with a single dendrite at one end and a single axon at the other are termed bipolar neurones. These are typically found in sensory systems such as the retina. Monopolar neurones have a single branch, which extends in two directions once it leaves the cell body. One end receives information while the other acts as the output region.

Neurones do not function in isolation. They are organised into ensembles called circuits that process specific types of information. The arrangements of circuits are varied but some features are characteristic to all. Nerve cells that carry information towards the central nervous system are termed afferent neurones, while those that carry information away from the brain and spinal cord are called efferent neurones. Nerve cells that only participate in the local aspects of a circuit, form connections only with other neurones and whose axons and dendrites are contained entirely within a single structure are termed interneurones. These three classes of neurones are all constituents of a neural circuit. Circuits, in turn, are combined into systems that serve broader functions. Sensory systems provide information on the environment, both internal and external. Motor systems respond to this information by generating movement.

To be able to acquire, coordinate and disseminate information, neurones have evolved a sophisticated means of generating electrical signals. There are two types of signalling mechanism – synaptic signals and ACTION POTENTIALS (APs). Synaptic signals permit information transfer by interconnecting multiple neurones. Action potentials allow information to travel along the entire length of a single nerve cell.

Transmission at most synapses is chemical. The presynaptic terminal liberates a chemical NEUROTRANSMITTER. In turn this binds to proteins on the POSTSYNAPTIC membrane to either directly or indirectly alter the electrical activity of the membrane (Weight 1971). At chemical synapses the flow of information is unidirectional – from PRESYNAPTIC to postsynaptic elements. Electrical synapses also occur at specialised sites called GAP JUNCTIONS. These allow direct passage of electrical current (Kumar and Gilula 1996). Current can pass equally well in both directions, hence these synapses are bidirectional. Gap junctions between adult mammalian neurones are relatively rare but they are common in non-neural cells, including glial cells.

Action potentials are brief electrical changes that travel rapidly along an axon in a chain-reaction fashion. They maintain a uniform size as they advance. Their generation depends on nerve cells having MEMBRANE POTENTIALS that can be changed in order to generate signals for transmission to other cells. These changes produce graded potentials at postsynaptic sites, which are also referred to as POSTSYNAPTIC POTENTIALS. These vary in size and duration. In contrast to the action potential, their size decreases with distance from the site of origin. Interaction between postsynaptic potentials, to generate action potentials, is the mechanism by which the nervous system processes and encodes information. *JAH*

Arroyo, E. J. and Scherer, S. S. 2000: On the molecular architecture of myelinated fibres. *Histochemistry and Cell Biology* 113, 1–18. Kumar, N. M. and Gilula, N. B. 1996: The gap junction communication channel. *Cell* 84, 381–8. Reddy, L. V., Koirala, S., Sugiura, Y., Herrera, A. A. and Ko, C. P. 2003: Glial cells maintain synaptic structure and function and promote development of the neuromuscular junction in vivo. *Neuron* 40, 563–80. Weight, F. F. 1971: Mechanisms of synaptic transmission. *Neuroscience Research* 4, 1–27. Williams, S. R. and Stuart, G. J. 2003: Role of dendritic synapse location in the control of action potential output. *Trends in Neurosciences* 26, 147–54.

cerebral aqueduct The part of the ventricular system that connects the third and fourth ventricles. *JAH*

cerebrospinal fluid Liquid found in the ventricles of the brain and the spinal canal of the spinal cord that is similar in composition to blood serum. *JAH*

cervical enlargement Expansion of the spinal cord, in the neck region, to accommodate the significant number of nerve cells and connections supplying the arms. *JAH*

channel protein Membrane-bound protein structure that forms a pore in the membrane through which specific ions can pass. *JAH*

chemical brain stimulation (CBS) Method of stimulating brain tissue by local application of chemicals (drugs, neurotransmitters) to affect brain function in some way. *SC*

cholecystokinin (CCK) Secreted by mucosa cells of the gut in response to ingested fat and protein. CCK provides a powerful within- and post-meal inhibitory signal terminating feeding behaviour and inhibiting subsequent intake. *JCGH*

cingulate gyrus Prominent ridge on the cerebral hemisphere, lying above the corpus callosum, which contributes to the limbic system. *JAH*

colliculi The two pairs of hillocks that characterise the dorsal surface of the midbrain (singular: colliculus). *JAH*

communication Communication is an essential part of the life of any organism, and not surprisingly it has been a central topic of research in animal behaviour. One of the striking features of animal behaviour is the extensive use of multi-modal channels of communication. Whereas language tends to be the primary means by which humans communicate, animals often use a combination of sound, scent, taste and vision.

Communication is said to occur when an individual sends a signal that other individuals respond to. Most usually the recipients of the signal are conspecifics, although interspecific communication is not uncommon. Furthermore, much of the communication conveys information about the individual sending the signal, but again there are many instances when signals correspond to events or stimuli in the external world. Most communication is assumed to function to share information between animals for their mutual benefit. This need not always be the case, however. In a Darwinian world where selfish organisms behave in ways that maximise their own inclusive fitness, there are obvious circumstances where we might expect an individual to manipulate the content of its signal to its own benefit but to the detriment of the recipient. For example, if animal 'A' habitually gives an alarm call when it detects a predator, other animals can benefit from the warning and take appropriate evasive action. Alternatively, if 'A' withholds its alarm call, it is possible that animal 'B' might get attacked and killed. In this case, 'A' benefits through reduced intraspecific competition with 'B', but 'B' gains no benefit at all. In fact, 'B' loses out altogether.

The three main modalities for communication are audition, vision and olfaction (Slater 1990), and each has its own advantages and disadvantages. Sound, for example, has the advantage of travelling across distance and around corners; the recipients of auditory communication don't have to be in direct sight, as is the case with visual communication. Sound also has the benefit of transmitting a large amount of information in a short space of time (Slater 1990). Olfactory communication, on the other hand, does not at first glance appear to be a very efficient means of communication. Once it lays down the scent, the signalling animal has little control over the message, since it then becomes reliant on wind to diffuse it. However, they have the advantage of persistence: they continue to provide information even after the signaller has left the area, and that is important in territory defence where the signalling animal cannot be in all parts of its territory at all times. *JL*

Slater, P. J. B. 1990: *An Introduction to Ethology*. Cambridge: Cambridge University Press.

configural processes

configural processes Many everyday situations require configural processes. For example, a request for 'a box of those bulbs' could be used – without confusion – in either a garden centre or an electrical retail shop. The ambiguous word 'bulb' has two meanings and its use must be determined on the basis of other signals. EXPERIMENTS (see s. 8) have confirmed, too, that many species of animal can solve a variety of configural problems. One example is the ambiguous-signal DISCRIMINATION (see s. 3 and s. 5) having the form A+; B–; AX–; BX+. The signal X (the ambiguous signal) is likened to the ambiguous word 'bulb': its meaning (whether or not it will be followed by the outcome) is dependent upon its co-occurrence with A or B. X will be followed by the outcome when it is presented with B but not when it is presented with A. In the absence of X, A and B announce the opposite outcome arrangement, which prevents the use of non-configural strategies. *JW-R*

Mackintosh, N. J. 1983: *Conditioning and Associative Learning*. Oxford: Clarendon Press. **Pearce, J. M.** 1997: *Animal Learning and Cognition* (2nd edn). Hove: Psychology Press.

constraints on learning

constraints on learning For some animals, LEARNING (see s. 3) is a more efficient means of acquiring information about the world [see INSTINCT AND LEARNING]. However, for most organisms, much of what goes on in the world is possibly irrelevant to their own survival and reproduction and therefore should not be attended to. Alternatively, there are some things that should definitely be attended to and learned. We should expect, therefore, that efficient learning might include some inbuilt predis-

position to learn some things and not others, or some things better than others. Animals should have an evolved tendency to learn only those things that have favoured survival, and thus they should have a genetic predisposition to channel their selective ATTENTION (see s. 3) towards some aspects of the environment more so than others (Byrne 1995). These kinds of constraints on learning have been well documented in bird song, where it has been shown that birds have a predisposition to listen to sounds that are similar to their species-specific song. The template model of birdsong assumes that birds hatch with an auditory template, which is a simple representation of their species-typical song. During subsequent phases of development, the template is believed to select, in a species-specific way, what songs the animal will learn. In other words, while the ability to learn might be present, the animal is constrained in what it can and will learn (Shettleworth 1998). IMPRINTING is also seen as an example of a constraint on learning. Some researchers have suggested that a similar kind of constraint on learning occurs in humans. We are very quick to learn to fear some animals, even though we might encounter them only rarely if indeed ever, whereas we are very slow to learn to fear things that we encounter far more frequently and which might arguably be as dangerous (e.g. cars, electricity sockets). One explanation is that the dangerous animals existed in the environment in which humans evolved, while cars and electricity did not, and hence we are more likely to be predisposed to learning the one category of dangerous things, but not the other (Byrne 1995). *JL*

Byrne, R. W. 1995: *The Thinking Ape: Evolutionary Origins of Intelligence*. Oxford: Oxford University Press. **Hinde, R. A.** 1982: *Ethology*. Oxford: Oxford University Press. **Shettleworth, S. J.** 1998: *Cognition, Evolution and Behaviour*. New York: Oxford University Press.

corpus callosum A large set of axons that connects the two hemispheres of the cerebral cortex. *JAH*

corticotropin-releasing hormone (CRH) Secreted by the hypothalamus in response to STRESS (see s. 7). Triggers the anterior pituitary to release ACTH, which in turn triggers cortisol release. *JCGH*

cortisol A glucocorticoid hormone secreted by the adrenal cortex in response to ACTH. Often termed the 'STRESS (see s. 7) hormone', cortisol is a metabolic hormone that increases energy availability to respond to threat. Chronically high cortisol levels can damage health and are associated with DEPRESSION (see s. 7). *JCGH*

cranial nerves The 12 pairs of cranial nerves arise from the brainstem and mostly innervate the head. They pass through small openings in the skull to enter or exit the brain. Each cranial nerve has a name and Roman numeral associated with it, being numbered in sequence from front to back. Some cranial nerves provide purely sensory pathways to the brain, such as the olfactory (I), optic (II) and vestibulocochlear (VIII) nerves. Others are exclusively motor pathways from the brain, with the oculomotor (III), trochlear (IV) and abducens (VI) nerves innervating the eye, the accessory (XI) nerves controlling the neck muscles and the hypoglossal nerves (XII) controlling the tongue. The remaining cranial nerves contain both sensory and motor fibres. For example, the trigeminal (V) nerve serves facial sensation and also controls chewing movements, the facial (VII) nerves control face muscles and receive taste sensation, while the glossopharyngeal (IX) nerves receive sensation from the throat and also control muscles there. The longest cranial nerves are the vagus (X) nerves that have both motor and sensory function and extend from the head to the gut (Chang, Mashimo and Goyal 2003). *JAH*

Chang, H. Y., Mashimo, H. and Goyal, R. K. 2003: Musings on the wanderer: what's new in our understanding of vago-vagal reflex? Current concepts of vagal efferent projections to the gut. *American Journal of Physiology* 284, G357–66.

D

dorsal Anatomical term referring to structures located at the back of the body or the top of the brain. *JAH*

drive Motivational construct referring both to a generalised activational effect and to more specific GOAL-DIRECTED BEHAVIOUR (see s. 3). *SC*

drug A substance with actions in biological systems, usually due to interactions with one or more receptors. *SC*

drug addiction The traditional pharmacological approach to drug addiction or dependence was to emphasise the effects of long-term (chronic) administration of drugs, the development of tolerance to the drugs' effects, and the occurrence of an abstinence syndrome if the drugs were withdrawn. A shift towards a behavioural account of drug dependence occurred in the 1960s and 1970s, when it was shown experimentally that animals would acquire instrumental responses to self-administer drugs. It was realised that drugs could function as reinforcers and could strengthen drug-taking behaviour. A wealth of research confirmed that drugs, which were abused by people, were capable of acting as effective reinforcers in a conventional instrumental LEARNING (see s. 3) PARADIGM (see s. 1) (e.g. amphetamines, barbiturates, cocaine, heroin, morphine, nicotine). Drug self-administration served, therefore, as a model for human drug-taking (Goldberg and Stolerman 1986). Moreover, it encouraged the search for common neural mechanisms which might underlie drug addiction and associated behavioural phenomena.

Roy Wise gave the lead in suggesting that brain dopamine mechanisms were responsible for the reinforcing effects of brain stimulation, natural rewards like food and, by extension, the reinforcing effects of self-administered drugs (Wise 1982, 1988). Most emphasis has been placed on dopamine (DA) neurotransmission in the nucleus accumbens [see NUCLEUS ACCUMBENS DOPAMINE AND BEHAVIOUR] (Wise 1996). Many authors have followed Wise in giving nucleus accumbens septi dopamine (NAS DA) a critical place in the development and maintenance of drug self-administration, although recent work points to two important extensions. Thus, Robinson and Berridge (2003) argue that abused drugs bring about SENSITISATION of an NAS DA-dependent incentive system, so that drugs are compulsively 'wanted'. Second, the NAS has been placed in a more extensive system of neural connections which may contribute to various aspects of drug-craving and addiction (Koob and Le Moal 2000). Recent work with human drug abusers suggests an involvement of prefrontal cortex in addiction (Volkow and Fowler 2000). The challenge remains to develop successful interventions to manage drug dependence and to alleviate drug 'cravings' and compulsive drug abuse. *SC*

Goldberg, S. R. and Stolerman, I. P. 1986: *Behavioral Analysis of Drug Dependence*. Orlando: Academic Press. **Koob, G.**

F. and Le Moal, M. 2000: Drug addiction, dysregulation of reward, and allostasis. *Neuropsychopharmacology* 24, 97–129. **Robinson, T. E. and Berridge, K. C.** 2003: Addiction. *Annual Review of Psychology* 54, 25–53. **Volkow, N. D. and Fowler, J. S.** 2000: Addiction, a disease of compulsion and drive: involvement of the orbitofrontal cortex. *Cerebral Cortex* 10, 318–25. **Wise, R. A.** 1982: Neuroleptics and operant behaviour: the anhedonia hypothesis. *Behavioural and Brain Sciences* 5, 39–87. **Wise, R. A.** 1988: The neurobiology of craving: implications for understanding and treatment of addiction. *Journal of Abnormal Psychology* 97, 118–32. **Wise, R. A.** 1996: Neurobiology of addiction. *Current Opinion in Neurobiology* 6, 243–51.

drug effects on CNS and behaviour It requires considerable interdisciplinary endeavour to integrate the information that exists, and continues to grow, dealing with drug action on the central nervous system (CNS), on the one hand, and their effects on psychological processes and behaviour on the other. The integrated field can be called neuropsychopharmacology (Feldman, Meyer and Quenzer 1997). Much of the focus of contemporary research falls on the drugs themselves: in the first instance, considerable interest is still invested in the development of new and improved therapeutic interventions for a wide variety of conditions (e.g. to treat ANXIETY – see s. 6 – conditions, SCHIZOPHRENIA (see s. 7), DEPRESSION (see s. 7), to arrest or slow down the decline in cognitive and psychomotor functions associated with neurodegenerative disorders, to reduce the effects of brain trauma such as stroke, or to deal with the growing problem of obesity linked with diabetes). Each of these problem areas sets therapeutic goals. In the second instance, though, drugs themselves are the issue, particularly in relation to addiction, or the adverse consequences associated with drug use. Alcohol, nicotine, amphetamines, cocaine, heroin, tranquillisers are examples of drugs which can have deleterious effects, and provide a major motive for trying to understand the mechanisms of action of such a wide variety of substances. There is a second sense in which research with drugs is conducted, and that is to use them as tools to investigate the relations between brain functions (on systems, cellular, subcellular and molecular levels) and psychological processes or behaviour. The focus here is not on drugs *per se*, but how they can be used to investigate linkages between brain and behaviour processes.

PSYCHOPHARMACOLOGY is a discipline which marries together pharmacology (the study of actions of drugs in biological systems) and psychology, a discipline which investigates mental processes (thought, PERCEPTION (see s. 1), MEMORY (see s. 1), LEARNING (see s. 3), etc.) and behaviour as outputs of such processes. Within psychology there is an enormous variety of methods and approaches on which to draw for psychopharmacological studies. A dominant and still enduring tradition has been BEHAVIOURISM (see s. 1), and the application of OPERANT CONDITIONING (see s. 3) concepts, procedures and types of measurement has had a major determining effect in behavioural pharmacology (McKim 2003). In contrast, a more ethological tradition has emphasised the observation of relatively unconstrained species-typical behaviour in naturalistic environments (Cooper and Hendrie 1994). Other approaches have placed greater emphasis on motivational constructs (e.g. appetite, drive), while others have investigated cognitive processes such as LEARNING (see s. 3) and memory (Cooper, Bloom and Roth 2003).

NEUROPHARMACOLOGY is the discipline which investigates drug actions within nervous systems, and here emphasis is placed on investigating both the increasing number of chemical neurotransmitters and the increasing variety of neurotransmitter RECEPTORS, and intracellular signalling and effector systems associated with them. The picture presented by this work is frequently far too complex to be incorporated within psychopharmacological investigations, which have to proceed with simplifying ASSUMPTIONS (see s. 8).   *SC*

Cooper, J. R., Bloom, F. E. and Roth, R. H. 2003: *The Biochemical Basis of Neuropharmacology* (8th edn). Oxford: Oxford University Press. **Cooper, S. J. and Hendrie, C. A.** (eds), 1994: *Ethology and Psychopharmacology*. Chichester: Wiley. **Feldman, R. S., Meyer, J. S. and Quenzer, L. F.** 1997: *Principles of Neuropsychopharmacology*. Sunderland MA: Sinauer. **McKim, W. A.** 2003: *Drugs and Behavior: An Introduction to Behavioral Pharmacology* (5th edn). New Jersey: Prentice Hall.

E

***

electrical brain stimulation (EBS) Method of stimulating electrically either cortex or subcortical brain structures through implanted electrodes. *SC*

electroencephalogram (EEG) Record of brain-wave activity obtained using scalp electrodes. Used to distinguish various stages of sleep. *SC*

emotion and the amygdala The amygdala (or amygdaloid complex) consists of a complex of nuclei, and their numerous subdivisions, which is lodged in the medial part of the temporal cortex (Pitkänen 2000). It is generally included in a group of interconnected brain structures called the LIMBIC SYSTEM. It has a very large number of connections within its nuclei, between its nuclei, receives input from many brain regions, including the cerebral cortex, and projects to many brain regions. It is neither neuroanatomically nor functionally homogeneous. Recently, the amygdala has attracted a great deal of research ATTENTION (see s. 3), both basic and clinical, because of its roles in EMOTION (see s. 6): emotional RECOGNITION (see s. 3), expression, LEARNING (see s. 3) and MEMORY (see s. 1) (Aggleton 2000).

Klüver and Bucy, in the 1930s, showed that bilateral removal of the temporal lobes in the rheus monkey gave rise to a condition described as 'psychic blindness', marked changes in emotional behaviour and increases in sexual activity. Weiskrantz, in 1956, identified the amygdala in relation to the emotional changes, and showed that amygdala lesions impaired AVOIDANCE LEARNING (see s. 3) in monkeys. Later, in the 1970s and early 1980s, Pavlovian (classical) fear conditioning was employed as a method to understand the amygdala's role in emotions (LeDoux 2000). In this learning PARADIGM (see s. 1), an emotionally neutral CS (conditional stimulus) is presented together with an aversive US (unconditional stimulus). After a number of pairings (one or more), the CS elicits responses indicative of fear: freezing responses, changes in autonomic indices (blood pressure, heart rate) and neuroendocrine responses (release of STRESS – see s. 7 – hormones).

Extended investigations by Joseph LeDoux, Michael Davis and others have yielded detailed information about the formation and mediation of the conditioned fear (or 'startle') responses (Davis 2000; LeDoux 2000). Sensory inputs (including auditory) terminate in the lateral nucleus of the amygdala (LA); the projection from the LA to the central nucleus of the amygdala (CeA) seems to be sufficient for conditioning to an auditory CS; outputs from the CeA appear responsible for the several conditioned fear responses – freezing, endocrine and autonomic changes.

The amygdala is likely to be involved in more emotions than simply fear, but human studies, using brain-imaging methodologies, have confirmed that the amygdala contributes in important ways to the recognition of fear signals and to expressions of fear (Zald 2003). So far, human studies have not attained the anatomical resolution to link specific nuclei within the amygdala with specific components of emotional conditioning, recognition or expression. *SC*

Aggleton, J. P. (ed.) 2000: *The Amygdala: A Functional Analysis* (2nd edn). Oxford: Oxford University Press. **Davis, M.** 2000: The role of the amygdala in conditioned and unconditioned fear and anxiety. In Aggleton, J. P. (ed.) 2000: *The Amygdala: A Functional Analysis* (2nd edn). Oxford: Oxford University Press. **LeDoux, J.** 2000: The amygdala and emotion: a view through fear. In Aggleton, J. P. (ed.) 2000: *The Amygdala: A Functional Analysis* (2nd edn). Oxford: Oxford University Press. **Pitkänen, A.** 2000: Connectivity of the rat amygdaloid complex. In Aggleton, J. P. (ed.) 2000: *The Amygdala: A Functional Analysis* (2nd edn). Oxford: Oxford University Press. **Zald, D. H.** 2003: The human amygdala and the emotional evaluation of sensory stimuli. *Brain Research Reviews* 41, 88–123.

environment of evolutionary adaptedness (EEA) The past environment in which aspects of human psychology were shaped. (See also s. 1, EVOLUTION AND PSYCHOLOGY) *JL*

ethology and sociobiology The modern study of animal behaviour is founded in large measure on the past contributions of both ethology and BEHAVIOURISM (see s. 1) in comparative psychology. Both of the latter two were concerned with the behaviour of animals, although they differed quite fundamentally with respect to the kind of questions they asked and how they went about finding the answers. The vast majority of behaviourists were concerned mainly with delineating principles of LEARNING (see s. 3), and for the most part focused on observable behaviours that they studied using a laboratory-based approach. Any reference to possible mental underpinnings of behaviour were deemed unnecessary, and only a few species were studied, mainly rats and pigeons. Behaviourists were concerned with identifying general laws of behaviour that held for all species, and possibly for humans as well. By contrast, ethologists are regarded as the intellectual descendants of natural historians on account of the fact that they were interested in the behaviour of a wide variety of animal species in their natural habitats. However, it was not simply a description of the naturalistic behaviour of animals. Ethologists concerned themselves with what they saw as the 'biological study of behaviour' and examined the ways that evolutionary processes shape behaviour in much the same way that they shape the morphological characteristics of an organism (Tomasello and Call 1997). To this end their studies focused on innate and species-specific patterns of behaviour (Eibl-Eibesfeldt 1970).

The kind of questions that behaviourists and ethologists addressed reflects the debate on the relative contributions of nature and nurture in development. For behaviourists, the search for a general law of learning placed them firmly on the side of nurture, while ethologists emphasised nature in their search for innate or instinctive species-typical behaviour. With time, however, ethologists came to realise that the behaviours they were watching were not necessarily fixed and invariant, but that learning and other environmental influences probably played a part.

The entire field of animal behaviour changed during the 1970s as the 'sociobiological revolution' took place (Wilson 1975). Within biology, the prevailing view that animals behaved 'for the good of the species' was swept aside and replaced with a focus at the level of the individual (or the gene). Since only the gene survived from generation to generation, the 'gene's-eye view' emphasised that organisms will behave in a way that promotes the survival and perpetuation of the gene. From this viewpoint, given that the individual was seen as the temporary vessel in which genes 'travelled', it follows that the vessel will have been designed by selection to further the interests of the genes that were being carried. Thus behaviour patterns were seen as strategic, with individuals choosing between alternative options while competing with others to ensure that their genes were represented in the next generation. Under the umbrella of this new theoretical framework there was an explosion of field and laboratory studies that all renewed the search for the biological functions of behaviour. Researchers started to look very closely at the function of behaviour, asking what is the adaptive significance of behaviour?

The modern study of animal behaviour is a truly interdisciplinary subject. Among others, it draws on disciplines such as genetics, anthropology, psychology, physiology, neurobiology, endocrinology and mathematics to provide an integrated account of behaviour. (See also s. 1, ETHOLOGY AND COMPARATIVE PSYCHOLOGY and SOCIOBIOLOGY) *JL*

Eibl-Eibesfeldt, I. 1970: *Ethology: The Biology of Behavior*. New York: Holt, Rinehart & Winston. **Manning, A. and Dawkins, M. S.** 1998: *An Introduction to Animal Behaviour*. Cambridge: Cambridge University Press. **Shettleworth, S. J.** 1998: *Cognition, Evolution and Behaviour*. New York: Oxford University Press. **Tomasello, M. and Call, J.** 1997: *Primate Cognition*. New York: Oxford University Press. **Wilson, E. O.** 1975: *Sociobiology. The New Synthesis*. Harvard: Belknap Press.

event-related potential (ERP) Recordings of scalp EEG which are time-locked to presented stimuli; multiple recordings are summated to improve signal-to-noise ratio. *SC*

evolutionary psychology Evolutionary psychology is a relatively new branch of psychology, and is concerned with understanding the mind and behaviour through the application of the principles of evolutionary biology. (See also s. 1, EVOLUTION AND PSYCHOLOGY) Underpinning evolutionary analyses of human behaviour is the assumption that we, like all other organisms, have evolved to maximise our reproductive success. However, while the logic of ADAPTATION (see s. 4) by NATURAL SELECTION provides the broad theoretical framework that guides the evolutionary social sciences, there is considerable disagreement between groups of researchers with respect to what constitutes the appropriate study of evolutionary human behaviour.

On the one hand there are those who identify themselves as evolutionary psychologists (EPs) and they are mainly interested in the structure and function of the human mind. To this end, they apply evolutionary theory to psychological phenomena, seeking to confirm the view

that the psychological mechanisms that underpin behaviour show evidence of 'good design'. In turn, evidence of good design points to the operation of selection in the past. Briefly, their central argument is that during the course of human evolutionary history, human ancestors faced a number of recurrent and intrusive problems that were relevant to survival and reproduction in the ancestral environment [see ENVIRONMENT OF EVOLUTIONARY ADAPTEDNESS (EEA)]. EPs take the view that the mind is composed of a large number of special-purpose mechanisms (or modules) that allowed individuals to solve these particular adaptive problems. Since the brain is energetically and metabolically very expensive to build and maintain, EPs argue that organisms cannot be good at all cognitive tasks, and that the particular tasks that they are good at will have been determined through the operation of natural selection. Therefore, the goal of EP is twofold: to uncover the psychological mechanisms that underpin (human) behaviour, and to identify the selection pressures that shaped those psychological mechanisms. For example, it has been argued that in the EEA, characterised as the Pleistocene world of nomadic foragers, social cheats probably posed a significant threat to relatively small, mobile social groups. They would have enjoyed the benefits of social living but reneged on the costs, and thereby would have undermined the reciprocal arrangements that are believed to have been at the core of Pleistocene social life. EPs argue, therefore, that Pleistocene hunter-gatherers should have been sensitive to those individuals who were unlikely to contribute or act in a reciprocal way, and this would ultimately have resulted in selection for a 'mental module' running a 'Darwinian ALGORITHM' (see s. 3) that solved the problem of cheat detection. Other discrete and specialised modules evolved to solve other intrusive problems, such as those concerned with mate choice, parental solicitude, distinguishing between appropriate and inappropriate food items, and incest-AVOIDANCE (see s. 7). From the EP perspective, humans are characterised as 'ADAPTATION (see s. 4) executors' in the sense that our responses to particular environmental cues in any specific domain are guided by the specific mental module that evolved in past environments to solve that particular category of problem (Smith et al. 2001).

Crucially, the EP concept of the EEA includes the assertion that the EEA does not include the last 10,000 years or so since the advent of agriculture. EPs claim that the pace of change during the last 10,000 years has been far too rapid for our brains, and hence our behaviour, to adapt. They argue that our brains are adapted to the world of the EEA, and that that world is radically different from the environments we currently find ourselves in. It follows, then, that EPs do not consider current behaviour to be adaptive. Modern environments confront our 'stone-age minds', and this adaptive lag means that any search for current fitness differentials is misguided. This position stands in stark contrast to that of human behavioural ecologists.

The second major approach to the evolutionary study of human behaviour is that adopted by human behavioural ecologists (HBEs). Whereas EPs consider a TRAIT (see s. 6) to be an adaptation if it shows evidence of good design, HBEs consider a trait to be biologically adapted if it increases the FITNESS of those individuals who bear the trait, relative to those who do not. Researchers who identify themselves as HBEs apply to human behaviour the same approach that is used to study the behavioural ecology of non-human animals, namely searching for reproductive differentials between individuals, or between groups of individuals, in relation to the behavioural strategies that each follows. Since reproductive differentials are the primary focus of interest, the HBE approach has been coined the 'counting babies' approach, and the babies that have been counted have traditionally been in those societies that are believed to be largely unaffected by western influences and CULTURE (see s. 1 and s. 5). These include hunter-gatherer peoples whose way of life is claimed to have remained relatively stable for thousands of years. That is not to say that modern industrialised societies are entirely ignored, since they are not, and there is a growing body of HBE research that focuses on modern societies.

HBE and EP differ quite fundamentally. Since they disagree on what constitutes an adaptation, that very disagreement means that they disagree on whether current behaviour is adaptive. For the EPs, the psychological mechanisms that humans possess today are adaptations to a world that no longer exists (i.e. the EEA), whereas HBEs argue that it is perfectly legitimate to consider current behaviour adaptive. HBEs are less concerned with the structure of the mind than they are with its output, and in so doing they make the not unsupported assumption that a large human brain means that we can adaptively adjust behaviour as necessitated by variable environments and circumstances. The HBE approach is premised on CONTINGENT (see s. 1) DECISION MAKING (see s. 3) of the kind, 'In situation A, do x, and when in situation B, do y'. As such, by looking at current reproductive differentials, HBEs are very much asking the question whether or not current behaviour is adaptive.   *JL*

Barkow, J. H., Cosmides, L. and Tooby, J. (eds) 1992: *The Adapted Mind: Evolutionary Psychology and the Generation of Culture*. New York: Oxford University Press. **Barrett, L., Dunbar, R. I. M. and Lycett, J. E.** 2002: *Human Evolutionary Psychology*. Houndmills: Palgrave MacMillan. **Smith, E. A., Borgerhoff Mulder, M. and Hill, K.** 2001: Controversies in the evolutionary social sciences: a guide for the perplexed. *Trends in Ecology and Evolution* 16(3), 128–35. **Winterhalder, B. and Smith, E. A.** 2000: Analysing adaptive strategies: human behavioural ecology at twenty five. *Evolutionary Anthropology*, 9, 51–72.

F

feeding and drinking Together, feeding and drinking are called ingestive behaviours. Deficits may give rise to motivational states – hunger and thirst, respectively – which lead to approaches to appropriate goal objects (food items or fluids), and then consumption. Once the relevant deficit has been removed, then the source of the MOTIVATION (see s. 6) disappears, and the ingestive behaviour ceases. This portrait of feeding and drinking relates to a homeostatic regulation of energy balance and fluid balance, respectively (Toates 2001; Mook 1996). It is conventional to distinguish the signals (internal and external) which initiate ingestion from those that terminate the behaviour.

In the case of feeding, prior food deprivation is a powerful stimulus to initiate the behaviour. Lowered levels of blood glucose may stimulate glucoreceptors, neurones which signal reduced glucose availability. In the case of satiety, several FACTORS (see s. 8) may contribute to feeding cessation: oral stimulation, stomach distension, preabsorptive chemoception, postabsorptive effects in the liver and elsewhere. Within the brain, the hypothalamus has been strongly implicated in the control of feeding behaviour. Neurochemically, a great variety of hypothalamic neuropeptides are involved in the control of feeding responses (Carlson 2004). Leptin is a peptide synthesised in adipose tissue which acts in the hypothalamus to inhibit appetite (Schwartz et al. 2000).

In the case of drinking, thirst can be generated as a result of water deficits in either the intracellular (osmometric thirst) or extracellular (volumetric thirst) fluid compartments: deprivation of water brings about removal of both deficits. Satiety occurs when water is consumed, and in anticipation of the restoration of the fluid deficits. In the brain, structures that border the anteroventral tip of the third ventricle (AV3V) integrate the signals for both osmometric and volumetric thirst (Carlson 2004).   *SC*

Carlson, N. R. 2004: *Physiology of Behavior* (8th edn). Boston: Pearson. **Mook, D. G.** 1996: *Motivation: The Organisation of Action* (2nd edn). New York: Norton. **Schwartz, M. W., Woods, S. C., Porte, D., jun., Seeley, R. J. and Raskin, D. G.** 2000: Central nervous system control of food intake. *Nature* 404, 661–71. **Toates, F.** 2001: *Biological Psychology: An Integrative Approach.* Harlow: Prentice Hall.

fertility The number of children produced by an individual in a given time period.   *JL*

fitness A measure of an individual's genetic contribution to future generations.   *JL*

follicle-stimulating hormone (FSH) A gonadotropic hormone released from the anterior pituitary. FSH stimulates the sexual development of males and females at PUBERTY (see s. 4). In females, FSH stimulates the development of ovarian follicles and oestrogen secretion. In males, FSH stimulates spermatogenesis.   *JCGH*

forebrain The forebrain is the most anterior and most prominent part of the mammalian brain. It can be subdivided (on the basis of its development) into the telencephalon, which contains the cerebral hemispheres, hippocampus and basal ganglia, and the diencephalon, which contains the thalamus and hypothalamus. The major components of the telencephalon are the two cerebral hemispheres. These form the surface of the forebrain and surround all other forebrain structures. Each hemisphere is designed to receive information from, and control muscles on, the contralateral (opposite) side of the body. The cerebral hemispheres are covered by a layer of tissue called the cerebral cortex and communicate with each other via two bundles of axons, the CORPUS CALLOSUM and the ANTERIOR COMMISSURE. About 90 per cent of human cerebral cortex is frequently referred to as neocortex, meaning of relatively recent evolution. However, this term is based on unfounded evolutionary arguments from the end of the nineteenth century, and the term isocortex is now preferred (Swanson 2003). The isocortex contains SIX LAMINAE (layers of cell bodies). These lie parallel to the cortex and vary in thickness and prominence from one part of the cortex to the next. The cells of the cortex are organised into columns perpendicular to the laminae. This vertical flow of information forms mini-circuits that perform a single function. The hippocampus is one important area of cortex that is not isocortex – it contains only three layers. It lies between the thalamus and the cerebral cortex and is connected to the hypothalamus by the fornix (a major axon tract). The basal ganglia are also within the cerebral hemispheres. These include the caudate nucleus, putamen, globus pallidus and amygdala. These nuclei innervate one another to form a neural system that is very important in certain aspects of motor control (Groenewegen 2003).

The other part of the forebrain, the diencephalon, contains the thalamus and hypothalamus. The thalamus is a large two-lobed structure that sits on top of the brainstem. It provides the main source of input to the cerebral cortex, with most sensory information going first to the thalamus. Located immediately under the thalamus is another paired structure termed the hypothalamus. It is a small area near the base of the brain, which contains a number of distinct nuclei. Activity of these nuclei controls daily rhythms of sleep as well as many aspects of motivated and emotional behaviour (Williams, Harrold and Cutler 2000). (See s. 1, EMOTION AND MOTIVATION) It also influences the pituitary gland (attached to the base of the hypothalamus) to control hormone secretion.

The LIMBIC SYSTEM is also contained within the forebrain. It is a widespread GROUP (see s. 5) of nuclei that innervate each other to form a network that is particularly important for motivational and emotional behaviours such as eating, drinking, sexual behaviour, AGGRESSION (see s. 5) and ANXIETY (see s. 6). It contains structures from both divisions of the forebrain, with the larger structures being the hippocampus, amygdala, hypothalamus,

OLFACTORY BULB and CINGULATE GYRUS of the cerebral cortex (Patterson and Schmidt 2003). *JAH*

Groenewegen, H. J. 2003: The basal ganglia and motor control. *Neural Plasticity* 10, 107–20. **Patterson, D. W. and Schmidt, L. A.** 2003: Neuroanatomy of the human affective system. *Brain and Cognition* 52, 24–6. **Swanson, L. W.** 2003: The cognitive system: Thinking and voluntary control of behaviour. In *Brain Architecture: Understanding the Basic Plan*. New York: Oxford University Press. **Williams, G., Harrold., J. A. and Cutler, D. J.** 2000: The hypothalamus and the regulation of energy homeostasis: lifting the lid on a black box. *Proceedings of the Nutritional Society* 59, 385–96.

G

---

ganglia Collections of thousands of neurones found outside the CNS along the course of peripheral nerves (singular: ganglion). *JAH*

gap junction A narrow gap between two cells that is spanned by channel proteins. These allow ions to pass directly from one cell to the next. *JAH*

genotype The particular combination of genes (or ALLELES – see s. 4) that an individual carries. *JL*

ghrelin A hormone secreted in the stomach that stimulates eating behaviour. Ghrelin appears to achieve this by stimulating the orexigenic (appetite stimulatory) circuits with the hypothalamus. Levels of endogenous ghrelin are suppressed by food intake. *JCGH*

glial cells Glial cells comprise diverse cell types with entirely different functions. Their common denomination is their major distinction from neurones – they do not participate directly in electrical signalling. However, some of their supportive functions help maintain the signalling abilities of neurones. They may also serve a nutritional role, providing a pathway to deliver raw materials from which neurones synthesise complex compounds. The morphology of glial cells also differs from neurones. Although glial cells can be complex in form, they are typically smaller than neurones and lack axons and dendrites.

There are four types of glial cells. *Astrocytes* are restricted to the brain and spinal cord. They have a star-like appearance due to the presence of elaborate local processes. Extensions of astrocytes form the dura mater, the tough sheets that coat the outer surface of the brain. They also fill the space between neurones. Astrocytes may play an active role in the functioning of the brain by maintaining an appropriate chemical environment for neuronal signalling. *Microglial* cells are smaller cells that share many properties with tissue MACROPHAGES. These cells migrate in large numbers to sites of neural damage and remove debris left by dead or regenerating neurones and glial cells. Oligodendrocytes and Schwann cells are the remaining glial cell types. Oligodendrocytes are restricted to the CNS, while Schwann cells are located in the peripheral nervous system. Both cell types lay down myelin (a laminated wrapping) around some axons. This accelerates the speed of conduction of neural impulses. Myelination by Schwann cells differs from that by oligodendrocytes. A single oligodendrocyte may myelinate several segments of the same axon or several different axons (Fanarraga et al. 1998), whereas each Swann cell myelinates only a single segment (typically no longer than 200 µM) of one axon. Between the myelin segments are small gaps where the axon is exposed. These are termed Nodes of Ranvier (Arroyo and Scherer 2000). *JAH*

Arroyo, E. J. and Scherer, S. S. 2000: On the molecular architecture of myelinated fibres. *Histochemistry and Cell Biology* 113, 1–18. Fanarraga, M. L., Griffiths, I. R., Zhao, M. and Duncan I. D. 1998: Oligodendrocytes are not inherently programmed to myelinate a specific size of axon. *The Journal of Comparative Neurology* 399, 94–100.

glucagon Secreted by pancreatic α cells in response to a fall in blood glucose. Stimulates the conversion of glycogen back into glucose restoring normal blood glucose levels. *JCGH*

gonads as endocrine organs Differentiated into either testes or ovaries during foetal development, the gonads release hormones which coordinate development and activate behaviour. In the male, testicular secretions of androgens such as TESTOSTERONE, dihydrotestosterone and androstenedione cause the development of masculine sexual characteristics. In the adult male, testosterone secretion also controls the production of sperm within the testes. In the female, secretion of OESTROGENS and PROGESTERONE from the ovaries causes the development of uterine and other feminine tissues, including the mammary glands. Oestrogen and progesterone release also regulates the development and release of ova every month during the female reproductive lifespan (Brook and Marshall 1996). *JCGH*

Brook, C. and Marshall, N. 1996: *Essential Endocrinology.* London: Blackwell Science.

G protein-coupled receptor [See METABOTROPIC RECEPTOR]

H

Hebbian synapse Term used in cognitive neuroscience and neurocomputation to refer to SYNAPTIC PLASTICITY, such that inputs and outputs become associated in an activity-dependent way; named after the psychologist Donald Hebb.   *SC*

hedonic evaluation ATTRIBUTION (see s. 5) of pleasantness or aversiveness to encountered stimuli (colloquially termed 'liking').   *SC*

hedonic evaluation and incentive motivation
Often, when we refer to 'reward', we assume that reward as 'incentive' is equivalent to reward as 'pleasure', and that 'pleasure' may represent a conscious, subjective counterpart to some underlying process of reward. Recent theoretical and EMPIRICAL (see s. 8) work has led to important distinctions in the use of the concept 'reward' (Berridge and Robinson 2003). Berridge (1996) drew a critical distinction between 'liking' (hedonic evaluation), on the one hand, and 'wanting' (incentive salience), on the other. Although the two may be linked (we may want something we like), they are nevertheless dissociable. Not only are these concepts psychologically and functionally distinct, but they are anatomically and neurochemically dissociable too.

Rats, primates and human infants demonstrate positive affective responses ('liking') to sweet tastes (Steiner et al. 2001). Two neuroanatomical locations with distinct neurochemical characteristics have been shown to be involved in the mediation of 'liking'. The first is the parabrachial nucleus in the lower brainstem: here, benzodiazepine drugs enhance the hedonic evaluation of sweet tastes (Peciña and Berridge 1996). The second is the nucleus accumbens (shell), where opioid drugs act to enhance sweet taste 'liking' (Peciña and Berridge, 2000). Berridge (2003) proposes that these subcortical systems may contribute to conscious experience of sensory pleasure.

In contrast, incentives refer to stimuli with motivational salience, which can be anticipated or expected by an organism. We can talk about 'wanting' such a reward. Berridge and Robinson (1998) argue that ventral striatal dopamine is critical to such incentive salience. Moreover, these authors propose that addictive drugs produce sensitisation of this dopaminergic incentive-salience system, to cause excessive 'wanting' or craving for the drugs (Robinson and Berridge 1993). Taken together, this work offers important insights into the ways in which emotions (or affective responses), like 'pleasure', are generated and how they may interface with motivational processes (or incentive salience and LEARNING (see s. 3)). (See s. 1, EMOTION AND MOTIVATION)   *SC*

Berridge, K. C. 1996: Food reward: brain substrates of wanting and liking. *Neuroscience and Biobehavioral Reviews* 20, 1–25. **Berridge, K. C.** 2003: Pleasures of the brain. *Brain and Cognition* 52, 106–28. **Berridge, K. C. and Robinson, T. E.** 1998: What is the role of dopamine in reward: hedonic impact, reward learning, or incentive salience? *Brain Research Reviews* 28, 309–69. **Berridge, K. C. and Robinson, T. E.** 2003: Parsing reward. *Trends in Neurosciences* 26, 507–13. **Peciña, S. and Berridge, K. C.** 1996: Brainstem mediates diazepam enhancement of palatability and feeding: microinjections into fourth ventricle versus lateral ventricle. *Brain Research* 727, 22–30. **Peciña, S. and Berridge, K. C.** 2000: Opioid eating site in accumbens shell mediates food intake and hedonic 'licking': map based on microinjection Fos plumes. *Brain Research* 863, 71–86. **Robinson, T. E. and Berridge, K. C.** 1993: The neural basis of drug craving: an incentive-sensitization theory of addiction. *Brain Research Reviews* 18, 247–91. **Steiner, J. E., Glaser, D., Hawilo, M. E. and Berridge, K. C.** 2001: Comparative expression of hedonic impact: affective reactions to taste by human infants and other primates. *Neuroscience and Biobehavioral Reviews* 25, 53–128.

hindbrain and spinal cord The hindbrain is the most posterior part of the brain. It can be divided into two component parts: the myelencephalon, which contains the medulla, and the metencephalon, which contains the pons and cerebellum. Along with the midbrain and certain central structures of the forebrain, these three hindbrain structures constitute the brainstem. The medulla forms the bottom of the brainstem and marks the transition from brainstem to spinal cord. It is composed largely of tracts carrying information from the brain to the rest of the body. However, it also controls a number of vital reflexes, including breathing, heart rate, sneezing and coughing (Nogues, Roncoroni and Benarroch 2002). Thus, damage to the medulla is typically fatal. This control is achieved via cranial nerves. The cranial nerves V through XII originate in the medulla and pons. The pons lies above the medulla. In Latin, the term *pons* means bridge, and the name reflects the fact that many axons cross from one side of the brain to the other within this region. The pons includes regions involved in motor control and sensory analysis. It also contains several groups of neurones that influence the spinal cord, primarily to regulate movement. The medulla and pons also contain the reticular formation and the raphe system. These two systems regulate arousal. While neither system provides sensory information, they act to enhance or reduce the brain's readiness to respond to other sources of information (Mesulam 1995).

The medulla can be considered as an elaborate extension of the spinal cord. This is the main route of information transfer from the skin, joints and muscles to the brain and vice versa. Severing of the spinal cord results in lack of feeling in the skin and paralysis of muscles in the body. Loss of sensation and motor control begin from the segment at which the spinal cord is cut and extend to all parts of the body served by that and lower segments.

The cerebellum is a large folded structure on the brainstem's dorsal surface. It has long been known to play a role in the control of movement. However, it is now believed that this region is more active in organising the sensory information that coordinates movements rather than in controlling the movement itself. Damage to the cerebellum results in problems switching between auditory and visual stimuli. Malformation of the cerebellum is common in autistic children (Courchesne et al. 1994).

JAH

Courchesne, E., Saitoh, O., Townsend, J. P., Yeung-Courchesne, R., Press, O., Lincoln, A. J., Haas, R. H. and Schriebman, L. 1994: Cerebellar hypoplasia and hyperplasia in infantile autism. *Lancet* 343, 63–4. **Mesulam, M. M.** 1995: Cholinergic pathways and ascending reticular activating system of the human brain. *Annals of the New York Academy of Sciences* 10, 169–79. **Nogues, M. A., Roncoroni, A. J. and Benarroch, E.** 2002: Breathing control in neurological diseases. *Clinical Autonomic Research* 12, 440–9.

histological methods

In EXPERIMENTS (see s. 8) on animals' brains (e.g. a lesion study or intracranial injection) it is critical to verify the location and extent of the lesion or to specify the site of injection, in relation to identifiable brain structures. To accomplish this, histological methods are used to fix, slice, stain and microscopically examine the brain tissue (Carlson 2004). First the brain is perfused with a fixative (usually formalin) which halts deterioration of the tissue and hardens it. Then the brain is sliced in very thin sections (e.g. 10–80 µm thickness), using a device called a microtome. Staining of the slices is important to reveal structural details, such as nerve cell bodies (e.g. cresyl violet), and then the sections are examined at high magnification using a light microscope. Identification of the structures under scrutiny relies on stereotaxic brain atlases (e.g. Swanson 1992).

SC

Carlson, N. R. 2004: *Physiology of Behavior* (8th edn). Boston: Pearson. **Swanson, L. W.** 1992: *Brain Maps: Structure of the Rat Brain*. New York: Elsevier.

homeostasis

Term introduced by the physiologist Walter Cannon to refer to a range of systems (behavioural, physiological, endocrine) which act in concert to ensure stable values of bodily functions essential to survival. *SC*

hormones and aggression

In animals AGGRESSION (see s. 5) is demonstrated in a variety of situations. It can be a response to threat (defensive aggression) or associated with reproductive competition (offensive aggression). Within species, offensive aggression (occurring particularly in birds and mammals) often occurs between males competing to attract females. The onset of offensive aggression in males tends to co-occur at the onset of sexual maturity. It is therefore common practice to castrate male livestock prior to PUBERTY (see s. 4) to make them easier and safer to handle. In animals, prenatal exposure to ANDROGENS seems to stimulate the development of TESTOSTERONE-sensitive neural circuits. Males exposed to excess androgens during development require less testosterone in later life to trigger aggression towards another male. Females exposed to androgens during development also show offensive aggression towards other females in adulthood. In contrast, offensive aggression in non-androgenised females is unusual. However, adult female rodents will demonstrate offensive aggression towards unfamiliar females after testosterone treatment. The main form of aggression normally observed in female rodents is defensive. Maternal aggression, which commences during pregnancy in rodents, appears to be dependent on the secretion of the hormone PROGESTERONE.

In humans, androgens may also be critical in the expression of aggressive behaviour. Certainly both aggression and antisocial behaviour are far more common in men. Again foetal exposure to androgens may contribute to these differences between males and females. However, it should be noted that females with congenital adrenal hyperplasia (CAH), exposed to excessive androgens during development, do not display increased aggression. Again human male aggression increases at puberty when the gonadotropin hormones stimulate a surge in testosterone release from the testes. When levels of hormones in prisoners convicted of violent crimes and non-violent crimes are compared, testosterone levels are higher in those who have shown criminal aggression. Moreover, it has been reported that castration can reduce aggression in men (Dabbs and Dabbs 2000; Mazur and Booth 1998). (See also s. 1, CRIME AND PSYCHOLOGY) *JCGH*

Dabbs, J. M. and Dabbs M. G. 2000: *Heroes, Rogues and Lovers: Testosterone and Behavior*. New York. McGraw-Hill. **Mazur, A. and Booth, A.** 1998: Testosterone and dominance in men. *Behavioral and Brain Sciences* 21, 353–71.

hormones and reproductive behaviour

The secretion of steroid hormones underpins reproductive behaviour. Hormones secreted from the ANTERIOR PITUITARY gland, FOLLICLE-STIMULATING HORMONE (FSH) and LUTEINISING HORMONE (LH) control the human menstrual cycle. Secretion of FSH triggers the growth of the ovarian follicle, usually around a single ovum. The rapidly maturing ovarian follicle in turn secretes OESTROGEN. Oestrogen has two effects. First, it thickens the uterus wall in preparation for ovulation, and second it triggers the release of LH from the anterior pituitary. The combination of LH and FSH triggers the release of the ovum (ovulation). The empty ovarian follicle then starts to secrete PROGESTERONE. Progesterone maintains the lining of the uterus and inhibits further follicle development in the ovaries. If sperm fertilises the ovum on its way to the uterus, and the fertilised cell reaches the uterus wall, the continued secretion of these gonadal hormones will maintain these conditions for the developing FOETUS (see s. 4).

In humans, the optimum point in the menstrual cycle for successful fertilisation is around the point of ovulation. It therefore would seem plausible that around this period human females should demonstrate a surge in sexual behaviour to take advantage of this period of fertility. Certainly the reproductive cycle in other female mammals, the oestrous cycle, does cause marked observable changes in the animal's behaviour. The rise in oestrogen prior to ovulation and the surge of progesterone immediately after causes the female to become more receptive to males. In rats this period is called lordosis. During lordosis the female no longer defends herself from male advances but instead positions herself for copulation. If this is not sufficient, her eagerness to mate will lead her to more actively elicit a sexual response. The removal of the ovaries (ovariectomy), stopping the secretion of oestrogen and progesterone, inhibits this sexual behaviour in the rodent. Interestingly the absence of olfactory and behaviour cues associated with the female's oestrous cycle diminishes male sexual interest in her. Therefore, in rodents, gonadal hormones affect both the female's capacity to successfully mate (fertility) and her willingness to engage in copulation. In humans, matters are less simple. However, levels of circulating hormones are still considered to be important in the expression of sexual behaviour. Women are more likely to initiate sexual activity around the point of ovulation. However, evidence also suggests that ANDROGENS release from the adrenal cortex may also stimulate female sexual behaviour. Moreover, ovariectomised human females given TESTOSTERONE report marked increases in sexual urges, behaviour and enjoyment (LeVay 1993; Bagatell and Bremner 1997).

In all male mammals, testosterone appears critical to the activation of sexual behaviour. In humans, as the level of testosterone fluctuates during their lifespan, so does sexual interest and activity. These peak in the human male during their twenties and decline over the rest of their lives. In rats, removal of the testes causes a rapid decline in both testosterone and sexual behaviour. Similarly, in humans, chemical blocking of testicular testosterone release also produces a marked decrease in sexual urges, behaviour and enjoyment. Chemical or physical castration of sex offenders also produces dramatic decreases in sexual desire in some but not all individuals. Studies demonstrate that surges of testosterone within the individual can be stimulated by anticipation of sex or erotic material (Robbins 1996). *JCGH*

Bagatell, C. J. and Bremner, W. J. 1997: Androgens and behaviour in men and women. *Endocrinologist*, 7, 97–102.
LeVay, S. 1993: *The Sexual Brain*. Cambridge, Mass: MIT.
Robbins A. 1996: Androgens and male sexual behaviour: From mice to men. *Trends in Endocrinology and Metabolism*, 76, 345–350.

hormones and stress   Organisms experience STRESS (see s. 7) in response to threat. In threatening situations the AUTONOMIC NERVOUS SYSTEM causes immediate changes in the body to enable an organism to rapidly deal with the situation (the flight-or-fright response). This autonomic response is characterised by release of ADRENALINE and noradrenaline from the adrenal medulla. Adrenaline released into the bloodstream quickly circulates around the body. Adrenaline acts to enhance sugar metabolism, increase heart rate, increase breathing rate and depth, and leads to changes within muscle tissue that delay the onset of FATIGUE (see s. 7). This activation serves to instantly shut down non-essential systems, to get oxygen and glucose to the muscles. Adrenaline also increases blood pressure through vasoconstriction. High blood pressure increases circulatory efficiency, ensuring oxygen and nutrients are quickly distributed to the muscles. More adrenaline than noradrenaline is released from the adrenal medulla in response to stress. However, the effects of noradrenaline and adrenaline appear to be similar. Adrenaline is a more potent heart rate and metabolic stimulator while noradrenaline is a more potent vasoconstrictor.

In addition, the hypothalamic pituitary axis (HPA) is also activated in response to stress. CORTICOTROPHIN-RELEASING HORMONE (CRH) is immediately released from the hypothalamus and travels to the ANTERIOR PITUITARY, stimulating the release of large amounts of the peptide ADRENOCORTICOTROPHIN HORMONE (ACTH) into the blood stream. ACTH travels to the adrenal cortex, stimulating the release of glucocorticoid hormones such as CORTISOL. Cortisol is a metabolic hormone that, like adrenaline,

enables the body to react to the stress by enabling the mobilisation of energy to muscles. It stimulates the liver to increase blood glucose concentrations (glucogenesis). Cortisol also alters metabolic activity and rate, converting proteins and stored fats to utilisable energy. Cortisol has an anti-inflammatory effect, delaying immune reactions that could inhibit an effective stress response. Finally, cortisol sustains adrenaline-induced high blood pressure. The relationship between cortisol and stress is so close that either blood or salivary levels of cortisol can be used to gauge a stress response. In the absence of threat and stress, circulating cortisol inhibits the further releases of CRH and ACTH (negative feedback). Prolonged stress in humans can cause serious effects on health (related to both adrenaline and cortisol). It should be noted that noradrenaline and CRH also act as NEUROTRANSMITTERS within the LIMBIC SYSTEM, critical in triggering and coordinating the behavioural response to stress (Brook and Marshall 1996).   *JCGH*

Brook, C. and Marshall, N. 1996: *Essential Endocrinology*. London: Blackwell Science.

hormones, appetite and energy regulation

Hormones perform two critical functions with regard to energy regulation. First, they provide the brain with current information on both nutrients recently ingested and the status of the body's existing energy stores. Second, they control the body's blood glucose levels, preventing either dangerous excesses or deficits. For the body to maintain energy balance, the energy expended through both metabolism and activity must be replaced through energy intake (eating). Some hormones appear to respond to energy deficit and signal the brain to initiate feeding behaviour. Others detect ingested nutrients and signal the brain to inhibit feeding behaviour. The hormone GHRELIN, for instance, is secreted in the gut prior to a meal. Ghrelin stimulates the hypothalamic feeding centres which initiates food intake. The consumption of food suppresses the ghrelin release (negative feedback), inhibiting this hunger signal (Wang et al. 2002). Alternatively, the release of gut hormone CHOLECYSTOKININ (CCK) is stimulated by the presence of fat and protein within the gastrointestinal tract. The detection of CCK release leads to the termination and subsequent suppression of eating behaviour (Silver and Morley 1991). Energy already stored within the body also acts to inhibit food intake. The hormone LEPTIN is secreted by the body's adipose tissue. As increasing levels of fat are stored, the circulating leptin levels rise (Bates and Myers 2003). Like CCK, a rise in leptin levels acts on the brain to suppress eating behaviour.

The antagonistic action of two pancreatic hormones, INSULIN and GLUCAGON, ensures blood glucose levels stay within safe parameters. Insulin secretion occurs in anticipation of and in response to rises in blood glucose, stimulating the liver and muscle to convert blood glucose to the inert storage substance glycogen. Without insulin, post-consumptive rises in blood glucose would damage body tissues and organs. Glucagon is a polypeptide hormone, secreted in response to a fall in blood glucose. Glucagon stimulates the conversion of glycogen back into glucose, restoring normal blood glucose levels. Without glucagon, falls in blood glucose would starve organs within the body, in particular the brain, of energy. Insulin and glucagon levels not only control blood glucose levels but are also detected by structures within the brain modulating feeding behaviour (Brook and Marshall 1996).

JCGH

Bates, S. H. and Myers, M. G. 2003: The role of leptin receptor signalling in feeding and neuroendocrine function. *Trends in Endocrinology and Metabolism* 14, 447–52. **Brook, C. and Marshall, N.** 1996: *Essential Endocrinology.* London: Blackwell Science. **Silver, A. J. and Morley, A. J.** 1991: Role of CCK in regulation of food intake. *Progress in Neurobiology* 36: 23–34. **Wang, G. Y., Lee, H. M., Englander, E. and Greeley, G. H.** 2002: Ghrelin – not just another stomach hormone. *Regulatory Peptides* 105, 75–81.

hormones: embryonic and early development

Humans, like most vertebrates and all mammals, are sexually dimorphic (i.e. there are two sexes). This enables genetic material to be mixed more effectively. Between conception and six weeks of development, male and female EMBRYOS (see s. 4) are identical, differing only chromosomally. At this stage hormones act to organise the development of both the sexual organs and the brain of the embryo. Hormones translate the chromosomal differences between male (XY) and female (XX) embryos into the development of internal sexual organs (the testes and seminal vesicles, or the ovaries, fallopian tubes and uterus) and primary external sexual characteristics (the penis and scrotum or the vagina and labia). These same hormones influence brain development in the embryo, SHAPING (see s. 3) sexually differentiated behaviour (gender stereotypical behaviour) and GENDER IDENTITY (see s. 4).

Prior to week six of development, both male and female embryos possess a pair of basic glands in the lower abdomen called the GONADS. These glands eventually develop into either the testes in males or the ovaries in females. The embryo also contains two dual-duct systems in the same location. These are the WOLFFIAN DUCTS, which are the precursors of the male internal organs, and the MÜLLERIAN DUCTS, which are the precursors of the female internal organs. In males, a gene on the Y chromosome, called the testis determination FACTOR (see s. 8) gene (also know as the Sex Region Y gene), produces testis

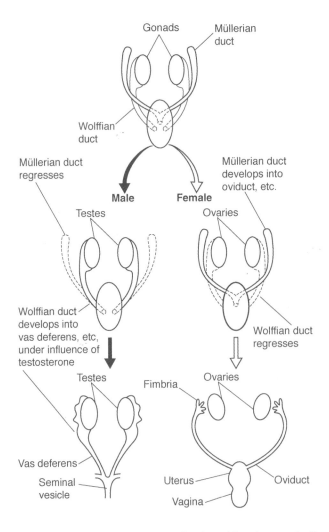

hormones: embryonic and early development *The development of male and female reproductive tracts from different precursor structures.*

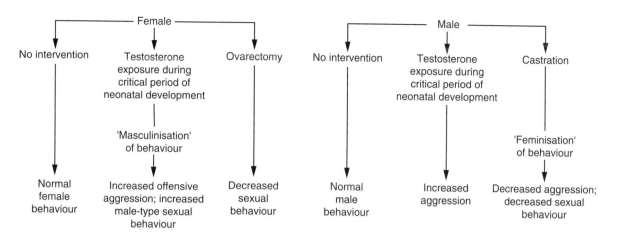

hormones: embryonic and early development *The permanent effect of either neonatal testosterone or gonad removal on adult rodent behaviour.*

determination factor (TDF) in the cells of the gonads. It is the presence of TDF that causes the gonads to develop into testes. The embryonic testes then start to produce TESTOSTERONE. Testosterone has a masculinising effect on the FOETUS (see s. 4), stimulating the Wolffian ducts to develop into male internal sexual organs (rete testes and epididymis involved in the production and storage of sperm, and seminal vesicles and vas deferens involved in sperm transmission). The testes also release another factor called ANTI-MÜLLERIAN HORMONE (AMH), which has a defeminising effect on sexual development. As the name suggests, AMH blocks the development of the Müllerian ducts into female internal organs. Female embryos have no Y chromosome and consequently no TDF, so their gonads develop into female organs (Fallopian tubes, uterus and inner vagina) as their Müllerian ducts are unimpeded by AMH. In the absence of testosterone, the Wolffian ducts regress (Nef and Parada 2000; Ostrer 2004). Anomalies during this process can lead to syndromes such as ANDROGEN insensitivity syndrome (AIS) or persistent Müllerian duct syndrome. In AIS, genetic males develop as females in external appearance (primary and SECONDARY SEXUAL CHARACTERISTICS – see s. 4) and often do not realise they are chromosomally male until they fail to menstruate or try to start a family. In persistent Müllerian duct syndrome, genetic males develop both female and male sexual organs (Wiener et al. 1997).

The hormones, which organise early sexual development, also contribute to the organisation of the developing brain that may underpin gender differences in reproductive and non-reproductive behaviours. In human beings, even prior to PUBERTY (see s. 4), the types of games children choose to play are differentiated by gender, suggesting biological sexual difference strongly influences natural behaviour. Boys' games, in particular, tend to be rougher and more violent. The case of David Reimer provides an eloquent demonstration of the effect of foetal androgen exposure on subsequent behaviour (Colapinto 2000). David suffered accidental mutilation while undergoing infant circumcision. Subsequently he was surgically altered and raised as a girl. However, 'she' exhibited 'tomboy' behaviour as a girl and in adulthood

totally rejected 'her' surgically assigned gender, reverting instead to living as a man. David's gender identity had obviously been set by the masculinising effect of androgens during his early development. Foetal androgen exposure on adult behaviour affects more than gender identity. There are subtle differences in males and females in the shape and size of certain brain regions, and also in the lateralisation of brain function between the two hemispheres (more marked in males, as are differences in hemispheric mass). There are also established gender differences in cognitive and perceptual task performance. (See also s. 1, GENDER AND SEXUALITY ISSUES) Males tend to perform better at spatial relations tasks and demonstrate on average better visuospatial ABILITIES (see s. 6); however, in females, perceptual systems seem to be more sensitive. Women with the condition congenital adrenal hyperplasia (CAH) are exposed to excessive androgens during foetal development. In both childhood and adulthood these women show more masculine behaviour and have more masculine interests. The fact that women with CAH tend to perform better in visuospatial tasks would support the notion that foetal androgen exposure is important in the development of a number of gender differences. For further reading, see Schefer and Goodfellow (1996) and Watchel (1984).

JCGH

Colapinto, J. 2000: *As Nature Made Him: The Boy Who Was Raised as a Girl*. New York: HarperCollins. Nef, S. and Parada, L. F. 2000: Hormones in male sexual development. *Genes and Development* 14, 3075–86. Ostrer, H. 2004: Alterations of sex differentiation in males: from candidate genes to diagnosis and treatments. *Current Pharmaceutical Design* 10, 501–11. Schefer, A. J. and Goodfellow, P. N. 1996: Sex determination in humans. *BioEssays* 18(12), 955–63. Watchel, S. S. 1984: Human sexual development. *Journal of Endocrinological Investigation* 7, 663–73. Wiener, J. S., Teague, J. L., Roth, D. R., Gozales, E. T. and Lamb, D. J. 1997: Molecular biology and function of the androgen receptor in genital development. *Journal of Urology* 157, 1377–86.

hormones: function and nature Hormones are a key chemical message system within the body. This system of hormones is called the endocrine system. The endocrine, like the nervous system, is a key control system of the body. It is responsible for regulating the body's internal states and its development and growth throughout life. The endocrine system operates by sending chemical messages via the circulatory system to target organs or structures. The endocrine system produces changes in behaviour that are generally far longer in duration than those produced by the nervous system. The chemical messengers of the endocrine system are termed *hormones*, from the Greek, meaning to excite or arouse. Hormones both initiate and inhibit biological responses and behaviour. The endocrine system is important in the control of both autonomic behaviour and motivated behaviour and acts together with the nervous system to co-ordinate appropriate behavioural responses to a variety of situations (Wagner 1999).

Hormones are secreted from endocrine cells, which often reside in endocrine glands located around the body. Hormones are also released from other organs and tissues including the gastrointestinal tract. The release of a hormone can be:

1. triggered by a direct signal from the nervous system (neuroendocrine). Glands directly stimulated by the nervous system include the POSTERIOR PITUITARY and adrenal medulla.

2. released in response to the detection of rises or falls of critical factors within the periphery, such as levels of blood glucose or blood, rate of blood flow-through, or ingested nutrients.

3. released in response to the detection of other circulating hormones. In fact, endocrine responses often rely initially on the secretion of another triggering hormone, which then circulates to other endocrine tissues causing the release of a variety of hormones.

The key endocrine glands in the human body include the pituitary and pineal glands in the head, the thyroid and parathyroid glands in the neck, the adrenal glands (consisting of adrenal cortex and medulla) on the kidneys, the pancreas and the gonads (ovaries in female and testes in men). The pituitary gland, often termed the 'master gland', is situated immediately below the hypothalamus and is connected to it by the pituitary stalk (or infundibulum). It is a small gland weighing less than a gram and consisting of two sections, termed the ANTERIOR PITUITARY and the posterior pituitary, which develop from two distinct embryonic structures (Marieb 1992; Brook and Marshall 1996).

There are three classes of hormone. Firstly, there are hormones derived from the amino acid tyrosine: they include ADRENALINE, noradrenaline, dopamine and thyroxine. The second class are hormones formed from chains of amino acids and termed peptides and protein hormones. Examples of peptide hormones include vasopressin and oxytocin. Small protein hormones include INSULIN. Larger protein hormones include FOLLICLE-STIMULATING HORMONE (FSH) and LUTEINISING HORMONE (LH). Finally, the third group are the steroid hormones, which are lipids formed from cholesterol. Steroid hormones include aldosterone, TESTOSTERONE, PROGESTERONE and OESTROGENS (Marieb 1992; Brook and Marshall 1996).

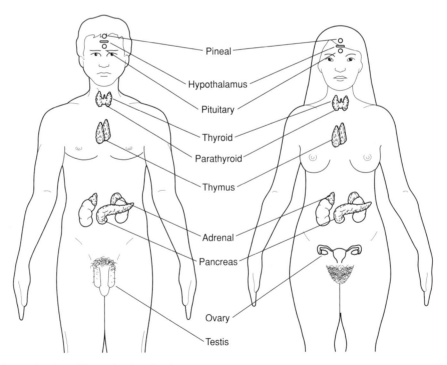

hormones: function and nature *The endocrine glands.*

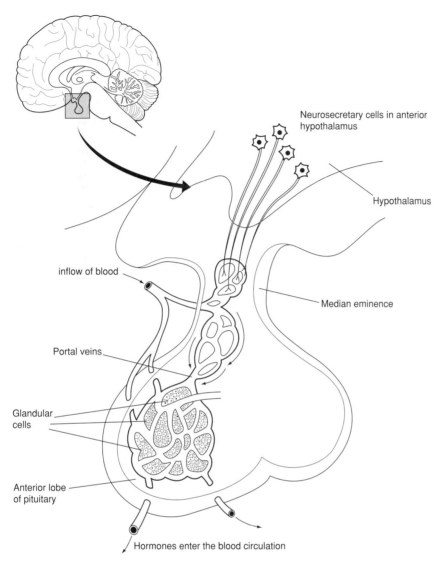

Neurosecretary cells in anterior hypothalamus

Hypothalamus

Median eminence

inflow of blood

Portal veins

Glandular cells

Anterior lobe of pituitary

Hormones enter the blood circulation

hormones: function and nature *The hypothalamus and anterior pituitary.*

In behavioural terms, structural differences in these classes of hormones are important. The smaller and simpler the hormone molecule, the faster acting it is, but also the briefer in duration its effect. The impact of transmitter-type hormones is generally instantaneous, and their release generally triggered directly by the nervous system. For example, it is necessary that the adrenaline response to threat is immediate to give the individual sufficient time to act in their defence ('flight or fight' response). The secretion of peptide hormones produces biological and behavioural responses in seconds or minutes. Again the effects are short-lived and diminish quickly after secretion stops. The biological effects of large protein and steroid hormones take minutes, hours or longer. Prolonged secretion of hormones such as steroids can produce permanent physical and behavioural effects. For example, peaks of testosterone released during PUBERTY (see s. 4) cause a marked change in the behaviour of males toward females,

as well as the more obvious physical changes (Wagner 1999).

In order to have any biological or behavioural effect, a hormone must first reach and then activate its target cell. In most cases these chemical messengers are carried to their target cells by the blood stream and travel all round the body, although notable exceptions include hormones secreted by the hypothalamus that travel directly to the pituitary. When passing by the target cell some of the hormone molecules bind to receptors on the target cell's surface in a process similar to the way NEUROTRANSMITTERS bind to RECEPTORS on neuronal membranes. Target cells exist not only on other endocrine glands, but also on tissues and organs throughout the body. Activation of these cells determines both the function and growth of the target tissue or organ (Marieb 1992; Brook and Marshall 1996).

The study of the role of hormonal mediation of behaviour has been comparatively neglected (compared to

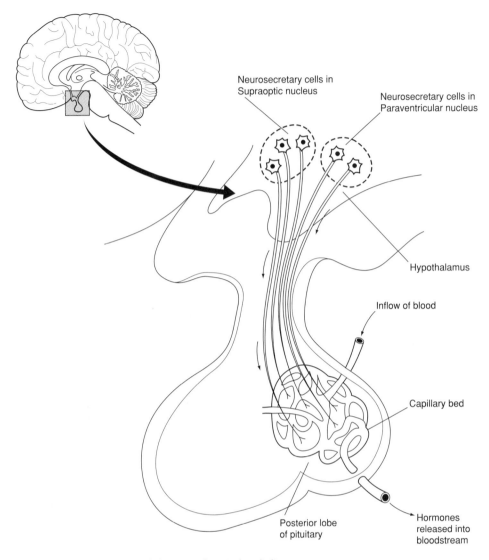

Neurosecretary cells in
Supraoptic nucleus

Neurosecretary cells in
Paraventricular nucleus

Hypothalamus

Inflow of blood

Capillary bed

Hormones
released into
bloodstream

Posterior lobe
of pituitary

hormones: function and nature *The hypothalamus and posterior pituitary.*

that of the nervous system). The endocrine system is highly responsive to external stimuli such as anticipated ingestion of food or the perception of threat. Moreover, hormonal fluxes contribute to the initiation of behavioural events (e.g. eating, drinking, conflict, sexual competition and initiation of mating) and changes in psychological state (e.g. mood, arousal, aggression, fear, hunger, thirst). From a developmental perspective, their organisational effects shape long-term behaviour. The secretion of hormones within the FOETUS (see s. 4) both stimulates and coordinates the development of tissues, including, critically, the nervous system. Moreover, they are necessary for the physical and behavioural differentiation of males and females. Lack of a key hormone or excessive exposure to one at this stage of development can have dramatic effects on behaviour later in life (Wagner 1999).

JCGH

Brook, C. and Marshall, N. 1996: *Essential Endocrinology.* London: Blackwell Science. **Marieb, E. N**. 1992: *Human Anatomy and Physiology.* California: Benjamin Cummings Publishing. **Vander, A., Sherman, J. and Luciano, D.** 1998: *Human Physiology: Theory, Treatment and Research.* Boston: McGraw Hill. **Wagner, H.** 1999: *The Psychobiology of Human Motivation.* London: Routledge.

hormones: pubertal development It is not only prior to birth that 'sex' hormones affect physical development and subsequent behaviour. At the onset of PUBERTY (see s. 4), the hypothalamus releases gonadotropin-releasing factor, which in turn stimulates the release of gonadotropic hormones – such as FOLLICLE STIMULATING HORMONE (FSH) and LUTEINISING HORMONE (LH) – from the anterior pituitary. In males, gonadotropic hormones induce a rapid increase in TESTOSTERONE release and cause the testes to start to produce sperm (spermatogenesis). In females, these hormones stimulate the ovaries to release the hormone OESTROGEN and eventually the ova as the menstrual cycle begins. At puberty the surge of gonadal

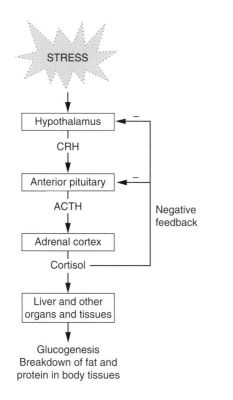

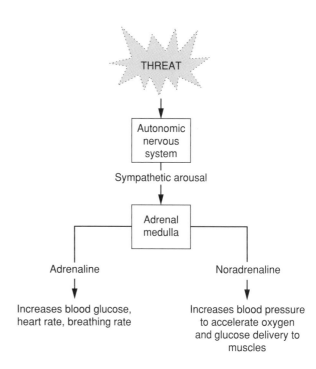

hormones: function and nature *The neuroendocrine response to stressors.*

hormones: function and nature *Flight, fright or fight: endocrine responses to immediate threat.*

hormones affects many areas of the body. They stimulate further differential development in males and females and activate sexual interest and behaviour. During this period the genitalia of males grow and those of females mature. In males, the development of the penis is triggered by the hormone dihydrotestosterone, which is produced from testosterone in the testes. SECONDARY SEXUAL CHARACTER-ISTICS (see s. 4) also begin to develop. In males these include the broadening out of the figure, the deepening of the voice and the development of facial, underarm and pubic hair. In females these include the development of breasts and change in figure due to adipose tissue increasing around the bottom and thighs. The development of underarm and pubic hair in females is stimulated by a surge of androgens released from the adrenal cortex. Critically, from the psychological perspective, the hormonal peaks at puberty mark obvious changes in the behaviour of both males and females. In particular, most adolescents develop an interest in sex. In males, peaks in testosterone levels also appear to correlate with a surge in sex drive. For further reading see Diamond et al. (1996), Romeo et al. (2002) and Spear (2000).   *JCGH*

Diamond, M., Binstosk, T. and Kohl, J. V. 1996: From fertilization to adult sexual behaviour. *Hormones and Behavior* 30, 333–53. **Romeo, R. D., Richardson, H. N. and Sisk, C. L.** 2002: Puberty and the maturation of the male brain and sexual behaviour: Recasting a behavioural potential. *Neuroscience and Biobehavioral Reviews* 26, 381–91. **Spear, L. P.** 2000: The adolescent brain and age-related behavioural manifestations. *Neuroscience and Biobehavioral Reviews* 24, 417–63.

human ethology   The questions and methods of ethology have not been confined only to the study of animal behaviour. Following the lead of Darwin, who expressly located human behaviour within an evolutionary framework and advocated the comparative approach as a means of understanding human nature, some ethologists focused their attention on human behaviour. The basic premise was much the same as that which underpinned the study of animal behaviour: that the behaviour of present-day humans is a product of evolutionary processes [see EVOLUTIONARY PSYCHOLOGY]. (See also s. 1, EVOLUTION AND PSYCHOLOGY) Human ethologists examined the extent to which ADAPTATIONS (see s. 4) pre-programme human behaviour (Eibl-Eibesfeldt 1970) and did so in a number of ways. One strategy was to compare behaviours across CULTURES (see s. 1 and s. 5), looking for similarities and differences that might indicate 'species characteristics', especially in cultures that were geographically separate from each other with little interaction. In addition, some ethologists directly compared human behaviour to that of non-human primates. Another means of uncovering the extent to which behaviour is inherited was to carry out research on newborn infants who had had little or no opportunity for LEARNING (see s. 3).

In many respects the ethologists who looked at human behaviour laid much of the groundwork for contemporary evolutionary analyses of human behaviour.   *JL*

Eibl-Eibesfeldt, I. 1970: *Ethology: The Biology of Behavior.* New York: Holt, Rinehart & Winston.

I

imprinting Imprinting represents a special case of LEARNING (see s. 3). Or, perhaps more accurately, imprinting is a case of 'programmed learning'. It was Konrad Lorenz, the other father of ethology, who demonstrated that when young birds hatch they do not have any innate knowledge of who their parents are; they do not immediately recognise them, either as individuals or even at a species-specific level. What Lorenz demonstrated is that shortly after hatching, there is a critical time period during which imprinting takes place. Imprinting is the process whereby a young precocial animal becomes attached to another individual, usually its mother. Some of the obvious behavioural manifestations of imprinting are the tendency of the young to attend to, and stay very close to, the animal they have imprinted on. The newborn is programmed to learn who its mother is, although as Lorenz revealed, the results can sometimes be quite startling. He showed that during the sensitive period, chicks would imprint upon *any* large moving object that they were exposed to, be it the mother, a moving block of wood, a dog, or even Lorenz himself.   *JL*

Byrne, R. W. 1995: *The Thinking Ape: Evolutionary Origins of Intelligence.* Oxford: Oxford University Press. **Eibl-Eibesfeldt, I.** 1970: *Ethology: The Biology of Behavior.* New York: Holt, Rinehart & Winston. **Slater, P. J. B.** 1990: *An Introduction to Ethology.* Cambridge: Cambridge University Press.

incentive motivation Refers principally to the motivational effects of expected or anticipated rewards.   *SC*

inclusive fitness A measure of an individual's total fitness, obtained by direct fitness (one's own genetic contribution to future generations through own offspring) and indirect fitness (by assisting in the reproduction of related individuals who share genes by common descent).   *JL*

information encoding Action potentials are described as an 'ALL-OR-NONE' response. Their size and shape are INDEPENDENT (see s. 8) of the intensity of the stimulus that initiated them. Consequently, the frequency and pattern of action potential firing, rather than the amplitude of the signal, encodes the intensity of stimulus. The rate of firing, the firing frequency, depends on the magnitude of the depolarising stimulus. Firing frequency increases with the magnitude of depolarisation. However, there is a limit to the rate at which neurones can generate action potentials. The rate-limiting step is called the refractory period (de Ruyter van Stevenick et al. 1997). It has two component parts. The first is referred to as the absolute refractory period. It is impossible to initiate another action potential during this period of time, which lasts approximately 1 msec. The relative refractory period lasts for a further 2–4 msec. The amount of current required to depolarise the neurone to reach threshold is elevated during this period, making it relatively more difficult to initiate an action potential. Consequently, if a neurone is subject to a continuous high level of stimulation, it will generate action potentials repeatedly following each absolute refractory period. However, if the level of stimulation is just sufficient to fire the neurone when at rest, it will not fire again until both the absolute and relative refractory periods are complete. Intermediate levels of stimulation produce intermediate rates of firing.

Additional information encoding flexibility is introduced by diverse characteristics of neurones. For example, nerve cells differ in impulse threshold, the amount of depolarisation required to initiate the generation of an action potential. Additionally, neurones vary in their relationship between the magnitude of depolarisation and the frequency of action potential firing. Consequently, small changes in membrane potential will result in action potential firing in some neurones, while in others the slope of the relationship is shallower. Finally, the form of an action potential (shape and duration) differs between neurones.   *JAH*

de Ruyter van Stevenick, R. R., Lewen, G. D., Strong, S. P., Koberle, R. and Bialek, W. 1997: Reliability and variability in neural spike trains. *Science* 275, 1805–8.

inhibitory conditioning The commonest procedure for establishing a signal, X, as a conditioned inhibitor is the feature-negative DISCRIMINATION (see s. 3 and s. 5): A+; AX–. The exciter, A, is followed by the outcome unless it is presented with the inhibitor, X. Animals will respond during A and – early in training – during AX too; but later responding to AX will become negligible. One explanation of INHIBITION (see s. 3) is that X gains an inhibitory association with a representation of the outcome; the alternative is that X gains an excitatory association with a representation of 'no outcome'. In either case, X will offset the excitation normally governed by A. Rescorla has recommended that *true* inhibition should affect both *performance* to other signals and new *learning*: the signal X will be found to suppress performance to a new exciter, B+ (despite it never having been directly trained before); pairing of X (alone) with outcome should result in slow rate of LEARNING (see s. 3).   *JW-R*

Mackintosh, N. J. 1983: *Conditioning and Associative Learning.* Oxford: Clarendon Press. **Pearce, J. M.** 1997: *Animal Learning and Cognition* (2nd edn). Hove: Psychology Press.

instinct and learning Consider the information demands of an organism, and how it goes about meeting them. On the one hand, an animal can be born with most or all of the information it requires to function in the world. Most probably, this kind of pre-programming will be advantageous for an organism that has a relatively short lifespan and lives a solitary life, with little generational overlap or parental care. Such an organism is likely to be time-constrained and therefore acquiring information through the potentially risky route of individual trial and ERROR (see s. 8) is unlikely to be an optimal solution. This kind of pre-programmed solution to information demands is what is broadly referred to as instinct, and has been described as an inherited, pre-set behavioural response (Manning and Dawkins 1998). Such instincts develop along with the organism's nervous system and are available for use the first time they are needed, without any apparent need for LEARNING (see s. 3).

On the other hand, there are much longer-lived animals that live in seasonal and unpredictable environments, and often in social groups. In these circumstances, social and environmental unpredictability makes pre-set patterns of behaviour a risky option. Here the ability to learn is probably a better solution. Learning has a number of advantages over inherited information: it can provide the organism with more detailed information, and it can replace old or outdated information, which is especially important when environmental circumstances have changed. Learning can occur individually through trial and error, or through social mediated learning. For the former, the animal is essentially interrogating the environment directly, and there are attendant risks. For example, in diet selection a young animal might need to avoid toxic and potentially life-threatening food items; socially mediated diet choice allows it to avoid certain food items since the presumably older and competent animals that it is learning from have solved that particular adaptive problem.

Implicit in this distinction between instincts and learning is the suggestion that one is flexible while the other is not. This might be the case, but not necessarily. It is not uncommon that the expression of learned, flexible behaviours can become as inflexible and stereotyped as instinctive behaviours (Manning and Dawkins 1998). There are instances where it is clear that an animal has learned a particular behaviour, but then carries it out in what appears to be an instinctive, inflexible, routine way. Furthermore, it is not appropriate to think of behaviour as either instinctive or learned. A complete explanation of behaviour should include an account of how both genetic and environmental FACTORS (see s. 8) interact to shape behaviour during development (Manning and Dawkins 1998).   *JL*

Byrne, R. W. 1995: *The Thinking Ape: Evolutionary Origins of Intelligence*. Oxford: Oxford University Press. **Hinde, R. A.** 1982: *Ethology*. Oxford: Oxford University Press. **Manning, A. and Dawkins, M. S.** 1998: *An Introduction to Animal Behaviour*. Cambridge: Cambridge University Press.

insulin   Secreted by pancreatic β cells in response to rises in blood glucose or in anticipation of food consumption. Triggers the liver and other tissue to convert excess glucose to glycogen. A high blood insulin level signifies energy storage and inhibits eating behaviour.   *JCGH*

internal resistance   The resistance to electrical current flowing longitudinally down a neurone.   *JAH*

intersexual selection   A form of sexual selection where female choice drives selection for male traits that are attractive to females.   *JL*

intrasexual selection   A form of sexual selection that is driven by same-sex competition for access to opposite-sex partners. Examples of intrasexually selected traits include large body size and canine teeth.   *JL*

ionotropic receptor   Receptor composed of multiple subunits surrounding a central pore; when activated, channel opens to allow passage of ions (e.g. Na^+, K^+, Ca^{++}, Cl^-).   *SC*

K

---

kin cooperation Organisms can enhance their fitness in two ways: they can do so directly by passing on their genes to their own offspring, or they can do so indirectly by assisting or promoting the reproduction of individuals with whom they share common genes (i.e. related individuals). Thus, if a given organism does not reproduce itself, assisting a genetic relative that shares the same gene to reproduce can still enhance its fitness. This THEORY (see s. 8), known as the theory of KIN SELECTION, explains how seemingly altruistic behaviour can evolve in the Darwinian world of the selfish gene where individuals are expected to behave in ways that enhance their own reproductive success. Hamilton's Rule, named after William Hamilton who solved the apparent paradox of individuals assisting other individuals at a cost to themselves, specifies that a gene for ALTRUISM (see s. 5) can evolve if the following inequality is satisfied: $r B > C$ where B is the benefit to the recipient of the altruistic act, C is the cost to the donor and r is the coefficient of relatedness between the actor and the beneficiary.

It should be obvious that if two individuals are unrelated, then $r = 0$, and the left-hand side of the formula is reduced to zero. Under those circumstances, the cost of the altruistic act is greater than the benefit, and thus altruistic behaviour should not occur.

Hamilton's Rule sets up a number of easily testable hypotheses. One of them is the expectation that individuals should discriminate between relatives on the basis of relatedness with respect to who should be the recipient of altruistic acts. Closely related individuals (e.g. SIBLINGS – see s. 4, parents; $r = 0.5$) should be treated differently from more distantly related individuals (e.g. cousins; $r = 0.125$), who should be treated differently from unrelated individuals ($r = 0$). Similarly, it has been argued that altruistic actors should be sensitive to the age of the recipient of altruistic acts, since helping an older non-reproductive individual is not likely to enhance the actor's indirect fitness, whereas helping a younger reproductive relative probably will (reviewed in Barrett et al. 2002). Although there have been a number of studies that demonstrate that people do behave in ways that are in accordance with the expectations of the theory of kin selection, most of them have not been able to rule out other possible explanations for the observed patterns. Nonetheless, one recent study has provided strong experimental evidence that humans do obey Hamilton's Rule (Tunney et al. under review). Subjects were asked to participate in an isometric skiing exercise for a financial reward, the amount of which depended on the amount of time they were able to participate in the exercise. Prior to starting the exercise, the experimenters had nominated who the recipient of the financial reward would be, and this varied by degrees of relatedness from SELF (see s. 1, s. 4 and s. 5) ($r = 1$) to a same-sex friend ($r = 0$). After a short time, participation in the exercise became painful, and thus subjects incurred a cost (PAIN – see also s. 7) to benefit themselves or other people. As predicted from Hamilton's Rule, both male and female subjects were prepared to endure more pain the more closely related to them the recipient was. *JL*

Barrett, L., Dunbar, R. I. M. and Lycett, J. E. 2002: *Human Evolutionary Psychology*. Houndmills: Palgrave MacMillan. **Tunney, R., Madsen, E., Fieldman, G., Plotkin, H. C., Dunbar, R. I. M., Robertson, J.-M. and McFarland, D. J.** under review: A cross-cultural experimental study of altruism.

kin selection A THEORY (see s. 8) stating that altruistic acts will be favoured by selection if the product of the benefit to the recipient and the degree of relatedness between donor and recipient exceeds the cost to the donor. *JL*

L

lamina Layers of cells that characterise the neocortex (isocortex) and hippocampus. *JAH*

language Human language is both qualitatively and quantitatively different from any kind of animal communication, although there have been – and continue to be – many attempts to draw parallels between the two. While most other species communicate to some extent, none of them does so on the scale that humans do through language. It is an open-ended system of communication that, on account of grammatical structure, allows complex information to be exchanged between people (Barrett et al. 2002). Conventional theories that explain the origin of language tend to focus on the purpose of language, which is the communication of information. Unfortunately, such explanations do not tell us why we have language, only what we use it for (Dunbar 1996). Recently there has been growing support for the idea that language is a product of evolution. In contrast to more conventional theories that emphasise information transfer, theories for the evolution of language focus on the social functions of language and argue that it evolved as a result of the complexities and pressures of social living (Deacon 1997; Dunbar 1996; Miller 2000). *JL*
Barrett, L., Dunbar, R. I. M. and Lycett, J. E. 2002: *Human Evolutionary Psychology*. Houndmills: Palgrave MacMillan. **Deacon, T.** 1997: *The Symbolic Species: The Coevolution of Language and the Human Brain*. Harmondsworth: Allen Lane. **Dunbar, R. I. M.** 1996: *Grooming, Gossip and the Evolution of Language*. London: Faber and Faber. **Miller, G. F.** 2000: *The Mating Mind*. London: Heinemann.

latent inhibition and attention-like processes Conditioning may be retarded by the exposure of the signal before it is paired with outcome (e.g. X–, then X+) – a finding that may be understood by assuming that the exposure processes reduced ATTENTION (see s. 3) to X. This phenomenon's term, latent inhibition, refers to the assumption that the (non-reinforced) exposure gives X a modicum of conditioned INHIBITION (see s. 3) which offsets subsequent conditioned excitation. The attentional account receives support over the inhibition account from the finding that exposure to X will also retard LEARNING (see s. 3) when it is subsequently used as an inhibitory signal (i.e. X–, then A+; AX–). The inhibitory account of latent inhibition incorrectly anticipates that the exposure should *enhance* subsequent inhibition; the fact that the opposite occurs is anticipated by the attentional account. *JW-R*
Mackintosh, N. J. 1983: *Conditioning and Associative Learning*. Oxford: Clarendon Press. **Pearce, J. M.** 1997: *Animal Learning and Cognition* (2nd edn). Hove: Psychology Press.

leptin (ob-protein) Secreted by fat cells within the body's adipose (fat) tissue. Circulating levels of leptin in the bloodstream inform the brain of the current status of the body's energy stores. High levels of leptin inhibit feeding behaviour controlled by orexigenic (appetite stimulatory) circuits within the hypothalamus. *JAH*

lesion Damage to tissue, arising by accident or by experimenter intervention. *SC*

lifetime reproductive success The total number of living offspring that an individual contributes to the next generation. *JL*

ligand-gated ion channel [See IONOTROPIC RECEPTOR]

limbic system A neuroanatomical term introduced by McLean to describe an interconnected system of medial brain structures involved in the emotions. *SC*

localisation of brain function A doctrine which postulates a close and specific relationship between brain regions and psychological/physiological processes. *SC*

localising neurotransmitters and receptors There are a variety of methods available to localise NEUROTRANSMITTERS in the brain (Watson and Cullinan 1995). NEUROPEPTIDES can be localised directly by immunocytochemical methods, by exposing brain slices to an antibody for the peptide, linked to a fluorescent dye. The slices can then be examined microscopically to determine neuronal axons and terminals containing the peptide. Another method is *in situ* hybridisation: neuropeptide precursors are genetically encoded and messenger RNA is generated to determine their synthesis in the cell. Exposure of the brain tissue to a radioactive RNA tracer binds to the messenger RNA and reveals indirectly the presence of the neuropeptide precursor. Since enzymes which are responsible for the synthesis of non-peptide neurotransmitters are themselves proteins, immunocytochemical methods can be used to detect the presence of the enzymes.

Receptors for neurotransmitters can be detected immunocytochemically, because they consist of protein molecules. An alternative method is to use autoradiography, in which slices of brain tissue are exposed to a radioactive ligand which binds selectively to the receptor. Autoradiographic methods are used to visualise the radioligand, which binds to the receptor and hence reveals the receptor location, typically distributed non-homogeneously in brain tissue. *SC*
Watson, S. J. and Cullinan, W. E. 1995: Cytology and circuitry. In Bloom, F. E. and Kupfer, D. J. (eds) *Psychopharmacology: The Fourth Generation of Progress*. New York: Raven Press.

long-term depression (LTD) Long-lasting decrease in synaptic efficiency in response to low-frequency stimulation of afferent nerve fibres; first observed in the hippocampus. *SC*

long-term potentiation (LTP) Long-lasting increase in synaptic efficiency in response to high-frequency stimulation of afferent nerve fibres; first observed in the hippocampus. (See also s. 3, LONG-TERM POTENTIATION)

SC

lumbar enlargement Expansion of the spinal cord, in the region of the lower back, to accommodate the significant number of nerve cells and connections supplying the legs.

JAH

luteinising hormone (LH) A gonadotropic hormone released from the ANTERIOR PITUITARY. Like FOLLICLE-STIMULATING HORMONE (FSH), LH stimulates the sexual development of males and females at PUBERTY (see s. 4). In males, LH stimulates the development of Leydig cells and TESTOSTERONE secretion. In females, LH triggers PROGESTERONE secretion.

JCGH

M

macrophages A cell that plays a role in immunity by ingesting foreign matter and cell debris. *JAH*

mate choice decisions Finding a suitable partner is the first step in the process of successful reproduction, and evolutionary-oriented researchers of human behaviour have enjoyed much success in uncovering the basis on which mate choice decisions are made. For both males and females, mate choice criteria closely match predictions derived from evolutionary first principles, and to interpret them we need to consider the cost of reproduction for mammals. There is a large gender asymmetry in the cost of reproduction for mammals: for males, reproduction is relatively cheap, since they contribute some sperm and little else. In general, mammalian males contribute little, if anything, towards postnatal care of offspring. For females, however, the costs are rather larger, since they gestate the FOETUS (see s. 4) and provide almost all the postnatal care, including the provision of milk through lactation. Since males contribute little by way of postnatal care, the best way for a male to enhance his reproductive success is by mating with as many females as he can. By contrast, since females are going to be left literally holding the baby, females should be more choosy about whom they mate with. Females should therefore select males on the basis of what they can offer the offspring: good genes (Barrett et al. 2002; Buss 1987, 1989; Buss and Barnes 1986).

In humans the situation is more complex, since most reproduction takes place within monogamous unions, and both males and females contribute directly to child-rearing. Under these circumstances, where males are constrained in their ability to mate with as many females as possible, it pays men to choose the best female they are able to attract. It follows that humans, both male and female, are choosy when it comes to mate selection. Females should choose males on the basis of the impact they might have in rearing children, while men should choose the most fertile female they can, and thus men should be sensitive to indicators of female fertility (Barrett et al. 2002). Cross-cultural studies of mate choice have revealed remarkably consistent patterns in most parts of the world: females are attentive to cues that indicate male status and/or wealth, while men's mate choice preferences are dominated by cues to female physical attributes that correlate with fertility. That is not to say that people do not also choose partners based on other criteria, since it is obvious that they do. However, the consistent and near universal finding that mate choice decisions conform with evolutionary predictions underlines the claim that marriage can be viewed as a reproductive contract, and the choices that men and women make when choosing a partner reflect this. *JL*

Barrett, L., Dunbar, R. I. M. and Lycett, J. E. 2002: *Human Evolutionary Psychology.* Houndmills: Palgrave MacMillan. **Buss, D. M.** 1987: Sex differences in human mate selection criteria: An evolutionary perspective. In Crawford, C., Krebs, D. and Smith, M. (eds) *Sociobiology and Psychology: Ideas, Issues and Applications.* Hillsdale NJ: Erlbaum, 335–52. **Buss, D. M.** 1989: Sex differences in human mate preferences. *Behavioral and Brain Sciences* 12, 1–49. **Buss, D. M. and Barnes, M. F.** 1986: Preferences in human mate selection. *Journal of Personality and Social Psychology* 50, 559–70.

membrane potential A neurone's membrane potential is the difference in electrical charge between the inside and the outside of the cell. This arises because the composition of the internal fluid environment differs from that of the external environment. Salts in the fluid can be separated into negatively and positively charged particles called ions. In a steady state the membrane potential of a neurone is -70 mV, as the ratio of negative to positive ions is greater inside the neurone than out. This is referred to as the resting membrane potential. This uneven distribution occurs as a combination of differential permeability of the membrane to ions and the presence of specialised pores, called ion channels, each of which allows the passage of particular ions (Mueller 1976).

With an uneven distribution of ions a cell is described as being polarised. The binding of a NEUROTRANSMITTER to a postsynaptic receptor can have one of two effects to this electrical POLARISATION (see s. 5). They may hyperpolarise the membrane or increase the resting membrane potential, making it more negative (for example from -70 mV to -75 mV). Alternatively, they may depolarise a membrane, which decreases the resting membrane potential, making it more positive (for example from -70 mV to -60 mV). When a membrane is depolarised sufficiently to allow the firing of an action potential, it has reached its threshold membrane potential. The effect achieved depends on how the neurotransmitter influences the passage of ions by either leading to the opening or closing of ion channel proteins. *JAH*

Mueller, P. 1976: Molecular aspects of electrical excitation in lipid bilayers and cell membranes. *Horizons in Biochemistry and Biophysics* 2, 230–84.

membrane resistance The resistance to electrical current flowing across the membrane of a neurone. *JAH*

memory: genetic studies Evidence indicates that genetic approaches in the study of MEMORY (see also s. 1) hold considerable promise and will be critical in elucidating important processes in LEARNING (see s. 3) and memory (Mayford and Kandel 1999). Kandel and his colleagues have found that a simple defensive reflex in the marine invertebrate aplysia can display several forms of learning, HABITUATION (see s. 3 and s. 4), sensitisation and associative (classical) conditioning [see NON-ASSOCIATIVE LEARNING]. During sensitisation, release of the NEUROTRANSMITTER *serotonin* (5-hydroxytryptamine or 5-HT) activates G PROTEIN-COUPLED RECEPTORS on sensory neurones, which in turn show an increase in cyclic adenosine monophosphate (cAMP) levels. This increase in cAMP appears to underlie sensitisation. If pulses of 5-HT are administered repeatedly, cAMP increase is maintained: protein kinase A (PKA) then recruits mitogen-activated protein (MAP) kinase, and together they move to the cell nucleus to bring about long-term strengthening of synaptic connections, or long-term facilitation. In the nucleus, cAMP-responsive transcription FACTOR (see s. 8) (CREB) is activated, and appears to be importantly involved in the conversion from short-term to LONG-TERM MEMORY (see s. 3). Silva et al. (1998) suggest that CREB, a nuclear protein, may be a universal modulator of cellular processes involved in the formation of memories. It seems possible that CREB is a component in mechanisms leading to the synthesis of proteins necessary for the development of LONG-TERM POTENTIATION (see also s. 3) [see SYNAPTIC PLASTICITY].

Genetic studies of memory in the mouse with targeted deletions in genes (knockout mice) have thrown considerable light on the biochemical and molecular biological basis of learning and memory (Chen and Tonegawa 1997; Matynia et al. 2002). The rather complex picture which emerges is that there are cascades of internal cellular signalling systems, which, together with genetic expression, mediate between stimulus events and long-term neural plasticity, which underlie learning and memory processes. *SC*

Chen, C. and Tonegawa, S. 1997: Molecular genetic analysis of synaptic plasticity, activity-dependent neural development, learning, and memory in the mammalian brain. *Annual Review of Neuroscience* 20, 157–84. Matynia, A., Kushner, S. A. and Silva, A. J. 2002: Genetic approaches to molecular and cellular cognition: a focus on LTP and learning and memory. *Annual Review of Genetics* 36, 687–720. Mayford, M. and Kandel, E. R. 1999: Genetic approaches to memory storage. *Trends in Genetics* 15, 463–70. Silva, A. J., Kogan, J. H., Frankland, P. W. and Kida, S. 1998: CREB and memory. *Annual Review of Neuroscience* 21, 127–48.

mesencephalon As the name suggests, the mesencephalon, or midbrain, starts in the middle of the brain. In adult mammals it is dwarfed and surrounded by the FOREBRAIN. It has two divisions – the tectum and the tegmentum. The tectum forms the roof of the midbrain. It has two swellings, COLLICULI, on each side. The posterior pair are the inferior colliculi and the anterior are the superior colliculi. Both pairs are important routes for sensory information. The inferior colliculi are concerned with auditory function and the superior colliculi have a visual function.

The tegmentum lies under the tectum. It contains the nuclei for the third and fourth cranial nerves. Also found within this division of the mesencephalon are parts of a network of neurones collectively referred to as the reticular formation. This extends from the midbrain to the medulla and has had various functions attributed to it, including sleep, arousal, temperature regulation and motor control (Steckler, Inglis, Winn and Sahgal 1994). Tracts of passage, extensions of the pathways between the forebrain and spinal cord or HINDBRAIN, also run through the tegmentum. In addition to these, the tegmentum contains three structures of interest to biopsychologists: the periaqueductal grey, the red nucleus and the substantia nigra. The periaqueductal grey is the grey matter surrounding the CEREBRAL AQUEDUCT – the duct connecting the third and fourth cerebral ventricles. It plays a role in mediating the analgesic effects of opiate drugs. The red

nucleus and substantia nigra are both important components of the sensorimotor system (Houk 1991). The substantia nigra is the structure that deteriorates in Parkinson's disease (Dauer and Przedborski 2003). *JAH*

Dauer, W. and Przedborski, S. 2003: Parkinson's disease: mechanisms and models. *Neuron* 39, 889–909. Houk, J. C. 1991: Red nucleus: role in motor control. *Current Opinions in Neurobiology* 1, 610–15. Steckler, T., Inglis, W., Winn, P. and Sahgal, A. 1994: The pedunculopontine tegmental nucleus: a role in cognitive processes? *Brain Research: Brain Research Reviews* 19, 298–318.

metabotropic receptor A family of guanine nucleotide-binding (G) proteins composed of α, β, γ–subunits in seven transmembrane domains. *SC*

methods in biological psychology In his acclaimed book, *The Organization of Behavior*, the psychologist Donald Hebb (1949) put forward a THEORY (see s. 8) of behaviour which he based as far as possible on the physiology of the nervous system. He embraced physiological psychology (later rebranded as behavioural neuroscience) and anticipated the rise of cognitive and affective neuroscience within the greater field of neuroscience – the study of the brain and nervous systems. Today, psychologists who accept the challenge of trying to relate ideas concerning psychological functions and experiences to brain structure, composition and function must work together with physiologists, neuroanatomists, neuropharmacologists, biochemists and neuroendocrinologists, and others, and understand, if not use directly, their methods and approaches. This does not imply deserting 'true' psychology, but, like Hebb, endeavours to root psychology in our ever-expanding understanding of the brain.

In the late eighteenth and early nineteenth centuries, there was a long-standing controversy concerning the LOCALISATION OF BRAIN FUNCTION (Clarke and Jacyna 1987). Franz Joseph Gall insisted that the mind was to be found in the brain, and that the various components of the mind were located within discrete parts of the brain's surface. This view was challenged by the Frenchman, Pierre Flourens, who believed that the cerebral hemispheres undertook specific functions, but that these were distributed in the hemispheres and not precisely localised. Flourens' views held sway for much of the nineteenth century, until Fritsch and Hitzig, in 1870, reported the localisation of the motor cortex (Finger 2000). Their method was to employ electrical stimulation of the exposed cortex. In today's psychological neuroscience, localisation of function remains a dominant research motif, although ideas of circuits, networks, etc. echo Flourens' ideas.

An equivalent long-standing controversy in electrophysiology concerned the supposed existence of ANIMAL ELECTRICITY. Luigi Galvani of Bologna proposed, at the end of the eighteenth century, a theory of animal electricity, the idea of intrinsic electricity in nerves and muscle. His views were opposed by his compatriot, Alessandro Volta, who argued that the source of electricity lay in non-organic materials, and that nerves and muscles were merely excited by it. Experimentation throughout the nineteenth century, particularly in the hands of the German physiologist, Emil du Bois-Reymond, decided in favour of Galvani, but it was not until the twentieth century that insight into ACTION POTENTIALS and POSTSYNAPTIC

POTENTIALS was achieved (Clarke and Jacyna 1987; Finger 2000). However, arising from these electrophysiological studies were two key approaches: neural tissue could be electrically activated, and neural electrical activity could be recorded. These approaches continue today.

The French physician, Paul Broca, reported in 1861 the case of a man who had lost his speech and whose brain showed damage in the frontal region of the left hemisphere (Finger 2000). This work not only supported the idea of local function, but also of hemispheric lateralisation. A research and clinical tradition of neuropsychology continues strongly today, and has fed into cognitive neuroscience.

A strong assumption underlying lesion techniques (removal of tissue, cutting connections, destroying neural tissue or fibres of passage, etc.) is that the ensuing loss of function can be linked directly with the damaged tissue. A related assumption occurs in NEUROPHARMACOLOGY, when a drug antagonist is administered locally within the brain to block the action of a specific NEUROTRANSMITTER, or the neurotransmitter's biosynthesis is blocked. Complementing this approach is the equally strongly held idea that stimulation techniques (electrical stimulation or chemical transmission) will excite underlying tissue to reveal or exaggerate their normal functions. Both of these approaches involve experimenter intervention. However, because neural tissue generates its animal electricity, recording techniques are available to determine electrical activity of POPULATIONS (see s. 8) of nerve cells – using ELECTROENCEPHALOGRAM (EEG), for example – down to the activity of single neurones (single-unit recording). Intrinsic neuronal activity also underpins the contemporary approaches of brain imaging, which allows reconstructions of regions of brain activity to be determined. Any one of these fundamental approaches has its limitations and drawbacks, and, therefore, wherever possible, investigators attempt to integrate findings in order to reach a coherent view of brain function in relation to psychological processes. Inevitably, however, new methodological advances not only provide richer data, but also often redefine research questions and challenge existing theories. *SC*

Clarke, E. and Jacyna, L. S. 1987: *Nineteenth-century Origins of Neuroscientific Concepts*. Berkeley: University of California. **Finger, S.** 2000: *Minds Behind the Brain: A History of the Pioneers and their Discoveries*. Oxford: Oxford University Press. **Hebb, D. O.** 1949: *The Organization of Behavior: A Neuropsychological Theory*. New York: John Wiley.

microfilament   A very small filament (7 nM in diameter) that determines the shape of cells.   *JAH*

microtubule   A small (20 nM in diameter), hollow, tube-shaped structure that is involved in axoplasmic transport.   *JAH*

monoamine transmitters   These include some of the most extensively studied NEUROTRANSMITTER systems in the central nervous system. They can be subdivided into catecholamines, norepinephrine (NE) or noradrenaline, epinephrine (E) or adrenaline, and dopamine (DA), and the indoleamine, 5-hydroxytryptamine (5-HT) or serotonin.

There are a number of cell groups in the brain which synthesise and utilise NE. The most prominent is the locus coeruleus (LC), which is found in the central grey of the caudal pons. Their axons form extensive collateral branches, which project to all areas of the cerebral cortex, thalamus and hypothalamus, hippocampus, amygdala, cerebellum, brainstem and spinal cord. There are far fewer E-containing neurones and these have their own discrete anatomical distribution. It appears that LC neurones have relatively general functions involved in aspects of ATTENTION (see s. 6), learning (see s. 3), and anxiety (see s. 3) (Robbins and Everitt 1995).

Dopamine NEUROTRANSMISSION has generated considerable interest because of its involvement in reward and motivational properties, in DRUG ADDICTION and in Parkinson's disease and SCHIZOPHRENIA (see s. 7). Central dopamine systems are more complex than the noradrenergic system. Apart from short- and intermediate-length projection systems, most interest has focused on long-projection systems. These systems connect cell groups in the ventral tegmentum and substantia nigra with target regions: the neostriatum, the limbic cortex and a variety of limbic structures. Dopamine receptors were originally classified as D_1 and D_2 receptors, with distinctive pharmacological characteristics. Cloning studies have now identified four sub-types of the D_2 receptor and two of the D_1 receptor (Mansour and Watson 1995). ANTIPSYCHOTIC DRUGS (see s. 7), which are used to treat symptoms of schizophrenia, function as dopamine receptor antagonists. Parkinson's disease is a progressive neurodegenerative disorder of the basal GANGLIA, leading to profound loss of dopamine-containing neurones. Abundant evidence links mechanisms of drug addiction to dopamine activity in the nucleus accumbens [see NUCLEUS ACCUMBENS DOPAMINE AND BEHAVIOUR and other FOREBRAIN structures (Robinson and Berridge 2000).

Serotonin-containing neurones are found in clusters lying in or near the midline or raphe regions of the pons and upper brainstem. Rostral cell groups provide the extensive 5-HT innervation of the forebrain; more caudal groups project largely to the medulla and spinal cord. Following early distinctions between 5-HT receptors, the existence of a comparatively large number of receptors has been recognised (Glennon and DuKat 1995). The majority belong to the G PROTEIN-COUPLED RECEPTOR superfamily, with the exception of $5-HT_3$ receptors, which are ligand-gated ion channel receptors. Drugs which selectively block serotonin reuptake mechanisms (e.g. fluoxetine, paroxetine) are widely used clinically as antidepressants.   *SC*

Glennon, R. A. and DuKat, M. 1995: Serotonin receptor subtypes. In Bloom, F. E. and Kupfer, D. J. (eds) *Psychopharmacology: The Fourth Generation of Progress*. New York: Raven Press. **Mansour, A. and Watson S. J.** 1995: Dopamine receptor expression in the central nervous system. In Bloom, F. E. and Kupfer, D. J. (eds) *Psychopharmacology: The Fourth Generation of Progress*. New York: Raven Press. **Robbins, T. W. and Everitt, B. J.** 1995: Central norepinephrine neurons and behaviour. In Bloom, F. E. and Kupfer, D. J. (eds) *Psychopharmacology: The Fourth Generation of Progress*. New York: Raven Press. **Robinson, T. E. and Berridge, K. C.** 2000: The psychology and neurobiology of addiction: an incentive-sensitization view. *Addiction*, 95, 91–117.

motivation and emotion: biological bases

MOTIVATION (see s. 6) and EMOTION (see s. 6) are two key

concepts in psychology; related but distinguishable. (See also s. 1, EMOTION AND MOTIVATION) Setting aside observable or experimenter-controlled stimuli, and observed responses, both terms are used to refer to internal states or conditions with important psychological functions. Both have activational or arousal aspects (from quiescence to excitement); both have positive or negative aspects (e.g. approach-AVOIDANCE (see s. 7); pleasure-fear); both have differentiated and distinguishable types of components (e.g. hunger or thirst; happiness or anger); both are goal-directed and adaptive (e.g. approach food when hungry; preparations for flight when attacked); both fluctuate in intensity over time, depending upon environmental FACTORS (see s. 8), past history, internal stimuli (e.g. hormones), deprivation and need, circadian periodicity, and so on. Disorders of emotion and mood (e.g. DEPRESSION – see s. 7 and ANXIETY – see s. 6) can be closely associated with loss of motivation or a heightened sensitivity to fear-inducing stimuli (Mook 1996; Toates 2001). How are they to be distinguished? One could argue that emotions are subjectively experienced and expressed. However, there are many data which argue for non-conscious processing of emotions, with common features shared between human beings and other animals (LeDoux 1996). Motivation implies an activational component together with a purpose or goal-directedness, which is not necessarily accompanied by specific emotional arousal. Emotion implies a widespread but integrated set of responses, including physiological, behavioural and endocrine responses, which reflect experience to a greater degree than intention. Together, these psychological concepts can be brought together in a unified biological approach, called affective neuroscience (Panksepp 1998; Rolls 1999).

Within the field of motivation, the DRIVE concept proved influential, referring to a generalised activational component and to more specific, goal-directed behavioural responses (Pfaff 1999). Also historically influential has been the concept of HOMEOSTASIS, introduced by the twentieth-century physiologist, Walter Cannon. This captures the many mechanisms available, both behavioural and physiological, to maintain key bodily VARIABLES (see s. 8) within certain limits, critical for survival (Saper et al. 2002). The link between the two ideas is that in response to homeostatic need, a drive might be engaged to motivate behaviour in ways to alleviate the need. Conscious awareness of motivational states was not a necessary feature of such schemes, and the field became heavily reliant on non-human animal experimentation.

The hypothalamus, a small structure situated in the ventral diencephalon, became the neuroanatomical focus for motivational studies. Stellar's (1954) THEORY (see s. 8) of 'The physiology of motivation' proved highly influential, postulating INDEPENDENT (see s. 8) excitatory and inhibitory controls of motivational states, associated with distinct nuclei within the hypothalamus. So, too, was the discovery by Olds and Milner (1954) of the powerful rewarding effects of electrical stimulation of the brain in awake animals. The brain's REWARD SYSTEM focused strongly on the hypothalamus. This hypothalamocentric view of reward and motivation held sway for decades, generating considerable research, and emphasising subcortical mechanisms common to people, primates or rodents.

Interest moved from an initial preoccupation with neuroanatomical localisation to major interest in NEUROTRANSMITTERS involved in reward and motivation (Mook 1996; Toates 2001). This led to a refocusing on other structures innervated by neurotransmitters such as dopamine or serotonin (5-hydroxytryptamine).

Dopamine, in particular, as a monoamine neurotransmitter, has attracted a great deal of scrutiny. Beginning with evidence that dopamine may be involved importantly in reward mechanisms, it has more recently been implicated in INCENTIVE MOTIVATION (Berridge and Robinson 1998) and DRUG ADDICTION (Robinson and Berridge 2003; Wise 1996). Dopamine innervation of the nucleus accumbens (ventral striatum) has been much emphasised [see NUCLEUS ACCUMBENS DOPAMINE AND BEHAVIOUR].

Darwin is credited with establishing the 'expression of emotions' as a serious topic for study in human beings as well as other animals. Early in the twentieth century, the neuroanatomist James Papez postulated an 'emotional circuit' in the brain; this idea was extended by MacLean, who introduced the term LIMBIC SYSTEM to describe an extended, and phylogenetically old, system of structures in the brain subserving emotions (LeDoux 1996). In recent years, there has been a considerable resurgence of interest in the study of emotions. On the one hand, animal studies have implicated the amygdala and related structures in fear-conditioning, and the brainstem in pleasure or HEDONIC EVALUATION. On the other, human brain-imaging studies (fMRI, PET) have led to fresh understanding of the separable neuroanatomical basis for human emotions such as fear or disgust (Critchley 2003). Emotions are firmly back on the research agenda, and one expects to see closer ties between human studies and those derived from other animals.   *SC*

Berridge, K. C. and Robinson, T. E. 1998: What is the role of dopamine in reward: hedonic impact, reward learning, or incentive salience? *Brain Research Reviews* 28, 309–69. **Critchley, H.** 2003: Emotion and its disorders. *British Medical Bulletin* 65, 35–47. **LeDoux, J.** 1996: *The Emotional Brain: The Mysterious Underpinnings of Emotional Life.* New York: Simon and Schuster. **Mook, D. G.** 1996: *Motivation: The Organization of Action* (2nd edn). New York: Norton. **Olds, J. and Milner, P.** 1954: Positive reinforcement produced by electrical stimulation of septal area and other regions of rat brain. *Journal of Comparative and Physiological Psychology* 47, 419–27. **Panksepp, J.** 1998: *Affective Neuroscience: The Foundations of Human and Animal Emotions.* New York: Oxford University Press. **Pfaff, D. W.** 1999: *Drive: Neurobiological and Molecular Mechanisms of Sexual Motivation.* Cambridge MA: MIT Press. **Robinson, T. E. and Berridge, K. C.** 2003: Addiction. *Annual Review of Psychology* 54, 25–53. **Rolls, E. T.** 1999: *The Brain and Emotion.* Oxford: Oxford University Press. **Saper, C. B., Chou, T. C. and Elmquist, J. K.** 2002: The need to feed: homeostatic and hedonic control of eating. *Neuron* 36, 199–211. **Stellar, E.** 1954: The physiology of motivation. *Psychological Review* 61, 5–22. **Toates, F.** 2001: *Biological Psychology: An Integrative Approach.* Harlow: Prentice Hall. **Wise, R. A.** 1996: Neurobiology of addiction. *Current Opinion in Neurobiology* 6, 243–51.

Müllerian duct Embryonic duct structure found in both males and females. The Müllerian duct will develop into female internal genitalia and inner labia if not inhibited by the defeminising ANTI-MÜLLERIAN HORMONE (AMH).   *JCGH*

N

---

natural selection Evolutionary approaches to the study of human behaviour are underpinned by the logic of ADAPTATION (see s. 4) by natural selection. Natural selection was Charles Darwin's great insight, although Alfred Russel Wallace came up with the same THEORY (see s. 8) almost simultaneously. It is a theory of how evolutionary change occurs, and follows from a number of postulates:

1. All species are capable of producing more offspring than there are resources available to support them.

2. Individuals of a species vary to some extent in the behavioural and physical traits that they possess.

3. At least part of that variation is heritable and is passed on from generation to generation.

4. In competition for scarce resources, individuals who bear a particular TRAIT (see s. 6) that better enables them to exploit resources will be more likely to survive and reproduce than those individuals who do not bear the trait.

It follows that some individuals in a POPULATION (see s. 8), on account of variation, will be better suited to exploit the available resources. They might be more efficient at finding food or mates, they might be better at avoiding predators, or they might be able to cope better with climatic conditions in an unpredictable environment. If the trait affords them an advantage over competitors who do not bear the trait, then those who enjoy the advantage are more likely to survive and reproduce, and natural selection will have taken place. Nature will have selected the individuals who were best suited to current conditions, and that heritable trait will become more common in successive generations. By contrast, traits that are disadvantageous to survival and reproduction will not be selected and will disappear from the population. *JL*

Darwin, C. 1859: *The Origin of Species*. London: Murray (1985: Harmondsworth: Penguin Books).

neural integration at synapses POSTSYNAPTIC POTENTIALS arising from the activity of a single SYNAPSE are well below the potential for generating a postsynaptic ACTION POTENTIAL. However, most neurones are innervated by thousands of synapses, and the multiple postsynaptic potentials produced integrate together to determine the overall behaviour of the POSTSYNAPTIC neurone. Summation of excitatory postsynaptic potentials (EPSPs) allows sub-threshold potentials to influence action potential production, while subtraction of inhibitory postsynaptic potentials (IPSPs) brings the membrane potential away from threshold. This process permits the cell to integrate the electrical information provided by all inhibitory and excitatory synapses acting at any one time. The balance between excitatory and inhibitory signals reaching the axon hillock determines whether an action potential is generated and thus whether the postsynaptic neurone becomes an active element in a neural circuit.

EPSPs summation represents the simplest form of integration in the central nervous system. There are two types of summation: spatial and temporal. Spatial summation is the adding together of EPSPs generated simultaneously by many different synapses on a dendrite (Price, McHaffie and Larson 1989). Temporal summation is the adding together of EPSPs occurring at a single synapse in rapid succession (within 1–15 msec). Whether an EPSP contributes to an action potential is also influenced by the distance of the synapse from the axon hillock and the properties of the dendritic membrane, particularly the INTERNAL RESISTANCE and MEMBRANE RESISTANCE. *JAH*

Price, D. D., McHaffie, J. G. and Larson, M. A. 1989: Spatial summation of heat-induced pain: influence of stimulus area and spatial separation of stimuli on perceived pain sensation intensity and unpleasantness. *Journal of Neurophysiology* 62, 1270–9.

neural pathway tracing A common strategy in neuroscience research is to determine the neural pathways which interconnect one or more identifiable brain structures or regions. Input pathways into a structure are called afferents; outputs from one structure projecting to another are called efferents. One important approach is to introduce a tracer into a neuronal POPULATION (see s. 8), which is then transported in an anterograde direction to the axon terminals. A tracer protein commonly used is Phaseolus vulgaris-leucoagglutinin (PHAL), which is detected with an antibody. Hence, the axons from the GROUP (see s. 5) of neurones at the injection site are clearly labelled (Swanson 2003). Tracing in the opposite direction can be accomplished using retrograde axonal transport of injected markers, including horseradish peroxidase (HRP). A combination of anterograde and retrograde tracer analysis is used to chart neural connections and networks. *SC*

Swanson, L. W. 2003: *Brain Architecture: Understanding the Basic Plan*. Oxford: Oxford University Press.

neuroanatomy of the central nervous system and peripheral nervous system The vertebrate nervous system is naturally subdivided into the central nervous system (CNS), which is located within the skull and spinal column, and the peripheral nervous system, which contains all the nervous system components lying outside these areas.

The CNS is composed of two divisions: the brain and the spinal cord. The brain is contained within the skull, and the spinal cord within the spinal column. These are the most protected organs in the body. They are encased in bone and covered by three protective membranes. The meninges [see VENTRICULAR SYSTEM: MENINGES] prevent

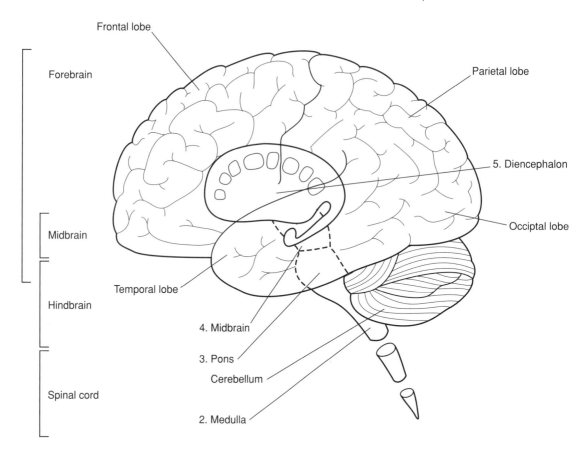

6. Cerebral hemisphere

Frontal lobe

Forebrain

Parietal lobe

5. Diencephalon

Occiptal lobe

Midbrain

Temporal lobe

Hindbrain

4. Midbrain

3. Pons

Cerebellum

Spinal cord

2. Medulla

neuroanatomy of the central nervous system and peripheral nervous system *The human central nervous system divided into six main parts: 1. spinal cord; 2. the medulla; 3. the pons and cerebellum; 4. the midbrain; 5. the diencephalons (hypothalamus and thalamus); 6. the cerebral hemispheres, divided into frontal, parietal, temporal and occipital lobes.*

the central nervous system from coming into direct contact with the overlying bone. Also protecting the central nervous system is the CEREBROSPINAL FLUID. This fills the central canal of the spinal cord and the cerebral ventricles, a series of chambers within the brain. It is a clear, colourless liquid that supports and cushions the structures within the CNS.

The blood-brain barrier is a further mechanism to protect the brain. It impedes the passage of many toxic substances from the blood into the brain. This barrier occurs as a consequence of the special structure of cerebral blood vessels. In the brain the cells of the blood vessels are tightly packed and thus offer much greater resistance to the passage of large molecules – particularly proteins – than capillaries elsewhere in the body (Goldstein and Betz 1986). However, the blood-brain barrier does not impede the passage of all large molecules. Molecules such as glucose, that are critical for normal brain function, are actively transported through cerebral blood vessel walls. Some areas of the brain are also selectively permeable to other large molecules; for example, sex hormones can readily enter parts of the brain involved in

sexual behaviour [see HORMONES AND REPRODUCTIVE BEHAVIOUR].

The adult brain consists of three major subdivisions: the FOREBRAIN, the midbrain [see MESENCEPHALON] and the HINDBRAIN. The forebrain and hindbrain can be further subdivided. The component parts of the forebrain are the telencephalon and diencephalon, while the metencephalon and myelencephalon constitute the hindbrain. Using this Greek terminology, where encephalon, meaning brain, comes from the Greek for 'in the head', the midbrain is known as the mesencephalon.

A small but important component structure of the forebrain is the hypothalamus. It contains many distinct NUCLEI, or cell groups, with vital functions. These form a longitudinal column that passes through the hypothalamus and includes the paraventricular nucleus, the ventromedial nucleus, the anterior hypothalamic nucleus and the medial preoptic nucleus. The nuclei play a role in the regulation of several motivated behaviours. The paraventricular and ventromedial nuclei contribute to the control mechanisms for ingestive behaviour (FEEDING AND DRINKING). Parts of the ventromedial nucleus, in combination

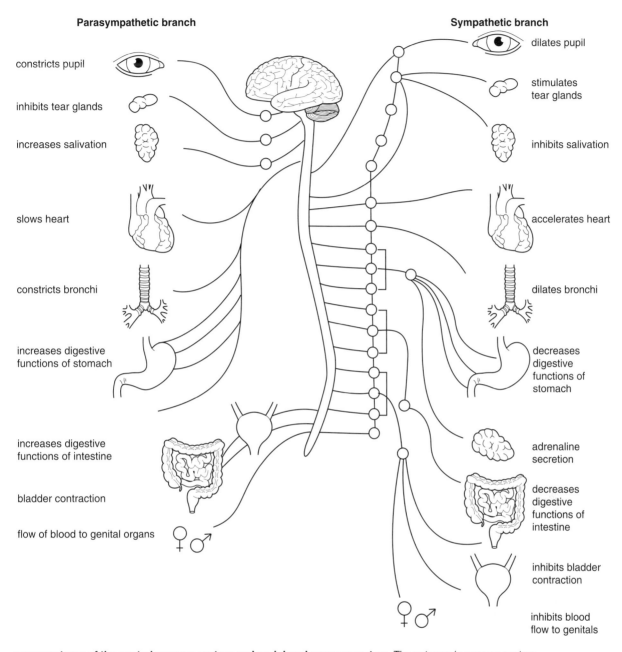

Parasympathetic branch

constricts pupil

inhibits tear glands

increases salivation

slows heart

constricts bronchi

increases digestive functions of stomach

increases digestive functions of intestine

bladder contraction

flow of blood to genital organs

Sympathetic branch

dilates pupil

stimulates tear glands

inhibits salivation

accelerates heart

dilates bronchi

decreases digestive functions of stomach

adrenaline secretion

decreases digestive functions of intestine

inhibits bladder contraction

inhibits blood flow to genitals

neuroanatomy of the central nervous system and peripheral nervous system *The autonomic nervous system.*

with the medial preoptic nucleus, also play a role in the organisation of sexual behaviour. Additionally, the control mechanism for defensive behaviour includes the anterior hypothalamic nucleus. Other nuclei are concerned with the regulation of body temperature or are sensitive to the products of the immune system (Maier and Watkins 1999). The hypothalamus also regulates the pituitary gland, which in turn controls almost all hormone secretion [see HORMONES: FUNCTION AND NATURE].

The spinal cord is composed of two different areas: the grey matter and the white matter. The grey matter is composed largely of cell bodies and in cross-section is apparent as an inner H-shaped core. It is surrounded by the white matter, which is largely composed of myelinated axons. The cord lies within the spinal or vertebral column, but is considerably shorter than the column. Both the cord and column are segmented and can be divided into cervical, thoracic, lumbar, sacral and coccygeal regions. Pairs of SPINAL NERVES are attached to the spinal cord – one on the left and one on the right – at 31 different levels. They innervate the body and are identified by the region from which they originate. Two regions of the spinal cord are enlarged to accommodate the significant number of nerve cells and connections required to process information related to the upper and lower limbs. The CERVICAL ENLARGEMENT lies at the level of the nerves to the arms, whilst the expansion at the level of the nerves to the legs is called the LUMBAR ENLARGEMENT.

In addition to the nerves that arise from the spinal cord there are 12 pairs of CRANIAL NERVES that project from the brain and innervate most of the head. Some of the cranial nerves are part of the central nervous system while others are part of the peripheral nervous system.

The peripheral nervous system also has two divisions: the somatic nervous system and the AUTONOMIC NERVOUS SYSTEM (ANS). The somatic nervous system contains the nerves that innervate the skin, joints and skeletal muscles that are under voluntary control. As such it interacts with the external environment. The ANS consists of nerves that innervate internal organs (smooth muscle), blood vessels and glands that are under involuntary control. It thus regulates the internal environment (Loewy and Spyer 1990).

Both divisions of the peripheral nervous system are composed of GANGLIA (accumulations of nerve cell bodies) and nerve fibres (bundles of nerve cell axons). The latter can be described as either afferent or efferent nerve fibres. Afferent fibres (inward-going) carry sensory information to the CNS. The efferent fibres (outward-going) emerge from the CNS and carry motor signals to muscles and glands.

The autonomic nervous system contains two kinds of efferent nerves: sympathetic nerves and parasympathetic nerves (Akasu and Nishimura 1995) [see AUTONOMIC NERVOUS SYSTEM (ANS) – SYMPATHETIC BRANCH and AUTONOMIC NERVOUS SYSTEM (ANS) – PARASYMPATHETIC BRANCH]. The sympathetic nervous system prepares the body for the 'fight-or-flight' response. It stimulates, mobilises and organises energy reserves to deal with threatening situations (Janig and McLachlan 1992). The functions of the parasympathetic nervous system generally oppose those of the sympathetic nervous system – it acts to conserve energy. Most autonomic organs receive both sympathetic and parasympathetic input, with their overall activity being governed by the relative levels of each. *JAH*

Akasu, T. and Nishimura, T. 1995: Synaptic transmission and function of parasympathetic ganglia. *Progress in Neurobiology* 45, 459–522. **Goldstein, G. W. and Betz, A. L.** 1986: The blood-brain barrier. *Scientific American* 255, 74–83. **Janig, W. and McLachlan, E. M.** 1992: Specialized functional pathways are the building blocks of the autonomic nervous system. *Journal of the Autonomic Nervous System* 41, 3–13. **Loewy, A. D. and Spyer, K. M.** 1990: *Central Regulation of Autonomic Functions.* New York: Oxford University Press. **Maier, S. F. and Watkins, L. R.** 1999: Bidirectional communication between the brain and the immune system: implications for behaviour. *Animal Behaviour* 57, 741–51.

neurofilaments A rod-like structure involved in the transport of materials within axons. *JAH*

neuromodulation Various mechanisms (e.g. presynaptic INHIBITION – see s. 3 – or NEUROTRANSMITTER reuptake) which modulate NEUROTRANSMISSION. *SC*

neuronal (or neural) networks Relates to the study of information processing in networks of elementary numerical processors; may be given varying degrees of biological realism. *SC*

neurones: basic structures Neurones are remarkably diverse in shape and size. These differences have implications for the way neurones process and integrate information. Despite this diversity, some structures are common to all nerve cells. Most neurones have three structural parts that are related to the property of the cell: the cell body, the dendrite and the axon. The cell body is the metabolic centre of the neurone. It is defined by the presence of the nucleus. It also contains numerous other organelles common to all animal cells. The cell body is enclosed within a semi-permeable membrane. This is composed of a lipid bilayer embedded in which are numerous protein molecules, for example CHANNEL PROTEINS and RECEPTOR PROTEINS, which are the basis of many of the membrane's functional properties.

Dendrites are short processes extending from the cell body. The variety of neuronal shapes arises from the variation in the form and shape of dendrites. They increase the surface area of the cell body onto which other neurones can make contact at synapses (Jan and Jan 2003). Neurones specialised for the transfer of information over long distances also have a single extension of a different type – the axon (Jan and Jan 2003). A typical axon has several regions that are structurally and functionally distinguishable. The cone-shaped region at the junction between the axon and the cell body is termed the axon hillock. This is the place where ACTION POTENTIALS are usually generated. Axons often divide into many branches called axon collaterals (Spenger et al. 1991). This enables a single nerve cell to influence numerous other cells. Towards its end, each axon or collateral divides into multiple fine branches called axon terminals. Specialised structures at the end of these form synapses, which enable connection to the next nerve cell (Jan and Jan 2003). Protein synthesis does not occur in the axon. All proteins needed in the axon for growth and function must originate in the cell body and be transported to distant regions in the axon. This movement of materials within the axon is referred to as axonal transport and is thought to involve elements of the cell's cytoskeleton.

SYNAPSES have two sides, PRESYNAPTIC and POSTSYNAPTIC. The presynaptic side consists of an axon terminal. Typically the axon swells at its terminal to form the synaptic bouton within which are synaptic vesicles. These contain a chemical called a NEUROTRANSMITTER, which is released by electrical activity in the axon (Ruegg 2001). The neurotransmitter flows across the space between the presynaptic and postsynaptic elements. This gap is termed the synaptic cleft and is typically 20–40 nM wide. The postsynaptic side is typically a dendrite or cell body of another cell. It is a specialised surface with a particularly dense covering of receptor proteins. Binding of the neurotransmitter to these receptor proteins results in an electrical change in the postsynaptic membrane. These changes are the basis of transmission of excitation or INHIBITION (see s. 3) from one cell to the next. *JAH*

Jan, Y. N. and Jan, L. Y. 2003: The control of dendrite development. *Neuron* 40, 229–42. **Ruegg, M. A.** 2001: Molecules involved in the formation of synaptic connection in muscle and brain. *Matrix Biology* 20, 3–12. **Spenger, C., Braschler, U. F., Streit, J. and Luscher, H. R.** 1991: An organotypic spinal cord – dorsal root ganglion – skeletal muscle coculture of embryonic rat. I. The morphological correlates of the spinal reflex arc. *European Journal of Neuroscience* 3, 1037–53.

neuropeptides It has been recognised for over 30 years that NEURONES can synthesise neuropeptides, which contribute to chemical NEUROTRANSMISSION within the central nervous system. The number of neuropeptides continues to grow, and only brief mention is possible here. An interesting characteristic of neuropeptides is that they typically co-localise with 'classical' NEUROTRANSMITTERS, like ACh, GABA, dopamine or 5-HT. The several families and varieties of peptides include: vasopressin and oxytocin; the tachykinins (including Substance P); VIP-related peptides; pancreatic polypeptide-related peptides; opioid peptides (including the enkephalins, β-endorphin, the dynorphins, nociceptin); somatostatin; CHOLECYSTOKININ (CCK); neurotensin; CORTICOTROPHIN-RELEASING HORMONE; galanin; cocaine- and amphetamine-regulated transcript (CART); melanin-concentrating hormone (MCH); and orexin/hypocretin (Cooper et al. 2003).

There is currently much interest in hypothalamic neuropeptides, which are involved in the control of food intake, energy balance and body weight. Neuropeptide Y (NPY) is a very potent stimulant of food intake, whereas α-melanocyte-stimulating hormone (α-MSH) acts to decrease food intake. Recently, orexin/hypocretin has been identified as a neuropeptide which stimulates food intake (Sakurai et al. 1998). *SC*

Cooper, J. R., Bloom, F. E. and Roth, R. H. 2003: *The Biochemical Basis of Neuropharmacology* (8th edn). Oxford: Oxford University Press. **Sakurai, T.** et al. 1998: Orexins and orexin receptors: a family of hypothalamic neuropeptides and G protein-coupled receptors that regulate feeding behavior. *Cell* 92, 573–85.

neuropharmacology The study of the actions of DRUGS on nerve cells and nervous systems. *SC*

neurotransmission Usually, release of a chemical messenger from storage vesicles in PRESYNAPTIC nerve terminals, which diffuses to produce a response in a POSTSYNAPTIC cell. *SC*

neurotransmitter Chemical located in vesicles within the synaptic bouton. When released by an ACTION POTENTIAL it travels across the synaptic cleft to react with the POSTSYNAPTIC membrane. *JAH*

neurotransmitter release and modulation Neurones communicate with each other using chemical signals or NEUROTRANSMITTERS, which are released at SYNAPSES and bring about consequent actions. Characteristically, neurotransmitter molecules are stored in vesicles which are localised at special release sites on PRESYNAPTIC membranes. The vesicles are primed to expel transmitter into the synapse in response to an influx of Ca^{++} ions, which is in turn triggered by depolarising ACTION POTENTIALS. The molecular events involved in neurotransmitter release are complex (Miller 1998). Neurotransmitters themselves may be involved in fast transmission, causing excitatory or inhibitory effects at POSTSYNAPTIC receptors (AMINO ACID TRANSMITTERS: glutamate-excitatory; GABA or glycine-inhibitory), or they may be involved in slower, more modulatory modes (MONOAMINE TRANSMITTERS, NEUROPEPTIDES, NOVEL NEURAL MODULATORS).

Importantly, neurotransmitter release itself is modulated through a variety of presynaptic receptor mechanisms (MacDermott et al. 1999; Miller, 1998). Presynaptic receptors may be either IONOTROPIC RECEPTORS or METABOTROPIC RECEPTORS. Examples of the former include GABA$_A$ receptors, most glutamate receptors, the 5-HT$_3$ receptor and the nicotinic acetylcholine receptor (nAChR). Effects on transmitter release at these receptors may either facilitate or inhibit neurotransmitter release. Examples of the latter include GABA$_B$ receptors, the muscarinic ACh receptor (mAChR) and monoamine receptors. Actions at these receptors are invariably inhibitory on neurotransmitter release.

There are two main sources of neurotransmitters which activate presynaptic modulatory receptors. First, the neurotransmitter may be released from the same presynaptic terminal where the receptors are localised. In this case, they are called autoreceptors. Second, the transmitter may be released from terminals distinct from those having the target presynaptic receptors. An example of this arrangement would occur at axo-axonic synapses, where release of transmitter from one axon terminal acts at presynaptic receptors on the target terminal.

Clearly such presynaptic modulation helps to control neurotransmitter availability and concentrations at synapses. In addition, transporter mechanisms prove effective in controlling functional extracellular concentrations of transmitter. Monoamine transporters have received considerable attention (Gainetdinov and Caron 2003). For monoamines, the major mechanism controlling extracellular concentrations is the reuptake by presynaptic neurones using membrane-bound monoamine transporters. These include transporters specific for dopamine (DAT), 5-HT or serotonin (SERT), and norepinephrine or noradrenaline (NET). Transporters also exist for a variety of other chemical neurotransmitters. Pharmacologically, cocaine and methylphenidate are inhibitors of DAT, while amphetamine affects not only dopamine, but also NE and 5-HT NEUROTRANSMISSION. DAT knockout (DAT-KO) mice are hyperactive, and have been considered as a possible model for human attention deficit hyperactivity disorder (ADHD) (Gainetdinov and Caron 2003). *SC*

Gainetdinov, R. R. and Caron, M. G. 2003: Monoamine transporters: from genes to behaviour. *Annual Review of Pharmacology and Toxicology* 43, 261–84. **MacDermott, A. B., Role, L. W. and Siegelbaum, S. A.** 1999: Presynaptic ionotropic receptors and the control of transmitter release. *Annual Review of Neuroscience* 22, 443–85. **Miller, R. J.** 1998: Presynaptic receptors. *Annual Review of Pharmacology and Toxicology* 38, 201–7.

NMDA-receptor complex Glutamate (Glu) IONOTROPIC RECEPTOR, which selectively recognises NMDA (N-methyl-D-aspartate), glycine (Gly) and D-serine. *SC*

non-associative learning One of the simplest forms of behavioural change (or LEARNING – see s. 3) which can take place is HABITUATION (see s. 3 and s. 4), which can be defined as a progressive decrease in response amplitude or frequency to a series of discrete and repetitive stimuli. Pavlov, the Russian physiologist, first described behavioural habituation, but it is a widespread phenomenon and can be described at a cellular level and in terms of SYNAPTIC PLASTICITY. Independent of this change is the opposite process of sensitisation, in which there occurs a progressive increase in response strength with repeated stimulation. Groves and Thompson (1970) dealt with both processes in terms of a DUAL-PROCESS THEORY (see s. 5).

Eric Kandel and his colleagues investigated these changes in EXPERIMENTS (see s. 8) involving the marine snail, *Aplysia californica*, which has a simple nervous system containing about 20,000 central nerve cells. In this animal, a mild touch to its siphon elicits withdrawal of both siphon and gill; with repeated stimulation, these reflex withdrawals habituate. The habituation of the response is closely associated with a decrease in synaptic transmission between sensory neurones and their targets – either interneurones or motor neurones. On the one hand, sensitisation appears to involve an enhancement of synaptic transmission (Kandel 1991). Long-term habituation and sensitisation may lead to synaptic biochemical and morphological changes, which may contribute towards the formation of stored memories.

The withdrawal reflexes of *Aplysia* has also been shown to be subject to CLASSICAL CONDITIONING (see s. 3) (or ASSOCIATIVE LEARNING). This requires activity in two pathways, which are closely associated in time. Stimulation of the tail (US) is applied together with stimulation of the mantle (CS); after training, the CS elicits a strong withdrawal response.   *SC*

Groves, P. M. and Thompson, R. F. 1970: Habituation: a dual-process theory. *Psychological Review* 77, 419–50. **Kandel, E. R.** 1991: Cellular mechanisms of learning and the biological basis of individuality. In Kandel, E. R., Schwartz, J. H. and Jessel, T. S. (eds) 1991: *Principles of Neural Science* (3rd edn). New York: Elsevier.

novel neural modulators   NEUROTRANSMITTERS such as MONOAMINE TRANSMITTERS, AMINO ACID TRANSMITTERS and NEUROPEPTIDES have been long established, giving rise to a 'typical' set of criteria for identifying and confirming neurotransmitter candidates. However, within the last decade, a number of substances have been discovered which do not conform to the stereotype of a classical transmitter and hence challenge earlier ASSUMPTIONS (see s. 8) about the nature and characteristics of neurotransmitters. 'Atypical' neural modulators include nitric oxide (NO), carbon monoxide (CO), hydrogen sulphide (H_2S) and the d-amino acid, D-serine (Boehning and Snyder 2003).

D-serine is not released from NEURONES, but occurs in and is released from astrocytes, a type of GLIAL CELL. D-serine is an endogenous ligand acting at the NMDA RECEPTOR COMPLEX; it acts as a co-transmitter with glutamate, the excitatory amino acid transmitter.

Nitric oxide (NO) is produced by neuronal nitric oxide synthase (nNOS), as required, and is not stored. NO can diffuse to neighbouring neurones to produce its effects. Carbon monoxide (CO) is generated by heme oxygenase (HO), an enzyme which degrades heme in red blood cells to give biliverdin, iron and CO. The best evidence for a role of CO in the central nervous system, to date, is in

olfactory neurones, where it modulates ADAPTATION (see s. 4) to odorants. Substantial levels of hydrogen sulphide (H_2S) exist in the brain, and it is formed from cysteine by the enzyme cystathionine β-synthase (CBS) and cystathionine γ-lyase (CSE). There is some evidence of involvement in the facilitation of LONG-TERM POTENTIATION (LTP) (see also s. 3) in the hippocampus.   *SC*

Boehning, D. and Snyder, S. H. 2003: Novel neural modulators. *Annual Review of Neuroscience* 26, 105–31.

nucleus   An anatomical collection of neurones within the central nervous system (plural: nuclei).   *JAH*

nucleus accumbens dopamine and behaviour

Neurones containing dopamine (DA), the cell bodies of which lie in the ventral tegmental area (VTA) of the midbrain [see MESENCEPHALON], project forward to innervate a variety of FOREBRAIN regions, including the nucleus accumbens septi (NAS) or VENTRAL striatum. Dopaminergic release in the NAS modulates glutamergic (excitatory) NEUROTRANSMISSION from the cerebral cortex. Drugs like amphetamine or cocaine enhance DA transmission in the NAS, whereas ANTIPSYCHOTIC DRUGS (see s. 7) or dopamine antagonists (e.g. pimoxide, haloperidol) block DA transmission in the NAS.

Roy Wise (1982) initiated two decades of intensive research into the functions of the DA innervation of the NAS with his proposal that brain DA plays a central role in reward phenomena (extended to include DRUG ADDICTION) and subjective pleasure. More recent work [see HEDONIC EVALUATION and INCENTIVE MOTIVATION] indicates that pleasure (or hedonics) is not dopamine-related, but many authors have endeavoured to account for dopamine's function in the ventral striatum.

Ikemoto and Panksepp (1999) propose that NAS DA transmission has two functions: to invigorate flexible approaches to stimuli and to allow the formation of incentive properties of stimulus representations, i.e. incentive LEARNING (see s. 3). Salamone and Correa (2002) argue that NAS DA is involved in the behavioural economics underlying decisions to meet a particular work requirement in relation to the anticipated reward or incentive. Both work requirement and the value of the reward are taken into consideration. Schultz and colleagues (2003) provide evidence that striatal NEURONES (including those in the NAS) respond to novel unpredicted rewards and contribute to the learning of the significance of stimuli which predict reward. Kelley (2004) argues that the NAS plays important roles in food MOTIVATION (see s. 6) and in neuronal plasticity underlying appetitive learning. Di Chiara (2002) and several other authors have argued for important roles of NAS DA transmission in relation to drug addiction. Cardinal and colleagues (2002) place the NAS in an extended brain system, which also includes the amygdala and prefrontal cortex, and which contributes significantly to motivation and EMOTION (see s. 6). (See also s. 1, EMOTION AND MOTIVATION)   *SC*

Cardinal, R. N., Parkinson, J. A., Hall, J. and Everitt, B. J. 2002: Emotion and motivation: the role of the amygdala, ventral striatum, and prefrontal cortex. *Neuroscience and Biobehavioral Reviews* 26, 321–52. **Di Chiara, G.** 2002: Nucleus accumbens shell and core dopamine: differential role in behaviour and addiction. *Behavioural Brain Research* 137, 75–114. **Ikemoto, S. and**

Panksepp, J. 1999: The role of nucleus accumbens in motivated behaviour: a unifying interpretation with special reference to reward-seeking. *Brain Research Reviews* 31, 6–14. **Kelley, A. E.** 2004: Ventral striatal control of appetitive motivation: role in ingestive behaviour and reward-related learning. *Neuroscience and Biobehavioral Reviews* 27, 765–76. **Salamone, J. D. and Correa, M.** 2002: Motivational views of reinforcement: implica-

tions for understanding the behavioural functions of nucleus accumbens dopamine. *Behavioral Brain Research* 137, 3–25. **Schultz, W., Tremblay, L. and Hollerman, J. R.** 2003: Changes in behaviour-related neuronal activity in the striatum during learning. *Trends in Neurosciences* 26, 321–8. **Wise, R. A.** 1982: Neuroleptics and operant behaviour: the anhedonia hypothesis. *Behavioral and Brain Sciences* 5, 39–87.

O

oestrogens Steroid hormones secreted by the ovaries (small amounts produced by adrenal cortex and by testes in men). In females they stimulate the growth of the uterus, breasts and fat deposition. During the menstrual cycle oestrogen stimulates ovarian and uterine changes prior to ovulation, and during pregnancy oestrogens cause the growth of breast ducts. In rodents and other non-primates peaks of oestrogen (and PROGESTERONE) coincide with peaks in sexual behaviour, ensuring copulation when the female is most fertile. *JCGH*

olfactory bulb A FOREBRAIN structure that, through small openings in the skull, provides receptors for smell. *JAH*

P

pain Pain can be described as a sensory or an emotional experience, which is unpleasant and motivates withdrawal and AVOIDANCE (see s. 7), and is associated with actual or potential tissue damage. Historically, there have been two broad views of the neural basis of pain. The first view is that pain is a distinct experience, represented by specialised neural elements both peripherally and in the central nervous system. In the late 1800s, researchers discovered that painful and thermal sensations could be elicited from discrete points on the skin. The other view stresses CONVERGENCE (see s. 3) and proposes that pain represents an integrated state, reflecting a pattern of convergent somatosensory activity. The 'gate control THEORY' (see s. 8) of Melzack and Wall (1965) is a prominent example of a convergent theory. Recently, Craig (2003) has advocated a specialised neural system, subserving pain. In his view, pain is represented in the FOREBRAIN and depends on a well-organised, hierarchical system which contributes to homeostatic functions. He describes a specific Lamina 1 (dorsal horn of the spinal cord) spino-thalamo-cortical system. He views pain as one aspect of physiological and behavioural systems which subserve homeostatic functions to maintain survival. Somewhat in contrast, Price et al. (2003) emphasise the exteroceptive functions of central NEURONES underlying pain experience, i.e. there is a cutaneous nociceptive system which signals potentially harmful stimuli affecting our bodies. They place greater emphasis on the role of wide dynamic range (WDR) neurones as distinct from highly specific nociceptive neurones.

It is well known that opiate DRUGS like morphine and its derivatives are powerful analgesic drugs (pain suppressants). They produce their analgesic effects by acting at specific opioid receptors present in the brain and spinal cord. Endogenous opioid peptides are believed to contribute to endogenous analgesic systems. It is interesting that opioid analgesia may share neural systems (including anterior cingulate cortex) with the analgesia associated with PLACEBO (see s. 8) treatments (Petrovic et al. 2002). (See also s. 7, PAIN) *SC*

Craig, A. D. 2003: Pain mechanism: labelled lines versus convergence in central processing. *Annual Review of Neuroscience* 26, 1–30. **Melzack, R. and Wall, P. D.** 1965: Pain mechanisms: a new theory. *Science* 150, 971–9. **Petrovic, P., Kalso, E., Petersson, K. M. and Ingvar, M.** 2002: Placebo and opioid analgesia – imaging a shared neuronal network. *Science* 295, 1737–40. **Price, D. D., Greenspan, J. D. and Dubrier, R.** 2003: Neurons involved in the exteroceptive function of pain. *Pain* 106, 215–19.

parental investment Any investment that parents make in an offspring that increases that offspring's chances of surviving. However, that investment imposes a cost to the parents as measured by their ability to invest in other offspring, current and future. *JL*

parental investment decisions PARENTAL INVESTMENT was defined by Robert Trivers as 'any investment by the parent in an individual offspring that increases the offspring's chance of surviving at the cost of the parent's ability to invest in other offspring' (Trivers 1972, 1974). Implicit in the concept of parental investment is the notion of finite resources. The resources that a parent might have to invest in one offspring are, necessarily, not available to invest in a different offspring, and parental investment decisions refer to the basis upon which parents decide which of their children, if indeed any, to invest in. There is a large body of research which shows that parents do not always invest equally in all their offspring and in some cases they might actively neglect or harm particular children. An extreme version of disinvestment is the cross-cultural finding that in almost all societies around the world, some parents occasionally deliberately kill their own offspring (Daly and Wilson 1988). Deliberately killing one's offspring, or even neglecting one in favour of others, appears to fly in the face of evolutionary predictions that organisms are selected to care for their offspring and ensure their survival. However, on closer examination of the circumstances that surrounds cases of infanticide, it seems that there are three main causes why parents kill their offspring: paternity uncertainty, poor offspring quality and lack of parental resources. In each case, parents balance the cost of continued investment in a given child against the expected outcome of that investment, and the latter might be measured in terms of the future survival and reproductive prospects of the child, or in terms of the ability of the parents themselves to reproduce in the future.

There are also strong theoretical grounds to expect that in certain circumstances parents will favour sons over daughters, or vice versa. The THEORY (see s. 8), known as the Trivers-Willard effect, predicts that parents should show sex-biased investment in conditions where one offspring gender has a greater VARIANCE (see s. 8) in reproductive success than the other (Trivers and Willard 1973). In other words, where the reproductive opportunities are not similar or equal for males and females, parents should BIAS (see s. 3, s. 6 and s. 8) their investment towards the gender with the greater variance in reproductive success; they should prefer the gender that is most likely to produce more grandchildren for them. There are a number of studies that have tested the Trivers-Willard HYPOTHESIS (see s. 3 and s. 8) in human POPULATIONS (see s. 8), and some of the results quite strongly support the predictions. Nonetheless, in other studies the results have been equivocal, and further research is necessary.

In general, studies of human parental investment decisions clearly show the conditional nature of the decisions that parents make, and they very closely match evolutionary predictions. *JL*

Barrett, L., Dunbar, R. I. M. and Lycett, J. E. 2002: *Human Evolutionary Psychology*. Houndmills: Palgrave MacMillan. **Daly, M. and Wilson, M.** 1988: *Homicide*. New York: Aldine de Gruyter. **Trivers, R. L.** 1972: Parental investment and sexual selection. In Campbell, B. (ed.) *Sexual Selection and the Descent of*

Man. Chicago: Aldine. **Trivers, R. L.** 1974: Parent-offspring conflict. *American Zoologist* 14, 249–64. **Trivers, R. L. and Willard, D.** 1973: Natural selection of parental ability to vary the sex ratio. *Science* 79, 90–2.

phenotype The behavioural and morphological traits that are displayed by an individual. Note that individuals who have very similar phenotypes do not necessarily have to have similar GENOTYPES. *JL*

phenylketonuria (PKU) Individuals with PKU are unable to metabolise phenylalanine, an amino acid which is found in many foods. High blood levels of phenylalanine cause severe brain damage, leading to cognitive dysfunction. These individuals are HOMOZYGOUS (see s. 4) for a recessive gene on chromosome 12, which is responsible for synthesising the enzyme that metabolises phenylalanine (Carlson et al. 2000). As this disturbed metabolism of phenylalanine can be detected in the urine it is possible to screen infants for PKU. If a low phenylalanine diet is then given, normal brain development will result. *JC*

Carlson, N. R., Busket, W. and Martin, G. N. 2000: *Psychology: The Science of Behaviour.* Harlow: Allyn and Bacon.

posterior pituitary The posterior pituitary develops in the EMBRYO (see s. 4) from a small outgrowth at the base of the brain and, unlike the ANTERIOR PITUITARY, it is neural in origin. Neurones project down from the paraventricular nucleus and supraoptic nucleus of the hypothalamus into the posterior pituitary. These neurones produce the hormones vasopressin and oxytocin. Unlike the hormones secreted by the anterior pituitary both vasopressin and oxytocin consist of far shorter peptide chains. They are carried down the neuronal axons into the posterior pituitary and stored in secretary vesicles located in the nerve cell terminals, and are then released into the bloodstream in response to neural impulses (Brook and Marshall 1996). *JCGH*

Brook, C. and Marshall, N. 1996: *Essential Endocrinology.* London: Blackwell Science.

postganglionic cells Cells of the AUTONOMIC NERVOUS SYSTEM that are located in autonomic GANGLIA and send axons to innervate target organs. *JAH*

postsynaptic Refers to a neurone on the receiving end of a synapse. *JAH*

postsynaptic potentials Unlike axons, dendrites and soma do not produce ACTION POTENTIALS. However, at a SYNAPSE, action potentials in the PRESYNAPTIC neurone (axon) can evoke changes in electrical potential across the POSTSYNAPTIC neurone (dendrite or soma) through the release of NEUROTRANSMITTERS. These postsynaptic potentials vary in magnitude and can be either positive or negative. Postsynaptic depolarisations are called excitatory postsynaptic potentials (EPSPs). They increase the LIKELIHOOD (see s. 8) of an action potential being generated. Postsynaptic hyperpolarisations reduce the likelihood of an action potential being generated. Hence, they are called inhibitory postsynaptic potentials (IPSPs).

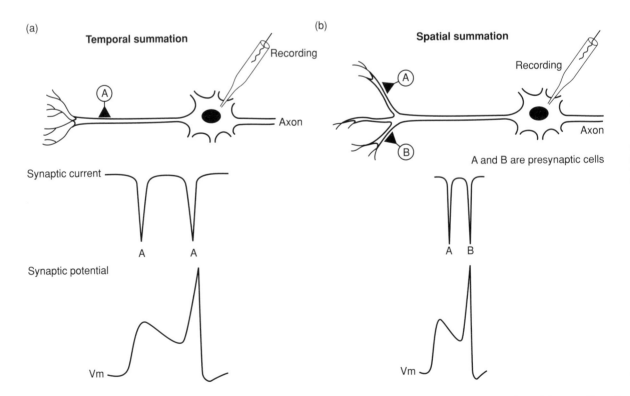

postsynaptic potentials *Central neurones can integrate a variety of synaptic inputs through temporal and spatial summation of synaptic potentials.*

The amplitude of both EPSPs and IPSPs is proportional to the signal that generated them. Consequently, they are referred to as graded responses and do not follow the 'ALL-OR-NONE' law. These changes in MEMBRANE POTENTIAL are conducted to adjacent areas of the same cell in a passive manner. This transmission has two important characteristics – it is rapid (almost instantaneous) but decremental, such that the potentials decrease in amplitude with distance from the site of initiation (Lev-Tov et al. 1983). Therefore synapses closest to the axon hillock, the site of initiation of an action potential (Coombs, Curtis and Eccles 1957), will have decayed the least and will thus have the most influence over the firing of the neurone (Williams and Stuart 2002, 2003).

Integration of these potentials, in the form of summation and subtraction, is the basis of information processing in the neurone. Generally, it takes the combined effect, the summation, of many excitatory inputs to elicit the all-or-none response of an action potential. However, every inhibitory input will subtract from this effect and take the membrane potential back towards the resting potential, thus decreasing the probability that an action potential will fire. Subtraction occurs because the polarity of an IPSP is opposite to that of an EPSP, i.e. hyperpolarisation rather than depolarisation. This is in contrast to action potentials of inhibitory presynaptic NEURONES. These action potentials look exactly like those of excitatory presynaptic fibres. INHIBITION (see s. 3) is achieved by the action potential initiating the passage of ions through the postsynaptic membrane in a manner that will hyperpolarise the membrane. *JAH*

Coombs, J. S., Curtis, D. R. and Eccles, J. C. 1957: The generation of impulses in the motoneurones. *Journal of Physiology-London* 139, 232–49. Lev-Tov, A., Miller, J. P., Burke, R. E. and Rall, W. 1983: Factors that control amplitude of EPSPs in dendritic neurons. *Journal of Neurophysiology* 50, 399–412. Williams, S. R. and Stuart, G. J. 2002: Voltage- and site-dependent control of the somatic impact of dendritic IPSPs. *Journal of Neuroscience* 23, 7358–67. Williams, S. R. and Stuart, G. J. 2003: Dependence of EPSP efficacy on synapse location in neocortical pyramidal neurons. *Science* 295, 1907–10.

preganglionic cells Cells of the AUTONOMIC NERVOUS SYSTEM that are located in the central nervous system and send axons to target autonomic GANGLIA. *JAH*

presynaptic Refers to the neurone on the releasing end of a SYNAPSE. *JAH*

progesterone A steroid hormone secreted by the ovaries in response to LUTEINISING HORMONE (LH). Progesterone secretion peaks after ovulation, causing the thickening of the uterus lining in preparation for pregnancy. *JCGH*

psychopharmacology The study of the actions of DRUGS on psychological (cognitive, affective) processes and behavioural outputs. *SC*

Q

quantitative trait loci (QTL) Multiple genes and environmental variation result in quantitative (continuous) distributions of PHENOTYPES. Quantitative genetics estimate the genetic and environmental contributions to phenotypic variation in a POPULATION (see s. 8) (Plomin et al. 1997). This is expressed as QTL, which are genes of various EFFECT SIZES (see s. 8) (the proportion of INDIVIDUAL DIFFERENCES – see s. 6 – accounted for by a particular FACTOR – see s. 8). *JC*

Plomin, R., DeFries, J. C., McClearn, G. E. and Rutter, M. 1997: *Behavioral Genetics* (3rd edn). New York: W. H. Freeman and Co.

R

receptor protein Membrane-bound protein structure to which specific NEUROTRANSMITTERS bind. *JAH*

receptors Early in the twentieth century, Langley introduced the notion of receptor substances on cells to account for specificity of the actions of DRUGS in biological systems. The concept of receptors for drugs became well established and was extended to include receptors for hormones and chemical NEUROTRANSMITTERS. An 'agonist' was defined as a drug which combines with a specific receptor to produce a biological response. In contrast, an 'antagonist' can combine with a receptor and prevent the response taking place. An antagonist will reduce the action of an agonist, either competitively or non-competitively. Recently, terminology has been extended to account for 'partial agonists' (cannot elicit as large an effect as a full agonist) and 'inverse agonists' (bind to receptors and reduce the fraction of them in an active conformation) (Neubig et al. 2003).

We now know that macromolecules can be isolated which fit the criteria for receptors. These macromolecules consist of a number of subunits and are typically found in association with cell membranes. Two large families of receptors can be distinguished: ionophore receptors, or LIGAND-GATED ION CHANNELS, and METABOTROPIC RECEPTORS or G PROTEIN-COUPLED RECEPTORS (guanine nucleotide-binding proteins). Ligand-gated channels consist of a number of transmembrane subunits enclosing a central pore: when opened this allows increased flux of ions (Na^+, K^+, Ca^{++}, Cl^-) across membranes. This permits very fast responses to take place. Included within this receptor family are nicotinic ACh, GABA, glycine, most glutamate and $5\text{-}HT_3$ receptors. Metabotropic receptors, on the other hand, mediate slower and more extended responses, allowing modulatory effects on faster signalling. Included within this family are muscarinic ACh, all catecholamine, NEUROPEPTIDES and most 5-HT receptors (Cooper, Bloom and Roth 2003).

Drugs can act as agonists, antagonists or inverse agonists at each of these many types of receptor. Depending upon the degree of receptor specificity, drugs therefore prove to be extremely useful tools in understanding the mechanisms of NEUROTRANSMISSION, with actions mediated at corresponding receptors, and the physiological and/or behavioural effects which ensue. *SC*

Cooper, J. R., Bloom, F. E. and Roth, R. H. 2003: *The Biochemical Basis of Neuropharmacology* (8th edn). Oxford: Oxford University Press. **Neubig, R. R., Spedding, M., Kenakin, T. and Christopoulus, A.** 2003: International Union of Pharmacology Committee on receptor nomenclature and drug classification. XXXVIII. Update on terms and symbols in quantitative pharmacology. *Pharmacological Reviews* 55, 597–606.

recording neural activity Nerve cell activity in the brain generates electrical activity which can be measured. At a large-scale level, the ELECTROENCEPHALOGRAM (EEG) is a familiar measurement tool, and records the summed activity of large POPULATIONS (see s. 8) of cortical NEURONES using affixed scalp electrodes and appropriate signal amplification. EEG can be used clinically to investigate epilepsy or the several stages of sleep. In human cognitive neuroscience, studies of EVENT-RELATED POTENTIAL (ERP) have become prominent: in this approach, EEG is recorded at numerous scalp locations in a way that is time-locked to some definable event. For example, memory processes can be studied using ERPs, and through an analysis of spatial distributions across the scalp, separation of cognitive processes involved in task performance can be achieved (Rugg and Coles 1995).

In animal studies, it is possible to investigate the activity of individual nerve cells (SINGLE-UNIT RECORDING) not only in cortical areas but at subcortical locations too. David Hubel and Torsten Wiesel shared the 1981 Nobel Prize in Physiology or Medicine for their work together at Harvard on the single-unit responses of cells in the cat visual system (Hubel and Wiesel 1962). In the UK, Edmund Rolls, working at Oxford, has been at the forefront in conducting single-unit studies in relation to reward, appetite, EMOTION (see s. 6), taste and olfaction (Rolls 1999). Studying the human nervous system at this level of detail is impracticable, although an approximation can be made in primate work. *SC*

Hubel, D. H. and Wiesel, T. N. 1962: Receptive fields, binocular interaction and functional architecture in the cat's visual cortex. *J. Physiol. (Lond.).*, 160, 106–154. **Rolls, E. T.** 1999: *The Brain and Emotion.* Oxford: Oxford University Press. **Rugg, M. D. and Coles, M. G. H.** 1995: *Electrophysiology of Mind: event-related brain potentials and cognition.* Oxford: Oxford University Press.

redundancy effects: overshadowing and blocking Animals will often fail to learn about signals when they are not the sole provider of information about a forthcoming outcome. Pairings of a signal, X, and an outcome would be anticipated to result in excitatory conditioning; but if these X+ pairings occurred in the presence of a second signal, A (i.e. AX+), when tested alone, X will often produce only a reduced ('overshadowed') CONDITIONED RESPONSE (see s. 3). A more profound diminution in the conditioned response seen to X on test is produced when A is paired with the outcome *before* the compound trials (i.e. A+, *then* AX+); LEARNING (see s. 3) is said to be 'blocked'. These widely found phenomena appear to demonstrate that animals are less inclined to learn about redundant signals than those that provide good sources of information. (See also s. 3, BLOCKING) *JW-R*

Mackintosh, N. J. 1983: *Conditioning and Associative Learning.* Oxford: Clarendon Press. **Pearce, J. M.** 1997: *Animal Learning and Cognition* (2nd edn). Hove: Psychology Press.

REM (or rapid eye-movement) sleep A distinctive stage of normal sleeping, characterised by desynchronised ELECTROENCEPHALOGRAM (EEG), rapid eye-movements and loss of muscle tone. *SC*

reward system Concept introduced by James Olds based on evidence that stimulation of certain brain structures (e.g. hypothalamus) can produce intense reward or REINFORCEMENT (see s. 3) effects. *SC*

ribosome The structure at which the cell synthesises new protein molecules. *JAH*

roots Two distinct branches of a spinal nerve, each of which serves a separate function. *JAH*

S

sensitisation A process of increasing responsivity following repeated stimulation.   *SC*

sexual selection Sexual selection is the second kind of selection that Darwin proposed. Whereas NATURAL SELECTION operates on phenotypic variation in both males and females and enhances their ability to survive and reproduce, sexual selection operates to increase the relative attractiveness of individuals as potential mates. Sexually selected traits do not necessarily increase an individual's survival prospects, and in some cases they might decrease them. They are, however, traits that are attractive to members of the opposite sex and, to the extent that they become a basis for MATE CHOICE DECISIONS, they are likely to be selected. They are traits that are advantageous in reproduction, but not necessarily survival. Perhaps the most famous example of a sexually selected TRAIT (see s. 6) is the peacock's tail: the tail itself probably reduces a male's survivorship, since it makes it extremely difficult to fly and so escape predation. However, females prefer to mate with males who have the most eyespots in their trains and so sexual selection operates on the peacock's tail. Sexually selected traits are likely to evolve in species where there is a gender asymmetry in the costs of reproduction, and hence in mate choosiness. If one sex is choosier than the other, then that sex can exert pressure on the less choosy sex.

Sexual selection can be subdivided into INTRASEXUAL SELECTION and INTERSEXUAL SELECTION. In the former, members of one sex compete among themselves for access to mates. This competition leads to the evolution of traits that increase competitive ability, such as large body size, horns, antlers or large canine teeth. In mammals, intrasexual competition occurs usually between males, and results in the evolution of sexual dimorphism. Intersexual selection, also known as 'female choice', occurs when one sex chooses to mate with members of the other sex primarily on the basis of characteristics or traits that the latter possesses. These characteristics might include: traits that confer direct benefits on the female and her ability to rear offspring, such as male ability to defend resources, territories or offspring; traits that indicate male genetic quality, and by mating with males who display these traits, a female ensures that her offspring will inherit the same good genes; and traits that are non-adaptive, but that make males more conspicuous to females. In the latter case, this might lead to the evolution of conspicuous colours, exaggerated morphological characters or complex courtship routines.

It remains unclear the extent to which aspects of human morphology have been shaped by sexual selection. However, it is generally accepted that there are some that appear to have been, and they are features that differ conspicuously between the sexes. The male beard and deep voice are candidate examples: they have no apparent survival value, since females and children do not have them, and they are clearly sexually dimorphic. If beards and deep voices are sexually selected traits, then females should prefer males who have those traits relative to men with little or no facial hair and high-pitched voices.   *JL*

Barber, N. 1995: The evolutionary psychology of physical attractiveness: sexual selection and human morphology. *Ethology and Sociobiology* 16, 395–424. **Darwin, C.** 1871: *The Descent of Man and Selection in Relation to Sex*. London: Murray (1998: New York: Prometheus Books).

single-unit recording Method of recording the electrical activity of individual nerve cells in the brain using fine microelectrodes.   *SC*

sleep and biological rhythms Sleep is not a homogeneous process: there are qualitative differences between stages of sleep, and sleep also exhibits cyclical patterns. Conventionally, sleep is divided into SLOW-WAVE SLEEP or non-rapid eye-movement (non-REM) sleep, on the one hand, and rapid eye-movement (REM) SLEEP, on the other. During a night's sleep, episodes of non-REM sleep alternate with episodes of REM sleep. Stages of sleep have been investigated in laboratories where records are taken of the sleeper's ELECTROENCEPHALOGRAM (EEG), electromyogram (EMG) and electro-oculogram (EOG). During wakefulness, the EEG (which records brainwave activity) exhibits alpha and beta activity (frequencies of 8–12 Hz and 13–30 Hz, respectively). With the onset of stage 1 sleep, theta activity is exhibited (3.5–7.5 Hz), and with stage 2 sleep, sleep spindles and K complexes are seen (less than 3.5 Hz). Together, these stages constitute non-REM sleep. After about 90 minutes of sleep, there is an abrupt change in physiological measure: the EEG becomes desynchronized, there are rapid movements of the eyes and there is a profound loss of muscle tone. These indicate the presence of REM sleep. During an eight-hour period of sleep, there may be four to five REM sleep episodes, alternating with non-REM sleep episodes (Horne 1988).

Sleep is not a passive process, but is actively controlled as part of a sleep-waking cycle. Several neuronal circuits are involved in the control of waking and arousal, including ACETYLCHOLINE (ACh), norepinephrine (NE), serotonin (5-HT), histamine and the newly described hypocretin. A structure particularly important in the control of non-REM sleep is the ventrolateral preoptic area (VLPA), rostral to the hypothalamus. The VLPA may act to inhibit each of the brain's arousal systems (Saper et al. 2001). The brain system most involved in the control of REM sleep is the GROUP (see s. 5) of acetylcholine-containing neurones of the peribrachial area, located in the brainstem (Jones and Beaudet 1987).

The sleep-waking is embedded within daily patterns following an approximately 24-hour cycle (circadian rhythms). The primary biological clock which determines this regular rhythmicity is found in the suprachiasmatic nucleus (SCN) of the hypothalamus. Damage to the SCN abolishes circadian patterns of activity and sleeping.

113

Changes in pattern, for example, changes in shift work or the jet lag associated with flying across time zones, can cause mood and sleep disturbances on a temporary basis, until the internal clock resets (Carlson 2004). *SC*

Carlson, N. R. 2004: *Physiology of Behavior* (8th edn). Boston: Prentice Hall. **Horne, J. A.** 1988: *Why We Sleep: The Functions of Sleep in Humans and Other Mammals.* Oxford: Oxford University Press. **Jones, B. E. and Beaudet, A.** 1987: Distribution of acetylcholine and catecholamine neurons in the cat brain stem studied by choline acetyltransferase and tyrosine hydroxylase immunohistochemistry. *Journal of Comparative Neurology* 261, 15–32. **Saper, C. B., Chou, T. C. and Scammell, T. E.** 2001: The sleep switch: hypothalamic control of sleep and wakefulness. *Trends in Neurosciences* 24, 726–31.

slow-wave sleep   Distinctive phases of normal sleeping, which alternate with REM SLEEP; characterised by high-amplitude, low-frequency ELECTROENCEPHALOGRAM (EEG) waveforms. *SC*

spinal nerves   The spinal cord communicates with the body via 31 pairs of spinal nerves, which are all part of the peripheral nervous system. The spinal nerves run along the length of the spinal cord and join it at regular intervals through notches between each VERTEBRA of the spinal column. Each nerve divides as it nears the cord such that it attaches by two functional distinct branches, or roots. The DORSAL (back) root consists of sensory pathways (peripheral afferents) bringing information into the spinal cord from the body. The VENTRAL (front) root consists of motor pathways (peripheral efferents) carrying information away from the spinal cord to the muscles (Jorgensen 2003). The name of the spinal nerve is the same as the segment of the spinal cord to which it is connected. The cervical regions gives rise to 8 cervical nerves (C1–C8), the thoracic to 12 thoracic nerves (T1–T12), the lumbar region to 5 lumbar nerves (L1–L5), the sacral region to 5 sacral nerves (S1–S5) and the coccygeal region to 1 coccygeal nerve. As the spinal cord is shorter than the spinal column, the lumbar and sacral nerves lie in the vertebral column for some distance, thus forming the CAUDA EQUINA. *JAH*

Jorgensen, C. B. 2003: Aspects of the history of the nerves: Bell's theory, the Bell-Magendie law and controversy, and two forgotten works by P.W. Lund and D.F. Eschricht. *Journal of the History of the Neurosciences*, 12, 229–249.

stereotaxic atlas   Atlas prepared to assist investigators in their investigations of brain structure and function; arranged as serial sections through the brain, set within a three-coordinate system. *SC*

stereotaxic surgery   In order to stimulate or lesion subcortical brain structures, it is necessary to use stereotaxic surgery. In 1908, Victor Horsley and Robert Clarke designed a stereotaxic instrument to maintain the head in a fixed position and orientation, and to locate the position of an electrode or cannula according to three sets of ORTHOGONAL (see s. 8) coordinates. Under general anaesthesia, an incision is made in the scalp and the skull is bared. A hole is drilled through the skull, and the electrode or cannula is lowered into the brain using a carrier on the stereotaxic instrument until the correct coordinate position is reached. The electrode or cannula can be cemented into position, attached to the skull, and follow-ing recovery from surgery, the animal can be used in chronic studies in the awake state. STEREOTAXIC ATLASES provide maps of the brain in which the three-dimensional coordinates are given for identified brain structures (e.g. Swanson 1992). *SC*

Swanson, L. W. 1992: *Brain Maps: Structure of the Rat Brain.* New York: Elsevier.

stress hormones, health and illness   Exposure to long-term STRESS (see s. 7) has been demonstrated to produce detrimental effects on health. Specifically, chronic stress increases the LIKELIHOOD (see s. 8) of suffering from non-communicable illnesses such as diabetes and cardiovascular disease, and also susceptibility to infection. Many of these effects are due to prolonged secretion of stress hormones, in particular glucocorticoids such as CORTISOL. Continuous excess cortisol production produces a wide range of damaging effects to the body. If stress is prolonged the cortisol-induced effects on blood pressure and the immune system leave the individual susceptible to both non-communicable diseases and infection. It should also be noted that elevated levels of cortisol are observed in severely depressed patients, suggesting some form of malfunction in the hypothalamic pituitary axis (HPA). *JCGH*

Ader, R. and Cohen, C. 1993: Psychoneuroimmunology; conditioning and stress. *Annual Review of Psychology* 4, 53–85. **Brown, E. S., Varghese, F. P. and McEwan, B. S.** 2004: Association of depression with medical illness. Does cortisol play a role? *Biological Psychiatry* 55, 1–9. **Padgett, D. A. and Glaser, R.** 2003: How stress influences the immune response. *Trends in Immunology* 24, 444–8. **Tafei, G. E. and Bermardini, R.** 2003: Psychoneuroendocrinological links between chronic stress and depression. *Progress in Neuro-Psychopharmacology & Biological Psychiatry* 27, 893–903.

synapse   Functional contact between a neurone and other cells, most commonly involved in chemical NEUROTRANSMISSION. *SC*

synaptic homeostasis   Mechanisms which act to ensure stability of neuronal activity. *SC*

synaptic plasticity   Donald Hebb's book *The Organization of Behavior* has had lasting value, and continues to be widely influential. In this book, he proposed a 'neurophysiological postulate' that: '*When an axon of cell A is near enough to excite a cell B and repeatedly or persistently takes part in firing it, some growth or metabolic change takes place in one or both cells such that A's efficiency, as one of the cells firing B, is increased.*' This postulate, which embodies a principle of synaptic change or plasticity which is activity-dependent, is now referred to as a HEBBIAN SYNAPSE. Hebb (1949) clearly intended that this type of synaptic plasticity would provide an account of the relative permanence of long-term memories. In a contemporary version of this fundamental idea, the synaptic plasticity and memory (SPM) HYPOTHESIS (see s. 3 and s. 8) states that: 'Activity-dependent synaptic plasticity is induced at appropriate SYNAPSES during memory formation, and is both necessary and sufficient for the information storage underlying the type of memory mediated by the brain area in which that plasticity is observed' (Martin et al. 2000: 650). Activity-dependent synaptic plasticity in relation to

LEARNING (see s. 3) and MEMORY (see s. 1) is not only of particular interest in psychology, but is of major importance in neuroscience generally. Synaptic plasticity is also of great interest in relation to the development of the nervous system when connections between nerve cells are formed, and also in relation to recovery of function following brain injury or neural degeneration.

The discovery of LONG-TERM POTENTIATION (LTP) in the hippocampus (Bliss and Lømo 1973) initiated an enormous research effort to understand the cellular and synaptic bases of a phenomenon which might hold the key to understanding fundamental mechanisms of learning and memory (Collingridge and Bliss 1995). The question – does LTP equal memory? (Stevens 1998) – is an oversimplification, although undoubtedly synaptic plasticity is necessary for learning and memory, even if it is not sufficient (Martin et al. 2000). A further important discovery was the evidence for the involvement of the NMDA (N-methyl-D-aspartate) RECEPTOR in LTP (Collingridge et al. 1983). Nowadays it is recognised that LTP is exhibited widely throughout the brain, and is not restricted to the hippocampus (e.g. cerebral cortex, amygdala), and that LTP can either be NMDA-dependent or NMDA-independent (Martin et al. 2000).

A related phenomenon, exemplifying synaptic plasticity, is LONG-TERM DEPRESSION (LTD), first reported in the CA1 field of the hippocampus (Lynch et al. 1977). Hence, in response to repetitive stimulation, either LTP or LTD may ensue as long-lasting traces of the stimulation. Both types of long-term synaptic change incorporate the associative or relational features of learning and memory, which characterise Hebbian synapses. Both are input-specific, and persist over time. Shors and Matzel (1997) have challenged that LTP is involved in learning, and instead propose that LTP serves as an arousal or attentional device. It is not easy on present experimental evidence to distinguish their view from the HYPOTHESIS (see s. 3 and s. 8) that LTP is necessary to learning and memory (Martin et al. 2000).

Recently, ATTENTION (see s. 3) has been paid to SYNAPTIC HOMEOSTASIS, which acts to stabilise neuronal activity, and may therefore act in opposition to Hebbian plasticity (Turrigiano and Nelson 2000). For NEURONAL NETWORKS to operate efficiently and effectively, a variety of homeostatic mechanisms are required to stabilise neural activity, and these themselves may incorporate examples of synaptic plasticity. Although the changes which underlie the function of Hebbian synapses can lead to long-term changes in nerve cell activity, the changes have to be regulated through the control exerted by homeostatic mechanisms. In this way, activities of nerve cells and neural network functions are maintained in normal physiologically relevant ranges (Burrone and Murthy 2003).

Hebb (1949) also introduced the idea of a cortical CELL-ASSEMBLY, in which 'any two nerve cells or systems of cells that are repeatedly active at the same time will tend to become "associated", so that the activity in one facilitates activity in the other'. It is a form of persistent, reverberatory circuit which may underlie LONG-TERM MEMORY (see s. 3) storage. Fuster and Alexander (1971) reported the existence of neural activity associated with delayed responses required in some SHORT-TERM MEMORY (see s. 3) tasks. Since their pioneering work, considerable interest has grown in the notion of SYNAPTIC REVERBERATION, as a form of persistent neural activity which may underlie memory processes (Amit and Mongillo 2003; Brunel 2003; Wang 2001). This contemporary interest, together with the established place of Hebbian synapses, serves to emphasise the enduring importance of Hebb's seminal insights. *SC*

Amit, D. J. and Mongillo, G. 2003: Selective delay activity in the cortex: phenomena and interpretation. *Cerebral Cortex* 13, 1139–50. **Bliss, T. V. P. and Lømo, T.** 1973: Long-lasting potentiation of synaptic transmission in the dentate area of the anaesthetized rabbit following stimulation of the perforant path. *Journal of Physiology – London* 232, 331–56. **Brunel, N.** 2003: Dynamics and plasticity of stimulus-selective persistent activity in cortical network models. *Cerebral Cortex* 13, 1151–61. **Burrone, J. and Murthy, V. N.** 2003: Synaptic gain control and homeostasis. *Current Opinion in Neurobiology* 13, 560–67. **Collingridge, G. L. and Bliss, T. V. P.** 1995: Memories of NMDA receptors and LTP. *Trends in Neurosciences* 18, 54–6. **Collingridge, G. L., Kehl, S. J. and McLennan, H.** 1983: Excitatory amino acids in synaptic transmission in the Schaeffer collateral-commissural pathway of the rat hippocampus. *Journal of Physiology – London* 334, 33–46. **Fuster, J. M. and Alexander, G. E.** 1971: Neuron activity related to short-term memory. *Science* 173, 652–4. **Hebb, D. O.** 1949: *The Organization of Behavior*. New York: John Wiley. **Lynch, G. S., Dunwiddie, T. and Cribkoff, V.** 1977: Heterosynaptic depression: a postsynaptic correlate of long-term potentiation. *Nature* 266, 737–9. **Martin, S. J., Grimwood, P. D. and Morris, R. G. M.** 2000: Synaptic plasticity and memory: an evaluation of the hypothesis. *Annual Review of Neuroscience* 23, 649–711. **Shors, T. J. and Matzel, L. D.** 1997: Long-term potentiation: what's learning got to do with it? *Behavioral and Brain Sciences* 20, 597–655. **Stevens, C. F.** 1998: A million dollar question: does LTP equal memory? *Neuron* 20, 1–2. **Turrigiano, G. G. and Nelson, S. B.** 2000: Hebb and homeostasis in neuronal plasticity. *Current Opinion in Neurobiology* 10, 358–64. **Wang, X.-J.** 2001: Synaptic reverberation underlying mnemonic persistent activity. *Trends in Neurosciences* 24, 455–63.

synaptic reverberation Persistent neural activity within networks of nerve cells. *SC*

synaptic transmission and psychopharmacology

The term SYNAPSE was introduced by the physiologist, Sir Charles Sherrington, in 1897, to describe the functional junction between NEURONES in the central and peripheral nervous systems. Both pharmacologists and physiologists recognised that certain DRUGS were effective in mimicking the effects of neural excitation, and speculated that neurones themselves may release chemical messengers or transmitters when excited. In the early 1920s, the pharmacologist, Otto Loewi, performed the first critical EXPERIMENTS (see s. 8) which showed that chemical release and transmission took place at neuronal synapses, and identified substances now known to be ACETYLCHOLINE (ACh) and noradrenaline (or norepinephrine, NE). In 1933, Sir Henry Dale introduced the terms 'cholinergic' and 'adrenergic' to refer to the nerves which released these transmitters, respectively. In 1936, Dale and Loewi were awarded a Nobel prize 'for their discoveries relating to chemical transmission of nerve impulses' (Finger 2000). It is now generally accepted that a principal means by which neurones exert effects on each other and on effector organs is by means of chemical transmission at synaptic junctions (Cooper, Bloom and Roth 2003).

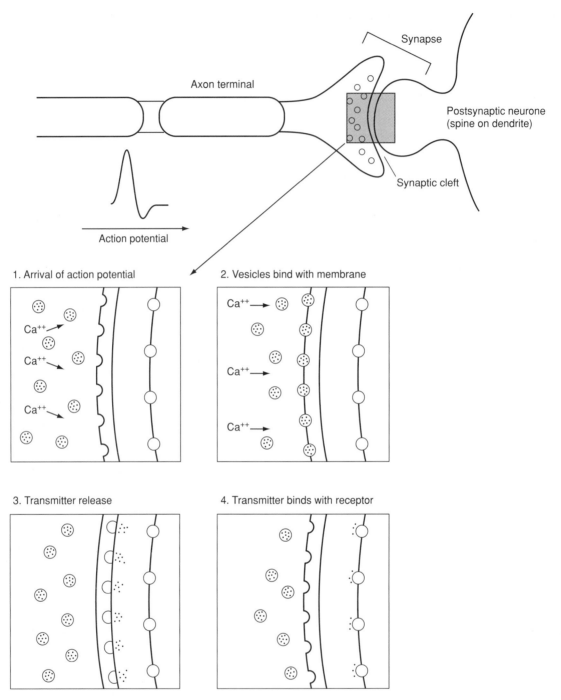

synaptic transmission and psychopharmacology *Neurotransmitter release at the synapse. When the action potential reaches the axon terminals, it causes voltage-gated calcium (Ca⁺⁺) channels to open (1), triggering vesicles containing neurotransmitter molecules to bind to the presynaptic membrane (2). Neurotransmitter is released into the synaptic cleft (3) and binds to receptors located in the postsynaptic membrane (4).*

Synaptic transmission in the mammalian central nervous system (CNS) typically involves a number of steps: within the secreting neurone, the chemical transmitter is synthesised, transported down the axon and placed in storage within synaptic vesicles at nerve endings. ACTION POTENTIALS, propagated along the axon, lead to changes in ion fluxes across terminal membranes, which lead in turn to release of transmitter molecules into the synaptic cleft, which separates the PRESYNAPTIC cell from the POSTSYNAPTIC target. The effects of the transmitter are mediated by interlocking with receptor proteins located at the postsynaptic surface. The effects on the postsynaptic cell can be either excitatory or inhibitory, depending upon the transmitter and the type of receptor(s) present on the postsynaptic membrane. If sufficient excitatory POSTSYNAPTIC POTENTIALS (EPSPs) summate, both spatially and temporally, then the postsynaptic cell will in turn generate its own action potentials. Conversely, a postsynaptic cell can be inhibited if inhibitory postsynaptic potentials (IPSPs) preponderate. This standard picture of synaptic transmission has been built up over several decades of intensive research, but recently, departures from this view have been described. Work on NOVEL NEURAL MODULATORS has revealed that certain gases, nitric oxide (NO), carbon monoxide (CO) and hydrogen sulphide (H_2S), may act as signalling molecules in the CNS. They are not stored in vesicles, and once synthesised, they diffuse to their target sites of action. These findings indicate that chemical transmission presents a richer and more varied picture than once thought.

In the late 1950s, the neuropharmacologist Bernard Brodie suggested that 5-hydroxytryptamine (5-HT or serotonin) functions as a NEUROTRANSMITTER. In the 1960s, dopamine (DA) was admitted into the neurotransmitter club. MONOAMINE TRANSMITTERS comprise NE, DA and 5-HT, and can be further subdivided into catecholamines (NE, DA) and the indoleamine (5-HT). Throughout the 1960s and 1970s, the pathways in the CNS utilising these chemical messengers were described in great detail, and the basic principles of organisation were established (Iversen, Iversen and Snyder 1978). Running in parallel with these important discoveries, drugs were discovered or developed which interacted in a wide variety of ways with each of these chemical transmission systems. A major impetus to research was to develop therapeutic drug treatments for use in PSYCHIATRY (see s. 7).

Later it was realised that single AMINO ACIDS could act as chemical transmitters, and, indeed, they function as the major excitatory and inhibitory neurotransmitters. Glutamate (Glu) is the principal excitatory neurotransmitter in the CNS, whereas γ-amino-butyric acid (GABA), and to a lesser extent glycine (Gly), function as the main inhibitory neurotransmitters. Seen from this perspective, the monoamines act to modulate excitatory and inhibitory neurotransmission. Beginning in the 1970s, and continuing to the present day, a more complex class of chemical messengers has become increasingly prominent. NEUROPEPTIDES are peptides synthesised with neurones and consist of 3–100 amino acid residues, linked by peptide bonds. Typically, they derive from larger precursor molecules which are divided enzymatically to give cleavage products. A single precursor molecule, such as pro-opiomelanocortin (POMC), can be cleaved into a multiplicity of products: adrenocorticotrophic hormone (ACTH), β-lipotropin (β-LPH), β-endorphin (β-END), melanocyte-stimulating hormone (α-MSH) and corticotrophin-like intermediate peptide (CLIP). These smaller fragments are frequently biologically active and can feature as neurotransmitters or modulators (Strand 1999).

One group of neuropeptides to attract considerable attention has been the opioid peptides (Snyder and Pasternak 2003). In the early 1970s, investigators detected the presence of receptors for opiate drugs like morphine or methadone in the CNS. This was followed by the discovery of enkephalins (meaning 'in the head'), two pentapeptides which bind stereospecifically and with high affinity to the opiate receptors. Further intensive work led to the discovery of β-endorphin and the dynorphins, further varieties of endogenous opioid peptides with distinctive distributions within the brain. Additionally, multiple opioid receptors were discovered, each with a distinctive pharmacology: mu (MOP), delta (DOP) and kappa (KOP) opioid peptide receptors. Major driving forces in research in this area have been the development of novel analgesic compounds and the desire to understand and effectively treat addiction to opioid drugs like heroin.

The neuropeptide family of chemical messengers is exceedingly large: 50 or more have been described and the number is likely to increase. As a general rule, neuropeptides also feature elsewhere, outside the central and peripheral nervous systems, and are involved in a wide variety of functions. Why so many are used in the CNS is not known, and how they interact with chemical transmission mediated by the amino acids and monoamines is far from being understood. Nevertheless, one general principle to emerge is that neuropeptides co-localise with other transmitters in the same neurones.

PSYCHOPHARMACOLOGY investigates the effects of drugs on the mind and behaviour, and is closely geared to the development of therapeutic drugs in relation to psychiatric conditions, neurological conditions, addictions and 'lifestyle' phenomena like the current obesity epidemic. There are a number of ways to classify drugs in psychopharmacology, but conventionally they can be distinguished as follows (Julien 2001; McKim 2003). Psychomotor stimulants include the amphetamines, methylphenidate, cocaine and cathinone. Amphetamines and related drugs are synthetics, but cocaine is extracted from the leaves of the coca tree, and cathinone is found in the leaves of a shrub (Catha edulis). These drugs interact strongly with monoamine transmitters. They induce mood changes (euphoria) and are addictive. In large doses, they can induce stereotyped behaviour and even forms of PSYCHOSIS (see s. 7). ANTIPSYCHOTIC DRUGS (see s. 7) are employed to treat symptoms of SCHIZOPHRENIA (see s. 7), and typically act to block dopamine (DA) neurotransmission in the brain. So-called 'atypical' antipsychotics (clozapine, quetiapine, olanzepine) cause fewer extrapyramidal side effects. Antidepressants are used to treat major mood disturbances, and typically interact with monoamine neurotransmission. Monoamine oxidase inhibitors (MAOIs) and TRICYCLIC ANTIDEPRESSANTS (see s. 7) (TCAs) elevate brain concentrations of monoamine. Second-generation antidepressants include the SELECTIVE SEROTONIN REUPTAKE INHIBITORS (SSRIs) (see s. 7), which selectively elevate 5-HT levels in the brain. These drugs include fluoxetine (Prozac) and paroxetine (Paxil). Tranquillisers or sedative-hypnotics include the synthetic drugs, barbiturates and benzodiazepines. These drugs reduce ANXIETY (see s. 6) and the effects of STRESS (see s. 7). They act centrally by enhancing the GABA neurotransmission. Alcohol has effects related to the sedative-hypnotics. It is not easy to identify the mechanism of action of alcohol, but it affects glutamate neurotransmission as well as GABA transmission. It produces euphoria and is highly addictive. Nicotine is a natural constituent of tobacco and stimulates nicotinic ACh receptors. It produces pleasurable effects and is addictive. Caffeine belongs to a family of drugs called methylxanthines, and is found in tea, coffee and chocolate. It has mild stimulant effects. Opiates, such as morphine, derive from the opium poppy (Papaver somniferum). Heroin is a semi-synthetic derivative of morphine. Synthetic opiates include meperidine, methadone, pethidine and fentanyl. They are powerfully analgesic, but also highly addictive. Cannabis is derived from the hemp plant (Cannabis sativa); the active ingredient is delta-9-tetrahydrocannabinol (Δ^9-THC). Two types of cannabinoid receptor have been discovered in the brain (CB_1 and CB_2), and endogenous ligands identified (e.g. ananamide) (Elphick and Egertová 2001). Hallucinogens include lysergic acid diethylamide (LSD), psilocybin, mescaline, phencyclidine and many others. Subjective effects are a defining feature and can include perceptual and mood changes. *SC*

Cooper, J. R., Bloom, F. E. and Roth, R. H. 2003: *The Biochemical Basis of Neuropharmacology* (8th edn). Oxford: Oxford University Press. **Elphick, M. R. and Egertová, M.** 2001: The neurobiology and evolution of cannabinoid signalling. *Philosophical Transactions of the Royal Society of London Series B–Biological Sciences* 356, 381–408. **Finger, S.** 2000: *Minds Behind the Brain: A History of the Pioneers and their Discoveries.* Oxford: Oxford University Press. **Hökfelt, T., Bartfai, T. and Bloom, F.** 2003: Neuropeptides: opportunities for drug discovery. *Lancet* 2, 463–72. **Iversen, L. L., Iversen, S. D. and Snyder, S. H.** 1978: *Chemical Pathways in the Brain. Volume 9. Handbook of Psychopharmacology.* New York: Plenum Press. **Julien, R. M.** 2001: *A Primer of Drug Action* (9th edn). New York: Worth. **McKim, W. A.** 2003: *Drugs and Behavior: An Introduction to Behavioral Pharmacology* (5th edn). New Jersey: Prentice Hall. **Snyder, S. H. and Pasternak, G. W.** 2003: Historical review: opioid receptors. *Trends in Pharmacological Sciences* 24, 198–205. **Strand, F. L.** 1999: *Neuropeptides: Regulators of Physiological Processes.* Cambridge MA: MIT Press.

T

testosterone Stimulates the development of male sexual characteristics at the foetal and pubertal stages. Also regulates spermatogenesis and is implicated in male sexual behaviour and AGGRESSION (see s. 5). *JCGH*

theories of associative learning: configural processes Non-configural problems such as the feature-negative DISCRIMINATION (see s. 3 and s. 5) (having the form A–; AX+) require only that training results in X having an associative strength of + 1.00 and A having an associative strength of .00 (thus the 'values' of A = .00 and AX = 1.00 correctly reflect the anticipated outcome, or its absence) [see THEORIES OF ASSOCIATIVE LEARNING: RESCORLA AND WAGNER (1972)]. Configural problems are not amenable to such an analysis; for example, no combination of numerical values can reflect the anticipated outcome of an ambiguous-signal discrimination (having the form A+; B–; AX–; BX+). A variety of solutions have been suggested to remedy this problem that currently receive experimental attention.

One account suggests that a 'unique cue' is created during presentation of compound stimuli. This would render ambiguous-signal discrimination an A+; B–; AXp–; BXq+ problem. The subsequent application of standard associative theorising [see THEORIES OF ASSOCIATIVE LEARNING: RESCORLA AND WAGNER (1972)] supplies a ready explanation of the discrimination: Solution occurs when the elements have the following values: A = 1.00; B = .00; X = .00; p = –.00; q = 1.00. The notion of a unique cue may strike the reader as somewhat abstract, but just a moment's consideration tells us that it is not. For example, a cappella and instrumental versions of even a very familiar song are often hard to place when we have become accustomed only to their fully combined form.

Wagner (2003) has recently suggested that compound presentation of cues will *remove* as well as *add* stimuli. For example, according to Wagner's 'replaced elements THEORY' (see s. 8) the ambiguous-signal discrimination may be coded as: Aa+; Bb–; AXp+; BXq–; that is ordinarily presentation of A results in production of pattern Aa. The presence of X 'turns on' element p, but turns off element a. Examination of Wagner's suggestion is beyond the scope of this brief entry, but the interested reader is advised to read the references below for a full appreciation of their benefits and the problems it is intended to overcome. *JW-R*

Pearce, J. M. 2002: Evaluation and development of a connectionist theory of configural learning. *Animal Learning and Behavior* 30, 73–95. **Wagner, A. R.** 2003: Context-sensitive elemental theory. *Quarterly Journal of Experimental Psychology* 56B, 7–29.

theories of associative learning: Rescorla and Wagner (1972) This THEORY (see s. 8) describes the changes in the strength of an association between representations of a signal (X) and outcome (+). The strength of an association is assumed to increase with diminishing increments until a maximal (asymptotic) value is reached. This LEARNING (see s. 3) is assumed to correspond directly to performance and, therefore, appropriately characterises a typical 'learning curve'. The expression below describes this growth:

$$\Delta V_X = \alpha.\beta\ (\lambda - \Sigma V_X)$$

ΔV_X = the change in associative strength of signal X on the trial in question; λ = the ultimate value of the association between X and the outcome (say, 1.00); ΣV_X = the running total value of associative strength for X on the trial in question; α and β = learning-rate parameters for, respectively, the signal and the outcome (say, .35 and .45). Note that the values of α, β and λ are arbitrary and cannot, therefore, be used to derive quantitative predictions about the outcome of particular ASSOCIATIVE LEARNING EXPERIMENTS (see s. 8, EXPERIMENT); but, as we shall see, they can be adjusted to capture qualitative features of learning.

The value of ΣV_X will be .00 before training and if we imagine that signal X is, for the first time, being paired with the outcome: $\Delta V_{X1} = \alpha.\beta\ (\lambda - \Sigma V_X) = .35 \times .45 \times (1.00 - .00) = .1576$. On Trial 2 the values are the same except for the value of ΣV_X which is now .1576; that is: $\Delta V_{X2} = .35 \times .45 \times (1.00 - .1576) = .1327$. On Trial 3 $\Delta V_{X3} = .35 \times .45 \times (1.00 - [.1576 + .1327]) = .1118$. The changes in associative strength for X diminish with each trial. Were you to compute values for more trials and draw a graph (Trial number on the abscissa; ΣV_X on the ordinate) a 'negatively accelerating' learning curve would be seen.

In a BLOCKING (see s. 3) [see REDUNDANCY EFFECTS: OVERSHADOWING AND BLOCKING] experiment (A+, then AX+), the model is modified to include A's associative strength on the compound trials: $\Delta V_X = \alpha.\beta\ (\lambda - [\Sigma V_X + \Sigma V_A])$. A's prior establishment as a signal for the outcome ensures that $\Sigma V_A = \lambda = 1$; the discrepancy between $(\lambda - [\Sigma V_X + \Sigma V_A])$ is zero, therefore LEARNING (see s. 3) about X cannot proceed. Rescorla and Wagner's success in accommodating phenomena such as blocking has led to its experimental scrutiny over the last four decades. *JW-R*

Pearce, J. M. and Bouton, M. E. 2001: Theories of associative learning in animals. *Annual Review of Psychology* 52, 111–39.

Tinbergen's four whys Asking the simple question 'why does the animal behave in that way?' might not result in an equally simple answer. Niko Tinbergen, one of the two founding fathers of ETHOLOGY (see s. 1), pointed out that there are at least four levels of explanation embedded in the question. The first is the proximate (or mechanistic) cause of behaviour, and simply addresses the question why an organism behaves in a particular way at a particular time. Proximate explanations of behaviour need not be evolutionary, since they are concerned only with finding out what motivated a particular behaviour there and then. Developmental (or ontogenetic) explanations of behaviour provide information on how the individual came to perform a given behaviour, and might make reference to LEARNING (see s. 3) over their lifespan, or the influence of any innate tendencies. The third cause of behaviour addresses the evolutionary history of a particular behaviour, and is known as the phylogenetic (or historical) cause of behaviour. This level of explanation attempts to understand why the behaviour evolved in the first place, and the answer might include a search for the presence or absence of the behaviour in related species. Finally, behaviour can be explained at an ultimate (or functional) level that addresses the issue of how and why a particular behaviour increases the survival and reproductive prospects of the organism. Thus ultimate explanations are evolutionary explanations.

The answer depends on the question. For example, there can be, and probably are, both proximate and ultimate explanations for most behaviours, and the trick is not to say which is the more correct, since they both might be. The real trick lies in not confusing levels of explanation and, for example, providing a proximate explanation when the question demands one at the ultimate level. *JL*

Eibl-Eibesfeldt, I. 1970: *Ethology: The Biology of Behavior.* New York: Holt, Rinehart & Winston. **Hinde, R. A.** 1982: *Ethology.* Oxford: Oxford University Press. **Manning, A. and Dawkins, M. S.** 1998: *An Introduction to Animal Behaviour.* Cambridge: Cambridge University Press. **Shettleworth, S. J.** 1998: *Cognition, Evolution and Behaviour.* New York: Oxford University Press.

V

ventral Anatomical term relating to structures towards the bottom of the brain or the front of the body.   *JAH*

ventricular system: meninges Three protective membranes, collectively called the meninges, cover the brain and spinal cord. The dura mater (tough mother) forms the tough, outer, inelastic bag. Immediately inside the dura is the fine arachnoid (spider-web) membrane. There is normally no space between these two layers. However, the arachnoid membrane is separated from the final membrane, the pia mater (gentle mother), by the subarachnoid space. This contains blood vessel and CERE-BROSPINAL FLUID. As the pia mater adheres to the surface of the central nervous system, the brain essentially floats inside this layer of fluid. The cerebrospinal fluid also fills the small central canal that runs the length of the spinal cord and the ventricular system of the brain. There are four cerebral ventricles (large chambers) in the brain. Each hemisphere contains a lateral ventricle. Cerebrospinal fluid is formed here by the choroid plexus – a network of small blood vessels that protrude from the pia mater (Spector and Johanson 1989). From here the fluid flows into the third and fourth ventricles at the core of the brainstem. Excess fluid is absorbed from the sub-arachnoid space by blood vessels. If this normal flow of cerebrospinal fluid is disrupted, pressure, occurring as a result of the build-up of fluid in the ventricles, can lead to brain damage.   *JAH*

Spector, R. and Johanson, C. E. 1989: The mammalian choroid plexus. *Scientific American* 261, 68–74.

vertebrae Component bones of the spinal column (singular: vertebra).   *JAH*

W

Wolffian duct Another embryonic dual duct structure, which, like the MÜLLERIAN DUCT, is found in both
males and females. The Wolffian duct will develop into
male internal organs if stimulated by the masculinising
hormone TESTOSTERONE (secreted by the embryonic
testes).   *JCGH*

Section 3

Cognitive Psychology

Introduction

'Cognition' comes from the Latin 'to know' or 'to get knowledge of'. This definition gives a good flavour of what a cognitive psychologist is interested in. *Webster's Dictionary* defines the term as 'the psychological result of perception and learning and reasoning', which again gives a good impression of the topic of study. However, cognitive psychologists themselves like to think of it more as an approach to the study of human behaviour and less as a set of topics of investigation. For the cognitive psychologist, the central notion is the study of human thought processes as information processing.

Other psychologists may use the term slightly differently, and not always in a way a cognitive psychologist would approve of. For instance, clinicians will often refer to 'cognitions', where the word 'thoughts' would probably do. Such use of the term borrows from the discipline of cognitive psychology, and 'cognitions' encapsulates mental representations and beliefs, both of which are important ideas for psychological therapies. Similarly, applied psychologists interested in the effect of nutrition on behaviour, for example, study the effect of glucose on 'cognition', where the term 'performance' would be better. This is because the study of cognition is about identifying information processes and systems in the mind, and not just the measurement of people's capabilities. Of course, cognitive theory is helpful to applied psychologists, otherwise it would not be such an important field of study; but the application is in the approach, using experimental methods and trying to identify how the mind operates. These conceptual ideas are discussed in the entries on COGNITIVE SCIENCE and MARR'S COMPUTATIONAL THEORY. As to how the approach evolved, see LEARNING APPROACH.

References

Introductory texts:

Eysenck, M. W. and Keane, M. T. 2001: *Cognitive Psychology*. Hove: Psychology Press. **Gazzaniga, M. S., Ivry, R. B. and Mangun, G. R.** 2002: *Cognitive Neuroscience*. New York: W.W. Norton & Company. **Solso, R. L.** 2000: *Cognitive Psychology*. Needham Heights MA: Pearson Education.

Advanced texts:

Baddeley, A. 1999: *Essentials of Human Memory*. Hove: Psychology Press. **Bruce, V., Green, P. R. and Georgeson, M. A.** 1996: *Visual Perception: Physiology, Psychology and Ecology* (3rd edn). Hove: Psychology Press. **Jay, T. B.** 2003: *The Psychology of Language*. Needham Heights MA: Pearson Education. **Manktelow, K.** 2000: *Reasoning and Thinking*. Hove: Psychology Press.

The term 'cognitive psychology' refers both to an area of study and to a specific theoretical approach within that area. Generally speaking, cognitive functions are those that underpin our ability to perceive and understand the world around us, to function intelligently in it, to communicate with one another and to carry out adaptive and appropriate actions. Cognitive psychology thus embraces the fields of perception, attention, learning and memory, language, thinking and problem solving. The 'cognitive approach' to these areas of research is one that seeks to understand these abilities in terms of mental processes interacting with the external environment via the senses on the one hand, and acting back into the outside world via decisions and motor responses on the other. The cognitive approach thus stands in contrast to behaviourism, whose adherents studied learning in terms of interactions between observable stimuli and responses, and also in contrast to the Gestalt psychologists, who studied perception in terms of generalised patterns and mental organisation.

Within cognitive psychology, research proceeds in a number of related ways. The most basic of these methods (but also the core of the discipline) is experimental psychology coupled with descriptive models of hypothesised mental structures and processes. Thus researchers have postulated a connected set of mechanisms and processes termed 'working memory' that underlie our ability to manipulate information held in conscious awareness, and have carried out a programme of experiments to confirm, disconfirm and extend the model. Other researchers construct computational and mathematically expressed models, often translated into computer simulations, whose validity is assessed by the similarity of the output to the behaviour of humans in similar circumstances. This computer-based approach is often referred to as COGNITIVE SCIENCE. *Other crucial clues to understanding cognitive processes come from clinical observations of patients with brain damage; this specialty is known as neuropsychology. Disorders of memory and of language, for example, have revealed a great deal about how these abilities normally function. The relations between brain and cognitive behaviours are still not well understood, although the study of cognitive deficits following specific areas of brain damage has provided some important clues. But the development of such neuro-imaging techniques as functional magnetic resonance imaging (fMRI), magnetic encephalography (MEG) and evoked response potentials (ERP) now enables researchers to study brain processes while the participant is carrying out various cognitive tasks. This new field of cognitive neuroscience is providing exciting insights into both brain mechanisms and the nature of cognitive processes themselves.*

Modern cognitive psychology had its origins in the notion that the brain may be regarded as an information-processing device. In a classic paper written in 1956, George Miller demonstrated that participants' ability to process choices and hold information in mind was surprisingly limited – unless the raw information was 'chunked' into larger meaningful units, such as words, phrases or well-known numerical sequences. The idea that people are information processors was developed by the British psychologist Donald Broadbent in his 1958 book Perception and Communication, *and extended into a comprehensive description of mental functioning in 1967 by Ulric Neisser in his* Cognitive Psychology.

Among the ideas that are central to the cognitive approach, possibly the most significant (and least well understood!) is the concept of conscious awareness. Intense efforts are under way at present to develop models that delineate the functions of consciousness and link these functions to areas of the brain. We can say, for example, that conscious decisions come into play to override automatic habits, and that the frontal lobes of the brain appear to be heavily involved in such conscious processing. Another central idea is the concept of mental representation, whereby aspects of the outside world come to be represented – as maps, images, words and abstract thoughts – inside the head. An animal that has such representations is no longer a passive reactor to the environment, but can plan ahead and become usefully detached from the here and now. A third important strand of cognitive psychology is the idea that various aspects of cognition (e.g. perception, ATTENTION, *memory and thinking) are highly interrelated. As just one example, when we encounter an unexpected scene, we perceive its various features, pay attention to those that seem most central, bring our past experience to bear on understanding its significance and in so doing create a new episodic memory of the event.*

There are many more interesting puzzles still to be solved. How do emotion and motivation interact with cognitive processes, for example? How does cognition develop in children and decline in the course of ageing? How do cognitive processes map onto brain structures and mechanisms? How can the findings of cognitive psychology be usefully applied in education, industry and in clinical settings? Answers to many of these important questions are to be found in this comprehensive and fascinating dictionary.

Professor Fergus Craik

My strategy with the cognitive section is to reflect the contemporary hot topics in cognition, while providing the student with a grounding in classic studies of cognitive psychology. For example, contemporary issues such as inhibitory mechanisms in memory are covered [see RETRIEVAL INHIBITION], but the section also gives coverage to well-established topics for the student and researcher: such as what visual illusions contribute to the study of perception [see VISUAL ILLUSION]. In addition, the contributors are aware of the rich heritage of cognitive psychology, and what it inherited from the experimental approach first espoused by the behaviourists [see LEARNING APPROACH]. In fact, for completeness many concepts are defined here that predate the cognitive approach (e.g. CLASSICAL CONDITIONING), but to miss these out would be like trying to explain the appeal of sliced bread without describing bread that does not come pre-sliced. Most of the larger entries have a historical slant, and demonstrate why cognitive theories and approaches were necessary to better understand human behaviour. One of the emergent and more contentious themes in cognitive psychology is its relation to consciousness. The contributors have not shied away from this complex topic (see entries under CONSCIOUSNESS, RECOLLECTIVE EXPERIENCE and BLINDSIGHT for examples of why consciousness is important to cognitive psychologists).

The recent advances in cognitive psychology are mostly to do with application. As such, this dictionary demonstrates how cognitive principles are applied to clinical populations (e.g. COGNITIVE BEHAVIOURAL THERAPY), the understanding of the function of the brain (e.g. MRI SCANNING) and computational models of human behaviour (e.g. CONNECTIONISM). Additionally, cognitive psychology is a lively field with many of the central concepts, such as WORKING MEMORY, still being hotly debated and continually refined. The contributors have been aware of this and included up-to-date references and modern critiques of the theories (e.g. the addition of the episodic buffer to the working memory model). These strategies have been reflected in the contributors to this section: they represent the second generation of cognitive researchers, applying the existing cognitive theories to understanding bilingualism, neurological impairment, the effects of alcohol and complex conceptual issues like the subjective experience of memory and the role of imagery in drawing.

Finally, by way of prioritisation, the entries were selected on the basis of student needs. The core areas of cognitive psychology were chosen: memory, perception, thinking and reasoning and language. The contributors have experience of teaching these topics, and based their examples on the demands of modern curricula. Additionally, some critical topics were included that tend to be underrepresented in standard texts, such as connectionism, cognitive science and cognitive psychology's roots in the learning approach. The overall aim was to give complete factual coverage, but with some more important topics covered in more critical detail. It is hoped that this gives a lively presentation of this important area of psychology and its links to other areas.

Dr Chris Moulin

A

abstract thought   Thought concerning symbolic or conceptual attributes. Abstract thought is generalisable across concepts or objects, such as redness. Consider a continuum, from relatively abstract (e.g. happiness) to more concrete concepts (e.g. tables).   *CM*

accessibility   Whether information can be retrieved from MEMORY (see s. 1). It contrasts with AVAILABILITY. When you cannot remember something one day, but can the next, it suggests it was always available, but not necessarily accessible.   *CM*

accommodation   In vision, this is the process where the lens of the eye adjusts to compensate for the distance of an object from the retina. (See also s. 4 and s. 6, ACCOMMODATION)   *CM*

action slips   Performance of an unintended action, usually occurring in a sequence of highly practised motor programmes that require little attentional monitoring. *AS*

agnosia   Derived from Greek, meaning 'absence of knowledge', the term refers to a broad class of recognition disorders, where individuals are typically able to sense the presence of a stimulus (e.g. an object) but are unable to link it to relevant semantic information (e.g. function). Usually acquired as a result of neurological pathology (e.g. cerebrovascular accident), recognition disorders can occur in most perceptual and cognitive systems, thus affecting a wide variety of functional skills, such as face perception (prosopagnosia) [see FACE RECOGNITION] and musical discrimination (amusia). Conceptual accounts of agnosia have mainly evolved through the study of visual disorders, with Lissauer (in the nineteenth century) being the first to distinguish between disturbed processing of stimulus form (apperceptive agnosia) and inability to attach meaning to accurately perceived forms (associative agnosia). Functional accounts of the agnosias have since fractionated them further, in line with developments in cognitive and neuropsychological theories.   *AS*

algorithm   A method of PROBLEM SOLVING that will definitely lead to the solution. It is an exhaustive but guaranteed method: a systematic search. Contrast with HEURISTIC, where no solution is guaranteed.   *CM*

Alzheimer's disease   Alzheimer's disease is a form of dementia, first described by Lois Alzheimer in 1904. It can be thought of as the common cold of memory impairment. It is caused by pronounced and progressive cell death in the brain of people typically over the age of 60. These dead cells agglomerate as plaques and tangles in the brain, particularly the temporal cortex. Alzheimer's disease results in poor LONG-TERM MEMORY and EXECUTIVE FUNCTION (see s. 4) [see DYSEXECUTIVE SYNDROME]. People with Alzheimer's disease will forget the names of their grandchildren, for example. For the cognitive psychologist, it is a way of exploring MEMORY (see s. 1) systems. For instance, people with Alzheimer's disease are thought to have intact IMPLICIT MEMORY but poor EXPLICIT MEMORY, and relatively preserved RECENCY but poor PRIMACY.   *CM*

Greene, J. D. W., Baddeley, A. D. and Hodges, J. R. 1996: Analysis of the episodic deficit in early Alzheimer's disease: Evidence from the doors and people test. *Neuropsychologia* 34, 527–51.

amnesia   Much of what we understand about how human MEMORY (see s. 1) works has come from the study of amnesia: memory loss. Memory loss can have many causes, but amnesia is most usually used to refer to memory loss due to brain damage. One of the most famous case studies in psychology, PATIENT HM, had ANTEROGRADE AMNESIA. He had a part of his brain cut to treat epilepsy, which resulted in damage to the hippocampus and surrounding temporal cortex of the brain. HM was left with memory loss that severely impaired his ability to live independently. He was unable to learn new information and could not recognise any of the people he met after surgery. Importantly, HM was able to remember information over very brief periods, indicating that he had intact SHORT-TERM MEMORY. Also, HM was able to complete learning tasks based on IMPLICIT MEMORY, such as mirror drawing. HM would get better and better at tests of mirror drawing, a skill that he acquired proficiently despite not being able to remember anything about being tested on the task before. These patterns of memory impairment and memory preservation tell us that these processes rely on different systems and different parts of the brain. A different type of amnesia is when people cannot remember any information from before their injury, RETROGRADE AMNESIA.

One often overlooked problem is that memory impairment can result in marked emotional difficulties and severe disruption of everyday life. Consider the amnesic Clive Waring, who had such bad memory impairment that when his wife left the room to make a cup of tea, he greeted her on her return with the level of emotion appropriate to having not seen her for years. Clive Waring's memory impairment is such that he constantly notes in his diary that he has just regained consciousness for the first time, crossing out the same entry from just minutes before. Unsurprisingly, observations like this and the fact that amnesics show intact implicit memory but not EXPLICIT MEMORY has led to the idea that amnesia is a disorder of CONSCIOUSNESS. Finally, amnesia can also be caused by psychosis, where people do not have brain damage but a form of memory loss due to psychological distress. This is known as psychogenic amnesia, or a psychogenic fugue. For instance, people often have amnesia for events of intense trauma, such as abuse, stress or committing a crime. Sometimes, this results in a fugue state, where people turn up miles from home not knowing who they are or how they arrived where they are.   *CM*

For a full account of patient HM see **Hilts, P. J.** 1995: *Memory's Ghost: The Strange Tale of Mr M. and the Nature of Memory.* New York: Simon and Schuster. For other accounts of memory disorder and amnesia (including Clive Waring) see **Campbell, R. and Conway, M. A.** 1995: *Broken Memories: Case Studies in Memory Impairment.* Oxford: Blackwell.

anterograde amnesia   MEMORY (see s. 1) loss for information acquired after the onset of amnesia.   *CM*

aphasia   Aphasia is a speech disorder caused by brain damage, resulting in difficulties in producing or comprehending speech. Aphasic speech disturbances are not attributable to deafness or to a simple motor deficit and must be relatively isolated. Two major classes of the disorder are Broca's and Wernicke's aphasias, so called to reflect the primary regions of brain damage. Broca's aphasia (Broca 1861) refers to a disruption of the ability to speak and consists of difficulties with word ordering (agrammatism), word finding (anomia) and articulation. It is characterised by slow, laborious and non-fluent speech, primarily reflecting mispronunciation (rather than misselection) of appropriate words. In contrast, Wernicke's aphasia (Wernicke 1874) refers to a disruption in the comprehension of speech, and consists of difficulties in recognising spoken words, comprehending the meaning of words and converting thoughts into words. Wernicke's aphasia is characterised by fluent and unlaboured speech, which is meaningless, although grammatically correct.   *AT*

Broca, P. 1861: Remarques sur le siège de la faculté de la parole articulée, suives d'une observation d'aphemie (perte de parole). *Bulletin de la Société d'Anatomie* 36, 330–57. **Wernicke, C.** 1874: *Der aphasische Symptomenkomplex.* Breslau: Cohn and Weigart (reprinted in translation in *Boston Studies in Philosophy of Science* 4, 34–97).

articulatory loop   The articulatory loop is a subsidiary slave-system of the WORKING MEMORY model (Baddeley and Hitch 1974), proposed to be responsible for the storage and manipulation of speech-based information in working memory. It comprises two subcomponents, the phonological store, which holds verbal material in a phonological (sound-based) code and a subvocal rehearsal process, responsible for refreshing decaying representations in the store and for converting visual input such as printed text into a phonological code for storage. Verbal material is thought to have direct and obligatory access to the phonological store. The rehearsal process is proposed to operate in real time and does not appear to require overt articulation. This component of working memory is thought to be critically involved in LANGUAGE (see s. 2) learning and, in particular, in the acquisition of vocabulary (Baddeley, Gathercole and Papagno 1998). The articulatory loop has more recently been renamed the phonological loop.   *AT*

Baddeley, A. D., Gathercole, S. E. and Papagno, C. 1998: The phonological loop as a language learning device. *Psychological Review* 105, 158–73. **Baddeley, A. D. and Hitch, G.** 1974: Working memory. In Bower, G. A. (ed.), *Recent Advances in Learning and Motivation* 8, 47–90. New York: Academic Press.

artificial intelligence (AI)   The study of artificial systems (usually computers) that have human-like qualities or INTELLIGENCE (see s. 4 and s. 6). The study of artificial intelligence has importance for cognitive psychology, since it allows researchers to test their theories by building a 'model' on a computer. The key point about artificial intelligence is that the model should be based on the system's own intelligence rather than that of a programmer. For example, based on what we know, it is possible to produce a computer simulation or model of WORKING MEMORY, where a pattern of data similar to that of humans is created on a computer. This would not be artificial intelligence, since the programmer would have put a set of rules into the model based on theory. Artificial intelligence should be able to think for itself. Many CONNECTIONIST NETWORKS can be thought of as artificial intelligence, since they order information for themselves, and are not explicitly told to process information in any particular way.

Alan Turing is often credited as the originator of artificial intelligence. He suggested in 1950 that computers would one day be able to think, and he originated what is known as the Turing test as a measure of artificial intelligence. This is an 'imitation game', where a human and a computer are interrogated under conditions where the interrogator does not know which is which. Turing argued that if it was not possible to distinguish the computer from the human, then you could call the computer intelligent. The question of how one might test for intelligence in non-human systems remains hotly contested.   *CM*

Turing, A. M. 1950: 1. Computing machinery and intelligence. *Mind: A Quarterly Review of Psychology and Philosophy* LIX (236), 433–60.

attention   A process that enables the selection of one stimulus from many. The term has been used to describe selectivity at all functional levels, from perceptual organisation to conscious ideation and the maintenance of an alert state. However, most research has been directed at the lower-level workings of attention, and in particular how we select elements from an information-rich environment for preferential processing. One real-world problem (the COCKTAIL PARTY PHENOMENON) was posed by Cherry in the 1950s: how do we follow one conversation when there are many others going on in the same room? By concurrently presenting different spoken messages to each ear, Cherry discovered that listeners make use of physical differences (e.g. location, the sex of the speaker) to select a single stream. When such differences were removed (i.e. the same voice in both ears), participants found it difficult to attend to the meaning of a single message. Cherry also carried out verbal shadowing experiments, where listeners had to repeat aloud one of the messages while it was playing. In these circumstances it seemed that very little information about the unattended message was processed: for example, listeners seldom noticed if it was spoken in a foreign LANGUAGE (see s. 2). This suggested that unattended stimuli received virtually no processing. A number of models were developed to account for such findings (e.g. Broadbent 1958) and they tended to favour an early-selection view: unattended information is discarded after physical features have been coded, and before stimulus identification. However, other researchers argued that non-selective information could be processed to a high level and demonstrated semantic interference from messages in the unattended channel. A familiar example of this phenomenon is the alarming ease with which we notice our name being mentioned in someone else's conversation. These data argued for a late-selection account of attention, whereby unattended information undergoes semantic analysis and is selected subsequent to identification.

In more recent years the majority of research has focused upon visual processes, with the VISUAL SEARCH paradigm being widely used to study how we orient attention to different items in the visual array. An influential account of visual selection has been the feature integration theory (Treisman and Gelade 1980), which explains findings observed in visual search and also offers an interpretation of the BINDING PROBLEM. An early pre-attentive stage is postulated to run in parallel across the entire visual field, extracting single primitive features from the array. The second attentive stage functions by integrating information from one part of the visual field at a time (i.e. serially). Duncan and Humphreys (1989) proposed an alternative explanation, with both attentional modes being part of the same mechanism. In their account, search time is dependent upon grouping between items in the visual field, and matching an item (or a GROUP – see s. 5 – of items) to a template held in MEMORY (see s. 1). Another debate has focused on whether visual attention operates upon spatial locations or objects. The space-based view holds that attention is directed to regions of space, and stimuli that fall within these regions are processed more efficiently than those in a non-selective region. In comparison, the object-based account holds that attention is not directed towards spatial locations, but the objects that occupy them.

As well as providing a means to single out a particular aspect of sensorial input for processing, attention can be divided between multiple tasks. The nature and success of this division is usually due to a number of FACTORS (see s. 8). One such influence is the degree of similarity between the tasks, with the standard of performance being less for tasks that are more similar. Another factor is the amount of practice one has had: for example, holding a conversation while driving can be difficult for learners, but becomes easier as the individual becomes a more proficient driver. Prolonged practice of a task can lead to 'automaticity' [see AUTOMATIC], meaning that its performance does not require focused attention, thus allowing the individual full attentional capacity in the performance of an additional task. Fractionating this distinction further, Norman and Shallice (1986) identified three levels of processing: fully automatic processing controlled by schemas, partially automatic processing involving unconscious resolution of schema conflict, and deliberate control by a SUPERVISORY ATTENTION SYSTEM.

The functional nature of attention is apparent on occasions when it goes awry. When one is not attending to an automatic task (e.g. chopping vegetables) there is the likelihood that ACTION SLIPS may occur at a decision point. Thus one might 'absent-mindedly' throw away the chopped vegetables and keep the peelings (Reason 1992). A more striking example is offered by studies of inattentional blindness, which have shown that observers engaged in attentionally demanding tasks can often fail to notice unexpected objects or events. Simons and Chabris (1999) asked observers to watch a video of two teams of basketball players passing a ball among themselves and count the number of passes made by either one of the teams. At one point in the video a person in a gorilla costume unexpectedly walked through the middle of proceedings, remaining clearly visible for five seconds, and then exited the display after beating its chest. The observers were later asked whether they had seen anything odd, and it transpired that 56 per cent of them had failed to notice the gorilla, even though it was obvious to anyone not engaged in the counting task. Selection can also be pathologically disrupted, such as in the acquired disorder of unilateral visual neglect, which has been characterised as a deficit of spatial attention. Patients have usually sustained damage to the right parietal lobe, and typically exhibit decreased awareness of objects and events in their left visual field (e.g. copying only one half of a picture, or failing to eat food from one side of the plate). Such behaviour is not due to any form of blindness, and patients can also neglect the left side of internally generated images [see IMAGERY]. Evidence suggests that the symptoms may be due to impaired orientation of attention to the contralesional hemispace, or in a difficulty disengaging attention from objects on the ipsilesional side. In support of this, neglect behaviours can be reduced when patients are cued to attend to the contralesional side of space (Robertson and Marshall 1993).

Attention is a particularly convoluted aspect of cognitive functioning; a fact that is belied by the multiplicity of systems that appear to be in operation, and the freedom with which the term is applied to a wide variety of processes. Not only are issues of selection and control important for gating of sensorial information and preparing for action, they are also central to most theories of CONSCIOUSNESS. Therefore, as we progress in our understanding of the mechanisms of attention, we may perhaps be advancing in our understanding of what it means to be conscious. *AS*

Broadbent, D. E. 1958: *Perception and Communication.* Oxford: Pergamon. **Duncan, J. and Humphreys, G. W.** 1989: A resemblance theory of visual search. *Psychological Review* 96, 433–58. **Norman, D. A. and Shallice, T.** 1986: Attention to action: willed and automatic control of behaviour. In Davidon, R. J. Schwartz, G. E. and Shapiro, D. (eds) *The Design of Everyday Things.* New York: Doubleday. **Reason, J. T.** 1992: Cognitive underspecifications: its variety and consequences. In Barrs, B. J. (ed.) *Experimental Slips and Human Error: Exploring the Architecture of Volition.* New York: Plenum Press. **Robertson, I. H. and Marshall, J. C.** 1993: *Unilateral Neglect: Clinical and Experimental Studies.* Hove: Lawrence Erlbaum Associates. **Simons, D. J. and Chabris, C. F.** 1999: Gorillas in our midst: sustained inattentional blindness for dynamic events. *Perception* 28, 1059–74. **Treisman, A. M. and Gelade, G.** 1980: A feature integration theory of attention. *Cognitive Psychology* 12, 97–136.

autobiographical memory

The psychological history of the SELF (see s. 1, s. 4 and s. 5). It consists of memories for specific personal experiences (EPISODIC MEMORIES) as well as knowledge of the self or autobiographical knowledge, such as schools we attended, people we had relationships with, places where we lived, holidays we enjoyed, and so on (Conway 2001). Because it is the psychological history of the self, it is critical for personal

IDENTITY (see s. 4 and s. 5) and a healthy functioning self. Autobiographical memory forms the basis of the self and binds self-conceptions to reality through remembered experiences and related autobiographical knowledge. In psychiatric illnesses and following brain damage the connection between self-conceptions and the history of the self can become disrupted or lost, leading to selves that lack the ability to change and, in some cases, self-conceptions imbued with DELUSIONS (see s. 7), confabulations and false beliefs.

Autobiographical information frequently comes to mind not as memories but rather in the form of statements, propositions, declarations and BELIEFS (see s. 5) about the self, often accompanied by generic and/or specific (mainly visual) images of details of prior experience: this is autobiographical knowledge. Autobiographical knowledge is distinct from sensory perceptual episodic memories, which represent specific details derived from actual experience. In the formation of a specific autobiographical memory, autobiographical knowledge becomes linked to episodic memories. When this occurs, the rememberer has a RECOLLECTIVE EXPERIENCE – a sense or feeling of the self in the past.

Autobiographical memory changes across the lifespan. Undoubtedly the self and autobiographical memory changes over the course of childhood and perhaps only stabilises into an enduring form in late ADOLESCENCE (see s. 4) and early adulthood (Erikson 1950). These periods of development of the self are reflected in the *lifespan retrieval curve* (see Figure), which is observed when older adults (about 35 years and older) recall autobiographical memories from their life (e.g. Rubin, Wetzler and Nebes 1986). Memories are plotted in terms of age at the time of the remembered experiences and the resulting lifespan retrieval curve typically takes a form similar to that shown in the Figure. The lifespan retrieval curve consists of three components: the period of childhood AMNESIA (from birth to approximately 5 years of age), the period of the reminiscence bump (from 10 to 30 years), and the period of recency (from the present declining back to the period of the reminiscence bump).

There are many explanations of childhood amnesia, but currently there is no generally accepted explanation for this component of the lifespan retrieval curve, and although not as mysterious as it once was, the period of childhood amnesia continues to present a challenge to autobiographical memory researchers. In particular, it is peculiar that children appear to have intact memory function at the time, but that this is not available to them later in life. Similarly, the reminiscence bump also has several plausible explanations. One is that this period is permeated by novel experiences and it is the novelty, preserved in some way in memory, of these experiences that ensures their enduring memorability. Somewhat counter to this proposal is the finding that of the experiences recalled from the period of the reminiscence bump, only a small proportion are of novel events. Instead, most are of idiosyncratic events peculiar to the life circumstances and interests of the individual rememberer. This suggests an alternative to the novelty hypothesis, which is that the high accessibility of memories from this period may be related to their enduring relation to the self. Possibly, many memories from the period of the reminiscence bump are of 'self-defining' experiences (Singer and

Salovey 1993) and have a powerful effect in binding the self to a specific reality. However, and as with current understanding of the period of childhood amnesia, there is as yet no generally accepted explanation of the reminiscence portion of the lifespan retrieval curve.

The final part of the lifespan retrieval curve, with forgetting and recency components, is less contentious: memories recently encoded remain accessible, whereas memories retained over a longer retention interval are subject to decay and/or interference and so become progressively less accessible. This is a pattern of retention familiar from laboratory studies and one which has been observed many times (see RECENCY).

Autobiographical memory can become impaired in many different ways following brain injury. Injuries to the frontal lobes often lead to a 'clouding' of memory and patients with these types of injuries cannot recall detailed memories. In more extreme cases patients may 'confabulate' and construct autobiographical knowledge into plausible but false memories. Patients with damage to the temporal lobes and underlying structures in the LIMBIC SYSTEM (see s. 2) (i.e. hippocampal formation) may lose the ability to form new memories while retaining access to at least some memories from the period before their brain injury. Yet other patients with damage to posterior regions of the brain, regions involved in visual processing (occipital lobes), may lose the ability to generate visual images of the past and because of this become amnesic. Their amnesia occurs because episodic content of autobiographical memories is predominately encoded in the form of visual images. When the ability to generate visual images is compromised or lost as a consequence of brain damage, access to specific details of the past held in episodic images is also lost and an amnesia for details of the past is the result.

In psychiatric illness a common occurrence is that of a severe clouding of autobiographical memory resulting in overgeneral memories. For instance, in clinical DEPRESSION (see s. 7) patients recall many memories that lack detail and are much more schematic than typical autobiographical memories. Thus, a patient asked to recall specific memories of his father could only recall general events such as 'walks in the park after Sunday lunch', but was unable to generate a specific memory of a single walk.

MC/CM

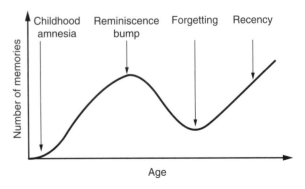

autobiographical memory *The lifespan retrieval curve.*

Conway, M. A. 2001: Sensory perceptual episodic memory and its context: autobiographical memory. *Philosophical Transactions of the Royal Society of London 356*, 1297–306. **Erikson, E. H.** 1950: *Childhood and Society.* New York: W. W. Norton & Company. **Rubin, D. C., Wetzler, S. E. and Nebes, R. D.** 1986: Autobiographical memory across the adult lifespan. In Rubin, D. C. (ed.) *Autobiographical Memory.* Cambridge: Cambridge University Press, 202–11. **Singer, J. A. and Salovey, P.** 1993: *The Remembered Self.* New York: The Free Press.

automatic   Strictly, actions that operate without control from another system. Cognitive psychology often refers to automatic processes as those that function without conscious control. For instance, in the STROOP EFFECT, the interference is caused by automatically reading the word, when actually one only wants to name the colour of the ink. *CM*

availability   In MEMORY (see s. 1), availability refers to whether an item has been stored or not. If it is available for retrieval from memory, it may or may not be accessible. *CM*

avoidance learning   Conditioning where an organism makes a response in order to avoid something unpleasant (e.g. a rat learns to press a lever to avoid an electric shock). This is of great theoretical importance because the learning is a response to anticipated outcomes, not a stimulus currently being sensed. *CM*

B

backward propagation of errors In CONNECTIONIST NETWORKS, this is a mechanism whereby the system compares its output with a known output, and corrects its internal representation. *CM*

bias From signal detection theory, the tendency to pick one response over another. A person would show bias if they constantly chose one option from a random set (e.g. constantly guessing that a die was going to land on six). (See also s. 6 and s. 8, BIAS) *CM*

binding problem Theories of PERCEPTION (see s. 1) suggest that different aspects of the system are devoted to different aspects of vision. Separate systems are said to deal with motion, colour and form. However, we never perceive an object separated from its colour. When an object moves, its colour and shape move with it, despite these representations being registered in different cells of the visual area of the brain. This leads to the binding problem: what binds these different representations together? Because we perceive these different ATTRIBUTIONS (see s. 5) as one, it suggests that the different cells are bound together at some stage. As yet, little is known about this problem, but it appears that the synchronous firing of nerve cells may serve to group these different attributes together (Zeki 1993). *CM*

Zeki, S. 1993: *A Vision of the Brain*. Oxford: Blackwell.

binocular cue A visual cue to depth PERCEPTION (see s. 1) that relies upon information from both eyes, such as retinal disparity or CONVERGENCE. *AS*

blindsight A term coined by Weiskrantz to describe visually guided behaviour in the absence of conscious visual awareness. Following damage to the primary visual cortex, patients are classed cortically blind as they fail to acknowledge seeing stimuli in the affected portion of their visual field (scotoma). However, individuals typically demonstrate spared visual capacities in response to the 'unseen' stimulus. Experiments have shown accurate reaching and grasping behaviour aimed towards objects in the blind field. Patients have also been found to discriminate motion, and even colour, in the region of the scotoma. The favoured explanation for these spared abilities is that visual information is received from subcortical structures, as well as from striate cortex, and therefore bypasses damaged areas: around 10 per cent of optic fibres terminate in the superior colliculus, a midbrain structure that has projections to areas controlling the apparently spared abilities. Note that not all individuals with scotoma demonstrate blindsight. *AS*

blocking This is where stimulus response training does not lead to the usual operant conditioning. Kamin trained rats to respond to one stimulus in the normal fashion, but then paired that stimulus with a new second stimulus. He showed that the first stimulus 'blocked' the second. (See s. 2, REDUNDANCY EFFECTS: OVERSHADOWING AND BLOCKING) *CM*

bottom-up processing Bottom-up processing is governed by stimulus information. In cognitive THEORY (see s. 8), bottom-up processes are governed by the information in the environment, which is why this is sometimes described as data-driven processing. An example is children's language learning. A bottom-up model would be one where children would first need to master all the individual sounds before piecing them into words, and then into sentences, before finally deriving meaning from sentences. A top-down model would be driven by meaning and thought processes rather than the constituent parts in the environment. In this case, a child would predict what an utterance meant, and from this higher-level representation of meaning, it would begin to understand what the lower-level units, such as individual sounds, meant. It is tempting to think of bottom-up processing as the poor relation in cognitive processing, but it can be thought of as governing TOP-DOWN PROCESSING. When trying to make sense of an ambiguous stimulus, bottom-up processing can identify individual aspects of the stimuli and constrain the top-down processes. For instance, in a conversation in a noisy room, you are listening to a conversation about a member of your friend's favourite band. If you fail to hear what it is that he does, you could make top-down inferences and guess that he is a guitarist. However, if you hear the fragment 'ummer', you will correctly generate 'drummer' from the combination of top-down and bottom-up processes. *CM*

C

category In LONG-TERM MEMORY, a category is a group of related semantic information, such as animals or vehicles. *CM*

central executive The central executive is a sub-component of the WORKING MEMORY model (Baddeley and Hitch 1974). It is a modality-independent, flexible but limited capacity processing resource that also serves as an interface between two slave-systems, the phonological loop (responsible for maintaining and manipulating verbal material) and the VISUO-SPATIAL SCRATCH PAD (used for storage and processing of visual and spatial information). Many different functions have been attributed to this component of working memory, including the regulation of information flow, the control of action, planning and goal-directed behaviour and the retrieval of information from LONG-TERM MEMORY. The central executive has also been implicated in the execution of specific strategies and specialised types of computation, such as mental arithmetic and logical reasoning. The role of coordination of information from the slave-systems and long-term memory has more recently been ascribed to a fourth component of working memory, the episodic buffer (Baddeley 2000). *AT*

Baddeley, A. D. 2000: The episodic buffer: a new component of working memory? *Trends in Cognitive Sciences* 4, 417–23. Baddeley, A. D. and Hitch, G. 1974: Working memory. In Bower, G. A. (ed.) *Recent Advances in Learning and Motivation* 8, 47–90. New York: Academic Press.

chunking Chunking is where information is better remembered by grouping it into smaller and/or more meaningful units. For instance, the difficult-to-remember number 501911747666 could be chunked into 501–911–747–666, or even better, Levi's jeans, Porsche sports car, jumbo jet, number of the beast. *CM*

classical conditioning The discovery of classical conditioning is attributed to Pavlov, who famously trained dogs to salivate when presented with a bell. Naturally, dogs will salivate when presented with food, in order to facilitate digestion. Pavlov demonstrated that dogs can be trained to salivate to only a ringing bell, in the absence of any food, so long as the dogs have previously learned the association of bell-ringing and food presentation. All classical conditioning operates like this. Before conditioning occurs, an unconditioned stimulus (food) and a conditioned stimulus (bell) operate separately. The dogs hear the bell, but make no association with the unconditioned response (salivation). During training, the dogs begin to associate the conditioned stimulus (bell) with the conditioned stimulus (food), to give the unconditioned response (salivation). Finally, after conditioning has occurred, we now term salivation the conditioned response, in that it is elicited by the conditioned stimulus alone (i.e. bell and no food). *CM*

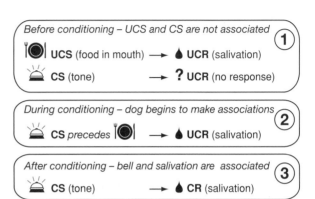

classical conditioning *Before conditioning – UCS and CS are not associated during conditioning – dog begins to make associations. After conditioning – bell and salivation are associated.*

cocktail party phenomenon The ability to pay ATTENTION to one conversation against a backdrop of other general noise and conversation. *CM*

cognitive behavioural therapy (CBT) CBT is an extremely successful and popular method of psychotherapy, loosely based on cognitive principles (see Hawton et al. 1989). Before CBT, behavioural therapy used rewards and the stimulus-response framework to interpret and treat people's psychopathologies. CBT, over and above behavioural therapy, considers not only people's behaviour, but also their BELIEFS (see s. 5). For example, CBT has proved very successful at treating panic attacks. In CBT, a person with panic attacks will confront their beliefs about their thoughts and the impacts their thoughts have on behaviour. This might involve explaining how panic can lead to hyperventilation, which can lead to sensations of dizziness, in turn increasing the level of panic. By addressing beliefs and cognitions about their problems, psychologists can break this vicious circle. Other examples come from theoretical models of how cognition is related to emotion. For instance, Beck suggested that DEPRESSION (see s. 7) can be caused by negative thought patterns, and therefore treated by restructuring and challenging habitual thought patterns. *CM*

Beck, A. and Emery, G. 1985: *Anxiety Disorders and Phobias: A Cognitive Perspective.* New York: Basic Books. Hawton, K., Salkovskis, P. M., Kirk, J. and Clark, D. M. 1989: *Cognitive Behavioural Therapy for Psychiatric Problems: A Practical Guide.* Oxford: Oxford University Press.

cognitive map A topographic mental representation of environmental spatial relations. Tolman coined the term to explain his observations of maze learning in rats. Tolman and Honzik (1930) reinforced one GROUP (see s. 5) of animals every time they successfully found their way through a maze to the food box, another group received no reinforcement, and a third only received reinforcement 11 days into the study (halfway through). As expected, the consistently reinforced group rapidly learned to efficiently navigate the maze, whereas the group without reinforcement demonstrated no learning effects. It was the third group that provoked interest: while they showed no learning in the first 10 days, upon reinforcement their performance immediately improved to a level equal to that of the consistently reinforced group. Clearly this group of rats had been learning the maze during the first 10 days, but it was latent, and not evident in their performance until an incentive was given by the reinforcement. Tolman went on to develop a place-learning (or 'sign-learning') THEORY (see s. 8): in this framework, rats learn expectations about which parts of the maze will lead to other parts. This was termed a cognitive map, and can be thought of as a primitive perceptual representation of spatial relations within the maze (or any environment). Support comes from observations that rats show advanced behaviour in a learned maze, such as taking short cuts or efficiently locating the food box from different starting points if the maze is rotated.

Later research concentrated on the neural mechanisms of cognitive maps: SINGLE-UNIT RECORDING (see s. 2) in freely moving animals demonstrated that individual NEURONES (see s. 2) in the hippocampus respond when the rat is in a particular location. These have been referred to as place cells. Their importance in representing space is evident when rats show particular impairments on navigation tasks following hippocampal damage. Similar impairments have been observed in humans who have undergone temporal lobotomies (including the hippocampal formation): they appear to have difficulties with spatial tasks that depend upon an allocentric representation of object arrays. This implicates the hippocampus in memory for the spatial relations between objects, and in providing a cognitive map for locations and landmarks within our environment (see Burgess, Jeffery and O'Keefe 1999).

AS

Burgess, N., Jeffery, K. J. and O'Keefe, J. 1999: *The Hippocampal and Parietal Foundations of Spatial Cognition*. Oxford: Oxford University Press. Tolman, E. C. and Honzik, C. H. 1930: Introduction and removal of reward and maze learning in rats. *University of California Publications in Psychology* 4, 257–75.

cognitive science At present, the precise differences between cognitive science and cognitive psychology are a little difficult to pinpoint. Generally, cognitive science can be thought of as a multi-disciplinary approach involving computer science, psychology, neuroscience and, to a lesser extent, philosophy. For the psychologist, cognitive science may appear like cognitive psychology with a good

deal more computational modelling [see ARTIFICIAL INTELLIGENCE and CONNECTIONIST NETWORK] and more input from neuro-imaging techniques such as MRI, PET and EEG. One important difference is that cognitive science, as opposed to more traditional cognitive psychology, has a greater emphasis on the structure of the brain, and the need to understand information processing in the context of the hardware of the system. In this way, MARR'S COMPUTATIONAL THEORY was crucial to the development of cognitive science. Marr suggested that scientists needed to understand information processing on several levels, one of which was the hardware – in the case of humans, the brain. By understanding the structure and performance of the brain, we can understand the constraints on information processing. The structure of the brain can help us understand cognition.

For many, however, the most important element of cognitive science is its use of computational models. Traditionally, cognitive psychology theories were rather poorly specified, such as, 'information enters SHORT-TERM MEMORY and then is transferred to LONG-TERM MEMORY'. Although this might have been a nice description of the data available at the time, this is a vague statement. How is information transferred? What information is not transferred? The box-and-arrow flow charts of cognitive psychologists were good generalisations of mental processes, but they were little more than that. What happens in the boxes? What travels down the arrows? (For an example of a classic box-and-arrow model, see Figure.)

Cognitive scientists tend to make computational models of information-processing models. These models are such that it is not possible to leave parts of the THEORY (see s. 8) unspecified. If one wanted to build a working model of a car, it would not be enough to say that the engine drives the wheels: we would need an understanding of the workings of the internal combustion engine. Thus, computational models leave no grey areas, at the very least they must make assumptions about certain processes or variables. Cognitive scientists can be thought of as interested in the 'software' of the human mind: 'What makes people smarter than machines? . . . One answer, perhaps the classic one we might expect from ARTIFICIAL INTELLIGENCE, is "software". If only we had the right computer programme, the argument goes, we might be able to capture the fluidity and adaptability of human information processing' (McClelland, Rumelhart and Hinton 1986: 3). However, McClelland and others realise that software is not the only part of the solution: it is also crucial to understand the cognitive architecture – this is why cognitive scientists are equally interested in the neuro-logical constraints and features that support cognitive processes.

There are a number of drawbacks to this contemporary

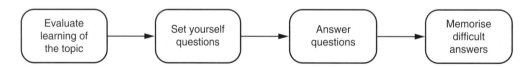

cognitive science *A box-and-arrow representation of a real-world task: revising for an exam. Although this is readily understood, what does it actually mean? What travels down the arrows? What's the difference between a box and an arrow? How does this differ from a description?*

cognitive science approach. One is that the cognitive scientist may actually get bogged down in processes that are not psychologically interesting. Palmer and Kimichi (1986) suggested that it should be possible to elucidate theories on several different levels, from descriptive statement, through flow chart to computational model. They also add that at some point you could draw a line, above which is psychologically relevant information, and below which is more specific, less relevant material. For instance, to build our working model of a car, we would need to mix fuel and air in the correct proportion in order to ensure combustion. Would we really need to understand the chemical composition of air and fuel in order to produce a fully functioning car? At what level do we decide to leave the details of psychological models to microbiologists or neuroscientists?

Finally, a criticism of the model-building approach is that it often leads to complex models with many parameters. Consider a large connectionist network with many units. The model is arguably so complex and built to such a specification that it might be difficult not to build a functioning model. The modellers can tweak so many parameters – the rate at which the model learns, the strength of the weights, the threshold of the units, the number of units, and so on – that it may be inevitable that it is possible to model any well-specified theory, whether it is ultimately psychologically correct or not. This is particularly true of neuropsychological uses of connectionist networks, where fiddling with any one of a set of parameters is likely to produce an impaired, 'brain-damaged' network. In response to this sort of criticism, the most exciting way computational models have been used is to make new predictions about human behaviour, which can then be tested in experimental situations with humans (e.g. Henson et al. 2003).

In summary, the best way of differentiating cognitive psychologists and cognitive scientists might be that the former use box-and-arrow models, whereas the latter use computational models, but this is a definition likely to upset and unhelpfully segregate a good many researchers.
CM

Henson, R., Hartley, T., Burgess, N., Hitch, G. and Flude, B. 2003: Selective interference with verbal short-term memory for serial order information: a new paradigm and tests of a timing-signal hypothesis. *Quarterly Journal of Experimental Psychology Section A – Human Experimental Psychology* 56, 1307–34. **McClelland, J. L., Rumelhart, D. E. and Hinton, G. E.** 1986: The appeal of parallel distributed processing. In Rumelhart, D. E. and McClelland, J. L. (eds) *Parallel Distributed Processing. Explorations in the Microstructure of Cognition (Vol. 1): Foundations.* Cambridge MA: MIT Press. **Palmer, S. E. and Kimichi, R.** 1986: The information processing approach to cognition. In Knapp, T. and Robertson, L. C. (eds) *Approaches to Cognition: Contrasts and Controversies.* Hillsdale NJ: Lawrence Erlbaum Associates.

colour vision The ability to see in colour. Normal human colour perception is based on three different types of cones (light-receptive cells in the retina). Each of the three cones responds maximally to a different wavelength (or colour) of light, hence human vision can be termed trichromatic. It is often thought that each type of cone only responds to one wavelength of light – in fact, each type of cone will respond to a whole range of wavelengths, and for any one wavelength, all three types may be activated, but at different rates. It is this firing at different rates that enables computations about colour. The Young-Helmholtz THEORY (see s. 8), put forward in the late 1800s, suggests that red light will activate one set of RECEPTORS (see s. 2) strongly, and the other types only weakly, and this gives rise to the sensation of redness, for example. This theory suggests that the three cone types are preferentially sensitive to red, green and blue, and all other colours are derived from a mixture of these primary colours. A television produces a range of colours in the same way, by having these three different colours of pixel. Colour blindness is caused by a lack of rods of a certain type (usually the red detector).

However, there are some problems with this theory. Most importantly, it does not explain the systematic pattern of how colours combine in the outside world to give rise to different resultant hues and how certain colours will cancel out to form grey (e.g. red and green, and orange and blue-green) according to set patterns. Nor does it explain why, when we stare at a yellow image, we get a blue after-image, or so on in a completely predictable manner. And, to human vision, yellow is a primary colour, but we know it to be perceived as a mixture at the physiological level. These observations and difficulties gave rise to the opponent-process theory (see Hurvich and Jameson 1957). According to this theory, the physiological properties of light are rendered into six 'psychological' primaries by another level of processing: red, green, yellow, blue, black and white. These are then set up as three opponent-process pairs: red-green, blue-yellow, black-white. Excitation of one half of the pair automatically inhibits the other. Thus, colours are viewed in relative amounts, where the more red something is, the less green it must be. Colours will be perceived on the basis of the balance of red-green and blue-yellow. If all four are equal, no colour will be perceived. If there is a red stimulus, the red-green channel will react, inhibiting the perception of green, whereas the blue-yellow channel will be unaffected. Initially just a theory based on observations of behaviour (such as after-images), this theory was supported by the discovery of opponent-process type activations in individual cells of the rhesus monkey brain (De Valois 1965).
CM

De Valois, R. L. 1965: Behavioural and electrophysiological studies of primate vision. In Neff, W. D. (ed.) *Contributions of Sensory Physiology.* New York: Academic Press, vol. 1. **Hurvich, L. M. and Jameson, D.** 1957: An opponent-process theory of colour vision. *Psychological Review* 64, 384–404.

concrete thought As opposed to abstract thought, based on concrete objects and concepts, i.e. specific based on one particular example. Concrete thought is one-dimensional and unlikely to lead to generalisations. *CM*

conditioned reinforcers A reinforcer in operant conditioning that is learnt itself. A dog biscuit is a reinforcer for a well-behaved dog. If you say 'good dog' when giving biscuits, the praise will eventually become the reinforcer in the absence of actual biscuits. The praise is the conditioned reinforcer. *CM*

conditioned response (CR) In conditioning, this is the new response (e.g. Pavlov's dogs salivating) that would not have occurred before the learning regime.

Strictly, this term should be restricted to classical conditioning, but will be found used for operant conditioning.

CM

conditioned stimulus (CS)   In conditioning (particularly classical) this is the stimulus that is originally neutral, but becomes associated with a new response (e.g. Pavlov's bell).

CM

confabulation   The unintentional production of incorrect material from memory. (See s. 1, FALSE MEMORY SYNDROME)

CM

connectionism   One of the methods used in the computational modelling approach, connectionism concerns the simulation of cognition through DISTRIBUTED REPRESENTATION. CONNECTIONIST NETWORKS are also known as NEURAL NETWORKS (see s. 2, NEURONAL (OR NEURAL) NETWORKS) or parallel distributed models. The main feature of a connectionist network as an approach to ARTIFICIAL INTELLIGENCE is that it can learn for itself. A connectionist network is not usually taught explicit rules by a programmer, but 'learns' information as a result of 'experience'. The mechanisms in connectionist networks are therefore presumed to be similar to the activation of NEURONES (see s. 2) in the brain, hence the term neural network. As such, connectionist networks can be thought of as using the sort of learning characterised by Hebb [see LONG-TERM POTENTIATION]. The following is a description of a typical network as used by psychologists. Many other varieties exist beyond the scope of this entry.

Connectionist networks take an input and manipulate it in a mathematical manner to produce an output. To give a human analogue, this might be represented as how we learn to read aloud. We look at the visual form of the word (the input), and some system in the brain learns to map this word onto speech (the output). We typically learn to read in the presence of another, who can tell us whether we are right (give feedback). If we see the word 'brain' but pronounce it as 'brine', feedback can tell us we are wrong, and we can use this information to change our response for next time we encounter the word. This idea of input and output and response to feedback is the essence of connectionism. Connectionist modellers just let the system sort itself out in any way that produces the desired result. In fact, such a model of speech production exists, NETtalk (Sejnowski and Rosenberg 1987).

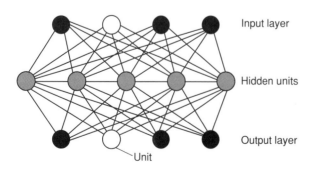

connectionism *A connectionist network.*

Connectionist networks (see Figure) usually have the following features (Rumelhart and McClelland 1986). The network is composed of individual units. The units connect up to several other units. The units act on each other through INHIBITION or excitation. Each unit considers what all the other units are feeding it, and if this value is over a certain amount, it produces a single output. A distributed representation can be built up over the units and a network can produce a wide range of different patterns across its units. Networks learn by receiving feedback and altering their internal mathematical rules (such as described in BACKWARD PROPAGATION OF ERRORS): the pattern of activations created by the mathematical rules are flexible and always changing. Connectionist networks are dynamic – they change their properties in response to their experience of input and feedback on output.

The key manner in which connectionist networks work is in the mathematical rules that the hidden units produce. Units act on the input they are given predictably. Each unit can be thought of as turned on $(+1)$ or turned off (-1) (either black or white in the Figure). In the example Figure, the task of the grey internal representation units is to produce a pattern of activation that yields the same output pattern as input pattern. For different patterns of input, the internal representation units will generate different patterns of activation and thus yield different responses. Hidden units have a threshold, which means that if the input is over a certain level, the unit will be activated and give $+1$ (excitation), otherwise it will give -1 (inhibition).

The hidden units work by considering all the values of the connected units, and adding them up to produce an output. For instance, a unit with a threshold of 1 might have one input of $+1$ and another of -1. It would respond with a -1 in this case, because $(+1) + (-1) = 0$, which is less than the threshold of 1. However, if both inputs were $+1$, it would respond with a $+1$. Units will respond differently if they have different thresholds: a network learns by adjusting all the thresholds across its hidden units in order to produce the correct input-to-output match. In our example, if the threshold were changed to 0, then the unit would produce a $+1$ value for inputs of $+1,+1$; $-1,+1$; $+1,-1$; but not $-1,-1$.

As well as thresholds, connectionist networks work by altering the weights. Threshold can be thought of as when a unit will be activated; the weight is how much it gives when it is activated. So instead of thinking just about -1 or $+1$ in the example above, units are also giving a range of values, such as $+2$, -0.5, etc. As well as adjusting thresholds, therefore, networks can learn by modifying their weights.

If connectionist networks are 'taught' to make the correct connections by giving them a variety of inputs and giving them feedback on their outputs, they can adjust these thresholds and weights to respond appropriately to the materials. This is why they can be described as learning for themselves: we do not tell them what thresholds to have in order to produce the correct output, the model itself determines the threshold values from feedback from its output. The most exciting aspect of connectionist networks is testing them on novel materials. It is usual to train a network on one set of materials and then test it on another. In the pronunciation example, the network would be trained with 'brain' and 'trout', for example, but the rules it learnt, held in the pattern of thresholds in the hidden units, would mean it could pronounce words it had not encountered before, such as 'train'. In this way, connectionist networks' performance is comparable to human abilities.

As models, connectionist networks have had many applications. Psychologists have sought to explain many different cognitive processes through this approach. A famous example shows how a connectionist network can model representations of semantic knowledge about people (using as an example two fictitious gangs of people, the Jets and the Sharks; McClelland and Rumelhart 1986). Smolensky (1987) reviews work on connectionist models of speech PERCEPTION (see s. 1), visual recognition, AMNESIA and the acquisition of the English past tense, for example. Much contemporary work on people with brain damage considers how damage to a connectionist network is similar to damage to the brain. Connectionist networks will be trained in the normal manner, and the researcher will examine the effect on performance of removing units or connections or altering thresholds and weights. *CM*

McClelland, J. L. and Rumelhart, D. E. 1986: *Parallel Distributed Processing. Explorations in the Microstructure of Cognition (Vol. 2): Psychological and Biological Models.* Cambridge MA: MIT Press. **Rumelhart, D. E. and McClelland, J. L.** 1986: *Parallel Distributed Processing. Explorations in the Microstructure of Cognition (Vol. 1): Foundations.* Cambridge MA: MIT Press. **Sejnowski, T. J. and Rosenberg, C. R.** 1987: Parallel networks that learn to pronounce English text. *Complex Systems* 1, 145–68. **Smolensky, P.** 1987: Connectionist AI, symbolic AI and the brain. *Artificial Intelligence Review* 1, 95–109.

connectionist network   [See CONNECTIONISM]

consciousness   Loosely, this is the STATE (see s. 6) of awareness, as in 'to regain consciousness', of which we all should have an understanding. However, it might be a wise idea for psychology to leave the description of this term to philosophers. Some cognitive psychologists (although rarely the authors of these models themselves) will describe very specific mechanisms and models as being like consciousness, such as WORKING MEMORY or the control mechanism that guides ATTENTION in the SUPERVISORY ATTENTION SYSTEM. Others may like to think of consciousness as METACOGNITION. It is because of better-defined constructs like these that many psychologists will avoid talking about consciousness wherever possible, and refer instead to these entities. Some prominent philosophers suggest that we will never understand the subjective nature of consciousness (Searle 1992), since its very subjective nature means it is not likely to be accommodated in objective scientific methods. One of the problems is that the idea of subjective awareness central to consciousness is poorly understood. For instance, if awareness is about monitoring a system and then acting on this information, we might describe a thermostat as being aware, since it can monitor the heat of a tank of water and control a heating element accordingly. But we would not describe a thermostat as possessing consciousness.

The whole area is further complicated by the fact that consciousness is often put forward as one of the differences between humans and all other species – the way religions have often talked about humans and souls. It is these kinds of issues that led BEHAVIOURISM (see s. 1) to reject the need to measure or consider consciousness at all, and instead focus on stimulus-response links. Thankfully, however, there is a growing GROUP (see s. 5) of credible researchers beginning to define and explore consciousness. Pinker (1997), for instance, has summarised consciousness into three distinct parts: sentience, access to information and self-knowledge. Sentience describes subjective experience, phenomenal awareness and feelings of what something seems like to you. Access to information considers the ability to report your ongoing mental experience or OPERATIONS (see s. 4). Self-knowledge considers whether an organism can know itself and its impact on the world. To paraphrase Steven Pinker: I cannot only say I feel happy and I can see red, I can say, 'Hey, here I am, Chris Moulin, feeling happy and seeing red.' These three facets of consciousness are beginning to be taken forward in research: illuminated by such things as AMNESIA, BLINDSIGHT and SPLIT-BRAIN patients. *CM*

Pinker, S. 1997: *How the Mind Works.* New York: W. W. Norton & Company. **Searle, J. R.** 1992: *The Rediscovery of Mind.* Cambridge MA: MIT Press.

constancy   The tendency for object properties to be perceived in a consistent manner, despite differences in viewing conditions (e.g. distance, illumination). *AS*

convergence   The movement of both eyes in order to maintain fixation of an object that has changed distance from the observer. *AS*

cybernetics   The study of artificial control mechanisms and COMMUNICATION (see s. 2) systems. (See also s. 1, CYBERNETICS AND SYSTEMS THEORY) *CM*

D

data-driven Any cognitive process that relies purely on information presented. There is no input from existing knowledge. Also known as BOTTOM-UP PROCESSING. *ES*

decision making Research has focused on the ways in which information about probabilities (how likely something is) can be combined with information about utility (how desirable an outcome is in relation to an individual's goals). Although there are various normative theories by which psychologists have assessed decision making, one of the major approaches has been to compare decisions with those that are suggested by subjective expected utility THEORY (see s. 8) (SEU). As the name implies, the approach attempts to assess the LIKELIHOOD (see s. 8) and usefulness of different decisions. The theory tries to characterise the trade-off that exists between utility (something's worth) and probability (something's likelihood). To compute SEU, the following formula is used:

$$SEU = \Sigma p_i U_i$$

This means that in order to correctly compute SEU one takes the probability of each outcome (p_i) and the utility of each outcome (U_i) and sums them (Σ). Consider the following example: I take a pack of cards and say that I will give you £2 every time you cut the pack and find a jack, a queen or a king, and £5 for an ace. All other cards yield no prize and I keep your £1 stake.

We can then use this information to compute the SEU for this gamble (SEU effectively sees decisions as 'gambles'). The chance of you cutting the pack and hitting a winning card is 16/52 (four of each kind of winning card) or 0.31. However, the utility differs depending on card type (some are worth more than others), so we need to compute these independently. For each card type the probability is 4/52 (or .077). The utility of the jack, queen and king is 2, and 5 for an ace. We multiply the utility by the probability. Thus for a jack, queen or king the utility is 0.154 (.077 × 2) and for an ace is 0.385 (.077 × 5). This gives a total SEU of 0.539. Thus for every £1 stake you stand to receive £0.539 back. This appears not to be the world's soundest gamble and yet people do still gamble: as is often the case in psychology, people deviate from normative theory. One of the biggest problems is that people rarely compute probabilities accurately, or the computations required are simply too complicated. *ES*

declarative memory Memory that is available for conscious report, such as facts and memory for one's own life. *CM*

deductive reasoning Deduction is a form of thinking that involves making what was previously implicit, explicit. Consider the following example from Rips (1994):

If Calvin deposits 50c then he gets a coke
Calvin deposits 50c
∴?

Given the two premises, most of us can successfully deduce the conclusion that 'Calvin gets a coke' (via application of the logic rule of MODUS PONENS). In this example we have added nothing to the premises at all; we have merely made the implicit, explicit. One of the important points about deductive reasoning is that if we follow the rules of logic in our thinking, then the conclusion must be true if the premises are true. That is, the nature of deduction is 'truth preserving'. When the form (or structure) of an argument is such that it always yields true conclusions from true premises, we can say that the argument form is valid. *ES*

Rips, L. 1994: *The Psychology of Proof.* Cambridge MA: MIT Press.

determinism The doctrine whereby every event has environmental causes, the implication being that human actions are beyond wilful control. Determinism can be thought of as the central belief behind behaviourist approaches to psychology. *CM*

dichotic presentation Presented to both ears simultaneously. *CM*

digit span A term for the maximum number of digits that an individual can consistently hold in SHORT-TERM MEMORY. *AT*

discrimination In conditioning, discrimination is the ability to determine between two or more stimuli. To show discrimination, one will respond to one stimulus (e.g. fear of Alsatians) but not another (no phobia for other types of dog). (See also s. 5, DISCRIMINATION) *CM*

distributed representation The idea that MENTAL REPRESENTATIONS or representations in a CONNECTIONIST NETWORK are distributed across a selection of units or NEURONES (see s. 2) in the network. A distributed network will not be catastrophically affected by the loss of any one neurone or unit. Consider that one neurone alone is responsible for holding your representation of a thing, such as your grandma. If you received an annoyingly accurate bump on the head, you may lose that one 'grandma' neurone and thereafter fail to recognise or remember your grandma. Thus, it seems much more likely that representations are distributed across a system. More technically, in connectionist networks, distributed representations are crucial, since they explain how we store different attributes within one system. A distributed representation is described as sub-symbolic (Smolensky 1988), because it is more fundamental than the label, or symbol, of a thing. A symbolic system, for example, would have to store concrete representations of chairs for different types of chair and for chairs viewed from different angles – one unit for each type of chair. This would be an unwieldy and inefficient system. A distributed representation merely needs a group of units to respond to the abstract concept of 'chair-ness', however it is encountered. The same units can respond in different patterns to different objects and representations also, since it is the pattern of the units' activation that gives rise to a representation. Finally, a distributed representation system does not need to be taught explicit rules: it can sort itself out by BACKWARD PROPAGATION OF ERRORS, for example. *CM*

Smolensky, P. 1988: On the proper treatment of connectionism. *Behavioural and Brain Sciences* 11, 1–74.

double dissociation

double dissociation Descriptive of a particular pattern of deficits demonstrated by brain-damaged patients, and generally used to infer the existence of separate cognitive functions. A single dissociation is observed when a patient is impaired at task X (testing one function), but performs normally on task Y (testing another function). In comparison, a double dissociation is usually obtained with two patients, when one patient is impaired at task X and normal at task Y, while the other patient is normal on task X but impaired on task Y. Whereas a single dissociation allows the inference that there is a cognitive function required by task X but not task Y, a double dissociation also allows the inference that an additional function is required by task Y but not task X. It is possible to obtain a double dissociation within one patient (e.g. written versus spoken input). A particularly important methodology in cognitive neuropsychology. *AS*

dysexecutive syndrome Also referred to as executive dysfunction, dysexecutive syndrome can be thought of as the group of cognitive symptoms that arise due to malfunction of or damage to the frontal lobes. Broadly speaking, frontal damage can be split into DORSAL (see s. 2) damage, leading to cognitive difficulties, and VENTRAL (see s. 2) damage, leading to emotional difficulties (Stuss and Levine 2002). Patients with frontal lobe damage will have difficulty coordinating, planning and initiating actions. They may also have particular difficulties with PROSPECTIVE MEMORY and INHIBITION. The frontal lobes are an extremely large area of the brain, and as a result they appear to be implicated in a whole range of deficits. For instance, executive dysfunction leads to difficulties in language fluency (producing the right words), but also wandering topics in conversation. It also leads to CONFABULATION in memory, and propensity to repeatedly respond in the same manner to tasks or questions (perseveration). These seemingly disparate symptoms can be well incorporated into Norman and Shallice's model of ATTENTION, the SUPERVISORY ATTENTION SYSTEM. In this, dysexecutive syndrome can be thought of as difficulty in initiating, switching and regulating actions: people with dysexecutive syndrome may be able to carry out routine tasks well, but may not be able to switch from one task to the next easily, or respond to novel situations.

Because EXECUTIVE FUNCTION (see s. 4) is such a nebulous entity, and with such importance for day-to-day tasks, some important work has been conducted in order to ensure tests of dysexecutive function have appropriate ECOLOGICAL VALIDITY (see also s. 8). For instance, one contemporary test of executive function is the multiple errands shopping task (Shallice and Burgess 1991), which examines the ability to carry out a range of tasks in a hypothetical shopping trip. Other tasks which can be used to measure dysexecutive problems include tests of inhibition, such as the Hayling sentence completion task (Burgess and Shallice 1996), where participants have to suppress the usual response to a very predictable sentence, such as: 'Before you go to bed, turn off the _____.' Burgess and Shallice report that people with frontal lobe difficulties find this very difficult, usually not managing to overcome the usual response, such as 'lights' in the example above. They also report that frontal patients are more likely to use related words or obscenities to complete the sentences, such as: 'The whole town came to hear the mayor FART THROUGH A MEGAPHONE.' Finally, care should be taken with the use of the term CENTRAL EXECUTIVE, which although executive in nature, specifically applies to only the control of the WORKING MEMORY system. *CM*

Burgess, P. W. and Shallice, T. 1996: Response suppression, initiation and strategy use following frontal lobe lesions. *Neuropsychologia* 34, 263–72. Shallice, T. and Burgess, P. W. 1991: Deficits in strategy application following frontal-lobe damage in man. *Brain* 114, 727–41. Stuss, D. T. and Levine, B. 2002: Adult clinical neuropsychology: lessons from studies of the frontal lobes. *Annual Review of Psychology* 53, 401–33.

E

---

echoic memory   The extremely brief store of auditory information in sensory memory.   *CM*

ecological validity   Applicable to the real world, an accurate reflection of everyday processes. A persistent criticism of cognitive psychology is that it lacks ecological validity, i.e. its findings cannot be readily incorporated into real life. The central issue here is about experimental control. Cognitive psychologists often wish to reduce the effects of EXTRANEOUS VARIABLES (see s. 8) by testing cognitive processes in contrived laboratory settings. For instance, memory for made-up words is tested in perfect silence. This is a situation nothing like how we encounter and try to memorise important information. Ecological validity became something of a holy grail for memory researchers, leading to many interesting, ecologically valid, but obscure experiments (some of which are reviewed by Banaji and Crowder 1989). For instance, one researcher tested his wife's memory for the cycling holiday that they had enjoyed, with the unsurprising finding that she, who had actually been on the holiday, could remember the events of the holiday better than a CONTROL GROUP (see s. 8) who had not been on it.

Because one of the thrusts of cognitive psychology is to better understand the failures of cognition seen in brain damage and human ageing, there is a move towards tests of cognitive function that are more ecologically valid [see DYSEXECUTIVE SYNDROME]. For instance, the Rivermead behavioural memory test has many real-world memory tasks, such as remembering a series of people's names or remembering an appointment (Wilson, Cockburn, Baddeley and Hiorns 1989).

Debate rages over the issue of ecological validity, and the sensible view to hold would be that theoretical development in the laboratory needs to be demonstrated in the field, but without either, psychology as a whole suffers. Eysenck and Keane (1995) dispatch the issue carefully but concisely (p. 465): 'Although many experimental cognitive psychologists are aware that much of their research is somewhat lacking in ecological validity, they are rightly sceptical of a wholesale abandonment of experimental rigour and control in favour of a totally naturalistic approach.' (See s. 8)   *CM*

Banaji, M. R. and Crowder, R. G. 1989: The bankruptcy of everyday memory. *American Psychologist* 44, 1185–93. Eysenck, M. W. and Keane, M. T. 1995: *Cognitive Psychology: A Student's Handbook*. Hove: Lawrence Erlbaum Associates. Wilson, B. A., Cockburn, J., Baddeley, A. D. and Hiorns, R. 1989: The development and validation of a test battery for detecting and monitoring everyday memory problems. *Journal of Clinical and Experimental Neuropsychology* 11, 855–70.

EEG scanning   ELECTROENCEPHALOGRAM (see s. 2) scanning (EEG) is where tiny electrical impulses (related to the firing of NEURONES – see s. 2) are measured in the brain. Electric fields are detected by electrodes attached to the scalp. EEG scanning is of particular interest to cogni-

tive scientists when the pattern of electrical activity is studied for a particular task (called event-related potentials). From this, it is possible to infer what regions of the brain are used for the task in question. EEG recordings are not very good at locating precise areas in the brain, but they can measure change in time very accurately. As such they can be used to show how activation changes in the brain when one is recalling information from AUTOBIOGRAPHICAL MEMORY, for example. Over a couple of seconds, activation can be seen to move from the frontal lobes, where a search process is set up, to the parietal and occipital lobes of the brain, where visual imagery and other detail is added (Conway et al. 2001).   *CM*

Conway, M. A., Pleydell-Pearce, C. W. and Whitecross, S. E. (2001): The neuroanatomy of autobiographical memory: a slow cortical potential study (SCP) of autobiographical memory retrieval. *Journal of Memory and Language* 45, 493–524. For a description of electrophysiological investigation of cognition, see Rugg, M. D. and Coles, M. G. H. 1996: *Electrophysiology of Mind – Event-related Brain Potentials and Cognition*. Oxford: Oxford University Press.

elaboration   The process of memorisation by extending meaning or making links. In the example for the CHUNKING entry, elaboration is the use of meaning for the three-digit chunks.   *CM*

encoding specificity   This is the notion that a cue to remembering will only be effective if it was encoded at the time of learning the material. Tulving and Thomson (1973) used this term to describe how to-be-remembered material is encoded with information about the context and the material itself – with the result being a unique MEMORY (see s. 1) trace. The implication of this mechanism is that material will be particularly well recalled if the context between encoding and retrieval is constant. Most famously, Godden and Baddeley (1975) showed that divers had superior memory performance for material encountered underwater when tested underwater (or when material learnt on land was tested on land). Recall was around 50 per cent better when context was the same at encoding as retrieval. In laboratory conditions, encoding specificity can be demonstrated using cue-target word pairs, such as green – HORSE. The word HORSE will be much better recalled in its original context (i.e. paired with the cue, green). The effects of the encoding specificity principle are pretty much confined to RECALL tests, with RECOGNITION being far less sensitive to context effects. Encoding specificity is the mechanism by which STATE-DEPENDENT LEARNING can be thought to occur. *CM*

Godden, D. R. and Baddeley, A. D. 1975: Context-dependent memory in two natural environments: on land and under water. *British Journal of Psychology* 66, 325–31. Tulving, E. and Thomson, D. M. 1973: Encoding specificity and retrieval processes in episodic memory. *Psychological Review* 80, 352–73.

episodic memory   Episodic memory can be defined either on the basis of subjective experience or content matter. In either case, it is distinct from SEMANTIC MEMORY. On the basis of subjective experience, episodic memory is memory that generates a special first-person sense of remembering. Events that you recall from episodic memory will be rich, evocative memories, possibly with associated feelings and links to other memories [see RECOLLECTIVE EXPERIENCE]. On the basis of content, episodic memory is MEMORY (see s. 1) with contextual information attached; it is memory for information with a sense of SELF (see s. 1, s. 4 and s. 5). AUTOBIOGRAPHICAL MEMORY can be thought of as drawing on episodic memory. In the laboratory, episodic memory is defined as memory for information from a study phase. For example, giving people a list of fruits to study and then asking them to recall as many as they can remember from that list is a TEST (see s. 6) of episodic memory. Just asking them to list as many different fruits as they can think of is a test of semantic memory.

Episodic memory has become something of a hot topic in cognition (see Baddeley, Conway and Aggleton 2002). This is presumably because as memory associated with the sensation of self, or as self in the past, it may be able to illuminate our understanding of consciousness. In fact, many researchers argue that the purpose of episodic memory is to maintain a sense of self. Despite this, episodic memory is not deemed to be a uniquely human ability. Animals' feats of remembering, such as how elephants in the Namib Desert walk for days and days to a waterhole, are considered to be episodic in nature [see COGNITIVE MAP]. It is suggested that the neuropsychological basis for episodic memory is in the medial temporal lobes (especially the hippocampus), but with the frontal lobes necessary for appropriate control and monitoring of the contents of retrieval and the organisation of material for effective learning. *CM*

Baddeley, A. D., Conway, M. A. and Aggleton, J. P. 2002: *Episodic Memory: New Directions in Research*. Oxford: Oxford University Press.

expertise   The study of expertise has focused on what it is that converts 'novices' into 'experts'. Fitts and Posner (1967) outlined three stages in the development of expertise. The first stage is known as the cognitive stage. During this stage the learner commits to MEMORY (see s. 1) the information necessary to perform the required skill. Performance here is very slow, as the required knowledge is still stored in a declarative format. The second stage is the associative stage, when there is a reduction in the number of errors, and links between the required elements are strengthened. The final stage in this development is the autonomous stage. Here the required skill becomes increasingly AUTOMATIC. This means that it requires few resources to perform the task successfully. Two of the main features of this stage are an increase in both speed and accuracy, making it possible to perform two skills at once – such as driving and talking. *ES*

Fitts, P. M. and Posner, M. I. 1967: *Learning and Skilled Performance in Human Performance*. Belmont CA: Brock-Cole.

explicit memory   Synonymous with declarative memory, this is MEMORY (see also s. 1) that is available for conscious report. *CM*

extinction   (1) A disorder of visual ATTENTION resulting from brain pathology (e.g. cerebrovascular accident). A patient demonstrating extinction can detect a single item in the left and right visual fields, but when two items are placed simultaneously in each field (bilateral double simultaneous stimulation) the patient fails to detect the item on one side of space (usually the one contralateral to the LESION – see s. 2). This behaviour contrasts with unilateral visual neglect, as the perceptual impairment occurs only upon bilateral presentation. This also demonstrates that the effects are not due to a visual field deficit (hemianopia). Usually observed following damage to the right parietal lobe, extinction is also one of the hallmarks of Balint-Holmes syndrome, which results from bilateral parietal damage. The attentional basis of extinction has been demonstrated in various PARADIGMS (see s. 1): for example, if the two items can be grouped according to Gestalt principles (e.g. good continuation) then there are fewer omission errors. (2) In conditioning, this is where the conditioned stimulus no longer produces the conditioned response. *AS*

eyewitness memory   The study of real-world memory skills focusing on people's memory for information related to crime, e.g. the ability to recognise the face of an attacker. *CM*

F

face recognition   The ability to identify a face (and to reproduce information about it). Face recognition is not the mere process of PERCEPTION (see s. 1). People interested in face recognition tend to consider how one produces information about a person when given their face as a cue. Face recognition, therefore, considers the perception of a face, but also the processing that matches the face to a stored representation, and the access from the face to semantic and name information in LONG-TERM MEMORY. Because of its clear real-world basis, and the applications of this THEORY (see s. 8) to everyday life, face recognition research is often held up as an example of cognitive psychology with high ECOLOGICAL VALIDITY (see also s. 8). It is clearly of interest to those interested in EYEWITNESS MEMORY, where people may be asked to pick out a perpetrator of a crime from a set of lures or distracters. In fact, this is also a good description of how face recognition experiments work.

As with the influence of AMNESIA on our understanding of MEMORY (see also s. 1), face recognition has been illuminated by the study of prosopagnosia, the inability to recognise faces. Prosopagnosics will fail to recognise very familiar people – they will walk past their spouse on the street, if they encounter them in an unusual context, for example. Nonetheless, they will be able to identify meaningfully other categories and classes of objects, including animals and buildings. Prosopagnosia, therefore, suggests that there is a special system for face processing.

It is established that face processing relies on two types of information about the face: featural information and configural information. Featural information considers what each individual aspect is like: eye colour, nose size, lip shape, etc. Configural information considers how these individual features are aligned. Manipulating the features or the configuration of a face will affect your ability to recognise the face.

Bruce and Young (1986) developed a model of how face processing is carried out. Their ambitious model involves the perceptual identification of face features and configuration, right through to the naming of a face and retrieval of associated information. A major feature of their model is that it suggests that processing of familiar and unfamiliar faces occurs in different parts of the system: this has been supported by DOUBLE DISSOCIATIONS in the prosopagnosia literature. Crudely, Bruce and Young's model takes visual information (including the movements we make when we speak, or facial expressions and complex structural analysis such as described by MARR'S COMPUTATIONAL THEORY of perception) and compares this information to stored representations (face recognition units), which activates person IDENTITY (see s. 4 and s. 5) nodes (context-free abstract representations of people) and semantic information units (concrete information about people, such as their name or occupation). In the model, there is basically a flow of information from BOTTOM-UP PROCESSING from the visual characteristics of a face, and a corresponding flow of TOP-DOWN PROCESSING

concerning people's characteristics and representations of people that are view-INDEPENDENT (see s. 8) (exactly like Marr's theories about view-independence). The model makes some interesting predictions because it has a linear, SERIAL PROCESSING structure: it is more difficult to produce some information about a person over and above just recognising them, and it is more difficult still to produce a name to a face rather than some other information (occupation, hobby, etc.). These predictions have been borne out in data from errors made in everyday life (Young, Hay and Ellis 1985) and from tightly controlled experiments taking REACTION TIME measures (Young, McWeeny, Hay and Ellis 1986).

Current research has the aim of using computational modelling to test these earlier box-and-arrow theories. Burton, Bruce and Hancock (1999), for instance, have used a statistical technique, PRINCIPAL COMPONENTS ANALYSIS (see s. 8), as the lower-level perceptual tasks of face recognition, and joined it to a simple CONNECTIONIST NETWORK type of system to represent knowledge structures. Although modelling at a more complex level, the ethos is the same as the earlier models – face processing is different for familiar and novel faces, and knowledge structures are important for identifying faces.

Other interesting foci for research includes eyewitness memory and face-bias, with a consensus that people are better at recognising faces from their own race (e.g. Wright, Boyd and Tredoux 2001) and age group (e.g. Wright and Stroud 2002) and work on Capgras delusion (e.g. Ellis and Lewis 2001). Capgras delusion involves the belief that someone has been replaced by an impostor (usually a person or a robot); that is, the person looks the same, but the sufferer believes the person not to be the same. Such peculiar neuropsychological cases suggest that the mechanisms of person identification (in perceptual terms) are distinct from the mechanisms of person recognition (in semantic or emotional terms).

In summary, face recognition is good cognitive psychology in a nutshell. The researchers in this field have worked well in an applied context, making clear applications of their work to eyewitness theory and practice, and they have generated theories with sound EMPIRICAL (see s. 8) evidence from a range of sources: neuropsychology, experimental tasks, diary studies of errors and computational modelling.   *CM*

Bruce, V. and Young, A. W. 1986: Understanding face recognition. *British Journal of Psychology* 77, 305–27. **Burton, A. M., Bruce, V. and Hancock, P. J. B.** 1999: From pixels to people: a model of familiar face recognition. *Cognitive Science* 23, 1–31. **Ellis, H. D. and Lewis, M. B.** 2001: Capgras delusion: a window on face recognition. *Trends in Cognitive Sciences* 149–56. **Wright, D. B., Boyd, C. E. and Tredoux, C. G.** 2001: A field study of own-race bias in South Africa and England. *Psychology, Public Policy, and Law* 7, 119–33. **Wright, D. B. and Stroud, J. N.** 2002: Age differences in lineup identification accuracy: people are better with their own age. *Law and Human Behavior* 26, 641–54. **Young, A. W., Hay, D.C. and Ellis, A. W.** 1985: The faces that launched a thousand slips: everyday difficulties and errors in recognising people. *British Journal of Psychology* 76, 495–523. **Young, A. W., McWeeny, K. H., Hay, D. C. and Ellis, A. W.** 1986: Naming and categorisation latencies for faces and written names. *Quarterly Journal of Experimental Psychology* 38A, 297–318.

fixed reinforcement schedule

In OPERANT CONDITIONING, this is where reinforcers are given at set time intervals (fixed interval) or after a set number of correct performances (fixed ratio). Generally, fixed schedules of reward do not produce as strong conditioning as variable schedules.   *CM*

flashbulb memory

A particularly vivid MEMORY (see s. 1), usually for a public event of great importance. Typically, we will all have a memory for where we were and what we were doing (if we were born) when we heard about the events of 11 September 2001, the death of Diana, Princess of Wales, Margaret Thatcher's resignation or the assassination of President Kennedy. Brown and Kulik (1977) first used the term 'flashbulb' to describe the vividness and detail with which these surprising events are 'burnt' into memory. Knowledge of this sort of powerful memory is not that recent: the first systematic study of memory like this was carried out on memory for the assassination of President Lincoln (Colegrove 1899). Colegrove found that 127 of his 179 participants were able to remember something of the event – which had occurred 33 years before.

The contentious issue in contemporary flashbulb memory literature is whether the memories are special in some way. Brown and Kulik contended that they were, suggesting that when an event is highly novel or unexpected, it is more likely to be of biological importance and thus encoding of the memory involves more of the 'lower' brain areas involved in EMOTION (see s. 6) and flight-or-fight mechanisms. We remember vividly the mundane events surrounding our memory of the news event, because they are given a particular significance to our well-being. It is evolutionarily important to be able to remember well the circumstances of surprising and emotional events.

Neisser (1982) put forward of a strong critique of the concept of flashbulb memories. His argument hinged on the fact that flashbulb memories are prone to distortion, reconstruction and inconsistencies, just like any other memory. If flashbulb memories are produced by a special encoding mechanism, then they should not be prone to error – one should just catch a snapshot of the actual events occurring at the time. Neisser also suggested that

the critical FACTOR (see s. 8) in flashbulb memories is rehearsal. These memories for events have particular social value, and are likely to be repeatedly retrieved and refreshed by news reports and anniversaries. How many times have you re-discussed the events of 11 September 2001? No one debates that flashbulb memories are particularly persistent, vivid memories – they are even intact in ALZHEIMER'S DISEASE.   *CM*

Brown, R. and Kulik, J. 1977: Flashbulb memories. *Cognition* 5, 73–99. **Colegrove, F. W.** 1899: Individual memories. *American Journal of Psychology* 10, 228–55. **Neisser, U.** 1982: Snapshots or benchmarks? In Neisser, U. (ed.), *Memory Observed: Remembering in Natural Contexts*. San Francisco: Freeman.

forgetting

Where we cannot remember something that we once could. Theories of forgetting can be divided into two different camps. One suggests that nothing is actually lost, but interference prevents us accessing the information. The other suggests that information decays slowly over time, in the manner that a hot mug of coffee will gradually lose heat.   *CM*

fovea

The central region of the retina, which offers the highest degree of visual acuity due to densely packed photoreceptor cells.   *AS*

fuzzy logic

A logic based on the idea that propositions can be graded in value, rather than simply being true or false. Degree of truth is represented by a value between 0 (perfectly false) to 1 (perfectly true). It was devised in the 1960s as a technique for analysing situations in which probabilities cannot be determined, and where the combination of probabilities does not follow a predictable pattern. As such, fuzzy logic principles are of interest to those engaged in computational modelling. Clearly, a system that can produce a range of values rather than just have binary states is going to be more flexible and have a higher number of permutations. Fuzzy logic systems are more complex and are also thought to match more closely the sorts of biological changes that occur in living neural systems. Neurones do not only fire or not fire, they can fire at different rates, for example. Fuzzy logic models exist in many domains of cognitive psychology, most notably for perception (Crowther, Batchelder and Hu 1995).   *CM*

Crowther, C. S., Batchelder, W. H. and Hu, X. 1995: A measurement-theoretic analysis of the fuzzy logic model of perception. *Psychological Review* 102, 396–408.

G

geons Basic shape components (e.g. blocks, spheres) that, according to Biederman's theory, can be combined to form all visual object descriptions. *AS*

Gestalt psychology A PARADIGM (see s. 1) for the study of visual PERCEPTION (see s. 1) (not to be confused with Gestalt therapy). The Gestalt school was founded by a group of German psychologists (including Kohler and Wertheimer) in the 1920s, and based itself upon a holistic approach to perceptual organisation. This is encapsulated in the notion that the whole (or, the 'Gestalt') is greater than the sum of its parts. Thus a triangle, for example, is more than a simple arrangement of lines: it has certain qualities that emerge only subsequent to its assembly. The Gestalt psychologists defined a number of principles that govern the organisation of simple elements into coherent wholes, and these can be mostly summarised under the 'Law of Prägnanz', which states that of several possible arrangements, elements will be organised under the one that possesses the most stable and simple shape.

Principles of organisation can be broadly delineated as follows: a) proximity – elements that appear close together (spatially or temporally) tend to be perceived together; b) closure – incomplete figures will be perceived as closed in order to obtain their familiar meaning; c) continuity – similar elements which appear in straight or curved lines will be perceived as a single entity; d) similarity – elements that are alike tend to be perceived as belonging to the same arrangement; e) figure-ground – some aspects of the stimulus will be grouped as the figure, while remaining elements will be perceived as background. Most of these principles are derived from two-dimensional static images, whereas another principle, common fate, applies to moving stimuli: elements that appear to move together (e.g. in the same direction) are grouped. This is demonstrated particularly well in experiments where lights are attached to the joints of an actor, who is filmed in a darkened room.

Observers are unable to make sense of the lights when the actor is still, but once movement is present (e.g. walking) then the stimulus is instantly identifiable as a human being.

Whilst the Gestalt principles make intuitive sense, they are descriptive statements and therefore cannot explain the mechanisms of perceptual organisation. Those explanations that were attempted by the school (i.e. that electrical fields in the brain precisely mirror perceptual events) have long since been discredited. (See also s. 1, GESTALT PSYCHOLOGY) *AS*

goal-directed behaviour Tolman emphasised a LEARNING APPROACH where all human behaviour 'reeks of purpose'. That is, we learn and adapt to the environment in order to fulfil some goal. At about the same time, experimentalists were realising that rats could behave in anticipation of an aversive stimulus (e.g. AVOIDANCE LEARNING). The philosophical notion that our behaviour (like evolution) is guided by purpose, combined with the empirical observation that organisms can anticipate events, led to the theory that higher order cognitions exist in order that organisms can achieve internalised goals. Thus, like MENTAL REPRESENTATION, goal-directed behaviour can be seen as one of the cornerstones of contemporary cognitive psychology.

For the modern psychology student, goal-directed behaviour will most likely be encountered in relation to PROBLEM SOLVING, as typified by means-end analysis. In these kinds of theories, people are focused on what their goals are, and move towards these by setting sub-goals. Problem solving becomes difficult when a sub-goal appears to conflict with the main goal (e.g. the Tower of Hanoi) [see PROBLEM SOLVING]. It is important to note that most day-to-day behaviours can be described in goal and sub-goal routines. I have the goal of drinking a cup of tea. This will involve a series of sub-goals – go downstairs, put the kettle on, find a mug, and so on. It may even include

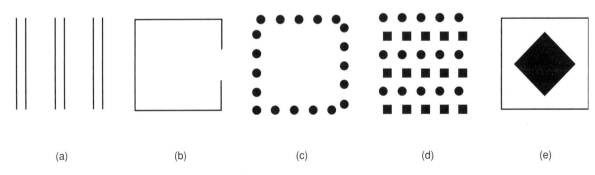

(a)   (b)   (c)   (d)   (e)

Gestalt psychology *Some principles of Gestalt theory.*

some sub-goals that actually, at surface value, take me further from my ultimate goal (e.g. coming back upstairs to get a mug, because I've left all of them for the past week by the side of my bed). Central to cognitive approaches to PSYCHOPATHOLOGY (see s. 7) are the ideas that it is our goal structures that can be dysfunctional, as well as our behav-

iours. For instance, an anorexic's failure to eat could be based on a dysfunctional goal of weighing 6 stone [see COGNITIVE BEHAVIOURAL THERAPY]. *CM*

grapheme A term for the smallest meaningful unit in a writing system. *AT*

H

habituation The process of diminishing response or sensitivity to a repeatedly encountered stimulus. Generally, this is the process of adaptation to events in the environment. Examples include becoming less aware of the intrusion of sound, such as air conditioning or background traffic noise. In the laboratory, studies of habituation are often described as demonstrating desensitisation – where one may be startled by a loud noise on its first presentation, but become progressively less startled by it on successive presentations. This laboratory observation has led to the use of habituation in the desensitisation procedure, where people with PHOBIAS (see s. 7) are treated for their disorder using gradual increments in presentation of the feared stimulus. Developmentally, habituation is an important means of understanding how infants orient their attention to important events. Because of the natural process of habituation, attention can be directed to more important, novel stimuli. (See also s. 4, HABITUATION) *CM*

hemispheric encoding retrieval assymetry (HERA) A description of the pattern of results found for the learning of verbal materials in PET SCANNING. It describes how the left frontal lobe is differentially activated for the encoding of material, whereas in contrast, the right frontal lobe is activated more during retrieval from EPISODIC MEMORY. This is a particularly robust finding, with many studies finding this left-sided encoding, right-sided retrieval pattern (for a review, see Cabeza and Nyberg 1997). However, it is a good illustration of a descriptive theory that has little generalisability. For instance, neuropsychological investigations of left and right frontal-damage patients do not support this asymmetric model. Moreover, if one uses MRI SCANNING and not PET scanning, the pattern disappears completely (although the frontal lobes are important generally, there is no asymmetry). As such, although the model generated much excitement at first, it has not yielded any great new insights into EPISODIC MEMORY function and can be taken as an example of the limitations of neuro-imaging [see discussion under MRI SCANNING].

Two more interesting issues come out of the HERA findings. One is that any verbal stimulus that is ultimately well remembered, regardless of instruction, will yield higher activation in the left frontal lobes when it is first encountered. So, in an incidental memory task, where people are not instructed to study for recall (such as the LEVELS OF PROCESSING task), higher left frontal activations will be seen in the conditions that lead to higher memory performance. Second, on a related note, retrieval from SEMANTIC MEMORY leads to predominantly left frontal activation. This suggests that episodic learning may involve semantic networks, encoding the item on the basis of its meaning, retrieving semantically related information to integrate the episodic memory into. Such observations are a possible way in which PET imaging can inform the cognitive psychologist. *CM*

Cabeza, R. and Nyberg, L. 1997: Imaging cognition: an empirical review of PET studies with normal subjects. *Journal of Cognitive Neuroscience* 9, 1–26.

heuristic A 'rule of thumb' used in PROBLEM SOLVING. Will not always be correct, but is quick and easy. [See ALGORITHM] *ES*

hidden units In a CONNECTIONIST NETWORK, hidden units make a network more flexible and powerful – they are another layer of units between input and output, and thus allow more complex patterns of activation and association. *CM*

human factors The study of man–machine interface. It is the application of information processing to artificial devices such as the layout of an aeroplane's cabin or the knobs on a cooker. *CM*

hypothesis A proposed explanation of facts, a testable assumption or THEORY (see s. 8). (See also s. 8, HYPOTHESIS) *CM*

I

iconic memory   The extremely brief visual store in sensory memory.   *CM*

imagery   Mental imagery occurs when one accesses perceptual information from memory and experiences it in an indirect way (e.g. 'seeing with the mind's eye'). Unlike PERCEPTION (see s. 1), imagery does not require concurrent sensory stimulation, and we can combine and manipulate information in novel ways. The study of imagery has a chequered history, due to its inherently private nature; and the very existence of mental images has been questioned. However, following developments in cognitive psychology and functional imaging, advances have been made in understanding the processes that may be involved. A particular focus has been upon the apparent commonality between imagery and direct perceptual experience, and especially the ways in which imagery engages brain mechanisms that are used in perception and action.

Visual imagery has been the most widely studied modality, and mental rotation provides a good example of these issues. In a typical experiment, participants are presented with an alphanumeric item in either its normal form, or in a mirror-reversed form. The task is then to compare the figure with a rotated version and ascertain whether they represent the same form (or mirror images). Researchers find that the further the test figure has been rotated from upright, the longer participants take to make their judgement. This is taken as evidence for an analogue mental-rotation process that obeys the laws of normal perceptual experience, and suggests that people rotate the image in the same way that they would an object in the real world. The relationship is further accentuated by neuro-imaging studies that report brain activation in visual and motor cortices during mental rotation (see Kosslyn 2001).

Motor images are also seen to be endowed with the same properties as the corresponding motor representation: for example, it has been found that mental simulation of the rotation of one's hand is directly related to actual movement time and the limits of hand joints (Parsons 1994). The fact that mental imagery can activate systems in this way may help to explain the beneficial effects of mental practice (e.g. of a golf swing): imagining movements relies on the same brain areas as performing them, and may therefore be a form of exercise in itself.   *AS*

Kosslyn, S. M. 2001: Neural foundations of imagery. *Nature Reviews Neuroscience* 2, 635–42. **Parsons, L. M.** 1994: Temporal and kinematic properties of motor behaviour reflected in mentally simulated action. *Journal of Experimental Psychology: Human Perception and Performance* 20, 709–30.

implicit learning   Implicit learning typically refers to the learning, without conscious awareness, of a complex rule. In the real world, implicit learning is thought to be the process by which children acquire abstract rules about GRAMMAR (see s. 4) through exposure to LANGUAGE (see

s. 2), and without ever being presented with abstract rules. Most famously, Berry and Broadbent (1984) demonstrated implicit learning by asking participants to manage a hypothetical sugar factory, by changing controls and parameters. They showed that participants gained an implicit knowledge of the rules governing optimal sugar production. That is, they became better and better at carrying out the complex task, but most were not able to report how. Implicit learning is an important demonstration of how information can be processed in the mind without deliberate control, insight or overt organisation. For the experimentalist, it underlies the problems in studying behaviour only through INTROSPECTION (see s. 1) – even complex skilful behaviours can be unavailable for report.   *CM*

Berry, D. C. and Broadbent, D. E. 1984: On the relationship between task performance and associated verbalisable knowledge. *Quarterly Journal of Experimental Psychology* 36A, 209–31.

implicit memory   Memory for a previously encountered stimulus that is not available for conscious report. Mostly, the term is used interchangeably with PROCEDURAL MEMORY, although the term does not tend to be used for all forms of non-declarative memory, such as skills memory. For instance, it would be more normal to describe memory for riding a bike as procedural, rather than implicit, but there is no great distinction in the literature. The wide range of implicit memory phenomena includes PRIMING, with faster reaction times for previously studied items than non-studied items in lexical decision tasks [see SEMANTIC PRIMING]. Other implicit memory demonstrations include perceptual identification, where participants can accurately identify a visually degraded word or picture stimulus, stem completion and fragment completion, and category generation.

Stem completion is where a previously studied word is used to complete a word stem. For instance, if you previously studied the word 'television' on a memory task, you would be much more likely to complete the stem 'tele' to make the word 'television' than 'telephone'. Similarly, fragment completion, a slightly more tricky task, is where you have to fill in the blanks to make a real word, such as 't_l__is__n', which can be completed with 'television'. Category generation is a task where people might be told to study a list of fruits, but rather than being instructed to remember all the ones that they studied (as in EXPLICIT MEMORY tasks), they are asked to write down all the fruits that they can think of. They are more likely to complete this task with fruits that they have just encountered.

The central issue with all these implicit memory tasks is that people need not be able to explicitly remember the item in order to demonstrate their memory. Even though they may not be able to remember 'television', they will be able to complete a task more efficiently where it is the target. There are some methodological issues, such as whether the tasks can be 'contaminated' by explicit memory processes, and some theoretical issues, such as whether the implicit memory is based on processing benefits in perceptual (how it looks) or conceptual (what it means) processes (e.g. Schacter 1994). *CM*

Schacter, D. L. 1994: Priming and multiple memory systems: perceptual mechanisms of implicit memory. In Schacter, D. L. and Tulving, E. (eds) *Memory Systems*. Cambridge MA: MIT Press.

impossible figures   Objects that cannot be physically realised in the real world. Local relations appear correct, but are incongruous across wider areas. *AS*

impossible figures

inductive reasoning   When we engage in inductive reasoning we are making a generalisation from a specific example. We may consider that all swans are white because all the swans we have seen have been white. It would only require us to see one black swan to know that this generalisation is not true (Cygnus atratus is a black swan). Whereas in DEDUCTIVE REASONING one is concerned with what is certain given any piece of information, in inductive reasoning one is concerned with ascertaining what is probable in relation to that information.

Psychologists use Bayes' theorem as the THEORY (see s. 8) by which the performance of participants can be judged as being correct or not on inductive tasks. It is far more common that we engage in inductive reasoning as there are few times when everything is certain. Therefore it is likely that we are often making judgements about probability rather than engaging in deduction. *ES*

inhibition   Inhibition is the suppression or dampening of an active process or stimulus. Freud's concept of REPRESSION (see s. 7) can be thought of as an inhibitory process. Most notably in the area of memory, the study of inhibition has recently come to the fore in cognitive psychology (e.g. Anderson and Bjork 1994). The oft-cited example of an everyday inhibitory process is that of suppressing where you parked your car yesterday, in order to proficiently remember where you parked it today. Other inhibitory tasks consider ironic mental control, such as encapsulated in the white bear task (Wegner 1994). In this task, participants are instructed to free-associate, or think aloud, and told not to think about a white bear. Participants are instructed to ring a bell every time they think of a white bear. Despite being told not to think of them, participants tend to generate white bears as an ironic process set up to check that they are not being thought about. It has been found that intrusions of white bears occur more frequently when someone is given another concurrent task to perform. This suggests that the inhibition of white bears is dependent on executive resources. One of the reasons that inhibition receives so much attention in cognitive research is that a failure of inhibition has been proposed as being central to the cognitive decline shown in older adults (Hasher and Zacks 1988). *CM*

Anderson, M. C. and Bjork, R. A. 1994: Mechanisms of inhibition in long-term memory: a new taxonomy. In Dagenbach, D. and Carr, T. H. (eds) *Inhibitory Processes in Attention, Memory and Language*. San Diego: Academic Press, 265–325. **Hasher, L. and Zacks, R. T.** 1988: Working memory, comprehension, and aging: a review and a new view. In Bower, G. H. (ed.) *The Psychology of Learning and Motivation*. San Diego: Academic Press, vol. 22, 193–225. **Wegner, D. M.** 1994: Ironic processes of mental control. *Psychological Review* 101, 34–52.

insight learning   Nicely captured in the phrase 'a-ha! experience', this is learning by a sudden realisation, as opposed to gradual association. *CM*

instrumental conditioning   [See OPERANT CONDITIONING] *CM*

K

Korsakoff's syndrome Korsakoff's syndrome is a form of AMNESIA caused by long-term alcohol abuse. It is of interest to memory researchers because it is a form of memory loss associated mostly with the thalamus and hippocampus.
CM

L

---

language comprehension   A term for the ability to understand the meaning conveyed by written or spoken LANGUAGE (see s. 2).   *AT*

language production   A term for the ability to produce LANGUAGE (see s. 2) in written or spoken form.   *AT*

law of contiguity   Contiguity refers to the close proximity of two events or stimuli in time or space. This closeness between two events has long been known to be of critical importance in learning associations, and was first reported by Aristotle. More recently, BEHAVIOURISM (see s. 1) explored the parameters by which associations would be made. Of course, simple contiguity is not enough to form an association; otherwise it would not be necessary to reward and shape behaviours in CLASSICAL CONDITIONING and OPERANT CONDITIONING. Of course, we can also make associations between distant events from LONG-TERM MEMORY and events in the present, although some people argue that this is due to an act of retrieval making these two events contiguous in the mind.   *CM*

law of effect   This law, attributed to Thorndike, says that behaviours with good outcomes get repeated, but behaviours with bad outcomes do not get repeated. It is a fundamental law of the LEARNING APPROACH to psychology.   *CM*

learned helplessness   A THEORY (see s. 8) of behaviour in which helplessness (often thought of as DEPRESSION – see s. 7) arises due to the exposure to noxious stimuli from which one cannot escape (e.g. Seligman 1975). This is another concept that was generated from research using the learning approach using animals (see s. 1, BEHAVIOURISM). In a classic experiment, dogs in two groups were given electric shocks. One GROUP (see s. 5) of dogs (X) could exert control and could stop the shock by pressing a lever. The dogs in the second group (Y) could not exert any control over the shock. Dogs were in a yoked control condition: each dog in the X group was paired with a dog in the Y condition so that the dogs received identical levels of electric shocks. The X group learned to avoid the shock by pressing a lever, as predicted by AVOIDANCE LEARNING. Seligman was interested in what this learning experience meant for later behaviour. In a second, crucial part of the experiment, all dogs from both groups encountered electric shocks in a novel situation. In this task, dogs could avoid electric shock by jumping from one compartment to another. The X dogs learned this task easily, but the Y dogs did not learn to avoid the shock. They only lay down and accepted the shocks, whining quietly. The interpretation is that in the initial phase of the experiment the Y dogs learned to be helpless. Interestingly, subsequent work has shown that just a few trials where the Y group dogs *can* avoid shock are enough to prevent learned helplessness developing.

Seligman believed that this type of learning could explain many cases of depression in humans, where the depressed patient can be seen to be impassive to misfortune and difficulty, like the helpless dog. The idea is that the person believes that there is no connection between behaviour and outcomes, and thus there is no point in taking action. This theory is open to debate. In favour of the theory, antidepressant medications that reduce symptoms in humans reduce helplessness in dogs: the animals can learn to avoid electric shock. Those who argue against the theory point out that depression usually includes feelings of self-hatred. If you are truly helpless, and events are beyond your control: why hate yourself?   *CM*

Seligman, M. E. P. 1975: *Helplessness: On Depression, Development, and Death.* San Francisco: Freeman.

learning   A relatively permanent change in behaviour, through experience; an increase in knowledge. For the psychologist, learning is a jargonised term reflecting how an organism responds to the environment to produce changes in behaviour. Learning has also been used as a general approach to understanding complex behaviours [see LEARNING APPROACH]. For most, learning will be almost synonymous with memory, with memory being the result of learning. In fact, many of the stimulus-response type conditioning experiments [see CLASSICAL CONDITIONING and OPERANT CONDITIONING] have human analogues in verbal learning tasks, such as learning lists of paired words (e.g. blue – lotus). Through this focus on memory, learning as the gathering of declarative knowledge has been emphasised, and this is how we think about learning as students. However, we also learn other non-declarative skills, such as driving a car, juggling or swimming. Social learning theory (e.g. Bandura and Walters 1963) contends that social behaviours and PERSONALITY (see s. 1 and s. 6) are the outcomes of learnt behaviours that arise through conditioning.   *CM*

Bandura, A. and Walters, R. H. 1963: *Social Learning and Personality Development.* New York: Holt, Rinehart & Winston.

learning approach   An approach to psychology that focuses on organisms' learning, most often used to refer to the work of the BEHAVIOURISM (see s. 1) movement. Central to the learning approach are the means by which organisms build associations between stimuli and their responses.

In its most extreme form, proponents of this approach argue that there is no need for CONSCIOUSNESS and that humans operate solely on the basis of learned associations between the stimulus and the response they need to make. This idea is captured well in Pavlov's famous study of dogs' salivation, which demonstrates CLASSICAL CONDITIONING. Pavlov showed that dogs learned to associate the sound of the bell (stimulus) with the arrival of their food (response). At first, the dogs salivated only when presented with their food, but after a period of learning they salivated not when the food was presented, but when the bell announcing their food was rung. Thus, they learned a new association between a stimulus and its response. In short, they learnt to associate the sound of a bell with food. In humans, this sort of learning can be harnessed to stop alcoholics from drinking. An emetic (a DRUG – see s. 2 – that makes you nauseous) can be presented at the same time as a drink, so that the alcoholic begins to associate drinking with the feeling of sickness, and so learns not to like alcohol.

Moving on from Pavlov's work on association in classical conditioning, Thorndike and Skinner developed more complex ASSOCIATIVE LEARNING (see s. 2) (OPERANT or INSTRUMENTAL CONDITIONING), where new repertoires of behaviour were learnt for voluntary actions. In classical conditioning, dogs' salivation is an automatic, reflexive action and the dog merely learns to associate this old trick with a new stimulus. In operant conditioning, a new behaviour, such as raising a paw, can be taught to a dog, even though it is not part of the usual behavioural response to a stimulus. Other extremely important behaviourist theories include the LAW OF EFFECT, which, in essence, is the driving force of behaviourism: organisms repeat behaviours with good outcomes but do not repeat behaviours with bad outcomes; and HABITUATION (see also s. 4), whereby organisms become less sensitive to repeatedly encountered stimuli.

Behaviourism was most prominent during the early twentieth century. However, it has been responsible for a number of themes that remain central to the notion of modern psychology. Thorndike, for instance, was a pioneer in using animals in EXPERIMENTS (see s. 8) to infer what basic processes might be at work in humans. Skinner, meanwhile, was determined to rid the science of psychology of 'magical ideas' and focus on the study of what was directly observable. Watson (1924, 1970) nicely summarises these ideas: 'Behaviorism, as I tried to develop it in my lectures at Columbia in 1912 and in my earliest writings, was an attempt to do one thing – to apply to the experimental study of man the same kind of procedure and the same language of description that many research men had found useful for so many years in the study of animals lower than man. We believed then, as we do now, that man is an animal different from other animals only in the types of behaviour he displays' (Watson 1970: 4). Skinner, Watson and Thorndike all advocated the use of an approach that emphasised an organism's response to its environment. This was the foundation of modern experimental psychology: one can make inferences about the internal processes of an organism by considering how it alters its behaviour in response to external factors.

There are numerous criticisms of the learning approach, and although there are many practising researchers who would describe themselves as using behaviourist tasks and theories, the branch of psychology has been largely accommodated into cognitive psychology. As experiments progressed, it became clear that a number of phenomena were not readily explained solely by stimulus-response links. For example, Kohler (1927) studied how chimpanzees solved various problems, with the observation that they suddenly solved problems and by new means. The fact that they could use objects in a novel way suggested that they were not merely working on associations that were pre-existing in the environment: they showed insight. Such INSIGHT LEARNING is evidence

that not all learning is through gradual associative mechanisms. The recognition of insight learning suggested that organisms have internal thought processes, or cognition.

Further evidence against mere stimulus response psychology was to come from studies of rats in mazes by experimentalists such as Tolman. Rat navigation through mazes was largely thought to be due to associative processes such as operant conditioning, where they learnt a route through trial and ERROR (see s. 8) and by gradually acquiring an association between which turn led to where and where the reward was to be found. However, it was found that if the walls of the maze were moved, rats could very quickly and correctly find their way to their reward. If they were working on association alone, rats would be utterly confused by a different configuration of the maze. The fact that they could find their way when the walls changed meant that they had learnt the geography of the maze: they had a COGNITIVE MAP, or a MENTAL REPRESENTATION of the outside world. Moreover, rats could even learn the layout of a maze passively. They could be pulled around the maze in carts, and still learn the route, again suggesting it was unlikely that learning was merely due to associative learning through experience, but rather the generation of an internal representation.

Finally, this approach has led to many applications. CLINICAL PSYCHOLOGY (see s. 1 and s. 7) uses behavioural interventions to alter behaviour. For example, in AUTISM (see s. 6), where children often fail to use appropriate social eye contact, clinical psychologists can use a REWARD SYSTEM (see s. 2) based on operant conditioning to greatly improve behaviour. In this case, a psychologist may present a child with a sweet every time they make appropriate eye contact (e.g. looking in the eye while listening). At first, the child will carry out this behaviour just for reward, but in time, they will learn the association between eye contact and listening, and the sweet reward can be withdrawn. Even 'common-sense' interventions (e.g. where people with arachnophobia are treated by gradually being introduced to spiders) have a sound behaviourist rationale (e.g. Ost et al. 1991). People unlearn negative associations between a stimulus (spider) and response (fear), and in one sense they HABITUATE to the noxious stimulus.   CM

Kohler, W. 1927: *The Mentality of Apes* (2nd edn). New York: Harcourt Brace. **Ost, L. G., Salkovskis, P. M. and Hellstrom, K.** 1991: One-session therapist-directed exposure vs. self-exposure in the treatment of spider phobia. *Behavior Therapy* 22, 407–22. **Watson, J. B.** 1924: *Behaviourism* (1970 edn). New York: W.W. Norton & Company.

levels of processing

Levels of processing THEORY (see s. 8) (Craik and Lockhart 1972) contends that a stimulus that is more deeply encoded will be better remembered than a less deeply encoded stimulus. For example, given a list of words which we are told to process meaningfully, such as judging how pleasant the words are, compared to a list where shallow processing occurs, such as merely counting the number of vowels, memory will be far superior for the words judged for pleasantness, even if there has been no explicit instruction to remember the items. At the time, Craik's levels of processing approach revolutionised the study of memory, because until that point theory had tended to concentrate on memory as the storage of information. Craik's theory, however, suggested that memory was a by-product of processing information and was more about how it was processed than in what hypothetical store it was retained. For everyday life, levels of processing theory indicates the importance of the relationship between meaning and memory. Encounter an important stimulus, even incidentally, and you are more likely to remember it, especially if you spend mental effort relating the information to yourself. *CM*

Craik, F. I. M. and Lockhart, R. S. 1972: Levels of processing: a framework for memory research. *Journal of Verbal Learning and Verbal Behaviour* 11, 671–84.

lexicon In psycholinguistics (see s. 1, LANGUAGE AND PSYCHOLINGUISTICS) the term 'lexicon' is used to refer to a kind of 'mental dictionary' of all the words an individual knows (Aitchison 1994). Each entry in the lexicon is thought to consist of a modality-independent representation of a word's syntactic (what part of speech the word is) and semantic (how the word is interpreted) attributes, as well as its phonological properties (how the word is pronounced and stressed). Rather than comprising an entire listing of every unique word, the standard view is that the lexicon is a listing of all the morphemes (words that cannot be further subdivided) an individual knows. Semantically related words appear to be structurally connected in the lexicon, such that retrieval of one inevitably leads to retrieval of the other (in part or in whole). Neuropsychological data from, for example, anomic patients (who experience word-finding difficulties) suggest we have separate input (recognition) and output (production) lexicons. *AT*

Aitchison, J. 1994: *Words in the Mind: An Introduction to the Mental Lexicon* (2nd edn). Oxford: Blackwell.

light A form of electromagnetic radiation. Particles travel in a straight line, releasing light energy (photons) as they strike other particles. *AS*

local representation In computational modelling, this is where one unit represents one entire concept or meaningful entity. This is as opposed to DISTRIBUTED REPRESENTATION. *CM*

logogens Small units of verbal information. (Imagens, much less frequently discussed, are small units of non-verbal information.) Such units explain how a concept like 'table' links up with its phonological and lexical information. *CM*

long-term memory A general term for the store of any material that is not in SHORT-TERM MEMORY, primary memory or WORKING MEMORY. [See EPISODIC MEMORY, SEMANTIC MEMORY, PROCEDURAL MEMORY, DECLARATIVE MEMORY and IMPLICIT MEMORY, all of which are constituents of long-term memory in one framework or another] *CM*

long-term potentiation (LTP) A cellular model of memory formation, based on brain plasticity. The most basic and earliest model of how NEURONES (see s. 2) represent memories is Hebbian learning (see s. 2, HEBBIAN SYNAPSE). Hebb's law states that if one SYNAPSE (see s. 2) is active, and another neurone connected to it is also active, then the link between the two will be strengthened [see also CONNECTIONISM]. LTP works along a similar line: there is a long-term cellular change on the basis of a cell's activation. Working in the rabbit brain, Bliss and Lomo (1973) found that brief stimulation of one part of the hippocampus led to long-term increases in the excitation of connected synapses in other parts of the brain, confirming Hebb's earlier ideas. To demonstrate the role of LTP in memory, researchers chemically blocked the LTP process in the hippocampus of mice, with the result that learning was impaired (but see Saucier and Cain 1995 for conflicting evidence). Research into LTP is ongoing, and it is still hoped that it may provide a sound biological/physiological basis for LONG-TERM MEMORY. (See also s. 2, LONG-TERM POTENTIATION) *CM*

Bliss, T. V. P. and Lomo, T. 1973: Long-lasting potentiation of synaptic transmission in the dentate area of the anaesthetized rabbit following stimulation of the preforant pathway. *Journal of Physiology – London* 232, 331–56. **Saucier, D. and Cain, D. P.** 1995: Spatial learning without NMDA receptor-dependent long-term potentiation. *Nature* 378, 186–9.

M

mach bands An edge-enhancement VISUAL ILLUSION. Uniform bands appear to change in brightness at the region near a lighter or darker band. *AS*

mach bands

magno cells A class of ganglion cells characterised by large RECEPTIVE FIELDS, high-contrast sensitivity, and selectivity for form and movement information. *AS*

Marr's computational theory A general THEORY (see s. 8) of cognition that states that one needs to understand three different levels of explanation (Marr 1982). These three explanations are the computational, algorithmic and hardware levels. For a car, you could describe it at the computational level (its function, to get you from A to B), at the algorithmic level (the operations of the spark plug, the importance of the explosive fuel-air mixture) and the hardware level (the components, such as tyres, spark plugs, radiator). Marr used his theory to describe human PERCEPTION (see s. 1).

Somewhat separately, Marr also explains how the process of perceiving an image on the retina gives rise to three different levels of representation: the primal sketch, the 2½D sketch and the 3D model. The primal sketch is the most basic, with just 2D patterns of light and dark, with edges and basic shapes [see SINE-WAVE GRATING]. The 2½D sketch adds information about depth and orientation of surfaces, but is still a representation based on the observer's point of view. The 3D sketch is the most complete representation of the scheme, describing objects in the environment and their relation to each other, without recourse to the observer's viewpoint. This is a crucial perceptual operation, since it explains how we can recognise familiar objects from novel angles, which is particularly important for models of FACE RECOGNITION. The perceiver builds up a MENTAL REPRESENTATION of the scene following input from these three stages. *CM*

Marr, D. 1982: *Vision: A Computational Investigation into the Human Representation and Processing of Visual Information.* San Francisco: W. H. Freeman.

masking In PERCEPTION (see s. 1) experiments, masking is the covering of one stimulus with another, with the result of making the first more difficult to perceive. *CM*

massed practice This is where to-be-remembered information is repeatedly rehearsed over a short period of time, and typically with no other intervening activity. It results in memory performance far poorer than DISTRIBUTED PRACTICE. *CM*

mental representation The central construct to cognitive psychology, mental representation contends that knowledge about the world is reproduced in some form in the mind. The need to think in terms of mental representation largely arose from work such as Tolman's on how rats navigate in mazes. The fact that rats could proficiently navigate through a maze even when the layout of the maze was changed suggested that the rats were not just storing a programmed sequence of directions. Moreover, the fact that rats did not need to actively navigate through the maze but could also learn the correct route through passive observation also indicated that the rat was creating a COGNITIVE MAP, not just a complex sequence of stimulus-response links. This idea gradually led to the cognitive revolution, and the study of thought as flows of information and internal representations of the outside world. So much so that clinical psychologists often use the term 'cognitive' to refer to people's mental representations. The concept has allowed CLINICAL PSYCHOLOGY (see s. 1 and s. 7) to move beyond mere manipulation of behaviour, by considering how an individual's representation of the world may be pathological. *CM*

metacognition Generally, thinking about thinking. Metacognition refers to the higher order cognitive thoughts that coordinate proficient information processing. The study of metacognition has largely focused on memory, such as the processes by which we regulate cognition in order to improve our memory. Nelson and Narens (1990) present a framework of metacognition consisting of two flows of information between the object level (the stimulus in the environment) and the meta-level (the MENTAL REPRESENTATION) of the item. These flows are monitoring (where the object level informs the meta-level) and control (where the meta-level modifies the object level). For instance, when studying for an exam, we will have an idealised notion of performance (at the meta-level) and we will have some to-be-learned material (at the object level). We will monitor our learning of the material and control it through allocating more or less study or effort. Thus, through metacognition, we will reflect on our performance and modify behaviour accordingly, terminating study when monitoring tells us that information is well learnt. *CM*

Nelson, T. O. and Narens, L. 1990: Metamemory: a theoretical framework and some new findings. In Bower, G. H. (ed.) *The Psychology of Learning and Motivation.* San Diego: Academic Press, vol. 26.

misinformation effect An extremely famous effect, reported by Elizabeth Loftus, whereby memory for an event is changed by the subsequent questions asked about the event. *CM*

mnemonic A device or thought that is used to improve one's memory. OIL RIG is a popular mnemonic used in chemistry – representing Oxygen Is Loss, Reduction Is Gain. *CM*

modus ponens A form of logical statement, which affirms. For example: If Monday is the 4th, then Friday must be the 7th. Monday is the 4th. Therefore, Friday is the 7th. *CM*

modus tollens A form of logical statement, based on indirect proof. For example: If it had rained this morning, then the grass would still be wet. But the grass is not wet. Therefore, it did not rain this morning. *CM*

monocular cue A perceptual cue that gives an impression of depth or distance which is not to do with both eyes working together (e.g. things look smaller when they are further away). *CM*

MRI scanning Magnetic resonance imaging. MRI is an imaging or brain scanning technique which uses water molecules' reaction to being in an extremely strong magnetic field to measure densities of brain tissue, oxygenation of blood or blood flow in the brain. In fMRI studies, the 'f' stands for functional; in this case, it measures the brain's reaction to being involved in a particular task or function. For most, the implication is that by studying the tiny but significant differences in blood flow associated with an event, it is possible to build or test models of how the mind works. For instance, fMRI studies have indicated that the frontal lobes of the brain are used in checking responses to a MEMORY (see s. 1) task, and can be thought of as organising and monitoring memory retrieval. Although fMRI and other imaging techniques are undoubtedly revolutionising our understanding of the brain, and what different brain regions are associated with which different cognitive functions, the approach is not without its critics. For instance, many argue that we do not understand enough yet about behaviour and function alone, so we may not be asking the right questions and designing the right experiments when we have people in the brain scanner. Another problem is that we still do not know what a particular 'activation' means. The brain may well have increased blood flow to a particular area, but how does that translate into feelings or PERCEPTIONS (see s. 1) , or even the storage of memories?

For the most part, MRI methodologies are a powerful means of testing theories: if two different cognitive processes stem from activations in two distinct regions, it can be thought of as converging evidence, support for the cognitive theory. Popular studies using MRI methodologies include one which considers the neural basis of romantic love (Bartels and Zeki 2000), and another, which uses volumetric MRI, demonstrates the relationship between size of the hippocampus and route knowledge in London taxi drivers (Maguire et al. 2003). *CM*

Bartels, A. and Zeki, S. 2000: The neural basis of romantic love. *Neuroreport* 11, 3829–34. **Maguire, E. A., Spiers, H. J., Good, C. D., Hartley T., Frackowiak, R. S. and Burgess, N.** 2003: Navigation expertise and the human hippocampus: a structural brain imaging analysis. *Hippocampus* 13, 250–9.

N

negative priming In standard priming PARADIGMS (see s. 1), there is a benefit in processing performance as a result of previously processing a related experience. In negative priming, the effect is reversed. Negative priming is the decrease in performance caused by previously having to *not* respond to a stimulus. For instance, if you are asked on one trial to name a picture of a tree, but ignore a picture of a dog, you will be slower on the next trial if asked to name the picture of a dog and ignore a picture of a car. Experiments on negative priming are important because its existence demonstrates the need for INHIBITION in ATTENTION and MEMORY (see s. 1) systems. That is, our attention is slower to return to a location or idea that it previously has had to ignore or avoid. *CM*

nonword A term for an item that has no meaning but has the correct structure to be a word in a given language. *AT*

O

operant conditioning Usually synonymous with INSTRUMENTAL CONDITIONING, this is the process of learning a new behaviour through reinforcement, generally attributed to Skinner. In contrast to CLASSICAL CONDITIONING, in operant conditioning the behaviour produced is new, and not part of the animal's usual repertoire. For instance, a dog will always salivate to food – but you can make it salivate to another stimulus (classical conditioning). Dogs will not normally stop at the edge of one surface or another, but you can train them through rewards to not stray from the kerb, off the pavement and into the road. Staying on the pavement is not part of a dog's behavioural repertoire normally, but it can certainly acquire this behaviour.

The main experimental distinction is that in classical conditioning, the reinforcer always follows every stimulus, until the association is learnt. In operant conditioning, the reinforcer is only given for the desired response. In this way, it is possible to 'shape' behaviour, by rewarding only certain behaviours, which is how the dog could learn, for example, to answer the phone, or not to stray into the road. The mechanism behind this learning is the LAW OF EFFECT.

In an experimental situation, an organism is given free reign to behave in any manner. When it does something that is desirable, such as accidentally press the red button in its cage (UNCONDITIONED RESPONSE), it will be given a food reward. Gradually, it will learn the association between the red button and the food, and when learning is complete, the button press can be described as the CONDITIONED RESPONSE. It was exactly in this manner that Thorndike first studied animal learning, examining how long a cat took to escape from a 'puzzle box' by pulling a piece of string to gain a reward of food outside the box. Skinner developed this idea, using cages that contained stimuli and reward mechanisms, so that escape was not part of the learning process – a Skinner box. For humans, operant conditioning can be seen as the mechanism by which we gain many voluntary behaviours, learn new ways of thinking and skills. Parents will shape a child's behaviour by rewarding good behaviours and punishing bad behaviours in exactly the same way that rats can be conditioned in Skinner boxes. Operant conditioning, a more powerful explanation of complex behaviours than classical conditioning, is central to BEHAVIOURISM (see s. 1) and the LEARNING APPROACH. *CM*

P

parallel processing Information processing can be described as either SERIAL PROCESSING or parallel processing. Crudely, this considers whether we can perform two or more tasks at once, or only one after the other. For instance, popular belief is that men are particularly poor at conducting two tasks at once, whereas women can multi-task, and are thus capable of parallel processing. There is some element of automaticity [see AUTOMATIC] in parallel processing, with one or more tasks being controlled outside the focus of ATTENTION. Where tasks are conflicting, or use similar cognitive resources, processing will have to be serial, as attention moves from one task to the next. For those interested in modelling human behaviour, a major consideration will be whether operations occur serially or in parallel. *CM*

partial reinforcement A schedule of reinforcement in OPERANT CONDITIONING where the desired response is only sometimes rewarded. *CM*

parvo cells A class of ganglion cells characterised by small RECEPTIVE FIELDS, low-contrast sensitivity and selectivity for colour-opponent information. *AS*

patient HM One of the most famous cases in psychology, HM was an amnesic patient. He had severe epilepsy as a boy in the 1940s and did not respond well to standard treatment. In 1953, he underwent a temporal lobotomy, removing part of his temporal lobe – the area around (and including) the hippocampus. This surgical procedure was carried out in order to reduce epileptic symptoms; surgeons had recently discovered that removing part of the brain involved in epileptic seizures reduced the symptoms significantly. Although HM's epileptic symptoms were reduced somewhat, he was left with a profound MEMORY (see s. 1) disorder. HM has become a one-man focus for research into memory. Presumably this is partly because his was a relatively pure and well-defined LESION (see s. 2) within the brain (unlike head injury amnesics), but it must also partly be due to the fact that HM was prepared to patiently endure so many memory tests; the field is indebted to him.

HM had, for the most part, ANTEROGRADE AMNESIA, where he could not acquire new memories, even though he could remember events prior to his surgery. He was not, however, impaired generally: LANGUAGE (see s. 2) and intellectual function were above average, and actually better after surgery than before. At the time, the two most interesting facts about HM's memory impairment were that his SHORT-TERM MEMORY seemed intact (he could repeat a series of digits immediately), but his long-term retention was virtually nil; and also that he could not recall instances of previous test sessions, but he could 'learn' new procedural tasks like mirror drawing.

The fact that his short-term memory (STM) was intact but LONG-TERM MEMORY (LTM) was impaired led to the conclusion that HM failed to transfer information from STM to LTM, and therefore that the hippocampus was involved in memory consolidation. This fitted well into the contemporary THEORY (see s. 8), Atkinson and Shiffrin's (1968) modal model, whereby information flows from a sensory register into short-term storage and then into long-term storage. This idea has largely been discredited, since there are also patients who have intact LTM, but impaired STM (e.g. Basso et al. 1982). This DOUBLE DISSOCIATION suggests that LTM and STM must be two separate systems. HM also showed intact PROCEDURAL MEMORY, but impaired DECLARATIVE MEMORY, supporting the notion of two distinct memory systems, and the role of the hippocampus in rising memory to conscious awareness (see Corkin 2002). This idea has proved more robust, and data from HM still contributes a lot to this IMPLICIT MEMORY literature.

For more about memory impairment and HM, see AMNESIA. *CM*

Atkinson, R. C. and Shiffrin, R. M. 1968: Human memory: a proposed system and its control processes. In K. W. Spence and J. T. Spence (eds), *The Psychology of Learning and Motivation* vol. 2, New York: Academic Press. **Basso, A., Spinnler, H., Vallar, G. and Zanobio, M. E.** 1982: Left hemisphere damage and selective impairment of auditory-verbal short-term memory. *Neuropsychologia* 20, 263–74. **Corkin, S.** 2002: What's new with the amnesic patient HM? *Nature Reviews Neuroscience* 3, 153–60.

perspective A monocular (or pictorial) cue to depth PERCEPTION (see s. 1) based upon distortion of the image as a function of viewing position. *AS*

PET scanning Positron emission tomography scanning is a neuro-imaging technique that involves injecting a radioactive isotope into the blood stream and then measuring blood flow in the brain using x-ray technology. PET scanning, as opposed to fMRI SCANNING, has poorer temporal resolution, but better spatial resolution. This means that it is better at isolating structures in the brain, but much worse at unearthing the time course of activity in the brain. One of the major findings to come out of PET scanning was the HEMISPHERIC ENCODING RETRIEVAL ASYMMETRY effect, but it has great applications in all areas of cognition. Of course, many of the arguments against MRI scanning can be applied to PET studies. For a review of PET findings in cognitive neuroscience, consider Cabeza and Nyberg (2000). *CM*

Cabeza, R. and Nyberg, L. 2000: Imaging cognition II: an empirical review of 275 PET and fMRI studies. *Journal of Cognitive Neuroscience* 12, 1–47.

Phineas Gage Like PATIENT HM, Phineas Gage is a famous case in cognitive neuropsychology. However, unlike HM, Phineas Gage did not take part in a series of EXPERIMENTS (see s. 8) and inform contemporary THEORY (see s. 8). Phineas Gage received his famous injury in September 1848, over 30 years before the start of psychology (Wundt's laboratory was created in 1879). Phineas

Gage was a railway construction worker at the level of foreman who, in an accidental explosion, survived a metre-long iron bar being speared clean through his head, allegedly landing about 9 metres behind him. The bar destroyed most of the frontal lobes of his brain, particularly on the left side (Macmillan 2000a). This event left Phineas Gage with a marked PERSONALITY (see s. 1 and s. 6) change and presumably little or no intellectual impairment. His friends described him as 'No longer Gage'. Gage was evidently an efficient foreman pre-morbidly. After the injury he was fitful, irreverent and unable to settle on any of the many plans he devised, but he continued to work, although not at the level of a foreman. Phineas Gage died in 1860.

It is almost certainly the case that most textbook reports of Gage include inaccuracies and exaggerations of his case and descriptions of his pathology (Macmillan 2000b), because simply, not enough contemporary reports of his case exist. For instance, there is no documentary support to the popular notion that he became a drunkard and sexually disinhibited after the injury. He has been an extremely inspiring (but not insightful) patient because many of the descriptions of his behaviour (whether true or not) are consistent with current views of frontal lobe dysfunction [see DYSEXECUTIVE SYNDROME]. He has undoubtedly done more for spicing up the teaching of psychology than he has for the understanding of the human mind. Possibly the most remarkable thing about Gage is that he survived the accident at all.   *CM*

Macmillan, M. 2000a: *An Odd Kind of Fame: Stories of Phineas Gage.* Cambridge MA: MIT Press. **Macmillan, M.** 2000b: *Restoring Phineas Gage: a 150th retrospective. Journal of the History of the Neurosciences* 9, 46–66.

phoneme A term for the smallest unit of sound that distinguishes one word from another in a language.   *AT*

phonemic restoration effect A psycholinguistic term for the phenomenon of 'filling in' missing sounds when listening to spoken words, although unaware of doing so.   *AT*

phonemic similarity effect A term for the deleterious effect on SHORT-TERM MEMORY capacity of memory items sharing common phonemes.   *AT*

phonological mediation Where written forms must be converted into speech before meaning is achieved. *CM*

pixel The smallest unit of PERCEPTION (see s. 1). An image can be thought of as comprised of numerous pixels.   *CM*

pop-out Efficient detection, in VISUAL SEARCH, of a target defined by a single feature. REACTION TIME is independent of display size.   *AS*

power function A law which mathematically describes the magnitude of a physical entity and its resultant sensory intensity.   *CM*

practice For the cognitive psychologist, practice can be conceptualised as the repetition of processing with the aim of improving performance. In the study of EXPERTISE,

it has long been known that massive levels of practice are necessary to become skilled at an action. Fitts (1964) provides a model of skill acquisition describing how practice leads to qualitatively different performance, starting with deliberate wilful actions, and resulting in quick, efficient, automatic stimulus-response associations. In the study of memory, it has long been known (since the late nineteenth century) that DISTRIBUTED PRACTICE rather than MASSED PRACTICE leads to greater benefits to memory. Distributed practice is where items are practised at spaced intervals with intervening tasks, whereas massed practice is where repetition happens all at once. Thus, it is best not to cram for your exams.   *CM*

Fitts, P. M. 1964: *Perceptual motor skill learning. In Melton, A. W. (ed.) Categories of Human Learning.* New York: Academic Press.

primacy Superior MEMORY (see s. 1) for the first part of a list of words, or more generally the first part of any set or sequence (see figure).   *CM*

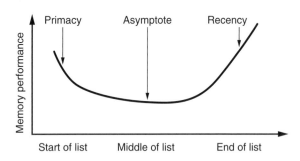

primacy *A serial position curve, showing memory performance for a list of words.*

priming The term priming comes from the idea of making ready for action – in the way that a pump is primed ready to produce water, by the first few movements of the handle filling the pump with water before it is actually produced. In cognitive psychology, priming is the benefit to processing one stimulus as a result of already having encountered that stimulus or one similar. In semantic priming, one would show a benefit (faster REACTION TIME) in making a decision about whether 'horse' was an animal or not if they had been primed with the word 'pony' rather than being primed with an unrelated word. In phonological priming, one would be quicker to produce the word 'horse' if one had just been primed with the rhyming word 'course' (e.g. Rastle and Coltheart 1999). These experimental findings suggest that information is organised in the mind on the basis of LANGUAGE (see s. 2) sounds and semantic information.

Repetition priming is a behavioural change associated with the repeated processing of a stimulus and, like HABITUATION (see also s. 4), shows how the mind is geared up to learn and to respond differently to novel stimuli. Repetition priming is a manifestation of IMPLICIT MEMORY. Priming has often been used subliminally, where people can be given cues that they are not consciously aware of that nonetheless affect future performance.

For the most part, priming is an experimental tool for understanding how the mind is organised (e.g. Henson 2003). Priming is one of the main tasks at the disposal of the experimental psychologist, but it has also been harnessed to try to improve performance in people with cognitive dysfunction. For example, repetition priming and semantic priming have been combined to successfully improve naming objects in ANOMIA (e.g. Cornelissen et al. 2003). (See also s. 5, PRIMING) *CM*

Cornelissen, K., Laine, M., Tarkiainen, A. et al. 2003: Adult brain plasticity elicited by anomia treatment. *Journal of Cognitive Neuroscience* 15: 444–61. **Henson, R. N. A.** 2003: Neuroimaging studies of priming. *Progress in Neurobiology* 70, 53–81. **Rastle, K. and Coltheart, M.** 1999: Lexical and non-lexical phonological priming in reading aloud. *Journal of Experimental Psychology-Human Perception and Performance* 25, 461–481.

problem solving The study of problem solving in psychology has its beginnings in the Gestalt school. Gestalt psychologists established many early principles of problem solving, many of which are considered relevant today. Much of this research was conducted during the early twentieth century and was discredited during the rise of BEHAVIOURISM (see s. 1). It was not until the cognitive revolution of the late twentieth century that problem solving was once again studied extensively. Many of the ideas from GESTALT PSYCHOLOGY have been reinterpreted within the information-processing PARADIGM (see s. 1).

Ironically, early research within problem solving was based on the work of one of the great behaviourists: Thorndike. He had noted that a cat could escape from a 'puzzle box' with increasing speed over time. Successful escape from a puzzle box required the cat to hit a pole in the box. Initially the animal thrashed around aimlessly until chancing upon the pole. Over many trials the animal would learn that hitting the pole was the key and eventually would go straight to the pole and escape. Thus it appeared that early explanations of problem solving relied on trial-and-error behaviour. Much of the work of the Gestalt psychologists looked at such trial-and-error routes to problem solving. Early work conducted by Kohler on apes led to claims that problems could be restructured and this involved some form of 'insight' that led to the correct solution. Kohler watched an ape reach a banana that was outside its cage by using two sticks joined together. This occurred after a period of contemplation, hence it was argued that there had been some thinking that had led to the insight.

The notions of insight and restructuring form the basis of the Gestalt approach. The approach suggests that problem solving can take two forms – it can be reproductive or productive. Reproductive behaviour relies on the problem solver using prior experience and this can hinder problem solving. Productive problem solving, on the other hand, is where there is insight and the problem is restructured in a productive manner.

These concepts can help us to explain the behaviour that we observe in a classic problem: Duncker's (1945) candle problem. In this task the participant is presented with a candle, a box of tacks and a book of matches, among other things. The task is to fix the candle to the wall in such a way that wax will not drip onto the floor (this means that banging a six-inch nail through the candle and into the lab wall is *not* the correct solution!). Here we observe classic reproductive behaviour, characterised by what Duncker referred to as 'functional fixedness'. The correct solution requires participants to empty the box of tacks, fix it to the wall and use it as a platform to support the candle. Duncker explained poor performance by arguing that participants became fixated on the function of the box (holding tacks). Thus the reproductive behaviour (using what has been seen before – that tack boxes hold tacks) inhibits the correct solution.

The Gestalt ideas were innovative and are attractive in terms of their intuitive appeal – we have all experienced the solution of problems that seem to involve some sudden 'a-ha' type experience or insight that allows us to view the problem (and its solution) in a restructured manner. However, as scientific constructs, the concepts of insight and restructuring are weak. They lack any clear definition and thus elude testing.

One of the great successes in cognitive psychology is the problem space theory of Newell and Simon (1972). In essence, the theory is quite simple but it accounts for masses of the data that have been collected on problem solving. The theory and its ideas are well illustrated using a common example – the Tower of Hanoi problem (see Figure).

In the Tower of Hanoi problem participants must move from the initial state to the goal state (as shown in Figure). At no time must a large disc be placed on a smaller disc and only one disc can be moved at a time. Newell and Simon argued that there are mental states that relate to these actual states. Thus there is an initial knowledge state and an initial goal state and there are mental operators – these are the legal moves that can be made from wherever the participant is in the problem at that time. From the initial state we can see that there are two possible moves: the small disc can move to the middle peg or the end peg; from here the middle disc could move to the end peg or

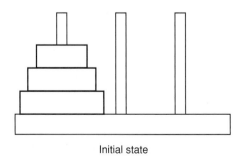

Initial state

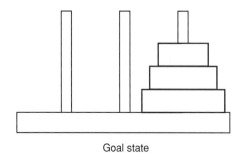

Goal state

problem solving *The Tower of Hanoi problem.*

the middle peg (depending on where the first disc has gone to). As more moves are made there are more alternatives available. The result of all of this is that there is a whole space of possible states through which a problem solver can move. This is the problem space.

Newell and Simon suggested that when solving problems people use HEURISTICS. These are short cuts that may not always give the correct solution but usually do and are low on cognitive effort. The most important of these is means-ends analysis. This is simply noting the difference between the current state and the goal state, creating a sub-goal that reduces that difference and then applying the appropriate operator to achieve the sub-goal. Egan and Greeno (1974) found evidence to support means-ends analysis through exposing participants to a three- and four-disc version of the task before giving them a five-disc version (the problem space here is very large). Participants showed benefits from prior exposure because it helped them establish sub-goals.

It should be noted that while problem space theory can account for much of the laboratory work on problem solving, one can question its generality. Problems used in the laboratory are well-defined problems in that their initial state and goal state are clear. Unfortunately, in the real world, problems are not always so clear and are thus referred to as ill-defined problems. *ES*

Duncker, K. 1945: On problem solving (translated by L. S. Lees). *Psychological Monographs* 58(270). **Egan, D. W. and Greeno, J. G.** 1974: Theories of rule induction: knowledge acquired in concept learning, serial pattern learning and problem solving. In Gregg, W. G. (ed.) *Knowledge and Cognition*. Hillsdale NJ: Lawrence Erlbaum Associates Inc. **Newell, A. and Simon, H. A.** 1972: *Human Problem Solving*. Englewood Cliffs NJ: Prentice-Hall.

procedural memory Procedural memory is strictly speaking memory for skills and procedures, sometimes referred to as 'knowing how'. It should be thought of as the opposing store to DECLARATIVE MEMORY, as part of Cohen and Squire's (1980) conception of LONG-TERM MEMORY. Because procedural memory is not available for conscious report, the term is often used interchangeably with IMPLICIT MEMORY and is also sometimes called non-declarative memory, in order to emphasise the distinction from declarative memory. Examples include knowing how to ride a bike, how to play the piano and being able to remember your PIN number at a cashpoint only by the sequence of finger movements on the pad. Interestingly, in many amnesic disorders, including ALZHEIMER'S DISEASE, skills such as ballroom dancing are well retained. *CM*

Cohen, N. J. and Squire, L. R. 1980: Preserved learning and retention of pattern analysing skill in amnesia using perceptual learning. *Cortex* 17, 273–8.

propositional reasoning REASONING based on the relationship between propositions.

[See also DEDUCTIVE REASONING, INDUCTIVE REASONING and SYLLOGISM] *CM*

prosody A term for the patterns of stress and intonation in a language. *AT*

prospective memory Memory to carry out a future action. This particular type of memory can be thought of as our ability to remember an appointment in three weeks' time, the memory for the items that you wish to buy on your way home from work, and your representation of the intention to phone your mother once you have finished eating dinner. As such, it is clearly an important part of everyday life, and somewhat proportionately underresearched in comparison to work on retrospective memory. One significant laboratory finding characterises our knowledge of prospective memory: the intention superiority effect, where to-be-performed actions are more highly activated in memory than other actions (e.g. Dockree and Ellis 2001). Neuropsychologically, prospective memory appears to be a task that requires planning aspects of the frontal lobes (Daum and Mayes 2000), since patients with frontal lobe dysfunction are highly susceptible to difficulties in this area of cognition. *CM*

Daum, I. and Mayes, A. R. 2000: Memory and executive function impairments after frontal or posterior cortex lesions. *Behavioural Neurology* 12, 161–73. **Dockree, P. M. and Ellis, J. A.** 2001: Forming and canceling everyday intentions: implications for prospective remembering. *Memory and Cognition* 29, 1139–45.

prototype The best exemplar of a category, the most typical example of class of things. An apple is a prototypical fruit, as is an orange. A kumquat is definitely not. *CM*

pseudoword Another term for a NONWORD, an item that could be a real word in a given language but has no meaning. *AT*

puzzle box A device associated with Thorndike, where an animal has to escape from a box to receive a reward. Most famously, it was a cat in a box with a door that was released by a piece of string or pole hanging down. *CM*

R

reaction time (RT) The whole of experimental psychology can be thought of as resting on two main measures of function – ERRORS (see s. 8) and reaction times. Cattel is often credited as the first to measure thought processes using reaction time, before which time psychological measurement had relied on subjective report. For the experimentalist, reaction time can be used as an index of depth of processing or automaticity (see s. 5) [see AUTOMATIC]. For instance, psychological theories about FACE RECOGNITION have used evidence from reaction time EXPERIMENTS (see s. 8) to show that people take longer to name a person when given a face than to give a fact about that person (Young, McWeeny, Hay and Ellis 1986). This suggests that naming a face is processed later in the face recognition system than semantic information. Alternatively, long and short RTs in the Stroop task [see STROOP EFFECT], for example, indicate processing which is effortful and subject to interference (long RT) and automatic (short RT). Finally, RT measures have been used to show how words in the lexicon are stored and processed according to the age at which we first encountered them (Morrison, Ellis and Quinlan 1992).   *CM*

Morrison, C. M., Ellis, A. W. and Quinlan, P. T. 1992: Age of acquisition, not word-frequency, affects object naming, not object recognition. *Memory and Cognition* 20, 705–14. **Young, A. W., McWeeny, K. H., Hay, D. C. and Ellis, A. W.** 1986: Naming and categorisation latencies for faces and written names. *Quarterly Journal of Experimental Psychology* 38A, 297–318.

reasoning There are two types of reasoning: inductive and deductive. There are many definitions of both of these, but in order to distinguish between them the following definition from Garnham and Oakhill (1994) will be used: An inductive process leads to an increase in semantic information whereas a deductive process does not, deduction makes explicit what was previously implicit.

The study of reasoning in humans has a history far greater than that of cognitive psychology. Over 2000 years ago, Aristotle considered the nature of human reasoning and the way that we think has occupied philosophers and psychologists ever since. The psychological study of reasoning can be dated back to the work of Peter Wason in the early 1960s (although there had been some work on syllogistic reasoning [see SYLLOGISM] before this). The standard approach by psychologists interested in reasoning is to consider the reasoning that is observed in humans and then to compare this to the dictates of formal logic. We then look to see whether there is any DEVIATION (see s. 8) from logic. Many psychologists have noted that our ability to reason is the one thing that makes us distinct from animals (Garnham and Oakhill 1994), but psychology has often shown that deductive reasoning does deviate from that which logic would say is correct. Although there have been many studies on the nature and accuracy of deductive processes and there are contrasting findings, there is some consistent evidence. The evidence shows that while we find some valid inferences easy (such as MODUS PONENS) others are hard and made less frequently (MODUS TOLLENS). In addition to this, we often endorse invalid inferences such as affirmation of the consequent and denial of the antecedent (see Evans, Newstead and Byrne 1993).

The study of INDUCTIVE REASONING is not so straightforward as there is really no formal normative THEORY (see s. 8) that can be used as an INDEPENDENT (see s. 8) assessment of 'correctness'. However, as much of what is classed as induction involves the ability to compute probability accurately, much of the work has centred on probability theory. Work in this area is also closely linked to the study of PROBLEM SOLVING.   *ES*

Garnham, A. and Oakhill, J. V. 1994: *Thinking and Reasoning.* Oxford: Blackwell. **Evans, J. St. B. T., Newstead, S. E. and Byrne, R. M. J.** 1993: *Human Reasoning: The Psychology of Deduction.* Hove: Lawrence Erlbaum Associates Ltd.

recall Recall is the reproduction of previously encountered information. As a measure of LONG-TERM MEMORY, it is often compared with RECOGNITION.   *CM*

recency As opposed to PRIMACY, the superior memory for the last portion of a list, or set of items, events, etc. (See Figure under PRIMACY)   *CM*

receptive field A region of the retina that affects the firing rate of a given nerve cell when stimulated by light. Photoreceptors in the vertebrate retina are grouped into functional units, and individual cells in the visual system code particular changes in light intensity through their output. Some spatial regions are selectively excited by an increment in light intensity, whereas other regions are excited by a decrement. These regions are typically circular, and can be combined to form a receptive field that is selective for increments of light in its centre, and for decrements in the surround zone (known as centre-on), or vice versa (centre-off). The responses of each region oppose each other and form an efficient means of detecting contours from variations in luminance: for example, cells in primary visual cortex have receptive fields with elongated zones and are organised to respond particularly well to bars of an appropriate orientation. [See SINE WAVE GRATING]   *AS*

recognition Recognition is the correct identification, on re-encountering it, of a previously encountered stimulus. It is often compared with RECALL, with the finding that recognition for materials is much better. For instance, in EYEWITNESS MEMORY, you may find it difficult to remember the face of a perpetrator, finding it impossible to generate a description of the man. However, you may very well be able to recognise the same man in a line-up, despite recall being so poor. This well-established phenomenon has lead to a number of theories of memory retrieval. The most important of these is the two-process theory (Watkins and Gardiner 1979), which states that recall is comprised of two processes, a search or retrieval process, followed by a decision process. Recognition only involves the second of these processes and is therefore less likely to lead to errors. The decision process inherent in recognition itself is thought to reflect contributions from two separate processes: recollection and familiarity [see RECOLLECTIVE EXPERIENCE]. Recollection is a decision based on the AVAILABILITY of the item in memory (like RECALL), whereas familiarity is a judgement based on the stimulus merely appearing familiar. Empirically comparing recall and recognition can distinguish items' ACCESSIBILITY from availability. *CM*

Watkins, M. J. and Gardiner, J. M. 1979: An appreciation of the generate-recognise theory of recall. *Journal of Verbal Learning and Verbal Behaviour* 18, 687–704.

recollective experience   Recollective experience is a subjective report of the sensations attached to the retrieval of an item from memory. Basically, it distinguishes between sensations of 'remembering' and 'knowing'. It can be considered in two ways: as reflecting episodic versus semantic storage (Tulving 1985) and differentiating recollection and mere familiarity with a stimulus. The former is the original notion, that CONSCIOUSNESS surrounding retrieval separates EPISODIC MEMORY (remembering) and SEMANTIC MEMORY (knowing). Remembering from episodic memory includes a subjective state of pastness, and knowledge about the memory's context and source. For example, I may like to think about my recent holiday to Greece. I can remember who I went there with, and the sights and the smells of the place I stayed, and how I felt at the time. As I dwell on the memory, I begin to recall more detail about it, and I may enjoy the sensation of reminiscence. On the other hand, *knowing* about information and recalling it from semantic memory only involves the retrieval of information. There is no rich contextual information, or a sense of pastness, I just *know* the information that I have retrieved. For example, if someone asks me the capital of Greece, I can tell them that the answer is Athens. I cannot remember how I encountered this information and it doesn't necessarily evoke any feeling in me: it is just a well-established fact. Some psychologists use

these subjective reports to discriminate recollection from familiarity, as discussed under RECOGNITION. We know that information tends to be episodic in nature at first (giving rise to remembering), but as it is used more often and established in semantic memory, it is retrieved as 'knowing'. Psychology students who perform better in exams report more 'knowing' of the facts than 'remembering' (Conway et al. 1997). *CM*

Conway, M. A., Gardiner, J. M., Perfect, T. J., Anderson, S. J. and Cohen, G. M. 1997: Changes in memory awareness during learning: the acquisition of knowledge by psychology undergraduates. *Journal of Experimental Psychology – General* 126, 393–413. **Tulving, E.** 1985: How many memory systems are there? *American Psychologist* 40, 385–98.

reinforcement   In behaviourist approaches, reinforcement is where rewards are given to alter or 'shape' behaviour. *CM*

retention   The storage of information. In a MEMORY (see s. 1) TEST (see s. 6), participants may be asked to retain information over a retention interval of a week. *CM*

retrieval inhibition   The suppression of to-be-remembered information at the stage of reproduction from MEMORY (see s. 1). The notion central to retrieval inhibition is that material in memory has AVAILABILITY, but through some INHIBITION process, it is inaccessible for retrieval. Such ideas are contemporary (and empirically supported) reworkings of Freud's notions of REPRESSION (see s. 7). Anderson, Bjork and Bjork (1994) provide a framework for discussing inhibition in LONG-TERM MEMORY, and describe how such inhibitory processes are a natural part of efficient remembering. If one wants to retrieve one piece of information, it would be beneficial to temporarily inhibit the ACCESSIBILITY of related information.

Anderson, M. C., Bjork, R. A. and Bjork, E. L. 1994: Remembering Can Cause Forgetting – Retrieval Dynamics in Long-Term Memory. *Journal of Experimental Psychology–Learning, Memory and Cognition* 20, 1063–87.

retrograde amnesia   Memory loss for information encountered before the onset of AMNESIA.

CM

S

saccades A quick eye-movement from one fixation point to another. Saccades are easily seen when watching the flickering eye-movements of someone looking at the passing scenery through the window of a moving vehicle. You may also be aware of little saccadic jumps as you are reading this text. Saccades are interesting because they are an example of active vision: how brain processes operate on PERCEPTION (see s. 1) through TOP-DOWN PROCESSING in order to deliver information to cognition in meaningful chunks. Indeed, in the rare event that someone cannot make saccadic eye-movements, the mind will 'need' to make the same type of head or neck movement to produce the same sort of saccades, in order that perceptual information arrives in the mind in the correct form (Gilchrist et al. 1998). *CM*

Gilchrist, I. D., Brown, V., Findlay, J. M. and Clarke, M. P. 1998: Using the eye-movement system to control the head. *Proceedings of the Royal Society of London Series B–Biological Sciences* 265, 1831–6.

savings An often overlooked measure of memory, this is the time taken (or effort required) to relearn material that has been previously learnt (and presumably forgotten). *CM*

schema A plan or outline of behaviour. Schemata (or schemas) are cognitive mental plans that serve as guides for action. They are abstract representations [see ABSTRACT THOUGHTS] that enable one to operate across a range of novel situations. Generally, you can have schemata for how to read a sentence, how to ride a bike, how to order a pint of beer in a bar and all manner of other tasks. More specifically, however, you are likely to encounter the term as used in memory, as a way of organising and summarising life events. [See also SCRIPT] *CM*

script A standard sequence of events which have become over-learned through repeated use. These are plans, like schemata [see SCHEMA], which can be stored and called into use in certain situations. Consider making your friend a cup of tea: boil the kettle, steep the teabag, add some milk, stir the drink and offer them some sugar. Scripts are a more detailed, less abstract form of schema, and are more predictable. As with schemata, they are a way of summarising behaviours for manageable storage. *CM*

second-order conditioning This occurs in CLASSICAL CONDITIONING, where a CONDITIONED STIMULUS (e.g. a bell ring) is now paired with a new response as an UNCONDITIONED STIMULUS (e.g. pairing the bell ring with giving exercise, not feeding). *CM*

selective attention Selection of one item, from among others, for preferential processing. May be considered a redundant term, in favour of ATTENTION. *AS*

semantic memory Semantic memory can be thought of as our store of factual information. In contrast to EPISODIC MEMORY, semantic memory has no rich contextual cues or any first-person sense of pastness [see RECOLLECTIVE EXPERIENCE]. Semantic memory is a large part of our DECLARATIVE MEMORY, the store of language [see LEXICON] and conceptual information, such as categories [see CATEGORY]. The study of semantic memory sometimes concerns language processes and often the way in which we classify and categorise the world. This, of course, makes semantic memory a focal point of how MENTAL REPRESENTATIONS are formed and stored – the cornerstone of cognitive psychology. Semantic memory can also be thought of as the interface between LANGUAGE (see s. 2) and memory processes. Central to the notion of semantic memory is the semantic network. This can be thought of as the store of semantic knowledge, and semantic memory as the process that taps this store.

The semantic network can be thought of as a hierarchy of concepts and categories (e.g. Collins and Quillian 1969). We might have the category of animals, in which we store birds. Within birds we will have flightless birds, including ostriches and penguins, and more typical birds, such as canaries and sparrows. REACTION TIMES change from one level of the network to another – the less distance between these classifications, the quicker we are to verify the pair as true (e.g. animal – bird processed faster than animal – sparrow). We also know that this semantic network is structured somewhat according to typicality. We are quicker to access information about more typical birds than atypical ones, and can verify that a canary is a bird quicker than we can a penguin.

The structure and function of semantic memory has recently been researched with reference to semantic dementia (a form of dementia not dissimilar to ALZHEIMER'S DISEASE, but affecting semantic and not episodic memory predominantly). People with semantic dementia find it extremely difficult to name objects and classify objects (for instance, what certain vegetables are, and even whether they are edible). So much so, that their disorder often appears more like a problem of language than of memory (Hodges et al. 1992). *CM*

Collins, A. M. and Quillian, M. R. 1969: Retrieval time from semantic memory. *Journal of Verbal Learning and Verbal Behavior* 8, 240–8. Hodges, J. R., Patterson, K., Oxbury, S. and Funnell, E. 1992: Semantic dementia – progressive fluent aphasia with temporal-lobe atrophy. *Brain* 115, 1783–806.

semantic priming This is the benefit in performance as a consequence of having recently encountered a stimulus that is related in meaning, usually measured as a decrease in REACTION TIME. Studies of semantic priming have been insightful as to the structure of the mental LEXICON. One widely used task is lexical decision, where people simply have to decide whether a stimulus is a word or not. Participants are presented pairs of words, where the first word (the cue) is always a real word, and the second word (the target) can either be a real word (e.g. truck) or a nonword (e.g. gruck). It has been shown that the reaction time to identify the target as a word (truck) is much faster if people are given a semantically related cue (e.g. car), rather than an unrelated cue (e.g. apple). This indicates that the mental lexicon is in some way organised on the basis of SEMANTICS (see s. 4). *CM*

serial processing Processing that occurs in single file, one task after another. *CM*

shape constancy The tendency to perceive the shape of a rigid object in a consistent manner, despite variations in viewing position. *AS*

shaping In OPERANT CONDITIONING, this is training by rewarding successive approximations (e.g. training a dog to offer its paw by giving it a reward every time it merely moves that paw, and then shaping until only the exact gesture is rewarded). *CM*

short-term memory A term for the system responsible for the temporary storage of information prior to that information either being forgotten or transferred to LONG-TERM MEMORY. *AT*

sine-wave grating A grating is a grid of lines (see Figure). A sine-wave grating is one where the regions of light and dark modulate smoothly, like in the smooth rounded shape of the sine-wave. Sine-wave gratings are of importance to PERCEPTION (see s. 1), because they have been associated with MARR'S COMPUTATIONAL THEORY, explaining how the most basic of light intensity changes can be computed in vision. Any visual scene, therefore, can be broken down into a complex interaction of overlaid sine-wave gratings (Fourier analysis). This might be one way in which we detect edges of objects and boundaries of scenes (especially given the structure of RECEPTIVE FIELDS). Imagine moving a single photocell across a scene in a line so that it just detects one PIXEL of light. As you moved the cell across the scene it would pick up different levels of light, and you could plot that on a graph. This would produce a curve showing how light changed across the scene. (For the grating in the Figure, this would be a perfect sine wave.) The unique way the light changed across the scene can be thought of as a series of overlaid sine waves. If we decomposed the main complicated

sine-wave grating

wave, we could show how it was just built up of more simple underlying patterns of how light changed across the scene. Unsurprisingly, sine-wave gratings have been used as a stimulus in PERCEPTION (see s. 1) EXPERIMENTS (see s. 8). *CM/AS*

size constancy The tendency to perceive the size of a rigid object in a consistent manner, despite variations in viewing distance. *AS*

skill The ability to carry out complex, well-organised patterns of behaviour, usually motor tasks (e.g. dribbling a football). [See also PROCEDURAL MEMORY and PRACTICE] *CM*

speech errors ERRORS (see s. 8) made in fluent speech by normal adult speakers are relatively common. The term 'speech error' is used specifically to refer to those errors that reflect unintentional use of sounds or words, or placement of an intended sound or word in an unintended location. These are errors of performance, not of knowledge (the speaker is not ignorant of the correct form of the intended message), and relate to fluently produced utterances, so distinguishing them from errors involving things like hesitations, false starts and misarticulations. The most common type of speech errors are exchange errors, and perhaps the most famous of these is the Spoonerism, named after Reverend William Archibald Spooner (1844–1930). Dean and Warden of New College, Oxford. Rev. Spooner was famous for making verbal slips involving the transposition of sounds from two or more words (phoneme exchange errors), often to humorous effect. For example, a likely Spoonerism would be, 'You've hissed all my mystery lectures', for 'You've missed all my history lectures'.

Other types of common speech errors include 1) deletion errors – a sound or word from the intended utterance is omitted (e.g. backjack for blackjack); 2) anticipation or perseveration errors – a sound or word occurs both in the right place and earlier/later in the utterance (e.g. fastidious rule becomes fastidious fool; shopping bag becomes bopping bag); 3) blend errors – two words combine (e.g. 'chung', a blend of children and young); and 4) substitution errors – a word is substituted for a different word (e.g. 'give me a fridge' for 'give me a fork').

Freud (1901) believed speech errors were motivated by thoughts related to unconscious wishes or desires. However, speech errors are almost always indifferent to the meaning of the resultant utterance. The causes of speech errors are instead now believed to be either 'noise' or 'competition' based (Butterworth 1982). For example, competition between children and young might give rise to a blend error like 'chung'. Analysis of speech errors can tell us a great deal about the LANGUAGE (see s. 2) system, and particularly about the role played by monitoring devices in speech production. *AT*

Butterworth, B. 1982: Speech errors: old data in search of new theories. In Cutler, A. (ed.) *Slips of the Tongue.* Amsterdam: Mouton. **Freud, S.** 1901: The psychopathology of everyday life. *Monatschrift fur Psychiatrie und Neurologie* 10, 1–13.

split-brain Split-brain patients are those who have had the CORPUS CALLOSUM (see s. 2) severed, and thus have two unconnected, independent hemispheres of the brain.

Study of people with split-brains has illuminated our understanding of the cognitive processes devoted to each hemisphere and the interplay between the two sides of the brain.

Split-brain procedures are usually carried out to ameliorate electrical abnormalities in the brains of people with epilepsy, so that the seizure will not spread from one hemisphere to another. After surgery, split-brain patients typically retain their intellectual function and PERSONALITY (see s. 1 and s. 6) but show striking patterns of behaviour on experimental tasks. For instance, if you present objects to the left hemisphere, they can be named. However, the right hemisphere fails to name the same objects – and the person will claim they see nothing. On tasks with a definite hemispheric focus, such as arranging blocks into a pattern, the left hand will be able to do the task (which is controlled by the right hemisphere and is good at such spatial tasks), whereas the right will not. The two hands may even compete on the task, and the split-brain patient may have to sit on their right hand in order to carry out the task (e.g. Gazzaniga 1967). From such studies, our notions of cognitive specialisms in each of the hemispheres has been enhanced. Hemispheric differences in cognitive processes are supported by experimental studies on healthy participants, who can be shown to show similar specialisms for material presented very quickly in one side of the visual field or the other.

More recently, split-brain patients have been used to investigate the SELF (see s. 1, s. 4 and s. 5) and CONSCIOUSNESS. It has been shown that split-brain patients are better at recognising images of themselves presented to the left hemisphere than to the right. The idea is that the self is generated by the need to integrate the two halves of the brain, with the left half acting as 'interpreter', and this left side being the possible source of consciousness (Turk et al. 2003). *CM*

Gazzaniga, M. S. 1967: The split brain in man. *Scientific American* 217, 24–9. **Turk, D. J., Heatherton, T. F., Macrae, C. N., Kelley, W. M. and Gazzaniga, M. S.** 2003: Out of contact, out of mind – the distributed nature of the self. Self: from soul to brain. *Annals of the New York Academy of Sciences* 1001, 65–78.

spontaneous recovery In learning contexts, this is where a stimulus-response association has disappeared, but reappears without further training after a delay. *CM*

state-dependent learning Largely synonymous with ENCODING SPECIFICITY, this form of learning contends that material encountered in one setting will be much better retrieved in the same setting. If there is a difference in the use of the two terms, it is that state-dependent learning is often used with much more reference to internal states, such as intoxication or mood. A tired, dubious favourite example for students is that information learned while drunk, or high, is better retrieved when drunk or high again (e.g. Baddeley 1982). With regard to mood, studies have shown that mood congruence between encoding and retrieval leads to higher levels of recall. This has been put forward as a reason why depressed people remain depressed: when sad, they cannot help but retrieve sad memories, which in turn makes them sadder, and so on. Some experimental problems exist with this line of thinking. Due to ELABORATION, emotional memories are probably better encoded anyway [see FLASHBULB MEMORY]. *CM*

Baddeley, A. D. 1982: Domains of recollection. *Psychological Review* 89, 708–29.

stereopsis The ability to see with both eyes; stereoscopic vision. *CM*

Sternberg task A SHORT-TERM MEMORY or WORKING MEMORY task, where a small set of items is presented and participants must report at test whether an item appeared in that set or not. *CM*

stimulus generalisation In learning, this is where one stimulus becomes confused with other similar stimuli: such as having a bad experience on one plane trip, and becoming scared of flying, or even all modes of transport. *CM*

stimulus-response A term referring to the learning processes captured in BEHAVIOURISM (see s. 1). *CM*

Stroop effect Typically, the Stroop effect occurs when trying to ignore word forms in processing a stimulus. Stroop (1935) found that participants found it extremely difficult (as measured by REACTION TIME) to name the colour of ink that a colour name word was written in. For example, participants take longer to say 'red' for the word 'green' written in red ink than they do for a row of red 'X's. This is because the written word form 'green' interferes with the AUTOMATIC response that should be made to the ink: red [see ATTENTION]. This colour word version of Stroop is the most researched, but other forms exist (see Figure), all based on the same idea of interference between one automatically processed attribute (e.g. the WORD) and one less commonly attended-to attribute (the colour of the ink). In the figure-ground Stroop, your task is to name the big 'F', while ignoring the small 'H's. In the arrow Stroop, your task is to ignore the word 'RIGHT' in the arrow, and report which way the arrow is pointing, left in this case.

The Stroop effect has received a great deal of research attention; it has been mentioned in over 800 scientific papers since the year 2000. One major advance has been in the use of the Stroop task to consider the relationship between COGNITION AND EMOTION (see s. 6). This use of the Stroop effect (e.g. McKenna and Sharma 1995) involves presenting participants with emotional words, and again

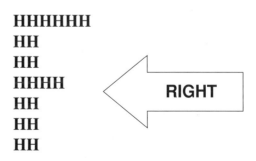

stroop effect *A figure-ground Stroop (left) and an arrow Stroop (right).*

measuring the reaction time to the name of the colour of the word. For words with particular emotional importance, the reaction time will be slowed. For example, Watts, McKenna, Sharrock and Treize (1986) reported slowed colour-naming reaction times for spider-related words in people who were arachnophobes. This suggests that attention is guided by personally relevant information in the environment. Further use of the Stroop PARADIGM (see s. 1) has been in trying to examine the difficulties in attention and INHIBITION in older adults, where arguably older adults are slower at this task than young people (e.g. Shilling, Chetwynd and Rabbitt 2002). *CM*

McKenna, F. P. and Sharma, D. 1995: Intrusive cognitions: an investigation of the emotional Stroop task. *Journal of Experimental Psychology: Learning, Memory and Cognition* 21, 1595–1607. **Shilling, V. M., Chetwynd, A. and Rabbitt, P. M. A.** 2002: Individual inconsistency across measures of inhibition: an investigation of the construct validity of inhibition in older adults. *Neuropsychologia* 40, 605–19. **Stroop, J. R.** 1935: Studies of interference in serial verbal reactions. *Journal of Experimental Psychology* 28, 643–62. **Watts, F. N., McKenna, F. P., Sharrock, R. and Treize, L.** 1986: Colour naming of phobia-related words. *British Journal of Psychology* 77, 97–108.

subliminal perception Subliminal refers to information that is below the threshold of conscious experience. Subliminal perception refers to occasions where a stimulus (usually visual) is processed, but the perceiver has no awareness of it. For example, in subliminal PRIMING EXPERIMENTS (see s. 8), a cue word can be presented very briefly (typically less than 50 ms, and often masked [see MASKING]), and although the participant has no awareness that they have seen the word, they will show benefits in processing a subsequent target (e.g. Marcel 1983). Of course, such instances of perception without awareness (something of an oxymoron) are insightful about the properties and purposes of CONSCIOUSNESS. In the 1960s and onwards, there was much excitement about whether subliminal priming could be used for advertising or other illicit message transmission, for instance, piping subliminal messages into store music about being honest and not stealing. Despite the ban on subliminal presentation of images in advertising, there is actually little evidence that subliminal perception affects ATTITUDES (see s. 5) or preferences, or has any long-term consequences. However, more modern researchers have successfully used subliminal means to activate noxious STEREOTYPES (see s. 5) in undergraduate populations (e.g. Bargh et al. 1996). *CM*

Bargh, J. A., Chen, M. and Burrows, L. 1996: Automaticity of social behavior: direct effects of trait construct and stereotype activation on action. *Journal of Personality and Social Psychology* 7, 230–44. **Marcel, A.** 1983: Conscious and unconscious perception: experiments on visual masking and word recognition. *Cognitive Psychology* 15, 197–237.

supervisory attention system A model of ATTENTION, based on data from everyday absent-mindedness and studies of patients with brain damage [see DYSEXECUTIVE SYNDROME]. This model sets AUTOMATIC, routine processes in opposition to more wilful actions, with control of these two processes through a supervisory system. *CM*

syllogism A valid deductive statement comprising three arguments, such as: all definitions in this book are correct; this is a definition from this book; therefore this definition is correct. *CM*

syntax A term for the set of rules governing the arrangement of words and phrases into sentences in a language. *AT*

T

texture gradient A monocular (or pictorial) cue to depth PERCEPTION (see s. 1) based upon decreased textural detail as a function of greater viewing distance.   *AS*

tip-of-the-tongue state The frustrating sensation of being unable to produce a known word. It is a momentary state where one cannot access information. That we cannot find the word but know its meaning, know that we know it, and even know how it may

sound, is evidence for METACOGNITION and crudely, of an abstract, meaning-based LANGUAGE (see s. 2) system.
CM

top-down processing Perception or processing governed by expectations or high-level representations. [For a discussion, see BOTTOM-UP PROCESSING]
CM

texture gradient *Source:* Photodisc

U

unconditioned response In CLASSICAL CONDITION-ING this is the behaviour that, pre-learning, is only associ-ated with the unconditioned stimulus (e.g. a dog salivating to the sight of food).   *CM*

unconditioned stimulus This is the stimulus that, pre-learning, is not associated with any specified outcome (e.g. the sight of food causing a dog to salivate).   *CM*

V

variable reinforcement schedule A schedule of REINFORCEMENT where rewards are delivered in a random fashion, with a variable interval between the behaviour and response.   *CM*

visual illusion An erroneous interpretation of perceptual data. Visual illusions (see Figures) are instances where perceptual systems 'see' something other than the mere data in the environment. They are a normal product of the visual system, and most if not all people will be susceptible to them. Illusions have been split into two types, those which distort reality, and those which arise from ambiguous figures.

Of the illusions that distort reality, the most well-researched is the Muller-Lyer illusion (or arrowhead illusion), which was described first in 1889. In this illusion,

the arrowheads serve to distort our PERCEPTION (see s. 1) of length, even though the two lines are the same. Gregory (1968), who was influential in harnessing illusions to make inferences about how human perception was arranged, offered an explanation of the illusion. He suggested that the illusion was caused by TOP-DOWN PROCESS-ING and the need to make sense of the stimulus. He suggested that the arrowheads represented the converging and diverging lines of a 3D object. (In the Figure, imagine that the line on the right is formed by looking into the corner of a room, with the V of the arrowheads representing the floor and ceiling. The line on the left could similarly be viewed as the external corner of a box or building, with the top and bottom faces going away from us.)

Gregory suggested that the illusion was formed by size constancy scaling, which is a perceptual process that makes up for differences in size of the image formed on the retina, in order to yield sensible sizes. We do not think that cows viewed from afar are small cows, we know that they are standard size cows viewed from a distance. For the Muller-Lyer illusion, this means that the mind compensates for the arrowheads on the right, presuming that

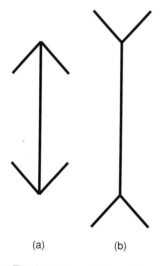

(a)   (b)

visual illusion *The Muller-Lyer illusion: the vertical lines are exactly the same length, but appear to be different lengths because of the 'arrowheads' at either end.*

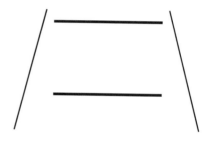

visual illusion *The Ponzo illusion: the two horizontal lines are actually the same length.*

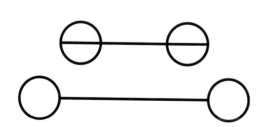

visual illusion *The Muller-Lyer illusion with shapes other than arrowheads.*

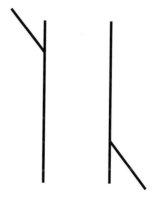

visual illusion *The Poggendorf illusion: the broken diagonal line actually line up perfectly – check it with a straight edge.*

visual illusion *An ambiguous figure: is it two men shouting at close quarters or an ornate chalice?*

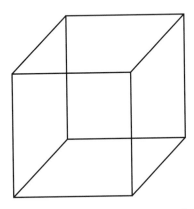

visual illusion *A Necker cube: an ambiguous figure – is the cube coming towards you or going away from you?*

this line is further away. There are some problems with this interpretation, however, since the Muller-Lyer illusion (see Figure) also works with non-arrowhead shapes at the end of the lines (Virsu 1971). Those who argue with the size constancy interpretation say that the illusion is formed by low-level processes that operate to find the centre of a stimulus (for example) and that the features at the end of the lines change the relative perception of the line itself.

Other distortions of reality are formed by size constancy scaling, such as the similar Ponzo illusion (see Figure). In this case, we interpret the converging lines as a 3D plane going into the distance. The two horizontal lines are the same length, but again, overcompensation from size constancy scaling leads to the 'further' line appearing longer than the 'nearer' one. The Poggendorf (see Figure) also is a distortion, where the diagonal appears not to line up very well. Other illusions in this category include MACH BANDS.

Visual illusions also arise where there are ambiguous stimuli. A very famous example of this is Ruben's vase (an example of which is given in the Figure), an ambiguous figure which can be seen as either two faces looking at each other, or a candlestick-like ornamental vase. Something of a psychology cliché, and the favourite of management training exercises, it is more useful as an

example of a figure-ground illusion. In figure-ground illusions, one can either perceive one interpretation of the data or another; one cannot perceive both at once. Such observations are of interest to those researching Gestalt principles. The Necker cube (see Figure) is another ambiguous illusion. The cube can either be seen pointing towards or away, and will change as you look at it: the image is said to vacillate. Again, both interpretations cannot be seen at once, even though both interpretations arise from exactly the same visual input.

For the cognitive psychologist, a fruitful way of thinking about how visual illusions arise is to consider top-down and BOTTOM-UP PROCESSING. Visual illusions tend to arise when there are conflicts between bottom-up and top-down interpretations of the visual scene. Moreover, some illusions seem to be the result of low-level DATA-DRIVEN processes (such as are seen in mach bands), whereas others are to do with higher-level perceptual processes that need to resolve an image to one perception out of two competing representations.   *CM*

Gregory, R. L. 1968: Visual illusions. In *Psychology in Progress: Readings from* Scientific American. San Francisco: Freeman. **Virsu, V.** 1971: Tendencies to eye movement, and misperception of curvature, direction and length. *Perception and Psychophysics* 9, 65–72.

visual search An experimental PARADIGM (see s. 1) used to study visual attentional processes. In the real world we are often presented with the task of looking for an item from an array (e.g. searching for a jigsaw piece) and visual search experiments are designed to characterise the processes that engender search of our surroundings. In a standard task, subjects look for a target item among a number of distracter items. Typically, there is a target present in half the number of the trials, and in the other half only distracters are present. Participants are required to make a response to indicate that there is a target present or that no target has been found, and their REACTION TIME (RT) is taken as a dependent measure. When participants search for a target defined by a simple feature (e.g. a red item among green distracters), their RT is unrelated to the number of distracters present. That is, they are equally fast to locate the target (or report its absence) when there are 5 distracters as when there are 50 distracters. This phenomenon is known as 'pop-out' and is usually used to infer that elements in the scene have been searched efficiently, or in parallel. In comparison, when participants must search for a target defined by a more subtle difference (e.g. an '8' item among 'B' distracters), then their RT increases linearly with the number of distracters present. This is consistent with an inefficient, or serial, search of the elements that is self-terminating. When there is a target present it may be the first item to be attended to or it may be the last, and therefore half the items will be searched on average. However, when there is no target present, all the items will be searched in order to confirm that there is no target present. In this case, the cost of increasing the number of distracters is twice as great for target-absent trials. A number of theories have been proposed to explain the difference between these two forms of search, and the paradigm has been widely used to assess the specificity and sensitivity of visual and attentional systems.   *AS*

visuo-spatial scratch pad The visuo-spatial scratch pad is a subsidiary slave-system of the WORKING MEMORY model (Baddeley and Hitch 1974), responsible for the maintenance and manipulation of visual and spatial information in working memory. Logie (1995) proposed that the visuo-spatial scratch pad has two sub-components: a visual store in which the physical characteristics of MEMORY (see s. 1) information are represented (termed the visual cache) and a spatial mechanism that can be used for planning movements and that may also serve as a rehearsal process to refresh the contents of the visual store (termed the inner scribe). Although in practice it is extremely difficult to dissoci-ate visual from spatial information, evidence of selective interference from spatial or visual distraction on tasks requiring the short-term retention of spatial or visual information, respectively, suggests that the two sub-components of the visuo-spatial scratch pad are functionally separable. The visuo-spatial scratchpad has more recently been renamed the visuo-spatial sketch-pad.

AT

Baddeley, A. D. and Hitch, G. 1974: Working memory. In Bower, G. A. (ed.) *Recent Advances in Learning and Motivation.* New York: Academic Press vol. 8, 47–90. **Logie, R. H.** 1995: *Visuo-spatial Working Memory.* Hove: Lawrence Erlbaum Associates.

W

Whorfian hypothesis Boldly, the theory that our language abilities govern our thought. The Whorfian hypothesis is that we think in words, and that the language we use determines our perception and representation of the world. Whorf (1941) based his theory on the study of the Hopi language of a native North American people. He argued that their language had only crude terms for time, whereas western languages can give precise terms for past, present and future. This led to differences in how speakers of these two languages perceive time. The strength of this argument is that Hopi concepts are in fact very difficult to understand from our perspective. However, this need not only be because of language, but also because of our social context and the mental representations we have acquired. A clichéd example is that of Eskimos and snow. Whorf described how Eskimos have many different words for snow, and thus can think about snow in a much more complex way. However, just because our language does not differentiate snow for igloo building and snow for sledging, it seems unreasonable to conclude that faced with the different types of snow, and their qualities (e.g. coldness, powdery-ness, wetness), we could not think about them in a more complex manner.   *CM*

Whorf, B. L. 1941: The relation of habitual thought and behaviour to language. In Spier, L. (ed.) *Language, Culture and Personality*. Provo: University of Utah Press.

word superiority effect A term for the phenomenon whereby letters are identified faster when embedded in a word.   *AT*

working memory Working memory (WM) can be thought of as a set of cognitive functions that allows a person to hold and manipulate information over short periods of time. Central to the notion of WM is the view that the temporary storage of information is an active process which is an integral part of general cognitive functioning. In fact, WM has been described as the 'hub of cognition' (Haberlandt 1997: 212), reflecting the pivotal role that very short-term maintenance and manipulation of information plays in cognitive processes. WM is thought to support many everyday tasks, from involvement in simple activities, such as remembering a telephone number, to the support of more complex cognitive processing, such as reasoning, problem solving and mental arithmetic. WM may also play a critical role in LANGUAGE (see s. 2) learning.

Theories of WM have been developed from EMPIRICAL (see s. 8) studies of healthy adults and children and from neuropsychological investigations of individuals who suffer from cognitive deficits as a result of brain damage. Most theories agree that WM is a limited capacity system that maintains information over periods of seconds. There is also general agreement that the contents of WM are subject to displacement by new input, and that WM interacts with and is supported by other parts of the cognitive system, such as stored knowledge or the products of PERCEPTION (see s. 1). However, theories differ as to the detailed architecture and functioning of the WM system.

Broadly, there are two classes of WM THEORY (see s. 8). One type of theory views WM as an embedded component of a single unitary memory system. By this view, the contents of WM reflect what is currently activated from LONG-TERM MEMORY, with an attentional mechanism providing a means of focusing on task-relevant activated information (Cowan 1995). Although this view of WM

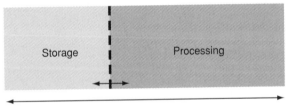

Total WM resources available

working memory *A schematic representation of the 'resource-sharing' view of working memory; by this view, as storage demands increase, resources available for processing decrease and vice versa. Source: A. D. Baddeley, Human Memory: Theory and Practice (1990), Psychology Press.*

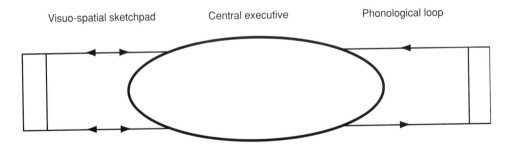

working memory *A simplified representation of the working memory model.*

can successfully explain why EXPERTISE in a particular field apparently enhances WM capacity (for example, taxi drivers are particularly good at WM tasks involving familiar street names), it does not easily account for the retention and manipulation of novel material in WM. In addition, the view that WM is no more than the activation of information in long-term memory is not consistent with the selective impairment of memory resources observed in individuals who suffer from cognitive deficits as a result of brain damage (Warrington 1982). For example, some individuals demonstrate very poor performance on immediate memory tasks, but normal performance on memory tasks involving the long-term retention of information. Conversely, others have shown normal immediate memory performance with poor retrieval from long-term memory, or poor long-term learning. This type of dissociation is not consistent with the theory that WM comprises temporary activation of information from long-term memory, since this would predict that if long-term memory access is impaired then temporary activation of long-term knowledge should also be impaired.

Neuropsychological dissociations in the functioning of long- and SHORT-TERM MEMORY systems are more readily accounted for by the second type of theoretical approach, which views WM as a functionally separate cognitive system. There are two principal versions of this view. The first is that WM functioning involves a single flexible system that provides both temporary storage and on-line processing, with a fixed allocation of resources that are shared between storage and processing (Engle 1996) (see Figure). A number of tasks have been developed to tap simultaneous storage and processing, such as the reading span task, in which individuals are required to read a series of sentences and subsequently recall the terminal words from the sentences, in their order of presentation. Performance on tasks like these has been found to correlate well with other measures of cognitive ability, such as reading comprehension and mental arithmetic, leading to the suggestion that INDIVIDUAL DIFFERENCES (see s. 6) in such activities reflect individual differences in resource-sharing capacity. An alternative interpretation though is that tests like the reading span task tap a range of cognitive functions that are also involved in more complex cognitive tasks.

The second approach to WM as a functionally dissociable memory system explicitly embodies the notion of separable components of WM. The most influential multi-component model of WM was proposed by two British scientists, Alan Baddeley and Graham Hitch, in 1974. A schematic representation of the original formulation of the model is shown in the Figure. In this model, information in the auditory and visual modalities is served by separable systems, both controlled by a central processor. The central processor, known as the CENTRAL EXECU-

TIVE, is a modality-INDEPENDENT (see s. 8) attentional system. Functions attributed to the central executive include the regulation of information flow, the control of action, planning and GOAL-DIRECTED BEHAVIOUR, the allocation of attention and the implementation of strategies and HEURISTICS used in PROBLEM SOLVING (Baddeley 1986). The first 'slave-system', the phonological loop (originally termed the articulatory loop), is responsible for maintaining and manipulating speech-based information, while the second 'slave-system', the visuo-spatial sketchpad (originally termed the VISUO-SPATIAL SCRATCH PAD), holds and manipulates visual and spatial information. The fractionation of WM into specialised, modality-specific components is supported by findings of selective interference on immediate memory tasks involving WM for visual and verbal information: visual secondary tasks and unattended visual material interfere with immediate memory for visual but not verbal information, while verbal secondary tasks interfere with the retention of verbal but not visual information. Further support for separable verbal and visual components of WM is provided by neuro-imaging studies, which indicate that anatomically and functionally distinct systems serve the temporary storage and manipulation of verbal and visuospatial material (Smith and Jonides 1997).

A recent development of the working memory model has seen the addition of a fourth component, the episodic buffer, proposed to be controlled by the central executive (Baddeley 2000). The episodic buffer is assumed to be a limited-capacity temporary storage system that binds information from the slave-systems and from long-term memory into a unitary MULTIMODAL (see s. 8) episodic representation. This component of working memory is proposed to play an important part in the process of CHUNKING, and thereby in LANGUAGE (see s. 2) comprehension, problem solving and planning. *AT*

Baddeley, A. D. 1986: *Working Memory*. Oxford: Oxford University Press. **Baddeley, A. D.** (1990). *Human Memory: Theory and Practice*. Hove, UK: Psychology Press. **Baddeley, A. D.** 2000: The episodic buffer: a new component of working memory? *Trends in Cognitive Sciences* 4, 417–23. **Baddeley, A. D. and Hitch, G.** 1974: Working memory. In Bower, G. A. (ed.) *Recent Advances in Learning and Motivation*. New York: Academic Press, vol. 8, 47–90. **Cowan, N.** 1995: *Attention and Memory: An Integrated Framework*. New York: Oxford University Press. **Engle, R. W.** 1996: Working memory and retrieval: an inhibition-resource approach. In Richardson, J. T. E., Engle, R., Hasher, L., Logie, R., Stolzfus, E. and Zacks, R. (eds) *Working Memory and Cognition*. New York: Oxford University Press, 89–120. **Haberlandt, K.** 1997: *Cognitive Psychology* (2nd edn). Boston: Allyn & Bacon. **Smith, E. E. and Jonides, J.** 1997: Working memory: a view from neuroimaging. *Cognitive Psychology* 33, 5–42. **Warrington, E. K.** 1982: The double dissociation of short- and long-term memory deficits. In Cermak, L. S. (ed.) *Human Memory and Amnesia*. Hillsdale NJ: Lawrence Erlbaum Associates, 61–76.

Section 4

Developmental Psychology

Introduction

The way in which people change and grow over the course of their lives is the provenance of developmental psychology. Developmental psychology is an exceptionally broad sub-discipline of psychology, because it spans change over the entire life-course, and is thus not synonymous with child development. It is true to say, however, that the majority of research within developmental psychology concerns infants, children or adolescents, and this bias is reflected within this volume. The sub-discipline includes cognitive and language development, social development, and their intersection, social-cognitive development. Consideration is also given to the effects that contextual factors can have on development. That is, children grow up within families, alongside peers at school and in particular subcultures.

A unique aspect of developmental psychology is that attention is paid to both *normative* development and *individual differences*. Normative development is the study of the way in which human children normally develop. This spans the development of everything from the acquisition of rules of grammar, to the understanding of moral transgressions. The defining nature of this body of work is that it seeks to explain and chart the developmental progression of humans from conception through to old age. It does not, however, involve the examination of individual differences between infants or children. This type of work involves specifying, for example, the age-range at which children acquire a certain rule of grammar, or the different levels of moral understanding displayed by a large sample of ten-year-olds. Some of the most sophisticated work in developmental psychology combines both of these approaches. Therefore, some researchers study large groups of children as they grow up, documenting normative developmental patterns as well as individual differences in these developmental trajectories. Work in this area also seeks to reveal the mechanisms underlying normative development and the variations between children.

There are literally hundreds of developmental psychology texts on the market that provide comprehensive coverage of the area. Here, I will recommend just a few. Rudolph Schaffer has written a really excellent introductory text that is clear and accessible, and contains the core themes and examples of new directions for research (Schaffer 2004). More advanced treatments of infant development (Bremner and Fogel 2001), childhood social development (Smith and Hart 2002), childhood cognitive development (Goswami 2002) and adolescent development (Adams and Berzonsky 2002) are provided in an impressive series of volumes. Each contains 25–30 chapters by international leaders in the field.

References

Adams, G. and Berzonsky, M. 2002: *Blackwell Handbook of Adolescent Development*. Oxford: Blackwell Publishing.

Bremner, G. and Fogel, A. (eds) 2001: *Blackwell Handbook of Infant Development*. Oxford: Blackwell Publishing.

Goswami, U. (eds) 2002: *Blackwell Handbook of Cognitive Development*. Oxford: Blackwell Publishing.

Schaffer, H. R. 2004: *Introducing Child Psychology*. Oxford: Blackwell Publishing.

Smith, P. K. and Hart, C. H. (eds) 2002: *Blackwell Handbook of Social Development*. Oxford: Blackwell Publishing.

Recent developments in developmental psychology

Any science of human behaviour and functioning is inextricably linked to the study of human development. Who we are, and the environments that surround us, change remarkably over our lifespan. Some of the changes are erratic and very difficult to trace, while others are systematic and robust, thus lending themselves more readily to empirical investigation. Advancing our knowledge of human development is not merely an academic pursuit. Doing so not only increases understanding of our selves and others, but leads to innovations in social policy, health care and education – with demonstrable positive impact on the lives of children and adults alike.

Today's science regards human development as shifts in integration across many levels of functioning, from the microscopic (e.g. genes and neurones), to activity of entire brain regions, conscious perception of self and others, action and behaviour or the behaviours of small and large groups. The entire field of psychology, like many other areas of inquiry in the human sciences, is experiencing an exciting and challenging shift towards examination of integration across these multiple levels of analysis. Studies that examine development simultaneously at the individual's behavioural, neural and genetic levels are now possible, and will become increasingly common. These studies will answer many old questions, while raising new ones with regard to how and why human development occurs.

With this consideration of multiple systems of functioning comes the related idea of human development as changes in regulation. Our developing capacities and limitations increasingly are viewed not as temporal shifts in otherwise static and isolated components or traits, but as alterations in the organisation of systems of components. For instance, young children's developing capacity to control or regulate their thoughts, emotions and actions is strongly linked to their ability to understand their own and others' thoughts, emotions and actions [see EMOTIONAL SELF-REGULATION, EXECUTIVE FUNCTION, SELF and THEORY OF MIND].

This growing emphasis on regulation is not limited to the individual, however. Self-regulation is thought to emerge from sensitive, coherent co-regulation of behaviour in human interaction. A number of theories place strong emphasis on a central role of predictable, sensitive and age-appropriate parent – child interaction in infancy and early childhood, for children's concurrent and subsequent healthy self-regulation of emotions and behaviours [see ATTACHMENT, INTERSUBJECTIVITY and INTERACTIONAL SYNCHRONY].

Psychologists also are studying culture and its impact on how we develop, and how individual differences emerge and shift as we develop. We share a genome and a planet, but there is truly remarkable variation in our experiences that arises from differences in time, birthplace, nation, ethnicity, and so on. Whether and how this variation meaningfully affects specific aspects of development is an empirical question – one that cross-cultural researchers tackle in earnest. For example, are the parental, sibling and peer influences on child and adolescent cognitive and social-emotional development comparable across cultural groups? Do particular behaviours, such as expression of anger or eye contact during conversation, 'mean' the same thing or different things across cultural groups? When scientists find cultural variations in developmental mechanisms, what are the causes and consequences of those differences?

Developmental psychology also is becoming a science that addresses the connections between domains of development that traditionally have been studied separately. Examples of this abound, including interest in the links between SOCIAL COGNITION and numerous aspects of social-emotional development. For instance, what are the costs and benefits of efficient and accurate INFORMATION PROCESSING to our developing social skills and maladaptive behaviours (e.g. prosocial behaviour, aggression)? What are the connections between children's and adolescents' social-emotional health, their SPECIFIC COGNITIVE ABILITIES, LANGUAGE DEVELOPMENT and ACADEMIC ACHIEVEMENT? Clearly, individuals and their developing capacities are best represented by a science that recognises and examines the whole person – cognitions, emotions and behaviours, and biology and environment. The answers to our questions lie not in consideration of which domain matters most, but how transactions between these domains operate to produce stability and change in functioning.

Dr Kirby Deater-Deckard

In choosing the entries for the Developmental Psychology section, a balance was struck between areas of study that have been core to developmental psychologists for many years, and the inclusion of material representing more recent advances in the field. Entries span five main areas: biological foundations and prenatal development; early learning and emotional development in infancy; cognitive and language development; social development (the self, moral and gender development); and contexts for development. Contributors within these areas include academics from the USA and the UK, reflecting international expertise in their fields.

Entries for the biological foundations and prenatal development section were contributed by Fred Holtz, and edited by Kirby Deater-Deckard, both from the University of Oregon. These entries cover the basics of our genetic and biological heritage, as well as introducing themes that represent new developments in molecular and quantitative genetics, set to revolutionise our understanding of the nature and nurture of development.

Infants provide researchers with many challenges methodologically, and Brenda Todd describes the ways in which researchers have overcome these barriers in order to explain infant learning, as well as infants' attachments to their caregivers. Bowlby's theory of attachment is one of the few truly 'grand' theories in developmental psychology, generating a vast amount of research as well as public debate. The basic tenets of the theory, as well as the debate surrounding its practical implications, are well reflected in this set of entries. Finally, entries edited by Kimberley Saudino at Boston University provide insight into normative emotional development, as well as individual differences in infant temperament.

The other 'grand theories' within developmental psychology feature within the areas of cognitive and language development. Kathleen Petrill outlines Piagetian theory, and Vygotsky's sociocultural theory and Chomsky's theory of language acquisition are also explained. More recent developments, such as the information-processing approach, are also included, as is the field of intelligence that considers individual differences in children's cognitive abilities. Such grand theories of development do not characterise social development beyond attachment, however, core areas such as 'the self', moral development and gender development have been the focus of research activity over many years, and this work is well documented by Robin Banerjee, Dawn Watling and Anna Harrison.

Children's development does not occur in a vacuum, and the final area covered within this section is the contexts in which children develop. Socialisation theories emphasise the influence of individuals and environmental experiences on children's well-being and adaptation to life's challenges. Beth Manke from the California State University at Long Beach coordinated and edited the entries for this section, which include family, peer, school and media influences. Here, social factors that contribute to individual differences in children's development are highlighted. Such factors range from Diana Baumrind's typology of parenting styles (a traditional theory of parental influence) to the effects of a child's popularity, to the novel role that computers are playing in schools today.

It is my hope that this introduction to the key themes in developmental psychology will spark a lifelong interest in the theory, research and practical implications of this far-reaching discipline.

Dr Alison Pike

A

academic achievement As well as having higher IQ [see INTELLIGENCE QUOTIENT] scores, high achievers believe in themselves, regulate their own LEARNING (see s. 3), try hard, persist in the face of difficulties and seek help when necessary. Children who are high achievers also tend to be intrinsically motivated, investing in schoolwork because of personal interest, the desire to improve their skills and the joy of seeing a job well done. Low achievers are more likely to be extrinsically motivated, achieving only enough to obtain an external reward or to prove, not improve, their skills. Achieving children typically have parents who are actively involved in their children's schooling. They use an AUTHORITATIVE PARENTING style, rather than an authoritarian or permissive approach [see AUTHORITARIAN PARENTING and PERMISSIVE PARENTING] (Glasgow, Dornbusch, Troyer, Steinberg and Ritter 1997). Children are also aware of teachers' expectations of them and tend to perform at a level consistent with those expectations. Teachers who enhance student achievement engage in practices that demonstrate confidence in each individual child's capability to succeed. *SH/BM*

Glasgow, K. L., Dornbusch, S. M., Troyer, L., Steinberg, L. and Ritter, P. L. 1997: Parenting styles, adolescents' ATTRIBUTIONS (see s. 5), and educational outcomes in nine heterogeneous high schools. *Child Development* 68, 507–29.

accommodation In PIAGETIAN THEORY, the process of interpreting experiences by modifying existing mental SCHEMES to fit realities in the environment. *KP*

adaptation In PIAGETIAN THEORY, the twofold process of fitting new information into current schemes (ASSIMILATION) and modifying existing schemes to fit new realities (ACCOMMODATION). *KP*

adolescence The developmental period of adolescence is a historically recent concept used to describe the 'growing up' period between childhood and adulthood. There is no consensus as to the beginning and end points of adolescence, some authors focusing on the biological process of PUBERTY, and others on the cultural construction of adolescence. To illustrate, an early maturing girl may enter puberty at age 9, and thus begin adolescence, while a 25-year-old university student may be reliant on financial support from her parents and still considered an adolescent by many developmental psychologists. This extended period (especially in the western world) of change involves development across three domains. First, the biological changes of puberty require adolescents to adjust to a new body shape and size, as well as sexual maturity. The physical changes of puberty are protracted (on average lasting four years), and there is also a wide range of age of onset (some seven years), with girls entering puberty on average two to three years prior to boys (Tanner 1990). PUBERTAL TIMING plays a role in adolescent adjustment, especially in the case of girls (Caspi and

Moffitt 1991). Research has shown that girls who mature early dislike it, and are at increased risk for delinquency; for boys it is the late maturers who dislike their status. Second, cognitive developments mean that ADOLESCENT THOUGHT is more mature than children's thought; however this does not come without pitfalls. That is, although adolescents are able to think abstractly and engage in metacognition (think about their own thinking), adolescents are also likely to become self-absorbed, leading to cognitive distortions (Enright, Lapsley and Shukla 1979). Third, adolescents strive for socio-emotional maturity and financial independence. Although adolescence is often portrayed as a period of storm and STRESS (see s. 7), as well as rebellion against parental authority, the vast majority of adolescents remain closely connected with their parents, and continue to be influenced by their parents about life goals and VALUES (see s. 5). On the other hand, by late adolescence (age 17–18), teenagers spend the majority of their non-classroom time with same-age peers rather than with family members (Csikszentmihalyi and Larson 1984). This social independence, coupled with financial independence, defines adulthood in most western societies. *AP*

Caspi, A. and Moffitt, T. E. 1991: Individual differences are accentuated during periods of social change: the sample case of girls at puberty. *Journal of Personality and Social Psychology* 61, 157–68. **Csikszentmihalyi, M. and Larson, R.** 1984: *Being Adolescent: Conflict and Growth in the Teenage Years*. New York: Basic Books. **Enright, R. D., Lapsley, D. K. and Shukla, D.** 1979: Adolescent egocentrism in early and late adolescence. *Adolescence* 14, 687–95. **Tanner, J. M.** 1990: *Foetus into Man* (2nd edn.). Cambridge MA: Harvard University Press.

adolescent thought PIAGETIAN THEORY proposes that adolescents between the ages of 11 and 15 achieve the highest level of cognitive development, the FORMAL OPERATIONAL STAGE (Ginsburg and Opper 1988). This is characterised by ABSTRACT THOUGHT (see s. 3), idealism and propositional logic (hypothetical deductive reasoning). For Piaget, the hallmark of this stage is that adolescents are able to logically deduce solutions to abstract problems, making tasks such as algebra possible. Critics, however, have criticised the stage-like progression as being too simplistic – some abilities emerge earlier and their development is more prolonged. In addition, training is possible, and culture and education do influence adolescents' performance on Piagetian tasks. Research has also shown that only 33 per cent of 14-year-olds consistently use formal operational thought patterns (Strahan 1983). Another major theory of cognitive development, VYGOTSKY'S SOCIOCULTURAL THEORY, proposes that advances in thinking are guided by more skilled individuals. This perspective emphasises context, and underlines all of the non-academic avenues through which adolescents develop their cognitive abilities and acquire information, for example peers, media, computers, etc. Finally, the INFORMATION PROCESSING APPROACH focuses on quantitative increases in abilities. In particular, Keating (1990) proposes that specific gains are made in adolescence: improved ability to pay attention, improved memory, quicker speed of information processing and improved organisational strategies.

Regardless of the theoretical perspective taken, adolescent thought *does* demonstrate developmental change from the thinking of children. First, adolescents are better able to generate multiple possibilities, and to judge these alternatives rather than simply perceiving the present reality. Related to this, adolescents are able to think beyond concrete and observable phenomena and think abstractly. Adolescents are also able to think about their own thinking (METACOGNITION – see s. 3), and about their own emotions (INTROSPECTION (see s. 1)). This new-found ability, to think about the process of thinking itself, can lead to self-absorption (EGOCENTRISM). Elkind and Bowen (1979) proposed that cognitive distortions thus arise, namely the IMAGINARY AUDIENCE (the view that many adolescents hold that they are at the centre of everyone's attention) and PERSONAL FABLE (the belief that one is unique, coupled with an over-inflated sense of importance). *AP*

Elkind, D. and Bowen, R. 1979: Imaginary audience behaviour in children and adolescents. *Developmental Psychology* 15, 33–44. **Ginsburg, H. P. and Opper, S.** 1988: *Piaget's Theory of Intellectual Development* (3rd edn.). Englewood Cliffs NJ: Prentice Hall. **Keating, D.** 1990: Adolescent thinking. In Feldman, S. S. and Elliott, G. R. (eds), *At the Threshold.* Cambridge MA: Harvard University Press, 54–89. **Strahan, D. B.** 1983: The teacher and ethnography: observational sources of information for educators. *Elementary School Journal* 83, 195–203.

allele   Some genes have alternative forms, alleles, which are recognised by differences in their expression in characteristics such as eye colour or blood type.   *FH*

a-not-b search error   The A-not-B error is a searching behaviour an infant displays when looking for an object at location A, even though witnessing the object, originally hidden at location A, moved to a new hiding place, location B. According to Piaget, the error occurs in the SENSORIMOTOR STAGE because the infant does not realise objects exist independently from their action of looking at the location first associated with the object (Galotti 1999). Disappearance of the searching error means the toddler can systematically look for an object at locations A, then B, even though movement to the new hiding place was not observed. PIAGETIAN THEORY proposes this indicates the toddler has gained the mental capacity to understand OBJECT PERMANENCE (Goswami 1998). Some researchers question this assertion given the effects of A-trial repetitions and task difficulties on A-not-B search outcomes (Marcovitch, Zelazo and Schmuckler 2002).   *KP*

Galotti, K. M. 1999: *Cognitive psychology in and out of the laboratory* (2nd ed). Belmont, CA: Brooks/Cole Publishing Co. **Goswami, U.** 1998: *Cognition in Children.* Hove, East Sussex: Psychology Press Ltd. **Marcovitch, S., Zelazo, P. D. and Schmuckler, M. A.** 2002: The effect of the number of A trials on performance on the A-not-B task. *Infancy* 3(4), 519–29.

assimilation   In Piaget's theory, the process of interpreting experiences by fitting information into new/current mental SCHEMES for understanding the world.   *KP*

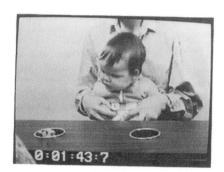

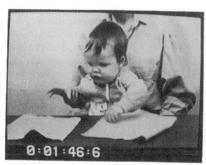 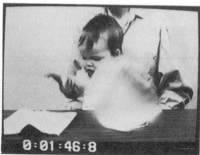 

a-not-b search error *The A-not-B search error. Source: D Bukatko and M W Daehler,* Child Development: A Thematic Approach *(5th ed), © 2004 by Houghton Mifflin Company. Used by permission.*

attachment   Attachment is defined as an enduring and emotionally meaningful relationship between individuals who support one another through the everyday and more challenging experiences of life. In developmental psychology, attachment refers to the relationship between a baby or child and a caregiver to whom the child turns for love and protection, especially when fear or anxiety is experienced. The attachment figure will ideally provide a SECURE BASE from which the child can set out and explore their environment, safe in the understanding that the person will be available and willing to provide responsive support on their return. This function is said to be critical to developing cognitive abilities.

The evolutionary significance of attachment was thought to be protection from predators and attachment behaviour is defined as any form of behaviour resulting in attaining or maintaining proximity to another individual who is predisposed to provide protection (Bowlby 1988). Although attachment behaviours can be seen in people of any age, they are most associated with babies and young children.

The hypothesis that early relationships were central to emotional development across the lifespan was elaborated and refined by John Bowlby over a number of years (Bowlby, 1951, 1969; 1988). Bowlby's thinking was influenced by his training in PSYCHOANALYSIS (see s. 1, PSYCHOANALYSIS AND RELATED SCHOOLS) and understanding of ETHOLOGICAL THEORY and SYSTEMS THEORY (see s. 1). Early in his career, he became convinced of the importance of family life to healthy emotional development after working with groups of young people who had experienced MATERNAL DEPRIVATION.

The attachment bond is said to develop during infancy, beginning with a 'pre-attachment' phase when eye contact, crying and finally smiling serve to keep the caregiver physically close and attentive to the baby. In the second, 'indiscriminate' attachment phase, babies are comforted by attention from any sensitive person who satisfies their needs and it is not until the age of about eight or nine months when attachment behaviours become 'specific', being directed at particular familiar individuals, especially the mother. At this age, babies begin to show STRANGER ANXIETY and experience SEPARATION ANXIETY when they are parted from their primary caregiver. Older children will try to maintain proximity by clinging or following.

It is not only the existence of an attachment relationship that is important; the quality of the relationship or degree of MATERNAL SENSITIVITY experienced is critical to later development. In Bowlby's theory, a secure attachment relationship is thought to pave the way for healthy emotional and social development through the medium of INTERNAL WORKING MODELS of the self in relation to other people. Children who have experienced sensitive parenting learn to expect care and consideration in future social relationships. The persistence of the early model of relationships has clinical significance. When attachments are secure, future relationships are likely to be fulfilling and rewarding, but attachment insecurity gives rise to relationships that are prone to anxiety, jealousy and discontent.

Much research has stemmed from measurement of the attachment bond in the STRANGE SITUATION technique, devised by Mary Ainsworth and her colleagues in 1978 and modified by Main and Solomon in 1986. Ainsworth categorised the main types of attachment. The SECURE ATTACHMENT type was identified when children were able to play and explore happily in the caregiver's presence and readily accept comfort after a separation. Three insecure attachments types, AVOIDANT ATTACHMENT, RESISTANT ATTACHMENT and DISORGANISED ATTACHMENT, were proposed according to the kinds of reaction children showed in the separation and reunion phases of the procedure.

Maternal attachment was central to Bowlby's concept of monotropy – the importance of a special relationship to the mother or one permanent mother substitute. Later researchers have allowed for multiple attachments, especially to the father, siblings and grandparents. The value of alternative attachments may depend on the amount of time that person spends with the child, the sensitivity they show and the enjoyment they find in the relationship.

Attachment theory has implications for child-rearing practice, both for individual parents and in social policy. Bowlby stressed the importance of maternal care within the family; this was especially pertinent as he developed his theory during times when World War II had seriously disrupted family life and many orphans of the war needed appropriate care. In recent decades, the debate on the provision of satisfactory childcare has been focused on the provision of day care for children of working parents. Research in this area is hampered by the multiplicity of FACTORS (see s. 8) involved. For example, the number of hours away from the parent, quality and type of alternative care, reason for choosing care and age at which it is initiated vary considerably. Unsurprisingly, the studies also vary in the outcomes they predict and the results remain controversial. There is some evidence that only early, repeated and prolonged separations are associated with poor developmental and attachment outcomes (e.g. Belsky 1988). The points are critical, however, as they inform both parental practice and social policy on childcare provision. Naturally, outcomes will also depend on the quality of care parents provide alongside day care, and experience outside the home may be *beneficial* in developing a child's confidence and sociability (NICHD Early Child Care Research Network 2001).

Many professionals working in this research area are themselves working mothers, and Goldberg (2000) points out that they may therefore be motivated to reassure themselves and others that non-maternal care is not detrimental to children's development. However, where separations are the norm, being both frequent and predictable, they may be much less traumatic to the child than the disruption of one central bond. Multiple attachments are likely to develop, but many of these may be relatively short-lived and superficial and shared with many other children. The child's own family are the people most likely to have a deeper emotional investment in their welfare.

Attachment is a complex and far-reaching concept that continues to be researched and developed in terms of developmental outcomes, clinical contexts, parenting practice and social policy.   *BT*

Ainsworth, M. D., Blehar, M. C., Waters, E. and Wall, S. 1978: *Patterns of Attachment: Assessed in the Strange Situation.* Hillsdale NJ: Erlbaum. **Belsky, J.** 1988: The 'effects' of infant day care reconsidered. *Early Child Research Quarterly* 3, 929–49. **Bowlby, J.** 1951: *Maternal Care and Mental Health. Report to the World Health Organisation.* New York: Shocken Books. **Bowlby, J.** 1969: *Attachment and Loss.* Harmondsworth: Pelican Books, vol. 1. **Bowlby, J.** 1988: *A Secure Base*. London: Routledge. **Goldberg, S.** 2000: *Attachment and Development*. London: Arnold. **Main, M. and Solomon, J.** 1986: Discovery of a new, insecure-disorganised/disoriented, attachment pattern. In Brazleton, T. B. and Yogman, M. (eds), *Affective Development in Infancy*. Norwood NJ: Ablex, 95–124. **NICHD Early Child Care Research Network** 2001: Nonmaternal care and family factors in early development: an overview of the NICHD Study of Early Child Care. *Journal of Applied Developmental Psychology* 22, 457–92.

authoritarian parenting This parenting style is characterised by high demands, high control and little warmth. Children are expected to obey without question.
AE

authoritative parenting This parenting style is characterised by high demands and high warmth. Parents have high expectations and set rules, but explain reasons. *AE*

autonomous morality Autonomous morality is the second stage of Piaget's theory [see PIAGETIAN THEORY] of moral development. At this stage children, approximately ten years of age, begin to question if the rules which they are expected to abide by are also rules that others are expected to abide by. These children understand that rules are made by people and therefore they should consider the actor's intentions as well as the consequences when judging what is good and bad behaviour (Piaget 1932). Additionally, children's social understanding is enhanced through their peer RELATIONSHIPS (see s. 5); indeed, they take part in RECIPROCITY, thus sharing ideas and points of view on the appropriateness of behaviours. From their interactions, children's perceptions of the rigidity of rules are challenged and changed, allowing them to understand their own ideas of what is right or wrong, as well as to understand the importance of motivations and fairness in social interactions. *DW*

Piaget, J. 1932: *The Moral Judgment of the Child*. New York: Harcourt Brace.

autosomes All CHROMOSOMES that are not SEX CHROMOSOMES are called autosomes. Humans have 22 pairs of autosomes and 1 pair of sex chromosomes. *FH*

avoidant attachment An insecure ATTACHMENT type (Type A) classified by Ainsworth and her colleagues (1978) in the STRANGE SITUATION task and found to apply to approximately 20 per cent of children.

Avoidant attachment is characterised by the child showing minimal distress at separation from the mother (or other attachment figure), failing to seek proximity with her on reunion and rejecting her attempts to comfort him/her. In the pre-separation phase, the avoidant child may appear indifferent to the mother's presence, sometimes showing more interest and warmth towards the stranger than the mother or treating both in the same way.

The child has no confidence that they will elicit responsive care when it is sought and expects to be rejected or excluded. This leads to a persistent INTERNAL WORKING MODEL of the self as unlikely to warrant loving attention, which predicts relationship styles of avoiding closeness and maintaining emotional self-sufficiency. *BT*

Ainsworth, M. D., Blehar, M. C., Waters, E. and Wall, S. 1978: *Patterns of Attachment: Assessed in the Strange Situation*. Hillsdale NJ: Erlbaum.

B

basic emotions The basic emotions, happiness, surprise, fear, sadness, disgust, anger and interest, are those emotions that are cross-culturally recognised from facial expressions. There is evidence that these emotions are present early on in infancy (Izard et al. 1995), and over the first six months of life they become more organised and may reliably indicate the internal emotions of the infant (Weinberg and Tronick 1994).

The basic emotions that have been most frequently researched are happiness, fear, sadness and anger. Happiness, which has been noticed as early as a few weeks after birth, helps with parent-child bonding. An infant's smiles and expressions of joy serve as reinforcement for the caregiver's affection towards the infant, thus enabling a positive relationship between parent and child. Fear develops later in the first year of life as a protective mechanism to help infants avoid potentially dangerous situations. Both sadness and anger are first expressed around four to six months of age and are exhibited as reactions to unpleasant situations.

SC

Izard, C. E., Fantauzzo, C. A., Castle, J. M., Haynes, O. M., Rayias, M. F. and Putnam, P. H. 1995: The ontogeny and significance of infants' facial expressions in the first 9 months of life. *Developmental Psychology* 31(6), 997–1013. Weinberg, M. K. and Tronick, E. Z. 1994: Beyond the face: an empirical study of infant affective configurations of facial, vocal, gestural, and regulatory behaviors. *Child Development* 65(5), 1503–15.

Baumrind's parenting typology

One of the most well-known and widely used methods of classifying parenting styles is Baumrind's parenting typology. Diana Baumrind began her research in the 1960s. Her goal was to discover which parental characteristics were most likely to lead to competent children. In her initial studies, she examined middle-class, white, North American preschoolers and their parents. Based on interviews, tests and home visits, she identified three parenting styles based on parental demandingness and responsiveness: AUTHORITATIVE PARENTING, AUTHORITARIAN PARENTING and PERMISSIVE PARENTING (Mandara 2003). She also identified child behaviour correlates for each parenting style. Children of authoritative parents (i.e. parents that are warm but firm) are the most competent, self-controlled and self-reliant. They typically do well in school and get along with peers. Boys of authoritarian parents (i.e. parents that are demanding and lack compassion) are often hostile and rebellious, while girls with authoritarian parents tend to be dependent and easily overwhelmed by difficult tasks. Children of permissive parents (i.e. parents that are warm but fail to set limits) are immature, impulsive and may have difficulty following rules. A fourth parenting style was later introduced, NEGLECTFUL PARENTING. Due to financial stress or DEPRESSION (see s. 7), some parents have little time for their children, and therefore may be uninvolved with them. These children tend to display low social responsibility, low social assertiveness and experience the most behaviour problems (Baumrind 1991).

basic emotions *According to some research, three-day-old infants are capable of imitating expressions for happiness, sadness and surprise when they are modelled by an adult.*

	Demandingness	
	High	Low
Responses High	Authoritative	Permissive
Responses Low	Authoritarian	Neglectful

Baumrind's parenting typology

Although most research over the past 30 years has confirmed much of Baumrind's initial findings, studies focusing on different ethnic groups suggest that authoritative parenting may not always be the best style. In Asian-American families, obedience and strictness is associated with caring and concern (Chao 1994). Common in African-American families is a style situated between authoritarian and authoritative parenting, referred to as 'no-nonsense parenting' (Brody and Flor 1998). No-nonsense parents are warm and affectionate, but demand immediate obedience and exercise firm control. This style is most effective in low socio-economic status families living in dangerous neighbourhoods, where strict adherence to rules is necessary for survival. Finally, it is important to recognise that most research on parenting styles is cross-sectional, and thus cannot determine the causal direction between parenting behaviours and child outcomes. It is also possible that children's TEMPERAMENT elicits parenting behaviours. *AE*

Baumrind, D. 1991: The influences of parenting style on adolescent competence and substance use. *Journal of Early Adolescence* 11, 56–95. **Brody, G. H. and Flor, D. L.** 1998: Maternal resources, parenting practices, and child competence in rural, single-parent African American families. *Child Development* 70, 1197–208. **Chao, R. K.** 1994: Beyond parental control and authoritarian parenting style: understanding Chinese parenting through cultural notion of training. *Child Development* 65, 1111–19. **Mandara, J.** 2003: The typological approach in child and family psychology: a review of theory, methods, and research. *Clinical Child and Family Psychology Review* 6, 129–46.

bilingualism Bilingualism is the ability to communicate effectively in two languages (multilingual, for more than two), with more or less the same degree of proficiency. Children can become bilingual either through simultaneous acquisition (acquiring both languages at the same time in early childhood) or through consecutive acquisition (LEARNING (see s. 3) a second language after the first). Bilingual children appear to develop vocabulary more slowly than monolingual children; however, often when scores from vocabulary tests of the two languages are combined, bilingual children compare more favourably.

Contrary to early research which proposed that bilingualism had a negative effect on children's intellectual development, more recent studies show that it actually has a positive impact, e.g. on tests of analytical reasoning and cognitive flexibility (Hakuta, Ferdman and Diaz 1987). Bilingual children also tend to develop skills which enhance their reading achievement (Bialystock 1997). Studies on bilingualism, however, are often fraught with methodological problems, particularly in reference to defining 'simultaneous' acquisition. *JC*

Bialystock, E. 1997: Effects of bilingualism and biliteracy on children's emerging concepts of print. *Developmental Psychology* 33, 429–40. **Hakuta, K., Ferdman, B. M. and Diaz, R. M.** 1987: Bilingualism and cognitive development: three perspectives. In Rosenberg, S. (ed.), *Advances in Applied Psycholinguistics: Vol. 2. Reading, Writing and Language Learning.* New York: Cambridge University Press, 284–319.

birth order Many believe that first-born children are more assertive, intelligent and self-centred, whereas later-borns are more submissive, dependent and altruistic (Wallace 1999). Current research, however, does not support most notions concerning inherent birth order differences in children's PERSONALITY (see s. 1 and s. 6) and social and emotional functioning. When birth order differences do exist, it appears that a more fruitful way to understand these differences is to examine family processes that evolve as additional children are born. For example, according to the resource dilution model, parents have limited resources (time, energy, money). First-born children may benefit intellectually from having their parents' undivided attention, at least until a sibling is born (Zajonc 2001). As a result of greater resources, first-borns may also develop a sense of entitlement. Later-born children, in contrast, must always share parental resources and thus may adopt more altruistic or submissive roles. (See s. 2, PARENTAL INVESTMENT DECISIONS) *BM*

Wallace, M. 1999: *Birth Order Blues: How Parents Can Help their Children Meet the Challenges of Birth Order.* New York: Henry Holt. **Zajonc, R. B.** 2001: The family dynamics of intellectual development. *American Psychologist* 56, 490–6.

C

canalisation Canalisation refers to the tendency of genes to restrict the influence of the environment on development. A highly canalised trait, therefore, is relatively immune to the effects of the environment. However, the degree to which a trait is canalised can change over the course of development. Originally developed by Waddington (1957) to explain findings in EXPERIMENTS (see s. 8) with fruit-flies (drosophilia), in psychology the term is often used when discussing the stability of psychological characteristics, such as intelligence or temperament, across development.

Recently, canalisation has also been used as a model for explaining the development of some kinds of PSYCHOPATHOLOGY (see s. 7). Disorders such as DEPRESSION (see s. 7) or SCHIZOPHRENIA (see s. 7), which have moderate HERITABILITY and a diverse set of environmental correlates, may arise in a canalised manner into a finite number of behaviour patterns typical of such disorders (Grossman et al. 2003).   FH

Grossman, A. W., Churchill, J. D., McKinney, B. C., Kodish, I. M, Otte, S. L. and Greenbough, W. T. 2003: Experience effects on brain development: possible contributions to psychopathology. *Journal of Child Psychology and Psychiatry and Allied Disciplines* 44, 33–63. Waddington, C. H. 1957: *The Strategy of the Genes*. London: Allen and Unwin.

carrier A person who possesses the recessive ALLELE for a genetically transmitted disease, but is HETEROZYGOUS for that allele, is a carrier of that disease.   FH

categorical self The SELF as described in terms of basic categories or dimensions (e.g. gender, age, physical characteristics) that are salient for younger children. RB

Chomsky's nativist perspective In 1957, Noam Chomsky critically reviewed the behaviourist theory of language learning which held that language is learnt through OPERANT CONDITIONING (see s. 3). He argued that the rules of sentence organisation were too complex to be directly taught, modelled or independently discovered by young children. He stressed the tacit knowledge most people have of the structure of their own language, even though they cannot describe the structures. Chomsky (1976) proposed that humans are born with a biologically based innate system called the LANGUAGE ACQUISITION DEVICE (LAD), which aids children's language learning and is triggered by verbal input from the environment. His theory emphasised features which the world's languages have in common and assumes that differences between them can nonetheless be reduced to a set of underlying rules. The LAD allows for the development of any language (assuming exposure to utterances from that language) and through this process, GRAMMAR is also acquired.

Evidence which might support Chomsky's theory includes the fact that, from birth, babies are sensitive to speech sounds and are able to perceive regularities in their language before they are able to produce them, as well as the fact that children across the world reach the major milestones of language development in a similar order.

However, although it is now widely accepted that humans are to some extent biologically predisposed to language learning, his account has been questioned and no one has yet been able to produce a single set of rules which apply to all languages.   JC

Chomsky, N. 1976: *Reflections on Language*. London: Temple Smith.

chromosomes A chromosome is a long strand of DNA (deoxyribonucleic acid) that has bundled itself together in order to replicate. Within the nucleus of every human cell (except gametes – egg and sperm cells) there are 46 chromosomes, which together contain all an individual's genetic information. There are two kinds of chromosomes, AUTOSOMES and SEX CHROMOSOMES. The autosomes are essentially 22 pairs of duplicate chromosomes, with each member derived from each parent. The 23rd pair, called sex chromosomes, determines the sex of the individual. Gametes contain only 23 chromosomes (one half-set). New sets of chromosomes are produced when cells divide or when gametes are joined in fertilisation. A complete map of the genetic code contained in a set of human chromosomes (over 3 billion pieces of information) has recently been completed, and future studies in psychology will examine how components of this code relate to human PHENOTYPES (see s. 2) (Plomin, DeFries, Craig and McGuffin 2003).   FH

Plomin, R., DeFries, J. C., Craig, I. W. and McGuffin, P. 2003: *Behavioral Genetics in the Postgenomic Era*. Washington, DC: American Psychological Association.

co-dominance The inheritance of traits where two different ALLELES (HETEROZYGOUS genes) are simultaneously expressed in offspring.   FH

cognitive development Cognitive development is the sequence of change in human thinking occurring over time. The study of cognitive development has traditionally focused on the time period from infancy to adulthood. Several influential perspectives have emerged.

One of the most dominant perspectives has been the constructivist theory formulated by Swiss psychologist, Jean Piaget. PIAGETIAN THEORY proposes children actively participate in constructing their mental worlds. As children interact with the environment, the inborn tendency for organisation prepares them to create and order mental SCHEMES about their experiences. They also come into the world equipped to interpret their experiences through the process of intellectual ADAPTATION, the ASSIMILATION of new information into existing understandings of the world and ACCOMMODATION of current understandings to fit new realities. According to Piaget's theory, cognitive development of all children involves these change mechanisms, entails similar cognitive gains and follows identical stage

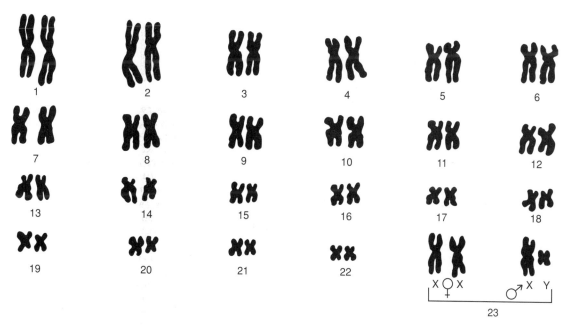

chromosomes *Every human cell nucleus contains twenty-three pairs of chromosomes. J. W. Vander Zanden, T. L. Crandell and C. Haines Crandell,* Human Development *(7th ed), 2000, McGraw Hill, reproduced with permission of the McGraw-Hill Companies.*

advancements (Smith 1999). In the SENSORIMOTOR STAGE (birth–2 years), infants combine schemes for sensory/motor experiences and acquire OBJECT PERMANENCE. They understand objects exist independently from personal sensory/motor activities. Throughout the PREOPERATIONAL STAGE (2–7 years), young children advance their cognitive worlds through organisation of MENTAL REPRESENTATIONS (see s. 3) to symbolise things/events. Language and pretend play emerge. But EGOCENTRISM still limits thinking to their views of the world. During the CONCRETE OPERATIONAL STAGE (7–11 years), children can use mental OPERATIONS to think logically about concrete experiences and objects physically present or imagined as existing. Within the FORMAL OPERATIONAL STAGE (11+ years), adolescents can generate abstract ideas and apply HYPOTHETICO-DEDUCTIVE REASONING to logically create, test and evaluate imagined possibilities. Piaget's theory has stimulated learner-centred curricula and cognitive-oriented research (Henson 2003; Smith 2003). Nevertheless, critics question the invariance of suggested stages, timing of predicted advancements, difficulty of measurement tasks (McDonald and Stuart-Hamilton 2003) and lack of sociocultural considerations.

Like Piaget, Russian psychologist Lev Vygotsky envisioned children as active constructors of their knowledge. However, in contrast to Piaget's view, Vygotsky's perspective stresses the impact of CULTURE (see s. 1 and s. 5) and social relations on cognitive development. VYGOTSKY'S SOCIOCULTURAL THEORY proposes these influences operate in two ways. First, children create their cognitive worlds within a cultural context, regularly transmitting information deemed important to learn. Second, social interactions in this environment guide children's LEARNING (see s. 3) towards acquisition of new cognitive ABILITIES (see s. 6). Via SCAFFOLDING, adults and more skilled peers help

children move through the ZONE OF PROXIMAL DEVELOPMENT and master cognitive tasks too difficult to achieve alone. Through dialogue, child and 'teacher' reach a point of INTERSUBJECTIVITY and share a common understanding. Vygotsky's perspective further suggests cognitive development is best studied by examining changes in children's utilisation of language for interpersonal dialogue and private speech for self-regulation. Vygotsky's theory has provided a framework for investigating the association between language performance and cognitive change, as well as the relationship between cooperative learning and knowledge acquisition (Henson 2003; Johnson-Pynn and Nisbet 2002).

ARTIFICIAL INTELLIGENCE (see s. 3) research fostered the emergence of the INFORMATION-PROCESSING APPROACH to the study of cognitive development. Using a model analogous to computer operations, the approach focuses on how the mind functions as a processing system. Children are viewed as actively participating in the input, transformation and management of information. However, cognitive advances are linked to maturation-related changes in the physical brain ('hardware') and process-related changes in system functioning ('software'). Changes in memory are seen as particularly relevant (Galotti 1999). Cognitive gains are linked to memory improvements facilitated by neurone (see s. 2, NEURONES: BASIC STRUCTURES) development in various brain regions and more efficient flow of information through the sensory, short- and long-term memory components. Brain maturation also leads to better functioning of several control processes, including attention management, content retrieval and strategy usage. Hence the approach perceives cognitive development as a series of continuous increases in the mind's ability to manage information from the individual's internal and external worlds.

More specific in context, theories of SOCIAL COGNITION (see also s. 5) focus on learning and developmental changes in the ways individuals think about their own and others' behaviours. Interactions between environment, behaviour and cognition are particularly relevant. Children acquire many behaviours via observation. However, this learning depends on several cognitive abilities, including thinking about environmental responses to actions of SELF and others (Green and Piel 2002). Children's THEORY OF MIND, inner thoughts about others' thinking processes, also affects their interpretations of the world. Research using location change tasks (e.g. SALLY-ANNE TASK) indicates that very young children fail to recognise another person's FALSE BELIEF. They still associate others' inner thoughts with physical experiences. From approximately age four, children gradually understand their own and others' mental activities, transform information about the world and affect interactions with the world. Social interactions, including shared discourse (Lohmann and Tomasello 2003) and joint attention (Budwig 1999), contribute to and are affected by these changes in the child's theory of mind. Understanding emotions, intentions and mental states also advances with increased cognitive abilities for EXECUTIVE FUNCTION and corresponding improvements in planning and monitoring one's own mental activity.

INTELLIGENCE, the ability to learn from and adapt to the environment, continues to be the primary focus of many researchers and theorists interested in cognitive development. In contrast to other perspectives, the study of individual differences is viewed as essential for understanding cognitive function. The traditional PSYCHOMETRIC APPROACH focuses on the assessment of individual differences in intelligence. Measurement instruments developed by this approach help identify children functioning at different levels of GIFTEDNESS or MENTAL RETARDATION. However, research evidence also suggests, across infancy through adolescence, earlier assessment outcomes serve as poor predictors of later INTELLIGENCE QUOTIENT (IQ) scores. Explanations of this instability, as well as other VARIANCES (see s. 8), depend on how intelligence is defined. Some theorists relate functionality to differences in a single, unitary GENERAL ABILITY (see s. 6) ('g'). Other theorists associate functioning with variances in SPECIFIC COGNITIVE ABILITIES. Both conceptions of individual differences in intelligence are addressed by current research (Petrill 2003), designed to examine how genetic and environment (shared/non-shared) processes operate in discrete and interactive ways to influence cognitive functioning. Collectively, studies of intelligence and research generated by theorists from each perspective broaden behavioural science's knowledge about cognitive development. *KP*

Budwig, N. 1999: The contribution of language to the study of mind: a tool for researchers and children. *Human Development* 42, 362–8. **Galotti, K. M.** 1999: *Cognitive Psychology in and out of the Laboratory* (2nd edn). Belmont CA: Brooks/Cole-Wadsworth Publishing Company. **Green, M. and Piel, J. A.** 2002: *Theories of Human Development: A Comparative Approach*. Allyn & Bacon. **Henson, K. T.** 2003: Foundations for learner-centered education: a knowledge base. *Education* 124(1), 5–12. **Johnson-Pynn, J. S. and Nisbet, V. S.** 2002: Preschoolers effectively tutor novice classmates in a block construction task. *Child Study Journal* 32(4), 241–55. **Lohmann, H. and Tomasello, M.** 2003: Language and social understanding: commentary on Nelson et al. *Human Development* 46, 47–50. **McDonald, L. and Stuart-Hamilton, I.** 2003: Egocentrism in older adults: Piaget's three mountains task revisited. *Educational Gerontology* 29, 417–25. **Petrill, S. A.** 2003: The development of intelligence: behavioural genetic approaches. In Sternberg, R. J., Lautrey, J. and Lubart, T. I. (eds), *Models of Intelligence: International Perspectives*. Washington, DC: American Psychological Association, 81–9. **Smith, L.** 1999: Eight good questions for developmental epistemology and psychology. *New Ideas in Psychology* 17, 137–47. **Smith, L.** 2003: Teaching reasoning in a constructivist epistemology. *Educational and Child Psychology* 20(2), 31–50.

computer use in schools According to the National Center for Education Statistics, 81 per cent of children use computers in US schools. However, schools demonstrate differences with regard to computer resources, including student/computer and computer/classroom ratios, both of which affect the availability and convenience of computer access. Traditional uses include drill and practice, computer simulations (e.g. science demonstrations), on-line testing, internet access for research and email communication between schools and parents (Haugland and Wright 1997). Computers are increasingly being used to conduct higher-order tasks, such as social emotional learning and character development. For example, MindOH! is a series of character education and discipline management modules that stream Flash and Real Media over the internet to teach students concepts such as respect and responsibility in decision making. *BC*

Haugland, S. W. and Wright, J. L. 1997: *Young Children and Technology: A World of Discovery*. Boston: Allyn & Bacon.

computer use in schools

concordance Concordance refers to the degree that siblings are similar for a trait. IDENTICAL TWINS will have a higher concordance of a higher heritable trait compared to FRATERNAL TWINS. *FH*

concrete operational stage In PIAGETIAN THEORY, the concrete operational stage (7–11 years) is the third major period of cognitive development. This stage begins when the child can perform mental OPERATIONS on concrete objects actually or imagined to be physically experienced (Green and Piel 2002). Thinking is characterised by several cognitive advances. The abilities to decentre and focus on multiple dimensions reduce EGOCENTRISM. Being able to mentally invert the order of operations makes reversibility in thinking possible. Both advances facilitate acquisition of CONSERVATION and the resultant understanding of the presence or absence of transformational change. Categorisation becomes more refined. REASONING (see s. 3) involves transitivity (logical combining of isolated relations) and includes seriation (logical ordering of related elements). Thinking moves beyond the realm of direct perceptions (Solso 2001). Nevertheless, mental processing remains limited to thoughts about concrete reality. Creation of abstract ideas signals the end of concrete operational thinking and the development of the FORMAL OPERATIONAL STAGE. *KP*

Green, M. and Piel, J. A. 2002: *Theories of Human Development: A Comparative Approach.* Boston MA: Allyn & Bacon. Solso, R. L. 2001: *Cognitive Psychology* (6th edn). Boston MA: Allyn & Bacon.

conservation Conservation is Piaget's term for a child's (or adult's) ability to recognise what basic properties of a physically present or imagined concrete object are not changed by certain transformations in the object's form (Thomas 1999). For example, presented with identical glasses A and B, filled with equal amounts of water, the child knows pouring glass A's water into a taller glass C does not make the amounts of water in glasses C and B unequal. This realisation occurs because the child can simultaneously appreciate multiple dimensions and mentally reverse procedural steps. However, conservation for different properties (e.g. conservation of length, number,

etc.) follows a pattern of horizontal *décalage* and emerges unevenly across the CONCRETE OPERATIONAL STAGE of COGNITIVE DEVELOPMENT. The child cannot quickly transfer and apply gains in conservation ability to another domain. According to PIAGETIAN THEORY, thinking remains linked to specific, concrete objects and events (Ginsberg and Opper 1988). *KP*

Ginsberg, H. P. and Opper, S. 1988: *Piaget's Theory of Intellectual Development* (3rd edn). Englewood Cliffs NJ: Prentice Hall. Thomas, R. M. 1999: *Human Development Theories: Windows on Culture.* Thousand Oaks CA: Sage Publications. Inc.

controversial children These children are both liked and disliked by their peers; they tend to be highly aggressive but possess better social and cognitive skills than REJECTED CHILDREN. *AC*

conventional level The conventional level is the second major level of Kohlberg's theory of MORAL DEVELOPMENT. At this level individuals will conform and endorse the rules imposed by their SOCIETY (see s. 5) or some authority simply because these are the rules, expectations and conventions (Kohlberg 1984). Indeed, individuals at this level have internalised the rules and conventions of their society and authorities. This level encompasses two stages of moral understanding: the 'GOOD GIRL' AND 'NICE BOY' ORIENTATION and the 'LAW AND ORDER' ORIENTATION. *DW*

Kohlberg, L. 1984: *The Psychology of Moral Development: The Nature and Validity of Moral Stages.* San Francisco: Harper & Row, vol. 2.

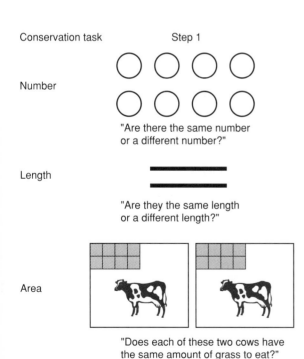
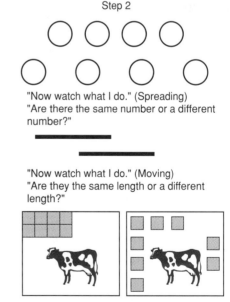

conservation *Some Piagetian conservation tasks. Source: D Bukatko and M W Daehler,* Child Development: A Thematic Approach *(5th ed), © 2004 by Houghton Mifflin Company. Used by permission.*

D

difficult child A child whose temperament reflects irregular routines, intense and generally negative reactions, and some resistance to new experiences. *JG*

dishabituation Dishabituation occurs when a habituated response increases following exposure to a novel stimulus (Kahn-D'Angelo 1987). This phenomenon can serve as a test to determine whether an infant's decreased physiological response to a given stimulus following repeated presentations is specific to that stimulus (HABITUATION – see also s. 3) or rather occurs because of non-stimulus-related general fatigue. There are two ways that dishabituation can be assessed. The first involves the presentation of a novel, usually more intense, stimulus immediately following habituation to an initial stimulus. The infant is then re-exposed to the initial stimulus. If the infant's response to the original stimulus on this final trial exceeds that elicited by the original stimulus on the preceding trial, dishabituation is said to occur. Dishabituation can also be elicited following multiple presentations of a habituated stimulus by subsequently presenting one or more instances of a new, similarly intense stimulus. Dishabituation occurs if the infant's response to the new stimulus exceeds that elicited by the last trial of the initial stimulus (Osofsky 1979). *SF*

Kahn-D'Angelo, L. A. 1987: Infant habituation: a review of the literature. *Physical and Occupational Therapy in Pediatrics* 7, 41–55. **Osofsky, J. D. (ed.)** 1979: *The Handbook of Infant Development.* Oxford: John Wiley and Sons.

disorganised attachment This ATTACHMENT category (Type D) was devised to cover a minority of infants (approximately 5–10 per cent) who showed little consistency in their strategies for coping with the separations and reunions of the STRANGE SITUATION task and therefore did not fit the three original types.

It was added by Main and Solomon (1986) to include children whose behaviour was disoriented and contradictory, displaying features of both AVOIDANCE (see s. 7) and resistance. The children appeared to lack any clear goal and behaviours were variable. Proximity seeking might be accompanied by a depressed and dazed appearance and followed by avoidance.

This attachment type is said to reflect the greatest insecurity and is found most commonly in children at high social risk, for example where there is parent pathology, neglect or abuse. Because of the disorganised and varied features of this type, it is difficult to characterise the INTERNAL WORKING MODEL or predict outcomes. *BT*

Ainsworth, M. D., Blehar, M. C., Waters, E. and Wall, S. 1978: *Patterns of Attachment: Assessed in the Strange Situation.* Hillsdale NJ: Erlbaum. **Main, M. and Solomon, J.** 1986: Discovery of a new, insecure-disorganised/disoriented, attachment pattern. In Brazleton, T.B. and Yogman, M. (eds), *Affective Development in Infancy.* Norwood NJ: Ablex, 95–124.

dominant-recessive inheritance Dominant-recessive inheritance is a pattern in which dominant ALLELES are always expressed in the presence of recessive alleles, and recessive traits will only be expressed if recessive alleles are paired with one another. Alleles occur in pairs, one from each parent [see CHROMOSOMES] (Plomin, DeFries, McClearn and McGuffin 2001). For instance, the Type A blood gene is dominant whereas the Type O blood gene is recessive. If a child receives a Type A gene from one parent and a Type O gene from the other, the child will express the dominant gene and have Type A blood. It can be inferred that all people with Type O blood have two Type O blood genes. A person with Type A blood can have either two Type A genes or one Type A and one Type O. *FH*

Plomin, R., DeFries, J. C., McClearn, G. E. and McGuffin, P. 2001: *Behavioral Genetics.* New York: Worth Publishers.

E

easy child A child whose temperament reflects a regular routine in infancy, general exuberance, and unproblematic adaptation to new experiences. *JRG*

egocentrism In PIAGETIAN THEORY, a term for the cognitive inability to distinguish between one's own and others' perspectives. *KP*

embryo A term for the prenatal organism during the period from the third to the eighth week after conception. *FH*

emotion, a functional approach The functionalist approach describes a group of theories that individually explain the purpose of EMOTION (see s. 6) as it relates to fulfilling a goal or initiating an action (Barrett and Campos 1987). Accordingly, emotions serve a major role in life by organising and regulating our behaviour, cognitive processing and physical health. Emotions are also integral in the development of the infant's sense of SELF, in that the infant's emotional state helps them to develop a sense of self and, in turn, this emerging sense of self enables the infant to experience new and different emotions.

Another factor in the functionalist approach is that as emotion develops, it becomes more susceptible to external social experience while also coming under voluntary control. The infant must learn how to control and when to express his or her emotions according to what is appropriate in his or her CULTURE (see s. 1 and s. 5). *SC*
Barrett, K. C. and Campos, J. J. 1987: Perspectives on emotional development II: a functionalist approach to emotions. In Osofsky, J. D. (ed.), *Handbook of Infant Development* (2nd edn). *Wiley Series on Personality Processes.* Oxford: John Wiley & Sons, 555–78.

emotional development Emotional development refers to how children learn to appropriately express their own emotions, as well as how children learn to understand and respond to the emotions of others. From birth, infants are able to recognise emotion, and the development of the ways in which they express EMOTION (see s. 6) are tied to the development of their understanding of the emotions of others. Infants are born both with the ability to express nearly all the BASIC EMOTIONS (joy, interest, anger, disgust, sadness) (Lewis 2000) and the ability to match the emotions of another person with whom they are in face-to-face contact (Haviland and Lewicka 1987). Within the first six months of life, infants develop the SOCIAL SMILE and laughter (see s. 6, HUMOUR AND LAUGHTER). Additionally, during these first six months, emotional expression becomes linked to the social environment and social development of the infant.

In the second six months of life, anger and fear are reflected in STRANGER ANXIETY. In addition, the ability to gauge others' emotions and their meanings improves. SOCIAL REFERENCING also develops at this time, with infants using trusted caregivers' emotional reactions to appraise new or unfamiliar situations. Between the 12th and the 24th months, children begin to develop SELF-CONSCIOUS EMOTIONS, such as shame and guilt. Children also begin to understand that people may experience emotion differently, leading to the appearance and development of EMPATHY at this age (Eisenberg and Fabes 1999).

In the pre-school years, emotional development progresses, and children acquire additional methods of emotional regulation with advances in COGNITIVE DEVELOPMENT and LANGUAGE DEVELOPMENT. Additionally, children begin to learn how to display emotions they do not feel; to this end, they are also able to understand more about what causes certain emotions and how to read them from the behaviour of others. Ultimately, school-aged children develop the understanding that they and others can have mixed feelings and that a person's outward expression of emotion may not be a true indicator of how that person really feels (Eisenberg and Fabes 1999). *SC*
Eisenberg, N. and Fabes, R. A. 1999: Emotion, emotion-related regulation, and quality of socioemotional functioning. In Balter, L. and Tamis-LeMonda, C. S. (eds), *Child Psychology: A Handbook of Contemporary Issues.* Philadelphia: Psychology Press, 318–35. **Haviland, J. M. and Lewicka, M.** 1987: The induced affect response: 10-week-old infants' responses to three emotion expressions. *Developmental Psychology* 23(1), 97–104. **Lewis, M.** 2000: The emergence of human emotions. In Lewis, M. and Haviland-Jones, J. M. (eds) *Handbook of Emotions* (2nd edn). New York: The Guilford Press, 265–80.

emotional display rules These are implicit rules that indicate how, when and where it is appropriate to express emotion in a given culture or society. (See also s. 5, DISPLAY RULES) *SC*

emotional self-regulation In order to be able to go about our lives and conduct our daily duties as necessary, we must maintain our emotional state at a tolerable level. Emotional self-regulation involves those methods and tactics that help to manage our emotions. Behavioural and cognitive INHIBITION (see s. 3), as well as attentional focusing and shifting, are necessary capacities for emotional self-regulation (Thompson 1994). For example, deciding to avoid a confrontational situation that may cause stress and anxiety is an act of emotional self-regulation.

Emotional self-regulation develops throughout the lifespan. In the first few months, infants have very little ability to control their emotions, and as a consequence, are easily overwhelmed by intense stimuli. Though they can turn away from something unpleasant, they cannot control or leave their environment, and require external soothing to deal with their heightened emotions. By the age of four months, infants begin to develop the capacity to shift their attention and their emotional self-regulation improves, and by one year, infants can typically crawl and walk, making them then able to physically remove themselves from an environment that they do not like, hence allowing

emotional self-regulation

them to learn to calm themselves. By the end of the second year, gains in LANGUAGE (see s. 2) and cognitive capacities provide the child with more ways to regulate their emotions. Children can self-distract and redirect their attention from something that causes negative emotions. Though their language capabilities are not sophisticated enough to verbally soothe themselves (Grolnick, Bridges and Connell 1996), they can verbally help their parents or caregivers in their attempts to soothe the child.

Once children are able to verbally express their emotions at around age two, they can then begin to realise how to regulate them. However, in early childhood, the external environment is still very important in the emotions children feel.

When children enter school, they have a whole new set of experiences to deal with and their emotional self-regulation abilities develop further. Additionally, the child's CULTURE (see s. 1 and s. 5) begins to play a role in emotional self-regulation at this point (Ollendick et al. 1996). Cognitive development throughout the school years also improves children's abilities to rationalise stimuli and, therefore, the emotions these stimuli arouse.   *SC*

Grolnick, W. S., Bridges, L. J. and Connell, J. P. 1996: Emotion regulation in two-year-olds: strategies and emotional expression in four contexts. *Child Development* 67(3), 928–41. **Ollendick, T. H., Yang, B., King, N. J., Dong, Q. and Akande, A.** 1996: Fears in American, Australian, Chinese, and Nigerian children and adolescents: a cross-cultural study. *Journal of Child Psychology and Psychiatry and Allied Disciplines* 37(2), 213–20. **Thompson, R. A.** 1994: Emotion regulation: a theme in search of definition. *Monographs of the Society for Research in Child Development* 59(2–3), 25–52, 250–83.

empathy   An understanding of, or ability to relate to, the experiences and feelings of another.   *SC*

equilibration   In PIAGETIAN THEORY, balancing cycles of ASSIMILATION/ACCOMMODATION in order to achieve congruence between existing mental SCHEMES and new experiences.   *KP*

ethological theory (of attachment)   John Bowlby's ATTACHMENT theory developed out of his understanding of the significance of the biological functions of behaviour, outlined in ETHOLOGY (see s. 1, ETHOLOGY AND COMPARATIVE PSYCHOLOGY and s. 2, ETHOLOGY AND SOCIOBIOLOGY). In particular, he applied concepts of IMPRINTING (see s. 2) and critical periods in animal development to the bond between human babies and their mothers. Although Bowlby was trained in PSYCHOANALYSIS (see s. 1, PSYCHOANALYSIS AND RELATED SCHOOLS), this approach formed an alternative to the Freudian view that emotional attachment is based on the mother's ability to satisfy the infant's basic need to be fed.

Bowlby was influenced by Konrad Lorenz's (1935) work on the survival value of imprinting in birds. Imprinting is the mechanism by which newly hatched chicks rapidly learn the specific characteristics of the mother, which enables them to recognise and follow her. Although bonding processes in human newborns are very different, they are analogous to imprinting in that attachment ensures that the parent stays close and responsive to their needs.

Bowlby theorised that crying, smiling and proximity seeking are species-specific action patterns that emerged in human evolutionary history because they promote infant survival (Bowlby 1969). When experiencing pain, fatigue or fear, the infant is predetermined to behave in ways that evoke protection. In turn, parenting behaviours evolved to respond to such stimuli, so providing a reciprocal system of giving and receiving care and protection.

A further feature of imprinting is that it takes place during a restricted time interval during which the chick is able to acquire specific adaptive behaviours. According to Bowlby, there is also a sensitive period for the formation of attachment relationships in young children. This period begins to develop when infants can distinguish their parents from other people (research conducted since Bowlby's original work suggests that this occurs much earlier than he envisaged). Attachment is established at about eight months of age, as wariness of strangers increases and infants begin to protest on separation from their attachment figures. The sensitive period extends over the first few years of life, and failure to form attachments at this time results in a serious detrimental effect on the child's emotional and social development, which Bowlby termed MATERNAL DEPRIVATION.   *BT*

Bowlby, J. 1969: *Attachment and Loss*. Harmondsworth: Pelican Books, vol. 1. **Lorenz, K. Z.** 1935: Der kumpen in der umvelt des vogels. English translation in Schiller, C. H. (ed.), *Instinctive Behaviour*. New York: International Universities Press. 1957.

executive function   Executive function refers to a number of processes, associated with the prefrontal cortex, that are involved in flexible GOAL-DIRECTED BEHAVIOUR (see s. 3), including planning, INHIBITION (see s. 3), WORKING

MEMORY (see s. 3) and attentional control. A widely used test of executive function (EF) is the Wisconsin card sorting test, where individuals must sort cards for a number of trials using one rule (e.g. colour) and then sort cards using a different rule (e.g. shape); this requires a shift in attention and a capacity to inhibit an established response pattern. EF impairment is evident in certain developmental psychopathologies, such as AUTISM (see s. 6) and attention deficit hyperactivity disorder (Pennington and Ozonoff 1996). In addition, the development of EF abilities in young children is associated with the emergence of THEORY OF MIND (e.g. Hughes 1998), a finding that has led to varying interpretations of children's performance on standard theory of mind tasks, such as those testing FALSE BELIEF understanding. *RB*

Hughes, C. 1998: Executive function in preschoolers: links with theory of mind and verbal ability. *British Journal of Developmental Psychology* 16(2), 233–54. **Pennington, B. F. and Ozonoff, S.** 1996: Executive functions and developmental psychopathology. *Journal of Child Psychology and Psychiatry* 37(1), 51–87.

expressive traits Expressive traits are personality traits in adults that are culturally associated with femininity, for example, being sympathetic and warm. *AH*

F

false belief A cognitive representation of the world that is inaccurate, understanding of which is tested using the SALLY-ANNE TASK. [See also THEORY OF MIND] *RB*

fast-mapping Fast-mapping is a process in word learning of connecting a new word onto an underlying concept after very brief exposure to it (e.g. hearing it once or twice). *JC*

father absence Father absence refers to the legal and physical absence of fathers from their children's lives. Father absence and its potential effects on child development are primarily studied in the context of parental divorce; however, father absence resulting from parents never having established a relationship, desertion, parental separation or paternal death has also been investigated. The effects of father absence on children are generally considered negative (particularly for boys) (Amato and Booth 1996). Some recent inquiries hypothesise that father absence is not always harmful and in some contexts (e.g. domestic violence) may be beneficial, especially if it reduces the amount of STRESS (see s. 7) to which children are exposed (Wallerstein, Lewis and Blakeslee 2000). Non-custodial fathers who are authoritative parents [see AUTHORITATIVE PARENTING] and maintain a cordial relationship with their children's mother, are more likely to have children who develop strong identities, positive self-worth and a record of academic achievement (Marsiglio, Amato, Day and Lamb 2000). *MD*

Amato, P. R. and Booth, A. 1996: A prospective study of divorce and parent-child relationships. *Journal of Marriage and the Family* 58(2), 356–65. Marsiglio, W., Amato, P., Day, R. D. and Lamb, M. E. 2000: Scholarship on fatherhood in the 1990s and beyond. *Journal of Marriage and the Family* 62, 1173–91. Wallerstein, J., Lewis, J. and Blakeslee, S. 2000: *The Unexpected Legacy of Divorce*. New York: Hyperion.

foetal alcohol syndrome Prenatal exposure to alcohol can cause a number of defects in the developing organism, known collectively as foetal alcohol syndrome [see TERATOGENS]. Common effects include low birth weight, brain damage, MENTAL RETARDATION, facial abnormalities, stunted growth, hyperactivity and attention problems, among many others. Prenatal alcohol exposure affects development directly by entering the foetus and damaging the developing nervous system and other tissues. Alcohol can indirectly affect prenatal development by restricting the blood supply from the mother. Aside from the fragility of the foetus, damage from alcohol is often severe because both the foetus and its environment in the womb store alcohol for a longer time and in higher concentrations than in the mother's bloodstream (Nulman, O'Hayon, Gladstone and Koren 1998). *FH*

Nulman, I., O'Hayon, B., Gladstone, J. and Koren, G. 1998: The effects of alcohol on the fetal brain: the central nervous system tragedy. In Slikker, W. and Chang, L. W. (eds), *Handbook of Developmental Neurotoxicology*. San Diego: Academic Press.

foetus A term for the prenatal organism from the ninth week after conception until birth. *FH*

formal operational stage In PIAGETIAN THEORY, the formal operational stage is the fourth major period of cognitive development. The stage begins at approximately 11 years of age, when the pre-adolescent's thoughts move from constraints of physical reality to freedom of abstract ideas. HYPOTHETICO-DEDUCTIVE REASONING emerges and probable outcomes of possibilities are imaged. PROPOSITIONAL THOUGHT enables analyses of logical relationships embedded within statements (Muller, Sokol and Overton 1999). Development of recursive thought (Green and Piel 2002) means abstract reflections can centre on one's own thinking. Corresponding focus on being observed and judged by others (termed IMAGINARY AUDIENCE) fosters a slight increase in EGOCENTRISM. Thinking about thoughts also produces new knowledge. Varied research findings have led some theorists to propose abstract thinking occurs at an earlier age than Piaget predicted. Other theorists suggest this higher-ordered thinking first appears in adult years of COGNITIVE DEVELOPMENT or within contexts of formal education (Goswami 1998). *KP*

Green, M. and Piel, J. A. 2002: *Series of human development: a comparative approach*. Boston MA: Allyn and Bacon. Goswami, U. 1998: *Cognition in Children*. Hove, East Sussex: Psychology Press Ltd. Muller, U., Sokol, B. and Overton, W. F. 1999: Developmental sequences in class reasoning and propositional reasoning. *Journal of Experimental Child Psychology* 74, 69–106.

fraternal (dizygotic) twins Fraternal twins occur when two eggs are each fertilised by different sperm at nearly the same time. The resulting twins share the same genetic similarity as full siblings with an age gap. *FH*

friendship influence A term referring to FRIENDSHIP SIMILARITY due to the great influence friends can have on one another, both positive, such as increasing social competence, and negative, such as peer pressure to smoke or drink. *AC*

friendship selection A term referring to FRIENDSHIP SIMILARITY due to friends choosing one another for reasons such as proximity, common needs, interests or personality traits. *AC*

friendship similarity Similarity among friends plays an important role in both the selection and maintenance of friendships. Children tend to select friends of the same age, gender, socio-economic status, and ETHNICITY. Children also befriend those with similar PERSONALITY TRAITS (see s. 6), popularity status, interests and levels of ACADEMIC ACHIEVEMENT (Haselager, Hartup, van Lieshout and Riken-Walraven 1998). In addition, children are attracted to those with similar attitudes and values regarding drug use and alcohol consumption. Since friends both influence and reinforce one another's behaviours, attitudes and interests, friends are likely to become increasingly similar over time. However, as adolescents begin to develop and maintain their own identities, they are more likely to befriend those different from themselves. *AC/AE*

Haselager, J. T., Hartup, W. W., van Lieshout, C. F. M. and Riken-Walraven, J. M. A. 1998: Similarities between friends and nonfriends in middle childhood. *Child Development* 69, 1198–208.

G

gender consistency By six years, children understand that sex is permanent across time and context and are no longer confused by superficial changes in appearance. *AH*

gender constancy Gender constancy is the central idea underpinning Kohlberg's (1966) cognitive-developmental theory which is based on the assumption that children's understanding about gender emerges within a framework of general COGNITIVE DEVELOPMENT. It is children's understanding of gender that initiates GENDER DEVELOPMENT. Slaby and Frey (1975) outlined three stages in the development of children's understanding about gender: GENDER LABELLING, GENDER STABILITY and GENDER CONSISTENCY. After the final stage, children achieve gender constancy, that is, a fully formed gender concept. However, there are mixed findings about the age at which children achieve gender constancy, and increased awareness of gender constancy does not necessarily result in increased preference for same-sex toys or activities. *AH*

Kohlberg, L. A. 1966: A cognitive-developmental analysis of children's sex-role concepts and attitudes. In Maccoby, E.E. (ed.), *The Development of Sex Differences*. Stanford CA: Stanford University Press, 82–173. **Slaby, R. G. and Frey, K. S.** 1975: Development of gender constancy and selective attention to same-sex models. *Child Development* 46, 849–56.

gender development Theoretical accounts of gender development can be broadly divided into cognitive and socialisation accounts. Two ways in which the theories differ are: whether children are conceptualised as active or passive participants in gender development; and the relationship described between GENDER STEREOTYPES and gender-related preferences. In cognitive theories (e.g. GENDER SCHEMA THEORY), the child is an active participant and awareness of gender stereotypes occurs prior to and influences gender-stereotyped behaviour. However, in social theories, the child is a passive participant and awareness of gender stereotypes arises from the child acquiring gender-related preferences by observing and modelling others. These theoretical accounts are outlined in the sections relating to GENDER CONSTANCY, gender schema theory and SOCIAL LEARNING OF GENDER theories.

Gender is a multidimensional construct (Huston 1983), comprising gender stereotypes, activity and interest preferences, personal-social attributes (e.g. personality traits, gender-based social relationships (e.g. gender of friends) and stylistic and symbolic characteristics (e.g. gestures, non-verbal behaviour). The main focus of this section will be on the development of gender-related preferences and gender stereotypes in children.

Children demonstrate consistent gender-related preferences (e.g. for toys, play activities) by three years of age (see Eisenberg et al. 1996). By four to five years of age, children often avoid toys associated with the other sex, even when they are appealing, for example, being new (e.g. Hartup, Moore and Sager 1963). Trautner (1992) identified two patterns in the development of gender-stereotyped preferences. Children show either a large increase in gender-stereotyped preferences until the age of seven years, after which preferences stabilise or,

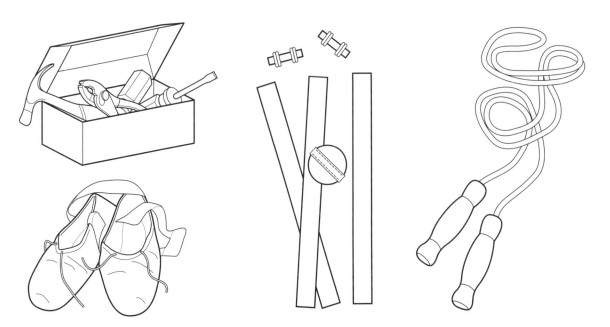

gender development *Stimuli used to ask children about their preferences.*

gender development *Both boys and girls may engage in cross-gender activities. However, it is usually easier for girls to cross gender boundaries than for boys.*

alternatively, they already have strongly stereotyped preferences by the age of five years. Boys' preferences for masculine activities typically increase with age, whereas girls' preferences for feminine activities increase until the age of five or six years, after which girls show declining interest in feminine activities and increasing interest in masculine activities (e.g. Huston 1985). Part of boys' gender development is the avoidance of activities seen to be feminine (Archer 1992), which emerges as early as two years of age and persists into adulthood. A similar process does not occur in girls until adolescence (Hill and Lynch 1982). A consequence of this developmental difference is that boys avoid feminine activities to a greater extent than girls avoid masculine activities, at least until adolescence. Concepts of 'gender boundary maintenance' (Sroufe et al. 1993) explain this difference in adherence to gender-stereotyped preferences as it reaffirms the boundaries of girls' and boys' groups. Boys are more likely to monitor their behaviour on grounds of gender because they are more likely than girls to experience negative reactions by 'straying' across the gender boundary. For example, Levy, Taylor and Gelman (1995) reported that both boys and girls viewed boys with feminine preferences more negatively than they did girls with masculine preferences.

Even three-year-old children hold gender-stereotyped beliefs about objects and activities (e.g. Huston, 1983). Stereotyped beliefs about activities and occupations increase between three and five years of age and reach ceiling levels by seven years (e.g. Martin, Wood and Little 1990). Gender stereotypes in the more abstract domain of personality traits emerge at a later age. Five-year-olds believe that boys are more aggressive, independent and ambitious than girls, and that girls are more sentimental, dependent and emotional. By ten years, their STEREOTYPES (see s. 5) match those of adults (e.g. Williams, Bennett and Best 1985).

Two key changes in gender stereotypes occur during middle childhood. First, stereotyped beliefs become increasingly flexible, and second, they become increasingly complex. Flexibility refers to the extent to which children believe that gender-stereotyped activities or roles are appropriate for both females and males. There is a curvilinear relationship between age and flexibility (Trautner 1992). Very young children show more flexibility before they learn stereotypes, which decreases as stereotypes are learned, but increases again by seven years of age. Typically, girls have more flexible stereotypes than boys by middle childhood. Importantly, though, while flexibility reflects cognitive changes in children's understanding of females' and males' engagement in certain activities, it does not necessarily reflect changes in beliefs about the *appropriateness* of such behaviour (Carter and McCloskey 1984). The second change is the increasing complexity of gender stereotypes. Martin (1989, 1993) conceptualised gender stereotypes as comprising two types of associations that link gender-related information. First, vertical associations are beliefs that link biological sex with gender-related attributes (e.g. that trucks are for boys) and develop at an early age. Second, horizontal associations link together gender-related attributes by a shared relation with masculinity and femininity, allowing us to infer directly that a child who likes trucks would also like cars, even when we do not know the sex of that child. Horizontal associations develop initially for own-sex relevant information (by approximately four to six years of age), and become established for both own- and other-sex relevant information by the age of eight years.

One way of examining children's understanding of horizontal associations is by telling them about children with either masculine or feminine interests and asking them to decide what other activities those children might like. The

193

focus is the judgements that children make when the gender-stereotyping of the target child's interest is inconsistent with their biological sex (e.g. a girl who likes playing with trucks). Adults' judgements about the preferences of another person are based primarily on that person's actual behaviour rather than on stereotypes about what men or women like doing. In contrast, children's judgements are (at least until the age of eight years) based primarily on biological sex (Martin 1989; Martin et al. 1990). When four-to six-year-olds are asked how much a girl would like masculine toys, they do not differentiate between a girl with a masculine interest (e.g. likes trucks) and a girl with a feminine interest (e.g. likes dolls); they rely on the target child's sex as more diagnostic of possible interests than the child's *actual* interests. In contrast, children older than eight years use both sources of information; they predict that the girl who likes trucks would like other masculine toys *more* than would the girl who likes dolls. Older children draw upon horizontal associations in making judgements about other children, and understand that 'masculinity' and 'femininity' are constructs separate from biological sex. In summary, children's preferences remain strongly gender-stereotyped in middle childhood. When they start to become more flexible, this is typically true for girls only. Finally, gender stereotypes become increasingly flexible throughout middle childhood, but also become increasingly complex in structure. *AH*

Archer, J. 1992: Childhood gender roles: social context and organisation. In McGurk, H. (ed.), *Childhood Social Development: Contemporary Perspectives*. Hove: Lawrence Erlbaum Associates. **Carter, D. B. and McCloskey, L. A.** 1984: Peers and the maintenance of sex-typed behaviour: the development of children's conceptions of cross-gender behaviour in their peers. *Social Cognition* 2(4), 294–314. **Eisenberg, N., Martin, C. L. and Fabes, R. A.** 1996: Gender development and gender effects. In Berliner, D. and Calfee, R. C. (eds), *Handbook of Educational Psychology*. London: Prentice-Hall International, 358–96. **Hartup, W. W., Moore, S. G. and Sager, G.** 1963: Avoidance of inappropriate sex-typing by young children. *Journal of Consulting Psychology* 27, 467–73. **Hill, J. P. and Lynch, M. E.** 1982: The intensification of gender-related expectations during early adolescence. In Brooks-Gunn, J. and Petersen, A. C. (eds), *Girls at Puberty: Biological and Psychological Perspectives*. New York and London: Plenum. **Huston, A. C.** 1983: Sex-typing. In Mussen, P. H. and Hetherington, E. M. (eds), *Handbook of Child Psychology: Socialisation, Personality and Social Behaviour*. vol. 4, 387–467. New York: Wiley. **Huston, A. C.** 1985: The development of sex typing: themes from recent research. *Developmental Review* 5, 1–17. **Levy, G. D., Taylor, M. G. and Gelman, S. A.** 1995: Traditional and evaluative aspects of flexibility in gender roles, social conventions, moral rules and physical laws. *Child Development* 66, 515–31. **Martin, C. L.** 1989: Children's use of gender-related information in making social judgments. *Developmental Psychology* 25, 80–88. **Martin, C. L.** 1993: New directions for investigating children's gender knowledge. *Developmental Review* 13, 184–204. **Martin, C. L., Wood, C. H. and Little, J. K.** 1990: The development of gender stereotype components. *Child Development* 61, 1891–904. **Sroufe, L. A., Bennett, C., Englund, M. and Urban, J.** 1993: The significance of gender boundaries and preadolescence: contemporary correlates and antecedents of boundary violation and maintenance. *Child Development* 64, 455–66. **Trautner, H. M.** 1992: The development of sex-typing in children: a longitudinal analysis. *The German Journal of Psychology* 16(3), 182–99. **Williams, J. J., Bennett, S. M. and Best, D. L.** 1985: Awareness and expression of sex-stereotypes in young children. *Developmental Psychology* 11, 635–42.

gender identity Gender identity refers to gendered self-perception and comprises several components, including our sense of masculinity or femininity, self-perception of our activities, traits, interests, abilities and behaviour (see Huston 1983; Ruble and Martin 1998). By the age of eight to nine years, children describe themselves as possessing gender-typed personality traits, with self-perceptions of INSTRUMENTAL TRAITS and EXPRESSIVE TRAITS becoming increasingly gender-typed until early adolescence (Boldizar 1991). Cognitive theories of GENDER DEVELOPMENT emphasise gender identity as being a key motivator for gender-typed behaviour. By approximately two and a half years old, children identify correctly the sex of others and can identify their own sex. This knowledge is assumed to influence children's construction of gender schema [see GENDER SCHEMA THEORY]. *AH*

Boldizar, J. P. 1991: Assessing sex-typing and androgyny in children: the Children's Sex Role Inventory. *Developmental Psychology* 27(3), 505–15. **Huston, A. C.** 1983: Sex-typing. In Mussen, P. H. and Hetherington, E. M., (eds), *Handbook of Child Psychology. Volume 4: Socialization, Personality and Social Development*, 387–467. New York: Wiley. **Ruble, D. N. and Martin, C. L.** 1998: Gender development. In Eisenberg, N. (ed.), *Handbook of Child Psychology. Volume 3: Social, Emotional and Personality Development*. New York: John Wiley & Sons, Inc.

gender labelling By approximately two and a half years old, children can identify correctly the sex of others and identify their own sex. *AH*

gender roles Gender roles refer to the adoption of gender-related activities and characteristics which are culturally defined as masculine (e.g. assertiveness, playing football) or feminine (e.g. being passive, doing ballet) (see Huston 1983). In children, the earliest signs of gender roles are the adoption of same-sex toy preferences. By the age of three years, children demonstrate consistent preferences for toys stereotyped as being appropriate for their own sex (see Eisenberg et al. 1996). By the age of four to five years, children tend to avoid toys associated with the other sex even when they are attractive (e.g. new toys). Girls typically show a wider range of preferences than boys. *AH*

Eisenberg, N., Martin, C. L. and Fabes, R. A. 1996: Gender development and gender effects. In Berliner, D. and Calfee, R. C. (eds), *Handbook of Educational Psychology*. London: Prentice-Hall International, 358–96. **Huston, A. C.** 1983: Sex-typing. In Mussen, P. H. and Hetherington, E. M. (eds), *Handbook of Child Psychology*: Socialisation, Personality and Social Behaviour. vol. 4, 387–467.

gender schema theory Gender schema theories offer an attractive means by which to conceptualise the cognitive organisation of gender-related information (e.g. Bem 1981; Martin and Halverson 1981). Children are seen as active participants in the gendering process and are considered to be motivated to discover more about their gender group once they achieve GENDER LABELLING (this is in contrast to cognitive developmental theory in which children are seen as seeking out information associated with their gender group once they achieve GENDER CONSTANCY). Networks of gender-related information are considered to guide behaviour and gender-typed processing of information. Gender schema comprise diverse information associated with gender and provide the basis for interpreting the environment and selecting appropriate behaviour to adopt. Children learn first about objects and behaviours associated with their own sex, and then about those associated with the other sex. Gender schema affect attention, organisation and memory for gender-related information. There are wide individual differences in the use of gender schemas (Jacklin and Reynolds 1993). Some individuals are highly schematised and rely heavily on GENDER STEREOTYPES when processing information, whereas others are more likely to employ other dimensions. An attractive aspect of this theory is its ability to explain why gender-stereotyped beliefs are so resistant to change. Individuals are prone to either disregard or distort information that is inconsistent with their schema. For example, when children observe individuals engaging in behaviours that are stereotypically associated with the other sex (e.g. a male nurse or female doctor), they tend to distort the information and report that the nurse was female and that the doctor was male (Carter and Levy 1988). A problem for gender schema theories is that the relationship between gender stereotypes and behaviour is largely inconsistent. If cognitions are the major determinants of gender-role development, we would expect to find a relationship between gender-stereotype knowledge and behaviour. However, this relationship is often weak, and although girls and boys acquire gender stereotypes at the same time and pace, there are considerable differences in the flexibility of their STEREOTYPES (see s. 5) and behaviour. *AH*

Bem, S. L. 1981: Gender schema theory: a cognitive account of sex-typing. *Psychological Review* 4, 354–64. Carter, D. B. and Levy, G. D. 1988: Cognitive aspects of children's early sex-role development: the influence of gender schemas on pre-schoolers' memories and preferences for sex-typed toys and activities. *Child Development* 59, 782–93. Jacklin, C. N. and Reynolds, C. 1993: Gender and childhood socialisation. In Beall, A. E. and Sternberg, R. J. (eds), *The Psychology of Gender*. London: Guilford Press. Martin, C. L. and Halverson, C. F. 1981: A schematic processing model of sex-typing and stereotyping in children. *Child Development* 52, 1119–34.

gender stability By three and a half years old, children recognise that sex remains stable over time, but are confused by superficial changes in appearance (e.g. a boy wearing a dress). *AH*

gender stereotypes Gender stereotypes are beliefs relating to gender which consist of culturally relevant expectations about characteristics (e.g. personality traits, activity preferences) that are considered to be appropriate for males and females. The stereotyping process is one of 'applying a stereotypical judgment such as rendering those individuals interchangeable with other members of the category' (Leyens, Yzerbyt and Schadron 1994). For example, assuming that we hold a stereotyped belief that men are good at car maintenance, we might assume that any man is more likely to be adept at repairing cars than a woman. Of course, stereotyped beliefs do not necessarily reflect accurately the actual behaviour and characteristics of males and females. As such, while stereotypes help us categorise a complex world into more coherent and understandable structures (Tajfel 1969), their outcome can be undesirable given that they can deprive individuals of opportunity, for example, restricting the range of activ-

ities from which children are prepared to choose. Martin (1989, 1993) conceptualised gender stereotypes as comprising two types of associations. First, vertical associations are beliefs that link biological sex with gender-related attributes (e.g. trucks are for boys). Even three-year-olds consider specific toys to be 'for boys' or 'for girls'. Second, horizontal associations link together gender-related attributes by a shared relation with masculinity and femininity, and allow us to infer directly that a child who likes trucks would also like cars, even when we do not know the sex of that child. Horizontal associations develop initially for own-sex relevant information (by approximately four to six years of age), and become established for both own- and other-sex relevant information by the age of eight years. In this way, we can use gender stereotypes to make judgements about others based either on their biological sex (e.g. that a boy would like cars) or their interests (e.g. that a child who likes cars would also like tool sets). *AH*

Leyens, L. S., Yzerbyt, V. and Schadron, G. 1994: *Stereotypes and Social Cognition*. London: Sage Publications. Martin, C. L. 1989: Children's use of gender-related information in making social judgments. *Developmental Psychology* 25, 80–8. Martin, C. L. 1993: New directions for investigating children's gender knowledge. *Developmental Review* 13, 184–204. Tajfel, H. 1969: Cognitive aspects of prejudice. *Journal of Psychological Issues* 25, 79–97.

general factor, 'g' General factor 'g' is the theoretical term denoting a single pervasive factor or neurological mental energy that underlies the ability to do all intellectual work. *EE*

generalised other A notion of the collective view or perspective of other people, especially with regard to how others see us. *RB*

giftedness Giftedness is used to describe individuals with extraordinary ability in some area(s), with 'schoolhouse giftedness' and 'creative-productive giftedness' being the two main broad categories (Gregory 2000). Academic or schoolhouse giftedness exists in varying degrees and is often applied to those individuals who score within the top 1 per cent on standard intelligence tests such as the STANFORD-BINET (see s. 6) or WECHSLER SCALES (see s. 6), which translates to an IQ [see INTELLIGENCE QUOTIENT] of approximately 135 or above (Gregory 2000). School grades and teacher recommendations may also be considered in the identification of academic giftedness (Gregory 2000). Creative-productive giftedness refers to children and adults who excel in the development of original products and materials, and is typically considered to be the confluence of above average ability, evidence of creativity and of task commitment (Gregory 2000). *EE*

Gregory, R. J. 2000: *Psychological Testing: History, Principles and Applications* (3rd edn). London: Allyn & Bacon.

'good girl' and 'nice boy' orientation At Kohlberg's stage 3 [see MORAL DEVELOPMENT], children judge behaviour with regard to what makes others happy or helps others, and think about the motivations and intentions behind behaviour. *DW*

195

goodness-of-fit Goodness-of-fit is a model that Thomas and Chess (1977) proposed to describe how child TEMPERAMENT and environmental factors can interact to produce specific outcomes. Goodness-of-fit involves the formation of child-rearing practices and environments that reflect the temperament of the child and promote adaptive functioning. When there is a poor fit, developmental outcomes are distorted and maladjusted. This model illustrates why a child with a difficult temperament [see DIFFICULT CHILD] is at a higher risk for behaviour problems later in development. Children with difficult temperaments are less likely to receive sensitive caregiving and encouragement to try new experiences, and by the age of two, they receive more punitive discipline than other children. Many children respond to this parenting style with defiance and disobedience, leading to more inconsistent parenting and increased irritability and conflict in the parent–child relationship. When parents remain positive and establish a stable environment for their difficult child, these negative behaviours decline (Belsky, Fish and Isabella 1991). *JG*

Belsky, J., Fish, M. and Isabella, R. A. 1991: Continuity and discontinuity in infant negative and positive emotionality: family antecedents and attachment consequences. *Developmental Psychology* 27, 421–31. Thomas, A. and Chess, S. 1977: *Temperament and Development*. New York: Brunner/Mazel.

grammar Grammar is the study of word structures (morphology) and the rules by which words are combined and ordered to form a sentence (SYNTAX – see s. 3). *JC*

grammatical development Grammatical development requires that a child uses more than one word in a single utterance. After the vocabulary spurt [see also SEMANTIC DEVELOPMENT] between the ages of 18 and 24 months, children start to combine two words (e.g. 'Daddy car'). These first sentences are referred to as 'telegraphic speech' as they focus on high-content words and do not include smaller, less important ones. Between two and three years of age, children start using three- and four-word sentences. A rapid increase in the use of grammatical rules also takes place. These sentences adopt the word order of the LANGUAGE (see s. 2) to which the child is exposed (Maratsos 1998). Children also start to add grammatical morphemes (small units of speech which change the meaning of a sentence, e.g. plural markers, 'Daddy's car', and tense markers, 'Mummy walked') and start to be able to form questions and negative statements. At this stage children tend to extend some of these grammatical morphemes to words which are exceptions (e.g. 'mouses' or 'Mummy runned') – a process known as over-regularisation. By the age of two and a half, children can create sentences containing different forms of speech (adjectives, verbs, prepositions, articles, etc.) used in the correct way. Between the ages of three and six, children are starting to use more complex forms of GRAMMAR, and although by six years old they have mastered most of the grammar in their language, their understanding and use of grammar continues to improve throughout their school years. There is debate regarding how grammatical development takes place – whether it is innate [see CHOMSKY'S NATIVIST PERSPECTIVE] or dependent on general COGNITIVE DEVELOPMENT; and about how exactly it takes place. Some theorists believe development takes place as a result of direct observation of the structure of language (Braine 1992). Others take a more nativist approach and argue that children have a specific language-making capacity (Slobin 1985) which helps them to analyse language. Yet another approach – semantic bootstrapping – suggests that children rely on semantic properties of words to work out basic grammatical rules. *JC*

Braine, M. D. S. 1992: What sort of innate structure is needed to 'bootstrap' into syntax? *Cognition* 45, 77–100. Maratsos, M. 1998: The acquisition of grammar. In Kuhn, D. and Siegler, R. S. (eds), *Handbook of Child Psychology: Cognition, Perception and Language* (5th edn). New York: Wiley, vol. 2, 421–66. Slobin, D. I. 1985: Crosslinguistic evidence for the language-making capacity. In Slobin, D. I. (ed.), *The Cross-Linguistic Study of Language Acquisition: Theoretical Issues*. Hillsdale NJ: Erlbaum, vol. 2, 1157–256.

H

habituation Considered the most basic form of LEARNING (see s. 3) (Feldman 2003; Osofsky 1979), habituation refers to a decrease in physiological response to a visual, tactile, auditory or olfactory stimulus following repeated exposure to that stimulus. Physiological reactions may include AUTONOMIC NERVOUS SYSTEM (ANS) (see s. 2 – PARASYMPATHETIC BRANCH AND SYMPATHETIC BRANCH) responses such as heart rate or galvanic skin response changes, or motor reflexes, such as limb movement or eye-blink (Kahn-D'Angelo 1987). When presented with a novel stimulus, infants generally become quiet and more attentive, as well as exhibiting a decreased heart rate, a reaction also known as an orienting response. With repeated exposure to the stimulus, this orienting response gradually disappears. When a new and different stimulus is subsequently presented, infants will respond once again with an orienting response. This DISHABITUATION indicates the infant's ability to distinguish between novel and familiar stimuli. Linked to both physical and COGNITIVE DEVELOPMENT, the capacity for learning through habituation is present at birth and gradually becomes stronger over the course of early infancy. Problems with habituation in infancy can thus be indicative of a larger developmental issue (Feldman 2003). (See also s. 3, HABITUATION) *SF*

Feldman, R. S. 2003: *Child Development* (3rd edn). Upper Saddle River NJ: Prentice-Hall. **Kahn-D'Angelo, L. A.** 1987: Infant habituation: a review of the literature. *Physical and Occupational Therapy in Pediatrics* 7, 41–55. **Osofsky, J. D.** (ed.) 1979: *The Handbook of Infant Development*. Oxford: John Wiley & Sons.

heritability Heritability refers to the influence of genes in the development and expression of a person's traits and behaviours. An estimate of heritability is often derived by comparing family members who differ in their genetic relatedness. For a heritable trait, researchers expect that people who are more similar in that trait also are genetically more similar. INTELLIGENCE is a common example of a heritable trait, estimated to have about 50 per cent heritability (Plomin, DeFries, McClearn and McGuffin 2001). This means that about half of the variability in IQ [see INTELLIGENCE QUOTIENT] scores for the general population can be accounted for by genetic differences between people, and the other half can be accounted for by environmental differences between people (as well as MEASUREMENT ERROR – see s. 8). It is also worth noting that heritability estimates are derived from specific SAMPLES (see s. 8), and may not generalise across ethnic or social groups. *FH*

Plomin, R., DeFries, J. C., McClearn, G. E. and McGuffin, P. 2001: *Behavioral Genetics* (4th edn). New York: Worth Publishers.

heteronomous morality Heteronomous morality is the first stage of the PIAGETIAN THEORY of MORAL DEVELOPMENT. At this stage, children in middle childhood understand that there are rules of behaviour they are expected to follow. Children believe that these rules are developed and maintained by adults or God (external to the SELF), and are thereby understood as unchangeable (moral realism). Children at this stage judge behaviour on the basis of the consequences of the behaviour and not on the intentions of the behaviour. For instance, children judge that a child who breaks 15 cups by accident should be punished more than a child who breaks 1 cup on purpose (Piaget 1932). Additionally, children at this stage believe that punishment is inevitable and will occur immediately following a broken rule; indeed, this is what Piaget (1932) defined as children's belief in immanent justice. *DW*

Piaget, J. 1932: *The Moral Judgment of the Child*. New York: Harcourt Brace.

heterozygous When an individual possesses two different ALLELES for a gene, the gene pair is heterozygous. *FH*

homozygous When an individual possesses two identical ALLELES for a gene, the gene pair is homozygous. *FH*

hypothetico-deductive reasoning A cognitive ability Piaget associated with formal operational thought [see FORMAL OPERATIONAL STAGE] that involves systematically deducing the probable outcomes of all imagined possibilities (hypotheses). *KP*

I

identical (monozygotic) twins Identical twins are the result of a ZYGOTE duplicating itself, producing a pair of zygotes with the exact same genes. *FH*

identity Erik Erikson (1902–94) departed from Freud's teachings by emphasising societal factors in development. His main contribution to the theory of psychosocial development was to extend across the life-span, dividing the life-course into eight stages, each with a specific 'crisis' to resolve. By far the most influential stage to emerge from this formulation was the identity 'crisis' during ADOLESCENCE. Erikson defined identity as 'confidence in one's inner continuity amid change' (Erikson 1968). Furthermore, Erikson proposed that men must achieve a stable identity *prior* to intimacy, whereas women's identity is defined through their intimate roles of wife and mother. Such a formulation was clearly influenced by the historical time and culture in which the theory emerged! From this initial foundation, however, much EMPIRICAL (see s. 8) work has sprung [see also the SELF] (see also s. 1 and s. 5).

Marcia's follow-on work from Erikson has been particularly fruitful (e.g. Marcia 1980). Marcia proposed that individuals may pass through a series of identity statuses, characterised by high versus low levels of exploration and commitment. Such exploration and commitment concern life decisions, such as educational decisions, and religious and political affiliations. Marcia proposed that a typical progression is from IDENTITY DIFFUSION (little sense of commitment without actively seeking to make decisions) to IDENTITY FORECLOSURE (high level of commitment from an authority without exploration of options), to MORATORIUM (active exploration before commitment), to IDENTITY ACHIEVEMENT (firm commitments made after exploration). Subsequent research has found that a cycle from moratorium to achievement, back to moratorium, etc. is also common (Archer 1989), and that development continues well into adulthood.

Parental influences have also been linked to identity (Grotevant and Cooper 1985). In particular, attachment to parents in concert with freedom to voice opinions fosters achievement or moratorium. Overly close bonds without separation are associated with identity foreclosure, and low warmth with open communication is linked to identity diffusion. Finally, historical and cultural influences are highlighted by the fact that full-fledged identity development is being achieved at older ages now than in the past (Archer 1989). (See also s. 5, IDENTITY)
AP

Archer, S. L. 1989: The status of identity: reflections on the need for intervention. *Journal of Adolescence* 12, 345–59. **Erikson, E. H.** 1968: *Identity, Youth, and Crisis*. New York: Norton. **Grotevant, H. D. and Cooper, C. R.** 1985: Patterns of interaction in family relationships and the development of identity exploration in adolescence. *Child Development* 56, 415–28. **Marcia, J. E.** 1980: Identity in adolescence. In Adelson, J. (ed.), *Handbook of Adolescent Psychology*. New York: Wiley, 159–87.

identity achievement The status of having committed to a particular identity or life choices after exploring many options [see IDENTITY]. *AP*

identity diffusion Identity diffusion characterises individuals who have neither committed to a particular identity or life choices, nor are actively exploring options [see IDENTITY]. *AP*

identity foreclosure The status of having committed to a particular identity or life choices prematurely – adopting an identity from an authority figure without having explored alternatives [see IDENTITY]. *AP*

imaginary audience This refers to the view held by many adolescents that they are at the centre of everyone's attention. *AP*

imitation Imitation refers to the performance of specific motor or verbal behaviours that are like those previously enacted by a model. Imitation is an important mechanism for the acquisition of new behavioural repertoires in infancy, and may additionally serve as a basis for the infant's future social interactions (Meltzoff and Moore 1999). Though imitation was originally believed to be a behavioural characteristic only of infants at later stages of COGNITIVE DEVELOPMENT, subsequent research has demonstrated that the capacity to imitate is present as early as a few minutes after birth, indicating that the potential for imitative behaviour may in fact be an innate human characteristic (Meltzoff and Moore 1999). Newborn infants have been found to imitate a range of simple facial gestures, such as mouth opening, smiling and frowning, in response to an adult model, and are able to distinguish between and subsequently approximate adult expressions of happiness, sadness and surprise (Field 1983).

Deferred imitation is a term used to describe imitative behaviour performed following a significant time delay, separating the target action from the response period. Infants as young as 6 weeks of age exhibit deferred imitation following a 24-hour delay, and infants at 14 months are capable of deferred imitation following temporal delays of up to 4 months (Meltzoff 1995). LONGITUDINAL RESEARCH (see s. 1) examining deferred imitation in young infants has found that infants who exhibit poor retention on a deferred imitation task at age 9 months, likewise perform poorly on a later deferred imitation task administered at 15 months – a finding suggestive of a relationship between imitative behaviour and stable cognitive characteristics (Meltzoff and Moore 1999).

Though imitative behaviour is clearly associated with learning, it does not require REINFORCEMENT (see s. 3) or association with an UNCONDITIONED STIMULUS (see s. 3) in order to occur. Early studies of imitation from a social

imitation

physical development allowing for the performance of learned behaviours (Bornstein and Lamb 1992).

HABITUATION is perhaps the most basic and primitive form of learning (Osofsky 1979). The capacity for habituation is present from birth and continues to develop over the first few weeks of life (Feldman 2003). This mechanism for learning occurs following repeated presentation of the same stimulus, and is evidenced by a decrease in physiological response (also referred to as orienting response) to the stimulus with increased exposure. If the infant is subsequently presented with a novel stimulus, the new stimulus should once again elicit an orienting response, a phenomenon known as DISHABITUATION (Kahn-D'Angelo 1987).

As early as a few hours post-birth, infants also demonstrate learning of behaviours via CLASSICAL CONDITIONING (see s. 3). Classical conditioning occurs when a neutral stimulus (the CONDITIONED STIMULUS (see s. 3), or CS) is repeatedly paired with a second stimulus (the UNCONDITIONED STIMULUS (see s. 3), or UCS) that naturally elicits a certain emotional or behavioural response, until exposure to the CS eventually elicits that response when presented alone (Pavlov 1927; Osofsky 1979). Classical conditioning can produce both pleasant and aversive responses to previously neutral stimuli (Feldman 2003). One famous example of classical conditioning in a young infant can be found in Watson and Rayner's 1920 research involving 11-month-old 'Little Albert', who was classically conditioned to fear a white rat after repeated presentations of the rat accompanied by a loud and startling noise. Though he had demonstrated no initial apprehension or fear when presented with the rat prior to this manipulation, the infant eventually began to cry and become fearful when presented with the rat, even in the absence of the unpleasant sound. This fear subsequently generalised to other white, furry objects including a white rabbit and a Santa Claus mask (Watson and Rayner 1920).

Most classical conditioning of newborn behaviour involves pairing a previously neutral stimulus with one that naturally elicits a reflex response such as sucking or startle (Smith 1999), or head-turning (Papousek 1967). For instance, newborn infants who are repeatedly stroked on the head (UCS) prior to being given a small amount of sweet-tasting liquid (CS) eventually learn to turn their heads and suck in response to head-stroking alone (Blass, Ganchrow and Steiner 1984). Similarly, four- to six-week-old infants appear to show a classically conditioned head-turning (rooting) response to an auditory stimulus after the auditory stimulus (CS) has been repeatedly paired with tactile pressure at the corner of the mouth (UCS), a technique that elicits the rooting response, in addition to a nutritive substance (Papousek 1959). Eye-blink is another reflexive response which can be elicited in infants through classical conditioning. For example, 20–24-month-old infants can learn to respond to the sound of a bell by blinking their eyes following repeated pairings of the bell (CS) with a blink-eliciting puff of air (UCS) (Horowitz 1968).

The infant's classically CONDITIONED RESPONSE (see s. 3) may gradually dissipate as a result of EXTINCTION (see s. 3), where repeated presentations of the CS fail to elicit the UCS. When infants in one of the aforementioned studies underwent a series of trials wherein they received ten sec-

learning perspective found that children were most likely to imitate positively reinforced behaviours of a model, yet there exists evidence to suggest that imitation draws upon different cognitive mechanisms to conditioned behaviours. Infants and young children spontaneously imitate observed behaviours even in the absence of clear reinforcers, and are able to transfer these behaviours more easily to new situations and contexts (Hanna and Meltzoff 1993).   *SF*

Field, T. M. 1983: Discrimination and imitation of facial expressions by term and preterm neonates. *Infant Behaviour and Development* 6, 485–9. **Hanna, E. and Meltzoff, A. N.** 1993: Peer imitation by toddlers in laboratory, home, and day care contexts: implications for social learning and memory. *Developmental Psychology* 29, 701–16. **Meltzoff, A. N.** 1995: Understanding the intentions of others: reenactment of intended acts by 18-month old children. *Developmental Psychology* 31, 838–50. **Meltzoff, A. N. and Moore, M. K.** 1999: Persons and representation: why infant imitation is important for theories of human development. In Nadel, J. and Butterworth, G. (eds), *Imitation in Infancy*. New York: Cambridge University Press.

infant learning   Learning refers to a relatively enduring change in behaviour that comes about through practice (Kimble 1961). Learning in infancy is generally thought to occur through one of several cognitive processes, including HABITUATION (see also s. 3), CLASSICAL CONDITIONING (see s. 3), operant (or instrumental) conditioning and IMITATION. It has been suggested that the effectiveness of each of these processes may be limited by the infant's ability to pay attention to or perceive certain stimuli, motivation to perform the learned behaviour and

onds of head-stroking with no subsequent dose of sweet liquid, they eventually ceased to turn their heads and suck in response to head-stroking altogether (Blass, Ganchrow and Steiner 1984).

In addition to habituation and classical conditioning, infants are capable of learning via OPERANT CONDITIONING (see s. 3), the eliciting of a desired behaviour through REINFORCEMENT (see s. 3). This form of learning occurs when certain behaviours are rewarded, either by presenting a desirable stimulus (positive reinforcement) or removing an aversive stimulus (negative reinforcement), thus increasing the likelihood that the behaviour will occur again in the future. Similarly, undesirable behaviours may be halted through punishment, or the presentation of an aversive stimulus (Feldman 2003). As with classical conditioning, behaviours elicited through operant conditioning can be extinguished after several consecutive trials where reinforcement ceases to be given for the conditioned behaviour.

Operantly conditioned responses are voluntary, and are strengthened or weakened according to the nature of the positive or negative reinforcers associated with them. For example, operant conditioning has been used to elicit behavioural change in newborn infants, who learn to suck on a non-nutritive nipple when positively reinforced for this behaviour by hearing the sound of their mothers reading a story (DeCasper and Fifer 1980). Comparable results have been obtained with two-day-old infants, who are also able to learn to alter their patterns of sucking according to whether they are reinforced with the sound of their mothers' voices (Moon and Fifer 1990).

Parents may even be able to manipulate and eventually change their infants' sleep patterns via an operant conditioning PARADIGM (see s. 1). Following an eight-week period wherein parents maintained a consistent schedule of feeding at set intervals and occasionally substituting another caretaking behaviour, such as diapering, for feedings at undesirable times during the night, 100 per cent of infants were induced to sleep through the night, compared to only 23 per cent of infants whose parents had not used this operant conditioning schedule (Feldman 2003).

Finally, learning in infancy may occur via the imitation of others' behaviour. This phenomenon has been demonstrated in infants as early as a few minutes post-partum (Meltzoff and Moore 1997), and is thought to mediate early learning processes such as SCAFFOLDING, in which the infant's initial mimicry of another's behaviour leads to reciprocal imitation by the model, adding to the child's behavioural repertoire by moving a step beyond the child's cognitive starting point. Additionally, imitation is thought to serve as a tool for understanding how objects function and can aid in the understanding and efficient performance of GOAL-DIRECTED BEHAVIOUR (see s. 3) (Meltzoff and Gopnik 1993). *SF*

Blass, E. M., Ganchrow, J. R. and Steiner, J. E. 1984: Classical conditioning in newborn humans 2–48 hours of age. *Infant Behaviour and Development* 7, 223–35. **Bornstein, M. H. and Lamb, M. E.** 1992: *Development in Infancy: An Introduction* (3rd edn). New York: McGraw-Hill Book Company. **DeCasper, A. J. and Fifer, W. P.** 1980: Of human bonding: newborns prefer their mothers' voices. *Science* 208, 1174–6. **Feldman, R. S.** 2003: *Child Development* (3rd edn). Upper Saddle River NJ: Prentice-Hall. **Horowitz, F. D.** 1968: Infant learning and development: retrospect and prospect. *Merrill-Palmer Quarterly* 14, 100–20. **Kahn-D'Angelo, L. A.** 1987: Infant habituation: a review of the literature. *Physical and Occupational Therapy in Pediatrics* 7, 41–55. **Kimble, G. A. (ed.)** 1961: *Hilgard and Marquis' 'Conditioning and Learning'*. East Norwalk CT: Appleton-Century-Crofts. **Meltzoff, A. N. and Gopnik, A.** 1993: The role of imitation in understanding persons and developing a theory of mind. In Baron-Cohen, S. and Tager-Flausberg, H. (eds), *Understanding Other Minds: Perspectives from Autism*. London: Oxford University Press, 335–66. **Meltzoff, A. N. and Moore, M. K.** 1997: Explaining facial imitation: a theoretical model. *Early Development and Parenting* 6, 179–92. **Moon, C. and Fifer, W. P.** 1990: Syllables as signals for 2-day-old infants. *Infant Behaviour and Development* 13, 377–90. **Osofsky, J. D. (ed.)** 1979: *The Handbook of Infant Development*. Oxford: John Wiley and Sons. **Papousek, H.** 1959: A method of studying conditioned food reflexes in young children up to the age of 6 months. *Pavlov Journal of Higher Nervous Activities* 9, 136–40. **Papousek, H.** 1967: Experimental studies of appetitional behaviour in human newborns and infants. In Stevenson, H. W., Hess, E. H. and Rheingold, H. L. (eds), *Early Behaviour*. New York: Wiley. **Pavlov, I.** 1927: *Conditioned Reflexes*. New York: Oxford University Press. **Smith, L. B.** 1999: Do infants possess innate knowledge structures? The con side. *Developmental Science* 2, 133–44. **Watson, J. B. and Rayner, R.** 1920: Conditioned emotional reactions. *Journal of Experimental Psychology* 3(1), 1–14.

information-processing approach This approach is better characterised as a framework for understanding cognition rather than a singular THEORY (see s. 8). In contrast to PIAGETIAN THEORY, information-processing theories agree that COGNITIVE DEVELOPMENT is quantitative, entailing small changes in children's processing speed, processing capacity and amount of general knowledge (Bjorklund 1997). The mind is conceived as a mechanism where different kinds of information are processed with certain constraints and limits. Information stores have been proposed (Atkinson and Shiffrin 1968), along with executive processes thought to be responsible for the control of the flow of information. However, information processing occurs in more complex ways than accounted for by the store model. For example, we engage in PARALLEL PROCESSING (see s. 3) (Bjorklund 1997), namely performing cognitive functions simultaneously rather than carrying out one cognitive activity at a time. The following main factors in cognitive development lead to increasing speed, accuracy and efficiency in cognitive growth (Kail 1997). The capacity of working memory increases with age (Case 1991). Older children have a greater capacity and therefore their WORKING MEMORY (see s. 3) is free to engage in other cognitive operations. Case (1991) examines the interplay between children's processing capacity and their ability to perform more complex tasks with age. Second, children use memory strategies more efficiently with age. The encoding, storing and retrieval of information becomes more effective over time. The capacity for metamemory also develops with age (Gathercole 1999). Metamemory is the ability to think about cognitive processes and strategies. Older children show an increasing ability to select more appropriate strategies for processing information (Kail 1993). Fourth, older children have acquired a larger knowledge base that improves their ability to learn new, and remember stored, information. Most researchers focus on increasing memory span (e.g. Case 1991) and processing speed (e.g. Kail 1997) to account for development, yet there is no overall consensus on the relative roles of other processing capacities in facilitating cognitive development.

EB

Atkinson, R. C. and Shiffrin, R. M. 1968: Human Memory: a proposed system and its control processes. In Spence, K. W. and Spence, J. T. (eds) *The Psychology of Learning and Motivation*. New York: Academic Press. **Bjorklund, D. F.** 1997: In search of a metatheory for cognitive development. *Child Development* 68, 144–8. **Case, R.** 1991: *The Mind's Staircase: Exploring the Conceptual Underpinnings of Children's Thought and Knowledge*. New Jersey: Lawrence Erlbaum. **Gathercole, S.** 1999: Cognitive approaches to the development of short-term memory. *Trends in Cognitive Sciences* 3, 410–19. **Kail, R.** 1993: The role of a global mechanism in developmental change in speed of processing. In Howe, M. L. and Pasnak, R. (eds), *Emerging Themes in Cognitive Development: Foundations*. New York: Springer-Verlag, vol. 1, 97–119. **Kail, R.** 1997: Processing time, imagery, and spatial memory. *Journal of Experimental Child Psychology* 64, 67–78.

inheritance   Inheritance refers to the role of genetics in the development and expression of traits and behaviours. Inheritance can be divided into two broad categories. The first involves inheritance as determined by single genes. Examples include eye colour, hair colour or diseases such as Huntington's disease. The second is inheritance determined by the interactions of many genes. These 'polygenic' influences contribute to complex physical characteristics such as height or weight, and psychological characteristics such as shyness, aggressiveness and intelligence.

The same basic genetic principles are at work in both single-gene and polygenic inheritance. To start with, each person is endowed with a GENOTYPE (see s. 2), or set of genes, composed of strands of DNA (deoxyribonucleic acid) bundled together into a set of 23 pairs of CHROMOSOMES. Upon the fertilisation of an egg cell by a sperm cell, chromosomes from the mother and father are combined so that one half of an offspring's genotype is derived from

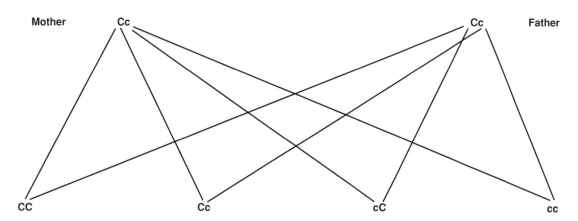

inheritance *Recessive inheritance of cystic fibrosis: CC individuals are affected by the disease; Cc/cC individuals are carriers of the disease; cc individuals are unaffected.*

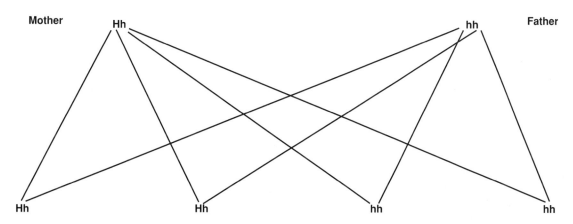

inheritance *Dominant inheritance of Huntington's disease: Hh individuals are affected by the disease; hh individuals are not affected.*

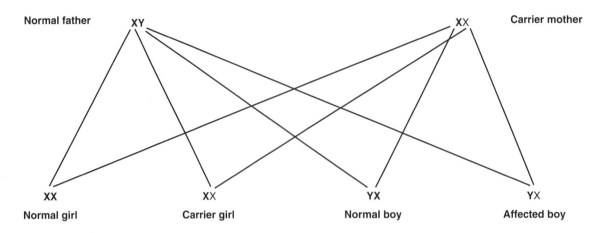

Normal father XY   XX **Carrier mother**

XX   XX   YX   YX

Normal girl   **Carrier girl**   **Normal boy**   **Affected boy**

inheritance *X-linked inheritance of haemophilia.*

each parent. Because genes are paired, they are either redundant or different. A system of DOMINANT-RECESSIVE INHERITANCE, a pattern of inheritance where a dominant gene will always be expressed in the presence of a recessive gene and a recessive gene will only be expressed if paired with another, matching, recessive gene, resolves this problem. Typical dominant gene traits include brown eyes and straight hair, and recessive gene traits include blue eyes and curly hair. Although they are rare, there are genetic disorders that also follow the dominant-recessive patterns of inheritance.

Most single-gene genetic disorders are recessive. This means that many people may be CARRIERS of a disease without ever expressing the disease. Understanding dominant-recessive inheritance has allowed the prediction of the likelihood of passing on disorders that are related to single genes. Any child of two carriers will have a 25 per cent chance that he or she will have the disease, a 50 per cent chance to be a carrier and a 25 per cent chance that the recessive gene will not be present. Examples of recessive gene disorders include PHENYLKETONURIA (PKU) (see s. 2), Tay–Sachs disease and cystic fibrosis.

Serious genetic disorders related to dominant genes are rare because a person who possesses such a disorder would be unlikely to reproduce and pass the gene to the next generation. One notable exception is Huntington's disease. This fatal disease attacks the nervous system, and persists because it usually does not appear before a person is 30 years old. Any offspring of parents where one parent has the disorder and one does not will have a 50 per cent chance of inheriting the disorder.

X-linked inheritance involves traits or disorders whose genes are contained on the female or 'X' SEX CHROMOSOME. Recessive genetic disorders found on the X chromosome include haemophilia, colour blindness and muscular dystrophy. Although these genetic disorders also follow the rule of dominant-recessive inheritance, X-linked inheritance produces a different set of genetic predictions because only females have redundant (XX) sex chromosomes. Because males lack the redundant X chromosome (they are XY), they are vulnerable to any recessive disorders contained on the maternal X chromosome.

Therefore, the daughter of a carrier of haemophilia has a 50 per cent chance of being a carrier. A son has a 50 per cent chance of being a haemophiliac and a 50 per cent chance of not having the gene.

It is also important to note that genetic disorders can occur in a manner unrelated to dominant-recessive inheritance. Problems can occur during the process of cell division that can produce abnormal chromosome configurations. Examples of disorders related to deleted, damaged or extra chromosomes include Turner's syndrome, where there is one X sex chromosome but no second X or Y; Klinefelter's syndrome, characterised by sex chromosomes XXY; and Down's syndrome, where there is an extra 21st chromosome. Chemicals and radiation exposure can also harm chromosomes, leading to serious birth defects [see TERATOGENS].

Polygenic traits arise as the result of the actions of many genes over time. The environment plays an important role in shaping the phenotypic expression of polygenic traits. Because of these many influences, polygenic traits occur across a normally distributed continuum, which means that most people are found to be near the average, and fewer have these traits in extreme forms. Polygenic traits can be physical (e.g. height or weight) or psychological (e.g. INTELLIGENCE or TEMPERAMENT).

Research into the inheritance of psychological tendencies is conducted under the aegis of 'BEHAVIOURAL GENETICS' (see s. 2), a field that studies the dynamic interplay of genes and environments in psychology. Behavioural geneticists use the basic principles of inheritance to predict the role of genes in behaviour. For instance, it is known that IDENTICAL (MONOZYGOTIC) TWINS share 100 per cent of their genes, whereas FRATERNAL (DIZYGOTIC) TWINS share only 50 per cent on average. Therefore, for any heritable trait, monozygotic twins should be more similar than dizygotic twins. An estimate of HERITABILITY (termed 'h²', representing a percentage from 0 to 100) can be determined for each characteristic measured in such studies. Heritability estimates for IQ [see INTELLIGENCE QUOTIENT] in children from western cultures average around $h^2 = .50$. These findings must be interpreted carefully. For instance, h² = .50 does not mean that 50 per cent of any particular child's intelligence is due to genes; it is impossible to generalise from a population estimate to an individual. It is also impossible to separate the influences of genes from the influences of environment. What it does tell us is that genes and environment each account for half the VARIANCE (see s. 8) in IQ scores across the measured population (Plomin, DeFries, McClearn, and McGuffin 2001).

Heritability estimates have been derived for many serious psychological disorders. The genetics of SCHIZOPHRENIA (see s. 7) are the most thoroughly studied. The average person has about a 1 per cent chance of developing the disease. Siblings of someone with schizophrenia have about a 10 per cent chance, and offspring about a 13 per cent chance of developing the disorder (Owen and O'Donovan 2003). TWIN STUDIES (see s. 7) have estimated the heritability of schizophrenia at around 80 per cent (Cardno and Gottesman 2000). Though behavioural genetics can help discern the basic interplay of genes and environments, the exact mechanisms of such interactions are the focus of the related field of behavioural genomics (Plomin, DeFries, Craig and McGuffin 2003). This emerging field combines recent advances in molecular genetics (the science that explores DNA sequences) and behaviour genetics. Researchers in this field continue to identify the specific genes and their functions as they relate to schizophrenia and other psychological disorders.

FH

Cardno, A. G. and Gottesman, I. I. 2000: Twin studies of schizophrenia: from bow-and-arrow concordances to star wars Mx and functional genomics. *American Journal of Medical Genetics* 97, 12–17. Owen, M. J. and O'Donovan, M. C. 2003: Schizophrenia and genetics. In Plomin, R., DeFries, J. C., Craig, I. W. and McGuffin, P. (eds), *Behavioural Genetics in the Postgenomic Era*. Washington, DC: American Psychological Association. Plomin, R., DeFries, J. C., McClearn, G. E. and McGuffin, P. 2001: *Behavioural Genetics*. New York: Worth Publishers.

instrumental purpose orientation At Kohlberg's stage 2 [see MORAL DEVELOPMENT], children judge behaviour with regard to if it is 'fair' and/or satisfies a personal need.

DW

instrumental traits Instrumental traits are PERSONALITY TRAITS (see s. 6) in adults that are culturally associated with masculinity, for example, assertiveness and independence.

AH

intelligence Many different definitions of intelligence exist, but most agree that intelligence is an individual's capacity to solve problems, or a logical reasoning ability used to negotiate in the world (Kline 1991). Intelligence is thus quite distinct from LEARNING (see s. 3), but is rather concerned with individual's *capacity* to learn, or rate of learning. Another key point is that intelligence tests, and researchers concerned with intelligence, are focused on INDIVIDUAL DIFFERENCES (see s. 6) between people in their cognitive ability, and from this perspective, the study of individual differences is viewed as essential for understanding cognitive function.

The traditional PSYCHOMETRIC APPROACH focuses on the assessment of intelligence, and yields IQ scores [see INTELLIGENCE QUOTIENT]. Measurement instruments developed by this approach help identify children functioning at different levels of GIFTEDNESS or MENTAL RETARDATION. However, research evidence also suggests, across infancy through adolescence, earlier assessment outcomes serve as poor predictors of later intelligence quotient (IQ) scores. Explanations of this instability, as well as other variances, depend on how intelligence is defined. Some theorists relate functionality to differences in a single, unitary general ability ('g'). Other theorists associate functioning with variances in SPECIFIC COGNITIVE ABILITIES. Both conceptions of individual differences in intelligence are addressed by current research (Petrill 2003) designed to examine how genetic and environment (shared/non-shared) processes operate in discrete and interactive ways to influence cognitive functioning. In its simplest form, behavioural genetic research [see INHERITANCE] indicates that about half of the variability seen in people's IQ scores is due to genetic differences between people, and half due to differences in people's environments (Plomin, DeFries, McClearn and McGuffin 2001).

Assessments of intelligence have also been used to predict future academic achievement (Kline 1991). Summarising across studies, the average correlation between IQ and academic achievement is approximately 0.5. This correlation decreases from primary school ($r = .6$) through college ($r = .4$). In addition, subjects requiring more abstract reasoning and logic (e.g. natural sciences and mathematics) correlate more highly with tests of 'g' than other subjects (e.g. social sciences, history). (See also s. 6, intelligence)

KP

Kline, P. 1991: *Intelligence: The Psychometric View*. London: Routledge. Petrill, S. A. 2003: The development of intelligence: behavioural genetic approaches. In Sternberg, R. J., Lautrey, J. and Lubart, T. I. (eds), *Models of Intelligence: International Perspectives*. Washington, DC: American Psychological Association, 81–9. Plomin, R., DeFries, J. C., McClearn, G. E. and McGuffin, P. 2001: *Behavioural Genetics*. New York: Worth Publishers.

intelligence quotient (IQ) Intelligence quotient (IQ) scores indicate people's level of ability on standardised INTELLIGENCE tests. The construction of IQ scores allows comparisons across different ability tests and different ages and is an assessment of individual differences between people (as opposed to general shifts in children's COGNITIVE DEVELOPMENT). IQ scores were traditionally calculated as a ratio (mental age divided by chronological age, multiplied by 100). Difficulties with this approach include the inherent assumption that cognitive development is linear across age, and application of the method to adults. In recent years, some suggest that 'deviation IQ' represents a better index (see Cooper 2002). Deviation IQ represents the transformation of intelligence test scores to an average score (based on the population of 100, and a STANDARD DEVIATION (see s. 8) of 15. The resulting distribution of scores has the properties of the NORMAL DISTRIBUTION (see s. 8). (See also s. 6, IQ).

EE

Cooper, C. 2002: *Individual Differences* (2nd edn). Arnold Publishers: London.

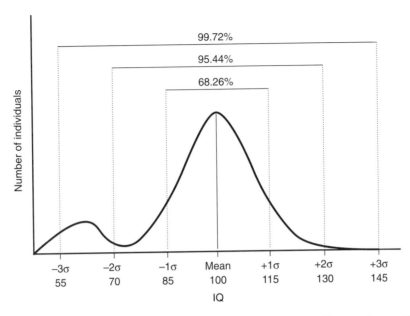

intelligence quotient (IQ) *How intelligence is distributed in the general population of intelligence. Source: D. Bukatko and M. W. Daehler,* Child Development: A Thematic Approach *(5th edn), © 2004 by Houghton Mifflin Company. Used by permission.*

interactional synchrony Mutual and reciprocal interplay of social behaviours or turn-taking observed in pleasurable communicative exchanges between adults and young babies. *BT*

internal working model A central concept of ATTACHMENT theory, defined by Bowlby (1988), was that young children form internalised models or representations of aspects of their experience. In particular, internal working models provide the mechanism by which an understanding of the SELF's relationship to others arises from early interactions with the parents. In infancy, an image of our primary attachment relationship is built up through the way we are treated and what is said to us. This representation works to shape our future RELATIONSHIPS (see s. 5) by setting up an expectation about our treatment by, and our responses to, others.

This includes the way we act, think and feel about the interactions.

The concept was based in psychoanalytical understanding of the infant's relationship with the primary caregiver, involving the manipulation of 'internal objects'. Because the model is said to exist outside of CONSCIOUSNESS (see s. 3), it is resistant to change but can evolve through experiences in subsequent relationships. *BT*

Bowlby, J. 1988: *A Secure Base*. London: Routledge.

intersubjectivity This is a collaborative process where two or more people learn through an activity where knowledge and responsibility are shared. *EB*

I-self A sense of the SELF as knower, distinct from others, continuous over time, and capable of its own actions. [See also ME-SELF] *RB*

J

joint attention A sharing of attention on some common focus between two or more individuals, typically raised in the context of infant–caregiver interaction. *RB*

L

language acquisition device Chomsky (1976) proposed that humans are born with a biologically based innate system called the language acquisition device (LAD). The system aids children's language learning and is triggered by verbal input from the environment. According to Chomsky, the LAD contains a set of universal grammatical rules common to all languages, which means that it can acquire any language provided it is exposed to utterances of that language. The LAD is able to 'perceive' regularities in these utterances and, as long as children have sufficient vocabulary, these rules enable them to produce grammatically consistent novel sentences and to understand the meaning of sentences they hear. The vast diversity of the world's languages has, however, called into question the existence of a set of 'universal grammatical rules' which form the basis of the LAD. [See also CHOMSKY'S NATIVIST PERSPECTIVE].   *JC*

Chomsky, N. 1976: *Reflections on Language*. London: Temple Smith.

language development   Language development can be broken down into development in four main areas: PHONOLOGY (the rules of sound), GRAMMAR (or SYNTAX – see s. 3), SEMANTICS (meaning) and PRAGMATICS (context in which language is used). On average, typically developing children say their first words around the age of 12 months. By the time they are 6 years old, they have a vocabulary of around 10,000 words and can speak in elaborate, grammatically correct sentences. Before children actually produce their first words, they begin to develop some of the skills needed for language and to communicate non-verbally [see PRELINGUISTIC DEVELOPMENT]. The different developmental milestones in phonology, grammar and semantics are described in the relevant entries [see PHONOLOGICAL DEVELOPMENT, GRAMMATICAL DEVELOPMENT and SEMANTIC DEVELOPMENT]. The field of language development began one of the most fierce NATURE-NURTURE (see s. 1, NATURE-NURTURE ISSUE) debates in child development. The behaviourist perspective was championed by B. F. Skinner (1957) who proposed that language is acquired through the process of OPERANT CONDITIONING (see s. 3) whereby something is learnt through REINFORCEMENT (see s. 3). He argued that when children produced sounds that resembled words, this was 'rewarded' by parents, who would smile, hug, clap, etc. Other LEARNING (see s. 3) theorists have suggested that language is learnt in part through imitation (Bandura 1971). There is little support for this perspective today, though it should be noted that adult responsiveness can support children's language learning, even if it cannot explain it. On the other side of the debate was Noam Chomsky [see CHOMSKY'S NATIVIST PERSPECTIVE], who focused on the universal properties of language and argued that language is too complicated to be learnt purely through conditioning or imitation. He proposed that humans are born with a LANGUAGE ACQUISITION DEVICE (Chomsky 1976) which contains a set of underlying rules for any language and which is triggered by verbal input. This theory prompted a huge amount of research suggesting that children's language learning seems to be governed by rules and does develop in systematic ways. However, more recent research and theories tend to lie between the two perspectives and emphasise the interaction between innate predispositions and the environment. Debate still exists as to the nature of these innate dispositions and whether they are specifically for language learning or whether they apply general cognitive tools to the task of language learning (Tomasello 1995).   *JC*

Bandura, A. 1971: An analysis of modeling processes. In Bandura, A. (Ed.), *Psychological Modeling*. New York: Lieber-Atherton. **Chomsky, N.** 1976: *Reflections on Language*. London: Temple Smith. **Skinner, B. F.** 1957: *Verbal Behavior*. New York: Appleton-Century-Crofts. **Tomasello, M.** 1995: Language is not an instinct. *Cognitive Development* 10, 131–56.

'law and order' orientation   At Kohlberg's stage 4 [see MORAL DEVELOPMENT], children judge behaviour based on whether it adheres to rules implemented by authority (authority must be respected and social order maintained).   *DW*

M

maternal deprivation Maternal deprivation syndrome was identified by John Bowlby and associated with infants who have been deprived of a close and continuous ATTACHMENT relationship with a mother figure. The consequences include long-term damage to EMOTIONAL DEVELOPMENT and COGNITIVE DEVELOPMENT. Deprivation could be partial or complete; the former being associated with ANXIETY (see s. 6) and excessive need for love and the latter with MENTAL ILLNESS (see s. 7) and an inability to relate to others.

In developing his theory, Bowlby was influenced by his training in PSYCHOANALYSIS (see s. 1, PSYCHOANALYSIS AND RELATED SCHOOLS and ETHOLOGICAL THEORY), and by studies of the effects of toxins and viruses on an embryo, where the extent of the damage often depends on the timing of its occurrence. He claimed that mother love in early childhood is as important for mental health as vitamins and proteins are for physical health (Bowlby 1951).

Adverse outcomes of children raised in institutions, or who suffered periods of separation from their mothers in early childhood, appeared to confirm Bowlby's hypothesis. Further support came from primate research (e.g. Harlow and Harlow 1969); baby monkeys who were reared in prolonged isolation became extremely disturbed and subsequently failed to care adequately for their own infants. Bowlby was highly critical of care outside the family, claiming, controversially, 'children thrive better in bad homes than in good institutions' (Bowlby 1951: 68).

Later research has failed to substantiate a straightforward link between early separation from the mother and such serious consequences. Michael Rutter (1981) argues that it is important also to consider the antecedents to deprivation and that inadequate substitute care interacts with other stressors. Children who have most difficulties are likely to be those who have never had an attachment relationship (maternal 'privation'). Where maternal care is lost, or 'disrupted', for example through death of the mother in a previously intact family, children's development was not as seriously impaired as when 'distortion' of relationships occurred and children experience ambivalence, violence or neglect.

Current thinking suggests that maternal deprivation is less influential and more modifiable than Bowlby proposed, and the protective effects of secure attachment relationships to caregivers other than the mother have been demonstrated. *BT*

Bowlby, J. 1951: *Maternal Care and Mental Health. Report to the World Health Organisation.* New York: Shocken Books. **Harlow, H. and Harlow, M.** 1969: Effects on various mother-infant relationships on rhesus monkey behaviours. In Foss, B. M. (ed.), *Determinants of Infant Behaviour.* London: Methuen. **Rutter, M.** 1981: *Maternal Deprivation Reassessed* (2nd edn). Harmondsworth: Penguin.

maternal sensitivity A mother's appropriate responsiveness to an infant's physical, emotional and social needs as distinct from her physical availability. *BT*

mental retardation 'Mental retardation refers to substantial limitations in present functioning. It is characterized by significantly sub-average intellectual functioning, existing concurrently with related limitations in two or more of the following applicable adaptive skill areas: COMMUNICATION (see s. 2), self-care, home living, SOCIAL SKILLS (see s. 5), community use, self-direction, health and safety, functional academics, leisure and work. Mental retardation manifests itself before age 18' (American Association on Mental Retardation (AAMR), 1992; cited in Gregory 2000: 231). AAMR considers sub-average intellectual functioning to be an IQ [see INTELLIGENCE QUOTIENT] of 70 to 75 or below, but affirms the importance of professional judgement in individual cases (Gregory 2000). Current diagnostic procedures focus on a hierarchy of 'intensities of needed supports' and rehabilitation needs rather than the shortcomings of the person and their level of retardation (Gregory 2000). (See also s. 7, MENTAL RETARDATION) *EE*

Gregory, R. J. 2000: *Psychological Testing: History, Principles and Applications* (3rd edn). London: Allyn & Bacon.

me-self A sense of the SELF as known, characterised by a set of physical, psychological and material attributes. [See also I-SELF]. *RB*

moral development Moral development refers to how individuals learn, understand and comply with rules and conventions in their interactions with others. Indeed, moral development is one area of social understanding. There are various theories of moral development: biological theories (focused on the inherent goodness of individuals), social learning theories (focused on REINFORCEMENT – see s. 3, punishment and observational learning), cognitive developmental theories (focused on children's moral reasoning as an aspect of their COGNITIVE DEVELOPMENT). The most accepted theories are those with a cognitive developmental basis.

In 1932 Piaget introduced his cognitive developmental theory of moral development. Piaget argued that children's moral development was a result of their cognitive development. The PIAGETIAN THEORY of moral development includes two stages: HETERONOMOUS MORALITY, characterising children's moral understanding in middle childhood, and AUTONOMOUS MORALITY, characterising children's moral understanding in late childhood through adulthood. Piaget's (1932) interview with young boys about the rules of marbles demonstrated that in middle childhood (the PREOPERATIONAL STAGE) rules were believed to be inflexible, while in late childhood (the CONCRETE OPERATIONAL STAGE) rules were believed to be mutually agreed upon social conventions that can change. Piaget also interviewed children using hypothetical dilemmas, such as: John accidentally broke 15 cups. Henry purposely broke 1 cup. Who is naughtier, John or Henry? The younger children believed that John was naughtier because he broke more cups, whereas the older children believed that Henry was naughtier because he *intended* to break the 1 cup, whereas John did not intend to break the 15 cups.

Kohlberg also used hypothetical dilemmas in expanding Piaget's theory of moral development. Kohlberg modified Piaget's interview methodology to standardise the interview process. For example, one of Kohlberg's well-known stories is: 'In Europe, a woman was near death from a special kind of cancer. There was one drug that the doctors thought might save her. It was a form of radium that a druggist in the same town had recently discovered. The drug was expensive to make, but the druggist was charging ten times what the drug cost him to make. He paid $200 for the radium and charged $2,000 for a small dose of the drug. The sick woman's husband, Heinz, went to everyone he knew to borrow the money, but he could only get together $1,000 which is half of what it cost. He told the druggist that his wife was dying and asked him to sell it cheaper or let him pay later. But the druggist said, "No, I discovered the drug, and I am going to make money from it." So Heinz got desperate and broke into the man's store to steal the drug for his wife.' (Kohlberg, 1969: 379)

After hearing the story, children were asked a series of questions (e.g. should Heinz have stolen the drug? Was stealing it right or wrong? Why?). From the interviews, Kohlberg developed his stage theory of moral development. Kohlberg's theory was similar to Piaget's, but offered more detail of moral development through adulthood. Kohlberg proposed three levels of moral development with two stages within each level: 1) PRECONVENTIONAL LEVEL, similar to Piaget's heteronomous morality, with a PUNISHMENT AND OBEDIENCE ORIENTATION and an INSTRUMENTAL PURPOSE ORIENTATION 2) CONVENTIONAL LEVEL, similar to Piaget's autonomous morality, with a 'GOOD GIRL' AND 'NICE BOY' ORIENTATION and a 'LAW AND ORDER' ORIENTATION; 3) POSTCONVENTIONAL LEVEL, with a SOCIAL CONTRACT ORIENTATION and a UNIVERSAL ETHICAL PRINCIPLE ORIENTATION. Both Piaget and Kohlberg believed that children's interactions with their peers enhanced their moral understanding through the process of RECIPROCITY (mutual give-and-take).

Although there is evidence demonstrating that children do have higher moral reasoning as they age (Rest 1983), there are critics of Kohlberg's theory. Turiel (1983) challenged the stage theory proposal that the moral stages are the same for all types of social rules. Turiel argued that rules are arranged in different domains; in particular, there is the moral domain that encompasses issues in relation to welfare, justice and rights, based on the understanding that behaviours have consequences for other individuals (e.g. one is not supposed to hit another person). Additionally, there is the social conventional domain that encompasses issues in relation to behaviours that are mutually defined by SOCIETY (see s. 5) and are based on the understanding that behaviours have consequences because of the expectations of society (e.g. one should eat one's food with a fork), but that these expectations may change by mutual consent (e.g. one can eat French fries with one's fingers). Research has demonstrated that young children do see these two sets of rules differently, with moral transgressions judged as more serious than social conventional transgressions (e.g. Arsenio and Ford 1985; Tisak and Turiel 1988). Turiel proposed that mod-

els of moral development may be incorrect in stating that moral understanding occurs late in childhood or adolescence; indeed, Turiel stated that such models demonstrate the development of social conventional rule understanding, and that moral rule understanding occurs earlier in childhood (Turiel 1983).

A further criticism of Piaget's and Kohlberg's theories of moral development is that their theories were developed through interviews with boys, leading to what Gilligan (1982) argued was a justice perspective. The justice perspective primarily focuses on the rights of individuals to make moral choices. Gilligan introduced the care perspective, which focuses on communication, relationships and concern for other individuals. Gilligan proposed that girls would demonstrate more of a care perspective to moral understanding. Gilligan and Attanucci (1988) demonstrated that when asked to think about and rate moral dilemmas that they had experienced, both boys and girls focused on both types of concerns, but boys focused more on the justice concerns and girls focused more on the care concerns. *DW*

Arsenio, W. and Ford, M. 1985: The role of affective information in social-cognitive development: children's differentiation of moral and conventional events. *Merrill-Palmer Quarterly* 31, 1–17. **Gilligan, C.** 1982: *In a Different Voice.* Cambridge MA: Harvard University Press. **Gilligan, C. and Attanucci, J.** 1988: Two moral orientations: gender differences and similarities. *Merrill-Palmer Quarterly* 34, 223–37. **Kohlberg, L.** 1969: Stage and sequence: the cognitive-developmental approach to socialization. In Goslin, D. A. (ed.), *Handbook of Socialization Theory and Research.* Chicago: Rand McNally. **Kohlberg, L.** 1984: *The Psychology of Moral Development: The Nature and Validity of Moral Stages.* San Francisco: Harper & Row, vol. 2. **Piaget, J.** 1932: *The Moral Judgment of the Child.* New York: Harcourt Brace. **Rest, J.** 1983: Morality. In Flavell, J. H. and Markman, E. M. (eds), *Handbook of Child Psychology: Cognitive Development.* New York: Wiley, vol. 3. **Tisak, M. and Turiel, E.** 1988: Variation in seriousness of transgressions and children's moral and conventional concepts. *Developmental Psychology* 24(3), 352–7. **Turiel, E.** 1983: *The Development of Social Knowledge: Morality and Convention.* Cambridge: Cambridge University Press.

moral understanding Moral understanding is the comprehension of moral rules. Piaget and Kohlberg developed theories to explain children's moral reasoning about various dilemmas [see MORAL DEVELOPMENT]. Turiel (1983) argued that moral rule understanding occurred earlier than both Piaget and Kohlberg had proposed. However, it is possible that moral understanding is present prior to children's ability to articulate their understanding. Dunn (1987) focused on the ability of two-year-old children to understand social rules. Children at this age were able to make reference to a sibling violation of an expectation or unwritten rule in conflict situations (e.g. being bumped), and were also able to make moral judgements about behaviour (e.g. using words such as bad, naughty, nice). At three years of age children demonstrate an understanding of being accountable for behaviours, for example, by blaming others or denying responsibility for their actions (Dunn 1988). In understanding accountability, children are demonstrating that they have a concept of SELF and are able to combine this with a concept of goodness. Children's use of excuses or justifications demonstrates that they also understand that rules may differ for different people. Additionally, these young children tend to question why rules apply to some, but not to others (Dunn 1988).

Research has also demonstrated that five-year-old children are able to differentiate between different types of transgressions and that their responses change as they age. For example, from age five to age six, the belief that cheating is a more serious offence than hitting someone increased significantly (Dunn, Brown and Maguire 1995). Parental factors are also linked to moral understanding. Children of mothers who demonstrated more effective methods of conflict resolution demonstrated higher levels of moral understanding than did children of less effective mothers. Specifically, these mothers were more likely to explain conflicts by considering their three-year-old child's perspective. Additionally, Dunn et al. (1995) demonstrated that children's ability to assess how others feel (emotion understanding) was related to how they respond to moral issues.   *DW*

Dunn, J. 1987: The beginnings of moral understanding: development in the second year. In Kagan, J. and Lamb, S. (eds), *The Emergence of Morality in Young Children*. London: The University of Chicago Press. **Dunn, J.** 1988: *The Beginnings of Social Understanding*. Oxford: Blackwell Publishers. **Dunn, J., Brown, J. and Maguire, M.** 1995: The development of children's moral sensibility: individual differences and emotion understanding. *Developmental Psychology* 31(4), 649–59. **Turiel, E.** 1983: *The Development of Social Knowledge: Morality and Convention*. Cambridge: Cambridge University Press.

moratorium The identity status characterised by being in the midst of exploring several alternative identities or life-choices. [See also IDENTITY]   *AP*

N

neglected children These children are neither liked nor disliked by their peers; they are unsociable, but are not necessarily shy or aggressive and can be well adjusted.
AC/AE

neglectful parenting Also known as uninvolved parenting, this parenting style is characterised by low demands and low warmth. Parents are withdrawn and indifferent to children.
AE

O

object permanence Object permanence is the cognitive understanding that objects continue to exist independent from one's actions and/or direct sensory experiences. In PIAGETIAN THEORY, awareness of object permanence is a milestone in cognitive advancement. At the start of the SENSORIMOTOR STAGE, the infant associates the existence of objects with self-generated actions and/or visual perceptions. What the infant's mind conceives is what the infant's eyes can see and actions can produce. Understanding object permanence means the toddler can think about images of a world filled with many permanent objects, including an independent SELF (Crain 2000). Piagetian theory, asserting partial comprehension of object permanence, begins at approximately 8–12 months of age and full understanding occurs at 18–24 months of age. Studies exploring Piaget's proposals suggest object permanence develops at an earlier chronological age (Solso 2001).

KP

Crain, W. 2000: *Theories of Development: Concepts and Applications* (4th edn). Upper Saddle River NJ: Prentice-Hall, Inc. **Solso, R. L.** 2001: *Cognitive Psychology* (6th edn). Boston: Allyn & Bacon.

operations In PIAGETIAN THEORY, a term for reversible mental actions that enable the individual to logically transform, separate and combine information. *KP*

overextension Overextension in word learning is the opposite of UNDEREXTENSION, involving children applying a learnt word to a wider set of circumstances, events or objects than it should be used for (e.g. 'dog' to refer to all animals).

JC

P

---

parenting Parents are the first and perhaps primary socialising agents for children. This powerful influence can be seen in numerous areas of development, such as children's learning of GENDER ROLES, MORAL DEVELOPMENT, social-emotional functioning and cognitive growth. As a result, much ATTENTION (see s. 3) is paid to pinpointing optimal family structures and parenting practices. Increasingly, fewer children grow up in two-parent, traditional homes; many children live in stepfamilies, with single parents, in gay and lesbian families and in grandparent-headed households. Although some research suggests children fare better in two-parent households, any home that is stable and nurturing, regardless of type, can yield competent and well-adjusted children (Golombok 2000).

At different stages in a child's life, different challenges exist for parents. In infancy, parents are often concerned about the adjustment to the new baby and bonding. There has been much discussion about the importance of early bonding with an infant; however, research suggests there is no critical period for bonding with human babies. This means that adoptive parents or parents separated from their babies shortly after birth have just as many opportunities to create close connections with their babies as other parents. Early infant–parent relationships are important and can lead to different types of ATTACHMENT. The mothers of securely attached babies are high in responsiveness and sensitive to their babies' needs.

In adolescence, new challenges emerge when parents deal with adolescent children and their increasing desires for freedom. Research shows there are variations among families in the amount of ensuing conflict. White-American parents generally experience more conflict with their teenagers than African-American or Latino-American parents (Barber 1994). Parents who have clear expectations yet are willing to consider children's opinions also experience less discord with their adolescent children. Even as teenagers, these children are more competent in school and less likely to use drugs or alcohol.

One of the greatest challenges parents face, regardless of the child's age, is learning how and when to discipline. Research suggests children learn better behaviour through REINFORCEMENT (see s. 3) than punishment. Three general types of discipline strategies have been identified: power assertion, inductive techniques and withdrawal of love (Grusec and Goodnow 1994). Power assertion, including smacking and threatening, is the attempt to get children to obey through physical or verbal force. There is much debate over the effectiveness of smacking, with growing research supporting the idea that parental aggression only increases children's aggressive behaviour (Kazdin and Benjet 2003). Inductive techniques focus on reasoning as the method for producing desirable behaviour in children. In an attempt to get a child to behave, parents may also withdraw their love from that child by ignoring or showing dislike. Of the three, induction is the most effective, particularly with older children, and power assertion is the least.

Unfortunately, some parents abuse their children. Four major types of abuse are commonly identified: physical abuse, sexual abuse, emotional maltreatment and neglect (Cicchetti and Toth 1998). In some cases, however, it is difficult to distinguish abuse from normative parenting or discipline strategies, as parents may not consider certain practices as abusive. For example, in Cambodia, fever is often treated by rubbing hot coins over the child's back or chest, a practice that would be considered abusive in many other cultures. Parents who are more likely to abuse their children are those who themselves were abused as children, lack control, believe in harsh punishment and feel personally incompetent. Children who are more likely to be abused are those that are often sick, were born with low birth weight or other medical problems and have difficult TEMPERAMENTS. Fortunately, child abuse can be prevented through education, community support and addressing larger social problems like poverty, drug abuse and teen pregnancy.

Many researchers look for models to classify parenting styles and pinpoint optimal strategies; the most famous is BAUMRIND'S PARENTING TYPOLOGY. Baumrind identified four parenting styles based on parental demandingness and responsiveness: AUTHORITARIAN PARENTING, AUTHORITATIVE PARENTING, PERMISSIVE PARENTING and NEGLECTFUL PARENTING. Authoritative parenting, marked by high but realistic demands and high warmth, is largely agreed on as the most effective style for raising competent children. Cultural context also plays a role in parenting styles and practices. For example, in collectivist societies, including much of Africa and Japan, indulgent care of infants is common. This care includes co-sleeping, feeding on demand and constantly attending to crying babies. In contrast, in individualistic cultures, such as the USA, independence is stressed over interdependence; thus infants often sleep in separate rooms, are fed on a schedule and are thought to be spoiled if picked up every time they cry (Small 1998). Neither way is inherently better, as both aim to instil in children the important VALUES (see s. 5) of that particular culture.

Throughout the life-course, parents may face special challenges as they attempt to provide for their families. Chief among these are the difficulties balancing work and family responsibilities. Unemployed parents are more prone to DEPRESSION (see s. 7) and more likely to punish their children, in turn leading to more behavioural problems in the children. Many families, where both parents work outside the home, place their children in day care and after-school programmes. Although there are mixed findings about the impact of early childcare [see ATTACHMENT], some research suggests that young children who spend much time in day care are more aggressive and less securely attached to their parents. Other studies point to the possible positive effects, especially for low-income families who lack educational resources. In a landmark study, The Abecedarian Project (Ramey and Campbell 1999) found that underprivileged children who received quality day care scored higher on reading and maths and were more likely to graduate from college than a comparison group of low-income infants who did not attend quality day care. Results from this study suggest that the quality of the day care, rather than the number of hours spent in day care, determines whether children experience positive or negative effects. In sum, parenting is a complex and varying task. There is no universally right way to raise children; different parental, child and cultural characteristics interact to produce effective parenting.

Barber, B. K. 1994: Cultural, family, and personal contexts of parent-adolescent conflicts. *Journal of Marriage and the Family* 56, 375–86. **Cicchetti, D. and Toth, S.** 1998: Perspectives on research and practice in developmental psychopathology. In Damon, W. (series ed.) and Sigel, I. and Renningerg, K. (volume eds), *Handbook of Child Psychology: Child Psychology in Practice.* New York: John Wiley, vol. 4. **Golombok, S.** 2000: *Parenting: What Really Counts?* New York: Routledge. **Grusec, J. E. and Goodnow, J. J.** 1994: Impact of parental discipline methods on the child's internalization of values: a reconceptualization of current points of view. *Developmental Psychology* 30, 4–19. **Kazdin, A. E. and Benjet, C.** 2003: Spanking children: evidence and issues. *Current Directions in Psychology Science* 12, 99–103. **Ramey, C. and Campbell, F.** 1999: Effects of early intervention on intellectual and academic achievement: a follow-up study of children from low income families. *Child Development* 63, 684–98. **Small, M. F.** 1998: *Our Babies, Ourselves.* New York: Anchor Books/Doubleday.

partners in crime Children with close sibling relationships may encourage and promote each other's delinquency by engaging in deviant acts together.

BM

paternal interaction Paternal interaction refers to the extent fathers are actually involved in hands-on child-rearing tasks, nurturing or play activities, as opposed to simply physical presence. *MD*

paternal involvement Greater attention is currently being paid to the distinct role fathers play in the lives of their children, and the impact of that role on the father, his children and the family as a whole (Pruett 1993). Contemporary research recognises the varied yet distinct roles fathers play within the family, ranging from the traditional, distant, 'breadwinner' father, to the contemporary figure who takes a more active role in child-rearing duties. In general, greater paternal involvement is beneficial for children's well-being and academic success. Fathers who are confident in their child-rearing skills, have positive marital relations and adopt realistic expectations for their children are especially effective in promoting positive child development. In some areas of development, such as gender-role socialisation, fathers contribute more than mothers do (Leve and Fagot 1997).

MD

Leve, L. D. and Fagot, B. I. 1997: Gender-role socialization and discipline processes in one- and two-parent families. *Sex Roles* 36, 1–21. **Pruett, K. D.** 1993: The paternal presence. *Families in Society* 74(1), 46–50.

paternal presence Paternal presence refers to the emotional and physical availability of fathers in their children's lives and how this affects children's development. This is often examined in the context of divorce. *MD*

paternal responsibility Paternal responsibility refers to the conventional expectation of the father as the breadwinner and protector. *MD*

peer relationships Being accepted by the wider peer group is different from having close friends. Sociometric ratings [see SOCIOMETRIC STATUS] are used to determine whether individuals are considered POPULAR CHILDREN, REJECTED CHILDREN, NEGLECTED CHILDREN or CONTROVERSIAL CHILDREN within the larger peer group. Although popular children find it easier to establish close friends, many unpopular children manage to enter into at least one reciprocal friendship. Having at least one close friend is associated with better psychological adjustment (e.g. less lonely and greater sense of self worth).

Children's concepts of friendships, and the ways they behave with friends, change with age, reflecting cognitive and emotional growth (Hartup and Stevens 1999). Younger children tend to describe their friends by referencing physical characteristics and shared activities (e.g. 'We like to play football together'), whereas adolescents describe their friends' personalities, shared VALUES (see s. 5) and mutual loyalty (Rubin, Bukowski and Parker 1998). As children mature they spend more time with peers and less with parents. Being able to confide in friends and get both emotional and instrumental assistance becomes more important as children get older. Girls tend to report higher levels of intimacy in their friendships than boys do, and they achieve emotional intimacy in their cross-sex friendships at earlier ages.

Although friendships are typically based on FRIENDSHIP SIMILARITY and personal choice, parents still influence children's choice of peers. Through their socialisation practices and child-rearing styles, parents communicate values and ATTITUDES (see s. 5). Children often adopt similar values and attitudes and use them to select friends. Parents further influence their children's choice of friends by planning and supervising children's activities. Finally, the quality of a child's attachment to their parents can influence the quality of children's current and future peer relationships. Specifically, children who are securely attached to their parents, who are independent yet emotionally close, tend to have more positive interactions with peers.

In short, peer relationships provide a source of SOCIAL SUPPORT (see s. 5) and companionship for children and are crucial for children's cognitive, behavioural and EMOTIONAL DEVELOPMENT. Further, good peer relations in childhood are predictive of healthy development in adulthood.

AC/BM

Ducharme, J. and Doyle, A. 2002: Attachment security with mother and father: associations with adolescents' reports of interpersonal behaviour with parents and peers. *Journal of Social and Personal Relationships* 19(2), 203–31. **Hartup, W. W. and Stevens, N.** 1999: Friendships and adaptation across the life span. *Current Directions in Psychological Science* 8, 76–9. **Rubin, K. H., Bukowski, W. and Parker, J. G.** 1998: Peer interactions, relationships, and groups. In Damon, W. and Eisenberg,

N. (eds) *Handbook of Child Psychology: Social, Emotional, and Personality Development*. New York: Wiley, vol. 3, 619–700.

permissive parenting
Also known as indulgent parenting, this parenting style is characterised by low demands and high warmth. Parents don't set many rules and rarely punish children.   *AE*

personal fable
A cognitive distortion held by many adolescents that they are unique, coupled with an over-inflated sense of importance.   *AP*

phonological development
Phonological development refers to the acquisition of the sounds appropriate to a LANGUAGE (see s. 2) and their organisation into speech patterns. Observations of children's first words indicate that early phonological and SEMANTIC DEVELOPMENT are related; children are influenced in part to say what they can actually pronounce, hence the first words tend to start with consonants and end with vowels ('mama', 'dada'). Phonological strategies start to appear in the middle of the second year when children start to try different sounds. At this stage their pronunciation is not always right, but research has shown that their errors are consistent and follow a general developmental pattern (Vihman 1996). At first children focus on the stressed syllable of a word, after which they add ending consonants, unstressed syllables and adjust the vowel length. Eventually they are able to produce the whole word with a correct stress pattern (Demuth 1996). Phonological development continues during the pre-school years, and by the time children go to school it is almost complete.   *JC*

Demuth, K. 1996: The prosodic structure of early words. In Morgan, J. and Demuth, K. (eds) *From Signal to Syntax*. Mahwah NJ: Erlbaum, 171–84. **Vihman, M. M.** 1996: *Phonological Development*. London: Blackwell.

phonology
Phonology is the study of speech sounds in a LANGUAGE (see s. 2), and of how these units of sound (PHONEMES – see s. 3) can be combined and organised within a language.   *JC*

Piagetian theory
Piagetian theory is a set of inter-related concepts put forth by the Swiss psychologist, Jean Piaget (1896–1980) to describe and explain how human cognition develops. According to Piaget's theory, children actively participate in constructing their understandings of the world. Heredity endows all children with two tendencies for constructing this understanding (Ginsburg and Opper 1988). The first tendency, organisation, facilitates ordering of mental structures, or SCHEMES, into meaningful systems. A second tendency, ADAPTATION, involves the twofold process of interpreting experiences through ASSIMILATION of new information into mental structures and through ACCOMMODATION of existing mental structures to fit new realities. Different experiences create a state of mental disequilibrium between what is known and what is encountered. The EQUILIBRATION of going back and forth from assimilation to accommodation brings mental equilibrium and cognitive advancement (Green and Piel 2002). Piagetian theory further suggests that COGNITIVE DEVELOPMENT of all children involves these change mechanisms, encompasses similar mental gains and proceeds through identical stages. During the SENSORIMOTOR STAGE (birth–2 years), infants coordinate sensory and motor schemes to construct an initial understanding of the world. By the end of this period, young children acquire OBJECT PERMANENCE and know objects exist independently from personal actions and sensory experiences. In the PREOPERATIONAL STAGE (2–7 years), young children can further organise MENTAL REPRESENTATIONS (see s. 3) into symbolic schemes for words and images. Towards the end of this stage, thinking is less constrained by EGOCENTRISM, as the ability to distinguish between one's own and others' perspectives emerges. Throughout the CONCRETE OPERATIONAL STAGE (7–11 years), school-aged children develop mental abilities for logically thinking about, as well as systematically classifying, concrete objects and events. Within the FORMAL OPERATIONAL STAGE (11+ years), adolescents apply logical thinking and abstract reasoning to ideas and hypothetical possibilities. Across each stage, acquisition of new mental abilities depends on prior cognitive advancements. Some theorists question the invariance of predicted stages, timing of cognitive advances and universality of formal operational processes. Nevertheless, the cognitive abilities identified by Piaget continue to be acknowledged (Galotti 1999). The theory's influence on education reform (Smith 2003) and cognitive research remains unparalleled.   *KP*

Galotti, K. M. 1999: *Cognitive Psychology in and out of the Laboratory* (2nd edn). Belmont CA: Brooks/Cole-Wadsworth Publishing Company. **Ginsburg, H. P. and Opper, S.** 1988: *Piaget's Theory of Intellectual Development* (3rd edn). Englewood Cliffs NJ: Prentice Hall. **Green, M. and Piel, J. A.** 2002: *Theories of Human Development: A Comparative Approach*. Boston MA: Allyn & Bacon. **Smith, L.** 2003: Teaching reasoning in a constructivist epistemology. *Educational and Child Psychology*, 20(2), 31–50.

popular children
These children are well liked by their peers; physically attractive children and those with good SOCIAL SKILLS (see s. 5) are overrepresented in this group.   *AC/AE*

postconventional level
The postconventional level is the third major level of Kohlberg's theory of MORAL DEVELOPMENT. Kohlberg (1984: 173) stated that at this level individuals understand and accept societal rules, but that 'acceptance of society's rules is based on formulating and accepting the general moral principles that underlie those rules.' Indeed, these principles may conflict with specific rules and the individual at this level will make judgements about behaviour on these principles rather than on the rules. At this level individuals will have separated their own VALUES (see s. 5) and beliefs about right and wrong from those values and beliefs of others, and will judge behaviour on the basis of their own values and beliefs. Kohlberg (1984) further stated that few adults ever reach this level of moral reasoning, and if they do it is after 20 years of age. Within this level Kohlberg proposed two stages (SOCIAL CONTRACT ORIENTATION and UNIVERSAL ETHICAL PRINCIPLE ORIENTATION).   *DW*

Kohlberg, L. 1984: *The Psychology of Moral Development: The Nature and Validity of Moral Stages*. San Francisco: Harper & Row, vol. 2.

post-formal thought Piaget proposed the final (fourth) stage of COGNITIVE DEVELOPMENT to be formal operations, during adolescence. Psychologists have since proposed that cognitive development continues throughout the life-course, and in particular that a fifth stage, coined post-formal operational thought, characterises many people's thinking in adulthood (Demtrious 1988). Adults no longer view all information as absolute truth, but acknowledge that multiple views can be valid. That is, post-formal thought recognises that knowledge can be relativistic and socially constructed. Post-formal thought also encourages tolerance towards seemingly opposing world-views and information systems. This stems from experience in the real world, and the everyday tasks of deciding between multiple alternatives. Finally, adults integrate such contradictory knowledge in order to formulate a coherent understanding of life's experiences; hence the real development during this stage is the tempering of adolescent idealism by real-world practicalities.   *AP*

Demtrious, A. (ed.) 1988: *The Neo-Piagetian Theories of Cognitive Development: Toward an Integration.* Amsterdam: North-Holland.

pragmatics Pragmatics is the study of the relationship between LANGUAGE (see s. 2) and the context in which it is used.   *JC*

preconventional level The preconventional level is the first major level of Kohlberg's theory of MORAL DEVELOPMENT. At this level individuals do not yet have an understanding and do not endorse conventional or societal rules and expectations (Kohlberg 1984). With no internalisation of moral values, moral reasoning at this level is controlled by external rewards and punishment. Individuals who are at this level of moral understanding are usually under nine years of age, although they may also be older. This level encompasses two stages of moral understanding: the PUNISHMENT AND OBEDIENCE ORIENTATION and the INSTRUMENTAL PURPOSE ORIENTATION.   *DW*

Kohlberg, L. 1984: *The Psychology of Moral Development: The Nature and Validity of Moral Stages.* San Francisco: Harper & Row, vol. 2.

prelinguistic development Research has shown that, on average, typically developing children say their first words around the age of 12 months. However, children seem prepared to acquire language from birth, and during their first year biological predispositions, cognitive and biological maturation and a responsive social environment all help to prepare a child for language development. From birth, babies are especially sensitive to the pitch range of the human voice and seem to prefer speech to any other sound. Within the first few days after birth, they are also able to distinguish their own language from other languages (Moon, Cooper and Fifer 1993). At around two months of age, children start making vowel-like sounds (cooing). Gradually they add consonants and at around 4–6 months they begin babbling (repeating consonant-vowel combinations, e.g. 'bababa'). The timing of this appears to be due to maturation as all babies (including deaf children) start to babble at around the same time (Stoel-Gammon and Otomo 1986). For speech to develop further, children must be exposed to human speech. At around seven months of age, babies' babbling starts to include the sounds of mature spoken languages. There is, however, disagreement between researchers about the extent to which babbling and later speech are related, and babbling often continues for four or five months after a child has said its first word.

At the same time as these developments are taking place, children are also making other prelinguistic developments. At around four months, infants start to gaze in the same direction as adults. When this happens, parents often follow the child's gaze and comment (Collis and Schaffer 1975), and this 'JOINT ATTENTION' has been shown to help infants talk earlier and develop their vocabulary quicker. By about nine months, babies are able to understand pointing and they are pointing themselves by the end of their first year. This also aids joint attention and preverbal communication between babies and others. By the end of the first year, babies are more capable of intentional behaviour and can use two preverbal gestures to influence others' behaviour: the protodeclarative gesture involves the child drawing others' attention to an object by touching it, pointing at it or holding it up; the protoimperative gesture involves the child getting another person to do something by reaching, pointing or making sounds (Carpenter, Nagell and Tomasello 1998).   *JC*

Carpenter, M., Nagell, K. and Tomasello, M. 1998: Social cognition, joint attention, and communicative competence from 9 to 15 months of age. *Monographs of the Society for Research in Child Development*, 63(4), 176. **Collis, G. M. and Schaffer, H. R.** 1975: Synchronization of visual attention in mother-infant pairs. *Journal of Child Psychology and Psychiatry and Allied Disciplines*, 16(4), 315–20. **Moon, C., Cooper, R. P. and Fifer, W. P.** 1993: Two-day-olds prefer their native language. *Infant Behavior and Development*, 16(4), 495–500. **Stoel-Gammon, C. and Otomo, K.** 1986: Babbling development of hearing impaired and normally hearing subjects. *Journal of Speech and Hearing Disorders*, 51, 33–41.

preoperational stage In PIAGETIAN THEORY, the preoperational stage (ages 2–7 years) is the second major period of COGNITIVE DEVELOPMENT. During this stage, the child's cognitive advancement proceeds through two phases, each encompassing unique modes of thought (Thomas 1999). The first phase (ages 2–4 years) is characterised by the pre-school-aged child's acquisition of semiotic function, the ability to use mental symbols to represent or replace things (Green and Piel 2002). This capacity for symbolic thought broadens the child's mental experiences. Language develops and enriches communication. Pretend play emerges and expands ideas. However, the child's thinking is still limited by EGOCENTRISM, the inability to distinguish between one's own and others' viewpoints. Further limitations are imposed by the persistence of animism in thinking, the childlike belief that inanimate objects have qualities and actions of living organisms. The second phase (ages 4–7 years) of the preoperational stage is characterised by the child's use of intuitive thought. At the start of this transitional phase, the young child constructs simple logic by using transductive, irreversible REASONING (see s. 3) rather than using systematic mental operations. Thought is also centred and constrained by the child's inability to focus on multiple aspects of events. These cognitive limitations are readily evident in the child's lack of CONSERVATION, the ability to understand that properties of objects do not change with alterations in the object's form. For example, using a typical Piagetian conservation task, a child at this stage believes the amount of water changes because the liquid is poured from a short, wide bottle into a tall, narrow container. Piaget designed several tasks to assess children's progress in developing and using conservation across various dimensions (e.g. conservation of length, number, etc.). His studies indicated that acquisition of conservation follows a pattern of horizontal *décalage* and emerges at different points throughout the next period, the CONCRETE OPERATIONAL STAGE, of cognitive development. Some researchers contend difficult tasks (Galotti 1999) rather than limited mental abilities constrain children's performances, and, thus, the logic needed for conservation in thinking may occur at an earlier point in the development of cognition.   *KP*

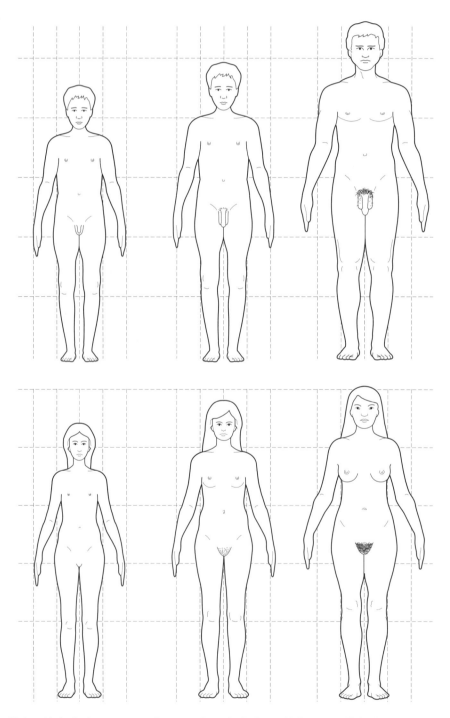

pubertal timing *All the girls in the lower row are the same chronological age: 12.75 years. All the boys in the upper row are also the same chronological age: 14.75 years. Source: J. M. Tanner, 'Growing Up' in* Scientific American *229, 1973.*

Galotti, K. M. 1999: *Cognitive Psychology in and out of the Laboratory* (2nd edn). Belmont CA: Brooks/Cole-Wadsworth Publishing Company. **Green, M. and Piel, J. A.** 2002: *Theories of Human Development: A Comparative Approach.* Boston MA: Allyn & Bacon. **Thomas, R. M.** 1999: *Human Development Theories: Windows on Culture.* Thousand Oaks CA: Sage Publications, Inc.

primary sex characteristics Reproductive features that physically differentiate males and females, such as the penis and vagina. *AP*

propositional thought A cognitive ability Piaget associated with formal operational thought [see FORMAL OPERATIONAL STAGE] that involves analysing the logical relationships embedded within verbal statements (e.g. either-or). *KP*

psychometric approach The psychometric approach refers to the development and evaluation of tests in either psychology or education (Gregory 2000). A test is a standardised procedure for SAMPLING (see s. 8) the behaviour or psychological characteristics of an individual or a group, and describing it with categories or scores (Gregory 2000). Statistical analyses are often applied to test results to examine group and individual differences. Most tests have norms or standards by which the results can be used to predict other behaviours. Psychometric tests typically focus on a wide domain of non-observable constructs, including but not restricted to PERSONALITY (see s. 1 and s. 6) and INTELLIGENCE. There is a wide variety of formats and applications of psychometric tests; however, standardised procedures, behaviour sampling, scores or categories, norms or standards, and prediction of non-test behaviours are defining features of most psychometric tests. *EE*

Gregory, R. J. 2000: *Psychological Testing: History, Principles and Applications* (3rd edn). London: Allyn & Bacon.

pubertal timing The biological changes of PUBERTY require adolescents to adjust to a new body shape and size, as well as sexual maturity. The physical changes of puberty are protracted (on average lasting four years), and there is also a wide range of age of onset (some seven years), with girls entering puberty on average two to three years prior to boys (Tanner 1990). Pubertal timing plays a role in adolescent adjustment, especially in the case of girls (Caspi and Moffitt 1991). Research has shown that girls who mature early dislike it, and are at increased risk of delinquency; for boys, it is the late maturers who dislike their status. Findings concerning the consequences of pubertal timing are equivocal; however, an impressive LONGITUDINAL RESEARCH (see s. 1) programme found that early maturing girls are more likely to associate with older peers, which was in turn linked to higher rates of delinquency (Magnusson 1988). *AP*

Caspi, A. and Moffitt, T. E. 1991: Individual differences are accentuated during periods of social change: the sample case of girls at puberty. *Journal of Personality and Social Psychology* 61, 157–68. **Magnusson, D.** 1988: *Individual Development from an Interactional Perspective: A Longitudinal Study.* Hillsdale NJ: Lawrence Erlbaum. **Tanner, J. M.** 1990: *Foetus into Man* (2nd ed). Cambridge, MA: Harvard University Press.

puberty The physical and biological changes during the transition from childhood to adulthood that result in sexual maturity. [See also ADOLESCENCE] *AP*

punishment and obedience orientation At Kohlberg's stage 1, children believe that rules should be obeyed, and their behaviour is controlled by the threat of punishment. *DW*

R

---

reaction range Reaction range refers to the variety of possible PHENOTYPES (see s. 2) a GENOTYPE (see s. 2) may produce in response to the environment [see also HERITABILITY, CANALISATION]. This concept describes how differing environments can produce a range of individual differences that is restricted by genes. Because reactions to the environment differ, individuals with different genes and different experiences may end up with very similar traits, and, conversely, individuals with similar experiences may develop very different traits (Gottesman 1963). Reaction ranges are complex and can vary by age. For instance, research has shown that genes play a greater role in the expression of antisocial behaviour for adults than for adolescents (Plomin, DeFries, McClearn and McGuffin 2001). Reaction ranges also can differ across contexts. For instance, recent research suggests that the environment plays a greater role in shaping the intelligence of children living in poverty compared to children from more affluent families (Turkheimer et al. 2003). *FH*

Gottesman, I. I. 1963: Heritability of personality: a demonstration. *Psychological Monographs* 77 (No. 572). **Plomin, R., DeFries, J. C., McClearn, G. E. and McGuffin, P.** 2001: *Behavioral Genetics* (4th edn). New York: Worth Publishers. **Turkheimer, E., Haley, A., Waldron, M., D'Onofrio, B. and Gottesman, I. I.** 2003: Socioeconomic status modifies heritability of IQ in young children. *Psychological Science* 14, 623–8.

reciprocity The idea of fairness in relationships through mutual give-and-take (e.g. disagreements are discussed, reasoned and subsequently settled). *DW*

rejected children These children are disliked by their peers, often because they are either aggressive or withdrawn. *AC/AE*

remembered self An autobiographical narrative about the SELF, informed by conversations with adults about the past. *RB*

resistant attachment This insecure ATTACHMENT type (Type C) was classified by Ainsworth and colleagues (1978) in the STRANGE SITUATION task and found to apply to approximately 10–15 per cent of children. It is sometimes described as an anxious resistant or anxious ambivalent type.

Resistant attachments are characterised by ambiguity towards the mother (or other attachment figure). In the strange situation task, the child is unlikely to explore the environment and appears unsettled with both mother and stranger. They may become upset or angry at separation and prove difficult to comfort on reunion, seeming to be torn between resisting contact and seeking proximity.

Resistant children are generally anxious about separations and exploring the world. Uncertainty about whether or not the parent will be responsive to their needs gives rise to an INTERNAL WORKING MODEL of relationships as problematic and unpredictable.

This model predicts instability in future relationships, with fluctuation between closeness and distance. *BT*

Ainsworth, M. D., Blehar, M. C., Waters, E. and Wall, S. 1978: *Patterns of Attachment: Assessed in the Strange Situation.* Hillsdale NJ: Erlbaum.

S

Sally-Anne task A task used to test children's understanding of FALSE BELIEF, involving a story enacted by puppets or dolls. *RB*

scaffolding This is a supportive facilitative learning structure that enables learners to build on current knowledge and skills and take more responsibility in the learning activity. *EB*

scheme In PIAGETIAN THEORY, a cognitive representation of an action and its consequences that provides procedures to follow in similar situations. *KP*

schooling Schools serve many functions. They impart knowledge, promote advanced COGNITIVE DEVELOPMENT and provide children with social opportunities. Because children spend, on average, 1000 hours per year in school, optimal school configurations and teaching practices have been the focus of much debate. Although most children attend publically funded schools, a growing number of parents are choosing other options, such as independent schools and home schooling. More important than type of school, however, are factors such as school size and learning climate. Research has repeatedly found that children attending small schools are more involved in school activities and are more likely to develop close relationships with teachers.

Differing cultural values and goals influence how different societies structure the school environment. Asian cultures, for example, place a high value on education and thus require that children attend school more days per year than most western cultures. In addition, students in many Asian societies spend more class time on academic topics, and more time participating in group learning activities rather than working alone (Stevenson, Chen and Lee 1993).

A related aspect of school structure that impacts children's well-being is the transitions that take place from primary/elementary school to middle school and then again from middle to secondary/high school. During these transitions, students may experience a decline in ACADEMIC ACHIEVEMENT and SELF-ESTEEM (see s. 5 and s. 7). Declines are most likely due to the change in classroom structure (i.e. a move from one classroom with one teacher to several classrooms and teachers) and the concomitant developmental changes associated with PUBERTY (Wigfield and Eccles 1994). Several strategies have been found to ease school transitions, including organising teachers and students into teams so that teachers can work together to balance the demands of different subjects, assess problems of individual students and promote parent involvement.

Recent efforts to reform the structure of schools have focused on the creation of full-service schools. These schools integrate education, medical, social and human services on school grounds to meet the wide range of needs of children and their families (Dryfoos 1995).

Specific components of this comprehensive approach to schooling include on-campus health centres, vocational guidance, counselling services, and community collaborations and referrals. (See also s. 6, SCHOOLING AND INTELLIGENCE) *SH*

Dryfoos, J. G. 1995: Full service schools: A revolution or fad? *Journal of Research on Adolescence* 5, 149–50. **Stevenson, H. W., Chen, C. and Lee, S.** 1993: Mathematics achievement of Chinese, Japanese and American children: Ten years later. *Science* 258, 53–8. **Wigfield, A. and Eccles, J. S.** (1994). Children's competence beliefs, achievement values, and general self-esteem: Change across elementary and middle school. *Journal of Early Adolescence* 14(2), 107–38.

secondary sex characteristics Physical features that differentiate sexually mature males and females (e.g. facial hair for men and breast development in women), but that are not directly involved in reproduction. [See also PRIMARY SEX CHARACTERISTICS] *AP*

secure attachment The most common and advantageous pattern of ATTACHMENT (Type B) classified by Ainsworth and her colleagues (1978) in the STRANGE SITUATION task and found to apply to approximately 60–70 per cent of children.

The securely attached child is confident that the mother or other attachment figure will be available and responsive to their physical and emotional needs and so happily explores the 'strange' situation. The child may protest at separation from the mother, but greet her positively on reunion, seeking proximity and comfort. On the stranger's arrival, exploratory behaviour is reduced, but the child does not show overt distress.

The securely attached child is said to have an INTERNAL WORKING MODEL of the SELF as worthy of love and care, which arises from positive early experience. This sense of security allows for confident exploration of the environment, so enhancing the potential for cognitive as well as emotional and social development. *BT*

Ainsworth, M. D., Blehar, M. C., Waters, E. and Wall, S. 1978: *Patterns of Attachment: Assessed in the Strange Situation.* Hillsdale NJ: Erlbaum.

secure base A key aspect of ATTACHMENT theory whereby parents provide psychological and physical security that enables infants to explore their world. *BT*

self The 'self' is a term encompassing the unique individuality of a person. William James (1890) distinguished between two fundamental aspects, the I-SELF (self as subject) and the ME-SELF (self as object). In contemporary reformulations, the awareness of the self as a distinct entity, separate from the environment and other people, existing continuously over time and capable of acting on the environment as a causal agent, is often presented as distinct from cognitive representations of the self in terms of physical, psychological, social and material characteristics. [See also SELF-AWARENESS and SELF-CONCEPT] – see also s. 5. Neisser (1988) outlines several facets of the self. The ecological self refers to the self as perceived in relation to the physical environment, while the interpersonal self corresponds to the sense of self that emerges in the context of interactions with social partners, such as caregivers. Observing that one's own actions map onto perceivable outcomes in the physical environment or in social interactions provides a basic sense of AGENCY (see s. 1), a key aspect of the I-self. Because this contingency between self and environment can be perceived in infancy, recent perspectives on the developing sense of self tend to oppose the traditional view that young infants make no differentiation between self and other. Moving on to other aspects of self, cognitive representations of self include a REMEMBERED SELF based on a narrative of memories and information about past events, as well as a self-concept consisting of the characteristics and attributes we see as defining who we are.

Our explicit self-descriptions vary across the course of development [see SELF-CONCEPT], and are influenced by social factors such as the attitudes of other people, or the GENERALISED OTHER. These self-descriptions involve a significant evaluative component, SELF-ESTEEM (see s. 5 and s. 7), which relates to how we feel about ourselves. This in turn is linked with self-discrepancies between our 'real' and 'ideal' selves (Higgins 1987). Although early work on the development of self-concept was mostly focused on changes in the content of self-descriptions, more recent research has emphasised the structural organisation of individuals' representations of self (Harter 1998). One issue involves seeing our concepts of self as multidimensional, involving a profile of self-evaluations that may vary across domains, rather than assuming a global, unidimensional construct. On a related note, the notion that the self involves multiple facets has led to ambiguity about how multiple self-representations are integrated with each other. The possibility of multiple selves, emerging and receding according to the demands of changing social contexts, has been raised particularly in discussions of adolescence, when different images of the self are considered appropriate in different circumstances. Although some of these self-images may be thought of as deliberately portrayed false selves that are different from the 'true' self, much of the variability in self-images may simply reflect flexible choices regarding portrayal of different aspects of the private self-concept. However, it seems that some individuals display much greater responsiveness to perceived situational demands than others in their portrayals of self. These 'high self-monitors' are less consistent in their behaviour across situations than those individuals who are low in SELF-MONITORING (see s. 5) (Snyder 1987).

Research has addressed a proliferation of terms with self as a prefix, including self-consciousness, self-efficacy, SELF-REGULATION (see s. 5), and SELF-PRESENTATION (see s. 5). SELF-CONSCIOUS EMOTIONS, such as EMBARRASSMENT, (see s. 5) are often conceptualised as founded on cognitive representations of the self as perceived by others, but research on coyness in infancy (Reddy 2000) suggests that early affective experiences of others' attention to the self may be developmentally connected to such self-conscious cognitions.

Self-efficacy, as conceived in Bandura's (1994) social-cognitive theory, refers to confidence in one's ability to accomplish a given task or solve a given problem. Like appraisals of the self, perceived self-efficacy is likely to be experienced by individuals to varying extents across different domains of activity, and this specificity may be an advantage when it comes to explaining differences in achievement.

A substantial literature has examined how individuals come to regulate or control their own actions and mental states. Children are known to improve in their self-control as they grow older, and thus become better between 18 and 30 months in delay-of-gratification tasks where they must wait for a given period of time before obtaining a tempting object or performing some desired action (Vaughn, Kopp and Krakow 1984). Although self-regulation is likely to occur first in the form of compliance in response to externally imposed rules, children become increasingly able to direct their own behaviour. Similar trends can be observed in emotional self-regulation, as children develop effective strategies for managing negative emotions. If avoidance of the cause of the negative emotion is not possible, early regulation of one's emotional state often involves gaining comfort from caregivers or making concrete attempts to remediate the problematic situation. Later, children become able to call on internal strategies to redefine or reappraise situations in less negative ways, even if the situation itself is uncontrollable. Such mentalistic strategies for EMOTIONAL SELF-REGULATION are linked to children's developing understanding of mental states. [See also THEORY OF MIND]

Children also regulate the public self that is observed and evaluated by others. In the context of emotions, such regulation takes the form of EMOTIONAL DISPLAY RULES (e.g. looking happy when receiving a disappointing present). Children become increasingly able to use and understand emotional displays that are discrepant from real emotion. This corresponds to a general increase in children's appreciation of self-presentation, which involves efforts to control the way one is evaluated by others. Banerjee (2002) has suggested that self-presentation in children is associated both with their understanding of mental states and with the motivational concerns about social evaluation that underlie feelings of embarrassment. Attention to such self-presentational motives, in addition to individuals' private self-concepts, has been helpful for making sense of diverse social phenomena (Baumeister 1982). (See also s. 1 and s. 5, SELF) *RB*

Bandura, A. 1994: *Self-efficacy: The Exercise of Control.* New York: Freeman. **Banerjee, R.** 2002: Children's understanding of self-presentational behaviour: links with mental-state reasoning and the attribution of embarrassment. *Merrill-Palmer Quarterly* 48, 378–404. **Baumeister, R. F.** 1982: A self-presentational view of social phenomena. *Psychological Bulletin* 91, 3–26. **Harter, S.** 1998: The development of self-representations. In Eisenberg, N. (ed.), *Handbook of Child Psychology: Social, Emotional, and Personality Development* (5th edn). New York: Wiley, vol. 3. **Higgins, E. T.** 1987: Self-discrepancy: A theory relating self and affect. *Psychological Review* 94, 319–40. **James, W.** 1890: *Principles of Psychology.* Chicago: Encyclopedia Britannica. **Neisser, U.** 1988: Five kinds of self knowledge. *Philosophical Psychology* 1, 35–59. **Reddy, V.** 2000: Coyness in early infancy. *Developmental Science* 3(2), 186–92. **Snyder, M.** 1987: *Public Appearances, Private Realities: The Psychology of Self-Monitoring.* New York: Freeman. **Vaughn, B. E., Kopp, C. B. and Krakow, J. B.** 1984: The emergence and consolidation of self-control from eighteen to thirty months of age: normative trends and individual differences. *Child Development* 55, 990–1004.

self-awareness Recognition of the SELF (see also s. 1 and s. 5) as a distinct entity, separate from others, with its own thoughts, feelings and characteristics. In developmental psychology, many research investigations have addressed the thorny question of when infants can be said to be self-aware. There are strong indications that babies early on develop a sense that they are distinct from the environment, but visual recognition of their own physical form and features (SELF-RECOGNITION) is usually demonstrated in the second year of life. Kagan (1981) has argued that a number of different behaviours exhibited at this age indicate a growing cognitive appreciation of the self in relation to certain standards (e.g. non-social 'mastery' smiles produced upon attaining a goal). The development of self-awareness is related to SELF-CONSCIOUS EMOTIONS, such as EMBARRASSMENT (see s. 5), pride and guilt, which involve reflections on the self in relation to personal or social standards. As children's capacity for language increases, they become increasingly able to describe explicitly their physical, material and psychological states and attributes. [See also SELF-CONCEPT – see also s. 5.]   *RB*

Kagan, J. 1981: *The Second Year: The Emergence of Self-awareness.* Cambridge MA: Harvard University Press.

self-concept A component of SELF (see also s. 1 and s. 5) referring to the set of physical, psychological and material attributes that an individual believes is characteristic of him or her [see ME-SELF]. A basic form of self-concept is evident when children are able to recognise their physical features, as in mirror SELF-RECOGNITION tasks. As children become more proficient in language, verbal self-descriptions can also be examined in order to identify developmental trends in self-understanding (e.g. Damon and Hart 1988). Although young children often refer to their own mental states, their spontaneous self-descriptions mainly focus on categorical identifications of physical attributes and membership of basic categories like age and gender groups (CATEGORICAL SELF). In middle childhood, spontaneous self-descriptions are more likely to include references to psychological traits and dispositions. In addition, the increasing tendency to compare the self with others leads to comparative judgements about the self, especially in terms of competencies and abilities (Ruble and Frey 1991). This in turn leads to changes in children's self-evaluations and SELF-ESTEEM (see s. 5 and s. 7), as they recognise their relative strengths and weaknesses. In early adolescence, the features of one's self-concept are frequently described in terms of their implications for social interactions, but among older adolescents, the self-concept becomes increasingly tied to broader systems of BELIEFS (see s. 5) and VALUES (see s. 5). Throughout development, social factors are likely to have

self-concept *Self-concept assessment for young children, using puppets.*

a significant influence on children's self-concepts. Consistent with Cooley's (1902) idea of a 'LOOKING-GLASS SELF' (see s. 5), children's notion of how they are seen by significant others and by the GENERALISED OTHER contributes to the way they see themselves. In addition, several investigations indicate that concepts of self differ across CULTURES (see s. 1 and s. 5), with varying emphases on individualistic traits and social roles (Markus and Kitayama 1991). Techniques used to measure self-concept range from open-ended questions that elicit spontaneous self-descriptions, to detailed questionnaires designed to yield a profile of an individual's perceived competence in different domains. More recently, puppet interviews (see Photo) have been developed to assess the self-conceptions of children as young as four years old (Measelle, Ablow, Cowan and Cowan 1998). Our actual self-concepts may be discrepant with the way we think we ought to be ('ought self'), the way we would ideally like to be ('ideal self'), and the way we present ourselves to other people ('public self'). (See also s. 5, SELF-CONCEPT) *RB*

Cooley, C. H. 1902: *Human Nature and the Social Order.* New York: Charles Scribner's Sons. **Damon, W. and Hart, D.** 1988: *Self-understanding in Childhood and Adolescence.* New York: Cambridge University Press. **Markus, H. and Kitayama, S.** 1991: Culture and the self: implications for cognition, emotion, and motivation. *Psychological Review* 98, 224–53. **Measelle, J. R., Ablow, J. C., Cowan, P. A. and Cowan, C. P.** 1998: Assessing young children's views of their academic, social and emotional lives; an evaluation of the self-perception scales of the Berkeley Puppet Interview. *Child Development* 69, 1483–702. **Ruble, D. N. and Frey, K. S.** 1991: Changing patterns of comparative behaviour as skills are acquired: a functional model of self-evaluation. In Suls, J. and Wills, T. A. (eds) *Social Comparison: Contemporary Theory and Research.* Hillsdale NJ: Erlbaum.

self-conscious emotions Self-conscious emotions are emotions that are experienced in relation to the SELF (see also s. 1 and s. 5). They include guilt, pride and shame. For example, if a person feels positively about his own behaviour, they may experience pride. These emotions generally develop during the second half of the second year of life, paralleling the development of the sense of self. Self-conscious emotions are not innate and require some socialisation by adults. Thus, the situations that would elicit a certain self-conscious emotion are not cross-cultural; the expression of self-conscious emotions varies among different CULTURES (see s. 1 and s. 5) and societies (Lewis 1992). The expression of self-conscious emotions also varies with age; pre-school-aged children show self-conscious emotion as a response to others' reactions to their behaviour. However, as children age, they begin to express self-conscious emotions as an intrinsic response to their own behaviour itself, not how others react to it. Self-conscious emotions are essential for moral development as well as achievement-related behaviour. *SL*

Lewis, M. 1992: *Shame: The Exposed Self.* New York: Free Press.

self-recognition Recognition of the unique physical form and features of the SELF (see also s. 1), often tested in infants using mirrors, photographs or video recordings. *RB*

semantic development Semantic development refers to the development of a child's vocabulary. Typically developing children say their first words at around 12 months of age. They continue to utter single words for several months, before starting to produce novel word combinations. Children's first words tend to be almost exclusively terms for objects (mama, cat, car) and actions (go, up) which are commonly encountered in their environment (Nelson 1985). Between 12 and 18 months children tend to learn 1–3 new words a week, but at around 18 to 20 months they experience what is known as the 'vocabulary explosion', when the rate of new word learning suddenly increases (e.g. Bloom 1973). This is thought to be due to a process called FAST MAPPING. When children are learning new words they often apply the word too narrowly (UNDEREXTENSION) or too widely (OVEREXTENSION), but as their vocabulary and PHONOLOGY develop, these phenomena tend to disappear. By the end of their second year, English-speaking children start to use more verbs, and over the next six months they start to use state words to indicate possession (e.g. my toy), as well as adjectives, such as for size and colour. Children's vocabularies continue to expand and by the time they reach school age they know about 10,000 words. As children develop cognitively, their vocabulary continues to grow and becomes better organised. A number of strategies have been proposed to account for semantic development. Gleitman's (1989) syntactic bootstrapping hypothesis maintained that children work out the meaning of words through information provided by cues in SYNTAX (see s. 3). Other researchers maintain that children are guided by certain lexical principles; for example, Clark (1988, 1990) proposed the principles of conventionality (every word has a conventional meaning which is known to all speakers of that language and contrast (the assumption that a new word is different in meaning to any other word). *JL*

Bloom, L. 1973: *One Word at a Time.* The Hague: Mouton. **Clark, E. V.** 1988: On the logic of contrast. *Journal of Child Language* 15, 317–35. **Clark, E. V.** 1990: The pragmatics of contrast. *Journal of Child Language* 17, 417–31. **Gleitman, L.** 1989: The structural sources of verb meaning. *Papers and Reports on Child Language Development* 28, 1–48. **Nelson, K.** 1985: *Making Sense: The Acquisition of Shared Meaning.* New York: Academic Press.

semantics Semantics is the study of meaning in LANGUAGE (see s. 2). *JC*

sensorimotor stage In PIAGETIAN THEORY, the sensorimotor stage (birth–age 2 years) is the first major period of COGNITIVE DEVELOPMENT. During this stage, infants construct knowledge through the increased coordination of SCHEMES for sensory and motor experiences. Piaget believed these changes occur in six sub-stages. At birth, newborns' innate reflex behaviours and functional sensory systems provide the bases for interactions with the world (Goswami 1998). In the first sub-stage, a time of using reflexes, newborns develop and modify mental structures for these sensorimotor responses. These schemes become the framework for cognitive development. The second sub-stage, primary circular reactions (1–4 months), unfolds as infants start organising schemes for sensory and motor activities. Simple habits emerge. Actions are voluntarily repeated (primary circular reactions) to re-experience satisfying effects originally created by chance. However, infants' acts are still centred on bodily experiences and instinct satisfaction (Goswami 1998). Focus on the external world begins in the third sub-stage, secondary circular reactions (4–8 months). Babies develop schemes for repeating actions with interesting effects on objects and people in the world. In the fourth sub-stage, coordination of secondary circular reactions (8–12 months), infants organise a series of mental structures for various actions and develop intentionality of behaviour. Separate schemes for means and ends facilitate the accomplishment of simple goals. External-oriented attention generates the emergence of the fifth sub-stage, tertiary circular reactions (12–18 months). Now toddlers seek discovery of new information about how objects and people work. Several cognitive milestones occur in the sixth sub-stage, internalisation of schemes (18–24 months). OBJECT PERMANENCE is acquired and toddlers understand objects continue to exist independent from self-generated actions and sensory experiences. Toddlers can also mentally combine schemes for different action sequences and their consequences. These refined schemes and understandings mark the beginnings of mental representation and resultant capacities for deferred imitation and causal ideas (Galotti 1999). Some researchers question Piagetian assumptions about the timing of these abilities and methods for testing achievements (Marcovitch, Zelazo and Schmuckler 2002). But to Piaget, the developments within this period signal a child's cognitive freedom from purely sensorimotor experiences and movement towards symbolic thought. *KP*

Galotti, K. M. 1999: *Cognitive Psychology in and out of the Laboratory* (2nd edn). Belmont CA: Brooks/Cole-Wadsworth Publishing Company. **Goswami, U.** 1998: *Cognition in Children*. Hove, East Sussex: Psychology Press Ltd. **Marcovitch, S., Zelazo, P. D. and Schmuckler, M. A.** 2002: The effect of the number of A trials on performance on the A-not-B task. *Infancy* 3(4), 519–29.

separation anxiety   Distress felt in response to actual or feared separation from a parent or any object of attachment, especially in childhood. *BT*

sex chromosomes   There is a single pair of CHROMOSOMES (labelled X or Y) that determines the sex of an individual. In humans, females are XX and males are XY. *FH*

sibling deidentification   The process by which children in the same family intentionally adopt different interests, behaviours and roles in order to appear maximally different from their siblings. *BM*

siblings   Sibling relationships are the most enduring relationships, linking us to individuals who may share many of our genes and experiences. There are several different types of siblings, including full siblings, half-siblings, stepsiblings and adopted siblings. Although there is a secular trend towards smaller family sizes, most children still grow up with at least one sibling. The affective nature and function of sibling relations differ depending on cultural context. In industrial societies, close relationships among siblings tend to be optional, based on siblings' desires to be friendly towards each other. In non-industrial, primarily agrarian societies, sibling cooperation is necessary to accomplish tasks, to maintain family functioning and to attain economic growth. In general, sibling relations are friendlier when mothers and fathers respond sensitively to all of their children and do not consistently favour one over another (McHale, Updegraff, Jackson-Newman, Tucker and Crouter 2000).

Siblings can play critical roles in the socialisation of children (Parke and Buriel 1998). Older siblings, in particular, are likely to influence younger siblings' social and COGNITIVE DEVELOPMENT (e.g. GENDER ROLES, EMPATHY) by modelling behaviours for them to imitate. Younger siblings may also rely on their older siblings as a source of advice about life plans and personal problems (Tucker, Barber and Eccles 1997). Siblings may confide in and comfort one another during a parental divorce or may physically protect weaker siblings in the face of domestic violence. Nevertheless, sibling relationships can be negative. In fact, conflict constitutes a normal part of the sibling experience, even as children enter adolescence. It appears that conflict between siblings reflects the strains of group living; the most common themes of sibling conflict are personal property disputes (McGuire, Manke, Eftekhari and Dunn 2000). Levels of conflict typically decrease after early adolescence, as teenagers spend more time away from the family. Yet, prolonged aggressive conflict, especially conflict that includes physical aggression, can result in severe conduct problems and may escalate to sibling abuse and generalise to situations outside the family (Garcia, Shaw, Winslow and Yaggi 2000). *BM*

Garcia, M., Shaw, D., Winslow, E. and Yaggi, K. 2000: Destructive sibling conflict and the development of conduct problems in young boys. *Developmental Psychology* 36, 44–53. **McGuire, S., Manke, B., Eftekhari, A. and Dunn, J.** 2000: Children's perceptions of sibling conflict during middle childhood: issues and sibling (dis)similarity. *Social Development* 9, 173–90. **McHale, S. M., Updegraff, K. A., Jackson-Newman, J., Tucker, C. J. and Crouter, A. C.** 2000: When does parents' differential treatment have negative implications for siblings? *Social Development* 9, 149–72. **Parke, R. and Buriel, R.** 1998: Socialization in the family: ethnic and ecological perspectives. In Damon, W. (series ed.) and Eisenberg, N. (volume ed.), *Handbook of Child Psychology: Child Psychology in Practice*. New York: Wiley, vol. 3. **Tucker, C. J., Barber, B. L. and Eccles, J. S.** 1997: Advice about life plans and personal problems in late adolescent sibling relationships. *Journal of Youth and Adolescence* 26, 63–76.

slow-to-warm-up child   A child whose temperament reflects inactivity, mild reactions to external stimuli, negative mood and gradual adjustment to new experiences. *JG*

social cognition Social cognition refers to knowledge and thoughts about the social world and the people in it. This has been a major focus of attention in SOCIAL PSYCHOLOGY (see s. 1) and developmental psychology. With regard to the former, researchers over the last half-century have displayed a keen interest in formulating models of our everyday understanding of people and of social events. Heider's (1958) work on the 'naïve psychology' we all employ in making sense of people's behaviour has led to a substantial literature on how we perceive other people, how we attribute our own and others' behaviour to dispositional or situational causes, how we use HEURISTICS (see s. 3) to draw inferences about social events and other processes involved in our thinking about people and their social interactions (Fiske and Taylor 1991). In developmental work, research on social cognition has been dominated by work on children's THEORY OF MIND (see Flavell and Miller 1998), since our understanding of mental states is an essential foundation for understanding people and their behaviour. Most research in this area has focused on the period up to around five years of age, when children typically pass the FALSE BELIEF task. Work on social cognition in infancy has often dealt with how children relate to others' attentional and emotional states (e.g. JOINT ATTENTION and social referencing). Research on the understanding of mental states in early childhood has involved the use of experimental tasks (usually involving hypothetical stories, told using puppets/dolls or illustrations) to determine children's understanding of desires, emotions, beliefs and how they relate to each other and to behaviour. The most famous of these tasks is the false belief task (of which the SALLY-ANNE TASK is one variant). More recent research suggests that children beyond the age of five continue to develop an increasingly complex understanding of mental and social processes, and the narrow focus on three- to five-year-olds' understanding of belief has been complemented by a wider emphasis on issues such as children's understanding of traits and their appreciation of emotional display rules (see Hala 1996). (See also s. 5, SOCIAL COGNITION) *RB*

Fiske, S. and Taylor, S. 1991: *Social Cognition*. New York: McGraw-Hill. **Flavell, J. H. and Miller, P. H.** 1998: Social cognition. In Kuhn, D. and Siegler, R. (eds) *Handbook of Child Psychology: Cognition, Perception, and Language* (5th edn). New York: Wiley, vol. 2. **Hala, S.** (ed.) 1996: *The Development of Social Cognition*. Hove, East Sussex: Psychology Press. **Heider, F.** 1958: *The Psychology of Interpersonal Relations*. New York: Wiley.

social contract orientation At Kohlberg's stage 5 [see MORAL DEVELOPMENT], children judge behaviour based on whether it adheres to the norms and rules of society, recognising that different societies have different norms. *DW*

social learning of gender According to social learning theory (e.g. Mischel 1966), children learn GENDER ROLES because social agents (e.g. parents, peers, media) teach them through such processes as REINFORCEMENT (see s. 3) and modelling. The child is a passive recipient of gender-related knowledge, unlike the active role ascribed to children in later cognitive approaches (e.g. GENDER SCHEMA THEORY). Knowledge of GENDER STEREOTYPES is seen increasingly *as a result* of children developing gender-linked preferences, for example, girls learn that dolls are 'for girls' because they like playing with dolls. Differential reinforcement by adults encourages girls and boys to engage in own-sex behaviour but avoid other-sex behaviour. For example, fathers, but not mothers, were positive towards their pre-school children who engaged in own-sex play (e.g. boys playing with cars), but were critical of other-sex play (e.g. boys playing with dolls), particularly for sons (Langlois and Downs 1980). Modelling is another key process by which children gather information about social norms and expectations. However, children's gender-role behaviour is not strongly correlated with that of their parents (Huston 1983), so while parental modelling may make a contribution to their children's gender development, it cannot be the only explanation. Social cognitive theory (Bussey and Bandura 1999) integrates both social and cognitive factors. Three key influences are outlined: (1) modelling in the child's immediate environment provides information about the gender associations of roles and behaviours; (2) evaluative social reactions to gender-related behaviour promote the learning of these associations; (3) direct tuition may provide further information about these associations. The gendering process is initially governed by external factors (e.g. parental reinforcement) but shifts gradually to a self-regulated process. The major socio-cognitive regulator of gender-stereotype behaviour becomes the outcomes anticipated for engaging in that behaviour. The major problem for socialisation approaches is that they fail to account for developmental changes, assuming that learning processes are similar at all ages. They do not account well for children's gender-role beliefs changing considerably with age, or for children's beliefs often being much more rigid than those of their parents (whom they are supposed to model). *AH*

Bussey, K. and Bandura, A. 1999: Social cognitive theory of gender development and differentiation. *Psychological Review* 106(4), 676–713. **Huston, A. C.** 1983: Sex-typing. In Mussen, P. H. and Hetherington, E. M. (eds) *Handbook of Child Psychology: Socialisation, Personality and Social Behaviour.* New York: Wiley, vol. 4, 387–467. **Langlois, J. and Downs, A. C.** 1980: Mothers, fathers, and peers as socialisation agents of sex-typed play behaviours in young children. *Child Development* 51, 1237–47. **Mischel, W.** 1966: A social learning view of sex differences in behaviour. In Maccoby, E. E. (ed.). *The Development of Sex Differences*. Stanford: Stanford University Press.

social referencing Using the reactions and/or expressions of a person as a reference to determine how to act or feel in a specific situation. *SC*

social smile A smile that an infant younger than six months gives as a response to visual and auditory stimuli. It serves to engage the caregivers and make them feel more secure with and drawn to the infant. *SC*

social smile

grammes have been implemented to help rejected children learn SOCIAL SKILLS (see s. 5) and gain peer acceptance.

AC

Asher, S. R. and Coie, J. D. 1990: *Peer Rejection in Childhood.* New York: Cambridge University Press.

specific cognitive abilities Specific cognitive abilities are a variety of intellectual abilities unique to carrying out specific tasks. Opinion is divided on whether these relate to 'g' and to each other. *EE*

specific language impairment Specific language impairment is a developmental LANGUAGE (see s. 2) disorder in the absence of explanatory FACTORS (see s. 8) such as hearing impairment, non-verbal cognitive deficits, neurological damage or socio-emotional deficits. *JC*

stranger anxiety A wariness of unfamiliar adults developing during infancy alongside ATTACHMENT RELATIONSHIPS; it may be a pre-programmed DEFENCE MECHANISM (see s. 7). *BT*

sociometric status Sociometric techniques are methods for determining who is liked and disliked in a group. Nomination procedures, where children are asked who they like and do not like, is the technique most commonly used to assess sociometric status. Children are categorised into four groups: POPULAR CHILDREN, REJECTED CHILDREN, NEGLECTED CHILDREN and CONTROVERSIAL CHILDREN (Asher and Coie 1990). Popular children are well liked by most of their peers; rejected children are generally disliked; neglected children receive very few nominations, either positive or negative; and controversial children are both liked and disliked by their peers. Research suggests that neglected children have an easier time gaining peer acceptance than rejected children. Peer rejection can have long-term effects on children's SELF-ESTEEM (see s. 5 and s. 7), and can lead to an increased likelihood of poor academic performance, drop-out and delinquency. In response, a number of intervention pro-

strange situation The 'strange situation' methodology was designed to measure the quality of infants' ATTACHMENT RELATIONSHIPS). Mary Ainsworth and her colleagues (1978) devised the technique to observe the way infants interacted with their caregiver and a stranger in an unfamiliar setting, paying particular attention to separations and reunions with the caregiver.

In the standard procedure, which typically takes place in a playroom within a laboratory, a stranger enters the room where the caregiver and child are waiting. After a few minutes, the caregiver leaves the room and the child is left there with the stranger. The caregiver returns and the stranger departs again before the caregiver goes out for a second time leaving the child briefly alone in the room. The procedure consists of seven episodes, each taking approximately three minutes. The events are designed to become increasingly stressful for the child.

The child's response to each part of the procedure is coded in order to categorise the style of attachment relationship with the caregiver. Judgements are made about the child's ability to use the caregiver as a secure base for exploring the new environment, the degree of stress experienced on separation and the capacity to derive comfort from the caregiver or stranger. Ainsworth et al. (1978) made three main classifications: SECURE ATTACHMENT, insecure AVOIDANT ATTACHMENT and insecure RESISTANT ATTACHMENT. Main and Solomon (1986) later added an insecure DISORGANISED ATTACHMENT category. The types are considered to represent fundamental differences in the kind of INTERNAL WORKING MODEL of social relationships that children form.

The procedure has been criticised because the laboratory setting lacks ECOLOGICAL VALIDITY (see s. 3). Assessment fails to take account of individual differences in caregiver behaviour, infant temperament, or any particular circumstances, like tiredness or illness, at the time of the procedure. It is also argued that the method does not allow for cultural differences in child-rearing practice and that it is not standardised on children who experience regular separations from their parents. The

Positive peer nominations

	Many	Few
Many	Controversial	Rejected
Few	Popular	Neglected

(Negative peer nominations)

sociometric status *Classifications of peer status. Source: D. Bukatko and M. W. Daehler,* Child Development: A Thematic Approach *(5th edn), © 2004 by Houghton Mifflin Company. Used by permission.*

strange situation *The episodes of the strange situation*

Episode*	Persons present	Action	Attachment behaviours assessed
1	Caregiver, baby, observer	Observer introduces caregiver and baby to experimental room and leaves.	
2	Caregiver, baby	Baby explores and plays while caregiver is passive.	Secure base
3	Stranger, caregiver, baby	Stranger enters room, converses with caregiver and approaches baby.	Stranger anxiety
4	Stranger, baby	Caregiver leaves room unobtrusively.	Separation anxiety
5	Caregiver, baby	Caregiver returns and greets baby.	Reunion behaviour
6	Baby	Caregiver leaves room, saying 'bye-bye'.	Separation anxiety
7	Stranger, baby	Stranger enters and orients to baby.	Stranger anxiety
8	Caregiver, baby	Caregiver returns and greets baby.	Reunion behaviour

Each episode except the first lasts for about three minutes.

Source: D. Bukatko and M. W. Daehler, *Child Development: A Thematic Approach* (5th edn), © 2004 by Houghton Mifflin Company. Used by permission. Adapted from Ainsworth et al. 1978.

procedure is still widely used in standard or modified form, although a successful alternative method is the attachment Q-SORT (see s. 6), devised by Waters and Deane (1985). *BT*

Ainsworth, M. D., Blehar, M. C., Waters, E. and Wall, S. 1978: *Patterns of Attachment: Assessed in the Strange Situation.* Hillsdale NJ: Erlbaum. **Main, M. and Solomon, J.** 1986: Discovery of a new, insecure-disorganised/disoriented, attachment pattern. In Brazleton, T. B. and Yogman, M. (eds) *Affective Development in Infancy.* Norwood NJ: Ablex, 95–124. **Waters, E. and Deane, K. E.** 1985: Defining and assessing individual differences in attachment relationships: Q-methodology and the organisation of behaviour in infancy and early childhood. In Bretherton, I. and Waters, E. (eds) *Growing points of attachment theory and research. Monographs for the Society for Research in Child Development* 50, 41–64.

T

television   The word television has three definitions. It is a device and an industry, but primarily television is the content of its programmed broadcasts (Condry 1989). Since its initial dissemination in the 1950s, television has become an increasingly prominent force in the lives of adults and children. In many western societies over 90 per cent of homes include at least one television set, with almost 60 per cent of children having a television set in their bedrooms. Children often watch up to four hours of television per day, at least half of which is in children's rooms to relax before bedtime (Huston and Wright 1998). This suggests that children are watching television without adults sharing and monitoring the programmes. Although television may educate [see TELEVISION AND LEARNING] and entertain children, it also has the tendency to replace children's participation in physical activities. Because television watching is typically passive, it may contribute to obesity and other health-related problems, including ANXIETY (see s. 6) and sleep disturbances. Furthermore, the majority of research on television content over the last 40 years suggests that violence viewed on television contributes to children's aggressive behaviours. Critics of television violence maintain that television produces aggressive or violent behaviours in children because children tend to imitate the models they see and learn that violence is acceptable for resolving conflicts and achieving goals (Wilson et al. 2002). An association has been observed between the amount of time children watch television and greater withdrawal, social problems, AGGRESSION (see s. 5) and other negative behaviours (Miller 2003). Over 30 hours per week of television viewing interferes with academic achievement. According to the social cognitive theory, children who watch a lot of television are also more apt to develop distorted images, such as gender stereotyping with an unreal emphasis on beauty. Because television is so powerfully attractive to children and excessive television watching may have negative consequences for children's emotional and physical well-being, attempts have been made to regulate television content. One such effort is the Children's Television Act of 1990, which was established in the USA to serve the educational and informational needs of children.   *RA*

Condry, J. 1989: *The Psychology of Television*, Hillsdale NJ: Lawrence Erlbaum Associates Inc. **Huston, A. C. and Wright, J. C.** 1998: Mass media and children's development. In Damon, W. (ed. in chief) and Siegel, I. E. and Renninger, K. A. (eds) *Handbook of Child Psychology: Child Psychology in Practice* (5th edn). New York: Wiley, vol. 4, 999–1058. **Miller, K. E.** 2003: Children's behaviour correlates with television viewing. *American Family Physician* 67, 593. **Wilson, B. J., Smith, S. L., Potter, W. J., Kunkel, D., Linz, D., Colvin, C. M. et al.** 2002: Violence in children's programming: assessing the risks, *Journal of Communication* 52, 5–35.

television and learning   Children are said to actively process what they view. Thus, some claim that children can learn positive behaviours and important skills by watching TELEVISION. First, television viewing may offer the advantage of exposing children to learning experiences that they might not encounter in their own living environments. Recent studies indicate that watching educational programmes, such as *Barney and Friends* and *Sesame Street*, improves the counting and vocabulary skills of young children when supplemented with other activities in pre-school (Huston and Wright 1998). Slower-paced shows that contain simple, flowing storylines may also contribute to more elaborate make-believe play. Parents can play an active role in enhancing the educational value of what children see on television by discussing programme content with their children. Finally, television viewing in schoolrooms gives teachers an unprecedented opportunity to expand studies. This process requires teachers to use dedicated and creative teaching methods to effectively combine television with more traditional classroom curricula.   *RA*

Huston, A. C. and Wright, J. C. 1998: Mass media and children's development. In Damon, W. (ed. in chief) and Siegel, I. E. and Renninger, K. A. (eds) *Handbook of Child Psychology: Child Psychology in Practice* (5th edn). New York: Wiley, vol. 4, 999–1058.

television literacy   A term referring to children's understanding of television content, including the critical element of realistic versus fantastic content.   *AP*

temperament   Temperament is considered by many child development experts to be the foundation or the building blocks of PERSONALITY (see s. 1 and s. 6). It refers to behavioural tendencies rather than discrete behavioural

television *Young children in most families spend many hours watching television.*

acts, has a biological underpinning, usually focuses on early childhood and refers to INDIVIDUAL DIFFERENCES (see s. 6) as opposed to species-general characteristics (Goldsmith et al. 1987). Temperament traits tend to be less complex than personality traits, and temperament encompasses behaviour and EMOTION (see s. 6) while personality includes those concepts as well as ATTITUDES (see s. 5) and motives. Although temperament traits differ among the dominant theories, there are several core dimensions: negative emotionality, described as unpleasant or distressing behaviour; positive emotionality, happiness or exuberance; activity level, the tempo and vigour of motoric behaviour; sociability, the preference for being with others; shyness, inhibition to novel or intense stimuli; and attention span/persistence, the duration of orienting or interest. Research indicates that several temperament traits have genetic influences and HERITABILITY is moderate (Emde et al. 1992). In addition to genetic factors, environmental experiences specific to each child within a family also play a role in the development of temperament.

Temperament is considered important in development because it is related to multiple behaviours, traits and outcomes in child, adolescent and adult development, including cognitive ability, social behaviour and PSYCHOPATHOLOGY (see s. 7). The results of the New York Longitudinal Study, one of the earliest comprehensive investigations of infant temperament, indicated that temperament is a major factor in the chances of whether a child will experience psychological problems or not (Thomas and Chess 1977). Also, children were placed into three categories of temperament: EASY CHILD; DIFFICULT CHILD; and SLOW-TO-WARM-UP CHILD. The GOODNESS-OF-FIT model of temperament involves the formation of child-rearing practices and environments that reflect the temperament of the child and promote adaptive functioning. When there is a poor fit, developmental outcomes are distorted and maladjusted.

Temperament is assessed through parent interviews and reports, behavioural ratings by teachers, physicians and others familiar with the child, direct observations by researchers, and psychophysiological measures. Because of their convenience, parent ratings have been historically emphasised in temperament research. However, they have been criticised as being biased and subjective. Most researchers support a multi-method approach to studying temperament, emphasising objective modes of measurement. *JG*

Emde, R. N., Plomin, R., Robinson, J., Corley, R., DeFries, J., Fulker, D. W., Reznick, J. S., Campos, J., Kagan, J. and Zahn-Waxler, C. 1992: Temperament, emotion, and cognition at fourteen months: the MacArthur Longitudinal Twin Study. *Child Development* 63, 1437–55. Goldsmith, H. H., Buss, A. H., Plomin, R., Rothbart, M. K., Thomas, A., Chess, S., Hinde, R. A. and McCall, R. B. 1987: Roundtable: What is temperament? Four approaches. *Child Development* 58, 505–29. Thomas, A. and Chess, S. 1977: *Temperament and Development*. New York: Brunner/Mazel.

teratogens Any substance that damages a developing foetus is a teratogen. Many substances in the environment would have teratogenic effects, but for the natural protective barriers that surround the foetus and filter the mother's blood supply. Teratogens can cross these barri-

ers and can restrict the maternal oxygen and nutrient supply. Furthermore, during the early stages of prenatal development, the barriers and systems that protect infants and adults from harmful substances are not fully developed, allowing these substances access to sensitive areas, such as the developing brain.

Teratogens have uniquely harmful effects on prenatal developing organisms for many reasons. First, prenatal development is characterised by rapid and ubiquitous cell division, and cells and the CHROMOSOMES they contain are most vulnerable when they are dividing. Second, anatomical systems, especially in the brain, are organising themselves during this period, and damage to this process can affect the structure and, therefore, the function of systems. Perhaps most importantly, prenatal development happens in timed stages, where the development of one system sets the stage for the next (Cowan 1979). Damage to early forming structures can cause damage to subsequent, dependent structures. Because of these developmental characteristics, periods of sensitivity make the timing of teratogen exposure critical to determining its effects (Jensen and Catalano 1998).

There are many kinds of teratogens that can be found in food, air or water. Among the most common are lead, mercury, radiation and pesticides. Substance abuse provides another common source of teratogens. Harmful behaviours include the use of alcohol, nicotine, marijuana, opiates, methamphetamine, cocaine and phencyclidine (PCP). Physicians must be careful in prescribing pharmaceuticals to pregnant women because the teratogenic effects for many drugs are not well known (Bitiello 1998). The effects of the teratogens mentioned above are varied. Most severe effects cause death, physical malformations and brain damage. Lastly, much research has implicated teratogens in the development of some major psychological disorders such as AUTISM (see s. 6) and SCHIZOPHRENIA (see s. 7). Current research suggests that exposure to one or more teratogens, in combination with genetic vulnerability, can lead to a high risk for the development of psychological disorders. *FH*

Bitiello, B. 1998: Pediatric psychopharmacology and the interaction between drugs and the developing brain. *Canadian Journal of Psychiatry* 43, 582–4. Cowan, M. 1979: The development of the brain. *Scientific American* 241, 113–33. Jensen, K. F. and Catalano, S. M. 1998: Brain morphogenesis and developmental neurotoxicology. In Slikker, W., jun. and Chang, L. W. (eds) *Handbook of Developmental Neurotoxicology*. San Diego: Academic Press.

theory of mind The understanding of one's own and other people's mental states, often said to be impaired or absent in autistic individuals. The phrase was first used by Premack and Woodruff (1978) in their work with chimpanzees, and there is now a substantial literature on how children come to understand beliefs, desires and emotions. The THEORY THEORY view suggests that children's understanding of mind is similar to a scientific THEORY (see s. 8), while the simulation view implies that we understand others' minds by using our own experience to imagine what we would think or do under given circumstances. Controversy also surrounds the origins of theory of mind, with some researchers suggesting that there is a specific innate module, while others emphasise general cognitive abilities and the role of social experience.

Although early understanding of mind is likely to emerge in infancy (e.g. JOINT ATTENTION), children are usually said to have a theory of mind when they display an understanding that beliefs are representations of reality and thus can be false (Perner 1991). [See also FALSE BELIEF and SALLY-ANNE TASK]   *RB*

Perner, J. 1991: *Understanding the Representational Mind.* Cambridge MA: MIT Press. **Premack, D. and Woodruff, G.** 1978: Does the chimpanzee have a theory of mind? *Behavioral and Brain Sciences* 4, 515–26.

theory theory   The view that children's understanding of mind [see THEORY OF MIND] takes the form of a theory-like framework used to explain and predict people's thoughts and actions.   *RB*

U

underextension Underextension in word learning involves children applying a learnt word to a more select and specific category than it should be, that is, applying it to a narrower set of circumstances, events or objects (e.g. 'cat' only to their own pet, not all cats). *JC*

universal ethical principle orientation At Kohlberg's stage 6 [see MORAL DEVELOPMENT], children judge behaviour on universal abstract and ethical beliefs that should apply to all societies (e.g. human rights). *DW*

V

Vygotsky's sociocultural theory Lev Vygotsky (1978) integrated the influence of CULTURE (see s. 1 and s. 5) into his theory of development to a much more fundamental extent than Piaget's stage theory. Vygotsky saw development as originating in social and cultural interaction. Three core themes can be identified in Vygotsky's sociocultural theory of COGNITIVE DEVELOPMENT. First, he proposed that the best way to study and understand the mind is to examine when it changes. According to Vygotsky (1978) the mind is constantly changing as part of a dialectical relationship, with the environment influencing the individual and the individual influencing the world. He believed that this process, not the product, of change should be investigated. Second, Vygotsky proposed that all higher mental functions originate in social activity. Social interaction plays a fundamental role in the development of cognition (Wertsch 1985). The basic assumption of this approach is that action is mediated by, and cannot be separated from, the context in which it is carried out (Wertsch 1991). Vygotsky separated two main levels of cognitive functioning: lower-level mental functions, which he argued were genetically inherited and which enable us to react to the environment, and higher mental functions, which result from social interaction. These functions allow us to develop higher reasoning, such as instrumental and intentional action and complex symbolic thought. Development proceeds through mental processes, appearing first on a social level (interpersonal) and second on an individual level (intrapersonal) within the child. We learn from and through interaction with others and then individualise our learning. Vygotsky focused primarily on LANGUAGE DEVELOPMENT and the process whereby children progress from external speech to egocentric speech and finally to inner speech. The third main theme relates to how higher mental functions are mediated by signs and tools. For example, speech is one tool by which the child and the world interact and influence each other. Vygotsky also maintained that learning was most efficient when children engage in activities within a supportive environment, receiving appropriate guidance mediated by learning tools.

EB

Vygotsky, L. 1978: *Mind in Society. The Development of Higher Psychological Processes*. Cambridge MA: Harvard University Press.
Wertsch, J. V. 1985: *Culture, Communication, and Cognition: Vygotskian Perspectives*. Cambridge: Cambridge University Press.
Wertsch, J. V. 1991: *Voices of the Mind. A Sociocultural Approach to Mediated Action*. Cambridge MA: Harvard University Press.

Z

zone of proximal development A key concept in VYGOTSKY'S SOCIOCULTURAL THEORY is the zone of proximal development (ZPD). Vygotsky (1978) maintained that the potential for COGNITIVE DEVELOPMENT is limited to a certain timespan. On one side of this span, children have a certain level of skills and knowledge and, through engaging in an interactive learning activity with a more experienced peer or adult, children progress through their zone of proximal development to a higher level of development. They then progress through a task to a point where the tutor is no longer needed to perform that task. It could be thought of as the space between potential learning and actual learning. The ZPD is a useful framework for examining change and learning in many knowledge domains (Tharp and Gallimore 1988) and for investigating the dynamics necessary for effective learning (Scrimsher and Tudge 2003). *EB*

Scrimsher, S. and Tudge, J. 2003: The teaching/learning relationship in the first years of school: some revolutionary implications of Vygotsky's theory. *Early Education and Development* 14(3), 293–312. **Tharp, R. G. and Gallimore, R.** 1988: *Rousing Minds to Life: Teaching, Learning and Schooling in Social Context.* New York: Cambridge University Press. **Vygotsky, L.** 1978: *Mind in Society. The Development of Higher Psychological Processes.* Cambridge MA: Harvard University Press.

zygote A term for the cell that results from the fertilisation of an egg cell by a sperm cell. *FH*

Section 5

Social Psychology

Introduction

Social psychology is the application of psychological theories and concepts to an understanding of the relations between individuals and their social worlds. Social psychology is not the only discipline that seeks to make sense of social life. Sociology and anthropology also take this question as central, while many other disciplines and sciences, including biology, geography, history, philosophy, economics and political science, have had contributions to make. If anything sets social psychology apart from these others it is the aspiration to relate the various manifestations of collective existence to what goes on in the heads of individuals, in effect, to understand social life from the perspective of the individual social actor.

The beginnings of contemporary social psychology are sometimes located at the very end of the nineteenth century, with the appearance of the first experiments testing the effects on individuals of a social context. What is clear is that from around this time social psychology moved decisively from theorising supported largely by anecdote and speculation towards the systematic collection of data to test precisely defined hypotheses. The experimental method has become a dominating style, but social psychological inquiry has always been broader than this. Moreover, methodological innovation has played its own important part in the popularity of particular topics. For example, research into person perception, leadership and relationships declined towards the middle of the last century, but interest in each of these areas has been reinvigorated in recent years by the development of new and more sophisticated research designs, data collection techniques and statistical procedures.

Other trends have been more linear. Interest in the cognitive mechanisms and processes underlying the individual's relation to the social world has grown steadily from the mid-1950s. Distinctive phases have also been apparent here, starting with a fairly rational view of humans as processors of social information, moving to their characterisation as inherently flawed and fallible in this respect and thence to the idea that humans are frugal with their limited cognitive resources, and most recently to the idea that these resources are used tactically depending on the importance of the task at hand. Linked to this movement in theorising about socio-cognitive processes has been a shift from emphasis on conscious processes to those that are largely automatic and then to recognition that humans have access to multiple levels of functioning.

In this light, some other developments have begun to hamper progress. Experiments proliferated in the middle of the last century involving deceptions about the true nature of situations in which research participants found themselves – leading them to believe that they were giving others real electric shocks or that they were witnesses to real accidents. The cost of running such experiments, but more particularly a climate of greater concern about ethical procedures, now tends to rule out this kind of research. But it has also increased the difficulties in discovering how people will really behave in particular situations, as opposed to how they might anticipate they would behave.

Finally, if social psychology aspires to identify general truths, it also strongly reflects the influences of history and culture. In particular, its concerns continue to reflect the clashes of cultures and nations that have dominated the last 100 years, seen through the lens of the uncertainties of individuals in their relations with others in a multicultural world. In their different ways, all the big themes of social psychology reflect this.

References

A good introduction to the field can be found in Hewstone and Stroebe (2001). The handbook edited by Gilbert, Fiske and Lindzey (1998) is a more detailed and comprehensive treatment.

Gilbert, D. T., Fiske, S. and Lindzey, G. (eds) 1998: *The Handbook of Social Psychology* (4th edn). New York: McGraw-Hill, vol. 1. **Hewstone, M. and Stroebe, W.** (eds) 2001: *Introduction to Social Psychology* (3rd edn). Oxford: Blackwell.

Note

The level 1 entries correspond to major domains of inquiry in contemporary social psychology. These are the general themes around which textbook chapters tend to be organised. Typically, they embrace a range of phenomena, have stimulated a number of theoretical perspectives and are associated with a very substantial body of empirical research. Each of these entries has been contributed by an international expert, able to provide an overview of the ideas and research trends that have characterised the development of this domain, as well as an authoritative statement of the current state of play and of the questions now dominating research. The level 2 entries deal with broad social psychological processes and phenomena, such as aggression, cooperation, self-presentation and persuasion. Many of these entries have been contributed by social psychologists at the forefront of research. The fact that in these cases reference is made to their own published work is not vanity; it accurately reflects their inclusion as social psychologists making leading contributions to our understanding of these phenomena and processes.

The level 3 entries primarily cover the principle theories and concepts in social psychology, theories such as social identity theory, the theory of cognitive dissonance and equity theory, and concepts such as culture, norms and social skill. At this level also are entries dealing with a number of important phenomena such as polarisation and embarrassment. The decision to place these here rather than at level 2 has been based on their scope. Those covered at level 2 are usually broader classes of phenomena or they have attracted a larger volume of research and more extensive theorising. Finally, level 4 entries offer definitions of quite specific phenomena and processes such as the black-sheep effect or illusory correlation, as well as definitions of the technical terms one is likely to encounter in social psychology, and definitions of specific concepts and techniques such as deindividuation and forced compliance.

The cross-referencing allows the reader to explore the manner in which different topics, themes, issues and theories in social psychology are interlinked. Organisation of the entries into the four levels also means that by employing the cross-referencing the reader can follow a line of inquiry both from the most specific issue to the most general questions and vice versa. Thus, for example, definition of the minimal group at level 4 can take the interested reader to the level 3 entry on social identity theory. This is one of the theories dealing with more general classes of phenomena, such as identity and the self, covered in entries at level 2, but also one of a number of theories that has proved influential in the general domain of inquiry identified, at level 1, as intergroup relations. Alternatively, the reader might start with a broad area, such as pro-social behaviour, at level 1, be led thence to level 2 entries dealing with such processes as exchange, and then to a theory dealing with this process, equity theory, at level 3, and definition of a concept, distributive justice, at level 4. However, social psychology is not all neatly organised into a perfect hierarchy, and pursuit of the cross-references will sometimes take the reader in unexpected directions (or so the editor hopes). Finally, however, each entry is also intended to be self-contained and so to make sense by itself.

Professor Nick Emler

A

ad hoc group A GROUP of previously unacquainted individuals, often formed just for the purposes of an EXPERIMENT (see s. 8). *NE*

aggression Actions intended to harm another, either physically or psychologically, or to coerce them into COMPLIANCE. Psychological harm can involve threats to the person's SELF-ESTEEM and IDENTITY (for example, insults), or social exclusion. Human aggression has its evolutionary origins in animal fighting, which is widespread in animals, from those with simple nervous systems, such as sea anemones, to the great apes. The function of animal aggression is to protect the individual or its offspring from danger, to compete for resources or to remove a competitor. These broad functions apply to human aggression. In animals, aggression is associated with a characteristic form of EMOTIONAL EXPRESSION (anger), supported by specific brain mechanisms. These features are retained in human aggression, which is greatly elaborated in terms of the actions involved. Verbal aggression, based on the threat displays of animals, can be a basic expression of anger or an intended use of force. Or it may involve verbally sophisticated forms of challenges and put-downs, which in some masculine CULTURES (see also s. 1) require a physical response for the person's social identity to be maintained ('the culture of honour'; Nisbett and Cohen 1996).

These direct forms of aggression are more common in boys and men than in girls and women. Research on another form, termed indirect or relational aggression, has shown that this way of deliberately harming a person's social position, for example, by malicious gossip, is characteristic of girls, particularly during middle childhood and adolescence (Archer forthcoming). Indirect aggression can cause considerable psychological harm to its victims. Even a brief experience of social rejection produces wide-ranging effects in a person's self-concept and a lowering of their self-esteem, but little change in emotional expression, a pattern termed a 'deconstructed state' (Twenge, Catanese and Baumeister 2003).

High levels of damaging aggression ('violence') are associated with a number of individual and situational variables among groups of men, for example, a disinhibited personality or state, a male-biased sex ratio, lack of resources and societal status, a culture of honour and the availability of weapons. In modern western settings, higher levels of aggression are associated with watching media violence (Bushman and Anderson 2001). *JA*

Archer, J. forthcoming: Sex differences in aggression in real-world settings: a meta-analytic review. *Review of General Psychology.* Bushman, B. and Anderson, C. 2001: Media violence and the American public. *American Psychologist* 56, 477–89. Nisbett, R. E. and Cohen, D. 1996: *Culture of Honor: The Psychology of Violence in the South.* Boulder CO: Westview Press. Twenge, J. M., Catanese, K. R. and Baumeister, R. F. 2003: Social exclusion and the deconstructed state: time perception, meaninglessness, lethargy, lack of emotion, and self-

awareness. *Journal of Personality and Social Psychology* 85, 409–23.

altruism Action performed with the primary goal of benefiting another. The big debate in psychology has been whether altruism is biological (a natural capacity of the species) or cultural (a socially imposed standard of conduct; Bateson 1991). A difficulty for the first view is that NATURAL SELECTION (see s. 2) would appear to favour selfishness, not altruism. But if altruism is necessarily a product of CULTURE (see also s. 1), then some shocking failures of altruism publicised in 1960s North America suggested that the capacity of culture to limit selfishness is precarious at best. One research response was to document conditions moderating the impact of cultural NORMS enjoining altruism, as well as its high degree of cross-cultural variability. Thus the impact of generosity or social responsibility norms depends on their situational salience; for example, the presence of others may either increase their self-relevance [see also SELF-PRESENTATION] or reduce their impact [see also SOCIAL LOAFING, DIFFUSION OF RESPONSIBILITY]. Another response was to test to the limits the hypothesis that what appears to be altruism is invariably underpinned by more egoistic or self-serving motives. However, the alternative 'empathy-altruism' hypothesis – identifying an empathic emotional reaction to another's situation as the root of altruistic action – appears to have survived such tests (Piliavin and Charng 1990). [See also PERSPECTIVE TAKING]

A parallel enterprise in evolutionary psychology (see also s. 1, EVOLUTION AND PSYCHOLOGY) considered how altruism could be favoured by natural selection. Optimism seemed justified by the frequent observation of apparent altruism in non-human species, necessarily unattributable to any civilising force of culture. This enterprise has produced various promising answers, though some reduce altruism to COOPERATION. [See also PRISONER'S DILEMMA] An evolutionary analysis has, nonetheless, predicted that 'true' altruism – defined as help carrying a net cost for the actor – will be a function of the degree of genetic relatedness between helper and helped (Burnstein, Crandall and Kitayama 1994).

Consequences of this prediction – for example, that altruism will be more marked between kin – are also anticipated by more social psychological analyses, however. Thus, sacrifices benefiting other in-group members supposedly follow self-categorisation as a group member. [See also SELF-CATEGORISATION THEORY] However, this potentially shifts the definition of altruism to action benefiting the group. Campbell (1965) suggested precisely this, drawing the conclusion that ETHNOCENTRISM, given it entails self-sacrifice, is altruistic. *NE*

Bateson, D. 1991: *The Altruism Question: Toward a Social Psychological Answer.* Hillsdale NJ: Erlbaum. Burnstein, E., Crandall, C. and Kitayama, S. 1994: Some neo-Darwinian rules for altruism: weighing cues for inclusive fitness as a function of the biological importance of the decision. *Journal of Personality* and *Social Psychology* 67, 773–89. **Campbell, D. T.** 1965: Ethnocentric and other altruistic motives. In Levine, D. (ed.) *Nebraska Symposium on Motivation* 13, 283–311. Lincoln: University of Nebraska Press. **Piliavin, J. A. and Charng, H.-W.** 1990: Altruism: a review of recent theory and research. *American Sociological Review*, 16, 27–65.

altruism-empathy hypothesis Hypothesis linking acts motivated by a desire to improve another's welfare [see ALTRUISM] with felt empathic concern for the other rather than with the actor's own distress. *NE*

attitudes Like many other concepts that have been absorbed into scientific psychology from everyday language, the concept of attitude has had many definitions and variations in its long history in social psychology. But on some features there has been general agreement. Attitudes always have an 'object' (they are always about 'something': a material object, a person, a group, a policy, etc.), and in this way they are different from PERSONALITY TRAITS (see s. 6).

Attitudes have generally been thought of as 'evaluative tendencies'. This evaluative element distinguishes attitudes from BELIEFS. People could have the same belief, but have different attitudes. For example, two people may believe 'Eating chocolate cake makes me put on weight', but if one person thinks that putting on weight is good then they would have a positive attitude towards eating chocolate cake, while if another thought it was bad, they would have a negative attitude. Attitudes also admit of degrees, so that one person's attitude can be more strongly positive (or negative) than another's. Attitudes are expected to influence a wide range of psychological functioning, including MEMORY (see s. 1), interpretation and EMOTION (see s. 6), as well as what a person does. [See also STEREOTYPES]

The MEASUREMENT (see s. 1, MEASUREMENT AND STATISTICS) of attitudes, initiated by Thurstone in the 1920s, was one of the milestones in the development of social psychology since it showed that such concepts could be measured and scaled rigorously. One of the most common ways of measuring attitude still follows Thurstone's general lead of presenting respondents with statements and inviting them to express their agreement or disagreement with these. [See THURSTONE SCALING, LIKERT SCALE and, GUTTMAN SCALE] A much used alternative, the semantic differential, presents respondents with the relevant attitude object (e.g. 'cannabis use') and invites them to respond to the object on a series of bipolar evaluative scales (e.g. 'good – bad', 'pleasant – unpleasant').

Research into attitudes after World War II was dominated by two major sets of issues. One of these concerned PREJUDICE. Adorno et al.'s milestone work on the psychological roots of anti-Semitism tried to relate prejudiced attitudes towards Jews to attitudes towards other minority groups, to other economic and political views and to individual PERSONALITY (see s. 1 and s. 6) [see AUTHORITARIANISM and F-SCALE]. However, there were a wide range of conceptual and methodological criticisms of this work, and rather than look for the causes of prejudice in terms of individual personality, most research turned to looking for other explanations.

The other main area of research at the time was 'PERSUASION' research. Led by Carl Hovland, a highly influential group of social psychologists based at Yale University began a wide-ranging, systematic and largely experimental set of investigations into the factors underlying persuasion. They examined the effects of variables such as the order of the presentation of arguments and the effects of fear appeals. Other research on the formation of attitudes was based on general principles of LEARNING (see s. 3) such as conditioning and IMITATION (see s. 4) (see Bohner and Waenke 2002).

Later in the 1950s a number of related theoretical models were developed whose core concept was the notion of 'psychological consistency'. The general idea was that certain states of mind were more consistent than others and, further, that consistent states were generally stable and inconsistent states likely to change. These models were used extensively to understand and predict attitude change. The most influential of these was Festinger's theory of cognitive dissonance. [See COGNITIVE DISSONANCE; also BALANCE THEORY, FORCED COMPLIANCE, REACTANCE and COUNTER-ATTITUDINAL ROLE-PLAYING]

Since attitudes have been thought to have a causal influence on behaviour, a vast literature accumulated attempting to predict behaviour from attitude. By the late 1960s accumulating evidence suggested that the relationship might in fact be rather weak, and a number of researchers began to think that attitudes were not good predictors of behaviour (Wicker 1969).

One response to this was to move from a general level ('attitude to the object') to a more specific and behavioural level ('attitude to the act'). So instead of considering a person's attitude towards 'condoms', and expecting that to predict condom use with a particular new partner, this move considers attitude towards the behaviour of using condoms with that new partner. This idea is incorporated in the theory of reasoned action, put forward by Fishbein and Ajzen (Ajzen 1988). [See REASONED ACTION and PLANNED BEHAVIOUR] Another response involved trying to elaborate the conditions under which attitudes were and were not good predictors of behaviour. For instance, Fazio and Zanna (1981) showed that attitudes formed through direct experience with the attitude object were more likely to predict behaviour than attitudes which were formed indirectly. They explained this relationship in term of concepts drawn from an increasingly influential cognitive psychology such as salience and accessibility.

This increasing use of concepts and processes drawn from cognitive psychology has been a persistent feature of recent work in the attitude domain. Drawing on research on PRIMING (see also s. 3) and automatic activation, some researchers have developed implicit measures of attitude, based on measuring REACTION TIMES (see s. 3) (Fazio and Olson 2003). Research on attitude change has also been heavily influenced in this way. Calling on the idea of depth of processing, researchers began to distinguish between 'routes' to persuasion – a central route (which involved detailed information processing) and a peripheral route (which relied more on shortcuts) (Petty and Cacioppo 1986). [See also DUAL-PROCESS THEORY and ELABORATION LIKELIHOOD MODEL] Using these models, researchers have been increasingly able to specify what different factors would lead to attitude change under different conditions.

Some recent research has focused more on the processes involved when a person makes an attitudinal judgement. A number of studies have shown that attitudes are considerably dependent upon the context of their expression. For example, responses to questionnaire items can vary depending on what is salient at the time, including the mood of the respondent, their current goals, recent memories, the nature of the interviewing context and even the order of presentation of items (Schwarz and Bohner 2001). This work shows how attitudes are constructed on a particular occasion. The relationship between these situated constructions and attitudes as stable dispositions is currently being considered. *ML*

Ajzen, I. 1988: *Attitudes, Personality and Behavior*. Chicago: Dorsey. **Bohner, G. and Waenke, M.** 2002: *Attitudes and Attitude Change*. Hove: Psychology Press. **Eagly, A. H. and Chaiken, S.** 1993: *The Psychology of Attitudes*. Fort Worth TX: Harcourt Brace Jovanovich. **Fazio, R. H. and Olson, M. A.** 2003: Implicit measures in social cognition research: their meaning and use. *Annual Review of Psychology* 54, 297–327. **Fazio, R. H. and Zanna, M. P.** 1981: Direct experience and attitude-behavior consistency. *Advances in Experimental Social Psychology* 14, 161–202. **Petty, R. E. and Caccioppo, J. T.** 1986: The elaboration likelihood model of persuasion. *Advances in Experimental Social Psychology* 18, 124–203. **Schwarz, N. and Bohner, G.** 2001: The construction of attitudes. In Tesser, A. and Schwarz, N. (eds) *Blackwell Handbook of Social Psychology: Intraindividual Processes*. Oxford: Blackwell, vol. 1, 436–57. **Wicker, A. W.** 1969: Attitude versus action: the relationship of verbal and overt behavioral responses to attitude objects. *Journal of Social Issues* 25(4), 41–78.

attribution   The processes by which people make inferences from observations. The observations may be of actions (striking someone), reactions (blushing) or outcomes (passing an exam, a car crash). The inferences may be about the weight that should be assigned to different causal FACTORS (see s. 8), most notably whether something about the situation or about the person is the more significant causal factor [see CAUSAL ATTRIBUTION], or they may be about qualities (states or traits) of the person associated with the observed actions, reactions or outcomes. Attribution supports such fundamental human goals as prediction, through inferences about others (e.g. their PERSONALITY – see s. 1 and s. 6 – ATTITUDES, ABILITIES – see s. 6) and control, for example, through fixing moral responsibility (Shaver 1985).

The early social psychology of attribution was strongly influenced by Fritz Heider's (1958) conceptual analysis of social perception. Thus, CORRESPONDENT INFERENCE THEORY and COVARIATION THEORY set out models of how observers might reasonably make inferences from observations. But it quickly became apparent that observers frequently deviate from the reasonable procedures these models described. Evidence accumulated for various systematic biases in the way human observers interpret their observations, leading some authorities to conclude that humans are chronically error-prone in the business of social perception. [See FUNDAMENTAL ATTRIBUTION ERROR]

People also make self-attributions and these appear to differ systematically from observers' attributions. Thus, actors are more likely than observers to explain their own actions in terms of the situation. However, when the action is of a kind liable to be judged positively or negatively, actors may show a self-serving bias [see SELF-SERVING ATTRIBUTION], attributing successes and other positively valued actions to internal causes (e.g. their own ability or virtue), but negatively valued actions to external causes. [See also ULTIMATE ATTRIBUTION ERROR] The self-serving bias itself can vary with SELF-ESTEEM, those with very low self-esteem displaying an ATTRIBUTIONAL STYLE (see s. 7) in which the bias is reversed and failures are self-attributed, while successes are situationally attributed.

In recent years, research on attribution has fallen somewhat out of fashion. Doubts have grown about what can be learned from rather artificial tasks of the kind used in much attribution research, which have limited capacity to engage research participants. The basic questions addressed in attribution research about social perception remain important, however, but are now addressed in other frameworks within the field of SOCIAL COGNITION (see also s. 4) (Gilbert 1998). *NE*

Gilbert, D. 1998: Ordinary personology. In Gilbert, D, Fiske, S. and Lindzey, G. (eds) *The Handbook of Social Psychology* (4th edn). New York: McGraw-Hill, vol. 2, 415–469. **Heider, F.** 1958: *The Psychology of Interpersonal Relations*. New York: Wiley. **Shaver, K.** 1985: *The Attribution of Blame: Causality, Responsibility and Blameworthiness*. New York: Springer-Verlag.

augmenting   In CAUSAL ATTRIBUTION, stressing the importance of one cause when other plausible causes would have had the opposite of the effect observed. *NE*

authoritarianism   A cluster of ATTITUDES reflecting racist sentiments and other extreme right-wing views, identified originally as a PERSONALITY (see s. 1 and s. 6) syndrome. Adorno et al. (1950), in a study of the psychological roots of anti-Semitism, concluded that it is underpinned by excessive need to defer to IN-GROUP authority, rigid adherence to conventional standards, and a hostile punitive attitude to those seen as failing to conform to group NORMS. They proposed a psychoanalytic interpretation in which the attitudes defining an authoritarian personality arise from repressed hostility to parental authority. Their research was subject to an unprecedented level of methodological criticism, while the THEORY (see s. 8) suffered from a more general falling from favour of both psychoanalytic concepts and personality-based explanations for PREJUDICE. However, more recent work by Altemeyer (1996) has resurrected the concept of authoritarianism, defining the syndrome more precisely, elaborating a social learning interpretation of its origins and documenting a range of behavioural consequences. *NE*

Adorno, T. W., Frenkel-Brunswik, E., Levinson, D. and Sanford, N. 1950: *The Authoritarian Personality*. New York: Harper. **Altemeyer, B.** 1996: *The Authoritarian Specter*. Cambridge MA: Harvard University Press.

automaticity   In social psychology, a process that, once started, runs by itself without conscious guidance, is typically fast and efficient, requires only minimal cognitive resources and may not be amenable to conscious control (Wegner and Bargh 1998). It is an old idea in psychology that, as with many bodily functions such as breathing, mental functions, including some that are to begin with deliberate and conscious, can also occur quite automatically. Thus motor SKILL (see s. 3) acquisition was seen as a process of automatising a sequence of actions. This analysis was translated directly into social psychology with the concept of SOCIAL SKILL. More recently the idea has been extended to formation of ATTITUDES, stereotype activation [see STEREOTYPES], PREJUDICE, EMOTIONAL EXPRESSION and PERSON PERCEPTION (Wegner and Bargh 1998). [See also DUAL-PROCESS THEORY]   *NE*

Wegner, D. and Bargh, J. 1998: Control and automaticity in social life. In Gilbert, D., Fiske, S. and Lindzey, G. (eds) *The Handbook of Social Psychology* (4th edn). New York: McGraw-Hill, vol. 2.

B

balance theory A set of propositions about the relations, such as ATTITUDES, between objects of perception and the consequences of different combinations of such relations. Heider (1958) originally worked out the details of the THEORY (see s. 8) in terms of a triad of perceiver (P), another person (O) and an object (X – which could be a third person), and of positive or negative relations between them (e.g. for attitudes, those of P towards O, P towards X, and O towards X). Heider argued that the triad of attitudes could either be balanced, and therefore stable and resistant to change, or unbalanced, and therefore unstable and readily changed. The theory has also been applied to the development of INTERPERSONAL ATTRACTION, based on attitude similarity and difference. More generally, balance theory assumes, in common with

the notion of COGNITIVE DISSONANCE, a basic human preference for sets cognitions, perceptions and evaluations that are internally consistent.   *NE*

Heider, F. 1958: *The Psychology of Interpersonal Relations.* New York: Wiley.

bargaining theory A theory of coalition formation and resource division in situations in which at least three parties compete for a limited resource but no one of them alone has sufficient power to resolve the competition. Bargaining theory (Komorita and Chertkoff 1973) was an attempt to resolve limitations of preceding theories of coalition formation proposing that parties will choose to join the coalition that will give them the largest resource

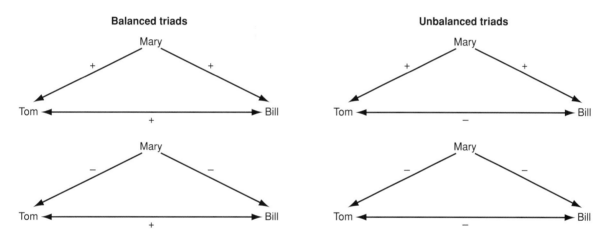

balance theory *Some examples of balanced and unbalanced triads. From Social Psychology by John Sabini. Copyright © 1992 by John Sabini. Used by permission of W. W. Norton & Company, Inc.*

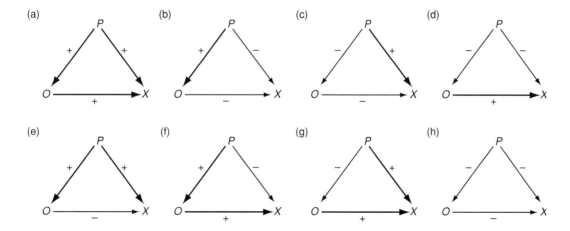

balance theory *Balanced (a to d) and unbalanced (e to h) cognitive triads according to balance theory. Source: M. Hewstone and W. Stroebe,* Introduction to Social Psychology: A European Perspective, *3rd ed, Blackwell (2001).*

share consistent with equity. [See EQUITY THEORY] According to Komorita and Chertkoff, the importance to parties of equity diminishes as they gain experience over repeated attempts to form coalitions; bargaining will become more competitive, and the coalition that finally proves stable will reflect the maximisation of outcomes independent of equity. *NE*

Komorita, S. S. and Chertkoff, J. M. 1973: A bargaining theory of coalition formation. *Psychological Review* 80, 1491–62.

basking in reflected glory A SELF-PRESENTATION strategy involving public identification with a successful person or group. *NE*

beliefs In theories of ATTITUDES, the more purely cognitive as opposed to evaluative elements of attitudes, as in the belief that some property is associated with some object, sometimes assessed as a probability judgement. [See also REASONED ACTION] *NE*

black-sheep effect The tendency to regard nonconforming IN-GROUP members even more negatively than members of an OUT-GROUP, thereby confirming the superior standards of the in-group. *NE*

bogus pipeline A method for assessing ATTITUDES stripped of social desirability bias, based on deceiving respondents into thinking that apparatus to which they are connected can detect untruthful responses. *NE*

brainstorming A method for promoting creativity in a GROUP by encouraging quantity of idea production without concern for quality, this supposedly reducing the inhibiting effects of anticipated criticism. *NE*

bystander intervention A focus for research on ALTRUISM, testing, often through experiment, the reasons for non-intervention in emergencies to help strangers. *NE*

C

causal attribution   The process by which an observer arrives at a conclusion about the causes of an actor's behaviour (Hewstone 1989). An initial focus of research was upon judgements as to whether causes internal to an actor (such as their ABILITIES – see s. 6 – or desires) or external (such as the difficulty of a task or social pressures) should be emphasised. Then attention shifted to biases in attribution, such as the FUNDAMENTAL ATTRIBUTION ERROR, when it seemed that people frequently fail to assess the relative weight of internal and external causes in ways anticipated by theoretical models such as COVARIATION THEORY. Weiner (1986) proposes a more complex model of causal attribution, arguing that people typically seek to decide not just whether a cause is internal to the actor or external, but also whether it is stable or unstable, and whether or not it is controllable. [See also ATTRIBUTION and ULTIMATE ATTRIBUTION ERROR]   *NE*

Hewstone, M. 1989: *Causal Attribution: From Cognitive Processes to Collective Beliefs.* Oxford: Blackwell. **Weiner, B.** 1986: *An Attributional Theory of Motivation and Emotion.* New York: Springer Verlag.

cognitive dissonance   A state of being aware that one simultaneously believes or knows two things that are mutually inconsistent. This state is distressing, motivating the individual to distort one or both cognitions to restore consistency. As a theory of attitude change (Festinger 1957), the concept was tested in experiments in which participants were induced via such techniques as FORCED COMPLIANCE and COUNTER-ATTITUDINAL ROLE-PLAYING, to do or say things contrary to their existing attitudes. This supposedly created a state of dissonance they could only reduce by modifying their original attitudes. The theory was criticised for being too imprecise to test, and alternative explanations for experimental findings have been advanced in terms of SELF-PRESENTATION. Nonetheless, the theory has continued both to evolve and to inspire research (Joule and Beauvois 1998). Moreover, newer research has helped to specify the conditions under which dissonance as a discrepancy between attitudes and actions produces attitude change: actions must have consequences perceived to be negative, the actor must feel personally responsible and arousal must be both experienced and linked to the dissonance. [See also EQUITY THEORY]   *NE*

Festinger, L. 1957: *A Theory of Cognitive Dissonance.* Stanford CA: Stanford University Press. **Joule, R. and Beauvois, L.** 1998: Cognitive dissonance theory: a radical view. *European Review of Social Psychology* 8, 1–32.

cognitive miser   View that people are chronically disposed to adopt low-effort, low-cost cognitive processes in preference to more accurate but higher cost alternatives (contrasts with MOTIVATED TACTICIAN).   *NE*

cohesion of groups   Attraction of group members to the GROUP, sometimes measured as their unwillingness voluntarily to abandon their membership; reflected in willingness to strive on behalf of the group.   *NE*

collectivism   Notion that the GROUP or community as a whole is more important than the individual, supposedly a dominant NORM [see NORMS] in certain CULTURES (see also s. 1).   *NE*

communal orientation   An inclination to show concern for meeting the needs of others with whom one has a close personal relationship [see RELATIONSHIPS], contrasted with 'exchange orientation' as greater concern for a fair balance of contributions and benefits. [See also EQUITY THEORY and EXCHANGE PROCESSES]   *NE*

compliance   CONFORMITY in deeds rather than BELIEFS, typically when conformity can be verified by others controlling rewards or punishments.   *NE*

confirmatory bias   The tendency for perceivers to seek or pay attention to information confirming a belief they hold, for example, about a minority group, in preference to information that could disconfirm the belief. [See also ATTRIBUTION]   *NE*

conformity   Aligning one's actions, expressed opinions or judgements with those of the majority. The classic work of Sherif (1936) demonstrated a version of this inclination

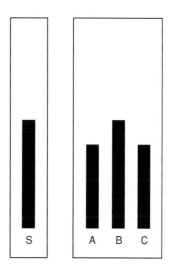

conformity *Stimulus cards similar to those used in Asch's experiment in which the subject faces a simple question and a majority who unanimously adopt the wrong answer. Source: John Sabini, Social Psychology, W. W. Norton & Co (1992).*

with respect to GROUP-created perceptual judgement NORMS; judgements converged on the average and, crucially, this convergence persisted even when others were not present. Sherif's studies suggested that conformity is primarily a response to initial uncertainty; in so far as the task is ambiguous or difficult, this increases individuals' dependence on majority opinion as a best guess concerning the correct response. However, Asch (1956) showed that initial uncertainty is not absolutely necessary; a lone individual can sometimes be induced to adopt a majority response that is unambiguously wrong. But this tendency is clearest when the majority is unanimous, substantially reducing if it is not (and virtually disappearing if the response is given privately). Schachter's (1951) work on the reactions of majorities to dissenting minorities clarifies why public conformity might be such a strong inclination; he showed that non-conformity risks attracting extreme social costs, including ridicule and exclusion.

Behind social psychology's analysis of conformity has been a larger debate about the individual – SOCIETY relationship. On one side is the view that individuals, left to their own devices, are inclined to variability in judgement and action; conformity therefore corrects error in DECISION MAKING (see s. 3), ensures adoption of optimal responses (outside the experiment, the majority will more often be right than wrong) and achieves the unity of purpose needed for effective joint action. On the other side is the view that a civilised and progressive society requires individual moral and intellectual autonomy; conformity suppresses autonomy, thereby inhibiting the collective's capacity for innovation and adaptive change, and at worst secures acquiescence in the persecution of minorities (Asch's own view).

In the longer run, a synthesis of these positions is emerging. It is recognised that a human bias towards conformity is adaptive and affords social groups needed stability and inertia, but is balanced by at least limited openness to novelty and change. Moscovici's analysis of how minorities can lead people to question established wisdom [see MAJORITY/MINORITY] offers one view of how innovations may be introduced into social systems (for another, see Rogers 2003).   *NE*

Asch, S. E. 1956: Studies of independence and conformity: I. A minority of one against a unanimous majority. *Psychological Monographs* 70 (9, Whole No. 416). Rogers, E. M. 2003: *Diffusion of Innovations* (5th edn). New York: Free Press. Schachter, S. 1951: Deviation, rejection and communication. *Journal of Abnormal and Social Psychology* 46, 109–207. Sherif, M. 1936: *The Psychology of Social Norms*. New York: Harper.

consensus   Level of agreement within a GROUP regarding a judgement, OPINION or course of action.   *NE*

contact hypothesis   The hypothesis (Allport 1954) that STEREOTYPES can be modified, PREJUDICE overcome, DISCRIMINATION reduced and INTER-GROUP RELATIONS generally improved by contact between members of different GROUPS. Research has not endorsed the simplest version of the hypothesis that any contact is beneficial; contact has positive effects only under certain conditions. Among the most important are that: 1) contact occurs with social and institutional support; 2) contact is sufficiently frequent, extended and intimate for personal RELATIONSHIPS to develop; 3) contact is on the basis of equality of SOCIAL

STATUS; and 4) the contact involves COOPERATION in pursuit of common goals. Some work also indicates that contact with OUT-GROUP members is more beneficial if they are seen as typical rather than atypical of their group (see Hewstone and Brown 1986).   *NE*

Allport, G. 1954: *The Nature of Prejudice*. Reading MA: Addison-Wesley. Hewstone, M. and Brown, R. (eds) 1986: *Contact and Conflict in Intergroup Encounters*. Oxford: Blackwell.

contingency theory (of leadership)   A theory (Fiedler 1978) that LEADERSHIP effects on GROUP performance depend on three 'contingencies' (see s. 1) – leader–member relations (good–bad), task (structured–unstructured) and leader's POWER (weak–strong) – and their moderating effect on leadership style. For Fiedler, the relevant dimension of style was the extent of concern with good interpersonal relations as opposed to productivity, assessed in terms of attitude to the least preferred co-worker; the less positive this attitude, the greater the relative concern with productivity. The theory was advanced as a counter to PERSONALITY (see s. 1)-based explanations of leadership effectiveness. Its complexity has made the theory difficult to test, and support has been mixed (Schriesheim, Tepper and Tetrault 1994) but it has been influential in the argument that no one leadership style is invariably most effective; what works best depends on a variety of circumstances.   *NE*

Fiedler, F. 1978: The contingency model and the dynamics of the leadership process. In Berkowitz, L. (ed.) *Advances in Experimental Social Psychology*. New York: Academic Press, vol. 11, 59–112. Schriesheim, C., Tepper, B. and Tetrault, L. 1994: Least preferred co-worker score, situational control and leadership effectiveness: a meta-analysis of contingency model performance predictions. *Journal of Applied Psychology* 79, 561–73.

cooperation   Cooperation is often conceptualised in relation to other interpersonal MOTIVATIONS (see s. 6) or orientations, such as ALTRUISM, individualism, competition and AGGRESSION. Cooperation can be defined by the tendency to maximise outcomes for SELF (see s. 1 and s. 4) and others ('doing well together'), thereby assigning positive weight to outcomes for both self and others. In contrast, competition is defined by the tendency to maximise relative advantage over others ('doing better than others'), thereby assigning positive weight to outcomes for self in combination with assigning negative weight to outcomes for others. Whereas cooperation and competition include taking account of outcomes for SELF (see also s. 1) *and* outcomes for others, three other important orientations do not. Kelley, Holmes, Kerr, Reis, Rusbult and Van Lange (2003) propose that individualism can be defined by the tendency to maximise outcomes for self, with no or very little regard for outcomes for others, altruism by the tendency to maximise outcomes for others, with no or very little regard for outcomes for self, and aggression by the tendency to minimise outcomes for others.

Cooperation is often studied in the well-known PRISONER'S DILEMMA, a form of social dilemma representing a conflict between that which is good for the dyad or group (i.e. a cooperative choice) and that which is good for the individual, at least in the short term (i.e. a non-cooperative choice). Research has shown that cooperative motivation can be influenced by a variety of factors, including dispositional, relational and situational variables (Komorita and Parks 1995). For example, cooperative behaviour is more likely among individuals with a so-called pro-social orientation [see PRO-SOCIAL BEHAVIOUR] than among those with individualistic or competitive orientations; such dispositions are partially rooted in past social interaction experiences (e.g. pro-socials tend to have more SIBLINGS – see s. 4, especially sisters, than individualists and competitors; Van Lange, Otten, De Bruin and Joireman 1997). At the relationship level, cooperative behaviour is more likely among friends (rather than strangers), in communal [see COMMUNAL ORIENTATION] RELATIONSHIPS (rather than exchange relationships) and relationships characterised by strong (rather than weak) commitment. Finally, several situational variables affect cooperation, such as group size (more cooperation in smaller groups), the possibility of COMMUNICATION (see s. 2) about the social dilemma, public (versus anonymous) response, and circumstances that foster trust, perceived efficacy or commitment to or identification with the GROUP (see Kelley et al. 2003). *PVL*

Kelley, H. H., Holmes, J. W., Kerr, N. L., Reis, H. T., Rusbult, C. E. and Van Lange, P. A. M. 2003: *An Atlas of Interpersonal Situations*. New York: Cambridge. Komorita, S. S. and Parks, C. D. 1995: Interpersonal relations: mixed-motive interaction. *Annual Review of Psychology* 46, 183–207. Van Lange, P. A. M., Otten, W., De Bruin, E. M. N. and Joireman, J. A. 1997: Development of prosocial, individualistic, and competitive orientations: theory and preliminary evidence. *Journal of Personality and Social Psychology* 73, 733–46.

correspondence bias The tendency for perceivers to treat observations of others' actions and reactions as corresponding to or informative about underlying traits of the actor; the term is sometimes used in preference to FUNDAMENTAL ATTRIBUTION ERROR. [See also CORRESPONDENT INFERENCE THEORY] *NE*

correspondent inference theory A theory of dispositional or TRAIT (see s. 6) ATTRIBUTION, specifying conditions under which perceivers will infer that an observed action corresponds to an underlying trait of the actor (Jones and Davis 1965). Jones and Davis argued that, because actions can have multiple effects, only one of which may have been their primary intention, such inferences depend on deciding what the actor was intending to do, applying a principle of 'non-common effects' (which of the effects observed is unique to the action chosen). Judgements of intentions are additionally based on a 'knowledge criterion' (could the actor have foreseen this effect?) and an 'ability criterion' (was he/she capable of producing this effect as a matter of choice?). However, if the intended effect or outcome has high social desirability, it is unlikely to be seen as informative about dispositions peculiar to the actor. [See also DIAGNOSTICITY] Tests of the theory were mainly of significance in drawing attention to biases in attribution. [See also FUNDAMENTAL ATTRIBUTION ERROR and COVARIATION THEORY] *NE*

Jones, E. and Davis, K. 1965: From acts to dispositions: the attribution process in person perception. In Berkowitz, L. (ed.) *Advances in Experimental Social Psychology*. New York: Academic Press, vol. 7, 219–66.

counter-attitudinal role-playing Rehearsing, usually publicly, an attitude [see ATTITUDES] position contrary to one's own, a technique used to test predictions from COGNITIVE DISSONANCE theory. *NE*

covariation theory A theory of CAUSAL ATTRIBUTION, broader than CORRESPONDENT INFERENCE THEORY in treating all behavioural responses, reactions as well as intentional actions, as evidence from which inferences can be drawn about the dispositions of actors. Kelley (1967) argued that perceivers proceed like scientists, making multiple observations and drawing conclusions from 'covariations' between behaviour and potential causes. Kelley proposed perceivers consider three aspects of covariations, to what extent the observed behaviour or reaction is (1) uniquely associated with a particular actor (low consensus), (2) consistently associated with this actor, and (3) distinctively associated with certain

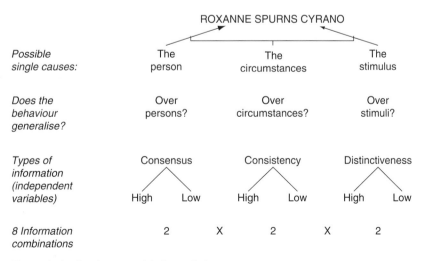

covariation theory *The analysis of variance model of covariation.*

contexts. The theory has been criticised for an overly rational view of information processing given research evidence suggesting that perceivers are rarely such systematic observers. *NE*

Kelley, H. 1967: Attribution theory in social psychology. In Levine, D. (ed.) *Nebraska Symposium on Motivation*. Lincoln NA: University of Nebraska Press, vol. 13, 192–240.

crowd behaviour Crowd psychology emerged in the late nineteenth century when the rise of trade unionism and socialism led to widespread fears about the masses among social elites. This was reflected in theories portraying crowd members as mindless and barbaric. Most famously, Gustav Le Bon (1895) argued that people become anonymous in the crowd, lose their individual IDENTITY (see also s. 4) and revert to a primitive group mind. Consequently their behaviours are uncontrolled, emotional and brutal. These ideas have been incorporated into modern DEINDIVIDUATION theories.

Many theorists, such as Floyd Allport, criticised the very idea of a 'group mind'. Allport initiated a tradition which proposes that individuality is not lost but maintained or even accentuated in collective settings. Thus violent crowds result from the convergence of violent people. Such theories maintain the idea that crowd behaviour, and particularly crowd conflict, are pathological and meaningless. However, they locate pathology in the character of particular individuals rather than a crowd process that can affect anyone.

While crowd behaviour often challenges dominant social standards, this does not make it senseless. Rather it might be based on alternative standards. Turner and Killian's (1987) 'emergent norm theory' suggests that crowds form their own NORMS during events through a process of interaction and the intervention of prominent 'keynoters'. However, this approach has been criticised for its failure to specify either what becomes normative or the speed with which norms form and change during crowd events.

Social identity models [see SELF-CATEGORISATION THEORY] of crowds also focus on the normative nature of crowd action, but argue that norms are not created from scratch (e.g. Reicher 1984). The core assumption is that people do not lose identity in the crowd but shift from personal identity to social identity. Hence control is not lost in the crowd but shifts from individual values, beliefs and understandings to those associated with the specific social category of which the crowd forms part. Recently, this insight has been developed into an 'elaborated social identity model' of crowds (Reicher 2001), which examines how collective norms are formed and changed in the interactions between crowds and others (notably the police) as events unfold over time. *SR*

Le Bon, G. 1895/1947: *The Crowd: A Study of the Popular Mind*. London: Ernest Benn. **Reicher, S.** 1984: The St. Pauls riot: an explanation of the limits of crowd action in terms of a social identity model. *European Journal of Social Psychology* 14, 1–21. **Reicher, S.** 2001: The psychology of crowd dynamics. In Hogg, M. and Tindale, S. (eds) *Blackwell Handbook of Social Psychology: Group Processes*. Oxford: Blackwell. **Turner, R. H. and Killian, L. M.** 1987: *Collective Behaviour* (3rd edn). Englewood Cliffs NJ: Prentice Hall.

culture A distinctive, relatively enduring way of living, shared by a definable population. The term is sometimes used interchangeably with 'SOCIETY', though it is clearly more reasonable to talk of societies having CULTURES (see also s. 1) than the reverse. However, across the social sciences there is a distinct lack of definitional consensus, and some definitions include the human-made material features and elements of the local environment in so far as these support a particular way of living. Within social psychology, however, the focus has been on behavioural and psychological phenomena that might be expected to vary across cultures and therefore constitute, or at least sustain, the distinctiveness of each. Thus variations have been expected in NORMS or standards of behaviour, in systems of BELIEFS and VALUES, in styles of NON-VERBAL COMMUNICATION and expression, in the routine practices around which daily life is structured and, through a specific LANGUAGE (see s. 2), in the meanings attributed to actions and events. [See also ATTRIBUTION] Cultural differences in these phenomena have, however, more often turned out to be matters of degree than categorical differences. [See also COLLECTIVISM] (See also s. 1, CULTURE) *NE*

Fiske, A., Kitayama, S., Markus, H. and Nisbett, R. 1998: The cultural matrix of social psychology. In Gilbert, D., Fiske, S. and Lindzey, G. (eds) *The Handbook of Social Psychology* (4th edn). New York: McGraw-Hill, vol. 2.

D

deception   Research reveals that deception or lying, particularly about feelings, is a universal and regular activity (DePaulo, Kashy, Kirkendol, Wyer and Epstein 1996), in effect, a routine feature of competent SELF-PRESENTATION. Research has also considered whether people are able to conceal lies successfully and, correspondingly, how reliably observers can detect lies, particularly from non-verbal cues. [See also NON-VERBAL COMMUNICATION] Ekman (1992) has endorsed both possibilities, arguing that lies can be almost impossible to detect, but also that true feelings can be difficult to conceal entirely, deceptions being revealed by poorly controlled non-verbal behaviour. [See also EMOTIONAL EXPRESSION] (See also s. 8, DECEPTION)   *NE*

DePaulo, B., Kashy, D., Kirkendol, S., Wyer, M. and Epstein, J. 1996: Lying in everyday life. *Journal of Personality and Social Psychology* 70, 979–93. Ekman, P. 1992: *Telling Lies* (2nd edn). New York: Norton.

deindividuation   Conditions exaggerating individual anonymity, supposedly arising naturally whenever people are in a GROUP, and leading to increased AGGRESSION.   *NE*

depersonalisation   The psychological state created by self-categorisation as a GROUP member. [See SELF-CATEGORISATION THEORY]   *NE*

diagnosticity   A characteristic of information able to clarify something specific to a particular person, sometimes contrasted with base-rate information, which describes a population rather than its individual members.   *NE*

diffusion of responsibility   The effect of the presence of others in reducing the tendency of any individual to take the initiative, or take responsibility for action or intervention, particularly in emergencies. Latané and Darley (1970) discovered that the witnesses to a murder who failed to intervene or act to help the victim were not callous and indifferent, but instead uncertain about their responsibility to act. Experimental research by the same authors established that witnesses to an emergency are less likely to intervene if others are also present, suggesting that others' presence spreads the feeling of responsibility more widely and so weakens its impact on any one individual. Subsequent work indicated its effects are moderated by individuals' degree of commitment to NORMS of social responsibility. [See also ALTRUISM, helping behaviour, PRO-SOCIAL BEHAVIOUR, SOCIAL IMPACT THEORY, PLURALISTIC IGNORANCE]   *NE*

Latané, B. and Darley, J. 1970: *The Unresponsive Bystander: Why Doesn't He Help?* New York: Appleton-Century-Crofts.

direct read-out view (of emotional expression)   The view that expressions, particularly facial, of emotions are direct and reflexive products of internal emotional states, largely unaffected by social context (contrasts with SOCIAL COMMUNICATION VIEW).   *NE*

discounting   In CAUSAL ATTRIBUTION, ruling out one cause when other more likely causes are present.   *NE*

discrimination   The effects of actions or policies upon the distribution of social (rights, respect, opportunities) and material goods, such that their allocation is sensitive to the social category memberships of the recipients (distinguished from PREJUDICE). [See also INTER-GROUP RELATIONS and SOCIAL DOMINANCE THEORY]   *NE*

display rules   The NORMS of a GROUP or CULTURE (see also s. 1) regulating public EMOTIONAL EXPRESSION, most often thought to apply to facial expressions. (See also s. 4, EMOTIONAL DISPLAY RULES)   *NE*

distributive justice   The fairness of decisions about distribution, usually of resources, but can also apply to distribution of burdens, obligations and punishments. [See also SOCIAL JUSTICE and EQUITY THEORY]   *NE*

dual-process theory   A number of theories of social psychological phenomena postulate the operation of contrasting psychological processes (see Chaiken and Trope 1999). Examples include the ELABORATION LIKELIHOOD MODEL and HEURISTIC-SYSTEMATIC MODEL of persuasion, the theory of REASONED ACTION and theoretical accounts of POLARISATION in GROUP DECISION MAKING (see s. 3). The typical contrast is between a low-effort process, which may also run automatically [see AUTOMATICITY], and a high-effort process, which may also be more deliberately or consciously controlled. In some theoretical accounts, the two processes are also alternatives – either one or the other operates, but not both – while in others it is acknowledged that they may operate in parallel. Use of the high-effort process is typically assumed to be constrained by MOTIVATION (see s. 6) and availability of necessary psychological resources. Thus a resource such as ATTENTION (see s. 3) may be temporarily limited by its allocation to other tasks or more chronically limited by intellectual capacity.   *NE*

Chaiken, S. and Trope, Y. (eds) 1999: *Dual Process Theories in Social Psychology*. New York: Guilford Press.

E

ego depletion Idea that humans' capacity for volition (SELF-REGULATION, choice) is limited and depleted by use, leading to attempts to conserve remaining resources until they have an opportunity to regenerate. *NE*

elaboration likelihood model A DUAL-PROCESS THEORY of PERSUASION or attitude [see ATTITUDES] change that specifies conditions under which close inspection (elaboration) of the argument in a persuasive message is more or less likely (Petty and Caccioppo 1986). MOTIVATION (see s. 6) and ability determine the likelihood of such elaboration. To the extent that elaboration occurs, strong arguments are more persuasive than weak arguments, but they have no advantage if elaboration does not occur. It is not clear, however, what features of arguments make them strong or weak. Petty and Caccioppo describe elaboration of message content as the 'central route' to persuasion, and anticipate that its effects will be more enduring than those of persuasion via the alternative 'peripheral route', based on considerations other than message content. [See also HEURISTIC-SYSTEMATIC MODEL] *NE*

Petty, J. and Caccioppo, J. 1986: The elaboration likelihood model of persuasion. In *Berkowitz, L.* (ed.) *Advances in Experimental Social Psychology*. New York: Academic Press, vol. 19, 123–205.

embarrassment Goffman (1956) identified embarrassment as the powerful distress that overtakes someone when they are unable to continue performing the ROLE they have adopted in a social encounter [see also SELF-PRESENTATION, WORKING CONSENSUS]; he proposed it is so distressing that people will accept all manner of other costs to avoid it. Non-verbal expression of embarrassment, notably blushing, suggests it is quite distinct from ANXIETY (see s. 6) or fear, which are associated with very different facial reactions. Keltner and Buswell (1997) argue that embarrassment is also distinguishable from emotions such as shame and guilt in terms of antecedents, experience and display [see also EXPRESSION OF EMOTION] and suggest its display serves an appeasement function, seeking to repair social relations one has damaged. *NE*

Goffman, E. 1956: Embarrassment and social organisation. *American Journal of Sociology* 62, 264–71. **Keltner, D. and Buswell, B.** [1997]: Embarrassment: its distinctive form and appeasement functions. *Psychological Bulletin* 122, 250–70.

emotional expression Refers to any sign, verbal or non-verbal, by which emotions are revealed, displayed or communicated to others. However, research in social psychology has tended to concentrate on NON-VERBAL COMMUNICATION of emotions.

It is well established that voice and speech cues may

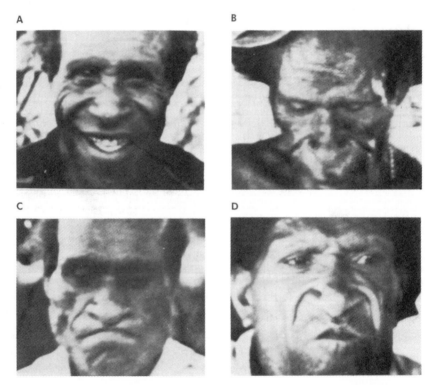

emotional expression *Photographs of facial expressions in members of a tribal society in New Guinea that had little prior contact with the outside world. © Paul Ekman, 1971.*

communicate emotions independent of verbal content. Emotion-specific vocalisation has been shown to be recognised across boundaries of LANGUAGE (see s. 2) and CULTURE (see also s. 1). Similarities in vocalisation across species indicate that vocal expression is biologically determined and that it has its origins in animal COMMUNICATION (see s. 2). Anger and hostility are typically expressed by loud, harsh vocalisation, while fear and helplessness are expressed by high-pitch, shrill vocalisation.

Emotion-specific bodily postures and gestures have so far received little attention. A few studies have examined the general bodily postures associated with the emotions of anger (tense, erect posture), sadness (slumped posture), happiness (expansive, relaxed posture) and fear (stiff body posture).

The vast majority of research on emotional communication has been concerned with facial expression. According to Darwin (1872/1998), human facial expressions of emotions evolved from animal expressions; they are innate and thus universal. Many studies have found cross-cultural similarities in the display and recognition of facial expression of the BASIC EMOTIONS (see s. 4) of anger, disgust, sadness, happiness, surprise and fear. Photographs of posed (but to a lesser extent spontaneous) facial expressions of emotions are identified in the same way by people of different cultures, even by those never exposed to western media (Ekman and Friesen 1971). The biologically based, universal character of facial expression is also supported in studies of congenitally blind and deaf children and infants. However, some psychologists point to a number of methodological shortcomings in the cross-cultural evidence (see Russell in Fridlund, 1994).

According to the read-out view [see DIRECT READ-OUT VIEW], facial expressions reveal people's emotional state to others, except when social and cultural NORMS require their control [see DISPLAY RULES], while bodily signs may betray emotional states even when facial expressions are controlled. [See also DECEPTION] Facial expressions can also act back on emotional states, influencing the intensity or quality of emotional feelings. [See FACIAL FEEDBACK HYPOTHESIS] Some psychologists contest the direct relationship between facial expression and subjective emotional experience. According to Fridlund's (1994) SOCIAL COMMUNICATION VIEW, facial expressions occur for the purpose of communicating context-specific social motives. More recent models strive to integrate the social and emotional functions of facial expression (Manstead, Fischer and Jacobs 1999). *SK-G*

Darwin, C. 1872/1998: *The Expression of Emotion in Man and Animals.* Oxford: Oxford University Press. **Ekman, P. and Friesen, W.** 1971: Constants across culture in the face and emotion. *Journal of Personality and Social Psychology* 17, 124–9. **Fridlund, A.** 1994: *Human Facial Expression: An Evolutionary View.* San Diego CA: Academic Press. **Manstead, A., Fischer, A. and Jacobs, E.** 1999: The social and emotional functions of facial display. In Philippot, P., Feldman, R. and Coats, E. (eds) *The Social Context of Nonverbal Behavior.* Cambridge: Cambridge University Press, 287–313.

equity theory A social psychological theory of DISTRIBUTIVE JUSTICE (Adams 1965). The theory builds upon theories of social exchange [see EXCHANGE PROCESSES], SOCIAL COMPARISON and COGNITIVE DISSO-

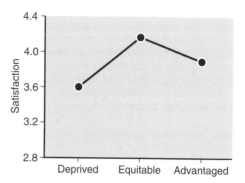

equity theory *Equity and satisfaction in intimate relationships. Source: M. Hewstone and W. Stroebe,* Introduction to Social Psychology: A European Perspective, *Blackwell (2001) (based on Buunk & VanYperen, 1991).*

NANCE. It assumes that people consider what they contribute to an interaction with others (their inputs) and what they get in return (their outcomes). People assess the given degree of equity (i.e. justice) by comparing the ratio of their own outcomes and inputs with the outcome-input ratio of others. If the two ratios do not match, people experience inequity, an aversive state of distress that motivates them to restore equity. Equity can be restored either behaviourally, by means of compensation or retaliation, or by cognitive reconstruction. Equity theory was originally developed to explain people's reactions to underpayment and overpayment in work organisations. Walster, Walster and Berscheid (1978) expanded equity theory to other kinds of interactions and relationships, as for instance intimate relationships. [See also SOCIAL JUSTICE] *GM*

Adams, J. S. 1965: Inequity in social exchange. In Berkowitz, L. (ed.) *Advances in Experimental Social Psychology.* New York: Academic Press, vol. 2, 267–99. **Walster, E., Walster, G. W. and Berscheid, E.** 1978: *Equity: Theory and Research.* Boston MA: Allyn and Bacon.

ethnocentrism Set of reactions in which preference for the CULTURE (see also s. 1) of the IN-GROUP is coupled with hostility to one or more OUT-GROUPS. [See also AUTHORITARIANISM and REALISTIC GROUP CONFLICT THEORY] *NE*

evaluation apprehension Arousal resulting from the anticipation that one's performance will be subject to critical evaluation. [See also SOCIAL FACILITATION] *NE*

exchange processes Processes involving reciprocal transfer of benefits. Social exchange differs from pure ALTRUISM in that a benefit derived by one party from another is at some point reciprocated and, crucially, both parties recognise this as an obligation (Gouldner 1960). Most social psychological analyses of exchange processes incorporate three key economic ideas, profit, equivalence and market (e.g. Thibaut and Kelley 1959).

First, exchange requires the expectation by both parties of profit; the cost that each incurs must be less than the value of the benefit each gains. Second, exchange is governed by NORMS of equivalence; there should be some correspondence in the profit each party derives from the transaction. [See also EQUITY THEORY] Money as a medium of exchange gives precision to equivalence, but some authorities argue that social exchange differs crucially from money-based or commercial transactions in avoiding explicit equivalence values. Equivalence expectations are not absent, but ambiguity around the definition of equivalence is left deliberately unresolved. This ambiguity is exploited to sustain exchange RELATIONSHIPS; exchanges continue between the same parties partly because the precise balance of credit and debt remains chronically in doubt. An advantage derived from such continuity is the opportunity also to avoid specificity about the timeframe for reciprocation; effectively, the parties allow one another to optimise the value of a benefit owed by selecting the timing and content of reciprocation, and trust one another to honour the obligation (Boissevain 1974). [See also SOCIAL CAPITAL]

Exchange within close relationships is complicated both by the variety of benefits exchanged, further exaggerating equivalence problems, and by its coexistence with other processes, such as COOPERATION and altruism, from which the parties benefit. This has led some to argue that an exchange orientation is ultimately incompatible with such relationships, but for others the evidence points to the opposite conclusion: without a long-term balancing out in exchanges, both satisfaction and relationship survival are threatened (see Buunk and Schaufeli 1999).

Third, however, market conditions – the balance of 'buyers' to 'sellers' in a population – influence both the profitability and equivalence values of particular exchange relationships. Partners, for example, the male as compared to the female in a heterosexual relationship, may differ in their respective dependence on this as an exchange relationship, accepting substantial differences in profit because they differ in realistic alternative suppliers of the same benefits.   *NE*

Boissevain, J. 1974: *Friends of Friends: Networks, Manipulators and Coalitions*. Oxford: Blackwell. **Buunk, B. and Schaufeli, W.** 1999: Reciprocity in interpersonal relations: An evolutionary perspective on its importance for health and well-being. In Stroebe, W. and Hewstone, M. (eds) *European Review of Social Psychology*. Chichester: Wiley, vol. 10. **Gouldner, A.** 1960: The norm of reciprocity: a preliminary statement. *American Sociological Review* 25, 161–78. **Thibaut, J. and Kelley, H.** 1959: *The Social Psychology of Groups*. New York: Wiley.

expectancy-value model A family of rational choice theories, treating decision making as a multiplicative function of the probability (expectancy) of various outcomes and the value attached to each. [See also REASONED ACTION]   *NE*

experimenter expectancy effects Effects on experimental results of implicit messages that may be communicated to participants as to what response the experimenter expects or would prefer.   *NE*

F

facial feedback hypothesis The proposition that affective state is influenced by facial expression, based on the notion that our faces give us feedback about what we are feeling. One version of the hypothesis, namely that facial expression affects which particular EMOTION (see s. 6) is subjectively experienced, has found less EMPIRICAL (see s. 8) support than a version holding that the influence is limited to the intensity with which an emotion is felt (McIntosh 1996). A basic problem in testing the hypothesis, namely how to induce people to pose facial expressions without simultaneously creating EXPERIMENTER EXPECTANCY EFFECTS by suggesting the emotion to be expressed, has been ingeniously solved in experiments such as those by Strack, Stepper and Martin (1988). [See also EMOTIONAL EXPRESSION] *NE*

McIntosh, D. (1996): Facial feedback hypothesis: evidence, implications and directions. *Motivation and Emotion* 20, 121–47.
Strack, F., Stepper, L. and Martin, S. 1988: Inhibiting and facilitating effects of the human smile: a non-obtrusive test of the facial feedback hypothesis. *Journal of Personality and Social Psychology* 54, 768–77.

FACS Facial Action Coding System, devised to measure muscle-based facial movements from video recordings of facial EMOTIONAL EXPRESSIONS. [See also FAST] *NE*

false consensus effect The tendency to believe that one's own attitudes and inclinations are more widely shared by the population at large than is the case. *NE*

FAST Facial Affect Scoring Technique, a precursor to FACS, based on matching photographs of facial EMOTIONAL EXPRESSIONS with standard illustrations for three facial areas. *NE*

foot-in-the-door technique A SOCIAL INFLUENCE technique, based on preceding larger requests with trivial ones to which the influence target is likely to accede. *NE*

forced compliance Set of techniques for studying COGNITIVE DISSONANCE by inducing people to do or say things contrary to their true BELIEFS or ATTITUDES. [See also COUNTER-ATTITUDINAL ROLE-PLAYING] *NE*

free rider One using public goods, or benefiting from collective efforts, without contributing, supposedly a tendency enhanced by the DIFFUSION OF RESPONSIBILITY effects of other contributors. *NE*

frustration-aggression hypothesis Hypothesis that frustration of attempts to achieve a goal leads to AGGRESSION, which may be displaced onto a safer target than the source of the frustration, also offered as an explanation of violence towards minorities. *NE*

F-scale The Fascism or implicit anti-democratic trends scale of opinions constructed to measure AUTHORITARIANISM. *NE*

fundamental attribution error (FAE) The inclination of observers to exaggerate the importance of causes internal to the actor, such as PERSONALITY (see s. 1 and s. 6) or ATTITUDES, at the expense of causes external to the actor (sometimes identified as correspondence bias). An experiment (Jones and Harris 1967) in which participants attributed attitudes to the writer of an essay despite being told the writer had been instructed to adopt the line expressed, is typical of many appearing to show that

A

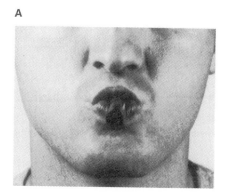

B

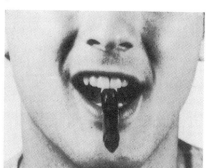

facial feedback hypothesis *A procedure to test the facial feedback hypothesis wherein subjects were asked to hold a magic marker in their mouths: holding it with their teeth but not their lips produced a smile; holding it with their lips but not their teeth produced a frown. Source: Strack et al. 1988.*

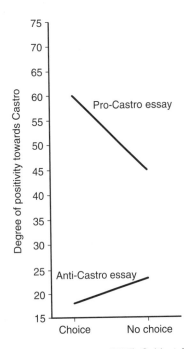

fundamental attribution error (FAE) *Subjects' estimates of the essay writer's true attitude towards Castro, as indicated by the degree of positivity towards Castro. Source: John Sabini,* Social Psychology, *W. W. Norton & Co (1992). Data from Jones and Harris, 1967.*

people routinely neglect the significance of situational constraints on behaviour when they make ATTRIBUTIONS. [See also CAUSAL ATTRIBUTION] Proponents of the situationist critique of personality psychology [see SITUATIONISM] invoked the FAE as accounting for the widespread belief in an illusion – that personality explains behaviour. The implication that human social perception is chronically and incorrigibly flawed in this way was later modified in the light of evidence that such attributions can reflect adaptive HEURISTICS (see s. 3) (cognitively efficient short cuts) which may primarily produce errors in the special conditions created within experiments (Funder 1987). [See also ULTIMATE ATTRIBUTION ERROR] *NE*

Funder, D. (1987): Errors and mistakes: evaluating the accuracy of social judgment. *Psychological Bulletin* 101, 75–90. **Jones, E. and Harris, V.** (1967). The attribution of attitudes. *Journal of Experimental Social Psychology* 3, 1–24.

G

group   In social psychology the term has been applied to virtually all collective entities with which individuals can be identified, including families, gangs, crowds, teams, committees, juries, parliaments, communities, tribes, clubs, associations, organisations, nation states and even culturally or biologically defined categories. Virtually every social psychological process of any consequence is thought to be affected by the particular group or groups to which individuals belong or with which they identify, making 'group' a fundamental analytic category for the discipline. Despite this, it has not been easy to identify the crucial defining features of a group or decide what, psychologically speaking, all groups have in common.

Around the turn of the twentieth century several influential arguments (LeBon, McDougall, Freud) converged on the idea that, at the very least, the behaviour of people in groups is qualitatively different from their behaviour as individuals, and that perhaps groups should be regarded as distinct psychological entities, possessing a 'group mind' and acting virtually as discrete sentient organisms. [See CROWD BEHAVIOUR] This was soon to be challenged by Floyd Allport (1924) with the claim that behaviour can only be analysed at the level of the individual. His challenge provoked, from the 1930s, a range of initiatives to demonstrate experimentally that group phenomena are not reducible to individual behaviour, e.g. studies of NORMS, CONFORMITY, POLARISATION (e.g. Sherif 1936).

But pinning down the defining features of groups has remained a problem. Among the features proposed have been common fate or interdependence, internal structure (distinctions of ROLE and SOCIAL STATUS) and face-to-face interaction. However, it has also been argued that all these are variable features and none is necessary. [See also MINIMAL GROUP] One response has been the proposal that group is essentially a psychological construct in the minds of individuals, a way individuals think about themselves and their relation to the social world. Thus, SELF-CATEGORISATION THEORY (Turner 1987) treats group as a categorisation of the SELF (see also s. 1 and s. 4) at a higher level of inclusion than individual, arguing that a fundamental shift in psychological functioning follows when this occurs.

Another response has been to study the processes and outcomes that can be observed in particular kinds of groups, typically relatively small face-to-face groups, and treat as empirical questions the effects of variables such as size, group age or degree of internal structure (Levine and Moreland 1998). This approach does suggest that relationships between two people are quite distinct from all larger groups. [See also GROUP PROCESSES]   NE

Allport, F. 1924: *Social Psychology*. New York: Houghton Mifflin. **Levine, J. and Moreland, R. L.** (1998): Small groups. In Gilbert, D., Fiske, S. and Lindzey, G. (eds), *The Handbook of Social Psychology* (4th edn). New York: McGraw-Hill, vol. 2, 415–69. **Sherif, M.** 1936: *The Psychology of Social Norms*. New York: Harper. **Turner, J.** 1987: *Rediscovering the Social Group*. Oxford: Blackwell.

group processes   Dozens of definitions of GROUPS have been offered over the years. These have emphasised such diverse criteria as the level of COMMUNICATION (see s. 2), INFLUENCE (see s. 1) or interaction among members; the degree to which members share common goals and are interdependent for achieving them; the impact of structural factors (e.g. NORMS, ROLES and SOCIAL STATUS) on how members behave; and members' thoughts and feelings about one another and the group as a whole (e.g. shared IDENTITY (see also s. 4), cohesion). For present purposes, we will define the prototypical group as containing a small number of members who interact freely on a wide range of activities, are highly interdependent and have a remembered past and an anticipated future.

Groups of this kind are a ubiquitous feature of human society because they satisfy several fundamental needs. For example, groups facilitate child-rearing, acquisition of food and shelter, and defence against enemies; they allow members to avoid loneliness and maintain a positive image of themselves; and they help members understand the world they live in and their own capabilities. Although group membership does not always satisfy all of these needs, the rewards of membership typically cause people to belong to groups of one sort or another throughout their lives.

The 1930s marked the beginning of systematic research on small groups by social psychologists, and several notable research projects were conducted prior to World War II. These included Sherif's laboratory EXPERIMENTS (see s. 8) on the development of group norms under conditions of uncertainty [see SOCIAL INFLUENCE and CONFORMITY]; Lewin, Lippitt and White's (1939) field experiments on how adult LEADERSHIP style influenced children's aggressive behaviour; and Whyte's (1943) participant observation research on the social dynamics of Italian-American gangs in Boston.

Interest in small groups surged after the WAR (see also s. 1, WAR AND PSYCHOLOGY) and remained strong during the 1950s, as indicated by the many important theoretical, EMPIRICAL (see s. 8) and methodological advances of that period. By the early 1960s, however, many social psychologists were losing enthusiasm for group research, perhaps because theoretical developments were not keeping pace with empirical findings. Though important work on groups was done during the next 30 years, the field as a whole languished until the middle 1980s. Since that time, the amount of published research on groups has increased dramatically. Though much of the newer work by social psychologists has dealt with inter-group processes [see INTERGROUP RELATIONS], recent work by organisational psychologists has focused primarily on intra-group processes, especially group performance and conflict within groups.

The large literature on intra-group processes can be organised into five major topic areas (Levine and Moreland 1998): (1) group composition, which involves the causes and consequences of variations in the number and characteristics of people who belong to the group; (2) group structure, which concerns the origins and implications of enduring patterns of relations among members (e.g. status hierarchies, norms, roles); (3) conflict in groups, which involves members' efforts to deal with various forms of competition (e.g. social dilemmas, negotiation, coalition formation, MAJORITY/MINORITY influence); (4) group performance, which concerns members' ability to achieve common goals through collaborative work (e.g. DECISION MAKING (see s. 3), productivity, LEADERSHIP); and (5) group ecology, which involves the impact of the group's physical, social and temporal environments on group processes and outcomes.

Within each of these topic areas, some research questions are currently receiving more attention than others. For example, in regard to group composition, there is substantial interest in the impact of diversity (i.e. variability in members' demographic characteristics, tenure in the group, SKILLS – see s. 3) on group dynamics and performance. Evidence suggests that diversity is often a double-edged sword, reducing members' interpersonal comfort and COMMUNICATION (see s. 2) but enhancing their ability to perform certain tasks, such as developing innovative ideas (Milliken, Bartel and Kurtzberg 2003). Regarding group structure, research indicates that certain characteristics of social norms, such as their salience, have substantial impact on conformity to these norms (Cialdini and Trost 1998). Regarding conflict in groups, several factors have been shown to influence the likelihood of cooperative responses (which enhance collective welfare at the expense of individual welfare) in social dilemma situations. These include the pay-off structure, the presence of sanctioning systems, the size of the group, social norms relevant to cooperation and the opportunity for communication among group members (Pruitt 1998). Regarding group performance, interest in enhancing the productivity of work teams in organisations, has stimulated efforts to answer a wide range of questions. These include how to select and train team members, how to manage personnel turnover, how to enhance members' communication, how to develop an optimal balance of distributed and shared knowledge and EXPERTISE (see s. 3), and how to manage time pressure and STRESS (see s. 7) (Guzzo, Salas and Associates 1995). Finally, regarding group ecology, researchers have devoted attention to specialised roles that work groups in organisations use to enhance their effectiveness, as well as the impact of group mergers on social IDENTITY (see also s. 4) and inter-group relations (Gaertner, Bachman, Dovidio and Banker 2001).

Research seeking to clarify group phenomena frequently employs the individual as the unit of analysis, focusing on the cognitions of individual respondents. An example is research on majority and minority influence, which shows that people given information about the responses of numerical minorities to problems generate more creative ideas than do those exposed to the responses of numerical majorities (Nemeth and Nemeth-Brown 2003). A welcome trend in recent research is an emphasis on 'group cognition', or cognitive activity that occurs at the level of the social aggregate. Although early social psychologists were uncomfortable with the notion of 'group mind', several lines of contemporary research seek to clarify how groups create, conserve, transmit and use information to make decisions and carry out other tasks (Tindale, Meisenhelder, Dykema-Engblade and Hogg 2001). Examples include work on shared reality, social representations, transactive memory and team mental models. This work is noteworthy because it reflects an expanded conception of human cognition that is likely to enrich cognitive as well as social psychology.

JL

Cialdini, R. B. and Trost, M. R. 1998: Social influence: social norms, conformity, and compliance. In Gilbert, D. L., Fiske, S. T. and Lindzey, G. (eds) *The Handbook of Social Psychology* (4th edn). Boston MA: McGraw-Hill, vol. 2, 151–92. **Gaertner, S. L., Bachman, B. A., Dovidio, J. and Banker, B. S.** 2001: Corporate mergers and stepfamily marriages: identity, harmony, and commitment. In Hogg, M. A. and Terry, D. J. (eds) *Social Identity Processes in Organizational Contexts*. Philadelphia PA: Psychology Press, 265–82. **Guzzo, R. A., Salas, E. and Associates** (eds) 1995: *Team Effectiveness and Decision Making in Organizations*. San Francisco CA: Jossey-Bass. **Levine, J. M. and Moreland, R. L.** 1998: Small groups. In Gilbert, D. L., Fiske, S. T. and Lindzey, G. (eds) *The Handbook of Social Psychology* (4th edn). Boston MA: McGraw-Hill, vol. 2, 415–69. **Lewin, K., Lippitt, R. and White, R.** 1939: Patterns of aggressive behavior in experimentally created 'social climates'. *Journal of Social Psychology* 10, 271–99. **Milliken, F. J., Bartel, C. A. and Kurtzberg, T. R.** 2003: Diversity and creativity in work groups: a dynamic perspective on the affective and cognitive processes that link diversity and performance. In Paulus, P. B. and Nijstad, B. A. (eds) *Group Creativity: Innovation Through Collaboration*. Oxford: Oxford University Press, 32–62. **Nemeth, C. J., and Nemeth-Brown, B.** 2003: Better than individuals? The potential benefits of dissent and diversity for group creativity. In Paulus, P. B. and Nijstad, B. A. (eds) *Group Creativity: Innovation Through Collaboration*. Oxford: Oxford University Press, 63–84. **Pruitt, D. G.** 1998: Social conflict. In Gilbert, D. L., Fiske, S. T. and Lindzey, G. (eds) *The Handbook of Social Psychology* (4th edn). Boston MA: McGraw-Hill, vol. 2, 470–503. **Tindale, R. S., Meisenhelder, H. M., Dykema-Engblade, A. A. and Hogg, M. A.** 2001: Shared cognition in small groups. In Hogg, M. A. and Tindale, R. S. (eds) *Blackwell Handbook of Social Psychology: Group Processes*. Malden MA: Blackwell, 1–30. **Whyte, W. F.** 1943: *Street Corner Society*. Chicago: University of Chicago Press.

groupthink Tendency for GROUPS that isolate themselves from the wider community to come adrift from moral standards and reality in their DECISION MAKING (see s. 3). [See also RISKY SHIFT] *NE*

Guttman scale A scale to measure attitudes that maximises 'reproducibility', meaning that identical total scores reflect identical response patterns across scale items. *NE*

H

---

heuristic-systematic model (of persuasion)
Like the ELABORATION LIKELIHOOD MODEL (ELM), this contrasts two processes of PERSUASION that can lead to changes in ATTITUDES (Chaiken 1987). One involves systematic processing of relevant information and requires considerable cognitive effort; the other relies on use of information as a cue or HEURISTIC (see s. 3), in effect a short cut to an answer that minimises cognitive effort. Similar to the ELM, Chaiken argues that people are more likely to engage in systematic processing to the extent that the issue is important to them, but also when they are not suffi-ciently confident in their existing attitude. Overall, however, the model generates few predictions not also derivable from the ELM, which is also slightly more comprehensive. *NE*

Chaiken, S. 1987: The heuristic model of persuasion. In Zanna, M., Olson, J. and Herman, C. (eds) *Social Influence: The Ontario Symposium*. Hillsdale NJ: Erlbaum, vol. 5, 3–39.

homogamy The norm [see NORMS that MATE SELEC-TION should occur within one's own social or cultural group. *NE*

identity A concept used throughout the social sciences relating to self-understanding and the SELF-CONCEPT. It is sometimes used to refer to an individual's experience of personal continuity over time, and sometimes to refer to the perception and experience of a commonality with others (and the self-understanding that arises from group belonging). In the social sciences the (collective or social) identities derived from group memberships (e.g. national identity) have attracted particular attention. Whereas lay theorising often conceives of such identities in essentialist terms, the social scientific literature emphasises the constructed nature of social identities (Brubaker and Cooper 2000). This does not mean that such identities are of little psychological or behavioural consequence. Rather it draws attention to the social processes through which individuals come to adopt a common collective identification with others. For example, analyses of national identity explore the everyday social practices through which self-understandings based upon national categories are produced and reproduced (Reicher and Hopkins, 2001).

SELF-CATEGORISATION THEORY provides an account of the social psychological processes of identification. According to the theory, the SELF (see also s. 1 and s. 4) may be defined at different levels of abstraction. Sometimes, it may be in terms of individual uniqueness. At other times, it may be in terms of a specific group membership. This psychological shift from individual uniqueness to collective identity underlies the behavioural shift from inter-individual to inter-group action. Specifically, when a collective identity is salient, group members' behaviour conforms to the contents of the IN-GROUP stereotype. Rather than implying a dichotomy between collective and personal identities in which social

processes are only relevant to the former, the theory conceives of identification (at whatever degree of abstraction) as socially determined and as (psychologically speaking) equally 'real' (Haslam 2001).

Self-categorisation theory uses 'identity' as an analytic category to theorise the psychological processes involved in the diverse phenomena of group life (e.g. SOCIAL INFLUENCE and STEREOTYPING (see also s. 1)). Others (e.g. Antaki and Widdicombe 1998), working with the logic of DISCOURSE ANALYSIS (see s. 8), adopt a radically different approach. Rather than viewing identity as an analytic category, they view identity as a discursive topic and as being accomplished in the context of interaction as people negotiate issues of blame and responsibility. (See also s. 4, IDENTITY) *NH*

Antaki. C. and Widdicombe, S. 1998: *Identities in Talk.* London: Sage. **Brubaker, R. and Cooper, F.** 2000: Beyond 'identity'. *Theory and Society,* 29, 1–47. **Haslam, S. A.** 2001: *Psychology in Organizations: The Social Identity Approach.* London: Sage. **Reicher, S. and Hopkins, N.** 2001: *Self and Nation.* London: Sage.

ideology An integrated set of ATTITUDES more or less consciously organised around core VALUES, sometimes underpinning a SOCIAL IDENTITY, and often legitimising a programme of collective action. *NE*

ideosyncrasy credit Theory that an individual's capacity to change the NORMS of a GROUP is a function of their degree of prior CONFORMITY. [See also LEADERSHIP] *NE*

illusory correlation The mistaken perception or RECALL (see s. 3) of an association between infrequently

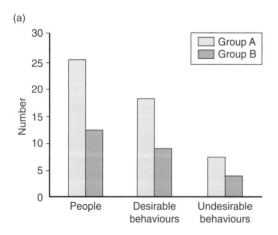

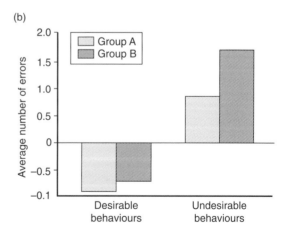

illusory correlation *(a) The stimuli presented to groups A and B: there are twice as many desirable and undesirable behaviours in group A, but there are also twice as many people in group A as in group B. (b) Errors in recall of the frequency of stimuli. Subjects are especially prone to overestimate the number of rare (undesirable) behaviours in the rare (B) group. Source: John Sabini,* Social Psychology, *W. W. Norton & Co (1992). (Data from Hamilton & Gifford, 'Illusory correlations in interpersonal perception',* Journal of Experimental Social Psychology, *39, 1976.)*

observed phenomena, for example, between CRIME (see s. 1, CRIME AND PSYCHOLOGY) and OUT-GROUP membership; seen as contributing to the formation of negative ethnic STEREOTYPES. *NE*

implicit personality theory People's sets of assumptions about the relations between PERSONALITY TRAITS (see s. 6). In impression formation, we will draw upon this implicit theory to infer the presence of traits in another on the basis of what we already know about them. Thus we may infer that someone is generous if we already believe them to be warm. The theoretically interesting issue concerns the origins of these theories given that they do not appear to be idiosyncratic. According to one view (Shweder 1980), they are shared illusions generated by the semantic structure of a shared language (and so should vary in content from one LANGUAGE (see s. 2) group or CULTURE (see also s. 1) to another). According to another, the semantic structure of personality terms merely reflects the ways in which traits naturally co-occur and so such theories should be similar across cultures (see Jackson, Chan and Striker 1979). *NE*

Jackson, D., Chan, D. and Striker, L. 1979: Implicit personality theory: Is it illusory? *Journal of Personality* 47, 1–10. **Shweder, R.** 1980: Facts and fictions in person perception: a reply to Lamielle, Foss, and Cavenne. *Journal of Personality* 48, 74–81.

impression formation The processes by which different pieces of knowledge about another are combined into a global or summary impression. Asch's (1946) classic research on how people integrate information about PERSONALITY TRAITS (see s. 6) indicated that some traits (e.g. 'warm' versus 'cold') are central to overall impressions, disproportionately influencing interpretation of other traits. Likewise, information encountered earlier affects interpretation of information encountered later (the PRIMACY – see s. 3 – effect). Asch offered a constructivist view of impression formation; perceivers strive to form meaningful impressions, such that one piece of information affects the meaning of others. The contrasting approach treats impressions as primarily 'DATA-DRIVEN' (see s. 3), shaped by the information available such that new pieces of information are added to what is already known so that impressions continually evolve (e.g. Anderson 1981). Others have argued both processes can operate, but that their relative contributions to impressions formed will depend on such factors as the motives of the perceiver. [See also SOCIAL COGNITION – see also s. 4 – and STEREOTYPING] *NE*

Anderson, N. 1981: *Foundations of Information Integration Theory.* New York: Academic Press. **Asch, S. E.** 1946: Forming impressions of personality. *Journal of Abnormal and Social Psychology* 41, 1230–40.

impression management Following Goffman (1959), impression management can be defined as anything people use or do to encourage an audience to accept a particular interpretation of what is before them. Though the term is often employed interchangeably with SELF-PRESENTATION, Goffman argues it covers many matters in addition to an audience's view of a particular actor. One such matter is the definition of the situation: what kind of event is in progress? Without knowing this, for example,

there can exist no WORKING CONSENSUS on what identities or roles people can adopt in the situation. Goffman starts from the position that the meaning of events is not necessarily straightforward or transparent and may therefore have to be dramatised for an audience. His 'dramaturgical' analysis proposes that people (actors) will often use the devices of staged dramas, such as appropriate props and scenery, to achieve these ends. His discussion of 'normal appearances' (Goffman 1971) draws attention to an impression management goal that arises when individuals are in public places, namely to dramatise or 'explain' to others present that nothing alarming is about to happen. *NE*

Goffman, E. 1959: *The Presentation of Self in Everyday Life.* New York: Doubleday. **Goffman, E.** 1971: *Relations in Public.* New York: Harper & Row.

ingratiation A strategy of SELF-PRESENTATION, the goal of which is to have an audience believe the actor is likeable. *NE*

in-group A GROUP that is distinguished from other groups or OUT-GROUPS for the individual in so far as the individual defines him/herself as a member. *NE*

interaction process analysis A system for classifying behaviour in face-to-face GROUP interactions, distinguishing between affective (or relationship-oriented) and cognitive (or task-oriented) contributions. *NE*

inter-group relations Involve behaviour and PERCEPTIONS (see s. 1) between people that are based on their belonging to different social groups and categories (Hogg and Abrams 2003; Hewstone, Rubin and Willis 2002). Historically, social psychological theory and research has focused on negative features of such relations, including PREJUDICE, conflict, oppression and rebellion.

One early theme concerned collective protest, emphasising its irrational character. Le Bon's (1895/1995) theory of CROWD BEHAVIOUR held that anonymity, contagion and suggestibility combined to unleash primitive, barbaric and instinctual acts that characterised crowd violence. Similarly, the notion of DEINDIVIDUATION (Diener 1980) holds that anonymity and lack of identifiability combine to reduce people's SELF-AWARENESS (see s. 4) and result in unconstrained actions and aggression.

In the 1930s the FRUSTRATION-AGGRESSION HYPOTHESIS was offered as an explanation of inter-group conflict, a line of reasoning sustained in Berkowitz's (1967) idea that frustration combines with aversive environmental stimuli and aggressive cues to cause collective violence such as rioting. More rationalist explanations for collective protest are provided by theories of RELATIVE DEPRIVATION; these propose that protest follows when people's expectations are higher than their attainments. Early versions of these theories emphasised objective differences in material wealth, but subsequently evidence has pointed to the importance of subjective perceptions of differences based on SOCIAL COMPARISONS with particular individuals (egoistic deprivation) or groups (fraternalisic deprivation; Runciman 1966); fraternalistic deprivation plays the greater role in collective unrest. More recent formulations also draw a distinction between wanting and deserving or entitlement. [See SOCIAL JUSTICE] Additionally, theorists have argued that reactions to unfairness are more sensitive to PROCEDURAL JUSTICE than to DISTRIBUTIVE JUSTICE. Others have emphasised that collective protest requires organisation, COMMUNICATION (see s. 2) and the expectation of success among group members.

A quite different view of ETHNOCENTRISM and generally negative attitudes to OUT-GROUPS regards socialisation experiences and individual PERSONALITY (see s. 1 and s. 6) as important. Thus, Adorno et al. (1950) identified AUTHORITARIANISM as a personality syndrome that may have underpinned the rise of Fascism in pre-war Germany. More recently, Sidanius has argued that individuals vary in their social dominance orientation such that some are more likely to endorse the idea of a highly structured division between groups of different power and status. [See SOCIAL DOMINANCE THEORY]

In contrast, REALISTIC GROUP CONFLICT THEORY treats inter-group conflict and hostility as rational responses to realistically identified threats to IN-GROUP interests. Sherif (1966) demonstrated that when groups find themselves competing for resources they develop increased solidarity and an ethnocentric orientation to their competitors. Research on game playing, such as the PRISONER'S DILEMMA, has revealed an individual-group discontinuity effect; level of competition (or non-cooperation) increases significantly when the games are between groups rather than between individuals. However, a superordinate goal – effectively, a situation in which neither group can succeed without the cooperation of the other – introduces more harmony into inter-group ATTITUDES and behaviour.

Other evidence indicates that mere social categorisation of people can be sufficient to cause them to favour their own category (or in-group) over a different category (out-group). This was demonstrated by the MINIMAL GROUP PARADIGM, first devised by Rabbie and Horwitz (1969) and researched extensively by Henri Tajfel and his colleagues. Even in the absence of competition and when group members are completely anonymous and do not interact with one another, they still demonstrate in-group bias and favouritism, for example, in allocation of rewards or points to members of each category. Subsequent research indicated that this cannot easily be explained in terms of experimental demand or implicit NORMS. Instead the explanation seems to reside in participants' social identification with their own category. But there is an asymmetry (Mummendey et al. 1992); in-group bias is reduced if participants have to remove positive resources or allocate negative resources.

SOCIAL IDENTITY THEORY explains inter-group relations in terms of the extent to which people identify with their group or social category, and their desire to sustain positive distinctiveness and SELF-ESTEEM from other groups (Tajfel and Turner 1986). Depending on the stability and perceived legitimacy of status differences between groups, members may hold a 'social change' or 'social mobility' belief structure, the former corresponding to BELIEFS that one's self-image can be improved only by enhancing the group's relative position, the latter that it can only be improved by joining a different group. When the in-group finds it difficult to compete directly with an out-group, its members may use 'social creativity' strategies, which involve finding different dimensions of social comparison on which it may be judged more favourably. Choice of these strategies may depend on the level of threat to social identity that is present, and the degree of uncertainty within the situation. A motivational perspective is offered by optimal distinctiveness theory, which holds that people desire a balance between assimilation within groups and a degree of differentiation from others. Other, evolutionary, approaches suggest that when mortality is salient, people may become more intolerant of differences both between groups and within the in-group. [See TERROR MANAGEMENT THEORY]

The cognitive underpinnings of social IDENTITY (see also s. 4) are explained by SELF-CATEGORISATION THEORY. In particular, based on earlier theories of category accentuation [see SOCIAL CATEGORISATION], the 'meta-contrast ratio' of differences within categories to differences between categories, together with the extent to which these categories fit the normative context, is thought to explain when and why people apply social categorisations to themselves and others. When people are perceived as category members they are depersonalised. [See DEPERSONALISATION] Prototypical positions for social categories tend to be polarised away from those of contrasting groups.

Other cognitive approaches dwell on the processes by which stereotypes are formed and changed. [See SOCIAL COGNITION – see also s. 4] These include processes of ILLUSORY CORRELATION between category memberships and particular characteristics. Stereotypes may change through a process of 'bookkeeping' (gradual change as new information arrives), 'conversion' (change based on critical items of information) or 'sub-typing' (creating new variations for different subsets of the main social category). [See also STEREOTYPING] Stereotypes affect inter-group relations by determining the assumptions people make, either consciously or unconsciously, about members of out-groups. These assumptions can, in turn, result in prejudice, which may be explicit or implicit, and expressed without awareness [see PREJUDICE], or may be expressed through biased attributions. [See ULTIMATE ATTRIBUTION ERROR] Some forms of prejudice have a positive tone, such as 'benevolent sexism'. These forms of prejudice reinforce positive stereotypes that also hold group members in a subordinate or lower status situation (e.g. women are regarded positively as carers but not as managers).

Inter-group relations are also affected by the cultural context and history of relationships between groups. An important feature of many groups is their LANGUAGE (see s. 2) and ethnolinguistic vitality. Positive relationships between groups may be marked by more convergence in speech styles [see SPEECH ACCOMMODATION THEORY], but also by integrationist views on acculturation. Inter-group communication also requires a degree of contact [see CONTACT HYPOTHESIS], but research suggests that positive outcomes of contact depend on members of different categories recognising that they also share some superordinate categorisation. [See also COMMUNAL ORIENTATION and COLLECTIVISM]   DA

Adorno, T. W., Frenkel-Brunswik, E., Levinson, D. J. and Sanford, R. M. 1950: *The Authoritarian Personality*. New York: Harper. **Berkowitz, L.** 1967: Frustrations, comparisons and other sources of emotion arousal as contributors to social unrest. *Journal of Social Issues* 28, 77–91. **Diener, E.** 1980: Deindividuation: the absence of self-awareness and self-regulation in group members. In Paulus, P. B. (ed.) *The Psychology of Group Influence*. Hillsdale NJ: Lawrence Erlbaum, 209–42. **Hewstone, M., Rubin, M. and Willis, H.** 2002: Intergroup bias. *Annual Review of Psychology* 53, 575–604. **Hogg, M. A. and Abrams, D.** 2003: Intergroup behaviour and social identity. In Hogg, M. A. and Cooper, J. (eds) *Handbook of Social Psychology*. California: Sage, 407–31. **Le Bon, G.** 1895/1995: *The Crowd: A Study of the Popular Mind*. London: Transaction Publishers. **Mummendey, A., Simon, B., Dietze, C., Grunert, M., Haeger, G., Kessler, S., Lettgen, S. and Shaferhoff, S.** 1992: Categorization is not enough: intergroup discrimination in negative outcome allocation. *Journal of Experimental Social Psychology* 28, 124–44. **Rabbie, J. M. and Horwitz, M.** 1969: Arousal of ingroup-outgroup bias by a chance win or loss. *Journal of Personality and Social Psychology* 13, 269–77. **Runciman, W. G.** 1966: *Relative Deprivation and Social Justice*. London: Routledge and Kegan Paul. **Sherif, M.** 1966: *In Common Predicament: Social Psychology of Intergroup Conflict and Cooperation*. Boston MA: Houghton Mifflin. **Tajfel, H. and Turner, J. C.** 1986: An integrative theory of intergroup conflict. In Austin, W. G. and Worchel, S. (eds) *Psychology of Intergroup Relations*. Chicago: Nelson Hall, 7–24.

interpersonal attraction

Can refer both to whether or not one person is attracted to or has a favourable attitude towards another person and the extent to which this occurs. It may be thought of as a single bipolar dimension, with intense love or attraction at one end, moving through liking, indifference and disliking, to intense hatred or hostility at the other end (Swensen 1972). This kind of dimension is included in circular or circumplex models of interpersonal behaviour in which the other major bipolar dimension is dominance versus submission. Although the range of this construct is potentially large and may include whether an individual has a positive attitude towards a head of state or expresses an intention to vote for a political candidate, in practice the topic has been primarily concerned with explaining the development and dissolution of friendships and romantic- or marital-type RELATIONSHIPS, more research addressing these latter kinds of relationship. Many attempts have been made to distinguish different aspects of interpersonal attraction, such as loving and liking or intimacy, passion and commitment (Hendrick and Hendrick 1989), but, as yet, without any consensus about these distinctions.

Various theories have been put forward to explain interpersonal attraction (Cramer 1998). These include CLASSICAL CONDITIONING (see s. 3), complementarity, consistency, equity [see EQUITY THEORY], familiarity, interdependence, REINFORCEMENT (see s. 3), self-enhancement or SELF-ESTEEM, self-consistency or verification, similarity and social exchange theories. [See EXCHANGE PROCESSES] There is little or no evidence that married or dating partners are complementary with respect to psychological characteristics. On the other hand, partners have been found to be highly correlated in terms of age, followed by physical attractiveness, ATTITUDES and INTELLIGENCE (see s. 4 and s. 6). The strongest and most consistent predictors of couples staying together is less negative conflict and lower psychological distress such as NEUROTICISM (see s. 6) and DEPRESSION (see s. 7) (Karney and Bradbury 1995). However, surprisingly few studies have investigated the association between interpersonal attraction and relationship satisfaction, possibly because these two factors have been found to be so closely related. Recently there has been considerable research on styles or dimensions of ATTACHMENT (see s. 4), particularly in adults, although these have often been assessed in terms of close relationships generally rather than a specific close relationship. *DC*

Cramer, D. 1998: *Close Relationships: The Study of Love and Friendship*. London: Arnold. **Hendrick, C. and Hendrick, S. S.** 1989: Research on love: Does it measure up? *Journal of Personality and Social Psychology* 56, 784–94. **Karney, B. R. and Bradbury, T. N.** 1995: The longitudinal course of marital quality and stability: a review of theory, method, and research. *Psychological Bulletin* 118, 3–34. **Swensen, C. H.** 1972: The behavior of love. In Otto, H. A. (ed.) *Love Today: A New Exploration*. New York: Association Press, 86–101.

interpersonal communication

Interpersonal COMMUNICATION (see s. 2) is of central importance to many aspects of human life. Yet it is only within the last century that it has become the focus of systematic scientific investigation. Such research has been conducted in a wide variety of academic disciplines, most notably social psychology, PSYCHIATRY (see s. 7), anthropology, linguistics, sociology, ETHOLOGY (see s. 1, ETHOLOGY AND COMPARATIVE PSYCHOLOGY and s. 2, ETHOLOGY AND SOCIOBIOLOGY and HUMAN ETHOLOGY) and communications. Within these disciplines, a number of distinctive approaches may be distinguished: in particular, conversation analysis (e.g. Sacks 1992), DISCOURSE ANALYSIS (see s. 8) (e.g. Potter and Wetherell 1987), speech act theory (Austin 1962), ethology (e.g. Fridlund 1997) and the SOCIAL SKILLS approach (e.g. Hargie 1997). Despite substantial disagreements and differences, these approaches do share a number of common assumptions. Of particular importance has been the belief in the value of studying social interaction through film, audiotape and videotape recordings. Because such research is based on the detailed ('micro') analysis of both speech and non-verbal behaviour, it may be referred to as the microanalytic approach (Bull 2002).

Microanalysis represents not only a distinctive methodology, but also a distinctive way of thinking about communication. Undoubtedly, the detailed analysis of film, audiotape and videotape recordings has facilitated discoveries which otherwise simply would not be possible. Indeed, the effect of the video recorder has been likened to that of the microscope in the biological sciences. Without recorded data which can repeatedly be examined, it is simply not possible to perform the kind of highly detailed analysis of both speech and NON-VERBAL COMMUNICATION so characteristic of the microanalytic approach.

But microanalysis did not develop simply as a consequence of innovations in technology. Film technology had been available since the beginning of the twentieth century; two of the earliest pioneers of cinematography, Muybridge and Marey, had a particular interest in analysing and recording movement patterns in animals and humans (Muybridge 1899, 1901; Marey 1895). The extensive use of this technology in the study of human social interaction has only really developed in the past few decades; its use reflects fundamental changes in the way in which we think about human communication (Kendon 1982). What may be seen as the key features of the microanalytic approach are listed below (Bull 2002):

1. Communication is studied as it actually occurs. This marked a radical shift from the traditional concern with the study of communication in terms of what it should be – for example, its efficiency, clarity or persuasiveness.

2. Communication can be studied as an activity in its own right. This feature contrasts with more traditional approaches, which were concerned with the study of communication not for its own sake but as a means of investigating other social processes, such as leadership, interpersonal relationships or power structures.

3. All features of interaction are potentially significant. A further distinguishing feature has been the expansion of what behaviour can be regarded as communicative. The remarkable development of interest in NONVERBAL COMMUNICATION can be regarded as one such manifestation. So, too, is the extraordinary detail in which conversation analysts seek in their transcripts to represent as exactly as possible the way in which conversation sounds. The underlying assumption is that all features of interaction are potentially significant, and therefore should not be dismissed out of hand as unworthy of investigation.

4. Communication has a structure. Although interaction may seem at first sight to be disorderly or even random, it cannot be assumed to be so, and one of the tasks of the investigator is to analyse whether an underlying structure can be discerned.

5. Conversation can be regarded as a form of action. According to speech act theory, LANGUAGE (see s. 2) does not simply describe some state of affairs or state some facts: it is in itself a form of action. This proposal has been profoundly influential. It underlies a great deal of research on the functions of conversation, on the ways in which conversational actions are accomplished.

6. Communication can be understood in an evolutionary context. This proposal is central to ethological and sociobiological approaches to communication analysis. Outside those traditions, it has had comparatively little influence, this is not a concern of approaches such as conversation analysis or discourse analysis. However, it has been of importance for social psychologists who study EMOTIONAL EXPRESSION.

7. Communication is best studied in naturally occurring contexts. This proposal is common to almost all approaches. The prime exception is experimental social psychology, whose proponents have traditionally made extensive use of laboratory-based experimentation as a means of studying communication. However, the trend in social psychology in recent years has also been towards naturalistic analysis.

8. Communication can be regarded as a form of SKILL (see s. 3). This proposal represents one of the main contributions of the social psychological approach to communication. Indeed, it has been so influential that the term 'communication skills' has passed into the wider CULTURE (see also s. 1).

9. Communication can be taught like any other skill. This again has been highly influential in the wider culture; social or communication skills training has been widely used in a variety of personal and occupational contexts.

10. Macro issues can be studied through microanalysis. Also of particular importance for the wider culture is the assumption that major (or macro) social issues such as racism, politics or feminism can be analysed through microanalysis.

Thus microanalysis represents a novel and distinctive way of thinking about communication. It has produced not only valuable insights into how we communicate, but is also of considerable practical significance. In contemporary research on interpersonal communication, microanalytic techniques are now of central importance. *PB*

Austin, J. 1962: *How To Do Things with Words*. Cambridge MA: Harvard University Press. **Bull, P.** 2002: *Communication under the Microscope: The Theory and Practice of Microanalysis*. London: Psychology Press. **Fridlund, A. J.** 1997: The new ethology of human facial expressions. In Russell, J. A. and Fernández-Dols, J. M. (eds) *The Psychology of Facial Expression*. New York: Cambridge University Press, 103–29. **Hargie, O. D. W.** 1997: Interpersonal communication: a theoretical framework. In Hargie, O. D. W. (ed.) *The Handbook of Communication Skills*, (2nd edn). London: Routledge, 29–63. **Kendon, A.** 1982: Organization of behaviour in face-to-face interaction. In Scherer, K. R. and Ekman, P. (eds) *Handbook of Methods in Nonverbal Behaviour Research*. Cambridge: Cambridge University Press, 440–505. **Marey, É. J.** 1895: *Movement*. New York: D. Appleton. **Muybridge, E.** 1899/1957: *Animals in Motion*. New York: Dover Publications. **Muybridge, E.** 1901/1957: *The Human Figure in Motion*. New York: Dover Publications. **Potter J. and Wetherell M.** 1987: *Discourse and Social Psychology: Beyond Attitudes and Behaviour*. London: Sage. **Sacks, H.** 1992: *Lectures on Conversation* (edited by Jefferson, G.). Cambridge MA: Blackwell.

ironic process One that has the opposite of its intended effect, applied to suppression of STEREOTYPES, such that the attempt at suppression itself causes stereotypical thoughts to become increasingly intrusive. *NE*

J

just world belief The need to believe that justice tends to prevail in the world such that people generally get what they deserve. The need produces distortions of perception. Thus, one interesting consequence is that witnesses to another's suffering are likely to derogate the victim if they think the suffering will continue and are powerless to prevent it. Lerner (1980) concluded that this response is an attempt by observers to protect their belief in a just world, a belief that has its roots in childhood rationalisations for delaying gratification. Individuals have been shown to differ in the strength of their inclination to believe in a just world. Stronger belief results in greater PRO-SOCIAL BEHAVIOUR when this is expected to be entirely effective, but otherwise reduces the likelihood of helping. [See also SOCIAL JUSTICE] *NE*

Lerner, M. 1980: *The Belief in a Just World: A Fundamental Delusion.* New York: Plenum.

L

leader-member exchange (LMX) theory Theory that LEADERSHIP is best analysed starting from the recognition that leaders develop different exchange relationships with different followers. *NE*

leadership A process of influence to attain group, organisational or societal goals. Leadership implies having status [see SOCIAL STATUS], prestige and POWER over others. Early research on leadership was concentrated on finding PERSONALITY TRAITS (see s. 6) that reliably distinguish leaders from non-leaders (TRAIT – see s. 6 – approach). Leadership is systematically, but weakly, correlated with such factors as age, sex, IQ (see s. 6), extroversion, ambition and SOCIAL SKILLS. This research line was attacked in the 1950s and 1960s, however, because it failed to consider sufficiently the demands of the situation [see SITUATIONISM] and of followers in leader emergence and performance (Hollander 1985). The effectiveness of leaders is certainly shaped by features of the task and group under consideration. CONTINGENCY (see s. 1) theorists [see CONTINGENCY THEORY] offered a compromise in the 1970s, arguing that leader effectiveness is dependent upon the interaction between leadership style and elements of the situation. Yet, the fairly specific hypotheses from some of these contingency models have so far received mixed EMPIRICAL (see s. 8) support. After a lull in research activity, the study of leadership regained popularity in the late 1980s and 1990s. This was primarily due to the influence of organisational psychologists, who started to look at leadership in teams and businesses. Out of this tradition comes the theory of TRANSACTIONAL/TRANSFORMATIONAL LEADERSHIP, which emphasises the charismatic qualities of leaders, as well as research on women leaders and leaders from ethnic minority groups. Another main impetus to leadership research has been given by SELF-CATEGORISATION THEORY, which accentuates the role of the GROUP in leader selection and effectiveness.

Looking to the future of leadership research, it is fair to say that this field is much in need of integration. There are a lot of findings and mini-theories on offer. Currently, however, a grand unifying theory of leadership is lacking. No doubt, new developments in research on GROUP PROCESSES, cultural and EVOLUTIONARY PSYCHOLOGY (see s. 2 and s. 1, EVOLUTION AND PSYCHOLOGY) and behavioural genetics will contribute to theoretical progress in this important field of inquiry. *MVV*

Hollander, E. P. 1985: Leadership and power. In Lindzey, G. and Aronson, E. (eds) *The Handbook of Social Psychology*. New York: Random House, 485–537. **Van Vugt, M. and De Cremer, D.** 2002: Leader endorsement in social dilemmas: comparing the instrumental and relational perspectives. *European Review of Social Psychology* 13, 155–84.

Likert scale Procedure for measuring ATTITUDES that seeks to maximise precision of MEASUREMENT (see s. 1, MEASUREMENT AND STATISTICS) (RELIABILITY – see s. 6 and s. 8). (See also s. 8, LIKERT SCALE) *NE*

looking-glass self The notion that evaluation of the SELF (see also s. 1, and s.4) is based on the anticipated reactions of others, and will be coloured by the perceived virtues of those others. *NE*

lost-letter technique Indirect method for assessing prevalence of particular ATTITUDES in a population, in terms of willingness of people to post a lost letter clearly associated with a particular moral or political position. *NE*

M

majority/minority Moscovici (1980) proposed that numerical minorities can exercise SOCIAL INFLUENCE on the PERCEPTIONS (see s. 1) and ATTITUDES of members of majorities when they adopt a behavioural style that is consistent, distinctive and characterised by consensus among minority group members. [See also COVARIATION THEORY] This proposal was intended to explain how innovations, by definition initially minority views, could be introduced into societies. It also served as a critique of views of influence equating it with CONFORMITY to majority group NORMS and requiring a relationship of dependence upon the source of influence (based on source attractiveness, SOCIAL STATUS, POWER or EXPERTISE – see s. 3). The claim that minority and majority influence are qualitatively distinct, the former involving a VALIDATION PROCESS, the latter a process of SOCIAL COMPARISON, parallels the central/peripheral distinction in the ELABORATION LIKELIHOOD MODEL. [See also SOCIAL IMPACT THEORY]   *NE*

Moscovici, S. 1980: Toward a theory of conversion behaviour. In Berkowitz, L. (ed.) *Advances in Experimental Social Psychology*. New York: Academic Press, vol. 13, 208–39.

matched guise technique A technique for distinguishing the STEREOTYPES evoked by particular accents from speaker PERSONALITY (see s. 1 and s. 6) effects, in which the same speaker is heard in different guises (using different accents).   *NE*

matching hypothesis Expectation that people will seek romantic partners who match them in net social value, based on their respective assets and liabilities, or more narrowly who will match them in physical attractiveness. [See also INTERPERSONAL ATTRACTION and MATE SELECTION]   *NE*

mate selection One of the most widely studied of topics in the field of personal RELATIONSHIPS. Systematic studies date back at least 60 years, with most studies examining either the characteristics an individual seeks in a (usually heterosexual) partner or the psychological, physiological or demographic characteristics of established couples. Two main theoretical approaches have dominated. Sociobiologists argue that a 'selective advantage' is afforded to those who prefer mates capable of reproductive investment, and therefore partners with preferred attributes are chosen for mating (e.g. Buss 1989). Social ROLE theorists focus on the link between desired partner characteristics and power differentials within societies (Bombar 1996). From this perspective, biological factors in partner choice should be considered alongside other sociological and more proximal psychological variables.

Mate selection across the world varies along a continuum, ranging from societies where marriage is always arranged to societies where individuals have complete freedom in mate choice, although few societies fall at either extremes of this division (Goodwin 1999). Despite an apparently wide range of eligible partners, western research has stressed the remarkable similarity in ATTITUDES, level of physical attractiveness, ethnic background, RACE (see s. 1, ETHNICITY AND RACE ISSUES) and educational level between couples in long-term relationships, with demographic compatibility likely to be more important in the longer relationship. Family and friends also exert a significant influence on mate choice, although this influence may be relatively covert.

In non-western, more 'collectively' orientated societies, the majority of marriages are by arrangement, with matchmakers and relatives having a more overt influence on partner selection. Marriage in such CULTURES (see also s. 1) is a strategic union of two, usually similar, families. Attraction and love are assumed to grow out of marriage, rather than to be a motivator for the formation of a relationship. Although there is some evidence of a worldwide movement towards the greater emphasis of 'love' in partner choice, this movement is uneven, with religion continuing to act as a major moderator in mate selection. As a result, new and 'adaptive' forms of mating opportunity (such as dating agencies for particular religious groups) are becoming increasingly common. [See also INTERPERSONAL ATTRACTION and s. 2, MATE CHOICE DECISIONS]   *RG*

Bombar, M. L. 1996: Putting biological approaches in context. *Bulletin of the International Society for the Study of Personal Relationships* 12, 3–6. **Buss, D. M.** 1989: Sex differences in human mate preferences: evolutionary hypotheses tested in 37 cultures. *Behavioral and Brain Sciences* 12, 1–14. **Goodwin, R. B.** 1999: *Personal Relationships Across Cultures*. London: Routledge.

mere exposure effect Attraction to what is familiar by virtue merely of frequent or extended exposure to it, a hypothesis concerning formation of favourable ATTITUDES.
                                                                  NE

minimal group A GROUP membership held by an individual on the most minimal basis possible, such as arbitrary assignment, shared with unknown others, to a meaningless category. [See SOCIAL IDENTITY THEORY] *NE*

mixed motive situation One in which the interests of the participants simultaneously coincide and conflict with one another, as in the PRISONER'S DILEMMA game.
                                                                  NE

modern racism scale Measures racist ATTITUDES that are expressed indirectly through approval of standards and policies that disadvantage other races. *NE*

motivated self Theoretical proposition that knowledge of the SELF (see also s. 1 and s. 4) contains complex, sometimes contradictory, information from which the individual selects what is perceived as situationally most desirable. *NE*

motivated tactician View that individuals invest their cognitive resources tactically according to their goals, so that more resources will be invested in judgements or decisions that are more consequential for the individual (contrasts with COGNITIVE MISER view). [See also DUAL-PROCESS THEORY] *NE*

N

negativity bias The tendency to regard negative information about an actor as more diagnostic of the actor's true character than positive information. *NE*

network density The proportion of theoretically possible links in a SOCIAL NETWORK that actually exist. *NE*

non-verbal communication (NVC) This term potentially covers all the non-linguistic means by which people communicate. NVC may be based on any of the sense modalities, including auditory (non-linguistic aspects of spoken LANGUAGE – see s. 2 – such as accent, pitch, tone, loudness), tactile, visual (appearance, body posture, bodily movements, gestures, facial expressions, eye-movements, interpersonal spacing) and chemical (Argyle 1988). The term 'body language', popularly applied to visual signals, is misleading; no form of NVC appears to have SYNTAX (see s. 3) (rules for combining elements to generate different meanings).

The 'sending capacity' (Ekman and Friesen 1969) of a class of signals (e.g. hand gestures) refers to its 'visibility' to observers, the number of different signals that can be distinguished and the speed with which one signal can follow another (average transmission time), and clarifies why different channels may serve different communicative goals. Hence appearance and accent (slow transmission) are suited to communicate matters that do not change rapidly, such as the communicator's IDENTITY (see also s. 4), while facial expressions (rapid transmission) communicate rapidly changing states in the communicator, such as moment-to-moment comprehension of a speaker.

NVC poses various difficulties of definition. It is sometimes applied to behaviours that seem merely informative to observers rather than signals to them. Shivering informs observers about one's body temperature, but one may also mimic shivering to signal this information. Restricting the term 'COMMUNICATION' (see s. 2) to intentionally informative behaviour is not necessarily helpful, however, given that NVC can often be unconscious or automatised [see AUTOMATICITY and SOCIAL SKILLS], while the criterion of intention poses problems for reflexive responses in other species – and probably humans as well – that appear primarily to serve communicative functions. The proposal that NVC, as distinct from signs, entails encoding and decoding (Weiner et al. 1972) confronts similar difficul-

ties of ambiguous cases. [See also EMOTIONAL EXPRESSION and SOCIAL COMMUNICATION VIEW]

Earlier research into NVC addressed such issues as the way receivers resolve conflicts between verbally and non-verbally transmitted meanings. Controversially, it was claimed (Argyle, Alkema and Gilmour, 1972) that receivers treat the latter as far more reliable evidence than the former in deciding a transmitter's true interpersonal ATTITUDES. [See also DECEPTION] The more recent research emphasis is on the close integration of NVC with speech (Bavelas and Chovil 2000). *NE*

Argyle, M. 1988: *Bodily Communication*, 2nd ed. New York: Methuen. **Argyle, M., Alkema, F. and Gilmour, R.** 1972: The communication of friendly and hostile attitudes by verbal and non-verbal signals. *European Journal of Social Psychology* 9, 2220–31. **Bavelas, J. and Chovil, N.** 2000: Visible acts of meaning: an integrated message model of language in face-to-face dialogue. *Journal of Language and Social Psychology* 19, 163–94. **Ekman P. and Friesen, W.** 1969: Non-verbal leakage and cues to deception. *Psychiatry* 32, 88–106. **Weiner, B., Devoe, S., Rubinow, S. and Geller, J.** 1972: Nonverbal behaviour and nonverbal communication. *Psychological Review* 79, 185–214.

norms Shared expectations, both implicit and explicit, concerning behaviour, judgements or standards of performance. Norms are the basic sources of coherence in human social life. The classic research on norms by Sherif (1935) demonstrated how implicit agreements emerge within GROUPS about an aspect of experience – in his experiments, how far a point of light moved in a given time (the apparent movement was actually an illusion). Sherif's emphasis on norms as group-created beliefs about what *is* the case contrasts with a later emphasis on norms as shared expectations about how people *should* behave (cf. Brown 1965). Brown described norms as 'fragments of CULTURE' (p. 49). Although norms can be highly group- and situation-specific, Brown also argued that some norms are universal; thus all LANGUAGES (see s. 2) have equivalent conventions of address for marking relations between people. [See SOCIAL STATUS] Also claimed to be universal is the moral norm of reciprocity in EXCHANGE PROCESSES. [See also SOCIAL INFLUENCE and ROLE and s. 6, NORMS] *NE*

Brown, R. 1965: *Social Psychology*. New York: Free Press. **Sherif, M.** 1935: A study of some social factors in perception. *Archives of Psychology* 2, 187.

O

obedience Milgram (1974) famously demonstrated that entirely normal people will show obedience to the instructions of an authority figure even when these conflict with their own conscience and appear to result in the suffering of an innocent other. Key to Milgram's analysis was the claim that when individuals interpret a situation as properly governed by authority relations, they cease to act autonomously, undergoing 'agentic shift', which also relieves them of feelings of responsibility for the consequences of the orders they follow. Another key idea was that extreme results of obedience to authority, such as the holocaust, are the end result of a habit of COMPLIANCE produced by commencing with orders entirely innocuous in their consequences. [See also FOOT-IN-THE-DOOR TECHNIQUE] Critics of Milgram's research have variously claimed that it lacks ECOLOGICAL VALIDITY (see s. 3 and s. 8, and also s. 1 and s. 8, DEMAND CHARACTERISTICS), and that it does not demonstrate unconditional obedience to an authority's instructions irrespective of their content (Blass 1991). [See also SOCIAL INFLUENCE] *NE*

Blass, T. 1991: Understanding behaviour in the Milgram obedience experiment. *Journal of Personality and Social Psychology* 60, 398–413. **Milgram, S.** 1974: *Obedience to Authority.* New York: Harper & Row.

objective self-awareness Being aware of oneself as the focus of others' perceptions, supposedly provoking distress as it tends to increase awareness of faults rather than of assets. *NE*

opinion Sometimes used to refer to ATTITUDES expressing a position on some social issue, social practice or matter of public controversy, or attitudes involving a judgement of approval/disapproval, as distinct from attitudes describing personal preferences or tastes. *NE*

opinionation The extent to which coherent and stable OPINIONS or ATTITUDES have been formed, most commonly applied with respect to social or political attitudes. *NE*

organisational citizenship behaviour Behaviour supporting organisational goals that goes beyond what is required by the contract of employment. *NE*

out-group Group identified as outside the boundaries of one's own. *NE*

out-group homogeneity effect Perception that the members of OUT-GROUPS are more similar to one another in VALUES, ATTITUDES, NORMS or patterns of behaviour than are the other members of one's IN-GROUP. *NE*

overjustification effect A decrease in free-choice interest in an activity following introduction of external constraints or inducements to engage in that activity. *NE*

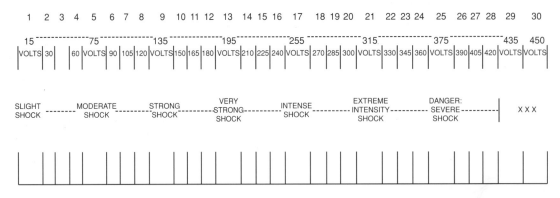

obedience *The legend below the switches on the Milgram shock machine. A high proportion of subjects progressed to give shocks of the highest voltage when ordered to do so. Image of voltage markings on Milgram shock machine, p. 28, from* Obedience to Authority: An Experimental View *by Stanley Milgram. Copyright © 1974 by Stanley Milgram. Reprinted by permission of HarperCollins Publishers.*

P

person perception The perception of both states (emotions, intentions) and traits (PERSONALITY – see s. 1 and s. 6, attitudes, ABILITIES – see s. 6) in others. Until the mid-1950s questions about the degree to which individuals differ in their capacity to make accurate judgements about others dominated research on person perception. Such research then virtually ceased, following Cronbach's (1955) claim that research designs had largely failed to match the complexity of the problem of determining accuracy. One response was to conclude that accuracy, at least in TRAIT (see s. 6) perception, is impossible because the quality in question – personality – is not a real property of the person perceived but a construction of the perceiver. [See also FUNDAMENTAL ATTRIBUTION ERROR] The research focus then shifted to questions such as the processes by which people assemble summary impressions of others from different elements [see IMPRESSION FORMATION] and the relative diagnosticity of different kinds of behavioural evidence for trait inferences (Skowronski and Carlston 1989). Perception of states such as emotions and intentions became more specialised domains of inquiry. [See also NON-VERBAL COMMUNICATION and CAUSAL ATTRIBUTION]

In the longer term, researchers have re-evaluated some of the more pessimistic conclusions drawn from Cronbach's critique. Kenny (1994) argues that Cronbach's analysis, which distinguishes different kinds of accuracy, can only properly be addressed in research designs allowing partitioning of VARIANCE (see s. 8) in perceptions among different sources, the principle ones being perceiver, target, their relationship and ERROR (see s. 8). Such designs require complex computations, incidentally underlining the importance of growth in computing power to this field, but do confirm that perceivers can make valid judgements of others' personalities. This and other work prompts questions about the factors that influence accuracy. Thus, Funder (1999) advocates consideration of such factors as those relating to the nature of the trait (some traits are more perceivable), the target (targets differ in their perceivability) and the quality of information available to a perceiver (as a consequence, for example, of degree of acquaintance with the target). Also related to the issue of information quality has been the emergence of a more interactive model of person perception in which the target actively contributes to construction of the perceiver's impression. [See also SELF-PRESENTATION]   *NE*

Cronbach, L. J. 1955: Processes affecting scores on 'understanding of others' and 'assumed similarity'. *Psychological Bulletin* 52, 177–93. **Funder, D.** 1999: *Personality Judgment: A Realistic Approach.* San Diego CA: Academic Press. **Kenny, D.** 1994: *Interpersonal Perception: A Social Relations Analysis.* New York: Guilford Press. **Skowronski, J. and Carlston, D.** 1989: Negativity and extremity biases in impression formation. *Psychological Bulletin* 105, 131–42.

perspective taking The basis for many social phenomena is that individuals are able to imagine or antici-pate how another sees or experiences the world. Thus, competent SELF-PRESENTATION requires that actors can anticipate how they will be seen by others. ALTRUISM, based on EMPATHY (see s. 4) with a victim of misfortune, appears to require anticipation of the victim's distress. Certain 'reflexive' emotional responses [see REFLEXIVE CONSCIOUSNESS], such as guilt, shame and embarrassment, supposedly stem from anticipation of others' reactions to one's behaviour. Some theories of the SELF-CONCEPT (see also s. 4) have also proposed that people's views of themselves stem from the anticipated judgements of others. [See also LOOKING-GLASS SELF] The theoretical significance of perspective taking in social life was first developed extensively by Mead (1934), while its early genesis in childhood as a cognitive SKILL (see s. 3) was described by Piaget and Inhelder (1948). It is sometimes regarded as a peculiarly human cognitive capacity, though a motivational element may also be involved. *NE*

Mead, G. H. (1934). *Mind, self and society.* Chicago: University of Chicago Press. **Piaget, J. and Inhelder, B.** (1948). *The child's conception of space.* London: Routledge.

persuasion Formation or change of ATTITUDES through information processing, usually in response to persuasive COMMUNICATION (see s. 2). Early persuasion research (1930s to 1950s) studied the effects of variables related to the elements of a persuasion setting – source, message, channel and recipient – on OUTCOME VARIABLES (see s. 8) such as RETENTION (see s. 3) of message content or acceptance of its conclusion. This eclectic approach yielded intriguing findings (e.g. the SLEEPER EFFECT), but also contradictory explanations, lacking a unifying theory. Persuasion research in the 1960s and 1970s was guided by broad theoretical frameworks (e.g. cognitive consistency and ATTRIBUTION), which explained how a few theoretically relevant variables (e.g. FORCED COMPLIANCE and PERCEPTION (see s. 1) of a communicator's self-interest) affect attitude change (McGuire 1985).

With the advent of the SOCIAL COGNITION paradigm in the 1980s, researchers developed comprehensive dual-process theories [see DUAL-PROCESS THEORY] of persuasion: the ELABORATION LIKELIHOOD MODEL and the HEURISTIC-SYSTEMATIC MODEL (Petty and Wegener 1998). Guided by the insight that people cannot equally scrutinise all the countless messages they encounter daily, these models distinguish between effortless ('peripheral-route' or 'heuristic') and effortful ('central-route' or 'systematic') processing modes. A person using low-effort strategies is influenced mainly by easily processed surface characteristics of a persuasion setting (e.g. perceived CONSENSUS or the mere number of arguments provided). A person using high-effort strategies, by contrast, actively evaluates a position's true merits. [See VALIDATION PROCESS] The most influential determinants of processing effort, broadly conceived, are the recipient's ability and MOTIVATION (see s. 6) to process extensively. [See MOTIVATED TACTICIAN]

Research in the dual-mode tradition is typically conducted in laboratory EXPERIMENTS (see s. 8). Researchers systematically vary participants' motivation and ability, the properties of a persuasive message and the context in which it is presented. In addition to participants' post-experimental attitudes, thought-listing protocols provide insight into the cognitive processes that took place. Research topics have included the biasing effects of specific motivations (e.g. IMPRESSION MANAGEMENT) and the interplay of low-effort and high-effort processing modes (Bohner, Moskowitz and Chaiken 1995). The recent proposal of a single-process 'unimodel of persuasion' by Kruglanski and his colleagues (Erb et al. 2003), which emphasises the continuous nature of effort expenditure, has sparked an ongoing controversy about the optimal conceptualisation of persuasion.   *FS/GB*

Bohner, G., Moskowitz, G. B. and Chaiken, S. 1995: The interplay of heuristic and systematic processing of social information. *European Review of Social Psychology* 6, 33–68. **Erb, H.-P., Kruglanski, A. W., Chun, W. Y., Pierro, A., Mannetti, L. and Spiegel, S.** 2003: Searching for commonalities in human judgment: The parametric unimodel and its dual mode alternatives. *European Review of Social Psychology* 14, 1–48. **McGuire, W. J.** 1985: Attitudes and attitude change. In Lindzey, G. and Aronson, E. (eds) *Handbook of Social Psychology* (3rd edn). New York: Random House, vol. 2. **Petty, R. E. and Wegener, D. T.** 1998: Attitude change: Multiple roles for persuasion variables. In Gilbert, D., Fiske, S. T. and Lindzey, G. (eds) *The Handbook of Social Psychology*. (4th edn). New York: McGraw-Hill, vol. 1, 323–90.

P.I.P. (*primus inter pares*) effect

The inclination to perceive, and present, oneself as above average in whatever respect appears to be socially valued in a particular context.   *NE*

planned behaviour (theory of)

An extension of the theory of REASONED ACTION to take account of the amount of control people believe they have over FACTORS (see s. 8) influencing their capacity to act on their intentions.   *NE*

pluralistic ignorance

A situation created by people's unwillingness to act publicly on their beliefs or preferences because each falsely believes they are in the minority; the situation sustains the influence of a norm [see NORMS] that most people privately reject.   *NE*

polarisation

The tendency for the decisions reached by GROUPS following discussion to shift (polarise) more decisively towards the option preferred individually and privately by most group members prior to discussion (Brown 1986). Originally thought only to characterise choices between more and less risky alternatives [see RISKY SHIFT], polarisation has proved to characterise group decisions of all kinds. It also characterises pre- to post-discussion shifts in individuals' private judgements. A variety of explanations have been proposed, drawing on concepts of SOCIAL INFLUENCE (including SOCIAL COMPARISON and PERSUASION) and self-categorisation. [See SELF-CATEGORISATION THEORY] Another effect of group discussion that appears to encourage polarisation is repeated expression of ATTITUDES (Brauer and Judd 1996). However, polarisation effects are much more often observed in experiments than in naturally occurring

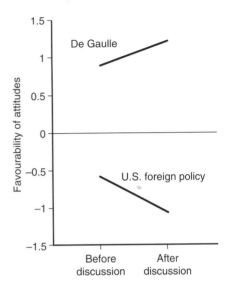

polarisation *Group discussion induced attitude polarisation. Positive attitudes (towards De Gaulle) became more positive and negative attitudes (towards U.S. foreign policy) became more negative after a group discussion. Source: John Sabini, Social Psychology, W. W. Norton & Co, 1992. (Data from Moscovici & Zavalloni, 'The group as a polarizer of attitudes?' in* Journal of Personality and Social Psychology, *12, 1969.)*

groups, suggesting they may require conditions found primarily in an AD HOC GROUP.   *NE*

Brown, R. (1986). *Social psychology: The second edition.* New York: Free Press. **Brauer, M. & Judd, C.** (1996) Group polarisation and repeated attitude expressions A new take on an old topic. *European Review of Social Psychology*, 7, 173–207.

power

The effects of power and its exercise on humans are extensive, affecting not only the target persons, but also the agents themselves and their approach- or inhibition-related affect, cognition and behaviour (Keltner, Gruenfeld and Anderson 2003; Ng 1980). For example, the successful exercise of power increases the agents' SELF-ESTEEM but devalues their PERCEPTION (see s. 1) of the target person, particularly when coercion has been used.

In 1934 Bertrand Russell proposed that 'power' is the fundamental concept in social science, just as energy is in physics. Broadly defined, power is the production of intended effects or, according to field theory, the possibility of inducing force to overcome resistance (e.g. OBEDIENCE). Forces can be induced on the basis of the agent's degree of control over positive (reward power) or negative (coercion power) outcomes for the target person. More subtly, forces can be derived from the target person's psychological state. For example, when a person identifies with or respects the influencing agent, this allows the agent to wield both referential and expert power. Still another category of power base is the persuasive content of the agent's COMMUNICATION (see s. 2) (as distinct from perceived communicator EXPERTISE – see s. 3), which gives rise to informational power (Raven 1992).

power *Types, sources, and mechanisms of social power.*

Type	Based on	Effective
Legitimate	Right to lead	Whether follower is under surveillance or not
Reward	Control over resources	Only with surveillance
Coercive	Control over punishments	Only with surveillance
Referent	Admiration	Whether follower is under surveillance or not
Expert	Perceived knowledge	Whether follower is under surveillance or not

Source: From BH Raven and JRP French, 'Legitimate power, coercive power and observability in social influence' in *Sociometry*, 21, 1958.

In contrast to a view of power in terms of force and its resistance, exchange theory locates power, defined as control, in the exchange of outcomes between interdependent participants. [See also EXCHANGE PROCESSES and SELF-PRESENTATION] Person X's control over person Y is derived from Y's dependence on X. Seemingly dyadic interpersonal power relationships actually involve third parties. Thus, when a third party who is attractive becomes available to Y, Y's relational dependence on X ceases, and with this, X's contact control over Y will end. The combined analysis of dependence and third-party effects gives rise to four mechanisms of power change: withdrawal, power networking, SOCIAL STATUS giving and coalition formation.

Discourse practices (e.g. ageist, sexist or racist talk) may simply reflect existing power relationships, but can also routinise and reproduce the relationships or, at the opposite extreme, subvert them through politicisation. In INTER-GROUP RELATIONS, politicisation of social identity through participation in collective action radicalises the SELF-CONCEPT (see also s. 4) and induces a sense of empowerment (Drury and Reicher 2000). (See also s. 8, POWER)   *SHN*

Drury, J. and Reicher, S. 2000: Collective action and psychological change: the emergence of new social identities. *British Journal of Social Psychology* 39, 579–604. **Keltner, D., Gruenfeld, D. H. and Anderson, C.** 2003: Power, approach, and inhibition. *Psychological Review* 110, 265–84. **Ng, S. H.** 1980: *The Social Psychology of Power.* London: Academic Press. **Raven, B. H.** 1992: A power/interaction model of interpersonal influence: French and Raven thirty years later. *Journal of Social Behavior and Personality* 7, 217–44.

prejudice

prejudice Antipathy or hatred felt towards others because of their category membership. Common categories associated with prejudice include those based on religion, ETHNICITY (see s. 1, ETHNICITY AND RACE ISSUES) and nationality. Prejudice has often been used interchangeably with both stereotyping [see STEREOTYPES] and DISCRIMINATION (and also with such terms as bigotry and intolerance). But a good case can be made for regarding negative emotions felt towards others as distinct from either beliefs about social categories (stereotypes) or biased treatment, given that measures of prejudice correlate only modestly with measures of discriminatory behaviour and even less with stereotype measures (Dovidio et al. 1996).

Research points to a secular decline in prejudice, and indeed in intolerance. Part of the decline may reflect effects of improving general levels of education, associated with shifting social NORMS about the (un)acceptability of expressing openly prejudiced views. However, some authorities argue that prejudice persists but is now expressed in other, more disguised ways. The notion of SUBTLE RACISM [see also MODERN RACISM SCALE] refers to prejudice expressed through support for values supposedly not shared by the OUT-GROUP (reflecting an older idea linking prejudice to perceived cultural value differences). The concept of aversive racism predicts that feelings of unease or ANXIETY (see s. 6) about out-groups can persist in people consciously committed to egalitarian principles, but will be expressed covertly or discreetly when circumstances can obscure their racist character.

Some recent work (Kleinpenning and Hagendoorn 1993) links these ideas by identifying them with different levels of prejudice, placing blatantly expressed hatred and bigotry at one extreme and aversive racism at the other. While this recognises some individuals are chronically more prejudiced than others towards out-groups in general, we are still far from understanding the origins of such differences. [See AUTHORITARIANISM] Several theoretical analyses focus on contextual FACTORS (see s. 8) likely to influence the manner and intensity of expression of prejudice. Among these are conditions affecting the degree of perceived threat to in-group interests or IDENTITY (see also s. 4) (e.g. REALISTIC GROUP CONFLICT THEORY and SOCIAL IDENTITY THEORY). Such analyses also draw attention to the susceptibility of secular trends to changing socio-political conditions. Research on prejudice reduction has considered the relevance of such experiences as inter-group contact. [See CONTACT HYPOTHESIS]   *NE*

Brown, R. 1995: *Prejudice: Its Social Psychology.* Oxford: Blackwell Publishers. **Dovidio, J., Brigham, J., Johnson, B. and Gaertner, S.** 1996: Stereotyping, prejudice and discrimination. In Macrae, N., Stangor, C. and Hewstone, M. (eds) *Stereotypes and Stereotyping.* New York: Guilford, 276–319. **Kinder, D. and Sears, R.** 1981: Symbolic racism versus racial threats to the good life. *Journal of Personality and Social Psychology* 40, 414–31. **Kleinpenning, G. and Hagendoorn, L.** 1993: Forms of racism and the cumulative dimension of ethnic attitudes. *Social Psychology Quarterly* 56, 21–36.

primary group

primary group The GROUP formed of close family members, typically those living together in a shared household.   *NE*

priming

priming In SOCIAL COGNITION (see also s. 4), the impact of prior recent use of an idea (e.g. ATTITUDES or STEREOTYPES) on the likelihood of its subsequent activation. (See also s. 3, PRIMING)   *NE*

prisoner's dilemma

prisoner's dilemma The basis for a two-player experimental game in which cooperation between players is pitted against their respective self-interest. The prisoner's dilemma game (PDG) is intended to capture the dilemma that self-interest can prevail over mutual COOPERATION, even when such cooperation is collectively more profitable, because individuals cannot be certain that if they cooperate others will also cooperate. The PDG has been extensively used in computer simulations, with different strategies played against one another to test hypotheses about the evolution of cooperation. Key features of these simulations are that the game is 'iterated' or repeated several times with the same players, who are kept in ignorance of how many repetitions there will be. In these simulations one of the most successful strategies is TIT-FOR-TAT. *NE*

Axelrod, R. 1984: *The Evolution of Cooperation.* New York: Basic Books.

procedural justice Fairness of the procedures by which decisions, whether about rewards or punishments, are reached. [See also DISTRIBUTIVE JUSTICE and SOCIAL JUSTICE] *NE*

propinquity effect Tendency for personal ties or RELATIONSHIPS to develop between people who are, by virtue of residence or ROLE, closest in physical space. [See also MATE SELECTION] *NE*

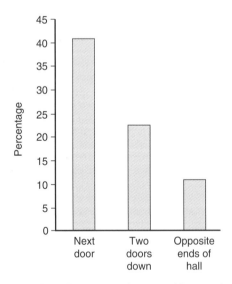

propinquity effect *Percentage of opportunities to make friends varied as a function of location. People were twice as likely to make friends with their next-door neighbours as they were to make friends with the people just two doors down. Source: John Sabini,* Social Psychology, *W. W. Norton & Co, 1992. (Data from Festinger, Schachter, & Back,* Social Pressures in Informal Groups, *Stanford University Press, 1950.)*

pro-social behaviour The term is used to refer to all acts that benefit another person. In the social sciences numerous definitions for pro-social behaviour have been advocated. A common denominator of many is that pro-social behaviour refers to intentional and voluntary acts

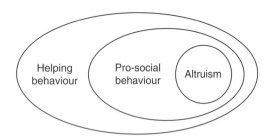

pro-social behaviour *Relationships between the concepts of helping, pro-social behaviour and altruism. Source: M. Hewstone and W. Stroebe,* Introduction to Social Psychology: A European Perspective, *3rd ed, Blackwell (2001).*

which potentially or actually benefit a recipient. An example is a person who helps his neighbour by watching his children when he is not at home. The ultimate goal of pro-social behaviour can be to benefit another person, or to benefit oneself, or both. Values of self-enhancement (e.g. hedonism) and self-transcendence (e.g. benevolence) may equally contribute to pro-social behaviour (Van de Vliert, Huang and Levine 2004). The first value orientation includes COOPERATION, EXCHANGE PROCESSES and SOCIAL SUPPORT in a SOCIAL NETWORK of RECIPROCITY (see s. 4), whereas self-transcendence is related to ALTRUISM. Note that 'helping behaviour' is an even broader term, including pro-social behaviour but also help that is given out of professional obligations (e.g. a nurse helping a patient). The psychology of pro-social behaviour (cf. Bierhoff 2002) is an important part of positive psychology, which focuses on human resources instead of human weaknesses.

If an emergency occurs [see BYSTANDER INTERVENTION] five decisions lead to giving help (Latané and Darley 1970): decide something has happened that deserves your attention; that an emergency has occurred; that you are personally responsible to intervene; the kind of help that is appropriate; and how it is to be implemented efficiently. Many studies indicate that the first three steps, in particular, in the decision-making process are crucial in determining whether an intervention occurs or not. For example, research shows if the cues clearly indicate that an emergency has taken place (e.g. the victim calls for help) and if the person considers himself responsible for intervention, the LIKELIHOOD (see s. 8) of intervention is quite high. Such findings indicate that many people are willing to sacrifice time and effort on behalf of others. On the negative side, FACTORS (see s. 8) that tend to interfere with the decision-making process (e.g. DIFFUSION OF RESPONSIBILITY as a result of many onlookers, each of whom could, in principle, intervene; PLURALISTIC IGNORANCE, when each passive bystander is a model for the other; and audience inhibition, because of fear of doing something wrong in public) can dramatically reduce intervention rates in emergencies.

What motivates pro-social behaviour? From the perspective of self-interest the answer refers to the expectation of positive and negative consequences, which may operate in an obvious or a subtle way. For example, the norm of reciprocity (Perugini et al. 2003), which is related to the goal to maximise joint outcomes in a situation of interdependence [see PRISONER'S DILEMMA] may either explicitly or implicitly enhance the willingness to offer help (e.g. among neighbours).

Other factors may also contribute to an egoistic motivation of pro-social behaviour (Batson, Ahmad, Lishner and Tsang 2002). One explanation in terms of egoism is that helping is in the service of aversive-arousal reduction. The encounter with another person in need may trigger feelings of personal distress in the observer. An appropriate COPING (see s. 7) response which reduces the level of STRESS (see s. 7) in the situation is helpful intervention. Note that the stress is more likely to be reduced by leaving the situation if such an escape is easily available.

Another such explanation invokes the guilt feelings that are aroused by not helping a victim who is dependent on the help. The anticipation of such guilt feelings may motivate an intervention with the goal of avoiding in advance internal processes of self-punishment. Guilt feelings, which originate in personal relationships that are characterised by mutual concern, are considered as pro-social emotions (Baumeister 1998). They are typically aroused when persons attribute the distress of others to their own failure, as in the case of personal neglect, which, for example, is represented by a potential helper who does not intervene although it would be easy to do so.

An additional self-serving motivation is based on empathy-specific rewards, which may occur because the helper feels that he or she has done something good and congratulates himself or herself for acting appropriately. The basic idea is that during socialisation children learn that helping is socially desirable behaviour because it corresponds with what society expects of them (Cialdini, Kenrick and Baumann 1982). A socialised observer of the misfortune of another person is likely to feel sad because of the suffering of the victim, and intervention has a mood-enhancing effect for such an observer.

In contrast, altruistic motivation is based on the primary goal to help the person in need. It is assumed that its source is empathic EMOTION (see s. 6), which is defined 'as an other-oriented emotional response elicited by and congruent with the perceived welfare of someone else' (Batson et al. 2002: 486). Knowing another person's internal STATE (see s. 6), projecting oneself into another's situation, imagining how another is feeling and role-taking may facilitate the occurrence of empathic emotion.

In addition, people may help because of felt obligation based on an internalised norm of social responsibility (Bierhoff 2002). Successful internalisation means that external demands are converted into personal expectations about what behaviour is in accordance with humanitarian goals.

New evidence indicates that the thermal climate may influence pro-social behaviour. Countries with uncomfortable climates (either cold or hot) tend to have inhabitants who act more pro-socially than countries with comfortable climates. From comfortable to uncomfortably cold but also uncomfortably hot climates, the average helpfulness of inhabitants of major cities across the world increases (van de Vliert, Huang and Levine 2004).

Besides situational determinants, pro-social behaviour is influenced by altruistic PERSONALITY (see s. 1 and s. 6), which is characterised by a high willingness to accept social responsibility, high dispositional EMPATHY (see s. 4), internal locus of control and other personality VARIABLES (see s. 8). Personality dimensions that are related to egoistically motivated helping differ from those that are related to altruistically motivated helping (Bierhoff and Rohmann forthcoming). *H-WB*

Batson, C. D., Ahmad, N., Lishner, D. A. and Tsang, J. A. 2002: Empathy and altruism. In Snyder, C. R. and Lopez, S. J. (eds) *Handbook of Positive Psychology.* Oxford: Oxford University Press, 485–98. **Baumeister, R. F.** 1998: Inducing guilt. In Bybee, J. (ed.) *Guilt and Children.* San Diego CA: Academic Press, 127–38. **Bierhoff, H. W.** 2002: *Prosocial Behaviour.* Hove: Psychology Press. **Bierhoff, H. W. and Rohmann, E.** forthcoming: Altruistic personality in the context of the empathy-altruism hypothesis. *European Journal of Personality* 18. **Cialdini, R. B., Kenrick, D. T. and Baumann, D. J.** 1982: Effects of mood on prosocial behavior in children and adults. In Eisenberg, N. (ed.) *The Development of Prosocial Behavior.* New York: Academic Press, 339–59. **Latané, B. and Darley, J. M.** 1970: *The Unresponsive Bystander: Why Doesn't He Help?* New York: Appleton. **Perugini, M., Callucci, M., Presaghi, F. and Ercolani, A. P.** 2003: The personal norm of reciprocity. *European Journal of Personality* 17, 251–83. **Van de Vliert, E., Huang, X. and Levine, R. V.** 2004: National wealth and thermal climate as predictors of motives for volunteer work. *Journal of Cross-Cultural Psychology* 35, 62–73.

prototypicality In SELF-CATEGORISATION THEORY, the degree to which an individual exemplifies NORMS of the IN-GROUP in terms of VALUES, OPINIONS or behaviour. *NE*

P. T. Barnum effect Inclination to accept flattering-sounding, but in reality vacuous, statements about oneself as genuine insights (basis for experimental manipulations involving false feedback to participants). *NE*

R

reactance Reassertion of autonomy by individuals after they have been induced to do or say something contrary to their own beliefs or inclinations. [See also COGNITIVE DISSONANCE] *NE*

realistic group conflict theory A THEORY (see s. 8) that ETHNOCENTRISM is a realistic collective response to competition with other GROUPS for scarce resources. Ethnocentrism is coupled with a realistic perception both that IN-GROUP interests are threatened and the particular OUT-GROUP source of this threat, and is a realistic or adaptive set of reactions for protecting these interests. Levine and Campbell (1972) developed the theory as a criticism of the view that conflict between groups is based on erroneous perceptions of each other as threats to in-group interests. They described ethnocentrism as a culturally evolved syndrome that includes increasingly contrasting valuations and STEREOTYPES of in-group and out-group, tightening of group boundaries, increased in-group cohesion and deference to the LEADERSHIP, and punitive treatment of in-group members not sharing in these reactions. Though many of its key claims have been verified empirically, critics [see also SOCIAL IDENTITY THEORY] point out that real competition with an out-group is not a necessary condition for DISCRIMINATION (see also s. 3) in favour of the in-group. *NE*

Levine, R. and Campbell, D. 1972: *Ethnocentrism: Theories of Conflict, Ethnic Attitudes and Group Behaviour.* New York: Wiley.

reasoned action (theory of) A THEORY (see s. 8) of the determinants of specific behavioural intentions, developed (Fishbein and Ajzen 1975) to show how ATTITUDES could predict particular behaviours. It is essentially an EXPECTANCY-VALUE MODEL of behavioural choice except that a distinction is made between consequences inherent in the action itself (the attitude component in the model) and consequences for others' approval or disapproval (the 'subjective norm' component). MEASUREMENT (see s. 1, MEASUREMENT AND STATISTICS) of these two components has successfully predicted a wide variety of behaviours, including health-related, consumer and political behaviour. Ajzen and Fishbein (2000) have recently responded to criticisms of the theory, particularly those proposing that much behaviour is a 'mindless' reflection of habit or product of AUTOMATIC (see s. 3) processes [see AUTOMATICITY] rather than intentional action based on reasons. [See also PLANNED BEHAVIOUR] *NE*

Ajzen, I. and Fishbein, M. 2000: Attitudes and the attitude-behavior relation: reasoned and automatic processes. *European Review of Social Psychology* 11, 1–29. **Fishbein, M. and Ajzen, I.** 1975: *Belief, Attitude, Intention and Behaviour: An Introduction to Theory and Research.* Reading MA: Addison-Wesley.

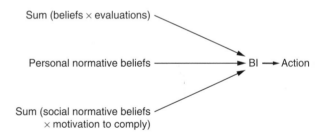

reasoned action (theory of) *Theory of Reasoned Action*

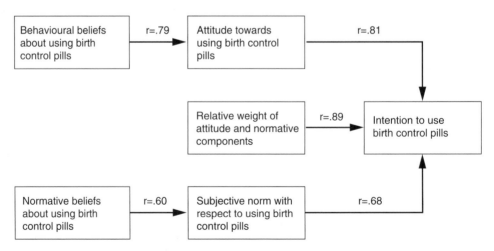

reasoned action (theory of) *Modified Theory of Reasoned Action.*

reference group A GROUP or social category selected by an individual for purposes of SOCIAL COMPARISON, particularly when judging personal entitlement. [See RELATIVE DEPRIVATION] *NE*

reflexive consciousness CONSCIOUSNESS (see s. 3) of the SELF (see also s. 1 and s. 4) as object, supposedly a distinctively human capacity. [See also PERSPECTIVE TAKING] *NE*

relationships A broadly defined term referring to a wide variety of personal relationships, including, but not limited to, friendships, workmates, marriages and dating or romantic partners. Curiously, studies of relatives, people with whom we have relationships not by choice but by accident of birth, are much less common. Perhaps more so than other social psychological topics, the study of relationships (sometimes referred to as close or intimate relationships) is interdisciplinary. Relationships are studied by psychologists, sociologists, anthropologists and by various scholars identified more by a topical focus (COMMUNICATION – see s. 2 – studies, marriage and FAMILY STUDIES – see s. 7, etc.) than by a discipline. The study of relationships began as a laboratory endeavour with a primary focus on simple interpersonal attraction (Byrne, Ervin and Lambeth 1970). Over time, researchers have used more naturalistic methods, such as diaries (Nezlek 1995), to study relationships *in vitro*, a change due in part to the recognition that it is difficult to create certain critical conditions in a laboratory (e.g. it is difficult to get people to fall in love during an EXPERIMENT – see s. 8).

Broadly speaking, the study of relationships tends to focus on how relationships are begun and maintained, on links between the quality of one's personal relationships and other domains, and differences in the 'style' of relationships. The initiation of relationships is typically conceptualised within the framework of INTERPERSONAL ATTRACTION, although relationships scholars pay more attention to the possibility that opposites attract (the complementarity HYPOTHESIS – see s. 3 and s. 8) than those who study interpersonal attraction, in which the emphasis is on the similarity hypothesis (birds of a feather flock together). The development of relationships is frequently conceptualised in terms of variations on the social penetration model (Altman and Taylor 1973), which posits that relationships tend to develop gradually as people reveal more and more about themselves to others. [See also SELF-DISCLOSURE]

One of the more enduring findings in the literature is the 'PROPINQUITY EFFECT' – people tend to form relationships with people who live near them or with whom they have more regular contact (Festinger, Schachter and Back 1951). This effect holds even for relationships such as marriage. The rationale for this effect is that contact is a necessary, but not sufficient, condition for the development of a relationship (i.e. you cannot form a relationship with people with whom you have no contact, but having contact with others does not necessarily lead to the development of relationships). However, the propinquity effect also indicates an inclination to economise on effort in the formation and maintenance of relationships (Catton and Smircich 1964).

Although there are some differences, research tends to find that people seek and receive similar rewards (e.g.

trust and acceptance) from different types of personal relationships (e.g. from friends and lovers). Moreover, although there are some important, perhaps evolutionarily based, differences between men and women in the attributes they value in the opposite sex, the similarities between the sexes outweigh the differences in the factors influencing choice of romantic partners. [See also MATE SELECTION]

One of the more prominent approaches to understanding relationship maintenance is the investment model (Rusbult 1983), which posits that people choose to leave or stay in relationships based upon how much they have invested in a relationship (emotionally and materially) and the availability and relative attractiveness of alternatives. [See also EXCHANGE PROCESSES] Other approaches emphasise how partners in relationships view each other's strengths and weaknesses with a sense that unrealistically positive views may be associated with more satisfying relationships. Aside from cases obviously to the contrary (e.g. abusive relationships), people in relationships tend to be healthier (both physically and mentally) than those who are not, an advantage probably provided by increased SOCIAL SUPPORT. There is a suspicion, however, that for heterosexual romantic relationships, such health benefits are more pronounced for men than for women.

Three important foci of research on relationship styles concern people's preferences for communal [see COMMUNAL ORIENTATION] versus exchange relationships, the sort of romantic relationships they prefer (e.g. passionate vs. companionate) and the extent to which adult patterns of relationships reflect childhood relationships with family members (typically parents). A prominent THEORY (see s. 8) involved in much of this research is attachment theory, which views INDIVIDUAL DIFFERENCES (see s. 6) in relationships as expressions of dispositional differences in basic patterns of relating (i.e. ATTACHMENT – see s. 4). One of the major considerations within such conceptualisations is the distinction between secure and insecure styles of attachment, and such distinctions have been linked to people's basic evaluations of the SELF (see also s. 1 and s. 4) and of others. For example, securely attached people view themselves and others positively, whereas 'dismissives' (those who do not desire close relationships) view themselves positively and others negatively (Bartholomew and Horowitz 1991). Most, but not all, research suggests that a SECURE ATTACHMENT (see s. 4) style is associated with greater well-being. What is not clear at this time is how closely the attachment styles individuals have as adults correspond to the attachment styles they had as children.

Recent trends in relationships research include a recognition of the importance of understanding relationships within a cultural context, a search for possible evolved mechanisms that might underlie the formation and maintenance of relationships, and an appreciation of the need to study 'non-traditional' relationships, such as homosexual romantic relationships. [See also MATCHING HYPOTHESIS and SOCIAL SUPPORT] *JN*

Altman, I. and Taylor, D. A. 1973: *Social Penetration: The Development of Interpersonal Relationships*. New York: Holt, Rinehart and Winston. **Bartholomew, K. and Horowitz, L. M.** 1991: Attachment style among young adults: a test of a four-category model. *Journal of Personality and Social Psychology* 61, 226–44. **Byrne, D., Ervin, C. R. and Lambeth, J.** 1970:

Continuity between the experimental study of attraction and 'real life' computer dating. *Journal of Personality and Social Psychology* 16, 157–65. **Catton, W. R. and Smircich, R. J.** 1964: A comparison of mathematical models for the effect of residential propinquity on mate selection. *American Sociological Review* 29, 522–9. **Festinger, L., Schachter, S. and Back, K.** 1951: *Social Pressures in Informal Groups: A Study of Human Factors in Housing*. New York: Harper. **Nezlek, J.** 1995: Social construction, gender/sex similarity and social interaction in close relationships. *Journal of Social and Personal Relationships* 12, 503–20. **Rusbult, C. E.** 1983: A longitudinal test of the investment model: the development and (deterioration) of satisfaction and commitment in heterosexual involvement. *Journal of Personality and Social Psychology* 45, 101–17.

relative deprivation The subjective feeling of deprivation relative to some standard of expectation or entitlement. This feeling is significant because it has so often proved to be a more important determinant of people's (dis)satisfaction with their lot than their absolute or objective deprivation. It has been invoked as one explanation of the observation that revolutionary movements often attract most support from among people whose conditions are either improving or who are not the most deprived in absolute terms (e.g. Davies 1962). The perceived entitlement underlying relative deprivation is supposedly derived from SOCIAL COMPARISON, but a difficulty in using relative deprivation as an explanatory concept lies in predicting how the REFERENCE GROUP is chosen for this comparison. However, Runciman (1966) argued that an important distinction exists between 'egoistic' deprivation based on interpersonal comparisons and 'fraternalistic' deprivation based on inter-group comparisons. [See also SOCIAL JUSTICE] *NE*

Davies, J. 1962: Towards a theory of revolution. *American Sociological Review* 27, 5–17. **Runciman, W.** 1966: *Relative Deprivation and Social Justice: A Study of Attitudes to Social Inequality in Twentieth-Century England*. Berkeley CA: University of California Press.

remedial exchange Actions, such as apologies, adopted by an individual to correct the otherwise negative impression of an audience, effectively a strategy of SELF-PRESENTATION. *NE*

Ringlemann effect The observation that effort exerted by a group is less than the sum of the individual parts. [See also SOCIAL LOAFING] *NE*

risky shift The tendency for decisions reached through GROUP discussion to be more risky than the average pre-discussion preference of individual group members. The phenomenon was first reported in studies comparing individual with group decisions about a range of problems in which the level of acceptable risk associated with pursuing an attractive opportunity had to be selected. The phenomenon was the basis for analysis of real-world decision-making disasters in terms of the GROUPTHINK concept. However, later work revealed, first, that some problems routinely produce a shift to caution when discussed in a group and, then, that both tendencies were likely to be instances of a more general phenomenon of POLARISATION (see Brown 1986). *NE*

Brown, R. 1986: *Social Psychology: The Second Edition*. New York: Free Press.

role A part played by an individual in a team, GROUP, institution or organisational setting, defined in terms of responsibilities (tasks) and NORMS for performance, and shaping the reactions of others to the role occupant. Goffman's analysis of SELF-PRESENTATION addresses the problem of how actors dramatise for audiences their FITNESS (see s. 2) to fill a particular, often occupational, role. However, his concept of 'role-distance' reflects self-presentation directed at expressing the non-equivalence of the role-player and the role played. Generally, role theory has been more influential as an explanatory framework in sociology than in social psychology, where it is now most often discussed with reference to GENDER (see s. 1, GENDER AND SEXUALITY ISSUES) (e.g. Eagly 1987). Nonetheless it remains a basic assumption that many GROUP PROCESSES are structured in terms of role-based relations between group members. *NE*

Eagly, A. 1987: *Sex Differences in Social Behaviour: A Social Role Interpretation*. Hillsdale NJ: Erlbaum.

S

satisficing Choice of a line of action that is minimally adequate to meet needs in preference to one that is optimal. *NE*

self The self is at once both utterly familiar and infinitely elusive. Everyone reading these words has a self or, perhaps more correctly, *is* a self, yet it is difficult to say what this means or amounts to, because, unlike other objects of scientific scrutiny, the self resists being pinned down or pointed out. In frustration, some philosophers have contended that the 'inner I' is an illusion, the product of outdated dualistic thinking or of misinterpreted personal pronouns. Even granting that the self does exist, two problems persist for the would-be empirical analyst: first, to define the self convincingly and conclusively in view of the hodgepodge of historical meanings it has assumed; and second, to identify worthwhile ways of studying the self in view of the well-established fallibility of verbal reports based upon INTROSPECTION (see s. 1).

To meet such challenges, social psychologists proceed pragmatically. They accept that REFLEXIVE CONSCIOUSNESS, the hallmark of human selfhood, is forever likely to elude full elucidation, but nonetheless note that, whatever its nature, it is still a key hub around which human psychology revolves. They maintain, moreover, that, even though the self, regarded as an arcane unity, may be empirically intractable, the subordinate phenomena associated with it, studied in a piecemeal way, need not be. Praxis proves, for example, that SELF-ESTEEM can be adequately conceptualised, reliably measured and fruitfully investigated, without having to specify exactly what is being esteemed. For scientific purposes, then, the self can be defined as the totality of psychological processes intimately intertwined with reflexive consciousness. It is not so much an object of scrutiny as an area of inquiry.

Social psychologists are consequently able to deploy a range of methodologies to investigate the self (Reis and Judd 2000). Common experimental techniques include short-term manipulations of self-related variables via the staging of social situations or the presentation of bogus feedback. Common MEASUREMENT (see s. 1, MEASUREMENT AND STATISTICS) techniques include not only psychometrically valid self-report inventories, but also objective indices borrowed from other disciplines, such as implicit measures from cognitive psychology and brain-imaging techniques from neuroscience.

The anatomy of the self

We conceptually dissect the self by adopting a classification scheme that maps on to the traditional division of mind into three faculties: knowing (cognition), feeling (affect) and doing (intention/action).

The knowing self. Compared to the rest of the animal kingdom, human beings possess a sophisticated intellect (Sedikides and Skowronski 2003). Moreover, reflexive self-consciousness allows them to use this intellect to make sense of themselves. The result is a rich tapestry of self-beliefs (Higgins 1996). These self-beliefs, in their entirety, make up the SELF-CONCEPT (see also s. 4). Social psychologists study both the content of these self-beliefs (the basis of personal and social IDENTITY – see also s. 4) and their associated properties (e.g. accuracy, consistency, generality, ACCESSIBILITY (see s. 3) and importance). Self-beliefs are only partly shaped by interpersonal feedback and cultural conditioning (contrary to the claims of LOOKING-GLASS SELF models) because people also interpret the world through their self-beliefs (Shrauger and Schoeneman 1989).

The feeling self. People do not, like indifferent androids, process self-related information dispassionately. Rather, they react to it affectively, delivering positive or negative evaluations and exhibiting agreeable or aversive emotions. People's overall affective reaction to themselves corresponds to their self-esteem. Having high self-esteem undeniably makes people's subjective lives brighter, but whether and to what extent it confers objective or interpersonal advantages is much debated (Baumeister, Campbell, Krueger and Vohs 2003). Social psychologists are interested not only in the quantity of self-esteem that people possess, but also in the quality of that esteem (e.g. how stable, unconditional or AUTOMATIC – see s. 3 – it is; Kernis 2003).

The doing self. People do not merely contemplate themselves and then react affectively; they also act. Indeed, self-reflexive thoughts and feelings arguably direct adaptive action. One key component of adaptive action is SELF-REGULATION, the executive management of spontaneous mental and behavioural inclinations. Such management is essential for attaining long-term goals and preserving psychological equilibrium. Consequently, social psychologists spend time studying the pitfalls of self-regulation, identifying particular sources of failure such as IRONIC PROCESSES and EGO DEPLETION, and building HEURISTIC (see s. 3) models of the self-regulation process as a whole (Carver and Scheier 2000).

Note that self-regulation can be either direct or oblique. When direct, an attempt is made to manage the mind from within (say, by trying to suppress feelings of worthlessness); when oblique, an attempt is made to manage the mind from without (say, by trying to impress others to feel worthwhile). Oblique self-regulation, as in the example given, is often accomplished by strategic SELF-PRESENTATION, a form of IMPRESSION MANAGEMENT that highlights the interplay between self and society. People also vary in their penchant for presenting a polished image to the world, an individual difference explored under the rubric of SELF-MONITORING.

The motives of the self

What is the psychological glue that binds the three domains of selfhood together? One plausible answer is

273

MOTIVATION (see s. 6): whenever people strive after something their self-directed thoughts, feelings and actions fuse. The cardinal motives of the self are manifold, operating sometimes in concert, sometimes in opposition (Sedikides and Strube 1997). For example, people seek, on occasions, to self-assess, because knowing the truth about themselves is salutary, whereas they seek, at other times, to self-enhance, because holding favourable illusions about themselves is gratifying. Multiple dispositional and situational FACTORS (see s. 8) determine which self-motive predominates. Nonetheless, the fact that self-enhancement manifests itself so variously and ubiquitously (e.g. in positivity bias, self-handicapping and self-serving attributions) suggests that the self is primitively experienced as an asset to be promoted or protected, either candidly or tactically, within the constraints of plausibility (Sedikides and Gregg 2003). Additional self-motives, possibly reducible to self-enhancement, include self-improvement and self-verification.

Several grand theories of self-related striving posit the existence of fundamental needs that must be met to maintain psychological stability and motivational systems designed to meet those needs (Pittman 1998). The SOCIOMETER HYPOTHESIS posits a need to belong to significant social groups; TERROR MANAGEMENT THEORY, to construct meaningful world-views; and self-determination theory, to act autonomously, accomplish goals effectively and bond closely with others. (See also s. 1 and s. 4, SELF)

CS/AG

Baumeister, R. F., Campbell, J. D., Krueger, J. I. and Vohs, K. D. 2003: Does high self-esteem cause better performance, interpersonal success, happiness, or healthier lifestyles? *Psychological Science in the Public Interest* 4, 1–44. Carver, C. S. and Scheier, M. F. 2000: On the structure of behavioral self-regulation. In Boekaerts, M., Pintrich, P. R. and Zeidner, M. (eds) *Handbook of Self-Regulation*. San Diego CA: Academic Press, 41–84. Higgins, E. T. 1996: The 'self digest': self-knowledge serving self-regulatory functions. *Journal of Personality and Social Psychology* 71, 1062–83. Kernis, M. H. 2003: Toward a conceptualization of optimal self-esteem. *Psychological Inquiry* 14, 1–26. Pittman, T. S. 1998: Motivation. In Gilbert, D. T., Fiske, S. T. and Lindzey, G. (eds) *The Handbook of Social Psychology* (4th edn). New York: McGraw-Hill, vol. 1, 549–90. Reis, H. T. and Judd, C. M. 2000: *Handbook of Research Methods in Social and Personality Psychology*. New York: Cambridge University Press. Sedikides, C. and Gregg, A. P. 2003: Portraits of the self. In Hogg, M. A. and Cooper, J. (eds) *Sage Handbook of Social Psychology*. London: Sage Publications, 110–38. Sedikides, C. and Skowronski, J. J. 2003: Evolution of the self: issues and prospects. In Leary, M. R. and Tangney, J. P. (eds) *Handbook of Self and Identity*. New York: Guilford, 594–609. Sedikides, C. and Strube, M. J. 1997: Self-evaluation: to thine own self be good, to thine own self be sure, to thine own self be true, and to thine own self be better. In Zanna, M. P. (ed) *Advances in Experimental Social Psychology* 29, 209–69. New York: Academic Press. Shrauger, J. S. and Schoeneman, T. J. 1979: Symbolic interactionist view of self-concept: through the looking glass darkly. *Psychological Bulletin* 86, 549–73.

self-categorisation theory (SCT)   A development from SOCIAL IDENTITY THEORY by Turner et al. (1987), distinguished from the former by emphasis on the consequences for individual thought and action of categorising the SELF (see also s. 1 and s. 4) in different ways. The THEORY (see s. 8) proceeds from the proposition that individuals possess a set of SELF-CONCEPTS. These concepts are

categorisations, varying both in content and in their level of inclusiveness; most interesting are the contrasting effects of categorisations at the personal versus group levels. [See also SOCIAL CATEGORISATION] Which particular categorisation (content and level) is selected at any moment will depend on its situational salience; SCT holds there is an inverse relation between salience of the personal and group levels. Group-level self-categorisation produces DEPERSONALISATION, which includes self-stereotyping as an exemplar of the category. SCT is an important attempt to specify the psychological meaning of the social GROUP. A detailed set of hypotheses derived from the assumptions of SCT (Turner et al. 1987) has been applied to a wide variety of phenomena, including SOCIAL INFLUENCE, POLARISATION, COHESION OF GROUPS, CROWD BEHAVIOUR and LEADERSHIP (see also Haslam 1999).   *NE*

Haslam, A. 1999: *Psychology in Organisations: The Social Identity Approach*. London: Sage. Turner, J., Hogg, M., Oakes, P., Reicher, S. and Wetherell, M. 1987: *Rediscovering the Social Group: A Self-categorization Theory*. Oxford: Blackwell.

self-concept   An individual's beliefs about the kind of person they are. Self-concepts appear to be, beyond childhood, fairly stable over time, despite subjective impressions of change. One view of self-concept formation, going back to William James, identifies the reactions of significant others – or reflected self-appraisals – as key. An argument more consistent with research evidence is that the self-concept is shaped by our capacity to guess how we appear from the point of view of others. [See PERSPECTIVE TAKING] Kenny and DePaulo (1993) show that these guesses are also quite accurate, arguing this is not because we accurately absorb reflected self-appraisals, but because the self-concept, on the one hand, drives the behaviour from which others' impressions are derived and, on the other hand, forms the basis for these guesses.

That others nonetheless play a role, particularly in calibrating self-concepts, is underlined by the concept of SOCIAL COMPARISON. One cannot know whether one is a competent swimmer, successful scholar or devout Catholic without comparing oneself with appropriate others. This also highlights the evaluative character of self-knowledge.

Contemporary theoretical analyses treat the self-concept as a complex body of knowledge about the SELF (see also s. 1 and s. 4), only particular elements of which will be salient, and hence potentially influence behaviour, at any moment (Baumeister 1998). Thus GENDER (see s. 1, GENDER AND SEXUALITY ISSUES) and nationality are elements of virtually everyone's self-concept, but their relative salience will vary across situations. For example, they may be highly salient at a given moment if everyone else present is of the opposite sex or a different nationality (cf. McGuire et al. 1978).

SELF-CATEGORISATION THEORY provides a systematic set of predictions as to which elements of the self-concept will be momentarily salient, and, in particular, whether these reflect distinguishing qualities of the self compared to other individuals (e.g. unique aspects of PERSONALITY (see s. 1 and s. 6)) or qualities shared with others by virtue of a common social IDENTITY (see also s. 4).

Markus and Nurius (1986) proposed that people can also envisage possible selves, which may be negative or positive, and which provide mental bridges between present and future, shaping the behaviour of the present self. (See also s. 4, SELF-CONCEPT) *NE*

Baumeister, R. 1998: The self. In Gilbert, D. T., Fiske, S. and Lindzey, G. (eds) *The Handbook of Social Psychology* (4th edn). New York: McGraw-Hill, vol. 1. **Kenny, D. and DePaulo, B.** 1993: Do people know how others view them? An empirical and theoretical account. *Psychological Bulletin* 102, 187–203. **Markus, H. and Nurius, P.** 1986: Possible selves. *American Psychologist* 41, 954–69. **McGuire, W. J., McGuire, C. V., Child, P. and Fujioka, T.** 1978: Salience of ethnicity in the spontaneous self-concept as a function of one's ethnic distinctiveness in the social environment. *Journal of Personality and Social Psychology* 36, 511–20.

self-disclosure

Revelation of personal details to another, supposedly important in the development of personal RELATIONSHIPS, and typically inviting reciprocation. *NE*

self-esteem

Individuals' ATTITUDES towards the SELF (see also s. 1 and s. 4). Rosenberg (1965) adopted a primarily emotional or affective definition as degree of liking or disliking for the self, in contrast to a more cognitive view of self-esteem as the summary of a set of evaluative judgements of the self as competent, successful, virtuous, etc. Self-esteem appears to be both a TRAIT (see s. 6) – individuals differ in their typical levels of self-esteem – and a STATE (see s. 6) that can fluctuate in response to circumstances. Despite the strong expectations of researchers, the trait of self-esteem appears to have very few behavioural consequences, except likelihood of self-harm (Emler 2001), but can strongly bias interpretation of self-relevant information. This biasing contributes to the relative immunity of high self-esteem to any long-term impact of a range of negative circumstances and experiences, and vice versa for low self-esteem. (See also s. 7, SELF-ESTEEM) *NE*

Emler, N. 2001: *Self Esteem: The Costs and Causes of Low Self-worth.* York: Joseph Rowntree Foundation. **Rosenberg, M.** 1965: *Society and the Adolescent Self-image.* Princeton NJ: Princeton University Press.

self-fulfilling prophecy

With respect to INTER-GROUP RELATIONS, the effects of STEREOTYPES in creating the circumstances they envisage. *NE*

self-handicapping

A strategy of SELF-PRESENTATION to excuse anticipated failure, based on adopting a handicap that can explain the failure; however, the objective may also be self-deception. *NE*

self-monitoring

A trait defined by the extent to which individuals engage in SELF-PRESENTATION, based on monitoring their own behaviour and others' reactions (Snyder 1979). Individuals high in self-monitoring are sensitive to the social appropriateness of their behaviour, and more likely to modify it to create a positive impression with their audience and cultivate different relationships for different purposes. Low self-monitors are more likely to behave consistently across situations, act in terms of their true ATTITUDES and say what they really think. However, low self-monitors may also have poorer SOCIAL SKILLS and

be less socially competent – high self-monitoring is, for example, positively associated with LEADERSHIP ratings. This is consistent with evidence that Snyder's self-monitoring scale assesses a mix of acting ability, sociability and concern with others' evaluations of the SELF (see also s. 1 and s. 4) (Briggs, Cheek and Buss 1980). *NE*

Briggs, S., Cheek, J. and Buss, A. 1980: An analysis of the self-monitoring scale. *Journal of Personality and Social Psychology* 36, 679–86. **Snyder, M.** 1979: Self-monitoring processes. In Berkowitz, L. (ed.) *Advances in Experimental Social Psychology.* New York: Academic Press, vol. 12, 85–128.

self-presentation

Actions, the goal of which is to create a particular impression of the SELF (see also s. 1 and s. 4) in the minds of an audience. Jones (1990) and Goffman (1959) offer contrasting views of this phenomenon. According to Jones, self-presentation serves the basic goals of people to augment their POWER in a face-to-face encounter and so derive more rewards from it than would be the case if others' impressions were accurate. As such, it is fundamentally manipulative; it entails persuading an audience to believe what is not in their interests to believe. Jones identified different strategic objectives in self-presentation, including SELF-PROMOTION, but argued that the most commonplace is INGRATIATION – seeking to persuade an audience one is likeable. He also argued that self-presentation is based on highly automatised behavioural repertoires [see AUTOMATICITY] that in adulthood tend not to benefit from deliberate rehearsal. Self-presentational tactics identified in research include SELF-HANDICAPPING and BASKING IN REFLECTED GLORY.

Goffman (1959) acknowledged that actors can present inauthentic selves, but often only because the audience does not wish to be presented with the truth. [See also DECEPTION] More frequently, however, the principle goal is to explain, or 'dramatise', to an audience matters about the self that could otherwise be misunderstood. [See also IMPRESSION MANAGEMENT] For Goffman, therefore, accuracy in PERSON PERCEPTION is as much a responsibility of the actor as it is of the perceiver. In this analysis, differences in the inclination to manage one's self-presentations [see also SELF-MONITORING] are differences in social competence, not authenticity. Goffman went on to identify a variety of problems actors face in self-presentation, such as manufacturing the appearance of spontaneity, conflicts between expressive and instrumental action, and threats to expressive control.

self-presentation *Self-presentation strategies.*

Strategy	Technique	Aim
Ingratiation	Flatter and agree	Be seen as likable
Self-promotion	Brag	Be seen as competent
Intimidation	Threaten	Be seen as dangerous
Exemplification	Brag and gossip	Be seen as morally pure
Supplication	Beseech	Be seen as weak

Source: Jones, E. E. and Pittman, T. S. (1982). Toward a general theory of strategic self-presentation. In J. Suls (ed.), *Psychological Perspectives on the Self*, vol. 1 (pp. 231–62). Hillsdale NJ: Lawrence Erlbaum Associates.

Baumeister (1982) reviews the wide range of phenomena that have been analysed in terms of self-presentation, including ALTRUISM, CONFORMITY, COGNITIVE DISSONANCE, EMOTIONAL EXPRESSION and AGGRESSION. [See also REACTANCE] A difficulty, however, lies in distinguishing between actions that are self-presentations and actions unmotivated in this way. The simple criterion normally adopted in research, whether the action is altered by the presence of an audience, does not necessarily rule out other audience effects on behaviour (e.g. SOCIAL FACILITATION).　　　　*NE*

Baumeister, R. 1982: A self-presentational view of social phenomena. *Psychological Bulletin* 91, 3–26. **Goffman, E.** 1959: *Presentation of Self in Everyday Life.* New York: Doubleday. **Jones, E.** 1990: *Interpersonal Perception.* New York: Freeman.

self-promotion

A strategy of SELF-PRESENTATION, the goal of which is to persuade an audience that the actor is highly competent, accomplished or successful.　　*NE*

self-regulation

This term is typically applied to internal control of behaviour to reach desired goals, often thought to include the inhibition of actions that would hinder achievement of these goals. Thus, self-regulation could involve inhibition of actions that are immediately rewarding (e.g. eating chocolate, watching TV rather than studying) in furtherance of goals providing a proportionately greater reward in the long term (e.g. being healthy, gaining qualifications). Carver and Scheier (1981) offered an influential analysis of the process of self-regulation as a system of control through feedback: people set goals for themselves which, when compared with actual behaviour, produce adjustments in the latter to reduce the ideal-real discrepancy. In this analysis, greater self-focused attention enhances the effectiveness of the feedback process. Bandura (1989) identifies self-efficacy beliefs as key moderators of self-regulation efforts. Bandura regards these as beliefs about one's capacity to perform behaviours relevant to specific goals.　　　　*NE*

Bandura, A. 1989: Human agency in social cognitive theory. *American Psychologist* 44, 1175–84. **Carver, C. S. and Scheier, M. S.** 1981: *Attention and Self-regulation: A Control Theory Approach to Social Behaviour.* New York: Springer-Verlag.

self-serving attribution

In perceptions of the SELF (see also s. 1 and s. 4) attributions that exaggerate the importance of internal causes of successes and external causes of failures.　　　　*NE*

situationism

A meta-theoretical perspective in social psychology, based on the view that attempting to explain social behaviour in terms of PERSONALITY TRAITS (see s. 6) is futile because all the important variations in social behaviour reflect conditions that vary across situations (Bowers 1973). The critique of traits ultimately backfired as it emerged that characteristics of situations manipulated in EXPERIMENTS (see s. 8) at best accounted for similarly limited proportions of VARIANCE (see s. 8) in social behaviour (Funder and Ozer 1983). This led some to argue for an interactionist position, on the grounds that the interaction between personal attributes and situational characteristics will explain most of the variance. However, situationism remains effectively the explanatory framework implicit in an experimental approach to social behaviour, as this necessarily tests hypotheses about the explanatory role of what can be manipulated experimentally, namely aspects of the situation. [See also FUNDAMENTAL ATTRIBUTION ERROR]　　*NE*

Bowers, K. 1973: Situationism in psychology: an analysis and critique. *Psychological Review* 80, 863–72. **Funder, D. and Ozer, D.** 1983: Behavior as a function of the situation. *Journal of Personality and Social Psychology* 44, 107–12.

sleeper effect

Delayed impact of persuasive messages, thought to depend on dissociation of message content from message source. [See also PERSUASION and SOCIAL INFLUENCE]　　　　*NE*

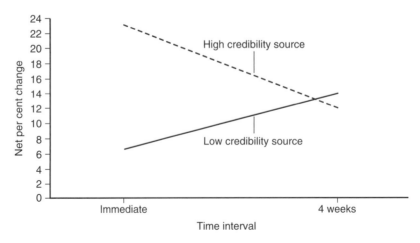

sleeper effect *Immediately after hearing a message, subjects are more likely to agree with the position of the high credibility source and less likely to agree with the low credibility source. Over time, however, the message becomes dissociated from its source, leading to less agreement with the high credibility source and more agreement with the low credibility source. (From C. I. Hovland and W. Weiss, 'The influence of source credibility on communication effectiveness' in* Public Opinion Quarterly, 1951, 15, pp. 635–50, by permission of Oxford University Press.)

small-world phenomenon Any two individuals in a large POPULATION (see s. 8) may be linked to one another through a relatively short chain of personal acquaintances; a consequence of the low NETWORK DENSITY of the population. [See also SOCIAL NETWORK] *NE*

social capital A quality of a SOCIAL NETWORK structure characterised by 'closure' such that network members are linked to one another indirectly – through mutual acquaintances – as well as through direct acquaintance (Coleman 1988). Because they are, consequently, not dependent on any single source of information about one another, it becomes more difficult for any one of them to violate NORMS without risking damage to a number of their relationships, and this disincentive increases trust within the network. This elevated net level of trust operates as 'social capital', allowing network members to engage in more extensive EXCHANGE PROCESSES that are also more profitable because they avoid costlier methods for ensuring norm compliance. Though the concept of social capital has been applied to a wide range of phenomena, critics have argued that in the process it has been overextended and has lost the definitional precision of Coleman's earlier conception (Baron, Field and Schuller 2000). *NE*

Baron, S., Field, J. and Schuller, T. (eds) 2000: *Social Capital: Critical Perspectives.* Oxford: Oxford University Press. Coleman, J. 1988: Social capital in the creation of human capital. *American Journal of Sociology* 94/Supplement, S95–S120.

social categorisation Given that people apply social as well as other kinds of categories to their experience, various predictions have been derived from cognitive tendencies inherent in the process of categorisation, particularly those of ASSIMILATION (see s. 4 and s. 6) and contrast. Categorisation imposes discontinuities on qualities of experience that are not naturally discontinuous. Thus skin colour varies on a continuum, but categorising people as black or white imposes an arbitrary division on this continuum. Assimilation is the tendency to exaggerate similarities within categories; contrast is the corresponding tendency to exaggerate differences across category boundaries, and this applies to social as well as other kinds of categorisation (Tajfel 1981). However, because descriptive social categorisation additionally implicates the SELF (see also s. 1 and s. 4) as member of at least one of the categories, it has additional consequences, for example, inducing corresponding evaluative and behavioural categorisations (Doise 1978). Such categorisation effects form important elements in SOCIAL IDENTITY THEORY and SELF-CATEGORISATION THEORY. [See also STEREOTYPES] *NE*

Doise, W. 1978: *Groups and Individuals: Explanations in Social Psychology.* Cambridge: Cambridge University Press. Tajfel, H. 1981: *Human Groups and Social Categories.* Cambridge: Cambridge University Press.

social cognition Social cognition is a relatively recent development in social psychology. It studies the processes involved in the construal of one's social environment where behaviours have to take place. Three periods can be distinguished, each prioritising a different research focus.

In the first period, researchers were especially interested in MEMORY (see s. 1). The classic IMPRESSION FORMATION paradigm belongs to this period, but researchers also sought to understand other aspects of how people access and retrieve knowledge about individuals and groups, and how this knowledge is represented in memory. Many studies were conducted on the encoding of inconsistent information. It was shown that performance varied with the kind of target. While inconsistent information was better remembered when this concerned individuals, consistent information was better encoded for groups. Because individuals are expected to behave coherently, inconsistent information about a specific person attracts attention and needs elaborative work to be integrated into a person-SCHEMA (see s. 3). This is not the case for groups composed of very different individuals for whom incongruence can be expected. As for representation of social information in memory, researchers are inclined to view it as different nodes that are linked or not, depending on the relation between the nodes. For some researchers, activation of a node automatically activates all the other connected nodes. For other investigators, the links between nodes may be excitatory or inhibitory. ILLUSORY CORRELATIONS constitute another example of the role, and deficiency, of (retrieved) memory for social information.

The second period represented social beings as COGNITIVE MISERS. This expression means that people do not use all their cognitive capacities because of laziness. REASONING (see s. 3) was the main centre of interest of this period. The misuse of different HEURISTICS (see s. 3) attracted particular attention. [See also ATTRIBUTION] Heuristics are rules of thumb used by laypersons to solve inferential tasks. These rules are not necessarily misleading, but need little effort. However, when misapplied, they can generate significant errors. People tend to rely on what comes most easily to mind (heuristic of ACCESSIBILITY – see s. 3); they are unduly influenced by immediately preceding information that is irrelevant (anchoring); and they too often think that similarity is synonymous to equivalence (representativeness). Besides undue reliance on heuristics, people also, perhaps too readily, trust implicit personality theories [see IMPLICIT PERSONALITY THEORY], such as in the case of the CORRESPONDENCE BIAS, as well as salient information. Thus, a single but vivid case can be more powerful than a mountain of statistics. Moreover, whenever people have to determine another's PERSONALITY (see s. 1 and s. 6), they seek out information that confirms their initial HYPOTHESIS (see s. 3 and s. 8). [See CONFIRMATORY BIAS] The cognitive miser perspective also led to a renewed interest in STEREOTYPES, which were considered the lazy device *par excellence* for describing members of social, and particularly stigmatised, groups.

Excluded during the cognitive miser era, MOTIVATION (see s. 6) reappeared during a third period in which individuals came to be conceived of as MOTIVATED TACTICIANS (Fiske and Taylor 1991). People may often reason inadequately and accept unduly a spurious correlation. However, when personally engaged, they will 'regain' their reasoning capacities. Such a phenomenon has been called motivated reasoning (Kunda 1999). Here is an example. A black physician bringing good news will be remembered as a physician; if the news is bad, it is the colour of the skin that will remain in memory. The reintroduction of motivation allowed new investigations of motivated reasoning (Kunda 1999), instances of which include use of more demanding reasoning processes when these provide better support for a personally desired conclusion. It also made it possible to reinterpret or further refine the implications of early studies from the cognitive miser era. Trying to confirm one's belief in an interview is not necessarily an error. On the contrary, when the belief is correct, a confirming approach by interviewees is preferable to a diagnostic one. When motivated to do so, people take situational cues into account and do not fall prey to the correspondence bias. Individuals do not always use category-based judgements to describe a target likely to be stereotyped. If there is sufficient motivation, if the information concerning the target is inconsistent and if cognitive resources are available to process this inconsistent information, perceivers will generate a more complex profile. The tactician metaphor also means that people think, feel and behave so that their interactions with other persons will be as rewarding as possible for them. For instance, systematically ignoring the tennis performances of one's best friend is a perceived means to retain their friendship and to avoid a competitor.

From its beginning, the most innovative import of social cognition may be the distinction between AUTOMATIC (see s. 3) and controlled processes. [See AUTOMATICITY] Social cognition allowed testing of the unconscious in EXPERIMENTS (see s. 8). It showed that judgements and behaviours are influenced by factors people are unaware of, have forgotten or do not consider plausible causes. Here are examples of these three possibilities. Without being aware of it, participants are first confronted with visual information or primes (e.g. faces of whites and blacks) presented subliminally; they then have to react as quickly as possible to clearly visible stimuli (e.g. positive and negative words). Usually, people will react faster to positive words after a white prime and to negative words after a black one than to a negative word after a white face and a positive word following a black prime (Leyens et al. 1994). Differences of REACTION TIMES (see s. 3) in such a procedure have become a classic measure of implicit racism. An instance of FORGETTING (see s. 3) is that people spontaneously infer the PERSONALITY TRAITS (see s. 6) of a target when reading the different behaviours of various targets. The third example is the rebound effect. When asked not to think about stereotypes of a specific group, people control their thoughts and comply, but after the interdiction is removed they unconsciously stereotype more than a CONTROL GROUP (see s. 8). [See IRONIC PROCESS] Obviously, most behaviours are neither completely AUTOMATIC (see s. 3) nor totally controlled and can be influenced at either or both levels (Chaiken and Trope 1999). To disentangle the automatic and controlled components of behaviours, a useful method has been developed by cognitive psychologist, Larry Jacoby (1991). (See also s. 4, SOCIAL COGNITION)

J-PL

Chaiken, S. and Trope, Y. 1999: *Dual-Process theories in Social Psychology.* New York: Guilford. **Fiedler, K. and Walther, E.** 2004: *Stereotyping as Inductive Hypothesis Testing.* Hove: Psychology Press. **Fiske, S. T. and Taylor, S. E.** 1991: *Social Cognition* (2nd edn). New York: McGraw-Hill (see also 1st edn, 1984, published by Addison Wesley). **Jacoby, L. L.** 1991: A process dissociation framework: separating automatic from intentional uses of memory. *Journal of Memory and Language* 30, 513–41. **Kunda, Z.** 1999: *Social Cognition. Making Sense of People.* Cambridge MA: MIT. **Leyens, J.-P., Yzerbyt, V. and Schadron, G.** 1994: *Stereotypes and Social Cognition.* London: Sage.

social communication view (of emotional expression) View that facial expressions of EMOTION (see s. 6) are COMMUNICATIONS (see s. 2) to an audience serving the social goals of the communicator and therefore likely to vary with context rather more than with internal emotional state (sometimes contrasted with the DIRECT READ-OUT VIEW).

NE

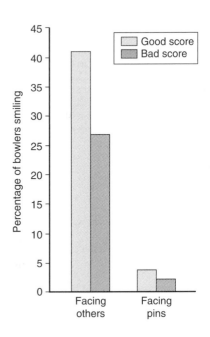

social communication view (of emotional expression) *Smiling from bowlers while facing the pins or other people with a good or bad score. Score matters little, but few bowlers smile while facing the pins. Source: John Sabini, Social Psychology, W. W. Norton & Co, 1992. (Data from R. E. Kraut & R. E. Johnston, 'Social and emotional messages of smiling' in Journal of Personality and Social Psychology, 45, 1979.)*

social comparison Refers to relating one's own characteristics to those of other real or imagined individuals and vice versa. Current theorising and research on social comparison can be traced to the pivotal paper on reference groups by Hyman (1942), who showed that the assessment of one's own status on such dimensions as financial position, intellectual capabilities and physical attractiveness, is dependent on the group with whom one compares oneself. It was, however, Festinger (1954) who coined the term 'social comparison' and theorised that when no objective standards are available, individuals will assess the validity of their OPINIONS and ABILITIES (see s. 6) by comparing these with those of others, and that in the case of abilities, there is an unidirectional drive upward, in that people tend to compare themselves with others doing better (upward comparisons).

In the first decades after the formulation of the theory, research on social comparison was relatively scarce, with a major focus on the factors determining the choice, particularly of upward comparison targets. Later, attention shifted towards the effects of social comparison, especially stimulated by Wills' (1981) now-classic paper on downward comparison theory; Wills argued that in situations producing a decrease in well-being, individuals will often compare with others who are thought to be worse off (downward comparisons) in an effort to improve their well-being, particularly when instrumental action is not possible. Further stimulated by work on cancer patients by Shelley Taylor and her colleagues, this paper led to an upsurge of research on social comparison processes among victimised populations, and eventually to recognition that in such populations upward comparisons may also contribute to COPING (see s. 7) by providing positive role models, and giving inspiration and hope.

Over the past decades, social comparison theory has undergone numerous transitions and reformulations, and has developed into a lively and varied area of research encompassing many different approaches, including basic work relating to social comparison to, among others, SOCIAL COGNITION (see also s. 4), social judgement, SOCIAL IDENTITY THEORY, EVOLUTIONARY PSYCHOLOGY (see s. 2 and s. 1, EVOLUTION AND PSYCHOLOGY), physiological processes and PERSONALITY (see s. 1 and s. 6), and applied work examining social comparison in relation to, among others, risk perception, EATING DISORDERS (see s. 7), advertising, coping with STRESS (see s. 7) and diseases, DEPRESSION (see s. 7) and SOCIAL JUSTICE (Buunk and Gibbons 1997; Suls and Wheeler 2000).   *BB*

Buunk, B. P. and Gibbons, F. X. (eds) 1997: *Health, Coping and Well-Being: Perspectives from Social Comparison Theory.* Hillsdale NJ: Erlbaum. **Festinger, L.** 1954: A theory of social comparison processes. *Human Relations* 7, 117–40. **Hyman, H.** 1942: The psychology of subjective status. *Psychological Bulletin* 39, 473–4. **Suls, J. and Wheeler, L.** 2000: *Handbook of Social Comparison: Theory and Research.* New York: Kluwer Academic. **Wills, T. A.** 1981: Downward comparison principles in social psychology. *Psychological Bulletin* 90, 245–71.

social constructivism   Theoretical framework treating CULTURES (see also s. 1) and moral systems as no more than arbitrary agreements among groups of individuals.
                                                    NE

social dominance theory   A theory of phenomena of oppression and DISCRIMINATION, attributing these to the tendency for human societies to be structured around 'group-based social hierarchies' (Sidanius and Pratto 1999: 31). Sidanius and Pratto argue that age- and gender-based hierarchies will be universal, but those based on 'arbitrary-set' (socially defined categories such as class, caste and ETHNICITY (see s. 1, ETHNICITY AND RACE ISSUES)) will arise in societies producing substantial and sustainable economic surplus. Arbitrary-set hierarchies are expected to produce more violent oppression, the degree of which will be a function of the COUNTERBALANCING (see s. 8) effect of hierarchy-attenuating forces and ideologies [see IDEOLOGY]. The processes through which social dominance occurs will include the aggregate effects of individual and institutional discrimination, regulated by legitimising myths (sets of beliefs that explain as natural the privileged position of a dominant group). Social dominance orientation as a TRAIT (see s. 6) reflects the degree to which an individual values non-egalitarian relationships among social groups such that certain among them are legitimately dominant over others.   *NE*

Sidanius, J. and Pratto, F. 1999: *Social Dominance: An Intergroup Theory of Social Hierarchy and Oppression.* Cambridge: Cambridge University Press.

social facilitation   Others' mere presence was originally thought to have non-specific arousal effects that enhance performance of tasks requiring well-learned responses but disrupt performance when the task requires non-dominant responses (Zajonc 1965). Subsequent research has confirmed the robustness of the effect, but indicates it is not large and may have other explanations.

social facilitation *To take advantage of social facilitation, practise alone and perform with an audience.*

The EVALUATION APPREHENSION explanation is that an audience is arousing because of a learned association of audience presence with evaluation leading to reward or punishment. A related explanation is that performers will divert some ATTENTION (see s. 3) from the task to the audience to check for evaluative feedback; the resulting attention conflict is arousing and benefits well-learned tasks (that tend to be automatised) [see AUTOMATICITY], but consumes cognitive resources, which is detrimental to performance of tasks that are not automatised (but see Huguet et al. 1999). *NE*

Huguet, P., Galvaing, M., Monteil, J.-M. and Dumas, F. 1999: Social presence effects in the Stroop task: further evidence for an attentional view of social facilitation. *Journal of Personality and Social Psychology* 77, 1011–25. **Zajonc, R.** 1965: Social facilitation. *Science* 149, 269–74.

social identity theory (SIT)   THEORY (see s. 8) that people, to an important degree, derive a sense of who they are and thus of their own worth (self-esteem) from the groups they belong to (Tajfel and Turner 1986). [See also SELF-CONCEPT and IDENTITY] Applied to INTER-GROUP RELATIONS, it explains DISCRIMINATION against OUT-GROUPS as the consequence of social competition for group status; the IN-GROUP and thus the SELF (see also s. 1) identified with it can only be seen positively *relative to* some outgroup. The classic study showed that individuals will display favouritism even towards meaningless in-groups [see MINIMAL GROUPS] in order to make these 'positively distinctive' in comparison to out-groups, and will do so even at the expense of in-group benefit in absolute terms. A central question for SIT, therefore, is how individuals respond to membership of low-prestige groups. However, it is not clear that need for self-esteem is the basic MOTIVATION (see s. 6) for social identification, and other motives, such as a search for meaning, may be more significant (see Brown 2000). The theory has proved extremely fertile in shedding light on a range of phenomena as well as inspiring new theoretical developments (e.g. SELF-CATEGORISATION THEORY and SPEECH ACCOMMODATION THEORY). *NE*

Brown, R. 2000: Social identity theory, past achievements, current problems, and future challenges. *European Journal of Social Psychology* 30, 745–78. **Tajfel, H. and Turner, J.** 1986: An integrative theory of social conflict. In Worchel, S. and Austin, W. (eds) *Psychology of Intergroup Relations*. Chicago IL: Nelson Hall.

social impact theory   A theory that SOCIAL INFLUENCE is a function of three features of the influence source: strength (e.g. perceived SOCIAL STATUS, EXPERTISE (see s. 3) relative to the target), immediacy (proximity to the target of influence or RECENCY (see s. 3) of target's exposure) and size (number of people making up the source relative to the target POPULATION – see s. 8) (Latane and Wolf 1981). The theory provides a single-process explanation of the influence of both majorities and minorities [see MAJORITY/MINORITY], proposing that numerical minority sources may be influential sometimes by virtue of their power and/or immediacy, despite lack of size. Regarding size, the theory postulates a negatively accelerating POWER FUNCTION (see s. 3); progressive increments in size do not lead to proportional increases in impact. The theory has also been applied to DIFFUSION OF RESPONSIBILITY and SOCIAL LOAFING, but with respect to social influence has difficulty accounting for the observation that minorities are better able than majorities to stimulate originality (Nemeth and Watchler 1983). *NE*

Latane, B. and Wolf, S. 1981: The social impact of majorities and minorities. *Psychological Review* 88, 438–53. **Nemeth, C. and Watchler, J.** 1983: Creative problem solving as a result of majority versus minority influence. *European Journal of Social Psychology* 13, 45–55.

social influence   Refers to the ways in which the judgements, OPINIONS and ATTITUDES of one person affect the judgements, opinions and attitudes of another person. Although influence can occur between individuals (e.g. LEADERSHIP, PERSUASION), *social* influence is widely seen to operate in the context of social GROUPS, where group members can be the source and recipients of influence from other group members. The aim of social influence is to affect group NORMS that refer to a set of rules and expectations of how people should behave. Norms can either be prescriptive, in that they indicate what behaviours should be performed, or proscriptive, in that they indicate behaviours to be avoided. Norms serve the purpose of helping groups to interact successfully and to avoid group conflict. Three forms of social influence occur within

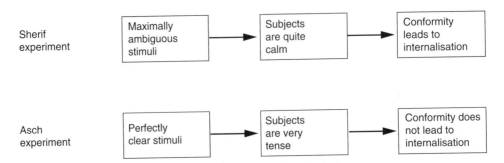

social influence *Comparison of Sherif and Asch experiments. Different stimuli lead to different reactions in subjects and a difference in whether the conformity is compliance or internalisation. From Social Psychology by John Sabini. Copyright © 1992 by John Sabini. Used by permission of W. W. Norton & Company, Inc.*

groups that serve the function of formation (normalisation), maintaining (social control) or changing (social change) group norms.

The first studies of social influence focused on how the opinions of group members converge to form a group norm. In a series of studies, Sherif (1936) asked groups of participants to judge the motion of a stationary dot of light which, in a darkened environment and with no frame of reference, appears to oscillate (known as the autokinetic effect). These studies showed that over a series of judgements, the judgements of group members tended to converge on a similar group judgement and that this judgement became a frame of reference for future judgements when people were outside the group. In ambiguous situations, where there is no norm for behaviour, people rely on other people's judgements to guide their own behaviour. The formation of group norms comes from the interaction between group members and the movement towards an accepted group position.

The dominant form of social control is CONFORMITY, that is, the process through which people accept (or comply with) the group's view. Since this examines how an individual conforms to the group, it is often referred to as majority influence. Unlike the process of normalisation, conformity refers to situations where group members change their opinions and attitudes to the majority position, and this can cause considerable conflict. This process is demonstrated in a series of studies by Asch (1951), where groups of participants took part in a line judgement task in which there was an objectively correct response. Several of the participants (the majority) were instructed to give the same wrong response. Faced with a majority opinion that was different from their own, many participants agreed with the erroneous majority. These studies show the power of the majority to make people conform to its position, even if that position is obviously incorrect. However, the change to the majority position was more likely when responses were made in public (and in front of the majority) than in private, showing that people complied with the new position without a real change in their judgements.

Deutsch and Gerard (1955) have suggested two reasons why people conform to a majority. People conform because they believe that a group of people can provide a more accurate judgement of reality than themselves (informational influence). People might reason that 'several pairs of eyes' are better than their own and believe the majority is more accurate than themselves. People also conform because they wish to get positive approval and to be accepted by the group and to avoid being seen as deviant (normative influence). Subsequent research has shown that the extent to which people conform can be increased or decreased by varying the informational or normative value attached to complying with the majority position (Allen 1975).

Another process of social control is OBEDIENCE, whereby individuals obey (often against their FREE WILL (see s. 1)) the requests of another person. Unlike conformity, where people can resist the majority position, obedience refers to situations where people are forced, or given very little choice, to agree with a particular position. Obedience is most likely to occur when the person requesting obedience is perceived to be in a position of legitimate authority, and therefore they are able to exert social POWER to

force people to believe something or to act in a certain way. Research by Milgram (1974) has shown that people will often obey the requests of a person in authority even if they believe that their behaviours could cause physical harm to someone else (for a review, see Blass 2000). For obedience to occur there must be some 'binding' factors between the authority figure and the recipient of influence that link them together in a particular ROLE relationship. In this relationship the recipient of influence enters an agentic state in that they believe they are acting as an agent for the authority figure and therefore they are not responsible for the outcomes of their behaviour.

Processes of social change typically originate from a small subsection of members of the group and therefore the process is often referred to as minority influence. [See MAJORITY/MINORITY] Since minorities lack status and power, they are unable to exert conformity to their position in the way that majorities can. According to Moscovici (1976, 1980), minorities need to adopt a particular behavioural style that shows it is committed and confident of its position and that it is a legitimate alternative to the group norm. By making people question the group norm, the minority position can become considered and this can lead to the group norm being changed. Unlike conformity, which can result in public compliance without genuine private change in opinions and attitudes, minorities can bring about conversion to their position which results in an enduring change in private (Wood, Lundgren, Ouellette, Busceme and Blackstone 1994).

Theories of social influence focus upon different processes involved in majority and minority influence, based, to differing extents, upon the concepts of informational and normative influence (Martin and Hewstone 2003). However, challenges to the dual-process theories emphasise the role of shared SOCIAL IDENTITY between the source and recipient of influence as being crucial for social influence to occur (Turner 1991).   *RM/PM*

Allen, V. L. 1975: Social support for nonconformity. In Berkowitz, L. (ed.) *Advances in Experimental Social Psychology.* New York: Academic Press, vol. 8, 1–43. **Asch, S. E.** 1951: Effects of group pressure upon the modification and distortion of judgments. In Guetzhow, H. (ed.) *Groups, Leadership, and Men.* Pittsburgh PA: Carnegie Press, 177–90. **Blass, T.** (ed.) 2000: *Obedience to Authority: Current Perspectives on the Milgram Paradigm.* Mahwah NJ: Lawrence Erlbaum Associates. **Deutsch, M. and Gerard, H. G.** 1955: A study of normative and informational social influence upon individual judgment. *Journal of Abnormal and Social Psychology* 51, 629–36. **Martin, R. and Hewstone, M.** 2003: Social influence processes of control and change: conformity, obedience to authority, and innovation. In Hogg, M. A. and Cooper, J. (eds) *Sage Handbook of Social Psychology.* London: Sage, 347–66. **Milgram, S.** 1974: *Obedience to Authority: An Experimental View.* New York: Harper & Row. **Moscovici, S.** 1976: *Social Influence and Social Change.* London: Academic Press. **Moscovici, S.** 1980: Toward a theory of conversion behavior. In Berkowitz, L. (ed.) *Advances in Experimental Social Psychology.* New York: Academic Press, vol. 13, 209–39. **Sherif, M.** 1936: *The Psychology of Social Norms.* New York: Harper. **Turner, J. C.** 1991: *Social Influence.* Milton Keynes: Open University Press. **Wood, W., Lundgren, S., Ouellette, J. A., Busceme, S. and Blackstone, T.** 1994: Minority influence: a meta-analytic review of social influence processes. *Psychological Bulletin* 115, 323–45.

social justice Justice means that people get what they deserve, or are entitled to, on the basis of who they are and what they have done. Social psychology's focus is on the subjective sense of justice and injustice and its impact on human action and judgement. Social psychologists study what people regard as just and unjust under given circumstances, how they react to situations that they regard as unjust, and under which circumstances, and why, people care about justice. Social psychology mainly deals with two different kinds of justice, distributive and procedural.

DISTRIBUTIVE JUSTICE refers to the perceived justice of the distribution of goods and benefits, but also burdens, obligations and punishments (Törnblom 1992), the basic notion being that people evaluate distribution outcomes relative to certain standards or rules rather than in absolute terms. [See also RELATIVE DEPRIVATION] Prominent among these rules are the contribution or equity rule ('to each according to his contributions'), the needs rule ('to each according to his needs') and the equality rule ('to each the same'). Different rules are regarded as just, and serve as principles of action and evaluation, under different circumstances.

PROCEDURAL JUSTICE relates to structural and social aspects of the procedures used in distribution and other decisions that affect people. Relevant criteria for the assessment of procedural justice include: participation of the affected parties in the decision making and the opportunity to express their opinions ('voice'), provision of accounts and explanations for the decision made and treatment of the affected parties with dignity and respect.

Perceiving justice has a variety of positive consequences. It improves people's satisfaction with the outcome they receive, acceptance of decisions and willingness to defer to authorities and cooperate with their group. Reactions to perceived injustice include behavioural attempts to restore justice by means of compensation or retaliation, psychological or cognitive restoration of justice by changing the interpretation of the situation, 'leaving the field' and non-acting or resignation. The subjective nature of justice evaluations allows divergent views about what is just and unjust, and can provoke social conflicts (cf. Mikula and Wenzel 2000). [See also EQUITY THEORY, JUST WORLD BELIEF and SOCIAL COMPARISON]   *GM*

Mikula, G. and Wenzel, M. 2000: Justice and social conflict. *International Journal of Psychology* 35, 126–35. **Miller, D. T.** 2001: Disrespect and the experience of injustice. *Annual Review of Psychology* 52, 527–53. **Törnblom, K.** 1992: The social psychology of distributive justice. In Scherer, K. (ed.) *Justice: Interdisciplinary Perspectives*. Cambridge: Cambridge University Press, 177–236. **Tyler, T. R. and Smith, H. J.** 1998: Social justice and social movement. In Gilbert, D. G., Fiske, S. T. and Lindzey, G. (eds) *The Handbook of Social Psychology* (4th edn). Boston MA: McGraw-Hill, vol. 2, 595–629.

social loafing   The tendency for individuals performing as part of a GROUP to reduce their efforts, especially when individual contributions are difficult to identify and there is no clear standard against which to compare overall group performance.   *NE*

social network   The pattern of connections linking people in a population. Social network theorists (e.g. Boissevain 1974) have emphasised connections based on personal acquaintance. Interest in social networks, developed partly as a critical response to the 'mass society thesis', that social life in the modern world is more likely to be ordered around impersonal social ROLES and social categories than on the basis of personal RELATIONSHIPS [see also SOCIAL CAPITAL], has reflected evidence that the pattern of personal links between people sheds light on a range of social phenomena, including occupational mobility, SOCIAL SUPPORT effects on health, PERSON PERCEPTION, coalition formation, SOCIAL INFLUENCE and innovation (Wasserman and Faust 1994). A key quality of social networks with respect to many of these phenomena is that normally only a minority of the theoretically possible connections in a population actually exist [see also NETWORK DENSITY]; effectively, many people have friends and acquaintances who are not themselves mutually acquainted, with the result that they are linked indirectly to friends of their friends. This is the basis for the SMALL-WORLD PHENOMENON.   *NE*

Boissevain, J. 1974: *Friends of Friends*. Oxford: Blackwell. **Wasserman, S. and Faust, K.** 1994: *Social Network Analysis: Methods and Applications*. Cambridge: Cambridge University Press.

social representation   Serge Moscovici (1961), expanding on Durkheim's concept of collective representations, developed a THEORY (see s. 8) of the production and elaboration of knowledge as social representation. In his seminal work on PSYCHOANALYSIS (see s. 1, PSYCHOANALYSIS AND RELATED SCHOOLS), Moscovici suggested that when a conceptual scientific framework (i.e. psychoanalysis) becomes an object of COMMUNICATION (see s. 2) and influence, it is transformed into a representation (see also Deaux and Philogene 2001).

Social representation involves two cognitive systems, an operational system that performs the basic cognitive operations (i.e. categorisations, associations, inclusions, DISCRIMINATIONS, deductions, etc.) and a meta-system, characterised by the social regulations of SOCIETY or CULTURE (see s. 1), guiding these operations by controlling, verifying and selecting informational content according to rules, both logical and otherwise. Two processes shape social representations: objectification transforms abstract concepts into concrete images, and anchoring labels new knowledge and classifies it into familiar frameworks. These processes operate within the meta-system to translate the social regulations and guide the cognitive operations (Lorenzi-Cioldi and Clemence 2001). Social representations are not individual mental activities but collective elaborations of knowledge and result from processes of SOCIAL INFLUENCE and communication.

The functions of social representations are:

1) To allow communication to take place, since it is important to have a common basis of shared knowledge to communicate.

2) To make the unfamiliar familiar and help people deal with novelty. When faced with unfamiliar events, people make sense of them by transforming abstract ideas into concrete images and by incorporating the new knowledge into familiar frameworks.

3) To 'locate' people within a social system. The fact that social representations are shared does not mean that each individual holds exactly the same views. It means

that the organisation of individual knowledge is influenced by common principles. According to Doise (1992), what differentiates people's positions are their other beliefs and VALUES (psychological anchoring), their different understandings of social regulations and experience of POWER asymmetries (social psychological anchoring), and their membership of different GROUPS (sociological anchoring).

The theory concerns both the processes that produce knowledge and the content of this knowledge. Social representations constitute the framework of people's worldviews, which helps them give meaning to their environment and guides their practices.   *XC*

Deaux, K. and Philogene, G. (eds) 2001: *Representations of the Social.* Oxford: Blackwell. **Doise, W.** 1992: L'ancrage sur les études sur les représentations sociales. *Bulletin de Psychologie* 405, 189–95. **Lorenzi-Cioldi, F. and Clemence, A.** 2001: Group processes and the construction of social representations. In Hogg, M. A. and Tindale, R. S. (eds) *Blackwell Handbook of Social Psychology: Group Processes.* Oxford: Blackwell, 311–33. **Moscovici, S.** 1961: *La Psychanalyse son image et son public.* Paris: Presses Universitaires de France.

social skill Argyle (1983) proposed that there is a direct analogy in social interaction to the motor SKILLS (see s. 3) underpinning physical action. Social skills, he argued, refer to the bodily movements supporting coherent face-to-face interaction. These can include the AUTOMATIC (see s. 3) gaze shifts accompanying conversation and supporting turn-taking, or the use of gestures, space and facial expressions to initiate and terminate interactions or regulate desired levels of intimacy. The point is that the skilled social performer does not have to think about what to do to achieve these ends; the necessary actions occur automatically. [See AUTOMATICITY] But, like motor skills, they must first be learned (and can be trained), and some performers achieve a higher level of proficiency than others. Argyle also anticipated that poorly developed social skills are at the root of difficulties in forming or developing close RELATIONSHIPS with others.   *NE*

Argyle, M. 1983: *The Psychology of Interpersonal Behaviour* (4th edn). Harmondsworth: Penguin.

social status The sociological analysis of status has tended to focus on stratification systems, such as class, and their consequences for the distribution of political power and material wealth. In contrast, social psychological interest has historically focused on subjective estimates of status based on comparisons with others (Hyman 1942) [See also SOCIAL COMPARISON] and on the fact that so many of the details of people's behaviour in face-to-face interactions are predicated on their relative social status. These include non-verbal behaviour [see NON-VERBAL COMMUNICATION], rules of address signalling the status relation between interactants [see NORMS], speech style (emphasising or de-emphasising status differences) [see SPEECH ACCOMMODATION THEORY] and asymmetry of influence [see LEADERSHIP]. Consequently, status inconsistency, a lack of correspondence in people's relative status positions across different status dimensions, creates significant difficulties for coherent social interaction (Homans 1961). Additionally, because status can be seen both as an invest-

ment and a reward [see also EQUITY THEORY], certain kinds of status inconsistency are associated with feelings of RELATIVE DEPRIVATION.   *NE*

Homans, G. C. 1961: *Social Behaviour: Its Elementary Forms.* London: Routledge. **Hyman, H.** 1942: The psychology of subjective status. *Psychological Bulletin* 39, 473–4.

social support Covers, potentially, the full range of support that individuals receive or believe they receive from other people, but particularly those with whom they have personal ties. Many different forms of social support have been defined and studied (Stroebe and Stroebe 1996), though they tend to fall into three broad categories: emotional, informational and instrumental. But because different kinds of support tend to covary – an individual who has access to one tends to have access to the others – it has been difficult to isolate the specific effects or benefits of one kind rather than another. Effects considered or hypothesised have included enhanced capacity to sustain a minority position [see CONFORMITY], but most interest has been shown in potential effects on health (e.g. Cohen 1988). Here there is some evidence that emotional support is particularly significant, but also that perceived support matters more than actual support. What remains unclear is the mechanism linking social support to health; earlier proposals that the effect of support is primarily to reduce the impact of STRESS (see s. 7) have received less empirical confirmation than a simple direct effect of social support on well-being. [See also PRO-SOCIAL BEHAVIOUR AND RELATIONSHIPS]   *NE*

Cohen, S. 1988: Psychosocial models of the role of social support in the etiology of physical disease. *Health Psychology* 7, 269–97. **Stroebe, W. and Stroebe, M.** 1996: The social psychology of social support, in Higgins, E. T. and Kruglanski, A. (eds) *Social Psychology: Handbook of Basic Principles*: New York: Guilford, 597–621.

society A collective enterprise within which complete lives can be lived. Many kinds of collective enterprise engage the individual partially, temporarily and sometimes regularly, but not normally totally from birth to death. This being so, society can be thought of as the totality of prevailing social arrangements and conditions in which lives are embedded. The concept of society forms a backdrop for social psychology, but it is rarely analysed directly, or even defined with any precision. Reference to 'human society' is typically made to highlight something distinctive about the social conditions of human lives as compared to those of other social animals. But more often 'society' serves as a summary term for the entire set of political, economic and interpersonal structures that surround, define and influence particular populations of individuals. Used in this way, it carries the connotation of boundaries and contrasts in conditions of life, sometimes made explicit by a qualifying adjective, as in 'British', 'tribal', 'industrialised' and 'nineteenth-century', used singly or in combination. [See also CULTURE]   *NE*

sociometer hypothesis The hypothesis that SELF-ESTEEM acts as a barometer of the state of one's RELATIONSHIPS with others and alerts the individual to possible social exclusion.   *NE*

sociometry A method to assess the structure of sentiments or personal RELATIONSHIPS within a GROUP; each member nominates, for example, their three best friends in the group. *NE*

speech accommodation theory (SAT) Theory that individuals use LANGUAGE (see s. 2) to achieve a desired social distance between SELF (see also s. 1 and s. 4) and others. The principle strategies to achieve this are convergence and divergence. SAT preceded from the observation that speakers, often unconsciously, adjust their speaking style towards (convergence) or away from (divergence) that of those they are speaking with, and that such adjustments have effects on the others' perceptions of the speaker (e.g. as more or less friendly). The aspects of style liable to adjustment in this way include, among others, accent, speech rate, dialect use and utterance length. In so far as these aspects of speech express or indicate social identity [see SOCIAL IDENTITY THEORY], their degree of similarity or difference between speakers marks the extent to which they do or do not share social identities. A more recent modification of SAT, communication accommodation theory (Shepard, Giles and Le Poire 2001), underlines that any aspect of face-to-face COMMUNICATION (see s. 2), including NON-VERBAL COMMUNICATION, may be manipulated to negotiate social distance. *NE*

Giles, H. 1973: Accent mobility: a model and some data. *Anthropological Linguistics* 15, 87–109. **Shepard, C., Giles, H. and Le Poire, B.** 2001: Communication accommodation theory. In Robinson, W. and Giles, H. (eds) *The New Handbook of Language and Social Psychology*. Chichester: Wiley.

stereotypes Shared BELIEFS about characteristics typifying categories of people, normally containing or implying evaluative judgements. Early views treated stereotypes as oversimplified, inaccurate representations based on limited knowledge of the target category, stemming from faulty thinking characteristic of particular types of people, and producing prejudice and DISCRIMINATION. Modern views challenge almost all these suppositions (Oakes et al. 1994).

Given that people have stereotypes of social categories with which they are very familiar, including those to which they themselves belong, it seems unlikely that these are merely substitutes for accurate knowledge. Thus one empirically well-supported view treats STEREOTYPING (see s. 1) as a direct and natural consequence of categorisation itself (Taylor 1981). The simplification involved in dividing the social world into categories in turn contributes to cognitive efficiency. [See also SOCIAL

CATEGORISATION] This 'cognitive economy' (or COGNITIVE MISER) view is also supported by evidence that stereotypes can be activated automatically, particularly when individuals are otherwise cognitively 'loaded' or busy. [See AUTOMATICITY].

Stereotypes have additionally been regarded as convenient guides to interaction, particularly when others can be rapidly categorised in relation to the SELF (see also s. 1 and s. 4) on the basis of highly visible personal features, such as sex, RACE (see s. 1, ETHNICITY AND RACE ISSUES) and age. This also bears on the accuracy issue; by guiding behavioural reactions to others, stereotypes can operate as self-fulfilling prophecies [see SELF-FULFILLING PROPHECY], creating the very attributes, both in self and others, that they supposedly anticipate. This parallels an interpretation of stereotypes as 'hypotheses' about social categories with a built-in CONFIRMATORY BIAS. [See also ILLUSORY CORRELATION]

An argument against the conclusion that negative stereotypes must inevitably lead to negative reactions, particularly discrimination, proposes that stereotypes are 'in the CULTURE' (see also s. 1) to the extent that we have some familiarity with their content without necessarily personally accepting them as true (Devine 1989). Other evidence, however, shows that stereotype content often changes rapidly when INTER-GROUP RELATIONS change, indicating they can also serve political-economic and ideological functions. Thus, advocates of REALISTIC GROUP CONFLICT THEORY argue that contrasting IN-GROUP/OUT-GROUP stereotypes serve to strengthen in-group solidarity, sharpen group boundaries and justify hostility towards a competitor out-group. Stereotype content can also legitimise the disadvantaged position of particular groups within one's own SOCIETY. [See also JUST WORLD BELIEFS] *NE*

Devine, P. G. 1989: Stereotypes and prejudice: their automatic and controlled components. *Journal of Personality and Social Psychology* 51, 629–36. **Oakes, P. J., Haslam, S. A. and Turner, J. C.** 1994: *Stereotyping and Social Reality*. Oxford: Blackwell. **Taylor, S. E.** 1981: A categorization approach to stereotyping. In Hamilton, D. L. (ed.) *Cognitive Processes in Stereotyping and Intergroup Behaviour*. Hillsdale NJ: Erlbaum, 88–114.

strategic interaction An interaction in which those involved, having conflicting interests, seek to influence one another to maximise their own outcomes. *NE*

subtle racism The expression of racist sentiment non-verbally, of interest because it can often characterise people who verbally endorse racial equality. *NE*

T

terror management theory Theory that humans, by virtue of capacity for awareness of their own mortality and the precariousness of life, are liable to overwhelming ANXIETY (see s. 6), the possibility of which they must manage in various ways (Solomon, Greenberg and Pyszczynski 1991). The principal management technique is commitment to a 'cultural world-view' that ascribes value to the individual adopting it. Circumstances increasing mortality salience induce punitive treatment of deviants and members of OUT-GROUPS because such people threaten the world-view on which terror management depends. The theory was first advanced as an account of people's need for SELF-ESTEEM, which was argued to provide protection against the anxiety otherwise aroused by awareness of mortality. *NE*

Solomon, S., Greenberg, J. and Pyszczynski, T. 1991: Terror management theory of social behaviour: the psychological functions of self-esteem and cultural world views. In Zanna, M. P. (ed.) *Advances in Experimental Social Psychology*. San Diego CA: Academic Press, vol. 24, 93–159.

T-group A procedure to train awareness of GROUP dynamics through unstructured group interactions. *NE*

Thurstone scaling Method for measuring ATTITUDES that seeks to identify specific OPINION statements to represent distinct numerical positions on a scale. *NE*

tit-for-tat A successful strategy in iterated versions of the PRISONER'S DILEMMA game, based on initial cooperation and then repetition of the other player's previous move; seen as significant to understanding the evolution of COOPERATION. *NE*

tragedy of the commons A situation in which rational pursuit of self-interest ultimately destroys a collective resource. [See also COOPERATION.] *NE*

transactional/transformational leadership A distinction (e.g. Bass 1998) between individuals who treat LEADERSHIP as primarily a matter of 'transactions', with followers to control their behaviour and correct errors in their performance, and those who augment this approach through a more transformational style. This latter has been defined in terms of charisma and communicating an inspiring vision, one that 'transforms' the mental framework of followers. Transformational leaders are expected to be more effective at motivating followers to work for the good of the group. *NE*

Bass, B. 1998: *Transformational Leadership: Industrial, Military and Educational Impact*. Hillsdale NJ: Erlbaum.

U

ultimate attribution error Causal attribution biased by in-group membership, such that positive in-group actions are over-attributed to internal causes, negative to external, and vice versa for out-group actions.

NE

V

---

validation process In SOCIAL INFLUENCE, cognitive activity directed at evaluating a persuasive message rather than its source. [See also MAJORITY/MINORITY]   *NE*

values General and abstract/ultimate goals that motivate action and that may also underpin more specific ATTITUDES. Values have also been defined as the general criteria against which actions, policies, people and states of affairs are judged (Schwartz 1992). Schwartz argues that values address three basic requirements of human existence: the needs of individuals as biological entities, the requirements of coordinated social interaction and the survival of human GROUPS or SOCIETIES [see SOCIETY]. From this analysis he derives ten value types expected to be universally endorsed, and provides extensive empirical support for this expectation. Differences between CULTURES (see also s. 1), he argues, exist not in their values so much as in the relative priority they give to each, particularly when values are in conflict with one another. Other work (e.g. Maio and Olson 1998) suggests values are akin to truisms; people endorse them unthinkingly, seldom examining their reasons for doing so, and such reasons are often lacking.   *NE*

Maio, G. and Olson, J. 1998: Values as truisms: evidence and implications. *Journal of Personality and Social Psychology* 74, 294–311. **Schwartz, S.** 1992: Universals in the content and structure of values: theoretical advances and empirical tests in 20 countries. In Zanna, M. (ed.) *Advances in Experimental Social Psychology.* New York: Academic Press, vol. 25, 1–65.

W

working consensus Informal agreement between participants in an interaction to accept one another's IDENTITY (see also s. 4) claims. *NE*

Section 6

Personality and Individual Differences

Introduction

Individual differences is more of a sub-discipline of psychology than a content area. Social psychologists may study how people generally behave when evaluating members of minority groups. Cognitive psychologists may study whether priming alters performance on a word-recognition task. Developmental psychologists may research how and when children become able to imagine something from another person's point of view. Perceptual psychologists may use information gleaned from visual illusions to determine how the visual system encodes information. All of these diverse branches of psychology focus on how people typically behave: data analysis typically involves comparing means between different conditions, and any person-to-person variation is usually treated as 'error'.

Individual difference psychologists, on the other hand, focus on systematic variations in behaviour from person to person, together with methods for their assessment (psychometrics). Thus rather than investigating whether members of a 'majority group' are viewed more or less favourably than members of a 'minority group', a psychologist studying individual differences may ask whether some people are more prejudiced than others – and develop theories to explain why this may be so. They may explore how and why some people consistently perform better than others on word-recognition tasks, why some children find it hard to view the world through someone else's eyes, and whether some people are more susceptible to visual illusions than others. These two approaches are, of course, complementary. At the very least, experimental psychologists should measure individual differences and treat them as covariates, as this will increase the sensitivity of their experiments by reducing the size of the ANOVA error term.

Individual differences are generally classified as mental (or cognitive) abilities, personality traits, mood states and motivational states, and the branch of statistics that has developed to assess them is known as psychometrics. Although we are inured to the idea, it is still surprising that performance on very diverse tasks should be related as it is difficult to see what cognitive processes are common to these tasks. Some are developed via the education system while others are not ... Whereas ability traits focus on a person's level of performance, personality traits describe their 'personal style'. Several very broad traits have been extensively researched – principally extroversion and neuroticism/anxiety. Several cognitive and biological models have been proposed to explain why people develop a characteristic level of each ability or personality trait: behaviour genetic research shows that family influences are far smaller than anyone suspected. Emotional intelligence – sensitivity in recognising and responding to other people's emotional states – is now being heavily researched.

Mood and motivation are transitory states, rather than enduring characteristics of the person: they thus vary from time to time and situation to situation. They are less well researched than personality or ability – perhaps because they are of less interest to occupational psychologists and other professionals who focus on traits. There is excellent evidence for two main dimensions of mood: positive affect and negative affect, although many authors misunderstand what positive affect is. Motivation is much less well understood, with only two main theories (by Apter and Cattell) focusing on transient motivational states.

Professor Nathan Brody, late of Wesleyan University, gives the following overview of the field.

Individual differences: in 50-year modules

From 1904

It is the centennial of the publication of Spearman's seminal paper on general intelligence. Spearman analysed a correlation matrix derived from relations among measures of sensory discrimination abilities and academic achievements. He assumed that all the relationships he obtained were primarily attributable to a latent trait – general intellectual ability. Contemporary research provides ample support for the presence of a general intellectual ability that is related to academic achievement. General intellectual ability can be assessed in childhood and remains relatively invariant over the lifespan. Recent research based on the Scottish Mental Surveys indicates that intelligence assessed at age 11 is remarkably predictive of intelligence in old age; and contemporary research provides ample support for Spearman's original finding that cognitive abilities are related to academic achievement. We now know that educational achievement, social mobility and even mortality are related to general intellectual abilities that can be assessed early in life. Spearman's g is alive and well!

Spearman's paper is also relevant to contemporary methodological developments. His theory allowed him to derive predictions about the properties of a correlation matrix representing correlations between different measures of intellectual ability. For much of the last century, the analysis of relationships among different individual difference measures initiated by Spearman was based on exploratory methods in which theoretical structures were imposed upon emerging patterns. The last two decades have seen a return to a more Spearmanian conception of multivariate research, in which theoretical assumptions are used to derive expected patterns of relationships among measures. This development permits one to test the 'fit' between theoretically expected patterns and obtained results.

From 1954

In the middle of the last century, Eysenck developed a theoretical integration of research on personality and psychopathology. He argued that there was a limited number of basic personality dimensions (initially two, extroversion and neuroticism) that were related to genetically determined differences in the structure and function of the nervous system. These biological characteristics influenced the response of individuals to the social situations they encountered. Individual difference psychology was a biosocial science reaching from biology to sociology. The last 50 years have provided ample support for this Eysenckian perspective. Taxonomic studies have provided support for the presence of a limited number of basic personality traits (perhaps three or five in number) that are relatively invariant over the adult lifespan of individuals. Behaviour genetic research based on twin and adoption studies has indicated that virtually all individual difference dimensions are heritable. These genotypically influenced traits determine the ways in which individuals respond to the social worlds they encounter.

From 2004

Caspi and his colleagues obtained data relating childhood abuse to the development of antisocial behaviour in adults (Science 2002, 297, 851–4). They found that a gene that regulates monoamine oxidase interacted with a history of childhood abuse to influence the development of antisocial behaviour. Individuals with the gene without the history of abuse were not likely to develop antisocial behaviour. Individuals with the gene who experienced childhood abuse were likely to develop antisocial behaviour. The study provides a model for the extension of the Eysenckian conception of a biosocial individual difference psychology in five ways:

1. *The study is longitudinal, relating experiences in early childhood to adult behaviours.*

2. *The study uses the techniques of molecular genetics to define genotypic characteristics.*

3. *Genotypic variations are related to biological hypotheses.*

4. *Biological reductionism is avoided. In order to understand the development of individual lives it is necessary to study the social experiences encountered by individuals.*

5. *Caspi's studies are based on the analysis of longitudinal data obtained from a population (not a sample) of individuals.*

I think that we shall see more longitudinal studies based on large and representative samples which use molecular genetic techniques to characterise genotypic characteristics of individuals that study the ways in which individuals respond to the social worlds they encounter. The search for genetic X environmental interactions will provide a new foundation for a biosocial science of individuality.

Professor Nathan Brody

Throughout this section on Personality and Individual Differences I have attempted to focus on the *important* issues rather than outdated theories. The face of personality research has changed substantially over the last century. 'Depth psychologies' such as the theories of Freud, Jung, Adler, Horney, etc., have more or less vanished from the mainstream journals because it is frequently difficult to use the scientific method to evaluate their merit, and where such attempts have been made (e.g. the effectiveness of psychoanalysis as a form of therapy), results have not been encouraging. The behaviourist tradition which swept away these theories has also waned, and most contemporary research seeks to understand the processes that cause people to develop different levels of traits such as anxiety or extroversion. This trend is reflected in the content of the encyclopaedia. There is little or no mention of pre-scientific theories, except where they are relevant for clinical practice today; hence terms from Rogers and

Kelly's theories are included, but there is no mention of repression, Oedipal fixation, etc.

Ability research has changed rather less (although some theorists like to give the opposite impression). The annual number of citations of Spearman's 1904 paper on general intelligence is still increasing exponentially, and there is now general agreement on a hierarchical structure of abilities. Interestingly, this model is also entirely consistent with Gardner's work on multiple intelligences, which has proved hugely influential among educators, despite a modest empirical basis. Some other theories have generated a brief flurry of interest before being discarded, Guilford's structure of intellect model being a prime example. Most research attempts to discover what causes some people to develop a particular, characteristic level of some ability (e.g. general ability or verbal ability). Biological models are currently popular, and so we include terms such as 'inspection time' and 'nerve conduction velocity' to reflect the zeitgeist.

Emotional intelligence turns out to have two faces. One deals with the ability to recognise emotion in others – a sort of ability. The other reflects skill and sensitivity when interacting with other people, which more closely resembles a personality trait. However, K. V. Petrides has recently shown that scores on emotional intelligence scales do indeed add something over and above personality scores when predicting emotional sensitivity. Understanding and assessing emotional intelligence is currently an extremely popular topic with both academic psychologists and occupational/industrial practitioners.

The cognitive style literature originated in the 1950s, but has re-emerged because of an interest in attempting to understand the processes that influence student learning. Carol McGuinness has a particular interest in these issues and offers several useful entries.

Mood and motivation research is, however, far less developed. We now know that there are very substantial individual differences in mood variability, some people remaining constant across time and situation while others' moods vary wildly. Chris McConville's research, however, shows that tying this down to personality is no simple matter. Others research day-to-day changes in mood and other cyclical activity. The entries in the encyclopaedia follow what seem to me to be important developments: thus rather than long descriptions of competing models of mood, the focus is on what causes mood to vary. Even less is known about the psychology of motivation. I have included more of Cattell's theory than is customary, if only because this seems to address several important issues. These include identifying a lattice of goals and sub-goals and some 20 basic motivational drives, together with a discussion about how motivation might reveal itself – through physiological responses, depth of knowledge, investment of time and money, and so on. There should be more to motivation research than hastily assembled attitude questionnaires.

Dr Colin Cooper

16PF A family of PERSONALITY QUESTIONNAIRES, developed initially by Raymond B. Cattell and originally intended to measure 16 personality TRAITS. However, several studies showed that the test failed to measure 16 traits, making its use questionable (Barrett and Kline 1982; Mathews 1989). Recent editions may prove more successful (Cattell, Cattell and Cattell 1994; Cattell and King 2000). *CC*

Barrett, P. and Kline, P. 1982: An item and radial parcel factor analysis of the 16PF questionnaire. *Personality and Individual Differences* 3, 259–70. **Cattell, R. B., Cattell, A. K. and Cattell, H. E. P.** 1994: *16PF Fifth Edition Technical Manual.* Urbana IL: Institute for Personality and Ability Testing. **Cattell, R. B. and King, J.** 2000: *16PF Industrial Version* (revised). Henley-on-Thames: The Test Agency. **Mathews, G.** 1989: The factor structure of the 16PF: 12 primary and 3 secondary factors. *Personality and Individual Differences* 10, 931–40.

360-degree appraisal Traditionally, performance appraisal is an evaluation and development exercise carried out by one's manager. 360-degree appraisal is an attempt to broaden this by also obtaining feedback from colleagues and subordinates. Although this broadens the evidence-base, collecting such data can create a significant additional burden. As might be expected, there is, at best, modest consistency between the appraisals given by different types of appraiser (Valle and Bozeman 2002), and negative feedback is often dismissed as being quirky or unreliable (Brett and Atwater 2001). Fletcher, Baldry and Cunningham-Snell (1998) outline the development and refinement of a typical instrument, and draw attention to some methodological issues. *CC*

Brett, J. F. and Atwater, L. E. 2001: 360 degrees feedback: accuracy, reactions, and perceptions of usefulness. *Journal of Applied Psychology* 86, 930–42. **Fletcher, C., Baldry, C. and Cunningham-Snell, N.** 1998: The psychometric properties of 360 degree feedback: an empirical study and a cautionary tale. *International Journal of Selection and Assessment* 6, 19–34. **Valle, M. and Bozeman, D. P.** 2002: Interrater agreement on employees' job performance: review and directions. *Psychological Reports* 90, 975–85.

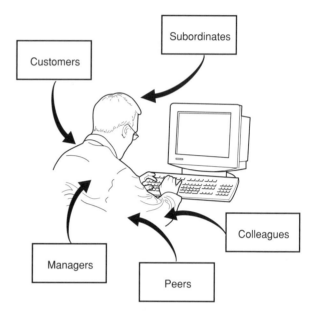

360-degree appraisal *360-degree feedback.*

A

abilities   Abilities reflect how well a person can perform some kind of cognitive operations, administered as a TEST under standard conditions. Although there are potentially an almost infinite number of abilities which could be assessed, the three-stratum model [see ABILITY: THREE-STRATUM MODEL] shows that it is possible to represent these in terms of a great number of PRIMARY MENTAL ABILITIES, several broad SECOND-ORDER ABILITY FACTORS and a FACTOR (see s. 8) of general intelligence, or *g* [see GENERAL ABILITY]. [See also BIAS AND GROUP DIFFERENCES, ABILITY: INDIVIDUAL TESTS OF, ABILITY: GROUP TESTS OF, INSPECTION TIME AND *G*, INTELLIGENCE AND HEALTH, INTELLIGENCE AND OCCUPATIONAL PERFORMANCE, BIOLOGICAL CORRELATES OF ABILITIES, LIFESPAN CHANGES IN ABILITIES, BEHAVIOUR GENETICS OF ABILITIES, the TRIARCHIC THEORY and the WECHSLER SCALES]   *CC*

abilities and cognitive processes   People may vary in the speed with which they can solve problems in ability tests, either because some individuals are faster than others in executing some of these cognitive OPERATIONS (see s. 4), or because some people use more efficient sequences of operations than do others (parallel vs. SERIAL PROCESSING (see s. 3), for example). Earl Hunt's work on verbal ability was designed to test the hypothesis that the speed with which a person can access their internal LEXICON (see s. 3) (i.e. extract the meaning of a letter of the alphabet) underpins verbal ability. Participants pressed one button if pairs of characters were physically identical (AA, bb vs. Ab, bB etc.) and another if they differed. This gave a measure of the time taken to read the letters, compare them, decide which response was appropriate and make the response. Then participants pressed one button if the characters represented the same letter of the alphabet (aA, Bb etc.) and another if not (bA etc.). The difference between these two conditions reflects the time taken to extract the meaning of the letters. Hunt hypothesised that this difference would be related to verbal ability; it was, although the correlations were only in the order of 0.3.

Other endeavours have included Carroll's (Carroll 1983) attempts to draw up a list of elementary cognitive operations, whose involvement in ability tasks could be inferred through correlation and regression analyses, and Sternberg's (Sternberg 1977) ingenious attempts to estimate the durations of cognitive components using regression analyses from tasks involving partial cuing. Neither was particularly successful, and there are probably three main reasons for this. First, it is not clear what constitutes a truly basic cognitive operation – one that proceeds autonomously once initiated, with a certain probability of concluding successfully. At which level should REDUCTIONISM (see s. 1) end? Second, the number of alternative flow charts that could be used to solve even a simple problem is potentially very great, and there is no way of knowing in advance which one a particular individual will use, or even if they use the same one consistently. Finally, this

basic analysis ignores what Sternberg (1985) in his TRIARCHIC THEORY calls metacomponents – the conscious strategies that individuals use when planning how to solve problems and relate them to previously encountered problems and knowledge.   *CC*

Carroll, J. B. 1983: Studying individual differences in cognitive abilities: through and beyond factor analysis. In Dillon, R. F. and Schmeck, R. R. (eds) *Individual Differences in Cognition.* New York: Academic, vol. 1. **Sternberg, R. J.** 1977: *Intelligence, Information Processing and Analogical Reasoning: The Componential Analysis of Human Abilities.* Hillsdale NJ: Erlbaum. **Sternberg, R. J.** 1985: *Beyond IQ.* Cambridge: Cambridge University Press.

ability: group tests of   These are tests of thinking, REASONING (see s. 3), memory, etc. which can be taken by several people at the same time. They are popular in PERSONNEL SELECTION as one psychologist can test a large number of people simultaneously. They usually comprise several sections of between 20 and 200 items, which are often arranged in order of difficulty. Participants are generally asked to solve as many items as possible, usually within a fixed time. Group tests of GENERAL ABILITY (*g*) include Raven's matrices and the Cattell culture-fair tests. Tests of PRIMARY MENTAL ABILITIES include the Ekstrom-French-Harman kit of factor-referenced cognitive tests, and the differential aptitude tests. Each includes example items, so that participants can check that they have understood what to do. However, there are limits to what can be measured using this format (e.g. the time taken to solve individual items; anything involving a response other than in writing, such as singing a note).   *CC*

Most, R. B. and Zeidner, M. 1995: Constructing personality and intelligence instruments: methods and issues. In Saklofske, D. H. and Zeidner, M. (eds) *International Handbook of Personality and Intelligence.* New York: Plenum.

ability: individual tests of   These are highly reliable [see RELIABILITY] tests which are designed to be administered to only one person at a time. They are widely used in educational, clinical and forensic psychology to provide valid estimates of IQ. Such applications demand the highest-quality assessment of thinking, REASONING (see s. 3), memory and performance, despite the extra costs of one-to-one testing. Individual tests of mental abilities include the WECHSLER SCALES: the Wechsler Intelligence Scale for Children (WISC; Wechsler 1992), the Wechsler Adult Intelligence Scale (WAIS; Wechsler 1999), the Stanford Binet test (Roid 2003) and the British Ability Scales (Elliott, Murray and Pearson 1996), the last being developed using RASCH SCALING. The three main advantages of individual testing are that: (a) a wider range of skills can be assessed than in group tests (e.g. ability to build shapes out of blocks; spoken language skills); (b) the testing relationship may better motivate the person being assessed; and (c) some tests allow the examiner to tailor the test to the examinee (e.g. if a person performs perfectly on a set

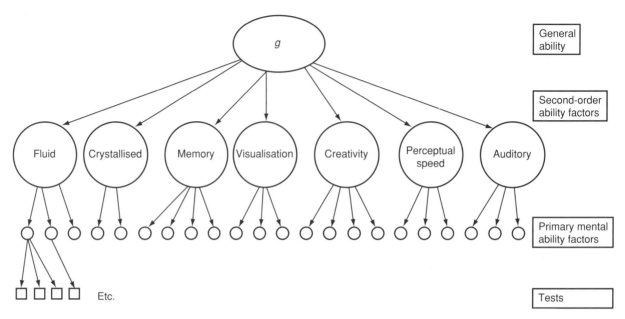

ability: three-stratum model *A hierarchical model of human abilities.*

of intermediate-difficulty vocabulary items, there is no need to give them a block of easier words). *CC*

Elliott, C. D., Murray, D. J. and Pearson, L. S. 1996: *British Ability Scales* (2nd edn). Windsor, Berkshire: NFER-Nelson. **Roid, G. H.** 2003: *Stanford-Binet Intelligence Scales* (5th edn). Itasca IL: Riverside Publishing. **Wechsler, D.** 1992: *WISC-III Manual*. New York: Psychological Corporation. **Wechsler, D.** 1999: *Wechsler Adult Intelligence Scale* (3rd UK edn – wais® -iii UK). London: Psychological Corporation.

ability: three-stratum model A hierarchical model of the structure of MENTAL ABILITIES developed by Carroll (1993), which incorporates GENERAL INTELLIGENCE (*g*), some six to eight SECOND-ORDER ABILITY FACTORS (including FLUID INTELLIGENCE, CRYSTALLISED INTELLIGENCE, memory, visual perception, auditory perception, speed and fluency/creativity) and numerous PRIMARY MENTAL ABILITIES. *CC*

Carroll, J. B. 1993: *Human Cognitive Abilities: A Survey of Factor-analytic Studies*. Cambridge: Cambridge University Press.

accommodation Accommodation is a learning style, as well as referring to a completely different concept in PIAGETIAN THEORY (see s. 4). It is one of four LEARNING STYLES assessed by Kolb's Learning Style Inventory. Kolb's learning styles are an extension of his more general theory of the learning cycle (Kolb 1984). Learning is conceived as cycling from concrete experiences and observations, to active exploration, to making abstract generalisations and then to more reflective observations, which give rise to new experiences and observations and so on. The model has two bipolar dimensions – concrete experience/abstract conceptualisation and active experimentation/reflective observation. A person with an accommodation learning style is one who is high on both concrete experience and active experimentation – who learns by doing, performs well when required to act in immediate circumstances, solves problems intuitively and takes risks. The construct VALIDITY (see also s. 8) of the styles has been questioned but there is more support for the bipolar dimensions (Loo 1999). Most reports comment on the pedagogical usefulness of the inventory to help students reflect on their learning styles and preferences. (See also s. 3 and s. 4, ACCOMMODATION) *CMG*

Kolb, D. A. 1984: *Experience as the Source of Learning and Development*. Englewood Cliffs NJ: Prentice-Hall. **Loo, R.** 1999: Confirmatory factor analyses of Kolb's Learning Style Inventory (LSI-1985). *British Journal of Educational Psychology* 69, 213–19.

achievement motivation Formulated by David McClelland, this refers to a form of MOTIVATION involving a competitive DRIVE (see s. 2) to meet standards of excellence first described by the personality theorist Henry A. Murray. McClelland's need theory of motivation distinguishes three types of need: the need for achievement (nAch), the need for affiliation and the need for POWER (see s. 5). McClelland was drawn to the analysis of nAch because he considered nAch to be a distinctively human motive and worthy of consideration for this reason alone; and nAch appeared to be a value that was central to many western societies (particularly North American society) and seemed to be widely regarded as a crucial determinant of actual accomplishment in many achievement situations. The practical impact of McClelland's work in organisational and educational settings stems from the fact that his reading of the societal significance of nAch was correct in the sense that the need to achieve is a core North American value. *NS*

McClelland, D. C. 1961: *Achieving Society*. New York: van Nostrand.

adaptive testing A perennial problem of conventional tests is that the difficulty level of the items in the test should broadly match the ability profile of the people taking the test. Suppose that one wants to determine the IQ of someone who is considerably more intelligent than average. It is virtually certain that they will get all the easy items in the test correct: such items provide no useful information about the individual. Indeed, they may feel bored by them and lose motivation. Likewise, the less able candidate may feel frustrated by struggling with items that are so hard that they have little chance of getting them correct.

Adaptive testing (also known as tailored testing) presents each candidate with items that are of appropriate difficulty for them (Van Der Linden and Glas 2000; Wainer, Dorans, Eignor, Flaugher, Green, Mislevy, Steinberg and Thissen 2000). The first step involves establishing the difficulty of test items (and perhaps their DISCRIMINATION (see s. 3 and s. 5) power and guessing parameters) by administering the items to a large SAMPLE (see s. 8) of the population and using standard methods of RASCH SCALING or ITEM RESPONSE THEORY (Hambleton and Swaminathan 1985) to estimate the item parameters. This information, along with the content of each item, is stored on a computer. A computer program then administers an item of moderate difficulty to a candidate and determines whether it is answered correctly. If so, it is likely that the person is of above-average ability; if not, they are more likely than not to be below-average. A statistic called the 'information function' can be calculated to determine what level of item difficulty will best help the program to refine its estimate of the candidate's ability. After administering each item and noting the response, the computer program calculates the information function and searches in its database for an item of appropriate difficulty to administer next. This procedure continues until either a set number of items has been administered or the computer program calculates that it has estimated the person's ability sufficiently accurately. Thus different people who take the test will probably receive very different sets of items. A high-ability candidate will be stretched by moderate and hard items, whereas a low-ability candidate will see only low-to-moderate difficulty items. As the properties of the items have been established using item response theory, it is possible to compare the abilities of individuals even though they may have been given completely different items by the adaptive testing computer program. *CC*

Hambleton, R. K. and Swaminathan, H. 1985: *Item Response Theory: Principles and Applications.* Boston: Kluwer-Nijhoff. **Van Der Linden, W. J. and Glas, C. A. W.** 2000: *Computerized Adaptive Testing: Theory and Practice.* Dordrecht and Boston: Kluwer Academic. **Wainer, H., Dorans, N. J., Eignor, D., Flaugher, R., Green, B. F., Mislevy, R. J., Steinberg, L. and Thissen, D.** 2000: *Computerized Adaptive Testing: A Primer* (2nd edn). Mahwah NJ: Lawrence Erlbaum Associates.

affect intensity Affect intensity has been defined as reflecting 'stable individual differences in the typical intensity with which individuals experience their emotions' (Larsen and Diener 1987). The theory proposes, for example, that a person who experiences positive moods as highly intense would also experience highly intense negative moods.

Some debate has arisen over how best to measure intensity of moods. Suggestions for indexing affect intensity include a person's mean level when measured over time, or the peaks and troughs of each day (see McConville and Cooper 1995). Not all the methods used to measure affect intensity indicate that it is an individual difference characteristic, and it may be that the degree of intensity is specific to each mood (McConville and Cooper 1995). Nonetheless, several self-report questionnaires purporting to assess this construct have been developed. *CM*

Larsen, R. J. and Diener, E. 1987: Affect intensity as an individual difference characteristic: a review. *Journal of Research in Personality* 21, 1–39. **McConville, C. and Cooper, C.** 1995: Is emotional intensity a general construct? *Personality and Individual Differences* 18, 425–7.

agreeableness Agreeableness is one of the five main personality factors found in the pioneering work of Tupes and Christal (Tupes and Christal 1992) and identified in many CULTURES (see s. 1 and s. 5) by Costa and McCrae (e.g. McCrae and Costa 1997), where it is a component of the FIVE-FACTOR MODEL OF PERSONALITY. It is usually assessed using the NEO-PI(R) or IPIP scales. An individual high in agreeableness is trusting, straightforward, altruistic, cooperative, modest and tender-minded. *CC*

McCrae, R. R. and Costa, P. T. 1997: Personality trait structure as a human universal. *American Psychologist* 52, 509–16. **Tupes, E. C. and Christal, R. E.** 1992: Recurrent personality-factors based on trait ratings. *Journal of Personality* 60, 225–51.

alexithymia A condition usually accompanying psychosomatic or somatoform illnesses whereby a person is unable to describe or recognise the emotions they experience. *AL*

anxiety Anxiety refers to an unpleasant emotional state that is not linked to a specific event or object in the past (fear) or irrationally to an object or event (phobia), although definitions such as 'TEST ANXIETY' muddy the water. Clinically and sub-clinically, anxiety is often associated with DEPRESSION (see s. 7), although the cognitive, biochemical and genetic mechanisms underlying these two traits are rather different. Hence authors such as Hans Eysenck have developed questionnaires to measure NEUROTICISM – a mixture of items measuring depression and anxiety – although others such as Charles Spielberger have developed scales to assess anxiety alone.

Anxiety exists as both a personality trait (the habitually anxious person) and mood STATE (brief elevation in anxiety). It is important for it has been shown that as well as being subjectively unpleasant, elevated levels of anxiety (particularly state anxiety) can impair performance on a great number of cognitive tasks, particularly those with a substantial WORKING MEMORY (see s. 3) component. It is thought that anxious individuals worry when performing the task, which reduces the working-memory capacity available for the task itself (Eysenck 1982). When asked to name the ink-colour of words (ignoring the meaning of the word itself) arachnophobes have been found to slow down when presented with spider-relevant words (e.g. 'web'), but not when they are shown matched neutral words; they inappropriately devote attention to reading and worrying about the threatening word (Martin, Horder and Jones 1992).

The physiological basis of anxiety has been extensively researched. For example, Jeffrey Gray's personality theory is based on the premise that anxious individuals are more sensitive to punishment than reward, via the ascending reticular formation (moderated by the hippocampus), the LIMBIC SYSTEM (see s. 2) and parts of the frontal cortex. *CC*

Eysenck, M. W. 1982: *Attention and Arousal, Cognition and Performance.* Berlin and New York: Springer-Verlag. **Martin, M., Horder, P. and Jones, G. V.** 1992: Integral bias in naming of phobia-related words. *Cognition and Emotion* 6, 479–86.

apperceptive personality test This PROJECTIVE TEST of personality is an updated version of the THEMATIC APPERCEPTION TEST, which incorporates an objective scoring system. *CC*

Karp, S. A., Holmstrom, R. W. and Silber, D. E. 1989: *The Apperceptive Personality Test Manual.* Worthington OH: International Diagnostic Systems.

assessment centres Assessment centres are centres used mainly by occupational psychologists to perform comprehensive assessments (e.g. in connection with PERSONNEL SELECTION or promotion of fairly senior staff, or staff for whom training costs are high, such as pilots). As well as standard PSYCHOMETRIC assessments (e.g. PERSONALITY TESTS, group tests of ability [see ABILITY: GROUP TESTS OF]), such centres frequently involve group-based work and other performance measures (such as IN-BASKET TECHNIQUES and LEADERSHIP – see s. 5 – exercises), and may involve managers or other members of the organisation as well as psychologists. The focus is often on competence-based assessments. *CC*

Lievens, F. 2002: Trying to understand the different pieces of the construct validity puzzle of assessment centers: An examination of assessor and assessee effects. *Journal of Applied Psychology* 87, 675–86.

assimilation Assimilation is a learning style, as well as referring to a completely different concept in PIAGETIAN THEORY (see s. 4). It is one of four LEARNING STYLES assessed by Kolb's Learning Style Inventory. Kolb's learning styles are an extension of his more general theory of the learning cycle (Kolb 1984). Learning is conceived as cycling from concrete experiences and observations to active exploration, to making abstract generalisations and then to more reflective observations, which give rise to new experiences and observations, and so on. The model has two bipolar dimensions – concrete experience/abstract conceptualisation and active experimentation/reflective observation. A person with an assimilation learning style is one who is high on both abstract conceptualisation and reflective observation – who has a strong tendency to create theoretical models, excels in INDUCTIVE REASONING (see s. 3) and is more concerned with abstract concepts than people. The construct VALIDITY (see also s. 8) of the styles has been questioned, but there is more support for the bipolar dimensions (Loo 1999). Most reports comment on the pedagogical usefulness of the inventory to help students reflect on their learning styles and preferences. (See also s. 4, ASSIMILATION) *CMG*

Kolb, D. A. 1984: *Experience as the Source of Learning and Development.* Englewood Cliffs NJ: Prentice-Hall. **Loo, R.** 1999: Confirmatory factor analyses of Kolb's Learning Style Inventory (LSI-1985). *British Journal of Educational Psychology* 69, 213–19.

autism A pattern of behaviour characterised by social isolation or inappropriate social interaction; elaborate repetitive routines and limited or inappropriate intonation and body language. *NS*

B

behaviour genetics of abilities At their simplest, behaviour-genetic studies examine whether individuals who share the same environment when they grow up, or who are genetically similar to each other, also tend to have similar scores on ability tests. This can reveal the extent to which the shared environment (parental ATTITUDES – see s. 5, behaviours and lifestyle, the availability of books, quality of nutrition, social class, etc.), the genes that children inherit from their parents and environmental influences which are not shared with other SIBLINGS (see s. 4) (e.g. influence of friends, the effects of illness, hobbies and other activities: the unique environment) influence various cognitive abilities.

More recently, STRUCTURAL EQUATION MODELLING (see s. 8) has allowed more complex relationships to be explored, such as the INTERACTION (see s. 8) between such VARIABLES (see s. 8) and the effects of the shared environment, genes and the unique environment at various stages of life, and whether the correlations between intelligence-test scores and other variables (such as nerve-conduction-velocity) arise because both are influenced by the same genes. Common research designs include the analysis of the test scores of pairs of IDENTICAL TWINS (see s. 4) who have been fostered/adopted shortly after birth and reared in different family environments, and studies involving pairs of non-identical twins and identical twins who have been brought up by their parents. In the former case, any similarity between the twins can only be due to the influence of genes: in the latter, it is possible to work out the relative importance of the family, genes and unique environment by studying the extent to which pairs of identical twins are more similar to each other than are pairs of non-identical twins.

Some early studies were technically flawed. However, recent studies have rectified these problems and produce consistent results. They show that the influence of genes on general intelligence is substantial, and endures throughout the lifespan. So, too, is the effect of the unique environment. The family environment influences children's INTELLIGENCE early in life, but declines and is effectively zero from late ADOLESCENCE (see s. 4) onwards.

CC

Bartels, M., Rietveld, M. J. H., Van Baal, G. C. M. and Boomsma, D. I. 2002: Genetic and environmental influences on the development of intelligence. *Behavior Genetics* 32, 237–49. **Plomin, R. and Petrill, S. A.** 1997: Genetics and intelligence: What's new? *Intelligence* 24, 53–77.

bell curve *The Bell Curve* (1994) was written by the late Harvard psychologist Richard Herrnstein and sociologist Charles Murray. The book was written for a general audience and mainly focuses on the social and policy implications of individual differences in cognitive ability. It comprises 22 chapters and is organised in four parts.

Part I argues that North American SOCIETY (see s. 5) is becoming increasingly stratified according to 'cognitive ability', with an emerging 'cognitive elite' dominating the most prestigious educational and occupational positions. The authors review data showing a substantial relationship between INTELLIGENCE AND OCCUPATIONAL PERFORMANCE and claim that the restriction of IQ testing in the workplace leads to severe macroeconomic costs in the North American economy.

Part II looks at the effects of cognitive ability on social behaviour and is largely based on data from the National Longitudinal Survey of Youth (USA). In successive chapters, the authors maintain that cognitive ability is a more powerful predictor than socio-economic status of socially untoward outcomes, such as poverty, unemployment and welfare dependency.

Part III focuses on group differences in intelligence [see INTELLIGENCE: GROUP DIFFERENCES] and is the most controversial in the book. It presents data showing that Asian-Americans tend to score higher on IQ tests than Caucasian Americans who, in turn, score higher than African-Americans. The authors believe that GROUP (see s. 5) differences in IQ are the result of a combination of genetic and environmental factors. They present analyses showing that many group differences in social and economic outcomes, including educational attainment and salaries, diminish considerably or are even reversed once variation in cognitive ability is taken into account. The authors claim that American society is experiencing 'dysgenic pressure' on cognitive ability levels, resulting from the higher reproductive rates of low-IQ women and an influx of immigrant cohorts with below-average IQ scores. [See BIAS AND GROUP DIFFERENCES]

Part IV begins by reviewing the effectiveness of intervention programmes aiming to boost IQ levels. The authors note encouraging research findings (notably from enhanced nutrition and early ADOPTION STUDIES – see s. 7), but conclude it is unlikely that effective interventions will appear in the foreseeable future. The last few chapters concentrate on implications and suggestions for social policy. The authors urge that public funds be shifted from programmes for the disadvantaged to support gifted students. Furthermore, they argue that the enforcement of affirmative action in higher education and in the workplace has long-term undesirable consequences. They propose that affirmative action be replaced by 'colour-blind' policies to promote individualism.

The authors close by presenting their view of where American society is headed in light of the rising 'cognitive elite' and the rapidly deteriorating fortunes of those at the low end of cognitive ability distribution. They predict the emergence of a 'cognitive underclass' that is likely to face increasingly difficult conditions in a job market that values information and intellectual abilities much more than low-skill labour. To forestall these developments, the authors maintain that North American society must come to terms with the reality of individual differences in cognitive ability, return to the principles of individualism and create opportunities that will allow all of its members to lead lives that are decent, meaningful and rewarding. *KP*

Fraser, S. 1995: *The Bell Curve Wars: Race, Intelligence, and the Future of America.* New York: Basic Books. **Herrnstein, R. J. and Murray, C.** 1994: *The Bell Curve: Intelligence and Class Structure in American Life.* New York: Free Press. **Neisser, U., Boodoo, G., Bouchard, T. J., Boykin, A. W., Brody, N., Ceci, S. J., Halpern, D. F., Loehlin, J. C., Perloff, R., Sternberg, R. J. and Urbina, S.** 1996: Intelligence: knowns and unknowns. *American Psychologist* 51, 77–101.

bias In statistical theory, bias refers to a systematic underestimation or overestimation of a POPULATION (see s. 8) parameter by a SAMPLE (see s. 8) statistic. In psychological testing, it generally refers to a systematic under- or overestimation of the true score of a group of test takers (e.g. males) on a construct (e.g. cognitive ability). Broadly speaking, test bias can be one of two types. INTERNAL BIAS concerns group differences in the internal properties of a MEASUREMENT (see s. 1, MEASUREMENT AND STATISTICS) instrument, including internal consistency, item facility values and item-total correlations. Across the groups of interest, an instrument should have similar internal consistencies, the items comprising it should have similar facility values and each item should have a similar correlation with the total scale score.

The second type of bias, EXTERNAL BIAS (or criterion or predictive test bias) concerns group differences in the relationship between a measurement instrument and a specific external criterion (e.g. IQ and job performance). Technically, an instrument of perfect RELIABILITY (see also s. 8) is said to be a biased predictor of a criterion if it leads to different regression lines or, less often, different standard errors of estimates for different groups of test takers. Differential regression lines may involve group differences in the intercepts or in the slopes (or in both parameters) of the equations. External test bias is always assessed in relation to specific criteria. Measurement instruments cannot be biased in an abstract sense (e.g. 'IQ tests are biased'), but only *vis-à-vis* specific criteria and groups of test takers. For instance, an IQ test may be an unbiased predictor of male mathematics performance, but consistently overestimate female English performance. Note that an unbiased predictor may appear to be biased with respect to a criterion, if the criterion itself is biased. For example, scores on a mathematics test may themselves be a biased indicator of underlying mathematical ability, in which case it makes little sense to use them as a criterion for validating an IQ test. In all cases, psychometric bias should be clearly distinguished from the notions of fairness and ethics, which mainly concern philosophical rather than statistical issues. (See also s. 3 and s. 8, BIAS) *KP*

Cooper, C. 2002: *Individual Differences* (2nd edn). London: Arnold. **Jensen, A. R.** 1980: *Bias in Mental Testing.* London: Methuen.

bias and group differences A test is biased if it systematically overestimates or underestimates the score of one or more groups. Consider this item from an IQ test. 'School is to GCSE as university is to (a) college, (b) RSPCA, (c) degree, (d) library.' Such an item would probably work well as a fairly easy verbal analogy item when used with 16-year-olds in the UK, who would know what 'GCSE' (and perhaps 'RSPCA') meant. For these individuals the difficulty of the item would be determined by whether they could recognise the relationship between the first and second term and apply it to the third term. However, anyone who lives outside England, Wales or Northern Ireland would probably not know that a GCSE is a type of educational qualification: they would be unlikely to get this item correct, not because they are unintelligent but because the item assumes knowledge which they do not have. This is an example of BIAS: the scores of people from outside the UK on a test built up of items such as these will underestimate their true levels of INTELLIGENCE (see also s. 4). There are several techniques available for detecting such biased items in tests, as discussed by Osterlind (1983), among others.

However, the presence of differences in the average scores of two or more groups of people does not necessarily mean that any items in the test are biased. For example, sex differences are often found in scales measuring AGGRESSION (see s. 5), emotional sensitivity, etc., and these probably reflect genuine differences between the sexes rather than any problem with the test, as the differences revealed by the tests are reflected in conviction rates for violence, etc. This creates problems when tests are used for PERSONNEL SELECTION. If a psychometric test assessing emotional sensitivity was used as part of an assessment procedure for counsellors (for example) it would almost certainly suggest that a greater proportion of female than male applicants were suitable for training. However, employment legislation assumes that no group differences of any kind exist – and if any are found, that these arise because the test/assessment procedure is flawed. This assumption is based on wishful thinking rather than hard evidence. Thus tests cannot be used for selection if they show substantial group differences – even if these appear to be genuine differences rather than apparent differences caused by biased items. *CC*

Osterlind, S. J. 1983: *Test Item Bias.* Beverly Hills: Sage Publications. **Reynolds, C. R.** 1995: Test bias and the assessment of intelligence and personality. In Saklofske, D. H. and Zeidner, M. (eds) *International Handbook of Personality and Intelligence.* New York: Plenum.

big five model of personality Another term for the particular variant of the FIVE-FACTOR MODEL OF PERSONALITY developed by Paul Costa and Robert McCrae. *CC*

biological correlates of abilities The high HERITABILITY (see s. 4) of INTELLIGENCE suggests a theory of mental ability accounted for by biological phenomena. Jensen and Sinha (1993) review investigations which demonstrate associations between IQ and physical correlates of intelligence including height, myopia, brain size and blood group. In terms of BRAIN FUNCTION (see s. 1, BRAIN FUNCTION AND NEUROPSYCHOLOGY), however, biological correlates such as nerve conduction velocity (NCV), electroencephalographic (EEG) (see s. 2, ELECTROENCEPHALOGRAM) waveforms, event-related potentials (ERPs) and the brain's metabolism of glucose provide estimates of nervous system functioning which are more readily interpreted within a neural efficiency model of intelligence (Vernon 1993). A number of studies have tested the hypothesis that the genetic basis of *g* [see GENERAL ABILITY] partly results from individual differences in NCV – speed at which electrical impulses are transmit-

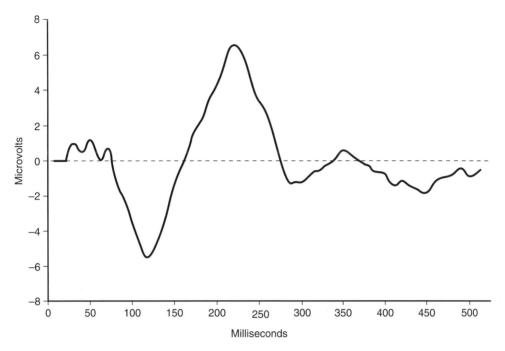

biological correlates of abilities *Typical auditory evoked potential showing change in brain electrical activity following a stimulus (a click), averaged over many trials. It has been suggested that variations in the shape of this waveform from person to person are related to intelligence.*

ted along nerve fibres and across SYNAPSES (see s. 2). Initial reports of moderately large correlations (0.42 to 0.48) suggest that those with high ability do indeed transmit information more quickly (Vernon and Mori 1992). Others, however, failed to replicate, and evidence relating intelligence to NCV is inconclusive. Two other similarly non-invasive estimates of neural activity are simple EEG waves, which record ongoing activity within the brain, and ERPs (referred to as average evoked potentials, or AEPs in earlier literature), which are derived by averaging electrical brain activity at one site of the brain following sensory stimulation. Deary and Caryl's (1993) review reports some consistent and substantial EEG-IQ correlations, but unequivocal conclusions have been hampered by small SAMPLE (see s. 8) sizes and few clear replications. Studies using ERPs provide the most consistent results, and significant negative correlations (–0.4 to –0.5) between IQ and ERP latency suggest brainwaves of higher IQ individuals respond more promptly to sensory stimuli. Positron emission tomography (PET) facilitates *in vivo* measures of brain activity, and Haier's (1993) review of the brain's glucose metabolic rate (via PET scan) demonstrates correlations between IQ and glucose metabolism, ranging from –0.7 to –0.8. Glucose is the brain's main source of energy, and higher IQ individuals seem to use less brain energy (indicated by amount of glucose uptake) to solve given problems. Recently, functional magnetic resonance imaging (fMRI) of the brain has redirected the search for association towards one of localisation, and current work attempts to identify neural circuits involved in IQ performance. *MM*

Deary, I. J. and Caryl, P. G. 1993: Intelligence, EEG and evoked potentials. In Vernon, P. A. (ed.) *Biological Approaches to the Study of Human Intelligence.* Norwood NJ: Ablex. **Haier, R. J.** 1993: Cerebral glucose metabolism and intelligence. In Vernon, P. A. (ed.) *Biological Approaches to the Study of Human Intelligence.* Norwood NJ: Ablex. **Jensen, A. R. and Sinha, S. N.** 1993: Physical correlates of human intelligence. In Vernon, P. A. (ed.) *Biological Approaches to the Study of Human Intelligence.* Norwood NJ: Ablex. **Vernon, P. A.** 1993: *Biological Approaches to the Study of Human Intelligence.* Norwood NJ: Ablex. **Vernon, P. A. and Mori, M.** 1992: Intelligence, reaction times and nerve conduction velocity. *Intelligence* 16 273–88.

C

Cannon-Bard theory A theory of EMOTION in which two parts of the brain, the thalamus and amygdala, are thought to play an essential role in interpreting an emotion-provoking situation. The error of the Cannon-Bard theory was to posit the existence of a brain centre – supposedly located in the thalamus – for emotions.   *NS*

cognition and emotion There are a large number of cognitively based theories of emotion, ranging from the general to the specific. [See also EMOTION: COGNITIVE APPRAISAL THEORIES] Central to this group of theories is the concept of emotional 'affect'. This is an explanation of emotion that emphasises the primacy of cognition. The central tenet of these theories is that ideas, BELIEFS (see s. 5), memories and expectations shape the interpretation of events around us and hence our emotional response to those events. Thus beliefs are thought to shape the way in which situations and events are cognitively appraised and it is the extent to which the individual feels they have control over an event that will influence their emotional response. For example, if a hungry lion is encountered in a controlled environment, such as a zoo or safari park, emotions such as delight and excitement will be experienced, whereas feelings of anxiety and dread would ensue were the animal encountered in a much less secure setting.

The AUTONOMIC NERVOUS SYSTEM (ANS) (see s. 2) influences many organs, including the brain, the lungs, the liver and the heart. It modulates activity, carrying blood to the heart and the digestive system, speeding up or slowing down the system as required. When we first experience an emotion it is the ANS that is responsible for our bodily reactions, such as widening eyes, sweating palms or raised heart rate. But how does the ANS 'know' which responses to trigger? To what extent does the brain send messages to the ANS about the type of emotional response required to particular stimuli? Which comes first, the physical emotional response or the perception of the bodily responses that tell the brain that an emotion is being experienced; do we run because we are afraid, or are we afraid because we run? Both the JAMES-LANGE THEORY and CANNON-BARD THEORY of emotion were some of the first systematic attempts to answer these questions.

One of the strongest criticisms of cognitive theories of emotion concerns the way in which they tend to *explain* rather than predict behaviour. Consequently, they tend to underplay the significance of behavioural and physiological aspects of emotion. Specifically, there is evidence that appraisal of a situation can occur without inducing an emotional experience or 'affect'. For example, we make daily AUTOMATIC (see s. 3) decisions about what we want, like or dislike: 'The table at which I am reading looks bigger and cleaner than the one over there.' Cognitive theories of emotion do not offer a strong explanation of reflex emotions such as fear or surprise. It is also very difficult to predict emotional experience from appraisals of a situa-

tion, yet paradoxically it is possible to experience an emotion simply by imagining a situation or observing someone else's emotional experience. *En face*, emotions associated with chronic DEPRESSION (see s. 7) and generalised anxiety seem to have no adaptive value – how, then, can they be based on appraisal of a situation (Griffiths 1997)?

Oatley and Johnson-Laird (1987) and Oatley (1992) have outlined an ambitious 'communicative' theory of emotion that addresses many of the concerns outlined by Griffiths (1997). For example, is it necessary for a stimulus to be processed cognitively for an emotional experience and action (affect) to occur? Oatley and Johnson-Laird (1987) explain emotional experience through an account of both the subjective experience of emotion, changes in body posture and facial expression, and the affective component of emotion, i.e. action. This theory is particularly useful since it focuses on goals rather than behaviour. This means that emotional evaluation can be considered separately from other types of situational evaluation. Within their theory, emotions are processed and exchanged both across various parts of the cognitive system and also across the social environment. Emotions are thought to have evolved to facilitate and guide the cognitive functions that are necessary to coordinate our plans and goals: goals are what the individual wishes to achieve and plans are the way in which those goals can be attained. By drawing on physiological evidence, cross-cultural EMOTIONAL EXPRESSION (see s. 5) and eliciting conditions, Oatley and Johnson-Laird named five BASIC EMOTIONS (see s. 4): happiness, success on a current goal; sadness, failure on a current goal; fear, threat to self-preservation; anger, frustration at inability to attain current goal; and disgust, violation of a gustatory or taste goal. [See EMOTIONS: BASIC]

There is conflict between each of these emotions, with an emotional experience only occurring when the cognitive system is settled in one mode. This would explain why we can only experience one basic emotion at any time. This suggests that a modular system operates in emotional experience with different parts of the system having specific functions. Information is processed in two ways, either as an early warning system for the control of cognition or for the processing of messages that require semantic interpretation.

The control signals do not provide any information about what has actually occurred or what action to take. In this context, the emotion controls the cognitive system, without actually providing any meaning. This low-level processing occurs through a simple early warning system that overrides all other cognitive activities, thus providing an evolutionary advantage in making available a fast response to situations such as immediate attack (Oatley 1992).

Conscious appraisal of a situation (goal and plan evaluation) is also necessary for emotional experience to occur. This occurs through an evaluation of the signals received at a cognitive level. These signals help give meaning to the emotional experience and this in turn triggers a voluntary action. Such messages require semantic interpretation and allow for the control and organisation of plans and processing which occur hierarchically through high-level cognitive modules. For example, a difficult situation, such as poor exam performance, generates a negative emotion. This emotion sends information to other parts of the cognitive system that enables the individual to take action, such as studying harder.

How can cognition be explained in the experience of emotions that serve no real useful purpose, such as depression and anxiety? In this context, Oatley and Johnson-Laird describe an emotional experience that becomes jammed, somewhere between the control signals and semantic messaging. Since emotions facilitate the transition of motivational states, any break in messaging between basic control signals and the relevant semantic messages that inform the emotion of its purpose will result in a system that is unable to move and a mood or TEMPERAMENT (see s. 4) ensues.

Finally, Oatley and Johnson Laird (1987) argue for the importance of social exchanges in emotional experience. Our emotional (and verbal) behaviour influences the emotions and behaviours of others. There are considerable individual and cross-cultural differences in the ways in which this occurs, but generally facial expressions – as well as body posture and vocal tone – have developed to provide us with a social reference. Grins, sneers, frowns, smiles and stares communicate excitement, anger, happiness, confusion and a host of other information that can be used to reduce ambiguity in uncertain situations. *AF*

Griffiths, P. E. 1997: *What Emotions Really Are*. Chicago: University of Chicago Press. **Oatley, K.** 1992: *Best Laid Schemes*. Cambridge: Cambridge University Press. **Oatley, K. and Johnson-Laird, P. N.** 1987: Towards a cognitive theory of emotions. *Cognition and Emotion* 4, 29–50.

cognitive style and learning style

The word 'style' is normally understood to refer to a set of stable and consistent characteristics about a person. Cognitive style refers to a person's habitual or consistent way of processing information that is largely independent of the information being handled. It is presumed to operate across a range of tasks and situations, as well as across time. The terms 'cognitive style' and 'learning style' are often used interchangeably, but there are importance differences in their meaning, largely due to the research traditions from which they grew and their intellectual heritage.

Cognitive style researchers tend to see style as an inbuilt and AUTOMATIC (see s. 3) way of cognitive processing that develops early in life (perhaps with a biological basis), appears as a pervasive feature of the person and is not amenable to change and SELF-REGULATION (see s. 5) (Riding and Rayner 1998). In contrast, learning style researchers tend to see style as being more flexible and open to change and self-management. Consequently, their work is more readily linked with research on LEARNING (see s. 3) strategies, approaches to learning and conceptions of learning (e.g. Tait and Entwistle 1996; Vermunt 1998). Indeed, Sternberg (1997) introduced the term, thinking style, to capture an aspect of style relating to mental management and mental self-government.

Cognitive style research emerged as a distinctive area during the 1950s and 1960s and a long list of styles were identified (e.g. field dependence/independence, levelling-sharpening, conceptual tempo (impulsivity/reflectivity), category width, cognitive complexity). At that time, cognitive style provided a new construct to bridge the gap between the more traditional dimensions of INDIVIDUAL DIFFERENCES – cognitive ability and PERSONALITY. One of the most widely researched cognitive styles is FIELD DEPENDENCE/independence, which refers to a person's ability to perceive an object (a geometric figure, an object in space or one's own body) as separate from the surrounding perceptual field (Witkin et al. 1962). This perceptual style was seen as indicative of a wider psychological mode of functioning called psychological differentiation or sense of separate IDENTITY (see s. 4 and s. 5). Field independence was measured either by an embedded figures tests (extracting a simple figure from a more complex one) or by the rod and frame test (ability to identify the true vertical in the context of a tilted frame). One of the criticisms of many tests of cognitive style is that they measure only a single pole of the dimension and cannot be distinguished from a more traditional measure of cognitive ability. For example, it is argued that measures of field independence are simply measures of spatial ability.

There have been several attempts to synthesise and/or categorise the burgeoning number of cognitive and learning styles that have been reported (believed to be over 70). In a review of the area, Sternberg and Grigorenko (1997) classified different kinds of cognitive style according to whether they were cognition-centred (e.g. field independence, conceptual tempo), personality-centred (e.g. deriving from a types theory of personality, such as the Myers-Briggs Type Indicator), or learning activity-centred (as in learning styles such as deep/surface processors, active experimenters/reflective observers, serialists/wholists). Riding and Cheema (1991) concluded that the various style labels can be accommodated within two independent dimensions: (1) wholistic vs. analytic, or the tendency to organise information into wholes and parts; and (2) verbal-imagery, or the tendency to mentally represent information either verbally or in mental pictures. Using their Cognitive Styles Analysis (CSA) with school-aged children, they generated a prolific programme of research showing the impact of cognitive style on classroom behaviour, teaching style and educational achievements (Riding and Rayner 1998).

Within the learning styles tradition, the methods for assessing style are primarily self-rating on questionnaires and inventories rather than performance on specific information-processing tasks. Some of the most extensively discussed are the learning styles derived from Kolb's experiential learning theory and learning cycle (Kolb 1984). The model has two bipolar dimensions – concrete experience/abstractive conceptualisation and active experimentation/reflective observation. Four learning styles are identified representing the combined poles of these two dimensions: ACCOMMODATION (high on concrete experience/active experimentation), ASSIMILATION (high on abstract conceptualising/reflective observation), converging (high on abstract conceptualisation/active experimentation) and diverging (high on concrete experience/reflective observation). Another important distinction is between deep processing (the tendency to extract meaning from information, exemplify, make connections and be intrinsically motivated) and surface processing (the tendency to fragment learning, engage in rote processing and be extrinsically motivated). These have formed the basis of extended programmes of research on students' learning in higher education in the United Kingdom (Tait and Entwistle 1996) and similar constructs have been investigated in Europe (Vermunt 1998).

Critiques of cognitive and learning style research generally point to their extensive number, their construct VALIDITY (see also s. 8), and whether they contribute anything to the predictive value of more traditional measures of individual differences (e.g. intellectual ability and personality traits). In educational research, important questions have been raised about their implications for pedagogy. There is no disagreement that teachers should recognise a variety of learning styles, orientations and preferences. Beyond that, it is difficult to judge how best to optimise learning conditions. For example, should teaching methods match the styles of learners or should efforts be made to extend the learner's repertoire? In this context, the question of whether cognitive and learning styles are flexible and open to self-management is crucial.

A recent collection of readings gives a comprehensive account of both current and historical research on cognitive, learning and thinking styles (Sternberg and Zhang 2001).   *CMG*

Kolb, D. A. 1984: *Experience as the Source of Learning and Development*. Englewood Cliffs NJ: Prentice-Hall. Riding, R. and Cheema, I. 1991: Cognitive styles – an overview and integration. *Educational Psychology* 11, 193–215. Riding, R. and Rayner, S. 1998: *Cognitive Styles and Learning Strategies*. London: David Fulton. Sternberg, R. J. 1997: *Thinking Styles*. New York: Cambridge University Press. Sternberg, R. J. and Grigorenko, E. L. 1997: Are cognitive styles still in style? *American Psychologist* 52(7), 700–12. Sternberg, R. J. and Zhang, L. F. (eds) 2001: *Perspectives on Thinking, Learning and Cognitive Styles*. Mahwah NJ: Lawrence Erlbaum. Tait, H. and Entwistle, N. 1996: Identifying students at risk through ineffective study strategies. *Higher Education* 31, 97–116. Vermunt, J. D. 1998: The regulation of constructive learning processes. *British Journal of Educational Psychology* 68, 149–71. Witkin, H. A., Dyk, R. B., Faterson, H. F., Goodenough, D. R. and Karp, S. A. 1962: *Psychological Differentiation*. New York: Wiley.

competence-based assessment Rather than assessing potential, competence-based assessments assess purely whether an individual possesses a sufficient level of EXPERTISE (see s. 3) to perform some task (e.g. the LEVEL A ACCREDITATION for test use). Such assessments produce an end decision that the individual is either competent or not yet competent. The driving test is one common example of competence-based assessment.

Competence-based assessment has several stages. First, there must be a clear definition of the behaviours to be assessed, together with a clear understanding of the minimum acceptable level of each of these behaviours: the 'standard'. Second, an assessment procedure must be developed which allows for the accurate assessment of performance. Evidence is then gathered about one or more individuals and the evidence is compared with the standard.

The approach is particularly appealing where the behaviours can be objectively assessed, and where relatively few different behaviours have to be assessed in order to demonstrate competency. Otherwise the presence of

significant MEASUREMENT ERROR (see s. 8) alone can ensure that rather few individuals meet the minimum standard on all behaviours, unless the minimum standards are set at a very low level.   *CC*

Wolf, A. 1995: *Competence-based Assessment*. Buckingham: Open University Press.

confluence model Zajonc's model (now seriously questioned) linking INTELLIGENCE AND BIRTH ORDER.   *CC*

conscientiousness Conscientiousness, or attention to detail, is one of the personality traits at the core of Costa and McCrae's FIVE-FACTOR MODEL OF PERSONALITY. It is negatively related to PSYCHOTICISM in EYSENCK'S THREE-FACTOR MODEL of personality, and is usually assessed using the IPIP scales or the NEO-PI(R). Clinically, high scores on this FACTOR (see s. 8) have been linked with OBSESSIVE-COMPULSIVE DISORDER (see s. 7) (Larstone, Jang, Livesley, Vernon and Wolf 2002) and reduced incidence of risky sexual behaviours (Trobst, Wiggins, Costa, Herbst, McCrae and Masters 2000). According the NEO-PI(R), conscientiousness involves competency, orderliness, a sense of duty, achievement motivation, self-discipline and forethought.   *CC*

Larstone, R. M., Jang, K. L., Livesley, W. J., Vernon, P. A. and Wolf, H. 2002: The relationship between Eysenck's P-E-N model of personality, the five-factor model of personality, and traits delineating personality dysfunction. *Personality and Individual Differences* 33, 25–37. Trobst, K. K., Wiggins, J. S., Costa, P. T., Herbst, J. H., McCrae, R. R. and Masters, H. L. 2000: Personality psychology and problem behaviors: HIV risk and the five-factor model. *Journal of Personality* 68, 1233–52.

continuity hypothesis The continuity hypothesis centres on the relationship between normal levels of TRAITS and clinical conditions. Whereas the disease model assumes that psychiatric syndromes, such as SCHIZOPHRENIA (see s. 7) or clinical DEPRESSION (see s. 7), are qualitatively different from 'normal' behaviour, the continuity hypothesis suggests that there is no qualitative difference, and that in many cases, the same basic mechanisms may be used to describe both normal behaviour and clinical conditions (Claridge 1985). For example, depressed mood may simply be a milder version of clinical depression, perhaps sharing the same biological, social and cognitive mechanisms. SCHIZOTYPY is another example of this approach. There is evidence that some of the cognitive deficits that differentiate schizophrenics from non-schizophrenics (e.g. impaired RECOGNITION (see s. 3) of emotions or faces) may be found when comparing 'normal' individuals high and low on schizotypy.   *CC*

Claridge, G. S. 1985: *Origins of Mental Illness*. Oxford: Blackwell.

control design The use of the principles of ergonomics in the design of devices such as switches, keyboards, etc., to control machines or processes.   *NS*

converging Distantly related to the process of converging in Guilford's structure of intellect model, converging is one of four LEARNING STYLES assessed by Kolb's Learning Style Inventory. Kolb's learning styles are an extension of his more general theory of the learning cycle (Kolb 1984). Learning is conceived as cycling from concrete experiences and observations to active exploration, to making abstract generalisations, and then to more reflective observations, which give rise to new experiences and observations, and so on. The model has two bipolar dimensions – concrete experience/abstract conceptualisation and active experimentation/reflective observation. A person with a converging learning style is one who is high on both abstract conceptualisation and active experimentation – can focus on hypothetical-deductive REASONING (see s. 3), is strong in the practical application of ideas, is relatively unemotional and has narrow interests. The construct VALIDITY (see also s. 8) of the styles has been questioned, but there is more support for the bipolar dimensions (Loo 1999). Most reports comment on the pedagogical usefulness of the inventory to help students reflect on their learning styles and preferences. *CMG*

Kolb, D. A. 1984: *Experience as the Source of Learning and Development*. Englewood Cliffs NJ: Prentice-Hall. **Loo, R.** 1999: Confirmatory factor analyses of Kolb's Learning Style Inventory (LSI-1985). *British Journal of Educational Psychology* 69, 213–19.

crystallised intelligence A SECOND-ORDER ABILITY FACTOR in Cattell's model of INTELLIGENCE (see also s. 4) and the three-stratum model [see ABILITY: THREE-STRATUM MODEL], this reflects intelligence as invested in LEARNING (see s. 3) and knowledge (e.g. vocabulary, information and numerical abilities). *CC*

D

display design The use of principles of ergonomics in the design of visual display hardware such as computer displays. *NS*

diverging Distantly related to the process of divergent thinking in Guilford's structure of the intellect model, diverging is one of four LEARNING STYLES assessed by Kolb's Learning Style Inventory. Kolb's learning styles are an extension of his more general theory of the learning cycle (Kolb 1984). Learning is conceived as cycling from concrete experiences and observations to active exploration, to making abstract generalisations and then to more reflective observations, which give rise to new experiences and observations, and so on. The model has two bipolar dimensions – concrete experience/abstract conceptualisation and active experimentation/reflective observation. A person with a diverging learning style is one who is high on both concrete experience and reflective observation – who is strong on imaginative ability, good at generating ideas and sees things from different perspectives, is interested in people and has broad interests. The construct VALIDITY (see also s. 8) of the styles has been questioned but there is more support for the bipolar dimensions (Loo 1999). Most reports comment on the pedagogical usefulness of the inventory to help students reflect on their learning styles and preferences. *CMG*

Kolb, D. A. 1984: *Experience as the Source of Learning and Development.* Englewood Cliffs NJ: Prentice-Hall. **Loo, R.** 1999: Confirmatory factor analyses of Kolb's Learning Style Inventory (LSI-1985). *British Journal of Educational Psychology* 69, 213–19.

drive reduction theories DRIVE (see s. 2) reduction theory is based on Hull's (1943) assertion that drives are internal states of arousal or tension that must be reduced in order to return to HOMEOSTASIS (see s. 2) or a balanced physiological state. Therefore, individuals are motivated to reduce these drives which produce energised behaviour. For example, if we feel hungry we are driven to reduce this feeling, that is, we are motivated. (Notice that in this model the drive only energises the behaviour, the actual behaviour is directed through LEARNING – see s. 3 – and REINFORCEMENT – see s. 3.) Primary drives are unlearned biological needs such as the drive for food to satisfy hunger. Secondary drives are learned needs and are often associated between a primary drive (food) and another variable (the money to buy the food). Later, Hull introduced the concept of incentives to explain why different types of external stimuli (e.g. different types of food) influenced motivation. Although popular, this theory also had limitations. It failed to adequately explain why motive could exist without biological need (eating a dessert when full) or why non-physiological motives could energise behaviour (refusing food when hungry). *DH*

Hull, C. L. 1943: *Principles of Behaviour.* New York: Appleton-Century-Crofts.

Duchenne smile The smile is used in many situations to mask true feelings, such as dislike or EMBARRASS-MENT (see s. 5), or to hide a lie. The Duchenne smile is a genuine spontaneous expression of happiness. There is uniqueness in the pattern of facial muscles associated with the Duchenne smile that cannot be replicated in a posed smile. Lip curling, raised cheeks and the wrinkles that branch out from the eye area are all characteristic of a genuine smile (Ekman and Friesen 1982). The eye area is particularly important in the Duchenne smile. While lip curling and raised cheeks can be replicated in a false smile the orbicularis oculi muscle around the eye is almost always motionless. A posed smile is also much more intense, asymmetrical and tends to differ in timing. Ekman and Friesen report that the posed smile will usually appear abruptly and last longer than a genuine smile. *AF*

Ekman, P. and Friesen, W. V. 1982: Felt, false and miserable similes. *Journal of Nonverbal Behaviour* 6(4), 238–52.

E

---

embedded figures test A standardised measure of the cognitive style of FIELD DEPENDENCE involving the ability to locate simple geometric forms which are embedded in larger figures (Witkin, Oltman, Raskin and Karp 1971). *NS*

Witkin, H. A., Oltman, P. K., Raskin, E. and Karp, S. A. 1971: *Embedded Figures Test, Children's Embedded Figures Test, Group Embedded Figures Test Manual.* Palo Alto CA: Consulting Psychologists Press.

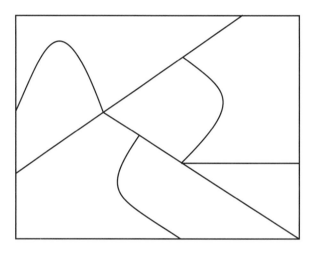

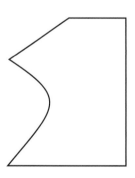

embedded figures test *A typical embedded figures item: whereabouts in the top shape would you find the bottom shape?*

emotion A complex personal response to a subjective cognitive state, resulting in transitory changes in bodily responses, expressive behaviours and motivated actions. *AF*

emotional change over time The area of EMOTIONAL DEVELOPMENT (see s. 4) is theoretically rich. Several theories have been put forward to explain the way in which EMOTION may change over time and these tend to place emphasis on the contribution of both the biological and the social to emotional development. T. Izard and his colleagues (Izard and Malatesta 1987; Malatesta-Magai, Izard and Camras 1991; Abe and Izard 1999) proposed the most thorough theories of emotional change. Basic emotional responses, such as happiness, sadness or fear [see EMOTIONS: BASIC], are present from birth until old age, and many theorists believe that these emotional experiences are experienced consistently over time (Izard and Malatesta 1987). In other words, both the adult and the aged experience the same emotional experience as the infant. Izard stresses that while we may be aware that our feelings have changed over time towards a situation or individual, it does not necessarily follow that our emotions have changed. Rather it is that we have a new set of emotions directed towards that person or situation.

While the infant may not have the same memories or thoughts as the adult, the expression of emotions is very similar. The same transitory changes in bodily responses and expressive behaviours occur, the same facial muscles contract and, most importantly, there is a separate expressive action for each BASIC EMOTION (see s. 4). Both the infant and the adult show the same 'long face' when experiencing sadness or the same lowered eyebrows during anger. Second, movement, posture and, particularly, facial expression all carry emotional information, and the communicative advantage of such a system makes it very unlikely that emotions *per se* could change over time, although attempts at manipulating emotions may be made [see EMOTIONS: MANIPULATION OF]. If there were no invariance or consistency over time, then there would be no evolutionary advantage. For example, sadness is communicated to others through facial expressions and body posture (Izard 1991). This expression informs others that something is wrong and may elicit both EMPATHY (see s. 4) and help from others.

The final piece of evidence that emotions cannot change over time is the sense of SELF (see s. 1, s. 4 and s. 5). Despite constant change from infancy to adulthood to old age, individuals retain a core sense of self; the idea that we are today the same person that we were yesterday (Izard 1991). The knowledge that some experiences – such as being close to a loved one – will bring us great joy and that other experiences will bring us great sadness provides invariance to emotional experience. Rather than changing emotions over time, the knowledge that these experiences will elicit similar emotional experiences in the future ensures that our emotional experiences are consistent. *AF*

Abe, J. A. and Izard, C. E. 1999: The developmental function of emotions: an analysis in terms of differential emotions theory. *Cognition and Emotion* 13(5), 523–49. **Izard, C.** 1991: *The Psychology of Emotions.* New York: Plenum Press. **Izard, C. and Malatesta, C.** 1987: Perspectives on emotional development: 1. Differential emotions theory of early emotional development. In

Osofsky J. D. (ed.) *Handbook in Infant Development* (2nd edn). New York: John Wiley and Sons, 494–554. **Malatesta-Magai, C., Izard, C. E. and Camras, L.** 1991: Conceptualizing early infant affect: emotions as fact, fiction or artifact? In Strongman K. T. (ed.) *International Review of Studies on Emotion*. Chichester: John Wiley and Sons, vol. 1, 1–36.

emotional intelligence The construct of emotional intelligence (EI) posits the existence of actual or perceived differences in the extent to which people attend to, process and utilise affect-laden information. The distal roots of EI are in E. L. Thorndike's (1920) construct of 'social intelligence,' which concerns the ability to understand and manage people and to act wisely in human relations. Its proximal roots are in Gardner's (1983) two personal intelligences (*intra*personal and *inter*personal) [see MULTIPLE INTELLIGENCES], which concern the ability to understand the emotions and mental states in one's own SELF (see s. 1) and in other people, respectively. The term 'emotional intelligence' appeared several times in the literature before Salovey and Mayer (1990) proposed the formal definition and model of the construct. The field was essentially launched by Goleman's (1995) best-selling book that influenced most subsequent models of EI.

Early work on EI failed to appreciate the crucial role of MEASUREMENT (see s. 1, MEASUREMENT AND STATISTICS) in the operationalisation of the construct. More specifically, the fundamental distinction between self-report and maximum-performance measurement went unheeded, thus leading to conceptual confusion and contradictory results. The choice of measurement method has a direct and significant influence on the operationalisation process and, thence, on EMPIRICAL (see s. 8) findings. The measurement of EI through maximum performance tests will not yield the same findings as its measurement through self-report inventories, just as the measurement of cognitive ability through IQ tests does not yield the same findings as its measurement through self-report questionnaires.

Petrides and Furnham (2001) proposed a conceptual distinction between two types of EI, based on the measurement method used to operationalise them. Ability EI (or cognitive-emotional ability) concerns the actual ability to perceive, process and utilise affect-laden information. This construct pertains primarily to the realm of cognitive ability and should be measured via maximum-performance tests. Trait EI (or emotional self-efficacy) concerns a constellation of emotion-related self-perceptions and dispositions. This construct pertains primarily to the realm of personality and should be measured via self-report questionnaires. It is important to understand that ability EI and trait EI are two distinct constructs, differentiated by the respective measurement methods used to operationalise them rather than by the content of their SAMPLING (see s. 8) domains. That is to say, even if the two methods were used to assess exactly the same sampling domains, the resultant operationalisations would be fundamentally different.

The measurement of ability EI is problematic because the inherently subjective nature of emotional experience undermines the effort to develop test items along cognitive ability lines, such as those used in standard IQ tests. In other words, it is not obvious how to create comprehensive tests based on truly objective criteria that can cover the entire sampling domain of the construct. For example, much of the intrapersonal component of ability EI (i.e. those facets concerning people's internal emotional states) is not amenable to objective scoring because the information required for such scoring is available only to the test taker.

To circumvent this problem, ability EI tests have employed scoring procedures that attempt to create correct options among the various alternatives. According to the general consensus scoring criterion, an item response is considered correct if it has been endorsed by the majority of participants in a normative SAMPLE (see s. 8), whereas the expert consensus scoring criterion relies on consensus among experts (as opposed to randomly selected individuals) in order to identify correct responses. These scoring procedures have many shortcomings and have not been especially successful in operationalising cognate constructs, like social intelligence. Nevertheless, tests of ability EI, of which the Mayer-Salovey-Caruso Emotional Intelligence Test (MSCEIT) is the most prominent, continue to be researched and the jury is still out on their VALIDITY (see also s. 8).

The measurement of trait EI is more straightforward because the construct consists of self-perceptions and behavioural dispositions, which are compatible with the subjective nature of emotions. There exist many trait EI measures, although most of them erroneously claim to assess EI as a cognitive ability. Petrides and Furnham (2001) presented the first systematically derived sampling domain of trait EI based on a content analysis of salient models. They identified the following 15 facets, which have provided the basis for the Trait Emotional Intelligence Questionnaire (TEIQue): adaptability, assertiveness, emotion perception, emotion expression, emotion management (others), emotion regulation, impulsiveness (low), relationship skills, SELF-ESTEEM (see s. 5 and s. 7), self-motivation, social competence, STRESS (see s. 7) management, trait empathy, trait happiness and trait optimism.

Factor analytic studies (see FACTOR ANALYSIS and also s. 8) have shown that the constellation of self-perceptions and dispositions that trait EI encompasses forms a distinct composite construct at the lower levels of the Eysenckian and five-factor personality taxonomies [see EYSENCK'S THREE-FACTOR MODEL and FIVE-FACTOR MODEL OF PERSONALITY]. An increasing number of empirical studies have supported the validity of the construct. Thus, it has been demonstrated that trait EI has incremental validity over the major personality dimensions predicting numerous criteria, such as DEPRESSION (see s. 7), life satisfaction, COPING (see s. 7) styles and truancy. It has also been found that individuals with high-trait EI are faster at recognising EMOTIONAL EXPRESSIONS (see s. 5) and are more sensitive to mood-induction procedures compared to their low-trait EI peers. Overall, trait EI has received more empirical support than ability EI; however, neither construct has hitherto shown effects commensurate with expectations in the popular literature. Research in the field of EI is still at a relatively early stage, although significant progress has been achieved since the early models were introduced. Future research must develop within the framework of the distinction between ability EI and trait EI. As expected, a different set of questions is facing the two constructs.

Ability EI research must overcome measurement problems, investigate the nature of the construct's relationship to the *g* [see GENERAL ABILITY] FACTOR, and demonstrate its relevance in real-life settings. Trait EI research must focus on the sociobiological bases of the construct, its implications and development over the lifespan and the design and evaluation of scientifically based intervention programmes.   *KP*

Goleman, D. 1995: *Emotional Intelligence: Why it Can Matter More than IQ*. London: Bloomsbury. Matthews, G., Zeidner, M. and Roberts, R. D. 2002: *Emotional Intelligence: Science and Myth*. Cambridge MA: MIT Press. Mayer, J. D., Caruso, D. R. and Salovey, P. 1999: Emotional intelligence meets traditional standards for an intelligence. *Intelligence* 27, 267–98. Petrides, K. V. and Furnham, A. 2001: Trait emotional intelligence: psychometric investigation with reference to established trait taxonomies. *European Journal of Personality* 15, 425–48. Salovey, P. and Mayer, J. D. 1990: Emotional intelligence. *Imagination, Cognition and Personality* 9, 185–211. Thorndike, E. L. 1920: Intelligence and its uses. *Harper's Magazine* 140, 227–35.

emotion and brain structures Early research implicated four basic brain mechanisms to be the emotional networks of the brain (Papez 1937): the hypothalamus with its mamillary bodies, the anterior thalamic nucleus, the CINGULATE GYRUS (see s. 2) and the hippocampus. Later the orbitofrontal and medialfrontal cortices (prefrontal area), the parahippocampal gyrus and important subcortical groupings like the amygdala, the medial thalamic nucleus, the septal area, prosencephalic basal NUCLEI (see s. 2) (the most anterior area of the brain) and a few brainstem formations were added (MacLean 1952).

More recent developments have identified the amygdala as the brain's emotional computer (see s. 2, EMOTION AND THE AMYGDALA). Animal studies have shown that when this general area (temporal lobe) is damaged, behaviour becomes erratic (Kluver and Bucy 1937); for example, appetite changes including the eating of faeces and rocks have been reported, as well as attempts to copulate with members of the wrong species. Damage to this area also results in a failure to show a fear response to threatening stimuli. More specific damage to the amygdala itself interferes with the ability to regulate the significance of a stimulus, in particular its reward value (see LeDoux and Phelps 2000 for a review). However, there is no single brain structure that is responsible for the production, control or regulation of emotions. There are areas that mediate different emotional and motivational experiences, but the complex interactions that take place between these and other neural and cognitive functions make specific identification difficult.

Panksepp (2000) offers one of the clearest neural taxonomies of emotion, by separating emotions into three categories: reflexive, grade-A and higher sentiments. Reflexive affects are immediate and AUTOMATIC (see s. 3) emotional responses, such as hunger, PAIN (see s. 2 and s. 7) and pleasure. These represent some of the earliest evolutionary EMOTIONAL DEVELOPMENTS (see s. 4) and seem to be organised quite low in the brainstem. Panksepp describes these reflexive affects as 'time-locked'. 'Blue ribbon' grade-A emotions are longer-lasting emotions that initiate behavioural, psychological, cognitive and affective consequences and several separate and interrelated brain areas are implicated. For example, motivation or explorative behaviour enables animals to explore their environments and seek out rewards and REINFORCEMENT (see s. 3). The most enthusiastic seeking behaviour triggers electrical activity along the ascending brain (mesolimbic and mesocortical) dopamine system. It is believed that fluctuations in this system enable the direct encoding of reinforcement. This sensitivity to LEARNING (see s. 3) and goal-directed behaviour – regardless of reward – means that the system facilitates learning, even the learning of FALSE BELIEFS (see s. 4); hence explaining its activation in certain types of DRUG ADDICTION (see s. 2) and schizophrenic DELUSIONS (see s. 7). Third, Panksepp describes the *higher sentiments* as recent evolutionary developments in the FOREBRAIN (see s. 2); these include emotions such as shame, guilt, envy or humour. These categories do not necessarily represent natural kinds, but are useful for examining emotional and affective phenomena more clearly.   *AF*

Kluver, H. and Bucy, P. C. 1937: 'Psychic blindness' and other symptoms following bilateral temporal lobectomy in rhesus monkeys. *American Journal of Physiology* 119, 352–3. LeDoux, J. E. and Phelps, E. A. 2000: Emotional networks in the brain. In Lewis, M. and Haviland-Jones, J. M. (eds) *Handbook of Emotions*. New York: Guilford Press. MacLean, P. D. 1952: Psychosomatic disease and the 'visceral brain': recent developments bearing on the Papez theory of emotion. *Psychosomatic Medicine* 11, 338–53. Panksepp, J. 2000: Emotions as natural kinds in the brain. In Lewis, M. and Haviland-Jones, J. M. (eds) *Handbook of Emotions*. New York: Guilford Press. Papez, J. W. 1937: A proposed mechanism of emotion. *Archives of Neurology and Psychiatry* 79, 217–24.

emotion and neurochemistry There are two major approaches in understanding the links between neurochemistry and EMOTION. One starts from a theoretical basis of understanding emotion and the second from understanding disorders of emotion and assessing the underlying neurochemistry. These two strands of research link together.

Scientists have not yet agreed on a clear definition of emotion. Two early theories of emotion are the JAMES-LANGE THEORY and the CANNON-BARD THEORY. A more recent approach attempts to link EMOTION AND MOTIVATION (see MOTIVATION and s. 1, EMOTION AND MOTIVATION and s. 2, MOTIVATION AND EMOTION: BIOLOGICAL BASES) and, thereby, understanding the reward and punishment systems that underlie them. Emotional behaviour is a means for an individual or an animal to communicate its motivational state to another. Many of the brain regions responsible for HOMEOSTASIS (see s. 2) and rhythms of the body also produce emotional experiences: it is well established that pharmacological manipulations of both dopamine and noradrenaline mediate the exhilaration that people seek in taking cocaine and amphetamines by altering self-stimulation rates (Rolls 1975).

Many neurochemicals and agents have been implicated in mood and emotion, such as serotonin, noradrenaline, dopamine, ACETYLCHOLINE (see s. 2) and NEUROPEPTIDES (see s. 2). Much of the work supporting these relationships is from clinical studies, from animal and experimental studies which have investigated disorders of emotion. One of the most common disorders of emotion is DEPRESSION (see s. 7). Serotonin is one of the main neurochemicals which is implicated in depression. This is evidenced by a number of mechanisms, for instance, effective treatment of depression using drugs (SELECTIVE SEROTONIN REUPTAKE INHIBITORS – see s. 7, e.g. Prozac) (Boyer and Feighner 1996), genetic studies and experimental manipulation of levels of serotonin.   *MS*

Boyer, W. F. and Feighner, J. P. (eds) 1996: *Efficacy of Selective Serotonin Re-uptake Inhibitors in Acute Depression.* New York: John Wiley and sons. **Rolls, E. T.** 1975: *The Brain and Reward.* Oxford: Pergamon Press.

emotion and performance
EMOTIONS such as anxiety, anger, fear and EMBARRASSMENT (see s. 5) can all enhance or impede personal performance, but the emotion-performance link is most obvious in sport. One of the most comprehensive and influential accounts of the role of emotion in sport comes from Weiner's (1986) attributional model of emotion. This theory argues that the outcome of an activity (i.e. win or lose) is equated with success or failure. This outcome can then become externalised or internalised depending on (i) the locus of the event, (ii) the degree to which the individual feels they have control over the outcome and (iii) the stability of the outcome. Losers are more likely to experience negative emotions such as guilt, anger and sadness; winners, more positive emotions such as joy and pride. If the outcome event becomes linked with negative emotions, uncontrollable events and/or possible event reoccurrence, the individual is likely to internalise the outcome cause. These cognitions can then influence expectations about events in the future (Willimczik and Rethorst 1995).   *AF*

Weiner, B. 1986: *An Attributional Theory of Emotion and Motivation.* New York: Springer Verlag. **Willimczik, K. and Rethorst, S.** 1995: Cognitions and emotions in sport achievement situations. In Biddle, J. H. (ed.) *European Perspectives on Exercise and Sport Psychology.* Leeds: Human Kinetics, 218–44.

emotion: cognitive appraisal theory
Cognitive appraisal theory emphasises the way in which ideas, memories, BELIEFS (see s. 5) and expectations influence the interpretation of events and hence our emotional response to those events. The extent to which the individual feels they have control over an event will influence their emotional response. This cognitive appraisal is thought to involve a two-stage process: physiological arousal in response to an event or situation, followed by the interpretation and labelling of the physiological experience (Schachter and Singer 1962). This means that emotional experiences will ultimately depend on what aspects of the situation are attended to and the way in which those aspects are evaluated. An approaching lion may elicit physical arousal, but this will differ depending on whether it is observed captive in a zoo or running loose on the street. This theory also suggests that similar physiological states of arousal could be labelled and hence experienced (e.g. anger and joy) as any other emotion. *AF*

Schachter, S. and Singer, J. E. 1962: Cognitive, social, and physiological determinants of emotional states. *Psychological Review* 69(5), 379–99.

emotion: computational models
If the brain is an information-processing system, then it is possible to understand emotions from a perspective that they are programs that have evolved to facilitate many of the brain's functions. Essentially, computational models of emotion are an evolutionary approach that attempts to examine the architecture of emotions.

It is a basic engineering consideration that different systems are designed to perform different functions. If this analogy is applied to the way in which humans are designed, it suggests that different parts of our anatomy must have evolved to perform certain functions better than others. In other words, human beings have evolved a modular system, where different components perform different bodily operations; the digestive system is perfectly designed for providing nutrients to the body, the heart is designed to pump blood around the body, the lungs for oxygen. It follows that a specialised system for behaviour guidance should be equally well designed; an expert system that reacts, learns, motivates, problem-solves and regulates itself.

There is a body of evidence that emotional systems have evolved to facilitate REASONING (see s. 3) about numbers, LANGUAGE (see s. 2), the physical and biological world, as well as the mediating inference systems that allow us to understand the BELIEFS (see s. 5) and motivations of others (see Cosmides and Tooby 2000 for a review). The way in which this system processes emotional information is unclear, but there is some suggestion that perceptual data processing occurs through a general processing ALGORITHM (see s. 3) (or set of rules) that facilitates activities such as reasoning. Expert/novice studies possibly provide the best evidence that such computational systems exist. Experts have available a larger number of alternative mental models and – based on these models – are able to develop HEURISTICS (see s. 3) (or rules of thumb) that permit PROBLEM SOLVING (see s. 3). For example, expert chess players have more knowledge than novice players about possible board positions. This accumulation of knowledge influences both the speed at which board positions can be evaluated and decisions about the implications of particular strategic decisions (Chase and Simon 1973; Gobet and Simon 1996).   *AF*

Chase, W. G. and Simon, H. A. 1973: Perception in chess. *Cognitive Psychology* 4, 55–81. **Cosmides, L. and Tooby, J.** 2000: Evolutionary psychology and the emotions. In Lewis, M. and Haviland-Jones, J. M. (eds) *Handbook of Emotions.* New York: Guilford Press. **Gobet, F. and Simon, H. A.** 1996: Recall of rapidly presented random board positions is function of skill. *Psychonomic Bulletin and Review* 3, 159–63.

emotions and facial expressions
Charles Darwin (1872) was one of the first to demonstrate the universality of expressions and the consistency of these expressions in both man and animals. Darwin proposed that EMOTIONAL EXPRESSIONS (see s. 5) and their accompanying facial actions are innate and maintained because of their communicative advantage. There is considerable disagreement about what Darwin actually meant when he wrote about facial expressions and his early ideas now play no part in modern research into facial behaviour. However, while disagreeing about the actual nature of EMOTION, the key investigators of facial expression – Izard, Camras, Zajonc and Ekman – agree that much of what is considered basic emotional expression is innately programmed (Strongman 2003). There are facial expressions that appear to be characteristic of emotions such as anger, joy, shame and sadness. Each of the BASIC EMOTIONS (see s. 4) – sadness, joy, anger, surprise – has distinctive, charac-

istic facial expressions (Ekman and Friesen 1982) and these expressions appear spontaneously in the very young, the congenitally blind and across different CULTURES (see s. 1 and s. 5). [See EMOTIONS: BASIC] For example, NEGATIVE EMOTIONS, such as anger or disgust, are usually associated with a furrowed brow (frown) and sadness with a slackened muscle tone or 'long face', whereas the smile is generally associated with the COMMUNICATION (see s. 2) of happiness or pleasure. There is uniqueness in the pattern of facial muscles associated with the DUCHENNE SMILE that cannot be replicated in a posed smile. A genuine smile is composed not only of raised lips and cheeks, but also of wrinkling around the eye area. 'Lying smiles' can be differentiated from genuine smiles by the absence of this wrinkled area.

These fundamental facial expressions are also present cross-culturally: different cultures use the same visual cues when making decisions about the emotional expression of others. Ekman and Friesen (1982) compared the intensity of differing facial expressions across ten different cultures, with universal agreement about which of the two expressions were the most intense. Through an examination of both within-culture and across-culture expression and within-gender and across-gender expression, Matsumoto and Ekman (1989) extended these findings, reporting that, despite differences in facial structure, RACE (see s. 1, ETHNICITY AND RACE ISSUES), GENDER (see s. 1, GENDER AND SEXUALITY ISSUES) and cultures, there is much homogeneity in the ways in which different cultures judge the emotional expressions of others.

However, while many aspects of emotional expression are innate, emotional expressions *per se* are not always an accurate indication of emotional states. The smile is used in many situations to mask true feelings, such as dislike or EMBARRASSMENT (see s. 5), or to hide a lie, and while universals in emotional expression exist (Ekman 1992) there are also many subtle individual and cross-cultural differences in the way in which emotion is communicated. Through a process of socialisation the individual is taught the NORMS (see also s. 5) that govern the way in which emotion can be expressed. These behavioural norms may emphasise the intensity of one facial expression over another or even the non-expression of a particular facial expression. One of the most comprehensive cross-cultural studies (Ekman 1972) examined differences in the facial expression of North American and Japanese students. Students watched film clips that included neutral or stressful scenes. American students were reported as expressing more facial 'surprise' in response to stressful stimuli, whereas the facial behaviour of the Japanese students reflected a sad emotional expression.

These findings have led Ekman and Friesen (1982) to develop a theory of facial expression that acknowledges that facial expressions do not always match emotions because emotional expression involves multiple signals, not just facial expression. Nonetheless facial expressions are central to the emotional experience and changing your facial expression can alter your emotions. Ekman argues that cognition, facial expression and AUTONOMIC NERVOUS SYSTEM (see s. 2) processing are separate but interrelated systems. While cognition may mediate an emotional experience, it is facial expression that has the most direct influence on how we feel. Basic emotions have distinctive facial expressions and these occur universally. Timing and intensity of the emotional experience – and hence emotional expression – reflect the details and strength of a particular emotional experience. Like Darwin, Ekman argues that these pan-human qualities mean that emotion has a specific adaptive advantage. For example, negative emotions such as anger and fear act as early warning systems, enabling us to respond quickly to threatening situations. The facial expressions associated with these emotions communicate vital information about how an individual is feeling, informing others that something is wrong and/or eliciting both EMPATHY (see s. 4) and help from others. *AF*

Darwin, C. 1872: *The Expression of the Emotions in Man and Animals with Photographic and Other Illustrations*. London: J. Murray. **Ekman, P.** 1972: Universals and cultural differences in facial expressions of emotion. In Cole, J. (ed.) *Nebraska Symposium on Motivation*. Lincoln: University of Nebraska Press, vol. 19, 207–83. **Ekman, P.** 1992: Facial expressions of emotions: new findings, new questions. *Psychological Science* 3, 34–8. **Ekman, P. and Friesen, W. V.** 1982: Felt, false and miserable similes. *Journal of Nonverbal Behaviour* 6(4), 238–52. **Matsumoto, D.** 1987: The role of facial response in the experience of emotion: more methodological problems and meta-analysis. *Journal of Personality and Social Psychology* 52(4), 769–74. **Matsumoto, D. and Ekman, P.** 1989: American-Japanese cultural differences in intensity ratings of facial expressions of emotion. *Motivation and Emotion* 13, 143–57. **Strongman K. T.** 2003: *The Psychology of Emotion* (5th edn). London: John Wiley.

emotions: basic BASIC EMOTIONS (see s. 4) are the primitive forms from which all other emotional experiences are derived. There are generally thought to be between six and ten basic emotions; these include happiness, interest, surprise, fear, anger, sorrow and disgust (Ekman 1992). Distinctions can be made between these primitive expressions and other 'derived' emotions through the unique way in which these emotions are expressed; all basic emotions differ in motivational, behavioural and physiological characteristics, and have their own unique facial expression. Evidence for the existence of these basic emotions comes from observations of emotional 'universals'. People from different CULTURES (see s. 1 and s. 5) display similar facial responses to similar emotional stimuli, leading to the argument that there is an evolutionary basis for their existence (Plutchik 1993). For example, the smile is generally associated with the COMMUNICATION (see s. 2) of positive emotional expression (happiness, pleasure), the frown with negative emotional expression (dislike, anger). *AF*

Ekman, P. 1992: An argument for basic emotions. In Stein, N. and Oatley, K. (eds) *Basic Emotions*. Hove: Lawrence Erlbaum, 169–200. **Plutchik, R.** 1993: Emotions and their vicissitudes: emotions and psychopathology. In Lewis, M. and Haviland-Jones, J. M. (eds) *Handbook of Emotions*. New York: Guilford Press.

emotions: clinical aspects Effectively managing our emotions facilitates understanding of the relationship between the SELF (see s. 1, s. 4 and s. 5) and the environment and fosters greater psychological well-being (Erber 1996). This emotional management involves emotional perception, appraisal, expression and self-reflection. The individual must be able to perceive acutely the emotion that they are experiencing and identify that emotion in others. When we are unable to regulate and communicate our emotions, dysregulation occurs; the system 'goes wrong'. Emotional dysfunction is considered a key component in PSYCHOPATHOLOGY (see s. 7); poor emotional regulation appears in all the DSM (see s. 7) II disorders and over 50 per cent of Axis I disorders (Gross 1998).

What does seem to be important is the ability to recognise and articulate our emotional experiences. Individuals who have difficulty articulating their emotions are less empathetic to others and more likely to suffer from DEPRESSION (see s. 7) (Salovey et al. 2000). ALEXITHYMIA sufferers are unable to describe or recognise emotions in either themselves or others. This condition is often found in both physical and psychiatric disorders, including EATING DISORDERS (see s. 7), anxiety and depression.

There are a number of approaches to understanding emotional dysfunction: psychoanalytic, behavioural, physiological, phenomenological and cognitive theories all contribute to our understanding of the way in which emotional behaviours are linked to particular pathologies. The way in which emotion influences our TEMPERAMENT (see s. 4) is of particular interest to clinical theory; individuals who present high levels of negative affect will often present symptoms of anxiety and/or depression. One of the most comprehensive theories of emotional disorders emphasises the links between emotional disorders and cognition (Barlow 1991, 2000).

While acknowledging the influences of factors such as biology, early life experiences and LEARNING (see s. 3), Barlow argues that what is essential to the establishment of an emotional disorder is uncertainty. Barlow sees four types of disorder – MANIA (see s. 7), uncontrollable anger, panic and depression – as being linked to both background conditions (e.g. STRESS – see s. 7) and transitory emotional experiences (e.g. panic, fear, anger). Stress anxiety or chronic states of dysthymia can interact with more temporary emotional experiences (panic, fear or anger). If transitory states are experienced suddenly or in an unexpected way, the individual will experience the emotion as being out of control. For example, panic attacks are a fear-related disorder. All individuals at some point experience fear, often unexpectedly; in panic attacks, however, an anxious apprehension of fear develops. The individual becomes worried about when and where the next attack will happen. Here we can see that the cognitive component of the panic attack disorder is the preoccupation with the attack itself. This preoccupation leads to the whole emotional process becoming circular and out of control. [See also EMOTIONS: MANAGEMENT OF]   AF

Barlow, D. H. 1991: Disorders of emotion. *Psychological Inquiry* 2(1), 58–71. Barlow, D. H. 2000: Unravelling the mysteries of anxiety and its disorders from the perspective of emotion theory. *American Psychologist* 55(1), 1245–63. Erber, R. 1996: The self-regulation of moods. In Martin, L. L. and Tesser, A. (eds) *Striving and Feeling: Interactions among Goals, Affect and Self-regulation*. Hillsdale NJ: Lawrence Erlbaum, 251–75. Gross, J. J. 1998: The emerging field of emotion regulation: an integrative review. *Review of General Psychology* 2(3), 271–99. Salovey, P., Bedell, B. T., Detweiler, J. B. and Mayer, J. D. 2000: Current directions in emotional intelligence research. In Lewis, M. and Haviland-Jones, J. M. (eds) *Handbook of Emotions*. New York: Guilford Press.

emotions: management of

Emotional management allows us to seek out activities that will bring about POSITIVE EMOTIONS such as pleasure or happiness and avoid activities that will bring about NEGATIVE EMOTIONS. The complexity of emotions and the ways in which they can combine in both forceful and subtle ways means that emotional management requires openness to emotional feelings and the ability to continually monitor and reflect on the emotional experience. The individual must be able to understand and analyse why certain experiences bring about a positive mood, whereas other experiences do not. Effective emotional management facilitates understanding of the relationship between the SELF (see s. 1, s. 4 and s. 5) and the environment and fosters greater psychological well-being (Erber 1996).

Emotional management comes through a process of emotional perception, appraisal, expression and self-reflection. The individual must be able to acutely perceive the EMOTION they are experiencing and identify that emotion in others. For example, individuals who have difficulty articulating their emotions are less empathetic to others and more likely to suffer from DEPRESSION (see s. 7) (Salovey et al. 2000).

Thinking about and understanding the emotional experience facilitates evaluation and prioritisation of emotions. To effectively appraise the emotional experience (EMOTIONAL INTELLIGENCE), the individual must learn to understand how different emotions are related and recognise the consequences of certain emotional responses. For example, experiencing guilt because of directing anger at a loved one regulates the intensity of the anger emotion. Understanding the relationship between anger and guilt allows us to perceive the causes and consequences of our actions, making it less likely that we will express inappropriate levels of anger in the future. Emotional knowledge such as this also enables us in managing emotions of others. Recognising that certain situations bring us great joy motivates us to seek out those experiences, and encourage others to do likewise. This desire to want to make others feel better is essential to the forming of bonds, particularly between loved ones.   *AF*

Erber, R. 1996: The self-regulation of moods. In Martin, L. L. and Tesser, A. (eds) *Striving and Feeling: Interactions among Goals, Affect, and Self-regulation*. Hillside NJ: Erlbaum. Salovey, P., Bedell, B. T., Detweiler, J. B. and Mayer, J. D. 2000: Current directions in emotional intelligence research. In Lewis, M. and Haviland-Jones, J. M. (eds) *Handbook of Emotions*. New York: Guilford Press.

emotions: manipulation of

It is interesting that while EMOTION plays an important part in everything we do, CULTURE (see s. 1 and s. 5) imposes certain restrictions on emotional behaviour. Parents quickly teach their crying children other ways to communicate their emotions and hence control their distress; likewise with the development of information-processing skills, SELF-AWARENESS (see s. 4) increases and the tendency to control, mask and suppress EMOTIONAL EXPRESSION (see s. 5) emerges. For example, the smile is used in many situations to mask true feelings, such as dislike and EMBARRASSMENT (see s. 5), or to hide a lie. The DUCHENNE SMILE is a genuine spontaneous expression of happiness. There is uniqueness in the pattern of facial muscles associated with the Duchenne smile that cannot be replicated in a posed smile. This emotional manipulation is one way in which we conform to cultural expectations of emotion; there is, however, another aspect to the way in which we can manipulate our emotions.

Ekman, Levenson and Friesen (1983) have argued that while cognition may mediate an emotional experience, it is facial expression that has the most direct influence on how we feel. By manipulating our facial expression, we can change how we feel. In other words, by smiling we can ensure a positive emotional experience. This 'FACIAL FEED-BACK' HYPOTHESIS (see s. 5) argues that the feedback from facial expressions influences, creates and sustains the type of emotion that we experience. Other researchers have found some support for this hypothesis (Izard 1990; Matsumoto 1987); however, there remains some disagreement over the nature of the physiological and cognitive mechanisms that would support such a system. [See also EMOTIONS: MANAGEMENT OF] *AF*

Ekman, P., Levenson, R. W. and Friesen, W. V. 1983: Autonomic nervous system activity distinguishes among emotions. *Science* 221(4616), 1208–10. Izard, C. E. 1990: Facial expressions and the regulation of emotions. *Journal of Personality and Social Psychology* 58(3), 487–98. Matsumoto, D. 1987: The role of facial response in the experience of emotion: more methodological problems and meta-analysis. *Journal of Personality and Social Psychology* 52(4), 769–74.

emotions: nature and language of Providing a framework for what exactly constitutes the nature of EMO-TION is elusive because emotions are not overt behaviours that can be measured easily. Emotions seem to be composed of a multitude of components, including bodily changes, feelings, thoughts and actions. Emotions are not specific thoughts, moods, TEMPERAMENTS (see s. 4) or actions, but transitory STATES induced by environmental stimuli, memories of past events or expectations of new experiences. These states involve some sort of physiological change, such as increased heart rate, sweating, blushing, changes in posture and facial expression.

Emotions have an important function in helping us deal effectively and rapidly with changes in our environment. For example, emotions such as ANXIETY, anger, fear, shame and EMBARRASSMENT (see s. 5) can all enhance or impede personal performance. [See EMOTION AND PERFORMANCE] NEGATIVE EMOTIONS such as anger and fear act as early warning systems, enabling us to respond quickly to threatening situations. They can also help to moderate behaviour and re-evaluate courses of action. For example, moderate levels of anxiety over examination performance may motivate students into working harder, whereas high levels of anxiety may be overwhelming and make it difficult to prepare adequately. More POSITIVE EMOTIONS, such as happiness, indicate that things are going well and may motivate us in our pursuit of a goal. Emotional experiences are thought to have direction, from positive to negative, and this directionality is referred to as emotional valence.

Cognition is also important to emotional experience. [See EMOTION: COGNITIVE APPRAISAL THEORIES] Our BELIEFS (see s. 5), expectations and memories influence the interpretation of events and hence our emotional response to those events. For example, first-time flyers will often experience negative emotions such as feeling apprehensive or fearful. As flying experience increases, however, thoughts and memories surrounding the flying experiences will begin to shape the emotional responses. If the experiences are generally positive – such as familiarity with the noise of the aircraft or the cabin crew routine – negative emotional responses will gradually become replaced by more positive emotions, such as a general enjoyment of the flying experience.

Humans have evolved a variety of ways to communicate emotion non-verbally: movement, posture and particularly facial expression carry emotional information. For example, sadness can be communicated to others through particular facial expressions and bodily postures (Izard 1991). Such non-verbal expressions can indicate to others that something is wrong and may elicit responses of EMPA-THY (see s. 4) and help from others. Thus the social implications of EMOTIONAL EXPRESSION (see s. 5) are dependent on the ability of others to detect and interpret non-verbal cues to covert emotional states. This has prompted questions concerning the extent to which the COMMUNICATION (see s. 2) of emotion is like LANGUAGE (see s. 2) (i.e. the extent to which it is based on a conventional set of symbols organised according to specific rules). If emotions are language-like then there should be some degree of meaning-making embedded in similar social structures. The concept of emotional universals is often used in support of this idea, in particular, evidence that people from different cultures display similar facial responses to similar emotional stimuli (Plutchik 1993). Each of the BASIC EMOTIONS (see s. 4) [see EMOTIONS: BASIC] – of which there are generally considered to be between six and ten – has a distinctive characteristic expression associated with it, and these expressions are elicited universally by the same stimuli (Ekman and Friesen 1982). For example, the smile is generally associated with the communication of positive emotional expression (happiness, pleasure), the frown with negative emotional expression (dislike, anger). Different CULTURES (see s. 1 and s. 5) use the same visual cues when making decisions about the emotional expression of others. Ekman et al. (1987) compared the intensity of differing facial expressions across ten cultures and found universal agreement about which two expressions were the most intense. Through an examination of both within-culture and cross-culture expression and within-gender and across-gender expression, Matsumoto (1987) found that there is much homogeneity in the ways in which different cultures judge the emotional expressions of others, despite differences in facial structure, RACE (see s. 1, ETHNICITY AND RACE ISSUES), GENDER (see s. 1, GENDER AND SEXUALITY ISSUES) and cultures.

Observations of others' facial expressions play a very important part in the overall 'language of emotions'; the emotional expression of one person shapes the responses of another. As studies of the congenitally blind have shown, when no facial feedback is available, facial expressions of emotion gradually become less animated over time (Izard and Malatesta 1987). This is because facial expressions – as well as body posture and vocal tone – provide us with a social reference. Grins, sneers, frowns, smiles and stares communicate excitement, anger, happiness, confusion and a host of other information that can be used to reduce ambiguity in uncertain situations.

While many aspects of emotional expression are innate, emotional expressions *per se* are not always an accurate indication of emotional states. The problem with the study of emotional expression is that particular emotional states are capable of being controlled and masked. For example, the emotional anguish of suicidal people can often go undetected by family and friends because true emotions are concealed by the controlled expression of more positive emotional states. The control of emotional expression follows a complex developmental course. Parents can teach their crying, angry children other ways to communicate and hence control their distress, for example, pointing or asking for a desired toy. As motor SKILLS (see s. 3) increase, children will begin to use locomotive responses in response to emotional stimuli, such as running away from a fearful situation (Lewis 1993). Likewise with the development of information-processing skills there is an increase in SELF-AWARENESS (see s. 4) and the capacity to control emotional expression emerges. For example, the smile is used in many situations to mask true feelings, such as dislike or embarrassment, or to hide a lie. The DUCHENNE SMILE is a genuine spontaneous expression of happiness. There is uniqueness in the pattern of facial muscles associated with the Duchenne smile that cannot be replicated in a posed smile. *AF*

Ekman, P and Friesen, W. V. 1982: Felt, false and miserable smiles. *Journal of Nonverbal Behaviour* 6(4), 238–52. **Ekman, P., Friesen, W. V., O'Sullivan, M., Chan, A., Diacoyanni-Tarlatzis, I., Heider, K., Krause, R., LeCompte, W. A., Pitcairn, T., Ricci-Bitti, P. E., Scherer, K., Tomita, M. and Tzavaras, A.** 1987: Universals and cultural differences in the judgments of facial expressions of emotion. *Journal of Personality and Social Psychology* 53(4), 712–17. **Izard, C. E.** 1991: *The Psychology of Emotions.* New York: Plenum. **Izard, C. and Malatesta, C.** 1987: Perspectives on emotional development: 1. Differential emotions theory of early emotional development. In Osofsky, J. D. (ed.) *Handbook in Infant Development* (2nd edn). New York: John Wiley and Sons, 494–554. **Lewis, M.** 1993: The emergence of human emotions. In Lewis, M. and Haviland, J. M. (eds) *Handbook of Emotions.* New York: Guilford Press. **Matsumoto, D.** 1987: The role of facial response in the experience of emotion: more methodological problems and a meta-analysis. *Journal of Personality and Social Psychology* 52(4), 769–74. **Plutchik, R.** 1993: Emotions and their vicissitudes: emotions and psychopathology. In Lewis, M. and Haviland-Jones, J. M. (eds) *Handbook of Emotions.* New York: Guilford Press.

emotions: negative and positive An emotion can never be considered entirely positive or negative, good or bad, desirable or undesirable. While being generally considered negative, emotions such as anger, fear, guilt and sadness have important survival, moral and social functions. For example, sadness at the death of a loved one is part of the psychological process that allows humans to bond closely with one another. Sadness is also communicated to others, through facial expressions and body posture (Izard 1991). This expression informs others that something is wrong and may elicit both EMPATHY (see s. 4) and help from others (e. g. the reaction of compassion in a mother to the sadness of a child). Izard argues that, rather than a negative emotion, sadness motivates the SELF (see s. 1, s. 4 and s. 5) to deal with problems, increase altruistic behaviour and strengthen bonds with others.

It is more accurate, then, to say that some emotions lead to constructive behaviour, while others lead to psychological entropy. For example, poorly regulated sadness can lead to destructive behaviour such as physical gratification through consuming large quantities of fast food, sugar, caffeine or alcohol. This in turn can lead to weight control problems, feelings of helplessness and DEPRESSION (see s. 7) (Izard 1991). Other emotions, such as happi-

ness, tend to promote the exploration and enjoyment of new experiences. This desire for activities that foster enjoyment or positive emotion helps maintain a positive or optimistic emotional experience. There is evidence that this type of emotional state can facilitate the consideration of a wide range of solutions and OPINIONS (see s. 5), thus enabling creative problem solving and complex decision making (Isen 1993). *AF*

Isen, A. M. 1993: Positive effect and decision making. In Lewis, M. and Haviland-Jones, J. M. (eds) *Handbook of Emotions.* New York: Guilford Press. **Izard, C.** 1991: *The Psychology of Emotions.* New York: Plenum Press.

EPQ-R The Eysenck Personality Questionnaire (Revised) is a personality test measuring the personality traits of neuroticism, extroversion and psychoticism, together with a lie scale to detect cheating. *CC*

Eysenck, S. B., Eysenck, H. J. and Barrett, P. 1985: A revised version of the psychoticism scale. *Personality and Individual Differences* 6, 21–9.

ergonomics and work design Ergonomics is the scientific study of methods to allow humans to interact effectively with machines, of all kinds. These principles are usually applied to increase operators' performance (e.g. quickly locating and opening a computer file; allowing air-traffic controllers to identify and discriminate aircraft; devising easily discriminable warning signals that alert pilots to danger), health, comfort or safety (e.g. positioning chairs and computer equipment so as to avoid back pain; design of workstations to minimise the effects of repetitive strain injury or eyestrain; arranging patterns of shiftwork so as to minimise the adverse effects of diurnal rhythms). The effects of special environmental and physiological factors (e.g. sleeplessness, medication, noise, distractions) may also be analysed, and organisational ergonomics includes work design, teamwork, personnel resource management, and design of working times.

Identifying and applying ergonomic principles thus involves many branches of psychology, physiology, computer science engineering, management and sociology. What is more, Broadbent (1958) famously argued that solving the real-world problems, revealed when humans have difficulty performing some apparently simple operation involving equipment, may highlight issues of considerable theoretical interest.

The psychology of visual perception can, for example, identify the colours to which the eye is most sensitive, for use in warning signals. Control theory offers some insights as to possible control laws linking an operator's movement of a pointing device (mouse or joystick) to the position of a cursor on a screen (or the position of a missile-sight), so that the cursor may be quickly moved to the appropriate region and then finely manoeuvred. The optimal control law may incorporate velocity and acceleration components instead of just reflecting the position of the pointing device.

The design of computer interfaces is of particular importance. Good ergonomic principles for display design have been established for over a decade (Hix and Hartson 1993). These broad principles include consistency (e.g. CTRL-X should have the same effect in any application; the RETURN and ENTER keys should either be treated as being identical by all applications or as different by all applications), breaking complex tasks into simpler ones (hence 'wizards', etc.) and minimising MEMORY (see s. 1) demands (e.g. showing users their level of progress through a complex sequence). Software should use 'real-world' metaphors where possible, such as desktops, and error messages should not make minor mistakes seem catastrophic. It should be possible to 'undo' mistakes, and colour should be used consistently, avoiding too many attention-grabbing alerts – flashing red icons, etc. However, the growing complexity of designing and facilitating navigation through entire virtual worlds will soon make such issues appear primitive. *CC*

Broadbent, D. E. 1958: *Perception and Communication.* New York: Pergamon Press. Hix, D. and Hartson, H. R. 1993: *Developing User Interfaces: Ensuring Usability Through Product and Process.* New York: J. Wiley.

ergs Ergs are biological DRIVES (see s. 2) in Cattell's model of MOTIVATION. [See MOTIVATION STRUCTURE and MOTIVATIONAL THEORIES] Examples include hunger and sex. *CC*

Cattell, R. B. and Child, D. 1975: *Motivation and Dynamic Structure.* London: Holt, Rinehart & Winston.

external bias If MULTIPLE REGRESSION (see s. 8) is used to predict job performance from test scores for two or more groups of people, external bias is inferred if the groups show regression lines having different slopes and/or INTERCEPTS (see s. 8). It implies that the relationship between test score and job performance is different for members of different groups. *CC*

Berk, R. A. (ed.) 1982: *Handbook of Methods for Detecting Test Bias.* Baltimore: The Johns Hopkins University Press.

extroversion The trait of extroversion is central to the current conceptualisations of trait psychology. Someone who scores high on extroversion is generally described as sociable, friendly, lively, assertive, carefree and active. However, it is not a new concept; its roots extend back to the work of James and Jung at the start of the twentieth century. Extroversion can be found across CULTURES (see s. 1 and s. 5) and is common to most of the well-known PERSONALITY QUESTIONNAIRES (Kline and Barrett 1983). Extroversion is a broad, higher-order trait – which means that it may be made up of distinct facets. Although there is broad agreement as to the general nature of the trait, researchers disagree as to the exact make-up of the facets, which may include sociability, impulsivity and reward sensitivity. Extroversion correlates positively with average levels of POSITIVE AFFECT and is a significant predictor of subjective well-being and happiness.

Because of its moderate HERITABILITY (see s. 4), extroversion is thought to be biologically based. However, to date there is little solid evidence for the mechanisms involved. Eysenck (1967) proposed that introversion/extroversion differences are based upon levels of activity of the cortico-reticular loop, with introverts having higher levels of activity than extroverts and thus being chronically more aroused. Due to this over-arousal, introverts will prefer non-stimulating behaviours such as reading in solitude, whereas under-aroused extroverts will seek social stimulation. Psychophysiological measures, such as EEG

and electrodermal response, have traditionally been used to test this theory as they give indices of arousal: the results are equivocal. The other main area of research to the biological basis of extroversion is neurochemical. This area is based predominantly on animal studies and Depue and Collins (1999) suggest that extroverts demonstrate an increased sensitivity to reward signals. In a review of evidence relating dopamine (DA) to extroversion, they concede that: 'There is a paucity of work on individual differences in DA functioning in normal humans'. Costa and McCrae (1980) suggest that: 'We may all be on hedonic treadmills ... [but] ... the treadmills of adjusted extroverts are much happier places to be.' *MS*

Costa, P. T. Junr. and McCrae, R. R. 1980: Influence of extroversion and neuroticism on subjective well-being: Happy and unhappy people. *Journal of Personality and Social Psychology* 38, 668–78. Depue, R. A. and Collins, P. F. 1999: Neurobiology of the structure of personality: dopamine, facilitation of incentive motivation, and extroversion. *Behavioural and Brain Sciences* 22, 491–569. Eysenck, H. J. 1967: *The Biological Basis of Personality.* Springfield IL: Charles C. Thomas. Kline, P. and Barrett, P. 1983: The factors in personality questionnaires among normal subjects. *Advances in Behavioural Research and Therapy* 5, 141–202.

Eysenck's three-factor model H. J. Eysenck's personality theory is one of the most influential ever to emerge in the field. It is hypothetico-deductive and has its origins in the clinical and experimental literatures, in contrast to big-five theories that are descriptive and have their origins in adjective ratings. Eysenck advocated a natural science approach to the study of personality. His theory falls within the NOMOTHETIC (see s. 8 and also s. 1, NOMOTHETIC METHODS) trait tradition and has been developed and modified over the years in response to EMPIRICAL (see s. 8) evidence gleaned through the application of the scientific method.

Eysenckian theory originally postulated two ORTHOGONAL (see s. 8) (i.e. uncorrelated) dimensions. The first dimension is NEUROTICISM–stability, described by 'tense', 'moody' and 'anxious' at one end and 'calm', 'confident' and 'relaxed' at the other. The second dimension is EXTROVERSION–introversion, described by 'active', 'outgoing' and 'sociable' at one end and 'restrained', 'unsociable' and 'withdrawn' at the other. In 1976, Eysenck added a third orthogonal dimension to his system, following evidence that neuroticism and extroversion could not differentiate between normal adults and borderline schizophrenics. PSYCHOTICISM–normality differentiates between 'aggressive', 'hostile' and 'psychopathic' individuals at one end and 'conformist', 'empathic' and 'socialised' individuals at the other.

A major advantage of Eysenckian theory is that it attempts to identify the origins of each of the three dimensions it comprises. The theory proposes that the dimension of neuroticism emerges because of individual differences in the AUTONOMIC NERVOUS SYSTEM (see s. 2), with neurotic individuals having systems that are more labile. With respect to extroversion, it postulates individual differences in cortical arousal, with extroverts experiencing lower levels of arousal. The theory is somewhat vague in relation to psychoticism, hinting at a possible involvement of male hormone levels based on the fact that males consistently show higher scores on this dimension than females. Although empirical support for these biological mechanisms has been mixed, Eysenck's foresight to seek the roots of personality in physiology was ahead of its time and continues to shape the field to the present day.

The development of the measures used to operationalise the Eysenckian dimensions has mirrored the development of the underlying theory. The best operationalisation of the model is provided by the revised version of the Eysenck Personality Questionnaire (EPQ-R), one of the most widely used psychological instruments in the world. Eysenckian theory has received considerable empirical support, including replicable evidence supporting the HERITABILITY (see s. 4) and universality of the three basic dimensions. In addition, it has provided the basis for several related theories of personality, the most influential of which was developed by Eysenck's student, J. A. Gray.

KP

Barrett, P. T., Petrides, K. V., Eysenck, S. B. G. and Eysenck, H. J. 1998: The Eysenck Personality Questionnaire: an examination of the factorial similarity of P, E, N, and L across 34 countries. *Personality and Individual Differences* 25, 805–19. **Eysenck, H. J.** 1967: *The Biological Basis of Personality.* Springfield IL: Charles C. Thomas. **Eysenck, H. J.** 1997: Personality and experimental psychology: the unification of psychology and the possibility of a paradigm. *Journal of Personality and Social Psychology* 73, 1224–37. **Eysenck, H. J. and Eysenck, M. W.** 1985: *Personality and Individual Differences: A Natural Science Approach.* New York: Plenum.

F

factor analysis Factor analysis is a statistical technique which is widely used in psychometric analyses [see PSYCHOMETRICS] to determine how many distinct traits are measured by a set of items or tests. Suppose that a psychologist has written a 30-item PERSONALITY QUESTIONNAIRE, but has no idea of how many different dimensions of personality there are. If these items are given to a large (minimum of 200) representative SAMPLE (see s. 8) of the population and the responses factor-analysed using a standard statistical package, the technique will show (a) how many different aspects ('traits' or 'factors') of personality are measured by the 30 items, and (b) which items measure which FACTOR (see s. 8).

Unfortunately, determining the number of factors that underlie a set of data is not straightforward. Simulation studies (Zwick and Velicer 1986) show that Cattell's (Cattell 1966) graphical scree test is often effective, although lacking a sound statistical rationale. At least a dozen other techniques have been proposed, but frequently give contradictory indications.

Once the factor analysis has been performed, it is necessary to name the factors by scrutinising the items that are the best indicators of each factor (highest 'factor loadings'). For example, if the items 'Do you have a good sense of humour?' and 'Are you generous?' are the best indicators of a factor, some theorists would label the factor as 'social adeptness'. This is inadequate. As being dour and mean are not sociably desirable characteristics, the factor might well just measure whether people are being honest when answering the questionnaire! It is essential to validate [see VALIDITY] factors, in the same way that one validates a test, before concluding that the label is correct.

Factor analysis has been used to explore the structure of human abilities at all levels (g [see GENERAL ABILITY], PRIMARY MENTAL ABILITIES, second-order abilities [see SECOND-ORDER ABILITY FACTORS]) using the three-stratum model [see ABILITY: THREE-STRATUM MODEL]. It has also been used to discover the main PERSONALITY TRAITS and STATES (e.g. Cattell 1973; the BIG-FIVE MODEL OF PERSONALITY) and is also useful in determining whether a test is well-constructed: if the scoring key for a test shows that items 1, 3 and 5 measure one trait and items 2, 4 and 6 another, when responses to the items are factor-analysed, two factors should be found, one comprising items 1, 3 and 5 and the other items 2, 4 and 6. (See also s. 8, FACTOR ANALYSIS)   *CC*

Carroll, J. B. 1993: *Human Cognitive Abilities: A Survey of Factor-analytic Studies.* Cambridge: Cambridge University Press. **Cattell, R. B.** 1966: The scree test for the number of factors. *Multivariate Behavioral Research* 1, 140–61. **Cattell, R. B.** 1973: *Personality and Mood by Questionnaire.* San Francisco: Jossey-Bass. **Comrey, A. L. and Lee, H. B.** 1992: *A First Course in Factor Analysis* (2nd edn). Hillsdale NJ: Lawrence Erlbaum Associates. **Zwick, W. R. and Velicer, W. F.** 1986: Comparison of five rules for determining the number of components to retain. *Psychological Bulletin* 99, 432–42.

field dependence Field dependence is a cognitive style [see COGNITIVE STYLE AND LEARNING STYLE] and refers to a person's ability to perceive an object (a geometric figure, an object in space or one's own body) as separate from the surrounding field (Witkin et al. 1962). According to Witkin, this perceptual style is indicative of a broader mode of personal functioning called psychological differentiation or sense of separate IDENTITY (see s. 4 and s. 5). Field dependence is normally measured by the EMBEDDED FIGURES TEST or by the rod and frame test. Completing the embedded figures test (sometimes called hidden figures) involves extracting a simple figure that is hidden in a more complex one. For those who are more field independent the simple figure seems to just 'pop out'. The rod and frame test requires an ability to adjust the rod to the true vertical when surrounded by a tilted frame. Those who are field independent can ignore the context and adjust the rod, while those who are field-dependent are more influenced by the tilted frame. One of the criticisms of the tests is that they measure a single pole of the dimension and cannot be distinguished from more conventional measures of cognitive ability. It has been argued that measures of field dependence/independence are simply measures of spatial ability (McLeod at al. 1986).

Despite these criticisms, field dependence has been one of the most intensively studied cognitive styles, and appeals to those with an interest in group differences in ABILITIES or group differences in PERSONALITY. Because of its relationship to spatial REASONING (see s. 3), it has attracted the interest of GENDER (see s. 1, GENDER AND SEXUALITY ISSUES) differences researchers, with considerable critique (Haaken 1988). Similarly, because the construct refers to an aspect of analytical vs. global style of information processing, it has been used to study various hypotheses about cross-cultural differences. For example, in a recent cross-cultural study, Kuehnen et al. (2001) reported that individualist CULTURES (see s. 1 and s. 5) (USA and Germany) are more likely to be field independent than collectivist cultures (Russia and Malaysia).

Although the construct has been studied for some 50 years, the cognitive processes involved are not yet fully specified. Recent research has attempted to relate performance on field-dependent tasks to visuo-spatial and executive components of WORKING MEMORY (see s. 3) (Miyake et al. 2001).   *CMG*

Haaken, J. 1988: Field dependence research: a historical analysis of a psychological construct. *Signs* 13(2), 311–30. **Kuehnen, U., Hannover, B., Roeder, U., Shah, A. A., Schubert, B., Upmeyer, A. and Zakaria, S.** 2001: Cross-cultural variations in identifying embedded figures: comparisons from the United States, Germany, Russia, and Malaysia. *Journal of Cross-Cultural Psychology* 32(3), 365–71. **McLeod, C. M., Jackson, R. A. and Palmer, J.** 1986: On the relation between spatial ability and field dependence. *Intelligence* 10, 141–51. **Miyake, A., Witzke, A. H., Emerson, M. J.** 2001: Field dependence-independence from a working memory perspective: a dual-task investigation of the hidden figures test. *Memory* 9(4–6), 445–57. **Witkin, H. A.,**

Dyk, R. B., Faterson, H. F., Goodenough, D. R. and Karp, S. A. 1962: *Psychological Differentiation*. New York: Wiley.

five-factor model of personality

Raymond Cattell has long argued (e.g. Cattell 1946) that careful ratings of behaviour could form the foundation of a comprehensive THEORY (see s. 8) of PERSONALITY. Applying the method of FACTOR ANALYSIS (see also s. 8) to a large number of such ratings should reveal the basic source traits of personality. Tupes and Christal (1992) found five such FACTORS (see s. 8) when analysing ratings of behaviour, although somewhat alarmingly the same factors were found when raters evaluated complete strangers (Passini and Norman 1966), raising the possibility that Tupes and Christal's raters were producing STEREOTYPES (see s. 5) rather than accurate ratings of how people actually behaved. Nevertheless, Norman (1967) produced 75 rating scales to measure the Tupes and Christal factors. Costa and McCrae were late converts to the model. They discovered (Costa and McCrae 1976) that EXTROVERSION and NEUROTICISM emerged when the scales of Cattell's 16PF questionnaire were factor analysed, as had others such as Hundleby and Connor (1968). Costa and McCrae also found another small factor, added more items and named it 'OPENNESS to experience', then later added two more factors from Goldberg's development of Norman's work – 'AGREEABLENESS' and 'CONSCIENTIOUSNESS' – altering Goldberg's factor of 'intellect' so that it corresponded with their factor of 'openness' in the process. Two questionnaires, the NEO-PI(R) and the shorter version, known as the five-factor inventory (Costa and McCrae 1992), were developed to measure these traits.

Despite its somewhat arbitrary nature (shaped at least as much by determination to discover five factors, each represented by six facets, as by the results of factor analysing the correlations between observed or self-reported behaviour), Costa and McCrae's five-factor model is enormously influential; the factors have been found to emerge when translations of the questionnaire are used, and several of the factors predict behaviour. [See PERSONALITY AND EVERYDAY LIFE] *CC*

Cattell, R. B. 1946: *Description and Measurement of Personality*. New York: World Book Company. Costa, P. T. and McCrae, R. R. 1976: Age differences in personality structure: a cluster-analytic approach. *Journal of Gerontology* 31, 564–70. Costa, P. T. and McCrae, R. R. 1992: *NEO-PI(R) Professional Manual*. Odessa FL: Psychological Assessment Resources. Hundleby, J. D. and Connor, W. H. 1968: Interrelationships between personality inventories: the 16PF, MMPI and MPI. *Journal of Consulting and Clinical Psychology* 32, 152–7. Norman, W. T. 1967: *2800 Personality Trait Descriptors: Normative Operating Characteristics for a University Population*. Ann Arbor: University of Michigan, Department of Psychological Sciences. Passini, F. T. and Norman, W. T. 1966: A universal conception of personality structure? *Journal of Personality and Social Psychology* 4, 44–9. Tupes, E. C. and Christal, R. E. 1992: Recurrent personality-factors based on trait ratings. *Journal of Personality* 60, 225–51.

fixed-role therapy

This is a form of therapy stemming from George Kelly's PERSONAL CONSTRUCT THEORY. The first stage involves establishing a patient's system of constructs using REPERTORY GRID TECHNIQUES. The person's own position on each of the constructs is established (by using 'me' as one of the elements in the repertory grid). So, too, is the person's ideal position on each of the constructs ('me as I would like to be'). Fixed-role therapy then involves the client acting as if they were their ideal SELF (see s. 1, s. 4 and s. 5) for a prolonged time. For example, someone with debilitating shyness who wanted to become a loud extrovert would simply act as if they were an extrovert in their daily life, to see what it felt like. A subsequent session would evaluate whether the person found that doing so proved useful in improving their problem. This is in stark contrast to approaches such as Rogers' self theory, where the emphasis is on understanding a relatively fixed self. *CC*

Kelly, G. A. 1955: *The Psychology of Personal Constructs*. New York: Norton, vols 1 and 2. Kelly, G. A. 1963: *A Theory of Personality*. New York: Norton.

fluid intelligence

A SECOND-ORDER ABILITY FACTOR of abstract thinking ability discovered by Raymond Cattell and found in the three-stratum model of mental abilities [see ABILITY: THREE-STRATUM MODEL]. Some authors find that it is almost identical to Spearman's GENERAL ABILITY factor, *g*. *CC*

Flynn effect

James Flynn's discovery that FLUID INTELLIGENCE test scores for any particular age group increase by about three IQ points (0.2 STANDARD DEVIATIONS – see s. 8) per decade, worldwide, summarised in Flynn (1999). *CC*

Flynn, J. R. 1999: Searching for justice – the discovery of IQ gains over time. *American Psychologist* 54, 5–20.

G

gender differences in neuroticism and psychoticism

Gender differences in NEUROTICISM and PSYCHOTICISM are well documented, females scoring somewhat higher than males on neuroticism and appreciably lower on psychoticism (Eysenck and Eysenck 1975). In terms of the FIVE-FACTOR MODEL OF PERSONALITY, women score higher on neuroticism, AGREEABLENESS, warmth and OPENNESS to feelings, and lower on assertiveness and openness to ideas (Costa, Terracciano and McCrae 2001), and these sex differences were most pronounced in western societies. An older META-ANALYSIS (see s. 8) of several PERSONALITY QUESTIONNAIRES found that males are more assertive, with higher self-esteem than females, and that females are higher than males in EXTROVERSION, ANXIETY, trust and (especially) tender-mindedness. The consistent differences in neuroticism/anxiety and tough-mindedness/psychoticism led Lynn (1995) to argue that sex differences in scores on personality questionnaires stem from the biologically determined higher levels of AGGRESSION (see s. 5) shown by men.

Cross-cultural studies are harder to interpret because of the possibility that differences between groups may be due to response biases or differences in nuance between translated items rather than genuine differences in personality. Lynn (1981) found that economically developed countries generally showed lower scores on neuroticism and psychoticism, and suggests that this is due to the STRESS (see s. 7) of poverty; controversially, he has recently suggested that differences in psychoticism are substantial and may reflect genetic differences (Lynn 2002; Skeem, Edens, Sanford and Colwell 2003; Zuckerman 2003). It also seems that cross-cultural differences in personality are reflected in value systems (Hofstede and McCrae 2004).

CC

Costa, P. T., Terracciano, A. and McCrae, R. R. 2001: Gender differences in personality traits across cultures: robust and surprising findings. *Journal of Personality and Social Psychology* 81, 322–31. **Eysenck, H. J. and Eysenck, S. B. J.** 1975: *Manual of the Eysenck Personality Questionnaire*. London: Hodder and Stoughton. **Hofstede, G. and McCrae, R. R.** 2004: Personality and culture revisited: linking traits and dimensions of culture. *Cross-Cultural Research* 38, 52–88. **Lynn, R.** 1981: Cross-cultural differences in neuroticism, extroversion and psychoticism. In Lynn, R. (ed.) *Dimensions of Personality*. Oxford: Pergamon. **Lynn, R.** 1995: Cross-cultural differences in intelligence and personality. In Saklofske, D. H. and Zeidner, M. (eds) *International Handbook of Personality and Intelligence*. New York: Plenum. **Lynn, R.** 2002: Racial and ethnic differences in psychopathic personality. *Personality and Individual Differences* 32, 273–316. **Skeem, J. L., Edens, J. F., Sanford, G. M. and Colwell, L. H.** 2003: Psychopathic personality and racial/ethnic differences reconsidered: a reply to Lynn (2002). *Personality and Individual Differences* 35, 1439–62. **Zuckerman, M.** 2003: Are there racial and ethnic differences in psychopathic personality? A critique of Lynn's (2002) racial and ethnic differences in psychopathic personality. *Personality and Individual Differences* 35, 1463–9.

general ability

Otherwise known as general intelligence or *g*. A pervasive FACTOR (see s. 8) of mental ability discovered by Spearman (1904) and a feature of most modern structures of mental ability (e.g. the three-stratum model [see ABILITY: THREE-STRATUM MODEL]), three notable exceptions being multiple intelligence theory [see MULTIPLE INTELLIGENCES], TRIARCHIC THEORY and the STRUCTURE OF INTELLECT MODEL.

CC

Spearman, C. 1904: General intelligence objectively determined and measured. *American Journal of Psychology* 15, 201–93.

generalisability theory

Generalisability theory (Brennan 2001; Cronbach, Gleser, Nanda and Rajaratnam 1972) is a psychometric [see PSYCHOMETRICS] method which offers an alternative to traditional RELIABILITY theory. Suppose that it is assumed that a test consists of a number of items, randomly sampled from the (perhaps near-infinite) number of items that could have been written to assess a trait. Assume also that the people taking the test form a random SAMPLE (see s. 8) of the population, and the scored data are cast into a table where rows represent people, and columns items. Generalisability theory simply suggests that the variability in the table may be described by five terms: a student effect (describing the variation between rows: some students have higher ability than others), an item effect (variability between columns: some items are harder than others), a term describing the student-by-item INTERACTION (see s. 8) (as in ANALYSIS OF VARIANCE – see s. 8), a constant and a term describing the amount of MEASUREMENT ERROR (see s. 8).

Unfortunately it is not possible to estimate each of these parameters separately: as each person answers each item only once, the measurement error term and the interaction term are confounded (i.e. incapable of being independently estimated). If the sum of the interaction term and the measurement error is called the RESIDUAL (see s. 8), and it is assumed that the student effect, the item effect and the residual effect are INDEPENDENT (see s. 8) of each other and that their EXPECTED VALUES (see s. 8) are zero, then conventional analysis of variance techniques may be used to obtain unbiased estimates of these three parameters. The relative size of these terms is all-important. For example, is most of the variation due to differences between people – or the residual? It is also possible to extend this basic model, for example, to consider the case where the scores reflect the marks assigned by different markers. It is also possible to develop the model so that it will handle missing data.

CC

Brennan, R. L. 2001: *Generalizability Theory*. New York: Springer. **Cronbach, L. J., Gleser, G. C., Nanda, H. and Rajaratnam, N.** 1972: *The Dependability of Behavioral Measurements*. New York: Wiley.

H

humour and laughter Humour and laughter are spontaneous social behaviours that play a prominent role in our everyday lives. We create opportunities to experience humour and laughter through magazines, newspapers, the radio and television. We have only the weakest voluntary control over the laughter reflex: we cannot genuinely laugh on command and, likewise, it is also very difficult to inhibit the laughter reflex once it is triggered. Laughter can trigger laughter; it is a contagious phenomenon. One of the most fascinating stories of the power of laughter was reported in Tanganyika, where an epidemic of laughter spread among 12- to 19-year-olds, resulting in the closure of schools (Rankin and Philip 1963). The infectious nature of laughter explains the success of 'canned laughter'. The mere presence of laughter is enough to educe laughter from radio and television show audiences.

Recognising that certain situations bring us great joy motivates us to seek out those experiences, and encourage others to do likewise. This human capacity to make others feel better is essential to the forming of bonds, particularly between loved ones. Some of the strongest evidence that laughter has a social function comes from studies that show that laughter rarely interrupts normal speech patterns, generally occurring only at the end of a phrase. This suggests that there is some degree of neurological programming that ensures that LANGUAGE (see s. 2) takes precedence over laughter (Provine 1993). Laughter disappears when the individual is placed in solitary situations. In addition, comedy programmes heard in a GROUP (see s. 5) setting will seem more humorous and generate more laughter than when they are viewed in isolation. Most laughter is not generated through manufactured forms of humour, such as comedy shows or cartoons. Rather it is integrated into our day-to-day interactions with others, through speech, facial expressions and gestures (Provine 1993, 1996).

Finally, our EMOTIONS have a direct effect on immune system activity. NEGATIVE EMOTIONS and negative moods (DEPRESSION – see s. 7, anxiety and distress) have been shown to evoke tenseness, enhanced cardiovascular activity and elevated plasma hormone (CORTISOL – see s. 2, prolactin and beta-endorphines), as well as changes in immunological parameters (Booth and Pennebaker 2000). Booth and Pennebaker report several studies that suggest that positive emotional states, such as humour and laughter, have a positive effect on our immune system. For example, compared to participants who viewed an educational video, participants who watched a humorous videotape presented elevated levels of an immune VARIABLE (see s. 8) (sIgA). *AF*

Booth, R. J. and Pennebaker, J. W. 2000: Emotions and immunity. In Lewis, M. and Haviland-Jones, J. M. (eds) *Handbook of Emotions*. New York: Guilford Press. **Provine, R. R.** 1993: Laughter punctuates speech: linguistic, social and gender contexts of laughter. *Ethology* 95, 291–8. **Provine, R. R.** 1996: Laughter. *American Scientist* 84, 34–45. **Rankin, A. M. and Philip, P. J.** 1963: An epidemic of laughing in the Bukoba District of Tanganyika. *Central African Journal of Medicine* 9, 167–70.

I

impulsivity This trait of impulsivity has been identified in several authors' models of personality, where it is associated with low levels of arousal. Empirically, this lack of behavioural INHIBITION (see s. 3) is correlated positively with EXTROVERSION, NEUROTICISM and PSYCHOTICISM in EYSENCK'S THREE-FACTOR MODEL of personality (Eysenck and Eysenck 1985), emerges as a component of SENSATION SEEKING (Zuckerman 1994) and again in the context of cognitive performance, where high levels of self-reported impulsivity are linked to poor performance on a very wide range of cognitive tasks (Brunas-Wagstaff, Bergquist and Wagstaff 1994). Dickman (2000) has suggested that there are in fact two distinct components of impulsivity. Acting on impulse without thinking through the possible negative consequences of the action is known as dysfunctional impulsivity. Functional impulsivity is more of a cognitive style – a preference for solving cognitive problems extremely fast (but with some errors) rather than slowly and accurately. However, it is unclear whether the underlying mechanisms of these two variants are different. Others suggest that impulsivity reflects an inability to focus ATTENTION (see s. 3) on the task in hand.

Elevated levels of self-reported impulsivity are also associated with a number of real-life behaviours, ranging from EEG P300 activity to an increased incidence of suicide attempts, AGGRESSION (see s. 5), problem gambling, behavioural dysregulation, substance use disorder, PERSONALITY DISORDERS (see s. 7) and attention deficit disorder (Moeller, Barratt, Dougherty, Schmitz and Swann 2001). Research issues include the adequacy of current self-report measures, determining the most appropriate of several theoretical models of impulsivity and its relation to arousal, time of day etc., and determining whether impulsivity has a causal role in the clinical-relevant behaviours listed above. *CC*

Brunas-Wagstaff, J., Bergquist, A. and Wagstaff, G. F. 1994: Cognitive correlates of functional and dysfunctional impulsivity. *Personality and Individual Differences* 17, 289–92. **Dickman, S. J.** 2000: Impulsivity, arousal and attention. *Personality and Individual Differences* 28, 563–81. **Eysenck, H. J. and Eysenck, M. W.** 1985: *Personality and Individual Differences.* New York: Plenum Press. **Moeller, F. G., Barratt, E. S., Dougherty, D. M., Schmitz, J. M. and Swann, A. C.** 2001: Psychiatric aspects of impulsivity. *American Journal of Psychiatry* 158, 1783–93. **Zuckerman, M.** 1994: *Behavioral Expressions and Biosocial Bases of Sensation Seeking.* Cambridge: Cambridge University Press.

in-basket techniques In-basket techniques for PERSONNEL SELECTION eschew formal psychological ability tests. Rather than administering a standard set of psychological tests, chosen on the basis of a job analysis, they instead involve assessing how well candidates perform when presented with tasks and challenges similar to those which they would encounter if appointed – a typical 'in-basket'. For a management post these challenges might involve responding to letters of complaint, drawing some inferences from a report, task prioritisation, appropriate delegation and dealing with personnel problems. Applicants would each be given the same set of typical problems to solve, and their performance would be appraised by experienced managers.

This approach is straightforward, and the VALIDITY (see also s. 8) of in-basket techniques is similar to that of standard aptitude tests (Schippmann, Prien and Katz 1990). Furthermore it is clear to the applicants that the technique is relevant to the post (has 'face validity'). However, it is not without its problems. Traditional aptitude tests assess potential rather than current performance, and it is unclear how much past experience in a similar post will impact on how well candidates perform on the in-basket exercises. The in-basket techniques may assess a mixture of knowledge and aptitude. Second, it is necessary to ensure that the in-basket techniques cover all aspects of the post. This will probably make them fairly lengthy, and the type of job analysis to ensure this is not dissimilar to that which would be required were standard psychological tests to be used. Third, assessing the quality of candidates' answers may be problematical, as it may be hard to quantify some aspects of their responses. Fourth, if the type of post within the organisation is likely to change over time then the SKILLS (see s. 3) for which the person was selected into the organisation may cease to become relevant; on the other hand, it is well-established that traditional ability tests predict performance in a wide range of different posts (Hunter 1986). *CC*

Hunter, J. E. 1986: Cognitive ability, cognitive attitudes, job knowledge and job performance. *Journal of Vocational Behavior* 29, 340–62. **Schippmann, J. S., Prien, E. P. and Katz, J. A.** 1990: Reliability and validity of in-basket performance-measures. *Personnel Psychology* 43, 837–59.

individual differences The branch of psychology which studies the ways in which people differ, and the origins and mechanisms of these differences. It includes the study of many STATES AND TRAITS, including PERSONALITY TRAITS, MOOD AND EMOTION, MOTIVATION STRUCTURE, MOTIVATIONAL THEORIES, the structure of MENTAL ABILITIES, BEHAVIOUR GENETICS OF ABILITIES and PERSONALITY. It also deals with group differences in intelligence [see INTELLIGENCE: GROUP DIFFERENCES], group differences in PERSONALITY and the assessment of these characteristics using individual tests of ability [see ABILITY: INDIVIDUAL TESTS OF], group tests of ability [see ABILITY: GROUP TESTS OF], PERSONALITY TESTS and MOOD SCALES. Measuring individual differences is an important component of PERSONNEL SELECTION. *CC*

inspection time and *g* Several theorists have proposed that *g*, or general mental ability, is a measure of the overall neural efficiency of the brain (e.g. Eysenck 1986). The inspection time PARADIGM (see s. 1) explores this hypothesis by investigating relationships between indirect measures of speed/efficiency of brain functioning and *g*. Inspection time (IT) is the time required for a stimulus to

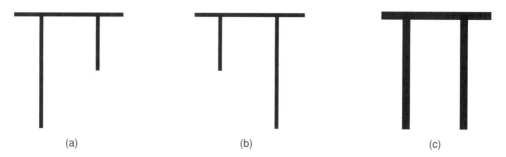

inspection time and g *In the most commonly used inspection time task, participants are shown either (a) or (b) for a very short time and asked to decide whether the left or right leg was the longer. This procedure is repeated for different durations in order to determine how long the shapes must be presented in order for them to have a particular probability (e.g. 75%) of being correctly recognised. To make the task harder, a backward mask (c) is often shown after each presentation.*

be processed in sufficient detail to allow a discriminative judgement (Vickers, Nettelbeck and Willson 1972). A typical visual IT stimulus consists of briefly presenting two parallel lines, each differing in length (see Figure). This is immediately followed by a 'mask' (see Figure), which prevents further processing of the original stimulus. The participant is required to state which of the original two lines is longer. If the theory is correct, high INTELLIGENCE (see also s. 4) individuals should be able to encode visual stimuli more quickly than others (Vickers et al. 1972). Significant associations with a variety of ability measures have been reported (Deary and Stough 1996), albeit these are more modest than earlier claims, and there is less evidence of a relationship with verbal IQ than with performance tests. Grudnik and Kranzler's (2001) updated meta-analysis concludes an overall IT-*g* correlation of −0.51, following correction for RELIABILITY (see also s. 8) and restriction of range. Alternative paradigms have been devised and generally report similar results. Empirically, the relationship is substantial and reliable. Theoretically, however, the basis of the association is less clear. Criticism that IT-*g* correlations may be influenced by cognitive strategy such as flicker detection (illusion of movement of the shorter line after it has been masked) seems to discredit IT as a sufficiently low-level task. Nonetheless, the exclusion of those reporting this strategy actually increases correlations (Grudnik and Kranzler 2001). More problematic are indications that, contrary to providing a measure of the biological basis of *g*, visual inspection time is simply associated with a group ability FACTOR (see s. 8) of processing speed (Deary and Crawford 1998). Clarification requires replication in studies using a more extensive battery of IQ tests. Current research, meanwhile, considers whether IT contributes to psychometric *g* (Deary and Stough 1996) by exploring the contribution of genetic and biological correlates. [See BEHAVIOUR GENETICS OF ABILITIES and BIOLOGICAL CORRELATES OF ABILITIES] *MM*

Deary, I. J. and Crawford, J. R. 1998: A triarchic theory of Jensenism: persistent, conservative reductionism. *Intelligence* 26, 273–82. **Deary, I. J. and Stough, C.** 1996: Intelligence and inspection time: achievements, prospects and problems. *American Psychologist* 51, 599–608. **Eysenck, H. J.** 1986: The theory of intelligence and the neurophysiology of cognition. In Sternberg, R. J. (ed.) *Advances in the Psychology of Human Intelligence*. Hillsdale NJ: Erlbaum. **Grudnik, J. L. and Kranzler, J. H.** 2001: Meta-analysis of the relationship between inspection time and intelligence. *Intelligence* 29, 523–35. **Vickers, D., Nettelbeck, T. and Willson, R. J.** 1972: Perceptual indices of performance: The measurement of 'inspection time' and 'noise' in the visual system. *Perception* 1, 263–95.

instinct theories of motivation These theories view the underlying processes that direct behaviour as emanating from instincts. Instincts (or fixed-action patterns) are unlearned behaviour patterns that are released in the presence of specific sign stimuli. For example, the stimuli of redness in a male stickleback will release an aggressive territorial behaviour from another male stickleback. Perhaps the most eminent proponent of this theory was William McDougall, who in 1908, influenced by the work of William James and Charles Darwin, proposed 12 human instincts, including the desire for food, self-assertion and reproduction. McDougall's list gradually expanded to 18 instincts, which claimed to initiate all human action, and which rather closely resembles that stemming from Cattell's later motivational theory [see MOTIVATIONAL THEORIES]. However, the number of potential instincts proposed in the literature soon spiralled out of control into the thousands (Dunlap 1919). The theory did adequately describe some simple patterns of behaviours in humans and other animals, but it did not explain the behaviour or account for learned behaviour. Crucially, the circular REASONING (see s. 3) it employed prevented the theory from being scientifically tested or falsified. *DH*

Dunlap, K. 1919: Are there any instincts? *Journal of Abnormal Psychology* 14, 35–50.

intelligence [See ABILITIES, GENERAL ABILITY and MULTIPLE INTELLIGENCES] (See also s. 4, INTELLIGENCE)

intelligence and birth order Zajonc's CONFLUENCE THEORY attempts to explain why older children in large families may be more intelligent than later-born children. However the data and statistical methods have recently been questioned (Rodgers, Cleveland, Van Den Oord and Rowe 2000), and within-family studies cast doubt on the claim that family resources are diluted as the number of children increases. Instead the data favour a model where more intelligent parents have fewer children. *CC*

Rodgers, J. L., Cleveland, H. H., Van Den Oord, E. and Rowe, D. C. 2000: Resolving the debate over birth order, family size, and intelligence. *American Psychologist* 55, 599–612.

intelligence and health Recent work conducted in Scotland has produced some interesting results concerning the relationship between INTELLIGENCE (see also s. 4), mental and physical health. The scores of a GROUP (see s. 5) of 11-year-old children who sat an intelligence test in 1932 were discovered in the 1990s by Ian Deary and his colleagues. These children happened to form a reasonably representative SAMPLE (see s. 8) of the Scottish population and Deary and his co-workers tracked them down 66 years later and obtained much useful information about their lives, health and psychological well-being. Of these individuals, 938 also took part in a health survey during the 1970s, when they were middle-aged. Intelligence was significantly related to longevity, in both old age and middle age, even when social factors were controlled (Hart, Taylor, Smith, Whalley, Starr, Hole, Wilson and Deary 2003). Those in the lowest QUARTILE (see s. 8) were particularly likely to die early. (People killed during World War II were excluded from this analysis.) A high level of intelligence in childhood was also found to be related to a lower incidence of psychiatric problems during adulthood (Walker, McConville, Hunter, Deary and Whalley 2002); other studies have shown that as well as intelligence (*g*), physical activity and low IMPULSIVITY are important. The higher a person's intelligence, the lower is their chance of experiencing dementia in later life. (High intelligence was not associated with a reduced incidence of early-onset dementia.) Childhood intelligence also predicts quality of life in old age (Bain, Lemmon, Teunisse, Starr, Fox, Deary and Whalley 2003) and the Barthel Index – a measure of self-sufficiency in old age.

It even seems that 'accidents' may not be entirely accidental. A study by O'Toole and Stankov (1992) followed up over 46,000 Australian men who left the army, where their general intelligence had been assessed. More than 500 of them died other than in combat before age 34, mostly in road accidents. It was found that both for all deaths and those killed on the roads, those with lower IQs were almost twice as likely to die in such circumstances as those with IQs above 100; the few with IQs below 85 were almost three times as likely to die as those with at least average intelligence. *CC*

Bain, G. H., Lemmon, H., Teunisse, S., Starr, J. M., Fox, H. C., Deary, I. J. and Whalley, L. J. 2003: Quality of life in healthy old age: relationships with childhood IQ, minor psychological symptoms and optimism. *Social Psychiatry and Psychiatric Epidemiology* 38, 632–6. **Gottfredson, L.** 2003: *g*, jobs and life. In Nyborg, H. (ed.) *Scientific Study of General Intelligence*. Oxford: Pergamon. **Hart, C. L., Taylor, M. D., Smith, G. D., Whalley, L. J., Starr, J. M., Hole, D. J., Wilson, V. and Deary, I. J.** 2003: Childhood IQ, social class, deprivation, and their relationships with mortality and morbidity risk in later life: prospective observational study linking the Scottish mental survey 1932 and the midspan studies. *Psychosomatic Medicine* 65, 877–83. **O'Toole, B. I. and Stankov, L.** 1992: Ultimate validity of psychological tests. *Personality and Individual Differences* 13(6), 699–716. **Walker, N. P., McConville, P. M., Hunter, D., Deary, I. J. and Whalley, L. J.** 2002: Childhood mental ability and lifetime psychiatric contact – a 66-year follow-up study of the 1932 Scottish mental ability survey. *Intelligence* 30, 233–45.

intelligence and occupational performance

Ability tests are widely used as part of PERSONNEL SELECTION procedures, where they frequently show substantial PREDICTIVE VALIDITY (see s. 7) against a wide range of occupational criteria, as shown by the meta-analyses of Schmidt and Hunter (1998). Even in World War II, American army recruits who had professional posts (accountants, lawyers, etc.) showed average IQs in the high 120s; those who were farm workers and labourers showed average IQs in the 90s. However, this does not show that it is necessary to have high *g* [see GENERAL ABILITY] in order to succeed as an accountant (for example). Because scores on INTELLIGENCE (see also s. 4) tests are substantially correlated with length of education and educational qualifications, it might be the case that only the highly intelligent children gained the educational qualifications which would allow them into professional training: it is arguably possible that anyone might be capable of benefiting from such training were they allowed to enter the system. Evidence that this is not so is given by Hunter and Hunter (1984), who report correlations between intelligence and performance within various occupations. The correlations are invariably positive: the intelligent manager, salesman or delivery driver tends to perform better than the less intelligent one.

Some interesting recent work has examined the merits of using test of *g* for personnel selection rather than the more popular specialised tests of job-relevant abilities. Given the ubiquity of the hierarchical model of abilities (e.g. the three-stratum model) [see ABILITY: THREE-STRATUM MODEL], it is practically impossible to devise any ability test that does not measure general intelligence to some extent. It is therefore quite possible that tests of clerical aptitude, computer-programming potential, critical REASONING (see s. 3) and all the other abilities beloved by occupational psychologists may work because they are all imperfect measures of general intelligence rather than because they assess narrow, job-related SKILLS (see s. 3). This possibility was tested by Thorndike (1985) and Jensen (1998) using somewhat different methods of analyses. Thorndike found that once general intelligence was removed from selection tests using PARTIAL CORRELATION (see s. 8), the test almost always lost all its predictive validity. Jensen noted that the tests that were the best measures of general intelligence were generally the ones with the highest validity coefficients. Thus it is possible to make a reasonable case for selecting employees using a test of general ability, rather than any task-related aptitude. *CC*

Hunter, J. E. and Hunter, R. F. 1984. Validity and utility of alternative predictors of job performance. *Psychological Bulletin* 96, 72–98. **Jensen, A. R.** 1998: *The g Factor*. Westport CT: Praeger. **Schmidt, F. L. and Hunter, J. E.** 1998: The validity and utility of selection methods in personnel psychology: practical and theoretical implications of 85 years of research findings. *Psychological Bulletin* 124, 262–74. **Thorndike, R. L.** 1985: The central role of general ability in prediction. *Multivariate Behavioral Research* 1985, 241–54.

intelligence: boosting There is a moderately strong relationship between IQ and social class. Working under the assumption that social deprivation is a direct cause of low INTELLIGENCE (see also s. 4), there have been several attempts to enhance the early environments of groups of socially deprived children in order to boost their intelligence and school performance. Unfortunately the whole area has become politicised, with those favouring social explanations of intelligence (which includes most of the researchers who conduct the studies) arguing for their utility, while others point to problems with the statistical analyses and observe that the supposed IQ gains do not appear to endure or be reflected in school performance.

Prior to the 1970s several intervention studies had been performed without spectacular success, as observed in Jensen's (1969) controversial paper. However, it is always possible that these failed because the intervention was insufficiently intensive, occurred too late or was suboptimal in terms of content. Two studies have involved substantial stimulation of socially deprived children.

The Milwaukee and Abecedarian projects used intensive stimulation programmes, starting at three months and lasting until the children started school. They included a wide range of interventions designed by educational psychologists, and children who received the intervention were compared with members of a CONTROL GROUP (see s. 8) at several ages. Both programmes appeared to work well, and when they entered school, the children who had received the intervention outperformed those in the control groups. Over the following years the difference between the groups declined somewhat – though in the Milwaukee project it was still well above that of the control group. However, these improvements were not reflected in measures of school performance, where both groups were well below average. (The 'intervention' children attended schools of at least average quality, so poor teaching was not the explanation.) The children who received the Abecedarian intervention outperformed the controls from a very early age (e.g. one STANDARD DEVIATION – see s. 8) and the difference was still evident at age 21, when the average IQs were 90 vs. 85. This raises the question of whether the intervention really did all its good work in the very early months, or whether the groups were not properly matched at the outset.   *CC*

Gorey, K. M. 2001: Early childhood education: a meta-analytic affirmation of the short- and long-term benefits of educational opportunity. *School Psychology Quarterly* 16, 9–30. **Jensen, A. R.** 1969: How much can we boost IQ and scholastic achievement? *Harvard Educational Review* 39, 1–123. **Spitz, H. H.** 1999: Attempts to raise intelligence. In Anderson, M. (ed.) *The Development of Intelligence*. Hove: Psychology Press.

intelligence: development of

Several issues must be considered when discussing the development of INTELLIGENCE (see also s. 4) and other cognitive abilities. Whether development appears continuous or increasing in spurts will probably depend to some extent on the choice of tests and timeframe. Thatcher, Walker and Giudice (1987) and others have shown that the VARIANCE (see s. 8) in intelligence test scores increases markedly between the ages of about 11 and 15, suggesting that individuals vary in their rate of COGNITIVE DEVELOPMENT (see s. 4) during this period. This work could logically imply that there are few or no reliable individual differences in intelligence during childhood: those observed in cross-sectional data (such as the tables of NORMS – see also s. 5 – of ability tests) may simply reflect the tendency of some children to mature quicker than others, or to be able to perform qualitatively different cognitive OPERATIONS (see s. 4) (in the Piagetian sense) somewhat earlier or later

than others. However, given that once-measured differences in childhood ability are appreciably correlated with individual differences in intelligence later in childhood and in adulthood and that this stability is genetically mediated (Bartels, Rietveld, Van Baal and Boomsma 2002), this position is not supported by fact: it appears that a child's level of REASONING (see s. 3) ability relative to their peers stays reasonably constant through childhood and adulthood.

Highly reliable [see RELIABILITY] tests that used to be used to assess the intelligence of very young children (e.g. the Bayley scales) show rather small correlations with scores on intelligence tests administered later, suggesting that there may well be massive discontinuities in cognitive development between birth and the age of about five or six (e.g. McCall and Carriger 1993). However, scales such as the Bayley measure ATTENTION (see s. 3) and psychomotor development, and it is quite possible that differences in developmental profile during the early months of life may account for this result. More recently, individual differences in the gaze preference of young infants have been studied and related to cognitive performance later in life. These tasks typically assess the extent to which the young infant prefers to look at a novel (rather than familiar) stimulus, or the rate at which the infant's looking response habituates when the same stimulus is presented repeatedly. Studies consistently show that individual differences in these VARIABLES (see s. 8) are reflected in cognitive performance in mid-childhood (Slater 1995; Smith, Fagan and Ulvund 2002), but although significant, the correlations are fairly modest in size until corrected for the unreliability of the infant measures.   *CC*

Bartels, M., Rietveld, M. J. H., Van Baal, G. C. M. and Boomsma, D. I. 2002: Genetic and environmental influences on the development of intelligence. *Behavior Genetics* 32, 237–49. **McCall, R. B. and Carriger, M. S.** 1993: A meta-analysis of infant habituation and recognition memory performance as predictors of later IQ. *Child Development* 64(1), 57–79. **Slater, A.** 1995: Individual-differences in infancy and later IQ. *Journal of Child Psychology and Psychiatry and Allied Disciplines* 36, 69–112. **Smith, L., Fagan, J. F. and Ulvund, S. E.** 2002: The relation of recognition memory in infancy and parental socioeconomic status to later intellectual competence. *Intelligence* 30, 247–59. **Thatcher, R. W., Walker, R. A. and Giudice, S.** 1987: Human cerebral hemispheres develop at different rates and ages. *Science* 236(4805), 1110–13.

intelligence: group differences

Few topics in psychology are as controversial as certain GROUP (see s. 5) differences in IQ. During World War I it was found that black American army recruits performed substantially less well on tests measuring IQ or g [see GENERAL ABILITY] than did white recruits – the difference being approximately one STANDARD DEVIATION (see s. 8). The difference is still found (Kaufman and Wang 1992). Sidestepping the debate about whether and how racial groups should be defined, three main explanations have been offered for this observation. First, the tests which were used may have been flawed (showing BIAS); having been designed by and for middle-class whites, the tests may have used language and/or concepts which made the items much harder for members of the black community. Second, the differences may be caused by cultural differences and/or social deprivation. For example, the difference may have arisen because of differences in the quality of education offered to black and white Americans at the time, or because black recruits may not have been so strongly motivated to perform well on the test, had lower SELF-ESTEEM (see s. 5 and s. 7) or did not expect to perform well (perhaps as a result of negative feedback from teachers). Finally, there may perhaps have been a genuine difference between the groups.

There is not space to evaluate the issues in detail, but research suggests that bias is not the whole explanation for these differences. Whether the difference is entirely due to sociocultural differences is still a controversial issue (e.g. there is some uncertainty as to whether the white-black difference is reducing, reflecting the improvement in black Americans' living standards over the past century).

Sex differences in general intelligence are generally small, although there is some evidence that women outperform men on tasks involving language, and men outperform women on tasks that involve the visualisation of shapes. Social class differences are more marked, but once again it is difficult to infer CAUSALITY (see s. 8). Do highly intelligent people obtain better jobs and move up the social scale or do the opportunities afforded to children of rich parents (good school, more support, etc.) boost their INTELLIGENCE (see also s. 4)? *CC*

Jensen, A. R. and McGurk, F. C. J. 1987: Black-white bias in cultural and noncultural test items. *Personality and Individual Differences* 8, 295–301. **Kaufman, A. S. and Wang, J. J.** 1992: Gender, race, and education differences on the K-BIT at ages 4 to 90 years. *Journal of Psychoeducational Assessment* 10, 219–29.

intelligence: stability of

There is excellent evidence that GENERAL INTELLIGENCE (*g*) is a stable characteristic of the individual; intelligent children generally develop into intelligent adults. One of the most convincing studies is that of Deary, Whalley, Lemmon, Crawford and Starr (2000). This is based on a SAMPLE (see s. 8) of 101 Scots children, whose general intelligence was assessed in 1932 when they were aged 11 and again (using the same test) 66 years later. Even before correcting for the RELIABILITY of the INTELLIGENCE used and restriction of RANGE (see s. 8) of scores of the 77-year-olds, the correlation between the two sets of scores was 0.63. This finding is consistent with other work which has studied the stability of general intelligence over shorter time periods. *CC*

Deary, I. J., Whalley, L. J., Lemmon, H., Crawford, J. R. and Starr, J. M. 2000: The stability of individual differences in mental ability from childhood to old age: follow-up of the 1932 Scottish mental survey. *Intelligence* 28, 49–55.

internal bias

Techniques for detecting BIAS (see also s. 3 and s. 8) which do not compare test scores with job performance. An example would be determining whether the item parameters are the same when ITEM RESPONSE THEORY is applied to the test scores of two or more groups of people. *CC*

Berk, R. A. (ed.) 1982: *Handbook of Methods for Detecting Test Bias*. Baltimore: The Johns Hopkins University Press. **Osterlind, S. J.** 1983: *Test Item Bias*. Beverly Hills: Sage Publications.

IPIP scales

Because their development costs are high, and most are copyrighted and published as commercial ventures, PERSONALITY TESTS and other psychological tests are frequently very expensive to buy and use. It also means that only the authors can refine and improve the scales. Lew Goldberg (Goldberg 1999) developed the FIVE-FACTOR MODEL OF PERSONALITY during the 1990s and made his items publicly available via the internet, where they are known as the International Personality Item Pool (IPIP). These items are in the public domain, and the plan is to allow all scientists to help refine and modify the scales. The website contains items that have been validated against scales such as the NEO-PI(R) and other commercial personality tests, together with details of the scale correlations and other psychometric data. *CC*

Goldberg, L. R. 1999: A broad-bandwidth, public domain, personality inventory measuring the lower-level facets of several five-factor models. In Mervielde, I., Deary, I., Fruyt, F. D. and Ostendorf, F. (eds) *Personality Psychology in Europe*. Tilburg: Tilburg University Press, vol. 7.

IQ

IQ is an abbreviation of 'INTELLIGENCE QUOTIENT' (see s. 4). The concept of the intelligence quotient was introduced in 1912 by William Stern, who devised an index of INTELLIGENCE (see also s. 4) based on the ratio (quotient) of mental age (measured by intelligence tests) to chronological age. The first modern intelligence TEST was developed by Alfred Binet in 1905. Louis Terman, who is credited with coining the term 'IQ', suggested that the index be multiplied by 100 to remove the decimals and to set the average score within each age band equal to 100. This definition is known as ratio IQ. The modern statistical definition of IQ, as a normally distributed VARIABLE (see s. 8) with a mean of 100 and a STANDARD DEVIATION (see s. 8) of 15, was introduced by David Wechsler in 1939 and is known as deviation IQ. Strictly speaking, IQ is measured on an ordinal scale, which allows rank-ordering scores, but not interval-based comparisons. For example, it is not possible to say whether the difference between 95 and 100 IQ points is the same as the difference between 100 and 105 IQ points. However, by making the reasonable assumption that IQ is normally distributed in the population and by developing tests that yield NORMAL DISTRIBUTIONS (see s. 8), it is possible to generate scores with interval level properties. There is a plethora of IQ tests, of which the WECHSLER SCALES and Raven's progressive matrices are the most well-established. (See also s. 4, INTELLIGENCE QUOTIENT) *KP*

Brody, N. 1992: *Intelligence* (2nd edn). New York: Academic Press. **Deary, I. J.** 2000: *Looking Down on Human Intelligence: From Psychometrics to the Brain*. Oxford: Oxford University Press. **Jensen, A. R.** 1998: *The g Factor*. Westport CT: Praeger. **Mackintosh, N. J.** 1998: *IQ and Human Intelligence*. Oxford: Oxford University Press.

IRT

[See ITEM RESPONSE THEORY] A statistical procedure that simultaneously estimates item properties (difficulty, etc.) and the abilities of people who have taken a test. *CC*

item response theory

Ability tests are conventionally scored by awarding one point for each correct answer and zero (or sometimes negative) points for each incorrect answer, and then summing the scores. Although intuitive, this effectively ignores all information about the difficulty of the items: a person who gets ten easy items and five hard items correct would obtain the same score as someone who gets five easy items and ten hard items correct.

Item response theory instead attempts to model what goes on when people solve test items. The simplest form (the '1-parameteter' or RASCH SCALING model) assumes that whether or not a person gets an item correct depends solely on the ability of that person and the difficulty of the item. Item response theory estimates the ability of each person who took the test and the difficulty of each item in the test. If 208 people took a 40-item test, and the responses were scored such that '1' represented a correct answer and '0' an incorrect answer, a computer program would estimate from this table of 0s and 1s the most likely values for the 208 abilities, plus the 40 item difficulties – a total of 248 parameters.

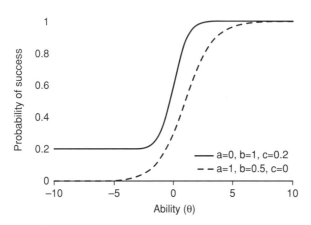

item response theory *Item Characteristic Curve showing the probability that a candidate with ability θ will pass each of two items.*

Unfortunately, items vary in terms of their discrimination power (the Rasch model assumes that they are all identical) and in the case of multiple-choice tests, even very low-ability individuals will have an above-zero chance of getting an item correct because of random guessing. Researchers have thus developed two-parameter and three-parameter models, which also estimate the discrimination power of each item and the chances that very low-ability participants will be able to guess the correct answer to the item. Thus the probability that a person with a particular level of ability will answer an item correctly can be plotted as shown in the Figure – a graph known as the Item Characteristic Curve (ICC). The Figure shows ICCs of two items, one having a discrimination (a) of 0, a difficulty (b) of 1 and with a guessing parameter (c) of 0.2, implying that a very low-ability candidate has a 0.2 chance of getting the item correct. The second item has a = 1, b = 0.5 and c = 0. Note how the item difficulty determines the position of the curve along the graph, while discrimination reflects the steepness of the curve.

Once the three item parameters have been estimated (by giving a test to a large SAMPLE (see s. 8) of people), candidates can be given different sets of items from the 'item bank' – and although they have sat completely different tests, it is possible to compare their abilities, something which would not be possible if 'ability' was defined in terms of the number of items correctly answered. Items are often presented using 'ADAPTIVE TESTING', whereby a person is initially given an item of moderate difficulty: if they get it wrong, the next item is easier; if correct, the next item is harder. *CC*

Hambleton, R. K., Swaminathan, H. and Rogers, H. J. 1991: *Fundamentals of Item Response Theory*. Newbury Park CA: Sage. **Thissen, D. and Wainer, H.** 2001: *Test Scoring*. Mahwah NJ: L. Erlbaum Associates.

J

James-Lange theory If we see a bear in a forest, do we run because we are scared or are we scared because we run? The psychologist William James (1884) and the physician Carl Lange (1885) proposed a theory of EMOTION based on the way in which autonomic responses are related to the experience of emotion. According to this theory, the brain first interprets a situation and then physiological responses follow. Once these physiological responses are triggered, the emotion enters CONSCIOUSNESS (see s. 3). This means that emotion does not occur during the initial neural response of the central nervous system; the PERCEPTION (see s. 1) of peripheral bodily responses, such as increased heart rate and perspiration, precede the emotional experience. The brain monitors these peripheral responses and the emotion is entered into consciousness. For example, we perspire and tremble and as a result we feel anxious.

The James-Lange theory was one of the first theories to consider that emotions could have distinct patterns of physiological responses. If these responses could not be distinguished from one another, then there was no basis to assume the existence of discrete emotions and there is good evidence that this is the case. For example, Ekman, Levenson and Friesen (1983) report that while fear reduces blood flow to the hands and feet, anger is associated with an increased blood flow to those areas. Ekman et al. also report that changes in facial activity will produce different patterns of autonomic activity. Participants requested to contract the facial muscles that correspond with the fear emotion (i.e. raise eyebrows, upper eyelids and stretch lips horizontally) also produced changes in heart rate that corresponded with changes in genuine experiences of fear. This would explain why it is possible to elicit similar emotional experiences by mimicking the facial expressions of others, for example in an expression of EMPATHY (see s. 4).

The importance of peripheral feedback in emotional experience has been questioned through studies of spinal injury. Individuals who suffer from spinal injury should report less intense emotions. However, there appears to be very little difference between the emotional experiences of patients with spinal cord injury and control participants (Cobos et al. 2002), suggesting a more integrated theory of emotional processing that considers simultaneous processing of peripheral and central processes in the experience of emotion. *AF*

Cobos, P., Sánchez, M., García, C., Nieves Vera, M. and Vila, J. 2002: Revisiting the James versus Cannon debate on emotion: startle and autonomic modulation in patients with spinal cord injuries. *Biological Psychology* 61(3), 251–69. **Ekman, P., Levenson, R. W. and Friesen, W. V.** 1983: Autonomic nervous system activity distinguishes among emotions. *Science* 221, 1208–10. **James, W.** 1884: What is an emotion? *Mind* 9, 188–205. **Lange, C.** 1885: *The Emotions.* Baltimore: Williams and Wilkens (English translation 1922).

L

learning style See COGNITIVE STYLE AND LEARNING STYLE

Level A accreditation In the UK, Level A accreditation awarded by the BRITISH PSYCHOLOGICAL SOCIETY (see s. 1) indicates that an individual has proved competent in the choice, administration and basic interpretation of some tests: for example, group-administered ability tests [see ABILITY: GROUP TESTS OF] in the field of OCCUPATIONAL PSYCHOLOGY (see also s. 1, INDUSTRIAL AND OCCUPATIONAL PSYCHOLOGY).   *CC*

Level B accreditation In the UK, Level B accreditation awarded by the BRITISH PSYCHOLOGICAL SOCIETY (see s. 1) indicates that an individual already holding Level A accreditation has proved competent in the choice, administration and basic interpretation of some other tests: for example, group-administered PERSONALITY TESTS in the field of OCCUPATIONAL PSYCHOLOGY (see also s. 1, INDUSTRIAL AND OCCUPATIONAL PSYCHOLOGY).   *CC*

lifespan changes in abilities Early research into how cognitive abilities change over the lifespan generally used a cross-sectional design, and concluded that most abilities increase through childhood, reaching their peak when an individual is in their twenties, thereafter staying stable until age 50 or 60 and then declining (Ryan, Sattler and Lopez 2000). CRYSTALLISED INTELLIGENCE (e.g. language skills) declined much less than did REASONING (see s. 3) skills (FLUID INTELLIGENCE) or speed of response. The discovery of the FLYNN EFFECT (e.g. Flynn 1999) has complicated the picture. Flynn and others observed that there was a steady increase in fluid intelligence from generation to generation for much of the past century: 30-year-olds now perform better at IQ tests than did 30-year-olds 20 years ago, for example. This means that reasoning skills may not show a marked decline in old age as was originally thought, and that our abilities may peak somewhat later than in our twenties.   *CC*

Flynn, J. R. 1999: Searching for justice – the discovery of IQ gains over time. *American Psychologist* 54, 5–20. **Ryan, J. J., Sattler, J. M. and Lopez, S. J.** 2000: Age effects on Wechsler adult intelligence scale-III subtests. *Archives of Clinical Neuropsychology* 15, 311–17.

M

mental abilities The three basic postulates of the psychology of human cognitive abilities are as follows. First, it is assumed that a very great number of different types of problems may be devised, each requiring thought for its successful completion. Second, the number of cognitive abilities that characterise people is unknown, but is believed to be rather smaller than the number of types of potential problems. Finally, it is assumed that performance on each type of problem may be influenced by one or many different cognitive abilities. Much of the twentieth century was spent trying to determine roughly how many different mental abilities exist, and their interrelationships.

The huge bulk of research into the nature of human INTELLIGENCE (see also s. 4) relies on the statistical method of FACTOR ANALYSIS (see also s. 8) to determine how many distinct cognitive abilities run through a set of data. The basic principle is straightforward. Ideally, one would develop a great number of tests, measuring every conceivable type of problem that depends on thought for its successful solution. All of these tests would be given to an enormously large SAMPLE (see s. 8) of people, forming a random sample of the population. Their scores on each of the tests would be intercorrelated and then factor-analysed. Unfortunately, real-life restrictions mean that this ideal EXPERIMENT (see s. 8) has never been carried out: the number of potential tests is probably so enormous that the statistical demands of factor analysis would require millions of people to take part for hundreds of hours testing each. In real life the number of tests administered to the same GROUP (see s. 5) of people rarely exceeds 20, and the people taking the test usually do not form a random sample of the population, being instead students, military recruits or potential employees. This means that the structure of abilities has often been determined piecemeal.

The first THEORY (see s. 8) dates back to Spearman (1904). Having gathered data on samples of schoolchildren (and invented factor analysis to analyse the results), Spearman found that children who performed well above average on one of his tests also excelled at others; likewise those who were well below average in one area tended to be below average in all the others. The interesting point about this discovery is that this occurred even though it appeared as if all the tests measured quite different things – for example, a test of accuracy of pitch PERCEPTION (see s. 1), a test of MEMORY (see s. 1) and a test of mathematical SKILLS (see s. 3). It is not at all obvious which cognitive processes these tasks may share, yet for some reason, such tasks show a positive correlation (POSITIVE MANIFOLD). Spearman showed that the correlations between the tests could be explained by a single FACTOR (see s. 8) of intelligence: it is as if a person's performance on each of the tests is influenced partly by some sort of general cognitive ability plus something unique to each test. Hence Spearman's theory is sometimes called a 'two-factor' theory, a term which causes confusion as it is really only the GENERAL

FACTOR (see s. 4) which influences performance on all the tests which is of interest. Spearman named this factor general intelligence (*g*), and argued that it reflected a task-independent capacity for thought. [See GENERAL ABILITY]

Thurstone (1938), in the USA, used different methods of factor analysis on different tests in different samples (college students) and came to rather different conclusions. Rather than one factor, he found about eight or nine 'PRIMARY MENTAL ABILITIES' (PMAs) such as verbal ability, spatial ability, memory, etc. According to Thurstone's initial analyses, it would be totally wrong to view test performance as being influenced by *g* and some test-specific factors. Instead, there are eight or nine quite distinct abilities each of which influences performance on tests.

The position became clarified during the 1950s and 1960s, when it was appreciated that Thurstone's PMAs were themselves substantially intercorrelated. It was therefore possible to factor-analyse the correlations between the PMAs to obtain SECOND-ORDER ABILITY FACTORS, and to factor-analyse the correlations between the second-order factors to produce 'third-order factors'. John B. Carroll's retirement project was to re-analyse 467 sets of data from the previous 90 years, using modern methods of factor analysis, in order to draw up a definitive list of the number and nature of human ability factors. Carroll (Carroll 1993) shows that there is excellent evidence for a hierarchical ('three-stratum') model of abilities. [See ABILITY: THREE-STRATUM MODEL] At the bottom of a three-level pyramid are a great many (probably well over 50) PMAs, much as envisaged by Thurstone: these reflect rather narrow abilities. Next in the hierarchy are about seven main broad 'second-order' abilities – FLUID INTELLIGENCE (abstract reasoning), CRYSTALLISED INTELLIGENCE (intelligence applied to knowledge, e.g. vocabulary), memory, visual perception, auditory perception, retrieval (creativity) and mental speed. Each of these second-order abilities influences several of the PMAs e.g. the memory factor influences performance on PMAs measuring associative memory, free RECALL (see s. 3), visual memory, etc. At the top of the pyramid is general intelligence, much as Spearman envisaged it: a measure of 'raw cognitive power' that influences every single lower-level ability – just as the speed of a single-processor computer's CPU affects the speed of every operation which it performs.

The Figure on page 294 shows just four PMAs and two second-order abilities, plus general ability. A line indicates that a higher-level ability influences a lower-level ability. Hence general ability influences both the memory and visual perception second-order abilities, and the memory second-order ability affects the associative memory, memory span and visual memory PMAs – but not scanning. It is possible to estimate a person's score on each of the factors (and also the size of the relationships between the factors indicated by the lines: some may be larger than others) and so it is possible to test how well such a model fits the data. Several such analyses have been reported (e.g. Undheim 1981) – and the fit is rather good. There is thus now good agreement about the structure of human cognitive abilities – the number and nature of the main ability factors.

Several other approaches have been followed, some based on a theoretical analysis, others on a literature review, and others on the analysis of EMPIRICAL (see s. 8) data. Gardner's MULTIPLE INTELLIGENCES model and the STRUCTURE OF INTELLECT MODEL are discussed elsewhere.

CC

Carroll, J. B. 1993: *Human Cognitive Abilities: A Survey of Factor-analytic Studies*. Cambridge: Cambridge University Press. **Spearman, C.** 1904: General intelligence objectively determined and measured. *American Journal of Psychology* 15, 201–93. **Thurstone, L. L.** 1938: *Primary Mental Abilities*. Chicago: University of Chicago Press. **Undheim, J. O.** 1981: On intelligence i: Broad ability factors in 15-year-old children and Cattell's theory of fluid and crystallised intelligence. *Scandinavian Journal of Psychology* 22, 171–9.

mood and cognition

Moods can influence cognitive processes such as PERCEPTION (see s. 1) and MEMORY (see s. 1). Parkinson, Totterdell, Briner and Reynolds (1996) review the research behind these phenomena. Research has indicated that if we feel good then we see the world around us in a positive way. It is believed that we process mood-congruent information more easily (that is, material that has an emotional tone consistent with the current mood state). Good moods influence us to pick out (and possibly exaggerate) the positive aspects of the environment. When in a bad mood we may be more likely to focus on the negative aspects of our environment and evaluate them in less than positive ways.

The effects of mood state on memory can be in the form of mood-congruent processes or state-dependent processes. Mood-congruency effects refer to the capacity for individuals to encode or retrieve information that is consistent in emotional tone with their current mood state. State-dependent mood effects refer to the capacity for better retrieval of information when the mood at the time of retrieval is consistent with the prevailing mood at the time of encoding. Parkinson et al. (1996) reviewed the evidence for the existence of both types of effect. Mood-congruency effects are generally more consistent for positive affects than for negative affects; it has been suggested that this is because people may actively adopt mood repair strategies when faced with negative moods, and thereby ignore bad memories. However, overall the evidence for mood-congruent effects is substantial, especially when the material to be remembered is relevant to the person. The state-dependent effect of improved memory for material learned in a similar mood state is not as well supported by the research. Ellis and Ashbrook (1991) suggest that this effect is most likely to occur if there is interference between originally LEARNING (see s. 3) the material and having to RECALL (see s. 3) it in the same mood. In this case, the person has to rely more heavily on mood-cues than on cues related to the material.

CM

Ellis, H. C. and Ashbrook, P. W. 1991: The 'state' of mood and memory research: a selective review. In Kuiken, D. (ed.) *Mood and Memory: Theory, Research and Application*. Newbury Park: Sage. **Parkinson, B., Totterdell, P., Briner, R. B. and Reynolds, S.** 1996: *Changing Moods: The Psychology of Mood and Mood Regulation*. London: Longman.

mood and emotion

It is difficult to distinguish objectively between moods and EMOTIONS. Izard (1991) opines that moods are 'emotion(s) that endure', perhaps for months (according to Plutchik 1994), which are less intense than emotions and may be 'tonic and not centred about an object or event' (Frijda 1986). However, it is not hard to find short-lived emotional states that are not linked to objects (e.g. a panic attack). As PERSONALITY TRAITS resemble averaged moods, by defining mood as being long-lived, emotion theorists may inadvertently reinvent the personality trait. Isen (1984), for example, views 'irritability' not as a personality trait but as a type of mood. In addition, the scales used in experimental studies of emotions are usually the same as those in mood research. Several theorists (e.g. Bower 1981; Watson and Tellegen 1985) use the terms 'emotion' and 'mood' interchangeably, and there seems to be scant EMPIRICAL (see s. 8) data that suggest that one should do otherwise.

CC

Bower, G. H. 1981: Mood and memory. *American Psychologist* 36, 129–48. **Frijda, N. H.** 1986: *The Emotions*. Cambridge: Cambridge University Press. **Isen, A. M.** 1984: Towards understanding the role of affect in cognition. In Wyer, R. S. and Srull, T. K. (eds) *Handbook of Social Cognition*. Hillsdale NJ: Erlbaum. **Izard, C. E.** 1991: *The Psychology of Emotions*. New York: Plenum. **Plutchik, R.** 1994: *The Psychology and Biology of Emotion*. New York: Harper Collins. **Watson, D. and Tellegen, A.** 1985: Towards a consensual structure of mood. *Psychological Bulletin* 98, 219–35.

mood and life events

Outside events can influence moods and, conversely, the tone of our mood can influence how we interpret an event. For the large majority of people the prevailing mood is generally positive in tone. This can often be enough to override the impact of minor negative events. Thayer (1996) emphasises the role of our bodily state when interpreting the impact of a life event. For instance, a negative reaction to an event is likely to be more pronounced in the morning or late evening than in the afternoon, as POSITIVE AFFECT is highest in the afternoon. In this respect, a person could overestimate the effect of a LIFE EVENT (see s. 7) on their moods. Watson (2000) reports that NEGATIVE AFFECT levels are generally low for most people and increase sharply at times when a threat occurs, such as impending surgery or an imminent examination. Stressful events such as these do not appear to have a significant impact on positive affect levels. Increased positive affect, on the other hand, is highly correlated with social interaction. Here, increased interaction promotes higher pleasant arousal, and the reverse also appears to be true, that elevated positive affect leads to more social engagement.

Thayer (1996) has shown that one of the best ways to increase positive affect, and reduce negative affect, is to engage in moderate exercise. It has also been shown that some depressed individuals can benefit from a regular exercise routine (Watson 2000). Positive affect is heavily influenced by activity, and Watson argues that positive affect is much easier to induce with action, while negative affect can be influenced strongly by thinking about, and ruminating over, negative personal issues.

Watson (2000) has reviewed the literature on the impact of weather on our moods and concluded that, contrary to popular belief, it has little impact. Sometimes people will attribute their low mood to the inclement weather, or attribute their good mood to the warm summer's day. Yet, when moods are assessed over time, without reference to the weather, there is no evidence that low moods predominate on gloomy days or that sunny days necessarily produce good moods. *CM*

Thayer, R. E. 1996: *The Origin of Everyday Moods.* New York: Oxford University Press. Watson, D. 2000: *Mood and Temperament.* New York: Guilford Press.

mood cycles

Moods may occur in cycles. These patterns may arise through socially entrained factors or because we have certain endogenous rhythms that operate according to the oscillations of a 'biological clock' (Watson 2000). Some of our moods arise out of regularities in our lifestyles. So, if consistently someone experiences strong NEGATIVE AFFECT a particular day of the week it may be due to certain unpleasant events that occur each week on that day. Yet not all mood patterns are externally caused. Some patterns of mood appear to arise endogenously. Most weekly (seven-day) rhythms appear to be linked to social factors, with studies showing that days at the weekend are generally associated with better moods. However, there is some suggestion that there may be a weekly cycle entrained by biological factors (Larsen and Kasimatis 1990).

Diurnal mood variation appears to be most strongly influenced by endogenous factors. Essentially, POSITIVE AFFECT is reported to be at its peak around halfway between waking up for the day and returning to sleep (see s. 2, SLEEP AND BIOLOGICAL RHYTHMS) that evening (regardless of actual timing of waking and falling asleep). Thus, a diurnal cycle in positive affect can be charted in the form of the familiar inverted-U. In support of the biological nature of this pattern is the finding that it is closely associated with the temperature cycle, as well as being linked to the sleep-wake cycle (Watson 2000). That positive affect has a daily cycle is consistent with an evolutionary explanation of behaviour. The positive emotions are likely to accompany motivation for behaviours such as sex, FEEDING (see s. 2, FEEDING AND DRINKING) and preparing shelter. At night, when we are less likely to be active, our body accommodates the need to conserve energy, and positive affect is lowered. Negative affect appears to show no strong pattern, diurnal or otherwise. With negative affect believed to exist as part of the reaction to threat, it should not be constrained by any endogenous rhythm. Watson (2000) has shown that negative emotions generally lack any predictable pattern in expression, and do not appear to accompany any of the biological oscillations linked with positive affect. *CM*

Larsen, R. J. and Kasimatis, M. 1990: Individual differences in entrainment of mood to the weekly calendar. *Journal of Personality and Social Psychology* 58, 164–N71. Watson, D. 2000: *Mood and Temperament.* New York: Guilford Press.

mood disorders

Ordinarily, people experience a wide range of moods, ranging from highs to lows, happy to sad, energised to fatigued. MOOD VARIABILITY research shows that people differ appreciably in their day-to-day variability of moods, and there is also considerable variation in average level of mood. Mood STATES can be viewed as comparatively short-lived processes (e.g. a momentary surprise, a flash of anger) rather than as durable dispositions or TRAITS.

Mood disorders are, however, the most frequently occurring mental health problem. DEPRESSION (see s. 7) (or unipolar affective disorder) affects thoughts, feelings, physical health and behaviours of more than 20 per cent of the adult population at some time during their adult lives. It is more than being sad or feeling grief after a loss. A depressive episode must have a certain level of severity and for DSM-IV (see s. 7) criteria a lowered mood state or loss of interest or pleasure in nearly all things must persist for a minimum of two weeks.

Bipolar affective disorder (or manic depression) is a disturbance of mood that is characterised by cycles of both depression and MANIA (see s. 7). A person with BIPOLAR DISORDER (see s. 7) may experience mood swings that can occur both gradually and, occasionally, with rapidity. There are a number of forms of bipolar disorder, depending on the symptoms. During the depressed phase, a person may experience some or all of the symptoms of depression. Symptoms of mania include elation, irritability, decreased need for sleep (see s. 2, SLEEP AND BIOLOGICAL RHYTHMS) and racing thoughts. Symptoms of mania can affect judgement, thinking and behaviour, leading to potential problems. *MS*

American Psychiatric Association 1994: *Diagnostic and Statistical Manual of Mental Disorders* (4th edn). Washington, DC.

mood scales

Mood scales used in normal volunteers and those used in clinical POPULATIONS (see s. 8) can overlap; however, the definitions and descriptions of mood can vary. Techniques of MEASUREMENT (see s. 1, MEASUREMENT AND STATISTICS) range from observer-rated scales and structured interviews to self-report. Within healthy normal controls, different researchers have proposed that mood falls into different categories. Particular aspects of mood do cluster together and may form dimensions; however, the structure of mood has yet to be adequately defined. For instance, McNair et al. (1992) claim six dimensions for normal mood. These are tension-anxiety, depression-dejection, anger-hostility, vigour, FATIGUE (see s. 7) and confusion-bewilderment, for which they have developed a measurement scale. Other researchers claim either a two- or three-FACTOR (see s. 8) structure for mood (Watson, Wiese, Vaidya and Tellegen 1999). The timeframe of mood measures may vary from weeks to minutes. Where the timeframe is over a longer period of time, this could represent more of a TRAIT measure than a STATE measure. Scales in the clinical field range from diagnostic tools to scales which assess severity of illness and change. Self-report questionnaires have been designed to screen individuals in the community for psychiatric disorder (Goldberg 1978). Other measures are available for assessing severity of depression, which give higher LEVELS OF MEASUREMENT (see s. 8) rather than a categorical measure, and others which are more sensitive to change over time. The Hamilton Depression Rating Scale (HDRS) is an observer-rated scale for measuring the severity of depression (Hamilton 1960). It is used widely and generally has high inter-rater RELIABILITY (see also s. 8) and correlates highly against psychiatrists' global ratings of severity. Self-report scales require less manpower and are extremely quick and easy to administer. However, they have their drawbacks: patients or volunteers may not use words in the way intended by the experimenter; an individual may interpret a word in a different way and use it in terms of their own experience; and some severely ill patients may have difficulties completing a self-report measure. It is difficult to measure reliability on many of these scales. For instance, when measuring mood, it is often expected that this will change, which makes measuring test-retest reliability difficult. *MS*

Goldberg, D. 1978: *General Health Questionnaire.* Windsor: NFER Publishing Company. **Hamilton, M.** 1960: A rating scale for depression. *Journal of Neurology, Neurosurgery and Psychiatry* 23, 56–62. **McNair, D. M., Lorr, M. and Droppleman, L. F.** 1992: *Profile of Mood States* (revised). San Diego: EdITS/Educational and Industrial Testing Service. **Watson, D., Wiese, D., Vaidya, J. and Tellegen, A.** 1999: The two general activation systems of affect: structural findings, evolutionary considerations, and psychobiological evidence. *Journal of Personality and Social Psychology* 76(5), 820–38.

mood structure

It is now widely accepted that the best way to describe moods is in terms of the INDEPENDENT (see s. 8) dimensions of POSITIVE AFFECT and NEGATIVE AFFECT (e.g. Watson and Tellegen 1985). Asked to describe one's mood at any point in time a person may say they feel 'happy' or 'calm' or 'excited' or even 'dull' or 'lively'. In so doing, the person is describing how they feel in terms of positive affect. If one describes their moods as 'angry' or 'sad' or even 'scared' or 'lonely', they are reporting that their feelings are dominated by negative affect. The independent nature of these affects means that one can be simultaneously high on both moods (the fear and thrill one gets from doing something daring) or low on both moods (unemotional and quiet). The intermediate combinations of these moods are more common experiences, however. So, feeling low on positive affect but high on negative affect is the depressed experience, yet to experience high positive affect together with low negative affect is to feel on top of the world (Watson 2000).

The structure of mood may indeed be dominated by the two broad dimensions termed positive and negative affect, but common parlance does not make use of such terms when describing everyday moods. Instead, people often claim to feel 'sad' or 'stressed', or maybe 'happy' or even 'relaxed'. A number of researchers have invested considerable effort in measuring discrete moods such as these, and indicated quite correctly that the number of moods we experience is considerably higher than two (e.g. Lorr and McNair 1988). However, most of the negative moods are highly correlated so that a person who reports experiencing high STRESS (see s. 7) is also very likely to report the simultaneous feeling of high anxiety and even sadness. Likewise, the positive moods that we experience often come as a package. In other words, all the negative moods may be combined into a single dimension of negative affect, and the positive moods into a single dimension of positive affect (Watson 2000) as second-order FACTORS (see s. 8) when the correlations between mood scales are subjected to FACTOR ANALYSIS (see also s. 8). *CM*

Lorr, M. and McNair, D. M. 1988: *Manual, Profile of Mood States, Bipolar Form.* San Diego CA: Educational and Industrial Testing Service. **Watson, D.** 2000: *Mood and Temperament.* New York: Guilford Press. **Watson, D. and Tellegen, A.** 1985: Toward a consensual structure of mood. *Psychological Bulletin* 98, 219–35.

mood theories

Explanations for mood experiences typically involve the firmly established connections between STATES and TRAITS. Eysenck and Eysenck (1985) proposed that positive moods largely arose from biological underpinnings of trait extroversion and that negative moods reflected the emotionality that characterises NEUROTICISM. Combinations of these traits were said to produce four types of MOOD VARIABILITY. So, for example, low neuroticism combined with high EXTROVERSION is said to produce a generally cheerful ('sanguine') person, and the unemotional ('phlegmatic') person is said to be characterised by scoring low on both these traits. While research has confirmed that one's mean level of positive affect measured over time is predicted by extroversion, and negative affect level is predicted by neuroticism, the model did not provide a good explanation for the existence of mood variability (e.g. McConville and Cooper 1999).

Watson (2000) has suggested that moods are tied to 'affective traits' consistent with the above model (that is, positive affect mood also exists as a trait version similar to extroversion, and negative affect has a corresponding trait version similar to neuroticism). It is further proposed that POSITIVE AFFECT and NEGATIVE AFFECT may have arisen as a consequence of evolutionary pressures. Watson has shown that positive affect shows a variety of cyclical patterns that are consistent with the HYPOTHESIS (see s. 3 and s. 8) that we should be active and motivated when we require such things as food, sex and shelter. There is no adaptive advantage in having our negative moods tied to purported biological oscillators, and negative affect is believed to be a reactive response to threats or impending harm. As predicted, Watson found that negative affect does not have any rhythmical patterns.

Thayer (1996), too, invokes the biological and evolutionary underpinnings of moods, but is one of a number of theorists who stress that cognitive components are also important. [See MOOD AND COGNITION] Thayer argues that we experience mood as a conscious awareness of the body's current state of general arousal. Integrating the physiological and cognitive aspects of mood has important applications. For example, various techniques for SELF-REGULATION (see s. 5) of mood can be applied to help overcome some of the physiological effects of poor moods. *CM*

Eysenck, H. J. and Eysenck, M. W. 1985: *Personality and Individual Differences.* New York: Plenum. **McConville, C. and Cooper, C.** 1999: Personality correlates of variable moods. *Personality and Individual Differences* 26, 65–78. **Thayer, R. E.** 1996: *The Origin of Everyday Moods.* New York: Oxford University Press. **Watson, D.** 2000: *Mood and Temperament.* New York: Guilford Press.

mood variability

Among the most interesting and important characteristics of moods is their capacity to change. Mood variability is the term used to describe a particular index of this change (Wessman and Ricks 1966). Assessment of moods is commonly conducted by having people report their moods on short mood scales over many occasions. A variety of useful STATISTICS (see s. 1, MEASUREMENT AND STATISTICS) can arise from this rich source of data. For instance, one can ascertain how positive a person's moods have been, on average, across a week or more. Yet this tells us nothing about how they experienced these moods. One person may have had generally positive feelings all week long, and another person with the same average level may have experienced upward and downward shifts in their moods across the week. A good measure of this mood change can be arrived at from summarising the swings around a person's mean level with the STANDARD DEVIATION (see s. 8) of the mood scale scores.

If scales assessing the two main moods (POSITIVE AFFECT and NEGATIVE AFFECT) are administered repeatedly to the same individuals, it is possible to derive two measures of mood variability, one for each mood. Interestingly, although the occasion-to-occasion levels of the moods have been found to display statistical independence, this is not the case for these two indices of mood variability. It is commonly found that variability in positive affect and the variability in negative affect correlate together positively and substantially (e.g. Cooper and McConville 1990). In other words, mood variability is a general characteristic of the individual. Furthermore, this FACTOR (see s. 8) of mood variability has been shown to be consistent over time, and is not entirely explained by our major personality traits. Somewhat curiously, mood variability levels are raised in some instances of DEPRESSION (see s. 7) (e.g. Hall, Sing and Romanoski 1991), and high mood variability is a characteristic disturbance in borderline personality (Cowdry, Gardner, O'Leary, Leibenluft and Rubinow 1991).

In sum, regardless of the mood valence, an individual's moods tend to vary to a characteristic extent. Some people's lives are dominated by their ever-changing moods, and some people rarely experience emotional highs and lows.   *CM*

Cooper, C. and McConville, C. 1990: Interpreting mood scores: clinical implications of individual differences in mood variability. *British Journal of Medical Psychology* 63, 215–25. **Cowdry, R. W., Gardner, D. L., O'Leary, K. M., Leibenluft, E. and Rubinow, D. R.** 1991: Mood variability: a study of four groups. *American Journal of Psychiatry* 148(11), 1505–11. **Hall, D. P., Sing, H. C. and Romanoski, A. J.** 1991: Identification and characterisation of greater mood variance in depression. *American Journal of Psychiatry* 148(10), 1341–5. **Wessman, A. E. and Ricks, D. F.** 1966: *Mood and Personality*. New York: Holt, Rinehart and Winston.

moods   [See STATES AND TRAITS, MOOD AND EMOTION, MOOD AND COGNITION, MOOD AND LIFE EVENTS, MOOD DISORDERS, MOOD SCALES, MOOD STRUCTURE, MOOD THEORIES and MOOD VARIABILITY]

motivation   MOTIVATIONAL THEORIES (such as INSTINCT THEORIES OF MOTIVATION, DRIVE REDUCTION THEORIES and more recently REVERSAL THEORY (see also s. 1)) stem from both the study of humans and animal models of motivation [see MOTIVATION: ANIMAL MODELS], which stress the physiology of motivation [see MOTIVATION: PHYSIOLOGY OF]. They attempt to explain MOTIVATIONAL STRUCTURE, how to best manipulate levels of motivation, and the links between MOTIVATION AND INTERESTS. MOTIVATION AND ADVERTISING and MOTIVATION AND SPORT are two major applications of this work.   *CC*

motivational theories   Motivation refers to the processes that energise and direct behaviour; it attempts to explain why people behave in a particular way. The importance of motivation is that, as a latent, intervening VARIABLE (see s. 8) it can act as an explanatory link between internal and external stimuli and behavioural responses (Reeve 1997). For example, hunger pangs or attractive cooking aromas can lead to a hunger motivational factor or motive which explains why the person will purchase a snack. The stimuli that elicit motivation can have a physiological (e.g. hunger), emotional (e.g. fear), social (e.g. cultural NORMS – see also s. 5) or cognitive basis (e.g. learnt relationships).

The origin of motivational force has been a subject of debate since the times of the ancient Greeks. It was, however, only in a post-Darwinian context that psychologists were able to move away from the philosophical concept of 'will' and adopt the biological motivational theories of instinct. These theories allowed psychologists to explain what motivation was and where it emanated from – something philosophers were unable to achieve. INSTINCT THEORIES OF MOTIVATION, pioneered by William James and William McDougall, did successfully account (descriptively at least) for human reflexive behaviour present at birth. However, it failed to survive as an all-encompassing theory of motivation as it did not explain learned behaviour satisfactorily.

The biologically based behavioural approaches then gained popularity, replacing the instinct with concepts of DRIVE (see s. 2) and incentives. These included DRIVE REDUCTION THEORIES, arousal theories and incentive theories. The drive reduction theories of motivation postulated that physiological imbalances created a psychological drive which activated behaviour to alleviate the imbalance and hence reduce the drive. This approach did successfully address many of the shortcomings that the instinct theories failed to address, namely, learnt behaviours and external incentives. The main limitation of the drive reduction model is that it cannot adequately account for behaviours which do not directly reduce drives, for example, SENSATION-SEEKING behaviours. These behaviours do not appear to reduce drives, but increase arousal. Arousal theory states that each person attempts to maintain a fixed level of physiological arousal at which they feel most comfortable and perform best (Hebb 1955). If the arousal state of the individual is too low (e.g. when almost asleep) or too high (e.g. when extremely anxious or thirsty), performance is impaired (this relationship is described by the Yerkes-Dodson law). People are therefore motivated to maintain an optimal level of arousal, which will vary between individuals. In contrast to the aforementioned approaches, incentive theory does not focus on the internal physiological stimuli, but external factors (Cofer 1972). Behaviours are motivated towards incentives that the individuals value. These values are influenced by each person's individual cognitive appraisal of the incentive (e.g. whether or not they like apples and how much expense should be used in obtaining apples) as well as biological factors (e.g. how hungry the person is).

There have also been motivational theories stressing the importance of cognition in the stimulus–reaction relationship. These include EQUITY THEORY (see s. 5), expectancy theory and the theory of achievement motivation. Adams' equity theory (1963) suggests that we are motivated to maintain cognitive consistency, that is, a consistent or equitable relationship between cognition and behaviour. Therefore, we are motivated to reduce COGNITIVE DISSONANCE (see s. 5) or the tension that is resultant from inconsistencies between cognition and our views. There is limited evidence of the PREDICTIVE VALIDITY (see s. 7) of this theory in applied contexts. Vroom (1964) proposed an expectancy theory in which motivation force could be calculated using expectancy (the perceived amount of effort to achieve an effective outcome), instrumentality (the probability that a successful outcome would lead to recognition or reward) and valence (the affective value of recognition or reward for the individual). Due to this model's design it has been the basis for extensive testing, but has received little EMPIRICAL (see s. 8) support. Another cognitive approach focuses on the need to achieve (and the need to avoid failure). However, an individual's behaviour will also be influenced by the probability of success and the incentives for success. This 'need achievement' demonstrates gender differences even at early ages. Those individuals with high need achievement generally enjoy responsibility and PROBLEM SOLVING (see s. 3), challenging but attainable goals, and the desire for performance feedback (Atkinson and Birsch 1978).

Other motivation theories include Cattell's dynamic calculus (Cattell and Child 1975) and Apter's REVERSAL THEORY (see also s. 1) (Apter 1982). Cattell's model integrates ERGS (basic drives) and learned metaergs (acquired sentiments and ATTITUDES – see s. 5) which influence behaviour. The dynamic structure proposed by Cattell includes both unintegrated (STATE) and integrated (TRAIT) factors. Apter's theory is based on the premise that psychological needs exist in opposite pairs, e.g. opposite to the need of sensation seeking is the need of security. People then 'reverse' between these different needs and demonstrate different motivational styles at different times.

Abraham Maslow (1943) adopted a different approach and instead of attempting to explain motivation, created a hierarchy of motives (sometimes referred to as a humanistic or interactive approach). Maslow's hierarchy assumes that the motives at the lower levels must be satisfied before people can become motivated by higher-level goals. For example, people must have their physiological needs, for food and water, met before they will be motivated to seek belongingness and love. Not everyone adheres to this linear hierarchy, for example individuals with fervent political and moral BELIEFS (see s. 5) often strive for high-level needs while basic lower-level needs (e.g. food or freedom from PAIN – see s. 2 and s. 7) remain unmet.

There has been a wide range of motivational theories proposed. The number of actual motives that exist varies between the competing theories (e.g. reversal theory proposes five pairs while instinct theories have suggested thousands of possible motives). Some theories have been more successful than others in explaining human behaviour, but it should be noted that many of the theories are not mutually exclusive and each adds to our still limited understanding of the causes of human behaviour.   *DH*

Adams, J. S. 1963: Towards an understanding of inequity. *Journal of Abnormal and Social Psychology* 67, 422–36. **Apter, M. J.** 1982: *The Experience of Motivation: The Theory of Psychological Reversals*. London: Academic Press. **Atkinson, J. W. and Birsch, D.** 1978: *Introduction to Motivation*. New York: Van Nostrand. **Cattell, R. B. and Child, D.** 1975: *Motivation and Dynamic Structure*. London: Holt, Rinehart and Winston. **Cofer, C. N.** 1972: *Motivation and Emotion*. Illinois: Scott, Foresman and Company. **Hebb, D. O.** 1955: Drives and the C.N.S.: conceptual nervous system. *Psychological Review* 62, 245–54. **Maslow, A. H.** 1943: A theory of human motivation. *Psychological Review* 50, 370–96. **Reeve, J. M.** 1997: *Understanding Motivation and Emotion*. Texas: Harcourt Brace College. **Vroom, V. H.** 1964: *Work and Motivation*. New York: Wiley.

motivation and advertising   The level to which an individual processes an advertisement is thought to be mediated by their motivational level, as well as the opportunity and ability to process the information. The motivation levels in this context refers to the consumer's arousal or desire to process the information that is presented to them during the advertisement, that is, the person is motivated to allocate processing resources to the message (MacInnis, Moorman and Jaworski 1991). These levels at which the consumer focuses on the message can be basic categorisation (when MOTIVATION is low), meaning analysis (indicating moderate motivation) or information integration (when motivation is high) (MacInnis and Jaworski 1989). Even though motivational levels exist before an individual is exposed to an advertisement, the advertisement can itself affect motivation. Advertisements often seek to increase a person's motivation to attend to the message and to process the message. Strategies employed by advertisers to attract attention to the adverts include featuring hedonistic material (e.g. sexual images), introducing novel stimuli (e.g. varying the length or voices used), including prominent stimuli (e.g. famous people or action sequences) and increasing complexity (e.g. editing in many varied scenes).

Similarly, strategies can also be employed to increase the consumers' motivation to process the information contained in the advertisement: making the message applicable to the individual (e.g. rhetorical questions or fear appeals), using cues to increase curiosity (e.g. suspense or humour: MacInnis, Moorman and Jaworski 1991).

It should be noted that while people may be motivated to attend and process the advertisement, it does not mean they will be motivated to behave in a favourable manner towards the product (e.g. purchase it). It has been shown that while novel advertisements are on average watched for longer and processed in more depth, it does not mean that the product or message was liked. In fact if the advertisement was too inconsistent with previous knowledge or views, the message would be rejected (Goodstein 1993).   *DH*

Goodstein, R. C. 1993: Category-based applications and extensions in advertising: motivating more extensive ad processing. *Journal of Consumer Research* 20, 87–99. **MacInnis, D. C. and Jaworski, B. J.** 1989: Information processing from advertisements: toward an integrative framework. *Journal of Marketing* 53, 1–23. **MacInnis, D. C., Moorman, C. and Jaworski, B. J.** 1991: Enhancing and measuring consumers' motivation, opportunity and ability to process brand information from ads. *Journal of Marketing* 55, 32–53.

motivation and interests   MOTIVATION and interests can play an influential role in how individuals spend their time and the degree to which they succeed with tasks. The need to achieve (and avoid failure) is encapsulated in the theory of ACHIEVEMENT MOTIVATION. [See also MOTIVATION THEORIES] This theory suggests individuals tend to be interested in moderately difficult tasks, persist longer with challenges and enjoy entrepreneurial pursuits. For example, individuals who score highly on questionnaires assessing sporting motives tend to show more interest and participate more in sporting activities. These results also show GENDER (see s. 1, GENDER AND SEXUALITY ISSUES) and experience differences, with female and recreational athletes typically displaying higher levels of intrinsic motivation (internal satisfaction) than males and competitive athletes who value extrinsic motivation (external reward) (Fortier, Vallerand, Briere and Provencher 1995). Motivation and interest can also influence academic performance of schoolchildren. Although FACTORS (see s. 8) such as cognitive abilities are important predictors of performance, motivation and interest in the subjects also appear to be related to ACADEMIC ACHIEVEMENT (see s. 4) (Singh, Granville and Dika 2002).

Many of the extreme behaviours in which people participate can also be explained by arousal theory. [See MOTIVATION THEORIES and SENSATION SEEKING] Arousal theory proposes that people are motivated to maintain their own specific physiological arousal level. For example, after a day's studying, one individual may be content to relax at home while another will be motivated to seek stimulation at the gym or the cinema. The behaviours at the extreme arousal end of the scale are known as sensation-seeking behaviours and include increased sexual activity, experimentation with DRUGS (see s. 2) and gambling (Zuckerman, Bone, Neary, Mangelsdorff and Brustman 1972). It is thought that these behaviours are acquired through an opponent process where the reaction to a stimulus is followed by an opposite reaction (Solomon 1980). For example, the fear experienced when first attempting a parachute jump is replaced and associated with the excitement it brings. *DH*

Fortier, M. S., Vallerand, R. J., Briere, N. M. and Provencher, P. J. 1995: Competitive and recreational sport structures and gender – a test of their relationship with sport motivation. *International Journal of Sport Psychology* 26, 24–39. **Singh, K., Granville, M. and Dika, S.** 2002: Mathematics and science achievements: effects of motivation, interest, and academic engagement. *Journal of Educational Research* 95, 323–32. **Solomon, R. L.** 1980: The opponent-process theory of motivation: the cost of pleasure and the benefits of pain. *American Psychologist* 35, 691–712. **Zuckerman, M., Bone, R. N., Neary, R., Mangelsdorff, D. and Brustman, B.** 1972: What is the sensation seeker? Personality trait and experience correlates of the sensation seeking scale. *Journal of Consulting and Clinical Psychology* 39, 308–21.

motivation and sport Motivation can offer explanations about needs, desires, ambition, achievement striving, persistence, competitiveness and contextual climates: concepts that are particularly salient when applied to participation in sport. The sport or exercise participant may typically encounter feelings relating to success and failure in SKILL (see s. 3) acquisition, SOCIAL COMPARISON (see s. 5), feedback from others (such as parents, coaches and peers) and conflict from alternative activities. The behaviour of participation in a sport or exercise may vary from season to season, activity to activity and according to the level at which they participate (recreational, competitive or elite). Participation may result in continued participation, or the participant choosing to leave the activity to try another, or total rejection of all physical activities, be it temporary or permanent withdrawal. Terms such as 'dropout' and 'burnout' are commonly used in sporting contexts to describe different types of withdrawal. Extensive descriptive research has documented the reasons people cite for participation and withdrawal from physical activity. The five common motives for participation are competence, affiliation, FITNESS (see s. 2), fun and success. The five common motives for withdrawal are a lack of progress or skill improvement, interest in and conflict with other activities, a lack of fun or boredom, lack of playing time, excessive pressure from others and increased time commitment. Statistical measures are also in abundance, measuring differences according to age, GENDER (see s. 1, GENDER AND SEXUALITY ISSUES), cultural background, type of and level of involvement (Biddle 1998).

Recent theories are mainly of a social cognitive nature, looking at the environmental factors and personal cognitions that influence MOTIVATION. The most popular of these theories among researchers are perceived competence theory (Harter 1978), self-determination theory (for a review, Vallerand 2001) and achievement goal theory (for a review, Roberts 2001). This reflects a move away from the traditional PSYCHOANALYTIC, humanistic and behavioural theories, which tended to emphasise either an exclusively mechanistic or organismic perspective. However, in recent years a number of integrated models, combining aspects of the traditional models, have emerged in response to calls for clarity and theoretical harmony. *RL*

Biddle, S. 1998: Sport and exercise motivation: a brief review of antecedent factors and psychological outcomes of participation. In Green, K. and Hardman, K. (eds) *Physical Education: A Reader.* Aachen, Germany: Meyer and Meyer. **Harter, S.** 1978: Effectance motivation reconsidered: towards a developmental model. *Human Development* 21, 34–64. **Roberts, G. C.** 2001: Understanding the dynamics of motivation in physical activity: the influence of achievement goals on motivational processes. In Roberts, G. C. (ed.) *Advances in Motivation in Sport and Exercise.* Champaign IL: Human Kinetics, 1–50. **Vallerand, R. J.** 2001: A hierarchical model of intrinsic and extrinsic motivation in sport and exercise. In Roberts, G. C. (ed.) *Advances in Motivation in Sport and Exercise.* Champaign IL: Human Kinetics, 263–319.

motivation: animal models Perhaps the most widely studied animal model of MOTIVATION is Konrad Lorenz's (1950) psycho-hydraulic model. This deterministic model proposes that a reservoir of motivational energy is continually building up inside an organism. This causes pressure on the releasing mechanism (which can be thought of as a tap or valve attached to the bottom of the reservoir of energy); the valve is held in opposing tension by inhibitory mechanisms (like a spring trying to keep the valve shut). The energy can be released by a stimulus (pulling the valve open) or simply by the pressure caused by the build-up of energy (pushing the valve open). For example, it has been shown in calves that the stimulus of a teat releases the energy to suck (Rushen and de Passille 1995). However, in this study it was noted that motivational energy did not always build up as proposed in the psycho-hydraulic model, instead it only started to build up when milk was present. It was also reported that the sucking motivation decreased after time even if the behaviour was not performed. This indicated that the motivational state decayed with time, not just with the release of energy. Lorenz's model has since been revised, allowing the 'reservoir' to have multiple sources of energy and dissipate this energy in various ways (Hogan 1997).

Another model was proposed by the ethologist Tinbergen (see s. 2, TINBERGEN'S FOUR WHYS) that focused on the flow of energy through hierarchical neural structures. However, this model is now accepted as inconsistent with current neurological and physiological knowledge. Yet another approach was proposed by Deutsch (1960). In this model a physiological imbalance is detected and excites a 'link', which, in turn, excites the motor system and produces behaviour. The benefit of this model is that it accounts for the results of sham-eating experiments (where the animal's stomach is filled externally without the animal engaging in eating behaviours) better than the psycho-hydraulic model. In sham-eating experiments the animals tend not to eat (as their stomachs are externally filled). Lorenz's model would predict the animals would perform eating behaviours whereas Deutsch's model predicts correctly that the animals would not eat. *DH*

Deutsch, J. A. 1960: *The Structural Basis of Behaviour.* Cambridge: Cambridge University Press. **Hogan, J. A.** 1997: Energy models of motivation: a reconsideration. *Applied Animal Behaviour Science* 53, 89–105. **Lorenz, K.** 1950: The comparative method in studying innate behaviour. *Symposium of the Society of Experimental Biology* 4, 221–68. **Rushen, J. and de Passille, A. M.** 1995: The motivation of non-nutritive sucking in calves. *Applied Animal Behaviour Science* 49, 1503–10.

motivation: physiology of

motivation: physiology of Physiological deprivation of a VARIABLE (see s. 8) (for example, food, water, sleep – see s. 2, SLEEP AND BIOLOGICAL RHYTHMS, etc.) gives rise to a biological imbalance or a need. A need can be defined as a deficiency-satisfying condition that produces behavioural energy and direction (Reeve 1997). This physiological need (if it continues and is of a certain magnitude) may give rise to a conscious psychological DRIVE (see s. 2). This drive promotes a deficiency-satisfying behaviour in an attempt to return the body to a physiological balanced state or HOMEOSTASIS (see s. 2). That is, the individual satisfies the physiological need and hence removes the conscious drive and therefore returns to an unmotivated state. After a period of time the physiological deprived state may reoccur and the process will be repeated. For example, intracellular water deprivation (and to a lesser extent extracellular water deprivation) can be classified as a physiological need. The hypothalamus detects the intercellular shrinkage due to the water deprivation and is responsible for the drive, that is, the sensation of thirst (Reeve 1997). This motivates the individual to perform a deficiency-satisfying behaviour (for example, drinking – see s. 2, FEEDING AND DRINKING – a glass of water). The individual returns to an unmotivated state when the cells become rehydrated; however, other thirst-inhibitory mechanisms may also influence the motivational state, including the number of swallows taken and the amount of water to enter the stomach (Blass and Hall

1976). These physiological cues do not act in isolation and learned associations or the flavour of the liquid may also influence the amount consumed.

Research on hunger has also highlighted the role of the hypothalamus in motivation. It is this area that monitors the nutrients and hormones in the blood to determine when food is needed (known as short-term hunger). Evidence suggests that the lateral hypothalamus controls the 'start eating signals' and the ventromedial nucleus controls the 'stop eating signals'. The paraventricular nucleus, affected by NEUROTRANSMITTERS (see s. 2) and hormones, will also influence hunger and the selection of specific food types (Keesey and Powley 1975). As with thirst, external FACTORS (see s. 8), including social and environmental factors, will also be in effect. (See s. 2, HORMONES, APPETITE AND ENERGY REGULATION) *DH*

Blass, E. M. and Hall, W. G. 1976: Drinking termination: interaction among hydrational, orogasic and behavioural control in rats. *Psychological Review* 83, 356–74. **Keesey, R. E. and Powley, T. L.** 1975: Hypothalamic regulation of body weight. *American Scientist* 63, 558–65. **Reeve, J. M.** 1997: *Understanding Motivation and Emotion.* Texas: Harcourt Brace College.

motivation structure

motivation structure There is considerable confusion about what, precisely, is meant by motivation in psychology – or the number of distinct motivators that exist. There are several MOTIVATION THEORIES. INSTINCT THEORIES OF MOTIVATION offered a circular definition in that they 'explained' any behaviour by suggesting that a person behaved that way because they had an instinct to do so: an unhelpful start. Many psychologists choose to view 'motivation' towards a particular goal as a personality trait (e.g. 'ACHIEVEMENT MOTIVATION') (McClelland 1961). It is hence unsurprising to find that the tests which assess such variables show some overlap with well-known personality dimensions (Judge and Ilies 2002). However, it is also likely that this approach suffers from the same problem of circularity as the older instinct theories. Psychologists such as Cattell (Cattell 1957) suggest that it is more useful to view motivation as a changeable STATE rather than a stable characteristic of the individual: a person is motivated to seek out food when hungry, but after eating their interest in food will wane.

Cattell argued that motivation should be understood through analysing the strength of many interests, and observing which covary together over time. However, it is possible that each interest can simultaneously satisfy several motives. For example, someone with a penchant for vintage cars will enjoy an opportunity to socialise with other like-minded individuals and engage in engineering challenges (when repairing them); they may derive aesthetic pleasure from them and/or enjoy being the centre of attention when driving around. To discover the basic dimensions of motivation it is necessary to ask people to describe their motives: ultimately they will not be able to identify a more basic goal (some things are just intrinsically rewarding) and these may be the basic DRIVES (see s. 2).

Strength of interest may itself show up in several ways (68, according to Cattell and Child 1975), not all of which are necessarily conscious. As well as expressing a conscious interest, the person's heart may race when they view a rare car; they will have a more extensive knowledge of car-related facts than does someone of similar INTELLIGENCE (see also s. 4) who has different interests; and their interest may perhaps display itself through occasional slips of the tongue and errors of PERCEPTION (see s. 1). This is a complicated model. However Cattell and Child (1975) claim to have identified several basic biological motivational states ('ERGS'), including sex, hunger, fear, gregariousness, exploration, self-assertion, pugnacity, narcissism and acquisitiveness, together with several culturally determined 'SENTIMENTS', such as a desire to perform well in one's job, please parents, please one's partner, obey one's conscience, follow religious BELIEFS (see s. 5), take part in sport, scientific interest, money and aesthetics. Unfortunately, the only test that has been developed to assess these ergs and sentiments (Cattell et al. 1970) shows lamentable psychometric properties (Cooper and Kline 1982) [see PSYCHOMETRICS].

Maslow's (1968) hierarchy of needs is a rather straightforward theory, based on observational studies of primate and human behaviour, which proves rather hard to test empirically. It suggests that there are several categories of 'need', the most numerous (and most urgent) being physiological needs. Once these physiological needs are satisfied, the individual tries to satisfy their need for safety/security, then their need for belonging, then their need for self-esteem, then cognitive needs, and finally their aesthetic needs. Finally (once these are all satisfied), the individual 'self-actualises' – that is, explores and tries to develop their inner potential. Assessing self-actualisation is not a trivial exercise, and it is not clear precisely how many distinct needs there are, or how they should be classified. As Cattell pointed out, most behaviours fulfil multiple needs. This makes it difficult to refute Maslow's theory, as without pure measures of needs it is difficult to test whether any purely 'cognitive' need (for example) is ever undertaken before all the lower-level needs are satisfied. The theory holds rather little sway today.

Apter's REVERSAL THEORY (see also s. 1) of motivation suggests that there are five 'metamotivational states' which guide how we view tasks. We may do something because it is a means to an end or, alternatively, because it is intrinsically rewarding – and indeed our view of the same task can change quickly along this 'telic/paratelic' dimension. Likewise we can focus on rules or give our imaginations free reign and play as we solve a problem ('conformist/challenging'). We can seek to control or appear attractive ('autic mastery' vs. 'autic sympathy'). We align ourselves with others, or nurture others ('alloic mastery'/'alloic sympathy') and we may seek peace or excitement ('tranquil/arousal seeking'). These five dimensions are the sorts of COGNITIVE STYLES AND LEARNING STYLES which determine how individuals approach tasks – but not directly why they choose to follow a certain course of action. Most research has focused on the telic/paratelic, which has been shown to correlate very substantially with EXTROVERSION (negatively) and NEUROTICISM (Apter, Mallows and Williams 1998), so it is questionable whether it is any more than a mixture of these two personality traits. Thus despite its popularity in sports and OCCUPATIONAL PSYCHOLOGY (see also s. 1, INDUSTRIAL AND OCCUPATIONAL PSYCHOLOGY), it is not clear that Apter's theory is a useful measure of motivation.

The psychology of motivation is far less advanced than other branches of individual differences, with few (if any) well-accepted theories, little clear evidence of the basic motivational 'source states' which combine to influence a person's choice of behaviour, and no well-accepted tools for assessing motivational states. *CC*

Apter, M. J., Mallows, R. and Williams, S. 1998: The development of the motivational style profile. *Personality and Individual Differences* 24, 7–18. **Cattell, R. B.** 1957: *Personality and Motivation Structure and Measurement*. Yonkers: New World. **Cattell, R. B. and Child, D.** 1975: *Motivation and Dynamic Structure*. London: Holt, Rinehart and Winston. **Cattell, R. B., Horn, J. L. and Sweney, A. B.** 1970: *Manual for the Motivation Analysis Test*. Champaign IL: Institute for Personality and Ability Testing. **Cooper, C. and Kline, P.** 1982: The internal structure of the motivation analysis test. *British Journal of Educational Psychology* 52, 228–33. **Judge, T. A. and Ilies, R.** 2002: Relationship of personality to performance motivation: a meta-analytic review. *Journal of Applied Psychology* 87, 797–807. **Maslow, A. H.** 1968: *Toward a Psychology of Being* (2nd edn). Princeton NJ: Van Nostrand. **McClelland, D. C.** 1961: *Achieving Society*. New York: Van Nostrand.

multiple intelligences The theory of multiple intelligences (MI) was proposed by Gardner (1983) as an alternative perspective on human cognitive ability. MI theory originally posited seven distinct types of INTELLIGENCE (see also s. 4), which are briefly described below. Linguistic intelligence is the ability to understand and use LANGUAGE (see s. 2) and words. Logical-mathematical intelligence is the ability to understand and use numbers and mathematical concepts. Musical intelligence reflects the ability to compose, understand and respond to musical compositions. Spatial intelligence concerns the ability to perceive and represent visuo-spatial relationships in different contexts. Bodily kinesthetic intelligence is the ability to appreciate the aesthetics of the body and to coordinate motor movements. There are also two personal intelligences which are the direct precursors of the construct of EMOTIONAL INTELLIGENCE and comprise intrapersonal intelligence (the ability to understand one's own emotions and mental states and to have insight into personal strengths and weaknesses) and interpersonal intelligence, which is the ability to understand and manage other people's emotions and mental states.

Gardner later posited two additional intelligences: naturalist intelligence, which is the ability to recognise and classify natural objects, like plants and animals, and existentialist intelligence, which is the ability to comprehend and contemplate the profound questions in existence (e.g. the meaning of life).

Gardner suggested eight conditions that may serve as criteria for identifying new intelligences, including isolation by brain damage, evolutionary plausibility and the existence of prodigies or idiot savants in the intelligence. However, many of the suggested criteria are vague and not amenable to quantification, such that it is unclear how existing intelligences satisfy them and easily imaginable how other candidate intelligences might (e.g. sexual intelligence).

MI theory has enjoyed considerable popularity in educational practice, but its conceptual confusion and dearth of supporting EMPIRICAL (see s. 8) evidence has prevented it from achieving scientific status. More generally, the influx of new intelligences (multiple intelligences, emotional intelligence, practical intelligence, etc.) has served to further dilute the meaning of the word rather than to expand the domain of human cognitive ability. To be considered scientific, any new theory of intelligence in the cognitive ability tradition must be either fully compatible or at least as powerful and parsimonious as the current theory of the g [see GENERAL ABILITY] factor.

KP

Gardner, H. 1983: *Frames of Mind: The Theory of Multiple Intelligences*. New York: Basic Books. **Jensen, A. R.** 1998: *The g Factor*. Westport CT: Praeger.

N

negative affect   A term used to convey an unpleasant emotional STATE, such as DEPRESSION (see s. 7), anxiety and tension; often associated with MOOD AND EMOTIONS.   *RL*

negative emotions   A generalisation that emotions such as anger or guilt have undesirable characteristics, this division overlooks the adaptive advantage of emotions (i.e. survival and social VALUES – see s. 5).   *AF*

NEO-PI(R)   A commercial personality test assessing the FIVE-FACTOR MODEL OF PERSONALITY: EXTROVERSION, NEUROTICISM, OPENNESS to experience, CONSCIENTIOUSNESS and AGREEABLENESS (Costa and McCrae 1992). An alternative to the IPIP.   *CC*

Costa, P. T. and McCrae, R. R. 1992: *NEO-PI(R) Professional Manual*. Odessa FL: Psychological Assessment Resources.

neuroticism   Neuroticism can be found across CULTURES (see s. 1 and s. 5) and is common to most of the well-known personality questionnaires (Kline and Barrett 1983). Someone who scored highly on neuroticism could be described as a worrier, emotional, moody, shy and anxious. Eysenck (1967) postulated that neuroticism is related to the activity of the visceral brain, which incorporates the hippocampus, amygdala, singulum, septum and hypothalamus and has interconnections to the cerebral cortex. Activity of the visceral brain produces autonomic arousal. Those who score highly on the neuroticism scale are more likely than low scorers to become autonomically aroused. Thus the high scorers are more likely to become agitated when faced with stressful situations. This biological theory is attractive in that it is testable. However, one of the problems when testing individuals is the environment in which they are tested. Individuals who are already autonomically aroused (high N scorers) will react to a situation differently.

Neuroticism is highly related to level of mood. Those who score high on neuroticism are more likely to be associated with more NEGATIVE AFFECT. Neuroticism scores are also related to clinical conditions such as DEPRESSION (see s. 7), anxiety and EATING DISORDERS (see s. 7). Neuroticism scores are higher in patients with depression and in patients in remission from a major depressive episode. High neuroticism scores predict depression in previously never ill controls and are related to a lifetime prevalence of depression (Kendler, Neale, Kessler, Heath and Eaves 1994).

Neuroticism, in this way, has been associated with the monoamine system (serotonin, noradrenaline and dopamine are all monoamines), however, studies to date have been correlational and have not shown firm evidence. (See s. 2, MONOAMINE TRANSMITTERS)

Neuroticism may also affect performance. [See PERSONALITY AND EVERYDAY LIFE] TEST ANXIETY is mediated by personality FACTORS (see s. 8) (McIlroy, Bunting and Adamson 2000). Increased levels of STRESS (see s. 7) can lead to improved performance due to increased cognitive effort in the low anxious individual or, conversely, in the anxious individual increased anxiety can lead to a decrement in performance (Hardy 1999).   *MS*

Eysenck, H. J. 1967: *The Biological Basis of Personality*: Springfield IL: Charles C. Thomas. **Hardy, L.** 1999: Stress, anxiety and performance. *Journal of Science and Medicine in Sport* 2(3), 227–33. **Kendler, K. S., Neale, M. C., Kessler, R. C., Heath, A. C. and Eaves, L. J.** 1994: Clinical characteristics of familial generalized anxiety disorder. *Anxiety* 1(4), 186–91. **Kline, P. and Barrett, P.** 1983: The factors in personality questionnaires among normal subjects. *Advances in Behavioural Research and Therapy* 5, 141–202. **McIlroy, D., Bunting, B. and Adamson, G.** 2000: An evaluation of the factor structure and predictive utility of a test anxiety scale with reference to students' past performance and personality indices. *British Journal of Educational Psychology* 70, 17–32.

norms   Unless a TEST has been developed using ITEM RESPONSE THEORY, an individual's score on the test can only be interpreted by relating it to the distribution of scores typically obtained by similar people. This is because item difficulty and ability are confounded: thus if a person scores 30 out of 60 on a particular vocabulary test, it is impossible to tell whether this score is good, average or poor unless one also knows the distribution of scores within the POPULATION (see s. 8). Norms are simply the tables showing these scores. They allow the test-user to convert the raw score from the test into a PERCENTILE (see s. 8), for example, indicating that a score of 30 places a 9-year-old child into the 82nd percentile (indicating that 82 per cent of the population of 9-year-old-children are likely to score 30 or less on this test).

When constructing tables of norms for tests of cognitive abilities, it is necessary to develop separate tables for children of different ages, as cognitive abilities increase steadily throughout childhood. Tests such as the WECHSLER SCALES have norms for each three-month age interval. Normative data are gathered by giving the test to a sample which is carefully recruited in order to form a stratified SAMPLE (see s. 8) of the population. Each normative GROUP (see s. 5) typically resembles the population in terms of age, geographical area of residence, socioeconomic status, GENDER [see s. 1, GENDER AND SEXUALITY ISSUES], urban/rural location and ethnic origin. Each normative group should comprise several hundred individuals, to ensure that the distribution of scores in the normative group closely resembles the distribution of scores in the population. The INTELLIGENCE QUOTIENT (IQ) (see s. 4) offers an example of how test scores may be compared with those of a normative group for several different age bands.

Tests used in OCCUPATIONAL PSYCHOLOGY (see also s. 1, INDUSTRIAL AND OCCUPATIONAL PSYCHOLOGY) are frequently normed much less carefully. Some test manuals contain tables outlining norms for tiny samples of 'managers' for example – but without knowing more details it is impossible to tell whether the data from such convenience samples are appropriate. It is vital to ensure that the tables of norms that are used to give meaning to a person's score are representative of some appropriate group (e.g. the population of the UK or the population of applicants to the UK's police forces in 2004, if one is selecting police officers in 2004).

While it is vital to use an appropriate table of norms if an individual's test score is to be interpreted, it is not necessary to use norms in order to predict job performance from test scores for a homogeneous group (21 to 25-year-old graduates, for example). Indeed, doing so may lead to non-NORMAL DISTRIBUTIONS (see s. 8) of scores. (See also s. 5, NORMS)

CC

Anastasi, A. 1961: *Psychological Testing.* New York: Macmillan.
Cronbach, L. J. 1994: *Essentials of Psychological Testing* (5th edn). New York: Harper-Collins.

O

objective tests The term 'objective test' is used in two ways. Raymond Cattell uses it to describe any test where the person cannot easily fake their response – either because they do not know what the correct response should be or because they are physically unable to do so. The former might involve asking job applicants to sketch a house. They would be unaware how the test is scored, and so could not fake their response. The latter might involve measuring skin resistance when people hear a standard loud noise; they will be physically unable to modify their startle response. Cattell designed two batteries of objective tests to assess mood (Cattell, Horn and Sweney 1970) and personality (Cattell and Schuerger 1978) in situations where participants may try to distort their scores (e.g. PERSONNEL SELECTION). Unfortunately, they have been shown to have extremely low VALIDITY (see also s. 8) (Cooper and Kline 1982; Kline and Cooper 1984).

Some authors also use the term to refer to questionnaires that can be scored with near-perfect accuracy, using a template. *CC*

Cattell, R. B., Horn, J. L. and Sweney, A. B. 1970: *Manual for the Motivation Analysis Test*. Champaign IL: Institute for Personality and Ability Testing. **Cattell, R. B. and Schuerger, J. M.** 1978: *Personality Theory in Action*. Champaign IL: IPAT. **Cooper, C. and Kline, P.** 1982. The internal structure of the motivation analysis test. *British Journal of Educational Psychology*, 52, 228–33. **Kline, P. and Cooper, C.** 1984. A construct validation of the objective-analytic test battery (OATB). *Personality and Individual Differences* 5, 323–37.

openness Originally identified by Goldberg (1990) where it was named 'intellect', openness to experience is one of the three (later five) major personality traits identified by Costa and McCrae (McCrae and Costa 1997) as a component of their FIVE-FACTOR MODEL OF PERSONALITY. These days it is usually measured using the NEO-PI(R) or the IPIP personality scales. Openness reflects interests in art, fantasy, willingness to try new experiences, tolerance and emotional sensitivity, and is significantly correlated with CRYSTALLISED INTELLIGENCE (Ashton, Lee, Vernon and Jang 2000). Like the other FACTORS (see s. 8) in this model of personality, it has been identified in extensive cross-cultural research using translations of the NEO-PI(R) (McCrae and Costa 1997). *CC*

Ashton, M. C., Lee, K., Vernon, P. A. and Jang, K. L. 2000: Fluid intelligence, crystallized intelligence, and the openness/intellect factor. *Journal of Research in Personality* 34, 198–207. **Goldberg, L. R.** 1990: An alternative 'description of personality': the big-five structure. *Journal of Personality and Social Psychology* 59, 1216–29. **McCrae, R. R. and Costa, P. T.** 1997: Personality trait structure as a human universal. *American Psychologist* 52, 509–16.

P

PANAS scale A self-report mood scale which has ten words relating to POSITIVE AFFECT and ten words to negative affect on a LIKERT SCALE (see s. 5 and s. 8) (Watson, Clark and Tellegen 1988). *MS*

Watson, D., Clark, L. A. and Tellegen, A. 1988: Development and validation of a brief measure of positive and negative affect: the PANAS scales. *Journal of Personality and Social Psychology* 54, 1063–70.

personal construct theory Clinicians and counsellors often seek to understand the unique phenomenological world of an individual; to attempt to view the world through their eyes. George Kelly (1955) developed a cognitive theory of PERSONALITY together with clinical tools (such as REPERTORY GRID TECHNIQUES) and a method of therapy (FIXED-ROLE THERAPY). The basic premise is simple: we all try to make sense of the world (including our own roles in it) and develop 'personal constructs' to help us predict the future. This, rather than past traumas or biological dispositions, may be the core of personality.

A personal construct is simply a way of categorising people (or objects) which a person uses to make predictions about them (e.g. 'talkative vs. quiet' or 'law-abiding vs. criminal'). Different individuals will probably develop different personal constructs, and we each categorise other individuals on these constructs and develop 'rules of thumb' which help us predict how these constructs relate to behaviour. For example, we may have noted in the past that talkative people generally make good company, and so we would predict (other constructs being equal) that a night out with a new person whom we have construed as highly talkative would be more enjoyable than a night out with someone whom we construed as being quiet. If these predictions fail we experience ANXIETY and may either review the model linking constructs to behaviour, reconstrue individual people or elaborate the model by developing new constructs. Exploring a person's repertoire of constructs, their interrelationships and the links between constructs and expected behaviour may allow the clinician to understand a patient's cognitive processes and their unique model of how the world operates. A good, more modern account of the theory and applications is given by Bannister and Fransella (1989). *CC*

Bannister, D. and Fransella, F. 1989: *Inquiring Man: The Psychology of Personal Constructs*. London: Croom Helm. Kelly, G. A. 1955: *The Psychology of Personal Constructs*. New York: Norton, vols I and II.

personality Personality is a branch of INDIVIDUAL DIFFERENCES which seeks to understand how people vary in their 'personal style' – the number and nature of the main PERSONALITY TRAITS, the biology of personality [see PERSONALITY: THE BIOLOGY OF], etc. using various PERSONALITY TESTS developed using PSYCHOMETRICS. (See also s. 1, PERSONALITY) *CC*

personality and cognition Those who eschew THE SOCIAL CONSTRUCTION OF PERSONALITY and therefore believe that PERSONALITY TRAITS have their origins within each individual person have frequently attempted to discover links between personality and cognitive processes. However the term 'cognition' is used in two rather distinct senses. Some theorists use the term rather tightly to describe low-level cognitive OPERATIONS (see s. 4) that are not necessarily conscious, but which are associated with certain personality types. Others use it to describe SOCIAL COGNITION (see s. 4 and s. 5) applied to the 'SELF' (see s. 1, s. 4 and s. 5) – for example, to understand how the SELF-CONCEPT (see s. 4 and s. 5) develops and changes (McCann and Sato 2000).

Michael Eysenck reports a cognitive model of ANXIETY (Eysenck 1997), which attempts to integrate the clinical and mood literature [see MOOD AND COGNITION] with that which regards anxiety as a personality trait. It argues that four types of information influence levels of anxiety: cognitions (such as ruminations about future events), external stimuli (e.g. a demanding deadline), the appraisal of one's own behaviour and internal physiological stimuli. Laboratory studies have suggested that highly anxious individuals show a cognitive BIAS (see also s. 3 and s. 8) which leads them to overestimate the threat in all four of these types of information, while individuals who tend to deny their feelings (repressors) show a pattern of cognitive biases which makes them systematically underestimate the threat-value information arriving via each of these channels.

Although it is impossible to give a full account here, there is evidence that several other personality traits and behaviours are linked to cognitive processes, biases and BELIEFS (see s. 5). For example, conservatism is linked to fear of death; shyness is (unsurprisingly) related to PERCEPTIONS (see s. 1) of social self-efficacy; and when a negative emotional state is induced, only individuals with low SELF-ESTEEM (see s. 5 and s. 7) show mood-congruent RECALL (see s. 3). Thus unlike the biological bases of personality, it seems that individual differences in cognitive processes may sometimes be consequences and sometimes causes of personality traits. *CC*

Eysenck, M. W. 1997: *Anxiety and Cognition: A Unified Theory*. Hove, East Sussex: Psychology Press. McCann, D. and Sato, T. 2000: Personality, cognition, and the self. *European Journal of Personality* 14, 449–61.

personality and everyday life While scores on ability tests can make reasonably good predictions about many important real-life behaviours (e.g. educational and job performance), PERSONALITY TRAITS generally show more modest relationships (Robertson and Kinder 1993). This is probably because, unlike group tests of ability and individual tests of ability [see ABILITY: GROUP TESTS OF and ABILITY: INDIVIDUAL TESTS OF], where performance must actually be demonstrated in order to achieve a high mark, personality tests rely on self-report, with fairly transparent items. Thus any reasonably intelligent job applicant is unlikely to admit to being slapdash, easily bored, etc., and this will reduce the PREDICTIVE VALIDITY (see s. 7) of the scale. Nevertheless, several PERSONALITY TESTS (e.g. Bernreuter Inventory, Occupational Personality Questionnaire) have been developed specifically for use in OCCUPATIONAL PSYCHOLOGY (see also s. 1, INDUSTRIAL AND OCCUPATIONAL PSYCHOLOGY).

Personality scales show several correlations with health behaviours (Contrada, Cather and O'Leary 1999), but it is important to try to distinguish between personality traits that may predispose a person towards illness or 'risky' behaviour, and elevated scores on questionnaires that arise as a consequence of disease. An example of the former might be the lack of concern about safe sex or the consequences of drug use shown by a person with high levels of PSYCHOTICISM; an example of the latter might be elevated levels of NEUROTICISM following a debilitating or life-threatening illness. Contrada et al. (1999) outline a plausible model, which incorporates personality traits alongside disease VARIABLES (see s. 8), the social environment, responses to stressors, the physical disease itself and reactions to illness, although the model itself does not appear to have been comprehensively tested.

There is a substantial literature relating the Type A personality to coronary-proneness. However, this research has failed to live up to its early promise, perhaps because the Type A personality is a composite of several personality dimensions, some of which (e.g. hostility) may be more predictive than others (Helmer, Ragland and Syme 1991). A META-ANALYSIS (see s. 8) (Miller, Smith, Turner, Guijarro and Hallet 1996) certainly suggests that measures of hostility obtained from a structured interview are related to coronary heart disease, although the EFFECT SIZES (see s. 8) are not large. *CC*

Contrada, R. J., Cather, C. and O'Leary, A. 1999: Personality and health: dispositions and processes. In Pervin, L. A. and John, O. P. (eds) *Handbook of Personality: Theory and Research*. New York: Guilford Press. **Helmer, D. C., Ragland, D. R. and Syme, S. L.** 1991: Hostility and coronary-artery disease. *American Journal of Epidemiology* 133, 112–22. **Miller, T. Q., Smith, T. W., Turner, C. W., Guijarro, M. L. and Hallet, A. J.** 1996: A meta-analytic review of research on hostility and physical health. *Psychological Bulletin* 119, 322–48. **Robertson, I. T. and Kinder, A.** 1993: Personality and job competences – the criterion-related validity of some personality-variables. *Journal of Occupational and Organizational Psychology* 66, 225–44.

personality questionnaires

Information about an individual's personality may be collected by a variety of methods. Personality questionnaires are much favoured, as a reliable questionnaire can be constructed and NORMS (see also s. 5) established quite easily. A questionnaire can have good internal consistency and high test-retest RELIABILITY (see also s. 8), but reliability does not ensure VALIDITY (see also s. 8). Questionnaires can be derived from many different theories and assess different aspects of personality. By studying personality we are attempting to simplify and categorise aspects of the persona by MEASUREMENT (see s. 1, MEASUREMENT AND STATISTICS) and assessment. There are two main approaches to assessing personality: NOMOTHETIC (see also s. 1, NOMOTHETIC METHODS) versus IDIOGRAPHIC (see s. 8 and also s. 1, IDIOGRAPHIC METHODS). Within the nomothetic approach there are two main ways to describe personality: by personality types or personality traits. The idiographic approach gives a portrait of the person.

Trait theories of personality suggest there are a number of dimensions which allow us to characterise people by underlying basic traits. Trait measures prove to be one of the most reliable and stable instruments in psychology (Matthews and Deary 1998). There are several possible types of PERSONALITY TESTS, but personality questionnaires tend to be the instruments of choice, with PSYCHOMETRICS (see also s. 1) providing statistical techniques to aid with judgements of reliability, validity and stability. A questionnaire can be made up of a number of items (questions) and scales. There are a number of models of personality which suggest a different number of personality traits. One of the most well-supported questionnaires within trait theory of personality is the FIVE-FACTOR MODEL OF PERSONALITY of Costa and McCrae (1992), measuring NEUROTICISM, EXTROVERSION, OPENNESS, AGREEABLENESS and CONSCIENTIOUSNESS.

An alternative model was derived by Eysenck. The Eysenck Personality Questionnaire contains three broad FACTORS (see s. 8) – extroversion (E), neuroticism (N) and PSYCHOTICISM (P). EYSENCK'S THREE-FACTOR MODEL is derived from psychiatric concepts. It is unusual in being linked to a clear model of the biology of personality, which has been extensively studied. Eysenck's questionnaires have also been revised, culminating in the EPQ-R (Eysenck et al. 1985). *MS*

Costa, P. T. and McCrae, R. R. 1992: *Revised NEO Personality Inventory (NEO PI-RTM) and NEO Five-Factor Inventory (NEO-FFI)*. Odessa FL: Psychological Assessment Resources, Inc. **Eysenck, S. B. G., Eysenck, H. J. and Barrett, P.** 1985: A revised version of the psychoticism scale. *Personality and Individual Differences* 6, 21–9. **Matthews, G. and Deary, I. J.** 1998: *Personality Traits*. Cambridge: Cambridge University Press.

personality tests

PERSONALITY reflects an individual's personal style (rather than their level of performance: an ABILITY) which is a relatively enduring characteristic of the individual across situations and over time. There are four main ways of assessing personality. These involve the use of carefully constructed and validated PERSONALITY QUESTIONNAIRES, PROJECTIVE TESTS, OBJECTIVE TESTS, ratings of behaviour and self-report.

Personality questionnaires (such as the 16PF, the NEO-PI(R) and the EPQ-R) are constructed by using FACTOR ANALYSIS (see also s. 8) to determine which different behaviours (e.g. feeling optimistic and liking social gatherings) covary from person to person and hence form 'source traits' (Cattell 1973). Items are retailed purely on the basis of their statistical relationship with other items and the proven VALIDITY (see also s. 8) of the resulting scale: in Cattell's terminology, they represent Q-data rather than Q' data, as the accuracy of the person's response is not assumed.

Projective tests ask people to interpret ambiguous stimuli, such as pictures or inkblots. Because of the problems associated with scoring and interpreting such responses, they are now little used. However, tests that use more objective scoring systems (Karp et al. 1989) may perhaps have some diagnostic value.

Objective tests, in Cattell's sense of the term, refers to tests whose purpose is not obvious to the person being assessed, or where the person being assessed is physically unable to modify their response. There were hopes that these would supplement or replace questionnaires for PERSONNEL SELECTION, where job applicants may tend to give socially desirable responses to questionnaire items. However, they are rarely valid (Kline and Cooper 1984).

Ratings of behaviour form the basis of at least one test (the 16PF) and involve a person being followed by a trained assessor, who notes their behaviour in a wide range of settings – or may just involve completing a standard personality questionnaire as they believe another person would.

Self-reports are typified by tests such as the '20 Statements Test'. Here individuals are simply asked to write 20 statements which describe them: these are then categorised and used to infer – inter alia – how individuals view themselves. The Q-SORT in Rogers' THEORY (see s. 8) is similar in intention and sophistication. The data emerging from such analyses are assumed to be accurate – Q' data rather than Q-data – and are taken at face value. CC

Cattell, R. B. 1973: *Personality and Mood by Questionnaire*. San Francisco: Jossey-Bass. **Karp, S. A., Holmstrom, R. W. and Silber, D. E.** 1989: *The Apperceptive Personality Test Manual*. Worthington OH: International Diagnostic Systems. **Kline, P. and Cooper, C.** 1984: A construct validation of the objective-analytic test battery (OATB). *Personality and Individual Differences* 5, 323–37.

personality: the biology of

Theories and measures of personality are well developed, however, there is a paucity of research on the biological basis of personality. Methods have ranged from TWIN STUDIES (see s. 7), which show that genes account for approximately 50 per cent of the VARIANCE (see s. 8) in most normally distributed personality traits, to drawing parallels between behaviour in animals and human personality traits (for a review, see Depue and Collins 1999).

Perhaps the most developed biological theory is that of Eysenck (1967). According to Eysenck's model, extroversion-introversion differences are largely determined by activity in the reticular formation-cortex arousal loop, with introverts hypothesised to have greater resting cortical arousal than extroverts so that they show greater arousability than extroverts to stimuli of weak intensity. Psychophysiological measures, such as EEG and electrodermal response, have traditionally been interpreted as indices of arousal. More recent research assesses EXTROVERSION's correlates with dopamine. Recently, studies have been carried out in humans which suggest that high but not low extroverts more readily acquire links between contextual stimuli and psychostimulant-induced reward and this is related to dopamine activity.

Individual differences in NEUROTICISM (or emotionality) are held to be due to differences in LIMBIC SYSTEM (see s. 2) functioning. The limbic system generates emotional reactions of fear and anxiety and helps people remember events from the world by pairing the event with an emotion. Those high on neuroticism have stronger limbic system responses, and will react in a stronger emotional manner which will persist for longer than those low on neuroticism.

Cloninger (1987) proposed (from animal research) that three personality traits – harm AVOIDANCE (see s. 7), reward dependence and novelty seeking (NS) – relate to the monoamine systems, serotonin, noradrenaline and dopamine, respectively. They are genetically INDEPENDENT (see s. 8), but the systems are interconnected. This model is attractive in that a trait is directly related to a monamine system. However, Cloninger's model must yet be shown to be both generalisable to humans and valid. (See s. 2, MONOAMINE TRANSMITTERS)

Zuckerman, one of the leading figures researching the biological basis of personality, suggests that any personality trait may relate to more than one brain system, and that a brain system may be related to more than one personality trait (Zuckerman 1991). This makes Zuckerman's model difficult to test empirically. *MS*

Cloninger, C. R. 1987: A systematic method for clinical description and classification of personality variants. A proposal. *Archives of General Psychiatry* 44(6), 573–88. **Depue, R. A. and Collins, P. F.** 1999: Neurobiology of the structure of personality: dopamine, facilitation of incentive motivation, and extraversion. *Behavioural and Brain Sciences* 22, 491–569. **Eysenck, H. J.** 1967: *The Biological Basis of Personality*. Springfield IL: Charles C. Thomas. **Zuckerman, M.** 1991: *Psychobiology of Personality*. Cambridge: Cambridge University Press.

personality traits

Modern TRAIT theories are rooted in the PSYCHOMETRIC [see PSYCHOMETRICS] APPROACH (see s. 4) to personality and focus on dispositional VARIABLES (see s. 8) that influence people's typical behavioural tendencies. For example, people high on NEUROTICISM tend to feel moody, anxious and vulnerable. Traits are decontextualised in that they are thought to exert an influence on behaviour, irrespective of the situation (context) in which the agent operates.

Trait theories can be either IDIOGRAPHIC (see s. 8 and also s. 1, IDIOGRAPHIC METHODS) or NOMOTHETIC (see s. 8 and also s. 1, NOMOTHETIC METHODS). The idiographic approach emphasises individuality and uniqueness, arguing that traits operate in unique ways within each person. The most influential exponent of idiographic trait theories was G. W. Allport. The nomothetic approach emphasises generality and seeks to identify universally valid personality dimensions. It is the dominant approach in the field and has been endorsed and developed by some of the greatest psychologists of all time. Major trait theories in the NOMOTHETIC (see also s. 1, NOMOTHETIC METHODS) tradition include R. B. Cattell's, H. J. EYSENCK's THREE-FACTOR MODEL and the BIG FIVE MODEL OF PERSONALITY.

Nomothetic trait theories attempt to answer two distinct, albeit interrelated, questions about personality, namely, how and why people differ. The various theories differ in the extent to which they emphasise these two questions. Big five models tend to focus on the 'how' question and are primarily descriptive in nature, aiming to yield a comprehensive map of individual differences in personality. They are DATA-DRIVEN (see s. 3) in that they have emerged from adjective ratings. Giant three models, of which H. J. Eysenck's is the most prominent, tend to focus on the 'why' question and are primarily hypothetico-deductive in nature, aiming to elucidate the origins of individual differences in personality. They are theory-driven in that they are predicated on EMPIRICAL (see s. 8) findings from the clinical and experimental literatures. Generally, big five models have the edge in terms of descriptive power, whereas giant three models have the edge in terms of explanatory power.

While there is still disagreement as to the number of basic dimensions necessary for the parsimonious description and explanation of normal adult personality (three versus five), there exist important commonalities between the various nomothetic trait theories. Their major common strength is that they are amenable to quantification and FALSIFICATION (see s. 1), in line with the precepts of the scientific method. A shared shortcoming is their limited ability to identify the psychological processes that link latent traits to manifest behaviours. [See PERSONALITY: THE BIOLOGY OF and PERSONALITY AND COGNITION]   *KP*

Kline, P. 1993: *Personality: The Psychometric View*. London: Routledge. Matthews, G., Deary, I. J. and Whiteman, M. C. 2003: *Personality Traits* (2nd edn). Cambridge: Cambridge University Press. Pervin, L. A. and John, O. P. 1999: *Handbook of Personality: Theory and Research* (2nd edn). New York: Guilford Press.

personnel selection The aim of any personnel selection system is to identify the candidate(s) who will perform best in a particular role (Kanfer, Ackerman and Goff 1995). The system must also be demonstrably fair (free from bias) and ensure that the costs of selection are outweighed by increases in employee performance over that which would be obtained by randomly selecting applicants. It is usually based on a job evaluation performed by an occupational psychologist – typically analysing the tasks that the person will be expected to perform and identifying the relevant psychological characteristics (e.g. cognitive abilities, personality traits, interpersonal SKILLS – see s. 3, task-specific knowledge) that are required. This job analysis may include interviewing existing employees as well as managers, perhaps using a variant of the REPERTORY GRID TECHNIQUES to determine which characteristics differentiate effective from ineffective colleagues. The psychologist then determines how the key characteristics might best be assessed, typically using psychometric tests [see PSYCHOMETRICS], data obtained from a carefully structured interview, and perhaps from other exercises such as group work or IN-BASKET TECHNIQUES, perhaps using an ASSESSMENT CENTRE. If the number of candidates for each position is likely to be very large, then consideration is also given to how the applicant pool may be reduced (e.g. by random selection or initial screening using one or more group-administered psychometric tests).

It is also necessary to determine how the information should be used: for example, whether a minimum acceptable level of performance should be set for each characteristic, or whether good performance on one measure should be allowed to compensate for poor performance on another. Recent work (Jensen 1998; Thorndike 1985) demonstrating that ability tests are effective because they are imperfect measures of general intelligence (rather than because they assess job-specific cognitive skills) suggests that a detailed analysis of the cognitive skills needed to perform a particular task is probably unnecessary, and that a standard test of GENERAL ABILITY (*g*) is likely to be at least as effective. However, this is not yet standard practice.   *CC*

Jensen, A. R. 1998: *The g Factor*. New York: Praeger. Kanfer, P. L., Ackerman, Y. M. and Goff, M. 1995: Personality and intelligence in industrial and organizational psychology. In Saklofske, D. H. and Zeidner, M. (eds) *International Handbook of Personality and Intelligence*. New York: Plenum. Thorndike, R. L. 1985: The central role of general ability in prediction. *Multivariate Behavioral Research* 1985, 241–54.

positive affect This is not the opposite of NEGATIVE AFFECT. It is a term used to indicate high levels of activity and arousal, and has links with EXTROVERSION.   *RL*

positive emotions A generalisation that emotions such as joy and interest have desirable characteristics; it is more accurate to argue that some emotions can elicit either constructive or destructive behaviour.   *AF*

positive manifold The consistent finding that all ability tests show positive correlations with all other ability tests, and hence may all be influenced by GENERAL ABILITY (*g*).   *CC*

practical intelligence Theories of practical intelligence as expounded by (for example) Sternberg (2000) argue that traditional INTELLIGENCE (see also s. 4) tests cannot always predict performance at day-to-day tasks, and that other measures of practical intelligence ('street-smartness' or common sense) may often be more appropriate. For example, in order to get something important done quickly in a hierarchical organisation, the 'smart' thing might well be to ignore the rulebook and bypass a rigid and unhelpful manager, while taking steps not to offend them in the process. In terms of the TRIARCHIC THEORY of intelligence, practical intelligence maps on to the experiential sub-theory, drawing and integrating threads from previous experiences to craft effective solutions to problems. Such tacit knowledge is highly specific to the task or organisation, is learned spontaneously rather than taught, and used to reach personal goals.

Sternberg's research shows that lay persons and experts seem to believe that both intelligence and tacit knowledge are important for success, and that they emerge as two distinct FACTORS (see s. 8) – which fits well with findings from OCCUPATIONAL PSYCHOLOGY (see also s. 1, INDUSTRIAL AND OCCUPATIONAL PSYCHOLOGY) that job knowledge predicts performance independently of cognitive ability (Hunter 1986). It is also argued that traditional intelligence tests are of little general applicability, and that tests of practical intelligence may be of more utility in predicting real-life behaviour. However, it is less than obvious that practical intelligence is completely different from general intelligence; it may resemble CRYSTALLISED INTELLIGENCE within the hierarchical model of abilities. Linda Gottfredson (2003) argues that the types of problems in conventional intelligence tests often require tacit knowledge (no one teaches children how to solve mazes, for example) and offers a detailed and extensive critique of Sternberg's work on practical intelligence in the context of hierarchical models of cognitive abilities such as the three-stratum model [see ABILITY: THREE-STRATUM MODEL].   *CC*

Gottfredson, L. S. 2003: Dissecting practical intelligence theory: its claims and evidence. *Intelligence* 31, 343–97. Hunter, J. E. 1986: Cognitive ability, cognitive attitudes, job knowledge and job performance. *Journal of Vocational Behavior* 29, 340–62. Sternberg, R. J. 2000: *Practical Intelligence in Everyday Life*. Cambridge and New York: Cambridge University Press. Sternberg, R. J. 2003: Our research program validating the triarchic theory of successful intelligence: Reply to Gottfredson. *Intelligence* 31, 399–413.

primary mental abilities (PMAS) Rather narrow mental abilities (e.g. ability to RECALL (see s. 3) lists of digits or rearrange a sequence of pictures so that they tell a story) which arise when responses to test items are factor-analysed (see FACTOR ANALYSIS and also s. 8). They form the bottom tier of Carroll's (1993) three-stratum model [see ABILITY: THREE-STRATUM MODEL], which determines the STRUCTURE OF MENTAL ABILITIES. *CC*

Carroll, J. B. 1993: *Human Cognitive Abilities: A Survey of Factor Analytic Studies.* Cambridge: Cambridge University Press.

projective tests Projective tests of personality spring from the Freudian and other depth-psychologists' belief that unconscious forces (repressed memories, hopes, DRIVES – see s. 2) influence how people interpret ambiguous stimuli. Projective tests involve presenting people with stimuli (usually pictures), which can potentially be interpreted in several ways, Rorschach's inkblots being a prime example. The person says what they see in each inkblot. These responses are then scored (for example, noting whether movement is reported, whether the person has focused on the whole inkblot, or whether a response is common or unusual). Curiously, these scoring procedures rarely have any theoretical foundation (why should it matter if people report movement?) and few projective tests set out to measure the core concepts of depth-psychology, such as level of Oedipal fixation. Other tests include the THEMATIC APPERCEPTION TEST (involving 20 pictures rather than inkblots) and the more recent APPERCEPTIVE PERSONALITY TEST (Karp, Holmstrom and Silber 1989), which can be scored reliably. There is little evidence for the VALIDITY (see also s. 8) of any projective tests, except, perhaps, for the last. Most also need to be administered and assessed by a psychologist who has undergone extensive specialised training, making it an expensive form of assessment. *CC*

Karon, B. P. 1978: Projective tests are valid. *American Psychologist* 33, 764–5. **Karp, S. A., Holmstrom, R. W. and Silber, D. E.** 1989: *The Apperceptive Personality Test Manual.* Worthington OH: International Diagnostic Systems. **Wood, J. M., Nezworski, M. T. and Stejskal, W. J.** 1997: The reliability of the comprehensive system for the Rorschach: a comment on Meyer (1997). *Psychological Assessment* 9, 490–4.

psychoanalytic theory A theory developed by Sigmund Freud which suggested that PERSONALITY and behaviour were largely governed by various forms of UNCONSCIOUS MOTIVATION, particularly sex and AGGRESSION

(see s. 5). Neither the theory itself, its research tools (PROJECTIVE TESTS), nor its method of therapy (PSYCHO-ANALYSIS (see also s. 1, PSYCHOANALYSIS AND RELATED SCHOOLS)) has stood up well to scientific scrutiny (Kline 1982), and so the theory is not now influential. *CC*

Kline, P. 1982: *Fact and Fantasy in Freudian Theory* (2nd edn). London: Methuen.

psychometrics A branch of STATISTICS (see s. 1, MEASUREMENT AND STATISTICS) that deals with the construction, evaluation and use of psychological tests, including PERSONALITY QUESTIONNAIRES, MOOD SCALES, group tests of ability [see ABILITY: GROUP TESTS OF] and individual tests of ability [see ABILITY: INDIVIDUAL TESTS OF]. Its methods include RELIABILITY (see also s. 8) theory, techniques for determining the VALIDITY (see also s. 8) of tests, FACTOR ANALYSIS, ITEM RESPONSE THEORY, ADAPTIVE TESTING and methods for the study of BIAS in mental tests. These feed into various codes of practice for testing (see also s. 1, PSYCHOMETRICS). [See TESTING: CODES OF PRACTICE] *CC*

psychoticism Psychoticism is one of the three bipolar personality FACTORS (see s. 8) proposed by Hans Eysenck [see also NEUROTICISM and EXTROVERSION] and is measured by the self-report EPQ-R PERSONALITY QUESTIONNAIRE. Eysenck regarded those who scored highly on psychoticism as 'egocentric, aggressive, impulsive, impersonal, cold, lacking in EMPATHY (see s. 4) and concern for others, and generally unconcerned about the rights and welfare of other people' (Eysenck 1982: 11). Respondents can vary from neurotic, indicating hostile and antisocial tendencies, to self-controlled, indicating more considerate and obedient individuals.

This scale was not created until some years after the other two and was included to provide a predictive measure for psychotic breakdown and distinguish between psychotic and normal individuals. A summary of the available research has shown that prisoners and juvenile delinquents score higher on the scale than psychotic patients (Zuckerman 1989). It has therefore been suggested that the scale should be renamed PSYCHOPATHOLOGY (see s. 7) to reflect the antisocial behaviour it measures. *DH*

Eysenck, H. J. 1982: *Personality, Genetics and Behaviour.* New York: Plenum. **Zuckerman, M.** 1989: Personality in the third dimension: a psychobiological approach. *Personality and Individual Differences* 10, 391–418.

Q

Q-sort The Q-sort is a technique designed to provide an objective assessment of SELF-CONCEPT (see s. 4 and s. 5). First introduced by Stephenson (1953), Q-sort derives from Rogers' (1959) SELF THEORY OF PERSONALITY as a method for defining a person's PERCEPTION (see s. 1, s. 4 and s. 5) of the SELF (see s. 1), ideal self and the degree of congruence between the two. Briefly, the Q-sort involves sorting 100–150 cards containing self-descriptors (e.g. 'I am shy') into a predefined number of piles, ranging from 'most like me' to 'least like me', typically forming a NORMAL DISTRIBUTION (see s. 8). The procedure can be repeated in relation to 'ideal self', and the difference between the two provides a quantifiable measure of self-ideal discrepancy. Q-sort can be used in a variety of settings (Block 1961), and can also be based on observer judgements. It has been useful in psychotherapy for testing improvement in self-perception – with small discrepancies between self and ideal self associated with better psychological well-being. Attempts to assess VALIDITY (see also s. 8), however, have been equivocal. *MM*

Block, J. 1961: *The Q-Sort Method in Personality Assessment and Psychiatric Research*. Springfield IL: Charles C. Thomas. **Rogers, C. R.** 1959: A theory of therapy, personality and interpersonal relationships, as developed in the client-centred framework. In Koch, S. (ed.) *Psychology: A Study of a Science*. New York: McGraw-Hill. **Stephenson, W.** 1953: *The Study of Behavior*. Chicago IL: University of Chicago Press.

R

Rasch scaling Rasch scaling is the simplest form of ITEM RESPONSE THEORY. It is a psychometric [see PSYCHO-METRICS] technique that simultaneously estimates the ability of each person taking a test and the difficulty of the items in a test according to the formula:

$$\text{Probability (correct)} = \left(\frac{1}{1 + e^{-(\theta - b)}} \right)$$

Here θ represents the ability of the person, and b the difficulty of the item. So (for example) the probability that a person with an ability level of 2 will get an item with difficulty level 3 correct is 0.27. Advocates of Rasch scaling observe that as long as the assumptions of the technique are not violated, estimates of item difficulties are not influenced by the distribution of abilities within the SAMPLE (see s. 8). It should not matter whether a test is given to a random sample of the population or a distinctly non-random sample: the estimates of item difficulties should be the same and so there is thus no need to compile tables of NORMS (see also s. 5) from carefully stratified samples of the population. This would not be the case for conventional difficulty indices, such as the proportion who correctly answer the item(s) or their total test score. However, it is difficult to find items that fit the assumptions of the Rasch model (particularly the assumption that all items have equal discrimination power) and so many prefer to use other methods of item response theory instead.   *CC*

Embretson, S. E. and Hershberger, S. L. 1999: *The New Rules of Measurement: What Every Psychologist and Educator Should Know.* Mahwah NJ: L. Erlbaum Associates. http://www.rasch.org/ (accessed September 2004)

reaction time and *g* Mental speed theories of INTEL-LIGENCE (see also s. 4) suggest that GENERAL ABILITY (*g*) is the result of a biological speed FACTOR (see s. 8) which is reflected in basic information-processing tasks. Initially proposed by Galton (1883) as an indirect measure of brain functioning, the REACTION TIME (RT) (see s. 3) PAR-ADIGM (see s. 1) was designed to elicit such measures. In comparison to inspection time (IT) [see INSPECTION TIME AND *g*], which estimates the time taken to perceive a stimulus, RT is a measure of the time taken to respond to a stimulus. MEASUREMENT (see s. 1, MEASUREMENT AND STATISTICS) of RT has been standardised around the procedure devised by Jensen and Munroe (1974), using eight lights in a semicircle with a 'home' button equidistant from each. The participant places their index finger on the 'home' button, and when one of the lights is illuminated, their task is to press the button below that light as quickly as possible. Simple reaction time (SRT) involves respond-ing to a single stimulus, whereas choice reaction time (CRT) involves having to choose between two or more different response alternatives. Reaction time is the time elapsing between stimulus onset and removal of the finger from the home button. Speed of processing theory [see BIOLOGICAL CORRELATES OF ABILITIES] predicts negative

correlations between RT and *g*, in that more intelligent individuals should be able to respond more rapidly. Fast reaction times do correlate with IQ test scores, with corre-lations tending to be weaker for SRT, becoming stronger as the number of choices increases (Jensen 1987). However, although robust, RT-*g* correlations are modest, and few studies report correlations stronger than –0.35. Therefore, even if response speed does reflect some underlying biological process, it can only account for a small proportion of the variability within the population. There is also criticism that RT is not the simple task originally assumed, and that more intelligent individuals may be better able to focus ATTENTION (see s. 3) or devise cognitive strategies for responding rapidly (Longstreth 1984). These arguments are theoretically important as they provide alternative explanations for the RT-IQ corre-lation in terms of TOP-DOWN PROCESSING (see s. 3). While not rejecting the processing speed hypothesis, it is possible that fast reaction times are a consequence of high intelli-gence, and not a reflection of any underlying biological cause.   *MM*

Galton, F. 1883: *Inquiries into Human Faculty and its Development.* London: Macmillan. **Jensen, A. R.** 1987: Individual differences in the Hick paradigm. In Vernon, P. A. (ed.) *Speed of Information Processing and Intelligence.* Norwood NJ: Ablex. **Jensen, A. R. and Munroe, E.** 1974: Reaction time, movement time and intelligence. *Intelligence* 3, 121–6. **Longstreth, L. E.** 1984: Jensen's reaction time investigations: a critique. *Intelligence* 8, 139–60.

Register of Competence in Occupational Testing (RCOT) In the UK, an individual (not neces-sarily a psychologist) appearing on this register (main-tained by the BRITISH PSYCHOLOGICAL SOCIETY (see s. 1)) has demonstrated the required competence to administer certain occupational tests. It is a lower-level qualification than LEVEL A ACCREDITATION or LEVEL B ACCREDITATION.   *CC*

reliability Broadly speaking, reliability refers to the dependability of MEASUREMENT (see s. 1, MEASUREMENT AND STATISTICS). More specifically, the index of reliability indicates the accuracy of measurement, which is given by the correlation between the observed scores on a measure-ment instrument and the hypothetical true scores on the construct. The square of the index of reliability gives the proportion of the total VARIANCE (see s. 8) in a set of test scores accounted for by true score variability, with the remainder constituting the ERROR (see s. 8) variance. The smaller the ratio of total-to-true variance, the more reliable the instrument. The reliability of a set of scores is a context-specific notion and concerns the administra-tion of a measurement instrument to a specific SAMPLE (see s. 8) at a specific point in time. It makes little sense to state that a test 'has been shown to be reliable', because relia-bility must be evaluated after each administration of the instrument. Reliability should be strictly distinguished from temporal stability, which is given by the correlation of scores from two administrations of the same instrument, usually separated by an interval of several weeks. Nevertheless, the stability of a measurement instrument is a function of its internal consistency reliability, such that unreliable test scores are necessarily unstable.

There are several different estimates of reliability. Internal consistency reliability involves a single administration of the instrument and is used to evaluate the consistency with which participants respond to its items. Internal consistency can also be conceived of as a test of homogeneity for the items in an instrument. It is most frequently given by CRONBACH'S ALPHA (see s. 8). SPLIT-HALF RELIABILITY (see s. 8) is estimated by randomly splitting a measurement instrument into two forms of equal length, correlating them and subsequently applying the Spearman-Brown prophecy formula. Parallel-forms reliability is estimated by creating two equal sets of equivalent items from the same SAMPLING (see s. 8) domain and correlating them.

Inter-rater (or inter-marker or inter-judge) reliability is applicable in situations where ratings or scores for the same construct are independently obtained from more than one source (e.g. a psychiatric diagnosis made by three different clinicians). Inter-rater reliability is estimated by correlating the ratings from the different rating sources. Test-retest reliability is a less preferable synonym for temporal stability. (See also s. 8, RELIABILITY) *KP*

Cronbach, L. J. 1990: *Essentials of Psychological Testing* (5th edn). New York: Harper Collins Publishers. **Kline, P.** 2000: *The Handbook of Psychological Testing* (2nd edn). London: Routledge. **Nunnally, J. C. and Bernstein, I. H.** 1994: *Psychometric Theory* (3rd edn). New York: McGraw-Hill.

repertory grid techniques

The repertory grid technique assesses the number and nature of a person's personal constructs in Kelly's PERSONAL CONSTRUCT THEORY. It involves identifying the names of about 12 people who play significant roles in the client's life, plus themselves, and possibly 'myself as I would like to be'. These names are known as 'elements'. The client is presented with three of these elements and is asked to give the most important psychological characteristic that differentiates any two elements from the third – and which is different from anything used before. The client is then asked to give the opposite of this term, and the process is repeated until several (typically between about 8 and 20) of these pairs of 'personal constructs' have been elected, or until the client is unable to think of any new construct. The person then rates the position of each of the elements on each of the constructs (e.g. using a five-point scale). These data are cast in a table with the poles of each construct in the first and last columns, the elements in between them: the repertory grid.

Some authors advocate FACTOR ANALYSIS (see also s. 8) of repertory grids, but this is statistically dubious. Other analyses range from simple scrutiny of the position of the SELF (see s. 1, s. 4 and s. 5) and ideal self on each of the constructs to computing measures of similarity between the constructs and between the elements. The former analysis may show, for example, that the client views intelligent people as being shy. The latter may show that someone's wife is construed in much the same way as their mother.

Although developed to assess constructs within Kelly's theory, the technique may be applied in any other areas to explore a person's phenomenological world. For example, it may be used in experimental aesthetics, where the elements are pictures or pieces of music, to discover how an individual categorises art. *CC*

Bannister, D. and Fransella, F. 1989: *Inquiring Man: The Psychology of Personal Constructs*. London: Croom Helm. **Fransella, F. and Bannister, D.** 1977: *A Manual for Repertory Grid Technique*. London: Academic Press. **Fransella, F. and Thomas, L. F.** (eds) 1988: *Experimenting with Personal Construct Psychology*. London: Routledge.

reversal theory

Michael Apter's (1982/1989) general theory of MOTIVATION, EMOTION and PERSONALITY provides a unitary account of a wide variety of seemingly contrasting unrelated psychological (including social, psychophysiological and psychopathological) phenomena. The theory attempts to explicate the structure of experience, and because a person might construe a given mental state of arousal (for example) as excitement or fear, it argues that it is important to find out what an individual is experiencing. The theory places considerable importance on four pairs of metamotivational states where, at any one time, one of each pair is operational and provides partial meaning of an event, and each pair exhibits multi-stability (each state is stable but can reverse to the other). The theory has stimulated a considerable body of EMPIRICAL (see s. 8) research by psychologists working in a number of different branches of the subject and an increasing number of practitioners have begun to adopt it in their work. (See also s. 1, REVERSAL THEORY) *NS*

Apter, M. J. 1982: *The Experience of Motivation: The Theory of Psychological Reversals*. London: Academic Press. **Apter, M. J.** 1989: *Reversal Theory: Motivation, Emotion and Personality*. London: Routledge.

repertory grid techniques

	Self	Mother	Father	Friend	
Kind	1	2	5	2	Cruel
Happy	2	1	5	5	Miserable

An example of a repertory grid, where ratings of 1–5 are used to show the position of each 'element' (self, mother, etc.) along each 'construct' (kind vs. cruel, etc.).

S

---

schizotypy Authors such as Claridge (1997) make the point that SCHIZOPHRENIA (see s. 7) may not exist as a discrete psychiatric category, but rather as a continuum along which every individual may be positioned: the CONTINUITY HYPOTHESIS. Schizotypy is the name given to milder versions of schizophrenic symptoms found in non-psychotic individuals, which may predispose the person to developing schizophrenia. It encompasses behaviours and BELIEFS (see s. 5) such as perceptual and cognitive distortions (such as fascination with the occult), solitary behaviour with dislike of intimacy, attentional disorders, unusual speech and odd behaviour. Questionnaires to measure the trait include the Oxford-Liverpool Inventory of Feelings and Experiences (Mason, Claridge and Jackson 1995). There is evidence that some of the physiological and cognitive processes that differentiate schizophrenics from non-schizophrenics are also related to scores on such questionnaires (e.g. P50 suppression in the EEG and cognitive INHIBITION – see s. 3).   *CC*

Claridge, G. 1997: *Schizotypy: Implications for Illness and Health.* Oxford and New York: Oxford University Press. **Mason, O., Claridge, G. and Jackson, M.** 1995: New scales for the assessment of schizotypy. *Personality and Individual Differences* 18, 7–13.

schooling and intelligence A very substantial body of research shows that measures of IQ and GENERAL INTELLIGENCE (*g*) have an appreciable and statistically significant correlation with both contemporary and future school performance (e.g. years of education and examination performance). Correlations are usually in the order of 0.5. Some critics have argued that this correlation is artefactual, as some INTELLIGENCE (see also s. 4) tests assess reading, LANGUAGE (see s. 2) and numerical SKILLS (see s. 3), which are also reflected in school performance indices. However, an analysis by Thorndike (1985) shows that these criticisms are not well supported by data, and that intelligence (rather than the narrower abilities) is all-important.

Education also enhances intelligence. Children who have missed school perform less well on intelligence tests. It is possible to identify children of nearly identical age who differ by 12 months in the amount of schooling they have received (Cahan and Cohen 1989). This is reflected in performance on intelligence tests. (See also s. 4, SCHOOLING)   *CC*

Cahan, S. and Cohen, N. 1989: Age versus schooling effects on intelligence development. *Child Development* 60, 1239–49. **Snow, R. E. and Yalow, E.** 1982: Education and intelligence. In Sternberg, R. J. (ed.) *Handbook of Human Intelligence.* Cambridge: Cambridge University Press. **Thorndike, R. L.** 1985: The central role of general ability in prediction. *Multivariate Behavioral Research* 1985, 241–54.

seasonal affective disorder A type of DEPRESSION (see s. 7) or similarly disabling illness typically associated with the winter season and less frequently linked with any of the other seasons. It is often considered to be caused by a biochemical imbalance in the hypothalamus due to the shortening of daylight hours and the lack of sunlight in winter.   *NS*

second-order ability factors Ability FACTORS (see s. 8) derived by applying FACTOR ANALYSIS (see also s. 8) to the table of correlations between several PRIMARY MENTAL ABILITIES. Carroll (1993) identified six to eight of these broad factors in his three-stratum model [see ABILITY: THREE-STRATUM MODEL] which determines the STRUCTURE OF MENTAL ABILITIES.   *CC*

Carroll, J. B. 1993: *Human Cognitive Abilities: A Survey of Factor-analytic Studies.* Cambridge: Cambridge University Press.

selection interviews Selection interviews are a popular component of most PERSONNEL SELECTION schemes, albeit a component which is expensive in terms of staff time, may introduce BIAS (see also s. 3 and s. 8) or PREJUDICE (see s. 5), and may vary in content from applicant to applicant, thereby providing a non-standardised assessment procedure. That said, a well-devised and closely monitored interview procedure is capable of eliciting information which is hard to discover by other means – such as whether the individual is likely to fit in with the ethos of the organisation or unit.

Research has consistently shown that structured interviews are more effective than free-ranging exchanges (Campion, Palmer and Campion 1997). Structured interviews have an agenda: a list of linked, clearly phrased questions related to important aspects of the job which are designed to elicit candidates' responses, reactions and OPINIONS (see s. 5), with little or no follow-up of the candidates' responses. The interview will generally be conducted by more than one trained interviewer, each independently following an explicit scheme for evaluating the quality of the candidate's responses (such as a behaviourally anchored rating scale), the final outcome being evaluated by statistically combining the ratings – perhaps after applying a standard set of weights reflecting the importance of each area, these being derived from a job analysis.

Behavioural interviews (also known as 'competency-based' or 'criterion-based' interviews) are also popular. Unlike structured interviews, these encourage exploration of the candidate's past behaviour: for example, how they actually behaved in the past when confronted with a work-related problem. Candidates do not have to speculate about how they might act in a hypothetical situation, and potential to verify the responses may lead to greater honesty from the interviewees, who are also less likely to produce rehearsed answers (Barclay 2001). However, young applicants may not be able to draw on a wealth of experience in order to demonstrate their behavioural competence.   *CC*

Barclay, J. M. 2001: Improving selection interviews with structure: Organisations' use of 'behavioural' interviews. *Personnel*

Review 30, 81–101. **Campion, M. A., Palmer, D. K. and Campion, J. E.** 1997: A review of structure in the selection interview. *Personnel Psychology* 50, 655–702.

self theories of personality

SELF (see s. 1) theories of PERSONALITY are based on the premise that a person's conscious thoughts and INTROSPECTIONS (see s. 1) are (a) likely to be accurate indicators of their true state of mind and (b) provide the best data for constructing a THEORY (see s. 8) of personality. Those with a PSYCHOANALYTIC THEORY or the psychology of PERSONALITY TRAITS will disagree with these ASSUMPTIONS (see s. 8), the former because of their emphasis on unconscious processes, and the latter because it is difficult to assess the VALIDITY (see also s. 8) of introspections. When a trait psychologist observes that someone has ticked a box claiming that they have an excellent sense of humour, that item is only of interest because it loads some broader FACTOR (see s. 8). They would not infer that the person really does laugh a lot.

Self theories have therefore developed out of CLINICAL (see s. 1, CLINICAL PSYCHOLOGY) and SOCIAL PSYCHOLOGY (see s. 1). Carl Rogers' theory suggests that we each have a unified sense of SELF (see s. 1, s. 4 and s. 5) ('self-concept'), which we supposedly consult in times of uncertainty. If law-abidingness forms an important part of someone's view of themselves, and a friend asks them to do something illegal, they will consult their SELF-CONCEPT (see s. 4 and s. 5) and not take part. (Or if they do, will subsequently revise their self-concept.) Feelings of STRESS (see s. 7) and guilt supposedly occur when behaviour is dissonant with the self-concept.

Several means have been developed to measure self-concept, such as the Q-SORT (Stephenson 1953). This involves giving a person a set of cards, each showing a different behaviour or trait name ('cries easily', 'generous', etc.). They then sort these into piles, ranging from 'very true of me' to 'very different from me', and the nature of the self-concept is inferred by examining the cards in the two extreme piles. Clinical interviews can also be used to assess the self-concept, where the therapist reflects back to the client the client's views of themselves in order to check their accuracy. The Twenty Statements Test simply asks people to write 20 words or phrases to describe themselves. If 'self' is used as an element in a repertory grid, this, too, may be used to help a clinician understand a person's self-concept. *CC*

Rogers, C. R. 1967: *On Becoming a Person.* London: Constable. **Stephenson, W.** 1953: *The Study of Behavior.* Chicago: University of Chicago Press.

sensation seeking

A dimension of personality studied by Marvin Zuckerman, sensation seeking is a TRAIT which attempts to explain why some individuals are drawn to seek out novel, exciting experiences while others actively avoid them. Zuckerman has developed an intricate EYSENCK'S THREE-FACTOR MODEL of personality, linking sensation seeking to several physiological and biochemical systems. Questionnaire measures of sensation seeking, such as Zuckerman's (1991) sensation seeking scale, correlate positively with Eysenck's personality FACTORS (see s. 8) of PSYCHOTICISM and EXTROVERSION. *CC*

Zuckerman, M. 1991: *Psychobiology of Personality.* Cambridge: Cambridge University Press.

sentiments

Sentiments are socially determined DRIVES (see s. 2) in Cattell's model of motivation. They include desire to perform well at work and to please one's partner. *CC*

Cattell, R. B. and Child, D. 1975: *Motivation and Dynamic Structure.* London: Holt, Rinehart & Winston.

situationalism

One of the key ASSUMPTIONS (see s. 8) of trait theory is that TRAITS reflect genuine characteristics of the individual, and that people show reasonable stability in their level of the trait from situation to situation and occasion to occasion. This is not to say that situations do not influence behaviour. Rather it means that the situation may affect the level of each individual's scores in the same way, so that the centile ranks stay fairly constant. This view is laid out in some detail by Cattell (1973), among others.

Mischel (1968), however, suggested that there is no cross-situational consistency in personality: that responses to PERSONALITY QUESTIONNAIRES were entirely determined by each person's PERCEPTION (see s. 1) of the situation. According to this view, personality traits simply do not exist. If this were true it is difficult to see how scores on personality traits could possibly correlate with any other VARIABLES (see s. 8) [see PERSONALITY AND COGNITION, PERSONALITY AND EVERYDAY LIFE, PERSONALITY: THE BIOLOGY OF] or show any genetic component. However, the data upon which some of these conclusions were based involve asking people how they might feel in imaginary situations (e.g. being alone in the wood at night), rather than repeatedly administering well-validated personality questionnaires to the same people in different situations. Mischel subsequently modified his views, focusing instead on the person by situation interaction. *CC*

Cattell, R. B. 1973: *Personality and Mood by Questionnaire.* San Francisco: Jossey-Bass. **Mischel, W.** 1968: *Personality and Assessment.* New York: Wiley.

social construction of personality

TRAIT theorists usually assume that the consistencies in behaviour which lead to PERSONALITY TRAITS (e.g. EXTROVERSION, SENSATION SEEKING) arise as a direct result of some internal feature of the individual – for example, as a consequence of the level of some NEUROTRANSMITTER (see s. 2), some cognitive set or some belief system. They therefore often try to identify lower-level biological, cognitive or social VARIABLES (see s. 8) which may explain why the individual shows a particular level of a certain trait.

Those favouring a social construction model, such as Hampson (1984), argue that this is fallacious. Rather than viewing personality as a characteristic of the individual, social constructionists focus on the processes by which personality ATTRIBUTIONS (see s. 5) are made. For example, why someone might choose to rate themselves as 'a worrier' when answering a personality questionnaire, or why they may sometimes explain behaviour by reference to some personality trait ('John is a snappy person') and sometimes the situation ('John is under STRESS' – see s. 7). To social constructionists, personality is not a reflection of some real, enduring, physically based characteristic of the individual, but the product of RELATIONSHIPS (see s. 5) and social encounters. It simply does not exist outside a particular social setting. We create rather than discover ourselves.

If the nihilistic view that nothing exists and life is but a social construction were true, then there is no reason why personality should be stable from situation to situation. Likewise, scores on personality tests could not possibly be linked to 'real' features of the physical body, such as genetic make-up or hormonal levels. Given that such effects are well-established, it is unclear that SOCIAL CONSTRUCTIONISM (see s. 1) offers a useful alternative to trait theory. *CC*

Hampson, S. E. 1984: The social construction of personality. In Bonarius, H., Van Heck, G. and Smid, N. (eds) *Personality Psychology in Europe: Theoretical and Empirical Developments.* Lisse: Swets and Zeitlinger.

social intelligence Social intelligence is not easy to distinguish from EMOTIONAL INTELLIGENCE. It was identified by E. L. Thorndike in 1920, and again by Howard Gardner (1983), and reflects a person's ability to interact sensitively and effectively with others. More recent research shows that social competence is largely distinct from general intelligence (*g*) [see GENERAL ABILITY], with many intelligent individuals showing poor interpersonal SKILLS (see s. 3). However, verbal skills are important for social competence. In addition, rather than being a single dimension, Schneider et al. (1996) have shown that questionnaires measuring social intelligence comprise some seven fairly distinct personality traits (extroversion, warmth, LEADERSHIP (see s. 5) or influence, social insight, openness to others, knowledge of appropriate social behaviour and social maladjustment/complaining). *CC*

Gardner, H. 1983: *Frames of Mind* (1st edn). New York: Basic Books. **Schneider, R. J., Ackerman, P. L. and Kanfer, R.** 1996: To 'act wisely in human relations': exploring the dimensions of social competence. *Personality and Individual Differences* 21, 469–81.

Stanford-Binet The Simon-Binet tests of INTELLIGENCE (see also s. 4) were developed in France and revised in a North American edition to take account of the fact that some items were too easy and others too difficult. 'Stanford-Binet' indicates the work was done at Stanford University. *NS*

state A state is a short-lived EMOTION, mood [see MOODS] or DRIVE (see s. 2), which may often be influenced by external events. A TRAIT may be an average level of some state. Examples of states are feelings of ANXIETY following a near-miss when driving, or hunger. *CC*

states and traits TRAITS refer to the measurable, stable aspects of behaviour. For example, we expect a person's trait INTELLIGENCE (see also s. 4) score to remain relatively consistent from one month to the next. Therefore, traits are hypothetical constructs which are used to account for personality and ability consistencies which may exist, influence and predict behaviour. These enduring traits are sometimes referred to as predispositions in the literature and may be accounted for through

environmental LEARNING (see s. 3) and genetic INHERITANCE (see s. 4).

The concept of traits is, however, less helpful in explaining the more volatile and changeable concepts of MOTIVATION and mood [see MOODS]. Motivation and mood can be regarded as STATES, that is, they vary over time and change according to internal and external stimuli. For example, an individual's motivational state to sleep (see s. 2, SLEEP AND BIOLOGICAL RHYTHMS) will differ depending on the time of day or whether they are in a warm bed or cold lecture theatre. States are therefore much harder to measure than traits (Cooper 1998). *DH*

Cooper, C. 1998: *Individual Differences*. London: Arnold.

structure of intellect model Guilford's (1967) structure of intellect model was an attempt to define all types of ability test that could logically exist; Guilford then developed tests to assess each of these abilities. The model sprang from the realisation that any task could be described in terms of some cognitive operation being applied to data to produce some kind of product. According to Guilford, all that is needed is to define the various cognitive OPERATIONS (see s. 4) that exist, produce a list of types of data to which they can be applied, and a list of products, and one would have defined all possible ability tests. For example, one type of test might involve applying MEMORY (see s. 1) to symbols (e.g. letters, numbers, shapes) and then using convergent production to produce the correct answer when asked what the second symbol was. Guilford claimed that there were four types of 'content' of test items, five basic mental operations that could be applied to these data, and the problem could produce one of six types of result. Hence there are $4 \times 5 \times 6 = 120$ distinct abilities.

There are several obvious problems with this approach. First, it is unscientific in the sense that it cannot be falsified. Problems *must* involve applying some thought process to some content and producing some thought; that is the definition of a problem. Second, it seems unlikely that humans are only capable of performing five types of mental operation – and the types of operation that are considered depends on the current trends in cognitive psychology. Third, where is the evidence that applying some operation to one kind of symbol (e.g. road signs) involves the same cognitive processes as applying it to others (e.g. letters of the alphabet, musical notes)? The number of types of contents, operations and products (and hence the number of human abilities) depends entirely on whether one chooses a broad or narrow categorisation (memory or rote memory; symbols or letters), and this is essentially arbitrary, unless one chooses to revert to the factor-analytic model which Guilford eschewed (see FACTOR ANALYSIS and also s. 8). Carroll (1993: 30) terms the theory an 'eccentric aberration', and it is hard to disagree, though it still holds sway with some educationalists. *CC*

Carroll, J. B. 1993: *Human Cognitive Abilities: A Survey of Factor-analytic Studies.* Cambridge: Cambridge University Press. **Guilford, J. P.** 1967: *The Nature of Human Intelligence.* New York: McGraw-Hill.

T

TAT [See THEMATIC APPERCEPTION TEST]

telic dominance Describes one of a pair of metamotivational, psychological STATES (its opposite state being paratelic) derived from the REVERSAL THEORY (see also s. 1) of MOTIVATION (Apter 1982; 1989). These states are thought to act as the catalyst for motives such as arousal, shelter and love. Apter describes four pairs of opposite metamotivational states that explain how people experience motives (telic and paratelic, conformist and negativistic, mastery and sympathy and autic and alloic). A person's metamotivational state will reflect one of the opposing pair but could switch or reverse rapidly to the other at any given time. The telic–paratelic pair is concerned with a person's somatic arousal (as is the conformist and negativistic pair) rather than interactions with other people or objects, which are referred to as transactional states (the latter two pairs). Individuals with a dominant metamotivational state have a predisposition to spend more time in that state rather than its opposite; therefore telic-dominant individuals are serious and goal-orientated, whereas those who are paratelic-dominant are playful and activity-orientated. A telic-dominant person will plan strategically rather than acting on impulse; their response to arousal is anxiety rather than excitement. Dominance is not analogous to a stable personality TRAIT; rather, individuals have the potential to switch from the dominant state to its opposite at any time during an activity or may react differently to similar situations at different times. The Telic Dominance Scale described by Apter (1982) measures three concepts of serious-mindedness, arousal AVOIDANCE (see s. 7) and planning orientation. Recent research has focused on risk-taking behaviour and, particularly, involvement in high-risk sports. Those who take part in low-risk sports (badminton) are lower in telic dominance than those who participate in high-risk sports (snowboarding) in terms of arousal avoidance and serious-mindedness, but not in terms of planning orientation (Cogan and Brown 1999). Matsuura (2002) discovered that telic-dominant participants experienced greater arousal of the sympathetic nervous system (see s. 2, AUTONOMIC NERVOUS SYSTEM (ANS) – SYMPATHETIC BRANCH) while music was played.   *RL*

Apter, M. J. 1982: *The Experience of Motivation: The Theory of Psychological Reversals*. London: Academic Press. **Apter, M. J.** 1989: *Reversal Theory: Motivation, Emotion and Personality*. London: Routledge. **Cogan, N. and Brown, R. I. F.** 1999: Metamotivational dominance, states and injuries in risk and safe sports. *Personality and Individual Differences* 27, 503–18. **Matsuura M.** 2002: Metamotivational states displayed using differential digital photoplethysmograms while listening to music and noise. *Perceptual and Motor Skills* 94, 607–22.

test A psychological test is simply any situation where STATES AND TRAITS or other aspects of behaviour are assessed under standard conditions; that is, where instructions, time limits, etc. are meticulously controlled. Tests are properly constructed using the principles of PSYCHOMETRICS (see also s. 1), which should ensure that their RELIABILITY (see also s. 8) and VALIDITY (see also s. 8) are known. [See also TESTS: LOCATING, 360-DEGREE APPRAISAL, PERSONALITY TESTS, BIAS (see also s. 3 and s. 8), INTELLIGENCE: GROUP DIFFERENCES, ABILITY: INDIVIDUAL TESTS OF, ABILITY: GROUP TESTS OF, ADAPTIVE TESTING and NORMS (see also s. 5)]   *CC*

test anxiety Better termed 'test fear' or 'test phobia', this refers to an unpleasant emotional STATE linked to the prospect of sitting psychological assessments or other tests such as examinations. Meta-analyses (Seipp 1991) show a fairly weak correlation in the order of − 0.2 between scores on questionnaires designed to measure test anxiety and cognitive or educational performance. This is usually taken to imply that test anxiety lowers performance, although it could equally be the case that test anxiety levels rise when one is aware that one is unlikely to perform well. Test anxiety is believed to comprise two correlated though distinct components: worry and emotionality. Some evidence suggests that test anxiety influences performance by reducing the amount of ATTENTION (see s. 3) paid to the test: test-anxious individuals instead begin to think about themselves.   *CC*

Seipp, B. 1991: Anxiety and academic performance: a meta-analysis of findings. *Anxiety Research* 4, 27–41.

testing: codes of practice National psychological societies almost invariably produce codes of practice to govern the use of PERSONALITY TESTS, group tests of ability and individual tests of ability [see ABILITY: GROUP TESTS OF and ABILITY: INDIVIDUAL TESTS OF] when used for PERSONNEL SELECTION, guidance, clinical or educational assessment, etc. This is because even though the results of a well-chosen TEST, which has been carefully administered and scored by trained personnel, may provide information which may be useful for a wide range of purposes, a great many factors can make the results of such assessments meaningless. For this reason test publishers will usually only supply psychometric [see PSYCHOMETRICS] tests to users who have undergone appropriate accredited training in their use and interpretation – such as LEVEL A ACCREDITATION or LEVEL B ACCREDITATION in the UK.

Many things can make the scores on psychological tests valueless. If the test was developed in a different country, using different groups (e.g. students rather than prisoners) or for different purposes (e.g. career guidance rather than suitability for rehabilitation), its VALIDITY (see also s. 8) needs to be demonstrated, rather than assumed. Many tests show psychometric problems such as low RELIABILITY (see also s. 8), low or unproven validity for their chosen purpose or clear evidence of BIAS (see also s. 3 and s. 8) for or against certain social or cultural groups. It is necessary to be fully conversant with these issues before deciding whether a particular test may be appropriate for a

351

particular application. There may be no NORMS (see also s. 5) for the POPULATION (see s. 8) in which it is being used. The use of untrained staff who deviate from standard procedures in administering, scoring or interpreting the results from the test can lead to scores which are valueless – hence the REGISTER OF COMPETENCE IN OCCUPATIONAL TESTING. Codes of practice will usually also cover issues of INFORMED CONSENT (see s. 8), the way in which scores from psychometric tests are integrated with other information (e.g. that stemming from a selection interview), issues of confidentiality and test security, the needs of disabled candidates, and the nature of feedback which is given to the participants. If computer programs are used to provide narrative interpretations of test scores, great care must be taken to ensure that these descriptions are accurate: some tend to overinterpret very small DEVIATIONS (see s. 8) from the norm. *CC*

British Psychological Society 2002: *Code of Good Practice for Psychological Testing*. Leicester: British Psychological Society. **National Council for Measurement in Education** 1988: *Code of Fair Testing Practices in Education*. Washington, DC: National Council for Measurement in Education.

tests: locating

Psychological tests fall into two main categories: those which are commercially published and those which are published in journal articles, the internet or elsewhere. Educational Testing Service (ETS) is a major test developer, with a library of over 20,000 tests. Their website contains a searchable index of these tests (commercially published and other), together with information about the publisher or source (e.g. a journal reference). The ETS site is an extremely useful resource for locating tests, however, it does not evaluate their technical quality in any way.

The Buros Institute publishes Mental Measurement Yearbooks approximately every two years (Plake, Impara and Spies 2003). These contain detailed reviews of commercially published tests, written by MEASUREMENT (see s. 1, MEASUREMENT AND STATISTICS) experts, along with details of the publisher and pricing information. It is possible to search this index via the Buros Institute's website, and if the test has been reviewed in the Mental Measurement Yearbooks, this search will give the publisher's contact details. The Psychological Testing Centre of the BRITISH PSYCHOLOGICAL SOCIETY (see s. 1) also publishes online reviews of tests, and the index of these reviews is also freely available: it too shows details of the publisher of each test that has been reviewed. Although they do not appear to allow on-line access at the time of writing, *Test Critiques* (Keyser and Sweetland 1994) and *Commissioned Reviews of 250 Psychological Tests* (Maltby, Lewis and Hill 2000) also provide publisher contact details as well as reviews of tests.

It is often difficult to locate tests that are very old, or which have not been published as commercial ventures. If the author's name is known then a citation search using PsychInfo or a similar database is useful: as tests tend to be heavily cited, it is likely that a heavily cited article may contain the test of interest. Many universities' test libraries are now online, and so an internet search for the test title may prove useful. *CC*

Keyser, D. J. and Sweetland, R. C. (eds) 1994: *Test Critiques*. Kansas City: Test Corporation of America. **Maltby, J., Lewis, C. A. and Hill, A.** (eds) 2000: *Commissioned Reviews of 250*

Psychological Tests. New York: Edwin Mellen Press. **Plake, B. S., Impara, J. C. and Spies, R. A.** (eds) 2003: *The Fifteenth Mental Measurements Yearbook*. Lincoln NB: University of Nebraska Press.

thematic apperception test (TAT)

A PROJECTIVE TEST of personality (Murray 1938) in which participants describe what is happening in 20 ambiguous pictures. It is supposed to reveal the individual's wants and needs. *CC*

Murray, H. A. 1938: *Explorations in Personality*. New York: Oxford University Press.

trait

A trait is any psychological characteristic of an individual which is fairly consistent over time and situations (e.g. general intelligence, sociability or meanness). *CC*

triarchic theory

Robert Sternberg (1985) suggested that instead of examining performance on a (fairly arbitrary) set of tasks, it may be better to view INTELLIGENCE (see also s. 4) as a process of ADAPTATION (see s. 4), which draws on past experience, the context of the problem and the cognitive components used in producing a solution. This led to his triarchic theory of intelligence, which comprises three distinct sub-theories.

The experiential sub-theory considers the role of previous experience in PROBLEM SOLVING (see s. 3): for example, recognising that the methods used to solve a previous problem may prove useful in solving another, and examining the role of AUTOMATICITY (see s. 5). The componential sub-theory attempts to describe the mechanisms that are used to solve problems. These comprise low-level 'performance components', which describe the basic cognitive SKILLS (see s. 3) (e.g. mental rotation, comprehension of text) used to solve a particular problem, strategic planning metacomponents, which allow us to determine the nature of the problem, which strategies should be used to try to solve it, how progress should be monitored, when a different method should be attempted, and so on, and 'knowledge acquisition components', which refer to the active encoding of novel information – sifting out irrelevant detail, spotting similarities. The contextual sub-theory considers problem solving as a means of adapting oneself to environmental demands, adapting the environment to suit one's needs or changing environments.

It is clear that Sternberg's approach provides a framework which may allow the study of 'real-life' problems rather than the abstract ones of little practical relevance which appear in most ability tests. (No one ever starved because they could not solve a verbal analogy item; the question of what to do when the harvest fails is an entirely different matter.) The problem is that it is difficult to test whether the theory is correct or not – as one reviewer pointed out, rather than being a refutable scientific theory, it is more like a set of chapter headings in a book. Obviously, if a problem is presented to someone, they must use some types of cognitive components to plan, solve and evaluate the solution. Without specifying the number, nature and mode of operation of these components, it is difficult to see what this 'high-level' theory offers, and so although vigorously promoted by Sternberg, it has generated rather little research interest. *CC*

Sternberg, R. J. 1985: *Beyond IQ*. Cambridge: Cambridge University Press.

U

unconscious motivation   Although the unconscious is important in many explanations of motivation it is Freud's (1932) PSYCHOANALYTIC THEORY that focuses on this area exclusively. Freud viewed motivation as emanating from the subconscious id and directed by two DRIVES (see s. 2), namely, Eros (the instincts for life as characterised by the sex drive) and Thanatos (the instincts for death as characterised by AGGRESSION – see s. 5). Freud hypothesised a model based on hydraulics; energy from Eros (libido) and Thanatos (mortido) would build up inside individuals and have to be released. The unconscious operated on the pleasure principle, directing behaviour towards satisfying these drives, and would have to be controlled by the ego. Psychoanalysts attempt to access clients' unconscious motives through FREE ASSOCIATION (see s. 7) or PROJECTIVE TESTS and attempt to direct behaviour through hypnosis. This theory is open to the main criticisms of much of Freud's work; it lacks external VALIDITY (see also s. 8) and testability.   *DH*

Freud, S. 1932: *New Introductory Lectures on Psychoanalysis.* Harmondsworth: Penguin.

V

---

validity Validity concerns the extent to which a MEASUREMENT (see s. 1, MEASUREMENT AND STATISTICS) instrument measures what it is intended to measure. It is not a dichotomous (valid versus invalid) or quantitative (more versus less valid) notion, but rather a context-specific one. Thus the same instrument may show evidence of validity in one situation, but not in another. There are many different types of validity.

Construct validity is a general type of validity that encompasses several of the more specific types. It concerns the accuracy with which a measurement instrument operationalises a construct. In contrast to other types of validity (e.g. concurrent, criterion and predictive), construct validity is important from a scientific perspective because it is predicated on the psychological THEORY (see s. 8) underpinning the instrument. The construct VALIDATION PROCESS (see s. 5) involves deriving hypotheses from the theory and subsequently testing them to determine their veracity.

Concurrent validity refers to the correlations between new and extant measures of a construct. It is a weak type of validity because extant measures may themselves have low validity. Occasionally, the term is used to refer to correlations between test and criterion scores when they are obtained around the same time, but this use of the term overlaps with CRITERION VALIDITY (see s. 8) and is less preferable.

Criterion validity concerns the extent to which a measurement instrument correlates with VARIABLES (see s. 8) external to itself (i.e. the criteria). It is important primarily from a practical perspective that does not necessarily entail understanding the nature and processes that give rise to associations between test and criterion scores. The sole prerequisite for demonstrating criterion validity is a statistically significant relationship, which may or may not be theoretically meaningful, between test and criterion scores.

Face validity entails an assessment by experts of the items in a measurement instrument with a view to determining whether they are valid 'on their face'. It is a weak form of validity without significant implications from a psychometric perspective.

PREDICTIVE VALIDITY (see s. 7) refers to the ability of a measurement instrument to predict future performance on a criterion.

CONTENT VALIDITY (see s. 8) involves an evaluation of the extent to which the contents of a measurement instrument are representative of the construct being operationalised. It is similar to face validity in that it is largely subjective, but more important psychometrically because it is evaluated with explicit reference to the SAMPLING (see s. 8) domain of the construct.

Convergent validity concerns the degree to which a measurement instrument correlates with variables with which it is expected to correlate (e.g. IQ and academic performance).

Discriminant validity concerns the extent to which a measurement instrument does not correlate with variables with which it is not expected to correlate (e.g. IQ and PERSONALITY).

Incremental validity refers to the degree to which a measurement instrument improves on the decisions or predictions that can be made based on existing information. The assessment of incremental validity usually involves examining whether the addition of the instrument in question leads to an increase in the multiple or PARTIAL CORRELATION (see s. 8) with a criterion. (See also s. 8, VALIDITY)   *KP*

Cronbach, L. J. 1990: *Essentials of Psychological Testing* (5th edn). New York: Harper Collins Publishers. **Kline, P.** 2000: *The Handbook of Psychological Testing* (2nd edn). London: Routledge. **Nunnally, J. C. and Bernstein, I. H.** 1994: *Psychometric Theory* (3rd edn). New York: McGraw-Hill.

Velten technique The Velten Mood Induction Procedure (VMIP) is a task designed to induce depressed, elated or neutral mood [see MOODS] states. It involves the volunteer reading self-referent statements, generally of a depressing or elating nature, and asked to 'try and feel the mood suggested' (Velten 1968). Statements for the depressed mood state condition include self-referent statements evocative self-devaluation and somatic characteristics of clinical DEPRESSION (see s. 7). The elated mood state condition contains self-referent statements evocative of elevated mood. Statements for the neutral mood condition contain statements that are unlikely to be associated with either depressed or elated mood. Each mood-induction phase takes approximately 20 minutes for the subjects to complete. The same subject can take part in each of the phases and it is normal to counterbalance the sessions. The Velten procedure produces significant changes in both self-report and non-self-report measures of mood (Larsen and Sinnett 1991).   *MS*

Larsen, R. J. and Sinnett, L. M. 1991: Meta-analysis of experimental manipulations: some factors affecting the Velten mood induction procedure. *Personality and Social Psychology Bulletin* 17, 323–34. **Velten, E. J.** 1968: A laboratory task for induction of mood states. *Behaviour Research and Therapy* 6, 473–82.

W

Wechsler scales: the WISC, WAIS and WPPSI

David Wechsler devised the Wechsler-Bellvue intelligence test in 1939 as a means of estimating the INTELLIGENCE (IQ) (see also s. 4) of adults and adolescents. It was an individually administered test comprising 11 sub-tests: 6 involving LANGUAGE (see s. 2) ('verbal' scales) and 5 nonverbal or performance scales. The tests have undergone relatively minor revisions since then, spawning a children's version, the WISC (Wechsler Intelligence Scale for Children) for children aged between 6 and 16, the Wechsler Pre-school and Primary Scale of Intelligence (WPPSI) for children aged between about 3 and 7, and the Wechsler Adult Intelligence Scale (WAIS) for those aged between 16 and 89. The latest versions are the WPPSI-III (Wechsler 2004), WAIS-III (Wechsler 1999) and WISC-III (Wechsler 1992). The WAIS and the WISC, in particular, show excellent psychometric [see PSYCHOMETRICS] properties, with internal consistency RELIABILITY (see also s. 8) well above 0.9 and substantial correlations with other ability tests. Much effort has also been invested in norming the test by administering it to large, representative SAMPLES (see s. 8) of the USA, UK and other populations. This ensures that the IQ estimates are accurate.

The verbal scales of the WAIS-III measure vocabulary, similarities, arithmetic, DIGIT SPAN (see s. 3), information, comprehension, letter-number sequencing and the nonverbal scales, picture completion, digit symbol-coding, block design, matrix reasoning, picture arrangement, symbol search and object assembly. The Wechsler tests are widely used in EDUCATIONAL PSYCHOLOGY (see s. 1), where a marked discrepancy between scores on the verbal and performance tests is often used as an indicator of dyslexia. However, modern factor-analytic evidence (see FACTOR ANALYSIS and also s. 8) suggests that four FACTORS (see s. 8) (not two) underlie the test. In addition, the make-up of the tests is somewhat arbitrary and welded to previous versions of the test rather than to modern evidence about the number and nature of human cognitive abilities. While Carroll (1993) has drawn up a comprehensive list of the best-established human cognitive abilities in the three-stratum model [see ABILITY: THREE-STRATUM MODEL], the Wechsler tests still do not attempt to assess all of the main ability factors that have been identified. For example, nothing in the Wechsler scales measures creative thinking or auditory PERCEPTION (see s. 1), and the only MEMORY (see s. 1) test is for lists of numbers. *CC*

Carroll, J. B. 1993: *Human Cognitive Abilities: A Survey of Factor-analytic Studies.* Cambridge: Cambridge University Press. **Cooper, C.** 1995: Inside the WISC-III(UK). *Educational Psychology in Practice* 10, 215–19. **Wechsler, D.** 1992: *Wechsler Intelligence Scale for Children*® (3rd UK edn, WISC®-iii UK). London: Psychological Corporation. **Wechsler, D.** 1999: *Wechsler Adult Intelligence Scale* (3rd UK edn, WAIS® -iii UK). London: Psychological Corporation. **Wechsler, D.** 2004: *Wechsler Pre-school and Primary Scale of Intelligence* (3rd UK edn, WPPSI-iii UK). London: Psychological Corporation.

work motivation

MOTIVATION to perform well in one's job is one of the SENTIMENTS in Cattell's model of motivation. Several occupational psychologists have developed scales to assess a TRAIT of work motivation; these can show appreciable overlap with conventional PERSONALITY TRAITS (Furnham, Forde and Ferrari 1999), but prove useful in PERSONNEL SELECTION (see Wood 2000 and other papers in that volume). Katzell and Thompson (1990) offer a useful overview. *CC*

Furnham, A., Forde, L. and Ferrari, K. 1999: Personality and work motivation. *Personality and Individual Differences* 26, 1035–43. **Katzell, R. A. and Thompson, D. E.** 1990: Work motivation – theory and practice. *American Psychologist* 45, 144–53. **Wood, R. E.** 2000: Work motivation: theory, research and practice – introduction to the special issue. *Applied Psychology – an International Review – Psychologie Appliquée-Revue Internationale* 49, 317–18.

Section 7

Abnormal, Clinical and Health Psychology

Introduction

Abnormal, clinical and health psychology are fields that share a common general purpose, namely, the application of psychological theories to the understanding and treatment of clinical phenomena. However, in other ways they are quite different. In the case of abnormal psychology, the older of these fields, the clinical phenomena of interest – abnormal mental states – are primarily psychological in nature, and despite more than a century of scientific investigation, serious disputes remain about how these phenomena are best construed. In the case of the relative newcomer, health psychology, the clinical phenomena of interest are mainly bodily diseases, as conventionally understood by physical medicine; there is very little dispute about how these phenomena are to be construed and the psychologist's interest is mainly in how they are influenced by social and psychological factors.

It has always been difficult to draw a clear line between abnormal psychology and the medical specialty of psychiatry. Indeed, much of the research which has been published in abnormal psychology (or psychopathology, as it is sometimes known) has been carried out by psychiatrists. It would be tempting to distinguish between the two disciplines on the basis of the kinds of models employed. For example, it is commonly assumed that psychologists favour dimensional models of mental illness (in which there is no clear dividing line between mental illness and normal functioning), whereas psychiatrists prefer a categorical approach to classification; and that psychologists are primarily interested in social and environmental determinants of abnormal behaviour, whereas psychiatrists favour explanations in terms of genes or cerebral dysfunction. However, even the most cursory examination of recent textbooks in abnormal psychology (for good examples, see Bennett 2003 and Davidson, Neale and Kring 2003) and psychiatry will reveal, for the most part, few differences. In the main, this reflects the current theoretical hegemony of the American Psychiatric Association's DSM system of classification, which is often used to organise knowledge in textbooks written by members of either discipline.

The publication of the third edition of the DSM in 1980 is rightly seen as a watershed in the history of abnormal psychology. Before that time, not only was there widespread disagreement about the classification of psychiatric conditions, but there were also some who even argued against the right of psychiatry to exist. (Some radical psychiatrists in the 1960s and 1970s called themselves 'antipsychiatrists' in order to emphasise their rejection of the ideological and theoretical framework of their own profession). Following the publication of DSM-III, these disagreements seemed to fade away. Whereas, beforehand, even those clinical psychologists (for example, those trained in the behavioural approach) who prided themselves on being scientific distanced themselves from psychiatry, many modern clinical psychologists have embraced the DSM system in its totality, and are as happy to focus on biological determinants of abnormal behaviour as their medical colleagues.

The current agreement about the subject matter of abnormal psychology is probably illusory, not least because the DSM system of classification is the product of consensus discussions, mainly involving distinguished psychiatrists, rather than scientific research. In fact, when scientific studies are conducted to test the validity of DSM diagnoses (for example, whether symptoms cluster as suggested by the diagnoses, whether different diagnoses predict outcome or response to different kinds of treatment) the diagnoses are almost always found wanting. Moreover, epidemiological studies conducted in the last ten years have shown that abnormal mental states (even hallucinations and delusions) are much more common in the general population than was previously thought, and that many people who experience these symptoms cope well without any psychiatric or psychological assistance. The implication of these observations is that the DSM system simply fails to describe abnormal mental states adequately for scientific purposes. Assuming these deficiencies cannot be avoided, it is a fair bet that fundamental disputes about the nature of psychiatric phenomena will resurface in the near future.

If this is the case, it is reasonable to ask from what quarter a resolution to these disputes might arise. The

357

conventional answer to this question is neuroscience. Recent developments in neuro-imaging and molecular genetics have certainly yielded insights into brain functioning that would have been unimaginable even twenty years ago, and it is not difficult to believe that the application of this knowledge will result in quantum leaps in our understanding of abnormal mental states. And yet the problem with the neuroscience approach is that it relies on existing methods of psychiatric classification (to select patients for the brain scanner or for genetic analysis) and therefore cannot provide the solution to this very problem. An alternative possibility is that great strides forwards in abnormal psychology will be made by psychologists working in the cognitive-behavioural tradition, who have already shown how testable scientific theories of abnormal mental states (especially anxiety and depression) can be woven using concepts borrowed from mainstream cognitive and social psychology. Recently, this same strategy has been extended to psychotic phenomena, such as delusions and hallucinations (Bentall 2003), and also the so-called personality disorders. In attempting to analyse these conditions, cognitive-behavioural investigators, for the most part, have not allowed themselves to be confined by existing approaches to psychiatric classification, and have elucidated processes (for example, dysfunctional self-schemas, biases in attention and memory) that cut across a range of apparently different phenomena.

Whether this optimism is justified or not, abnormal psychology continues to be a challenging field, which brings together scientific methods and the humanitarian values of the clinical professions. Its study will surely continue to reward further generations of psychologists.

References

Bennett, P. 2003: *Abnormal Psychology*. Milton Keynes: Open University Press. **Bentall, R. P.** 2003: *Madness Explained: Psychosis and Human Nature*. London: Penguin. **Davidson, G. C., Neale, J. M. and Kring, A.** 2003: *Abnormal Psychology* (9th edn). New York: Wiley.

INTRODUCTORY REMARKS

In terms of the number of students and practising professionals, clinical psychology is the largest sub-discipline of psychology as a whole. Over the last 30 years, the field has witnessed important developments. Until the 1970s, diagnoses were notoriously unreliable and effects of treatment were hardly documented. Many theories were around, but they were hard to test and few efforts to test them were undertaken. Inspection of the major journals and handbooks illustrates that, at the beginning of the twenty-first century, clinical and abnormal psychology became firmly rooted in scientific theories and methods.

Diagnosis

For many decades, diagnosis in clinical psychology and in psychiatry was largely dependent on the theoretical orientation of the clinician. A major development was the third edition of the Diagnostic and Statistical Manual of the American Psychiatric Association in 1980. The manual allows for a reliable classification of disorders while the classification is atheoretical and relies not on hypothetical explanations but on the presence or absence of actual symptoms. This 'DSM-III' and its successors allowed for reliable descriptive diagnosis; they became the international standard in research and they are used in clinical practice all over the world.

Research in individual differences showed that personality is largely composed of five traits. The trait that is most relevant to clinical psychology is 'neuroticism' or 'negative affectivity'. To a large extent, neuroticism is under genetic control and people who are high on neuroticism are vulnerable to the development of one of the disorders that are most prevalent in the western world: anxiety disorders and depression. While anxious and depressed patients are invariably high on neuroticism, most people high on neuroticism do not develop mental disorders.

Explanation

Clinical psychology research draws heavily on insights from other psychological sub-disciplines like social psychology, developmental psychology, experimental psychology, etc. An important development was the study of how people with a certain disorder respond to stimuli with a specific meaning. Depressed patients proved to have a surprisingly good memory for negative information. Anxious patients are somewhat less attentive, but they are very attentive to potential threat. Many psychological problems appeared to be associated with biased processing of specific types of information and these processing biases may serve to maintain the disorder. In the presence of problems, people tend to take measures to reduce their discomfort, but some of these measures are unproductive or even counter-productive and they may, like cognitive biases, add to the persistence of the disorder. Examples are taking drugs to overcome withdrawal effects, avoiding phobic situations, purging after binge eating, etc. Generally speaking, less is known about the origin of disorders than about how the disorders persist.

Treatment

Until the 1970s, treatment studies were largely naturalistic and documented the effects of non-standardised clinical routines that were inspired by theories from the various 'therapy schools'. These naturalistic studies were not very informative: patient groups were heterogeneous, the nature of the treatment was unclear, there were no proper control groups, etc. To overcome these problems, naturalistic studies were largely replaced by controlled outcome trials that compare the effects of two or more standardised treatments. Treatment packages that proved effective were subject to 'dismantling' studies, testing what treatment components are crucial for progress.

Most of these studies tested interventions from cognitive behaviour therapy and it seems that, at least in academic clinical psychology, cognitive behaviour therapy became the dominant approach to treatment. There is increasing pressure on health care workers to concentrate on evidence-based manuals. Though many believe the contrary, there is no evidence that 'tailor-made' therapy is more effective than conventional approaches laid out in treatment manuals.

Professor Marcel van den Hout

Given the range of phenomena covered by the fields of abnormal and health psychology (modern textbooks of abnormal psychology often run to many hundreds of pages) it was inevitable that many possible topics had to be left uncovered. The selection of the abnormal psychology items was made mainly by myself, but for the health psychology entries I obtained considerable assistance from my colleague, Alison Wearden. Perhaps because I am a clinical psychologist with an interest in the psychotic disorders, but also because abnormal psychology is longer established than health psychology, the greater share of the entries has gone to abnormal psychology.

When selecting these entries, a balance was sought between classifying the material according to the standard DSM approach (with definitions reflecting different diagnoses) and the need to assist the reader's awareness of the historical context in which the conventional approach to abnormal psychology has arisen. Two of the level 1 definitions (MENTAL ILLNESS: CONCEPTS OF and PSYCHIATRIC CLASSIFICATION) reflect this historical context and the different ways in which abnormal mental states have been described and explained, whereas six represent major categories of psychiatric disorder. Some of the definitions at Levels 2, 3 and 4 provide further information about clinical phenomena subsumed within these major categories (for example, particular ANXIETY DISORDERS, or types of PERSONALITY DISORDER, or particular symptoms such as HALLUCINATIONS and DELUSIONS), whereas others pertain to major constructs or research methods that have been used to understand these phenomena (varying from biological constructs, for example, from psychiatric genetics or psychopharmacology, to psychological constructs, such as learned helplessness or self-discrepancy theory). The remaining abnormal psychology entries concern treatment methods, mostly modern, but with the occasional mention of discredited therapies such as insulin coma and the prefrontal leucotomy. I have tried to strike a balance between biological and psychological treatments, with entries for the major types of psychiatric drugs and ECT, as well as different kinds of psychotherapy. Within the psychotherapy entries, I have tried to represent both cognitive-behavioural and psychodynamic approaches. The entries also address methods of evaluating the effectiveness of treatments, for example, with definitions for RANDOMISED CONTROLLED TRIALS, MULTIPLE BASELINE EXPERIMENTS and META-ANALYSIS (see s. 8).

Two health psychology definitions were written at Level 1, one for HEALTH PSYCHOLOGY itself and the other for STRESS (a construct that obviously has implications for understanding psychiatric disorders). The remaining health psychology entries reflect topics of current importance, for example PAIN, SOMATISATION and HEALTH BELIEFS.

Professor Richard Bentall

A

adoption studies The assumption behind adoption studies is that, if a child is removed from their biological parent soon after birth and raised by someone unrelated, then any similarity between the biological parent and the child must be due to genetic rather than environmental factors. In practice, two types of studies are carried out – either the adopted away children of individuals with the trait of interest are traced and compared with the adopted away children of parents who lack the trait, or the biological parents of affected adoptees are traced and compared with the biological parents of adoptees that are not affected. Adoption studies have been claimed to provide convincing evidence of the INHERITANCE (see s. 4) of a number of conditions, especially schizophrenia. However, critics point out that they are beset with many difficulties, including selective adoption effects (the tendency for children to be assigned to adoptive parents who are similar to their biological parents) (Joseph 2003). A recent study overcame this difficulty by measuring important characteristics of the adopting family, and found evidence of a gene x environment interaction in the causation of thought disorder (Wahlberg et al. 1997).   *RB*

Joseph, J. 2003: *The Gene Illusion: Genetic Research in Psychology and Psychiatry under the Microscope.* Ross-on-Wye: PCCS Books. **Wahlberg, K.-E., Wynne, L. C., Oja, H., Keskitalo, P., Pykalainen, L., Lahti, I., Moring, J., Naarala, N., Sorri, A., Seitamaa, M., Laksy, K., Kolassa, J. and Tienari, P.** 1997: Gene-environment interaction in vulnerability to schizophrenia: findings from the Finnish Adoptive Family Study of Schizophrenia. *American Journal of Psychiatry* 154, 355–62.

anger management training A cognitive behavioural treatment approach [see COGNITIVE (BEHAVIOUR) THERAPY] including SOCIAL SKILLS TRAINING, ASSERTIVENESS TRAINING and problem-solving enhancement in an effort to reduce problems of anger and AGGRESSION (see s. 5).

AO'K

anhedonia The inability to experience pleasure; a negative symptom sometimes thought to be a core feature of SCHIZOPHRENIA, but also found in patients with other diagnoses, especially DEPRESSION.   *RB*

antidepressant drugs A range of DRUGS (see s. 2) are available for the treatment of depression, although, as the same medications are used in the treatment of ANXIETY DISORDERS, SOMATISATION, chronic PAIN (see also s. 2) and migraine headaches, the term 'antidepressant' may be misleading (Hedaya 1996).

The oldest classes of antidepressants are the tricyclics [see TRICYCLIC ANTIDEPRESSANTS] such as imipramine and amatriptyline, and the monoamine oxydase inhibitors (MAOs) such as phenelzine. Common side effects include dry mouth, constipation, blurred vision, sedation and dizziness. MAOs have an additional disadvantage, in that they require dietary restrictions to avoid the risk of a sudden elevation in blood pressure.

More recent antidepressants include the SELECTIVE SEROTONIN REUPTAKE INHIBITORS (SSRIs) such as fluoxetine. These usually have less severe side effects, but there have been concerns about whether they can provoke either suicidal or homicidal acts in a very small minority of patients; claims that they can have led to several high-profile court cases.

Despite their widespread use, recent meta-analyses of published and unpublished clinical trial data have led some investigators to question the efficacy of antidepressant drug treatment for preventing suicide (Khan, Warner and Brown 2000).   *RB*

Hedaya, R. J. 1996: *Understanding Biological Psychiatry.* New York: Norton. **Khan, A., Warner, H. A. and Brown, W. A.** 2000: Symptom reduction and suicide risk in patients treated with placebo in antidepressant clinical trials: an analysis of the Food and Drug Administration database. *Archives of General Psychiatry* 57, 311–17.

antipsychiatry A loosely defined movement of clinicians (often psychiatrists; for example, R. D. Laing, 1927–89) and radical thinkers that objected to conventional psychiatric theories and treatments as dehumanising, and who often advocated more romantic conceptions of psychiatric difficulties (e.g. that such difficulties might be creative experiences or rational responses to an irrational world). The antipsychiatric movement was influential in the 1960s and 1970s, but has had very little lasting impact on psychiatric theory or practice.   *RB*

antipsychotic drugs The antipsychotics are DRUGS (see s. 2) that can be used in the treatment of psychotic disorders (disorders in which the individual experiences HALLUCINATIONS and DELUSIONS), especially SCHIZOPHRENIA. The first antipsychotic, chlorpromazine, was discovered adventitiously in the early 1950s and is still used today. They are recommended for continuous prophylactic use in patients who have a history of psychotic episodes, as numerous RANDOMISED CONTROLLED TRIALS have established that they are most effective at preventing psychotic episodes when used in this way (Thornley, Adams and Award 2001).

Following the discovery of chlorpromazine, many similar compounds were discovered. It was subsequently found that the potency of these compounds correlated with their capacity to block the dopamine D2 receptor (see s. 2, RECEPTORS) (Carlsson and Lindqvist 1963), a discovery that was a major stimulus for the DOPAMINE THEORY OF SCHIZOPHRENIA. The main disadvantage of all of the typical (conventional) antipsychotics is that they have numerous side effects, including extra-pyramidal side effects (Parkinsonism, dystonias, akathisia and tardive dyskinesia), weight gain and sexual dysfunction. The discovery that clozapine [see CLOZARIL] had an antipsychotic affect with very few extra-pyramidal side effects led to the synthesis of a new class of ATYPICAL ANTIPSYCHOTIC DRUGS, which are less specific in blocking the D2 receptor and which are better tolerated by patients. *RB*

Carlsson, A. and Lindqvist, M. 1963: Effect of chlorpromazine or haloperidol on formation of 3-methoxytyramine and normetanephrine in mouse brain. *Acta Pharmacologica et Toxicologica* 20, 140–4. **Thornley, B., Adams, C. E. and Award, G.** 2001: *Chlorpromazine Versus Placebo for Schizophrenia: Cochrane Review.*

antisocial personality disorder Antisocial Personality Disorder is defined in DSM-IV (American Psychiatric Association 1994) as 'a pervasive pattern of disregard for and violation of the rights of others'. To qualify for the diagnosis, a person must have (since the age of 15) repeatedly committed criminal acts, been deceitful, shown IMPULSIVITY (see s. 6), irritability and aggressiveness, shown a reckless disregard for safety of self or other people, demonstrated consistent irresponsibility, or shown lack of remorse for people that may have been hurt or mistreated.

About 2–3 per cent of the general population meets the criteria for antisocial personality disorder. It is more common in men, younger people, less well-off people, single people and people with more limited education. Antisocial personality disorder is very common in the prison population. As with most personality disorders, people with the diagnosis have often experienced abuse or ill-treatment during childhood. Although interventions for antisocial personality disorder are difficult and time-consuming, a variety of treatment approaches (including approaches used by probation services for reducing offending behaviour) can be successful. These are most likely to be successful if they are well structured, have a clear focus and are theoretically coherent, are well integrated with other services, continue for a relatively long period and involve a good treatment alliance between therapist and patient. *PK*

Bateman, A. and Tyrer, P. 2002: *Effective Management of Personality Disorder.* London: National Institute for Mental Health in England/Department of Health.

anxiety disorders ANXIETY (see s. 6) is a feeling of apprehension or fear, usually resulting from the anticipation of a threatening event; it is a common experience which may vary in intensity depending on the situation in which it is experienced. It is often accompanied by various physiological symptoms such as muscle tension, dry mouth, perspiring, trembling and difficulty swallowing. In its more chronic form, dizziness, chronic fatigue, sleeping difficulties, rapid or irregular heartbeat, diarrhoea or a persistent need to urinate, sexual problems, and nightmares may also accompany anxiety. In both healthy and clinical samples, intensity of anxiety usually correlates highly with intensity of DEPRESSION (Goldberg and Huxley 1992), and some EMOTION (see s. 6) theorists have argued that they are both manifestations of an underlying dimension of NEGATIVE AFFECT (see s. 6). The content of cognitions is often used to distinguish the two, as depression is associated with preoccupations about loss or failure, rather than threat. However, patients can often feel threatened and failing at the same time.

Most anxiety reactions are perfectly natural, and are essential for effective performance in challenging circum-

stances. However, anxiety can become so intense or attached to inappropriate events or situations, that it becomes maladaptive and problematic for the individual. This is when an anxiety disorder may develop. An anxiety disorder is an excessive or aroused state characterised by feelings of apprehension, uncertainty and fear. The anxiety response (1) may be out of proportion to the threat posed by the situation or event (e.g. in specific PHOBIAS), (2) may not be easily attributable to any specific threat (e.g. in GENERALISED ANXIETY DISORDER, or some forms of PANIC DISORDER), and (3) may persist chronically and be so disabling that the individual is unable to continue normal day-to-day living.

In DSM-IV there are six principal categories of anxiety disorder: specific phobias, panic disorder, generalised anxiety disorder (GAD), OBSESSIVE-COMPULSIVE DISORDER (OCD), POST-TRAUMATIC STRESS DISORDER (PTSD) and acute STRESS disorder.

Studies have shown that 17 per cent of adults in the USA have at least one type of diagnosable anxiety disorder in any year (Kessler et al. 1994), and this is higher than prevalence rates for both MOOD DISORDERS (see s. 6) and substance abuse disorders.

Theoretical explanations of the aetiology of anxiety disorders tend to focus on particular disorders, which may be acquired and maintained in different ways (Barlow 2001). However, anxiety disorders generally have a number of characteristics in common. First, the anxiety experienced by sufferers is usually severe enough to disrupt normal daily living and to cause significant emotional distress. As a consequence, sufferers often develop a core set of dysfunctional beliefs about the source of the anxiety (e.g. individuals with panic disorder believe many ambiguous bodily sensations predict an imminent threat, such as a heart attack), and also develop AVOIDANCE strategies. Although such strategies allow the individual to avoid the immediate source of the anxiety, they often help to maintain the dysfunctional beliefs.

Second, anxiety disorders are often associated with information-processing biases, such that sufferers (a) have a pre-attentional bias towards attending to threatening stimuli, (b) a tendency to interpret ambiguous information as threatening, and (c) have a bias towards accessing anxiety- and threat-related information in MEMORY (see s. 1) (Mathews and MacLeod 1994; Williams et al. 1997). Research suggests that these information-processing biases maintain hyper-vigilance for threat, create further sources for worry and thereby maintain anxiety. For example, individuals with anxiety disorders appear to have an information-processing bias that causes them to pre-attentively (i.e. rapidly and unconsciously) focus in on any threat-related stimulus (Mogg and Bradley 1998). This characteristic has been demonstrated using a number of experimental techniques such as the emotional Stroop PARADIGM (see s. 1) and the dot-probe procedure. It is not yet clear whether these information-processing biases are consequences of anxiety or whether individuals who develop anxiety disorders permanently display these biases, which then makes them vulnerable to acquiring these disorders (Williams, Watts, MacLeod and Mathews 1997). However, if they do not represent a vulnerability factor, they are certainly an important factor in the maintenance of anxious psychopathology.

Third, all anxiety disorders are characterised by increased levels of cognitive activity associated with anxiety, including worrying (Davey and Tallis 1994) – which is a cardinal diagnostic feature of generalised anxiety disorder – intrusive and pessimistic thoughts, anxious apprehension and a pervading sense of uncontrollability of both the thoughts and the anxiety (Barlow 1991).

A range of different therapeutic methods can be used to treat anxiety disorders. The symptoms of these disorders have often beeen treated with anxiolytics (tranquillisers) such as the BENZODIAZEPINES (which include the well-known tranquilliser, valium), and they have their effect by increasing the level of the NEUROTRANSMITTER (see s. 2) GABA at SYNAPSES (see s. 2) in the brain. Benzodiazepines are usually prescribed for only short periods because they can encourage dependence if taken over a longer period, and can also be abused if available in large doses. Moreover, it is important to be aware that anxiolytics usually offer only symptom relief, and do not address the psychological and cognitive factors that may be maintaining the anxiety. RANDOMISED CONTROLLED TRIALS have demonstrated that antidepressant medication can be at least as effective in the treatment of anxiety disorders as anxiolytics, and this kind of treatment is now the preferred medical approach. In recent years, a range of cognitive-behavioural therapies (CBTs) have been developed to treat individual anxiety disorders, and these are usually based on the need to modify and restructure the dysfunctional cognitions that maintain individual anxiety disorders (Wells 1997). [See COGNITIVE (BEHAVIOUR) THERAPY]   *GD*

Barlow, D. H. 1991: Disorders of emotion. *Psychological Inquiry* 2, 58–71. **Barlow, D. H.** 2001: *Anxiety and its Disorders: The Nature and Treatment of Anxiety and Panic*. New York: Guilford. **Davey, G. C. L. and Tallis, F.** 1994: *Worrying: Perspectives on Theory, Assessment and Treatment*. Chichester: Wiley. **Goldberg, D. and Huxley, P.** 1992: *Common Mental Disorders: A Bio-social Model*. London: Routledge. **Kessler, R. C., McGonagle, K. A., Zhao, S., Nelson, C. R., Highes, M., Eshleman, S., Wittchen, H. and Kendler, K. S.** 1994: Lifetime and 12-month prevalence of DSM-III-R psychiatric disorders in the United States: Results from the National Comorbidity Survey. *Archives of General Psychiatry* 51, 620–31. **Mathews, A. and MacLeod, C.** 1994: Cognitive approaches to emotion and emotional disorders. *Annual Review of Psychology* 45, 25–50. **Mogg, K. and Bradley, B. P.** 1998: A cognitive-motivational analysis of anxiety. *Behaviour Research & Therapy* 36, 809–48. **Wells, A.** 1997: *Cognitive Therapy of Anxiety*. Chichester: Wiley. **Williams, J. M. G., Watts, F. N., MacLeod, C. and Mathews, A.** 1997: *Cognitive Psychology and Emotional Disorders*. Chichester: Wiley.

anxiety management   A treatment approach for the amelioration of anxiety disorders that combines a number of cognitive behavioural [see COGNITIVE (BEHAVIOUR) THERAPY] techniques.

AO'K

assertiveness training   A cognitive behavioural [see COGNITIVE (BEHAVIOUR) THERAPY] treatment approach designed to help people become appropriately assertive (as opposed to being either timid or aggressive); typically involves role-playing strategies for non-aggressively asserting rights in difficult interpersonal situations.   *AO'K*

attention-deficit   hyperactivity   disorder   Attention-deficit hyperactivity disorder (ADHD) effects approximately 50 per cent of children referred for clinical assessment, and approximately 3–5 per cent of all primary schoolchildren, with an overrepresentation of boys of 3 : 1 (Scheres et al. 2003). Behavioural symptoms include inattention, impulsiveness and hyperactivity, all of which have shown to be relatively stable traits encompassing the lifespan. ADHD has been the focus of a wealth of psychological research, with various deficits being proposed; it is now generally accepted that the primary deficit is a component of executive control (Scheres et al. 2003). Barkley (1997) proposed that the primary deficit in ADHD was not ATTENTION (see s. 3), but behavioural INHIBITION (see s. 3) (sometimes referred to as response inhibition), because children with ADHD reliably demonstrate impairments on authenticated measures of inhibition. Current clinical interventions favour the efficacy of pharmaceutical treatments, but if behavioural inhibition is the primary deficit, it may be possible to develop cognitive behavioural therapies to treat the disorder. [See COGNITIVE (BEHAVIOUR) THERAPY]

RB

Barkley, R. 1997: Behavioural inhibition, sustained attention and executive functions: constructing a unifying theory of ADHD. *Psychological Bulletin* 12, 65–94. **Scheres, A., Oosterlaan, J., Guerts, H., Morein-Zamir, S., Meiran, N., Schut, H., Vlasveld, L. and Sergeant, J. A.** 2003: Executive functioning in boys with ADHD: primarily an inhibition deficit? *Archives of Clinical Neuropsychology.*

attributional style   A person's style of explaining significant life events; a pessimistic style (in which the individual attributes negative events to internal, stable and global causes) is thought to be a trait-like vulnerability factor for depression.   *RB*

atypical   antipsychotic   drugs   ANTIPSYCHOTIC (neuroleptic) DRUGS (see also s. 2, DRUG) that are less selective at blocking the dopamine D2 receptor (see s. 2, RECEPTORS) than traditional neuroleptics, [see NEUROLEPTIC MEDICATION] and which ameliorate psychotic symptoms with less extra-pyramidal side effects. Examples include clozapine (marketed as CLOZARIL) and olanzapine (Zyprexa).   *RB*

avoidance   Avoidance is a significant feature of many psychological disorders, and in particular, ANXIETY DISORDERS. Individuals suffering anxiety disorders will usually develop strategies for avoiding those situations, stimuli and events that give cause to their ANXIETY (see s. 6). For example, the arachnophobe will avoid all places where they believe they might find a spider, and the obsessive-compulsive will usually strive to avoid dirt and contamination (often developing very elaborate, complex and time-consuming cleaning rituals) or avoid situations where checking is demanded. These avoid responses can have a number of effects. First, they may prevent the anxiety sufferer from disconfirming the dysfunctional beliefs that maintain the anxiety disorder (e.g. they prevent the arachnophobe from ever finding out that spiders are harmless). Second, the anxiety reduction experienced as a consequence of avoidance may act to reinforce avoidance behaviours generally and maintain the disorder (e.g. Mowrer 1947).

Most behaviour and cognitive therapies for anxiety disorders usually include a component (such as exposure) designed to prevent or extinguish avoidance responses. *GD*

Mowrer, O. H. 1947: On the dual nature of learning: a reinterpretation of 'conditioning' and 'problem-solving'. *Harvard Educational Review* 17, 102–48.

avolition Apathy or lack of MOTIVATION (see s. 6); regarded as one of the negative symptoms of SCHIZOPHRENIA. *RB*

B

---

behavioural experiment A COGNITIVE (BEHAVIOUR) THERAPY technique, in which the patient is asked to make a prediction and then carry out an observation to test it; for example, a patient who is socially anxious may be asked to predict how others will react to him or her in a particular social situation, and then to go to the situation and observe what happens. *RB*

behavioural family therapy A type of family therapy developed specifically for working with the families of patients diagnosed as suffering from SCHIZOPHRENIA, which includes education about schizophrenia and help with problem-solving family disputes, aimed at reducing levels of EXPRESSED EMOTION in carers. *RB*

behaviour therapy Behaviour therapy is a psychological treatment approach which was developed, mainly after World War II and mainly (but certainly not exclusively) by clinical psychologists, and which was based on the application of learning theory. In the UK, the development of behaviour therapy techniques played an important role in establishing CLINICAL PSYCHOLOGY (see also s. 1) as a profession; prior to the development of these techniques the role of the clinical psychologist was mainly to administer psychological tests under the direction of a psychiatrist.

The origins of behaviour therapy can be traced to early experiments by the behaviourist John Brodus Watson (1878–1958) and his colleagues. Watson and Rayner (1920) demonstrated that it was possible to establish a phobia to a small animal in an infant child by making a frightening noise whenever the infant handled the small animal. Later, (Jones 1924) demonstrated that it was possible to remove an animal phobia in a small child by a process of counter-conditioning, in which the child was given sweets in the presence of the animal. The implications of these experiments were largely neglected until the South African psychiatrist Joseph Wolpe (1958) (1936–79) and the British (but German-born) psychologist H. J. Eysenck (1959) (1916–97) began to advocate the explicit application of learning theory (mainly Pavlovian – see s. 1, PAVLOV SCHOOL) principles in the clinical setting. Wolpe's treatment for phobias, SYSTEMATIC DESENSITISATION, which is highly effective and still in use today, is the quintessential behaviour therapy intervention. However, behaviour therapy interventions were soon developed for a wide range of ANXIETY DISORDERS. In addition to these were added behaviour modification techniques, based on OPERANT CONDITIONING (see s. 3) principles, developed by North American psychologists, inspired by B. F. Skinner (1904–90). (Since this time, the terms behaviour therapy and behaviour modification have often been used interchangeably.)

Kazdin and Hersen (1980) susggested that the four main features of behaviour therapy/modification are a strong commitment to evaluating treatment techniques; the principle that therapeutic techniques should provide opportunities to learn adaptive or pro-social behaviour; specification of treatment techniques in operational terms; and evaluation of treatment effects in multiple modalities, especially by the measurement (see s. 1, MEASUREMENT AND STATISTICS) of overt behaviour.

Although behaviour therapists insisted that their techniques were based on learning principles, critics pointed out that they included cognitive techniques all along. For example, systematic desensitisation is usually conducted with the patient imagining the feared stimulus. The emergence of cognitive therapy in the late 1970s and afterwards saw a decline in the number of practitioners who described themselves as behaviour therapists, although the new generation of cognitive-behaviour therapists often used behavioural techniques as a component of their therapeutic interventions. *RB*

Eysenck, H. J. 1959: Learning theory and behaviour therapy. *Journal of Mental Science* 105, 61–75. **Jones, M. C.** 1924: A laboratory study of fear: the case of Peter. *Pedagogical Seminary* 31, 308–15. **Kazdin, A. E. and Hersen, M.** 1980: The current status of behaviour therapy. *Behavior Modification* 4, 283–302. **Watson, J. B. and Rayner, R.** 1920: Conditioned emotional reactions. *Journal of Experimental Psychology* 3, 1–14. **Wolpe, J.** 1958: *Psychotherapy by Reciprocal Inhibition*. Stanford CA: Stanford University Press.

benzodiazapines A class of DRUGS (see s. 2) (sometimes referred to as minor tranquillisers) including lorazepam (marketed as Ativan) and diazepam (Valium) that are believed to act on the GABA neurotransmitter-receptor system, and which have marked short-term affects on ANXIETY (see s. 6). Although well tolerated, continued use can lead to dependency and severe withdrawal problems. For this reason, these drugs are now recommended only for short-term use in the treatment of ANXIETY DISORDERS and other conditions. *RB*

bipolar disorder Bipolar disorder or 'manic depression' is a mood (affective) disorder. It is a chronic and disabling mental illness, considered to be lifelong (Chen et al. 1998), and involves unpredictable shifts between periods of DEPRESSION, MANIA, HYPOMANIA, mixed affective episodes (in which the individual experiences both depression and manic symptoms) and normal functioning. Although the idea that mania is an end state of depression can be traced back to Roman physicians, bipolar disorder and unipolar depression were included in a single category of manic depression in the diagnostic system of Emil Kraepelin (1856–1926), whose work formed the basis of most modern classifications of psychiatric disorders. It was only following work by Karl Leohnard (1904–88) in the 1950s that bipolar disorder became recognised as a separate condition to unipolar depression.

Nonetheless, some researchers continue to argue that no clear dividing line can be drawn between the affective psychoses (psychotic depression and bipolar disorder) and SCHIZOPHRENIA. Consistent with this unitary psychosis hypothesis, many patients present with a mixture of schizophrenia and bipolar symptoms; in the DSM system the term SCHIZO-AFFECTIVE DISORDER is used to describe this combination of symptoms.

In the DSM system, a distinction is now made between bipolar-1 disorder (in which there is a history of both depression and mania) and bipolar-2 disorder (in which there is a history of depression and hypomania but an absence of full manic episodes). Contrary to common thinking, mood during mania is more often irritable than euphoric, and manic patients often evidence high levels of dysphoria (depression) (Goodwin and Jamison, 1990). Often manic episodes begin with feelings of euphoria, but proceed to panic, irritability and psychotic symptoms (HALLUCINATIONS and DELUSIONS).

Bipolar disorder affects approximately 1.5 per cent of the adult population (American Psychiatric Association 1994), males and females equally, and often begins in adolescence, with a mean age of onset of 21 years (Smith and Weissman 1992). Symptoms can begin much earlier in childhood and, as a result, can go undiagnosed for many years. The course of the disorder is most likely to be severe, with people suffering multiple episodes that usually have longer duration as the individual gets older. These episodes of severe mood disturbance can result in extreme alterations to the sufferer's behaviours and thinking, often with undesirable consequences. The risk of attempted and completed suicide is high.

The personal and social costs of bipolar disorder are immense, having a particularly detrimental impact on areas such as interpersonal RELATIONSHIPS (see s. 5), social and occupational functioning. People often start to become unwell at a time in their life when they would usually be establishing careers and developing meaningful adult relationships. Although most sufferers experience periods of relatively normal functioning between episodes of mood disturbance, they often have decreased social functioning and are never entirely symptom-free. Caregivers of those affected often experience substantial burden and distress (Woods 2000).

There is evidence from twin and family studies of a substantial genetic contribution to bipolar disorder (Torrey et al. 1994). However, the accidental discovery that lithium carbonate stabilises mood in bipolar patients, reducing the risk of relapse, has yet to lead to a clear understanding of the brain biochemistry of the disorder. Investigation of neurocognitive functioning in bipolar patients has consistently revealed evidence of mild neurocognitive deficits, but it is not yet known whether these precede the onset of illness.

Several psychological theories of bipolar disorder have been proposed. The MANIC DEFENCE HYPOTHESIS, first proposed by the psychoanalyst Karl Abraham (1911/1927), hypothesises that mania arises from extreme attempts to avoid depression. This can be restated as the hypothesis that, in an attempt to avoid feelings of depression, bipolar patients engage in dysfunctional coping strategies such as indulging in high-risk and stimulating activities, leading to mania. Recent psychological research, showing depression-like performance on cognitive tests in both remitted and currently manic bipolar patients, is consistent with this hypothesis (Lyon et al. 1999; Scott et al. 2000). It has also been argued that mania is triggered by sleep (see s. 2, SLEEP AND BIOLOGICAL RHYTHMS) disturbance. Consistent

with this idea, the onset of mania sometimes occurs following life events that disrupt social rhythms, for example, international travel or the birth of a child (Malkoff-Schwartz et al. 2000). It has also been argued that oversensitivity of the behavioural activation system (the brain system that mediates response to REINFORCEMENT – see s. 3) confers vulnerability to depression, and consistent with this idea, manic episodes are sometimes triggered by positive life events involving goal attainment (Johnson et al. 2000).

The treatment of bipolar disorder has usually involved the prescription of medications such as mood stabilisers and antipsychotics. However, greater understanding of the psychological mechanisms involved in mood disturbance has resulted in a wide range of psychological therapies proving to be successful in the management of bipolar disorder. Cognitive behavioural therapy [see COGNITIVE (BEHAVIOUR) THERAPY], interpersonal and social rhythm therapy and family therapy have recently been studied as psychological interventions for bipolar patients, and there is some preliminary evidence that these can be effective.

ST

Abraham, K. 1911/1927: Notes on the psychoanalytic investigation and treatment of manic-depressive insanity and allied conditions. In Jones, E. (ed.), *Selected Papers of Karl Abraham.* London: Hogarth. **American Psychiatric Association** 1994: *Diagnostic and Statistical Manual of Mental Disorders* (revised, 4th edn). Washington, DC: American Psychiatric Association. **Chen, Y. R., Swann, A. C. and Johnson, B. A.** 1998: Stability of diagnosis in bipolar disorder. *The Journal of Nervous and Mental Disease* 186, 17–23. **Johnson, S. L., Sandow, D., Meyer, B., Winters, R., Miller, I., Solomon, D. and Keitner, G.** 2000: Increases in manic symptoms after life events involving goal attainment. *Journal of Abnormal Psychology* 109, 721–7. **Lyon, H., Startup, M. and Bentall, R. P.** 1999: Social cognition and the manic defense. *Journal of Abnormal Psychology* 108, 273–82. **Malkoff-Schwartz, S., Frank, E., Anderson, B. P., Hlastala, S. A., Luther, J. F., Sherrill, J. T. and Kupfer, D. J.** 2000: Social rhythm disruption and stressful life events in the onset of bipolar and unipolar episodes. *Psychological Medicine* 30, 1005–16. **Scott, J., Stanton, B., Garland, A. and Ferrier, N.** 2000: Cognitive vulnerability in patients with bipolar disorder. *Psychological Medicine* 30, 467–72. **Smith, A. L. and Weissman, M. M.** 1992: National Study of Professional Activities. *American Journal of Psychiatry* 11, 1499–505. **Woods, S. W.** 2000: The economic burden of bipolar disease. *Journal of Clinical Psychiatry* 61 (suppl. 13), 38–41. **Torrey, E. F., Bowler, A. E., Taylor, E. H. and Gottesman, I. I.** 1994: *Schizophrenia and Manic-depressive Disorder.* New York: Basic Books.

borderline personality disorder

Borderline personality disorder is defined in DSM-IV (American Psychiatric Association 1994) as 'a pervasive pattern of instability of interpersonal RELATIONSHIPS (see s. 5), self-image, and affects, and marked IMPULSIVITY' (see s. 6). The disorder is so named because, as originally conceived by psychoanalytic theorists, it lies at the borderline between neurosis and PSYCHOSIS, making engagement in the process of PSYCHOANALYSIS (see s. 1) very difficult. People described as having the disorder are impulsive and have highly unstable SELF-CONCEPTS (see s. 4 and s. 5). They may be highly concerned about possible abandonment by partners and attempt extreme measures to avoid this. They often have extremely variable moods, oscillating between feelings of depression and euphoria in response to changes in their perceptions of other people, and also experiencing ANXIETY (see s. 6), irritability and anger. They are at high risk of attempting suicide or self-harm.

There is no pharmacological treatment for borderline personality disorder, although drugs may be prescribed in an effort to manage particular symptoms. It is accepted that psychological treatment may have to be long-term, and both psychoanalytic therapy and cognitive behav-ioural therapy have been recommended for borderline patients. Recently, some psychological interventions have been developed specifically for this purpose (Linehan 1993; Ryle 1991). [See COGNITIVE (BEHAVIOUR) THERAPY]

PK

Linehan, M. 1993: *Cognitive-behavioral Treatment of Borderline Personality Disorder*. London: Guilford Press. **Ryle, A.** 1991: *Cognitive-analytic Therapy: Active Participation in Change*. London: Wiley.

C

Camberwell family interview (CFI) A structured interview for assessing EXPRESSED EMOTION in the spouses, relatives or close associates of psychiatric patients, developed by Brown and Rutter (1966). The interview is scored for critical comments (criticisms of particular actions by the patient, which are counted), hostility (general criticisms of the patient, for example, 'He's so lazy', scored on a 1–5 scale), emotional over-involvement (extreme emotional distress accompanied by self-sacrificing and overprotective behaviour towards the patient, scored on a 1–5 scale), positive comments (statements of praise for particular actions, which are counted) and warmth (general positive remarks about the patient, scored on a 1–5 scale). In practice, only the critical comments, hostility and emotional over-involvement scales are used, as high scores on these scales have been shown to predict the likelihood that the patient will relapse.   *RB*

Brown, G. W. and Rutter, M. 1966. The measurement of family activities and relationships: a methodological study. *Human Relations* 19, 241–63.

Capgras syndrome Capgras syndrome is the most prevalent of a group of specific DELUSIONS referred to as the delusional misidentification syndromes. It involves the belief that familiar others have been replaced by imposters. People with Capgras syndrome will argue that these imposters look more or less the same as the replaced individual, but often claim to be able to discern small differences in appearance. The syndrome is named after the French psychiatrist Joseph Capgras, who first described the case of Madam M., who believed that her children, husband and doctor, among others, had been replaced by imposters (Capgras and Reboul-Lachaux 1923/1994).

Capgras delusions can occur in the context of several neurological and psychiatric conditions, but are most often seen in people with SCHIZOPHRENIA. In recent years, psychologists have attempted to understand Capgras syndrome in terms of a subtle impairment of face recognition at an emotional level, causing sufferers to lack a feeling of familiarity when seeing people they know well (Ellis and Lewis, 2001).   *RC*

Capgras, J. and Reboul-Lachaux, J. 1923/1994: L'illusion des 'sosies' dans un delire systematise chronique. *History of Psychiatry* 5, 117–30. **Ellis, H. D. and Lewis, M. B.** 2001. Capgras delusion: a window on face recognition. *Trends in Cognitive Sciences* 5, 149–56.

case formulation An individually tailored model of a patient's psychological difficulties; used by (especially cognitive-behavioural) therapists to guide treatment interventions.   *RB*

categorical model The general approach to classifying psychiatric disorders that separates them into different categories of illness, such as SCHIZOPHRENIA and BIPOLAR DISORDER. To be contrasted with other, for example, dimensional, approaches to psychiatric classification. *RB*

childhood neurological disorders Child neurological disorders are a consequence of developmental impairments or acquired damage to the central nervous system (Aicardi 1998). Neurological disorders that are typically present at birth include cerebral palsy, epilepsy and genetic conditions. Trauma to the central nervous system, such as head injuries and infections, can also cause neurological disorders. The effect of these disorders is considered in terms of their impact on health, motor and sensory function, cognition, social development and behaviour. Neurodevelopmental disorders, such as AUTISM (see s. 6), ATTENTION-DEFICIT HYPERACTIVITY DISORDER (ADHD) and dyspraxia are defined primarily by their behavioural effects.   *PR*

Aicardi, J. 1998: *Diseases of the Nervous System in Childhood* (2nd edn). Cambridge: Cambridge University Press.

chronic fatigue syndrome (CFS) Also known as myalgic encephalomyelitis (ME), CFS is an illness characterised by severe fatigue of unknown origin, lasting for six months or more, and causing substantial impairment to functioning. Other symptoms such as muscle PAIN, sleep (see s. 2, SLEEP AND BIOLOGICAL RHYTHMS) disturbance and memory problems may be present. CFS is diagnosed in accordance with agreed symptom criteria, after medical and psychiatric explanations for the fatigue have been ruled out. People with CFS experience severe disruption to their lives, often giving up work and social activities. The cause of CFS is unknown; some commentators believe that there are likely to be a variety of triggering factors, including acute illness or trauma, but that once the condition has become established, other factors such as limiting activity to avoid exacerbation of symptoms, may play a role in maintaining the condition (see Afari and Buchwald 2003, for a recent review of CFS). At present, it appears that the best treatment for CFS is COGNITIVE (BEHAVIOUR) THERAPY, with carefully graded increases in activity (Whiting et al. 2001).

Afari, N. and Buchwald, D. 2003: Chronic fatigue syndrome: a review. *American Journal of Psychiatry* 160, 221–36. **Whiting, P., Bagnall, A. M., Sowden, A. J. et al.** 2001: Interventions for the treatment and management of chronic fatigue syndrome – a systematic review. *Journal of the American Medical Association* 286, 1360–8.

cingulotomy A type of PSYCHOSURGERY sometimes recommended for patients suffering from OBSESSIVE-COMPULSIVE DISORDER who have failed to respond to psychological or pharmacological treatments.   *RB*

circadian dysrhythmia Disregulation of the circadian rhythm, leading to lack of synchrony between feelings of alertness and fatigue and the rhythm of daily events; thought to play a role in DEPRESSION, BIPOLAR DISORDER and CHRONIC FATIGUE SYNDROME.   *RB*

client-centred psychotherapy

Client-centred PSYCHOTHERAPY is a type of psychological treatment developed by Carl Rogers (1902–87). The therapy is highly non-directive, in that patients ('clients') are not given advice or homework assignments, but are encouraged to explore their own thoughts and feelings in the context of a relationship of acceptance. One of the main techniques used by the therapist is reflection; by rephrasing the patient's statements and reflecting them back, the therapist hopes to facilitate self-understanding.

Rogers (1951) believed that all individuals have the capacity for personal growth, and that this will occur if certain essential conditions are met. He believed that the therapist could provide these essential conditions in the context of a relationship characterised by genuineness, unconditional positive regard and empathic understanding.

Client-centred therapy is widely used by counsellors to help people who are experiencing problems of living. It is rarely used to treat serious psychiatric conditions and is usually considered ineffective for this purpose.   *RB*

Rogers, C. 1951. *Client-centered Therapy: Its Current Practice.* Boston: Houghton Mifflin.

clinical psychology

Clinical psychology is the branch of psychology concerned with the application of psychological theories and methods to clinical problems. Most clinical psychologists are involved in the direct assessment and treatment of patients, but some also undertake a supervisory or consultancy role with other professional groups.

Clinical psychology became established as a profession in Britain and the United States soon after World War II (see s. 1, WAR AND PSYCHOLOGY), but has been established more recently elsewhere. Entry into the profession generally requires a first degree in psychology followed by further training. In the USA, a doctoral level qualification was required at the outset, whereas the earliest British clinical psychology training schemes led either to masters degrees or a diploma awarded by the BRITISH PSYCHOLOGICAL SOCIETY (see s. 1); the current three-year postgraduate training leading to a professional doctorate (e.g. D.Clin.Psych.) only became standard in the UK in the 1990s. In both countries the actual professional role of clinical psychologists has evolved markedly, from an early focus on assessment and psychometric testing to a current role on intervention and therapy. In some states of the USA there is even a move towards allowing specially trained clinical psychologists 'prescription privileges' (the legal right to prescribe psychiatric drugs). Similarly, in the early days of the profession, clinical psychologists mostly worked under the direction of psychiatrists (in large psychiatric hospitals, often responding as technicians to requests for PERSONALITY (see s. 1 and s. 6) or INTELLIGENCE (see s. 4) assessments), whereas now they work as independent professionals, either as members of multidisciplinary teams or on their own in psychology clinics (the UK National Health Service has departments of clinical psychology in most parts of the country) or private practice. Whereas in the past psychiatrists often insisted that they should screen all patients prior to referral to a clinical psychologist, today referrals may be taken from family doctors, psychiatrists, other physicians, or patients may even refer themselves directly. It is fair to say that these changes have been hard won, and have required considerable lobbying by clinical psychologists, usually against resistance from organised psychiatry. In the United States, clinical psychologists have often resorted to the courts in order to obtain the right to describe themselves as competent in treating psychiatric disorders, to train in PSYCHOANALYSIS (see s. 1) and to continue to treat their own patients after admission to hospitals – all practices at one time opposed by the American Psychiatric Association.

There are many areas of specialisation within the profession of clinical psychology, including adult mental health, child mental health, MENTAL RETARDATION (see also s. 4), clinical neuropsychology, forensic clinical psychology (working with offenders) and clinical health psychology (working with patients who have physical problems). In the USA some degree of specialisation is possible during the doctoral-level training, but the UK doctoral qualification is generic (trainees do not specialise and acquire some experience and training in each of the major areas of practice) and graduates must therefore acquire further specialist training after qualifying (usually during their first few years of practice).

Guidance for those thinking of pursuing careers in clinical psychology is available in books by Marzillier and Hall (1999) (for UK training) and Sayette, Mayne and Norcross (2004) (for training in the USA). (See also s. 1, CLINICAL PSYCHOLOGY)   *RB*

Marzillier, J. and Hall, J. (eds) 1999: *What is Clinical Psychology?* Oxford: Oxford University Press. **Sayette, M. A., Mayne, T. J. and Norcross, J. C. (eds)** 2004: *Insider's Guide to Graduate Programs in Clinical and Counselling Psychology.* New York: Guilford Press.

clozaril (clozapine)

An ATYPICAL ANTIPSYCHOTIC DRUG first synthesised in the 1960s but rarely used before the 1990s because of fears of agranularcytosis (proliferation of the white blood cells), a potential fatal side effect. Its reintroduction followed the discovery that clozapine produced few extra-pyramidal side effects, and could be used to treat patients who had not responded to other ANTIPSYCHOTIC DRUGS. Regular blood tests are now used to detect the onset of agranularcytosis, in which case use of the drug must be discontinued immediately.   *RB*

cognitive (behaviour) therapy

The term COGNITIVE (see s. 1, COGNITIVE PSYCHOLOGY) therapy refers specifically to the psychotherapeutic approach developed by the American psychiatrist Aron T. Beck (1976) and his followers. Cognitive behaviour therapy is a generic term for a broad therapeutic approach that combines the cognitive techniques of Beck and others with the BEHAVIOUR THERAPY intervention strategies developed by an earlier generation of psychotherapists. Treatment typically includes the use of techniques designed to help patients become aware of and change their dysfunctional appraisals of their experiences, and also practical exercises such as BEHAVIOURAL EXPERIMENTS, designed to help patients learn new ways of coping. Cognitive behaviour therapy is practiced by a wide range of practitioners, especially clinical psychologists, but also some psychiatrists and specially trained nurses.

The origins of cognitive behaviour therapy can be traced to the work of Beck and also the American psychologist Albert Ellis (1962). Beck and Ellis independently began to introduce cognitive techniques into their practice as a result of dissatisfaction with the effectiveness of psychodynamic techniques. Beck's approach became known as cognitive therapy whereas Ellis's became known as rational emotive therapy. Common to both are the assumptions that psychological distress is a consequence of maladaptive interpretations of events, and that patients can learn to recognise these interpretations and substitute them with interpretations that are more adaptive. Early indications of the success of these approaches occurred just as behaviour therapists were questioning whether their techniques really conformed to learning principles derived from the animal laboratory, and also with the rise of the cognitive approach within mainstream psychology (Mahoney 1974). It was for these reasons that many behaviour therapists embraced the new cognitive strategies.

Beck's therapy originally focused on depression and assumed that episodes of negative mood are triggered by negative automatic thoughts [see NEGATIVE THOUGHT DISORDER] about the SELF (see s. 1, s. 4 and s. 5), the world and the future, which were, in turn, the product of distortions of REASONING (see s. 3) and mental SCHEMAS (see s. 3) that served to bias the individual towards pessimistic interpretations of events. Ellis's approach has focused on challenging 'irrational' BELIEFS (see s. 5) that are said to be common to a range of psychopathologies. Although both approaches are still in use today, it is Beck's that has been the most influential and subjected to most research. Since its inception, cognitive behaviour therapy has proven to be a highly adaptable approach, and has been used to treat ANXIETY DISORDERS (Wells 1997), PERSONALITY DISORDERS (Young 1999) and even psychotic disorders, such as BIPOLAR DISORDER (Basco and Rush 1996) and SCHIZOPHRENIA (Morrison, Renton, Dunn, Williams and Bentall 2003). *RB*

Basco, M. R. and Rush, A. J. 1996: *Cognitive-behavioral Therapy for Bipolar Disorder.* New York: Guilford Press. **Beck, A. T.** 1976: *Cognitive Therapy and the Emotional Disorders.* New York: International Universities Press. **Ellis, A.** 1962: *Reason and Emotion in Psychotherapy.* New York: Lyle Stuart. **Mahoney, M. J.** 1974: *Cognition and Behavior Modification.* Cambridge MA: Ballinger. **Morrison, A. P., Renton, J. C., Dunn, H., Williams, S., and Bentall, R. P.** 2003: *Cognitive Therapy for Psychosis: A Formulation-based Approach.* London: Brunner-Routledge. **Wells, A.** 1997: *Cognitive Therapy of Anxiety.* Chichester: Wiley. **Young, J. E.** 1999: *Cognitive Therapy for Personality Disorders: A Schema-focused Approach* (3rd edn). Sarasota FL: Professional Resource Press.

collective unconscious The concept of the 'collective unconscious' was proposed by Carl Justav Jung (1875–1961), a disciple of Freud who broke away to form his own school of psychotherapy. Noting similar themes in the mythology and literature of many cultures, and also that these themes were evident in his patients' dreams, Jung proposed that, in addition to the individual unconscious, there is an inherited or collective unconscious. The collective unconscious contains 'archetypes' – common ideas or patterns of thinking that are evident in dreams, legends, story-telling and art. *RB*

compliance/adherence/concordance The patient's adherence to a programme of treatment prescribed by a doctor or PSYCHOTHERAPIST; use of the term 'compliance' is sometimes thought to be ethically questionable because it seems to imply a duty by the patient to follow the advice of the clinician under any circumstances. The terms 'adherence' (to describe the degree to which the patient follows treatment) or 'concordance' (to describe the agreement between the clinician and patient about the treatment) are therefore often preferred. *RB*

conduct disorder Conduct disorder is a childhood condition consisting of persistent antisocial behaviour that violates the rights of other people, including aggressive behaviour, destruction of property, deceitfulness or theft and violation of rules. It is almost four times more common in boys than girls. It is commonly found together with ATTENTION-DEFICIT HYPERACTIVITY DISORDER (ADHD) and this co-morbidity is associated with neuropsychological impairment in EXECUTIVE FUNCTIONing (see s. 4). There is no single cause of conduct disorder and it is difficult to identify primary risk factors because of the complex transactions that occur across time in which the child affects their environment and the environment affects the child. However, child TEMPERAMENT (see s. 4) and coercive PARENTING (see s. 4) practices are key risk factors that can be identified early and these predict long-term outcome of antisocial behaviour in adult life. Two developmental pathways of antisocial behaviour have been identified, 'life-course persistent' and 'adolescence-limited', that are distinguishable in terms of age of onset, biological basis, maladaptiveness and prognosis (Caspi and Moffitt 1995). *RB*

Caspi, A. and Moffitt, T. 1995: The continuity of maladaptive behaviour: from description to understanding in the study of antisocial behaviour. In Cicchetti, D. and Cohen, D. J. (eds), *Developmental Psychopathology, Vol 2: Risk, Disorder and Adaptation* New York: Wiley, 472–511.

coping Modern research on coping has proliferated alongside the development of the transactional model of stress (e.g. Lazarus and Folkman 1984). This model suggests that when people are faced with negative or potentially threatening events, the way in which they cope with the events plays an important role in determining their appraisal of the events, their emotional responses to them and, ultimately, their physical and psychological well-being.

Folkman et al. (1986) defined coping as 'the person's cognitive and behavioural efforts to manage (reduce, minimise, master or tolerate) the internal and external demands of the person-environment transaction that is appraised as taxing or exceeding the resources of the person.' While it is important to note that a simple classification of coping behaviours vastly understates the complex and dynamic relationship between stress and coping, much of the research effort on coping has gone into describing different dimensions of coping strategies, and the effects of implementing these strategies (Endler and Parker 1990). One broad categorisation is the division of coping strategies into those which function to try to ame-liorate the harm caused by the problem (problem-focused coping), and those which function to regulate the distress engendered by the problem (emotion-focused coping). Endler and Parker (1990) have suggested that there is another underlying dimension of coping to be taken into account, namely, avoidance coping (for example, going out for a drink rather than getting on with stressful work such as studying for an exam).

There is a debate in the literature about the extent to which it is sensible to describe generic and persistent cop-ing styles (dispositional coping), as opposed to describing coping attempts in different situations (situational cop-ing); however, there is some evidence for the contention that people have habitual styles of coping. Unfortunately, few general conclusions can be drawn about the effective-ness or adaptiveness of different coping strategies, proba-bly because different strategies are effective for different problems, in different contexts and at different stages of dealing with a problem (Zeidner and Saklofske 1996).

Endler, N. S. and Parker, D. A. 1990: Multidimensional assessment of coping: a critical evaluation. *Journal of Personality and Social Psychology* 58, 844–54. **Folkman, S., Lazarus, R. S., Dunkel-Schetter, C., DeLongis, A. and Gruen, R. J.** 1986: The dynamics of a stressful encounter: cognitive appraisal, coping and encounter outcomes. *Journal of Personality and Social Psychology* 50, 992–103. **Lazarus, R. S. and Folkman, S.** 1984: *Stress Appraisal and Coping.* New York: Springer. **Zeidner, M. and Saklofske, D.** 1996: Adaptive and maladaptive coping. In Zeidner, M. and Endler, N. S. (eds), *Handbook of Coping. Theory, Research and Applications.* New York: Wiley, 505–31.

Cotard syndrome

When Cotard (1882) originally described the syndrome that now bears his name, he chose the term 'delire de negation' – nihilistic DELUSIONS – to reflect its most prominent characteristic. The original patient, Mlle X., denied the existence of many parts of her body, claimed that she did not need to eat and felt she was damned.

Cotard syndrome patients experience feelings of unreal-ity and nihilistic delusions. In the most severe but very rare form, patients believe that they are dead. It is unclear whether the syndrome is best understood as a form of psy-chotic DEPRESSION. What is clear is that all cases with Cotard syndrome score highly for depression, have suici-dal thoughts and suffer from delusions which are depres-sive in nature. Young and Leafhead (1996) have argued that patients with this syndrome also display the charac-teristic attributional style associated with depression. *RC*

Cotard, J. 1882: Du delires des negations. *Archives de Neurologie* 4, 152–70. **Young, A. W. and Leafhead, K. M.** 1996: Betwixt life and death: case studies of the Cotard delusion. In Halligan, P. W. and Marshall, J. C. (eds), *Method in Madness: Case Studies in Cognitive Neuropsychiatry.* Hove: Psychology Press.

counter-transference

A term used by psychody-namic therapists to describe the therapist's positive or negative emotional response to the patient. *RB*

culture-bound syndromes

The culture-bound syndromes are psychiatric disorders that appear to be restricted to a particular CULTURE (see s. 1 and s. 5) (Helman 1994). Examples include koro (an illness suf-fered by Chinese people, usually males, who believe that their sexual organs are shrinking), latah (experienced by Indonesians and characterised by an exaggerated startle response, which includes shouting rude words and mim-icking the behaviour of those nearby) and witiko psy-chosis (a rare disorder in which Algonkian-speaking Indians of Canada believe themselves to be possessed by vampires).

The culture-bound syndromes have been a source of much controversy amongst psychopathologists. They are relevant to a larger debate about whether and to what extent psychiatric disorders are universal phenomena (Klienman 1988). Some assume that the culture-bound syndromes are atypical and culturally shaped expressions of psychiatric disorders that are present in all cultures. For example, it is claimed that witiko psychosis is an atypical form of SCHIZOPHRENIA. However, anthropologists tend to be critical of the assumption that psychological distress presents in universal forms and that these forms have been uniquely and accurately described by western psychiatry. It has also been objected that, when attempt-ing to accommodate the culture-bound syndromes within a western framework, psychiatrists typically ignore spe-cific local factors that may have shaped the observed behaviour. For example, there is evidence that latah evolved as a way of mimicking the unintelligible demands of European colonialists. It is also often forgotten that disorders widely recognised in some parts of the developed world might actually be culture-bound because they are not seen elsewhere. Anorexia nervosa and chronic fatigue syndrome may well be culture-bound syndromes.

During the preparation of the fourth edition of the DSM, the US National Institute of Mental Health set up a task force to develop proposals for including cultural information (Mezzich, Fabrega and Klienman 1992). Most of the recommendations of the task force were ignored but a list of culture-bound syndromes was included as an appendix. *RB*

Helman, C. G. 1994: *Culture, Health and Illness* (3rd edn). London: Butterworth and Heinemann. **Klienman, A.** 1988: *Rethinking Psychiatry.* New York: Free Press. **Mezzich, J. E., Fabrega, H. and Klienman, A.** 1992: Cultural validity and DSM-IV. *Journal of Nervous and Mental Disease* 180, 4.

D

defence mechanisms The concept of 'defence mechanisms' originates in PSYCHOANALYSIS (see s. 1) and refers to psychological processes which serve to protect the individual from being consciously aware of undesirable impulses or thoughts. Within PSYCHOANALYTIC THEORY (see s. 6), the function of a defence is to protect the ego, and defence mechanisms may be triggered by ANXIETY (see s. 6) due to increases in instinctual tension, anxiety due to a bad conscience or realistic threats (Rycroft 1968). Neurosis may result from maladaptive defence mechanisms.

The concept of defence is now widely accepted by psychotherapists of many schools. Specific defence mechanisms include regression (motivated FORGETTING – see s. 3), denial (refusal to believe what is obvious to others), projection (attributing one's own undesirable traits and emotions to others), displacement (transference of EMOTION (see s. 6) from an object to a more acceptable object), rationalisation (inventing a logical justification for an emotional act), regression (a flight from reality by assuming a more infantile state) and sublimation (the diverting of primitive impulses into socially acceptable channels).

RB

Rycroft, C. 1968: *A Critical Dictionary of Psychoanalysis.* Harmondsworth: Penguin.

delusional disorder A psychiatric disorder in which the main symptom is a persistent and usually systematised set of DELUSIONS, usually involving persecutory BELIEFS (see s. 5) and/or grandiose ideas.

When Kraepelin (1896–1926) attempted to create a categorical system of classifying psychiatric disorders, he divided the severe disorders (what we would now call the psychoses) into two main categories of dementia praecox (SCHIZOPHRENIA) and manic depression (encompassing what are now known as unipolar depression and BIPOLAR DISORDER). However, he came to believe that there was a third major type of PSYCHOSIS, in which only delusions were evident and the outcome was relatively good, and used the term 'PARANOIA' to describe this condition. Paranoia was held to be distinct from the paranoid sub-type of dementia praecox/schizophrenia, in which delusions were also prominent, but in which other psychotic symptoms (for example, HALLUCINATIONS) were evident. Whether or not this condition is truly separate from schizophrenia remains a matter of dispute (Munro 1997); however, the diagnosis was included in the DSM system and the term 'paranoia' was replaced with delusional disorder in the revised third edition (DSM-III-R), published in 1987. *RB*

Munro, A. 1997: Paranoia or delusional disorder. In Bhugra, D. and Munro, A. (eds), *Troublesome Disguises: Underdiagnosed Psychiatric Syndromes.* Oxford: Blackwell, 24–51.

delusional misidentification syndromes A class of delusions in which the central theme is the misidentification of others; includes the CAPGRAS SYNDROME and FREGOLI SYNDROME. *RB*

delusions A delusion has been defined as 'a false personal belief based on incorrect inference about external reality and firmly sustained in spite of what almost everyone else believes and in spite of what usually constitutes incontrovertible and obvious proof or evidence to the contrary'; (the delusion) 'is not ordinarily accepted by other members of the person's culture or subculture' (American Psychiatric Association 1994).

Delusions can be a feature of a range of neurological and psychiatric diagnoses, but are consistently associated with the psychotic disorders of SCHIZOPHRENIA, BIPOLAR DISORDER and psychotic DEPRESSION. In schizophrenia the most common forms of delusions are persecutory or paranoid (in which it is believed that other people mean one harm) and delusions of control (in which it is believed that one's thoughts or actions are under the control of some alien force or power). Sartorius, Shapiro and Jablensky (1974) found that 65 per cent of a large sample of people with schizophrenia, collected internationally, suffered from delusions of persecution. In the affective disorders delusions tend to be mood congruent (e.g. delusions of guilt).

Delusions can vary from full delusions, in which the person is completely convinced about the truth of their belief, to partial delusions in which some doubt is expressed. Some delusions extend to envelop all aspects of life, forming a 'delusional system', while others are highly specific and relate only to certain people or situations. Historically it has been argued that delusions tend to be incorrigible (resistant to change), but with the increased acknowledgement of the benefits of COGNITIVE (BEHAVIOUR) THERAPY for psychotic disorders, this is no longer such a widely held view (Rector and Beck 2001). Similarly, the argument that delusions are 'un-understandable' (Jaspers 1913/1963) or meaningless is no longer widely accepted.

Several psychological theories have been proposed to account for delusion formation. Some delusions seem to arise from attempts to explain anomalous perceptual experiences (Maher 1992). Deluded patients in general seem to 'jump to conclusions' when reasoning about sequentially presented information, but show no evidence of deficits on more formal measures of reasoning (Garety and Freeman 1999). THEORY OF MIND (see s. 4) deficits (problems in understanding the beliefs and intentions of others) and an abnormal ATTRIBUTIONAL STYLE have been implicated in persecutory delusions (Bentall, Corcoran, Howard, Blackwood and Kinderman 2001).

RB

American Psychiatric Association 1994: *Diagnostic and Statistical Manual for Mental Disorders* (4th edn). Washington, DC: APA. **Bentall, R. P., Corcoran, R., Howard, R., Blackwood, R. and Kinderman, P.** 2001: Persecutory delusions: a review and theoretical integration. *Clinical Psychology Review* 21, 1143–92. **Garety, P. and Freeman, D.** 1999: Cognitive approaches to delusions: a critical review of theories and evidence. *British Journal of Clinical Psychology.* **Jaspers, K.**

1913/1963: *General Psychopathology* (translated by J. Hoenig and M. W. Hamilton). Manchester: Manchester University Press. **Maher, B. A.** 1992: Models and methods for the study of reasoning in delusions. *Revue Européenne de Psychologie Appliqée* 42, 97–102. **Rector, N. A. and Beck, A. T.** 2001: Cognitive behavioural therapy for schizophrenia: an empirical review. *Journal of Nervous and Mental Disease* 189, 278–87. **Sartorius, N., Shapiro, R. and Jablensky, A.** 1974: The international pilot study of schizophrenia. *Schizophrenia Bulletin* 1, 21–5.

depression Depression is a negative, unpleasant mood state experienced to some extent, and usually transiently, by most people, and which has therefore been dubbed 'the common cold of PSYCHIATRY' (Rosenhan and Seligman 1989). However, more severe depression is experienced by patients suffering from a wide range of psychiatric disorders. Depression is regarded as a mood disorder in its own right when negative mood is seen as the primary and most distressing symptom experienced by a patient. In the DSM system, patients suffering from this form of depression are given the diagnosis of major depressive disorder. Other symptoms include cognitive features (low SELF-ESTEEM (see also s. 5), hopelessness) and somatic symptoms, including fatigue, insomnia, weight loss and loss of libido). In extreme cases, depression can become psychotic, in which case the individual experiences HALLUCINATIONS and DELUSIONS that are congruent with negative mood (e.g. abusive voices; beliefs about responsibility for crimes of historic proportions). There is a high risk of suicide associated with severe depression, especially when the patient feels hopeless about the future (Beck, Steer, Kovacs and Garrison 1985).

Despite the apparent transparency of the concept of depression, it has evolved in meaning over time. The term was originally introduced into psychiatry in the middle of the nineteenth century to signify the opposite mood state to excitement and agitation, and only entered common usage in the early twentieth century (Berrios 1995). In both patient samples and the normal population, severity of depression usually correlates very highly with severity of ANXIETY (see s. 6) (Goldberg and Huxley 1992), and it can sometimes be difficult to decide which diagnosis is merited. However, the patient whose primary problem is depression is usually preoccupied by thoughts about loss or failure, whereas the anxious patient is usually preoccupied by future threats (of course, patients can be concerned about both). Most attempts to sub-type depression into different sub-types – for example, reactive (said to involve mainly cognitive symptoms and to occur in reaction to negative life events) and endogenous (said to largely involve somatic symptoms arising from within and unrelated to life events) – have never been convincing and have been abandoned by most researchers. However, following the work of the Austrian psychiatrist Karl Leonhard (1904–88), the distinction between unipolar depression (major depression in the absence of a history of MANIA or HYPOMANIA) and BIPOLAR DISORDER (in which recurring episodes of depression and either mania or hypomania are experienced) is now widely accepted. There has also been considerable interest in the hypothesis of a specific sub-type of depression – SEASONAL AFFECTIVE DISORDER (see s. 6) – that occurs in the winter months, and which may be triggered by inadequate exposure to daylight.

Many theories of depression have been proposed, putting weight on a variety of biological, psychological and environmental factors. Genetic research indicates that there are constitutional differences in vulnerability to depressive episodes, although the HERITABILITY (see s. 4) of unipolar depression appears to be less than for bipolar disorder (Trimble 1996). Neurochemical research, on the other hand, has highlighted the role of the serotonergic system. The apparent efficacy of SELECTIVE SEROTONIN REUPTAKE INHIBITORS as ANTIDEPRESSANTS provides some support for this hypothesis. Some biological investigators have focused their attention on sleep (see s. 2, SLEEP AND BIOLOGICAL RHYTHMS), arguing that desynchrony of the circadian rhythm [see CIRCADIAN DYSRYTHMIA] can cause persistent fatigue which, in turn, engenders a feeling of failure and hopelessness, which in turn leads to depression (Healy 1987).

Research into the role of life events has consistently shown that episodes of depression tend to follow adverse experiences. In a landmark study by Brown and Harris (1978), it was found that women who became depressed typically experienced an adverse event in the weeks prior to an episode, but that only a proportion of women who experienced such events became depressed. This finding, which has been well replicated in both male and female samples, raises the question of why some people are more vulnerable to depression than others. In Brown and Harris's study, they attempted to identify social vulnerability factors, finding that women who had lost their mothers at an early age, who were unemployed and had small children at home, and who lacked a supportive, confiding relationship were especially vulnerable to the INFLUENCE (see s. 1) of adverse events. However, most psychologists have focused their attention on cognitive and PERSONALITY (see s. 1 and s. 6) characteristics that might confer vulnerability to depression, and three main theories have attracted particular attention from researchers.

The LEARNED HELPLESSNESS (see s. 3) theory of depression has evolved from early behavioural models, which assumed that the main characteristic of the disorder is lack of behaviour, consequent on a loss of social REINFORCEMENT (see s. 3). In its latest form (Abramson, Metalsky and Alloy 1989), the theory proposes that people who are vulnerable to depression have an abnormal ATTRIBUTIONAL STYLE, so that they tend to attribute negative experiences to causes that are internal (to do with the self), global (affecting all areas of life) and stable (unchangeable). For this reason they become hopeless and depressed when faced with adverse life events. This model has been supported by comparisons between depressed patients and others and also in some prospective studies. A quite similar approach, known as the cognitive model of depression, was proposed by the psychiatrist Aron T. Beck, on the basis of his clinical experience developing COGNITIVE (BEHAVIOUR) THERAPY for depressed patients (Beck, Rush, Shaw and Emery 1979). According to this model, negative automatic thoughts about the self, the world and the future (the negative cognitive triad) are the immediate cause of depressed mood, but these thoughts arise as a consequence of systematic errors of thinking (for example, the tendency towards 'black and white' absolutist dichotomous thinking), and mental SCHEMAS (see s. 3) that serve to maintain a negative bias in MEMORY (see s. 1) and PERCEPTION (see s. 1). This model also enjoys considerable support, both from studies showing a bias towards the RECALL (see s. 3) of negative information in depressed people, and also from clinical studies which show cognitive behaviour therapy to be an effective treatment. Research initiated by Nolem-Hoeksema, on the other hand, has emphasised the different ways in which people respond to depressed mood, arguing that, as depression is very common, the ability to recover may distinguish depressed patients from others. In a series of experimental, naturalistic and even prospective studies (e.g. Nolen-Hoeksema and Morrow 1991), she has shown that ruminating about a depressed mood tends to prolong it, whereas engaging in distracting or problem-solving activities may have the opposite effect.

The first ANTIDEPRESSANT DRUGS, the tricyclics [see TRICYCLIC ANTIDEPRESSANTS] such as imipramine, were discovered by accident. Today, drug treatment for depression is more likely to involve the use of SELECTIVE SEROTONIN REUPTAKE INHIBITORS, such as fluoxetine (Prozac), which have a kinder side-effect profile than earlier medications, but which are probably no more effective at relieving symptoms. In cases of severe depression, ELECTOCONVULSIVE THERAPY (ECT) is sometimes used. However, a number of psychological therapies have been shown to be effective for depression, including COGNITIVE BEHAVIOUR THERAPY, and interpersonal therapy (a form of brief psychodynamic treatment). *RB*

Abramson, L. Y., Metalsky, G. I. and Alloy, L. B. 1989: Hopelessness depression: a theory-based subtype of depression. *Psychological Review* 96, 358–72. Beck, A. T., Rush, A. J., Shaw, B. F. and Emery, G. 1979: *Cognitive Therapy of Depression*. New York: Guilford Press. Beck, A. T., Steer, R. A., Kovacs, M. and Garrison, B. 1985: Hopelessness and eventual suicide: a ten-year prospective study of patients hospitalized with suicidal ideation. *American Journal of Psychiatry* 142, 559–63. Berrios, G. E. 1995: Mood disorders. In Berrios, G. and Porter, R. (eds), *A History of Clinical Psychiatry*. London: Athlone Press, 384–408. Brown, G. W. and Harris, T. 1978: *Social Origins of Depression*. New York: Free Press. Goldberg, D. and Huxley, P. 1992: *Common Mental Disorders: A Bio-social Model*. London: Routledge. Healy, D. 1987: Rhythm and blues: neurochemical, neuropharmacological and neuropsychological implications of a hypothesis of circadian rhythm dysfunction in the affective disorders. *Psychopharmacology* 93, 271–85. Nolen-Hoeksema, S. and Morrow, J. 1991: A prospective study of depression and post-traumatic stress symptoms after a natural disaster: the 1989 Loma Prieta earthquake. *Journal of Personality and Social Psychology* 61, 115–21. Rosenhan, D. L. and Seligman, M. E. P. 1989: *Abnormal Psychology* (2nd edn). New York: W. W. Norton. Trimble, M. 1996: *Biological Psychiatry* (2nd edn). Chichester: Wiley.

developmental disorders Developmental disorders are those conditions, normally identified by behavioural signs, which seriously disrupt the course of normal psychological development. The psychological study of developmental disorders has two major goals: (1) understanding the condition of interest in order to prevent or help future cases; (2) using these examples of how development can go awry to deepen understanding of typical development. Developmental disorders are defined by DSM-IV as clinical conditions that are first diagnosed in infancy, childhood or adolescence. Examples include autistic spectrum disorders (ASD), ATTENTION-DEFICIT HYPERACTIVITY DISORDER (ADHD) and dyslexia. Deficits are found in domains as varied as ATTENTION (see s. 3), SOCIAL COGNITION (see s. 4 and s. 5), PERCEPTION (see s. 1), LANGUAGE (see s. 2) and motor coordination.

Historically, the study of developmental disorders has been greatly influenced by cognitive neuroscience models, which use cases of specific brain injury to explore the relationship between brain areas and cognitive functions. Such cases include Paul Broca's famous patient 'Tan', so-called because this was the only syllable he could utter (Gleitman 1991). Tan's expressive APHASIA (see s. 3) resulted from a LESION (see s. 2) of the left fontal lobe in a region now known as Broca's area.

Cognitive neuropsychology has therefore produced models which suggest that specific functions, such as WORKING MEMORY (see s. 3) or language, are found in corresponding specific brain modules (Fodor 1983). These findings support a relatively nativist approach to understanding developmental disorders in which impairments arise from damage to modules either prenatally or early in life. This approach can be exemplified by the popular theory that ASD results from damage to an innately specified THEORY OF MIND (see s. 4) module (Segal 1996). It is suggested that theory of mind underpins all social cognition and gives rise to the deficits in social interaction and communication which are used to define ASD.

Most recently, the psychological approach to developmental disorders has been characterised by developmental psychopathology, which invokes developmental, genetic, neuropsychological, cognitive, evolutionary and cultural risk factors for developmental disorders. One of the most useful conceptualisations of this multifaceted approach to understanding developmental disorders is Waddington's (1975) epigenetic landscape. Waddington envisions the child as a ball rolling over an undulating surface. Most children will follow the simplest path, pulled onwards by time. However, some individuals may be pushed off course by neural insult, interactions with parents and SIBLINGS (see s. 4), or even extreme deprivation. Likewise, some children may not even begin life in the usual starting place, due to genetic or prenatal factors. The eventual resting place of the individual depends on a wealth of influences: the same resting place may be achieved by following different paths, while overlapping paths may lead to quite different ends.

Many researchers in developmental psychopathology have suggested that childhood developmental disorders cannot be described using models gleaned from adult data (Bishop 1997). The approach suggests that time is the crucial factor in the study of developmental disorders and that such conditions can only be understood with reference to continuous processes and the child's interaction with the world (Karmiloff-Smith 1998). Such models are known as transactional, since they are based on a concept of transactions between genes and the environment, and between the child and other individuals. Within this category of approaches, social-affective models are also gaining credence, with their focus on connections between EMOTION (see s. 6) and cognition (Hobson 2002).

Constructivism is a key transactional approach which uses cutting-edge neural modelling techniques to explore influences on the development of cognitive processes such as language (Elman et al. 2001). This technique has permitted researchers to explore how apparent steps in development may result from a single LEARNING (see s. 3) ALGORITHM (see s. 3) rather than two separate mechanisms. By replicating neural insult or introducing biased learning rules, these models can illuminate the effect of abnormal initial constraints on COGNITIVE DEVELOPMENT (see s. 4). Exponents believe that this method promises to be an invaluable tool for the future of developmental PSYCHOPATHOLOGY, though critics suggest that neural models cannot confirm or deny theories in the same way as data from real cases.

Another exciting new approach is dynamic SYSTEMS THEORY (see s. 1), which aims to model development using mathematical equations (van Geert 1998). This method has been criticised for its opaqueness, since understanding requires a high standard of mathematical knowledge. However, early findings suggest that the technique may be important in suggesting how different constraints relate to development.

Whatever approach is followed, the study of developmental disorders shares many characteristics and faces frequent obstacles. The first is that most developmental disorders are defined by a selection of co-occurring symptoms and therefore exhibit a high level of heterogeneity. This heterogeneity is further exacerbated by the fact that very many developmental disorders (e.g. ADHD and dyslexia) show co-morbidity with other conditions. Co-morbidity and heterogeneity mean that it is very difficult to compare findings across different studies, a problem made more serious by the fact that developmental disorders normally occur relatively rarely in the population. As such, findings about developmental disorders are often weakened by small samples and difficulty replicating results.

Second, research into developmental disorders is usually preoccupied with cause; the goal is often to understand how a particular pattern of behaviour arose and thus understand how it can be addressed in future. Most psychologists address a single level of cause, such as the COGNITIVE (see s. 1, COGNITIVE PSYCHOLOGY) basis for a disorder. However, a strong theory must incorporate influences at genetic, biological, structural, cognitive, emotional and environmental levels.

Finally, psychological approaches to researching developmental disorders remain cut off from clinical research and treatment. This gulf between theory and practice not only conceals potential treatment techniques from disordered individuals, but also dampens the inspirational effect of clinical cases on development of theory.   *SW*

Bishop, D. V. M. 1997: Cognitive neuropsychology and developmental disorders: uncomfortable bedfellows *Quarterly Journal of Experimental Psychology* 50A: 4, 899–923. **Elman, J. L., Bates, E. A., Johnson, M. A., Karmiloff-Smith, A., Parisi, D. and Plunkett, K.** 2001: *Rethinking Innateness: A Connectionist Perspective on Development.* Cambridge MA: Bradford Books, MIT Press. **Fodor, J. A.** 1983: *The Modularity of Mind.* Cambridge MA: Bradford Books. **Gleitman, H.** 1991: *Psychology.* New York: Norton. **Hobson, P.** 2002: *The Cradle of Thought.* London: Macmillan. **Karmiloff-Smith, A.** 1998: Development itself is the key to understanding developmental disorders. *Trends in Cognitive Sciences* 2, 389–97. **Segal, G.** 1996: The modularity of theory of mind. In Carruthers, P. and Smith, P. K. (eds), *Theories of Theories of Mind.* Cambridge: Cambridge University Press. **van Geert, P.** 1998: A dynamic systems model of basic developmental mechanisms: Piaget,

Vygotsky, and beyond. *Psychological Review* 105, 634–77. **Waddington, C. H.** 1975: *The Evolution of an Evolutionist.* Ithaca NY: Cornell University Press.

dimensional models of psychiatric disorder

Dimensional models of psychiatric classification have waxed and waned in popularity in response to dissatisfaction with the more conventional categorical approach outlined in manuals such as the DSM and the ICD [see INTERNATIONAL CLASSIFICATION OF DISEASE]. Some dimensional approaches, such as that of the German psychiatrist Ernest Kretschmer (1888–1964) and the British (but German-born) psychologist H. J. Eysenck (1916–97), have assumed that mental illness is the extreme end of a NORMAL DISTRIBUTION (see s. 8) of PERSONALITY TRAITS (see s. 6). According to Eysenck, affective disorders reflect an extreme manifestation of NEUROTICISM (see s. 6), whereas the psychotic disorders reflect an extreme manifestation of PSYCHOTICISM (see s. 6), also conceived of as a PERSONALITY (see s. 1 and s. 6) dimension. In fact, although high neuroticism does seem to confer vulnerability to a wide range of psychiatric problems, Eysenck's psychoticism dimension is not clearly related to psychotic illness (Claridge and Davis 2003).

Other dimensional approaches have been proposed by psychopathologists who have been struck by the widespread presence of subclinical symptoms in population samples, or because this concept has helped resolve confusion about the genetics of psychiatric disorder – the diagnostic concept of SCHIZOTYPAL PERSONALITY DISORDER was proposed for these reasons.   *RB*

Claridge, G. and Davis, C. 2003: *Personality and Psychological Disorders.* London: Arnold.

dissociative disorders

Dissociation is a psychological mechanism, usually considered to be a defence, in which there is an apparent failure of the integration and processing of information. Under these circumstances, the human mind continues to carry out complex mental activities in channels that are apparently split off from awareness. It can be evident in normal circumstances, especially when too much awareness would hamper performance (e.g. when driving long distances and being unable to RECALL (see s. 3) the journey), or when fatigued or under stress. In fact, most people experience dissociative experiences of some type or another (Ross 1997). The observation of these phenomena has led some theorists to claim that, 'The unity of CONSCIOUSNESS (see s. 3) is illusory. Man does more than one thing at a time – all the time – and the conscious representation of these actions is never complete' (Hilgard 1977: 1).

There was considerable interest in dissociation in Victorian times, followed by a decline during the period of BEHAVIOURISM (see s. 1). Interest was resumed following Ernest Hilgard's (1977) demonstration that dissociative phenomena could be induced by hypnosis.

Clinically, dissociation is evident in cognitive phenomena such as AMNESIA (see s. 3), depersonalisation (when one's sense of one's own SELF – see s. 1, s. 4 and s. 5 – is temporarily lost) and derealisation (when one's sense of the reality of the external world is temporarily lost), but also has somatoform features (e.g. changes in PAIN – see also s. 2 – thresholds). In extreme forms, it manifests as a number of dissociative disorders (dissociative amnesia – a severe but usually temporary failure to recall previously stored information, such as life history or IDENTITY (see s. 4 and s. 5), that cannot be attributed to ordinary FORGETTING (see s. 3) or neuropsychological impairment; dissociative fugue – in which there is not only amnesia but the individual also departs from their normal surroundings and assumes a new identity; and depersonalisation disorder – in which the individual repeatedly feels detached from their own body and mental processes, as if observing them from outside) and, in its most extreme and relatively rare form, as DISSOCIATIVE IDENTITY DISORDER (formerly known as MULTIPLE PERSONALITY DISORDER, see s. 1), in which the patient apparently has several personalities which become evident at different times, may have different names and may even have amnesia for each other.

Extreme forms of dissociation appear to be a consequence of traumatic experiences that are too painful to process or to integrate with other experiences. Dissociative disorders are commonly a consequence of childhood abuse. *GW*

Hilgard, E. R. 1977: *Divided Consciousness: Multiple Controls in Human Thought and Action.* New York: Wiley. Kihlstrom, J. F. 2001: Dissociative disorders. In Sutker, P. B. and Adams, H. E. (eds), *Comprehensive Handbook of Psychopathology* (3rd edn). New York: Plenum. Ross, C. A. 1997. *Dissociative Identity Disorder.* New York: Wiley.

dissociative identity (multiple personality) disorder

Dissociative identity disorder (DID) has been one of the most controversial diagnostic categories in the history of PSYCHIATRY. According to conventional definitions, it occurs when an individual acquires separate, multiple identities, some of which may be amnesic for others and some of which may have full awareness of the others. Lay interest in the phenomenon has been stimulated by popular books describing cases studies, such as *Sybil* (Schreiber 1973).

Reports of DID increased rapidly in the 1980s and afterwards; before this time only about 200 cases were recorded in the literature (Ross 1996). The fact that dissociative identity disorder is much more common in the United States than elsewhere, and has been described differently during different historical periods, has suggested to some commentators that it is a CULTURE-BOUND SYNDROME, or even a social psychological phenomenon induced by therapists' suggestions to highly suggestible, fantasy-prone patients (Spanos 1996). (See also s. 1, MULTIPLE PERSONALITY DISORDER) *GW*

Ross, C. A. 1996: *Dissociative Identity Disorder.* New York: Wiley. Schreiber, F. R. 1973: *Sybil.* New York: Warner Paperback. Spanos, N. P. 1996: *Multiple Identities and False Memories: A Sociocognitive Perspective.* Washington, DC: American Psychological Association.

distraction

A way of responding to negative mood, characterised by the focusing of ATTENTION (see s. 3) away from unhappiness and its causes and on to pleasant or neutral stimuli that are engaging enough to prevent thoughts returning to the source of distress. Individuals with this RESPONSE STYLE may throw themselves into their work or seek out pleasant social activities when depressed. *RB*

dodo bird verdict on psychotherapeutic outcomes

Adherents of a wide variety of psychotherapeutic approaches, from mainstream psychodynamic therapy, BEHAVIOUR THERAPY and COGNITIVE THERAPY, to more esoteric methods, claim success in treating psychological disorders. Although some approaches are better supported by outcome research than others, early meta-analyses of outcome data indicated that all main therapeutic approaches are equally effective, known as the 'dodo bird' verdict (so named after a character in Lewis Carol's *Alice Through the Looking-glass*, who declares that 'Everybody has won and all must have prizes').

The dodo bird verdict has remained controversial, but has been supported by some more recent meta-analyses (Wampold et al. 1997). However, critics point out that the conclusion is based on a selective reading of meta-analytic findings, and that most analyses point to the superiority of cognitive behavioural over psychodynamic therapies for most conditions (Hunsley and Di Guilo 2002). Nonetheless, it is clear from the evidence that patient improvement is heavily influenced by common factors shared by all psychotherapies. *RB*

Hunsley, J. and Di Guilo, G. 2002: Dodo bird: phoenix or urban legend? *The Scientific Review of Mental Health Practice* 1. Wampold, B. E., Mondin, G. W., Moody, M., Stich, F., Benson, K. and Ahn, H. 1997: A meta-analysis of outcome studies comparing bona fide psychotherapies: empirically, 'all must have prizes'. *Psychological Bulletin* 122, 203–15.

dopamine theory of schizophrenia

The dopamine theory of SCHIZOPHRENIA was inspired by the discovery that ANTIPSYCHOTIC DRUGS all blocked the dopamine D2 receptor (see s. 2, RECEPTORS), and by the observation that excessive use of amphetamine (which increases the turnover of dopamine in the brain) induced a schizophrenia-like PSYCHOSIS in healthy people. Together, these findings suggested that schizophrenia was caused by an abnormality in the dopaminergic pathways in the brain. Further evidence for the theory came from patients with Parkinson's disease, who sometimes experience psychotic symptoms as a consequence of taking drugs designed to increase the availability of dopamine in the brain; conversely, schizophrenia patients treated with antipsychotic drugs often experience Parkinsonian symptoms (stiffness, tremor) as a side effect.

Despite early enthusiasm for the theory in the 1970s, the search for dopamine abnormalities in the brains of schizophrenia patients has been very slow to yield results. For example, studies of the metabolites of dopamine have suggested that dopamine turnover is usually normal in schizophrenia patients. This led to a revised version of the theory in which it was proposed that schizophrenia patients have too many D2 receptors. Testing this hypothesis proved complicated because animal studies have shown that consumption of antipsychotic drugs leads to an increase in D2 receptor density. An early positron emission tomography study showing abnormal D2 receptor density in drug-naïve schizophrenia patients (Wong et al. 1986) has not been replicated, and some studies show no relation between receptor density and symptoms (Syvaelahti, Raekkoelaeinen, Aaltonen, Lehtinen and Hietala, 2000). Reviewing the theory, one of its main authors recently concluded that it continues to be unproven (Carlsson 1995). Moreover, he noted that, as the effects of antipsychotic drugs are not confined to patients with a diagnosis of schizophrenia, the theory should more correctly be called the dopamine theory of psychosis.

Recently, the dopamine theory has enjoyed something of a revival, partly following a study by Laruelle and Abi-Dargham (1999), who measured dopamine synthesis following the adminstration of amphetamine, finding increased synthesis in schizophrenia patients who were currently unwell and not those who had remitted. This finding suggests that dysregulation of the dopaminergic system may be closely related to the production of psychotic symptoms, but not to vulnerability to severe mental illness.   *RB*

Carlsson, A. 1995: The dopamine theory revisited. In Hirsch, S. R. and Weinberger, D. R. (eds), *Schizophrenia*. Oxford: Blackwell 379–400. **Laruelle, M. and Abi-Dargham, A.** 1999: Dopamine as the wind in the psychotic fire: new evidence from brain imaging studies. *Journal of Psychopharmacology* 13, 358–71. **Syvaelahti, E. K. G., Raekkoelaeinen, V., Aaltonen, J., Lehtinen, V. and Hietala, J.** 2000: Striatal D-sub-2 dopamine receptor density and psychotic symptoms in schizophrenia: a longitudinal study. *Schizophrenia Research* 43, 159–61. **Wong, D. F., Wagner, H. N., Tune, L. E., Dannals, R. F., Pearlson, G. D. and Links, J. M.** 1986: Positron emission tomography reveals elevated D2 dopamine receptors in drug-naive schizophrenics. *Science* 234, 1558–63.

DSM (Diagnostic and Statistical Manual of mental disorders)

The DSM is a manual outlining diagnostic criteria for psychiatric disorders, published by the American Psychiatric Association. Currently in its fourth revision (DSM-IV; APA 1994), the manual is widely used to classify patients and select them for research on particular disorders.

The first edition of the DSM was published in 1952, in response to the apparent lack of consensus among North American psychiatrists about the criteria for various psychiatric disorders, which had become particularly evident during World War II (see s. 1, WAR AND PSYCHOLOGY). A draft manual was circulated among American Psychiatric Association members for approval and the final version included a simple definition of each disorder, usually accompanied by a thumbnail sketch. DSM-II, published in 1968, was designed to be consistent with the eighth edition of the World Health Organization's INTERNATIONAL CLASSIFICATION OF DISEASE.

DSM-III, published in 1980 in response to continuing concerns about the RELIABILITY (see s. 6 and s. 8) of psychiatric diagnoses, had an almost revolutionary impact on psychiatrists' and psychologists' attitudes towards psychiatric diagnosis. In order to improve agreement between clinicians, each diagnosis was defined using a 'Chinese menu' system, in which precise combinations of carefully defined symptoms were required for each disorder. By comparison, the revisions in the fourth edition were not major, and the policy of including precise operational definitions has been maintained.

A competing diagnostic system, the International Classification of Disease (ICD) is published by the World Health Organization. Critics of the DSM system point to the fact that, despite their apparent precision, the definitions continue to be agreed by consensus, that patients often fulfil the criteria for multiple disorders (a phenomenon known as co-morbidity), that the number of diagnoses has greatly increased in successive editions, and that evidence of the VALIDITY (see s. 6 and s. 8) of DSM diagnoses remains largely absent (Bentall 2003).   *RB*

American Psychiatric Association 1994: *Diagnostic and Statistical Manual for Mental Disorders* (4th edn). Washington, DC: APA. **Bentall, R. P.** 2003. *Madness Explained: Psychosis and Human Nature*. London: Penguin.

E

eating disorders   The eating disorders are characterised by overvalued BELIEFS (see s. 5) about the importance of body weight and shape. Typical cognitions will be, 'I cannot eat normally because I will gain weight', and, 'If my weight begins to increase, then it will spiral out of control' (Fairburn, Cooper and Shafran 2003). These patterns of behaviour manifest in anorexia nervosa (in which there is a refusal to maintain body weight), bulimia nervosa (in which periods of binge eating alternate with extreme attempts to prevent weight gain) and the 'atypical' eating disorders (including binge-eating disorder, in which periods of overeating are not followed by purging but may be followed by repetitive diets).

In fact, the atypical eating disorders make up nearly half of all cases, and diagnoses are not stable within the individual (Fairburn and Harrison 2003). The majority of cases have a mixture of restrictive and bulimic features, manifesting in extreme fasting, binge eating and compensatory behaviours (e.g. exercise, self-induced vomiting). The restrictive element helps patients to feel in control of their own lives, by giving them something that they feel successful at: the bulimic features are sometimes a response to the restrictive behaviours (e.g. due to hunger and craving), but are more often reported to be associated with the reduction of NEGATIVE AFFECT (see s. 6) (Meyer, Waller and Watson 2000).

The eating disorders are commonly co-morbid with a variety of other psychological problems (e.g. OBSESSIVE-COMPULSIVE DISORDER, self harm) and are associated with severe physical health risks (e.g. osteoporosis, electrolyte imbalance). Prevalence is higher among women than men. There is little concrete evidence that prevalence is rising, though case identification has become better. Causality is commonly multifactorial.

COGNITIVE (BEHAVIOUR) THERAPY is the treatment of choice for bulimia nervosa and binge-eating disorder, with moderate effectiveness rates. However, the position is less clear in anorexia nervosa, with lower treatment effectiveness rates and no clear predominant therapy for adult cases (although family therapy is recommended for younger cases of a shorter duration). There is almost no evidence base regarding treatments for atypical cases. Medication can have a short-term role in the treatment of bulimia nervosa, but is not proven to be effective in anorexia. Most cases can be treated on an outpatient basis, though some require hospital treatment.   *GW*

Fairburn, C., Cooper, Z. and Shafran, R. 2003: Cognitive behaviour therapy for eating disorders: a 'transdiagnostic' theory and treatment. *Behaviour Research and Therapy* 41, 509–28. **Fairburn, C. and Harrison, P. J.** 2003: Eating disorders. *Lancet* 361, 407–16. **Meyer, C., Waller, G. and Watson, D.** 2000: Cognitive avoidance and bulimic psychopathology: the relevance of temporal factors in a non-clinical population. *International Journal of Eating Disorders* 27, 405–10.

electroconvulsive therapy (ECT)   ECT is a treatment for psychiatric disorders, especially refractory DEPRESSION, involving the application of electric shocks to the brain. The shocks have to be of sufficient intensity to provoke seizures, and patients today are therefore prepared for the procedure by being first administered a muscle relaxant (to prevent damage to the muscles and bones during the seizure itself – fractures and dislocations sometimes occurred during the early use of ECT) and an anaesthetic. A typical course of ECT would be 6–12 shocks over a number of weeks. Unilateral ECT, applied to the non-dominant hemisphere, is preferred over bilateral ECT, because of the reduced risk of MEMORY (see s. 1) loss.

ECT was originally developed in 1938 as a treatment for SCHIZOPHRENIA by two Italian psychiatrists, Ugo Cerletti and Lucio Bini, who erroneously believed that schizophrenia and epilepsy rarely occurred together. Observations of improved mood after ECT led to its use as a treatment for depression.

Advocates of ECT argue that it is no more invasive than many other medical treatments and claim that it has been shown to be effective in numerous RANDOMISED CONTROLLED TRIALS (Fink 2001). Critics have argued that few or no studies have demonstrated a therapeutic benefit over PLACEBO (see s. 8) lasting more than a few weeks (Read 2004).   *RB*

Fink, M. 2001: Convulsive therapy: a review of the first 55 years. *Journal of Affective Disorders* 63, 1–15. **Read, J.** 2004: Electroconvulsive therapy. In Read, J., Mosher, L. and Bentall, R. P. (eds), *Models of Madness: Psychological, Social and Biological Approaches to Schizophrenia*. London: Brunner-Routledge, 85–99.

exposure therapy   A class of treatments for ANXIETY DISORDERS in which the patient is exposed to the feared object or situation; includes SYSTEMATIC DESENSITISATION and FLOODING.   *RB*

expressed emotion   Whether or not an individual recovering from a psychiatric disorder goes on to suffer a further episode may depend on the social environment, as high levels of stress will increase the probability that a RELAPSE will occur. It has been shown that frequent exposure to other people who are critical, hostile or overcontrolling can have this effect. Such people are said to exhibit high 'expressed emotion' (EE).

Research on EE began with a study by Brown, Carstairs and Topping (1958), who followed up a large group of men (mainly suffering from SCHIZOPHRENIA) discharged from psychiatric hospital. Contrary to expectation, patients who went to live with wives or parents were more likely to relapse than those leaving hospital to live in lodgings or with brothers and sisters. Of those who had been married, patients who were widowed, separated or divorced were less likely to relapse than those who left hospital to live with their spouses. This discovery led to the search for those characteristics of close relatives that might be damaging to patients.

Subsequent research led Brown and Rutter (1966) to develop the CAMBERWELL FAMILY INTERVIEW, which is designed to assess high expressed emotion characteristics, particularly criticism, hostility and emotional over-involvement. In one well-known study, Vaughn and Leff (1976) studied the joint influences of family environment and ANTIPSYCHOTIC DRUGS in 128 schizophrenia patients discharged from hospital. Patients were very likely to relapse if they did not take medication and were in frequent face-to-face contact with a high EE relative. Vaughn and Leff showed that depressed patients were even more vulnerable than schizophrenia patients to the effects of exposure to a high EE environment, a finding which has been well replicated (e.g. by Hooley, Orley and Teasdale 1989). As risk of relapse in other psychiatric disorders (e.g. BIPOLAR DISORDER; Miklowitz, Goldstein, Nuechterlein, Snyder and Mintz 1988) is also influenced by exposure to a high EE environment, this appears to be a general phenomenon. Recent studies have extended the concept of expressed emotion to apply to psychiatric staff; patients are more likely to try and leave psychiatric hostels staffed by high EE carers than hostels staffed by low EE carers (Ball, Moore and Kuipers 1992). Most investigators assume that high EE behaviour, while playing a role in relapse, plays little role in the initial onset of psychiatric disorders. However, in the only study directly addressing this issue, Goldstein (1998) found that non-psychotic adolescents referred to a child guidance service were more likely to be suffering from a schizophrenia spectrum disorder 15 years later if their parents were classified as high EE at the beginning of the study.

The discovery of the effects of expressed emotion has led to novel interventions, especially behavioural family therapy designed to reduce high EE behaviour in the relatives of patients. Studies show that this kind of intervention can markedly reduce the risk of relapse in schizophrenia patients (Pitschel, Leucht, Baeumil, Kissling and Engel 2001). *RB*

Ball, R. A., Moore, E. and Kuipers, L. 1992: Expressed emotion in community care staff: a comparison of patient outcome in a nine month follow-up of two hostels. *Social Psychiatry and Psychiatric Epidemiology* 27, 35–9. **Brown, G. W., Carstairs, M. and Topping, G.** 1958: Post hospital adjustment of chronic mental patients. *Lancet* ii, 685–9. **Brown, G. W. and Rutter, M.** 1966: The measurement of family activities and relationships: a methodological study. *Human Relations* 19, 241–63. **Goldstein, M. J.** 1998: Adolescent behavioral and intrafamilial precursors of schizophrenia spectrum disorders. *International Clinical Psychopharmacology* 13 (suppl. 1), 101. **Hooley, J. M., Orley, J. and Teasdale, J. D.** 1989: Predictors of relapse in unipolar depressives: expressed emotion, marital distress and perceived criticism. *Journal of Abnormal Psychology* 98, 229–37. **Miklowitz, D. J., Goldstein, M. J., Nuechterlein, K. H., Snyder, K. S. and Mintz, J.** 1988: Family factors and the course of bipolar affective disorder. *Archives of General Psychiatry* 45, 225–31. **Pitschel, W. G., Leucht, S., Baeumil, J., Kissling, W. and Engel, R. R.** 2001: The effects of family interventions on relapse and rehospitalisation in schizophrenia: a meta-analysis. *Schizophrenia Bulletin* 27, 73–92. **Vaughn, C. E. and Leff, J.** 1976: The influence of family and social factors on the course of psychiatric illness: a comparison of schizophrenic and depressed neurotic patients. *British Journal of Psychiatry* 129, 125–37.

expressivity (of genes causing psychiatric disorders)

A gene may have variable expressivity for a particular TRAIT (see s. 6) (disease or psychiatric disorder) if those carrying the gene have the trait to varying degrees; for example, neurofibromatosis is a disease which affects all those carrying a particular gene, but the disease may be very mild (a few small brown spots on the skin) or severely disfiguring, according to other genetic or environmental influences. *RB*

F

family studies Family studies are carried out to estimate the extent to which psychiatric disorders are inherited. It is assumed that, if this is the case, a first-degree relative (mother, father, sibling, son or daughter) of an affected person will have a higher probability of being mentally ill compared to second- or third-degree relatives, or members of the general population. In general, family studies show greater than expected levels of psychiatric disorder in the first-degree relatives of patients suffering from a wide range of conditions. However, one problem in interpreting these findings is that family studies do not exclude the possibility of non-genetic mechanisms of transmission (for example, the children become mentally ill as a result of being neglected by their mentally ill parents), which is why researchers have turned to other methods such as TWIN STUDIES and ADOPTION STUDIES.

Family studies can also be used to determine if psychiatric disorders 'breed true' within families, which is an important method of validating systems of PSYCHIATRIC CLASSIFICATION. The results of these kinds of investigations have not been particularly clear-cut. For example, some findings have not supported a clear separation between SCHIZOPHRENIA and BIPOLAR DISORDER (Crow 1991). *RB*

Crow, T. 1991: The failure of the binary concept and the psychosis gene. In Kerr, A. and McClelland, H. (eds), *Concepts of Mental Disorder: A Continuing Debate*. London: Gaskell.

family therapy Family therapy adopts a view of psychological problems as relational rather than as located within persons. The core theoretical conceptualisation is drawn from SYSTEMS THEORY (see s. 1) in the analogy of a family as like a self-regulating biological system. Family members are seen to interact in such a way that their joint actions serve to produce and maintain problems or symptoms. This is a counter-intuitive view of problems which argues that, despite the typical protestations of family members that they desperately want to be rid of the problems, usually seen to be resident within one of their members, they in fact interact in ways that serve to ensure that the problems are maintained. Typically, the initial stages of therapy are concerned with attempting to understand what the positive functions of the symptoms may be. A core concept is 'triangulation', for example, where a child's distress and subsequent symptoms are seen to result from and also serve to detour the parents' conflictual relationship.

The practice of family therapy consists of meetings with all relevant family members. With their full permission, the therapy is usually conducted in a team setting, usually with the therapist in a room with the family and with the rest of the team offering live supervision, watching from behind a one-way screen in an observation room. The supervision team may phone in to make suggestions. Alternatively, in an increasingly popular approach, reflecting team conversation is used, in which the observers join the therapist and the family. The family is then invited to listen while the team have a conversation about the progress of the therapy. The family, in turn, are invited to discuss and reflect back on this discussion.

Various activities, such as homework tasks, may also be employed, for example, for members to observe their patterns of interacting at home or to engage in experiments such as the parents swapping roles. Underlying all these activities is the aim of promoting new patterns of interactions and helping family members to see their problems as interpersonal rather than due to individual deficits. *RD*

Anderson, T. 1990: *The Reflecting Team*. New York: Norton. **Dallos, R. and Draper, R.** 2002: *An Introduction to Family Therapy: Systemic Theory and Practice*. Buckingham: Open University Press. **Haley, J.** 1987: *Problem-solving Therapy*. San Francisco: Jossey Bass. **Hoffman, L.** 1981: *Foundations of Family Therapy*. New York: Basic Books.

fatigue Fatigue is such a common and ubiquitous experience that it might be thought to be easy to define. However, the definition of fatigue is complicated by the fact that the word 'fatigue' is used in everyday discourse in a number of different ways (Wessely, Hotopf and Sharpe 1998). Sometimes 'fatigue' is used to refer to a subjective, usually unpleasant, feeling of aversion to effort; on other occasions 'fatigue' refers to observable physical or mental performance decrements that are expected to occur after prolonged periods of effort, and which might or might not be accompanied by the subjective feeling of fatigue. (To complicate matters, occasionally 'fatigue' also refers to the hypothesised process of moving from one subjective or objective state to another.)

Over the years, psychologists such as the late Donald Broadbent have expended some effort in trying to work out both the correlations between subjective feelings of fatigue and performance changes, and the conditions under which the two aspects of fatigue occur, often with only limited success (Broadbent 1979). However, it is known that the feeling of fatigue is a common and familiar experience, which can be measured by asking people about how they feel, and which lies on a continuum from no fatigue to extreme fatigue (Pawlikowska et al. 1994). It is also known that fatigue is usually expected to resolve itself in a short period of time, with adequate relief from whatever demands led to the fatigue in the first place, but that there are a number of cases in which fatigue does not readily resolve itself. These cases include fatigue associated with medical conditions such as cancer or multiple sclerosis, or with psychiatric illnesses such as DEPRESSION. Furthermore, some people experience pathologically severe, long-lasting fatigue, which does not respond to rest, and for which there is no obvious antecedent condition or medical or psychiatric explanation. Conditions such as this are known as 'fatigue syndromes' (Wessely, Hotopf and Sharpe 1998). This pathological fatigue is often associated with other physical symptoms, high levels of distress and substantial disability, for example, in the case of CHRONIC FATIGUE SYNDROME (CFS) or ME. *AW*

Broadbent, D. E. 1979: Is a fatigue test now possible? *Ergonomics* 22, 1277–90. Pawlikowska, T., Chalder, T., Hirsch, S. R. et al. 1994: Population based study of fatigue and psychological distress. *British Medical Journal* 308, 763–6. Wessely, S., Hotopf, M. and Sharpe, M. 1998. *Chronic Fatigue and its Syndromes*. Oxford: Oxford University Press.

flooding A type of EXPOSURE THERAPY, in which a patient suffering from a PHOBIA is asked to confront the feared stimulus until the fear has subsided. *RB*

free association A therapeutic technique employed in psychodynamic therapy (especially PSYCHOANALYSIS – see s. 1) in which the patient is encouraged to allow their mind to wander freely, and to report whatever comes to mind. *RB*

Fregoli syndrome One of the delusional misidentification syndromes in which it is believed that unfamiliar people disguise themselves as people familiar to the patient. *RC*

functional analysis An approach to analysing and explaining psychological problems by hypothesising and identifying sometimes complex functional relationships between the problems and various factors thought to influence their development or prevent remission. Very often, a functional analysis will be written as a flow diagram, showing how the different variables influence each other.

Generic functional analyses may be constructed to illustrate interactions between factors thought to be responsible for a particular condition. However, they may be individualised in the form of a CASE FORMULATION of the difficulties suffered by a particular patient, which the therapist can then use to select an intervention. The apparently similar problems of two patients may be analysed in terms of two quite different functional analyses, pointing to quite different interventions. For example, one patient's anger problem may be judged to be mainly a consequence of a lack of assertiveness, whereas another's may be judged to be a consequence of an inability to regulate EMOTION (see s. 6).

Most advocates of functional analysis, for example Owens and Ashcroft (1982), have worked within the behavioural tradition. *RB*

Owens, R. G. and Ashcroft, J. B. 1982: Functional analysis in applied psychology. *British Journal of Clinical Psychology* 21, 181–9.

G

generalised anxiety disorder (GAD) The cardinal diagnostic criterion for GAD is excessive or uncontrollable chronic worry that has lasted for at least six months. An individual with GAD usually finds it difficult to control their ANXIETY (see s. 6) and their worry, and this may be accompanied by physical symptoms such as fatigue, trembling, muscle tension, headache and nausea. GAD is twice as common in women than in men, and can often be a disorder that lasts from adolescence to old age (Heimberg, Turk and Mennin 2003).

Over 5 per cent of the population will be diagnosed with GAD at some point in their lifetime, and over 12 per cent of those who attend anxiety disorder clinics will present with GAD.

There is some evidence for a genetic component to both anxiety generally and GAD specifically, which suggests that GAD has an inherited component. However, the challenge in explaining GAD is to understand why individuals with the disorder worry chronically and pathologically, while many other individuals – often with more stressful lifestyles – worry significantly less (Davey and Tallis 1994). The chronic worrying of those with GAD possesses two important features: it is always associated with high levels of anxious and depressed mood, and it is perceived by the individual as uncontrollable.

The worrying of GAD sufferers appears to be driven by a set of BELIEFS (see s. 5) that worrying is an important and necessary thing to do to avoid 'bad' things happening (Wells 1995; Borkovec and Roemer 1995). This suggests that, for pathological worriers, worrying serves a very specific function, and this gives rise to the rather paradoxical situation where worriers feel the need to worry, but yet are aware that it causes them a good deal of emotional discomfort. Although it is not clear yet what developmental factors help to fashion these global beliefs about worry, COGNITIVE (BEHAVIOUR) THERAPY techniques are being developed which attempt to change these dysfunctional beliefs about worry into functional ones (Wells 1997).

GD

Borkovec, T. D. and Roemer, L. 1995: Perceived functions of worry among generalized anxiety disorder subjects: distraction from more emotionally distressing topics. *Journal of Behavior Therapy & Experimental Psychiatry* 26, 25–30. **Davey, G. C. L. and Tallis, F.** 1994: *Worrying: Perspectives on Theory, Assessment and Treatment.* Chichester: Wiley. **Heimberg, R. G., Turk, C. L. and Mennin, D. S.** 2003: *Generalized Anxiety Disorder: Advances in Research and Practice.* New York: Guilford Press. **Wells, A.** 1997: *Cognitive Therapy of Anxiety.* Chichester: Wiley.

goal attainment life event Any life event that involves the achievement of a goal, for example, finding a new love partner or gaining entrance to university; associated with the onset of mania. *RB*

grandiose delusion A type of delusional belief in which the individual irrationally believes that he or she has a special IDENTITY (see s. 4 and s. 5) (e.g. 'I am Jesus Christ'), special powers or achievements ('I invented the helicopter') or great wealth, despite all evidence to the contrary. This type of DELUSION is common in the manic phase of BIPOLAR DISORDER. *RB*

group therapy Any therapy carried out with a group of patients; group therapies may be psychodynamic, behavioural or cognitive behavioural in orientation, and have the advantage of maximising the number of patients who can be treated by a PSYCHOTHERAPIST. *RB*

H

hallucinations A hallucination can be defined as 'A sensory PERCEPTION (see s. 1) that has the compelling sense of reality of a true perception but that occurs without external stimulation of the relevant sensory organ' (American Psychiatric Association 1994). A French psychiatrist, Jean-Etienne Esquirol, in a paper published in 1832, first observed that the hallucinating person, 'Ascribes a body and actuality to images that the memory recalls without the intervention of the senses', in this way distinguishing between hallucinations and illusions (roughly, the misperception of objects which are present).

Hallucinations can be experienced in all perceptual modalities. They are reported by people suffering from a variety of organic conditions, including intoxication (for example, from alcohol or psychoactive DRUGS – see s. 2 – such as LSD), confusional states and fever. They are also commonly reported by patients suffering from psychotic disorders, especially those diagnosed as suffering from SCHIZOPHRENIA. Recent epidemiological studies have found that a surprising proportion of the population (as many as 10 per cent) experience hallucinations at some point in their lives, and many people with these experiences are able to cope well with them and do not seek psychiatric treatment (van Os, Hanssen, Bijl and Ravelli 2000).

Organic hallucinations are most often experienced in the visual modality; in the case of LSD intoxication, for example, they typically consist of intense visual experiences involving bright colours and explosive, concentric, rotational or pulsating movements (Siegel and Jarvick 1975). In psychiatric patients, however, they are most commonly reported in the auditory modality, and often consist of a voice or voices speaking to the patient (including offering either reassurance or abuse), commenting on the patient's actions or even issuing instructions. They may be experienced as originating in the body or from within the head, but nonetheless alien (Slade and Bentall 1988). Although clinicians often note that patients' hallucinations are distressing, many patients report that their voices have positive content and express reluctance about losing them (Miller, O'Connor and DePasquale 1993).

Current psychological theories have focused on auditory-verbal hallucinations, and there is a consensus that these occur when an individual fails to accurately discriminate the source of their experiences, thereby attributing 'inner speech' (verbal thought) to a source alien to the SELF (see s. 1, s. 4 and s. 5) (Bentall 2000). This insight has led to new COGNITIVE (BEHAVIOUR) THERAPY treatments for patients who otherwise have only been treatable with ANTIPSYCHOTIC DRUGS.   *RB*

American Psychiatric Association 1994: *Diagnostic and Statistical Manual for Mental Disorders* (4th edn). Washington, DC: APA. **Bentall, R. P.** 2000: Hallucinatory experiences. In Cardena, E., Lynn, S. J. and Krippner, S. (eds), *Varieties of Anomalous Experience: Examining the Scientific Evidence*. Washington, DC: American Psychological Association, 85–120.

Miller, L. J., O'Connor, E. and DePasquale, T. 1993: Patients' attitudes to hallucinations. *American Journal of Psychiatry* 150, 584–8. **Siegel, R. K. and Jarvick, M. E.** 1975: Drug-induced hallucinations in animals and man. In Siegel, R. K. and West, L. J. (eds), *Hallucinations: Behavior, Experience and Theory*. New York: Wiley. **Slade, P. D. and Bentall, R. P.** 1988: Sensory deception: a scientific analysis of hallucination. London: Croom-Helm. **van Os, J., Hanssen, M., Bijl, R. V. and Ravelli, A.** 2000: Strauss (1969) revisited: a psychosis continuum in the normal population? *Schizophrenia Research* 45, 11–20.

health beliefs The term 'health beliefs' is used to refer to a broad set of cognitions about health, held by patients and health professionals. Health beliefs are of interest to health psychologists because people's BELIEFS (see s. 5) have been shown to interact with their emotional responses to health threats, and also, importantly, to affect their health-related behaviours. For example, the health belief model (Rosenstock 1974; see Sheeran and Abraham 1996, for a recent review) was developed specifically to explain how certain types of health beliefs predict the practice of health-preventative behaviours such as attending for cancer screening or condom use. The model holds that people weigh up, in a cost-benefit analysis, their beliefs about a personal health threat (such as contracting a sexually transmitted disease) against their beliefs about the effectiveness of a course of action (such as wearing a condom). The health beliefs which contribute towards the evaluation of the threat are those about personal susceptibility to the threat and those about the likely severity or consequences of that threat. Beliefs in the effectiveness of the health behaviour (in this example, condom use) are comprised of beliefs about the perceived benefits of that behaviour and beliefs about the perceived barriers to carrying out the behaviour, with the latter often proving to be a particularly potent predictor of whether or not the health behaviour occurs. Health beliefs are also related to emotional and behavioural responses to illness. Leventhal and co-workers' self-regulatory, or common-sense, model of illness representations suggests that patients' beliefs about the identity, cause, timeline, consequences and controllability of an illness or other health threat (such as receipt of a diagnosis) will impact on the way they deal with the threat, and ultimately on emotional adjustment and other outcomes (Leventhal, Meyer and Nerenz 1980).

A recent meta-analytic review showed that a belief in the controllability of a health threat was associated with more adaptive COPING attempts and better psychological well-being, whereas beliefs that an illness would have a long timeline and severe consequences were associated with greater distress and more avoidant or emotion-focused coping (Hagger and Orbell 2003).   *AW*

Hagger, M. S. and Orbell, S. 2003: A meta-analytic review of the common-sense model of illness representations. *Psychology and Health* 8, 141–84. **Leventhal, H. Meyer, D. and Nerenz, D.** 1980: The common sense model of illness danger. In

Rachman, S. (ed.), *Medical Psychology*. New York: Pergamon, vol. 2, 7–30. **Rosenstock, I. M.** 1974: Historical origins of the health belief model. *Health Education Monographs* 2, 1–8. **Sheeran, P. and Abraham, C.** 1996: The health belief model. In Conner, M. and Norman, P. (eds), *Predicting Health Behaviour*. Buckingham: Open University Press.

health psychology Probably the most famous definition of health psychology is that of Matarazzo, who defined it as '. . . the aggregate of the specific educational, scientific and professional contributions of the discipline of psychology to the promotion and maintenance of health, the prevention and treatment of illness, the identification of etiologic and diagnostic correlates of health, illness and related dysfunction, and to the analysis and improvement of the health care system and health policy formation' (Matarazzo 1982: 4). This is a very broad definition, covering almost all the possible ways in which psychological inquiry can be applied to the topic of health. In recent years, in the UK, there has been a move to delineate health psychology from other areas of the discipline, particularly at the interface of health and CLINICAL PSYCHOLOGY (see also s. 1). While the bulk of clinical psychology training and practice is focused on treating mental health problems, it is not uncommon to find clinical psychologists working in settings such as cardiac rehabilitation services and PAIN (see also s. 2) clinics. At the same time, a career route for health psychologists, with extended training in theory and practice, has been developed by the BRITISH PSYCHOLOGICAL SOCIETY (see s. 1). Health psychology training now leads to chartered status, and enables health psychologists to work autonomously as practitioners and consultants within the health care system, in community settings and as advisors to government bodies and international health organisations (BPS – The Division of Health Psychology 2004). Increasingly, health psychology is carving out its own areas of expertise, some of which are reviewed below.

During the course of the twentieth century, life expectancy increased markedly in developed countries. Analysis of epidemiological data suggests that this change in life expectancy was due only in part to advances in the ability to control infection, and that factors such as improved public health, improved living standards and changes in nutrition and lifestyle were also key (McKeown 1979). Health psychologists have contributed greatly to our understanding of the factors which lead people to engage in behaviours which impact adversely or positively on health. Such behaviours include smoking and substance use, dietary habits, exercise and health-protective behaviours such as condom use or uptake of screening services. Much of this work has taken place within the framework of general models explaining how ATTITUDES (see s. 5) and BELIEFS (see s. 5) predict behavioural intention and, ultimately, behaviour (for example, the theories of REASONED ACTION (see s. 5) and PLANNED BEHAVIOUR – see s. 5), while health-specific models, such as the health belief model [see HEALTH BELIEFS] and protection motivation theory, have also been developed (see Conner and Norman 1996, for a review of models used in the prediction of health behaviours). Recent work has focused on how developing specific time-and-place action plans helps people to translate their intentions into action; and interventions which induce people to develop these 'implementation intentions' have been shown to be successful (Gollwitzer 1999).

Whereas the models of health behaviour outlined above focus on general processes such as attitude and intention formation, which are common to all, another major theme in health psychology has been the exploration of INDIVIDUAL DIFFERENCES (see s. 6) in relation to health. For example, while the often cited association between Type A behaviour (characterised by achievement orientation, a sense of time urgency and a tendency to interrupt) and coronary heart disease now appears to be more complicated than originally thought, a body of evidence suggests that one component of Type A behaviour, namely hostility, *is* an independent risk factor for coronary heart disease (Miller, Smith, Turner, Guijarro and Hallet 1996). DEPRESSION has been shown to influence the rate at which people with HIV infection progress to the development of AIDS, and is now accepted as a fairly robust predictor of poorer survival rates after myocardial infarction (Frasure-Smith et al. 2000). Recently, attention has turned to the study of why people with a bias towards optimistic BELIEFS (see s. 5) and a (sometimes illusory) sense of control over events in their lives appear to have more positive health outcomes. It has been suggested that optimistic beliefs may act as internal resources which can be drawn on when faced with stressful or even life-threatening events such as illness (Taylor, Kemeny, Reed, Bower and Gruenewald 2000).

Another important area of health psychology is the study of stress and health, in particular, the effects of STRESS on immune functioning and infection, or psychoneuroimmunology. Sheldon Cohen and colleagues have reported a series of studies in which volunteers were infected with cold viruses under carefully controlled conditions. They were able to demonstrate that people who scored high on a psychological stress index (a composite measure of the experience of unpleasant life events in the previous year, perceived inability to cope and NEGATIVE AFFECT – see s. 6) were more likely to develop colds (Cohen, Tyrrell and Smith 1991). Other work in a similar tradition, for example, that of Janice Keicolt-Glaser and colleagues, has not only demonstrated that stress can influence bodily processes such as infection and wound healing, but has also shown how particular types of stressors, for example, conflict in marital RELATIONSHIPS (see s. 5), can lead to measurable immunological changes (e.g. Kiecolt-Glaser, Glaser, Cacioppo and Malarkey 1998).

Research and practice in health psychology is particularly wide-ranging. At one end of the spectrum health psychologists concern themselves with trying to describe and understand the varieties of individual, subjective experiences of health and illness, often using qualitative techniques. Then there are the attempts to predict health behaviours or illness outcomes at the individual level, such as those described above. Health psychologists have also been concerned with the impact of wider social conditions on health, and in particular with attempting to explain health inequalities. A social gradient has been demonstrated for many symptoms and illnesses, such that those of lower socio-economic status are at greater risk than those from higher socio-economic groups (e.g. Marmot et al. 1991). Furthermore, while socio-economic status-related differences in health behaviours can explain some of this social gradient, it appears that other factors, such as social environments and job characteristics, are also implicated in health inequalities. *AW*

British Psychological Society – Division of Health Psychology 2004: www.health-psychology.org.uk. **Cohen, S., Tyrrell, D. A. J. and Smith, A. P.** 1991: Psychological stress and susceptibility to the common cold. *New England Journal of Medicine* 325, 606–12. **Conner, M. and Norman, P. (eds)** 1996: *Predicting Health Behaviour*. Buckingham: Open University Press. **Frasure-Smith, N., Lesperance, F., Gravel, G., Masson, A., Juneau, M., Talajic, M. and Bourassa, M.G.** 2000: Social support, depression and mortality during the first year after myocardial infarction. *Circulation* 101, 1919–24. **Gollwitzer, P. M.** 1999: Implementation intentions – strong effects of simple plans. *American Psychologist*, 45, 493–503. **Kiecolt-Glaser, J., Glaser, R., Cacioppo, J. T. and Malarkey, W. B.** 1998: Marital stress: immunologic, neuroendocrine and autonomic correlates. *Annals of the New York Academy of Sciences* 840, 656–63. **Marmot, M. G., Smith, G. D., Stansfield, S., Patel, C., North, F., Head, J., White, I., Brunner, E. and Feeney, A.** 1991: Health inequalities among British civil servants – The Whitehall II study. *Lancet* 337, 1387–93. **Matarazzo, J. D.** 1982: Behavioral health's challenge to academic, scientific and professional psychology. *American Psychologist* 37, 1–14. **McKeown, T.** 1979: *The Role of Medicine*. Oxford: Blackwell. **Miller, T. Q., Smith, T. W., Turner, C. W., Guijarro, M. L. and Hallet, A. J.** 1996: A meta-analytic review of research on hostility and physical health. *Psychological Bulletin* 119, 322–48. **Taylor, S. E., Kemeny, M. E., Reed, G. M., Bower, J. E. and Gruenewald, T. L.** 2000: Psychological resources, positive illusions and health. *American Psychologist* 55, 99–109.

high-risk studies   High-risk studies are carried out to investigate the determinants and development of psychiatric disorders. Although it is sometimes possible to investigate the aetiology of conditions using population cohorts, this is often impractical because of the small proportion of the population who will eventually develop the illnesses of interest. In a high-risk study, individuals (often children) known to be at high-risk of developing a disorder are studied, followed up and compared with individuals at low risk.

The most common type of high-risk study is genetic: the children of psychiatric patients are selected for study. Investigations of this kind have confirmed that children of schizophrenic parents are at high risk of developing the disorder. However, they have also shown that environmental factors (such as relationships with parents) can be important (Schiffman et al. 2002).

People at high risk of psychiatric disorders can also be selected using COGNITIVE (see s. 1, COGNITIVE PSYCHOLOGY) or PERSONALITY (see s. 1 and s. 6) measures; in the Temple-Wisconsin Cognitive Vulnerability to Depression Project, this approach was used to show that young people with dysfunctional self-schemas and a depressogenic attributional style were at high risk of becoming depressed (Alloy et al. 1999). *RB*

Alloy, L. B., Abramson, L. Y., Whitehouse, W. G., Hogan, M. E., Tashman, N. A., Steinberg, D. L., Rose, D. T. and Donovan, P. 1999: Depressogenic cognitive styles: predictive validity, information processing and personality characteristics, and developmental origins. *Behaviour Research and Therapy* 37, 503–31. **Schiffman, J., LaBrie, J., Carter, J., Tyrone, C., Schulsinger, F., Parnas, J. and Mednick, S.** 2002: Perception of parent-child relationships in high-risk families, and adult schizophrenia outcome of offspring. *Journal of Psychiatric Research* 36, 41–7.

hypofrontality hypothesis of schizophrenia

The hypothesis that SCHIZOPHRENIA is associated with reduced activation of the frontal lobes of the brain. Evidence from functional neuro-imaging studies suggests that schizophrenia patients may show less increase in frontal lobe activation when presented with appropriate tasks than controls, but generally no differences in frontal lobe activation are observed between patients and controls when at rest. *RB*

hypomania   A condition with the same symptoms as MANIA but with reduced severity and duration, no psychotic features, and less disruption to social and occupational functioning, making hospitalisation unlikely. *ST*

I

inferiority complex According to Alfred Adler (1870–1937), a disciple of Freud who broke away to form his own school of psychotherapy, individuals strive for goals of significance, superiority and success. Frustration of these goals can lead to chronic feelings of inferiority (the inferiority complex), which in turn can cause mental ill health. In some cases, effective attempts to compensate for an inferiority complex may lead to outstanding achievement. *RB*

insulin coma therapy A now defunct form of physical treatment, at one time advocated for SCHIZOPHRENIA patients, in which patients were repeatedly administered INSULIN (see s. 2) in order to induce a comatose state. Following the recognition that the treatment was ineffective and hazardous to life, its use was discontinued in the mid-1950s. *RB*

intention to treat analysis A method of analysing data from RANDOMISED CONTROLLED TRIALS, often preferred by health service planners, in which the outcomes for all patients who enter the study are considered, whether or not they complete treatment or remain in the study (patients who drop out are usually assumed to have a poor outcome). *RB*

International Classification of Disease (ICD)

The International Classification of Disease (or to use the full title of its current tenth edition, the *International Statistical Classification of Diseases and Related Health Problems*; World Health Organization 1992) is a manual providing criteria for the diagnosis of physical and psychiatric conditions, published by the World Health Organization. ICD diagnoses are widely used for administrative purposes and also for the purposes of selecting patients for research (although, in the case of psychiatric research, the competing DSM system, published by the American Psychiatric Association, is probably more extensively used).

The ICD began life as an International Classification of the Causes of Death, compiled in 1853 by the French government. On its creation in 1948, the World Health Organization took over responsibility for the manual and included non-fatal diseases in the sixth edition, published in 1951.

ICD-10 contains detailed operational criteria for physical and psychiatric conditions. Many of the criteria for psychiatric disorders are similar to those contained in the current fourth edition of the DSM. *RB*

World Health Organization 1992: *ICD-10: International Statistical Classification of Diseases and Related Health Problems* (10th rev. edn). Geneva: World Health Organization.

intrusive life event A life event that involves unwanted experiences being forced on the individual (examples include threats, burglaries and police investigations); implicated in episodes of SCHIZOPHRENIA and PARANOIA. *RB*

intrusive thoughts Thoughts that are intrusive, unbidden and distressing are a symptom of a wide range of psychological disorders, especially DEPRESSION (where they are usually known as NEGATIVE AUTOMATIC THOUGHTS and usually concern the self, the world and the future) and OBSESSIVE-COMPULSIVE DISORDER (in which they may be the main source of distress and often concern actions that the patient either fears doing or not doing).

Surveys of ordinary people have shown that intrusive thoughts are extremely common, but that most people are not distressed by them. Researchers have therefore addressed why intrusive thoughts may be a problem for some people and not others. One possible answer is that attempts to suppress unwanted thoughts often lead to their persistence (Wegner 1994). It also appears that people who are distressed by their intrusive thoughts have considerable feelings of guilt and an exaggerated sense of responsibility for their thoughts, sometimes believing that thinking about doing something is equivalent to doing it (Rachman 1993). *RB*

Rachman, S. 1993: Obsessions, responsibility and guilt. *Behaviour Research and Therapy* 31, 149–54. **Wegner, D. M.** 1994: *White Bears and Other Unwanted Thoughts: Supression, Obsession and the Psychology of Mental Control.* New York: Guilford.

L

life events The term 'life events' has been used to describe particular stressful events that may precipitate a psychiatric disorder or cause a vulnerable person to RELAPSE.

The causal role of life events in psychiatric symptoms is difficult to investigate, because symptoms can sometimes lead to life events (for example, when a depressed person becomes unable to work and then loses their job). Some researchers have attempted to study life events by devising questionnaires based on lists of experiences that are judged to be stressful to most people by a panel of experts (Holmes and Rahe 1965). Although this approach has generally found evidence of an association between life events and both psychiatric and physical diseases, it has been criticised for lack of sensitivity to individual circumstances and failure to establish that life events cause disorder rather than vice versa.

In a ground-breaking study, Brown and Harris (1978) demonstrated unequivocally that negative life events often play a role in precipitating episodes of DEPRESSION. They used the Life Events and Difficulty Schedule, a semi-structured interview. Studying women (both depressed patients and a community SAMPLE – see s. 8) living in Camberwell, an economically deprived area of London, Brown and Harris found that, even when those life events that might be influenced by symptoms were excluded, most episodes of depression were closely preceded by negative life events. Importantly, some women who experienced life events did not become depressed. Brown and Harris went on to explore social vulnerability factors, finding that women who lacked a close confiding relationship, were unemployed, had small children at home and who had suffered the loss of their mother during childhood were especially likely to become depressed if exposed to a negative life event.

This relationship between life events and depression has been replicated many times in both men and women, and the approach has been extended to other psychiatric conditions, yielding some evidence of specific relationships between types of events and types of disorders. Events associated with the loss of a goal, person or cherished belief tend to lead to depression, whereas threatening events tend to lead to ANXIETY (see s. 6) (Brown and Moran 1998). Although the relationship between life events and episodes of SCHIZOPHRENIA is less clear (Bebbington, Bowen, Hirsch and Kuipers 1995), there is some evidence that intrusive life events (involving unwanted experiences being forced on the individual) are associated with psychotic symptoms (Day et al. 1987). Recent research has shown that, in BIPOLAR DISORDER patients, life events involving goal attainment (Johnson et al. 2000) and/or disruption of daily rhythms (Malkoff-Schwartz et al. 2000) lead to manic episodes.   *RB*

Bebbington, P. E., Bowen, J., Hirsch, S. R. and Kuipers, E. A. 1995: Schizophrenia and psychosocial stresses. In Hirsch, S. R. and Weinberger, D. R. (eds), *Schizophrenia*. Oxford: Blackwell, 587–604. **Brown, G. W. and Harris, T.** 1978: *Social Origins of Depression*. New York: Free Press. **Brown, G. W. and Moran, P.** 1998: Emotion and the etiology of depressive disorders. In Flack, W. F. and Laird, J. D. (eds), *Emotions in Psychopathology: Theory and Research*. New York: Oxford University Press, 171–84. **Day, R., Neilsen, J. A., Korten, A., Ernberg, G., Dube, K. C., Gebhart, J., Jablensky, A., Leon, C., Marsella, A., Olatawura, M., Sartorius, N., Stromgren, E., Takahashi, R., Wig, N. and Wynne, L. C.** 1987: Stressful life events preceding the onset of acute schizophrenia: a cross-national study from the World Health Organization. *Culture, Medicine and Psychiatry* 11, 123–206. **Holmes, T. H. and Rahe, R. H.** 1965: The social readjustment scale. *Journal of Psychosomatic Research* 11, 213–18. **Johnson, S. L., Sandow, D., Meyer, B., Winters, R., Miller, I., Solomon, D. and Keitner, G.** 2000: Increases in manic symptoms after life events involving goal attainment. *Journal of Abnormal Psychology* 109, 721–7. **Malkoff-Schwartz, S., Frank, E., Anderson, B. P., Hlastala, S. A., Luther, J. F., Sherrill, J. T. and Kupfer, D. J.** 2000: Social rhythm disruption and stressful life events in the onset of bipolar and unipolar episodes. *Psychological Medicine* 30, 1005–16.

linkage studies Linkage studies are carried out to identify specific loci on the human CHROMOSOMES (see s. 4) that carry genes relating to diseases, including psychiatric disorders. This approach capitalises on existing knowledge about the location of certain marker genes. During the formation of gametes (sperm and egg cells) DNA may be swapped between corresponding sections of each pair of chromosomes, and one chromosome is then selected to enter each gamete; if a marker gene is close to a gene contributing to a psychiatric disorder then it is likely to end up in the same gametes. It follows that if, in a family in which many members suffer from a particular psychiatric disorder, a marker gene is found in association with the disorder, the gene responsible for the disorder will be located close to the marker gene. This approach has been successfully used to locate ALLELES (see s. 4) (variants of genes) that confer vulnerability to Alzheimer's disease (Farlow 1997), but has so far led to mostly inconsistent results when applied to serious psychiatric disorder (Crow 1997).   *RB*

Crow, T. J. 1997: Current status of linkage for schizophrenia: polygenes of vanishingly small effect or multiple false positives? *American Journal of Medical Genetics (Neuropsychiatric Genetics)* 74, 99–103. **Farlow, M.** 1997: Alzheimer's disease: clinical implications of the apolipoprotein E genotype. *Neurology* 48 (suppl. 6), s. 30–s. 34.

M

mania A manic episode is characterised by an abnormal, elevated, expansive or irritable mood, which is out of keeping with the current situation. Patients may appear euphoric at the same time as appearing distressed and highly dysphoric (Goodwin and Jamison 1990).

Manic patients often appear grandiose, with highly inflated SELF-ESTEEM (see also s. 5), often becoming distractible and over-involved in what is going on around them (hyperactivity). Alterations to behaviour are very obvious, as patients often engage in pleasurable and GOAL-DIRECTED BEHAVIOUR (see s. 3) that is high risk (e.g. sexual disinhibition) or become aggressive. Other symptoms can include reduced need for sleep (see s. 2, SLEEP AND BIOLOGICAL RHYTHMS) and abnormal appetite, flight of ideas and psychomotor agitation.

Disturbed speech and thought are often part of the manic presentation, including increased talkativeness at a rapid rate (pressure of speech), excessive volume and rapid changes in train of thought (flight of ideas). People can also experience DELUSIONS and HALLUCINATIONS. *ST*

Goodwin, F. K. and Jamison, K. R. 1990: *Manic-depressive Illness*. Oxford: Oxford University Press.

manic defence hypothesis

A theory stating that MANIA and DEPRESSION have similar underlying cognitive processes and that mania is a COPING response (defence) to help protect the individual from depression, first put forward by the psychoanalyst Karl Abraham (1911/1927). Modern studies showing that manic and remitted bipolar [see BIPOLAR DISORDER] patients have cognitive biases similar to those found in depression provide some support for the theory. *RB*

mental illness: concepts of

All CULTURES (see s. 1 and s. 5) distinguish between behaviour that is seen as 'sane' or 'rational' and behaviour that is seen as 'mad' or evidence of mental derangement. However, cultures vary considerably in the way that they construe abnormal behaviour, variously attributing it to spiritual or supernatural causes, moral failure, psychic disturbance or diseases of the nervous system.

The idea that abnormal behaviour should be seen as evidence of illness is certainly not recent – evidence of it can be found in the writing of Greek and Roman physicians (Porter 2002). However, it only became dominant in Europe and North America following the emergence of an organised profession of psychiatry as a branch of medicine at the beginning of the nineteenth century. In the following century, psychiatrists, especially in German-speaking Europe, attempted to identify different types of mental illness in order to construct a system of PSYCHIATRIC CLASSIFICATION. This approach is dominant today, and is enshrined in diagnostic manuals such as the DSM and ICD [see INTERNATIONAL CLASSIFICATION OF DISEASE]. Modern advocates of a medical approach to abnormal behaviour, such as Andreasen (2001), see psychiatric disorders as brain diseases and sometimes argue that, 'There is no such thing as a psychiatry that is too biological' (Guze 1989). They assume that medical treatment such as PHARMACOTHERAPY and ECT [see ELECTROCONVULSIVE THERAPY] are required in order to treat severe psychological distress, but do not discount the possibility that psychological interventions may help ameliorate less severe conditions, or help patients to cope with the disabilities imposed on them by the more severe forms of mental illness. The term 'medical model' has sometimes been used to describe this general approach, but it would be better described as a medical PARADIGM (see s. 1), using the term 'paradigm' in the sense proposed by the philosopher Thomas Kuhn (1970) to indicate a framework of assumptions that are often held implicitly but which guide the practices of those working in the area.

Although now widely accepted by mental health professionals and lay people alike, the medical paradigm has been criticised from many quarters. Sociologists such as Thomas Scheff (1966) have argued that the term 'mental illness' is used to describe types of behaviour that are deviant when judged according to the implicit rules of social interaction that are the norm in a SOCIETY (see s. 5). According to this argument, the concept of mental illness serves the function of legitimising efforts to restrain people who are 'residually deviant' in this way. R. D. Laing (1927–89) and other members of the ANTIPSYCHIATRY movement argued that the medical approach is dehumanising and advocated a more romantic conception of psychological disturbance. However, the most enduring critic of the medical approach has probably been the Hungarian-American psychiatrist Thomas Szasz (1960, 1979), who, in a series of publications over nearly half a century, has argued that the concept of mental illness is incoherent. Szasz bases this claim on the assumptions that illness requires evidence of physical pathology, and that no such evidence has been found in the case of SCHIZOPHRENIA or any of the other major mental illness categories. Like Scheff, he claims that the concept of mental illness continues to be used because it appears to justify the containment and control of people who are irritating to others without being outright lawbreakers. However, Szasz is a libertarian and explicitly rejects the 'antipsychiatry' label because he has, 'No objection to psychiatry between consenting adults' (Szasz and Kerr 1997).

Of course, defenders of the medical approach often point to evidence of abnormal brain structure or function in mentally ill patients in an attempt to refute Szasz's argument. Recent evidence from structural and functional neuro-imaging studies seems to be consistent with this argument. However, evidence of this kind is frequently much less clear-cut than is often supposed (Bentall 2004). This is partly because abnormal BRAIN FUNCTION (see s. 1, BRAIN FUNCTION AND NEUROPSYCHOLOGY) and structure might plausibly arise as a consequence of adverse experience rather than any direct damage to the brain, but also because, as the philosopher Peter Sedgwick (1982) pointed out, human values inevitably affect our judgement about what is pathological, even in physical medicine. (If a swelling of the appendix had positive consequences, appendicitis would not be judged an illness.)

Within the discipline of psychology, a number of alternatives to the medical approach have been advocated. Psychodynamically orientated researchers and clinicians, following Sigmund Freud (1856–1939), view abnormal behaviour as arising from intrapsychic conflict, which typically occurs at the unconscious level. On this argument, the treatment of mental illness requires extensive psychotherapy to resolve the underlying conflicts. Although Freud believed in the unity of mind and brain, he eventually came to believe that a medical training provided a poor background for the practice of PSYCHOANALYSIS (see s. 1), and defended the right of non-medically qualified practitioners to work with patients (Freud 1926/1959).

The humanistic approach to psychiatric disorder, exemplified by the work of Carl Rogers (1902–87), assumes that people have a natural tendency to seek ways of fulfilling their potential, and that obstacles to this process create the need for defensive processes that lead to ANXIETY (see s. 6) or, when the defences are completely overwhelmed, psychosis (Rogers 1951). Within this framework, psychological treatment aims to create the conditions in which personal growth again becomes possible.

The first person to apply the behaviourist approach to psychological difficulties was John Broadus Watson (1878–1958), who argued that abnormal behaviour arose from unfortunate LEARNING (see s. 3) experiences; for example, that phobias could be established by CLASSICAL CONDITIONING (see s. 3) in the presence of adverse stimuli (Watson and Rayner 1920). Later behaviourists working in the operant tradition and inspired by the theories of B. F. Skinner (1904–90) claimed that abnormal behaviour often arose as a consequence of contingencies (see s. 1, CONTINGENCY/CONTINGENT) of REINFORCEMENT (see s. 3). According to this argument, abnormal behaviour can be eliminated by teaching the patient less dysfunctional ways of behaving, for example, by manipulating reinforcement contingencies (Ayllon and Azrin 1968). More recent advocates of COGNITIVE (BEHAVIOUR) THERAPY, for example Aaron Beck (1976), have argued that patients' difficulties arise as a consequence of their misinterpretations of events, reflecting selective cognitive biases that have been established in childhood.

Many of the competing ways of conceptualising psychiatric disorder may not be as incompatible as they first appear. For example, recent advances in neuroscience, particularly the development of neuro-imaging technologies, have created the possibility of examining brain changes during psychotherapy, or examining the effects on the central nervous system of adverse experiences such as sexual abuse or other kinds of trauma.   *RB*

Andreasen, N. C. 2001: *Brave New Brain: Conquering Mental Illness in the Era of the Genome*. Oxford: Oxford University Press. **Ayllon, T. and Azrin, N. H.** 1968: *The Token Economy: A Motivational System for Therapy and Rehabilitation*. New York: Appleton-Century-Crofts. **Beck, A. T.** 1976: *Cognitive Therapy and the Emotional Disorders*. New York: International Universities Press. **Bentall, R. P.** 2004: Sideshow?: Schizophrenia as con-strued by Szasz and the neoKraepelinians. In Schaler, J. (ed.), *Szasz Under Fire*. Chicago: Open Court. **Freud, S.** 1926/1959: The question of lay analysis: conversations with an impartial person (translated by J. Strachey), *Collected works*. London: Hogarth Press. **Guze, S.** 1989: Biological psychiatry: is there any other kind? *Psychological Medicine* 19, 315–23. **Kuhn, T.** 1970: *The Structure of Scientific Revolutions* (2nd edn). Chicago: Chicago University Press. **Porter, R.** 2002: *Madness: A Brief History*. Oxford: Oxford University Press. **Rogers, C.** 1951: *Client-centered Therapy: Its Current Practice*. Boston: Houghton Mifflin. **Scheff, T.** 1966: *Being Mentally Ill: A Sociological Theory*. Chicago: Aldine. **Sedgwick, P.** 1982: *Psychopolitics*. London: Pluto Press. **Szasz, T. S.** 1960: The myth of mental illness. *American Psychologist* 15, 564–80. **Szasz, T. S.** 1979: *Schizophrenia: The Sacred Symbol of Psychiatry*. Oxford: Oxford University Press. **Szasz, T. and Kerr, A.** 1997: Thomas Szasz: in conversation with Alan Kerr. *Psychiatric Bulletin* 21, 39–44. **Watson, J. B. and Rayner, R.** 1920: Conditioned emotional reactions. *Journal of Experimental Psychology* 3, 1–14.

mental retardation Mental retardation has been consistently defined in terms of significant limitations in intellectual functioning (normally, an INTELLIGENCE QUOTIENT (see s. 4) of less than 70, affecting 1–2.5 per cent of the population). Increasingly, it is accepted that deficits in intellectual functioning must be accompanied by limitations in adaptive SKILLS (see s. 3) (life skills including personal care, SOCIAL SKILLS (see s. 5) academic skills and COMMUNICATION – see s. 2). Mental retardation is considered as a DEVELOPMENTAL DISORDER (i.e. it should first appear before approximately 18 years of age) and may not be a permanent condition. That is, most definitions emphasise the need for assessments of *present* functioning. This reflects the fact that people may improve. A classic example of such improvement is the developmental catch-up experienced by children removed from deprived environments (e.g. O'Connor et al. 2000).

Definitions of mental retardation are revised regularly with the lead provided by the American Association on Mental Retardation (AAMR 2002). Although the term is used in the major classification systems (DSM and ICD [see INTERNATIONAL CLASSIFICATION OF DISEASES]), various labels are used throughout the world to refer to the same condition. The most recent internationally used term is 'intellectual disability', but other terms such as 'mental handicap' might still be in use. In the UK, 'learning disability' or 'learning difficulty' are two commonly used terms but this can cause confusion internationally (e.g. 'learning disability' in the USA refers to problems in school learning more broadly).

The causes of mental retardation are known in perhaps 50 per cent or more of cases and are many and varied: genetic syndromes, infections, physical injury, environmental deprivation and metabolic disorders, among others. A two-group approach to mental retardation suggests that those with mild intellectual limitations (IQ – see s. 6 – approximately 50/55–70) might develop similarly to those of normal IQ, but more slowly or reaching only earlier developmental stages, while those with severe intellectual impairments might have different developmental profiles and ABILITIES (see s. 6) due to neurobiological abnormalities of various kinds (Burack et al. 1998). This has fuelled an interest in characterising the behavioural PHENOTYPES (see s. 2) for genetic syndromes associated with mental retardation, including Down's syndrome.

Children and adults with mental retardation appear to be at increased risk of psychological problems such as severe behaviour disorders and psychiatric conditions, including AUTISM (see s. 6) (Dykens 2000). (See also s. 4, MENTAL RETARDATION) *RH*

American Association on Mental Retardation 2002: *Mental Retardation: Definition, Classification, and Systems of Support* (10th edn). Washington, DC: AAMR. **Burack, J. A., Hodapp, R. M. and Zigler, E.** 1998: *Handbook of Mental Retardation and Development.* New York: Cambridge University Press. **Dykens, E. M.** 2000: Psychopathology in children with intellectual disability. *Journal of Child Psychology and Psychiatry* 41, 407–17. **O'Connor, T. G., Rutter, M., Beckett, C., Keaveney, L., Kreppner, J. M. and the English and Romanian Adoptees Study Team** 2000: The effects of global severe privation on cognitive competence: extension and longitudinal follow-up. *Child Development* 71, 376–90.

mental state examination and diagnostic assessment

In order to assign a diagnosis to a patient, or simply to determine the range and severity of the patient's difficulties, a psychiatrist will collect information about the patient's symptoms and history of illness. If a diagnosis is required, this information will then be used to compare the patient to various diagnostic criteria, ideally those given in a diagnostic manual such as the DSM or ICD [see INTERNATIONAL CLASSIFICATION OF DISEASES].

Although case notes and the testimony of friends or relatives of the patient may be useful for this purpose, the primary source of information about the patient's symptoms is usually a mental state examination, in which the patient is asked about various common symptoms and experiences. In routine clinical practice, this process may be fairly informal and unstructured. However, if the information is required to be reliable (for example, when diagnoses are being assigned for the purposes of research), a formal interview schedule may be followed.

Several interview schedules have been designed for this purpose. All require the patient to be cross-examined about particular types of experiences and behaviour, but are flexible enough to enable the interviewer to vary the order of questions or to make up questions when a patient's answers are unclear. Most have been developed following extensive field trials, designed to show that the schedules yield reliable data. Examples include the Present State Examination (PSE; Wing, Cooper and Sartorius 1974), the Structured Clinical Interview for DSM-IV (SCID; First, Spitzer, Gibbon and Williams 1995), the Brief Psychiatric Rating Scale (BPRS; Overall and Gorman 1962) and the Positive and Negative Syndromes Schedule (PANSS; Kay and Opler 1987).

The PSE, which was subsequently revised to form the Structured Clinical Assessment in Neuropsychiatry (World Health Organization 1997), contains questions about a wide range of symptoms, and is not tied to any particular diagnostic system. The SCID, on the other hand, presents questions in an order designed to facilitate the assignment of DSM diagnoses. In contrast to these schedules, the BPRS and the PANSS (a revision of the BPRS, designed to give more information about NEGATIVE SYMPTOMS) are specifically designed to yield information about the severity of psychotic symptoms. Because they are sensitive to change, they are widely used in RANDOMISED CONTROLLED TRIALS of treatments for SCHIZOPHRE-

NIA, but they do not yield enough information about non-psychotic symptoms to make diagnoses outside of the schizophrenia spectrum.

Administering these schedules typically takes between 40 minutes and 1 hour but may require more time in the case of severely ill patients. Their use requires a formal period of training (typically lasting one or two weeks) but, with sufficient experience, competence can be achieved by most graduate researchers and does not require a formal qualification in PSYCHIATRY or CLINICAL PSYCHOLOGY (see also s. 1). *RB*

First, M., Spitzer, R., Gibbon, M. and Williams, J. 1995: *Structured Clinical Interview for Axis I DSM-IV Disorders.* Washington, DC: American Psychiatric Association Press. **Kay, S. R. and Opler, L. A.** 1987: The Positive and Negative Syndrome Scale (PANSS) for schizophrenia. *Schizophrenia Bulletin* 13, 507–18. **Overall, J. E. and Gorman, D. R.** 1962: The Brief Psychiatric Rating Scale. *Psychological Reports* 10, 799–812. **Wing, J. K., Cooper, J. E. and Sartorius, N.** 1974: *The Measurement and Classification of Psychiatric Symptoms.* Cambridge: Cambridge University Press, vol. 9. **World Health Organization** 1997: *Schedules for Clinical Assessment in Neuropsychiatry, SCAN Version 2.* Geneva: WHO.

mood stabilisers

DRUGS (see s. 2) that stabilise mood, often used in the treatment of patients suffering from BIPOLAR DISORDER, in order to prevent episodes of MANIA. The most widely used mood stabiliser is lithium carbonate, but recent studies have shown that anticonvulsant medications, such as carbamazepine, can act as effective mood stabilisers. *RB*

morbid jealousy

Feelings of jealousy and ownership of a loved person are a common human experience. However, morbid jealousy is evident when the individual becomes preoccupied and distressed by such feelings to an extent that it interferes with normal functioning. In extreme cases, the patient may develop DELUSIONS of infidelity, believing, in the absence of evidence, that a partner is being unfaithful despite reasonable reassurance to the contrary. This type of delusion is especially common in alcoholic men, although the reason for this is unclear. *RB*

motivational interviewing

A non-confrontational type of interviewing carried out by cognitive behaviour therapists [see COGNITIVE (BEHAVIOUR) THERAPY], designed to encourage the patient's MOTIVATION (see s. 6) to change and engage in treatment; used often with patients who are alcoholic or who abuse other substances, but who are only partially aware of the damaging effects of their addiction. *RB*

multiple baseline experiments

Used to measure the effects of an intervention or sequence of interventions, with the advantage that only a small number of participants are required. These kinds of EXPERIMENTS (see s. 8) work on the assumption that, if change occurs when or very shortly after a treatment is applied and not beforehand, then the treatment caused the observed changes. Typically, the behaviours of interest are assessed over a baseline period of days or weeks before the first intervention, and then the assessment is continued during the intervention and for a follow-up period afterwards.

Multiple baseline experiments may be conducted using a single participant and by measuring several behaviours (a multiple baseline across behaviours design) (Morley 1989). Alternatively, multiple baseline experiments may be conducted across several participants (a multiple baseline across subjects design) with varying baseline periods, so that the intervention is introduced at different times (thus allowing a more precise estimation of the extent to which behaviour change coincides with the introduction of the intervention).   *RB*

Morley, S. 1989: Single case research. In Parry, G. and Watts, F. N. (eds), *Behavioural and Mental Health Research: A Handbook of Skills and Methods*. Hove: Erlbaum.

Munchausen syndrome by proxy   A controversial diagnosis, often made by paediatricians, to indicate that a caregiver (usually a parent) is deliberately making a child ill in order to gain attention. Critics point out that the diagnosis is sometimes made simply on the basis of the absence of a physical explanation for a child's difficulties, rather than on positive evidence of abuse.   *RB*

myalgic encephalomyelitis (ME)   An illness characterised by excessive post-exertion fatigue, together with MEMORY (see s. 1) and concentration problems, now more often referred to as CHRONIC FATIGUE SYNDROME. Other symptoms may also be present.   *AW*

N

---

narcissistic personality disorder A PERSONALITY DISORDER characterised by a grandiose sense of self-importance, preoccupation with one's own 'specialness' and a sense of entitlement. *PK*

negative symptoms of schizophrenia The term negative symptoms is used today to describe those SCHIZOPHRENIA symptoms that involve the absence of desirable attributes, ABILITIES (see s. 6) and behaviours. However, the distinction between negative and positive symptoms originated in neurology and can be traced back to the writings of the nineteenth-century British neurologist Hughlings Jackson, who argued that the former resulted from the loss of higher cortical functions, whereas the latter (marked by the presence of behaviours that would preferably be absent) resulted from the consequent disinhibition of lower brain regions.

The distinction between positive and negative symptoms was imported into PSYCHIATRY by Tim Crow (1980). According to Crow's formulation, schizophrenia is the consequence of two separate pathological processes, the positive symptoms of DELUSIONS and HALLUCINATIONS resulting from some kind of abnormality in the dopamine system, whereas the negative symptoms are a consequence of cortical atrophy. Andreasen (1989) developed the Scale for the Assessment of Negative Symptoms, an interview schedule which defined five main types of negative symptoms: affective blunting (usually called flat affect; the loss of the ability to express EMOTION – see s. 6), alogia (impoverished speech), ANHEDONIA-asociality (loss of the ability to experience pleasure), AVOLITION (or apathy) and attentional impairment.

There is strong evidence that antipsychotic medication [see ANTIPSYCHOTIC DRUGS] can exacerbate negative symptoms – the term neuroleptic-induced deficit syndrome (NIDS) has been coined to describe the long-term loss of energy and MOTIVATION (see s. 6) sometimes experienced by patients taking this type of medication (Lewander 1994). It has also been argued that some patients develop deficits in SOCIAL SKILLS (see s. 5) and motivation as a consequence of long-term hospitalisation, and psychiatric services now try to avoid this. However, it is widely believed that a core of negative symptoms – sometimes called deficit symptoms – are the result of some kind of endogeneous pathological process. Consistent with this hypothesis, patients sometimes develop negative symptoms very early in their illness, and retrospective studies of school and occupational reports show that such patients often function poorly before becoming ill (Pogue-Geile and Harrow 1987).

There have been few psychological studies of specific negative symptoms, which tend to be unresponsive to either pharmacological or psychological treatment. However, experiments in which patients suffering from flat affect have been shown emotionally stimulating materials have found that their subjective experience of emotions is normal, so the problem seems to be one of EMOTIONAL EXPRESSION (see s. 5) (Berenbaum and Oltmanns 1992). Anhedonia, on the other hand, seems to be associated with both a lack of POSITIVE AFFECT (see s. 6) and increased NEGATIVE AFFECT (see s. 6) (Blanchard, Bellack and Mueser 1994). *RB*

Andreasen, N. C. 1989: Scale for the Assessment of Negative Symptoms (SANS). *British Journal of Psychiatry* 155 (suppl. 7), 53–8. **Berenbaum, H. and Oltmanns, T. F.** 1992: Emotional experience and expression in schizophrenia and depression. *Journal of Abnormal Psychology* 101, 37–44. **Blanchard, J. J., Bellack, A. S. and Mueser, K. T.** 1994: Affective and social correlates of physical and social anhedonia in schizophrenia. *Journal of Abnormal Psychology* 103, 719–28. **Crow, T. J.** 1980: Molecular pathology of schizophrenia: more than one disease process? *British Medical Journal* 280, 66–8. **Lewander, T.** 1994: Neuroleptics and the neuroleptic-induced deficit syndrome. *Acta Psychiatrica Scandinavica* 89, 8–13. **Pogue-Geile, M. F. and Harrow, M.** 1987: Negative symptoms in schizophrenia: longitudinal characteristics and etiological hypotheses. In Harvey, P. D. and Walker, E. F. (eds), *Positive and Negative Symptoms of Psychosis: Description, Research and Future Directions.* Hillsdale NJ: Erlbaum.

negative thought disorder A type of THOUGHT DISORDER in which there is both poverty of speech (relatively little speech is generated) and poverty of content of speech (speech is vague). Often observed in patients with a diagnosis of SCHIZOPHRENIA. *RB*

neuroleptic medication An alternative term for ANTIPSYCHOTIC DRUGS. Neuroleptics are used in the long-term treatment of psychotic disorders, especially SCHIZOPHRENIA. *RB*

O

obsessive-compulsive disorder (OCD)   OCD is
a condition in which the individual experiences obsessional thoughts (intrusive and unwanted thoughts and
images), sometimes accompanied by compulsions (repetitive behaviours such as handwashing and checking or performing particular mental rituals). The most common
types of obsessions concern contamination (e.g. by dirt),
undesirable impulses (e.g. to hurt a child or violate a
moral code) and doubts (e.g. that the door has been left
unlocked). Compulsions are usually performed with the
intention of avoiding a feared situation (e.g. repeatedly
washing to avoid contamination, or checking again and
again to see whether a door has been left unlocked), or
reducing the distress associated with an obsession.
Typically, OCD patients experience high levels of ANXIETY
(see s. 6). [see also ANXIETY DISORDERS].

Biological theories implicate neural circuits from the
frontal cortex to the caudate nucleus, which are thought to
regulate the release of stereotyped behaviour to specific
stimuli. However, cognitive behaviour therapists have
argued that OCD patients tend to make absolutist moral
judgements about their own thoughts, fail to distinguish
between thinking about behaving and actually behaving,
and have unrealistic expectations about their ability to
control their own thought processes (Salkovskis 1998).

Treatment is usually with ANTIDEPRESSANTS and/or COG-
NITIVE (BEHAVIOUR) THERAPY (Franklin and Foa 2002). *RB*

Franklin, M. E. and Foa, E. B. 2002: Cognitive behavioural
treatments for obsessive compulsive disorder. In Nathan, P. E.
and Gorman, J. M. (eds), *A Guide to Treatments that Work*. New
York: Oxford University Press. **Salkovskis, P. M.** 1998:
Psychological approaches to the understanding of obsessional
problems. In Swinton, R. (ed.), *Obsessive Compulsive Disorder:
Theory, Research and Treatment*. New York: Guilford.

P

pain The term 'pain' comes from the Latin word 'poena', meaning for punishment or torment and is used in many ways in common language to cover a range of phenomena, from a symptom of physical disorder, uncomfortable somatic sensations or emotional distress, to an irritating person, object or deed. In psychology a basic distinction is made between nociception (activation of pain RECEPTORS – see s. 2) and the PERCEPTION (see s. 1) of pain. There are many examples that show there is not a direct relationship between nociception and perceived pain. For example, in combat and sporting events people often do not feel the full pain of injury until after the event is over.

Two models of pain have been particularly influential in our understanding of pain. The first is the gate control theory of pain (Melzack and Wall 1965), which provides a physiological basis for the influence of psychological factors on pain. The gate control theory says there is a neural 'gate' mechanism in the spine which modulates the passage of pain information from the peripheral receptors to the central nervous system. The gate can be opened or closed by stimulation to peripheral nerves (such as rubbing a hurt limb) and by downward impulses from the brain. Therefore, if a person is tense and focused on the pain, the neural gate is more likely to be open and their perceived pain will be greater than someone who is relaxed and focused on something other than the pain.

The second approach to pain that is currently influential is the multidimensional model of pain. This acknowledges that pain is a complex and dynamic process involving nociception, cognitive factors (e.g. appraisal), behavioural factors (e.g. pain behaviours, reduced activity), emotional factors (e.g. ANXIETY – see s. 6, distress) and sociocultural factors (e.g. social context, responses of others, cultural norms, etc.). There is a lot of evidence for the role of these factors in perceived pain and pain behaviours. For example, Fisher and Johnston (1996) manipulated anxiety in chronic pain patients by asking them to RECALL (see s. 3) upsetting or positive events, and found change in anxiety predicted changes in disability.

These models form the theoretical basis for psychological treatment programmes for chronic pain which are effective in helping people become more active, less disabled and develop more adaptive ways of COPING with pain. (See also s. 2, PAIN) *SA*

Fisher, K. and Johnston, M. 1996: Emotional distress as a mediator of the relationship between pain and disability: an experimental study. *British Journal of Health Psychology* 1, 207–18. **Melzack, R. and Wall, P. D.** 1965: Pain mechanisms: a new theory. *Science* 50, 971–9.

panic disorder Panic disorder is a condition in which the individual repeatedly experiences unexpected panic attacks, which may involve palpitations, dizziness, shortness of breath, sweating, DEPERSONALISATION (see s. 5), derealisation and the fear of losing control. Panic attacks may be distinguished from other forms of anxiety by their sudden onset, intensity and brevity. Patients with panic disorder are typically preoccupied with the fear of having another attack. In DSM-IV (APA 1994), a distinction is made between panic disorder with agoraphobia (fear of public places) and panic disorder without agoraphobia. Typically, panic disorder patients become agoraphobic as a consequence of avoiding situations in which they think a panic attack is likely. Patients experiencing panic attacks often interpret them in a catastrophic way (e.g. that they are having a heart attack).

It has been estimated that about 3.5 per cent of the US population have experienced panic disorder at some point in their lives, and the disorder appears to be more common in women than men (Kessler et al. 1994). Age of onset is typically in late adolescence or early adulthood, especially in males. Many panic disorder patients also suffer from other psychiatric conditions, especially DEPRESSION.

Various stimuli can elicit panic attacks, including infusions of sodium lactate (a substance similar to the lactate produced by the body during exercise) and inhalation of carbon dioxide. Panic disorder patients are much more likely to experience attacks under these circumstances than ordinary people. Although these findings have sometimes been interpreted as evidence of an underlying biological dysfunction, most researchers now recognise that they can be accommodated within a COGNITIVE (see s. 1, cognitive Psychology) model of the disorder. According to this model (Clark 1996), a triggering stimulus leads to the perception of threat, which in turn leads to apprehension and various bodily sensations (for example, lightheadedness, sweating, palpitations, as a consequence of hyperventilation). The individual's catastrophic interpretations of these bodily sensations then leads to further apprehension and so on.

Panic disorder is sometimes treated with BENZODIAZAPINE medications, which are quick-acting, but which lead to withdrawal problems in the long-term. ANTIDEPRESSANT DRUGS are now favoured for this reason. However, the most effective treatment is COGNITIVE (BEHAVIOUR) THERAPY (CBT), usually conducted over 10–15 sessions. There is some evidence that patients receiving combined pharmacotherapy and CBT do worse in the long-term than those treated with CBT alone (White and Barlow 2002). *GD*

American Psychiatric Association 1994: *Diagnostic and Statistical Manual for Mental Disorders* (4th edn). Washington, DC: Author. **Clark, D. M.** 1996: Panic disorder: from theory to therapy. In Rapee, R. M. (ed.), *Current Controversies in the Anxiety Disorders*. New York: Guilford. **Kessler, R. C., McGonagle, K. A., Zhao, S., Nelson, C. R., Highes, M., Eshleman, S., Wittchen, H. and Kendler, K. S.** 1994: Lifetime and 12-month prevalence of DSM-III-R psychiatric disorders in the United States: results from the National Comorbidity Survey. *Archives of General Psychiatry* 51, 620–31. **White, K. S. and Barlow, D. H.** 2002: In Barlow, D. H. (ed.), *Anxiety and its Disorders* (2nd edn). New York: Guilford.

paradoxical intervention   A psychological intervention in which the patient is prescribed some kind of behaviour with the intention of preventing the behaviour in the future; for example, a person with a stutter may be asked to practise stuttering. Paradoxical interventions are sometimes used by behaviour therapists, but more often by practitioners of some forms of family therapy.   *RB*

paranoia   Either a mental state characterised by extreme suspiciousness of the intentions of others, or a psychotic disorder in which DELUSIONS (especially of persecution) are the main and perhaps only symptom (the term DELUSIONAL DISORDER is now often used as an alternative to PARANOIA in this second sense).   *RB*

paranoid personality disorder   A PERSONALITY DISORDER characterised by distrust and suspiciousness of other people and their motives.   *PK*

paraphilias   The paraphilias are sexual disorders that involve abnormal means of obtaining sexual arousal, leading to clinically significant distress or impairment of functioning. (According to the DSM, unusual means of obtaining sexual arousal do not constitute disorders in the absence of distress or impairment.) Examples include exhibitionism (involving exposing the genitals to strangers), fetishism (in which sexual arousal is associated with particular objects or materials), frotteurism (arousal from touching a non-consenting person), sexual masochism (arousal from the experience of PAIN or suffering), sadism (arousal from the infliction of pain or suffering on others), voyeurism (arousal from observing sexual activity by others) and paedophilia (arousal or sexual behaviour involving prepubescent children). Paedophilia, in particular, is a focus of interest by law enforcement agencies, because of concerns about the protection of children from sexual assault.

Paraphilias, especially fetishism, have been explained in terms of CLASSICAL CONDITIONING (see s. 3) (Rachman and Hodgson 1968). However, modern theories of paedophilia tend to be multidimensional, emphasising childhood experience and other factors that lead to the development of unconventional sexual interests, as well as cognitive distortions that undermine self-control (Marshall 1997).   *RB*

Marshall, W. L. 1997: Pedophilia: psychopathology and theory. In Laws, D. R. and O'Donohue, W. (eds), *Sexual Deviance*. New York: Guilford. **Rachman, S. and Hodgson, S.** 1968: Experimentally induced 'sexual fetishism': replication and development. *Psychological Record* 18, 25–7.

penetrance (of genes for psychiatric disorders)

A gene may have low penetrance for a TRAIT (see s. 6) (disease or psychiatric disorder) if only some of those carrying the gene have the trait, because of the involvement of other genes or environmental influences.   *RB*

per-protocol analysis   An analysis of data from a RANDOMISED CONTROLLED TRIAL in which only data from those who complete an adequate course of treatment are included (patients who refuse treatment or who drop out for other reasons are therefore excluded). Critics argue that this kind of analysis is unrealistic, because patients offered a treatment in real-life clinical services may refuse or fail to complete it, and, in these cases, the treatment should be considered unsuccessful.   *RB*

personality disorders   Personality disorder is defined in the American Psychiatric Association's *Diagnostic and Statistical Manual* (DSM-IV; American Psychiatric Association 1994) as '. . . an enduring pattern of inner experience and behaviour that deviates markedly from the expectations of the individual's culture, is pervasive and inflexible, has an onset in adolescence or early adulthood, is stable over time, and leads to distress or impairment'. A similar definition is given in the World Health Organization's (1992) INTERNATIONAL CLASSIFICATION OF DISEASE. The DSM system places personality disorders on a separate axis (axis-2) to psychiatric disorders (axis-1), to emphasise that they are different and to encourage clinicians to assign both types of diagnoses to the same patients.

There are ten categories or sub-diagnoses of specific personality disorders in DSM-IV, grouped into three clusters (see Table). There are nine such categories in ICD-10, and the fact that these two major diagnostic schemes do not agree is one reason to doubt the scientific VALIDITY (see s. 6 and s. 8) of a categorical classification system (Pilgrim 2001). Another difficulty is that very many patients meet the criteria for two or more personality disorders, giving rise to the suspicion that the diagnoses do not describe separable conditions. Examination of the definitions of each of the individual categories reveals ambiguity about whether these disorders should be regarded as attenuated psychiatric illnesses (SCHIZOTYPAL PERSONALITY DISORDER, for example, appears to be an attenuated form of SCHIZOPHRENIA), extreme variants of normal PERSONALITY TRAITS (see s. 6), both or (as implied in the DSM system) neither. In recent years, considerable efforts have

personality disorders *DSM-IV personality disorders grouped into three clusters*

Cluster A (the 'odd or eccentric' types)	
Paranoid	distrusting and suspicious interpretation of the motives of others
Schizoid	social detachment and restricted emotional expression
Schizotypal	social discomfort, cognitive distortions, behavioural eccentricities

Cluster B (the 'dramatic, emotional or erratic' types)	
Histrionic	excessive emotionality and attention seeking
Narcissistic	grandiosity, need for admiration, lack of empathy
Antisocial	disregard for and violation of the rights of others
Borderline	unstable relationships, self-image and affects, and impulsivity

Cluster C (the 'anxious and fearful' types)	
Obsessive-compulsive	preoccupation with orderliness, perfectionism and control
Avoidant	socially inhibited, feelings of inadequacy, hypersensitivity to negative evaluation
Dependent	submissive behaviour, need to be taken care of

been made to relate the DSM personality disorder categories to the big five dimensions of PERSONALITY (see s. 1 and s. 6) of OPENNESS (see s. 6), CONSCIENTIOUSNESS (see s. 6), EXTROVERSION (see s. 6), AGREEABLENESS (see s. 6) and NEUROTICISM (see s. 6) (Costa and Widiger 2001). Some researchers have pursued this line of investigation in the hope of finding more reliable ways of diagnosing patients and assigning them to the various DSM categories, whereas others have hoped to devise an alternative dimensional classification system altogether. A recent META-ANALYSIS (see s. 8) found a strong association between most personality disorder categories and a combination of high neuroticism and low agreeableness (Saulsman and Page 2004). In the absence of agreement about an alternative classification system, most psychologists and psychiatrists continue to use categorical diagnoses within a psychological framework that implies some continuity with normal functioning.

However defined, personality disorder is a common problem. The prevalence in the general population has been estimated as being around 10 per cent and considerably higher in people with other forms of mental health problems (Moran et al. 2000). Personality disorder is most commonly diagnosed in people aged between 25 and 44 and is equally common in men and women. However, ANTISOCIAL PERSONALITY DISORDER is more commonly diagnosed in men, and BORDERLINE PERSONALITY DISORDER is more commonly diagnosed in women. People with personality disorder are likely to suffer from alcohol and drug problems, self-harm and suicide, and are also more likely than ordinary people to experience adverse life events, such as relationship difficulties, housing problems and long-term unemployment. Personality disorder is also associated with frequent uses of mental health services (Perry et al. 1987; Guthrie et al. 1999). This means that personality disorder is a serious challenge for mental health services (National Institute for Mental Health in England 2002).

Attempts have been made to explain personality disorders within evolutionary (see s. 1, EVOLUTION AND PSYCHOLOGY), psychodynamic, neurobiological and social-cognitive frameworks (Clarkin and Lenzenweger 1996). However, psychologists generally agree that personality disorder has its origins in childhood. Adults who are diagnosed with personality disorder have often been subjected to neglect or abuse or have experienced other problems during childhood. There is no proven pharmacological treatment for personality disorder (although drugs may be prescribed to alleviate symptoms such as DEPRESSION), so it is usually assumed that intensive psychological treatment, such as psychodynamic therapy (Guthrie et al. 1999), or an extended period of COGNITIVE BEHAVIOUR THERAPY (Young 1999) will be required.

Beck and Freeman's (1990) approach, extended from Beck's previous work on the cognitive processes involved in depression and other psychiatric disorders, reflects the broad philosophical and theoretical assumptions of the social-cognitive framework. They assume that individuals' perceptions and interpretations of situations shape their emotional and behavioural responses and that psychopathology therefore arises from systematic errors, biases and distortions in perceiving and interpreting events. These, in turn, are related to dysfunctional assumptions and core beliefs about the world. When this broad approach is applied to personality disorder, relatively greater emphasis is placed on core beliefs and dysfunctional assumptions than in the case of more episodic psychiatric disorders. Young (1999), in particular, has emphasised the importance of early maladaptive SCHEMAS (see s. 3), which are seen as the self-perpetuating consequences of negative experiences in early life. For this reason, it is expected that cognitive therapy for personality disorder will require more time than the treatment of DSM axis-1 conditions.   *PK*

American Psychiatric Association 1994: *Diagnostic and Statistical Manual for Mental Disorders* (4th edn). Washington, DC: APA. **Beck, A. T. and Freeman, A.** 1990: *Cognitive Therapy of Personality Disorders*. New York: Guilford Press. **Clarkin, J. F. and Lenzenweger, M. F.** (eds) 1996: *Major Theories of Personality Disorder*. New York: Guilford Press. **Costa, P. T. and Widiger, T. A.** (eds) 2001: *Personality Disorders and the Five-Factor Model of Personality* (2nd edn). Washington, DC: American Psychological Association. **Guthrie, E., Moorey, J., Margison, F. et al.** 1999: Cost-effectiveness of brief psychodynamic-interpersonal therapy in high utilizers of psychiatric services. *Archives of General Psychiatry* 56, 519–26. **Moran, P., Jenkins, R., Tylee, A., Blizard, R. and Mann, A.** 2000: The prevalence of personality disorder among UK primary care attenders. *Acta Psychiatrica Scandinavica* 102, 52–7. **National Institute for Mental Health in England** 2002: *Personality Disorder: No Longer a Diagnosis of Exclusion*. London: National Institute for Mental Health in England/Department of Health. **Perry, J. C., Lavori, P. W. and Hoke, L.** 1987: A Markov model for predicting levels of psychiatric service use in borderline and antisocial personality disorders and bipolar type II affective disorder. *Journal of Psychiatric Research* 21, 215–32. **Pilgrim, D.** 2001: Disordered personalities and disordered concepts. *Journal of Mental Health* 10, 253–65. **Saulsman, L. M. and Page, A. C.** 2004: The five-factor model and personality disorder empirical literature: a meta-analytic review. *Clinical Psychology Review* 23, 1055–85. **World Health Organization** 1992: *ICD-10: International Statistical Classification of Diseases and Related Health Problems* (10th rev. edn). Geneva: WHO. **Young, J. E.** (1999): *Cognitive Therapy for Personality Disorders: A Schema-Focused Approach* (3rd edn). Sarasota, FL: Professional Resource Press.

pharmacotherapy (drug treatment) for psychiatric disorders

DRUG (see s. 2) treatments have long been used in the management of psychiatric disorders; in Victorian times psychiatrists used a variety of sedatives and stimulants to quieten or activate patients as required. However, the first drug therapy proven to be effective was chlorpromazine (marketed as Largactil and Thorazine in the UK and USA respectively), which was introduced as a treatment for SCHIZOPHRENIA in the early 1950s (Shorter 1997). The accidental discovery that this compound could ameliorate psychotic symptoms and reduce the risk of a psychotic RELAPSE led to the search for other ANTIPSYCHOTIC DRUGS, and a large number of these compounds are now available. Shortly after the introduction of the antipsychotics, the ANTIDEPRESSANT effects of the tricyclic medications and monoamine oxidase inhibitors were discovered. During the 1960s, the BENZODIAZAPINES were discovered to have an anxiolytic (anti-anxiety) effect, and lithium carbonate was discovered to be an effective MOOD STABILISER.

Antipsychotics, antidepressants, anxiolytics and mood stabilisers remain the main types of psychiatric drugs in use today, but the range of compounds available in each of these categories has increased, most notably with the introduction of the ATYPICAL ANTIPSYCHOTIC DRUGS and SELECTIVE SEROTONIN REUPTAKE INHIBITORS (which have more tolerable side effects than the antipsychotic and anti-depressant drugs which they have respectively super-seded), and with the discovery that some anticonvulsant drugs have mood-stabilising properties. Advocates of pharmacotherapy for psychiatric disorders, while noting that most of the drugs in use today have been discovered either by accident or trial-and-error experimentation, argue that future medications will be designed on the basis of an understanding of the molecular genetics of psychiatric disorders and knowledge about the central nervous system (Barondes 2003).

Critics have noted that pharmaceutical companies now exert enormous influence over psychiatric practice (Moncrieff 2003) and that the introduction of new classes of psychiatric drugs has led to changing perceptions about the nature of psychiatric disorders that may not be entirely beneficial; for example, prior to the discovery of the TRICYCLIC ANTIDEPRESSANTS, DEPRESSION was not seen as a medical condition and, indeed, drug companies were reluctant to invest in research into depression (Healy 1997). In modern times, some psychiatrists have even advocated 'cosmetic PSYCHOPHARMACOLOGY' (see s. 2) to bring about changes in normal personality characteristics (Kramer 1993). *RB*

Barondes, S. H. 2003: *Better than Prozac: Creating the Next Generation of Psychiatric Drugs.* Oxford: Oxford University Press. **Healy, D.** 1997: *The Anti-Depressant Era.* Cambridge MA: Harvard University Press. **Kramer, P. D.** 1993: *Listening to Prozac.* New York: Viking Press. **Moncrieff, J.** 2003: *Is Psychiatry for Sale? (Maudsley Monograph).* London: Institute of Psychiatry. **Shorter, E.** 1997: *A History of Psychiatry.* New York: Wiley.

phobias A phobia involves intense fear, triggered by the presence or anticipation of a particular stimulus. Many different kinds of phobia have received special names, including acrophobia (fear of heights), agoraphobia (fear of public places), and claustrophobia (fear of confined spaces). However, DSM-IV (APA 1994) recognises four main types: fear of animals (e.g. snakes or spiders), fear of aspects of the natural environment (e.g. water, heights), fear of specific situations (e.g. aircraft, elevators) and fear of blood, injections or injury. It has been estimated that about 7 per cent of men and 16 per cent of women suffer from one or more phobias (Kessler et al. 1994).

Freud interpreted the horse phobia of a five-year-old boy, Little Hans, in terms of the Oedipus complex, arguing that the horse symbolised the father who the boy feared might castrate him. However, LEARNING (see s. 3) theorists have argued that the boy's fear could more easily be explained in terms of CLASSICAL CONDITIONING (see s. 3) (Wolpe and Rachman 1960). The behaviourist John Watson attempted to demonstrate the role of conditioning in phobias by establishing a fear of small animals in an infant, Little Albert, by making a frightening noise while the infant held a tame animal (Watson and Rayner 1920). Although this somewhat unethical (see s. 1, ETHICAL ISSUES IN RESEARCH) experiment was successful, the classical conditioning model of phobias has been criticised because most phobic patients cannot recall a traumatic event associated with the onset of their symptoms, and because

some phobias (e.g. of spiders and snakes) seem to be more readily acquired than others.

Seligman (1971) argued that some stimuli are more readily associated with fear because these associations are prepared by evolution (see s. 1, EVOLUTION AND PSYCHOLOGY). In support of preparedness theory, laboratory studies show that fear can more readily be conditioned to evolutionarily significant stimuli (e.g. snakes and insects) than to evolutionarily meaningless stimuli (e.g. shapes). There is also evidence that vicarious LEARNING (see s. 3) can lead to phobias, especially towards prepared stimuli; for example Mineka (e.g. Mineka and Cook 1993) has shown that rhesus monkeys readily acquire a fear of snakes by observing the already established fear reactions of other monkeys.

Exposure therapies are the most effective method of treating phobias. These treatments require the patient to tolerate the feared object in a safe environment until the fear subsides. This can be done by immediate and prolonged exposure to the feared stimulus (FLOODING) or by gradual exposure to progressively more frightening stimuli in a series of steps (SYSTEMATIC DESENSITISATION). *GD*

APA. 1994: *Diagnostic and Statistical Manual for Mental Disorders* (4th edn). Washington, DC: American Psychiatric Association. **Kessler, R. C., McGonagle, K. A., Zhao, S., Nelson, C. R., Highes, M., Eshleman, S., Wittchen, H. and Kendler, K. S.** 1994: Lifetime and 12-month prevalence of DSM-III-R psychiatric disorders in the United States: results from the National Comorbidity Survey. *Archives of General Psychiatry* 51, 620–31. **Mineka, S. and Cook, M.** 1993: Mechanisms underlying observational conditioning of fear in monkeys. *Journal of Experimental Psychology: General* 122, 23–38. **Seligman, M. E. P.** 1971: Phobias and preparedness. *Behavior Therapy* 2, 307–20. **Watson, J. B. and Rayner, R.** 1920: Conditioned emotional reactions. *Journal of Experimental Psychology* 3, 1–14. **Wolpe, J. and Rachman, S. J.** 1960: Psychoanalytic evidence: a critique based on Freud's case of Little Hans. *Journal of Nervous and Mental Disease* 131, 135–45.

positive symptoms Those symptoms of severe mental illness (PSYCHOSIS) that consist of behaviours and experiences that would preferably be absent, for example, HALLUCINATIONS and DELUSIONS. Contrasted with negative symptoms. *RB*

positive thought disorder A type of THOUGHT DISORDER in which speech becomes incoherent to the listener because, for example, it shows apparent tangentiality (oblique responses to questions), derailment (ideas slip off one track onto an unrelated track), blocking (speech ceases unexpectedly), clanging (sounds rather than meaningful relations seem to link words) and other features. Often observed in patients with SCHIZOPHRENIA or MANIA. *RB*

post-traumatic stress disorder (PTSD) A cluster of symptoms commonly experienced by individuals following life-threatening or otherwise extremely traumatic events, including: (i) persistent re-experiencing of the event, for example, in distressing recollections, emotional reactions to relevant cues or dreams; (ii) persistent avoidance of stimuli associated with the traumatic event and a feeling of emotional numbness, for example, as reflected in detachment from others and a failure to participate in significant activities; and (iii) persistent arousal, as evidenced by loss of sleep (see s. 2, SLEEP AND BIOLOGICAL RHYTHMS), irritability and difficulty concentrating. According to DSM-IV the symptoms must persist for one month or more. In fact, it is not uncommon for patients to experience the symptoms for more than a decade (Kessler et al. 1995).

Individuals who are highly neurotic and who lack SOCIAL SUPPORT (see s. 5) are most likely to develop PTSD following a traumatic experience (Galea et al. 2002). At a cognitive level, it appears that PTSD symptoms are related to a lack of emotional processing and a failure to integrate memories of the trauma with broader memories and beliefs (Ehlers and Clark 2000). *RB*

Ehlers, A. and Clark, D. M. 2000: A cognitive model of persistent post-traumatic stress disorder. *Behaviour Research and Therapy* 38, 319–45. **Galea, S., Ahern, J., Resnick, H., Kilpatrick, D., Bucuvalas, M., Gold, J. and Vlahov, D.** 2002: Psychological sequalae of the September 11 terrorist attacks. *New England Journal of Medicine* 346, 982–7.

predictive validity The ability of a diagnosis to predict important outcomes, such as the course of an illness without treatment (whether or not the patient will get better) or response to treatment (for example, which type of DRUG – see s. 2 – will produce therapeutic benefits). *RB*

projection A defence mechanism in which undesirable characteristics of the SELF (see s. 1, s. 4 and s. 5) are attributed to one or more other persons. *RB*

pseudohallucination A term sometimes used to describe either a hallucination that is experienced as originating inside the body, or a hallucination for which the patient retains insight (that is, the patient knows that the experience is not real). Both distinctions with full-blown hallucinations are not thought to be of diagnostic or clinical significance. *RB*

psychiatric classification No scientific endeavour can be successful without a meaningful system of classifying the phenomena of interest. Unfortunately, the classification of psychiatric disorders continues to be the subject of controversy (Blashfield 1984; Kendell 1975).

Traditionally, psychiatric classification has been dominated by a medical conception of psychiatric disorders, according to which patients are allocated a diagnosis. This approach, which is sometimes called a CATEGORICAL MODEL (because it divides patients into categories) became widely accepted as a result of the efforts of (mainly) German-speaking psychiatrists in the nineteenth century. Emil Kraepelin (1856–1926) was particularly influential in this regard, arguing that disorders should be classified according to the pattern of symptoms experienced by patients and their long-term outcome (that is, patients with the same symptoms and similar outcomes should have the same diagnosis). Kraepelin's work, and his attempt to identify clusters of symptoms that occurred naturally together and which had typical outcomes, became the template for later attempts to devise categorical systems of diagnoses. His diagnostic concepts of dementia praecox (now called SCHIZOPHRENIA), alleged to have a deteriorating course, and 'manic depression' (under which term he grouped together all severe disor-

ders of mood), with a better average outcome, are widely accepted today.

Diagnostic concepts have evolved and been elaborated since Kraepelin's time, and this process continues today. However, by the final quarter of the twentieth century a consensus scheme had emerged, in which adult disorders were divided into three main types: the psychoses (characterised by loss of touch with reality and severe disablement); the neuroses (characterised by abnormalities of mood, especially DEPRESSION and ANXIETY (see s. 6), with reality testing preserved) and the PERSONALITY DISORDERS (persistent maladaptive ways of functioning and relating to others). After World War II (see s. 1, WAR AND PSYCHOLOGY), efforts were increasingly made to define these diagnostic concepts using unambiguous criteria, and a number of rival diagnostic schemes were proposed. A watershed was reached with the American Psychiatric Association's publication of the third edition of its *Diagnostic and Statistical Manual* (DSM-III; American Psychiatric Association 1980), which attempted to specify operational rules for making each diagnosis. Today, the only rival to the DSM system (currently in its fourth edition, published in 1997) is a very similar system outlined in the World Health Organization's INTERNATIONAL CLASSIFICATION OF DISEASES, currently in its tenth edition (*ICD-10*; World Health Organization 1992).

Critics of the categorical model point out that these kinds of diagnostic systems fail to fulfil many of the functions for which they are designed. A minimum requirement of such a system is that it be reliable – different clinicians should agree about which diagnosis each patient should receive. Although DSM-III was introduced to solve problems of RELIABILITY (see s. 6 and s. 8) evident in earlier diagnostic schemes, it is doubtful whether this has been achieved (Kirk and Kutchins 1992). A further problem that affects both the ICD and DSM systems is known as 'co-morbidity' – patients typically meet the criteria for more than one disorder, leading to the suspicion that they are not separate conditions. Categorical systems have also been criticised because they fail to pass various VALIDITY (see s. 6 and s. 8) tests – for example, they are not good predictors of outcome and fail to predict which kind of treatment will be most effective (Clark, Watson and Reynolds 1995).

A number of alternatives to the categorical model have been advocated at different times. One approach, advocated by Foulds (1965) proposes a hierarchy of disorders, in which the psychoses are seen as more severe than the neuroses. Consistent with this model, most psychotic patients also experience neurotic symptoms such as depression and anxiety.

Some researchers have advocated DIMENSIONAL MODELS, in which patients' symptoms are classified according to various dimensions of psychopathology. This approach was advocated by the German psychiatrist Ernest Kretschmer (1888–1964), who argued that he could identify normal personality types that were attenuated forms of schizophrenia and manic depression (BIPOLAR DISORDER). Kretschmer believed that each PERSONALITY (see s. 1 and s. 6) type was associated with a particular type of physical constitution. The British (but German-born) psychologist H. J. Eysenck (1916–97) later developed this idea further, arguing that psychiatric disorders represented extreme variants of the normal personality dimensions of NEUROTICISM (see s. 6) (N), EXTROVERSION (see s. 6) (E) and PSYCHOTICISM (see s. 6) (P) (for example, manic depression was said to be a manifestation of high P and high E). Although there is now compelling evidence of a normally distributed spectrum of schizotypal traits (sometimes called psychosis-proneness; see SCHIZOTYPAL PERSONALITY DISORDER), Eysenck's scheme has been criticised because his P dimension seems to be unrelated to PSYCHOSIS and would be better characterised as 'tough-mindedness'. More recent dimensional schemes have been developed pragmatically, on the basis of factor analyses (see s. 6 and s. 8, FACTOR ANALYSIS) of patients' symptoms. A widely accepted model suggests that psychotic symptoms can be classified on three dimensions according to the severity of positive symptoms, negative symptoms and symptoms of cognitive disorganisation; there is some evidence that classification according to this scheme better predicts social functioning and outcome than classification according to traditional diagnoses (van Os et al. 1999).

Some clinicians and researchers have argued that the attempt to classify psychiatric disorders will never be entirely satisfactory. The American psychiatrist Adolf Meyer (1866–1950) objected that, 'we should not classify people as plants', believing that psychiatric diagnoses never did justice to patients' problems. Radical psychiatrists such as R. D. Laing (1927–89), who characterised themselves as 'antipsychiatrists', often dismissed the whole attempt to understand patients' problems in medical or scientific terms, and argued that psychotic experiences should be seen as creative experiences or rational responses to an irrational world. Psychologists working within the behaviourist or cognitive-behaviourist traditions have advocated the use of individually tailored CASE FORMULATIONS of patients' problems to understand their origins and direct treatment.

More recently, some psychologists have argued that many of the problems of psychiatric classification can be resolved by abandoning broad diagnoses such as 'schizophrenia' and instead classifying patients according to their symptoms (for example, whether or not they experience hallucinated voices or suffer from delusions) (Bentall 2003); these researchers point out that substantial progress has been made in understanding psychiatric problems and devising treatments when individual symptoms have been examined (for example, that research points to the involvement of particular psychological processes in delusions, and that this discovery has led to the development of novel cognitive-behavioural interventions).

In defence of the categorical model, some clinicians and researchers concede that it has little scientific credibility but argue that traditional diagnoses nonetheless have some clinical utility, as a kind of shorthand that allows clinicians to communicate about cases.   *RB*

American Psychiatric Association 1980: *Diagnostic and Statistical Manual of Mental Disorders* (3rd edn). Washington, DC: APA. Bentall, R. P. 2003: *Madness Explained: Psychosis and Human Nature*. London: Penguin. Blashfield, R. K. 1984: *The Classification of Psychopathology: NeoKraepelinian and Quantitative Approaches*. New York: Plenum. Clark, L. A., Watson, D. and Reynolds, S. 1995: Diagnosis and classification of psychopathology: challenges to the current system and future directions. *Annual Review of Psychology* 46, 121–53. Foulds, G. A. 1965: *Personality and Personal Illness*. London: Tavistock Press. Kendell, R. E. 1975: *The Role of Diagnosis in Psychiatry*. Oxford: Blackwell. Kirk, S. A. and Kutchins, H. 1992: *The Selling of DSM: The Rhetoric of Science in Psychiatry*. Hawthorne NY: Aldine de Gruyter. van Os, J., Gilvarry, C., Bale, R., van Horn, E., Tattan, T., White, I. and Murray, R. 1999: A comparison of the utility of dimensional and categorical representations of psychosis. *Psychological Medicine* 29, 595–606. World Health Organization 1992: *ICD-10: International Statistical Classification of Diseases and Related Health Problems* (10th rev. edn). Geneva: World Health Organization.

psychiatric treatment Treatment for psychiatric conditions may be administered by psychiatrists [see PSYCHIATRY], clinical psychologists [see CLINICAL PSYCHOLOGY] and a variety of other health care professionals. The actual range of treatments offered has increased considerably over the last half century, as has the evidence base that allows judgements to be made about their usefulness. RANDOMISED CONTROLLED TRIALS (RCTs) are commonly used to assess their efficacy (the extent to which they produce a therapeutic effect under experimentally controlled conditions), effectiveness (the extent to which they produce a therapeutic effect in the realworld conditions of a clinical service) and cost-effectiveness (the extent to which they can be judged value for money when compared with other types of treatments).

Treatments for psychiatric disorders can be divided in to two main types: physical or somatic, and psychological. Prior to the widespread introduction of RCTs in the 1970s, a variety of physical treatments became popular and then unpopular as the balance of OPINION (see s. 5) among psychiatrists shifted. Some of these treatments, such as INSULIN COMA THERAPY and the prefrontal leucotomy operation, posed considerable hazards for patients, appeared to have little therapeutic effect and were arguably cruel. In modern psychiatric practice, the main types of physical treatment available are ELECTROCONVULSIVE THERAPY (ECT) and PHARMACOTHERAPY (DRUG – see s. 2 – treatment).

Few psychological practitioners today would advocate Freudian PSYCHOANALYSIS (see s. 1) as a form of treatment because of doubts about its effectiveness and cost effectiveness (it is a very lengthy type of treatment). However, a (to some minds, bewildering) range of psychological treatments is available. Most of the individual treatments can be grouped into the categories of psychodynamic therapy (inspired by psychoanalysis but typically much briefer), BEHAVIOUR THERAPY (based on learning theory, and most often employed with ANXIETY DISORDERS) and COGNITIVE (BEHAVIOUR) THERAPY (combining behavioural strategies with techniques for challenging patients' dysfunctional BELIEFS (see s. 5), originally developed as a treatment for DEPRESSION but now used with most types of psychiatric disorders). GROUP THERAPY (in which a number of patients are treated at the same time) and FAMILY THERAPY (in which the therapist works with families) are also used.   *RB*

psychiatry Psychiatry is the branch of medicine concerned with the treatment of people suffering from psychiatric disorders. Psychiatrists therefore receive an initial training in general medicine before undergoing further specific training in psychiatry.

Psychiatrists embrace a wide range of opinions about the nature and treatment of psychiatric disorders. However, most regard psychiatric problems as illnesses comparable to illnesses in physical medicine [see MENTAL ILLNESS: CONCEPTS OF]. They are therefore concerned with issues of PSYCHIATRIC CLASSIFICATION, regard diagnostic assessment as the essential first stage of treatment and often use PHARMACOTHERAPY as the main line of treatment.

In most countries, psychiatrists are the only professional group licensed to prescribe psychiatric DRUGS (see s. 2), but this may change (in the USA some states have introduced legislation that will allow clinical psychologists to prescribe.) Also, in most countries, psychiatrists have unique legal powers and responsibilities, for example, the power to compel patients to come into hospital and/or receive treatment.   *RB*

psychopathology   The scientific study of mental illness; the term 'abnormal psychology' is preferred by some psychological researchers.   *RB*

psychosis   The general class of psychiatric disorders, in which the patient experiences HALLUCINATIONS and DELUSIONS and appears to lose contact with reality. SCHIZOPHRENIA, DELUSIONAL DISORDER and BIPOLAR DISORDER are regarded as psychotic disorders. Patients with severe depression may become psychotic, in which case they suffer from hallucinations and/or delusions that are congruent with their mood.   *RB*

psychosurgery   Psychosurgery, involving the surgical destruction of areas of the brain, is one of the most controversial treatments in the history of PSYCHIATRY. Its origins can be traced to the work of the Portuguese neurologist Egas Monitz, who in 1949 won the Nobel prize for medicine for his invention of the prefrontal leucotomy, a procedure in which the nerve tracts linking the frontal lobes to anterior regions of the brain are severed. This was widely used in the 1950s, especially in the USA, where progressively more economical versions were developed (Whitaker 2002). Walter Freeman eventually established a procedure that involved stunning the patient with ELECTROCONVULSIVE THERAPY (ECT) and then inserting an ice-pick-like device above the eye and through the bone of the orbit. The operation fell out of use following the discovery of ANTIPSYCHOTIC DRUGS.

Although psychosurgery is now used rarely, bilateral CINGULOTOMY is sometimes advocated for patients suffering from OBSESSIVE-COMPULSIVE DISORDER who have failed to respond to other kinds of treatment. Follow-ups of treated patients suggest that about 30–50 per cent receive some benefit (Dougherty et al. 2002).   *RB*

Dougherty, D. D., Baer, L., Cosgrove, G. R., Cassem, E. H., Price, B. H., Nirenberg, A. A., Jenike, M. A. and Rauch, S. L. 2002: Prospective long-term follow-up of 44 patients who received cingulotomy for treatment-refractory obsessive-compulsive disorder. *American Journal of Psychiatry* 159, 269–75. **Whitaker, R.** 2002: *Mad in America: Bad Science, Bad Medicine and the Enduring Mistreatment of the Mentally Ill.* New York: Perseus Books.

psychotherapist   A person who professes to carry out psychological treatments according to a particular theoretical model (as in psychodynamic psychotherapist, behavioural psychotherapist, etc.). In most countries, use of the term psychotherapist is not regulated and therefore does not identify a group of individuals with a particular training (or, indeed, any training). Clinical psychologists [see CLINICAL PSYCHOLOGY], psychiatrists [see PSYCHIATRY], social workers and psychiatric nurses may, in some circumstances, choose to describe themselves as psychotherapists.   *RB*

puerperal psychosis   A type of psychotic disorder occurring at or shortly following childbirth. Extreme mood symptoms are usually evident. The risk of puerperal psychosis is increased if the woman experiences unusual stress, for example, separates from the husband during pregnancy or gives birth to a stillborn child.   *RB*

R

randomised controlled trial (RCT) An EXPERI-MENT (see s. 8) to measure the efficacy (the extent to which it has a therapeutic effect under experimentally controlled conditions), effectiveness (the extent to which it has a therapeutic effect in real-world conditions) and cost-effectiveness (the extent to which it can be judged value for money when compared with alternatives) of an intervention. RCTs are most often used to evaluate treatments for physical or psychiatric disorders, but have also been used to investigate the effects of educational interventions and even agricultural methods.

Patients are randomly allocated to several alternative conditions or treatment arms, typically an experimental treatment, a PLACEBO (see s. 8) treatment and/or an already established treatment. (A placebo control treatment may be unethical (see s. 1, ETHICAL ISSUES IN RESEARCH) if the disorder of interest is life-threatening or if an established treatment is known to be effective.) Attempts are made to control any sources of BIAS (see s. 8) that might affect the interpretation of the results. In double-blind trials, both the patient and the researcher measuring the patient's therapeutic response are kept ignorant of which treatment the patient has received; in this way patients' and clinicians' expectations cannot affect the outcome. However, a double-blind design is usually impossible in the case of psychological treatments. In these circumstances, a single-blind design may be employed, in which only the researcher measuring the therapeutic response is kept ignorant of the treatment assignment. Open trials, in which all participants are aware of treatment allocation, are not to be trusted as they nearly always lead to inflated estimates of a treatment's effect (Schulz, Chalmers, Hayes and Altman 1995).

An INTENTION TO TREAT ANALYSIS of RCT data (in which data from all those entering the study are included) is usually preferred over PER-PROTOCOL ANALYSIS (in which only data from those successfully completing treatment are considered).

Health care costs place a considerable burden on modern societies – 14.6 per cent and 7.7 per cent of gross domestic product in the USA and UK respectively in 2002, according to the Organization for Economic Co-Operation and Development. Moreover, the need for health care is almost limitless, because of the increasing range of conditions deemed worthy of treatment and because of the spiralling cost of new health care technologies. For these reasons, health care providers (the National Health Service in the UK, insurance companies in the USA) rely on RCTs to determine the most cost-effective interventions. However, some critics have pointed out that RCTs are not always practical or ethical (Smith and Pell 2003) and that alternative methods, including simple observation, can often yield useful data about treatment effects. Single case studies and MULTIPLE BASELINE EXPERIMENTS can yield valuable information about efficacy, and these kinds of studies are often carried out before investing the considerable sums needed to carry out an RCT.

In recent years, the statistical method of META-ANALYSIS (see s. 8) has been used to combine data from a number of RCTs to provide an overall verdict on the value of different types of treatment. The Cochrane collaboration, an international collaboration between researchers and health care providers, publishes detailed systematic reviews and meta-analyses of treatments for a wide range of conditions, which are available on the internet (www.Cochrane.org – accessed September 2004). *RB*

Schulz, K. F., Chalmers, I., Hayes, R. J. and Altman, D. G. 1995: Empirical evidence of bias: dimensions of methodological quality associated with estimates of treatment effects in controlled trials. *Journal of the American Medical Association* 273, 408–12. **Smith, G. C. S. and Pell, J. P.** 2003: Parachute use to prevent death and major trauma related to gravitational challenge: systematic review of randomised controlled trials. *British Medical Journal* 327, 1459–61.

relapse An exacerbation of symptoms, such that a patient who has recovered from a disorder is classified as becoming unwell again. *RB*

relapse prevention Any therapeutic approach which has the main aim of preventing a RELAPSE in patients who have recovered or partially recovered from an episode of psychiatric disorder; relapse prevention programmes may include pharmacological and psychological (usually cognitive-behavioural) interventions. *RB*

repression A defence mechanism involving motivated FORGETTING (see s. 3), with the consequence that the individual lacks conscious awareness of anxiety-provoking events. *RB*

response styles The term 'response style' has been used to describe an individual's characteristic way of COPING with negative EMOTION (see s. 6), which is believed to have an impact on the severity and duration of the emotional experience. An extensive programme of research into response styles has been conducted by Susan Nolen-Hoeksema (1991), who has argued that they fall into four main types: RUMINATION (engaging in thoughts and behaviours that focus the individual's mind on feelings of distress), problem solving (searching for ways to alter the circumstances that have led to distress), DISTRACTION (focusing ATTENTION – see s. 3 – away from unhappiness and its causes and on to pleasant or neutral stimuli that are engaging enough to prevent thoughts returning to the source of distress) and dangerous activities (risk-taking behaviours, which might be thought of as an extreme form of distraction). In experimental and naturalistic studies, Nolen-Hoeksema has shown that rumination increases the duration of negative mood and inhibits problem-solving. *RB*

Nolen-Hoeksema, S. 1991: Responses to depression and their effects on the duration of depressed mood. *Journal of Abnormal Psychology* 100, 569–82.

rumination A RESPONSE STYLE to negative mood, characterised by engaging in thoughts and behaviours that focus the mind on distress, and which usually has the effect of prolonging episodes of ANXIETY (see s. 6) or DEPRESSION. People with this response style spend much of their time thinking about how badly they feel and pondering such questions as, 'Why am I in such a mess?' and 'Will I ever feel better?'   *RB*

S

safety behaviour A type of AVOIDANCE behaviour that has the function of making a patient feel safer, but which has the effect of preventing the patient from LEARNING (see s. 3) that feared events are unlikely; for example, a phobic patient who stays at home to avoid dogs may fail to discover that most dogs are friendly. *RB*

schizo-affective disorder The term schizo-affective disorder is used to describe psychiatric conditions that involve a combination of schizophrenic and affective symptoms.

Emil Kraepelin (1856–1926) identified two main types of psychotic disorder: SCHIZOPHRENIA and manic DEPRESSION (encompassing what are now known as BIPOLAR DISORDER and unipolar depression). However, as Kasanin (1933) pointed out, many patients present with symptoms that do not fall clearly into either of these two classes. Kasanin believed that the symptoms of these patients had a sudden onset in a period of marked emotional turmoil, and that the prognosis was good, with many patients recovering completely. Since that time, the concept of schizo-affective disorder has been debated extensively in psychiatric literature (Tsuang, Levitt and Simpson 1995).

Schizo-affective disorders have been defined in various ways, narrower definitions of schizophrenia and the affective psychoses requiring broader definitions of schizo-affective disorder and vice versa. Some definitions of schizo-affective disorder, for example, the DSM-IV definition (American Psychiatric Association 1994), require that schizophrenic symptoms (HALLUCINATIONS and DELUSIONS) dominate the clinical picture for a period of time but that co-occurrence of schizophrenia and mood symptoms is also recorded during the same episode. A complicating issue is that traditional descriptive PSYCHIATRY has probably underestimated the role of affect in schizophrenia symptoms, as research has shown that these symptoms tend to be most severe during periods of depression and ANXIETY (see s. 6) (Norman and Malla 1991) and that dysphoric mood often precedes the onset of florid schizophrenic symptoms (Herz and Melville 1980).

There is considerable controversy about the real nature of schizo-affective disorder. Kasanin believed it to be a third type of PSYCHOSIS, whereas other psychiatrists have argued that it is an atypical type of schizophrenia, or that schizo-affective patients, on further investigation, can be divided into true cases of schizophrenia and true cases of affective psychosis. However, a common view is that schizo-affective disorder represents the mid-point of a continuum of psychosis, with typical schizophrenia and typical affective psychosis lying at either end (i.e. that schizophrenia and the affective psychoses are not separate conditions). Some statistical studies of patients' symptoms support this continuum concept (Kendell and Gourlay 1970) and patients with a schizo-affective presentation tend to have outcomes that lie midway between the relatively poor outcomes of 'pure' schizophrenia patients and the relatively good outcomes of patients suffering from 'pure' affective psychosis (Kendell and Brockington 1980). Genetic evidence has also been interpreted as supporting the continuum or 'unitary psychosis' concept, as patients with a schizo-affective presentation have a greater than expected number of both schizophrenic and affectively disordered patients among their close relatives (Crow 1991). *RB*

American Psychiatric Association 1994: *Diagnostic and Statistical Manual for Mental Disorders* (4th edn). Washington, DC: Author. **Crow, T.** 1991: The failure of the binary concept and the psychosis gene. In Kerr, A. and McClelland, H. (eds), *Concepts of Mental Disorder: A Continuing Debate*. London: Gaskell. **Herz, M. I. and Melville, C.** 1980: Relapse in schizophrenia. *American Journal of Psychiatry* 127, 801–12. **Kasanin, J.** 1933: The acute schizoaffective psychoses. *American Journal of Psychiatry* 90, 97–126. **Kendell, R. E. and Brockington, I. F.** 1980: The identification of disease entities and the relationship between schizophrenic and affective psychoses. *British Journal of Psychiatry* 137, 324–31. **Kendell, R. E. and Gourlay, J. A.** 1970: The clinical distinction between the affective psychoses and schizophrenia. *British Journal of Psychiatry* 117, 261–6. **Norman, R. M. G. and Malla, A. K.** 1991: Dysphoric mood and symptomatology in schizophrenia. *Psychological Medicine* 21, 897–203. **Tsuang, M. T., Levitt, J. J. and Simpson, J. C.** 1995: Schizoaffective disorder. In Hirsch, S. R. and Weinberger, D. R. (eds), *Schizophrenia*. Oxford: Blackwell, 46–57.

schizoid personality disorder A PERSONALITY DISORDER characterised by detachment from close social relationships, a preference for solitary activities and emotional coldness or detachment. *PK*

schizophrenia Schizophrenia is a severe psychiatric disorder in which HALLUCINATIONS and DELUSIONS are usually the most prominent symptoms, and in which there are often also NEGATIVE SYMPTOMS such as social withdrawal, apathy and flat affect. Schizophrenia is usually thought to be one of the most severe and debilitating of psychiatric disorders, and affects between 0.5 and 1 per cent of the population worldwide (Jablensky et al. 1992) (but see below).

The concept of schizophrenia dates from the work of Emil Kraepelin (1856–1926), who first grouped together a number of psychiatric disorders under the single term dementia praecox (literally, senility of the young), under the assumption that they were manifestations of a single disease that typically became evident in late adolescence or early adulthood and which had a deteriorating course, so that there was no possibility of recovery. Eugen Bleuler (1911/1950) (1857–1939), a Swiss psychiatrist who was influenced by both Kraepelin and Freud, coined the term schizophrenia because he believed that the disorder did not invariably begin in early life (although it often does) and did not invariably lead to a chronic, deteriorated condition. Although this name has also led to confusion (with some people mistakenly thinking it refers to a split personality), it became widely adopted and is used in modern diagnostic manuals such as the

DSM and ICD [see INTERNATIONAL CLASSIFICATION OF DISEASES].

There have been some disputes about the core symptoms of the disorder. Kraepelin believed that cognitive impairments were a core feature, whereas Bleuler held that the most fundamental symptoms were subtle emotional characteristics: loosening of the associations, inappropriate affect, emotional ambivalence and autism (by which he meant a retreat into a preferred world of fantasy, not to be confused with modern usage). Modern concepts of schizophrenia date from the work of the German psychiatrist Kurt Schneider (1887–1967), whose work was rarely translated into English, but whose list of first-rank symptoms of schizophrenia nonetheless influenced diagnostic practices in the English-speaking world. This list of different kinds of hallucination, delusions and passivity experiences (beliefs about actions, emotions or thoughts being caused by an external force or agent) was meant to be a pragmatic guide to diagnosis and was not meant to identify those symptoms that were most important. However, contemporary diagnostic criteria for schizophrenia, for example those in the DSM and ICD, emphasise POSITIVE SYMPTOMS such as hallucinations and delusions.

Despite the pessimistic views of Kraepelin, modern research has highlighted the heterogeneous outcomes of schizophrenia. Research by Manfred Bleuler (1978), the son of Eugen, was among the first to show that only about a third of patients have the poor outcome described by Kraepelin. Others experience repeated episodes of illness (RELAPSES) or continue to experience attenuated symptoms after an acute episode. As many as a quarter of patients recover completely, but there are no known clinical predictors of this good outcome. Cross-cultural research has consistently shown that patients are more likely to experience partial or complete recovery in the developing world than in the industrialised nations (Jablensky et al. 1992). It is often assumed that this is because there are fewer sources of stress in such countries but this explanation is not universally accepted.

There have been many theories of schizophrenia. FAMILY STUDIES, TWIN STUDIES and ADOPTION STUDIES have consistently pointed to genetic INFLUENCES (see s. 1), but these do not seem to be strong enough to entirely account for the disorder and it is now widely believed that it is vulnerability to the illness, rather than the illness itself, that is inherited. Following the accidental discovery that certain (now called) ANTIPSYCHOTIC DRUGS ameliorated schizophrenia symptoms, and the subsequent discovery that all of these drugs blocked dopamine RECEPTORS (see s. 2) in the brain, it became widely accepted that schizophrenia is caused by some kind of abnormality in the dopamine system. However, no consistent evidence of an abnormal dopamine system has been identified in patients (Carlsson 1995), although variants of this hypothesis continue to attract attention (Laruelle and Abi-Dargham 1999). [See DOPAMINE THEORY OF SCHIZOPHRENIA]

Studies over the last two decades have pointed to the possible role of neuro-developmental abnormalities in patients. Structural abnormalities (for example, enlarged cerebral ventricles) and functional abnormalities (for example, reduced activity in the frontal lobes) of the brain have been detected in some adult patients using modern neuro-imaging techniques, but the aetiological significance and specificity of these findings remains unclear (Bentall 2003). As studies show that birth during the winter months confers a slightly increased risk of developing schizophrenia (and BIPOLAR DISORDER) in later life, it has been hypothesised that early viral infection (probably before birth) may play a role (Torrey, Miller, Rawlings and Yolken 1997). Birth cohort studies, in which large populations of children have been followed up into adulthood, have consistently shown that subtle intellectual, cognitive and emotional abnormalities (for example, slightly delayed acquisition of LANGUAGE – see s. 2) are associated with an increased risk of schizophrenia in adulthood (Jones and Done 1997).

In contrast, possible environmental causes of schizophrenia have been relatively neglected by researchers, partly following the rejection of psychoanalytic theories that proposed a role for schizophrenogenic mothers, which were seen as stigmatising. However, it has long been known that a patient living with a high EXPRESSED EMOTION relative (a relative who is highly critical or over-controlling) has a higher probability of relapse than one who does not (Bebbington, Bowen, Hirsch and Kuipers 1995). The recent discovery that ethnic minorities in the UK and elsewhere have much higher rates of schizophrenia than indigenous populations has suggested that migration or victimisation may increase the risk of schizophrenia (Bhurgra, Mallett and Leff 1999) and has rekindled interest in environmental influences. Several studies in which genetic risk and environmental variables have been measured suggest that those genetically at risk are more likely to become ill if they have poor relationships with their parents (Schiffman et al. 2002; Wahlberg et al. 1997). Recent studies have also pointed to high rates of trauma in the histories of schizophrenia patients (Mueser et al. 1998).

In recent years a number of investigators have argued that the concept of schizophrenia has outlived its usefulness, mainly because it encompasses patients with a wide range of problems with different aetiologies. Epidemiological research has also established that schizophrenia symptoms are much more widely experienced than was hitherto thought (van Os, Hanssen, Bijl and Ravelli 2000) giving support to those investigators who have argued that schizophrenia, as well as SCHIZOTYPAL PERSONALITY DISORDER, lies at the extreme end of a normally distributed dimension of PERSONALITY (see s. 1 and s. 6) characteristics (Claridge 1985). Some psychologists have argued that greater progress in understanding the nature and aetiology of these symptoms might be achieved if each different type of symptom is studied in its own right (Bentall 2003).

Until recently, the only proven treatment for schizophrenia has been antipsychotic medication. However, recent research has shown that FAMILY THERAPY may be used to reduce the toxic effects of expressed emotion and thereby reduce the probability of relapse (Pitschel, Leucht, Baeumil, Kissling and Engel 2001) and that COGNITIVE (BEHAVIOUR) THERAPY may be a useful treatment for symptoms such as hallucinations and delusions (Rector and Beck 2001).   *RB*

Bebbington, P. E., Bowen, J., Hirsch, S. R. and Kuipers, E. A. 1995: Schizophrenia and psychosocial stresses. In Hirsch, S. R. and Weinberger, D. R. (eds), *Schizophrenia*. Oxford:

Blackwell, 587–604. **Bentall, R. P.** 2003: *Madness Explained: Psychosis and Human Nature.* London: Penguin. **Bhurgra, D., Mallett, R. and Leff, J.** 1999: Schizophrenia and Afro-Caribbeans: a conceptual model of aetiology. *International Review of Psychiatry* 11, 145–52. **Bleuler, E.** 1911/1950: *Dementia Praecox or the Group of Schizophrenias* (translated by E. Zinkin). New York: International Universities Press. **Bleuler, M.** 1978: *The Schizophrenic Disorders.* New Haven: Yale University Press. **Carlsson, A.** 1995: The dopamine theory revisited. In Hirsch, S. R. and Weinberger, D. R. (eds), *Schizophrenia.* Oxford: Blackwell, 379–400. **Claridge, G. S.** 1985: *The Origins of Mental Illness.* Oxford: Blackwell. **Jablensky, A., Sartorius, N., Ernberg, G., Anker, M., Korten, A., Cooper, J. E., Day, R. and Bertelsen, A.** 1992: Schizophrenia: manifestations, incidence and course in different cultures. *Psychological Medicine* (suppl. 20), 1–97. **Jones, P. B. and Done, D. J.** 1997: From birth to onset: a developmental perspective of schizophrenia in two national birth cohorts. In Keshavan, M. S. and Murray, R. M. (eds), *Neurodevelopment and Adult Psychopathology.* Cambridge: Cambridge University Press, 119–36. **Laruelle, M. and Abi-Dargham, A.** 1999: Dopamine as the wind in the psychotic fire: new evidence from brain imaging studies. *Journal of Psychopharmacology* 13, 358–71. **Mueser, K. T., Goodman, L. B., Trumbetta, S. L., Rosenberg, S. D., Osher, F. C., Vidaver, R., Auciello, P. and Foy, D. W.** 1998: Trauma and post-traumatic stress disorder in severe mental illness. *Journal of Consulting and Clinical Psychology* 66, 493–9. **Pitschel, W. G., Leucht, S., Baeumil, J., Kissling, W. and Engel, R. R.** 2001: The effects of family interventions on relapse and rehospitalisation in schizophrenia: a meta-analysis. *Schizophrenia Bulletin* 27, 73–92. **Rector, N. A. and Beck, A. T.** 2001: Cognitive behavioural therapy for schizophrenia: an empirical review. *Journal of Nervous and Mental Disease* 189, 278–87. **Schiffman, J., LaBrie, J., Carter, J., Tyrone, C., Schulsinger, F., Parnas, J. and Mednick, S.** 2002: Perception of parent-child relationships in high-risk families, and adult schizophrenia outcome of offspring. *Journal of Psychiatric Research* 36, 41–7. **Torrey, E. F., Miller, J., Rawlings, R. and Yolken, R. H.** 1997: Seasonality of births in schizophrenia and bipolar disorder: a review of the literature. *Schizophrenia Research* 28, 1–38. **van Os, J., Hanssen, M., Bijl, R. V. and Ravelli, A.** 2000: Strauss (1969) revisited: a psychosis continuum in the normal population? *Schizophrenia Research* 45, 11–20. **Wahlberg, K.-E., Wynne, L. C., Oja, H., Keskitalo, P., Pykalainen, L., Lahti, I., Moring, J., Naarala, N., Sorri, A., Seitamaa, M., Laksy, K., Kolassa, J. and Tienari, P.** 1997: Gene-environment interaction in vulnerability to schizophrenia: findings from the Finnish Adoptive Family Study of Schizophrenia. *American Journal of Psychiatry* 154, 355–62.

schizotypal personality disorder

The concept of schizotypal personality disorder has two main origins: studies of the genetics of SCHIZOPHRENIA, which suggested that many of the relatives of schizophrenia patients have eccentric 'schizophrenia spectrum' characteristics, without showing frank symptoms of PSYCHOSIS (Meehl 1962), and research by PERSONALITY (see s. 1 and s. 6) theorists that has also suggested a continuum between schizophrenia and normal functioning (e.g. Claridge 1990). In the DSM system, a diagnosis of schizotypal PERSONALITY DISORDER requires that the person should experience (at least five of): ideas of reference, magical thinking or odd beliefs, odd perceptual experiences, odd thinking or speech, suspiciousness or PARANOIA, inappropriate moods, eccentric, odd or peculiar behaviour, few close friends and excessive social ANXIETY (see s. 6).

Many questionnaires exist for the measurement (see s. 1, MEASUREMENT AND STATISTICS) of schizotypal traits,

and FACTOR ANALYSIS (see s. 6 and s. 8) suggests that these measure three main domains of experience and behaviour: unusual experiences (corresponding to the positive symptoms of schizophrenia), introverted ANHEDONIA (corresponding to the negative symptoms), and subjective cognitive difficulties (probably corresponding to the schizophrenic disorganisation syndrome). *PK*

Claridge, G. S. 1990: Can a disease model of schizophrenia survive? In Bentall, R. P. (ed.), *Reconstructing Schizophrenia.* London: Routledge, 157–83. **Meehl, P.** 1962: Schizotaxia, schizotypia, schizophrenia. *American Psychologist* 17, 827–38.

selective serotonin reuptake inhibitors (SSRIs)

A class of psychiatric DRUGS (see s. 2) that inhibits the reuptake of serotonin into the pre-synaptic cleft, maintaining maximum availability of serotonin at the SYNAPSE (see s. 2). SSRIs are effective treatments for DEPRESSION and ANXIETY DISORDERS. *RB*

self-esteem

One's global sense of self-worth. Low self-esteem is associated with many types of psychiatric disorder, but especially DEPRESSION. Recent research has implicated low self-esteem in the POSITIVE SYMPTOMS of PSYCHOSIS, which are exacerbated when self-esteem is especially low. (See also s. 5, SELF-ESTEEM) *RB*

serotonin theory of depression

Interest in the role that the NEUROTRANSMITTER (see s. 2) serotonin plays in DEPRESSION was stimulated by the observation that the early ANTIDEPRESSANT DRUGS increased the amount of serotonin available at the SYNAPSE (see s. 2). This observation eventually led to a new class of antidepressants, the SELECTIVE SEROTONIN REUPTAKE INHIBITORS, which are specifically designed for this purpose.

Evidence that low levels of serotonin play a causal role in depression has been more difficult to achieve. However, a number of studies have shown low levels of the serotonin metabolite 5-hyroxyindoleacetic acid in the CEREBROSPINAL FLUID (see s. 2) of depressed patients. Other studies have shown that reduction of dietary tryptophan (which is synthesised into serotonin in the brain) leads to an increase in depressed mood, especially in people who have already experienced a depressive disorder, or who are at genetic risk of becoming depressed (Benkelfat, Ellenbogen, Dean, Palmour and Young, 1994) *RB*

Benkelfat, C., Ellenbogen, M. A., Dean, P., Palmour, R. M. and Young, S. N. 1994: Mood-lowering effect of tryptophan depletion: enhanced susceptibility in young men at genetic risk for major affective disorders. *Archives of General Psychiatry* 51, 687–700.

sexual dysfunction

Problems affecting sexual functioning are quite common. One survey found that 43 per cent of US women and 3 per cent of US men reported one or more such difficulties in the preceding 12 months. These difficulties can be divided into four main types: disorders of sexual desire (characterised by a deficiency of interest in sexual activity), disorders of sexual arousal (failure to maintain sexual excitement, as indicated by lubrication in the female and erection in the male), orgasmic disorders (delayed or absent ejaculation in the male; premature ejaculation in the male; delay or absence of orgasm in the female) and sexual PAIN (see also s. 2) disorders (dysareunia – pain during intercourse that is most often reported by women – and vaginismus – recurrent spasms of the vagina that make intercourse impossible).

Sexual dysfunction may be caused by physical factors such as hormone deficiencies, the effects of DRUGS (see s. 2) or fatigue. However, ANXIETY (see s. 6) and STRESS are very often responsible. A number of specific psychological treatment techniques are available in the latter instance (Bancroft 1989). *RB*

Bancroft, J. 1989: *Human Sexuality and its Problems* (2nd edn). Edinburgh: Churchill-Livingstone.

social functioning
The ability to function socially and to maintain effective RELATIONSHIPS (see s. 5) with partners, family, friends and acquaintances; a common outcome measure used in PSYCHIATRY. *RB*

social rhythm disrupting life event
Any life event that disrupts the normal pattern of daily rhythms and impacts on the sleep-wake cycle; implicated in the onset of MANIA. *RB*

social rhythm metric
A questionnaire measure designed to quantify daily social rhythms, which help to cognitively structure the day and provide time cues (zeitgebers) to control circadian rhythms (biological clock). [See also CIRCADIAN DYSRHYTHMIA] Used in the investigation of BIPOLAR DISORDER and other psychiatric conditions. *RB*

social skills training
A type of behaviour therapy in which the specific aim is to teach SOCIAL SKILLS (see s. 5) to patients who lack competence in this domain. Social skills training has been used with a wide range of patients, including shy adults, delinquent adolescents and chronically ill SCHIZOPHRENIA patients. *RB*

sociotropy and autonomy
According to Beck's cognitive theory of DEPRESSION, excessive sociotropy (the tendency to judge one's self-worth on the basis of RELATIONSHIPS (see s. 5) with other people) and/or excessive autonomy (the tendency to judge one's self-worth on the basis of achievement and freedom from constraint) are two types of dysfunctional self-schemas which confer vulnerability to depression in the face of particular kinds of negative events (rejection in the case of excessive sociotropy, failure in the case of excessive autonomy). *RB*

Socratic questioning
A method of interviewing used in COGNITIVE (BEHAVIOUR) THERAPY, in which the therapist asks a series of questions designed to lead the patient to awareness of their dysfunctional beliefs and assumptions. *RB*

somatisation
A term used to refer to both a diagnosis (Somatisation disorder) and a hypothesised process in which psychological distress is experienced or communicated in the form of somatic symptoms.

Somatisation disorder is characterised by a lengthy history of many physical symptoms, which have no obvious organic basis, experienced in different bodily systems, and which cause significant impairment and medical help seeking. The disorder is more commonly diagnosed in women than men, and is often co-morbid with ANXIETY DISORDERS or DEPRESSION disorders. Recent studies have linked somatisation disorder, and the experience of multiple unexplained physical symptoms in general, to a history of sexual abuse. The psychodynamic formulation of somatisation, which suggests that distress appears in the form of somatic symptoms when people are unable to admit to psychological conflicts, is poorly supported in the literature. Many studies, including ones from different cultures and with both community and medical care seeking samples, have reported a strong association between overt, acknowledged psychological distress and physical symptoms, thus casting doubt on the notion of somatic symptoms as a defence against awareness of psychological difficulties (Simon and VonKorff 1991). Indeed, the most plausible explanation for the correlation between psychological distress and somatic symptoms is that psychological distress is associated with a heightened awareness of bodily sensations, and thereby affects symptom reporting and health care seeking.

Recently, there has been a move away from the use of the term 'somatisation' towards more descriptive labels such as 'medically unexplained symptoms', which make no assumptions about the origins of symptoms. It has been pointed out that the construct of somatisation is problematical in that it artificially separates out physical and psychological symptoms, which patients may experience as a unified whole; indeed patients are often dissatisfied with the explanations given to them by their doctors (Salmon, Peters and Stanley 1999). Somatisation is considered difficult to treat, but current treatments include pharmacological therapies, particularly to address symptoms of depression (O'Malley et al. 1999), and variants of COGNITIVE (BEHAVIOUR) THERAPY to address patients' illness models and illness behaviours (Kroenke and Swindle 2000). *AW*

Kroenke, K. and Swindle, R. 2000: Cognitive-behavioral therapy for somatization and symptom syndromes: a critical review of controlled clinical trials. *Psychotherapy and Psychosomatics* 69, 205–15. **O'Malley, P. G., Jackson, J. L., Santoro, J., Tomkins, G., Balden, E. and Kroenke, K.** 1999: Antidepressant therapy for unexplained symptoms and symptom syndromes. *Journal of Family Practice* 48, 980–90. **Salmon, P., Peters, S. and Stanley, I.** 1999: Patients' perceptions of medical explanations for somatization disorders: qualitative analysis. *British Medical Journal* 318, 372–6. **Simon, G. E. and VonKorff, M.** 1991: Somatization and psychiatric disorder in the NIMH Epidemiologic Catchment Area Study. *American Journal of Psychiatry* 148, 1494–1500.

stress
The term 'stress' was originally used in physics to mean an external force applied to a system. It has since been used in many different disciplines, ranging from engineering to medicine, and has been defined in many ways. It has been argued that the concept of stress is no longer useful because it is so widely used and poorly defined. However, although the concept of stress can be vague, it is an important construct with the potential to unify different disciplines and help us understand the mind–body relationship. In HEALTH PSYCHOLOGY the term 'stress' is now used more to describe a field of research and theory looking at the processes involved in stress, rather than a single phenomenon.

When looking at the stress process, basic distinctions are made between stressors, stress responses, and strain. Stressors are external or internal factors that cause stress responses: for example, external events such as exams, or internal factors such as role conflict. Stress responses can be emotional, behavioural, cognitive or physiological. Emotional responses include distress, ANXIETY (see s. 6), fear, depression and other emotions. Behavioural responses are many and varied and can be active or passive. Behavioural stress responses that health psychologists are particularly interested in are those that directly influence health, for example, increased alcohol use. Cognitive responses include changes in PERCEPTION (see s. 1), ATTENTION (see s. 3), MEMORY (see s. 1) and DECISION MAKING (see s. 3) processes. Physiological stress responses include AUTONOMIC NERVOUS SYSTEM (see s. 2) responses, neuroendocrine responses and immunological responses. Strain is the combined negative impact of stress on an individual.

A number of different theoretical approaches have been taken to stress. These are not necessarily contradictory, but have tended to focus on different parts of the stress process. Chronologically, theories of stress have concentrated on stress as a response (the physical stress response); stress as a stimulus; and stress as an interaction or transaction. Response-based models were pioneered by Walter Cannon (1914) and Hans Selye (1956) and defined stress as a non-specific physiological response to any demand. Cannon detailed the physical fight-flight responses to stress. Selye built on this work to look at different phases of physical responses and proposed the General Adaptation Syndrome where there are three physiological phases in response to stressors: alarm, where the body activates the fight-flight response; resistance, where the body attempts to restore HOMEOSTASIS (see s. 2) but can remain at an increased level of arousal if the stressor is still present; and exhaustion, where the body's resources are overstretched and break down. Selye proposed that the stage of exhaustion would result in psychosomatic illness and perhaps death.

There is no doubt that these response-based approaches added greatly to our understanding of physical stress responses. However, research has since shown that the physical response to stress is not non-specific. First, there are particular characteristics of stressors that make them more stressful, such as novel situations, unpredictable situations, or situations in which we have no control. Second, individuals vary both in the way they respond physically to stress and in the magnitude of their response.

Stimulus-based models of stress dominated research in the 1970s and 1980s and defined stress as the amount of life change or adjustment a person went through. This approach is typically labelled the life change or LIFE EVENTS approach and it assumes that any change or adjustment uses a person's resources and is therefore stressful. Because this approach measured stress as life events (i.e. quasi-objective phenomena), it made it possible to separate exposure to stress from the consequences. Research has shown that negative life events are associated with a wide range of illnesses (morbidity) and with death (mortality). This approach was therefore influential in demonstrating the association between stressful events and health. However, it has been widely criticised for measuring stress with checklists of events and for ignoring psychological processes and moderating VARIABLES (see s. 8) such as COPING and SOCIAL SUPPORT (see s. 5).

Interactional models of stress take greater account of INDIVIDUAL DIFFERENCES (see s. 6) in perceived stress and the role of psychological processes. The interactional approach defines stress as arising from the interaction between the environment and an individual. For example, stress is more likely to arise if an individual is exposed to a situation they are not familiar with, or which does not match their coping SKILLS (see s. 3). The difference between interactional and transactional models of stress is subtle and is most simply understood through transactional models positing a more complex interaction, or transaction, where environmental stimuli will influence an individual and vice versa.

The transactional model proposed by Lazurus and Folkman (1984) dominates current stress research and defines stress as occurring when the environment is appraised by an individual as taxing or exceeding their resources to cope. COGNITIVE (see s. 1, COGNITIVE PSYCHOLOGY) appraisal is central to this model and a series of experimental studies has shown the importance of cognitive appraisal in stress responses. For example, if research participants are given an appraisal of denial (e.g. that a gruesome film is acted) or intellectualisation (e.g. the film is real but shown for educational purposes), these participants have smaller affective and physiological responses to the stressor than controls (e.g. Steptoe and Vögele 1986). Lazarus and Folkman propose that there are three stages of cognitive appraisal: primary appraisal, which is appraisal of the demands of the stressor; secondary appraisal, which is appraisal of available resources to cope; and reappraisal, after attempts to cope with the demands of the stressor have been made. Stress and coping are thereby seen as integral parts of a dynamic stress process.

Thus stress is currently seen to be a complex and dynamic process in which an individual's appraisal of environmental demands, psychosocial resources and efforts to cope will all affect the type and extent of stress response.   *SA*

Cannon, W. B. 1914: The interrelations of emotions as suggested by recent physiological researches. *American Journal of Psychology* 25, 256–82. **Lazarus, R. S. and Folkman, S.** 1984: *Stress, Appraisal and Coping.* New York: Springer. **Selye, H.** 1956: *The Stress of Life.* New York: McGraw-Hill. **Steptoe, A. and Vögele, C.** 1986: Are stress responses influenced by cognitive appraisal? An experimental comparison of coping strategies. *British Journal of Psychology* 77, 243–55.

stress-vulnerability models These models distinguish between vulnerability to psychiatric disorder, which is often (but not always) seen to be of biological origin, and stressful events (usually, but not always, psychological in nature) that actually trigger episodes of illness. Models of this kind assume that some individuals who are vulnerable to psychiatric disorder will not become ill because they are not exposed to critical stressful events. It is also often assumed that individuals vary in their degree of vulnerability, so that some people will become ill when exposed to relatively minor stressors.

Examples include Zubin and Spring's (1977) model of schizophrenia, which assumes an inherited vulnerability to illness, and attributional models of depression (e.g. Abramson, Metalsky and Alloy 1989), which assume a psychological vulnerability to the disorder in the form of a particular style of reasoning about negative events.   *RB*

Abramson, L. Y., Metalsky, G. I. and Alloy, L. B. 1989: Hopelessness depression: a theory-based subtype of depression. *Psychological Review* 96, 358–72. Zubin, J. and Spring, B. 1977: Vulnerability: a new view of schizophrenia. *Journal of Abnormal Psychology* 86, 103–26.

structural family therapy   A type of FAMILY THERAPY that focuses on the structural aspects of families, such as the family hierarchy and coalitions between members, and which aims to produce change by attempting to reorganise these. *RD*

systematic desensitisation   A treatment for PHOBIAS that is still widely used today and was one of the first BEHAVIOUR THERAPY techniques, developed by the South African psychiatrist Joseph Wolpe (1958). As usually practised, the technique involves the construction of a fear hierarchy – a list of progressively more frightening situations. The patient is then taught a series of brief exercises, designed to rapidly induce a state of physical relaxation, and is asked to imagine the least frightening scenario on the hierarchy. After the consequent ANXIETY (see s. 6) has subsided and a state of relaxation is re-established, the patient is asked to imagine the next most frightening scenario. The process is repeated over several sessions, until the patient is able to cope with the most frightening scenario. Where possible, many therapists prefer to use *in vivo* desensitisation, in which the patient is required to confront rather than imagine the feared object.

Research has shown that it is simply exposure to the feared stimulus without escape that produces the therapeutic change (Rachman 1990). Relaxation, and the gradual introduction of the feared stimulus, are not strictly necessary. FLOODING is an alternative, rapid, but less comfortable exposure therapy. *RB*

Rachman, S. J. 1990: The determinants and treatment of simple phobias. *Advances in Behaviour Research and Therapy* 12, 1–30. Wolpe, J. 1958: *Psychotherapy by Reciprocal Inhibition.* Stanford CA: Stanford University Press.

systemic family therapy   A type of FAMILY THERAPY that is aimed at helping to disrupt dysfunctional patterns or circularities. Techniques employed involve the use of strategic tasks and the use of reframing (redescribing problems in a way to promote change). *RD*

T

therapeutic alliance Also known as the working alliance, therapeutic relationship and therapeutic bond, the term refers to qualities of the relationship between the therapist and the patient that are believed to be essential for the good outcome of psychological treatment. The concept originates in PSYCHOANALYSIS (see s. 1). Freud believed the alliance has two aspects: the therapist's understanding and feeling of being well-disposed towards the patient and the therapist's encouragement of the patient's warm feelings toward the therapist. However, other accounts of the alliance emphasise the therapist's and patient's shared goals and understanding of the patient's difficulties.

The therapeutic alliance is now seen as important in all forms of therapy, including cognitive and behavioural [see COGNITIVE (BEHAVIOUR) THERAPY] approaches. Numerous studies show that the quality of the alliance, especially when rated by the patient rather than by the therapist, is a good predictor of therapeutic outcome (Orlinsky, Grawe and Parks 1994). *RB*

Orlinsky, D. E., Grawe, K. and Parks, B. K. 1994: Process and outcome in psychotherapy – noch einmal. In Bergin, A. E. and Garfield, S. L. (eds), *Handbook of Psychotherapy and Behavior Change* (4th edn). New York: Wiley, 270–376.

thought disorder Thought disorder is typically diagnosed when a patient's speech is incoherent and unintelligible to the listener. Eugen Bleuler, (1911/1950), who coined the term 'SCHIZOPHRENIA', believed it to be the consequence of 'loosening of the associations', which he argued is a fundamental symptom of the disorder. The following example of a patient's attempt to answer the question 'Why do you think people believe in God?' recorded by Chapman and Chapman (1973), illustrates the phenomenon:

> 'Uh, let's, I don't know why, let's see, balloon travel. He holds it up for you, the balloon. He don't let you fall out, your little legs sticking out down through the clouds. He's down to the smoke stack, looking through the smoke trying to get the balloon gassed up you know. Way they're flyin on top that way, legs sticking out, I don't know, looking down on the ground, heck, that'd make you so dizzy you just stay and sleep you know, hold down and sleep there. The balloon's His home you know up there. I used to be sleep out doors, you know, sleep out doors instead of going home.'

Bleuler's analysis led generations of psychologists to study cognitive and REASONING (see s. 3) impairments that might be responsible for thought disorder (Chapman and Chapman 1973), but the results of these efforts were largely inconclusive. In an influential book, Rochester and Martin (1979) argued that much of this work was misconceived because it assumed that thought disorder really was a disorder of thinking. They argued that researchers should consider why the speech of psychotic patients was unintelligible to the listener. Andreasen (1982) subse-

quently argued that the term 'thought disorder' should be replaced with 'thought, language and communication disorder'. She devised a system for rating 20 different types of abnormal speech and showed that, on FACTOR ANALYSIS (see s. 6 and s. 8), these fell into two main types: positive thought, language and communication disorder (incoherent speech) and negative thought, language and communication disorder (speech that is sparse and vague in content). Contrary to the (then) received wisdom, the positive type of disorder is more often seen in patients suffering from MANIA than in patients suffering from schizophrenia, whereas the negative type is most common in schizophrenia (Andreasen 1979).

In a series of studies by Docherty (e.g. Docherty, Evans, Sledge, Seibyl and Krystal 1994; Docherty and Hebert 1997), it has been shown that positive thought, language and communication disorder most often occurs when patients are discussing emotionally arousing topics, and that 'thought disordered' patients speak relatively normally at other times. The same seems to be true of manic patients (Tai, Haddock and Bentall 2004). Rochester and Martin (1979) argued that the distinctive linguistic feature of positive thought, language and communication disorder is a failure to use 'cohesive ties' that meaningfully link different parts of the speech message to others, but this analysis is not universally accepted (Chaika 1995). The linguistic features of this kind of speech have, in turn, been attributed to various cognitive difficulties, including, for example, working MEMORY (see s. 1) limitations (Goldberg and Weinberger 2000); patients' difficulty in distinguishing between their own speech and their own thoughts (Harvey 1985); and their inability to understand the mental state of the other person involved in the conversation (Sarfati and Hardy-Bayle 1999). *ST*

Andreasen, N. C. 1979: Thought, language and communication disorders: diagnostic significance. *Archives of General Psychiatry* 36, 1325–30. **Andreasen, N. C.** 1982: Should the term 'thought disorder' be revised? *Comprehensive Psychiatry* 23, 291–9. **Bleuler, E.** 1911/1950: *Dementia Praecox or the Group of Schizophrenias* (translated by E. Zinkin). New York: International Universities Press. **Chaika, E. O.** 1995: On analysing psychotic speech: what model should we use? In Sims, A. (ed.), *Speech and Language Disorders in Psychiatry*. London: Gaskell. **Chapman, L. J. and Chapman, J. P.** 1973: *Disordered Thought in Schizophrenia*. Englewood Cliffs NJ: Prentice-Hall. **Docherty, N. M., Evans, I. M., Sledge, W. H., Seibyl, J. P. and Krystal, J. H.** 1994: Affective reactivity of language in schizophrenia. *Journal of Nervous and Mental Disease* 182, 98–102. **Docherty, N. M. and Hebert, A. S.** 1997: Comparative affective reactivity of different types of communication disturbances in schizophrenia. *Journal of Abnormal Psychology* 106, 325–30. **Goldberg, T. E. and Weinberger, D. R.** 2000: Thought disorder in schizophrenia: a reappraisal of older formulations and an overview of some recent studies. *Cognitive Neuropsychiatry* 5, 1–19. **Harvey, P. D.** 1985: Reality monitoring in mania and schizophrenia: the association between thought disorder and performance. *Journal of Abnormal Psychology* 92, 368–77. **Rochester, S. and Martin, J. R.** 1979: *Crazy Talk: A Study of* the *Discourse of Psychotic Speakers*. New York: Plenum. **Sarfati, Y. and Hardy-Bayle, M. C.** 1999: How do people with schizophrenia explain the behaviour of others? A study of theory of mind and its relationship to thought and speech disorganization in schizophrenia. *Psychological Medicine* 29, 613–20. **Tai, S., Haddock, G. and Bentall, R. P.** 2004: The effects of emotional salience on thought disorder in patients with bipolar affective disorder. *Psychological Medicine*.

thought stopping   A BEHAVIOUR THERAPY technique designed to interrupt intrusive thoughts, especially in patients suffering from OBSESSIVE-COMPULSIVE DISORDER. The patient is trained to shout 'Stop!' immediately on being troubled by an intrusive thought.   *RB*

transference   Transference refers to the process whereby the psychotherapy patient develops ATTITUDES (see s. 5) and feelings towards the therapist that have, as their basis, feelings and attitudes held towards earlier (usually parental) figures. The concept of transference originates with Freud (see, for example, Freud 1915/1963), and interpretation of the transference relationship is seen as an important component of psychodynamic psychotherapy. In order to encourage the development of a transference relationship, the psychodynamic psychotherapist typically attempts to be a 'blank screen', disclosing nothing about him or herself to the patient. Patients may therefore develop intense feelings of love or hatred for the therapist, and it is by confronting and understanding these that progress is achieved.

Sometimes patients develop an extreme negative reaction to the therapy itself, which Freud called negative transference and which he believed was a response to the threat of uncovering unconscious processes. The term COUNTER-TRANSFERENCE was also used by Freud to describe the therapist's feelings towards the patient.   *RB*

Freud, S. 1915/1963: *Introductory Lectures on Psychoanalysis* (translated by J. Strachey: *The Standard Edition of the Complete Psychological Works of Sigmund Freud*, vols 15–16). London: Hogarth Press.

treatment adherence   Formerly termed 'treatment COMPLIANCE' (see s. 5), the extent to which people adhere to medical advice or treatment, and why people do or do not adhere to such treatment, has long been a topic of interest to health psychologists. The topic is important because there is evidence that patients often do not adhere to treatment recommended for them, and that this non-adherence is costly in terms of wasted medical resources and lost treatment opportunities (Sackett and Snow 1979).

Treatment adherence is not a unitary construct, and covers a wide range of patient behaviours, such as taking prescribed medicine or making prescribed lifestyle changes; the complexity of the behaviours subsumed under the heading of 'adherence', and the private setting in which such behaviours frequently take place, means that it often cannot be simply measured. For example, non-adherence to medication advice, which can occur even in life-threatening conditions, such as after an organ transplant (Wainwright and Gould 1997), can involve taking too much or too little medication, at the wrong time, or in the wrong dose. Some conditions require

patients to actively manage their condition in collaboration with health care professionals. In the case of diabetes for example, patients are advised on how and when to take medication, the components of a healthy diet, managing food intake and activity levels and monitoring blood sugar levels, among other things.

Psychologists have used a number of different approaches to understanding treatment adherence. Early work by Philip Ley established that patient satisfaction with the medical consultation is an important predictor of adherence to treatment, and that satisfaction is itself determined by patients' understanding of and RECALL (see s. 3) of the consultation (Ley 1988). Thus improving patient–doctor COMMUNICATION (see s. 2) may be important in improving adherence to treatment. More recently, working within the framework of Leventhal's self-regulatory model, researchers have shown the importance of patients' personal cognitive representations of their illness (for example, the cause of the illness and its likely consequences) in shaping their adherence behaviour; furthermore, cognitive representations of and BELIEFS (see s. 5) about medicines also influence adherence (Horne and Weinman 2002).   *AW*

Horne, R. and Weinman, J. 2002: Self-regulation and self-management in asthma: exploring the role of illness perceptions and treatment beliefs in explaining non-adherence to preventer medication. *Psychology and Health* 17, 17–32. **Ley, P.** 1988: *Communicating with Patients. Improving Communication, Satisfaction and Compliance*. London: Chapman & Hall. **Sackett, D. L. and Snow, J. C.** 1979: The magnitude of compliance and non-compliance. In Haynes, R. B., Taylor, D. W. and Sackett, D. L. (eds) *Compliance in Health Care*. Baltimore: Johns Hopkins University Press, 11–22. **Wainwright, S. P. and Gould, D.** 1997: Non-adherence with medications in organ transplant patients: a literature review. *Journal of Advanced Nursing* 26, 968–77.

tricyclic antidepressants   One of the oldest class of ANTIDEPRESSANT DRUGS, so-called because of their tricyclic molecular structure.   *RB*

twin studies   Human twins are of great interest to researchers studying the genetics of human traits, including psychiatric disorders. This is because identical or MONOZYGOTIC (see s. 4, IDENTICAL (MONOZYGOTIC) TWINS) (MZ) twins (created after fertilisation, when the ZYGOTE – see s. 4 – splits in two) are genetically identical, whereas non-identical or dyzygotic (DZ) twins (the result of two eggs being separately fertilised at the same time) share on average only 50 per cent of genes. For this reason, if a TRAIT (see s. 6) is in part genetically determined, the identical twin of an affected person will be very likely to carry the trait; the probability that a non-identical twin of an affected individual will carry the trait is much lower. Many twin studies have been carried out by psychologists and psychiatrists, and observations of higher CONCORDANCE (see s. 4) rates in MZ versus DZ twins have been interpreted as evidence for the genetic causation of a wide range of conditions, such as DEPRESSION, BIPOLAR DISORDER and schizophrenia. However, interpretation of these studies is not unproblematic, as twin studies can be beset by a number of methodological difficulties (Joseph 2003).   *RB*

Joseph, J. 2003: *The Gene Illusion: Genetic Research in Psychology and Psychiatry Under the Microscope*. Ross-on-Wye: PCCS Books.

type I bipolar disorder The major sub-type of BIPO-LAR DISORDER, in which a patient has experienced at least one manic episode in their history. *ST*

type II bipolar disorder A sub-type of BIPOLAR DISORDER in which the patient experiences major depressive episodes and hypomanic episodes, but has never met the criteria for a manic episode. *ST*

V

validity of psychiatric diagnoses In a seminal paper, Spitzer and Fliess (1974) defined the VALIDITY (see s. 6 and s. 8) of a diagnostic system as, '. . . The utility of the system for its various purposes. In the case of psychiatric diagnosis, the purposes of the classification system are communication about clinical features, aetiology, course of illness and treatment'.

Validity is the ultimate criterion for the scientific and clinical value of a diagnostic system. However, there is no simple validity test. Ideally, it should be possible to demonstrate that a diagnosis corresponds to a GROUP (see s. 5) of symptoms that cluster together and which have a common aetiology, that different methods of making the diagnosis identify the same people and that the diagnosis predicts the course of a disorder – whether or not the patient will get better over time – and which types of treatment are likely to be effective (PREDICTIVE VALIDITY).

As Spitzer and Fliess note, a diagnosis cannot be valid without first being reliable – unless there is agreement about which patients meet the criteria for which diagnoses, there is no possibility that validity tests will be met. *RB*

Spitzer, R. L. and Fliess, J. L. 1974: A reanalysis of the reliability of psychiatric diagnosis. *British Journal of Psychiatry* 123, 341–7.

ventricular enlargement Enlargement of the cerebral ventricles (fluid-filled cavities in the brain) found in some SCHIZOPHRENIA patients and also in some patients with other types of psychotic disorder. *RB*

Section 8

Research Methods and Statistics

Introduction

Research methods and statistics have changed little since the seminal contributions of Fisher and Pearson in the early part of the 1900s. Although there have been numerous advances in techniques (most notably multivariate techniques such as structural equation modelling), much of this new wisdom is based on the concepts introduced by the likes of Fisher and Pearson. In fact, scan your average psychology journal and you'll be amazed at how many multiple regressions, ANOVAs and factor analyses you find: techniques developed many decades ago. However, as the saying goes, 'if it isn't broken, don't fix it'. One of the major developments in the last decade or so has been serious consideration of the value of null hypothesis significance testing [see P-VALUE]. Although this foundation of social science statistics has been controversial since its conception, the psychological community has, until recently, buried its head in the sand. However, a task force put together by the American Psychological Association has recently produced guidelines encouraging the use of EFFECT SIZES, CONFIDENCE INTERVALS and techniques such as META-ANALYSIS, to drive research other than Fisher's, not in any way magical, 0.05.

The field of research methods and statistics is so vast that it is worthy of an encyclopaedic dictionary of its own, and for this reason this section has tended to be quite traditional in sticking with the commonly used tools in the psychologist's toolbox. Obviously there hasn't been room for many of the technical details and examples that can make teaching statistics so much fun, but many good books are available. I wear my biases on my sleeve and recommend Field and Hole (2003) for what I consider to be a good introduction to research methods in general and Field (2005a) as a book that goes from very basic to quite high-level statistical concepts. You'll notice most of my entries cite these as further reading. However, I do realise that you may consider this as very dubious behaviour and in the interest of fair play I want to mention four books with I think are absolutely wonderful and rarely gather dust in my office: Howell (2002), Pedhazur and Schmelkin (1991), Stevens (1992) and Tabachnick and Fidell (2001) should all be on your bookshelf.

As I have hinted, the entries in this section are somewhat traditional and tend towards statistics more than research methods. I took a top-down approach, which was to identify the small number of really key topics which underpin everything else. So, for example, MULTIPLE REGRESSION, CORRELATION COEFFICIENT, STRUCTURAL EQUATION MODELLING, ANALYSIS OF VARIANCE and GENERALISED LINEAR MODEL (GLM) were automatic choices for long entries because once you have grasped that all these things are the same and that most modern statistical models are just the same idea dressed up differently, then other concepts become much easier to grasp. For example, having explained the GLM, analysis of covariance really requires very little explanation. At the next level I tried to reflect modern trends by giving some extra space to concepts such as POWER, CONFIDENCE INTERVALS, EFFECT SIZE, META-ANALYSIS and HYPOTHESIS TESTING, all of which reflect current controversies and modern thinking (in the discipline of psychology at least) about how we should use statistics in our research. Also at this level were concepts with which students (my ones at any rate) struggle, such as ERROR BARS and DUMMY VARIABLES, and some procedures that simply require a lot of detail even to explain in a cursory way, such as DISCRIMINANT FUNCTION ANALYSIS and the CHI-SQUARE TEST. The remaining entries reflect the most commonly used procedures and research concepts that crop up in quantitative methods. You can treat the entries rather like RANDOM EFFECTS in that they are merely a sample of the population of entries that could have been selected, and selecting other samples would not have changed the overall question that we were trying to address. Having said that, it is probably best that I do not imply that it was a *random* sample: a lot of thought went into what to include!

At a time when everyone who has ever written anything about social science statistics was being asked to contribute to an encyclopaedia of behavioural statistics, I am grateful to Jeremy Miles, Graham Hole, Susanne Hempel and Michael Smithson for contributing to this one.

Dr Andy Field

A

---

acquiescence bias A tendency to give the same response to items on a survey irrespective of the content of the items. *AF*

α-level The probability of making a TYPE I ERROR (usually this value is 0.05). *AF*

alternative hypothesis The prediction that your experimental manipulation will have some effect or that certain variables will relate to each other. *AF*

analysis of covariance (ANCOVA) A statistical procedure that uses the *F*-RATIO to test the overall fit of a LINEAR MODEL, controlling for the effect that one or more COVARIATES have on the OUTCOME VARIABLE. In experimental research this linear model tends to be defined in terms of group means, and the resulting ANOVA is therefore an overall test of whether group means differ after the variance in the outcome variable explained by any covariates has been removed.

ANCOVA is an extension of ANALYSIS OF VARIANCE in which a continuous variable is entered into the model in addition to any categorical predictors. To take the example from the analysis of variance entry, if we were interested in group differences between the sperm counts of different groups of men, it might be important to consider the natural sperm count of the men involved. If you consider the situation as a linear model, then it is easy to conceptualise how in ANCOVA this model is extended to incorporate the covariate. The original model was:

$$\text{Sperm}_i = b_0 + b_1\text{Pocket}_i + b_2\text{Coat}_i + \varepsilon_i$$

By adding a covariate we get:

$$\text{Sperm}_i = b_0 + b_1\text{Pocket}_i + b_2\text{Coat}_i + b_3\text{Covariate}_i + \varepsilon_i$$

$$\text{Sperm}_i = b_0 + b_1\text{Pocket}_i + b_2\text{Coat}_i + b_3\text{Normal Sperm Count}_i + \varepsilon_i$$

In this model b_3 represents the impact that normal sperm counts have on sperm counts at the end of the study; however, b_1 is the difference between the mean sperm count of the group that had the phone in their pocket *adjusted* for the effect of natural sperm counts (the covariate) and the mean of the control group (no phone), also adjusted for the effect of the covariate. Likewise, b_2 is the difference between the *adjusted* mean sperm counts of the group that had the phone in their coat and the control group (no phone).

Like analysis of variance, the effects are tested using an *F*-ratio, but for the CATEGORICAL VARIABLE, this *F* represented the effect of the experimental manipulation (or dif-

ferences between group means) after the effects of any covariates have been considered. *AF*

Field 2005a; **Rutherford** 2000; **Wildt** 1978.

analysis of variance (ANOVA) A statistical procedure that uses the *F*-RATIO to test the overall fit of a LINEAR MODEL. In experimental research this linear model tends to be defined in terms of group means and the resulting ANOVA is therefore an overall test of whether group means differ.

The starting point for ANOVA is to discover how much variability there is in the observed data. To do this, the difference between each observed data point and the grand mean is calculated. These values are then squared and added together to give us the total SUM OF SQUARED ERROR (SS_T):

$$SS_T = \Sigma \, (x_i - \bar{x}_{\text{grand}})^2$$

Alternatively, this value can be calculated from the variance of all observations (the grand variance) by multiplying it by the sample size minus 1:

$$SS_T = s^2 \, (N - 1)$$

The DEGREES OF FREEDOM for this value are N–1.

Having established the total variance to be explained, this variance is partitioned into two parts: VARIANCE explained by the linear model fitted to the data (expressed as the model sum of squared error, SS_M) and variance that the model cannot explain (expressed as the residual sum of squared error, SS_R). The model sum of squares is the squared difference between the grand mean and the values predicted by the linear model. When analysing data from groups (i.e. when an experiment has been conducted), the linear model takes the form of the group means. The variance explained by the model is, therefore,

$$SS_M = \Sigma \, n_k \, (\bar{x}_k - \bar{x}_{\text{grand}})^2.$$

The degrees of freedom (df_M) are one less than the number of parameters estimated: when data from groups are analysed this is the number of groups minus 1 (which you will see denoted as k–1), and when continuous predictors are used, it is the number of predictors.

Finally, we need to establish the ERROR in the model, or the variance not explained by the model. This is simply the squared difference between the values predicted by the model, and the observed values. When analysing data from groups, the model used is the group means, so we are looking at the squared difference between the observed value and the mean of the group from which that observation came.

$$SS_R = \Sigma \, (x_{ik} - \bar{x}_k)^2$$

Alternatively, the value can be derived from $SS_R = SS_T - SS_M$. The degrees of freedom for SS_R (df_R) are the total degrees of freedom minus the degrees of freedom for the model ($df_R = df_T - df_M = 14 - 2 = 12$). Put another way, it is $N-k$: the total sample size, N, minus the number of groups, k.

SS_M tells us how much variation the linear model (e.g. the experimental manipulation) explains and SS_R tells us how much variation is due to extraneous factors. However, because both of these values are summed values they will be influenced by the number of scores that were summed. To eliminate this BIAS we can calculate the average sum of squared error – known as the MEAN SQUARED ERROR, (MS) – which is simply the sum of squares divided by the degrees of freedom:

$$MS_M = \frac{SS_M}{df_M}$$

$$MS_R = \frac{SS_R}{df_R}$$

MS_M represents the AVERAGE amount of variation explained by the model (e.g. the systematic variation), whereas MS_R is a gauge of the average amount of variation explained by extraneous variables (the unsystematic variation).

The F-ratio is a measure of the ratio of the variation explained by the model and the variation explained by unsystematic factors. It can be calculated by dividing the model mean squared error by the residual mean squared error.

$$F = \frac{MS_M}{MS_R}$$

The F-ratio is, therefore, a measure of the ratio of systematic variation to unsystematic variation, or, a comparison of how good the model is compared to how bad it is. In experimental scenarios it is the ratio of the experimental effect to the INDIVIDUAL DIFFERENCES (see s. 6) in performance. The observed F-ratio can be compared to critical values of F from a special distribution known as the F-DISTRIBUTION, which represents the values of F that can be expected at certain levels of probability. If the observed value exceeds the critical value for a small probability (typically 0.05), we tend to infer that the model is a significant fit of the observed data, or in the case of experiments, that the experimental manipulation has had a significant effect on performance.

As I have mentioned, when ANOVA is used to analyse data from groups it is a special case of a linear model. [See MULTIPLE REGRESSION and GENERALISED LINEAR MODEL]. Specifically, the linear model can be expressed in terms of DUMMY VARIABLES. Any categorical variable can be expressed as a series of BINARY VARIABLES; there will always be one less variable than there are groups, and each vari-

able compares each group against a base category (e.g. a CONTROL GROUP). There have been recent reports that mobile phones can lower sperm counts (if they are kept in your trouser pocket). Imagine we did an experiment. We had three groups of men who had not previously owned a mobile phone: the first group remained as they were, a second group were given a phone and asked to keep it in their front trouser pocket for a year, the final group were asked to keep the phone in their coat pocket (away from their genitals). After a year sperm counts were measured. The control group were the group not given a phone. This scenario can be represented by a standard regression equation:

$$\text{Sperm}_i = b_0 + b_1\text{Pocket}_i + b_2\text{Coat}_i + \varepsilon_i$$

in which Pocket is a binary variable coded 1 (phone kept in trouser pocket) and 0 (all other groups) and Coat is a binary variable coded 1 (phone kept in coat) and 0 (all other groups). It turns out that b_0 represents the mean of the control group (i.e. the sperm count when Pocket and Coat are both zero); b_1 is the difference between the mean sperm count of the group that had the phone in their pocket and the mean of the control group; and b_2 is the difference between the mean sperm count of the group that had the phone in their coat and the mean of the control group (no phone). [See GENERALISED LINEAR MODEL (GLM)].

For the F-ratio to be accurate the following ASSUMPTIONS must be met: (1) observations should be statistically independent [see INDEPENDENCE]; (2) data should be randomly sampled from the population of interest and measured at an interval level; (3) the outcome variable should be sampled from a NORMAL DISTRIBUTION; and (4) there must be HOMOGENEITY OF VARIANCE. When a REPEATED-MEASURES DESIGN is used, the assumption of independence is violated and this gives rise to an additional assumption of SPHERICITY. *AF*

Cohen 1968; **Field** 2005a.

association   The degree to which as one variable changes another variable also changes. [See CORRELATION COEFFICIENT] *AF*

assumptions   The conditions under which a TEST STATISTIC can be assumed to be accurate. *AF*

asymmetric distribution   [See SKEWNESS]

autocorrelation   When the RESIDUALS of two observations in a REGRESSION model are correlated. *AF*

average   [See MEAN]

B

backward elimination A method of model building (e.g. MULTIPLE REGRESSION and LOG-LINEAR MODELS) in which all predictors are initially included, but are then individually removed if their exclusion does not adversely affect the fit of the model. *AF*

balanced design An experimental design in which each treatment condition has an equal number of participants/observations. *AF*

bar chart A graph displaying some statistical property (FREQUENCY, MEAN, etc.) of an OUTCOME VARIABLE, for categories of data. *AF*

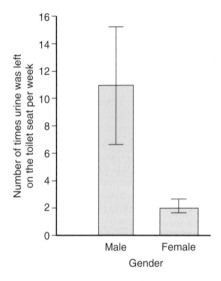

bar chart *graph of two means (with error bars)*

Bartlett's test A test of whether a VARIANCE-COVARIANCE MATRIX is proportional to an identity matrix: whether the diagonal elements are equal (i.e. group variances are the same), and the off-diagonal elements are approximately zero (i.e. the DEPENDENT VARIABLES are not correlated). *AF*

beta coefficient A general term for a regression coefficient. Unstandardised regression coefficients, b_i, represent the strength of relationship between a given predictor, i, and an outcome in the units of measurement of the predictor. It is the change in the outcome associated with a unit change in the predictor. Standardised regression coefficients, β_i, represent the strength of relationship between a given predictor, i, and an outcome in a *standardised* form. It is the change in the outcome (in standard deviations) associated with a one STANDARD DEVIATION change in the predictor. *AF*

β-level The probability of making a TYPE II ERROR (a maximum value of 0.2 is recommended). *AF*

between-groups design Any experimental design in which each condition is performed by a separate group of participants. (Also known as an INDEPENDENT-MEASURES DESIGN). *GH*

bias The degree to which a statistic fails to estimate or test whatever the researcher was trying to estimate or test. (See also s. 3, BIAS) *AF*

bimodal distribution A frequency distribution of observations that has two MODES. *AF*

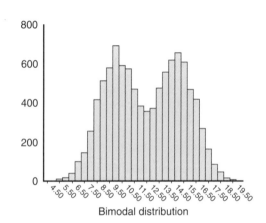

Bimodal distribution

bimodal distribution *(from Field and Hole 2003)*

binary variable A variable that consists of only two values: 0 and 1. Often used to represent DICHOTOMOUS VARIABLES. *AF*

biserial correlation A standardised measure of the strength of relationship between two variables when one is a DICHOTOMOUS VARIABLE and the other is a CONTINUOUS VARIABLE. The biserial correlation coefficient (r_b) is used when one variable is a continuous dichotomy (e.g. has an underlying continuum between the categories). An example is passing or failing your driving test: some people will only just fail (perhaps because of some small mistake), while others will fail by a large margin (perhaps because they ran over 26 pedestrians and a dog); likewise some people will scrape a pass while others will perform perfectly on the test. So although drivers fall into only two categories there is clearly an underlying continuum along which people lie.

A related measure is the point-biserial correlation coefficient (r_{pb}), which is used when the dichotomy is a discrete, or true, dichotomy (i.e. one for which there is no underlying continuum between the categories). An example of this is pregnancy: you can be either pregnant or not, there is no in-between. The point-biserial correlation is simply a PEARSON PRODUCT MOMENT CORRELATION COEFFICIENT when the dichotomous variable is a binary variable (i.e. coded with 0 for one category and 1 for the other) and is directly comparable to the t-TEST. The sign of the coefficient is completely dependent on which category you assign to which code and so all information about the direction of the relationship should be ignored.

The biserial correlation is based on the point-biserial correlation:

$$r_b = \frac{r_{pb} \sqrt{(p_1 p_2)}}{y}$$

in which P1 and P2 are the proportions of cases falling into categories 1 and 2 respectively. Imagine we wanted to look at the relationship between passing and failing your driving test and how nervous the person is before the test. Let us say that we had 24 per cent of drivers that passed and 76 per cent that failed, and for each driver we have an ANXIETY (see s. 6) score. If the point-biserial correlation between anxiety and the driving test was 0.34, then to discover y in the equation we look at the values of z [see Z-SCORES] from the NORMAL DISTRIBUTION (see Appendix), looking down the column labelled 'larger portion' for 0.76 (which is 76 per cent expressed as a proportion). The closest we find is 0.76115. Note that the smaller portion is .23885 (more or less .24 or 24 per cent). Now move to the final column labelled y and this is the value we need, in this case, 0.3101. The biserial correlation is, therefore:

$$r_b = \frac{r_{pb} \sqrt{p_1 p_2}}{y} = \frac{0.34 \sqrt{0.76 \times 0.24}}{0.3101} = 0.47$$

AF

Field 2005a; **Howell** 2002.

bivariate data   Measurements of two variables in a SAMPLE of entities. *AF*

block   A term used to describe a homogeneous group of some aspect of an experiment (be it participants, trials, measurements, etc.). *AF*

Bonferroni correction   A simple but effective correction applied to the α-LEVEL to control the overall TYPE I ERROR rate when multiple significance tests are carried out. Each test conducted should use a criterion of significance of the α-level (normally 0.05) divided by the number of tests conducted. *AF*

bootstrap   The bootstrap is a powerful resampling technique, introduced by Efron (1983; see also Efron and Tibshirani 1993) for statistical inference. What might be called 'traditional' statistical tests require that we know the sampling distribution of a test statistic under the NULL HYPOTHESIS. There are two occasions when we do not know this – one is where the assumptions (such as a NORMAL DISTRIBUTION) are violated, the second is where we do not know the sampling distribution of the statistic of interest, for example, the sampling distribution of the MEDIAN is not known (except in very large samples.) A large number of bootstrap samples is created by sampling, with replacement, from the original sample. The statistic of interest (e.g. the MEAN or the median) is calculated for each sample, to provide an estimated SAMPLING DISTRIBUTION. The STANDARD DEVIATION of the sampling distribution is used as the estimate of the standard error of the statistic, which can then be used to calculate CONFIDENCE INTERVALS and P-VALUES. *JM*

Efron 1983; **Efron and Tibshirani** 1993.

boredom effects   The possibility that performance at the end of a series of tasks, or one long task, is influenced by boredom. *AF*

boxplot   A boxplot, or box-whisker diagram, is a graphical representation of the MEDIAN, INTER-QUARTILE RANGE and RANGE of a set of observations.

The box in the Figure shows the inter-quartile range, so 50 per cent of the scores are bigger than the lowest line of the box but smaller than the top line of the box. The horizontal line within the box shows the value of the median. The top and bottom of the box also have whiskers. The top line of the upper whisker shows the highest score; therefore, the distance between the top edge of the box and the top of the upper whisker shows the upper quartile (i.e. the range within which the top 25 per cent of scores fall). The distance between the horizontal line at the bottom of the lower whisker and the horizontal line at the top of the upper whisker represents the range of scores. The strange blobs are OUTLIERS or extreme scores. *AF*

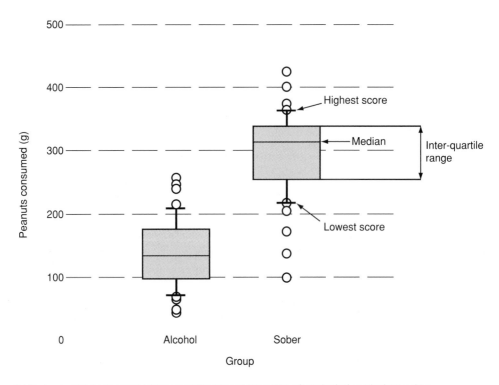

boxplot *a boxplot (or box-whisker diagram) of the quantity of peanuts eaten after alcohol, and when sober*

C

canonical correlation analysis A technique for exploring whether two sets of variables correlate. In effect, it can be viewed as an extension of MULTIPLE REGRESSION to situations in which there are several OUTCOME VARIABLES. The analysis works by finding the linear variates of the first set of variables and then those for the second set. It then calculates the correlation between these sets of variates. A high correlation tells us that some linear combination of one set of variables predicts a linear combination of the other set. For example, if we were interested in predictors of 'pop stardom', we might measure this in terms of records sold, concert tickets sold, popularity in an opinion poll and appearances in the media. These four variables would be used as indicators of 'pop stardom'. We might also have several predictors, such as innate talent, hours spent practising, amount spent on promotion and amount spent on image consultancy. Canonical correlation analysis would tell us whether a linear combination of these four variables predicts a linear combination of the variables chosen as indicators of 'pop stardom'. *AF*

Thompson 1985.

case study An in-depth study of either one entity (an individual, organisation, etc.) or a small number of entities. *JM*

categorical variable Any VARIABLE made up of categories of objects/entities. *AF*

causality The struggle to match causes to the effects they produce. Contemporary approaches to causality are based largely on Mill's (1865) three conditions necessary to infer cause: (1) cause has to precede effect; (2) cause and effect should correlate; and (3) all other explanations of the cause–effect relationship must be ruled out. This is achieved through manipulating proposed causes and observing the effect of the manipulation: scientists compare situations in which the cause is present with situations in which the cause is absent (see Field and Hole 2003). The condition in which the proposed cause is absent is typically called a CONTROL GROUP. For example, to discover whether drinking 'powerade' improves running performance, we should have a group who are given powerade before they run (cause present) and a group who are not given powerade before they run (cause absent). Any differences in performance between the groups is attributable to the drink they had *before* the run. *AF*

Field and Hole 2003; **Mill** 1865.

ceiling effect A ceiling effect occurs if performance on a measure is so good that scores are clustered around the top of the scale. This makes the measure insensitive, because it has little scope for variation (and is also more prone to REGRESSION TO THE MEAN). *GH*

central limit theorem The central limit theorem enables us to predict the properties of a SAMPLING DISTRIBUTION. The central limit theorem states that the sampling distribution will be normally distributed – no matter what the shape of the parent POPULATION of raw scores from which the SAMPLES were originally drawn. The sampling distribution increasingly approximates to a NORMAL DISTRIBUTION as the SAMPLE SIZE is increased. This theorem is important because it enables us to use the normal distribution as a 'model' for many different types of sampling distribution. As a result, we can make inferences about how samples might be related to populations even when we have no idea of the true DISTRIBUTION of scores in the parent population. *GH*

central tendency A generic term describing the centre of a FREQUENCY DISTRIBUTION of observations as measured by the MEAN, MODE and MEDIAN. *AF*

chi-squared distribution A PROBABILITY DISTRIBUTION of the sum of squares of several normally distributed variables. It tends to be used to test hypotheses about categorical data. The exact shape of the distribution is determined by the DEGREES OF FREEDOM of the TEST STATISTIC for which the distribution is being used. *AF*

chi-square goodness of fit This is a statistical test based on the chi-square statistic. It measures the extent to which an observed FREQUENCY DISTRIBUTION differs from the DISTRIBUTION that was expected (usually a rectangular distribution, where all categories have equal frequencies). For the formula, and constraints on the use of χ^2, see the entry on CHI-SQUARE TEST. The degrees of freedom are given by the number of categories minus 1. *GH*

chi-square test Chi-square (χ^2) is a measure of the discrepancy between a set of observed and expected frequencies. The formula is

$$\chi^2 = \sum_{i=1}^{r} \sum_{j=1}^{c} \left(\frac{(Observed_{ij} - Expected_{ij})^2}{Expected_{ij}} \right)$$

where *Observed* and *Expected* stand for observed and expected frequencies, respectively. There are a variety of tests based on the χ^2 statistic (see CHI-SQUARE GOODNESS OF FIT), but probably its most common use is in conjunction with a CONTINGENCY TABLE, to test whether there is an association between the two variables concerned. The larger the value of χ^2, the less likely the observed pattern of results is to have occurred by chance. In assessing the probability of obtaining a given value of χ^2 by chance, it is necessary to use a CHI-SQUARED DISTRIBUTION based on the DEGREES OF FREEDOM (DF). For a contingency table, this is obtained by adding the number of rows minus 1 to the number of columns minus 1. Special versions of χ^2 exist for when there is only 1 df. For χ^2 to be valid, no more than 20 per cent of the expected frequencies should be less than 5, and it is essential that all observations are independent events – each participant must contribute only a single score to a single category. *GH*

Field 2005a; **Howell** 2002.

cluster sampling A cluster sample takes a naturally occurring group (for example, children in a class or all general practitioners in Derbyshire). *JM*

Cochran's Q-test This test is an extension of MCNEMAR TEST and is basically a FRIEDMAN'S ANOVA for dichotomous data. So imagine you asked 20 men whether they would like to kiss Britney Spears, Madonna and Nicole Kidman and they could answer only yes or no. If we coded responses as 0 (no) and 1 (yes), we could do the Cochran test on these data to discover which of the three women was most kissable. The test is defined as:

$$Q = k(k-1) \frac{\sum_{j=1}^{k} \left(y_j - \frac{y}{k}\right)^2}{ky - \sum_{i=1}^{n} y_i^2}$$

in which k is the number of things being compared (in this case, three women), y_j is the number of '1' responses that a particular woman got (i.e. for each woman, it is the number of people who said they would kiss her), y is the total number of '1' responses across the entire data set, and y_i is the number of '1' responses a particular person gave (i.e. the number of people each man said they would like to kiss). *AF*

coefficient of determination This is the CORRELATION COEFFICIENT squared. In general terms it is the correlation between the values predicted by a REGRESSION model and the observed values and represents the amount of VARIANCE in the OUTCOME VARIABLE that is accounted for by the one or more predictors in the model. *GH/AF*

cohort study A study in which the behaviour of a particular group of individuals is measured repeatedly. For example, a LONGITUDINAL (see s. 1, LONGITUDINAL RESEARCH) study of people who were all born on the same day would be a cohort study. *GH*

collinearity [See MULTICOLLINEARITY]

confidence intervals A $100(1-\alpha)$ per cent confidence interval is an interval estimate around a POPULATION parameter θ that, under repeated random samples of size N, would be expected to include θ's true value $100(1-\alpha)$ per cent of the time. The confidence interval indicates the precision with which the population parameter is estimated by a SAMPLE statistic.

The confidence level, $100(1-\alpha)$ per cent, is chosen a priori. A two-sided confidence interval uses a lower limit L and upper limit U that each contain θ's true value $100(1-\alpha/2)$ per cent of the time, so that together they contain θ's true value $100(1-\alpha)$ per cent of the time. This interval often is written as $[L, U]$. The limits L and U are sample statistics, so L and U will vary from one sample to another under repeated random sampling.

The confidence interval is closely related to the significance test because a $100(1-\alpha)$ per cent confidence interval includes all hypothetical population parameter values that cannot be rejected by a significance test at a α significance level. In this respect, it provides more information than a significance test does (Schmidt 1996; Altman et al. 2000; Smithson 2003).

Suppose, for example, we have a random sample of $N = 50$ IQ (see s. 6) scores, with a sample mean of 102 and standard deviation $s = 15$. We will construct a two-sided 95 per cent confidence interval for the mean, θ. The t-statistic defined by

$$t = \frac{\overline{X} - \mu}{s_{err}}$$

where is $s_{err} = s/\sqrt{N}$, has a t-distribution with $df = N-1 = 49$. The value $t_{\alpha/2} = 2.0096$ cuts $\alpha/2 = .025$ from the upper tail of this t-distribution, and likewise $-t_{\alpha/2} = -2.0096$ cuts $\alpha/2 = .025$ from the lower tail. The sample standard error is $s_{err} = s/\sqrt{N} = 2.121$. So a t-distribution around $U = 102 + (2.0096)(2.121) = 106.26$ has .025 of its tail below 102, while a t-distribution around $L = 102-(2.0096)(2.121) = 97.74$ has .025 of its tail above 102. Therefore the 95 per cent confidence interval for μ is [97.74, 106.63], and these are the hypothetical values of the population mean IQ that we cannot reject.

Confidence intervals become narrower with larger sample size and/or lower confidence levels.

For central confidence intervals, the same standardised distribution (e.g. the NORMAL DISTRIBUTION) may be used regardless of the hypothetical value of the population parameter. However, non-central distributions change shape depending on the value of the parameter, so a unique distribution must be computed for every parameter value under consideration (see Steiger and Fouladi 1997, Smithson 2003). *MS*

Altman, Machin, Bryant and Gardner 2000; **Schmidt** 1996; **Smithson** 2003; **Steiger and Fouladi** 1997.

confirmatory factor analysis (CFA) [See STRUCTURAL EQUATION MODELLING]

confound variable A VARIABLE (that may or may not have been measured), other than the PREDICTOR VARIABLES in which we are interested, that potentially affects an OUTCOME VARIABLE. *AF*

consent [See INFORMED CONSENT]

conservative test A conservative test is often used to try to minimise the chances of committing a TYPE I ERROR. Conservative tests are often used when many tests need to be performed on the same data; under these circumstances there is an increased risk of making a type I error. By making it harder to attain statistical significance, conservative tests reduce the risk of a type I error – though at the cost of increasing the risk of a TYPE II ERROR. Examples of conservative tests include various POST HOC TESTS, such as the BONFERRONI CORRECTION, which are used after an ANOVA in order to make more specific comparisons between groups or conditions while preserving the type I error-rate at the .05 level of significance. *GH*

content validity   Evidence that the content of a test corresponds to the content of the construct it was designed to cover.   *SH*

contingency table   A table in which the rows represent values of one CATEGORICAL VARIABLE and the columns represent values of another. Each entry in the table represents the frequency with which that permutation of variables has occurred. In the Table below, the columns represent two levels of the categorical variable 'gender' and the rows represent three levels of another categorical variable, 'evening class course'. The cells in the table give the observed frequencies with which a sample of 200 men and women picked one of the three evening courses. The extent to which the two variables have a non-random association can be assessed by using a statistical test such as chi-square [see CHI-SQUARE TEST].   *GH*

contingency table *A contingency table showing the relationship between gender and evening class course*

	Male	*Female*	*total:*
Flower arranging	20	35	55
Karate	50	25	75
French	30	40	70
total:	100	100	200

continuity correction   [See YATES' CORRECTION FOR CONTINUITY]

continuous variable   A variable which (at least in theory) can be measured to any level of precision, e.g. REACTION TIME (see s. 3) (RT) is a continuous variable, because there is, in principle, no limit on how finely it could be measured. In contrast, 'number correct' is a discontinuous variable, because it can only take discrete integer values.   *GH*

contrast   Any linear function in which the coefficients sum to zero. Typically, contrasts are used to compare different levels of categorical variables [see PLANNED COMPARISONS] by adjusting the coefficients in such a way that certain categories are compared to certain other categories. Contrasts can be ORTHOGONAL, in which case the contrasts are independent and their coefficients cross-multiply to sum to zero, or *non-orthogonal*, in which case the same VARIANCE is used in more than one contrast and the contrasts are related.   *AF*
Field 2005a.

control group   The simplest experimental design involves randomly allocating participants to one of two groups, and then applying some manipulation to one group (the experimental group) but not to the other (the CONTROL GROUP). Performance of the latter provides a baseline against which to assess the effects of the treatment on the experimental group.   *GH*

correlation coefficient   Pearson's correlation coefficient is a standardised measure or the relationship between two variables and is the foundation of most statistical procedures in the social sciences. The simplest way to look at whether two variables are associated is to look at whether they covary. COVARIANCE is related to VARIANCE. The variance of a single VARIABLE represents the average amount that the data vary from the MEAN (see Field 2005a). Numerically, it is described by:

$$Variance\ (s^2) = \frac{\Sigma(x_i - \overline{x})^2}{N-1} = \frac{\Sigma(x_i - \overline{x})(x_i - \overline{x})}{N-1}$$

The mean of the sample is represented by, $\overline{x}$, x_i is the data point in question and N is the number of observations. To see if two variables are related, then, we are interested in whether changes in one variable are met with similar changes in the other variable. Therefore, as one variable deviates from its mean, the other should do so as well. If there is a relationship between two variables, then as one variable deviates from its mean the other variable should deviate from its mean in the same or the directly opposite way. If there is no relationship, then as one variable deviates from its mean the other will remain unchanged.

So, how do we measure the extent of this relationship? In the single variable case, we calculate the deviation from the mean for each observation and square these deviations to eliminate the problem of positive and negative differences cancelling out each other. When there are two variables, rather than squaring each deviation, we can multiply the deviation for one variable by the corresponding deviation for the second variable. If both deviations are positive or negative, this will give us a positive value (indicative of the deviations being in the same direction), but if one deviation is positive and one negative, the resulting product will be negative (indicative of the deviations being opposite in direction). If one variable simply doesn't deviate from the mean as the other one does, then the resulting product will be close to zero (or zero itself).

The results of multiplying the deviances of one variable by the corresponding differences of the second variable, are known as the cross-product deviations. If we were to sum these cross-product deviations we would have an estimate of the total relationship between two variables, however, this total would depend on the number of observations. Therefore, we tend to divide by the number of observations (actually we use $N-1$ when using a SAMPLE to estimate the relationship in the POPULATION of interest). The averaged sum of combined deviances is known as the covariance and is written as:

$$\text{cov}(x, y) = \frac{\Sigma(x_i - \overline{x})(y_i - \overline{y})}{N-1}$$

The covariance is a good way to assess whether two variables are related to each other. A positive covariance indicates that as one variable deviates from the mean, the other variable deviates in the same direction. On the other hand, a negative covariance indicates that as one variable deviates from the mean (e.g. increases), the other deviates from the mean in the opposite direction (e.g. decreases). However, one problem with covariance as a measure of the relationship between variables is that it depends upon the scales of measurement used. A covariance based on REACTION TIMES (see s. 3) in milliseconds will be much larger than the covariance for the same data if the reaction times are converted to seconds! This dependence on the scale of measurement is a problem because we cannot say whether a covariance is particularly large or small relative to another data set unless both data sets were measured in the same units.

To overcome this problem the covariance can be converted into a standard set of units [see STANDARDISATION]. The units we use are STANDARD DEVIATION units [see Z-SCORES] and the conversion is done simply by dividing by the standard deviation. However, because there are two variables and, hence, two standard deviations, we use both (in fact we multiply them together just like the deviations from the mean). The standardised covariance is known as *PEARSON PRODUCT MOMENT CORRELATION COEFFICIENT* (or *Pearson correlation coefficient*, for short) and is defined as:

$$r = \frac{cov_{xy}}{s_x s_y} = \frac{\Sigma(x_i - \overline{x})(y_i - \overline{y})}{(N-1)s_x s_y}$$

in which s_x is the standard deviation of the first variable and s_y is the standard deviation of the second variable (all other letters are the same as in the equation defining covariance).

By standardising the covariance we end up with a value that has to lie between –1 and +1. A coefficient of +1 indicates that the two variables are perfectly positively correlated, so as one variable increases, the other increases by a proportionate amount. Conversely, a coefficient of –1 indicates a perfect negative relationship: if one variable increases, the other decreases by a proportionate amount. A coefficient of zero indicates no linear relationship at all and so if one variable changes, the other stays the same. Also, because the correlation coefficient is a standardised measure of an observed effect, it is a commonly used EFFECT SIZE measure and values of ±0.1 represent a small effect, ±0.3 is a medium effect and ±0.5 is a large effect (Cohen 1988). *AF*

Cohen 1988; **Field** 2005a; **Wright** 2002.

correlation matrix A square matrix (i.e. same number of columns and rows) in which each column represents a measured VARIABLE and the rows represent the same variables as the columns and in the same order. The diagonal elements are all 1 (the CORRELATION COEFFICIENT of each variable with itself), whereas the off-diagonal elements are the correlation coefficients for pairs of variables. *AF*

counterbalancing In an experiment, counterbalancing is a technique used to ensure that order effects such as PRACTICE (EFFECTS) and BOREDOM (EFFECTS) do not affect performance systematically. As many participants experience the conditions in one order as experience them in the opposite order, e.g., with two conditions, half the participants perform the conditions in the order AB, and half in the order BA. *GH*

covariance [See CORRELATION COEFFICIENT]

covariance matrix [See VARIANCE-COVARIANCE MATRIX]

covariate A covariate is a VARIABLE which correlates with the OUTCOME VARIABLE that is of primary interest to an experimenter. The effects of a covariate can be examined in techniques such as ANALYSIS OF COVARIANCE. For example, an experiment on different methods of LEARNING (see s. 3) a LANGUAGE (see s. 2) (the main PREDICTOR VARIABLE) might want to adjust for the effects of IQ (see s. 6) (the covariate). *GH*

Cramer's V A variant of the PHI-COEFFICIENT that measures of the strength of association between two CATEGORICAL VARIABLES when one of these variables has more than two categories. It is used because when one or both of the categorical variables contain more than two categories, the phi-coefficient (which was designed for 2×2 CONTINGENCY TABLES) fails to reach its minimum value of zero (indicating no association). It is defined as:

$$V = \sqrt{\frac{\chi^2}{N(k-1)}},$$

which is simply the square root of the CHI-SQUARE TEST statistic divided by the sample size (N) multiplied by $k-1$, where k is the smaller of R (the number or rows in the contingency table) and C (the number of columns in the contingency table). The resulting value lies between 0 (no association) and 1 (complete association). *AF*

Howell 2002.

criterion validity Evidence that test scores predict or correspond with concurrent external criteria that are conceptually related to the measured construct. *SH*

critical value Most statistical tests involve calculating a value of a test statistic from the obtained data and then deciding how likely it would be to obtain this value by chance. This is done by comparing the obtained value to a critical value of the test statistic, generally the one that is likely to occur by chance with a probability of 0.05 (1 in 20 times). If the obtained value equals or exceeds the critical value, then it is unlikely to have arisen by chance. Other critical values may be used, e.g. 0.01, 0.001 or 0.0001. (Note that, in the case of some tests, such as the MANN-WHITNEY TEST, the obtained test statistic has to be *smaller* than the critical value in order to be unlikely to have arisen by chance). *GH*

Cronbach's α A measure of the reliability of a scale defined by:

$$\alpha = \frac{N^2 \overline{Cov}}{\sum s^2_{item} + \sum Cov_{item}}$$

In which the top half of the equation is simply the number of items (N) used in the scale squared multiplied by the average COVARIANCE between items on the scale (the average of the off-diagonal elements in the VARIANCE-COVARIANCE MATRIX of scale items). The bottom half is simply the sum of all the elements in the variance-covariance matrix of scale items.

A standardised version of the coefficient exists, which uses the same equation, except that correlations are used rather than covariances, and the bottom half of the equation uses the sum of the elements in the CORRELATION MATRIX of items (including the 1s that appear on the diagonal of that matrix). The normal alpha is appropriate when items on a scale are summed to produce a single score for that scale (the standardised α is not appropriate in these cases). The standardised alpha is useful, though, when items on a scale are standardised before being summed.

A value of 0.7–0.8 is regarded as an acceptable value for scale reliability, although Kline (1999) notes that when dealing with psychological constructs, values below 0.7 can, realistically, be expected. However, Cortina (1993) notes that general guidelines need to be used with caution because the value of alpha depends on the number of items on the scale (note that the top half of the equation for alpha includes the number of items squared). A second common interpretation of alpha is that it measures 'unidimensionality', or the extent to which the scale measures one underlying factor or construct. However, Grayson (2004) and Cortina (1993) demonstrate that data sets with the same alpha can have very different structures.

Indeed, Cronbach (1951) suggested that if several factors exist then the formula should be applied separately to items relating to different factors. *AF*

Cortina 1993; **Cronbach** 1951; **Field** 2005a; **Grayson** 2004; **Kline** 1999.

cross-sectional design An experimental design widely used in developmental research. Separate groups of participants are used to represent different levels of an INDEPENDENT VARIABLE, which would ideally be represented by a single group at different times. For example, in studying age differences, a cross-sectional design would involve using different groups of participants to represent different ages, rather than measuring the behaviour of a single group at different ages (a LONGITUDINAL – see s. 1, LONGITUDINAL RESEARCH – design). *GH*

D

deception Deliberately misleading participants about the purpose of the research (or some part of it) in which they are engaged. (See also s. 5, DECEPTION) *AF*

degrees of freedom (df) The number of items that are free to vary when calculating a statistic. Suppose we have a list of five numbers and a total. If the numbers are summed, then four of the numbers can be varied but the fifth will always be fixed: it is not free to vary because it *has* to be the difference between the total and the sum of the first four numbers. This lack of INDEPENDENCE among observations needs to be taken into account in many statistical tests. For example, in an independent T-TEST, the *df* are obtained by adding the number of scores in condition A minus one, to the number of scores in condition B minus one. In a CHI-SQUARE GOODNESS OF FIT test, the DF are the number of categories minus one. In each case, not taking DF into account would affect the statistic obtained because whichever value was entered into the calculations last would have its value determined by the values of the preceding items. *GH*

Field and Hole 2003; **Field** 2005a.

demand characteristic When a participant attempts to perform the task in the manner in which they think the experimenter would wish, they are responding to the demand characteristics of the study. (See also s. 1) *GH*

dependent variable Synonym for OUTCOME VARIABLE. This name is usually associated with experimental methodology (which is the only time it really makes sense) and is so-called because it is the VARIABLE that is not manipulated by the experimenter and so its value *depends* on the variables that have been manipulated. *AF*

deviation The difference between the observed value of a VARIABLE and the value of that variable predicted by a statistical model. For example, the deviation of an observation from the MEAN is simply the observed value minus the mean of all observations. *AF*

dichotomous variable A CATEGORICAL VARIABLE consisting of only two categories. *AF*

discourse analysis Discourse analysis operates on the basic assumption that by studying what we say (and how we interact) we can gain access to psychological processes. The starting point for a discourse analysis could be a transcribed individual interview (which has an advantage of control) or a group discussion (which has the advantage that you can look at natural interactions). Not all the material is analysed: topics or themes are identified, often through reading the material and looking for re-occurring features of conversation, or intuition about important parts of the dialogue. The transcripts would then be indexed according to the themes identified. The

material is scrutinised for counter-examples of things the researcher has identified. The analysis itself is based on writing an account of the identified themes and extracting data from the transcripts to support (or contradict) the researcher's ideas. Billig (1997) gives an excellent real-life example of the process. *AF*

Billig 1997.

discrete variable A VARIABLE having only integer values. *AF*

discriminant function analysis Also known as discriminant analysis, this is used to see whether groups of entities can be discriminated using a linear combination of several OUTCOME VARIABLES. Put more simply, like LOGISTIC REGRESSION, it seeks to determine group membership from a set of CONTINUOUS VARIABLES. The analysis identifies and describes the discriminant function variates of a set of variables. A discriminant function variate is a linear combination of variables created such that the differences between group means on the transformed variable is maximised. It takes the general form:

$$Variate_1 = b_1X_1 + b_2X_2 \ldots b_nX_n$$

For each variable measured we can calculate the SUM OF SQUARED ERROR (a measure of the VARIANCE within that VARIABLE) and a series of cross-products (a measure of the relationship between that variable and other measured variables). If we do this for all variables then we can create a square matrix for which the columns and rows represent the measured variables, the diagonal elements represent the variances within variables and the off-diagonal elements are the cross-products between variables. This is an SSCP matrix (it is simply a crude form of a VARIANCE-COVARIANCE MATRIX). If we calculate the model and residual sums of squares [see ANALYSIS OF VARIANCE] for each variable then we can place these in two SSCP matrices: H and E respectively. The HYPOTHESIS SSCP (H) represents the variance explained by the model, whereas the error SSCP (E) represents the variance unexplained by the model. By multiplying H by the inverse of E, we get a new matrix HE^{-1}, which is functionally equivalent to the F-RATIO in analysis of variance. As such, it is the ratio of explained to unexplained variance. The values of b for each variate is given by the elements of the EIGENVECTORS of HE^{-1}.

The first discriminant function is the linear combination of dependent variables that maximises the ratio of systematic to unsystematic variance (SS_M/SS_R); that is, it maximises the differences between groups. The number of variates that can be obtained is the smaller of p (the number of outcome variables) or k (the number of groups). Each variate can be significance-tested to see whether it significantly discriminates the groups, and if it does the resulting b values for each outcome variable can be used to interpret how the outcome variables contribute to group discrimination. Discriminant analysis is a useful way to follow up a MULTIVARIATE ANALYSIS OF VARIANCE.

AF

Field 2005a; **Klecka** 1980; **Stevens** 1992.

dispersion　The degree of DEVIATION of a set of observations from their MEAN.　　*AF*

distribution　[See FREQUENCY DISTRIBUTION]　　*AF*

distribution-free methods　Statistical procedures that do not depend on a specific form of the PROBABILITY DISTRIBUTION of observations. For example, these tests do not rely on the assumption that observations come from a normally distributed population and so are relatively less restrictive in their usage. In many cases, these tests operate on ranked data. [See RANKING DATA]　　*AF*

double-blind study　An experiment in which neither the experimenter nor the participant knows to which condition the participant has been assigned. This is important in DRUG (see s. 2) studies, for example, where either the experimenter or the participants' expectations might affect the results (e.g. by producing a PLACEBO EFFECT).　　*GH*

dummy variables　Dummy variables are a way of recoding a CATEGORICAL VARIABLE with more than two categories into a series of variables, all of which are dichotomous and can take on values of only 0 or 1. To create these variables: (1) count the number of groups or categories that you want to recode and subtract 1; (2) create as many new variables as the value you calculated in step 1 (these are the dummy variables); (3) choose one group or category as a baseline (this should be a group or category against which you want to compare all other groups) and assign that group values of 0 for all of your dummy variables; (4) for the first dummy variable, assign the value 1 to the first group that you want to compare against the baseline group and assign all other groups 0 for this variable); (5) for the second dummy variable assign the value 1 to the second group that you want to compare against the baseline group and assign all other groups 0 for this variable; and (6) repeat this process until you run out of dummy variables.

So, for example, if we had the categorical variable of 'soccer team' representing the soccer team that a person supports, and we had the categories of 'Arsenal', 'Liverpool', 'Manchester United' and 'Millwall', we could recode these in three dummy variables (see Table).

dummy variables

	Dummy Variable 1	Dummy Variable 2	Dummy Variable 3
Arsenal	1	0	0
Liverpool	0	1	0
Manchester United	0	0	1
Millwall	0	0	0

Imagine our outcome was some kind of measure of hooliganism, or crowd violence, we might use Millwall fans as our baseline category (as in the UK they have a, some would say unjustified, reputation for violence). The first dummy variable compares violence in Arsenal fans compared to Millwall fans, the second compares violence in Liverpool fans compared to Millwall fans, and so on. *AF*

Cohen 1968; **Field** 2005a.

Durbin-Watson test　A test for serial correlations between errors in REGRESSION models. It tests whether adjacent residuals are correlated, which is useful in assessing the assumption of independent errors. The test statistic can vary between 0 and 4, with a value of 2 meaning that the residuals are uncorrelated. A value greater than 2 indicates a negative correlation between adjacent residuals, whereas a value below 2 indicates a positive correlation. The size of the Durbin-Watson statistic depends upon the number of predictors in the model, and the number of observations. For accuracy, you should look up the exact acceptable values in Durbin and Watson's (1951) original paper. As a very conservative rule of thumb, Field (2005a) suggests that values less than 1 or greater than 3 are definitely cause for concern; however, values closer to 2 may still be problematic depending on your sample and model.　　*AF*

Durbin and Watson 1951; **Field** 2005a.

E

ecological validity Evidence that the results of a study, experiment or test can be applied, and allow inferences, to real-world conditions. (See also s. 3)

SH

effect size An effect size is simply an objective and standardised measure of the magnitude of observed effect. Many measures of effect size have been proposed, the most common of which are Cohen's, *d*, and Pearson's CORRELATION COEFFICIENT, *r* (although there are others, such as ODDS RATIOS).

Cohen's *d* is based on the standardised difference between two means:

$$d = \frac{M_1 - M_2}{\sigma}$$

So you simply subtract the MEAN of one group from the other and then standardise this difference by dividing by σ, which is the sum of squared errors (i.e. take the difference between each score and the mean, square it, and then add up all of these squared values) divided by the total number of scores.

The correlation coefficient is usually described within the context of measuring the strength of relationship between two continuous variables; however, it is also a very versatile measure of the strength of an experimental effect. [See GENERALISED LINEAR MODEL] J. Cohen (1988, 1992) has made some widely accepted suggestions about what constitutes a large or small effect:

- *r* = 0.10 (small effect): the effect explains 1 per cent of the total variance;

- *r* = 0.30 (medium effect): the effect accounts for 9 per cent of the total variance;

- *r* = 0.50 (large effect): the effect accounts for 25 per cent of the variance.

The equivalent values for *d* are 0.2 (small effect), 0.5 (medium effect) and 0.8 (large effect). We can use these guidelines to assess the importance of our effects (regardless of the significance of the TEST STATISTIC). *AF*

Cohen 1988, 1992; **Clark-Carter** 2003; **Field** 2005a; **Rosenthal** 1991.

eigenvalue [See EIGENVECTOR]

eigenvector Imagine you had two normally distributed variables: the number of Orange Smarties (M&Ms in North America) a child ate per hour and their hyperactivity. If we plot these variables on a SCATTERPLOT and they are correlated, the resulting data cloud will form an ellipse. The two lines that measure the length and height of this ellipse are *eigenvectors* of the original CORRELATION MATRIX for these two variables (a vector is just a set of numbers that tells us the location of a line in geometric

space). These lines will be perpendicular and, hence, they are independent from one another. We can extend this analogy to when three variables are plotted: a third dimension will be added to the scatterplot and the ellipse will become rugby-ball shaped (or American football shaped). A third eigenvector could then be drawn to measure the depth of the data cloud. The same logic applies if fourth and fifth variables are added, although it is harder to visualise. Each eigenvector has an EIGENVALUE that tells us its length (i.e. the distance from one end of the eigenvector to the other). So by looking at all of the eigenvalues for a data set, we know the dimensions of the data cloud. *AF*

Field 2005a.

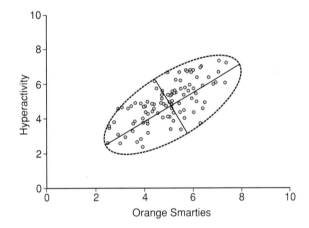

eigenvector

empirical Verifying ideas or theories by collecting data. *AF*

error The extent to which a statistic or model deviates from the thing it is attempting to estimate/model. *AF*

error bars Error bars are used to indicate how much variation is associated with each data point on a graph. Error bars are commonly used to denote two different types of variation, so it is important to label the graph clearly to show which is being used. Sometimes error bars show a MEAN and its associated STANDARD DEVIATION (SD) (see Figure). If so, the error bars tell the reader to what extent scores are spread out around the mean of those scores. Alternatively, error bars may show a mean and the STANDARD ERROR (SE) OF THE MEAN. In this case, the error bars show the extent to which the mean is likely to vary from SAMPLE to sample. Usually an error bar is shown by a line which extends from a marker placed at the value of the mean plus one sd (or se), to a marker placed at the value of the mean minus one sd (or se). However, in the interests of clarity, error bars may be limited to the mean

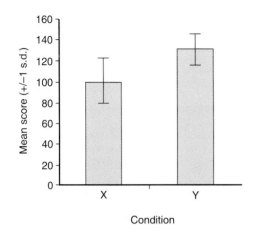

error bars *Mean test score.*

plus one SD (or SE) and the lower part of the error bar omitted. *GH*

Field 2005a; **Field and Hole** 2003.

estimation Using a SAMPLE to produce a value of some property of a POPULATION (e.g. the MEAN). *AF*

expected frequency The frequency we expect to find in a particular cell of a CONTINGENCY TABLE given the HYPOTHESIS (see also s. 3) of interest. *AF*

expected value The average value of a statistic from repeated sampling. *AF*

experiment A procedure which attempts to identify causal relationships between variables. At its simplest, the state of one VARIABLE (the INDEPENDENT VARIABLE) is varied systematically, and the effects of this are measured on another variable (the DEPENDENT VARIABLE). In a true experiment, as opposed to a quasi-experiment, the experimenter has complete control over allocation of participants to conditions and over the timing of the measurement of the dependent variable. *GH*

experimental hypothesis [See ALTERNATIVE HYPOTHESIS]

experimentwise error rate The probability of making a TYPE I ERROR in any experiment involving more than one significance test. *AF*

exploratory data analysis (EDA) Looking at data through graphical displays rather than formal statistics. Even when formal statistics are used this should be done first to get a 'feel' for the data. *AF*

exploratory factor analysis [See FACTOR ANALYSIS]

extraneous variable Any VARIABLE, measured or otherwise, that is not the primary PREDICTOR VARIABLE of interest, that has an influence over the OUTCOME VARIABLE. *AF*

F

---

factor A CATEGORICAL VARIABLE in an experiment, or another term for a LATENT VARIABLE in FACTOR ANALYSIS.

AF

factor analysis Factor analysis and PRINCIPAL COMPONENTS ANALYSIS are techniques for identifying groups or clusters of variables. The central idea is that relationships (CORRELATIONS) between observed variables stem from relations with other common underlying variables known as LATENT VARIABLES or FACTORS. These latent variables are similar to the discriminant variates in DISCRIMINANT FUNCTION ANALYSIS in that they take the form:

$$Factor_i = b_1 Variable_1 + b_1 Variable_2 + ... + b_n Variable_n + \varepsilon_i$$

in which *b* is a weight with which a particular observed variable loads onto a particular factor [see FACTOR LOADING]. The measured VARIABLES are made up of VARIANCE that is shared with other variables (*common variance*); and variance that is unique to that variable (*unique variance*); the proportion of shared variance in a variable is known as the *communality*. To find the latent variables underlying the data it is vital to know which variance is common. Principal components analysis begins by assuming all communalities are 1, that is, all variance is common; factor analysis is different in that the communalities are estimated using various methods (such as the multiple correlation between variables).

The factor loadings of the LATENT VARIABLES can be estimated in a variety of ways, but once estimated, decisions need to be made about which factors to retain. This decision is based on the EIGENVALUES of the latent variables (which represent the variance that a latent variable explains), either through cut-off points such as Kaiser's rule of retaining factors with eigenvalues greater than 1 (see Field 2005a), or the point of inflexion on a SCREE PLOT.

The retained latent variables are then usually subjected to FACTOR ROTATION to improve their interpretability. The result is a matrix of factor loadings that enable the researcher to decide which observed variables load onto which latent variables. In an ideal world, observed variables will have a large factor loading on one latent variable and small factor loadings on any others. By looking at factor loadings it is possible to see which observed variables related to which latent variables and as such make decisions about which observed variables cluster together. The exact value of a loading that constitutes an important relation between the observed measure and the latent variable depends on the SAMPLE SIZE (see Field 2005a), although Stevens (1992) suggests a value of 0.4. In psychology, these clusters of variables are usually then used to interpret the underlying variable (usually in terms of a psychological construct) although it is debatable whether this is justified! (See also s. 6, FACTOR ANALYSIS) *AF*

Field 2005a; **Pedhazur and Schmelkin** 1991; **Stevens** 1992; **Tabachnick and Fidell** 2001.

factorial designs Experimental designs in which there are more than one INDEPENDENT VARIABLE/predictor.

AF

factor loading Broadly speaking, factor loadings tell us about the relative contribution that a VARIABLE makes to a FACTOR in FACTOR ANALYSIS. The precise interpretation of factor loadings depends on the type of FACTOR ROTATION method used. When ORTHOGONAL rotation is used, the factor loading is the CORRELATION between the factor and the variable, but is *also* the REGRESSION coefficient. [See BETA COEFFICIENT] However, when oblique rotation is used, the resulting correlations between variables and factors will differ from the corresponding regression coefficients. In effect, two different sets of factor loadings emerge: the CORRELATION COEFFICIENTS between each variable and factor (which are put in a matrix called the factor structure matrix) and the regression coefficients for each variable on each factor (which are put in the factor pattern matrix). *AF*

Field 2005a; **Pedhazur and Schmelkin** 1991; **Tabachnick and Fidell** 2001.

factor rotation A technique used in FACTOR ANALYSIS to ease the interpretation of FACTORS. In essence, the aim is to maximise the FACTOR LOADINGS of each observed VARIABLE onto only one factor. There are two types of rotation that can be done: ORTHOGONAL rotation and oblique rotation. Orthogonal rotation ensures that factors remain independent (uncorrelated and perpendicular in geometric space), whereas oblique rotation allows factors to correlate. According to Field (2005a), the choice of rotation depends on whether there is a good theoretical reason to suppose that the factors should be related or independent, but in psychology there are rarely good grounds to assume that factors should be independent. Pedhazur and Schmelkin (1991) suggest that if the extracted factors appear to be negligibly correlated after oblique rotation, then it is reasonable to use the orthogonally rotated solution. Examples of orthogonal rotation techniques are varimax, quartimax and equamax, and examples of oblique rotations are direct oblimin and promax. *AF*

Field 2005a; **Pedhazur and Schmelkin** 1991; **Tabachnick and Fidell** 2001.

familywise error rate The probability of making a TYPE I ERROR in any family of tests involving more than one significance test. Some treat tests on the same data as a 'family' while others treat tests addressing the same specific research question as a 'family'. *AF*

***F*-distribution** Most famous for being the PROBABILITY DISTRIBUTION of the TEST STATISTIC in ANALYSIS OF VARIANCE. Imagine two independent random VARIABLES, both having a CHI-SQUARED DISTRIBUTION. If each of these variables is divided by its DEGREES OF FREEDOM and then the ratio of the resulting variables is calculated, it will have a probability distribution of F. *AF*

Fisher's z transformation A transformation applied to the CORRELATION COEFFICIENT to make its distribution normal (Fisher 1921). *AF*

$$Zr_i = \frac{1}{2} Log_e \left(\frac{1 + r_i}{1 - r_i} \right)$$

fixed effects The effect of a measure that has a fixed number of levels (for example, the effect of codeine and a PLACEBO drug on treating heroin addiction). Measures should be treated as fixed when changing one of the levels of the measures would significantly affect the research question (for example, replacing the codeine level with cheese changes the research question from 'does codeine help heroin addicts to stop taking heroin?' to 'does cheese help heroin addicts to stop taking heroin?'). *AF*

floor effect A floor effect occurs if performance on a measure is so poor that scores are clustered around the bottom of the scale. This makes the measure insensitive, because it has little scope for variation (and is also more prone to REGRESSION to the MEAN). *GH*

F-ratio The TEST STATISTIC produced in ANALYSIS OF VARIANCE. *GH*

frequency distribution A frequency distribution shows how often each of a RANGE of scores or things occurs. In the case of nominal (CATEGORICAL) DATA, a frequency distribution shows how often each category occurred. Thus, for data on 'preferred mode of transport', it might show how many people prefer walking, driving, cycling, etc. Where the data consist of scores on an ordinal, interval or ratio scale, the frequency distribution could, in principle, have as many categories as there are possible scores. This is usually undesirable, and so a grouped frequency distribution is used. The range of possible scores is divided into discrete categories, and then a record is made of how many of the observed scores fall into each of these categories. Thus, to obtain a frequency distribution of test scores, where any score can be obtained between 0 and 100, the range of possible scores might be divided into ten categories (0–10, 11–20, 21–30, and so on, up to 91–100). Each obtained score is then assigned to its appropriate category. In all cases, the categories used in a frequency distribution must cover the entire range of possible scores, with no omissions. The categories must also be mutually exclusive, so that an individual item is assigned to only one of them. In the case of scores, the width of the categories is a compromise. If they are too narrow, any patterns in the data may be difficult to see. However, excessively wide categories are also undesirable because information about individual scores is lost in the process of categorising them. Somewhere between 10 and 20 categories is usually best, although this will depend to a large extent on the number of observations. Raw frequency distributions can be converted into relative frequency distributions by dividing each category value by the total number of observations (and then multiplying this value by 100 to convert it into a percentage of the total number of observations). This facilitates comparisons between frequency distributions based on different numbers of observations; however, the raw frequencies should always be provided as well, because relative frequencies can be very misleading if they are based on small numbers of observations. *GH*

Field and Hole 2003; **Field** 2005a; **Wright** 2002.

Friedman's ANOVA A statistical test for determining whether there are any significant differences between three or more conditions in an experiment in which there is a single repeated-measures INDEPENDENT VARIABLE (i.e. all participants perform all conditions in the experiment). As with many DISTRIBUTION-FREE METHODS, FRIEDMAN'S ANOVA makes use of ranked data. Each participant's scores are ranked individually. These ranks are then summed for each condition, across participants. If the conditions differ markedly, then their rank totals will be different; if not, then high and low ranks will be distributed fairly randomly across conditions. The only requirements for using Friedman's ANOVA are that each participant provides scores measured on at least an ordinal scale. If the data meet the ASSUMPTIONS of PARAMETRIC METHODS then Friedman's ANOVA has less POWER than one-way repeated-measures ANOVA, and so the latter should be used in preference. The formula for Friedman's ANOVA is:

$$\chi r^2 = \left[\left(\frac{12}{N \times C \times (C + 1)} \right) \times \Sigma Tc^2 \right] - 3 \times N \times (C + 1)$$

where C is the number of conditions, N is the number of participants, and ΣTc^2 is the sum of the squared rank totals for each condition.

Assessing the statistical significance of χr^2 depends on the number of participants and the number of groups. If there are less than nine participants, special tables of critical values are available, against which to compare the obtained value of χr^2. If there are more than nine participants, compare the obtained χr^2 value to the critical value from the CHI-SQUARED DISTRIBUTION for the associated number of DEGREES OF FREEDOM (in this case the number of conditions minus 1). If the obtained value of χr^2 is *bigger* than the critical chi-square value, the difference between the conditions is statistically significant at the chosen level of significance. Note that Friedman's test can only indicate that some kind of difference exists between the conditions; inspection of the median score for each condition will usually be enough to show exactly where the difference lies. *GH*

Field 2005a; **Friedman** 1937.

G

generalised linear model (GLM) A term to describe a wide body of tests (ANALYSIS OF VARIANCE, MULTIPLE REGRESSION, LOG-LINEAR MODELS, STUDENT'S *T*-TEST, CHI-SQUARED TEST, to name but a few) that are different forms of a simple LINEAR MODEL (see Field 2005a, for descriptions of how all the listed procedures can be conceptualised as linear models). A linear model takes the form:

$$Y_i = b_0 + b_1 X_1 + b_2 X_2 \ldots b_n X_n + \varepsilon_i$$

in which Y is an OUTCOME VARIABLE, the Xs represent PREDICTOR VARIABLES, the bs are BETA COEFFICIENTS, and b_0 is the value of the outcome when all predictor variables are zero. If we take a simple two-group example then we can see how the independent *t*-test can be represented in this form (see Field 2005a; Wright 1997). Imagine we wanted to see whether people in the UK were happier in summer or winter. We could administer the Beck Depression Inventory (BDI) to a group of people in the middle of a beautiful sunny summer and then to a different group in the middle of a stormy, wet, windy winter. Also, imagine that the average BDI score for the sunny group was 33 and for the winter group was 63. The GLM for this scenario would be:

$$BDI_1 = b_0 + b_1 Weather_1 + \varepsilon_i$$

which just means that a person's BDI score can be predicted from some function (b_1) of the group to which they belonged and the baseline level of BDI (i.e. the value of BDI when the predictor is 0).

To discover what b_1 represents, all we have to do is place some values in the model. Before we do that, we have to think about how to represent our VARIABLE of *Weather*. This variable has two levels (summer and winter) and for this to work, we need to code these as a BINARY VARIABLE. That is, we use the values 0 and 1 to represent the groups. This is a form of dummy coding. Usually we code the group that we want to act as a baseline (the CONTROL GROUP) with 0, and the other group (often a group in which an experimental manipulation has been carried out) with 1. In this case, we do not have a control group as such; we are just interested in whether the groups differ. Therefore, we can assign 0 and 1 either way round. Let us code winter as 0 and summer as 1.

If we want to use this linear model to predict the BDI score of someone in the winter group, then the best prediction we can make is the MEAN of that group. Remember also that the Weather variable will be 0 for this person. Our model, therefore, becomes:

$$BDI_i = b_0 + b_1 Weather_1$$
$$\overline{X}_{Winter} = b_0 + (b_1 \times 0)$$
$$b_0 = \overline{X}_{Winter}$$

Therefore, we can see that b_0 merely represents the mean of the group coded with 0 (in this case, the winter group).

Now let us look at someone in the summer group. This time our prediction of BDI will be the mean of the summer group. We know also that b_0 is the mean of the winter group, and that the Weather variable will now be 1 (because we are looking at the summer group). The model now becomes:

$$BDI_i = b_0 + b_1 Weather_1$$
$$\overline{X}_{Summer} = b_0 + (b_1 \times 1)$$
$$b_1 = \overline{X}_{Summer} - \overline{X}_{Winter}$$

Therefore, b_1 represents the difference between the summer group and the baseline group (in this case, winter).

This example shows the basis for how linear models (like multiple regression) can be applied to a variety of situations, including when predictor variables are categorical. In regression models with 1 predictor, the resulting beta coefficient for the predictor is the same as the CORRELATION COEFFICIENT between the predictor and the outcome. It should be clear from this example that if a regression analysis was run on the data, the resulting r would, therefore, represent the difference between group means. Put another way, it represents the size of the difference between groups. In this way, r can be used as an effect size measure of group differences. [See EFFECT SIZE]

This basic idea can be extended to situations involving more than two groups (i.e. ANALYSIS OF VARIANCE). The analysis of variance entry described an experiment involving three groups of men who had not previously owned a mobile phone: the first group remained as they were; a second group was given a phone each and asked to keep it in their front trouser pocket for a year; and the final group was asked to keep the phone in their coat pocket (away from their genitals). The outcome was their sperm count after a year. This scenario can be represented by a standard linear model:

$$Sperm_i = b_0 + b_1 Pocket_i + b_2 Coat_i + \varepsilon_i$$

in which Pocket is a binary variable coded 1 (phone kept in trouser pocket) and 0 (all other groups), and Coat is a binary variable coded 1 (phone kept in coat) and 0 (all other groups). These are DUMMY VARIABLES.

If we take someone from the control group, then our best prediction of their sperm count is the mean of the control group. This group is represented by both dummy variables taking on a value of 0:

$$Sperm_i = b_0 + b_1 Pocket_i + b_2 Coat_i$$
$$\overline{X}_{Control} = b_0 + (b_1 \times 0) + (b_2 \times 0)$$
$$b_0 = \overline{X}_{Control}$$

Therefore, b_0 represents the mean of the control group (i.e. the sperm count when Pocket and Coat are both zero). If we now look at someone from the group who kept the phones in their pockets, our outcome is now the mean of that group. The dummy variable for Pocket will be 1, whereas the other is 0:

$$\text{Sperm}_i = b_0 + b_1\text{Pocket}_i + b_2\text{Coat}_i$$
$$\overline{X}_{Pocket} = \overline{X}_{Control} + (b_1 \times 1) + (b_2 \times 0)$$
$$b_1 = \overline{X}_{Pocket} - \overline{X}_{Control}$$

As such, b_1 is the difference between the mean sperm count of the group that had the phone in their pocket and the mean of the control group. Finally, if we now look at someone from the group who kept the phones in their coat, our outcome is now the mean of the coat group. The dummy variable for Coat will be 1, whereas the other is 0:

$$\text{Sperm}_i = b_0 + b_1\text{Pocket}_i + b_2\text{Coat}_i$$
$$\overline{X}_{Coat} = \overline{X}_{Control} + (b_1 \times 0) + (b_2 \times 1)$$
$$b_2 = \overline{X}_{Coat} - \overline{X}_{Control}$$

So, b_2 is the difference between the mean sperm count of the group that had the phone in their coat and the mean of the control group (no phone).

The basic logic described here can be extended to more complex analysis of variance and ANALYSIS OF COVARIANCE and also to CATEGORICAL MODELS (see s. 7) (see Field 2005a). *AF*

Cohen 1968; **Field** 2005a.

goodness-of-fit statistics These are tests of the agreement between a set of observed values from a SAMPLE and EXPECTED VALUES from the model of interest. The most widely known examples are probably the CHI-SQUARED TEST and the LIKELIHOOD RATIO. (See also s. 4, GOODNESS-OF-FIT) *AF*

Greenhouse-Geisser correction A correction applied to the DEGREES OF FREEDOM in repeated-measures ANALYSIS OF VARIANCE when the ASSUMPTION of SPHERICITY has been violated. Considered by some to be over-conservative. *AF*

H

harmonic mean An alternative to the MEAN that is sometimes used in situations in which groups contain unequal numbers of observations. It is defined as:

$$\overline{X}_{Harmonic} = \cfrac{1}{\cfrac{1}{n}\sum\limits_{i=1}^{n}\cfrac{1}{x_i}}$$

in which x_i is the ith observation (in psychology this would usually be the score of person i) and n is the number of people in the sample for which the mean is being calculated. The result is the same or smaller than the mean. *AF*

Hawthorne effect An early example of an EXPERI-MENTER EFFECT: researchers measuring the influence of various factors on factory workers' productivity found that merely observing the workers' behaviour appeared to affect their output. *GH*

Helmert contrast A planned contrast [see PLANNED COMPARISON] that compares each level (except the last) of a categorical predictor against the combined effect of all subsequent levels, e.g. with three categories there would be two contrasts: 1 vs (2 and 3), and 2 vs. 3. *AF*

heterogeneous Not the same. Used to indicate differences in a property. [See HOMOGENEITY OF VARIANCE] *AF*

hierarchical regression A method of MULTIPLE REGRESSION in which the researcher makes decisions about the order in which predictors should be entered into the model. *AF*

histogram A graphical representation of a FREQUENCY DISTRIBUTION in which bars represent the frequencies. *AF*

homogeneity of variance The ASSUMPTION that the VARIANCE of one VARIABLE is stable at all levels of another variable. If your PREDICTOR VARIABLE is categorical, this means that the variance of your OUTCOME VARIABLE or variables should be the same in each of these categories or groups. If you have collected continuous data (such as in correlational designs), this assumption means that the variance of one variable should be the same for all values of the other variable. It is generally tested with LEVENE'S TEST (see Field 2005a, for more detail). *AF*

Field 2005a.

Hotelling's T^2 [See MULTIVARIATE ANALYSIS OF VARIANCE]

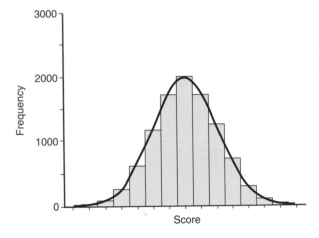

histogram *The normal distribution (the curve shows the idealised shape of the distribution)*

Huynh-Feldt correction A correction applied to the DEGREES OF FREEDOM in repeated-measures ANALYSIS OF VARIANCE when the ASSUMPTION of SPHERICITY has been violated. Considered by some to be too liberal. *AF*

hypothesis A testable statement, derived from theory, which is used to test that theory. (See also s. 3) *JM*

hypothesis testing The act of testing whether hypotheses about the POPULATION are true by assessing the extent to which observations in a SAMPLE are consistent with these hypotheses. Typically there is a NULL HYPOTHE-SIS, reflecting the absence of some form of effect, and an ALTERNATIVE HYPOTHESIS, predicting the presence of an effect. Hypothesis testing consists of designing some kind of research that will provide data that can be shown to be consistent or inconsistent with the alternative hypothesis. A statistical model is then fitted to the data (be it MULTIPLE REGRESSION, ANALYSIS OF VARIANCE or STUDENT'S *T*-TEST) and assessed. If the probability of getting the observed TEST STATISTIC under the null hypothesis is very small (typically less than 0.05), this is used as evidence that the alternative hypothesis is true (the effect is said to be 'significant'). There are several misconceptions about this process (see Cohen 1990, 1994). The first is that significance equates to importance – in fact it does not; the second is that non-significant effects suggest that the null hypothesis is true – it is *always* false because of SAMPLING ERROR; and, finally, that a significant result can be used to logically reason that the null hypothesis is false – it cannot, because hypothesis testing is based on probabilities. *AF*

Cohen 1990, 1994.

I

idiographic   Developing knowledge on a case-by-case basis. (See also s. 1, IDIOGRAPHIC METHODS)   *AF*

independence   Generally speaking, entities are independent if they have no effect on each other. This can be represented by linear functions that are perpendicular in geometric space, by a zero correlation between variables or by REASONING (see s. 3) that responses to one measure could not logically be influenced by responses to another.
   AF

independent-measures design   An experimental design in which different participants are allocated to different treatment conditions.   *AF*

independent *t*-test   [See STUDENT'S *T*-TEST]

independent variable   A VARIABLE, the values of which are systematically determined by a researcher to address a specific HYPOTHESIS (see also s. 3). A PREDICTOR VARIABLE.   *AF*

influence statistics   A family of statistics that estimate the extent to which a case is an INFLUENTIAL CASE. Most of these statistics work on the principle of estimating the model parameters with and without the case included. The difference between the parameters indicates the degree to which the case was influential. The main difference between the different methods is the 'parameter' they use to measure the change in the model. For example, the difference in the BETA COEFFICIENTS is referred to as DFBeta; the value of the predicted value for the

excluded case is known as the adjusted predicted value; the difference between this adjusted predicted value and the original predicted value is known as DFFit; and Cook's distance for a case, i, is a function of the summed adjusted predicted values for all cases when i is deleted. It is also possible to look at the effect on RESIDUALS. For example, the deleted residual is the residual based on the adjusted predicted value. Mahalanobis distances also measure overall influence by looking at the distance between an observation and the intersection (in geometric space) of the MEANS of all VARIABLES. LEVERAGE STATISTICS are also sometimes used; these are a function of the Mahalanobis distances.   *AF*
Field 2005a; **Fox** 1991.

influential cases   A case of data that has undue influence over the parameters of a statistical model (typically MULTIPLE REGRESSION).   *AF*

informed consent   The act of obtaining consent from individuals for research participation after full disclosure of the research (or at least disclosure of any details that might reasonably make someone unwilling to participate).
   AF

interaction   The combined effect of two or more PREDICTOR VARIABLES on an OUTCOME VARIABLE. Although most strongly associated with FACTORIAL DESIGNS, an interaction can be included in correlational models (such as MULTIPLE REGRESSION), the interaction term being a predictor variable that is the product of the variables within the interaction. In experimental designs, interactions are

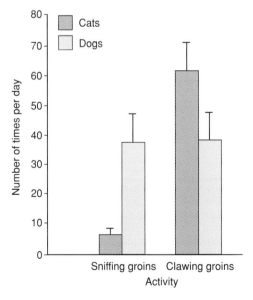
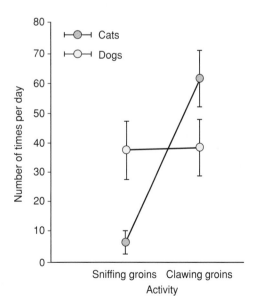

interaction *A line graph and a bar chart, each showing interaction effects with the same data*

typically illustrated with an interaction graph, in which the means of the combinations of treatment levels are plotted as bars or lines; with two predictor variables, levels of one VARIABLE are represented as points along the horizontal axis, and levels of the second variable are represented as different bars or lines. *AF*

Field 2005a.

intercept The parameter in a model that represents the predicted value of the OUTCOME VARIABLE when all predictors are zero. *AF*

inter-quartile range The RANGE of a set of observations when you ignore the upper and lower QUARTILE. The advantage of the inter-quartile range is that it is not affected by extreme scores at either end of the distribution. However, you lose a lot of data (half of it in fact!). Also cutting off the upper and lower 25 per cent of scores is completely arbitrary (why not the top and bottom 10 per cent or 5 per cent?). [See QUARTILES] *AF*

interval data Data measured on a scale, along the whole of which intervals are equal. *AF*

interviewer bias When an interviewer encourages certain responses from the interviewee through the wording of questions, prompting answers, body language or any other means. *AF*

intra-class correlation Commonly used correlations such as the PEARSON PRODUCT MOMENT CORRELATION COEFFICIENT measure the bivariate relation between variables of different measurement classes. By 'different measurement classes' we mean variables measuring different things. For example, we might look at the relation between listening to Norwegian death metal band Dimmu Borgir and Satanism; one of these variables represents a class of measures of the type of music a person likes, whereas the other represents the class of measurements of their religious beliefs. Intraclass correlations assess something different: the consistency between measures of the same class (that is, measures of the same thing). Two common uses are in comparing paired data (such as twins) on the same measure, and assessing the consistency between judges' ratings of a set of objects. The calculation of these correlations depends on whether a measure of consistency (in which the order of scores from a source is considered, but not the actual value around which the scores are anchored) or absolute agreement (in which both the order of scores and the relative values are considered), or whether the scores represent averages of many measures or just a single measure, is required. See Field (2005b) for more detail. *AF*

J

Jonckheere-Terpstra test A test for an ordered pattern of medians across independent groups. (See Field 2005a.) *AF*

K

Kaiser's criterion Used in FACTOR ANALYSIS to determine how many factors should be retained and interpreted. The criterion is that factors with EIGENVALUES greater than 1 should be retained. *AF*

kappa A measure of agreement between two judges assigning stimuli to different categories. Imagine two students had to assign lectures to categories of 'boring', 'very boring' and 'so boring I wanted to slit my own throat'. It would be possible to construct a CONTINGENCY TABLE showing how many lecturers fell into the various combinations of categories (see Table).

So for example, f_{bb} is the number of lectures that both judges rated as boring, and f_{vbb} is the number of lectures that judge 1 thought were boring and judge 2 thought were very boring. Likewise, T_{b1} is the total number of lecturers that Judge 1 thought were boring and T_{vb2} is the total number of lecturers that Judge 2 thought were very boring. N is the total number of lecturers that were rated.

There are two proportions we can calculate. The first is the proportion of observed agreement:

$$p_o = \frac{f_{bb} + f_{vbvb} + f_{tt}}{N}$$

This is the number of lecturers whom they placed in the same category (i.e. the sum of the frequencies in the diagonal of the contingency table) divided by the total number they categorised. The second proportion is the expected proportion of agreement:

$$p_e = \frac{1}{N}\left[\frac{T_{b1} \times T_{b2}}{N} + \frac{T_{vb1} \times T_{vb2}}{N} + \frac{T_{t1} \times T_{t2}}{N}\right]$$

This is based on the total number of lecturers that each judge placed into each category. Kappa is a function of these two proportions:

$$\kappa = \frac{p_o - p_e}{1 - p_e}$$

AF

Kendall's coefficient of concordance Kendall's coefficient of concordance, W, is a measure of the agreement between several judges who have rank-ordered several entities. It is defined by:

$$W = \frac{12 \times SS_{Rank\ Totals}}{k^2\ (n^3 - n)}$$

In which $SS_{Rank\ Totals}$ is the SUM OF SQUARED ERRORS of the total ranks of each of the things being judged, k is the number of judges and n is the number of things being judged. W represents the ratio of the observed variance of the total ranks of the ranked entities to the maximum possible variance of the total ranks. The significance of W can be tested by converting to a chi-squared statistic with $n - 1$ DEGREES OF FREEDOM:

$$\chi^2_W = k(n - 1)W$$

See Field (2005c) for more detail. *AF*
Field 2005c.

Kendall's tau A non-parametric correlation coefficient similar to Spearman's correlation coefficient, but should be used in preference when you have a small data set with a large number of tied ranks. [See also SPEARMAN'S RHO] *AF*
Field 2005a.

Kolmogorov-Smirnov test A test of whether a distribution of observations is significantly different from a NORMAL DISTRIBUTION. A significant value indicates a DEVIATION from normality, but this test is notoriously affected by large samples in which small deviations from normality yield significant results. *AF*
Field 2005a.

Kruskal-Wallis test A NON-PARAMETRIC TEST for comparing three or more conditions in a study with a wholly between-groups design (i.e. one in which each condition is performed by a separate group of participants). Its parametric equivalent is the one-way independent-measures ANOVA [see ONE-WAY ANOVA]. The formula is:

$$H = \frac{12}{N(N + 1)} \sum_{i=1}^{k} \frac{R_i^2}{n_i} - 3(N + 1)$$

where N is the total number of participants, R is the rank total for each group, and n is the number of participants in each group. There are special tables available that provide critical values of H for very small group sizes. However, in

kappa *Contingency table*

		Judge 2			
		Boring	*Very Boring*	*Throat*	*Total*
Judge 1	Boring	f_{bb}	F_{vbb}	f_{tb}	T_{b1}
	Very Boring	f_{bvb}	F_{vbvb}	F_{tvb}	T_{vb1}
	Throat	f_{bt}	F_{vbt}	f_{tt}	T_{t1}
	Total	T_{b2}	T_{vb2}	T_{t2}	N

most cases, H is compared to the critical value of a CHI-SQUARED DISTRIBUTION for the relevant DEGREES OF FREE-DOM (the number of groups minus 1). H is significant (unlikely to have arisen by chance) if it equals or exceeds this critical value. Note that the Kruskal-Wallis test only tests whether or not there is a difference of some kind between the groups; it says nothing about where that difference lies. Usually inspection of the group sum of ranks will enable this to be determined, or a follow-up test.   *GH*

Field 2005a.

kurtosis Kurtosis is the degree to which scores cluster in the tails of a FREQUENCY DISTRIBUTION. A *PLATYKURTIC* distribution has many scores in the tails (often called a heavy-tailed distribution) and so is quite flat, whereas a *LEPTOKURTIC* distribution is relatively thin in the tails and so looks quite pointy. We can measure kurtosis and, importantly, it should be 0 in a normal distribution. Therefore, if your frequency distribution has positive or negative values of kurtosis, this tells you that your distribution deviates somewhat from a NORMAL DISTRIBUTION.   *AF*

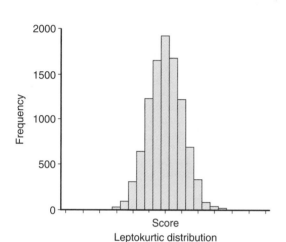

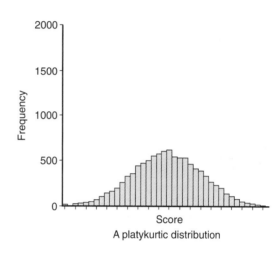

Kurtosis *Leptokurtic and platykurtic distributions*

L

latent variables   A VARIABLE that cannot be measured directly but instead is estimated from several variables that can. [See FACTOR ANALYSIS and STRUCTURAL EQUATION MODELLING]   *AF*

latin-square counterbalancing   A form of experimental design aimed at eliminating order and PRACTICE EFFECTS by adjusting the order in which different groups of participants undergo different treatments. In an experiment in which participants take part in two experimental tasks, A and B, the simplest form of this procedure would be to ensure that a randomly selected half of the participants do the tasks in the order AB, while the remainder do the tasks in order BA. In more complex designs a grid is made with an initial order at the top for the first group; for all subsequent groups the task in the last column of the grid is moved to the front (to be the first task) and all other tasks are shifted one space along to the right.

latin-square counterbalancing *Three- and four-task experiments*

	First Task	Second Task	Third Task
Group 1	A	B	C
Group 2	C	A	B
Group 3	B	C	A

	First Task	Second Task	Third Task	Fourth task
Group 1	A	B	C	D
Group 2	D	A	B	C
Group 3	C	D	A	B
Group 4	B	C	D	A

In doing so, every task appears at every temporal location, thus eliminating systematic BIAS (see also s. 3 and s. 6) from the order in which tasks are done.   *AF*

least significant difference test (LSD)   [See MULTIPLE COMPARISONS]

least squares estimation   A method for estimating parameters in a statistical model. It works through a process of minimisation in which the squared difference between the observed value and the value predicted by the model is minimised. As such, the parameters produced are for the model that best fits the data (because the error between observed and predicted values is the minimum it can be).   *AF*

leptokurtic   [See KURTOSIS]

levels (of a variable)   The categories of a CATEGORICAL VARIABLE are often referred to as levels (especially when these categories are determined as part of an experimental manipulation). For example, an EXPERIMENT that compares a drug intervention with a PLACEBO is said to have one variable (type of drug) with two levels. If we added a condition in which an alternative drug was used, there would still be one variable (type of drug) but it would now have three levels: placebo, drug A and drug B.   *AF*

levels of measurement   Different types of measurement scale exist, each with its own properties. Using a NOMINAL or categorical scale means that observations can merely be grouped into different categories. ORDINAL scale measurements consist of ranks – one can say that X is larger or smaller than Y, but not by how much. An INTERVAL scale consists of values that are equidistant, but there is no true zero on the scale. A RATIO scale consists of values that are equidistant and, additionally, has a true zero point on the scale.   *GH*

Levene's test   A test of the assumption of HOMOGENEITY OF VARIANCE that tests the HYPOTHESIS (see also s. 3) that the variances in different groups are equal (i.e. the difference between the variances is zero). A significant result indicates that the variances are significantly different – therefore, the ASSUMPTION of HOMOGENEITY OF VARIANCES has been violated. However, when samples sizes are large, small differences in group variances can produce a significant Levene's test. (See Field 2005a for more detail.)   *AF*
Field 2005a.

leverage statistics   [See INFLUENCE STATISTICS]

likelihood   The probability of obtaining a set of observations given the parameters of a model fitted to those observations.   *AF*

likelihood ratio   An alternative to the CHI-SQUARE TEST, which is based on maximum-likelihood theory. The statistic is based on comparing observed frequencies in row i and column j of a CONTINGENCY TABLE, with those predicted by a model fitted to the data (see Field 2005a):

$$L_{\chi^2} = 2 \sum Observed_{ij} \ln\left(\frac{Observed_{ij}}{Model_{ij}}\right)$$

AF

Field 2005a.

Likert scale   A rating scale with a fixed number of points (usually 5, 7 or 9). The mid-point of the scale represents neutrality about the property being rated; the highest and lowest points represent extreme opinions. Participants tick whichever point best represents their opinion, and the point's number is taken as their score. (See also s. 5, LIKERT SCALE)   *GH*

438

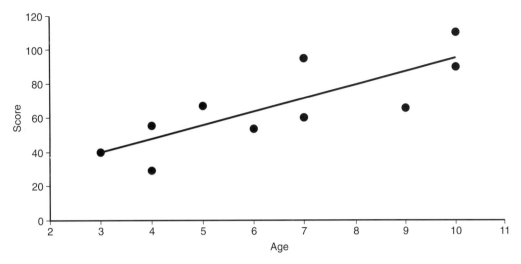

linear regression *Scatterplot showing relationship between age and score, with line of best fit*

linear model Any model based on the equation defining a straight line (or some extension of it). Models of this type have the form:

$$Y_i = b_0 + b_1X_1 + b_2X_2 \ldots b_nX_n + \varepsilon_i$$

AF

linear regression Linear regression is a statistical technique closely related to CORRELATION analysis, and extended into MULTIPLE REGRESSION. Linear regression is used where we have one predictor (which must be either binary or categorical) of one outcome measure (which must be continuous); for example, if we wish to predict the outcome on a TEST (see s. 6) of reading ability using the age of the child as a predictor, we would want to examine the relationship between age and the score. The aim of the regression analysis is to represent the relationship between age and score as a straight line on a scatterplot. (See Figure)

We could also show the line as an equation. The general form of the equation is:

$$Y_i = b_0 + b_1X_1$$

where y is the OUTCOME VARIABLE (score); x is the PREDICTOR VARIABLE (age); b_1 is the slope of the line (the regression coefficient); b_0 is the constant (also called the INTERCEPT), given to tell us the height of the line.

In this example, we would write this as:

Score = 15.2 + 7.9 × age

If you were to tell me the age of a child (sampled from the same POPULATION), I could tell you the score that they would be likely to get on the test, using that equation.

Linear regression has three uses:

1. Prediction: we can use linear regression to predict a score on an outcome variable, based on a predictor.

This may be used in applied psychology – we might be interested in how well a person will do a particular job (e.g. as a computer scientist), given a characteristic of that person (e.g. reasoning skills).

2. Explanation and theory testing: our theory may predict that people who score highly on one measure (e.g. locus of control) will score lower on another measure (e.g. DEPRESSION – see s. 7).

3. Diagnosis: we might want to explore whether people are scoring higher or lower than we would expect on an outcome, given the predictor (e.g. if a person has had one therapy session, we might not expect to see much improvement in their condition).

If a regression calculation is carried out on STANDARDISED VARIABLES, the constant will become 0 and the slope of the line will be equal to the correlation.

[See also MULTIPLE REGRESSION] *JM*

Field 2005a; **Miles and Shevlin** 2001.

linear trend A term usually associated with ANALYSIS OF VARIANCE, but relates to any set of grouped observations in which the central tendency (usually the MEAN or MEDIAN) of the groups changes across groups in a linear fashion. Such trends should only be investigated when the groups consist of meaningful ordered categories. For example, Field and Hole (2003) have an example of whether using text messages on mobile phones affects people's grammar. Imagine you had three groups of data, one measuring baseline grammar ability (as a percentage), and then data for grammar ability after one month and two months of using text messages. A linear trend would be represented by the means over time following a linear pattern (i.e. going up or down in such a way that a straight line, or approximately straight line, could connect the means). *AF*

439

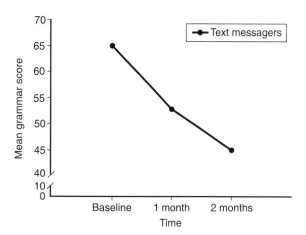

linear trend

line chart
A graph showing some property of a set of observations (usually the MEAN) across groups (along the horizontal axis) on which values of the property displayed are connected by a line. For the example used in the LINEAR TREND entry, the mean grammar ability was represented as a line chart (see Figure under LINEAR TREND).

These graphs can show data from a single set of groups (one line) or from multiple sets of groups (in which different lines represent different groups of observations). For example, if we added data from a control group to the example shown in the Figure in the LINEAR TREND entry (who did not write any text messages), we might get data as shown in Figure a. If means are then displayed, they may be accompanied by ERROR BARS (see Figure b).   *AF*

line of best fit
A term associated with LINEAR REGRESSION to refer to the regression line. It is so called because it is the LINEAR MODEL based on LEAST SQUARES ESTIMATION, and hence has the lowest error of all possible linear models that could be fitted to the data.   *AF*

logarithmic transformation
A TRANSFORMATION that is used to correct positive skew [see SKEWNESS] – the logarithm (usually to base *e*, i.e. the natural logarithm) of each value of a VARIABLE is taken.   *JM*

logistic regression
Logistic regression is MULTIPLE REGRESSION, but with an OUTCOME VARIABLE that is a DICHOTOMOUS VARIABLE and PREDICTOR VARIABLES that are CONTINUOUS VARIABLES or CATEGORICAL VARIABLES. It is based on a LINEAR MODEL of the form:

$$P(Y) = \frac{1}{1 + e^{-(b_0 + b_1 X_1 + b_2 X_2 + \ldots + b_n X_n + \varepsilon_i)}}$$

in which the outcome is the probability of the outcome variable occurring (in the sense that the outcome is usually coded as 1 for an event occurring and 0 for the event not occurring). The parameters (BETA COEFFICIENTS) of the model are much the same as multiple regression and are used to derive a TEST STATISTIC (the Wald statistic), which is derived in the same way as the *t* statistics in multiple regression. The significance of this statistic can be used to assess whether a particular predictor can explain a significant unique amount of VARIANCE in the outcome variable (although the Wald statistic is notorious for being underestimated when the beta values are large). However, for interpretation purposes the *exp b* is usually used, which is an indicator of the change in odds [see ODDS RATIO] resulting from a unit change in the predictor. As such, if *exp b* is greater than 1, it indicates that as the predictor increases, the odds of the outcome occurring increase; conversely, a value less than 1 indicates that as the predictor increases, the odds of the outcome occurring decrease.

As well as testing the unique contribution of predictors, the overall fit of the model has to be assessed. One way to do this is to calculate the LOG-LIKELIHOOD for different models and to compare these models by looking at the difference between their log-likelihoods. The difference between two log-likelihoods has a CHI-SQUARED DISTRIBUTION (see Field 2005a):

$$\chi^2 = 2[LL(New) - LL(Baseline)]$$

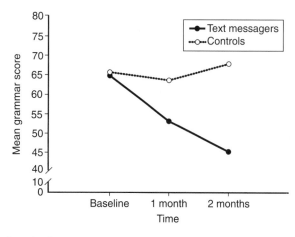

line chart *a*

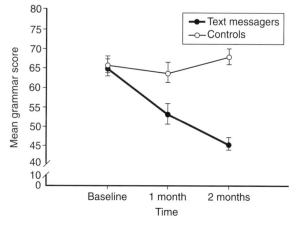

line chart *b*

It is also possible to calculate equivalents of r and r^2 from multiple regression. For example, r can be computed as follows:

$$R = \pm \sqrt{\left(\frac{\text{Wald} - (2 \times df)}{-2\text{LL(Original)}}\right)}$$

which is based on the Wald statistic and its associated DEGREES OF FREEDOM and the log-likelihood of the original model. Hosmer and Lemeshow (1989) suggest that r^2 for a model can be estimated from the − 2 log-likelihoods of the model and the model when only the INTERCEPT was included:

$$R_L^2 = \frac{-2LL(Model)}{-2LL(Original)}$$

However, there are other measures proposed by Cox and Snell, and Nagelkerke (see Field 2005a).

Like multiple regression, logistic regression can be carried out using STEPWISE REGRESSION and HIERARCHICAL REGRESSION. *AF*

Field 2005a; **Hosmer and Lemeshow** 1989.

log-likelihood
The log-likelihood statistic is analogous to the residual sum of squares in MULTIPLE REGRESSION and ANALYSIS OF VARIANCE, but for categorical OUTCOME VARIABLES. It is an indicator of how much unexplained information there is after the model has been fitted. Large values of the log-likelihood statistic indicate poorly fitting statistical models, because the larger the value of the log-likelihood, the more unexplained observations there are. The log-likelihood is calculated as follows:

$$\log-\text{likelihood} = \sum_{i=1}^{N} [Y_i \ln(P(Y_i)) + (1 - Y_i)\ln(1 - P(Y_i))]$$

in which $P(y_i)$ is the probability of the outcome for the ith case, and Y_i is the actual observed outcome for the ith case. *AF*

Field 2005a.

log-linear models
A family of procedures for testing associations between three or more categorical variables. These models are an extension of the GENERALISED LINEAR MODEL (GLM) (see Field 2005a), and hence are much the same as ANALYSIS OF VARIANCE, MULTIPLE REGRESSION and LOGISTIC REGRESSION, but for situations in which all PREDICTOR VARIABLES and the OUTCOME VARIABLE are categorical.

The process usually starts by fitting a saturated model, that is, a model in which all MAIN EFFECTS and INTERACTIONS are included. Imagine we had a three-variable example (variables A, B and C), then we would have three main effects (A, B and C), three interactions involving two variables (AB, AC and BC) and one interaction involving all three variables (ABC). The resulting linear model would be:

$$\ln(O_{ijk}) = (b_0 + b_1 A_i + b_2 B_j + b_3 C_k + b_4 AB_{ij} + b_5 AC_{ik} + b_6 BC_{jk} + b_7 ABC_{ijk}) + \ln(\varepsilon_{ijk})$$

When the saturated model is fitted to the data there will be no error in prediction (see Field 2005a). Log-linear analysis seeks to fit a simpler model to the data without any substantial loss of predictive POWER). This is done using backward elimination: we begin with all terms in the model, and then we remove a predictor from the model, use this new model to predict our observed data (calculate EXPECTED FREQUENCIES, just like in the CHI-SQUARE TEST), and then see how well the model fits the data (i.e. are the expected frequencies close to the observed frequencies?). If the fit of the new model is similar to the more complex model, then we abandon the complex model in favour of the simpler one: we assume the term we removed was not having a significant impact on the ability of our model to predict the observed data.

Terms are not removed randomly, but hierarchically. So, the first term to be removed is the highest-order interaction. If removing this interaction term has no effect on predictive ability of the model then it is discarded and lower-order interactions are removed. If removing these has no effect, then we carry on to any main effects until we find something that does affect the fit of the model if it is removed.

The LIKELIHOOD RATIO is used to assess each model. In this equation the observed values are the same throughout, and the model frequencies are simply the expected frequencies from the model being tested. For the saturated model, this statistic will always be 0 (see Field 2005a), but in other cases it will provide a measure of how well the model fits the observed frequencies. To test whether a new model has changed the likelihood ratio, all we need do is to take the likelihood ratio for a model and subtract from it the likelihood statistic for the previous model (provided the models are hierarchically structured):

$$L\chi^2_{\text{Change}} = L\chi^2_{\text{Current Model}} - L\chi^2_{\text{Previous Model}}$$

AF

Field 2005a; **Tabachnick and Fidell** 2001.

longitudinal study
A study in which observations of the same entities are made repeatedly over set time intervals. (See s. 1, LONGITUDINAL RESEARCH) *AF*

M

main effect A term usually used in ANALYSIS OF VARIANCE, but which applies in other domains (e.g. LOG-LINEAR MODELS) to refer to the unique effect of a predictor on the OUTCOME VARIABLE. For example, the main effect of gender on creativity would simply be the difference between creativity levels in men and women (in analysis of variance, the difference between the means of these two groups). *AF*

Mann-Whitney test A DISTRIBUTION-FREE METHOD for testing differences between two independent SAMPLES. It tests whether the POPULATIONS from which two samples are drawn have the same location. It is functionally the same as WILCOXON RANK SUM TEST, and both tests are distribution-free equivalents of the INDEPENDENT *T*-TEST. The test, like many distribution-free methods, works on the ranks of the data. The data are ranked irrespective of the group from which they came. The TEST STATISTIC is simply:

$$U = N_1 N_2 + \frac{N_1(N_1 + 1)}{2} - R_1$$

in which N_1 and N_2 are the number of observations in groups 1 and 2, respectively, and R_1 is the sum of the ranks for the data in group 1. *AF*
Field 2005a.

matched-design An experimental design involving different groups of entities that have been matched to control for EXTRANEOUS VARIABLES. An example would be two groups of people in which each person in one group has a corresponding person in the second group who has an identical IQ (see s. 6). *AF*

matched-pairs *t*-test [See STUDENT'S *T*-TEST]

Mauchly's test A test of the ASSUMPTION of SPHERICITY. If this test is significant then the assumption of sphericity has not been met and an appropriate correction (GREENHOUSE-GEISSER CORRECTION or HUYNH-FELDT CORRECTION) must be applied to the DEGREES OF FREEDOM of the *F*-RATIO in repeated measures ANALYSIS OF VARIANCE. The test works by comparing the VARIANCE-COVARIANCE MATRIX of the data to an identity matrix (that is, a square matrix with ones along the diagonal and zeros on the off-diagonal); if the variance-covariance matrix is a scalar multiple of an identity matrix then sphericity is met. See Field (2005a) for more detail. *AF*
Field 2005a.

maximum likelihood estimation A technique for estimating model parameters that is based on the general idea that the generated model is the one for which the probability of obtaining the observed set of observations is maximised. *AF*

McNemar test Tests differences between two related groups [see also WILCOXON SIGNED RANK TEST], when you have NOMINAL DATA. It compares the proportion of people who changed their response in one direction (i.e. scores increased) to those that changed in the opposite direction (scores decreased) and is used when there are two related DICHOTOMOUS VARIABLES. *AF*

mean The average of a set of observations. It is the sum of all scores divided by the number of scores:

$$\overline{X} = \frac{\sum_{i=1}^{N} x_i}{N}$$

GH

mean squared error (MS) A measure of average variability [see ANALYSIS OF VARIANCE]. For every SUM OF SQUARED ERROR (which measures the total variability) it is possible to create a MEAN square by dividing by the number of things used to calculate the sum of squares (or some function of it – usually the DEGREES OF FREEDOM). *AF*

measurement error The difference between the value of a VARIABLE given by a measure of that variable and the 'true' value of that variable. *AF*

median In a set of scores ranked in order of magnitude, the median is the middle score (if there is an odd number of scores) or the average of the two middle scores (if there is an even number of scores). *GH*

meta-analysis Meta-analysis is a statistical procedure for assimilating research findings. As scientists, we measure effects in SAMPLES to allow us to estimate the true size of the effect in a POPULATION to which we do not have direct access. Meta-analysis is based on the simple idea that we can take EFFECT SIZES from individual studies, quantify the observed effect in a standard way and then combine them to get a more accurate idea of the true effect in the population.

The first step in meta-analysis is to search the literature for studies that have addressed the same research question. It may make sense to have some kind of systematic criteria for including studies or rejecting studies (perhaps those that are methodologically weak).

Once appropriate articles have been collected, effect sizes need to be calculated (if not reported) for each paper that represents the same effect and are expressed in the same metric. If you were using *r*, this would mean obtaining a value for *r* for each paper you want to include in the meta-analysis. The main function of meta-analysis is to estimate the effect size in the population (the 'true' effect), using a weighted mean of the effect sizes. Although it is not the primary concern of meta-analysis, the significance of this mean can also be computed. The variability between effect sizes across studies (the homogeneity of effect sizes) can also be computed and explained using moderator variables (see Field 2003b).

There are two ways to conceptualise meta-analysis: FIXED EFFECTS and RANDOM EFFECTS models (Field 2001, 2003a, 2003b). These models differ not only in the theoretical assumptions that underlie them, but also in how the MEAN effect size and its significance are computed. The fixed-effect model assumes that all studies in a meta-analysis are sampled from a population in which the average effect size is fixed (Hunter and Schmidt 2000). The alternative assumption is that the studies in a meta-analysis come from populations that have different average effect sizes; so population effect sizes can be thought of as being sampled from a 'superpopulation' (Hedges 1992).

Three methods of meta-analysis have been popular: the methods devised by Hedges and colleagues (Hedges 1992; Hedges and Olkin 1985; Hedges and Vevea 1998), Rosenthal and Rubin's method (1978), or that of Hunter and Schmidt (1990). Hedges and colleagues have developed both fixed- and random-effects models for combining effect sizes; Rosenthal and Rubin have developed only a fixed-effects model; whereas Hunter and Schmidt label their method a random-effects model. The computations of these various methods differ, and the technical details of these differences are well documented elsewhere and are beyond the scope of this review (see Field 2001 for computational details). *AF*

Field 2001, 2003a, 2003b; **Hedges** 1992; **Hedges and Olkin** 1985; **Hedges and Vevea** 1998; **Hunter and Schmidt** 1990, 2000; **Rosenthal and Rubin** 1978.

mixed-effects model   A model involving both FIXED EFFECTS and RANDOM EFFECTS. *AF*

mixed-plot design   An experimental design using at least two PREDICTOR VARIABLES, at least one of which is measured using different participants and at least one of which is measured using the same participants. Often abbreviated to a mixed design. *AF*

mode   The most frequent score in a set of observations. *AF*

multicollinearity   Multicollinearity is the term used in MULTIPLE REGRESSION to indicate high correlations among the PREDICTOR VARIABLES. [See also VARIANCE INFLATION FACTOR (VIF) and TOLERANCE] *JM*

multimodal   A set of observations having more than one MODE. *AF*

multiple comparisons   A set of procedures for comparing differences between pairs of means, usually carried out when no specific hypotheses have been made about how groups will differ. They are usually used after an ANALYSIS OF VARIANCE, in which a significant effect has been found relating to several group means. Multiple comparisons are used to then determine which of the group means differ by comparing all combinations of pairs of group means. Typically, each test is a STUDENT'S T-TEST, but corrected for the fact that many tests are done. The simplest procedure is Fisher's LEAST SIGNIFICANT DIFFERENCE TEST (LSD), which uses standard student's t-tests, but only after a significant F-RATIO. The problem with this procedure is that every time a test is done, the probability of making a TYPE I ERROR is 0.05 (or 5 per

cent), and so when multiple t-tests are conducted, these errors add up. For example, with three t-tests, the probability of making at least one type I error (assuming a 0.05 α-level) is $1 - (0.95)^3 = 0.143$ or 14.3 per cent (see Field 2005a). Therefore, to ensure that the α-level is maintained at 0.05 across the whole family of tests, the t (or the probability at which significance is accepted) is adjusted.

The simplest adjustment is the BONFERRONI CORRECTION. However, a variety of other tests have been suggested. A large body of them are based on the studentised range statistic (q_r), which is a function of the difference between the largest and smallest group means and the residual MEAN squares [see ANALYSIS OF VARIANCE] and the SAMPLE SIZE per group:

$$q_r = \frac{\overline{X}_{largest} - \overline{X}_{smallest}}{\sqrt{\dfrac{MS_R}{n}}}$$

This statistic can be compared to critical values to assess the significance of the difference between the smallest and largest mean. However, it can also be computed for smaller ranges (for example, you could calculate the difference between the 3rd and 5th largest means – a range of 2 – or the 1st and 2nd largest means – a range of 1). Many POST HOC TESTS (for example, NEWMAN-KEULS TEST) are based on calculating studentised range statistics for all pairs of means and evaluating them against critical values corresponding to the RANGE for the particular comparison. This procedure does not always control the type I error rate, so tests such as Tukey's honestly significant difference (HSD) do much the same but compare each studentised range statistic against the critical value based on the critical value for the *maximum* possible range of means, rather than the value of the range for the particular comparison. An alternative to this is to use the studentised range statistic as is, but correct the probability at which the difference is accepted (rather like the Bonferroni correction) and tests such as the Ryan, Einot, Gabriel and Welsch Q (*REGWQ*) tests do this (see Howell 2002 for a beautiful description of these procedures).

A different procedure, based on the F-ratio, not the t-test or studentised range statistic, was proposed by Scheffé. The SCHEFFÉ TEST is based on constructing a CONFIDENCE INTERVAL for each comparison between means. In an ANALYSIS OF VARIANCE with k groups, a total sample size, N, and a residual mean squared error, MS_R, the confidence interval for the mean difference between two groups, i and j, is:

$$(\overline{X}_i - \overline{X}_j) \pm \sqrt{(k-1)F} \times \sqrt{MS_R \left(\frac{1}{n_i} + \frac{1}{n_j} \right)}$$

In which F is the F-ratio (at an appropriate α-level) with $k - 1$, and $N–k$ DEGREES OF FREEDOM.

There are also a whole range of tests designed to provide more accurate estimates when group sizes are unequal and when the ASSUMPTION of HOMOGENEITY OF VARIANCE is violated (e.g. the Games-Howell procedure).

In terms of which test to pick, Field (2005a) says that the Newman-Keuls procedure is a very liberal test and lacks control over the EXPERIMENTWISE ERROR RATE. Bonferroni's and Tukey's tests both control the type I error rate very well but lack POWER. Of the two, Bonferroni has more POWER when few comparisons are done, whereas

Tukey is more powerful when testing large numbers of means. Tukey generally has greater power than Scheffé. The REGWQ has good power, tight control of the type I error rate, and when you want to test all pairs of means is the best procedure. However, in unbalanced designs or when homogeneity of variance can not be assumed, these tests perform poorly. Of the various tests available, Field (2005a) recommends the Games-Howell test. [See MULTIPLE COMPARISONS, see also PLANNED COMPARISONS]

AF

Field 2005a; **Howell** 2002.

multiple correlation coefficient The CORRELATION COEFFICIENT between the observed values of the OUTCOME VARIABLE and the values predicted by a MULTIPLE REGRESSION model.

AF

multiple regression Multiple regression is a statistical technique closely related to LINEAR REGRESSION and CORRELATION. This entry will first consider linear regression in some detail, and will then examine how this generalises to multiple regression.

The entry on linear regression considers the relationship between children's age and their score on a TEST (see s. 6) of reading ability. The data for this analysis are shown in the Table.

multiple regression *Age and score on test of reading ability*

Age	Score	Predicted Score	Residual
3	40.0	38.9	1.1
4	29.2	46.8	−17.6
7	94.8	70.5	24.3
6	53.8	62.6	−8.8
4	55.5	46.8	8.7
5	67.0	54.7	12.3
9	65.5	86.3	−20.8
10	110.0	94.2	15.8
10	90.0	94.2	−4.2
7	60.0	70.5	−10.5

As well as the raw data, the Table shows the predicted score for each child, based on their age. This is found using the equation:

$$Y_i = b_0 + b_1 X_i + \varepsilon_i$$

where y is the OUTCOME VARIABLE, b_1 is a slope estimate, X_i is the value of the predictor for the ith observation and b_0 is the constant (or INTERCEPT).

$$\text{score} = 15.2 + 7.9 \times \text{age}$$

The final column of the Table shows the RESIDUAL – that is, the difference between the score that we would predict the child would get, using the regression equation, and the score that they actually did get. The definition of the LINE OF BEST FIT is the line that minimises the sum of the squared residuals. Hence regression is sometimes referred

to as *least squares regression*, or ORDINARY LEAST SQUARES (OLS) regression.

Many measures in psychology are measured on arbitrary scales – that is, the units of measurement are not informative. In this example, the PREDICTOR VARIABLE, age, is measured in what we might call 'real' units. One more year is meaningful – we understand the scale, and the units. One more point on the test is not meaningful – we do not know what it means, and hence the scale is arbitrary. If I decided to multiply all the scores by ten, such that one more point became ten more points, it would not make any difference to our interpretation. In addition, if we used a different test, with a different maximum score, we would find a very different regression equation, even if the substantive interpretation were the same. A solution to this problem is to use standardised variables in the regression. If we were to do this in this case, we would find that the regression equation was:

$$\text{score} = 0 + 0.80 \times \text{age}$$

The regression parameter (0.80) now represents the expected difference, in STANDARD DEVIATION units, in the test score associated with a standard deviation shift in age. If we were to calculate the CORRELATION COEFFICIENT we would find that the correlation was also $r = 0.80$. The correlation coefficient is the regression coefficient when using standardised variables – often called the standardised regression coefficient. We can also calculate the standardised coefficient using the (unstandardised) coefficient and the standard deviations of the VARIABLES. If we refer to the predictor as x, and the outcome as y, then the correlation (r) is given by:

$$r = \frac{b \times sd(x)}{sd(y)}$$

This is very convenient, because it means that if we can calculate r (and we can, because we know the formula), we can calculate the regression coefficient:

$$b = \frac{r \times sd(y)}{sd(x)}$$

The standardised coefficient, or correlation, can be thought of in other ways, which will prove useful when we move on to multiple regression.

First, we can consider the correlation in terms of VARIANCE. The variance of the residual scores is 224.0, the variance of the outcome is 629.4. We might consider that we had a certain amount of variance – 629.4 – to start with, and we have a certain amount – 224.0 – left. We have therefore explained 629.4 – 224.0 = 405.4. This value is the variance of the predicted scores. More useful than presenting this in raw units would be to ask what proportion of the variance we have explained (and hence what proportion remains).

The proportion of the variance explained is 405.4 / 629.4 = 0.64. The square root of this value is equal to 0.80, which is the CORRELATION COEFFICIENT. We therefore have a second way of considering the correlation – it is the square root of the proportion of variance explained.

We might also choose to calculate the correlation between the outcome variable and the predicted score on the outcome variable. This might seem (at first) like a curious thing to do, but if we did, the correlation would be equal to 0.80 – the same as the correlation between the variables. However, this gives us a third way to think of the correlation – it tells us how close our predictions are to the actual scores.

The statistic r can be tested for statistical significance, using the F-DISTRIBUTION, and the parameter estimates b_1 and b_0 have an associated STANDARD ERROR, which can be used to calculate CONFIDENCE INTERVALS, and can be tested for statistical significance using the t distribution.

In this example, for testing r, $F = 14.5$, with 1, 8 df, and $p = 0.005$. The standard error for the regression estimate (b) is equal to 2.07, giving us 95 per cent confidence intervals around the estimate (7.9) of 3.1 to 12.7. In addition, the value of t is given by the estimate divided by the standard error, $7.9/2.07 = 3.80$, which gives a P-VALUE of 0.005.

The value for F is equal to t^2, and the p-values are the same – which shouldn't surprise us, because the tests are testing the same NULL HYPOTHESIS.

The POWER of multiple regression comes from its ability to incorporate multiple predictors. The aim of the analysis is the same: to predict, explain and diagnose an outcome measure, but we are now attempting to use more than one predictor to do this. For example, we might examine the age of the children, their socio-economic group and their language ability at the age of two.

The basic procedure is still the same – the aim is to develop a regression equation, which minimises the sums of squares of the residuals, by finding the best values for the parameter estimates.

In this case, we now label the different parameters b_1, b_2, b_3, b_k, and will have an equation:

$$Y_i = b_0 + b_1X_1 + b_2X_2 \dots b_nX_n + \varepsilon_i$$

JM

Cohen, Cohen, Aiken and West 2003; **Field** 2005a; **Miles and Shevlin** 2001.

multivariate analysis of variance (MANOVA)

A family of tests that extend the basic ANALYSIS OF VARIANCE to situations in which more than one OUTCOME VARIABLE has been measured. The principles behind this analysis are directly analogous to analysis of variance except that matrices are used to represent variability instead of single values. When dealing with a single outcome variable [see ANALYSIS OF VARIANCE], we calculate a total SUM OF SQUARED ERROR (SS_T), a sum of squared error for the model (SS_M), and a residual sum of squared error, representing the error in the model (SS_R). When several outcome variables are used we get each of these values for each VARIABLE, therefore, we can create matrices representing the same things, but containing the multiple values of each. In addition, we can include in these matrices estimates of the relationships between variables in the form of cross-products [see CORRELATION CO-EFFICIENT]. As such, we get three square matrices, for which the columns and rows represent the measured variables, the diagonal elements represent the VARIANCES within variables and the off-diagonal elements are the cross-products between variables. This is a sum of squares and cross-product (SSCP) matrix and is simply a crude form of a VARIANCE-COVARIANCE MATRIX. Analogous to analysis of variance, we calculate a total SSCP (T), representing the total variability in the outcome variables, a model SSCP (H), representing the variance explained by the model, and a residual SSCP (E), representing the error in the model. In analysis of variance the TEST STATISTIC (F-RATIO) is proportionate to the model variability divided by error variability. In much the same way, the test statistic in MANOVA is based on dividing the model SSCP by the residual SSCP. However, because matrices are not divisible, rather than dividing H by E, it is necessary to do the functional equivalent, which is multiply H by the inverse of E (see Field 2005a). The result is a new matrix, HE^{-1}, which is functionally equivalent to the F-ratio in analysis of variance. This matrix contains multiple values, and so is reduced down to a single value for the test statistic. There are four proposed ways of doing this, resulting in four different test statistics. The simplest one is to take the biggest EIGENVALUE of the matrix HE^{-1} and this is known as ROY'S LARGEST ROOT (λ). This represents the proportion of explained variance to unexplained variance (SS_M/SS_R) for the first discriminant functions [see DISCRIMINANT FUNCTION ANALYSIS]. However, the matrix HE^{-1} will have several eigenvalues (as many as there are outcome variables, in fact), so an alternative is to not just look at the largest one, but to add them up. The result is known as HOTELLING'S T^2, and represents the proportion of explained variance to unexplained variance (SS_M/SS_R) for the all discriminant functions.

The two other test statistics are also functions of the eigenvalues from the matrix HE^{-1}. Wilk's Λ is given by:

$$\Lambda = \prod_{i=1}^{s} \frac{1}{1 + \lambda_i}$$

and represents the ratio of error variance to total variance (SS_R/SS_T) for the discriminant functions. [See WILK'S LAMBDA] The Pillai-Bartlett trace (V) is given by:

$$V = \sum_{i=1}^{s} \frac{\lambda_i}{1 + \lambda_i}$$

and is similar to the ratio of SS_M/SS_T (see Field 2005a).

MANOVA has similar assumptions to ANOVA but extended to the multivariate case: (1) observations should be statistically independent; (2) data should be randomly sampled from the POPULATION of interest and measured at an interval level; (3) we assume that the outcome variables (collectively) have multivariate normality within groups; and (4) we must assume HOMOGENEITY OF VARIANCE for each outcome variable, but also that the correlation between any two outcome variables is the same in all groups. When these assumptions are broken, the accuracy of the resulting multivariate test statistics is compromised.

Only when there is one underlying variate will the four test statistics necessarily be the same. Therefore, some advice is warranted on which test statistic to use. Field (2005a) noted, based on a review of the literature, that for small and moderate sample sizes the four statistics differ little in terms of POWER. If group differences are concentrated on the first variate (as will often be the case in social science research) the order of test power is Roy's largest root (because it takes into account only the first variate), Hotelling's T, Wilk's Λ and Pillai's trace. However, when groups differ along more than one variate, the power

445

ordering is the reverse. In terms of robustness, all four test statistics are relatively robust to violations of multivariate normality. Roy's root is affected by PLATYKURTIC distributions and is not robust when the homogeneity of covariance matrix assumption is untenable. Bray and Maxwell (1985) conclude that when sample sizes are equal, the Pillai-Bartlett trace is the most robust to violations of assumptions. However, when SAMPLE SIZES are unequal this statistic is affected by violations of the assumption of equal covariance matrices.

Although some recommend following up MANOVA with multiple analysis of variance (one on each outcome variable), doing so results in inflated EXPERIMENTWISE ERROR RATES and also ignores the information about the relationships between outcome variables on which the test statistics are partly based. For these reasons Field (2005a)

describes how to follow up MANOVA with discriminant function analysis. *AF*

Bray and Maxwell 1985; **Field** 2005a; **Stevens** 1992.

multivariate data   A set of observations consisting of multiple measures taken for each entity in a SAMPLE.   *AF*

multivariate normality   An extension of a NORMAL DISTRIBUTION to multiple variables. It is a PROBABILITY DISTRIBUTION of a set of variables $v' = [v_1, v_2 \ldots v_n]$ given by:

$$f(v_1, v_2 \ldots v_n) = 2\pi^{\frac{n}{2}} |\Sigma|^{\frac{1}{2}} \exp{-\frac{1}{2}(v - \mu)' \Sigma^{-1} (v - \mu)}$$

in which μ is the vector of means of the variables and Σ is the VARIANCE-COVARIANCE MATRIX.   *AF*

N

negative skew   [See SKEWNESS]

Newman-Keuls test   [See MULTIPLE COMPARISONS]

nominal data   Where numbers merely represent names, for example, the numbers on sports players' shirts: a player with the number 1 on their back is not necessarily worse than a player with a 2 on their back.   *AF*

nomothetic   Any theory that looks at general or abstract laws (rather than looking at the individual or unique) [see IDEOGRAPHIC]. The term tends to be associated with the acquisition of knowledge through experimentation (because the aim of experimental methods is to generate generalisable results). (See s. 1, NOMOTHETIC METHODS)   *AF*

non-parametric tests   Although an inaccurate term to describe them, it is usually used synonymously with DISTRIBUTION-FREE METHODS.   *AF*

normal distribution   A PROBABILITY DISTRIBUTION of a random variable that is known to have certain properties, namely, it is perfectly symmetrical and so has a SKEWNESS and KURTOSIS = 0. Technically, the distribution is described for any VARIABLE, v, as:

$$f(v) = \frac{1}{\sigma\sqrt{2\pi}} e^{\frac{(v-\mu)^2}{2\sigma^2}}$$

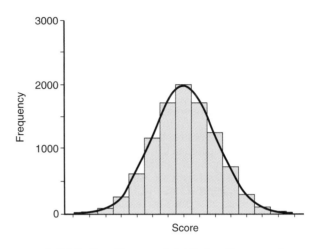

normal distribution *The normal distribution (the curve shows the idealised shape of the distribution)*

in which μ and σ are the MEAN and STANDARD DEVIATION, respectively, of the DISTRIBUTION. It is more easily thought of graphically as a bell-shaped curve (see Figure).   *AF*

null hypothesis   The reverse of the ALTERNATIVE HYPOTHESIS, that is, that your prediction is wrong and that the predicted effect does not exist. Incidentally, this HYPOTHESIS (see also s. 3) is never true. [See HYPOTHESIS TESTING]   *AF*

O

---

observational design   A general term for research in which the researcher does not intervene or exert control over events or variables. This can take the form of watching, recording and coding behaviour, or surveys and questionnaire research.   *AF*

odds   The probability of an event occurring divided by the probability of that event not occurring.   *AF*

odds ratio   The ratio of the ODDS of an event occurring in one group compared to another. So, for example, if the odds of worshipping Satan after listening to the band Cradle of Filth are 4, and the odds of worshipping Satan after not listening to Cradle of Filth are 0.25, then the odds ratio is 4/0.25 = 16. This means that if you listen to Cradle of Filth, you are 16 times more likely to worship Satan than if you do not. An odds ratio of 1 would indicate that the *odds* of a particular outcome are equal in both groups.   *AF*

one-tailed test   A test of a directional HYPOTHESIS. For example, the hypothesis 'the longer I write these statistical entries, the more I want to shoot the editor' requires a one-tailed test, because I have stated the direction of the relationship. Imagine we wanted to discover whether writing these entries made me want to shoot the editor. If we have no directional hypothesis then there are three possibilities: (1) writing these entries makes people want to shoot the editor (the MEAN for those writing entries minus the mean for those not writing entries is positive); (2) people who write entries do not want to shoot the

editor (the mean for those writing entries minus the mean for those not writing entries is negative); and (3) there is no difference between those writing entries and those not in their desire to shoot the editor. This final option is the NULL HYPOTHESIS.

The direction of the TEST STATISTIC (i.e. whether it is positive or negative) depends on whether the difference is positive or negative. Assuming there is a positive difference or relationship (writing these entries makes you want to shoot the editor), then to detect this difference we have to take account of the fact that the mean for contributors is bigger than for non-contributors. However, if we have predicted incorrectly and actually making contributions makes people want to shoot the editor less, then the test statistic will actually be negative.

If, at the 0.05 level, we needed to get a test statistic bigger than 20, for example, and the one we get is actually −12, then we would reject the hypothesis even though a difference does exist. To avoid this we can look at both ends (or tails) of the distribution of possible test statistics. This means we will catch both positive and negative test statistics. However, doing this has a price, because to keep our criterion probability of 0.05 we have to split this probability across the two tails: so we have 0.025 at the positive end of the distribution and 0.025 at the negative end. The Figure shows this situation – the grey areas are the areas above the test statistic needed at a 0.025 level of significance. Combine the probabilities at both ends and we get 0.05 – our criterion value. Now if we have made a prediction, then we put all our eggs in one basket and look only at one end of the distribution (either the positive or the

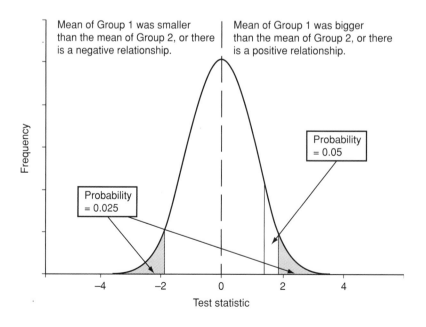

negative end, depending on the direction of the prediction we make). Consequently, we can just look for the value of the test statistic that would occur by chance with a probability of 0.05. The important point is that if we make a specific prediction then we need a smaller test statistic to find a significant result (because we are looking in only one tail), but if our prediction happens to be in the wrong direction then we will miss detecting the effect that does exist! See Field (2005a) for more detail.

[See also TWO-TAILED TEST] *AF*

Field 2005a.

one-way ANOVA An ANALYSIS OF VARIANCE in which there is only one PREDICTOR VARIABLE. *AF*

opportunity sample A SAMPLE of entities that happen to be available. *JM*

ordinal data Data that tell us not only that things have occurred, but also the order in which they occurred. These data tell us nothing about the differences between values. For example, gold, silver and bronze medals are ordinal: they tell us that the gold medallist was better than the silver medallist, however, they do not tell us how much better (was gold a lot better than silver, or were gold and silver very closely matched?). *AF*

ordinary least squares (OLS) [See LEAST SQUARES ESTIMATION]

orthogonal Statistically speaking, orthogonal is synonymous with INDEPENDENCE; that is, orthogonal entities are not correlated [see CORRELATION COEFFICIENT]. Mathematically speaking, it refers to matrices that, when multiplied by their transpose, produce an identity matrix (that is, a matrix with 1s on the diagonal and 0s on the off-diagonal), but in statistics we are typically using a VARIANCE-COVARIANCE MATRIX which means that the resulting matrix represents situations in which variables are not correlated (because the off-diagonal elements, which represent the covariances, are all 0). *AF*

outcome variable A VARIABLE whose values we are trying to predict from one or more PREDICTOR VARIABLES. Also known as DEPENDENT VARIABLE. *AF*

outlier An extreme score, which is unrepresentative of the scores to which it belongs. A common practice is to treat as outliers any scores which are more than 2 STANDARD DEVIATIONS from the MEAN of the set of scores. Outliers are common in REACTION TIME (see s. 3) data, where it is easy for a lapse of ATTENTION (see s. 3) to result in a spuriously long latency to respond on some trials. In this case, outliers can be treated in one of several ways. They can be discarded without replacement; replaced by the mean of the set to which they belong; or the entire data set can be subjected to a LOGARITHMIC TRANSFORMATION, which reduces the size of scores in proportion to their original magnitude and thus reduces the SKEWNESS of the original data set that is produced by large outliers. *GH*

P

paired-samples *t*-test [See STUDENT'S *t*-TEST]

parametric methods A test that requires data from one of the large catalogue of distributions that statisticians have described. Normally this term is used for parametric tests based on the NORMAL DISTRIBUTION, which require four basic ASSUMPTIONS that must be met for the test to be accurate: normally distributed data [see NORMAL DISTRIBUTION], HOMOGENEITY OF VARIANCE, interval or RATIO DATA and INDEPENDENCE. *AF*

partial correlation A measure of the relationship between two variables while 'controlling' the effect that one or more additional variables has on both. *AF*

Pearson product moment correlation coefficient [See CORRELATION COEFFICIENT]

Pearson's chi-squared statistic [See CHI-SQUARED TEST]

percentile The value that produces exactly 100 equal sub-groups of a set of continuous observations. Typically, percentiles are used to measure the proportion of scores above certain values or to identify cases in certain groups. For example, if the VARIABLE was psychopathy and you wanted to compare those high on psychopathy with those low on psychopathy then you might calculate the percentiles and then calculate the 25 per cent and 75 per cent values. You could then compare the top 25 per cent of psychopaths with the bottom 25 per cent just by looking at those that score above the 75th and 25th percentile respectively. *AF*

phi-coefficient, ϕ A measure of the strength of association between two DICHOTOMOUS VARIABLES. As such, phi is used with 2 × 2 CONTINGENCY TABLES. Phi is a variant of the chi-squared test, χ^2:

$$\phi = \sqrt{\frac{\chi^2}{n}},$$

in which n is the total number of observations. *AF*
Howell 2002.

pie chart A graphical technique for displaying frequencies. Typically this diagram takes the form of a circle (100 per cent), subdivided into smaller segments, with each segment representing a category of data. The size of the segment is proportionate to the frequency (or percentage) of data falling into that category. *AF*

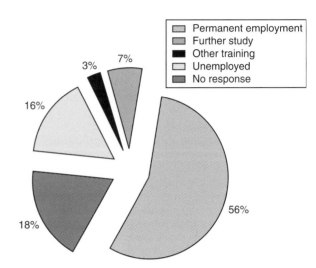

pie chart *Graduate destinations of Sussex University students*

pilot study A small-scale version of a final piece of research carried out to discover potential problems or to validate potential measures. *AF*

placebo An intervention designed to be like an active intervention in every way except for the fact it does not have an active component. For example, a placebo for alcohol should look, smell and taste like alcohol but not have any alcohol within the drink. *AF*

placebo effect A phenomenon in which participants given a PLACEBO respond in the same way as if they were given an active intervention. *AF*

planned comparisons A set of comparisons between group means that are constructed *before* any data are collected and are carried out after ANALYSIS OF VARIANCE. These are theory-led comparisons and are based on the idea of partitioning the VARIANCE created by the overall effect of group differences into gradually smaller portions of variance. For each contrast, two portions of variance are compared, and each portion may contain data from one or more groups. The aim is to split these portions until each group has appeared alone in one of the portions (after which it is not used in any further contrast). These contrasts usually have more POWER than MULTIPLE COMPARISONS.

Exactly how the variance is partitioned will depend upon the experimental hypotheses, however, as a general rule, the first contrast will compare all experimental conditions with any CONTROL GROUP or groups. For example, the analysis of variance entry described an experiment involving three groups of men who had not previously owned a mobile phone: the first group did not use a

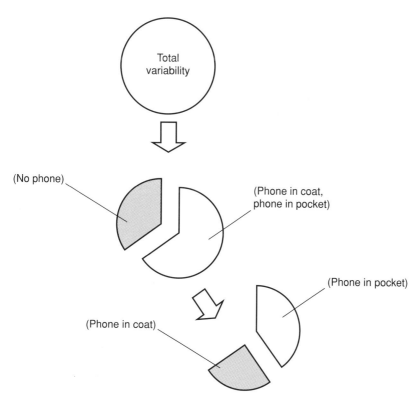

planned comparisons *Partitioning variance in planned comparisons.*

mobile phone (a control group), a second group were given a phone and asked to keep it in their front trouser pocket for a year and the final group were asked to keep the phone in their coat pocket (away from their genitals). The outcome was their sperm count after a year. One way to construct contrasts for this example would be to first compare having no phone to groups that did have a phone, and then to break apart the groups that used a phone. The Figure shows this scenario. The total variability (SS_T) [see ANALYSIS OF VARIANCE] is split into two chunks for the first contrast. This contrast compares the variability in the control group (no phone) to the variability in the other two conditions combined (phone in pocket and phone in coat). This, therefore, addresses the HYPOTHESIS 'using a phone affects your sperm count more than not having a phone'. Note how the contrast compares only two things; this is important for interpreting the contrast. This contrast contains a chunk of variation made up of two groups, and so the second contrast must break this variation up into its component parts. Therefore, contrast two compares the variability in the group who had the phone in their pocket to the variability in the group that had their phone in their coat. This addresses the hypothesis, 'having a phone in your trouser pocket affects your sperm count more than having a phone in your coat'.

This is not necessarily the 'correct' set of contrasts for this example. It would be equally valid to have contrast 1 comparing the phone in trouser group to the other two groups, and then have contrast two compare the no phone group to the phone in the coat group. However, these contrasts address slightly different hypotheses to the first contrasts. Contrast 1 would address the hypothesis, 'having a phone in your trouser pocket affects your sperm count more than not having a phone in your trouser pocket', and contrast two would be addressing the hypothesis, 'having a phone in your coat pocket affects your sperm count more than not having a phone at all'.

Because these contrasts merely partition variance, they control the TYPE I ERROR (provided they are independent). Mathematically these contrasts are significance-tested by using a SUM OF SQUARED ERROR for the contrast and using this in the usual way to obtain an F-RATIO. The sum of squared error for the contrast is defined as:

$$SS_{Contrast} = \frac{n\left(\sum_{i=1}^{k} w_i \overline{X}_i\right)^2}{\sum_{i=1}^{k} w_i^2}$$

In which, n is the number of observations per group, and the MEAN of each group is weighted by a value w. The values of w have to be determined by the experimenter to 'make' the contrast compare the groups that need to be compared. So, for a particular contrast, we assigned values of w to each group, and these values will differ in different contrasts. You can, of course, assign any values you like, but if you actually want to be able to interpret the contrast you should assign weights that address the hypothesis of interest. Also, the weights within a contrast should sum to 0, and the weights in different contrasts should cross-multiply to be zero if the contrasts are independent (which is important for controlling the TYPE I ERROR rate).

This all sounds hideously complex, but Field (2005a) suggests a way to achieve all this without too much stress. The hard part is designing the contrasts in the first place. The first rule is that any group that is singled out in a contrast must not be used in any subsequent contrasts and should be assigned a weight of 0 in all future contrasts. So, in the Figure, having singled out the 'no phone' group in the first contrast, we cannot use it in contrast 2, and the weight it receives in contrast 2 is 0 (which just means it is ignored). In terms of weights, in every contrast you should compare only two chunks of variance, you need to assign one chunk a positive weight and the other a negative (it does not matter which way round). The magnitude of the weight is then simply the number of groups in the *opposite* chunk of variance. (See Table for the weights in contrast 1)

	No phone	Phone in coat	Phone in pocket	Total
Contrast 1	−2	1	1	0
Contrast 2	0	−1	1	0
C1 × C2	0	−1	1	0

Note that for each contrast, the weights add up to zero, and if you cross-multiply the weights in each group, these also add up to zero. These two properties mean that these two contrasts are independent.

[See also MULTIPLE COMPARISONS] *AF*

Field 2005a.

platykurtic   [See KURTOSIS]

point-biserial correlation   [See BISERIAL CORRELATION]

population   In statistical terms, this usually refers to the collection of units (be they people, plankton, plants, cities, suicidal authors, etc.) to which we want to generalise a set of findings or a statistical model.   *AF*

positive skew   [See SKEWNESS]

post hoc tests   [See MULTIPLE COMPARISONS]

power   Power is the probability of rejecting the NULL HYPOTHESIS H_0 when it is actually false. Power = $1 - \beta$, where β is the probability of a TYPE II ERROR. In the Figure, suppose that if the null hypothesis were true, the MEAN would be $\mu = \mu_0$, but in reality the null hypothesis is false and the mean actually is $\mu = \mu_1$. The distribution around μ_0 is the SAMPLING DISTRIBUTION of the mean if the null hypothesis were true, and the distribution around μ_1 is the sampling distribution if the mean really equals μ_1.

The area under the darkly-shaded tail of the H_0 distribution is α, the probability of a TYPE I ERROR (for a ONE-TAILED TEST – otherwise it is $\alpha/2$). We will correctly reject H_0 if our SAMPLE mean falls in this area. The shaded area under the H_1 DISTRIBUTION is the probability that we will correctly reject H_0 if the mean really is μ_1, and that is the power to detect μ_1.

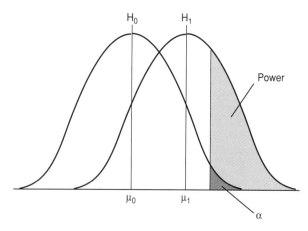

power

Given a random sample of 50 adult IQ (see s. 6) scores, suppose we want to know the power to detect $\mu = \mu_1 = 105$ when H_0 is $\mu = \mu_0 = 100$. Assume that we know the IQ scores are normally distributed with a STANDARD DEVIATION of 15. For N = 50 the standard error of the mean is $s_e = 15/\sqrt{50} = 4.2$. If we use a TWO-TAILED TEST with $\alpha = .05$, then we will reject H_0 given a sample mean greater than $100 + 1.96SE = 100 + 1.96 \times 4.2 = 104.16$. Power is the area beyond 104.16 under the normal curve when $\mu_1 = 105$ and sd $= 15/\sqrt{50}$. This area is .654, which is $1 - \beta$ or power.

Power depends on three things (Cohen 1988; Howell 2002). First, power increases with SAMPLE SIZE because the sampling distributions for the H_0 and H_1 distributions become narrower and more well-separated. If N = 100 instead of 50 then power would be .912. Second, power increases as the difference between μ_0 and μ_1 increases because the sampling distributions move farther apart. If $\mu_1 = 107$ instead of 105 then power would be .910. Third, power increases if we increase α because the border of the rejection region moves to the left, increasing both shaded areas. If $\alpha = .10$ instead of .05 then power would be .762.

MS

Cohen 1998; **Howell** 2002.

practice effects   The possibility that performance on a task changes (the assumption is for the better) when a task is performed more than once. This is a concern in REPEATED-MEASURES DESIGNS in which the OUTCOME VARIABLE is measured using the same task several times.   *AF*

predictor variable   A VARIABLE that is used to try to predict values of an OUTCOME VARIABLE. It is used synonymously (by me, at least) with INDEPENDENT VARIABLE.   *AF*

principal components analysis   A multivariate technique for identifying the linear components of a set of variables. The procedure has many similarities to FACTOR ANALYSIS and for the sake of cognitive efficiency they can be thought of as much the same thing (although those not labouring under the burden of the need for cognitive efficiency tend to have embolisms at the prospect of considering them as the same). The goal in principle

components analysis is to find the underlying linear variates in the data set in much the same way as DISCRIMINANT FUNCTION ANALYSIS. Therefore, unlike factor analysis, it begins by assuming all variables share all of their VARIANCE. Then, like factor analysis, decisions are made about which linear variates are important enough (statistically speaking) to retain, and the solution is optimised using FACTOR ROTATION. *AF*

Dunteman 1989; **Field** 2005a.

probability distribution A curve describing an idealised FREQUENCY DISTRIBUTION of a particular VARIABLE from which it is possible to ascertain the probability with which specific values of that variable will occur. For CATEGORICAL VARIABLES it is simply a formula yielding the probability with which each category occurs. *AF*

publication bias Refers to the fact that scientific journals have a tendency to publish positive findings rather than negative ones; hence the published literature may give a false impression of the robustness of findings, because failures to replicate seldom get published. *GH*

***p*-value** A probability value is used in the NULL HYPOTHESIS STATISTICAL TEST procedure (NHSTP). A statistical analysis is carried out, which gives rise to a test statistic (such as F in ANOVA, or r in correlation). The *p*-value is the probability of a test statistic at least that extreme occurring, if the null hypothesis is correct. While this seems like a simple statement, it is frequently misinterpreted – people understand the *p*-value to be the probability that the null hypothesis is correct; it is the probability of the test statistic occurring, if the null hypothesis is correct.

The first (correct) interpretation we could write as $p(H|D)$; the second, incorrect, interpretation as $p(D|H)$. An example might help to distinguish between them. If I am outside, and it is hot (H), it is probable that I will have a drink (D). If there was an 80 per cent chance that I would have a drink, we could write this as $p(D|H) = 0.8$. If you know this information, what information do you have about $p(H|D)$, that is, the probability that it is hot, given that I have a drink? The answer is that you have very little information.

Critics of NHSTP and *p*-values (e.g. Cohen 1994) suggest that the popularity of the procedure is based in part upon the lack of understanding that people have about the interpretation of a *p*-value – that it is a conditional value.

The use of *p*-values has also been criticised for other reasons: the null hypothesis has been described as a 'straw man' – all null hypotheses are false, and so the idea of rejection (or not) of something that we know to be false is meaningless. In addition, the simple use of a *p*-value to reject or fail to reject a null hypothesis is an oversimplistic decision – researchers should present EFFECT SIZES and CONFIDENCE INTERVALS, and use META-ANALYSIS to combine information from more than one study (Schmidt 1996). It should be noted that others have provided a robust defence of significance testing (see, for example, Chow 1996, and for arguments on both sides of the debate, Harlow, Mulaik and Steiger 1997). *JM*

Chow 1996; **Cohen** 1994; **Harlow, Mulaik and Steiger** 1997.

Q

qualitative methods Extrapolating evidence for a theory from what people say or write [see also QUANTITATIVE METHODS]. *AF*

quantitative methods Inferring evidence for a theory through measurement of variables that produce numeric outcomes [see also QUALITATIVE METHODS]. *AF*

quartiles Values of a set of ordered observations that split those observations into four equal-sized groups.

Imagine we counted how many darts a group of ten students threw at their statistics lecturer. First, arrange the scores into ascending order:

Number of darts: 21, 25, 28, 30, 32, 33, 36, 38, 44, 137

Next, split the data into four equal (or roughly equal) groups. The simplest way is to divide the number of scores, n, by 4. With ten scores, this gives us $n/2 = 10/4 = 2.5$. The first quartile (known as the lower quartile) should therefore contain the first 2.5 scores in your ordered list, the second quartile should contain the next 2.5 scores, the third quartile contains the next 2.5 scores, and the final quartile (known as the upper quartile) contains the final 2.5 scores. One obvious problem with our data is that you can not have 2.5 scores in each quartile,

you can have only two scores or three scores (we can not cut a score in half and put one half in one quartile and the other half in the next quartile). In these circumstances we would probably split the data as shown in the Figure.

In an ideal world, each quartile should have the same number of scores within it. Although there are more sophisticated ways of calculating quartiles, this gives you a simple flavour of what they represent. The bottom quartile contains the lowest 25 per cent of scores, the upper quartile contains the top 25 per cent, and the second and third quartiles collectively contain the remaining 50 per cent of the data. The INTERQUARTILE RANGE is simply the range when you ignore the upper and lower quartiles; put another way, it is the highest score of the third quartile minus the lowest score of the second quartile (in this case it would be $38-28 = 10$). *AF*

quasi-experimental design One in which the experimenter has no control over either the allocation of participants to conditions, or the timing of the experimental manipulations. *GH*

quota sampling A quota SAMPLE is an attempt to make a sample representative by having the same proportion of different groups of people in the sample and in the POPULATION. *JM*

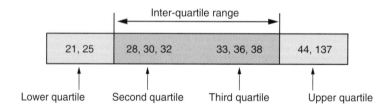

quartiles

R

---

random allocation   In the context of an experiment, this means that participants have been placed in one condition or another of the study in a non-systematic way. This reduces the risk of introducing systematic differences between conditions, other than those that the experimenter wishes to investigate.   *GH*

random effects   The effect of a measure that has a potentially infinite number of levels but of which only a random SAMPLE has been used in the study. Measures should be treated as random when changing one of the levels of the measure does not affect the research question. For example, if we explored the effect of SSRIs (a type of antidepressant) on DEPRESSION (see s. 7), there are many different brands of SSRIs produced by different companies. We could sample five of these: this is a random sample of a larger set of SSRIs that we could have chosen to study. Also, changing one of the five brands to a different randomly sampled brand does not change the research question, which is still 'do antidepressants reduce depression?'.   *AF*

range   The difference between the lowest and highest scores in a set of scores.   *GH*

ranking data   A common procedure used in DISTRIBUTION-FREE METHODS in which the data are placed in ascending or descending order and assigned values (called ranks) that reflect their relative position within this order. The ranks are then analysed instead of the raw data.   *AF*

ratio data   INTERVAL DATA, but with the additional property that ratios are meaningful (e.g. a score of 4 indicates twice as much of a property as a score of 2).   *AF*

reciprocal transformation   A TRANSFORMATION of values of a VARIABLE in which the transformed value is simply 1 divided by the original value:

$$y_i = \frac{1}{x_i}$$

This is used when the SAMPLE DISTRIBUTION is not a NORMAL DISTRIBUTION and is most useful when the problem is large values in the positive tail of the distribution.   *AF*

regression   [See LINEAR REGRESSION and MULTIPLE REGRESSION]

regression to the mean   A term applied to reflect the fact that scores at the extreme of the scale of measurement are more likely to be closer to the centre of the DISTRIBUTION upon subsequent measurement. For example, looking at a measure of statistical ANXIETY (see s. 6) that ranged from 0 (not at all anxious) to 100 (plucking the hair from my head with anxiety), if this scale has a NORMAL DISTRIBUTION with a MEAN of 50, then scores of 0 and 100 will be very unlikely (most people will have scores around

50). Therefore, if you took a group of students who were all highly anxious when initially tested, all of their scores are improbable (they are rare events). If you measure them a week later, probabilistically their scores are likely to be less simply because their initial scores are so high that it is more likely that their scores will go down than up (there is lots of room for scores to go down but no room for them to go up). This is particularly problematic if, for example, we introduced an intervention to reduce statistical anxiety. At the second measure it would be hard to tell whether scores had gone down because of the intervention, or simply because probabilistically they will 'regress' to the mean of the distribution.   *AF*

related *t*-test   Synonym for the dependent *t*-test. [See STUDENT'S *T*-TEST]

reliability   The ability of a measure to produce consistent results when the same entities are measured under the same conditions. One way to conceptualise this is that, other things being equal, a person should get the same score on a measure if they complete it at two different points in time (this is called TEST-RETEST RELIABILITY). Another way to think of it is that two people, who are the same in terms of the construct being measured, should get the same score.

There are several ways to measure reliability, the simplest is to use SPLIT-HALF RELIABILITY, and a more complex measure is the commonly used CRONBACH'S ALPHA. (See also s. 6)   *AF*
Field 2005a.

repeated-measures design   An experimental design in which each participant takes part in all of the conditions in the experiment. (Also known as a 'WITHIN-SUBJECTS' DESIGN.)   *GH*

residual   The difference between the value a model predicts and the value observed in the data on which the model is based.   *AF*

residual sum of squares   See ANALYSIS OF VARIANCE

robust methods   A term applied for a family of procedures to estimate statistics that are reliable even when the normal assumptions of the statistic are not met. Possibly the simplest example is a TRIMMED MEAN. The MEAN of a DISTRIBUTION is notoriously influenced by OUTLIERS (see Field 2005a). Imagine we had 20 scores representing the annual income of students (in thousands, rounded to the nearest thousand):

2, 2, 2, 2, 3, 3, 3, 3, 3, 4, 4, 4, 4, 4, 4, 4, 4, 4, 6, 35

If we work out the mean income we get 5 (£5000). Now this is silly because the vast majority of students earn less than this per year. This estimate is biased. However, there is an outlier in that one student is very wealthy. A trimmed mean is simply a mean based on the distribution of scores after some percentage of scores has been removed from each extreme of the distribution. So, a 10 per cent trimmed mean will remove 10 per cent of scores from the top and bottom before the mean is calculated. If we do this for our data, then with 20 scores, removing 10 per cent involves removing the top and bottom 2 scores. This gives us:

2, 2, 3, 3, 3, 3, 3, 4, 4, 4, 4, 4, 4, 4, 4, 4,

the mean of which is 3.44. This is much more representative of the sample. This is an example of a robust method: the mean depends on a symmetrical distribution to be accurate, but a trimmed mean produces accurate results even when the distribution is not symmetrical. There are more complex examples of robust methods, such as the BOOTSTRAP. *AF*

Roy's largest root [See MULTIVARIATE ANALYSIS OF VARIANCE]

S

sample A smaller (but hopefully representative) collection of units from a POPULATION used to determine truths about that population (for example, how a given population behaves in certain conditions). *AF*

sample size The number of entities within a SAMPLE. The value of this property has implications for the POWER of any statistical procedure applied to the resulting data. *AF*

sampling The process of selecting entities for a SAMPLE. *AF*

sampling distribution The PROBABILITY DISTRIBUTION of a statistic. You can think of this as follows: if we take a SAMPLE from a POPULATION and calculate some statistic (for example, the MEAN), there will be SAMPLING VARIATION. If, hypothetically, we took lots and lots of samples from the population and calculated the statistic of interest, we could create a FREQUENCY DISTRIBUTION of the values obtained. The resulting DISTRIBUTION is what the sampling distribution represents: the distribution of possible values of a given statistic that we could expect to get from a given population. *AF*

sampling error The DEVIATION of a SAMPLE parameter or statistic from the 'true' value in the POPULATION. *AF*

sampling variation The fact that the value of any statistic estimated from a SAMPLE will depend somewhat on the sample taken. As such, the statistic will vary slightly from sample to sample. *AF*

scatterplot A graph showing the relationship between two INDEPENDENT VARIABLES, X and Y. Each point on the graph represents an individual's permutation of X and Y values. *GH*

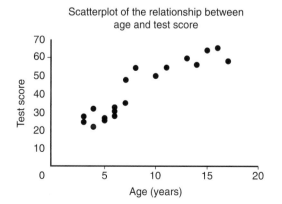

scatterplot

Scheffé test [See MULTIPLE COMPARISONS]

scree plot A plot of latent variables (*x*-axis) and their EIGENVALUES (*y*-axis) used in FACTOR ANALYSIS. *AF*

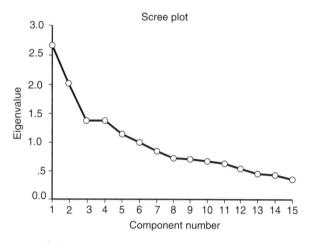

scree plot

significance [See HYPOTHESIS TESTING]

skewness The degree to which a FREQUENCY DISTRIBUTION is symmetrical. In a skewed distribution the most frequent scores (the tall bars on the graph) cluster at one end of the scale. In positively skewed [see POSITIVE SKEW] distributions, the frequent scores are clustered at the lower end and the tail of the distribution points towards the higher or more positive scores. In negatively skewed [see negative skew] distributions the opposite is true: frequent scores cluster at the higher end and the distribution tails off towards the lower, more negative, scores. We can measure skewness and, importantly, it should be 0 in a NORMAL DISTRIBUTION. Therefore, if your frequency distribution has positive or negative values of skew, this tells you that your distribution deviates somewhat from a normal distribution. *AF*

snowball sampling A snowball sample is used when a participant is used to introduce the researcher to further participants. *JM*

Spearman's rho Pearson's correlation coefficient [see CORRELATION COEFFICIENT] applied to ranked data [see RANKING DATA]. It is a distribution-free [see DISTRIBUTION-FREE METHODS] correlation coefficient and so can be used when the ASSUMPTIONS of PARAMETRIC METHODS have not been met. *AF*

sphericity The ASSUMPTION that the variances of the differences between data taken from the same participant (or other entity being tested) are equal (see Field 1998).

Skewness

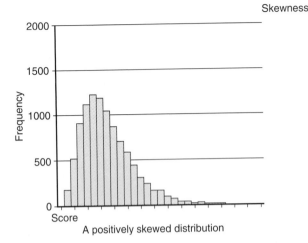

A positively skewed distribution

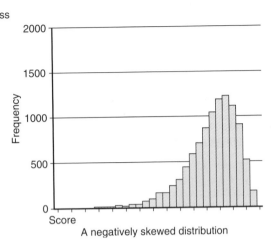

A negatively skewed distribution

skewness

This assumption is most commonly found in ANALYSIS OF VARIANCE when a REPEATED-MEASURES DESIGN is used and applies only when there are more than two points of data from the same participant (i.e. more than two LEVELS of the repeated-measures variable). The degree of sphericity can be assessed in different ways, the two most popular of which are estimates suggested by Greenhouse-Geisser and Huynh-Feldt (see Girden 1992 for computational details). The significance of departures from the assumption can be tested with MAUCHLY'S TEST. If the assumption is not met for an effect then the DEGREES OF FREEDOM for the resulting F-RATIO need to be corrected by multiplying them by one of the aforementioned estimates of sphericity [see GREENHOUSE-GEISSER CORRECTION and HUYNH-FELDT CORRECTION]. *AF*

Field 1998; **Field** 2005a; **Girden** 1992.

split-half reliability A means of assessing the reliability of a questionnaire or TEST (see s. 6): the correlation is measured between performance on one randomly selected half of the questionnaire/test and the other half (one method is to use odd- and even-numbered items). *GH*

square root transformation A TRANSFORMATION of values of a VARIABLE in which the transformed value is simply the square root of the original value:

$$y_i = \sqrt{x_i}$$

This is used when the SAMPLE DISTRIBUTION is not a NORMAL DISTRIBUTION and is useful for correcting SKEWNESS or stabilising variances. *AF*

standard deviation A measure of the spread of a set of scores around their MEAN: it is the average DEVIATION from the mean. As a description of a sample's properties, the formula is:

$$s = \sqrt{\frac{\sum_{i=1}^{n}(X_i - \overline{X})^2}{n}}$$

To use the SAMPLE s as an estimate of the POPULATION standard deviation, use n–1 as the denominator instead. *GH*

standard error of the mean (SE) This is the STANDARD DEVIATION of a set of SAMPLE means. Any sample MEAN is, in effect, a single estimate of the mean of the POPULATION from which the sample is drawn. Sample means are likely to vary from one sample to another [see SAMPLING VARIATION], and the standard error of the mean is a measure of this variability. In short, it is the standard deviation of the SAMPLING DISTRIBUTION. It indicates how much variation there is within a set of sample means, and hence the likely SAMPLING ERROR of the mean. The formula for the standard error is:

$$\sigma_{\bar{x}} = \frac{\sigma}{\sqrt{n}}$$

in which σ is the standard deviation in the population. Normally, because σ is unknown, the SE is estimated from our obtained sample data:

$$Estimated\ \sigma_{\bar{x}} = S_{\bar{x}} = \frac{s}{\sqrt{n-1}}$$

in which s is the standard deviation in the sample and n is the SAMPLE SIZE. The smaller the SE, the more likely it is that our obtained sample mean is similar to the true population mean. Note that increasing the sample size (n) reduces the size of the SE. Thus a sample mean based on 100 scores is likely to more *accurately* estimate the population mean than a sample mean based on 10 scores. *GH*

standardisation The process of converting a VARIABLE into a standard unit of measurement. The unit of measurement typically used is STANDARD DEVIATION units [see also z-SCORES]. Standardisation allows us to compare data when different units of measurement have been used (we could compare weight measured in Kg, with height measured in inches). *AF*

standardised regression coefficient [See BETA COEFFICIENT]

standardised residual The RESIDUAL of a model expressed in the STANDARD DEVIATION units [see STANDARDISATION]. Standardised residuals with an absolute value greater than about 3 are cause for concern because in an average sample a value this high is unlikely to happen by chance; if more than 1 per cent of our observations have standardised residuals with an absolute value greater than about 2.5 there is evidence that the level of error within our model is unacceptable (the model is a fairly poor fit of the SAMPLE data); and if more than 5 per cent of observations have standardised residuals with an absolute value greater than about 2 then there is also evidence that the model is a poor representation of the actual data.

See Field (2005a) for more specific and detailed advice.

AF

stepwise regression

stepwise regression   A method of MULTIPLE REGRESSION in which variables are entered into the model based on the semi-partial correlation with the OUTCOME VARIABLE. Once a new variable is entered into the model, all variables in the model are assessed to see whether they should be removed.

AF

structural equation modelling

structural equation modelling   Structural equation modelling (SEM) is a complex statistical technique, with its roots in FACTOR ANALYSIS and MULTIPLE REGRESSION. In most statistical techniques (such as *T*-TEST, REGRESSION, CORRELATION, factor analysis), your data are analysed, in an attempt to come up with a model – that model might be as simple as the MEAN value of a parameter, or the difference between two groups, or may be more complex, as in a multiple regression or a factor analysis. In SEM, the process is reversed – one starts with the model, and, in effect, asks 'could this model have generated my data?'

A structural equation model can be thought of as a system of equations, which can be represented more simply by using matrix algebra; however, it is usually easier and simpler to use a path diagram.

The model is represented in path diagram format using four basic elements: Correlations/COVARIANCES, represented by curved, two-headed arrows; regression estimates, represented by straight, single-headed arrows; measured variables, represented by rectangular boxes; and LATENT VARIABLES, represented by elliptical boxes.

A regression equation, with two predictors, x_1 and x_2, and a single outcome, y, could be written as:

$$y = b_1x_1 + b_2x_2 + e$$

The Figure shows the same regression equation, in path diagram format.

The two straight arrows labelled b_1 and b_2 are the regression coefficients, the curved arrow between x_1 and x_2 represents the correlation between the two predictor variables (note that, although this is not explicitly estimated in a regression equation, it is used in the calculation of the regression estimates and their standard errors.)

The variable e is a latent variable – this variable represents all of the other influences on the outcome that we have not measured – $R^2 = 1 - e$. While we do not usually think of R^2 in this way, it introduces the idea of a latent variable.

Using structural equation modelling to carry out a regression analysis will give the same results as if ordinary (least squares) regression were used; however SEM can also be used in situations where it would not be possible, or appropriate, to use other methods.

Perhaps the most common use of structural equation modelling is the confirmatory factor analysis (CFA). Confirmatory factor analysis is contrasted with exploratory factor analysis (EFA; usually just described as factor analysis; rarely shortened to FA). In EFA one explores the data to determine the structure. In CFA, one hypothesises that a certain structure exists, and attempts to explore the data to see if that structure can account for the data. The Figure shows a confirmatory factor analysis with 4 variables. We hypothesise that the latent variable (L) can account for the correlations between the measured variables.

The aim of the analysis is to find values for the loadings which reproduce as closely as possible the sample correlation or COVARIANCE MATRIX. (Note that it is usual to analyse covariance matrices).

The correlation matrix implied by the model presented in the Figure is found by multiplying the values in the paths that are used to travel from one variable to the next; the correlation between x_1 and x_2 is equal to $0.6 \times 0.7 = 0.42$. The full implied correlation matrix is as follows:

x_1	1			
x_2	0.42	1		
x_3	0.35	0.30	1	
x_4	0.28	0.24	0.20	1
	x_1	x_2	x_3	x_4

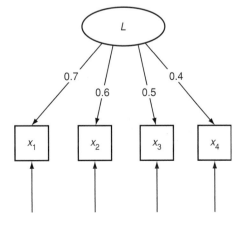

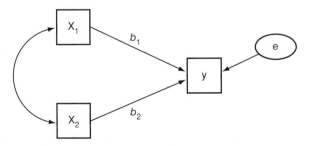

structural equation modelling *Path diagram representation of a simple regression*

structural equation modelling *Confirmatory factor analysis with 4 variables*

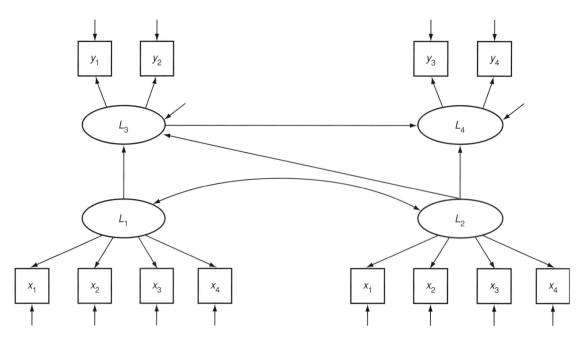

structural equation modelling *More complex path model*

The aim of the analysis is to find, via an iterative search, the values which give an implied covariance matrix as close as possible to the sample covariance matrix. The similarity between the two matrices can then be tested using a CHI-SQUARE TEST, which will give a probability value that the two matrices match (Bollen 1989). Low probability values (i.e. less than 0.05) imply that the model is incorrect.

More complex models, containing more than one latent variable, can be tested and the relations between these latent variables can include regression effects and correlations. The Figure contains a more complex model, in which 4 latent variables are represented, each measured by either 2 or 4 measured variables. The latent variables L_1 and L_2 are correlated. The variable L_3 is regressed on L_1 and L_2, the variable L_4 is regressed on L_2 and L_3. Note that L_1 and L_2 act as PREDICTOR (independent) VARIABLES, L_3 acts as both an outcome (dependent) and a predictor variable, and L_4 is only an outcome variable.

Probably the most controversial area in SEM is that of determining model fit. The χ^2 test, mentioned already, provides a probability associated with a particular model. However, the χ^2 has a number of problems associated with it. First, it can be sensitive to SAMPLE SIZE and model size. With large samples, the POWER of the χ^2 test to reject models can become excessive – if one were to rely solely on the χ^2 test, one would reject models which departed only trivially from the data. The power of the χ^2 test is also affected by the complexity of the model – more complex models (with higher *df*) have more power; and finally, the test is affected by the size of the correlations in the data – models with higher correlations have much higher power to reject the model.

A number of approaches have been developed to assist in the interpretation of model fit. The RMSEA is measure of fit that uses χ^2, along with the sample size and model complexity (*df*) – it can be thought of as a measure of

approximate fit. The incremental fit indices are a family of fit indices which compare the model with the null, or baseline model – that is, the worst model that is possible. The standardised root mean residual is a measure of the difference between the implied covariance matrix and the sample covariance matrix. In an important paper Hu and Bentler (1999) provided recommendations for combinations of fit indices that can be used to determine model fit.   *JM*

Bollen 1989; **Hoyle** 1995; **Hu and Bentler** 1999; **Miles and Shevlin** 2003.

student's *t*-test The *t*-test is used to determine whether two means differ significantly (i.e. differ to an extent that is unlikely to have occurred by chance). It is most commonly used to analyse the results from a simple two-condition experiment, but it is also the TEST STATISTIC used in a variety of other contexts (for the CORRELATION COEFFICIENT, the BETA COEFFICIENTS in REGRESSION and for PLANNED COMPARISONS).

There are two versions of the *t*-test. The dependent-means *t*-test (also known as the MATCHED-PAIRS *T*-TEST or repeated-measures *t*-test) is used when the same people participate in both conditions of an experiment. The INDE-PENDENT *T*-TEST (also known as an independent measures *t*-test) is used when there are two different groups of participants, one group performing one condition in the experiment, and the other group performing the other condition.

In both cases, there is one INDEPENDENT VARIABLE or PREDICTOR VARIABLE, with two levels (the two different conditions of the experiment); and a single DEPENDENT VARIABLE or OUTCOME VARIABLE (the measurement of the conditions' effects on performance). Each participant therefore produces either a single score (in the case of the independent-means *t*-test) or a pair of scores (in the case of the repeated-measures *t*-test).

Essentially, both formulae use the following logic. Consider the independent-means t-test first. In a proper experiment, participants are assigned randomly to group X or group Y. Therefore, initially, participants in group X come from the same POPULATION as those in group Y. If there is no effect of the experimental manipulation, scores from the two groups are effectively two samples of scores which have been drawn from the same population of scores. Another way to look at this is to say that group X is a SAMPLE from population X, and group Y is a sample from population Y – and that populations X and Y have identical characteristics (e.g. the same MEANS). The top line of the formula compares the *actual* difference between the mean of sample X and the mean of sample Y, to the *hypothesised* difference between the means of the two populations, X and Y, from which the samples are thought to come. (The latter is usually zero, because we assume that the two populations are identical; however, it is included in the formulae to allow for special cases when a systematic difference between population means is expected).

The difference between the observed and expected differences is divided by an estimate of the extent to which differences are likely to vary, based on the standard error of the differences between sample means. For independent samples t is:

$$t = \frac{(\overline{X} - \overline{Y}) - (\mu_X - \mu_Y)}{\sqrt{\left(\frac{(n_x - 1)s_x^2 + (n_y - 1)s_y^2}{n_x + n_y - 2}\right)\left(\frac{1}{n_x} + \frac{1}{n_y}\right)}}$$

In which n_x and n_y are the sample sizes of groups X and Y, s^2 represents the respective VARIANCES from these two groups, and μ represents the hypothesised population mean for each group.

The resultant value of t reflects the extent to which the difference between the two sample means is more extreme than one would expect if the two samples had come from identical populations: the larger the value of t, the less likely it is to have occurred by chance and the more plausible it is that it has arisen because the two samples did not in fact come from identical populations (which supports the ALTERNATIVE HYPOTHESIS). In practice, this is assessed by comparing the obtained t-value to the range of possible t-values that could occur: if the obtained t is larger than a critical value of t on this scale (normally the value of t which has a probability of occurring by chance of less than .05), then it is assumed that it is unlikely to have arisen by chance, and therefore that the difference between the sample means has occurred because they originated from different populations. (By chance, values of t have a frequency distribution that is similar to the normal distribution, but more LEPTOKURTIC, i.e., small values of t are highly likely to occur by chance; values of t that are much smaller or much larger than zero can occur by chance, but this is increasingly unlikely the larger the value of t).

The dependent-means t-test formula follows similar logic, but differs because it capitalises on the fact that the same people have participated in both conditions being compared. This means that variance between the conditions is likely to originate only from the effects of the experimenter's manipulations.

The formula for the repeated-measures t-test is:

$$t = \frac{\overline{D} - \mu_D}{S_{\overline{D}}}$$

where $\overline{D}$ is the mean difference between the two sets of scores, $S_{\overline{D}}$ is the standard error of the differences and μ_D is the hypothesised mean difference between conditions X and Y: this is normally set to zero, under the NULL HYPOTHESIS that the mean difference in the population of differences is zero.

The t-test is a PARAMETRIC METHOD and, in theory at least, it will only give meaningful results if the data meet the appropriate assumptions [see PARAMETRIC METHODS]. In practice, the t-test has been shown to be fairly robust with respect to violations of these ASSUMPTIONS, especially (in the case of the independent-measures version) if there are equal numbers of participants in the two conditions and the number of participants is reasonably large. Statistical programs such as SPSS usually offer alternative versions of the independent-measures t-test formula which do not assume HOMOGENEITY OF VARIANCE, if this is in doubt. However, if the data do not meet the requirements for a t-test, probably the best course of action is to use an alternative non-parametric test, such as the MANN-WHITNEY TEST or WILCOXON RANK SUM TEST (both equivalent to an independent-measures t-test) and the WILCOXON SIGNED RANK TEST (equivalent to a repeated-measures t-test). *GH*

Field 2005a; **Field and Hole** 2003.

sum of squared errors An estimate of total variability (spread) of a set of data. First the DEVIATION of each score from the MEAN is calculated, and then this value is squared. The sum of squared errors is the sum of these squared deviations from the mean:

$$ss = \sum_{i=1}^{n} (X_i - \overline{X})^2$$

The sum of squared errors is frequently used as a measure of variability, for example in ANALYSIS OF VARIANCE, MULTIVARIATE ANALYSIS OF VARIANCE, MULTIPLE REGRESSION, etc. *AF*

systematic sampling A systematic sample is a SAMPLE constructed by taking every nth individual from a list of names. *AF*

systematic variation Variation due to some genuine effect (e.g. the effect of an experimenter doing something to all of the participants in one sample but not in other samples). You can think of this as variation that can be explained by the model that has been fitted to the data. *AF*

461

T

test-retest reliability [See RELIABILITY]

test statistic A statistic with a known PROBABILITY DISTRIBUTION; that is, we know how frequently different values of this statistic occur. The observed value of such a statistic is typically used to test hypotheses [see HYPOTHESIS TESTING]. *AF*

theory Although it can be defined more formally, a theory is essentially a hypothesised general principle, or set of principles, that explains known findings about a topic and from which new hypotheses [see HYPOTHESIS] can be generated. *AF*

third variable problem The possibility that an apparent relationship between two variables is actually caused by the effect of a third VARIABLE on them both (often called a tertium quid). For example, in the 1970s there would have been a strong relationship between having long hair and taking drugs like LSD. Does this mean that taking LSD makes your hair grow? Probably not, and even if it did you could just cut it more regularly. Does it mean that having long hair overheats your brain and makes it desire LSD? Again, probably not. However, it is likely that both hair length and drug taking were influenced by a third variable, such as musical taste or, to be more precise, the NORMS (see s. 5 and s. 6) of certain social groups based around certain genres of music. *AF*

three-way design An experimental design in which there are three PREDICTOR VARIABLES (INDEPENDENT VARIABLES). *AF*

time series design Research involving measuring a VARIABLE (or variables) at (usually) regular intervals over a long period of time. *AF*

tolerance The tolerance is used in MULTIPLE REGRESSION to diagnose MULTICOLLINEARITY. It is calculated as $1-R^2$, where a regression is carried out on each of the PREDICTOR VARIABLES as an OUTCOME VARIABLE, and all of the other predictors as predictors. [See also VARIANCE INFLATION FACTOR (VIF)] *JM*

transformation The process of changing values of a VARIABLE to a new scale of measurement. It is typically done to correct distributional problems [see LOGARITHMIC TRANSFORMATION, RECIPROCAL TRANSFORMATION, SQUARE ROOT TRANSFORMATION]. *AF*

trend A pattern in a set of observations. The term can be used in two contexts. The first is when the data tend towards the predicted pattern but not significantly so, people will often say there is a 'trend'. However, more formally it relates to testing specific patterns in the data, for example, the pattern of means following ANALYSIS OF VARIANCE on groups that have a meaningful order. The simplest trend is a LINEAR TREND. However, it is possible to test for more complex trends, such as a quadratic trend, in which a curve with one change in direction can be fitted to the data (or ordered means), a cubic trend, in which a curve with two changes in direction can be fitted to the data (or ordered means), or a quartic trend, in which the curve fitted to the data has three changes in direction. See Field (2005a) for more detail. *AF*

trimmed mean [See ROBUST METHODS]

two-tailed test A test of a non-directional HYPOTHESIS. For example, the hypothesis, 'writing these entries has some effect on the degree to which I want to shoot the editor', requires a two-tailed test because it does not suggest the direction of the relationship. [See also ONE-TAILED TEST] *AF*

two-way design An experimental design in which there are two PREDICTOR VARIABLES (INDEPENDENT VARIABLES). *AF*

type I error Believing that there is a genuine effect in the POPULATION, when in reality no such effect exists. *AF*

type II error Believing that there is no effect in the POPULATION, when in reality there is. *AF*

U

univariate data Data involving a single measurement of each entity on a single OUTCOME VARIABLE. *AF*

unsystematic variance Variation in the OUTCOME VARIABLE that is not due to the effect in which we are interested. *AF*

V

validity Evidence that a study allows correct inferences to and a test measures what it set out to address conceptually. (See also s. 6, VALIDITY) *SH*

variable Anything that can be measured and can differ across entities or across time. *AF*

variance A measure of the average variability (spread) of scores that is not in the original units of measurement. The SUM OF SQUARED ERRORS is a measure of the total variability, and the variance is simply this value divided by the number of observations or values used to calculate that total. As such, it is given by:

$$s^2 = \frac{\sum_{i=1}^{n} (X_i - \overline{X})^2}{n}$$

However, in psychology we are usually interested in the POPULATION variance, not the SAMPLE variance. The equation above gives us the sample variance. However, the sample can be used to estimate the population by simply dividing by $n-1$ rather than n. In doing so we are dividing by the DEGREES OF FREEDOM for this estimate:

$$s^2 = \frac{\sum_{i=1}^{n} (X_i - \overline{X})^2}{n - 1}$$

It is important to understand that the sum of squared errors, the variance and the STANDARD DEVIATION are all proportionate: they are all measures of the variability or spread of scores. The sum of squared errors is based on the total variability, the variance is the average variability, and the standard deviation is simply the average variability but in the original units of measurement (remember that the sum of squared errors and variance are based on deviations squared and so are measured in the original units squared; the standard deviation returns things to the original units of measurement by taking the square root of the variance). *AF*

variance-covariance matrix A square matrix (i.e. same number of columns and rows) in which each column represents a measured VARIABLE and the rows represent the same variables as the columns and in the same order. The diagonal elements are the VARIANCES of each variable, whereas the off-diagonal elements are the COVARIANCES between pairs of variables. *AF*

variance inflation factor (VIF) The reciprocal of the TOLERANCE used in MULTIPLE REGRESSION to diagnose MULTICOLLINEARITY; it shows the amount the standard error of the parameter estimates has increased, as a result of multicollinearity. *JM*

visual analogue scale A way of measuring some psychological construct (such as ANXIETY – see s. 6) using a line with verbal anchors at the extremes (e.g. 'not at all anxious' and 'extremely anxious'). Participants place a mark on the line to indicate how they feel, the distance from one end of the line to the mark is measured and converted into a convenient scale (often a percentage). *AF*

volunteer sampling A SAMPLE consisting of people who have volunteered to take part in research. *AF*

W

weighted average   A MEAN in which observations are given a numeric weight reflecting their importance. For example, in META-ANALYSIS EFFECT SIZES are weighted by their SAMPLE SIZE because larger samples produce better estimates of the population effect size. The general form of a weighted average is:

$$\overline{X} = \frac{\sum\limits_{i=1}^{n} w_i x_i}{\sum\limits_{i=1}^{n} w_i}$$

in which w represents the weight for each observation.

AF

Wilcoxon rank sum test   A DISTRIBUTION-FREE METHOD for testing differences between two independent samples. It tests whether the populations from which two samples are drawn have the same location. It is functionally the same as the MANN-WHITNEY TEST, and both tests are distribution-free equivalents of the INDEPENDENT T-TEST. The test, like many distribution-free methods, works on the ranks of the data. The data are ranked irrespective of the group from which they came. The TEST STATISTIC is simply the sum of ranks for the smallest group, or when the groups are equal in size it is the smaller of the two summed ranks.

AF

Wilcoxon signed rank test   A DISTRIBUTION-FREE METHOD for testing differences between two dependent samples. It is the distribution-free version of the dependent t-test. It works in a fairly similar way to the dependent t-test in that it is based on the differences between scores in the two conditions being compared. Once these differences have been calculated they are ranked [see RANKING DATA], but the sign of the difference (positive or negative) is assigned to the rank. Finally, we add together the ranks that came from a positive difference, to get the sum of positive ranks (T_+), and we add up the ranks that came from negative differences to get the sum of negative ranks (T_-). The TEST STATISTIC, T, is the smaller of the two values. See Field (2005a) for more detail.

AF

Wilk's lambda   [See MULTIVARIATE ANALYSIS OF VARIANCE]

within-subjects design   [See REPEATED MEASURES DESIGN]

Y

Yates' correction for continuity A correction applied to Pearson's CHI-SQUARE TEST which tends to make a TYPE I ERROR when a 2×2 CONTINGENCY TABLE is used. Yates' continuity correction involves subtracting 0.5 when the DEVIATION from the model is calculated; Pearson's equation then becomes:

$$\chi^2 = \sum_{i=1}^{r} \sum_{j=1}^{c} \left(\frac{(\mid Observed_{ij} - Expected_{ij} \mid - 0.5)^2}{Expected_{ij}} \right)$$

This correction lowers the value of the chi-square statistic and, therefore, makes it less significant. There is a fair bit of evidence that this over-corrects and produces chi-square values that are too small (see Howell 2002).   *AF*

Field 2005a; **Howell** 2002.

Z

z-scores z-scores are a means of converting scores from their original raw score into a standardised format on a scale that is measured in STANDARD DEVIATIONS. The raw score is, therefore, expressed in terms of its standing relative to the MEAN of the set of scores from which it comes. z-scores are measurements on a scale which always has a mean of 0 and a standard deviation of 1. They make explicit the relationship of a score to the mean of the set of scores. They also provide a means by which scores measured on different scales can be made equivalent for ease of comparison.

The formula for converting a raw score into a z-score is:

$$z = \frac{X - \overline{X}}{s}$$

where X is the raw score, $\overline{X}$ is the mean of the sample of scores from which X originates, and s is the sample standard deviation. *GH*

z-test A STATISTICAL TEST to determine the probability of obtaining a given sample MEAN by chance, given knowledge of the parent POPULATION's mean and STANDARD DEVIATION. The sample mean is converted into a z-SCORE, so that it is expressed in terms of its difference from the population mean. It is then possible to assess how probable it is to obtain that value of z by chance. Differences between sample means and the mean of their parent population show a NORMAL DISTRIBUTION. Most sample means should be very similar to the population mean, and hence should produce z-scores which are close to zero. Large deviations between sample and population means (and hence large values of z) will occur by chance only rarely; they are more likely to arise because the sample did not in fact come from the hypothesised population at all. In practice, the z-test is rarely used, because the necessary population characteristics (mean and sd) are usually unknown and can only be estimated from the sample data – in which case the t-test is used. *GH*

REFERENCES FOR SECTION 8

Altman, D. G., Machin, D., Bryant, T. N. and Gardner, M. J. 2000: *Statistics with Confidence: Confidence Intervals and Statistical Guidelines* (2nd edn). London: British Medical Journal Books.

Billig, M. 1997: Rhetorical and discursive analysis: how families talk about the royal family. In Hayes, N. (ed.), *Doing Qualitative Analysis in Psychology*. Hove: Psychology Press, 39–54.

Bollen, K. A. 1989: *Structural Equations with Latent Variables*. Wiley.

Bray, J. H. and Maxwell, S. E. 1985: *Multivariate Analysis of Variance*. Newbury Park CA: Sage.

Chow, S. L. 1996: *Statistical Significance: Rationale, Validity and Utility*. London: Sage.

Clark-Carter, D. 2003: Effect size: the missing piece in the jigsaw. *The Psychologist* 16(12), 636–8.

Cohen, J. 1968: Multiple regression as a general data-analytic system. *Psychological Bulletin* 70(6), 426–43.

Cohen, J. 1988: *Statistical Power Analysis for the Behavioural Sciences* (2nd edn). New York: Academic Press.

Cohen, J. 1990: Things I have learned (so far). *American Psychologist* 45(12), 1304–12.

Cohen, J. 1992: A power primer. *Psychological Bulletin* 112(1), 155–9.

Cohen, J. 1994: The earth is round (p-less-than .05). *American Psychologist* 49(12), 997–1003.

Cohen, J., Cohen, P., Aiken, L. and West, S. 2003: *Applied Multiple Regression/Correlation Analysis for the Behavioural Sciences*. Hillsdale NJ: Erlbaum.

Cortina, J. M. 1993: What is coefficient alpha? An examination of theory and applications. *Journal of Applied Psychology* 78, 98–104.

Cronbach, L. J. 1951: Coefficient alpha and the internal structure of tests. *Psychometrika* 16, 297–334.

Dunteman, G. E. 1989: *Principal Components Analysis*. Newbury Park CA: Sage.

Durbin, J. and Watson, G. S. 1951: Testing for serial correlation in least squares regression, II. *Biometrika* 30, 159–78.

Efron, B. 1983: Computer intensive methods in statistics. *Scientific American* (May), 116–30.

Efron, B. and Tibshirani, R. 1993: *An Introduction to the Bootstrap*. New York: Chapman and Hall.

Field, A. P. 1998: A bluffer's guide to sphericity. *Newsletter of the Mathematical, Statistical and Computing Section of the British Psychological Society* 6(1), 13–22.

Field, A. P. 2001: Meta-analysis of correlation coefficients: a Monte Carlo comparison of fixed- and random-effects methods. *Psychological Methods* 6(2), 161–80.

Field, A. P. 2003a: Can meta-analysis be trusted? *Psychologist* 16(12), 642–5.

Field, A. P. 2003b: The problems in using fixed-effects models of meta-analysis on real-world data. *Understanding Statistics* 2, 77–96.

Field, A. P. 2005a: *Discovering Statistics Using SPSS* (2nd edn). London: Sage.

Field, A. P. 2005b: Intraclass Correlation. In Everitt, B. and Howell, D. C. (eds) *Encyclopedia of Behavioral Statistics*. New York: Wiley.

Field, A. P. 2005c: Kendall's Coefficient of Concordance. In Everitt, B. and Howell, D. C. (eds) *Encyclopedia of Behavioral Statistics*. New York: Wiley.

Field, A. P. and Hole, G. J. 2003: *How to Design and Report Experiments*. London: Sage.

Fisher, R. A. 1921: On the probable error of a coefficient of correlation deduced from a small sample. *Metron* 1, 3–32.

Fox, J. 1991: *Regression Diagnostics: An Introduction*. Newbury Park CA: Sage.

Friedman, M. 1937: The use of ranks to avoid the assumption of normality implicit in the analysis of variance. *Journal of the American Statistical Association* 32, 675–701.

Girden, E. R. 1992: *ANOVA: Repeated Measures*. Newbury Park CA: Sage.

Grayson, D. 2004: Some myths and legends in quantitative psychology. *Understanding Statistics* 3(1), 101–34.

Harlow, L. L., Mulaik, S. A. and Steiger, J. H. (eds) 1997: *What If There Were No Significance Tests?* Mahwah NJ: Lawrence Erlbaum Associates.

Hedges, L. V. 1992: Meta-analysis. *Journal of Educational Statistics* 17(4), 279–96.

Hedges, L. V. and Olkin, I. 1985: *Statistical Methods for Meta-analysis*. Orlando FL: Academic Press.

Hedges, L. V. and Vevea, J. L. 1998: Fixed- and random-effects models in meta-analysis. *Psychological Methods* 3(4), 486–504.

Hosmer, D. W. and Lemeshow, S. 1989: *Applied Logistic Regression*. New York: Wiley.

Howell, D. C. 2002: *Statistical Methods for Psychology* (5th edn). Belmont CA: Duxbury.

Hoyle, R. H. (ed.) 1995: *Structural Equation Modelling: Concepts, Issues and Applications*. Thousand Oaks CA: Sage.

Hu, L. and Bentler, P. M. 1999: Cutoff criteria for fit indexes in covariance structure analysis: conventional criteria versus new alternatives. *Structural Equation Modeling* 6, 1–55.

Hunter, J. E. and Schmidt, F. L. 1990: *Methods of Meta-analysis: Correcting Error and Bias in Research Findings*. Newbury Park CA: Sage.

Hunter, J. E. and Schmidt, F. L. 2000: Fixed effects versus random effects meta-analysis models: implications for cumulative knowledge in psychology. *International Journal of Selection and Assessment* 8, 275–92.

Klecka, W. R. 1980: *Discriminant Analysis*. Newbury Park CA: Sage.

Kline, P. 1999: *The Handbook of Psychological Testing* (2nd edn). London: Routledge.

Miles, J. and Shevlin, M. 2001: *Applying Regression and Correlation: A Guide for Students and Researchers*. London: Sage.

Miles, J. N. V. and Shevlin, M. 2003: Navigating spaghetti junction: structural equation models in psychological research. *The Psychologist* 16(12), 639–41.

Mill, J. S. 1865: *A System of Logic: Ratiocinative and Inductive*. London: Longmans, Green.

Pedhazur, E. and Schmelkin, L. 1991: *Measurement, Design and Analysis*. Hillsdale NJ: Erlbaum.

Rosenthal, R. 1991: *Meta-analytic Procedures for Social Research* (rev. edn). Newbury Park CA: Sage.

Rosenthal, R. and Rubin, D. 1978: Interpersonal expectancy effects: the first 345 studies. *Behavioral and Brain Sciences* 3, 377–415.

Rutherford, A. 2000: *Introducing ANOVA and ANCOVA: A GLM Approach.* London: Sage.

Schmidt, F. L. 1996: Statistical significance testing and cumulative knowledge in psychology: implications for training of researchers. *Psychological Methods* 1(2), 115–29.

Smithson, M. J. 2003: *Confidence Intervals.* Belmont CA: Sage.

Steiger, J. H. and Fouladi, R. T. 1997: Noncentrality interval estimation and the evaluation of statistical models. In Harlow, L., Mulaik, S. and Steiger, J. H. (eds), *What If There Were No Significance Tests?* Hillsdale NJ: Erlbaum, 222–57.

Stevens, J. P. 1992: *Applied Multivariate Statistics for the Social Sciences* (2nd edn). Hillsdale NJ: Erlbaum.

Tabachnick, B. G. and Fidell, L. S. 2001: *Using Multivariate Statistics* (4th edn). Boston: Allyn & Bacon.

Thompson, B. 1985: *Canonical Correlation Analysis: Uses and Interpretation.* Newbury Park CA: Sage.

Wildt, A. R. and Ahtola, O. T. 1978: *Analysis of Covariance.* Newbury Park CA: Sage.

Wright, D. B. 1997: *Understanding Statistics: An Introduction for the Social Sciences.* London: Sage.

Wright, D. B. 2002: *First Steps in Statistics.* London: Sage.

APPENDIX 1 Probability values of *z*-scores from the normal distribution (values calculated by Andy Field using SPSS version 11)

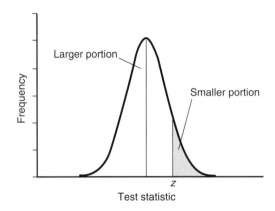

test statistic

z	Larger Portion	Smaller Portion	y		z	Larger Portion	Smaller Portion	y
.00	.50000	.50000	.3989		.38	.64803	.35197	.3712
.01	.50399	.49601	.3989		.39	.65173	.34827	.3697
.02	.50798	.49202	.3989		.40	.65542	.34458	.3683
.03	.51197	.48803	.3988		.41	.65910	.34090	.3668
.04	.51595	.48405	.3986		.42	.66276	.33724	.3653
.05	.51994	.48006	.3984		.43	.66640	.33360	.3637
.06	.52392	.47608	.3982		.44	.67003	.32997	.3621
.07	.52790	.47210	.3980		.45	.67364	.32636	.3605
.08	.53188	.46812	.3977		.46	.67724	.32276	.3589
.09	.53586	.46414	.3973		.47	.68082	.31918	.3572
.10	.53983	.46017	.3970		.48	.68439	.31561	.3555
.11	.54380	.45620	.3965		.49	.68793	.31207	.3538
.12	.54776	.45224	.3961		.50	.69146	.30854	.3521
.13	.55172	.44828	.3956		.51	.69497	.30503	.3503
.14	.55567	.44433	.3951		.52	.69847	.30153	.3485
.15	.55962	.44038	.3945		.53	.70194	.29806	.3467
.16	.56356	.43644	.3939		.54	.70540	.29460	.3448
.17	.56749	.43251	.3932		.55	.70884	.29116	.3429
.18	.57142	.42858	.3925		.56	.71226	.28774	.3410
.19	.57535	.42465	.3918		.57	.71566	.28434	.3391
.20	.57926	.42074	.3910		.58	.71904	.28096	.3372
.21	.58317	.41683	.3902		.59	.72240	.27760	.3352
.22	.58706	.41294	.3894		.60	.72575	.27425	.3332
.23	.59095	.40905	.3885		.61	.72907	.27093	.3312
.24	.59483	.40517	.3876		.62	.73237	.26763	.3292
.25	.59871	.40129	.3867		.63	.73565	.26435	.3271
.26	.60257	.39743	.3857		.64	.73891	.26109	.3251
.27	.60642	.39358	.3847		.65	.74215	.25785	.3230
.28	.61026	.38974	.3836		.66	.74537	.25463	.3209
.29	.61409	.38591	.3825		.67	.74857	.25143	.3187
.30	.61791	.38209	.3814		.68	.75175	.24825	.3166
.31	.62172	.37828	.3802		.69	.75490	.24510	.3144
.32	.62552	.37448	.3790		.70	.75804	.24196	.3123
.33	.62930	.37070	.3778		.71	.76115	.23885	.3101
.34	.63307	.36693	.3765		.72	.76424	.23576	.3079
.35	.63683	.36317	.3752		.73	.76730	.23270	.3056
.36	.64058	.35942	.3739		.74	.77035	.22965	.3034
.37	.64431	.35569	.3725		.75	.77337	.22663	.3011

z	Larger Portion	Smaller Portion	y	z	Larger Portion	Smaller Portion	y
.76	.77637	.22363	.2989	1.38	.91621	.08379	.1539
.77	.77935	.22065	.2966	1.39	.91774	.08226	.1518
.78	.78230	.21770	.2943	1.40	.91924	.08076	.1497
.79	.78524	.21476	.2920	1.41	.92073	.07927	.1476
.80	.78814	.21186	.2897	1.42	.92220	.07780	.1456
.81	.79103	.20897	.2874	1.43	.92364	.07636	.1435
.82	.79389	.20611	.2850	1.44	.92507	.07493	.1415
.83	.79673	.20327	.2827	1.45	.92647	.07353	.1394
.84	.79955	.20045	.2803	1.46	.92785	.07215	.1374
.85	.80234	.19766	.2780	1.47	.92922	.07078	.1354
.86	.80511	.19489	.2756	1.48	.93056	.06944	.1334
.87	.80785	.19215	.2732	1.49	.93189	.06811	.1315
.88	.81057	.18943	.2709	1.50	.93319	.06681	.1295
.89	.81327	.18673	.2685	1.51	.93448	.06552	.1276
.90	.81594	.18406	.2661	1.52	.93574	.06426	.1257
.91	.81859	.18141	.2637	1.53	.93699	.06301	.1238
.92	.82121	.17879	.2613	1.54	.93822	.06178	.1219
.93	.82381	.17619	.2589	1.55	.93943	.06057	.1200
.94	.82639	.17361	.2565	1.56	.94062	.05938	.1182
.95	.82894	.17106	.2541	1.57	.94179	.05821	.1163
.96	.83147	.16853	.2516	1.58	.94295	.05705	.1145
.97	.83398	.16602	.2492	1.59	.94408	.05592	.1127
.98	.83646	.16354	.2468	1.60	.94520	.05480	.1109
.99	.83891	.16109	.2444	1.61	.94630	.05370	.1092
1.00	.84134	.15866	.2420	1.62	.94738	.05262	.1074
1.01	.84375	.15625	.2396	1.63	.94845	.05155	.1057
1.02	.84614	.15386	.2371	1.64	.94950	.05050	.1040
1.03	.84849	.15151	.2347	1.65	.95053	.04947	.1023
1.04	.85083	.14917	.2323	1.66	.95154	.04846	.1006
1.05	.85314	.14686	.2299	1.67	.95254	.04746	.0989
1.06	.85543	.14457	.2275	1.68	.95352	.04648	.0973
1.07	.85769	.14231	.2251	1.69	.95449	.04551	.0957
1.08	.85993	.14007	.2227	1.70	.95543	.04457	.0940
1.09	.86214	.13786	.2203	1.71	.95637	.04363	.0925
1.10	.86433	.13567	.2179	1.72	.95728	.04272	.0909
1.11	.86650	.13350	.2155	1.73	.95818	.04182	.0893
1.12	.86864	.13136	.2131	1.74	.95907	.04093	.0878
1.13	.87076	.12924	.2107	1.75	.95994	.04006	.0863
1.14	.87286	.12714	.2083	1.76	.96080	.03920	.0848
1.15	.87493	.12507	.2059	1.77	.96164	.03836	.0833
1.16	.87698	.12302	.2036	1.78	.96246	.03754	.0818
1.17	.87900	.12100	.2012	1.79	.96327	.03673	.0804
1.18	.88100	.11900	.1989	1.80	.96407	.03593	.0790
1.19	.88298	.11702	.1965	1.81	.96485	.03515	.0775
1.20	.88493	.11507	.1942	1.82	.96562	.03438	.0761
1.21	.88686	.11314	.1919	1.83	.96638	.03362	.0748
1.22	.88877	.11123	.1895	1.84	.96712	.03288	.0734
1.23	.89065	.10935	.1872	1.85	.96784	.03216	.0721
1.24	.89251	.10749	.1849	1.86	.96856	.03144	.0707
1.25	.89435	.10565	.1826	1.87	.96926	.03074	.0694
1.26	.89617	.10383	.1804	1.88	.96995	.03005	.0681
1.27	.89796	.10204	.1781	1.89	.97062	.02938	.0669
1.28	.89973	.10027	.1758	1.90	.97128	.02872	.0656
1.29	.90147	.09853	.1736	1.91	.97193	.02807	.0644
1.30	.90320	.09680	.1714	1.92	.97257	.02743	.0632
1.31	.90490	.09510	.1691	1.93	.97320	.02680	.0620
1.32	.90658	.09342	.1669	1.94	.97381	.02619	.0608
1.33	.90824	.09176	.1647	1.95	.97441	.02559	.0596
1.34	.90988	.09012	.1626	1.96	.97500	.02500	.0584
1.35	.91149	.08851	.1604	1.97	.97558	.02442	.0573
1.36	.91309	.08691	.1582	1.98	.97615	.02385	.0562
1.37	.91466	.08534	.1561	1.99	.97670	.02330	.0551

z	Larger Portion	Smaller Portion	y	z	Larger Portion	Smaller Portion	y
2.00	.97725	.02275	.0540	2.54	.99446	.00554	.0158
2.01	.97778	.02222	.0529	2.55	.99461	.00539	.0154
2.02	.97831	.02169	.0519	2.56	.99477	.00523	.0151
2.03	.97882	.02118	.0508	2.57	.99492	.00508	0147
2.04	.97932	.02068	.0498	2.58	.99506	.00494	.0143
2.05	.97982	.02018	.0488	2.59	.99520	.00480	.0139
2.06	.98030	.01970	.0478	2.60	.99534	.00466	.0136
2.07	.98077	.01923	.0468	2.61	.99547	.00453	.0132
2.08	.98124	.01876	.0459	2.62	.99560	.00440	.0129
2.09	.98169	.01831	.0449	2.63	.99573	.00427	.0126
2.10	.98214	.01786	.0440	2.64	.99585	.00415	.0122
2.11	.98257	.01743	.0431	2.65	.99598	.00402	.0119
2.12	.98300	.01700	.0422	2.66	.99609	.00391	.0116
2.13	.98341	.01659	.0413	2.67	.99621	.00379	.0113
2.14	.98382	.01618	.0404	2.68	.99632	.00368	.0110
2.15	.98422	.01578	.0396	2.69	.99643	.00357	.0107
2.16	.98461	.01539	.0387	2.70	.99653	.00347	.0104
2.17	.98500	.01500	.0379	2.71	.99664	.00336	.0101
2.18	.98537	.01463	.0371	2.72	.99674	.00326	.0099
2.19	.98574	.01426	.0363	2.73	.99683	.00317	.0096
2.20	.98610	.01390	.0355	2.74	.99693	.00307	.0093
2.21	.98645	.01355	.0347	2.75	.99702	.00298	.0091
2.22	.98679	.01321	.0339	2.76	.99711	.00289	.0088
2.23	.98713	.01287	.0332	2.77	.99720	.00280	.0086
2.24	.98745	.01255	.0325	2.78	.99728	.00272	.0084
2.25	.98778	.01222	.0317	2.79	.99736	.00264	.0081
2.26	.98809	.01191	.0310	2.80	.99744	.00256	.0079
2.27	.98840	.01160	.0303	2.81	.99752	.00248	.0077
2.28	.98870	.01130	.0297	2.82	.99760	.00240	.0075
2.29	.98899	.01101	.0290	2.83	.99767	.00233	.0073
2.30	.98928	.01072	.0283	2.84	.99774	.00226	.0071
2.31	.98956	.01044	.0277	2.85	.99781	.00219	.0069
2.32	.98983	.01017	.0270	2.86	.99788	.00212	.0067
2.33	.99010	.00990	.0264	2.87	.99795	.00205	.0065
2.34	.99036	.00964	.0258	2.88	.99801	.00199	.0063
2.35	.99061	.00939	.0252	2.89	.99807	.00193	.0061
2.36	.99086	.00914	.0246	2.90	.99813	.00187	.0060
2.37	.99111	.00889	.0241	2.91	.99819	.00181	.0058
2.38	.99134	.00866	.0235	2.92	.99825	.00175	.0056
2.39	.99158	.00842	.0229	2.93	.99831	.00169	.0055
2.40	.99180	.00820	.0224	2.94	.99836	.00164	.0053
2.41	.99202	.00798	.0219	2.95	.99841	.00159	.0051
2.42	.99224	.00776	.0213	2.96	.99846	.00154	.0050
2.43	.99245	.00755	.0208	2.97	.99851	.00149	.0048
2.44	.99266	.00734	.0203	2.98	.99856	.00144	.0047
2.45	.99286	.00714	.0198	2.99	.99861	.00139	.0046
2.46	.99305	.00695	.0194	3.00	.99865	.00135	.0044
2.47	.99324	.00676	.0189	. . .	. . .	. . .	. . .
2.48	.99343	.00657	.0184	3.25	.99942	.00058	.0020
2.49	.99361	.00639	.0180	. . .	. . .	. . .	. . .
2.50	.99379	.00621	.0175	3.50	.99977	.00023	.0009
2.51	.99396	.00604	.0171	. . .	. . .	. . .	. . .
2.52	.99413	.00587	.0167	4.00	.99997	.00003	.0001
2.53	.99430	.00570	.1063				

Table taken from Field 2005a. Reprinted with permission from the author.

Index

This is an alphabetical index of all the entries in this book.